Internet and Telecommunications Regulation

Internet and Telecommunications Regulation

SECOND EDITION

Stuart Minor Benjamin
WILLIAM VAN ALSTYNE PROFESSOR OF LAW
DUKE UNIVERSITY SCHOOL OF LAW

Barak D. Richman
KATHARINE T. BARTLETT PROFESSOR OF LAW
DUKE UNIVERSITY SCHOOL OF LAW

James B. Speta
ELIZABETH FROEHLING HORNER PROFESSOR OF LAW
NORTHWESTERN UNIVERSITY PRITZKER SCHOOL OF LAW

CAROLINA ACADEMIC PRESS
Durham, North Carolina

ISBN 978-1-5310-2688-2
Looseleaf 978-1-5310-2700-1
eISBN 978-1-5310-2689-9
LCCN 2022949616

Carolina Academic Press
700 Kent Street
Durham, North Carolina 27701
(919) 489-7486
www.cap-press.com

Printed in the United States of America.

For Arti, Sophia, Anna, Laura, Ariella, Eden,
Izak, Denise, Mason, and Cameron

Contents

Table of Materials xv
Copyright Permissions xxiii
Preface xxv

Part One
Foundations

Chapter One · Introduction to Internet and Telecommunications Regulation 3
§ 1.A. Telecommunications as a "Regulated Industry" 6
§ 1.A.1. Justifications for Regulation 8
§ 1.A.1.a. Market Failure Justifications 8
§ 1.A.1.b. Noneconomic Justifications 13
§ 1.A.2. The Challenges of Regulation 15
§ 1.B. The Institutions of Telecommunications Policy 18
§ 1.B.1. Why Agencies? 18
§ 1.B.2. The Federal Communications Commission 21
§ 1.B.2.a. FCC Origins and Predecessors 21
§ 1.B.2.b. The Communications Act of 1934 22
§ 1.B.3. The FTC and DOJ 24
§ 1.B.3.a. The Mechanisms of Antitrust Enforcement 24
§ 1.B.4. Agency Actions and Legal Constraints 27
§ 1.C. A Policy Analysis Framework 29

Chapter Two · The Antitrust Laws and Their Regulation of Monopolies 31
§ 2.A. The History & Purpose of the Sherman Act 32
§ 2.B. The Rise of the Chicago School and the Consumer Welfare Standard 35
United States v. Syufy Enterprises 36
§ 2.C. Antitrust's Regulation of Monopolies 43
United States v. Aluminum Co. of America [*Alcoa*] 44

Chapter Three · First Amendment Coverage 49
§ 3.A. Industry-Specific Laws and the First Amendment 50
Turner Broadcasting System, Inc. v. FCC [*Turner I*] 51
Turner Broadcasting System, Inc. v. FCC [*Turner II*] 59
Sorrell v. IMS Health Inc. 64
§ 3.B. Antitrust and the First Amendment 73
FTC v. Superior Court Trial Lawyers Association 74

Part Two

Economic Regulation of Internet and Telecommunications

Chapter Four · Early Telephone Regulation Through Divestiture 83
§ 4.A. Telephone History 84
§ 4.B. Telephone Economics 89
§ 4.C. Telephone Regulation 90
§ 4.D. Precursors to Divestiture 91
§ 4.D.1. Competition in CPE 92
Federal Telecommunications Law 92
§ 4.D.2. Competition in Long-Distance Telephony 95
§ 4.D.3. Communications and Computer Convergence 96
§ 4.E. Breaking Up Bell: The 1984 Divestiture 98
§ 4.E.1. The MFJ 99
United States v. American Telephone & Telegraph Co. 99
§ 4.E.2. Discussion of the Government's Theory 106
§ 4.F. The 1996 Act 111

Chapter Five · Natural Monopoly Regulation 115
§ 5.A. Rate Regulation 117
§ 5.A.1. Rate of Return Regulation 117
§ 5.A.2. Price Cap Regulation 120
§ 5.A.3. Rate Regulation as Markets Become Competitive 121
§ 5.A.4. Price Regulation Strategies 123
§ 5.B. Access 126
§ 5.B.1. Interconnection Under the Telecommunications Act of 1996 127
§ 5.B.2. Common Carriage 131
Kinderstart.com LLC v. Google, Inc. 132
Joseph R. Biden v. Knight First Amendment Institute 139
§ 5.B.3. Nondiscrimination Obligations 144
Comcast Cable Communications v. FCC 145
§ 5.C. Vertical Prohibitions 152
§ 5.C.1. Regulation of Vertical Foreclosure by Television Networks 153
Schurz Communications, Inc. v. FCC 156
§ 5.C.2. Regulation of Vertical Foreclosure by Cable Companies 165
§ 5.C.2.a. The FCC's Program Access Rules 166
§ 5.C.2.b. MVPD Access to Buildings 167
National Cable & Telecommunications Ass'n v. FCC 168
§ 5.D. Unbundling 172
§ 5.D.1. Identifying Unbundled Elements 172
AT&T Corp. v. Iowa Utilities Board 172
United States Telecom Ass'n v. FCC [*USTA II*] 177

§ 5.D.2. Pricing Network Elements 184
Verizon Communications Inc. v. FCC 187
§ 5.E. Universal Service 196
§ 5.E.1. Achieving Universal Service Through Cross-Subsidies 197
§ 5.E.2. Universal Telephony Service After the 1996 Act 200
FCC 11-161 202
§ 5.E.3. Broadband Universal Service 211
FCC 11-161 213

Chapter Six · Regulating Internet Access 229
§ 6.A. Regulatory Characterization of Broadband Services 230
National Cable & Telecommunications Ass'n v. Brand X Internet Services 232
§ 6.B. Net Neutrality 241
Comcast Corp. v. FCC 243
Verizon v. FCC 249
Protecting and Promoting the Open Internet 252
United States Telecom Ass'n v. FCC 260
United States Telecom Ass'n v. FCC 273
Restoring Internet Freedom 280
Mozilla Corp. v. FCC 296

Chapter Seven · Federal or State Regulation? 317
§ 7.A. The 1934 Act: Spectrum and Telephony 317
§ 7.B. Jurisdiction to Implement the 1996 Act: Local Competition, National Regulation 320
United States Telecom Ass'n v. FCC [*USTA II*] 324
§ 7.C. Cable Television 325
§ 7.D. Jurisdiction to Promote Competition in MVPD Markets 332
§ 7.E. Internet Services 334
ACA Connects v. Bonta 336

Chapter Eight · Antitrust in Networked Industries 343
§ 8.A. Monopoly Leverage and Maintenance 344
§ 8.A.1. Market Definition in Digital Markets 344
FTC v. Facebook, Inc. 345
Epic Games, Inc. v. Apple, Inc. 353
§ 8.A.2. Interconnection 359
Otter Tail Power Company v. United States 360
Verizon Communications Inc. v. Law Offices of Curtis V. Trinko, LLP 365
§ 8.A.3. Vertical Restraints 372
United States v. Microsoft Corp. 372
United States v. Google LLC 384
Google Search (Shopping) 388

§ 8.B. Mergers 395
§ 8.B.1. Institutional and Statutory Landscape 397
Applications of Comcast Corp., General Electric Co., and NBC Universal, Inc. for Consent to Assign Licenses and Transfer Control of Licensees 398
§ 8.B.2. Horizontal Mergers 401
Satellite Sisters: XM and Sirius Satellite Radio Merger 402
Statement of the Department of Justice Antitrust Division on Its Decision to Close Its Investigation of XM Satellite Radio Holdings Inc.'s Merger with Sirius Satellite Radio Inc. 404
Commission Approves Transaction between Sirius Satellite Radio Holdings Inc. and XM Satellite Radio Holdings, Inc. Subject to Conditions 407
§ 8.B.3. Vertical Mergers 410
United States v. Comcast Corp. 411
United States v. AT&T 417
General Motors Corp. and Hughes Electronics Corp., Transferors, and the News Corp. Ltd, Transferee, for Authority to Transfer Control 429
§ 8.B.4. Acquisition of Nascent Competitors 435
Google/Double Click 436

Chapter Nine · Regulating the Spectrum 441
§ 9.A. Characteristics of Electromagnetic Waves 442
§ 9.A.1. Wires Versus Airwaves as a Means of Propagation 444
§ 9.A.2. The Spectrum as a Resource 446
§ 9.B. Rationales for Regulation: Scarcity/Interference 447
Why Not Use the Pricing System in the Broadcast Industry? 451
§ 9.C. Managing the Spectrum 455
§ 9.C.1. A Note on Tradeoffs: Allotment 457
§ 9.D. Allocating the Spectrum 459
§ 9.D.1. Models of Spectrum Control 460
Spectrum Policy Task Force Report 462
§ 9.D.2. Transitioning to Flexibility and Dealing with Incumbents 469
§ 9.D.3. Dedicating Spectrum to Unlicensed Uses 473
Some Economics of Wireless Communications 474
§ 9.D.4. Unlicensed Usage Without Dedicated Spectrum 480
§ 9.D.4.a. Unlicensed Devices on Vacant Frequencies 480
Unlicensed Operation in the TV Broadcast Bands and Additional Spectrum for Unlicensed Devices below 900 MHz and in the 3 GHz Band 481
§ 9.D.4.b. Spectrum Sharing and Government Spectrum 485

Realizing the Full Potential of Government-Held Spectrum to Spur Economic Growth 486
§ 9.E. Moving Licenses Closer to Property Rights 490
§ 9.E.1. Spectrum Subdivision and Leasing (and the Possibility of a Private Commons) 490
§ 9.E.2. License Transfer 491
§ 9.E.3. License Renewal 493
§ 9.F. Assignment Mechanisms 497
Using Auctions to Select FCC Licensees 499

Chapter Ten · Ownership Limits 509
§ 10.A. Cable Television Ownership Limits 510
Time Warner Entertainment Co. v. FCC [*Time Warner II*] 511
Comcast Corp. v. FCC 521
§ 10.B. Spectrum Ownership Limits 525
Policies Regarding Mobile Spectrum Holdings: Expanding the Economic and Innovation Opportunities of Spectrum Through Incentive Auctions 526
§ 10.C. Broadcast Ownership Limits 534
2014 Quadrennial Regulatory Review 537
FCC v. Prometheus Radio Project 540

Part Three

Noneconomic Regulation of Internet and Telecommunications

Chapter Eleven · Content-Based Regulations 551
§ 11.A. Mandating Carriage of Speech Deemed Valuable 552
Red Lion Broadcasting Co. v. FCC 552
Miami Herald Publishing Co. v. Tornillo 557
§ 11.B. Restrictions on Speech Deemed Harmful 569
§ 11.B.1. Indecency 570
§ 11.B.1.a. Regulation of Broadcast Indecency 570
FCC v. Pacifica Foundation 570
§ 11.B.1.b. Regulation of Cable Indecency 584
Denver Area Educational Telecommunications Consortium, Inc. v. FCC 585
§ 11.B.1.c. Regulation of Internet Indecency 601
Reno v. ACLU 602
Ashcroft v. ACLU [*Ashcroft II*] 610
§ 11.B.2. Violence 621
Brown v. Entertainment Merchants Association et al. 622
§ 11.B.3. False Statements 630

New York Times Co. v. Sullivan 631
United States v. Alvarez 636

Chapter Twelve · Regulating Algorithms 647
Stuart Minor Benjamin, Algorithms and Speech 649
Tim Wu, Machine Speech 659
Jian Zhang et al. v. Baidu.Com Inc. 671

Chapter Thirteen · Privacy Regulation 677
§ 13.A. Common Law Tort Protections 679
Jackson v. Mayweather 680
McDonald v. Kiloo ApS 685
§ 13.B. Protection by Contract 688
In re: Facebook Privacy Litigation 688
§ 13.C. FTC Privacy Supervision 692
Snapchat, Inc. 692
§ 13.D. Federal Statutory Privacy Protections 698
§ 13.D.1. Communications Act Privacy 698
Protecting the Privacy of Customers of Broadband and Other Telecommunications Services 698
§ 13.D.2. Other Federal Statutory Protections 701
Dinerstein v. Google, LLC 701
§ 13.E. Other Sources of Privacy Law 707
Google Spain SL v. Agencia Española de Protección de Datos (AEPD) 709

Chapter Fourteen · Copyright 717
§ 14.A. Copyright Basics 719
§ 14.B. Copyright and Traditional Communications Services 721
§ 14.B.1. Individual Programs 722
§ 14.B.1.a. Compulsory Copyright Licenses 722
§ 14.B.1.b. What Constitutes a Performance under Copyright Law? 726
American Broadcasting Companies, Inc. v. Aereo, Inc. 727
§ 14.B.2. Syndicated Exclusivity and Network Nonduplication 734
§ 14.B.3. Retransmission Consent 736
§ 14.C. Copyright and Internet Platforms 739
Metro-Goldwyn-Mayer Studios Inc. v. Grokster, Ltd. 740
Viacom International, Inc. v. YouTube, Inc. 752

Chapter Fifteen · General Protection for Intermediaries of User-Generated Content: Section 230 763
§ 15.A. Background and Foundation: Zeran v. America Online 764
Zeran v. America Online, Inc. 764
§ 15.B. Attributing Authorship: The Problem of Joint or Separate Production 769

Fair Housing Council of San Fernando Valley v. Roommates.com, LLC 770
Jones v. Dirty World Entertainment Recordings LLC 777
Barnes v. Yahoo!, Inc. 785
§ 15.C. The Limits of Protecting Bad Content 791
Doe v. Backpage.com 791

Conceptual Index and Glossary 799

Table of Materials

2014 Quadrennial Regulatory Review—Order on Reconsideration and Notice of Proposed Rulemaking, 32 FCC Rcd. 9802 (2017), 537

ACA Connects v. Bonta, 24 F.4th 1233 (9th Cir. 2022), 336
ACLU, *see also* Ashcroft v. ACLU *and* Reno v. ACLU
Aereo, Inc., *see* American Broadcasting Companies, Inc. v. Aereo, Inc.
Agencia Española de Protección de Datos (AEPD), *see* Google Spain SL v. Agencia Española de Protección de Datos (AEPD)
Alliance for Community Media v. FCC, 529 F.3d 763 (6th Cir. 2008), 332
Aluminum Co. of America (Alcoa), *see* United States v. Aluminum Co. of America (Alcoa)
Alvarez, *see* United States v. Alvarez
Amendment of the Commission's Rules Related to Retransmission Consent, Notice of Proposed Rulemaking, 26 FCC Rcd. 2718 (2011), 735
America Online, Inc., *see* Zeran v. America Online, Inc.
American Broadcasting Companies, Inc. v. Aereo, Inc., 573 U.S. 431 (2014), 727
American Telephone & Telegraph Co., *see* United States v. American Telephone & Telegraph Co.
Apple, Inc., *see* Epic Games, Inc. v. Apple, Inc.
Applications for Voluntary Assignments or Transfers of Control, 47 Fed. Reg. 985 (Jan. 8, 1982), 491
Applications of Comcast Corp., General Electric Co. and NBC Universal, Inc. for Consent to Assign Licenses and Transfer Control of Licensees, Memorandum Opinion and Order, 26 FCC Rcd. 4238 (2011), 398
Ashcroft v. ACLU [*Ashcroft I*], 535 U.S. 564 (2002), 608
Ashcroft v. ACLU [*Ashcroft II*], 542 U.S. 656 (2004), 610
AT&T Corp. v. Iowa Utilities Board, 525 U.S. 366 (1999), 172, 321
AT&T, *see also* United States v. AT&T

Backpage.com, *see* Doe v. Backpage.com
Baidu.Com Inc., *see* Zhang et al. v. Baidu .Com Inc.
Barnes v. Yahoo!, Inc., 570 F.3d 1096 (9th Cir. 2009), 785
Benjamin, Algorithms and Speech, 161 U. Penn. L. Rev. 1445 (2013), 519, 649
Benjamin, Transmitting, Editing, and Communicating: Determining What "The Freedom Of Speech" Encompasses, 60 Duke L.J. 1673 (2011), 279

Benkler, Some Economics of Wireless Communications, 16 Harv. J.L. & Tech. 25 (2002), 474

Berisha v. Lawson, 141 S. Ct. 2424 (2021), 635

Biden, Joseph R., v. Knight First Amendment Institute, 141 S. Ct. 1220 (2021), 139

Bonta, *see* ACA Connects v. Bonta

Bork, Legislative Intent and the Policy of the Sherman Act, 9 J.L. & Econ. 7 (1966), 35

Bork, The Antitrust Paradox: A Policy at War with Itself (1978), 40

Brand X Internet Services, *see* National Cable & Telecommunications Ass'n v. Brand X Internet Services

Brown v. Entertainment Merchants Association, 564 U.S. 786 (2011), 622

Caldwell, The Standard of Public Interest, Convenience or Necessity as Used in the Radio Act of 1927, 1 Air L. Rev. 295 (1930), 23

California v. FCC, 905 F.2d 1217 (9th Cir. 1990), 111

CBS Broadcasting Inc. v. PrimeTime 24 Joint Venture, 48 F. Supp. 2d 1342 (S.D. Fla. 1998), 724

Coase, Why Not Use the Pricing System in the Broadcast Industry? Testimony before the FCC, December 1959, *reprinted in* 4 Study of Radio & Television Network Broadcasting, 68, 451

Comcast Cable Communications v. FCC, 717 F.3d 982 (D.C. Cir. 2013), 145

Comcast Corp. v. FCC, 579 F.3d 1 (D.C. Cir. 2009), 521

Comcast Corp. v. FCC, 600 F.3d 642 (D.C. Cir. 2010), 243

Comcast Corp., *see also* Applications of Comcast Corp. *and* United States v. Comcast Corp.

Commission Approves Transaction between Sirius Satellite Radio Holdings Inc. and XM Satellite Radio Holdings, Inc. Subject to Conditions, Press Release, FCC (July 28, 2008), 2008 WL 2902112, 407

Competition in the Interstate Interexchange Marketplace, Notice of Proposed Rulemaking, 5 FCC Rcd. 2627 (1990), 109

Complaint of Syracuse Peace Council against Television Station WTVH Syracuse, New York, Memorandum Opinion and Order [*Syracuse Peace Council*], 2 FCC Rcd. 5043 (1987), 566

Customers of Broadband and Other Telecommunications Services, *see* Protecting the Privacy of Customers of Broadband and Other Telecommunications Services

Denver Area Educational Telecommunications Consortium, Inc. v. FCC, 518 U.S. 727 (1996), 585

Dinerstein v. Google, LLC, 484 F. Supp. 3d 561 (N.D. Ill. 2020), 701

Dirty World Entertainment Recordings LLC, *see* Jones v. Dirty World Entertainment Recordings LLC

Dissenting Statement of Commissioner Ajit Pai, 31 FCC Rcd. 6,327 (2016), 400

Doe v. Backpage.com, 817 F.3d 12 (1st Cir. 2016), 791

Double Click, *see* Google/Double Click

Entertainment Merchants Association, *see* Brown v. Entertainment Merchants Association

Epic Games, Inc. v. Apple, Inc., 559 F. Supp. 3d 898 (N.D. Cal., 2021), 353

Expanding the Economic and Innovation Opportunities of Spectrum

Through Incentive Auctions, Notice of Proposed Rulemaking, 27 FCC Rcd. 12,357 (2012), 507

Facebook, Inc., *see* FTC v. Facebook, Inc. *and* In re Facebook Privacy Litigation

Fair Housing Council of San Fernando Valley v. Roommates.com, LLC, 521 F.3d 1157 (9th Cir. 2008) (en banc), 770

FCC v. Fox Television Stations, Inc. [*Fox I*] 556 U.S. 502 (2009), 583

FCC, National Broadband Plan § 5.1 (2010), 212, 461, 473, 506

FCC v. Pacifica Foundation, 438 U.S. 726 (1978), 570

FCC v. Prometheus Radio Project, 141 S. Ct. 1150 (2021), 540

FCC Report to Congress on Spectrum Auctions, 1997 WL 629251 (1997), 504

FCC v. WNCN Listeners Guild, 450 U.S. 582 (1981), 562

FCC, *see also* Comcast Cable Communications v. FCC, Comcast Corp. v. FCC, Denver Area Educational Telecommunications Consortium, Inc. v. FCC, In re FCC 11-161, Mozilla Corp. v. FCC, National Cable & Telecommunications Ass'n v. FCC, Red Lion Broadcasting Co. v. FCC, Schurz Communications, Inc. v. FCC, Time Warner Entertainment Co. v. FCC, Turner Broadcasting System, Inc. v. FCC, United States Telecom Ass'n v. FCC, Verizon Communications Inc. v. FCC, Verizon v. FCC

FTC v. Facebook, Inc., 560 F. Supp. 3d 1 (D.D.C. 2021), 345

FTC v. Superior Court Trial Lawyers Association, 493 U.S. 411 (1990), 74

General Electric Co., *see* Applications of Comcast Corp.

General Motors Corp. and Hughes Electronics Corp., Transferors, and the News Corp. Ltd, Transferee, for Authority to Transfer Control, Memorandum Opinion and Order, 19 FCC Rcd. 473 (2004), 429

Google/Double Click, FTC File 071-0170, 2007 WL 4624893, Statement of the Federal Trade Commission, 436

Google LLC, *see* Dinerstein v. Google, LLC *and* Kinderstart.com LLC v. Google, Inc. *and* United States v. Google LLC

Google Search (Shopping), Commission Decision, Case AT.39740 (European Commission, June 27, 2017), 388

Google Spain SL v. Agencia Española de Protección de Datos (AEPD), ECLI:EU:C:2014:317 (May 13, 2014) [European Court of Justice], 709

Google, *see also* Dinerstein v. Google, LLC *and* Kinderstart.com LLC v. Google, Inc. *and* United States v. Google LLC

Grokster, *see* Metro-Goldwyn-Mayer Studios Inc. v. Grokster, Ltd.

Hovenkamp, Antitrust Policy After Chicago, 84 Mich. L. Rev. 213, 283–284 (1985), 40

Huber, Kellogg, and Thorne, Federal Telecommunications Law 663–70 (2d ed. 1999), 84, 92, 128

Hughes Electronics Corp., *see* General Motors Corp.

Implementation of Sections 11 and 13 of the Cable Television Consumer Protection and Competition Act of 1992: Horizontal and Vertical Ownership Limits, Second Report

and Order, 8 FCC Rcd. 8565 (1993), 520
Implementation of Sections 12 and 19 of the Cable Television Consumer Protection and Competition Act of 1992: Development of Competition and Diversity in Video Programming Distribution and Carriage, First Report and Order, 8 FCC Rcd. 3359 (1993), 165
In re Facebook Privacy Litigation, 192 F. Supp. 3d 1053 (N.D. Cal. 2016), 688
In re FCC 11-161, 753 F.3d 1015 (10th Cir. 2014), 202, 213
In the Matter of Snapchat, Inc., 2015-1 Trade Cas. ¶17,115 (F.T.C.) (2014), 692
Incentive Auctions, *see* Policies Regarding Mobile Spectrum Holdings
Inquiry Concerning High-Speed Access to the Internet Over Cable and Other Facilities, Declaratory Ruling and Notice of Proposed Rulemaking, 17 FCC Rcd. 4798 (2002), 231
Iowa Utilities Board, *see* AT&T Corp. v. Iowa Utilities Board

Jackson v. Mayweather, 217 Cal. Rptr. 3d 234 (Cal. App. 2 Dist. 2017), 680
Jones v. Dirty World Entertainment Recordings LLC, 755 F.3d 398 (6th Cir. 2014), 777

Kiloo ApS, *see* McDonald v. Kiloo ApS
Kinderstart.com LLC v. Google, Inc., No. C06-2057 JF (RS), 2006 WL 3246596 (N.D. Cal. July 13, 2006), 132
Knight First Amendment Institute, *see* Biden, Joseph R., v. Knight First Amendment Institute
Krattenmaker, The Telecommunications Act of 1996, 29 Conn. L. Rev. 123 (1996), 112
Kwerel and Felker, Using Auctions to Select FCC Licensees, FCC Office of Plans & Policy, Working Paper No. 16 (1985), 499

Lande, Wealth Transfers as the Original and Primary Concern of Antitrust: The Efficiency Interpretation Challenged, 34 Hastings L.J. 67 (1982), 42
Law Offices of Curtis V. Trinko, *see* Verizon Communications Inc. v. Law Offices of Curtis V. Trinko, LLP
Letwin, Congress and the Sherman Antitrust Law: 1887–1890, 23 U. Chi. L. Rev. 221 (1956), 32

Mayweather, *see* Jackson v. Mayweather
McDonald v. Kiloo ApS, 385 F. Supp. 3d 1022 (N.D. Cal. 2019), 685
Metro-Goldwyn-Mayer Studios Inc. v. Grokster, Ltd., 545 U.S. 913 (2005), 740
Miami Herald Publishing Co. v. Tornillo, 418 U.S. 241 (1974), 557
Microsoft Corp., *see* United States v. Microsoft Corp.
Mobile Spectrum Holdings, *see* Policies Regarding Mobile Spectrum Holdings
Mozilla Corp. v. FCC, 940 F.3d 1 (D.C. Cir. 2019), 296

National Cable & Telecommunications Ass'n v. Brand X Internet Services, 545 U.S. 967 (2005), 232
National Cable & Telecommunications Ass'n v. FCC, 567 F.3d 659 (D.C. Cir. 2009), 168
NBC v. United States, 319 U.S. 190 (1943), 450, 559

NBC Universal, Inc., *see* Applications of Comcast Corp.
New York Times Co. v. Sullivan, 376 U.S. 254 (1964), 631
News Corp., Ltd., *see* General Motors Corp.

Omega Satellite Prods. Co. v. Indianapolis, 694 F.2d 119 (7th Cir. 1982), 9
Otter Tail Power Company v. United States, 410 U.S. 366 (1973), 360

Pacifica Foundation, *see* FCC v. Pacifica Foundation
Packingham v. North Carolina, 137 S. Ct. 1730 (2017), 618
Policies Regarding Mobile Spectrum Holdings: Expanding the Economic and Innovation Opportunities of Spectrum Through Incentive Auctions, Report and Order, 29 FCC Rcd. 6133 (2014), 526
Policy and Rules Concerning Rates for Dominant Carriers, Report and Order and Second Further Notice of Proposed Rulemaking, 4 FCC Rcd. 2873 (1989), 119
Posner, Antitrust Law (2d ed. 2001), 36
Privacy, *see* In re Facebook Privacy Litigation *and* Protecting the Privacy of Customers of Broadband and Other Telecommunications Services
Prometheus Radio Project, *see* FCC v. Prometheus Radio Project
Protecting and Promoting the Open Internet, Report and Order on Remand, Declaratory Ruling, and Order, 30 FCC Rcd. 5601 (2015), 252
Protecting the Privacy of Customers of Broadband and Other Telecommunications Services, Report and Order, 31 FCC Rcd. 13,911 (2016), 698

Quadrennial Regulatory Review, Second Report and Order, 31 FCC Rcd. 9864 (2016), 536

Realizing the Full Potential of Government-Held Spectrum to Spur Economic Growth, President's Council of Advisors on Science and Technology (2012), 486
Redevelopment of Spectrum To Encourage Innovation in the Use of New Telecommunications Technologies, Notice of Proposed Rulemaking, 7 FCC Rcd. 1542 (1992), 472
Red Lion Broadcasting Co. v. FCC, 395 U.S. 367 (1969), 552
Reno v. ACLU, 521 U.S. 844 (1997), 602
Restoring Internet Freedom, Declaratory Ruling, Report and Order, and Order, 33 FCC Rcd. 311 (2018), 280
Review of the Prime Time Access Rule, Section 73.658(k) of the Commission's Rules, Report and Order, 11 FCC Rcd. 546 (1995), 155
Riley v. National Federation of the Blind, 487 U.S. 781 (1988), 563
Roommates.com, *see* Fair Housing Council of San Fernando Valley v. Roommates.com, LLC

Sable Communications of California, Inc. v. FCC, 492 U.S. 115 (1989), 600
Schurz Communications, Inc. v. FCC, 982 F.2d 1043 (7th Cir. 1992), 156
Sidak & Spulber, Deregulatory Takings and the Regulatory Contract (1997), 195
Sirius Satellite Radio Inc., *see* Commission Approves Transaction between Sirius Satellite Radio Holdings Inc. and XM Satellite Radio Holdings *and* Statement of the Department of Justice Antitrust Division

Snapchat, *see* In the Matter of Snapchat, Inc.
Sorrell v. IMS Health Inc., 564 U.S. 552 (2011), 64
Spectrum Policy Task Force Report, FCC, ET Docket No. 02-135 (Nov. 2002), 462
Spectrum, *see also* Realizing the Full Potential of Government-Held Spectrum to Spur Economic Growth
Statement of Chair Lina M. Khan, Commissioner Rohit Chopra, and Commissioner Rebecca Kelly Slaughter on the Withdrawal of the Vertical Merger Guidelines, Commission File No. P810034 (September 15, 2021), 43
Statement of the Department of Justice Antitrust Division on Its Decision to Close Its Investigation of XM Satellite Radio Holdings Inc.'s Merger with Sirius Satellite Radio Inc., Press Release, DOJ (Mar. 24, 2008), 404
Sullivan, *see* New York Times Co. v. Sullivan,
Superior Court Trial Lawyers Association, *see* FTC v. Superior Court Trial Lawyers Association
James Surowiecki, Satellite Sisters: XM and Sirius Satellite Radio Merger, The New Yorker (March 12, 2007), 402
Syufy Enterprises, *see* United States v. Syufy Enterprises

Time Warner Entertainment Co. v. FCC [*Time Warner II*], 240 F.3d 1126 (D.C. Cir. 2001), 511
Time Warner Entertainment Co. v. FCC [*Time Warner I*], 93 F.3d 957 (D.C. Cir. 1996), 329, 330, 519
Tornillo, *see* Miami Herald Publishing Co. v. Tornillo
Trinko, *see* Verizon Communications Inc. v. Law Offices of Curtis V. Trinko, LLP
Turner Broadcasting System, Inc. v. FCC [*Turner I*], 512 U.S. 622 (1994), 51, 58, 564
Turner Broadcasting System, Inc. v. FCC [*Turner II*], 520 U.S. 180 (1997), 58, 59, 564
TV Broadcast Bands, *see* Unlicensed Operation in the TV Broadcast Bands
Twentieth Century Music Corp. v. Aiken, 422 U. S. 151 (1975), 720

United States v. Aluminum Co. of America (Alcoa), 148 F.2d 416 (2d Cir. 1945), 44, 47
United States v. Alvarez, 567 U.S. 709 (2012), 636
United States v. American Library Ass'n, Inc., 539 U.S. 194 (2003), 620
United States v. American Telephone & Telegraph Co., 552 F. Supp. 131 (D.D.C. 1982), 16, 99
United States v. AT&T, 310 F. Supp. 3d 161 (D.D.C. 2018), 417
United States v. Comcast Corp., Civil Action No. 1:11CV00106 (D.D.C. Jan. 18, 2011), 411
United States v. Google LLC, No. 1:20-cv-03010 (D.D.C. Jan. 15, 2021), 384
United States v. Microsoft Corp., 253 F.3d 34 (D.C. Cir. 2001), 372
United States v. Syufy Enterprises, 903 F.2d 659 (9th Cir. 1990), 36
United States Telecom Ass'n v. FCC [*USTA II*], 359 F.3d 554 (D.C. Cir. 2004), 177, 324

United States Telecom Ass'n v. FCC, 825 F.3d 674 (D.C. Cir. 2016), 260
United States Telecom Ass'n v. FCC, 855 F.3d 381 (D.C. Cir. 2017), 273
United Video v. FCC, 890 F.2d 1173 (D.C. Cir. 1989), 735
Unlicensed Devices, *see* Unlicensed Operation in the TV Broadcast Bands
Unlicensed Operation in the TV Broadcast Bands and Additional Spectrum for Unlicensed Devices below 900 MHz and in the 3 GHz Band, Second Report and Order and Memorandum Opinion and Order, 23 FCC Rcd. 16,807 (2008), 481
U.S. Dept. of Justice & FTC, Horizontal Merger Guidelines, revised April 8, 1997, 402

Viacom International, Inc. v. YouTube, Inc., 676 F.3d 19 (2d Cir. 2012), 752
Verizon Communications Inc. v. FCC, 535 U.S. 467 (2002), 187
Verizon Communications Inc. v. Law Offices of Curtis V. Trinko, LLP, 540 U.S. 398 (2004), 48, 365
Verizon v. FCC, 740 F.3d 623 (D.C. Cir. 2014), 249

Wu, Machine Speech, 161 U. Penn. L. Rev. 1495 (2013), 659

XM Satellite Radio, *see* Commission Approves Transaction between Sirius Satellite Radio Holdings Inc. and XM Satellite Radio Holdings *and* Statement of the Department of Justice Antitrust Division

Yahoo!, Inc., *see* Barnes v. Yahoo!, Inc.
YouTube, *see* Viacom International, Inc. v. YouTube, Inc.

Zeran v. America Online, Inc., 129 F.3d 327 (4th Cir. 1997), 764
Zhang et al. v. Baidu .Com Inc., 10 F. Supp. 3d 433 (S.D.N.Y. 2014), 671

Copyright Permissions

Our sincere thanks go to the following copyright holders, who have granted permission for us to excerpt copyrighted materials in this book:

Aspen Publishers, Inc., for permission to excerpt Federal Telecommunications Law, Second Edition, by Peter W. Huber, Michael K. Kellogg, and John Thorne. Copyright 1999 by Peter W. Huber, Michael K. Kellogg, and John Thorne. All rights reserved.

Yochai Benkler and the Harvard Journal of Law and Technology for permission to excerpt Yochai Benkler, Some Economics of Wireless Communications, 16 Harv. J.L. & Tech. 25 (2002).

Ronald Coase for permission to excerpt Why Not Use the Pricing System in the Broadcast Industry? Testimony before the FCC (December 1959), reprinted in 4 Study of Radio & Television Broadcasting (No. 12,782) (1959).

Thomas Krattenmaker and Lucas Powe, for permission to adapt various sections of their book Regulating Broadcast Programming (1994). All rights reserved.

The New Yorker, for permission to excerpt James Surowiecki, Satellite Sisters (March 12, 2007).

Tim Wu, for permission to excerpt Machine Speech, 161 U. Penn. L. Rev. 1495 (2013).

Preface

This book is entitled *Internet and Telecommunications Regulation*, but if we could put "Internet" in a bigger font we would, because regulation of internet services is the heart of the book. The internet has become a centerpiece in the modern economy and is woven into most people's lives. Internet platforms in particular, including search engines, social media, marketplaces, app stores, etc. (which frequently blend into one another), have become central to modern life and business. In light of the internet's importance, this book devotes considerable attention to the regulation applicable to companies that provide internet services.

But this book is not just about the internet. It is also about broadcast, telephony, multichannel video like cable television, and other traditional telecommunications services. Why? There are three broad reasons. First, telecommunications services are important in their own right (as the smartphone that is probably within your reach can attest) and the law surrounding those services remain important. Second, internet access is built on the infrastructure of earlier technologies (particularly telephone and cable television). Third, and perhaps most relevant for a legal casebook, the regulation of internet services builds on the regulation of traditional telecommunications services. One cannot understand the regulation of internet services without understanding the telecommunications regulation that underpins it.

This relates to an important point: there is no comprehensive "law of the internet." Law surrounds the internet and all activity that takes place within it, but one of the most important changes in communications law has been the move from a sector-specific regime, with a defined set of statutes and a particular agency with explicit regulatory authority (the Federal Communications Commission), to an assortment of overlapping regimes with no dedicated regulator. Congress passed several generations of laws to govern telephony, telecommunications, cable, and other wired sectors, but Congress has not seen fit to regulate "the internet," and it is not clear what such regulation would look like. Instead, internet regulation has been confined to particular aspects of internet services. Prominent among these have been regulation of internet access service (the legal battle over which has turned on the interpretation of the word "telecommunications" in the federal statute regulating telephony, the Communications Act), regulation of wireless frequencies (also flowing from the Communications Act), and competition laws (including antitrust laws and those more specifically focused on particular telecommunications services).

Internet-focused laws have played a relatively small role in the regulation of internet services, with antitrust, telecommunications, and broad laws not specific to the internet (like privacy and copyright) playing a bigger role. This is not to say that there are no internet-focused statutes. The most prominent such law is 47 U.S.C. § 230, which has proved quite significant in providing fairly broad immunity for internet platforms with respect to third-party content. Congress has also attempted to regulate indecency on the internet (and every other form of telecommunications), but the Supreme Court has invalidated indecency regulation of every form of telecommunications other than broadcasting. This last point highlights an important constraint: the First Amendment, as interpreted, makes it difficult, if not impossible, for the government to regulate content. Users care deeply about the content that courses over internet and telecommunications services, but the government is largely disabled from regulating it.

In crafting this casebook, we focus on what we consider to be the centers of gravity for the legal and policy challenges concerning internet and telecommunications services. We believe there are common economic and policy challenges that characterize these services. There are common scale efficiencies, and thus a market tendency to slide towards concentrated ownership. There are common dangers, both economic and non-economic, to market concentration and to certain behaviors. There are common benefits to universal access. And there are common political dynamics, including a sense that wise regulation of the internet and telecommunications is important to our society and democracy (if only we could agree on what regulation is "wise").

These commonalities have persisted for much of the 20th and 21st century, and thus our casebook is not isolated to the issues of the current day. To the contrary, although both the law and its underlying policy priorities have changed, the challenges that we confront with the rise of today's internet platforms are informed by the challenges of the rise of the Bell System telephone monopoly. We believe that, normatively, today's policymakers can learn from the lessons of the past, and, descriptively, current law is somewhat historically determined by past law. For that reason, we organize our casebook conceptually around common policy challenges while adding frequent references to the statutes, cases, and regulatory efforts of the past.

Now, some acknowledgments. Doug Lichtman, Howard Shelanski, and Phil Weiser, who worked on a predecessor to this casebook, have provided invaluable help, as has Doug Sicker. Sincere thanks, too, to Carolina Academic Press, and particularly to Linda Lacy, who has been especially supportive of our work on this project. We genuinely appreciate everything you do for us and our readers. For this edition we owe a particular debt to Leanna Doty and Balfour Smith of Duke Law School, whose careful reading of the text helped it immeasurably, and to Duke Law students Gloria Han, Andrew Tisinger, and Wenyi Zhou for excellent research assistance.

One final word before we step aside: the materials included in this book have been ruthlessly edited for style, length, and clarity. To avoid clutter, we have left almost all those changes unmarked. While we are confident that none of our edits altered the meaning of the relevant passages, we do want to warn readers that the materials have been edited so as to maximize their value in the educational setting and, thus, attorneys looking to cite materials in court documents are advised to look to the original sources before quoting any of the materials excerpted here.

With that, we welcome you to the text. We hope you find your study of internet and telecommunications law to be a rewarding one.

Stuart Benjamin, Barak Richman, and Jim Speta

Part One

Foundations

Chapter 1

Introduction to Internet and Telecommunications Regulation

Telecommunications have been critically important to American life for at least the past century, even as the medium of communication has changed with new technologies. Similarly, the regulation of the telecommunications sector has been important to the American economy over that same time, even as the legal tools and policy strategies have changed. Both this technological history and its accompanying policy history are reflected in this book.

Telecommunications regulations, and the predecessors to this casebook, began with a focus on broadcasting, telephony, and radio spectrum. Then came mobile telephony, multichannel video programming (primarily via cable or satellite), and finally internet access. Telecommunications law, by and large, kept up, beginning most significantly with the Communications Act of 1934, Pub. L. No. 73-416, ch. 652, 48 Stat. 1064 (codified as amended at 47 U.S.C. §§ 151–609), and getting periodic updates from Congress, courts, and the agencies.

Today's economy still features broadcasting, telephony, video programming, and internet access, but one looms particularly large — the internet, of course. The centrality of the internet, in our culture, our economy, and our daily lives, elevates its significance and that of the business that comprise it, arguably far beyond its telecom predecessors. That means that a book on internet and telecommunications law requires a priority focus on internet regulation.

To be sure, this is not just a book about the internet, as the law governing those prior technologies and business models remain relevant. One reason is that traditional telecommunications services are still important in their own right. A second and perhaps more foundational reason is that current approaches to internet regulation have arisen out of earlier telecommunications regulation, so understanding the former requires familiarity with the latter. In the United States particularly, regulation still dominantly reflects the historical service categories, even as the technologies have changed. Thus, the first foundational challenge to contemporary communications law is the age-old conceptual challenge of applying old categories to new phenomena. As the telecommunications sector exhibits technological transformation, the current student or practitioner is nonetheless asked to apply principles for telephony to households that have no landline telephone service and rely instead on mobile phones or internet voice services or both. A legal field built atop a world of telephony, featuring one kind of wire and one kind of communication, now governs (just to name some examples) communications services transmitting combinations of voice, video, or data over multiple platforms using different technologies, and offering video entertainment via over-the-air broadcasting, cable television wires, satellite signals, or any device with an internet connection.

This challenge of translating old legal categories into contemporary meaning highlights a second foundational challenge: despite the unique and multiple policy challenges that the internet presents, the United States has no comprehensive internet law. The country is still chiefly governed by the Communications Act, which still has separate titles governing telephone service, broadcasting, and cable services, the platforms that provided rather distinct types of services when the Act was passed. When Congress enacted major revisions to the Communications Act (in 1996), it did not focus on the internet, and Congress has not revised the Act since. As a result, the Act — and the entire U.S. Code — lacks any comprehensive treatment of the internet.

This statutory and regulatory reality drives an important usage point, embedded in the title of the book. We will generally use "communications" to refer to the totality of electronic communications — i.e., the internet and the more traditionally regulated services (broadcast, telephony, and cable television). The latter group we will generally refer to as "telecommunications." The internet is of course a form of electronic communication that fits the dictionary definition of "telecommunications." Our separate reference to the internet reflects a common (though by no means universal) usage that distinguishes the internet from the other, more regulated services that this casebook covers. This naming convention itself reflects a framing of the internet as less regulated. There remains substantial debate about the degree to which aspects of the internet, such as broadband internet access services, should be regulated as ordinary telecommunications services, and indeed as common carriers akin to telephony providers.

Despite Congress's lack of focus on the internet, the internet's ubiquity has begun to raise genuine problems of "internet regulation." This book takes that term to mean something more limited than "internet law" or "cyberspace law," at least as those terms are more customarily used. Thus, this book addresses "internet regulation" as those bodies of statutory, agency-made, and court-made law that do, or could, address internet providers and internet platforms by virtue of the types of services that they provide, instead of simply the law applied to those whose transactions occur on the internet. While both private law (be it contract or tort) and public law (be it criminal law or government searches and seizures) have faced interesting and difficult problems adapting to the internet, this book does not include those within the scope of internet regulation.[1] Instead, the book uses the history and pol-

---

1. In the early days of the internet, Judge Frank Easterbrook famously asked whether there was any coherence to a "law of cyberspace" apart from the fact that legal problems arose on the internet. *See* Frank H. Easterbrook, Cyberspace and the Law of the Horse, 1996 U. Chi. Legal F. 207. Professor Lawrence Lessig responded by pointing to the institutional and cultural issues that a focus on

icy of telecommunications regulation as the basis for asking (among other things) whether a specialized body of regulation should be developed for the internet, and what that regulation might look like.

Lying beneath these demands to provide governance, mitigate abuses, and resolve disputes in the internet age is a set of policy tools and normative principles that we regularly, sometimes reflexively, rely upon in all matters of American law. These include the principles of competition economics, free speech, innovation policy, federalism, and individual safety, among others, that motivate the formation and implementation of law. As it becomes less clear how prior law should resolve new disputes, these underlying principles become arguably more prominent in guiding communications law across the traditional legal boundaries. These tenets assess the need for and effectiveness of regulation quite apart from the historical paths that led to the different statutory regimes.

This is the policy context into which this casebook steps. The reality is that the practitioner of communications policy—whether a representative of the Federal Communications Commission (FCC) or a regulated company or a member of the public seeking to influence policy—must make arguments at multiple levels. Effective arguments must account for the underlying technology and economics (and other policy dimensions) as well as place those arguments within an existing statutory, regulatory, and institutional structure that is tethered to history and its own internal precedents. Although this sounds daunting, it is also what makes this particular field so intellectually rich and challenging—in addition, of course, to the reality that communications remains one of the most important sectors in the modern economy.

Accordingly, Part One of this casebook begins with foundational chapters. The remainder of this chapter addresses fundamental questions about when and why a government issues regulations and the tradeoffs inherent in making regulatory policy. Chapter 2 then introduces antitrust law and Chapter 3 introduces principles of First Amendment jurisprudence that inform communications policy. We offer these at the outset because they pervade nearly the entirety of communications law and correspond to the two substantive sections of the book: antitrust law is a prelude to Part Two, which addresses economic regulation in the communications sector, and First Amendment law is a prelude to Part Three, which discusses noneconomic regulation.[2]

---

internet problems might illuminate. Lawrence Lessig, The Law of the Horse: What Cyberlaw Might Teach, 113 Harv. L. Rev. 501 (1999). Without denying Lessig's insights, this book's focus on "regulation" flows from a set of institutional and political ideas: that telecommunications regulation can be described and evaluated, and that telecommunications regulation provides, in large part, a foundation for possible internet regulation of a similar kind.

2. Although we organize the substantive chapters of this book according to economic and noneconomic regulations, we recognize that those categories overlap in important respects. Nearly all noneconomic regulations have important economic implications, and many economic regulations do not achieve their economic objectives, either from mistakenly relying on faulty economic

The chapters within each of those two parts follow a more traditional organization, framing issues largely within the context in which they arise. In Part Two, Chapters 4 through 7 review the history and assortment of traditional telecommunications regulations, and Chapters 8 through 10 discuss assorted legal and regulatory efforts to mitigate monopoly power. In Part Three, Chapters 11 and 12 discuss regulatory efforts to restrict certain content and the First Amendment restraints on those efforts, and Chapters 13 through 15 introduce assorted policies that have become central themes of internet policy: Chapter 13 on privacy, Chapter 14 on copyright, and Chapter 15 on immunities for internet intermediaries.

§ 1.A. Telecommunications as a "Regulated Industry"

Telecommunications has long been considered a "regulated industry." Telephony has been subject to special federal regulation since 1910 and broadcasting since 1927. But the fundamentals of communications regulation were established long before those dates. In fact, the key sections of Title II of the Communications Act of 1934 were lifted almost word for word from the Interstate Commerce Act of 1887, which subjected railroads to the specialized regulation of the Interstate Commerce Commission (ICC). The Interstate Commerce Act also served as the model for numerous other regulatory regimes, including air service (the Civil Aeronautics Act), trucking (the Motor Carriers Act), electricity (the Federal Power Act), and livestock (the Packers and Stockyards Act). Indeed, one could focus on regulated industries generally: the schemes of regulation governing railroads, electricity, communications, and many other industries have much in common. Communications regulation is thus a case study of a particular kind of regulation, shared at times by substantial portions of the economy.

All enterprises, of course, are subject to regulation. Even small businesses in competitive markets must adhere to contract and tort law, health and environmental prohibitions, and labor and safety regulations (among others). But describing an industry as a "regulated industry" has a particular meaning. At an institutional level, a regulated industry is typically supervised by a specialized administrative agency that implements sector-specific legislation. While the central features of regulated industries have changed over time, the classic model — the model of the Interstate Commerce Act and the original Communications Act — had three essential characteristics. First, the government (through a sector-specific, expert agency) limited entry into and exit from the market. The Communications Act of 1934, for

theory or because the regulation's economic motivation was pretextual. There certainly are other examples in which the categories bleed into each other. Still, we consider the categories to be useful pedagogical tools, as it is important to understand the motivation that underlies a regulation before either implementing or critiquing it.

example, prohibits anyone from providing interstate telephone service or transmitting using the airwaves without an appropriate license from the FCC. Second, the government regulated the key economic terms under which companies provided service. Under the 1934 Act, telephone companies were required to file, in advance of providing service, tariffs that set forth their rates and terms for all services, and the FCC was empowered to suspend, investigate, and reject those tariffs if it found them improper. This economic regulation is perhaps the hallmark of what was known as a regulated industry and became its most controversial feature. Third, government officials imposed obligations on regulated enterprises to pursue certain social policies, particularly the goal of ensuring "universal service," and had the authority to set rates to achieve those policies. Much of early telephony regulation included setting above-cost rates for some customers (e.g., businesses) to finance below-cost prices for others (e.g., residential consumers). By this definition, the Communications Act and the FCC are instruments of a sectoral regulatory framework, but the Sherman Act and the Federal Trade Commission (FTC) are not.

Much of today's telecommunications sector does not fit this description as a regulated industry. Some legacy sectors, like spectrum and cable, are still properly considered to be a regulated industry, and other areas, like broadband, have inherited some of the regulated status of their predecessors. But today's internet platforms, social media giants, and dominant software providers or device manufacturers are clearly not. The mix of regulated status of the various components of today's telecommunications sector reflects the diversity of their origins, the markets in which they operate, and the social and economic problems they are perceived to present. Moreover, today's mix might not reflect wise policy or even the policy preferences of the electorate, and there will always be a debate over whether currently unregulated activities should be regulated and vice versa. Therefore, to comprehensively examine communications regulation, one must not only identify economic areas that are regulated and those that are not; one must also appreciate the assorted economic, moral, and political motivations that prompt governments to regulate. Both policymakers and lawyers, whether interpreting regulations or designing regulatory improvements, benefit from linking the operation of a particular regulation to its normative motivation.

Below, we survey many of the common justifications for regulating the telecommunications sector. Consistent with the organization of this casebook, we organize these justifications by whether they serve economic versus noneconomic policy objectives. As we survey these justifications, we address their theoretical and factual bases, how well they have been translated into regulatory policy, and whether they remain valid as communications markets continually change. Many of these justifications are not unique to communications and can apply to many industries, just as the regulated industries model has governed many industries over time, and they also provide justifications for many non-sector-specific legal regimes, including antitrust and intellectual property law. Critically, many proffered justifications for regulations are merely pretextual, and it is critical both to recognize the politics of regulations and to scrutinize the alleged purpose, effect, and necessity of any given rule.

§ 1.A.1. Justifications for Regulation

One could argue that regulation does not need a justification, or, perhaps more precisely, that regulation needs no more justification than those with the ultimate power to regulate — generally Congress — deem adequate. At least since the New Deal and the overruling of Lochner v. New York, 198 U.S. 45 (1905),[3] courts have not considered themselves in the business of determining whether Congress had an *adequate* justification for regulating. Indeed, even during the so-called *Lochner* era, courts provided considerable leeway to regulators in industries "affected with a public interest."[4]

Recognizing that all regulation is essentially a political act does not make an inquiry into the justifications for regulation fruitless. And, indeed, in the regulated industries field, one can identify a more or less coherent set of justifications that have been offered for specialized regulation. Because political actors make arguments, they appeal to history, and they operate within a defined set of institutions. They also operate within a wider intellectual discourse, in which academics and other commentators assess both the arguments made for and the effectiveness of the regulation offered. At a more practical level, regulated industries law operates within the constraints of administrative law, which means that courts determine whether an agency has violated the Administrative Procedure Act (APA). This role requires the courts to decide whether an agency action is consistent with its statutory authority and whether the agency acted in a manner that is not "arbitrary [and] capricious." 5 U.S.C. § 706(2)(A).

In communications policy, the justifications for regulation can be broadly (and coarsely) divided into market-failure justifications and other justifications. Put more simply, some justifications for regulation are based on the notion that markets, if left unrestrained, will not achieve the desired and efficient outcomes of competitive prices and optimal output. Other justifications are based on the notion that, even if these markets can achieve these economic outcomes, they nevertheless do not provide the socially optimal level or mix of services.

§ 1.A.1.a. Market Failure Justifications

Markets can fail, and thus benefit from regulation, in a number of scenarios that do not characterize the communications sector. Factories that pollute impose costs on nonconsumers and are not easily factored into the costs of production, and these "negative externalities" are a common justification for environmental laws.

3. *See* West Coast Hotel Co. v. Parrish, 300 U.S. 379 (1937) (effectively overruling *Lochner*).

4. *See* German Alliance Ins. Co. v. Lewis, 233 U.S. 389 (1914) (holding that regulation of fire insurance rates is constitutional because fire insurance is "affected with a public interest").

Manufacturers of, say, pharmaceuticals are subject to disclosure and safety regulations because consumers cannot readily or efficiently identify the efficacy of the products. Although communications firms are affected by regulations that correct negative externalities and information asymmetries (for example, a smartphone manufacturer must abide by environmental laws, and a wireless provider must issue contracts with transparent pricing), these are not the market failure justifications that typify communications regulations.

Controlling Monopoly Power. The regulations that do typify the sector relate to the particular economic challenges — and the professed market failures — that are pervasive in communications. Historically, most regulation of communications firms, beginning with wireline companies, rested on concerns over monopoly. In market economies, the preferred method of supplying goods and services is to rely on competitive markets, with many firms offering substitutable goods and services to well-informed customers. Competition forces firms to price at the marginal cost — the cost of producing each additional unit — of the relevant good or service, which is the market price that generates the greatest economic welfare. Similarly, competition tends to reward firms that produce goods and services efficiently; because their costs are lower, these firms can underprice less efficient rivals. Ideally then, competition forces firms both to put their resources to their most productive uses (what economists sometimes call "productive efficiency") and to sell their products to anyone willing to pay a price equal to the firm's marginal costs of producing them (what economists sometimes call "allocative efficiency"). Monopoly is a market failure simply because monopolists maximize their profit by producing a lower quantity of goods or services and charging higher prices than what is generated in the competitive market.

There are several reasons, however, why monopolized markets have been a frequent presence in the telecommunications sector and in many instances are more economically desirable than competitive markets. The first reason, rooted in the logic of many sector-specific regulatory schemes, is that many telecommunications markets can be characterized as natural monopolies. What is a natural monopoly? Consider the following excerpt from Judge Richard Posner, taken from a case in which a would-be cable television franchisee accused the Indianapolis government of violating antitrust law by granting a de facto monopoly in the local cable market:

> The cost of the cable grid appears to be the biggest cost of a cable television system and to be largely invariant to the number of subscribers the system has. [O]nce the grid is in place — once every major street has a cable running above or below it that can be hooked up to the individual residences along the street — the cost of adding another subscriber probably is small. If so, the average cost of cable television would be minimized by having a single company in any given geographical area; for if there is more than one company and therefore more than one grid, the cost of each grid will be spread over a smaller number of subscribers, and the average cost per subscriber, and hence price, will be higher.

> If the foregoing accurately describes conditions in Indianapolis, it describes what economists call a "natural monopoly," wherein the benefits, and indeed the very possibility, of competition are limited. You can start with a competitive free-for-all — different cable television systems frantically building out their grids and signing up subscribers in an effort to bring down their average costs faster than their rivals — but eventually there will be only a single company, because until a company serves the whole market it will have an incentive to keep expanding in order to lower its average costs. In the interim there may be wasteful duplication of facilities. This duplication may lead not only to higher prices to cable television subscribers, at least in the short run, but also to higher costs to other users of the public ways, who must compete with the cable television companies for access to them. An alternative procedure is to pick the most efficient competitor at the outset, give him a monopoly, and extract from him in exchange a commitment to provide reasonable service at reasonable rates. In essence [the plaintiff's] antitrust allegations accuse the City of Indianapolis of having taken this alternative route to the monopoly that may be the inevitable destination to which all routes converge.

Omega Satellite Prods. Co. v. Indianapolis, 694 F.2d 119, 126 (7th Cir. 1982).

As Judge Posner pointed out, the presence of a natural monopoly turns the logic of competition on its head. A natural monopoly, in the rare cases where it occurs, is said to exist where the costs of production are such that it is less expensive for demand to be met by one firm than it would be for that same demand to be met by more than one firm. This occurs when, over a sufficiently large range of output, the addition of each new customer lowers the average cost of serving every other customer. *Total* costs for the natural monopoly firm increase as demand increases; the important feature is that the firm's average cost *per unit* of output declines with increasing demand. Critically, a natural monopoly is possible only if per-unit costs decline over *the range of output that the market will demand.* If per-unit costs continuously decline, then a single firm will always be able to produce at a lower average cost than any combination of multiple firms. Thus, the monopoly can both generate more output and profitably charge lower prices than a competitive market, making competition entirely undesirable and possibly futile.

Declining per-unit average cost typically occurs when a large fixed expense must be incurred no matter how many units are sold and then the incremental costs of adding units or users decreases as output expands. Many firms in the telecommunications sector arguably fit this description. A local telephone company, for example, had to build its network of wires, purchase switching machinery, create databases, and hire personnel before it could transmit its first call. But once it constructed its network, the cost of extending service to an additional location (little more than flipping a switch) was low, and because it gets easier adding households to an established network, the cost of adding each additional phone service thus declined as the number of callers on the network increases. The same economics likely apply to most other wired services like cable television and wired broadband internet.

However, even if a market is most efficiently serviced by a monopolist, consumers are vulnerable if the market is left unsupervised. First, the monopolist can price at will, especially if the good is a necessity (like water, electricity, and perhaps telephony). Second, the market might lose efficiency if a competitor enters. Thus, the typical regulatory framework for natural monopolies involves a quid-pro-quo with the government: the natural monopoly agrees to price regulation, and the government ensures that competitors will not enter the natural monopolist's market. Usually, more regulation then follows: the government usually feels compelled to monitor the quality of the service provided, make sure that its citizens are being treated fairly, complaints or repair requests are tended to swiftly, and the like. If typical market forces are precluded from forcing the monopolist to provide an optimal price-cost-quality service mix, then government regulations ostensibly fill the market's place.

In the following chapters, consider whether communications markets are, in fact, naturally monopolistic and whether the regulatory responses have been appropriate. There is reason to question, and perhaps be skeptical, of many claims that certain firms are natural monopolies and thereby require comprehensive regulation. Many industries, including automobile manufacturers, satellite companies, and biotechnology firms, exhibit high fixed costs and low marginal costs, but these sectors nonetheless appear to thrive with competition. Moreover, it is hard to imagine any industry exhibiting declining incremental costs for an endless range of output — eventually, marginal costs will go up (one more factory to build, one more technology to commercialize). One of the prevailing challenges of regulated industries is that both the government and the provider immensely enjoy elements of the arrangement: the government can assume additional powers, and the provider is protected from competition. For this reason, governments sometimes grant monopolies when there is little economic justification to do so (as we discuss in Chapter 7.C, many localities granted monopolies to cable television providers, until Congress prohibited it).

Navigating Network Effects. Perhaps the feature that distinguishes communications markets from other large industries with high fixed costs and declining marginal costs — and the reason that some communications markets have tended towards monopoly — is the phenomenon of network effects. Such effects arise when the value a consumer places on a good or service increases as the number of other consumers that simultaneously consume the good increases. The basic intuition is this: telephone service is not worth much to me if I am the only one with a telephone (or email account, social media account, or any number of other connectivity-based goods), and the value of having a telephone increases based on the number of people that I can call. If more than one network exists and the networks are not interconnected, then consumers will be drawn (all other things being equal) to the network with the greatest number of customers (or, more precisely, the network that consumers expect to have the greatest number of customers). And, eventually, smaller networks will either fail, be absorbed, or focus narrowly on niche services that are more highly valued by a small number of customers.

The telephone network, of course, provides the paradigmatic example of network effects: the more subscribers the network has, the more desirable it is to be on the network. Network effects can also arise in virtual networks and, in the internet age, have become increasingly common. For example, in the early days of the internet, the FCC determined that a then-dominant player (AOL) enjoyed powerful network effects in its instant messaging service.[5] More recently, some have argued that Facebook enjoys network effects for the same reasons—the value of a Facebook account is a function of the number of other Facebook accounts. And in many digital markets, where interoperability is critical (i.e., my computer needs to be able to read my software, or my web browser needs to read the webpage, or my data analysis client needs to read the database), certain technological standards generate valuable network effects. Microsoft's operating system was so valuable because programmers wrote software to run on that platform. And Apple's App Store is a platform for thousands of programs, which draws both more programmers and more iPhone purchases.

The presence of both scale economies (another way of describing high fixed costs and declining marginal costs) and network externalities in communications services explain the industries' strong tendency towards monopolies, and thus the comparative pervasiveness of regulation in the telecommunications sector compared to other industries. But when monopolies are not deemed to be natural, and competition is both possible and preferable, then generally applicable anti-monopoly and antitrust laws are likely preferable. Many markets, even in the presence of scale economies and network externalities, are better served by competition.

Supplying Public Goods. A third market failure justification on which much communications regulation—particularly of broadcasting—has been (at least historically) based is the "public goods" problem. A public good is any product or service for which demand is nonrivalrous (one consumer's consumption of a good does not affect any other person's ability to consume that same good) and nonexcludable (it is costly or impossible to exclude others from using the good). Classic examples of public goods include lighthouses and national defense. One person's watching a television broadcast, for example, does not affect any other person's ability to watch that same broadcast signal, unlike the manner in which, say, one person's consumption of a banana makes it impossible for anyone else to consume that same banana. The implication of nonrivalry is that the marginal cost of serving an additional customer is zero, which, in classic economics, suggests that the price for the good should be zero as well. That cannot be the case, of course, for television service has initial fixed costs, such as the costs of producing the programs, of erecting the

5. *See* Applications for Consent to the Transfer of Control of Licenses and Section 214 Authorizations by Time Warner Inc. and America Online, Inc., Transferors, to AOL Time Warner Inc., Transferee, Memorandum Opinion and Order, 16 FCC Rcd. 6547, 6627–29 (2001).

antennae, and of operating the station—and those costs need to be recovered. But a competitive market may underproduce public goods because of the difficulty of setting a price that recovers costs.

Nonexcludability compounds the problem. For instance, under the original broadcast technology, the owner of video programming had no technological means to exclude nonpaying customers. If a seller can exclude nonpaying buyers (and prevent resale), then the seller may be able to set a price above marginal cost. Still, in competitive markets, nonrivalry alone can result in underprovision, even if excludability is possible.

§ 1.A.1.b. Noneconomic Justifications

Market failures are, of course, not the only bases for communications regulation and, in many regards, not the most important. Many aspects of communications regulation respond to concerns that a well-functioning market is unlikely to provide a desired outcome without regulatory interventions.

Universal Service. One of the most salient and deeply rooted policy objectives in communications regulation is universal service. The term universal service was actually coined by the Bell System and its leader Theodore Vail, who operated the company under the motto "One Policy, One System, Universal Service."[6] From a regulatory perspective, no efficient market will provide service to everyone, for there will always be a set of customers unable or unwilling to pay the marginal cost of the service, even under a natural monopoly where marginal costs continue downwards. Nonetheless, a staple of telecommunications policy has been to extend access to all users.

Given the network externalities in most communications markets, universal service might be categorized as an economic justification since it enhances the value of any network to any individual user—and, as we will see, economic arguments have been deployed to justify universal service for basic communications. But most arguments for universal service, especially from representatives of rural communities, have been built atop notions of equity and citizenship. Communications service is hardly the only, or most obvious, basic good that must be distributed equally, as various government programs provide some level of food, housing, medical treatment, education, and certain other goods, but it is one of the services that has

6. The corporation was known as the Bell System or Bell but was named American Telephone & Telegraph, or AT&T, after AT&T bought American Bell (its parent company) in 1899. The current AT&T has fairly little in common with the AT&T that provided telephone services to most of the United States, usually as a regulated monopoly, from the late 19th century to 1984. To avoid confusion whether a reference to "AT&T" in the casebook is to the pre-1984 or post-1984 company, and because the network of companies that provided telephone services was often called the Bell System, in this casebook we generally refer to the pre-1984 dominant provider of telephone services as the Bell System or Bell. Similarly, we refer to the key component of the pre-1984 company—the telephony provider—as the Bell Telephone Company. When we refer to AT&T, we are generally talking about the post-1984 entity.

been successfully provided universally. One reason, surely, is that declining marginal costs make the economic burden of providing universal service manageable, but other core democratic values, including free speech and access to information, might also explain why universal communications access, particularly the provision of basic telephone service and free, over-the-air television, has been a longstanding policy priority.

Service Mix. Communications policy has also reflected policy values that prioritize some services or content over others, despite what the market might prefer. With respect to service mix, policymakers might prioritize local telephony over long-distance, or consider emergency 911 services to be essential. These policies have economic justifications — for example, educational programming and emergency services might be under-supplied public goods, or local service creates more valuable network effects than long distance — but the economic justifications only go so far, and the rhetoric supporting these policies tend to rely on the language of values more than the language of efficiency.

Content regulations also have economic justifications — for example, a reduction in indecent content might lead to a more productive workforce — but are typically supported by classic paternalistic arguments that focus on the individual consumer: the person who consumes good content will benefit from that consumption but will not consume as much absent regulation. (And the converse for bad content.) The underlying assumption is that individuals often do not know what is in their own long-term best interests, and perhaps even their future selves would be thankful for interventions that changed their earlier consumption patterns.

A different, though complementary, argument is based on externalities: one person's consumption of content may affect another person's well-being. For instance, as we discuss in Chapter 11, there are pervasive fears that individuals exposed to certain stimuli — indecent content, violence, or fake news — might then behave in antisocial ways. Similarly, some argue that individuals exposed to opposing viewpoints are likely to become more informed and thereby more thoughtful and balanced members of their community. Thus restrictions on content can be justified and framed in terms of paternalism, positive externalities, and/or public goods.

As this discussion illustrates, many policy debates implicate both economic and noneconomic arguments. One interesting example is the debate over network neutrality regulation (discussed in Chapter 6). Advocates of network neutrality regulation invoke market failure arguments, contending that broadband access markets are alarmingly concentrated and that this concentration gives broadband carriers the incentive and opportunity to foreclose access to some content and applications. They also make arguments relying on the logic of network externalities and public goods, suggesting that network access rules drive deployment of broadband services at lower prices, increasing the percentage of the public that subscribes to broadband. Finally (although this summary is far from exhaustive), advocates have invoked noneconomic justifications, saying that net neutrality regulation would advance a culture of participatory speech. Needless to say, sometimes economic justifications mask noneconomic motivations, and vice versa.

§ 1.A.2. The Challenges of Regulation

So far, we have discussed the benefits of regulation and its use as a set of legal tools designed to correct problems (real or perceived). But what of its costs? Part of the movement towards deregulation since the late 1970s reflects an increased appreciation for (or at least an increased focus on) the costs of regulation and the potential negatives of a regulatory system. In other words, modern regulatory analysis consists of a cost/benefit analysis not just of the industry that regulation seeks to address but also of regulation itself.

The most measurable cost of regulation is the cost of the regulatory structure itself. The FCC and FTC each have more than 1000 employees and a budget in the hundreds of millions of dollars. One can add to these sums the cost of parallel state regulators, judicial costs created by litigation under communications regulation, and industry expenditures on attorneys and other personnel to comply with regulation.

Beyond these direct costs is the recognition that regulation itself creates market distortions. Consider the following sequence under a typical regulatory regime: A regulated company wanting to enter a new business, offer a new service, or pursue a new business plan must first ask permission from the regulator. To do so, it must submit a plan and await permission, which imposes costly delays. Additionally, in going through the public regulatory process, it discloses its plans and creates certain opportunities for others. At a minimum, the disclosure required by the application process can eliminate a first-mover advantage in introducing an innovation. More problematically, the process can allow incumbents to oppose new applications that threaten their entrenched market positions. Whereas a free market would invite the innovator to pursue profit opportunities unilaterally, a regulated framework requires disclosure and delay.

Such a scenario highlights two additional problems. The first is the informational problems of regulation. Ideally, the regulator would approve of socially desirable business actions and prohibit or require revisions to undesirable actions, but that assumes that the regulator has the ability to investigate the relevant technological and market information and has the expertise and judgment to properly assess the evidence gathered. However — and practically by definition — the company knows more about itself than any regulator can. Information asymmetries mean not just that the regulator must engage in costly (in both time and expense) efforts to gather information, but also that it is possible that the regulator, from a social perspective, simply makes the wrong decision. This is a well-recognized limitation of regulation. In the opinion in which it approved the Bell breakup, the district court considered a behavioral injunction as an alternative remedy — essentially an order forbidding anticompetitive behavior that the court itself would supervise. In dismissing that option, the court commented on testimony that it had received on the effectiveness of FCC regulation:

> Two former chiefs of the FCC's Common Carrier Bureau, the agency charged with regulating AT&T, testified that the Commission is not and never has been capable of effective enforcement of the laws governing AT&T's behavior. In their view, this inability was due to structural, budgetary, and financial deficiencies within the FCC as well as to the difficulty in obtaining information from AT&T. Whatever the true cause, it seems clear that the problems of supervision by a relatively poorly-financed, poorly-staffed government agency over a gigantic corporation with almost unlimited resources in funds and gifted personnel are no more likely to be overcome in the future than they were in the past.

United States v. American Tel. & Tel. Co., 552 F. Supp. 131, 168 (1982). This is obviously not a sanguine perspective on the effectiveness of telecommunications regulation.

The second problem is the political realities of the regulatory state. The informational problems described above suggest that agencies make mistakes despite trying their best to issue rules that would lead to socially optimal outcomes. A political view of regulation, one sometimes called the positive view of regulation, recognizes that regulators are influenced by interested parties seeking to further their own interests. Thus, regulators might issue rules that harm consumers and the public not because of informational mistakes but because of pressures from the industry they regulate (or a combination of both, where the regulator is misinformed by the entity). It requires little imagination to realize that, when regulation exists, the regulated companies themselves will make arguments that serve their own narrow economic interests instead of the broader public interest.

Moreover, it is not just regulators — the agencies — that are subject to political influence. Legislators, the executive branch, judges, and other political actors have interests that do not neatly align with consumers or a broad public interest, and each of these parties in their own way can influence regulatory outcomes. "Public choice" economics began to evaluate regulatory systems from this perspective in the 1960s and 1970s and became part of the intellectual movement supporting deregulation. Public choice theory assumes that all government actors maximize, at least in part, their own private goals, so that the key question regarding public actors is what they want to maximize. Consider, first, legislators. The basic premise is that those who desire to become legislators (for whatever personal reasons) desire principally to remain legislators. In some cases, they may adopt policies that are broadly popular, even if they are not economically efficient. For example, legislators may demand that telephone companies subsidize prices for residential consumers and charge more for business service — reducing the price for a service that most voters would care very much about, even if this cross-subsidization causes inefficiently high prices for business services. Businesses don't vote; individual households do. In other cases, legislators may maximize their chances of being reelected by adopting policies that respond to industry desires, because industry is in a position to offer greater campaign contributions, and such contributions are necessary to reelection campaigns. Alternatively, rational legislators may threaten regulation against established businesses but, after raising campaign contributions, take no action at all.

Regulators may have similar personal interests. If one values being a regulator, then one may value even more being an "important" regulator, which means seeking to expand the regulatory scope of one's office or agency. Relatedly, an agency that regulates more or that charges higher industry fees may fund higher salaries or more non-salary perks, such as cars and drivers for busy commissioners. Alternatively, a rational regulator may recognize that most regulators serve limited terms and, in considering future employment options, may realize that employment within the regulated industry (or as a lawyer or lobbyist representing the industry) is the most likely and most remunerative path. This may constrain a regulator's desire to take actions adverse to industry. Even apart from narrow self-interest, industry may be more present in a regulator's life, due to better funding, better advocacy, and more frequent appearances. For all of these reasons, a regulatory body may become captured by the industry it regulates.

One can often see the costs of regulation, at least partly in hand with public choice theory, not just from the identification of a policy objective but from the selection of a particular policy instrument. If Congress, for example, wants more educational programming on television (aside: what might justify such an intervention in the television market? Does this have an economic rationale?), the simplest and most direct approach is to subsidize its production; an alternative is to tax non-educational programming (or auction the broadcast licenses) and use the funds for the government to produce educational programming. But under a regulatory regime in which licenses are issued to broadcasters, an easier alternative is to condition licenses on a pledge by licensees to broadcast educational programming. This is an example of what is called "taxation by regulation," which refers to any situation where the government imposes a financial burden on a regulated party not directly, but instead by requiring a particular unprofitable behavior. The phrase is designed to remind policymakers to consider the explicit alternative—namely, actually taxing the regulated parties in that same amount and then using those monies to further the policy goal at issue. There are myriad examples of taxation by regulation in this book. Most economists would argue that taxation by regulation is a costlier—i.e., less efficient and more distortive—manner of governing in the public interest, yet it's a technique that is replete in telecommunications regulation and elsewhere.

For their part, members of the industry should be expected to make arguments that are in their own economic interest. But the public choice perspective on the regulatory system takes this insight a step further. Regulation can give companies a competitive advantage just as surely as can a new technology or good advertising or any other business feature. In the context of traditional regulation, where companies are not permitted to provide service without a government license, legal barriers to entry are absolute and can be much more permanent than any economic barrier. As dominant as the Bell System was when long distance was provided by copper wire, the invention of microwave transmission technology radically changed the economics of long distance and made competition (more) possible. And yet new entrants into this field needed the FCC's permission to offer each new kind of service, which gave Bell the opportunity to fight. Simply stated, an incumbent usually likes barriers to entry, because they reduce competition. Similarly, a highly capitalized firm often likes regulations, if the costs of its own compliance are outweighed by the benefit (to the highly capitalized firm) of those compliance costs making it harder for other, less well capitalized firms to become threatening competitors.

The realities of the regulatory state thus are not just a cost or distortion in the marketplace, but they also are targets for corporate strategy. Regulation (and lobbying) is just another place in which companies invest, and they rationally invest in favorable regulatory outcomes (and perhaps outcomes that injure their competitors) just like they invest in product design or reducing manufacturing costs. In other words, companies will not simply live within pre-existing regulation and manage it in the best way possible. Companies will affirmatively seek legislation and regulation, and "public affairs" or "government relations" becomes important to corporate performance just as effective financing and marketing.

To be sure, public choice theory does not necessarily explain everything, and some notable legislative and regulatory acts (such as airline deregulation) defy public choice explanations. Moreover, we believe that legislators and regulators usually act in what they perceive to be the public's best interests, all things considered. Nonetheless, we also believe that the public choice lens is an important perspective to consider when evaluating any given policy.

§ 1.B. The Institutions of Telecommunications Policy

Having summarized the reasons for internet and telecommunications regulation, we now turn to the basic institutional choices that must be confronted in communications policymaking. What entities engage in regulation, how are they structured, and how do they shape regulatory policy?

§ 1.B.1. Why Agencies?

Just as there is no coherent body of "internet law," Congress also has not created an "internet agency." There is, however, an agency to which Congress has delegated authority over telecommunications, and that agency—the FCC—has used its authority over electronic communications to regulate aspects of the internet. The FCC is by no means the only agency relevant to internet policy. In particular, the FTC and the Department of Justice (DOJ) enforce the antitrust and consumer protection laws and accordingly play important roles in governing internet commerce.[7] We discuss these agencies briefly below, and throughout this casebook, but we start with a more fundamental question: why agencies?

Consider the regulation of the private use of wireless frequencies (often called "the spectrum"). Government regulation of the spectrum could have been achieved through a number of different mechanisms — utilizing courts, legislatures, and/or agencies, on the federal and/or state level. Admittedly, some approaches would have been more complicated than others. For example, leaving spectrum regulation to state entities might have introduced significant coordination, compliance, and enforcement costs because, whether intentionally or not, telecommunications transmissions (particularly broadcasts, which generally radiate in all directions) frequently cross state lines.[8]

As we discuss in Chapter 9, for a period in the 1920s, common law courts played a significant role in regulating the use of the spectrum. Pointing to such history, Professor Thomas Hazlett has suggested that, had the model of common law adjudication of wireless spectrum been allowed to develop, it would have led to more efficient uses of the wireless spectrum than under the oversight of the FCC. Thomas W. Hazlett, The Rationality of U.S. Regulation of the Broadcast Spectrum, 33 J.L. & Econ. 133 (1990). Interestingly, an evolution from common law to administrative law can be seen in telephony as well as spectrum: the English law of common carriage was a feature of the common law long before it was imposed by statute. *See* James B. Speta, A Common Carrier Approach to Internet Interconnection, 54 Fed. Comm. L.J. 225 (2002).

Even assuming a preference for regulators with a national purview, there were still several options on the federal level. Spectrum regulation could have been left, for example, to a specialized federal court with national jurisdiction (like the Court

---

7. Other agencies, in addition to the FCC and the antitrust agencies, play important roles in telecommunications policy. The National Telecommunications and Information Administration (NTIA), located within the Department of Commerce, manages all the spectrum assigned to the federal government (whereas the FCC manages private spectrum usage). The determination of which frequencies will be allocated for government versus private use (and thus between NTIA and FCC control) is jointly determined by the NTIA and FCC. 47 U.S.C. § 922. As we discuss in Chapter 9, given the large amount of spectrum occupied by the federal government, these decisions are particularly significant.

One international entity also bears mention. Radio waves do not respect geopolitical boundaries, so it is necessary for spectrum allocation in the United States to conform to rules established by the International Telecommunications Union (ITU), an organization established by treaty. Particularly for terrestrial transmission of radio waves, ITU regulations are typically not very confining. Usually, within any range of the spectrum, international standards permit a wide variety of uses. Further, international law does not restrict any spectrum usage within a country so long as that use does not radiate into other countries.

8. Spectrum does not respect national boundaries either, and yet we are governed by a federal commission and not a global one. Thus, while countries engage in bilateral coordination (say, between the U.S. and Mexico) as well as multilateral coordination through the International Telecommunications Union, the basic authority over spectrum rests at the national level.

of Appeals for the Federal Circuit, which hears all patent appeals). Or regulatory authority could have been vested in an agency directly controlled by the President rather than the more independent FCC that eventually was created.[9]

There is no ready answer to this basic question of institutional design. The main arguments that carried the day were twofold. First, it was widely believed that an independent administrative agency could develop relevant expertise. The argument was that judges are generalists with too few resources at hand, and, though Congress and the executive branch have greater resources at their disposal, they too lack the narrow focus that was thought to enhance the development of sound regulation in this complicated area.[10] Second, it was similarly believed that using an independent agency was the only way to sufficiently insulate spectrum decisions from the political process. During the period when the Federal Radio Commission (FRC) and, later, the FCC were created, there was widespread belief that politically insulated expert administrators would do a better job of managing complex regulatory undertakings than would their masters in Congress and the White House.[11]

Note that Congress could have given commissioners even more independence (life tenure?). But Congress showed no interest in offering that much independence. One person's insulation, after all, is another's unaccountability. Instead, Congress settled upon a commission with five commissioners each serving a five-year term of office. The President nominates commissioners, who are confirmed by the Senate, and designates one commissioner to serve as Chair, which effectively means that the Chair is from the President's party.[12]

---

9. Interestingly, in 1927 the House of Representatives wanted to leave licensing power with the Secretary of Commerce. The Senate did not, instead preferring an independent regulatory commission. The Radio Act of 1927 reflected a compromise between the two. For one year, a geographically balanced five-member commission was to exercise the government's licensing function; then that function would revert to the Secretary of Commerce. Senator Clarence Dill of Washington, the Senate's expert on radio and a key figure in drafting the Act, liked the compromise because, understanding both Congress and bureaucracy, he believed "if we ever got a commission, we would never get rid of it." Erik Barnouw, A Tower in Babel: A History of Broadcasting in the United States, Vol. 1 199 (1966). He was right. Congress ultimately abandoned the provision to return powers to the Commerce Department, and the successor to the "one year agency," the FCC, remains with us.

10. It is, of course, debatable whether a narrow focus is preferable. After all, what looks like admirable focus to one person may look like blinders to another. And note that, precisely because a narrowly focused agency deals with a smaller number of regulated entities than would an agency with a broader purview, the potential for the agency to be captured by the industry it regulates may be greater.

11. Although the FRC was created before the New Deal and the FCC was created during it, one commonality between the periods was a belief in the wisdom of governance via independent regulatory commissions. *See* Joseph B. Eastman, The Place of the Independent Commission, 12 Const. Rev. 95 (1928); James M. Landis, The Administrative Process (1938).

12. Replacements for commissioners who leave during their term serve only for the unexpired portion, and there can be no more than a bare majority of commissioners from any one political party. These and other structural details are codified at 47 U.S.C. § 154.

§ 1.B.2. The Federal Communications Commission

§ 1.B.2.a. FCC Origins and Predecessors

Before 1934, telegraph, telephone, and radio communications were governed by separate statutes and separate governmental bodies. Radio was first regulated by the Radio Act of 1912, which required all users of wireless frequencies (often called the spectrum) to obtain a license and placed licensing authority with the U.S. Secretary of Commerce.[13] Fifteen years later Congress passed the Radio Act of 1927, ch. 169, 44 Stat. 1162 (1927), which repealed the 1912 Act. Like its predecessor, the 1927 Act stipulated that spectrum could be used only upon grant of license. And, for the first time, it formally declared the electromagnetic spectrum to be government property and moved the authority for issuing such licenses from the Secretary of Commerce to a new Federal Radio Commission.

These statues did not address wireline communications such as telegraphy or telephony, and the regulation of such communications developed separately from regulation of radio. The first statute to regulate telephone service was the Mann-Elkins Act of 1910, ch. 309, 36 Stat. 539, enacted more than 15 years after the original Bell telephone patents had expired and well after numerous independent telephone carriers had entered into competition with the Bell System. The Mann-Elkins Act assigned regulatory jurisdiction over telephony to the ICC, which already had authority over the railroads as well as telegraphy and radiotelegraphy.

The mandate of the Mann-Elkins Act was fairly narrow by current standards. The Act categorized telephone service providers as "common carriers" — i.e., carriers that were "obligated to provide service on request at just and reasonable rates, without unjust discrimination or undue preference." Essential Communications Systems, Inc. v. AT&T, 610 F.2d 1114, 1118 (3d Cir. 1979); *see* Mann-Elkins Act, ch. 309, §§ 7 & 12. The ICC's charge was to enforce these common carrier requirements. The Mann-Elkins Act, however, neither required that telephone carriers file tariffs (rate plans) nor authorized the ICC to implement such a requirement. The Act thus gave the agency very limited authority, and the ICC, in turn, largely adopted a strategy of benign neglect towards telephone service, holding only four proceedings to investigate telephone rates between 1910 and 1934. Peter W. Huber, Michael K. Kellogg & John Thorne, Federal Telecommunications Law 215 (2d ed. 1999). To be sure, the ICC did try actively to regulate merger and acquisition behavior in the telephone industry. Nonetheless, the ICC was far more concerned with regulating railroads than with regulating telephones and did little to oversee the performance of the communications industry.

The ICC was not the only regulatory authority concerned with communications, however. Unlike radio, telephony was subject not just to federal oversight, but

13. Ch. 287, 37 Stat. 302 (1912) (repealed 1927). Congress had previously passed the Wireless Ship Act, ch. 379, 36 Stat. 629 (1910) (repealed 1954), which required all passenger ships to carry wireless sets.

to state regulation as well. State regulators reviewed rates, established accounting rules, and implemented service requirements related to local telephone service. The states' regulatory sphere was strictly limited to intrastate telephone service and its related facilities. But given that the vast bulk of telephone calls were typically local, this limitation did not mean that state commissions were weak or insignificant regulatory forces. The boundary between state and federal regulatory jurisdiction over telephone carriers has long been an area of vigorous dispute.[14]

§ 1.B.2.b. The Communications Act of 1934

The Communications Act of 1934 replaced the 1927 Act. The Act extended jurisdiction over communications to an agency focused on communications law rather than assigning such jurisdiction to entities that had other concerns, such as the ICC or the Department of Commerce. And instead of creating separate experts for each communications field, the 1934 Act provided for a single regulatory agency—the FCC—for wireline communication (like telephony) and wireless communication.[15]

The 1934 Act has been amended numerous times, and several of those amendments have been sufficiently extensive that they are often referred to as Acts in and of themselves, despite being incorporated into the 1934 Act. The most prominent example of these extensive amendments is the Telecommunications Act of 1996.[16] By convention "the Communications Act" refers to the 1934 Act and these later amendments, and we follow that convention.

The Communications Act is codified at Title 47 of the United States Code and is divided into seven subchapters or "Titles."[17] Of particular interest for our purposes are Titles I, II, III, and VI. Title I, 47 U.S.C. §§ 151–162, sets forth general provisions pertaining to the structure, jurisdiction, and operation of the FCC. Part of the significance of Title I is that it provides the FCC with some authority to impose some regulations on new technologies that are not covered by one of the other titles. Titles II, III, and VI differ in that they prescribe distinct sets of regulation for ostensibly distinct categories of services, service providers, and technologies.

---

14. We address jurisdictional issues primarily in Chapter 7.

15. On the 1934 Act's origins, see generally A Legislative History of the Communications Act of 1934 (Max D. Paglin ed. 1989); Speta, *supra*, at 261–65.

16. Pub. L. No. 104-104, 110 Stat. 56. Others include the Cable Communications Policy Act of 1984, Pub. L. No. 98-549, 98 Stat. 2779, the Cable Television Consumer Protection and Competition Act of 1992, Pub. L. No. 102-385, 106 Stat. 1460. In this book, we will often refer to those laws by their own names, but as we note above they are treated as statutory amendments to the Communications Act of 1934. The 1934 Act also abolished the FRC and repealed the Mann-Elkins Act.

17. For most of the provisions of the Communications Act, a reference to a section "of the Communications Act" corresponds to its location in 47 U.S.C. So, for example, § 201 of the Communications Act is codified at 47 U.S.C. § 201. This is not true of Title I (too old) or Title VI (too new). For Title I, § 1 of the Communications Act is codified at 47 U.S.C. § 151, § 2 is codified at 47 U.S.C. § 152, and so on. For Title VI, § 601 of the Communications Act is codified at 47 U.S.C. § 521, § 602 of the Communications Act is codified at 47 U.S.C. § 522, and so on.

Under Title II of the Act, *id.* §§ 201–276, were the telephone and telegraph companies that transmitted information by wire, operated as common carriers, and should therefore, it was assumed, be subject to classic public utility regulation. As such, Title II envisioned a role for the FCC in regulating the entry, rates, and services of common carriers, auditing their books, and assuring that they provided nondiscriminatory access to all.

Title III of the Act, *id.* §§ 301–399B, establishes the regulatory regime for regulating the private use of wireless frequencies. Under Title III, broadcasters were not to be regulated as (and indeed did not behave as) common carriers. It focuses on the licensing process — deciding who should be licensed to broadcast, on what frequencies, and in which communities. Notably, in contrast to Title II, Title III says nothing about controlling rates or providing equal access to broadcast stations. Finally, Title VI, *id.* §§ 521–573, addresses cable services and, obviously, governs the regulation of cable television as well as many other services provided over the cable infrastructure.[18]

Many provisions of the Communications Act authorize the FCC to make decisions that it finds consistent with the "public interest, convenience, or necessity."[19] This might sound like an enormous degree of discretion (and it is). Indeed, the first general counsel of the FRC (which was governed by similar language in the Radio Act of 1927) said

> [O]nly an indefinite and very elastic standard should be prescribed for the regulation of an art and a field of human endeavor which is progressing and changing at so rapid a pace as is radio communication. 'Public interest, convenience or necessity' means about as little as any phrase that the drafters of the Act could have used and still comply with the constitutional requirement that there be some standard to guide the administrative wisdom of the licensing authority.

Louis G. Caldwell, The Standard of Public Interest, Convenience or Necessity as Used in the Radio Act of 1927, 1 Air L. Rev. 295, 296 (1930). But there are constraints. First, the Communications Acts' provisions often give further guidance — they generally

---

18. Title VI was not, of course, part of the original 1934 Act because cable service did not then exist. It was added over time through amendments to the Act, notably in the 1984 and 1992 Cable Acts mentioned above. (Before that time, the FCC relied on its Title I authority to regulate cable television.)

19. Or sometimes "public convenience, interest, or necessity." *See, e.g.*, 47 U.S.C. § 303 (statutory section entitled "Powers and duties of Commission" that begins: "Except as otherwise provided in this chapter, the Commission from time to time, as public convenience, interest, or necessity requires, shall — (a) Classify radio stations; (b) Prescribe the nature of the service to be rendered by each class of licensed stations and each station within any class," etc.); 47 U.S.C. § 307(c)(1) (empowering the FCC to renew a broadcast license "if the Commission finds that public interest, convenience, and necessity would be served thereby"); 47 U.S.C. § 254(b) (laying out principles for universal service regulations, the last of which is "Such other principles as . . . are necessary and appropriate for the protection of the public interest, convenience, and necessity and are consistent with this chapter").

do not simply refer to the public interest, convenience, or necessity and leave it at that. Second, courts have interpreted the "public interest, convenience, or necessity" as itself imposing some limitations on the FCC. Most notably, in NBC v. United States, 319 U.S. 190, 216 (1943), the Supreme Court rejected the argument that "the public interest, convenience, or necessity" constituted an unconstitutional delegation of legislative power to the FCC, concluding that "the public interest, convenience, or necessity [is] a criterion which is as concrete as the complicated factors for judgment in such a field of delegated authority permit" and that the terms do not convey unlimited powers to the FCC, as they indicate that the FCC should be guided by, for example, "the ability of the licensee to render the best practicable service to the community reached by his broadcasts." (Citations and internal quotation marks omitted.)

§ 1.B.3. The FTC and DOJ

The FTC and DOJ are the principal antitrust enforcers in the federal government and have played a major role in communications policy for the past century. Indeed, one of the most important events in the history of American communications—the breakup of the Bell System in 1984—resulted not from anything in the Communications Act but from an antitrust suit brought by the DOJ (although the FCC was involved). Since 1996, the Department of Justice also has had primary responsibility for reviewing mergers and acquisitions in all sectors of the communications industry.

The nation's signature antitrust law, the Sherman Anti-Trust Act (which is discussed at length in the next chapter), was passed in 1890. But unlike the Communications Act, the Sherman Act did not create or authorize an agency to implement its statutory policy. To the contrary, the Sherman Act only prohibited certain conduct, and public enforcement of the Sherman Act first fell to the Department of Justice. In 1903, President Theodore Roosevelt—who gained fame for his calls for aggressive antitrust enforcement—obtained from Congress the first earmarked appropriation for antitrust enforcement, and when the Department of Justice was organized into divisions in 1919, the Antitrust Division was born.

In 1914, Congress passed the Federal Trade Commission Act, 15 U.S.C. §§ 41–58, which created the FTC as an independent agency authorized to bring cases under the Sherman Act. Like the FCC, the FTC has five commissioners appointed by the president, with three (including the chair) representing the president's party and two the opposition party. The Supreme Court has ruled that all violations of the Sherman Act also violate the FTC Act, and the FTC is fully empowered to punish Sherman Act violations.

§ 1.B.3.a. The Mechanisms of Antitrust Enforcement

With the creation of both the FTC and the Antitrust Division, federal enforcement of the antitrust laws is shared and usually coordinated between two differently structured agencies. Enforcement is also not limited to those agencies. State

Attorneys General may initiate actions under the Sherman Act (and under their respective state competition laws as well), and private parties that suffer financial injury from an antitrust violation can also bring antitrust actions.

Antitrust enforcement can also lead to an assortment of outcomes. The Department of Justice, though not the FTC, can bring criminal actions under the Sherman Act, and some prosecutions can lead to jailtime. Criminal and civil fines can be levied, and injunctive relief is routinely requested and is usually the centerpiece of any successful enforcement action or settlement.

The Sherman Act also imposes civil liability and awards private plaintiffs with treble damages and attorneys' fees. A common and lucrative strategy for plaintiff attorneys is to bring a private class action under the Act, thus pursuing treble damages on behalf of a large population. At the same time, antitrust lawsuits tend to be complex and expensive. Most cases require plaintiffs to prove that the defendant's conduct has inflicted economic harm on a particular market, a task that often requires gathering data, hiring experts, and submitting sophisticated reports. For these reasons, most substantial actions, especially actions under § 2 that target illegal monopolistic conduct (which, as we will see, are often the most complex) are led by either the FTC or the DOJ. It also means that private actions, especially class actions, commonly cherry-pick claims that are easy to prove, such as price fixing cases that feature "smoking guns" where proving a violation is easy, or follow-on cases to public enforcement, where a federal agency has already proven a violation. This interaction between public and private enforcement is an important feature of antitrust enforcement that has meaningful implications for antitrust policy.

Three other important features of federal antitrust enforcement are noteworthy. The first is merger review. In 1914, Congress passed the Clayton Act, 15 U.S.C. §§ 12–27, which prohibits mergers and acquisitions where the effect "may be to substantially lessen competition, or to tend to create a monopoly." *Id.* § 18. Most actions under the Clayton Act occur before the transaction takes place, and in 1976 the Hart-Scott-Rodino Act, Public Law 94-435, amended the Clayton Act to require companies planning large mergers or acquisitions to notify the government of their plans in advance. So-called "pre-merger review" is now a significant part of antitrust law practice and policy. After being notified by parties planning a merger or significant acquisition, the Hart-Scott-Rodino Act requires the FTC or Antitrust Division (the two agencies coordinate which body handles each merger) to determine whether effects of the merger are likely to cause competitive harm. In this critical respect, merger review in the U.S. is different from that in Europe and many other countries. In the U.S., the government must sue to block the merger and bears the burden of proving anticompetitive effects in court. Indeed, after the merger parties comply with the government's information requests, the statute provides that they may close the deal after 30 days unless the government sues (although, of course, the parties sometimes agree to "stand still" for a time). By contrast, merger review in Europe and many other countries is more classic administrative review, where the deal essentially may not be closed without the affirmative permission of the agency and, if the agency rules against the private parties, those private parties bear the burden of proof to convince the court that the agency has erred.

Although the agencies can take action post-merger if evidence suggests that the transaction increased prices or created harmful monopoly power, the strong preference is to stop parties from accumulating monopoly power at all, rather than punishing them afterwards. This means that pre-merger review is necessarily speculative (the agencies issue merger guidelines, discussed in Chapter 8, to signal the kinds of mergers they are likely to find problematic) and unavoidably reliant on market and technological assumptions. After challenging mergers, the agencies regularly reach settlements with the parties, which often entail divestitures or pledges to refrain from certain conduct. These negotiations and settlements often put the antitrust agencies in the role of active regulators and behavioral monitors, rather than in their standard role as enforcers-through-adjudication.

This leads to the second feature of antitrust enforcement that deserves emphasis. Unlike the FCC and several other agencies, neither the Antitrust Division nor the FTC have relied on rulemaking to make antitrust policy, and there is a vibrant debate over whether the FTC enjoys rulemaking authority at all.[20] Instead, the FTC and DOJ pursue their policy objectives as adjudicators, not rulemakers, so enforcement of the antitrust laws requires pursuing individualized actions.

The third feature, which is related to the second, is the scope of antitrust enforcement. Section 5 of the FTC Act authorizes the FTC, but not the Justice Department, to prohibit "unfair methods of competition" and "unfair or deceptive acts or practices," 15 U.S.C. § 45. This can extend to conduct that is otherwise permissible under the Sherman Act. The FTC uses its § 5 authority to pursue consumer protection actions or prohibit conduct that, though on its face might not harm competition, the FTC believes is "likely to cause reasonably foreseeable injury." 15 U.S.C. § 45(a)(4)(A). Those eager to see the FTC expand its enforcement purview argue that its § 5 authority extends to, for example, protecting consumer privacy and requiring corporate transparency. And those encouraging the FTC to exercise rulemaking authority are hopeful that rulemaking would implement policies under § 5 that reach beyond conduct that is policed by traditional adjudication.

This array of antitrust mechanisms — private and public actions, ex-ante merger review and ex-post adjudication, criminal and civil sanctions, and traditional Sherman Act enforcement with the uncertain supplemental authority under § 5 — distinguishes antitrust enforcement from the typical regulatory scheme that characterizes the Communications Act and the FCC. Throughout this casebook, we assess this menu of enforcement strategies and examine the merits and shortcomings of each.

---

20. *See* The FTC's Competition Rulemaking Authority, Congressional Research Service (2021), https://crsreports.congress.gov/product/pdf/LSB/LSB10635. At least two FTC Commissioners have argued forcefully that the FTC enjoys rulemaking authority and have encouraged the commission to use it aggressively. *See* Rohit Chopra & Lina Khan, The Case for "Unfair Methods of Competition" Rulemaking, 87 U. Chicago L. Rev. 357 (2020).

§ 1.B.4. Agency Actions and Legal Constraints

This is not an administrative law casebook, but we will very briefly outline the kinds of actions that agencies take and the legal constraints on them. The FCC, FTC, and DOJ are all agencies under the Administrative Procedure Act, Pub. L. No. 79-404, 60 Stat. 237 (1946). Under that statute, all agency actions are categorized as rulemaking (akin to legislation) or adjudication. In SEC v. Chenery Corp., 332 U.S. 194, 203 (1947), the Supreme Court made clear that, absent specific statutory language requiring adjudication or rulemaking, the choice is largely up to the agency.

Adjudications are most commonly used to decide disputes involving a small number of parties (often just one), and they are usually backward-looking (a common example is whether or not a given broadcaster violated indecency rules by airing a particular program). Agencies generally promulgate rules, by contrast, when they want to lay out prospective regulations that will apply broadly (e.g., laying out indecency rules in the first place). The rulemaking process formally begins with the agency issuing a Notice of Proposed Rulemaking (NPRM). An NPRM lays out the issues it is considering, discusses them, and proposes a response to them (sometimes accompanied by a set of proposed rules). The NPRM requests comments from interested parties on the proposed course of action. Parties often communicate with the agency before it issues an NPRM in the hope of influencing these proposals; after an NPRM is issued, however, there is a statutorily mandated comment period to ensure that everyone has an opportunity to comment before any regulation is adopted.

In some cases, an agency takes a prior step by issuing a Notice of Inquiry (NOI). The Administrative Procedure Act does not require, or even mention, NOIs (whereas it requires NPRMs), but agencies sometimes use them when they are not ready to issue an NPRM. An NOI raises the issue to be addressed and invites comments but usually does not propose any particular rules. An NOI generally functions to help the agency gather information on a particular topic.

Sometimes an agency takes no further action on a subject after an NOI or NPRM. And, of course, most of the ideas suggested to an agency are never the subject of any formal action. But if an agency wants to promulgate a substantive rule, then after issuing an NPRM (whether or not preceded by an NOI), the agency generally must respond to comments, formulate final rules, and write a statement of basis and purpose for those rules. The FCC often calls its documents containing the final rules, responses to comments, and explanation a Report and Order, but nothing turns on that terminology.

The rulemaking procedure outlined above may sound reasonably streamlined. In practice, however, it often is not. Frequently, an agency will issue an NPRM or NOI and later (in response to comments, on its own initiative, or in response to external events) decide to issue a further NPRM or NOI, calling for a new round of comments and responses on a defined set of issues. On the back end, a final order might not resolve all outstanding issues and might instead request comment on some additional matters. The result is that many rules are final rules as to some matters and an NPRM or NOI as to others. The possibility of multiple NPRMs and multiple rules, combined with the opportunities for communications to the agency not only during the official comment period but also before a rulemaking formally commences, makes for a more fluid rulemaking process than one might imagine from merely reading the statutory provisions.

As to adjudications, as we noted above, agencies generally use them to resolve disputes involving a single party. One form of adjudication that looms particularly large in the communications context is licensing decisions.[21]

In the wake of the enactment of the Communications Act, the decision whether to license a party to use the radio spectrum was invariably an important decision. The grant of a license to use spectrum entitled a firm to a privileged position in the market. A different licensing decision is also very important: the transfer of licenses in the context of a merger or acquisition. As we discuss in Chapter 8, in such cases not only do the antitrust authorities (i.e., the Department of Justice and FTC) review the transaction, but also the FCC by statute reviews the transfers under its public interest standard.

Most agency final actions (whether rulemakings or adjudications), and some decisions not to act, can be appealed to a federal court. Most agency findings of fact and policy judgments are subject to "arbitrary and capricious" review, under the catchall provision of the Administrative Procedure Act that empowers courts to "set aside agency action, findings, and conclusions found to be . . . arbitrary, capricious, an abuse of discretion, or otherwise not in accordance with law." 5 U.S.C. § 706(2). The court will consider whether the agency based its decision on substantial evidence, considered arguments on the opposite side, and explained the basis of its decision. The courts do not (or at least are not supposed to) substitute their judgments on the merits for those of the agency.

Legal interpretations made by the agency are subject to a slightly different form of review. When, as is usually the case, the agency makes such interpretations in a rulemaking, they are subject to *Chevron* analysis. Chevron U.S.A. Inc. v. Natural Resources Defense Council, Inc., 467 U.S. 837 (1984). Under *Chevron*, the court first determines "whether Congress has directly spoken to the precise question at issue. If the intent of Congress is clear, that is the end of the matter," and there will be no deference to the agency's determination. *Id.* at 842–43. But "if the statute is silent or ambiguous with respect to the specific issue, the question for the court is whether the agency's answer is based on a permissible construction of the statute," *id.* at 843, which entails quite considerable deference to the agency. If the agency makes a legal interpretation in a more informal context (such as an informal adjudication), then the deference accorded by a federal court will "'depend upon the thoroughness

21. You might wonder why licensing decisions are adjudications. The answer is that Congress so specified in the Administrative Procedure Act. 5 U.S.C. § 551(6).

evident in its consideration, the validity of its reasoning, its consistency with earlier and later pronouncements, and all those factors which give it power to persuade, if lacking power to control.'" United States v. Mead Corp., 533 U.S. 218, 228 (2001) (quoting Skidmore v. Swift & Co., 323 U.S. 134, 140 (1944)).

§ 1.C. A Policy Analysis Framework

This chapter is not meant to be exhaustive, only an introduction to some of the major issues that cut across all of communications policy. As we turn to specific legal and policy controversies in the chapters to come, we hope that the foregoing text provides something of a structure for considering specific areas of communications law and policy. The list below provides a checklist of sorts for considering particular issues using the framework set out above:

- What, if any, are the market failures said to justify the proposed government intervention? Do the asserted failures match up with a well understood economic theory? How do they match up with the historical bases for regulation?
- What are the other asserted justifications for the regulation? Who in particular is the regulation supposed to help?
- What will the government need to know in order to administer the proposed regulation effectively? Where will it gather this information, and how will it know whether it is reliable? Would reliance on expert agencies advance the policy goal?
- What are the likely shortcomings of the proposed regulation, and are there more effective regulatory alternatives? How does ex ante review compare with ex post adjudication? Should enforcement be private or public actions? Should sanctions be injunctive or damages?
- Might a policy alternative better meet the stated goal or reduce the costs of the regulatory intervention?
- Other than the intended consequences of the regulation (i.e., meeting the asserted needs), what are the likely market and nonmarket effects of the regulation? Is it possible that the regulation will entrench existing players and provide a barrier to entry to innovative upstarts? Will it put decision making in the appropriate hands?
- How will the government assess whether its regulation is working?
- Can the regulation be explained as a product of public choice theory—in the interests of the regulators and/or the regulated, narrowly conceived, rather than in the interests of the public generally?

Chapter 2

The Antitrust Laws and Their Regulation of Monopolies

Introduction

As we discussed in Chapter 1, among the prevailing justifications for regulation is the mitigation of the harm to markets and consumers caused by monopolies. One strategy to combat monopolies, pursued by both state and federal policymakers over many decades, is to develop sector-specific regulatory strategies to address monopolies in certain industrial sectors. This was the strategy pursued in the Communications Act of 1934, its predecessors, and its subsequent amendments to mitigate the harms of predicted monopolies in telephony, cable, and other telecommunications markets. An alternative strategy is reflected in the Sherman Act, the nation's chief anti-monopoly law, that applies throughout the economy. Because telecommunications and internet markets are frequently characterized by economic monopolies, and because the telecommunications regulation has historically intersected and paralleled both the application of and the motivations behind the Sherman Act of 1890, telecommunications companies, regulators, and attorneys require a familiarity with the Sherman Act and antitrust law in addition to relevant sector-specific laws.

This chapter offers an introduction to the nation's antitrust laws. It begins by describing their origins and the ideological debates that have shaped their enforcement. It then offers a primer on how they are applied to monopolies. More detail on how antitrust law is applied to the telecommunications sector, how it intersects with the Communications Act and other sector-specific regulatory regimes, and how it might play an increasingly prominent role in internet commerce are all discussed in Chapter 8.

§ 2.A. The History & Purpose of the Sherman Act

Congress passed the Sherman Anti-Trust Act in 1890 as a response to the rise of the unprecedented concentration of wealth and economic power that characterized the Gilded Age.[1] The era gets its name from an 1873 novel by Mark Twain and Charles Dudley Warner, which described the period following the Civil War as being rife with greed, materialism, and corruption in public life. Among the most salient features of the Gilded Age was the rise of unprecedentedly large economic conglomerates, colloquially known as the Trusts, that came to dominate post-Civil War industrial growth. Note that the Sherman Act is relatively contemporaneous with the first federal common carrier law: the Interstate Commerce Act of 1887. From the beginning, sector-specific regulation and general competition law lived side-by-side.

The trusts were targeted as the source of the age's economic excess and its rampant political corruption. Economic historian William Letwin wrote:

> In the years immediately before the Sherman Act, between 1888 and 1890, there were few who doubted that the public hated the trusts fervently. [B]ut since the public, despite its hostility, did not and could not suggest any specific solution to the problem, Congress was left very much to its own devices in deciding what was to be done.

William L. Letwin, Congress and the Sherman Antitrust Law: 1887–1890, 23 U. Chi. L. Rev. 221 (1956).

The legislation that Congress eventually passed in 1890, following a series of political compromises, was extremely terse. The Sherman Act's first two sections, which amount to the lion's share of substantive antitrust law, read in full as follows:

> **Sec. 1.** Every contract, combination in the form of trust or otherwise, or conspiracy, in restraint of trade or commerce among the several States, or with foreign nations, is hereby declared to be illegal. Every person who shall make any such contract or engage in any such combination or conspiracy, shall be deemed guilty of a misdemeanor, and, on conviction thereof, shall be punished by fine not exceeding five thousand dollars, or by imprisonment not exceeding one year, or by both said punishments, at the discretion of the court.
>
> **Sec. 2.** Every person who shall monopolize, or attempt to monopolize, or combine or conspire with any other person or persons, to monopolize any part of the trade or commerce among the several States, or with foreign

1. The Sherman Anti-Trust Act passed the Senate by a vote of 51–1 on April 8, 1890, and the House by a unanimous vote of 242–0 on June 20, 1890. President Benjamin Harrison signed the bill into law on July 2, 1890. The Act was named for Senator John Sherman of Ohio, who was then Chairman of the Senate Finance Committee.

> nations, shall be deemed guilty of a misdemeanor, and, on conviction thereof, shall be punished by fine not exceeding five thousand dollars, or by imprisonment not exceeding one year, or by both said punishments, in the discretion of the court.[2]

The brevity of the statute, combined with the enormity and complexity of the economic policies it aims to implement, has been interpreted as a deliberate delegation from Congress to the courts.[3] Although Congress has passed several additional antitrust statutes since 1890, antitrust law has largely been a product of federal common law.

Among the most consequential antitrust decisions by the Supreme Court was its 1911 ruling in Standard Oil Co. v. United States, 221 U.S. 1 (1911).[4] In the first decades following the Sherman Act's enactment, courts struggled over whether the Act was to be interpreted literally, to merely codify common law principles that were in force before 1890, or to stand for different principles. This seminal question was decided in *Standard Oil*, in which the basic question before the Court was how to interpret the word, "Every," the first word in both §1 and §2. If the Sherman Act were to be interpreted literally, a plain meaning would suggest that all restraints on commerce, including voluntary contracts, and all efforts to dominate a market, including by efficient firms, would be illegal. In an opinion by Chief Justice White, the Court rejected a literal approach and instead formulated what is now called the "Rule of Reason":

> [I]t was intended that the standard of reason which had been applied at the common law and in this country in dealing with subjects of the character embraced by the statute was intended to be the measure used for the purpose of determining whether, in a given case, a particular act had or had not brought about the wrong against which the statute provided.

Id. at 60. Although Chief Justice White offered few specifics in elaborating how a court should administer the Rule of Reason, he offered some direction in United States v. American Tobacco, a companion case to *Standard Oil*, by saying "[t]he Anti-Trust Act must have a reasonable construction" and thus it only prohibits "acts, contracts, agreements or combinations which operated to the prejudice of the public

---

2. U.S. Code, Title 15, §§1–2. Congress has periodically for corporations updated the statute's penalties. The statute currently authorizes fines up to $100,000,000 for corporation and $1,000,000 for individuals, and prison terms up to 10 years.

3. William Baxter, who led the Antitrust Division from 1981–1984, wrote:

> In failing to provide more guidance, the framers of our antitrust laws did not abdicate their responsibility any more than did the Framers of the Constitution. The antitrust laws were written with awareness of the diversity of business conduct and with the knowledge that the detailed statutes which would prohibit socially undesirable conduct would lack the flexibility needed to preserve (and at times even permit) desirable conduct.

William F. Baxter, Separation of Powers, Prosecutorial Discretion, and the "Common Law" Nature of Antitrust Law, 60 Tex. L. Rev. 661, 662–663 (1982).

4. For some background on the historic *Standard Oil* case, *see* James May, The Story of Standard Oil Co. v. United States, in Eleanor Fox & Daniel Crane (eds.), Antitrust Stories (2007).

interests by unduly restricting competition or by unduly obstructing due course of trade." 221 U.S. 106, 107 (1911).

Notes and Questions

1. Why Might Legislative History Be Important? The typical justification for studying legislative history is to infer legislators' intent behind enactment of a statute, which might be helpful in interpreting an ambiguity in the statutory text. Is this especially important when the statute in question, like the Sherman Act, is wholly ambiguous, or does the typical inquiry into legislative history then break down? And what if, as Letwin suggests, the legislative history is also ambiguous?

2. The Magna Carta of Free Enterprise. The Supreme Court has frequently used grandiose language to describe the Sherman Act. *See, e.g.*, Northern Pac. Ry. Co. v. United States, 356 U.S. 1, 4 (1958) ("The Sherman Act was designed to be a comprehensive charter of economic liberty aimed at preserving free and unfettered competition as the rule of trade."); United States v. Topco Assocs., Inc., 405 U.S. 596, 610 (1972) ("Antitrust laws in general, and the Sherman Act in particular, are the Magna Carta of free enterprise. They are as important to the preservation of economic freedom and our free enterprise system as the Bill of Rights is to the protection of our fundamental personal freedoms."). To some, this reverence gives the Act a quasi-constitutional status, and thus antitrust law addresses foundational questions of how to balance private and public power within a constitutional order. *See, e.g.*, Thomas B. Nachbar, The Antitrust Constitution, 99 Iowa L. Rev. 57 (2013).

Despite this reverence for the Act, or perhaps because of it, the Court over the past 150 years has offered multiple—and often conflicting—interpretations and applications of the statute. Do you see a connection between inconsistent applications of the Sherman Act and its quasi-constitutional status? What historical, political, or technological factors might influence antitrust jurisprudence?

3. Ida Tarbell and Standard Oil. One complicating factor in referencing the Sherman Act's legislative history might be, ironically, that there is so much history to choose from. Most of our popular conceptions of the Gilded Age were shaped by writings at the turn of the century, and among the most influential were investigative journalist Ida Tarbell's articles on Standard Oil in *McClure's Magazine* and her subsequent 1904 book, The History of the Standard Oil Company. Tarbell, whose father was an independent oilman who (Tarbell claimed) was driven out of business by Standard Oil, was credited for offering a vivid depiction of the excesses and ruthlessness of the Gilded Age and in capturing the popular anger against big business. Her writings are credited with encouraging the antitrust prosecution of Standard Oil that ultimately broke up the company into thirty-four smaller entities and for powering political demands that led to the Clayton Act. *See, e.g.*, Doris Kearns Goodwin, The Bully Pulpit: Theodore Roosevelt, William Howard Taft, and the Golden Age of Journalism (2013). Tarbell's writings offer two interesting challenges to uses of legislative history: First, how can a history that reveals widespread, deeply felt, and often visceral anger inform the interpretation of statutes? Second, how should contemporary writings be treated if they were not just reflections of, but also significantly shaped, popular opinion?

§ 2.B. The Rise of the Chicago School and the Consumer Welfare Standard

In the fifty years following the *Standard Oil* case, antitrust law reflected assorted ebbs and flows in enforcement rigor and seemed to embrace doctrines that many criticized for being either incoherent or ineffective in advancing any of the motivations that underlay the Sherman Act's passage. In the 1960s and 1970s, responding to antitrust confusion, some scholars at the University of Chicago argued that the Sherman Act should be interpreted to pursue only efficiency objectives, and thus should only prohibit conduct that reduced economic welfare. The so-called "Chicago School" and the "consumer welfare standard" were ultimately adopted by the Supreme Court in that late 1970s, and courts have ever since interpreted the Sherman Act and all subsequent antitrust laws to pursue the goal of market efficiency. This academic movement and its enormous influence on the law has been called an Antitrust Revolution.

The most influential Chicago School scholar was Robert Bork, who argued that antitrust law should pursue efficiency objectives because that is what Congress intended in 1890:

> Congress intended courts to implement (that is, to take into account in the decision of cases) only that value which we would today call consumer welfare. To put it another way, the policy the courts were intended to apply is the maximization of wealth or consumer want satisfaction. This requires courts to distinguish between agreements or activities that increase wealth through efficiency and those that decrease it through restriction of output.
>
> Not only was consumer welfare the predominant goal expressed by Congress but the evidence strongly indicates that, in case of conflict, other values were to give way before it. In short, since the legislative history of the Sherman Act shows consumer welfare to be the decisive value it should be treated by a court as the only value.

Robert H. Bork, Legislative Intent and the Policy of the Sherman Act, 9 J.L. & Econ. 7 (1966).

The Supreme Court's adoption of the consumer welfare standard, and more generally its embrace of economic analysis, transformed antitrust analysis such that it is often described as applied economic policy. The primacy of efficiency as the goal—and only goal—of antitrust law is best illustrated by the modern approach to monopoly. Richard Posner, who as a scholar was a pioneer in the Chicago School and as a federal circuit judge was a leading judicial implementer of Chicago-informed antitrust, wrote in his casebook:

> [T]o the extent that efficiency is the goal of antitrust enforcement, there is no justification for carrying enforcement into areas where competition is less efficient than monopoly because the costs of monopoly pricing are outweighed by the economies of centralizing production in one or a very few firms. That is why I referred to monopoly pricing as "presumptively" inefficient and as creating merely a "prima facie" case for having an antitrust policy. Nor is there any justification for using the antitrust laws to attain goals unrelated or antithetical to efficiency.

Richard A. Posner, Antitrust Law (2d ed. 2001), at 2.

Merger challenges can offer a useful lesson into the balance of monopoly and efficiency. Merging companies usually justify their union with efficiency justifications, arguing that their combination will reduce collective costs, generate synergies, or otherwise create a whole that is superior (i.e., creates more economic welfare) than the sum of the parts. At the same time, by definition, each merger inherently means more market consolidation and usually greater market power. If the antitrust laws were to prioritize combating the accumulation of economic power, then they would prohibit most mergers. Consider the approach employed below, which epitomizes much of modern antitrust law.

United States v. Syufy Enterprises

903 F.2d 659 (9th Cir. 1990)

Before WIGGINS and KOZINSKI, Circuit Judges, and QUACKENBUSH, District Judge.

KOZINSKI, Circuit Judge:

Gone are the days when a movie ticket cost a dime, popcorn a nickel and theatres had a single screen: This is the age of the multiplex. With more than 300 new films released every year — each potentially the next Batman or E.T. — many successful theatres today run a different film on each of their six, twelve or eighteen screens. The multiplex offers something for everyone: Moviegoers can choose from a wider selection of films; theatre operators are able to balance profits and losses from blockbusters and flops, and to reduce manpower by consolidating concession islands; the producers, of course, like having the extra screens on which to display their wares.

Raymond Syufy understood the formula well. In 1981, he entered the Las Vegas market with a splash by opening a six-screen theatre. Newly constructed and luxuriously furnished, it put existing facilities to shame. Syufy's entry into the Las Vegas market caused a stir, precipitating a titanic bidding war. Soon, theatres in Las Vegas were paying some of the highest license fees in the nation, while distributors sat back and watched the easy money roll in.

It is the nature of free enterprise that fierce, no holds barred competition will drive out the least effective participants in the market, providing the most efficient allocation of productive resources. And so it was in the Las Vegas movie market in 1982.

After a hard fought battle among several contenders, Syufy gained the upper hand. Two of his rivals, Mann Theatres and Plitt Theatres, saw their future as rocky and decided to sell out to Syufy. While Mann and Plitt are major exhibitors nationwide, neither had a large presence in Las Vegas. Mann operated two indoor theatres with a total of three screens; Plitt operated a single theatre with three screens. Things were relatively quiet until September 1984; in September, Syufy entered into earnest negotiations with Cragin Industries, his largest remaining competitor. Cragin sold out to Syufy midway through October, leaving Roberts Company, a small exhibitor of mostly second-run films, as Syufy's only competitor for first-run films in Las Vegas.

It is these three transactions—Syufy's purchases of the Mann, Plitt and Cragin theatres—that the Justice Department claims amount to antitrust violations. As government counsel explained at oral argument, the thrust of its case is that "you may not get monopoly power by buying out your competitors."

Competition is the driving force behind our free enterprise system. Unlike centrally planned economies, where decisions about production and allocation are made by government bureaucrats who ostensibly see the big picture and know to do the right thing, capitalism relies on decentralized planning—millions of producers and consumers making hundreds of millions of individual decisions each year—to determine what and how much will be produced. Competition plays the key role in this process: It imposes an essential discipline on producers and sellers of goods to provide the consumer with a better product at a lower cost; it drives out inefficient and marginal producers, releasing resources to higher-valued uses; it promotes diversity, giving consumers choices to fit a wide array of personal preferences; it avoids permanent concentrations of economic power, as even the largest firm can lose market share to a feistier and hungrier rival. If, as the metaphor goes, a market economy is governed by an invisible hand, competition is surely the brass knuckles by which it enforces its decisions.

When competition is impaired, producers may be able to reap monopoly profits, denying consumers many of the benefits of a free market. It is a simple but important truth, therefore, that our antitrust laws are designed to protect the integrity of the market system by assuring that competition reigns freely. While much has been said and written about the antitrust laws during the last century of their existence, ultimately the court must resolve a practical question in every monopolization case: Is this the type of situation where market forces are likely to cure the perceived problem within a reasonable period of time? Or, have barriers been erected to constrain the normal operation of the market, so that the problem is not likely to be self-correcting? In the latter situation, it might well be necessary for a court to correct the market imbalance; in the former, a court ought to exercise extreme caution because judicial intervention in a competitive situation can itself upset the balance of market forces, bringing about the very ills the antitrust laws were meant to prevent.

It is with these observations in mind that we turn to the case before us. It is true, of course, that when Syufy acquired Mann's, Plitt's and Cragin's theatres he temporarily diminished the number of competitors in the Las Vegas first-run film market. But this does not necessarily indicate foul play; many legitimate market arrangements diminish the number of competitors. It would be odd if they did not, as the nature of competition is to make winners and losers. If there are no significant barriers to entry, however, eliminating competitors will not enable the survivors to reap a monopoly profit; any attempt to raise prices above the competitive level will lure into the market new competitors able and willing to offer their commercial goods or personal services for less.

We bypass as surplusage the hundreds of pages of expert and lay testimony that support the district court's finding, and focus instead only on a single—to our minds conclusive—item. Immediately after Syufy bought out the last of his three competitors in October 1984, he was riding high, having captured 100% of the first-run film market in Las Vegas. But this utopia proved to be only a mirage. That same month, a major movie distributor, Orion, stopped doing business with Syufy, sending all of its first-run films to Roberts Company, a dark horse competitor previously relegated to the second-run market. Roberts Company took this as an invitation to step into the major league and, against all odds, began giving Syufy serious competition in the first-run market. By the end of 1987, Roberts was showing a larger percentage of first-run films than was the Redrock multiplex at the time Syufy bought it. Roberts then sold its theatres to United Artists, the largest theatre chain in the country, and Syufy continued losing ground. It all boils down to this: Syufy's acquisitions did not short circuit the operation of the natural market forces; Las Vegas' first-run film market was more competitive when this case came to trial than before Syufy bought out Mann, Plitt and Cragin.

The Justice Department correctly points out that Syufy still has a large market share, but attributes far too much importance to this fact. In evaluating monopoly power, it is not market share that counts, but the ability to *maintain* market share. Syufy seems unable to do this. In 1985, Syufy managed to lock up exclusive exhibition rights to 91% of all the first-run films in Las Vegas. By the first quarter of 1988, that percentage had fallen to 39%; United Artists had exclusive rights to another 25%, with the remaining 36% being played on both Syufy and UA screens.

Confronted with this record and the district court's clear findings, the government trots out a shopworn argument we had thought long abandoned: that efficient, aggressive competition is itself a structural barrier to entry. According to the government, competitors will be deterred from entering the market because they could not hope to turn a profit competing against Syufy. In the words of government counsel:

> There is no legal barrier. There is no law that says you can't come into this market, it's not that kind of barrier.... But, the fact of mere possibility in the literal sense, is not the appropriate test. Entry, after all, must, to be effective to dissipate the monopoly power that Syufy has, entry must hold some reasonable prospect of profitability for the entrant, or else the entrant will say, as Mann Theatres said ... this is not an attractive market to enter. There will be shelter. And the reason is very clear. You have to compete

> effectively in this market. And witness after witness testified you would need to build anywhere from 12 to 24 theatres, which is a very expensive and time consuming proposition. *And, you would then find yourself in a bidding war against Syufy.*

Tr. of Oral Arg. at 5 (emphasis added). It can't be said often enough that the antitrust laws protect competition, *not* competitors. As we noted earlier, competition is essential to the effective operation of the free market because it encourages efficiency, promotes consumer satisfaction and prevents the accumulation of monopoly profits. When a producer is shielded from competition, he is likely to provide lesser service at a higher price; the victim is the consumer who gets a raw deal. This is the evil the antitrust laws are meant to avert. But when a producer deters competitors by supplying a better product at a lower price, when he eschews monopoly profits, when he operates his business so as to meet consumer demand and increase consumer satisfaction, the goals of competition are served, even if no actual competitors see fit to enter the market at a particular time. While the successful competitor should not be raised above the law, neither should he be held down by law.

If a dominant supplier acts consistent with a competitive market—out of fear perhaps that potential competitors are ready and able to step in—the purpose of the antitrust laws is amply served. We make it clear today, if it was not before, that an efficient, vigorous, aggressive competitor is not the villain antitrust laws are aimed at eliminating. Fostering an environment where businesses fight it out using the weapon of efficiency and consumer goodwill is what the antitrust laws are meant to champion.

In this case, the government was suspicious because Syufy bought out the movie theatres of his retreating competitors. But, in a competitive market, buying out competitors is not merely permissible, it contributes to market stability and promotes the efficient allocation of resources. The fact is, a relentless, growing competitor is frequently the most logical buyer of a business that is declining. For competitors in a free market to fear buying each other out lest they be hit with the expense and misery of an antitrust enforcement action amounts to a burden only slightly less palpable than a direct governmental prohibition against such a purchase. In a free enterprise system decisions such as these should be made by market actors responding to market forces, not by government bureaucrats pursuing their notions of how the market should operate. Personal initiative, not government control, is the fountainhead of progress in a capitalist economy.

[Concurring opinion by District Judge QUACKENBUSH omitted.]

Notes and Questions

1. The Antitrust Revolution. What are the merits of the Chicago School's exclusive focus on economic welfare? What kinds of conduct does it not prohibit that one might find to be problematic? Why do you think the Chicago School was, from a jurisprudential perspective, such an astounding success?

2. *Syufy* and the Chicago School. In what ways is *Syufy* an illustration of the Chicago School in action? Does the opinion illuminate the reasons for the Chicago School's success? Does the opinion illustrate any of the shortcomings of the Chicago School?

3. Antitrust and Judicial Power. Robert Bork's advocacy of the consumer welfare standard was motivated by more than an affection for market efficiency. He worried that "[f]ailure to settle the issue of values has led inevitably to a degree of irresponsibility in the judicial process." Robert H. Bork, Legislative Intent and the Policy of the Sherman Act, 9 J.L. & Econ. 7, 7–8 (1966). Later in his enormously influential book, The Antitrust Paradox: A Policy at War with Itself (1978), Bork issued a dire warning if courts stray from (what he believed was) Congress' instruction to interpret the antitrust laws to exclusively promote economic welfare:

> We are right to be concerned about the integrity and legitimacy of that lawmaking process, both for its own sake and because ideas about the power and discretion proper to courts in one field of law will inevitably affect their performance elsewhere. At issue is the question central to democratic society: Who governs?
>
> Within the limited frame for observation provided by antitrust, therefore, it is worth noting that the general movement has been away from legislative decision by Congress and toward political choice by courts, away from the ideal of competition and toward the older idea of protected status for each producer, away from concern for the general welfare and toward concern for interest groups, and away from the ideal of liberty toward the ideal of enforced equality. No one can know how far these trends may go, but if, as I believe, they have already gone much too far in antitrust as elsewhere in our polity, they should be recognized and reversed, for they are ultimately incompatible with the preservation of a liberal capitalist social order.

Robert H. Bork, The Antitrust Paradox: A Policy at War with Itself (1978), at 10–11. Why does Bork think that so much is at stake if courts stray from this exclusive approach? Why, possibly, might he think that "the preservation of a liberal capitalist social order" is at stake?

4. Chicago versus Post-Chicago and the Efficiency Justifications in Antitrust. Modern antitrust law has embraced the use of economics and the lodestar of market efficiency to dictate antitrust disputes. That is not to say that there is widespread acceptance of the Chicago School of antitrust, and not long after the Supreme Court embraced market efficiency as the goal of antitrust law, a "post-Chicago School" emerged. Post-Chicago scholars did not critique the Chicago School's advocacy for economic welfare but instead targeted shortcomings of the kind of economics it used. Professor Herbert Hovenkamp, a Post-Chicago adherent and leader, wrote:

> The Chicago School of antitrust analysis has made an important and lasting contribution to antitrust policy. The School has placed an emphasis on economic analysis in antitrust jurisprudence that will likely never disappear.

> At the same time, however, the Chicago School's approach to antitrust is defective [because] the notion that public policymaking should be guided exclusively by a notion of efficiency based on the neoclassical market efficiency model is naïve. The neoclassical market efficiency model is itself too simple to account for or to predict business firm behavior in the real world. The model has proved to be particularly inept at identifying many forms of strategic behavior. In large part this is so because the market efficiency model is static and dwells too much on long-run effects. In the real world, short-run considerations are critical to business planning. Furthermore, the short run can be a very long time. In many industries a monopoly that lasts for only the short run can inflict great economic loss on society. By ignoring the short run, the market efficiency model fails to appreciate the social cost of many forms of monopolistic behavior.

Herbert Hovenkamp, Antitrust Policy After Chicago, 84 Mich. L. Rev. 213, 283–84 (1985).

In other words, the economic theory that underlies the Chicago School, according to Professor Hovenkamp, assumes that long-run market forces will dilute or punish most exclusionary conduct that reduces economic welfare, and therefore (since market participants know this) most restrictive economic behavior are really undergirded by efficiency motivations. Post-Chicago scholars, in contrast, developed models suggesting that many of those restrictive practices amount to strategic exercises of market power and reduce, rather than increase, economic welfare. The different approaches to economic theory led to sharp disputes over antitrust policy: whereas the Chicago School's assumptions suggest that antitrust's role in policing anticompetitive conduct should be limited, Post-Chicago adherents believe that anticompetitive conduct is much more widespread and that active antitrust enforcement is necessary to preserve competitive markets. Note, though, that the source of disagreement is not in whether to use economic theory, but how to use economic tools. These are alternative ways of evaluating economic welfare, not a debate over the primacy of economic welfare.

One might imagine Chicago versus Post-Chicago disagreements emerging in *Syufy*. If one accepts the stated facts, offered by the government and apparently accepted by Judge Kozinski, that after Syufy acquired its competitors and enjoyed a dominant market position, a new entrant would have to build between from 12 to 24 theatres in order to compete profitably with Syufy. Thus, after Syufy's acquisitions, profitable entry—and thus meaningful competition—would require a much larger investment. What might that reveal about Syufy's acquisition of its rivals and its effect on consumer welfare? Does it reflect additional efficiencies obtained by the incumbent, or added costs imposed upon a would-be entrant? Does this illustrate what Professor Hovenkamp critiqued as an over-emphasis on the long run and a failure to recognize short-term strategic behavior? Does it matter that, as the concurrence (deleted for space reasons) observes, Syufy "had a track record of monopolization, having been found, shortly before the commencement of this action, to have monopolized the exhibition of major feature films in the San Jose area."? *Syufy*, 903 F.3d at 674. Chicagoans and Post-Chicagoans are likely to offer different answers to these questions.

Why do you think that even those who oppose the Chicago School still accept the exclusivity of economic welfare as the prime directive in antitrust?

5. Noneconomic Values in the Sherman Act? Many scholars have resisted the exclusive use of economics to implement the Sherman Act, and in doing so, some have pointed to the Act's legislative history. Notably, Robert Lande argued that Congress was more concerned with the distributional consequences of monopolies, i.e., that monopolies — even efficient ones — charge higher prices than they would in a competitive market, and thus extract wealth from consumers. Lande wrote:

> [T]he legislative history of the Sherman Act reveals a total lack of concern for allocative inefficiency. Congress condemned firms with monopoly power despite their acknowledged efficiencies, and with the knowledge that this condemnation might not maximize society's economic efficiency. Indeed, the evidence suggests that Congress was unwilling to subordinate its distributive-based distaste for trusts and monopolists to the goal of corporate efficiency when the efficiency gains would be retained by the monopolist.

Robert H. Lande, Wealth Transfers as the Original and Primary Concern of Antitrust: The Efficiency Interpretation Challenged, 34 Hastings L.J. 67, 83 (1982). Lande therefore contended that, in passing the Sherman Act, Congress "condemned the unequal distribution of wealth resulting from monopolistic overcharges [and] decided that competitive prices were 'fair' whereas monopoly prices were not." *Id.* at 96. More specifically, he argued that Congress intended to "curb the social and political power of large businesses" and to "decentralize economic, social, and political decisionmaking" by taming corporate power. *Id.* at 96, 106.

Does Lande's legislative history seem more plausible than Bork's? Does either scholar's accurately capture Congress' intent when passing the Sherman Act? And how would you determine that intent? How, if at all, should Lande's representation of Congress's priorities in 1890 inform the priorities and objectives of antitrust policy?

Although most antitrust scholarship and policymaking has not put weight on Lande's concern for wealth transfers and corporate power, a majority of FTC commissioners in 2021, in voting to withdraw a policy from the previous administration, indicated a receptivity to some of these concerns. In advancing an interpretation of the Clayton Act's prohibition of mergers that "substantially lessen competition," the commissioners argued:

> The statute does not provide for a balancing test where an "efficient" merger is allowed even if it may lessen competition. Many "efficiencies" simply make the merged firm more profitable, without affecting the level of competition in the market. Yet under the statute, efficiencies are only relevant insofar as they shed light on the level of post-merger competition.

Statement of Chair Lina M. Khan, Commissioner Rohit Chopra, and Commissioner Rebecca Kelly Slaughter on the Withdrawal of the Vertical Merger Guidelines, Commission File No. P810034 (September 15, 2021). The statement implies a distinction between "competition" and "efficiency," such that mergers that enhance efficiency might nonetheless be illegal if those efficiencies translate into greater corporate profits without corresponding gains to consumers. Is this a plausible interpretation of the Clayton Act? Would Lande say it is a useful direction for antitrust law?

§ 2.C. Antitrust's Regulation of Monopolies

As we note above, substantive antitrust law falls into three general categories: prohibiting collusion (Sherman Act § 1), policing monopolies (Sherman Act § 2), and restricting problematic mergers (the Clayton Act, § 7). Thus, it should be clear that the Sherman Act and the nation's other antitrust laws do far more than regulate monopolies. But § 2 of the Sherman Act and its regulation of monopolies plays an especially important role in the telecommunications sector and in networked industries, and the principles that underlie it deserve greater elucidation.

Even though § 2's prohibition of monopoly might reflect the very essence of why the Sherman Act was passed, antitrust policymakers have always had difficulty articulating precisely what it prohibited. The primary cause for this difficulty is that aggressive competition often leads to monopoly. To consider a basic illustration: if a firm manufactures a market's best mousetrap, one that is so far superior and cost-effective than any other available mousetrap that all other manufacturers leave the marketplace, has that firm violated § 2 when it becomes a monopolist? Though one might expect that this foundational tension between competition and monopoly should have been anticipated by the framers of the Sherman Act, business scholar Hans Thorelli remarked, "Not until the antitrust policy had been confronted with stark realities did it dawn upon the public mind that to legislate against monopolies and restraints of trade may not necessarily be the same as to enforce, or maintain, free competition." Hans Thorelli, The Federal Antitrust Policy 226–27 (1954).

One of the early and effective articulations of what § 2 prohibits came from the pen of Learned Hand in the famous *Alcoa* case.

United States v. Aluminum Co. of America [*Alcoa*]

148 F.2d 416 (2d Cir. 1945)

Before L. HAND, SWAN, and A. HAND, Circuit Judges

L. HAND, Circuit Judge:

[T]he most important question in the case is whether the monopoly in "Alcoa's" production of "virgin" ingot, secured by the two patents until 1909, continued for the ensuing twenty-eight years; and whether, if it did, it was unlawful under § 2 of the Sherman Act. It is undisputed that throughout this period "Alcoa" continued to be the single producer of "virgin" ingot in the United States; and the plaintiff argues that this without more was enough to make it an unlawful monopoly. It also takes an alternative position: that in any event during this period "Alcoa" consistently pursued unlawful exclusionary practices, which made its dominant position certainly unlawful, even though it would not have been, had it been retained only by "natural growth."

There are various ways of computing "Alcoa's" control of the aluminum market as distinct from its production depending upon what one regards as competing in that market. We conclude therefore that "Alcoa's" control over the ingot market must be reckoned at over ninety per cent; that being the proportion which its production bears to imported "virgin" ingot. If the fraction which it did not supply were the produce of domestic manufacture there could be no doubt that this percentage gave it a monopoly lawful or unlawful, as the case might be. The producer of so large a proportion of the supply has complete control within certain limits. It is true that, if by raising the price he reduces the amount which can be marketed as always, or almost always, happens he may invite the expansion of the small producers who will try to fill the place left open; nevertheless, not only is there an inevitable lag in this, but the large producer is in a strong position to check such competition; and, indeed, if he has retained his old plant and personnel, he can inevitably do so. Was this a monopoly within the meaning of § 2? The judge found that, over the whole half century of its existence, "Alcoa's" profits upon capital invested, after payment of income taxes, had been only about ten per cent [which] could hardly be considered extortionate.

Having proved that "Alcoa" had a monopoly of the domestic ingot market, the plaintiff had gone far enough for it is no excuse for "monopolizing" a market that the monopoly has not been used to extract from the consumer more than a "fair" profit. The Act has wider purposes. Indeed, even though we disregarded all but economic considerations, it would by no means follow that such concentration of producing power is to be desired, when it has not been used extortionately. Many people believe that possession of unchallenged economic power deadens initiative, discourages thrift and depresses energy; that immunity from competition is a narcotic, and rivalry is a stimulant, to industrial progress; that the spur of constant stress is necessary to counteract an inevitable disposition to let well enough alone. Such people believe that competitors, versed in the craft as no consumer can be, will be quick to detect opportunities for saving and new shifts in production, and be eager to profit by them. In any event the mere fact that a producer, having command of the domestic market, has not been able to make more than a "fair" profit, is no evidence that a "fair" profit could not have been made at lower prices. True, it might have been thought adequate to condemn only those monopolies which could not show that they had exercised the highest possible ingenuity, had adopted every possible economy, had anticipated every conceivable improvement, stimulated every possible demand. No doubt, that would be one way of dealing with the matter, although it would imply constant scrutiny and constant supervision, such as courts are unable to provide.

Nevertheless, it is unquestionably true that from the very outset the courts have at least kept in reserve the possibility that the origin of a monopoly may be critical in determining its legality; and for this they had warrant in some of the congressional debates which accompanied the passage of the Act. This notion has usually been expressed by saying that size does not determine guilt; that there must be some "exclusion" of competitors; that the growth must be something else than "natural" or "normal"; that there must be a "wrongful intent," or some other specific intent; or that some "unduly" coercive means must be used. At times there has been emphasis upon the use of the active verb, "monopolize," as the judge noted in the case at bar. What engendered these compunctions is reasonably plain; persons may unwittingly find themselves in possession of a monopoly, automatically so to say: that is, without having intended either to put an end to existing competition, or to prevent competition from arising when none had existed; they may become monopolists by force of accident. Since the Act makes "monopolizing" a crime, as well as a civil wrong, it would be not only unfair, but presumably contrary to the intent of Congress, to include such instances. A market may, for example, be so limited that it is impossible to produce at all and meet the cost of production except by a plant large enough to supply the whole demand. Or there may be changes in taste or in cost which drive out all but one purveyor. A single producer may be the survivor out of a group of active competitors, merely by virtue of his superior skill, foresight and industry. In such cases a strong argument can be made that, although, the result may expose the public to the evils of monopoly, the Act does not mean to condemn the resultant of those very forces which it is its prime object to foster: *finis opus coronat*. The successful competitor, having been urged to compete, must not be turned upon when he wins.

It would completely misconstrue "Alcoa's" position in 1940 to hold that it was the passive beneficiary of a monopoly, following upon an involuntary elimination of competitors by automatically operative economic forces. Already in 1909, when its last lawful monopoly ended, it sought to strengthen its position by unlawful practices, and these concededly continued until 1912. In that year it had two plants in New York, at which it produced less than 42 million pounds of ingot; in 1934 it had five plants (the original two, enlarged; one in Tennessee; one in North Carolina; one in Washington), and its production had risen to about 327 million pounds, an increase of almost eight-fold. Meanwhile not a pound of ingot had been produced by anyone else in the United States. This increase and this continued and undisturbed control did not fall undesigned into "Alcoa's" lap; obviously it could not have done so. It could only have resulted, as it did result, from a persistent determination to maintain the control, with which it found itself vested in 1912. There were at least one or two abortive attempts to enter the industry, but "Alcoa" effectively anticipated and forestalled all competition, and succeeded in holding the field alone. So here, "Alcoa" meant to keep, and did keep, that complete and exclusive hold upon the ingot market with which it started. That was to "monopolize" that market, however innocently it otherwise proceeded. So far as the judgment held that it was not within § 2, it must be reversed.

Notes and Questions

1. Judge Learned Hand's Only Foray into Antitrust. For much of the 20th century, antitrust suits were appealed from federal district courts directly to the U.S. Supreme Court. For this reason, longtime federal circuit court judge Learned Hand was normally denied the opportunity to rule in a Sherman Act case. However, four Supreme Court justices recused themselves in United States v. Alcoa, thereby depriving the Court of a quorum, and the case was sent to the Second Circuit. It was the only time in history that the Second Circuit effectively sat by designation as the Supreme Court. Judge Hand knew this was a rare opportunity and reportedly made the most of it. For background, *see* Spencer Weber Waller, The Story of *Alcoa*: The Enduring Questions of Market Power, Conduct, and Remedy in Monopolization Cases, in Eleanor Fox & Daniel Crane (eds.), Antitrust Stories (2007).

2. What Is a Monopoly? Definitionally, a monopoly is a market with only one seller. Such markets are exceedingly rare, so courts have interpreted § 2 functionally. In *Alcoa*, Judge Hand ruled that Alcoa, with (only) 90% of the market was deemed to be a monopolist. He reached this conclusion not because 90 is close to 100, but because "[t]he producer of so large a proportion of the supply has complete control within certain limits." This forecasts the modern definition of monopoly power, which is *the power to control prices.* Judge Hand deemed Alcoa to be a monopolist because it could raise prices and "is in a strong position to check [any] such competition" from the remaining 10% of the market.

3. What Is an *Illegal* Monopoly? Even though Alcoa was deemed to be a monopoly, the question remained whether it was an illegal monopolist, i.e., that it violated § 2. The litigants and Judge Hand offered a number of different approaches to determine whether a monopolist violates § 2.

a) *Did the monopolist "extract from the consumer more than a 'fair' profit"?* Alcoa argued that it never imposed excessive prices onto consumers, and therefore could not have violated § 2. Judge Hand rejected this approach, arguing that "[t]he Act has wider purposes." What are those other purposes?

b) *Should monopolists be per se illegal?* The government originally argued that Alcoa was for a time the single producer of "virgin" ingot in the United

States and "this without more was enough to make it an unlawful monopoly." Judge Hand rejected this approach as well, noting that "size does not determine guilt; that there must be some "exclusion" of competitors." Do you think monopolies should be per se illegal? How does this approach reflect the 1890 Congressional intent, or the public sentiments that compelled Congress to pass the Sherman Act?

c) *Did the defendant both enjoy monopoly power and also engage in anticompetitive conduct?* Ultimately, Judge Hand concluded that Alcoa violated § 2 because it "effectively anticipated and forestalled all competition, and succeeded in holding the field alone." This is the rough standard that continues to direct § 2. Does this approach achieve what you think should be the goals of antitrust law?

4. The Mixed Incentives Surrounding Monopolies. The *Alcoa* opinion displays some of Judge Hand's signature eloquence, but some of his most expressive passages appear to offer some internal contradictions. On one hand, he wrote:

> Many people believe that possession of unchallenged economic power deadens initiative, discourages thrift and depresses energy; that immunity from competition is a narcotic, and rivalry is a stimulant, to industrial progress; that the spur of constant stress is necessary to counteract an inevitable disposition to let well enough alone.

But then he wrote later:

> A single producer may be the survivor out of a group of active competitors, merely by virtue of his superior skill, foresight and industry. [T]he Act does not mean to condemn the resultant of those very forces which it is its prime object to foster: *finis opus coronat.* The successful competitor, having been urged to compete, must not be turned upon when he wins.

Can these sentiments toward monopoly be reconciled?

5. Continued Difficulties in Defining § 2 Violations. Even after the *Alcoa* case, § 2 jurisprudence continued to suffer from ambiguity and confusion. After observing that "[m]onopolization doctrine is currently governed by vacuous standards and conclusory labels that provide no meaningful guidance about which conduct is condemned," Professor Einer Elhauge offered the following to provide some clarity:

> U.S. antitrust law does not merely require "monopoly power" in the abstract, but a causal connection between the challenged exclusionary conduct and the acquisition or maintenance of that power. Such a causal connection is implicit in the language of § 2, which makes it illegal to "monopolize," "attempt to monopolize," or "conspire . . . to monopolize." The "-ize" suffix proves crucial, for it indicates that the gravamen of the offense is the illicit creation or maintenance of a monopoly power that otherwise would not exist, at least not to the same degree. Thus, the statutory language calls for proof of some causal connection between the illicit conduct and the extent

> of monopoly power, or in the case of attempted monopolization, at least a dangerous threat of such a causal connection.

Einer Elhauge, Defining Better Monopoly Standards, 56 Stan. L. Rev. 253, 331 (2003). Is Professor Elhauge's formulation, which does not condemn monopolists who engage in illicit conduct but only monopolists who engage in illicit conduct that is enabled by their monopoly power, consistent with Judge Hand's opinion in *Alcoa*? Does this narrow the scope and focus of § 2?

6. An Ambivalence Towards Monopoly Power? Recall Judge Kozinski's tolerance, even admiration, for certain monopolies ("[W]hen a producer deters competitors by supplying a better product at a lower price, the goals of competition are served, even if no actual competitors see fit to enter the market at a particular time."). A similar attitude was echoed by Justice Antonin Scalia's influential decision in Verizon Commc'ns Inc. v. L. Offs. of Curtis V. Trinko, LLP, 540 U.S. 398, 407 (2004), excerpted in Chapter 8:

> The mere possession of monopoly power, and the concomitant charging of monopoly prices, is not only not unlawful; it is an important element of the free-market system. The opportunity to charge monopoly prices—at least for a short period—is what attracts "business acumen" in the first place; it induces risk taking that produces innovation and economic growth.

Id. at 407. How do these perspectives on monopoly power relate to the approach, or approaches, offered by Judge Hand? And which of these squares best with the formulation by Professor Elhauge? And are these characterizations of modern antitrust law consistent with the congressional intent and the original motivations that underlie the Sherman Act?

Chapter 3

First Amendment Coverage

Introduction

The First Amendment has a major role in internet and telecommunications regulation. This is perhaps unsurprising given that wires and spectrum carry bits of data. In light of the pervasiveness and importance of telecommunications technologies, if a legislature wants to regulate the content of communications, such regulation will include telecommunications services. And, as we will discuss in Chapter 11, Congress has passed legislation regulating the content of communications over every form of telecommunications service, and the Supreme Court has invalidated most of these laws.

In this chapter we focus not on the exact level of First Amendment scrutiny the Court applies (though the level of scrutiny is an element of these cases) but instead on the scope of First Amendment coverage. That is, we consider the question of what sorts of laws trigger any First Amendment scrutiny. What laws relevant to internet and telecommunications regulation implicate the First Amendment and thus are subject to some sort of First Amendment scrutiny, and which do not implicate the First Amendment in the first place? In this way, the cases present structural constraints that the First Amendment imposes on internet and telecommunications regulation.

It may seem obvious that a regulation limiting the communication of particular content (like depictions of sex) will trigger First Amendment scrutiny. The First Amendment provides that "Congress shall make no law . . . abridging the freedom of speech," and the Supreme Court has long interpreted words, pictures, and videos as speech for First Amendment purposes.[1] It is less obvious, however, that a cable television operator's decisions regarding which networks to offer to its subscribers is speech for First Amendment purposes. And yet all nine Supreme Court justices agreed with that proposition in Turner Broadcasting System, Inc. v. FCC, 512 U.S. 622 (1994) (*Turner I*).

1. The word "Congress" has not been limited to Congress. The Court has interpreted the First Amendment to apply to all government actors.

Our aim in this chapter is not to address all issues of First Amendment coverage but instead to focus on the coverage questions relevant to the regulation of the internet and telecommunications. Such a focus does not mean looking only at internet and telecommunications cases. Important cases like Sorrell v. IMS Health Inc., 564 U.S. 552 (2011), do not involve electronic communications but have important implications for the kinds of laws, such as privacy regulations, that interest policymakers. We include *Sorrell* and FTC v. Superior Court Trial Lawyers Association, 493 U.S. 411 (1990), because they are particularly important guideposts for possible and existing laws regulating the internet and telecommunications.

§ 3.A. Industry-Specific Laws and the First Amendment

We begin with *Turner I*. This case is useful for several purposes. It laid out some basic principles of the Court's First Amendment jurisprudence, such as the distinction between content-based and content-neutral speech regulations and the different scrutiny applied to each. It held that cable operators' decisions of which channels to carry implicates the First Amendment. And it dealt with a form of mandatory access regulation: Congress, articulating concerns about the power flowing to cable operators from their control of the wire carrying television channels, provided that local television stations can demand that the local cable provider retransmit their broadcast signals at no charge (this is known as must-carry). Cable operators are required to set aside up to one-third of their channels for commercial broadcast stations that request carriage and up to one-twelfth for local public broadcast television stations. Even if the cable provider does not want to retransmit these broadcasters, the must-carry statute compels it to do so. The logic behind must-carry is that the protected broadcasters could be significantly harmed were the cable operator to decide not to retransmit their signals and instead to devote that channel capacity to other programming. The sponsors of must-carry argued that must-carry would enhance the economic viability of local broadcasters, which would benefit those who do not subscribe to cable by helping to keep local broadcasters afloat. Thus there are two different forms of access at issue: local broadcasters' access to cable systems (which must-carry directly regulates) and the access of viewers who lack cable access to local broadcasters (a proffered indirect benefit of must-carry).

The must-carry provisions were considered by the Supreme Court twice. The first of those cases is excerpted below.

Turner Broadcasting System, Inc. v. FCC [*Turner I*]

512 U.S. 622 (1994)

KENNEDY, J., announced the judgment of the Court and delivered the opinion for a unanimous Court with respect to Part I, the opinion of the Court with respect to Parts II-A and II-B, in which REHNQUIST, C.J., and BLACKMUN, O'CONNOR, SCALIA, SOUTER, THOMAS, and GINSBURG, JJ., joined, the opinion of the Court with respect to Parts II-C, II-D, and III-A, in which REHNQUIST, C.J., and BLACKMUN, STEVENS, and SOUTER, JJ., joined, and an opinion with respect to Part III-B, in which REHNQUIST, C.J., and BLACKMUN and SOUTER, JJ., joined. BLACKMUN, J., filed a concurring opinion. STEVENS, J., filed an opinion concurring in part and concurring in the judgment. O'CONNOR, J., filed an opinion concurring in part and dissenting in part, in which SCALIA and GINSBURG, JJ., joined, and in Parts I and III of which THOMAS, J., joined. GINSBURG, J., filed an opinion concurring in part and dissenting in part.

JUSTICE KENNEDY announced the judgment of the Court and delivered the opinion of the Court, except as to Part III-B.

I C

Congress enacted the Cable Television Consumer Protection and Competition Act of 1992, Pub.L. 102–385, 106 Stat. 1460 (1992 Cable Act or Act), after conducting three years of hearings on the structure and operation of the cable television industry. The conclusions Congress drew from its factfinding process are recited in the text of the Act itself. In brief, Congress found that the physical characteristics of cable transmission, compounded by the increasing concentration of economic power in the cable industry, are endangering the ability of over-the-air broadcast television stations to compete for a viewing audience and thus for necessary operating revenues. Congress determined that regulation of the market for video programming was necessary to correct this competitive imbalance.

In particular, Congress found that over 60 percent of the households with television sets subscribe to cable, and for these households cable has replaced over-the-air broadcast television as the primary provider of video programming. This is so, Congress found, because "[m]ost subscribers to cable television systems do not or cannot maintain antennas to receive broadcast television services, do not have input selector switches to convert from a cable to antenna reception system, or cannot otherwise receive broadcast television services." § 2(a)(17). In addition, Congress concluded that due to "local franchising requirements and the extraordinary expense of constructing more than one cable television system to serve a particular geographic area," the overwhelming majority of cable operators exercise a monopoly over cable service. § 2(a)(2). "The result," Congress determined, "is undue market power for the cable operator as compared to that of consumers and video programmers." *Id.*

According to Congress, this market position gives cable operators the power and the incentive to harm broadcast competitors. The power derives from the cable operator's ability, as owner of the transmission facility, to "terminate the retransmission of the broadcast signal, refuse to carry new signals, or reposition a broadcast signal to a disadvantageous channel position." § 2(a)(15). The incentive derives from the economic reality that "[c]able television systems and broadcast television stations increasingly compete for television advertising revenues." § 2(a)(14). By refusing carriage of broadcasters' signals, cable operators, as a practical matter, can reduce the number of households that have access to the broadcasters' programming, and thereby capture advertising dollars that would otherwise go to broadcast stations. § 2(a)(15).

Congress found, in addition, that increased vertical integration in the cable industry is making it even harder for broadcasters to secure carriage on cable systems, because cable operators have a financial incentive to favor their affiliated programmers. § 2(a)(5). Congress also determined that the cable industry is characterized by horizontal concentration, with many cable operators sharing common ownership. This has resulted in greater "barriers to entry for new programmers and a reduction in the number of media voices available to consumers." § 2(a)(4).

In light of these technological and economic conditions, Congress concluded that unless cable operators are required to carry local broadcast stations, "[t]here is a substantial likelihood that . . . additional local broadcast signals will be deleted, repositioned, or not carried," § 2(a)(15); the "marked shift in market share" from broadcast to cable will continue to erode the advertising revenue base which sustains free local broadcast television, §§ 2(a)(13)–(14); and that, as a consequence, "the economic viability of free local broadcast television and its ability to originate quality local programming will be seriously jeopardized." § 2(a)(16).

II

There can be no disagreement on an initial premise: Cable programmers and cable operators engage in and transmit speech, and they are entitled to the protection of the speech and press provisions of the First Amendment. Through "original programming or by exercising editorial discretion over which stations or programs to include in its repertoire," cable programmers and operators "seek[] to communicate messages on a wide variety of topics and in a wide variety of formats." Los Angeles v. Preferred Communications, Inc., 476 U.S. 488, 494 (1986). By requiring cable systems to set aside a portion of their channels for local broadcasters, the must-carry rules regulate cable speech in two respects: The rules reduce the number of channels over which cable operators exercise unfettered control, and they render it more difficult for cable programmers to compete for carriage on the limited channels remaining. Nevertheless, because not every interference with speech triggers the same degree of scrutiny under the First Amendment, we must decide at the outset the level of scrutiny applicable to the must-carry provisions.

A

[T]he Government and some appellees maintain that the must-carry provisions are nothing more than industry-specific antitrust legislation, and thus warrant rational basis scrutiny under this Court's "precedents governing legislative efforts to correct market failure in a market whose commodity is speech," such as Associated Press v. United States, 326 U.S. 1 (1945), and Lorain Journal Co. v. United States, 342 U.S. 143 (1951). This contention is unavailing. *Associated Press* and *Lorain Journal* both involved actions against members of the press brought under the Sherman Antitrust Act, a law of general application. But while the enforcement of a generally applicable law may or may not be subject to heightened scrutiny under the First Amendment, laws that single out the press, or certain elements thereof, for special treatment "pose a particular danger of abuse by the State," Arkansas Writers' Project, Inc. v. Ragland, 481 U.S. 221, 228 (1987), and so are always subject to at least some degree of heightened First Amendment scrutiny. Because the must-carry provisions impose special obligations upon cable operators and special burdens upon cable programmers, some measure of heightened First Amendment scrutiny is demanded.

B

At the heart of the First Amendment lies the principle that each person should decide for himself or herself the ideas and beliefs deserving of expression, consideration, and adherence. Our political system and cultural life rest upon this ideal. Government action that stifles speech on account of its message, or that requires the utterance of a particular message favored by the Government, contravenes this essential right. Laws of this sort pose the inherent risk that the Government seeks not to advance a legitimate regulatory goal, but to suppress unpopular ideas or information or manipulate the public debate through coercion rather than persuasion.

For these reasons, the First Amendment, subject only to narrow and well-understood exceptions, does not countenance governmental control over the content of messages expressed by private individuals. Our precedents thus apply the most exacting scrutiny to regulations that suppress, disadvantage, or impose differential burdens upon speech because of its content. Laws that compel speakers to utter or distribute speech bearing a particular message are subject to the same rigorous scrutiny. In contrast, regulations that are unrelated to the content of speech are subject to an intermediate level of scrutiny, because in most cases they pose a less substantial risk of excising certain ideas or viewpoints from the public dialogue.

Deciding whether a particular regulation is content based or content neutral is not always a simple task. We have said that the "principal inquiry in determining content neutrality . . . is whether the government has adopted a regulation of speech because of [agreement or] disagreement with the message it conveys." Ward v. Rock Against Racism, 491 U.S. 781, 791 (1989). But while a content-based purpose may be sufficient in certain circumstances to show that a regulation is content based, it is not necessary to such a showing in all cases. Nor will the mere assertion of a content-neutral purpose be enough to save a law which, on its face, discriminates based on content.

As a general rule, laws that by their terms distinguish favored speech from disfavored speech on the basis of the ideas or views expressed are content based. By contrast, laws that confer benefits or impose burdens on speech without reference to the ideas or views expressed are in most instances content neutral.

C

It is true that the must-carry provisions distinguish between speakers in the television programming market. But they do so based only upon the manner in which speakers transmit their messages to viewers, and not upon the messages they carry: Broadcasters, which transmit over the airwaves, are favored, while cable programmers, which do not, are disfavored. Cable operators, too, are burdened by the carriage obligations, but only because they control access to the cable conduit. So long as they are not a subtle means of exercising a content preference, speaker distinctions of this nature are not presumed invalid under the First Amendment.

That the must-carry provisions, on their face, do not burden or benefit speech of a particular content does not end the inquiry. Our cases have recognized that even a regulation neutral on its face may be content based if its manifest purpose is to regulate speech because of the message it conveys.

Our review of the Act and its various findings persuades us that Congress' overriding objective in enacting must-carry was not to favor programming of a particular subject matter, viewpoint, or format, but rather to preserve access to free television programming for the 40 percent of Americans without cable.

In unusually detailed statutory findings, Congress explained that because cable systems and broadcast stations compete for local advertising revenue, §§ 2(a)(14)–(15), and because cable operators have a vested financial interest in favoring their affiliated programmers over broadcast stations, § 2(a)(5), cable operators have a built-in "economic incentive . . . to delete, reposition, or not carry local broadcast signals." § 2(a)(16). Congress concluded that absent a requirement that cable systems carry the signals of local broadcast stations, the continued availability of free local broadcast television would be threatened. *Id.* Congress sought to avoid the elimination of broadcast television because, in its words, "[s]uch programming is . . . free to those who own television sets and do not require cable transmission to receive broadcast television signals," § 2(a)(12), and because "[t]here is a substantial governmental interest in promoting the continued availability of such free television programming, especially for viewers who are unable to afford other means of receiving programming." *Id.*

Appellants and Justice O'Connor make much of the fact that, in the course of describing the purposes behind the Act, Congress referred to the value of broadcast programming. In particular, Congress noted that broadcast television is "an important source of local news[,] public affairs programming, and other local broadcast services critical to an informed electorate," § 2(a)(11), and that noncommercial television "provides educational and informational programming to the Nation's citizens." § 2(a)(3). We do not think, however, that such references cast any material doubt on the content-neutral character of must-carry. That Congress acknowledged the local orientation of broadcast programming and the role that noncommercial stations have played in educating the public does not indicate that Congress regarded broadcast programming as *more* valuable than cable programming. Rather, it reflects nothing more than the recognition that the services provided by broadcast television have some intrinsic value and, thus, are worth preserving against the threats posed by cable.

III A

[T]he must-carry provisions do not pose such inherent dangers to free expression, or present such potential for censorship or manipulation, as to justify application of the most exacting level of First Amendment scrutiny. [T]he appropriate standard by which to evaluate the constitutionality of must-carry is the intermediate level of scrutiny applicable to content-neutral restrictions that impose an incidental burden on speech.

Under United States v. O'Brien, 391 U.S. 367 (1968), a content-neutral regulation will be sustained if "it furthers an important or substantial governmental interest; if the governmental interest is unrelated to the suppression of free expression; and if the incidental restriction on alleged First Amendment freedoms is no greater than is essential to the furtherance of that interest." *Id.* at 377. To satisfy this standard, a regulation need not be the least speech-restrictive means of advancing the Government's interests. Narrow tailoring in this context requires that the means chosen do not "burden substantially more speech than is necessary to further the government's legitimate interests." Ward v. Rock Against Racism, 491 U.S. at 799.

Congress declared that the must-carry provisions serve three interrelated interests: (1) preserving the benefits of free, over-the-air local broadcast television, (2) promoting the widespread dissemination of information from a multiplicity of sources, and (3) promoting fair competition in the market for television programming. None of these interests is related to the "suppression of free expression," *O'Brien*, 391 U.S. at 377, or to the content of any speakers' messages. And viewed in the abstract, we have no difficulty concluding that each of them is an important governmental interest.

That the Government's asserted interests are important in the abstract does not mean, however, that the must-carry rules will in fact advance those interests. When the Government defends a regulation on speech as a means to redress past harms or prevent anticipated harms, it must do more than simply "posit the existence of the disease sought to be cured." Quincy Cable TV, Inc. v. FCC, 768 F.2d 1434, 1455 (D.C. Cir. 1985). It must demonstrate that the recited harms are real, not merely conjectural, and that the regulation will in fact alleviate these harms in a direct and material way.

Thus, in applying *O'Brien* scrutiny we must ask first whether the Government has adequately shown that the economic health of local broadcasting is in genuine jeopardy and in need of the protections afforded by must-carry. Assuming an affirmative answer to the foregoing question, the Government still bears the burden of showing that the remedy it has adopted does not "burden substantially more speech than is necessary to further the government's legitimate interests." *Ward*, 491 U.S. at 799. On the state of the record developed thus far, and in the absence of findings of fact from the District Court, we are unable to conclude that the Government has satisfied either inquiry.

[W]e think it necessary to permit the parties to develop a more thorough factual record, and to allow the District Court to resolve any factual disputes remaining, before passing upon the constitutional validity of the challenged provisions.

[Concurring opinions of JUSTICE BLACKMUN and of JUSTICE STEVENS are omitted.]

JUSTICE O'CONNOR, with whom JUSTICE SCALIA and JUSTICE GINSBURG join, and with whom JUSTICE THOMAS joins as to Parts I and III, concurring in part and dissenting in part.

I A

The 1992 Cable Act implicates the First Amendment rights of two classes of speakers. First, it tells cable operators which programmers they must carry, and keeps cable operators from carrying others that they might prefer. Though cable operators do not actually originate most of the programming they show, the Court correctly holds that they are, for First Amendment purposes, speakers. Selecting which speech to retransmit is, as we know from the example of publishing houses, movie theaters, bookstores, and "Reader's Digest," no less communication than is creating the speech in the first place.

Second, the Act deprives a certain class of video programmers — those who operate cable channels rather than broadcast stations — of access to over one-third of an entire medium. Cable programmers may compete only for those channels that are not set aside by the must-carry provisions. It is as if the government ordered all movie theaters to reserve at least one-third of their screening for films made by American production companies, or required all bookstores to devote one-third of their shelf space to nonprofit publishers. As the Court explains in Parts I, II-A, and II-B of its opinion, which I join, cable programmers and operators stand in the same position under the First Amendment as do the more traditional media.

But looking at the statute at issue, I cannot avoid the conclusion that its preference for broadcasters over cable programmers is justified with reference to content. The findings, enacted by Congress as § 2 of the Act, and which I must assume state the justifications for the law, make this clear. "There is a substantial governmental and First Amendment interest in promoting a diversity of views provided through multiple technology media." § 2(a)(6). "[P]ublic television provides educational and informational programming to the Nation's citizens, thereby advancing the Government's compelling interest in educating its citizens." § 2(a)(8)(A). "A primary objective and benefit of our Nation's system of regulation of television broadcasting is the local origination of programming. There is a substantial governmental interest in ensuring its continuation." § 2(a)(10). "Broadcast television stations continue to be an important source of local news and public affairs programming and other local broadcast services critical to an informed electorate." § 2(a)(11).

Similar justifications are reflected in the operative provisions of the Act. In determining whether a broadcast station should be eligible for must-carry in a particular market, the FCC must "afford particular attention to the value of localism by taking into account such factors as . . . whether any other [eligible station] provides news coverage of issues of concern to such community or provides carriage or coverage of sporting and other events of interest to the community." § 4.

Preferences for diversity of viewpoints, for localism, for educational programming, and for news and public affairs all make reference to content. They may not reflect hostility to particular points of view, or a desire to suppress certain subjects because they are controversial or offensive. They may be quite benignly motivated. But benign motivation, we have consistently held, is not enough to avoid the need for strict scrutiny of content based justifications. The First Amendment does more than just bar government from intentionally suppressing speech of which it disapproves. It also generally prohibits the government from excepting certain kinds of speech from regulation because it thinks the speech is especially valuable.

III

The question is not whether there will be control over who gets to speak over cable — the question is who will have this control. Under the FCC's view, the answer is Congress, acting within relatively broad limits. Under my view, the answer is the cable operator.

I have no doubt that there is danger in having a single cable operator decide what millions of subscribers can or cannot watch. And I have no doubt that Congress can act to relieve this danger. In other provisions of the Act, Congress has already taken steps to foster competition among cable systems. Congress can encourage the creation of new media, such as inexpensive satellite broadcasting, or fiber-optic networks with virtually unlimited channels, or even simple devices that would let people easily switch from cable to over-the-air broadcasting. And of course Congress can subsidize broadcasters that it thinks provide especially valuable programming.

But the First Amendment as we understand it today rests on the premise that it is government power, rather than private power, that is the main threat to free expression; and as a consequence, the Amendment imposes substantial limitations on the Government even when it is trying to serve concededly praiseworthy goals.

[Concurring and dissenting opinion of JUSTICE GINSBURG is omitted.]

Notes and Questions

1. Content-Based versus Content-Neutral Regulations, and Strict versus Intermediate Scrutiny. Part II-B laid out a central distinction in First Amendment jurisprudence, between content-based regulation (subject to strict scrutiny) and content-neutral regulation (subject to intermediate scrutiny). First Amendment strict scrutiny is almost always fatal, whereas intermediate scrutiny under the First Amendment is easier to satisfy. But both forms of scrutiny are substantially more difficult to satisfy than rational basis review and pose a significant hurdle for government regulation.

This is one of many cases articulating the distinction, and the Court was not making new law in this section. We include this section of the opinion to familiarize readers with this important distinction.

2. "There Can Be No Disagreement . . ." The most important element of *Turner I* was presented as obvious:

> There can be no disagreement on an initial premise: Cable programmers and cable operators engage in and transmit speech, and they are entitled to the protection of the speech and press provisions of the First Amendment. Through "original programming or by exercising editorial discretion over which stations or programs to include in its repertoire," cable programmers and operators "seek[] to communicate messages on a wide variety of topics and in a wide variety of formats." (Citation omitted.)

The dissenters made clear their agreement with this conclusion (and their dissent was premised on such agreement). Thus all nine Justices signed on to this proposition. The majority's assertion built on the cases it cited in this paragraph, but it stated the point with particular clarity: not only creating programming but also choosing which stations or programs to carry is speech for First Amendment purposes. This language suggests two—and only two—elements for First Amendment coverage: first, that cable programmers and operators either create programming or choose what to air; and, second, that in doing so they seek to communicate messages on a variety of topics.

And, as part II-A made clear, it does not change the First Amendment analysis to characterize a regulation as industry-specific antitrust legislation: even if the legislation is based on an anticompetitive rationale, if it singles out particular categories of speakers it will trigger First Amendment scrutiny. So even if (as the Court ultimately concluded in *Turner II*) Congress has antitrust-related reasons for passing legislation regulating particular categories of speakers, the Court will apply First Amendment scrutiny to such legislation.

As will become clear in this and following chapters, the quoted language from *Turner I* has enormous significance for internet and telecommunications regulation. Insofar as entities are exercising editorial discretion over what is communicated via their services, they will have a First Amendment argument for heightened scrutiny with respect to any industry-specific regulations of their exercise of that discretion.

Note that this places great importance on the question of exactly what constitutes editorial discretion, thus triggering First Amendment scrutiny. We address that question in Chapter 6 in the context of a prominent question in which this arose — net neutrality.

3. Content Neutral? Precisely why did the majority and dissenting opinions differ on the key question of whether the must-carry provisions are content neutral? Are you convinced by the majority's argument that the content-neutral criterion Congress used was "the manner in which speakers transmit their messages to viewers"? The 1992 Cable Act does not direct cable systems to carry all broadcasters or even a number of randomly selected ones; only local broadcasters were selected for must-carry status. On the other hand, were the dissenting Justices straining in finding a content-based explanation for must-carry provisions that appear more plainly to rest on an economic premise: that cable operators control a facility to which their rival broadcast stations need access in order to compete?

4. After Remand. The *Turner I* plurality did not apply intermediate scrutiny to the statutory regime and instead remanded. After remand, the Court issued its second opinion on the must-carry rules.

Turner Broadcasting System, Inc. v. FCC [*Turner II*]

520 U.S. 180 (1997)

KENNEDY, J., announced the judgment of the Court and delivered the opinion of the Court, except as to a portion of Part II-A-1. REHNQUIST, C.J., and STEVENS and SOUTER, JJ., joined that opinion in full, and BREYER, J., joined except insofar as Part II-A-1 relied on an anticompetitive rationale. STEVENS, J., filed a concurring opinion. BREYER, J., filed an opinion concurring in part. O'CONNOR, J., filed a dissenting opinion, in which SCALIA, THOMAS, and GINSBURG, JJ., joined.

JUSTICE KENNEDY delivered the opinion of the Court, except as to a portion of Part II-A-1.

II

As noted in *Turner [I]*, must-carry was designed to serve "three interrelated interests: (1) preserving the benefits of free, over-the-air local broadcast television, (2) promoting the widespread dissemination of information from a multiplicity of sources, and (3) promoting fair competition in the market for television programming." *Turner [I]*, 512 U.S. at 662. We decided then, and now reaffirm, that each of those is an important governmental interest.

A

The expanded record permits us to consider whether the must-carry provisions were designed to address a real harm, and whether those provisions will alleviate it in a material way. We turn first to the harm or risk which prompted Congress to act. The Government's assertion that "the economic health of local broadcasting is in genuine jeopardy and in need of the protections afforded by must-carry" rests on two component propositions: First, "significant numbers of broadcast stations will be refused carriage on cable systems" absent must-carry. *Id.* at 666. Second, "the broadcast stations denied carriage will either deteriorate to a substantial degree or fail altogether." *Id.*

1

We have no difficulty in finding a substantial basis to support Congress' conclusion that a real threat justified enactment of the must-carry provisions.

As to the evidence before Congress, there was specific support for its conclusion that cable operators had considerable and growing market power over local video programming markets. As Congress noted, § 2(a)(2), cable operators possess a local monopoly over cable households.

Evidence indicated the structure of the cable industry would give cable operators increasing ability and incentive to drop local broadcast stations from their systems, or reposition them to a less-viewed channel. Horizontal concentration was increasing as a small number of multiple system operators acquired large numbers of cable systems nationwide.

Vertical integration in the industry also was increasing. Extensive testimony indicated that cable operators would have an incentive to drop local broadcasters and to favor affiliated programmers.

After hearing years of testimony, and reviewing volumes of documentary evidence and studies offered by both sides, Congress concluded that the cable industry posed a threat to broadcast television. The Constitution gives to Congress the role of weighing conflicting evidence in the legislative process. Even when the resulting regulation touches on First Amendment concerns, we must give considerable deference, in examining the evidence, to Congress' findings and conclusions, including its findings and conclusions with respect to conflicting economic predictions. Furthermore, much of the testimony, though offered by interested parties, was supported by verifiable information and citation to independent sources.

In addition, evidence before Congress, supplemented on remand, indicated that cable systems would have incentives to drop local broadcasters in favor of other programmers less likely to compete with them for audience and advertisers. Empirical studies indicate that cable-carried broadcasters so enhance competition for advertising that even modest increases in the numbers of broadcast stations carried on cable are correlated with significant decreases in advertising revenue to cable systems. Thus, operators stand to benefit by dropping broadcast stations.

Cable systems also have more systemic reasons for seeking to disadvantage broadcast stations: Simply stated, cable has little interest in assisting, through carriage, a competing medium of communication.

It was more than a theoretical possibility in 1992 that cable operators would take actions adverse to local broadcasters; indeed, significant numbers of broadcasters had already been dropped. The record before Congress contained extensive anecdotal evidence about scores of adverse carriage decisions against broadcast stations.

The issue before us is whether, given conflicting views of the probable development of the television industry, Congress had substantial evidence for making the judgment that it did. We need not put our imprimatur on Congress' economic theory in order to validate the reasonableness of its judgment.

2

The harm Congress feared was that stations dropped or denied carriage would be at a "serious risk of financial difficulty" and would "deteriorate to a substantial degree or fail altogether." *Turner I* at 666. Congress had before it substantial evidence to support its conclusion. Congress was advised the viability of a broadcast station depends to a material extent on its ability to secure cable carriage.

III

Judgments about how competing economic interests are to be reconciled in the complex and fast-changing field of television are for Congress to make. Those judgments "cannot be ignored or undervalued simply because [appellants] cast[] [their] claims under the umbrella of the First Amendment." Columbia Broadcasting v. Democratic National Committee, 412 U.S. 94, 103 (1974). The judgment of the District Court is affirmed.

[Concurring opinion of JUSTICE STEVENS is omitted.]

JUSTICE BREYER, concurring in part.

I join the opinion of the Court except insofar as Part II-A-1 relies on an anticompetitive rationale. Whether or not the statute does or does not sensibly compensate for some significant market defect, it undoubtedly seeks to provide over-the-air viewers who *lack* cable with a rich mix of over-the-air programming by guaranteeing the over-the-air stations that provide such programming with the extra dollars that an additional cable audience will generate. I believe that this purpose — to assure the over-the-air public "access to a multiplicity of information sources" — provides sufficient basis for rejecting appellants' First Amendment claim.

I do not deny that the compulsory carriage that creates the "guarantee" extracts a serious First Amendment price. It interferes with the protected interests of the cable operators to choose their own programming; it prevents displaced cable program providers from obtaining an audience; and it will sometimes prevent some cable viewers from watching what, in its absence, would have been their preferred set of programs. This "price" amounts to a "suppression of speech."

But there are important First Amendment interests on the other side as well. The statute's basic noneconomic purpose is to prevent too precipitous a decline in the quality and quantity of programming choice for an ever-shrinking non-cable-subscribing segment of the public. This purpose reflects what "has long been a basic tenet of national communications policy," namely that "the widest possible dissemination of information from diverse and antagonistic sources is essential to the welfare of the public." *Turner I.* That policy, in turn, seeks to facilitate the public discussion and informed deliberation, which, as Justice Brandeis pointed out many years ago, democratic government presupposes and the First Amendment seeks to achieve.

With important First Amendment interests on both sides of the equation, the key question becomes one of proper fit. In particular, I note (and agree) that a cable system, physically dependent upon the availability of space along city streets, at present (perhaps less in the future) typically faces little competition, that it therefore constitutes a kind of bottleneck that controls the range of viewer choice (whether or not it uses any consequent economic power for economically predatory purposes), and that *some* degree—at least a limited degree—of governmental intervention and control through regulation can prove appropriate when justified under *O'Brien* (at least when not "content based"). I also agree that, without the statute, cable systems would likely carry significantly fewer over-the-air stations, that station revenues would therefore decline, and that the quality of over-the-air programming on such stations would almost inevitably suffer. I agree further that the burden the statute imposes upon the cable system, potential cable programmers, and cable viewers, is limited and will diminish as typical cable system capacity grows over time.

These and other similar factors discussed by the majority lead me to agree that the statute survives "intermediate scrutiny," whether or not the statute is properly tailored to Congress' purely economic objectives.

JUSTICE O'CONNOR, with whom JUSTICE SCALIA, JUSTICE THOMAS, and JUSTICE GINSBURG join, dissenting.

In sustaining the must-carry provisions against a First Amendment challenge by cable system operators and cable programmers, the Court errs in two crucial respects. First, the Court disregards one of the principal defenses of the statute urged by appellees on remand: that it serves a substantial interest in preserving "diverse," "quality" programming that is "responsive" to the needs of the local community. The course of this litigation on remand and the proffered defense strongly reinforce my view that the Court adopted the wrong analytic framework in the prior phase of this case. Second, the Court misapplies the "intermediate scrutiny" framework it adopts. Although we owe deference to Congress' predictive judgments and its evaluation of complex economic questions, we have an independent duty to identify with care the Government interests supporting the scheme, to inquire into the reasonableness of congressional findings regarding its necessity, and to examine the fit between its goals and its consequences. The Court fails to discharge its duty here.

Much of the principal opinion treats the must-carry provisions as a species of antitrust regulation enacted by Congress in response to a perceived threat that cable system operators would otherwise engage in various forms of anticompetitive conduct resulting in harm to broadcasters.

I fully agree that promoting fair competition is a legitimate and substantial Government goal. But the Court nowhere examines whether the breadth of the must-carry provisions comports with a goal of preventing anticompetitive harms.

I do not read Justice Breyer's opinion—which analyzes the must-carry rules in part as a "speech-enhancing" measure designed to ensure a "rich mix" of over-the-air programming—to treat the content of over-the-air programming as irrelevant to whether the Government's interest in promoting it is an important one. The net result appears to be that five Justices of this Court *do not* view must-carry as a narrowly tailored means of serving a substantial governmental interest in preventing anticompetitive behavior; and that five Justices of this Court *do* see the significance of the content of over-the-air programming to the Government's and appellees' efforts to defend the law. Under these circumstances, the must-carry provisions should be subject to strict scrutiny, which they surely fail.

Notes and Questions

1. Deference to Congress's Predictive Judgments. In both *Turner I* and *Turner II*, the Court suggested that the asserted harms to broadcast television had not yet occurred and that the legislative assertions of such harms were therefore predictions. A big part of the disagreement between the majority and the dissent was over the degree to which the Court should defer to Congress's predictive judgments. Should the predictive nature of these harms affect the constitutional analysis, and if so, how?

2. Breyer's Alternative Framing. Justice Breyer's concurrence encapsulates an alternative approach to First Amendment analysis that Breyer applied in other cases as well. Note that he placed First Amendment interests "on both sides of the equation" because he saw the government's interest in public discussion and informed deliberation as a First Amendment interest that the government can seek to effectuate. Supreme Court opinions have construed the First Amendment as a limitation on government power. Some academics and some Justices (Breyer being the most prominent recent Justice) have contended that this is a mistake, and that First Amendment interests also should be understood to empower Congress to regulate.

This relates to a second aspect of Breyer's concurrence—that must-carry is based not on an anticompetitive rationale but instead on the content that broadcasters offer, and that this focus on content is constitutionally permissible in this case. None of the other eight Justices accepted that framing: the plurality (in *Turner I* and *Turner II*) stated that must-carry is not content-based and is instead a content-neutral regulation reflecting anticompetitive concerns, and the dissent contended that must-carry is content-based and flunks strict scrutiny. The last paragraph of Justice O'Connor's dissent in *Turner II* reflected her apparent frustration that Breyer found the statute content-based but permissible anyway.

We highlight Breyer's approach because it represents an alternative to the way that the Supreme Court's jurisprudence has developed. If the Court treated the First

Amendment as empowering Congress and/or if the Court treated content-based regulations of speech as subject to intermediate (or less) scrutiny, the hurdles facing policymakers who wanted to regulate speech based on its content would be much lower.

3. Regulating the Marketing of Information. As we noted above, must-carry is a form of access regulation. A converse form of regulation prevents disclosure of information, at least for some purposes. The focus is not on access but on the denial thereof—keeping information out of the hands of those who might misuse it. Does the First Amendment apply to, and thus constrain, limits on disclosure of information? *Sorrell v. IMS Health Inc.*, excepted below, addresses that question. It is not a communications case, but it has relevance for the kinds of regulation that might be applied to the internet and telecommunications. More broadly, the *Turner* cases and *Sorrell* are the key cases regarding First Amendment coverage relevant to internet and telecommunications law. And, as the cases clarified, that coverage is quite broad.

Sorrell v. IMS Health Inc.

564 U.S. 552 (2011)

KENNEDY, J., delivered the opinion of the Court, in which ROBERTS, C.J., and SCALIA, THOMAS, ALITO, and SOTOMAYOR, JJ., joined. BREYER, J., filed a dissenting opinion, in which GINSBURG and KAGAN, JJ., joined.

JUSTICE KENNEDY delivered the opinion of the Court.

I A

Pharmaceutical manufacturers promote their drugs to doctors through a process called "detailing." This often involves a scheduled visit to a doctor's office to persuade the doctor to prescribe a particular pharmaceutical. Detailers bring drug samples as well as medical studies that explain the "details" and potential advantages of various prescription drugs. Interested physicians listen, ask questions, and receive followup data. Salespersons can be more effective when they know the background and purchasing preferences of their clientele, and pharmaceutical salespersons are no exception. Knowledge of a physician's prescription practices—called "prescriber-identifying information"—enables a detailer better to ascertain which doctors are likely to be interested in a particular drug and how best to present a particular sales message. Detailing is an expensive undertaking, so pharmaceutical companies most often use it to promote high-profit brand-name drugs protected by patent. Once a brand-name drug's patent expires, less expensive bioequivalent generic alternatives are manufactured and sold.

Pharmacies, as a matter of business routine and federal law, receive prescriber-identifying information when processing prescriptions. Many pharmacies sell this information to "data miners," firms that analyze prescriber-identifying information and produce reports on prescriber behavior. Data miners lease these reports to pharmaceutical manufacturers subject to nondisclosure agreements. Detailers, who represent the manufacturers, then use the reports to refine their marketing tactics and increase sales.

In 2007, Vermont enacted the Prescription Confidentiality Law. The measure is also referred to as Act 80. It has several components. The central provision of the present case is § 4631(d).

> A health insurer, a self-insured employer, an electronic transmission intermediary, a pharmacy, or other similar entity shall not sell, license, or exchange for value regulated records containing prescriber-identifiable information, nor permit the use of regulated records containing prescriber-identifiable information for marketing or promoting a prescription drug, unless the prescriber consents.... Pharmaceutical manufacturers and pharmaceutical marketers shall not use prescriber-identifiable information for marketing or promoting a prescription drug unless the prescriber consents....

II A 1

On its face, Vermont's law enacts content-and speaker-based restrictions on the sale, disclosure, and use of prescriber-identifying information. The provision first forbids sale subject to exceptions based in large part on the content of a purchaser's speech. For example, those who wish to engage in certain "educational communications," § 4631(e)(4), may purchase the information. The measure then bars any disclosure when recipient speakers will use the information for marketing. Finally, the provision's second sentence prohibits pharmaceutical manufacturers from using the information for marketing. The statute thus disfavors marketing, that is, speech with a particular content. More than that, the statute disfavors specific speakers, namely pharmaceutical manufacturers. As a result of these content- and speaker-based rules, detailers cannot obtain prescriber-identifying information, even though the information may be purchased or acquired by other speakers with diverse purposes and viewpoints. Detailers are likewise barred from using the information for marketing, even though the information may be used by a wide range of other speakers. For example, it appears that Vermont could supply academic organizations with prescriber-identifying information to use in countering the messages of brand-name pharmaceutical manufacturers and in promoting the prescription of generic drugs. But § 4631(d) leaves detailers no means of purchasing, acquiring, or using prescriber-identifying information. The law on its face burdens disfavored speech by disfavored speakers.

[Section 4631(d)] is designed to impose a specific, content-based burden on protected expression. It follows that heightened judicial scrutiny is warranted. The Court has recognized that the "distinction between laws burdening and laws banning speech is but a matter of degree" and that the "Government's content-based burdens must satisfy the same rigorous scrutiny as its content-based bans." United

States v. Playboy Entertainment Group, Inc., 529 U.S. 803, 812 (2000). Lawmakers may no more silence unwanted speech by burdening its utterance than by censoring its content.

The First Amendment requires heightened scrutiny whenever the government creates "a regulation of speech because of disagreement with the message it conveys." Ward v. Rock Against Racism, 491 U.S. 781, 791 (1989). A government bent on frustrating an impending demonstration might pass a law demanding two years' notice before the issuance of parade permits. Even if the hypothetical measure on its face appeared neutral as to content and speaker, its purpose to suppress speech and its unjustified burdens on expression would render it unconstitutional. Commercial speech is no exception. A "consumer's concern for the free flow of commercial speech often may be far keener than his concern for urgent political dialogue." Bates v. State Bar of Arizona, 433 U.S. 350, 364 (1977). That reality has great relevance in the fields of medicine and public health, where information can save lives.

2

The State argues that heightened judicial scrutiny is unwarranted because its law is a mere commercial regulation. It is true that restrictions on protected expression are distinct from restrictions on economic activity or, more generally, on nonexpressive conduct. It is also true that the First Amendment does not prevent restrictions directed at commerce or conduct from imposing incidental burdens on speech. That is why a ban on race-based hiring may require employers to remove "'White Applicants Only'" signs, Rumsfeld v. Forum for Academic and Institutional Rights, Inc., 547 U.S. 47, 62 (2006); why "an ordinance against outdoor fires" might forbid "burning a flag," R.A.V. v. St. Paul, 505 U.S. 377, 385 (1992); and why antitrust laws can prohibit "agreements in restraint of trade," Giboney v. Empire Storage & Ice Co., 336 U.S. 490, 502 (1949).

But § 4631(d) imposes more than an incidental burden on protected expression. Both on its face and in its practical operation, Vermont's law imposes a burden based on the content of speech and the identity of the speaker. While the burdened speech results from an economic motive, so too does a great deal of vital expression. Vermont's law does not simply have an effect on speech, but is directed at certain content and is aimed at particular speakers. The Constitution "does not enact Mr. Herbert Spencer's Social Statics." Lochner v. New York, 198 U.S. 45, 75 (1905) (Holmes, J., dissenting). It does enact the First Amendment.

The State contends that heightened judicial scrutiny is unwarranted in this case because sales, transfer, and use of prescriber-identifying information are conduct, not speech. Consistent with that submission, the United States Court of Appeals for the First Circuit has characterized prescriber-identifying information as a mere "commodity" with no greater entitlement to First Amendment protection than "beef jerky." IMS Health Inc. v. Ayotte, 550 F.3d 42, 52–53 (2008). In contrast the courts below concluded that a prohibition on the sale of prescriber-identifying information is a content-based rule akin to a ban on the sale of cookbooks, laboratory results, or train schedules.

This Court has held that the creation and dissemination of information are speech within the meaning of the First Amendment. Facts, after all, are the beginning point for much of the speech that is most essential to advance human knowledge and to conduct human affairs. There is thus a strong argument that prescriber-identifying information is speech for First Amendment purposes.

The State asks for an exception to the rule that information is speech, but there is no need to consider that request in this case. The State has imposed content- and speaker-based restrictions on the availability and use of prescriber-identifying information. So long as they do not engage in marketing, many speakers can obtain and use the information. But detailers cannot. Vermont's statute could be compared with a law prohibiting trade magazines from purchasing or using ink. Like that hypothetical law, § 4631(d) imposes a speaker- and content-based burden on protected expression, and that circumstance is sufficient to justify application of heightened scrutiny. As a consequence, this case can be resolved even assuming, as the State argues, that prescriber-identifying information is a mere commodity.

B

In the ordinary case it is all but dispositive to conclude that a law is content based and, in practice, viewpoint discriminatory. The State argues that a different analysis applies here because, assuming § 4631(d) burdens speech at all, it at most burdens only commercial speech. As in previous cases, however, the outcome is the same whether a special commercial speech inquiry or a stricter form of judicial scrutiny is applied. For the same reason there is no need to determine whether all speech hampered by § 4631(d) is commercial, as our cases have used that term.

Under a commercial speech inquiry, it is the State's burden to justify its content-based law as consistent with the First Amendment. To sustain the targeted, content-based burden § 4631(d) imposes on protected expression, the State must show at least that the statute directly advances a substantial governmental interest and that the measure is drawn to achieve that interest. There must be a "fit between the legislature's ends and the means chosen to accomplish those ends." Board of Trustees of State Univ. of N.Y. v. Fox, 492 U.S. 469, 480 (1989). As in other contexts, these standards ensure not only that the State's interests are proportional to the resulting burdens placed on speech but also that the law does not seek to suppress a disfavored message.

1

Vermont argues that its physicians have a "reasonable expectation" that their prescriber-identifying information "will not be used for purposes other than ... filling and processing" prescriptions. It may be assumed that, for many reasons, physicians have an interest in keeping their prescription decisions confidential. But

§ 4631(d) is not drawn to serve that interest. Under Vermont's law, pharmacies may share prescriber-identifying information with anyone for any reason save one: They must not allow the information to be used for marketing.

Vermont made prescriber-identifying information available to an almost limitless audience. The explicit structure of the statute allows the information to be studied and used by all but a narrow class of disfavored speakers. Given the information's widespread availability and many permissible uses, the State's asserted interest in physician confidentiality does not justify the burden that § 4631(d) places on protected expression.

The State points out that it allows doctors to forgo the advantages of § 4631(d) by consenting to the sale, disclosure, and use of their prescriber-identifying information. It is true that private decisionmaking can avoid governmental partiality and thus insulate privacy measures from First Amendment challenge. But that principle is inapposite here. Vermont has given its doctors a contrived choice: Either consent, which will allow your prescriber-identifying information to be disseminated and used without constraint; or, withhold consent, which will allow your information to be used by those speakers whose message the State supports. Section 4631(d) may offer a limited degree of privacy, but only on terms favorable to the speech the State prefers. This is not to say that all privacy measures must avoid content-based rules. Here, however, the State has conditioned privacy on acceptance of a content-based rule that is not drawn to serve the State's asserted interest. To obtain the limited privacy allowed by § 4631(d), Vermont physicians are forced to acquiesce in the State's goal of burdening disfavored speech by disfavored speakers.

The State also contends that § 4631(d) protects doctors from "harassing sales behaviors." "Some doctors in Vermont are experiencing an undesired increase in the aggressiveness of pharmaceutical sales representatives," the Vermont Legislature found, "and a few have reported that they felt coerced and harassed." It is doubtful that concern for "a few" physicians who may have "felt coerced and harassed" by pharmaceutical marketers can sustain a broad content-based rule like § 4631(d). Many are those who must endure speech they do not like, but that is a necessary cost of freedom. In any event the State offers no explanation why remedies other than content-based rules would be inadequate. Physicians can, and often do, simply decline to meet with detailers, including detailers who use prescriber-identifying information. Doctors who wish to forgo detailing altogether are free to give "No Solicitation" or "No Detailing" instructions to their office managers or to receptionists at their places of work.

Vermont argues that detailers' use of prescriber-identifying information undermines the doctor-patient relationship by allowing detailers to influence treatment decisions. According to the State, "unwanted pressure occurs" when doctors learn that their prescription decisions are being "monitored" by detailers. And Vermont claims that detailing makes people "anxious" about whether doctors have their patients' best interests at heart. If pharmaceutical marketing affects treatment decisions, it does so because doctors find it persuasive.

2

The State contends that § 4631(d) advances important public policy goals by lowering the costs of medical services and promoting public health. If prescriber-identifying information were available for use by detailers, the State contends, then detailing would be effective in promoting brand-name drugs that are more expensive and less safe than generic alternatives.

While Vermont's stated policy goals may be proper, § 4631(d) does not advance them in a permissible [and sufficiently direct] way. The State seeks to achieve its policy objectives through the indirect means of restraining certain speech by certain speakers — that is, by diminishing detailers' ability to influence prescription decisions. But the "fear that people would make bad decisions if given truthful information" cannot justify content-based burdens on speech. Virginia Bd. of Pharmacy v. Virginia Citizens Consumer Council, Inc., 425 U.S. 748, 769–770 (1976).

[T]he State defends the law by insisting that "pharmaceutical marketing has a strong influence on doctors' prescribing practices." This reasoning is incompatible with the First Amendment. In an attempt to reverse a disfavored trend in public opinion, a State could not ban campaigning with slogans, picketing with signs, or marching during the daytime. Likewise the State may not seek to remove a popular but disfavored product from the marketplace by prohibiting truthful, nonmisleading advertisements that contain impressive endorsements or catchy jingles.

The defect in Vermont's law is made clear by the fact that many listeners find detailing instructive. There are divergent views regarding detailing and the prescription of brand-name drugs. Under the Constitution, resolution of that debate must result from free and uninhibited speech. The choice "between the dangers of suppressing information, and the dangers of its misuse if it is freely available" is one that "the First Amendment makes for us." *Virginia Bd.*, 425 U.S. at 770.

Vermont may be displeased that detailers who use prescriber-identifying information are effective in promoting brand-name drugs. The State can express that view through its own speech. But [t]he State may not burden the speech of others in order to tilt public debate in a preferred direction.

The State nowhere contends that detailing is false or misleading within the meaning of this Court's First Amendment precedents. Nor does the State argue that the provision challenged here will prevent false or misleading speech. The State's interest in burdening the speech of detailers instead turns on nothing more than a difference of opinion.

JUSTICE BREYER, with whom JUSTICE GINSBURG and JUSTICE KAGAN join, dissenting.

In this case I would ask whether Vermont's regulatory provisions work harm to First Amendment interests that is disproportionate to their furtherance of legitimate regulatory objectives. And in doing so, I would give significant weight to legitimate commercial regulatory objectives. The far stricter, specially "heightened" First Amendment standards that the majority would apply to this instance of commercial regulation are out of place here.

[T]his Court has recognized that commercial speech including advertising has an "informational function" and is not "valueless in the marketplace of ideas." Central Hudson Gas & Electric Corp. v. Public Serv. Comm'n, 447 U.S. 557, 563 (1980). But at the same time it has applied a less than strict, "intermediate" First Amendment test when the government directly restricts commercial speech.

The Court has also normally applied a yet more lenient approach to ordinary commercial or regulatory legislation that affects speech in less direct ways. In doing so, the Court has taken account of the need in this area of law to defer significantly to legislative judgment—as the Court has done in cases involving the Commerce Clause or the Due Process Clause.

To apply a strict First Amendment standard virtually as a matter of course when a court reviews ordinary economic regulatory programs (even if that program has a modest impact upon a firm's ability to shape a commercial message) would work at cross-purposes with this more basic constitutional approach. Since ordinary regulatory programs can affect speech, particularly commercial speech, in myriad ways, to apply a "heightened" First Amendment standard of review whenever such a program burdens speech would transfer from legislatures to judges the primary power to weigh ends and to choose means, threatening to distort or undermine legitimate legislative objectives. To apply a "heightened" standard of review in such cases as a matter of course would risk what then-Justice Rehnquist, dissenting in *Central Hudson*, 447 U.S. at 589, described as a

> return[] to the bygone era of *Lochner*, in which it was common practice for this Court to strike down economic regulations adopted by a State based on the Court's own notions of the most appropriate means for the State to implement its considered policies.

There are several reasons why the Court should review Vermont's law "under the standard appropriate for the review of economic regulation," not "under a heightened standard appropriate for the review of First Amendment issues." Glickman v. Wileman Brothers & Elliott, Inc., 521 U.S. 457, 469 (1997). For one thing, Vermont's statute neither forbids nor requires anyone to say anything, to engage in any form of symbolic speech, or to endorse any particular point of view, whether ideological or related to the sale of a product.

For another thing, the same First Amendment standards that apply to Vermont here would apply to similar regulatory actions taken by other States or by the Federal Government acting, for example, through Food and Drug Administration (FDA) regulation. (And the Federal Government's ability to preempt state laws that interfere with existing or contemplated federal forms of regulation is here irrelevant.)

Further, the statute's requirements form part of a traditional, comprehensive regulatory regime. The pharmaceutical drug industry has been heavily regulated at least since 1906. Longstanding statutes and regulations require pharmaceutical companies to engage in complex drug testing to ensure that their drugs are both "safe" and "effective." 21 U.S.C. §§ 355(b)(1), (d). Only then can the drugs be marketed, at which point drug companies are subject to the FDA's exhaustive regulation of the content of drug labels and the manner in which drugs can be advertised and sold.

Finally, Vermont's statute is directed toward information that exists only by virtue of government regulation. Under federal law, certain drugs can be dispensed only by a pharmacist operating under the orders of a medical practitioner. Vermont regulates the qualifications, the fitness, and the practices of pharmacists themselves, and requires pharmacies to maintain a "patient record system" that, among other things, tracks who prescribed which drugs. But for these regulations, pharmacies would have no way to know who had told customers to buy which drugs (as is the case when a doctor tells a patient to take a daily dose of aspirin).

Regulators will often find it necessary to create tailored restrictions on the use of information subject to their regulatory jurisdiction. A car dealership that obtains credit scores for customers who want car loans can be prohibited from using credit data to search for new customers. Medical specialists who obtain medical records for their existing patients cannot purchase those records in order to identify new patients. Or, speaking hypothetically, a public utilities commission that directs local gas distributors to gather usage information for individual customers might permit the distributors to share the data with researchers (trying to lower energy costs) but forbid sales of the data to appliance manufacturers seeking to sell gas stoves.

Such regulatory actions are subject to judicial review, e.g., for compliance with applicable statutes. And they would normally be subject to review under the Administrative Procedure Act to make certain they are not "arbitrary, capricious, [or] an abuse of discretion." 5 U.S.C. § 706(2)(A). In an appropriate case, such review might be informed by First Amendment considerations. But regulatory actions of the kind present here have not previously been thought to raise serious additional constitutional concerns under the First Amendment. The ease with which one can point to actual or hypothetical examples with potentially adverse speech-related effects at least roughly comparable to those at issue here indicates the danger of applying a "heightened" or "intermediate" standard of First Amendment review where typical regulatory actions affect commercial speech (say, by withholding information that a commercial speaker might use to shape the content of a message).

Thus, it is not surprising that, until today, this Court has *never* found that the *First Amendment* prohibits the government from restricting the use of information gathered pursuant to a regulatory mandate — whether the information rests in government files or has remained in the hands of the private firms that gathered it. Nor has this Court *ever* previously applied any form of "heightened" scrutiny in any even roughly similar case.

At best the Court opens a Pandora's Box of First Amendment challenges to many ordinary regulatory practices that may only incidentally affect a commercial message. At worst, it reawakens *Lochner*'s pre-New Deal threat of substituting judicial for democratic decisionmaking where ordinary economic regulation is at issue.

Notes and Questions

1. Governmental Motive. As we noted in Question 2 after *Turner I*, the Court in the *Turner* cases concluded both that Congress's overriding objective in enacting must-carry was economic and that must-carry triggered First Amendment scrutiny. Similarly, in *Sorrell* the Vermont legislature's motives were irrelevant to the application of the First Amendment.

This is not new. The Court applies heightened scrutiny to laws singling out categories of speakers even if the legislature does not intend to suppress speech. For instance, in Minneapolis Star & Tribune Co. v. Minnesota Commissioner of Revenue, 460 U.S. 575 (1983), the Court applied heightened First Amendment scrutiny to a use tax applicable to publications even as it noted that there was no indication of any censorial or otherwise impermissible motive on the part of the legislature that enacted the tax. The Court stated:

> We need not and do not impugn the motives of the Minnesota legislature in passing the ink and paper tax. Illicit legislative intent is not the sine qua non of a violation of the First Amendment. We have long recognized that even regulations aimed at proper governmental concerns can restrict unduly the exercise of rights protected by the First Amendment. A tax that singles out the press, or that targets individual publications within the press, places a heavy burden on the State to justify its action.

Id. at 592–93.

In *Minneapolis Star* the Court invalidated a tax that, were it applied to almost any other form of economic activity, would have sailed through rational basis review.

This line of cases may help explain the fact that in *Sorrell* none of the Justices argued that the First Amendment is simply irrelevant to § 4631(d). That is, all the Justices agreed that some level of First Amendment scrutiny applies. The fact that § 4631(d) was apparently motivated by privacy considerations, and that the Vermont legislature apparently concluded that this was the best way to effectuate its privacy goals, did not protect § 4631(d) from First Amendment scrutiny. Should the dissenters have argued that the First Amendment is irrelevant to § 4631(d)?

2. Scrutiny. That said, the majority and the dissent disagreed sharply. The dissent argued for a very deferential form of First Amendment scrutiny akin to that applied to ordinary economic regulation, and the majority instead applied heightened scrutiny. So, although the dissent did not argue for the irrelevance of the First Amendment, it did argue that the applicable test is easy to satisfy. By contrast, the heightened scrutiny the Court applied is fairly difficult to satisfy. What is the best argument for applying heightened scrutiny? For applying lenient scrutiny?

3. Commercial and Ordinary Speech. As the majority indicated, the Court has held that commercial speech is a special category of speech for First Amendment purposes. The Court has defined it as "speech which does no more than propose a commercial transaction," thus basically encompassing commercial advertising. Bolger v. Youngs Drug Products Corp., 463 U.S. 60, 66 (1983) (internal quotations omitted). The Court did not decide whether § 4631(d) regulates only commercial speech because it held that the provision is unconstitutional whether considered noncommercial speech (which the Court sometimes calls "pure speech," *see* Board of Trustees of State University of New York v. Fox, 492 U.S. 469, 474 (1989)) or commercial speech. The Court presented the tests for commercial and noncommercial speech as fairly demanding. What evidence could Vermont have realistically presented that would have survived the level of scrutiny the Court applies?

4. How Broad is the Holding? The Court's holding obviously has significant implications for privacy laws. What other kinds of laws might *Sorrell* apply to? Can they survive this level of scrutiny?

5. Information as Speech. The majority noted that "[t]his Court has held that the creation and dissemination of information are speech within the meaning of the First Amendment," although it did not reach the question whether prescriber-identifying information is speech for First Amendment purposes. What are the implications of the principle that the creation and dissemination of information are speech, especially when combined with *Turner I*'s holding that exercising editorial discretion is speech? How much room does that leave for the government to regulate?

§ 3.B. Antitrust and the First Amendment

Turner I applied heightened scrutiny to "laws that single out the press, or certain elements thereof, for special treatment." What about antitrust laws, which are generally applicable rather than industry-specific? As *Turner I* and *Sorrell* indicated, the Supreme Court has held that antitrust laws can be applied to speakers without implicating the First Amendment. In Associated Press v. United States, 326 U.S. 1 (1945), the Court found the First Amendment inapplicable to an antitrust action challenging Associated Press rules prohibiting members from selling news to non-members and allowing members to block non-members from membership. The Court stated that "the First Amendment affords not the slightest support for the contention that a combination to restrain trade in news and views has any constitutional immunity" and that "[t]he fact that the publisher handles news while others handle food does not . . . afford the publisher a peculiar constitutional sanctuary in which he can with impunity violate laws regulating his business practices." *Id.* at 7, 20; *see also* Lorain Journal Co. v. United States, 342 U.S. 143, 156 (1951) ("Injunctive relief under . . . the Sherman Act is as appropriate a means of enforcing the Act against newspapers as it is against others.").

That said, under Eastern Railroad Presidents Conference v. Noerr Motor Freight, Inc., 365 U.S. 127 (1961), antitrust enforcement against actions aimed at changing regulations implicates the First Amendment. And politically motivated boycotts are covered by the First Amendment under NAACP v. Claiborne Hardware Co., 458 U.S. 886 (1982). *Noerr* construed the Sherman Act not to apply to conduct aimed at "influencing the passage or enforcement of laws" in light of the constitutional problems with a contrary construction—that regulation of such conduct would conflict with the First Amendment right to petition the government. *Claiborne Hardware*, meanwhile, emphasized that the challenged action (a boycott of white merchants by the NAACP in Mississippi during the civil rights movement) "sought to bring about political, social, and economic change. Through speech, assembly, and petition—rather than through riot or revolution—petitioners sought to change a social order that had consistently treated them as second-class citizens."

Does this mean that antitrust actions often will trigger First Amendment scrutiny? After all, many boycotts (and other group actions) have an expressive component. Below we excerpt the Supreme Court case that most directly addresses this question. It is not an internet or telecommunications case, but we include it because of its importance in discussing the application of the First Amendment to antitrust actions.

FTC v. Superior Court Trial Lawyers Association

493 U.S. 411 (1990)

STEVENS, J., delivered the opinion for a unanimous Court with respect to Parts I, II, III, and IV, and the opinion of the Court with respect to Parts V and VI in which REHNQUIST, C.J., and WHITE, O'CONNOR, SCALIA, and KENNEDY, JJ., joined. BRENNAN, J., filed an opinion concurring in part and dissenting in part, in which MARSHALL, J., joined. BLACKMUN, J., filed an opinion concurring in part and dissenting in part.

JUSTICE STEVENS delivered the opinion of the Court.

I

Beginning in 1982, respondents, the Superior Court Trial Lawyers Association (SCTLA) and its officers, and other bar groups sought to persuade the District [of Columbia] to increase [Criminal Justice Act (CJA)] rates [paid to lawyers representing indigent clients] to at least $35 per hour. Despite what appeared to be uniform support for the bill, it did not pass.

On August 11, 1983, about 100 CJA lawyers met and resolved not to accept any new cases after September 6 if legislation providing for an increase in their fees had not passed by that date.

On September 6, 1983, about 90 percent of the CJA regulars refused to accept any new assignments. Thereafter, SCTLA arranged a series of events to attract the attention of the news media and to obtain additional support.

II

[R]espondents' boycott "constituted a classic restraint of trade within the meaning of Section 1 of the Sherman Act." Superior Court Trial Lawyers Ass'n v. FTC, 856 F.2d 226, 234 (1988). As such, it also violated the prohibition against unfair methods of competition in §5 of the FTC Act. Prior to the boycott CJA lawyers were in competition with one another, each deciding independently whether and how often to offer to provide services to the District at CJA rates. The agreement among the CJA lawyers was designed to obtain higher prices for their services and was implemented by a concerted refusal to serve an important customer in the market for legal services and, indeed, the only customer in the market for the particular services that CJA regulars offered. "This constriction of supply is the essence of 'price-fixing,' whether it be accomplished by agreeing upon a price, which will decrease the quantity demanded, or by agreeing upon an output, which will increase the price offered." *Superior Court Trial Lawyers*, 856 F.2d at 234. The horizontal arrangement among these competitors was unquestionably a "naked restraint" on price and output.

Respondents' agreement is not outside the coverage of the Sherman Act simply because its objective was the enactment of favorable legislation.

Our decision in Eastern Railroad Presidents Conference v. Noerr Motor Freight in no way detracts from this conclusion. In *Noerr,* we "considered whether the Sherman Act prohibited a publicity campaign waged by railroads" and "designed to foster the adoption of laws destructive of the trucking business, to create an atmosphere of distaste for truckers among the general public, and to impair the relationships existing between truckers and their customers." NAACP v. Claiborne Hardware Co., 458 U.S. at 913. Interpreting the Sherman Act in the light of the First Amendment's Petition Clause, the Court noted that "at least insofar as the railroads' campaign was directed toward obtaining governmental action, its legality was not at all affected by any anticompetitive purpose it may have had." *Noerr,* 365 U.S. at 139–140.

It of course remains true that "no violation of the Act can be predicated upon mere attempts to influence the passage or enforcement of laws," *id.* at 135, even if the defendants' sole purpose is to impose a restraint upon the trade of their competitors. But in the *Noerr* case the alleged restraint of trade was the intended *consequence* of public action; in this case the boycott was the *means* by which respondents sought to obtain favorable legislation. The restraint of trade that was implemented while the boycott lasted would have had precisely the same anticompetitive consequences during that period even if no legislation had been enacted. In *Noerr,* the desired legislation would have created the restraint on the truckers' competition; in this case the emergency legislative response to the boycott put an end to the restraint.

Indeed, respondents' theory of *Noerr* was largely disposed of by our opinion in Allied Tube & Conduit Corp. v. Indian Head, Inc., 486 U.S. 492 (1988). We held that the *Noerr* doctrine does not extend to "every concerted effort that is genuinely intended to influence governmental action." *Id.* at 503. We explained:

> If all such conduct were immunized then, for example, competitors would be free to enter into horizontal price agreements as long as they wished to propose that price as an appropriate level for governmental ratemaking or price supports. Horizontal conspiracies or boycotts designed to exact higher prices or other economic advantages from the government would be immunized on the ground that they are genuinely intended to influence the government to agree to the conspirators' terms. Firms could claim immunity for boycotts or horizontal output restrictions on the ground that they are intended to dramatize the plight of their industry and spur legislative action.

Id.

IV

SCTLA argues that if its conduct would otherwise be prohibited by the Sherman Act and the Federal Trade Commission Act, it is nonetheless protected by the First Amendment rights recognized in *Claiborne Hardware.* That case arose after black citizens boycotted white merchants in Claiborne County, Mississippi. The white merchants sued under state law to recover losses from the boycott. We found that the "right of the States to regulate economic activity could not justify a complete prohibition against a nonviolent, politically motivated boycott designed to force governmental and economic change and to effectuate rights guaranteed by the Constitution itself." *Claiborne Hardware,* 458 U.S. at 914. We accordingly held that "the nonviolent elements of petitioners' activities are entitled to the protection of the First Amendment." *Id.* at 915.

SCTLA contends that because it, like the boycotters in *Claiborne Hardware,* sought to vindicate constitutional rights, it should enjoy a similar First Amendment protection. It is, of course, clear that the association's efforts to publicize the boycott, to explain the merits of its cause, and to lobby District officials to enact favorable legislation — like similar activities in *Claiborne Hardware* — were activities that were fully protected by the First Amendment. But nothing in the FTC's order would curtail such activities, and nothing in the FTC's reasoning condemned any of those activities.

The activity that the FTC order prohibits is a concerted refusal by CJA lawyers to accept any further assignments until they receive an increase in their compensation; the undenied objective of their boycott was an economic advantage for those who agreed to participate. It is true that the *Claiborne Hardware* case also involved a boycott. That boycott, however, differs in a decisive respect. Those who joined the *Claiborne Hardware* boycott sought no special advantage for themselves. They were black citizens in Port Gibson, Mississippi, who had been the victims of political, social, and economic discrimination for many years. They sought only the equal respect and equal treatment to which they were constitutionally entitled. They struggled "to change a social order that had consistently treated them as second class citizens." *Id.* at 912. As we observed, the campaign was not intended "to destroy legitimate competition." *Id.* at 914. Equality and freedom are preconditions of the free market, and not commodities to be haggled over within it.

The same cannot be said of attorney's fees. As we recently pointed out, our reasoning in *Claiborne Hardware* is not applicable to a boycott conducted by business competitors who "stand to profit financially from a lessening of competition in the boycotted market." *Allied Tube*, 486 U.S. at 508. No matter how altruistic the motives of respondents may have been, it is undisputed that their immediate objective was to increase the price that they would be paid for their services. Such an economic boycott is well within the category that was expressly distinguished in the *Claiborne Hardware* opinion itself.

Only after recognizing the well-settled validity of prohibitions against various economic boycotts did we conclude in *Claiborne Hardware* that "peaceful, political activity such as that found in the [Mississippi] boycott" are entitled to constitutional protection. We reaffirmed the government's "power to regulate [such] economic activity." 458 U.S. at 912–913. This conclusion applies with special force when a clear objective of the boycott is to economically advantage the participants.

V

Respondents' concerted action in refusing to accept further CJA assignments until their fees were increased was thus a plain violation of the antitrust laws. The exceptions derived from *Noerr* and *Claiborne Hardware* have no application to respondents' boycott. For these reasons we reject the arguments made by respondents in the cross-petition.

The Court of Appeals, however, crafted a new exception to the *per se* rules, and it is this exception which provoked the FTC's petition to this Court. The Court of Appeals derived its exception from *O'Brien*. In that case O'Brien had burned his Selective Service registration certificate on the steps of the South Boston Courthouse. He did so before a sizable crowd and with the purpose of advocating his antiwar beliefs. We affirmed his conviction. We held that the governmental interest in regulating the "nonspeech element" of his conduct adequately justified the incidental restriction on First Amendment freedoms. Specifically, we concluded that the statute's incidental restriction on O'Brien's freedom of expression was no greater than necessary to further the Government's interest in requiring registrants to have valid certificates continually available.

However, the Court of Appeals held that, in light of *O'Brien,* the expressive component of respondents' boycott compelled courts to apply the antitrust laws "prudently and with sensitivity," *Superior Court Trial Lawyers*, 856 F.2d at 233–234, with a "special solicitude for the First Amendment rights" of respondents. The Court of Appeals concluded that the governmental interest in prohibiting boycotts is not sufficient to justify a restriction on the communicative element of the boycott unless the FTC can prove, and not merely presume, that the boycotters have market power. Because the Court of Appeals imposed this special requirement upon the government, it ruled that *per se* antitrust analysis was inapplicable to boycotts having an expressive component.

There are at least two critical flaws in the Court of Appeals' antitrust analysis: it exaggerates the significance of the expressive component in respondents' boycott and it denigrates the importance of the rule of law that respondents violated. Implicit in the conclusion of the Court of Appeals are unstated assumptions that most economic boycotts do not have an expressive component, and that the categorical prohibitions against price fixing and boycotts are merely rules of "administrative convenience" that do not serve any substantial governmental interest unless the price-fixing competitors actually possess market power.

It would not much matter to the outcome of this case if these flawed assumptions were sound. *O'Brien* would offer respondents no protection even if their boycott were uniquely expressive and even if the purpose of the *per se* rules were purely that of administrative efficiency. We have recognized that the government's interest in adhering to a uniform rule may sometimes satisfy the *O'Brien* test even if making an exception to the rule in a particular case might cause no serious damage. The administrative efficiency interests in antitrust regulation are unusually compelling. The *per se* rules avoid "the necessity for an incredibly complicated and prolonged economic investigation into the entire history of the industry involved, as well as related industries, in an effort to determine at large whether a particular restraint has been unreasonable." Northern Pacific R. Co. v. United States, 356 U.S. 1, 5 (1958). If small parties "were allowed to prove lack of market power, all parties would have that right, thus introducing the enormous complexities of market definition into every price-fixing case." R. Bork, The Antitrust Paradox 269 (1978). For these reasons, it is at least possible that the *Claiborne Hardware* doctrine, which itself rests in part upon *O'Brien,* exhausts *O'Brien's* application to the antitrust statutes.

In any event, however, we cannot accept the Court of Appeals' characterization of this boycott or the antitrust laws. Every concerted refusal to do business with a potential customer or supplier has an expressive component. At one level, the competitors must exchange their views about their objectives and the means of obtaining them. The most blatant, naked price-fixing agreement is a product of communication, but that is surely not a reason for viewing it with special solicitude. At another level, after the terms of the boycotters' demands have been agreed upon, they must be communicated to its target: "[W]e will not do business until you do what we ask."

That expressive component of the boycott conducted by these respondents is surely not unique. On the contrary, it is the hallmark of every effective boycott.

At a third level, the boycotters may communicate with third parties to enlist public support for their objectives; to the extent that the boycott is newsworthy, it will facilitate the expression of the boycotters' ideas. But this level of expression is not an element of the boycott. Publicity may be generated by any other activity that is sufficiently newsworthy. Some activities, including the boycott here, may be newsworthy precisely for the reasons that they are prohibited: the harms they produce are matters of public concern. Certainly that is no reason for removing the prohibition.

In sum, there is thus nothing unique about the "expressive component" of respondents' boycott. A rule that requires courts to apply the antitrust laws "prudently and with sensitivity" whenever an economic boycott has an "expressive component" would create a gaping hole in the fabric of those laws. Respondents' boycott thus has no special characteristics meriting an exemption from the *per se* rules of antitrust law.

The judgment of the Court of Appeals is accordingly reversed insofar as that court held the *per se* rules inapplicable to the lawyers' boycott.

[Concurring and dissenting opinions of JUSTICE BRENNAN and of JUSTICE BLACKMUN are omitted.]

Notes and Questions

1. Distinguishing Among Boycotts. Are the distinctions the Court drew between this case and *Claiborne* meaningful as a constitutional matter? The superior court trial lawyers argued that in both cases those engaged in the boycott were seeking to help themselves and bring about a larger social change. How clear is the line that the Court drew between these two boycotts?

2. Are All Antitrust Actions Exempt from First Amendment Scrutiny? *Superior Court Trial Lawyers* emphasized the limits of *Noerr* and *Claiborne*, and it rejected the superior court trial lawyers' argument that the First Amendment modifies the treatment of their boycott. But it did not hold that all antitrust actions are exempt from First Amendment scrutiny. It left *Noerr* and *Claiborne* intact, and more generally focused on the nature of the trial lawyers' boycott. In contrast to *Turner I*'s broad statement that all laws singling out elements of the press are subject to heightened scrutiny, *Superior Court Trial Lawyers* did not state that the First Amendment is inapplicable to all applications of antitrust law. Nonetheless, the contrast with *Turner I* is clear: a statute that singles out a category of speakers is subject to heightened scrutiny even if it is grounded in anticompetitive concerns, but many antitrust actions can be brought against speakers (or groups of speakers) without implicating the First Amendment.

3. The Sherman Act versus Industry-Specific Antitrust Legislation. Is the Court's different treatment of applications of the Sherman Act and industry-specific antitrust legislation sensible? It is true that, in contrast to industry-specific statutes, the

Sherman Act was not written with the specific intention of regulating a particular industry, but does that distinction make a constitutional difference? Government actors like the FTC decide which antitrust actions to bring. How different is their exercise of discretion, in choosing which actions to bring, from Congress's exercise of discretion in choosing which industries to regulate? Is the difference that courts have taken on the role of overseeing the implementation of the Sherman Act and thus limiting the discretion of government actors?

4. A Different Outcome. If the distinction between the Sherman Act and industry-specific legislation is not sound, what then? Note that *Sorrell*, and the *Turner* cases, were decided after *Superior Court Trial Lawyers*. Should, and would, the later cases prevail if they cannot be reconciled with *Superior Court Trial Lawyers*? If so, that would entail the Court ruling that all antitrust actions trigger heightened First Amendment scrutiny in the same way that more specific regulations of speakers do. What would the implications of that be?

Part Two

Economic Regulation of Internet and Telecommunications

Chapter 4

Early Telephone Regulation Through Divestiture

Introduction

In this chapter, we introduce the fundamentals of telephone regulation and trace several key features up to and through the Bell System's divestiture. We start with some history, focusing in particular on the rise of the Bell Telephone Company and the important role played by Bell's refusal to interconnect with rival firms. Then, we turn to economics—the idea being to arm readers with both the words they will need to talk about telephone infrastructure and the associated intuitions about how that infrastructure affects market behavior. This discussion has two purposes: first, to explore telephone regulation itself; and, second, for the more general and important purpose of discussing these regulatory tools for addressing the problem of monopoly in communications networks (a project which continues into the next chapters). These regulatory techniques were best developed and were most extensively applied in telephony, but one can consider them for any communications market in which monopoly is a concern—as it was in cable television for a time and still is in the debate over internet regulation.

We then turn to the regulation preceding the breakup of the Bell System and the breakup itself. After Bell succeeded in securing monopoly franchises over local telephone service from state regulators across the United States, the company set about building an enterprise that controlled not only local phone service but also long-distance service, customer premises equipment, and network equipment like switches. A good way to think of Bell's scope is that the company controlled every service and piece of equipment involved in any telephone call in the United States.[1] We consider three important areas in which regulators and courts limited Bell's monopoly scope prior to the 1974 antitrust case. We first look at the process by which competition crept into the market for consumer premises equipment. We then examine the more important case of competition for interstate toll service. Finally, we discuss Bell's entry into computing and data processing. With those precursors under our belt, we move on to the most important event in the changing

1. This statement is not literally true. Many independent telephone companies existed alongside Bell even at its peak, but Bell did manufacture almost all network equipment, provide almost all long-distance service, and provide monopoly local service for the vast majority of people in the United States.

boundaries between competitive and monopoly telecommunications services: the 1984 divestiture of Bell and implementation of its governing consent decree.

Bell faced three major antitrust suits designed to scale back its monopoly. The first was a 1912 suit that resulted in the "Kingsbury Commitment" that purported to limit Bell's ability to acquire independent telephone companies but that ultimately did little to impede Bell's march. The second, filed in 1949 and aimed at Bell's control over the network equipment market, culminated in a 1956 consent decree under which Bell by and large agreed to refrain from manufacturing equipment other than for its own network and agreed to license its patents to other manufacturers upon payment of royalties. As the consent decree neither set prices for those royalties nor required Bell to buy any equipment from the third-party manufacturers, that decree, too, accomplished little in the telephone market (though it did prevent Bell from offering computer services, which seemed much less important at the time).

The third antitrust prosecution of the Bell System began in 1974. That suit, unlike the previous two, proved enormously effective; indeed, it would culminate a decade later in the breakup decree (divestiture) that split up the Bell System and significantly narrowed the scope of monopoly in the telephone industry. But the events that set the stage for the eventual breakup began well before 1974. By the time the decree was accepted by District Court Judge Harold Greene in 1982, "most of the events that would transform the shape of the industry" were already "well under way." Glen O. Robinson, The Titanic Remembered: AT&T and the Changing World of Telecommunications, 5 Yale J. on Reg. 517, 520 (1988) (book review).

§ 4.A. Telephone History

On March 10, 1876, Alexander Graham Bell declared, "Mr. Watson, come here, I want you," and with those words began what would be a technological revolution of extraordinary import. Mr. Bell knew it from early on, confidently predicting what must have sounded unthinkable at the time—that "a telephone in every house [would someday] be considered indispensable." Robert W. Garnet, The Telephone Enterprise: The Evolution of Bell System's Horizontal Structure 1876–1909, at 12 (1985).

Of course, even Alexander Graham Bell did not get all the details quite right. For example, he assumed that phones would be linked one-to-one instead of being linked together into web-like networks. From a legal standpoint, this is much more than a technical detail:

> Initially, telephones were linked one to one. It took until 1878, two years after the invention of the telephone itself, for the budding new telephone companies to grasp the necessity of a telephone "exchange." The telephone exchange—a simple switchboard at first—radically increased a telephone's utility by enabling each phone to reach any other phone connected to the same exchange. Demand for service increased dramatically.

> The advent of the telephone exchange gave rise to the first rumblings about the need for — or inevitability of — monopoly provision of telephone service. A central switchboard and the wires leading to it represented a large, fixed capital investment; the costs of an exchange seemed to decline rapidly as more subscribers were added. By fragmenting the market, competition appeared to drive up costs and nullify the key advantage of a central exchange, which was to connect everyone to everyone else.

Peter W. Huber et al., Federal Telecommunications Law 8 (2d ed. 1999).

But was monopoly provision really inevitable? Certainly not at the start: when the original Bell System patents expired in 1893–94, only about one in 250 Americans had a telephone. Bureau of the Census, Historical Statistics of the United States: Colonial Times to 1970, Part 2, 784 (1975). Free of patent limits, numerous independent companies entered the telephone business, and the spread of telephony grew rapidly. Indeed, the proportion of Americans with telephones more than doubled in the next five years and, by 1920, more than one third of all households had service. *Id.* New, independent carriers unaffiliated with Bell carried much of that expanding telephone traffic.

Part of the entrants' success came from serving markets ignored by Bell. Bell had been pursuing high-volume, business-generated traffic by connecting first the largest cities and then branching out to smaller ones. Milton Mueller, Universal Service in Telephone History: A Reconstruction, 17 Telecomm. Pol'y 352, 357 (1993). Bell's President, Theodore Vail, modeled his strategy on Western Union's 19th century linking of offices in commercial centers and envisioned that his company would control a nationwide network interconnecting all nodes of business activity.[2] As a result, in 1894 only 3% of Bell's subscribers were in rural areas, even though 62% of Americans lived in communities defined as rural. *Id.* at 357. Small independent phone companies, farming organizations, and rural cooperatives established thousands of local exchanges in areas not reached by Bell. *Id.* at 360.

In time, however, the Bell System was unable to avoid extending its operations into less dense regions. The independents — many of whom had joined in coalition — had accumulated enough customers in the urban periphery to make access to their systems valuable to the urban customers targeted by Bell. The dense population centers that Bell sought to monopolize became contested ground. To retain those markets, Bell had to satisfy urban customers who valued access to people served by the independents. Bell's management had discovered that "whenever you have the farmers tied to your exchange you have got the merchants where you want them."[3]

---

2. Mueller at 357. For a different take on Vail's model, *see* Paul Starr, The Creation of the Media 207 (2004) (arguing that Vail modeled Bell on the Post Office).

3. Cumberland Telephone Journal, Vol. 10, Jan. 15, 1904, at 12, AT&T-Bell Labs Archives, *quoted in* Mueller at 361.

In the first two decades of the 20th century, Bell and the independents invaded each other's territories to the point that over half of the U.S. population could choose between rival local telephone carriers. *Id.* at 359. Available data show that traffic was about equally divided between Bell and the independent carriers by 1908, when the Bell System carried an average of 16,029,000 conversations per day while independents together carried 15,956,000. Historical Statistics of the United States at 783. At least by this measure, the collective market share of competitive carriers had gone from zero to 50% in only fifteen years.

There was, however, an inherent instability in the way local telephone competition had developed. In general, customers of independent carriers and customers of Bell could not call each other because the competing networks did not interconnect to exchange customers' local calls. When phones were relatively rare and the bulk of one's calls went to one or a few parties whose service decisions could be coordinated, it may have been only a modest inconvenience that customers could only call other people served by the same carrier. But as the telephone became a more basic and ubiquitous tool for business and personal communication, people came increasingly to value not just connections between parties in regular contact who could coordinate to be on the same network, but also, in the words of Bell President Vail, "communication with some other one, who, until the particular necessity arose, might have been unknown and unthought of." Mueller at 364 (*quoting* Annual Report, AT&T 39 (1910)). In Vail's view, giving customers the ability to contact parties unknown to them when subscribing to a telephone network was justification for monopoly: "this necessity, impossible to predetermine, [makes] universal service the only perfect service." *Id.* By "universal service," Vail arguably meant one provider, not the term's modern connotation of telephone service that is available to everyone at affordable rates.[4]

Implicit in Vail's observation was the idea of network effects, which we discussed in Chapter 1—that, as more people can be reached through a given communications system, the more valuable that system is to any individual consumer. Competition that pulled subscribers to different, noninterconnected systems undermined this customer-side economy of scale.

Vail's basic argument, while grounds for increasing the number of telephones any given subscriber could reach, did not necessarily support a commitment to a government-protected monopoly. Mandatory interconnection of competing networks could have accomplished the same goal. The precedent for such a mandate was mixed, however. The Post Roads Act of 1866, ch. 230, 14 Stat. 221, *repealed by* Act of July 16, 1947, ch. 256, 61 Stat. 327, had required interconnection among competing or nonoverlapping telegraph systems,[5] but neither the statute nor its under-

4. *Id.* Paul Starr, in contrast to Mueller's account, believes that Vail indeed envisioned the subsidized service model as part of his "universal service" concept. *See* Starr, *supra* note 2, at 446.

5. *See* Western Union Telegraph Co. v. Pub. Serv. Comm'n of N.Y., 230 N.Y. 95, 101 (1920) ("[E]ach [telegraph carrier] represents the public when applying to the other for service and no

lying principle extended to common carriers (companies that carry goods, people, or information for all comers at set rates) generally. Indeed, the Supreme Court made clear in 1886 that common carriage did not generally encompass the traffic of other carriers — in the Court's words, there was no obligation to be a "common carrier of common carriers." St. Louis, I.M. & S. Ry Co. v. S. Express, 117 U.S. 1, 21 (1886). When the Mann-Elkins Act of 1910 deemed telephone companies to be common carriers, it did not specifically impose on them any interconnection obligations towards other phone companies, and state courts provided similarly little help to competitors seeking to interconnect with Bell.[6]

Of course, the Bell companies and independents could have chosen to interconnect, but they did not. Perhaps each side hoped that by standing its ground, it would eventually gain an edge that would make its network the most valuable to subscribers and push the competing network out of business. The data show such a stand to have been more plausible for Bell than for the independents. In 1910, Bell served about 4 million of the 7.6 million telephones in the United States. The remaining 3.6 million were served by the independents. Historical Statistics of the United States at 783. But this figure to some extent overstates the independents' competitiveness against the Bell companies. Not all independents competed against a Bell company; many served areas Bell did not want to serve.

Perhaps sensing its advantages over the independents, Bell pursued dominance of the telephone market. It was greatly helped in this quest by its acquisition in 1913 of the patents for amplification technology that vastly improved long-distance service. Bell refused to allow independents to interconnect to its improved long-lines network and many independents were forced to either merge into the Bell System or go out of business. *See* Roger G. Noll & Bruce M. Owen, The Anticompetitive Uses of Regulation: *United States v. AT&T*, *in* John E. Kwoka Jr. & Lawrence J. White (eds.), The Antitrust Revolution 291 (1989). Indeed, Bell's market share climbed steadily from 1910 on, with particularly rapid gains starting in 1913. Historical Statistics of the United States at 783.

As the Bell System acquired rivals, accumulated market share, and refused to interconnect either its local or long-distance networks with competitors, the enterprise not surprisingly attracted the trust-busting zeal of the times. On the heels of the government's victory over John D. Rockefeller and Standard Oil in 1911, Standard

---

discrimination can be made by either against the other, but each must render to the other the same services it renders to the rest of the community under the same conditions.").

6. *See* Home Tel. Co. v. People's Tel. & Tel. Co., 141 S.W. 845, 848 (Sup. Ct. Tenn. 1911). The distinction between a customer's access to a network under traditional common carrier law and a cocarrier's access to a network for interconnection purposes largely reflects (1) where interconnection may occur; (2) whether interconnection is comparable to what the carrier gives its own affiliates; and (3) what price the carrier may charge for interconnection. *See, e.g.*, Pacific Tel. & Tel. Co. v. Anderson, 196 F. 699, 703 (E.D. Wash. 1912) (holding that a cocarrier is not entitled to interconnection); *see also* James B. Speta, A Common Carrier Approach to Internet Interconnection, 54 Fed. Comm. L.J. 225, 258 (2002) (discussing the issue).

Oil Co. v. United States, 221 U.S. 1 (1911), one U.S. Attorney and several states sued Bell in 1912 and the Justice Department began a full-blown investigation.

The government's suit alleged that Bell had improperly leveraged its dominance in the long-distance market to force competing local carriers into closing down or merging with the Bell System. Bell advanced two kinds of arguments in its defense: one favoring monopoly, the other denigrating the alternatives. The pro-monopoly argument was essentially Vail's claim that a "universal" provider would benefit customers more than a divided system. Interconnection would also, of course, have delivered the same benefits to consumers, and would furthermore have preserved the additional benefits of competition. Against that alternative, Bell contended that technical incompatibility and coordination difficulties rendered interconnection among competing systems inferior to integrated monopoly, and that mandatory interconnection was furthermore unfair to the larger system which had undertaken the bulk of the facilities investment upon which smaller systems would be able to free ride.

Ultimately, in what came to be called the "Kingsbury Commitment," after the Bell vice president who negotiated with the government, the parties settled in 1914 on terms that proved enormously favorable for the Bell System. The government implicitly accepted Bell's arguments for a "universal service" monopoly and halted its pending antitrust action. In return, Bell promised to submit to a degree of regulatory oversight, to cease acquiring independent competitors, and to interconnect those competitors that remained to Bell's long-distance network. But the agreement also contained a great deal of built-in flexibility—"to conform to the development of telephony and to maintain the efficiency of the service"—that ultimately undermined some of the settlement's central parts, such as the nonacquisition provision. United States v. AT&T, 1 Decrees & Judgments in Civil Federal Antitrust Cases 554, ¶ 14 (D. Or. 1914) (No. 6082).

If the Kingsbury Commitment intended to preserve local competition from further erosion by prohibiting Bell from acquiring additional local companies, it was on the path to failure from the outset. Because the settlement required Bell to interconnect independents to its long-distance network, but not to its local system, subscribers to systems that competed with Bell still found themselves unable to call people on Bell's local networks, and vice versa. Ultimately, the continued existence of competition without interconnection proved untenable. Mueller recounts that "[a]s the nation became more urbanized and integrated, many telephone users, particularly small and medium sized businesses, found a divided service to be intolerable." Mueller at 365. With private incentives having failed to produce local interconnection, and with regulators having apparently abandoned the option, a transition began to occur in which an antitrust settlement that purported to preserve competition gave way to state and federal policies that embraced a monopoly model for telephone service.

In fairness to Bell's consolidation campaign, the inefficiency of separate, non-interconnecting telephone systems was burdensome to consumers. To reduce that burden, federal authorities allowed consolidation of competing carriers. The Department of Justice approved most of Bell's special applications to acquire local companies in the years the consent decree was in force. Huber et al. at 27 & n.113. And, in 1918, Congress and the President gave the Postmaster General emergency powers over the phone system which led to further consolidations. *Id.* Finally, in 1921, Congress suspended the nonacquisition provisions of the Kingsbury Commitment for good and gave the Interstate Commerce Commission authority to exempt telephone company mergers from the antitrust laws. Willis-Graham Act of 1921, Pub. L. No. 67-15, 42 Stat. 27 (codified as amended at 47 U.S.C. § 221(a)), *repealed by* The Telecommunications Act of 1996, § 601(b)(2), Pub. L. No. 104-104, 110 Stat. 56, 143. The resulting statute, the Willis-Graham Act, was aimed at eliminating the inefficient fragmentation of the phone system. *Id.*

An important effect of the Willis-Graham Act was to make the Bell System's conduct a matter for regulatory oversight as well as corporate strategy, leading in time to a system of regulated monopoly franchises. The "efficiency" from consolidation was the benefit to customers of being connected to the whole universe of other telephone subscribers. But other goals soon entered into consideration that further entrenched monopoly franchising in state and federal regulatory policy. The most prominent of those goals was making telephone service affordable to all Americans and thereby increasing the spread of telephony. As one commentary puts it, regulators aimed to put a "telephone within arm's reach of the chicken in every pot" — and to do it, in large part, by cooperating with and regulating a national, unified Bell Telephone Company. Huber et al. at 22.

In summary, then, from the late 1800s until the breakup order in 1982, regulatory policy put Vail and his successors in an enviable position. They were able to establish and maintain Bell's domination of the telephone industry, all the while arguing that Bell domination was actually in the public interest.

§ 4.B. Telephone Economics

Throughout his career, Theodore Vail argued that one firm — namely, his firm — should provide all telephone service nationwide. His argument was, of course, in part self-serving, but that does not necessarily mean that it was wrong.

First, the fact that the telephone system exhibits network properties is relatively uncontroversial; significantly more controversial are its implications. After all, while it might be true that, if left with the discretion to do so, a company like Bell would refuse to interconnect with competitors as a way of taking strategic advantage of any network externalities, it is also true (as hinted at above) that interconnection can be imposed even on unwilling firms. For one thing, subscribers can create de facto interconnection simply by purchasing access to multiple networks. If every family had both a Bell telephone with which to contact Bell customers and also, say, a Sprint telephone with which to contact all Sprint customers, there would be no need for interconnection between the Bell and Sprint networks. A more efficient and direct option might be to use legal rules to force Bell and Sprint to interconnect. The real question in both cases is whether the costs associated with interconnection are so great that competition/interconnection makes society worse off than would monopoly/no interconnection.

Second, a stronger argument in favor of Vail's monopoly vision was that, like the telegraph arguably had been in the past and as cable television would be considered in the future, the provision of telephone service was a natural monopoly. As we explained in more detail in Chapter 1, this means that — due to the structure of costs in this market — the cheapest way to provide nationwide telephone service might be to have a single firm provide service to all interested customers: to provide telephone service, a firm must incur a significant fixed investment (this time to build the initial network of wires, switches, and so on); but, once that investment has been made, the marginal cost of adding an additional phone customer is almost zero. There is an economy of scale, then, in having a single firm build the local loop instead of having multiple firms each build possibly overlapping networks.

Demand variability also bolsters this claim. An individual's demand for phone service varies significantly from moment to moment and day to day; yet, in order to provide adequate phone service, the phone company has to be ready to serve a given user whenever that user happens to pick up the telephone. By having a single firm serve a large number of users, the costs of providing phone service can be lowered dramatically. Several users can share a given amount of capacity, putting the equipment to better use since the variance in each consumer's demand would to some degree cancel out, leaving less of the phone system's capacity to sit idle at a given time.

Vail's vision of a single telephone company was supported not just by network externality arguments and not just by conventional natural monopoly arguments, but also by the concept of economies of scope. An economy of scope is said to exist in settings where a single firm can produce a given quantity of each of two or more goods more cheaply than multiple firms can produce those same total quantities. The economy of scope argument is not a straightforward natural monopoly argument. It suggests only that, if a company is in the business of selling one of two interrelated products, it likely makes sense for that same company to sell both. In telephony, a company can use much of the same infrastructure to provide both local and long-distance service, each more cheaply because of the dual use.

§ 4.C. Telephone Regulation

We have introduced some of the history and economics of the telephone system. We turn now to the regulatory issues. Specifically, we build here on the generalities of Chapter 1 and offer a brief overview of the types of telephone regulations that have been imposed over time. We will say much more about each of these categories in the chapters that follow. In Chapter 7, we consider the question of how federal and state authorities share regulatory power over telephone service.

As discussed in Chapter 1, the economics of the telephone system were for a long time interpreted to mean that the most efficient way to provide telephone service nationwide was to do so using a single monopoly provider. Thus, early regulations focused on ensuring that Bell or some other local telephone company would be the only telephone company in a given region. That, however, was only the tip of the regulatory iceberg, because a firm protected from competition would ultimately behave as any monopolist would: maximizing profits by charging consumers higher-than-competitive prices. To avoid this outcome, state public utility commissions regulated the rates that the local exchange carriers charged to consumers in their franchise areas and applied the other requirements of common carrier law.

As telephone service advanced and the Bell System grew, a second important area of telecommunications regulation was related to the scope of the monopoly franchise. The Bell System encompassed not just a state-by-state franchise over much local service, but also nationwide long-distance telephone service, the manufacture and sale of customer premises equipment (CPE), and the manufacture and sale of network equipment like switches and routers. Over how many of these different markets should Bell's monopoly extend? Both antitrust law and regulation played a role in answering this question, and, certainly by the mid-1930s, policing the boundaries of monopoly was a second significant regulatory task on the agenda.

The third major category of regulation involved universal service policies and responded directly to concerns that some citizens would not share in the benefits of telephone service because no carrier could serve them profitably. In granting monopoly franchises to Bell, state regulators found an opportunity to demand certain things in return; and one of the key conditions of the monopoly grants was that Bell would provide quality service to all consumers in a territory and do so at fair and generally equal rates. In the jargon of telecommunications regulation, this obligation is often referred to as the responsibility to be the carrier of last resort. If, for example, an individual moves to the top of a mountain in a given service territory, that individual has the right to request service at a fair rate (which is usually a statewide averaged rate) even if, in a competitive market, no firm would bother to serve such an awkwardly located and expensive-to-reach customer. Implementing and enforcing these policies was thus the third important focus of telephone regulation during the 20th century.

§ 4.D. Precursors to Divestiture

We now turn to the events preceding the Bell divestiture: three regulatory episodes that attempted, and to various degrees succeeded, in controlling the scope and impact of Bell's monopoly. In particular, we look at FCC efforts to inject competition into consumer premises equipment, into long-distance service, and into early versions of converged computer/telecommunications services.

§ 4.D.1. Competition in CPE

Federal Telecommunications Law

Peter W. Huber, Michael K. Kellogg & John Thorne, 663–70 (2d ed. 1999)

Bell did not sell equipment; it sold service. Its customers in turn bought service, and service alone. Thus, Bell supplied not only the wires and switches of the network, but also all CPE and inside wiring.[7] To freeze out alien CPE, Bell [prohibited subscribers from interconnecting any non-Bell product] with Bell's network. Such prohibitions appeared in private contracts with telephone subscribers as early as 1899, and they were incorporated in Bell company tariff schedules [public documents that described the services Bell offered and stipulated price and other conditions of service] by 1913. The ostensible purpose of these provisions was to protect the physical integrity of the network from dangers such as erratic voltage generation caused by defective equipment. Their practical effect was to eliminate all competitive suppliers of CPE.

It took some time before the FCC seriously questioned the equipment monopoly; the first suggestion that the link [between provision of equipment and provision of service] might not be inextricable did not come until 1948. That year, the Commission struck down "foreign attachment" provisions that prohibited the use of recording devices in connection with interstate service. [The FCC found that] [r]ecording devices could in fact be used without causing "any perceptible effect on the functioning of the telephone apparatus or the quality of the telephone service," Use of Recording Devices in Connection with Telephone Services, Report, 11 F.C.C. 1033, 1036 (1947); all federal tariffs purporting to bar the use of recording devices were therefore rejected.

[O]nly six years later, the Commission was in full retreat. That year it upheld Bell's refusal to permit the Jordaphone, [an early] answering machine, to be connected to the network. Unlike ordinary "recording devices," the Jordaphone "opens and closes the telephone circuit"; this was enough to justify different treatment. Jordaphone Corp. v. AT&T, Decision, 18 F.C.C. 644, 699 (1954). Bell had made no showing whatsoever that the network would suffer any substantial harm from Jordaphones. Nevertheless, the Commission decided that this kind of recording device would be used primarily with intrastate calls and should thus be left to the jurisdiction of individual state public utility commissions.

---

7. [At this time, most phone system subscribers rented their CPE from Bell instead of owning their CPE outright. This made the CPE more analogous to other Bell components — wires, switches, and so on — than it might seem to modern audiences. Eds.]

The following year the Commission issued perhaps its most comical order, revealing how a regulatory mind-set can sometimes overwhelm common sense. At issue was the "Hush-A-Phone," a metal device (packed with sound-muffling asbestos) that snapped onto the mouthpiece of the phone to provide some privacy and quiet in crowded office environments. Bell complained to the Commission that the Hush-A-Phone might muffle voices and lower the overall quality of telephone service; moreover, there was "no appreciable public demand" for the product. Hush-A-Phone Corp. v. AT&T, Decision, 20 F.C.C. 391, 397 (1955). The FCC agreed: "the unrestricted use of foreign attachments . . . may result in impairment to the quality and efficiency of telephone service, damage to telephone plant and facilities, or injury to telephone company personnel." *Id.* at 419. Foreign attachments would have to be analyzed one case at a time. And, after lengthy analysis, the Commission concluded that this particular snap-on cup would "be deleterious to the telephone system and injure the service rendered by it." *Id.* at 420. As a general principle, "telephone equipment should be supplied by and under control of the carrier itself." *Id.*

The D.C. Circuit sensibly reversed in a brief per curiam. The court found no support for the Commission's suggestion "that the use of a Hush-A-Phone affects more than the conversation of the user—that its influence pervades, in some fashion, the whole telephone system." Hush-A-Phone Corp. v. United States, 238 F.2d 266, 268 (D.C. Cir. 1956). But the court went on to establish a principle of much wider significance: it affirmed "the telephone subscriber's right reasonably to use his telephone in ways which are privately beneficial without being publicly detrimental." *Id.* at 269. Moreover, the court explained, "the mere fact that the telephone companies can provide a rival device would seem to be a poor reason for disregarding Hush-A-Phone's value in assuring a quiet line." *Id.* at 268, n.9.

The full implications of the D.C. Circuit's decision in *Hush-A-Phone* were not realized for over a decade, when the Commission handed down its 1968 *Carterfone* decision. Use of the Carterfone Device in Message Toll Telephone Service, Decision, 13 F.C.C. 2d 420 (1968). At issue was a device permitting direct communication between a mobile radio and the landline network.[8] True to form, Bell objected to the device, but failed to demonstrate that it would harm the network. The Commission rejected Bell's argument. Instead, the Commission ruled that the basic principle of *Hush-A-Phone* applied: any form of CPE could be attached to the network "so long as the interconnection does not adversely affect the telephone company's operations

8. [The FCC described the Carterfone device as follows: "The Carterfone is designed to be connected to a two-way radio at the base station serving a mobile radio system. When callers on the radio and on the telephone are both in contact with the base station operator, the handset of the operator's telephone is placed on a cradle in the Carterfone device. A voice control circuit in the Carterfone automatically switches on the radio transmitter when the telephone caller is speaking; when he stops speaking, the radio returns to a receiving condition. A separate speaker is attached to the Carterfone to allow the base station operator to monitor the conversation, adjust the voice volume, and hang up when the conversation has ended." *Carterfone*, 13 F.C.C. 2d at 420–21. Eds.]

or the telephone system's utility for others." *Id.* at 424. Unvarnished claims of threatened harm to the network would no longer suffice.

Even after *Carterfone*, competitive providers of CPE did not have unfettered access to the network. Bell responded to *Carterfone* by filing new tariffs, tariffs that permitted customers to connect to the telephone network, but only through interconnecting devices called "protective connecting arrangements" (PCAs) [that Bell itself would sell to interested parties]. Further, any "network control signaling" devices — devices, like the ordinary dial telephone, that actually put electronic signals onto the phone network — still had to be furnished, installed, and maintained by Bell. The Commission turned aside the immediate challenges to these tariffs. *Carterfone*, the Commission reasoned, permitted interconnections with — but not substitutions or replacements for — the "system," expansively defined. This substantially eviscerated *Carterfone*.

Notes and Questions

1. Subsequent Events. The FCC would ultimately reverse course. In 1972, the FCC began an inquiry into the issue of competitive CPE; that inquiry culminated in 1976 in a program of "technical registrations" for all CPE. Under this program, CPE suppliers had a choice: they could purchase a "protective connecting arrangement" (PCA) interface from Bell, or they could register their CPE with the FCC and show that the equipment would not harm the telephone network. Bell's stranglehold on the CPE market was thereby broken.

2. Ulterior Motives. In rejecting Bell's various technical justifications for its CPE tariff, the FCC apparently suspected Bell's ulterior motive was the desire to eliminate competition in the CPE market. But why would that be in Bell's interest? After all, Bell already controlled the phone network; why would it need two "stacked" monopolies — first the phone network, then the attached CPE? In fact, wouldn't Bell have been better off having competitive supply of CPE, since competitive supply would likely mean decreased costs and higher quality? Wouldn't those changes increase the profits Bell could make through its service monopoly? If telephone rates had been unregulated at the retail level, a good argument might be made that Bell could make up any profits lost due to CPE competition by raising the monopoly price of its services. But because telephone service itself was regulated, Bell not surprisingly looked to other, less regulated lines of business such as CPE as places to earn additional profits.

3. Bell/Microsoft/Apple. How similar is the Bell CPE issue to the more recent claims that Microsoft or Apple or Google has intentionally made it difficult for unaffiliated firms to develop or distribute software for the Windows operating system, the iPhone and iPad, or Android-based phones, respectively? That is, as we ask immediately above, would not Microsoft be better off allowing competition in the software market on the basis that high quality and low prices in the software market would drive demand for the operating system, making it in Microsoft's interest to allow competition in the software market so long as Microsoft could maintain its monopoly on the operating system? Or, in Apple's case, would it sell more products if it simply allowed all apps to be downloaded onto their devices? In 2018, the European Commission fined Google $5 billion for requiring its Chrome browser to be installed on phones running its Android operating system, even though the user could download other browsers. Note that none of these companies is price-regulated. How, if at all, might that fact make a difference?

§ 4.D.2. Competition in Long-Distance Telephony

At the same time that competition was emerging in the market for CPE, competition in the provision of interstate telephone service was also on the rise. This incipient competition resulted in part from the development of a new technology that eroded major barriers to entry in the long-distance market: microwave transmission.

Why was the introduction of this technology so important? To be sure, Bell's monopoly over long-distance telephony was supported by its control over local exchange service in most markets. But it was also supported by the high costs to an entrant of both obtaining the rights of way and digging the trenches needed to lay the transmission cable essential for providing telephone service. Microwave technology helped to reduce the entry barriers created by these two costs by greatly reducing the need to lay cable. A firm could transmit information by microwave, incurring only the more modest costs of constructing transmission and relay towers at sufficient intervals.

The FCC was at first resistant to new entry in the market for interstate communications. But in a 1959 decision, the FCC authorized the use of this new technology as part of a tailored form of interstate service called "private line service." Allocation of Frequencies in the Bands Above 890 MC., Report and Order, 27 F.C.C. 359 (1959). Private line service allowed large corporations to customize transmission capacity to meet their specialized needs. Instead of using the traditional telephone system, these firms could use their own "private" service to, for example, transmit information from one branch office to another. Importantly, private line service was not generic long-distance service. Private lines did not compete head-on with Bell's long-distance service because private lines served only particularly demanding users with peculiar transmission requirements.

Or so it was at first. Gradually, the FCC opened the door to more complete rival offerings. The coup de grace came in 1974 when the FCC required Bell to allow new private long-distance networks to connect to Bell's local telephone grids, thereby making it possible for Bell's local customers to use the private, non-Bell alternatives for long-distance (generally called "interexchange") communication. Bell resisted this last change quite heavily, and that resistance was one of the behaviors emphasized in the antitrust case that followed.

Bell, of course, was resisting in part for anticompetitive reasons. No monopolist is happy to see competition begin to emerge. It should be emphasized, however, that

Bell had a second reason to resist, and this one had much more policy allure. At the time, phone rates were heavily regulated, and those regulations intentionally pegged long-distance rates at a level above the competitive rate. The idea was to allow Bell to earn extra profit in the long-distance market such that local telephone rates could be kept artificially low. Given that, it is no surprise that private parties wanted to enter the long-distance market; prices there were, by design, quite high. But that was the regulator's choice, not Bell's. If competition were allowed to drive down long-distance prices, prices for local phone service would have either had to rise correspondingly or be subsidized through some other mechanism.

§ 4.D.3. Communications and Computer Convergence

A third area in which the FCC tried to delimit the scope of Bell's monopoly and which can be seen as a precursor to the Bell breakup involved the technological convergence of computer and communications technology. In 1949, the government filed its second antitrust action against Bell, this time arguing that Bell had impermissibly used its patents on telecommunications equipment to monopolize "almost the entire telephone operating and manufacturing fields." Huber et al. at 355 n.115 (quoting the government's complaint in United States v. Western Elec. Co., No. 17-49 (D.N.J. Jan. 14, 1949)). That case was settled in 1956, in large part because the Eisenhower administration was unsympathetic to the suit; the settlement at the time appeared to be a total victory for Bell. Under the settlement terms, Bell agreed that its manufacturing arm, Western Electric, would produce only equipment used in the provision of telecommunications services, and, further, that Bell itself would not engage "in any business other than the furnishing of common carrier communications services." United States v. Western Elec. Co., 1956 Trade Cas. (CCH) ¶ 68,246, ¶ 71,138 (D.N.J. 1956). These were seemingly token sacrifices; at the time, they represented Bell's approximate policies anyway.

As the market for computer services matured, however, the restrictions began to seem more binding. Bell scientists had invented the transistor — a key computer component — in 1947, and yet the 1956 decree seemed to bar Bell from participating in the industry that the transistor made possible. As Roger Noll and Bruce Owen put it, "with its leadership in semiconductor technology, Bell was positioned to be a very effective early competitor in computers; indeed, one can speculate that AT&T might well have been better off giving up the telephone but retaining its rights in transistors and computers." Noll & Owen, The Anticompetitive Uses of Regulation at 294. Bell sought to offer services in new areas, and on several occasions, most notably 1980, the question arose whether that 1956 agreement really did prohibit Bell from providing so-called "advanced" services.

For example, in the early 1980s, large mainframe computers were very expensive both to build and to operate. Because of this, many firms wanted to pool their resources, building a single large computer, and then sharing access to it. At the time, the easiest way to accomplish that sharing was to access the commonly owned computer over the telephone system, with each firm having a remote connection (a dummy terminal) that linked to the shared computer resource. But did the consent decree bar Bell from providing this sort of distributed computing service, or was this a permissible "common carrier communications service"? Questions like these did not admit easy answers, and as we will see later in Chapter 6, they continued to vex the FCC as it tried to decide the extent to which internet access should be considered a "telecommunications" service or something else for regulatory purposes.

With respect to the intersection of computing and telephone service in the 1970s and 1980s, the FCC recognized, on the one hand, that keeping Bell out of an unregulated market for data processing and computer services did not make sense. On the other hand, the FCC was concerned that Bell's control over the long-distance lines that connected users to mainframe computers, and those computers to each other, afforded Bell a potentially decisive advantage over other providers of computers and data processing services. The FCC tackled these thorny issues in its 1980 *Computer II* inquiry. Amendment of Section 64.702 of the FCC's Rules and Regulations (Second Computer Inquiry), Final Decision, 77 F.C.C. 2d 384 (1980) (*Computer II*).

In *Computer II,* the agency did two very important things: first, it deregulated all equipment used for "enhanced services" beyond basic telephone transmission and switching. This was good for firms providing computers and data processing services because they would not be regulated in their connections with the Bell System. Second, however, *Computer II* freed Bell to enter into the provision of such enhanced services. *Id.* To address concerns that Bell's control over the underlying telephone network would allow it to handicap its advanced-services rivals, the FCC required Bell to set up a wholly separate corporate subsidiary to provide CPE and enhanced services. *Id.*

Notes and Questions

1. **Structural Separation.** Did the FCC adequately balance the benefits and harms when it chose to abandon attempts at line drawing and instead rely on structural separation? The benefit, of course, was that structural separation allowed the FCC to defer to market forces in the markets for both CPE and "enhanced" services. But the harm was a possibly significant loss of the efficiencies that would have been possible had Bell been allowed to integrate its telecommunications and computer arms.

2. **Regulatory Competence.** Beyond the issue of correct policy, does the FCC's change in course enhance or detract from your confidence in the regulatory process? Going into the next section, which discusses the use of antitrust to break up the Bell System, think about the oddity of one part of the federal government (the Justice Department) bringing a lawsuit that essentially says that another part of the government (the FCC) has not been able to effectively regulate the anticompetitive behavior of a company.

§ 4.E. Breaking Up Bell: The 1984 Divestiture

The most dramatic effort to limit the scope of the Bell System's monopoly took place in 1984 when, pursuant to a consent decree with the Department of Justice, Bell was broken up into several completely independent companies. The breakup followed from the government's filing of its 1974 antitrust suit. The government was at that point dissatisfied with the state of competition and specifically complained that: (1) Bell was gaining an unfair advantage in the CPE, computer, and long-distance markets because it could discriminate against rivals who needed access to Bell's local telephone exchanges in order to compete effectively; and (2) that Bell was manipulating the regulatory environment to gain unfair cost advantages, specifically by assigning some costs to its regulated/monopolistic markets even though those were in fact incurred in unregulated/competitive markets. Anticompetitive discrimination in interconnection and predatory cross-subsidization through cost misallocation were thus the cornerstones of what would become the lawsuit that brought down Bell.

The antitrust case itself took until 1981 to come to trial, ultimately before Judge Harold Greene of the United States District Court in Washington, D.C. Part way through the trial, Bell and the government submitted to Judge Greene a proposed consent decree to settle the case. Judge Greene thus never had an opportunity to rule on the merits of the government's antitrust claims, although he did reject Bell's motions to dismiss and for judgment at the close of the government's case. *See* United States v. AT&T, 524 F. Supp. 1336 (D.D.C. 1981); United States v. AT&T, 461 F. Supp. 1314 (D.D.C. 1978). Under the Tunney Act (codified at 15 U.S.C. § 16), Greene could review the proposed consent decree only to determine whether its acceptance would be "in the public interest." Greene conducted that review, required several changes, and then accepted the decree as changed. That decree is known today as the "Modification of Final Judgment"—because it not only resolved the 1974 case but also modified the final judgment previously entered in 1956—and it is usually referred to simply as the MFJ.

The MFJ stripped Bell of its local exchange carriers but then freed the firm to provide long-distance service, to manufacture equipment, and indeed to compete in virtually any market. Meanwhile, the agreement imposed strict limitations upon the now-separate local exchange carriers (LECs) in terms of their business ventures outside the provision of basic local telephone service. All of these results stemmed from a desire to keep the computer, telephone equipment, long-distance, and enhanced services markets free of both discriminatory interconnection and predatory cross-subsidization.

The reading that follows is an excerpt from Judge Greene's opinion modifying, and then accepting as modified, the parties' proposed consent decree. On company names: As we noted in Chapter 1, we have referred to the pre-divestiture AT&T as the Bell System or Bell. We use "Bell" to make it easy for readers to distinguish the old monopolist from the post-divestiture AT&T. Judge Greene, meanwhile, refers to the pre-divestiture monopolist as "the American Telegraph & Telephone Company" or simply "AT&T."

As you parse the consent decree, be careful to keep track of exactly which entity is under consideration. The post-divestiture AT&T was no longer the entire Bell System, but instead became a long-distance carrier (AT&T) and, through its Western Electric subsidiary, an equipment company. (That company ceased to exist, by stages, in the 1990s and 2000s.) The Bell Operating Companies (BOCs), meanwhile, are the subdivisions of Bell that provided local exchange service and, after divestiture, were separated from the long-distance and equipment companies.

§ 4.E.1. The MFJ

United States v. American Telephone & Telegraph Co.

552 F. Supp. 131 (D.D.C. 1982), *aff'd sub nom.*, Maryland v. United States, 460 U.S. 1001 (1983)

GREENE, District Judge:

These actions are before the Court for a determination whether a consent decree proposed by the parties is in the "public interest" and should therefore be entered as the Court's judgment.

I. Preliminary Considerations

A. History of the Litigation

On January 14, 1949, the government filed an action in the District Court for the District of New Jersey against the Western Electric Company, Inc.[9] and the American Telephone and Telegraph Company, Inc. The complaint alleged that the defendants had monopolized and conspired to restrain trade in the manufacture, distribution, sale, and installation of telephones, telephone apparatus, equipment, materials, and supplies, in violation of the Sherman Act. The relief sought included the divestiture by AT&T of its stock ownership in Western Electric; termination of exclusive relationships between AT&T and Western Electric; divestiture by Western Electric of its fifty percent interest in the Bell Telephone Laboratories research facility; separation of telephone manufacturing from the provision of telephone service; and the compulsory licensing of patents owned by AT&T on a non-discriminatory basis.

9. Western Electric is the wholly owned subsidiary of AT&T that manufactures telecommunications equipment for AT&T's Long Lines Department and the Operating Companies. In addition, Western Electric provides telecommunications equipment and services to government agencies and, to a limited extent, the independent telephone companies.

The [1956] consent decree which was the product of this process included neither the divestiture of Western Electric nor any of the other structural relief originally requested by the government. Instead, an injunction was issued which precluded AT&T from engaging in any business other than the provision of common carrier communications services; precluded Western Electric from manufacturing equipment other than that used by the Bell System; and required the defendants to license their patents to all applicants upon the payment of appropriate royalties.

This was the status of the Western Electric suit when the government filed a separate antitrust action on November 20, 1974, in this Court against AT&T, Western Electric, and Bell Telephone Laboratories, Inc. The complaint in the new action alleged monopolization by the defendants with respect to a broad variety of telecommunications services and equipment in violation of § 2 of the Sherman Act. The government initially sought the divestiture from AT&T of the Bell Operating Companies (hereinafter generally referred to as Operating Companies or BOCs) as well as the divestiture and dissolution of Western Electric.

B. The Proposed Decree

Section I of the proposed decree would provide for significant structural changes in AT&T. In essence, it would remove from the Bell System the function of supplying local telephone service by requiring AT&T to divest itself of the portions of its twenty-two Operating Companies which perform that function.

Section II of the proposed decree would complement these structural changes by various restrictions which are said to be designed (1) to prevent the divested Operating Companies from discriminating against AT&T's competitors, and (2) to avoid a recurrence of the type of discrimination and cross-subsidization that were the basis of the AT&T lawsuit.

The first group of these provisions would require the divested Operating Companies to provide services to interexchange carriers equal in type, quality, and price to the services provided to AT&T and its affiliates. In addition, they would be prohibited from discriminating between AT&T and other companies in their procurement activities, the establishment of technical standards, the dissemination of technical information, their use of Operating Company facilities and charges for such use, and their network planning.

The second type of restriction imposed upon the Operating Companies is said to be intended to prevent them from engaging in any non-monopoly business so as to eliminate the possibility that they might use their control over exchange services to gain an improper advantage over competitors in such businesses. Thus, the Operating Companies would not be permitted (1) to manufacture or market telecommunications products and customer premises equipment; (2) to provide interexchange services; (3) to provide directory advertising such as the Yellow Pages; (4) to provide information services; and (5) to provide any other product or service that is not a "natural monopoly service actually regulated by tariff."

IV. The Divestiture

A. Conditions Necessitating Antitrust Relief

1. Evidence of Anticompetitive Actions by AT&T

The government asserted that AT&T monopolized the intercity telecommunications market and the telecommunications product market in a variety of ways in violation of the Sherman Act. The evidence that was produced during the AT&T trial indicates that, at least with respect to several of the government's claims, this charge may be well taken.

In its intercity case, the government alleged that AT&T used its control over its local monopoly to preclude competition in the intercity market. The government proved *inter alia* that after 1968 AT&T included a "customer premises" provision in its interconnection tariff which deterred potential competitors from entering that market; that it refused to provide FX and CCSA services to specialized common carriers and domestic satellite carriers until 1974 when the FCC specifically ordered it to do so;[10] and that it attempted to prevent competitors from offering metered long distance service that would compete with AT&T's own regular long distance service.

AT&T's basic rationale for these policies was that it was attempting to prevent competitors from "cream-skimming." As viewed by AT&T, it would have been able successfully to combat cream-skimming if it had priced each of its routes on the basis of the costs for operating that route. However, it concluded that the FCC had rejected this approach when it endorsed national rate averaging in the interest of promoting the goal of universal service. Accordingly, AT&T argued that, since rate averaging is inconsistent with competition, and since the basic rate averaging policy had been required by the FCC as being in the public interest, it was acting reasonably under the Communications Act in preventing competition as best and as long as it could.

What this line of reasoning fails to consider is that, at least by the mid-1970s, the FCC had clearly begun to promote competition in telecommunications. The government contended during the trial—correctly, in the Court's view—that AT&T had an obligation to follow the more recent FCC policy rather than previous policies which may have suited AT&T better, particularly since there was never a direct FCC rule against de-averaging.

---

10. FX (foreign exchange) service permits a customer to make or receive local calls through a distant switching center by effectively providing a long extension cord in the form of a dedicated line between the customer's location and a telephone company switching system in the distant location (the foreign exchange). *See* United States v. AT&T, 524 F. Supp. 1336, 1355 n.77 (D.D.C. 1981). CCSA (common control switching arrangement) is essentially a miniature AT&T long distance network, except for the fact that it is used by only one customer, albeit a customer, such as the federal government, with large telecommunications needs.

What is significant about these events is that AT&T was able to adopt the policies described above in large part because of its control over the local exchange facilities. For example, it was because of its ownership and control of the local Operating Companies—whose facilities were and are needed for interconnection purposes by AT&T's competitors—that AT&T was able to prevent these competitors from offering FX and CCSA services. Similarly, AT&T was able to deter competition by manipulating prices for access to the Operating Company networks.

AT&T's control over the local Operating Companies was central also to the anticompetitive behavior alleged with respect to the second facet of the government's case, that involving customer-provided terminal equipment.

The government proved that AT&T prohibited the attachment of competitors' equipment to the network except through a protective connecting arrangement (PCA). There was evidence that some experts (including a panel of the National Academy of Sciences) believed that such a PCA was necessary if the nationwide telephone network was to be protected from a variety of harms. On the other hand, the government's evidence indicated that AT&T required PCAs for equipment that in all probability could not harm the network; that there were delays in providing PCAs; that the PCAs were over-designed and over-engineered, and, thus, over-priced; that PCAs were required for competitive equipment while identical equipment sold by AT&T did not require their use; and that PCAs could not guard against all of the harms to the network that AT&T professed to fear.

Additionally, the alternative option of certification was available but never seriously pursued by AT&T. Moreover, when ultimately certification was directly mandated by the FCC as a substitute for the protective connecting arrangement, the telephone network did not cease to function in its customary fashion. Indeed, AT&T was unable during the trial to prove any actual harm to the network from the elimination of the PCAs.

In its procurement part of the case, the government alleged, and there was proof, that AT&T used its control over the local Operating Companies to force them to buy products from Western Electric even though other equipment manufacturers produced better products or products of identical quality at lower prices. Here, too, AT&T's control of the Operating Companies was central to the allegedly anticompetitive behavior.[11]

B. Effect of the Divestiture

[T]he ability of AT&T to engage in anticompetitive conduct stems largely from its control of the local Operating Companies. Absent such control, AT&T will not have the ability to disadvantage competitors in the interexchange and equipment markets.

11. It should be noted, however, that the government's procurement case was not extremely strong.

For example, with the divestiture of the Operating Companies, AT&T will not be able to discriminate against intercity competitors, either by subsidizing its own intercity services with revenues from the monopoly local exchange services, or by obstructing its competitors' access to the local exchange network. The local Operating Companies will not be providing interexchange services, and they will therefore have no incentive to discriminate. Moreover, AT&T's competitors will be guaranteed access that is equal to that provided to AT&T, and intercity carriers therefore will no longer be presented with the problems that confronted them in that area.

Abuses will also be unlikely in the equipment interconnection area, because the Operating Companies will not manufacture equipment and will therefore lack AT&T's incentive to favor the connection of one manufacturer's equipment over another's. Any pro-Western Electric bias on the part of these companies will be eliminated once the intra-enterprise relationship between the Operating Companies and Western Electric is broken.[12]

VII. Restrictions on the Divested Operating Companies

The proposed decree limits the Operating Companies, upon their divestiture, to the business of supplying local telephone service. In addition to a general prohibition against the provision of "any product or service that is not a natural monopoly service actually regulated by tariff," there are more specific restrictions that deny the Operating Companies the opportunity to engage in the following activities: (1) the provision of interexchange services; (2) the provision of information services; (3) the manufacture of telecommunications products and customer premises equipment; (4) the marketing of such equipment; and (5) directory advertising, including the production of the "Yellow Pages" directories.

A. Interexchange Services

To permit the Operating Companies to compete in this market would be to undermine the very purpose of the proposed decree—to create a truly competitive environment in the telecommunications industry. The key to interexchange competition is the full implementation of the decree's equal exchange access provisions. If the Operating Companies were free to provide interexchange service in competition with the other carriers, they would have substantial incentives to subvert these equal access requirements.

B. Information Services

The proposed decree prohibits the Operating Companies from providing information services, an umbrella description of a variety of services including electronic publishing and other enhanced uses of telecommunications.

All information services are provided directly via the telecommunications network. Here, too, the Operating Companies could discriminate by providing more

12. Any cross subsidization of AT&T's intercity services and equipment manufacturing operations with revenue from its monopoly local exchange services will likewise be eliminated.

favorable access to the local network for their own information services than to the information services provided by competitors, and here, too, they would be able to subsidize the prices of their services with revenues from the local exchange monopoly.

C. Manufacture of Equipment

There is a substantial likelihood that, should the Operating Companies be permitted to manufacture telecommunications equipment, nonaffiliated manufacturers would be disadvantaged in the sale of such equipment and the development of a competitive market would be frustrated. The Operating Companies would have an incentive to subsidize the prices of their equipment with the revenues from their monopoly services as well as to purchase their own equipment, even though it was more expensive and not of the highest quality. In that respect, the Operating Companies lack the competitive restraints that ordinarily prevent the typical vertically integrated company from engaging in such practices: the absence of competition in the end product market—exchange telecommunications—immunizes these purchasing decisions from competitive pressures. The Operating Companies therefore would be able to pay inflated prices for poor quality equipment and to reflect these costs in their rates without suffering a diminution in revenues.[13]

Moreover, if they were permitted to manufacture CPE, the Operating Companies would have substantial incentives to favor their own manufacturing arms by providing to them information regarding changes in network standards, thus permitting them to gain an advantage over non-affiliated manufacturers. In addition, they could subsidize the price of this equipment with revenues from the exchange monopoly.

F. Removal of the Restrictions

It is probable that, over time, the Operating Companies will lose the ability to leverage their monopoly power into the competitive markets from which they must now be barred. This change could occur as a result of technological developments which eliminate the Operating Companies' local exchange monopoly or from changes in the structures of the competitive markets. Thus, a restriction will be removed upon a showing that there is no substantial possibility that an Operating Company could use its monopoly power to impede competition in the relevant market.

XII. Conclusion

The American telecommunications industry is presently dominated by one company: AT&T. It provides local and long distance telephone service; it manufactures and markets the equipment used by telephone subscribers as well as that used in the

13. This rationale does not require the divestiture of Western Electric from the Bell System because AT&T's end products—interexchange services and information services—will be subject to competitive pressures. If AT&T paid a higher price for its equipment and that cost was reflected in higher rates, consumers would switch to a carrier with prices which reflected purchasing decisions based upon the principles of best quality and least cost.

telecommunications network; and it controls one of the leading communications research and development facilities in the world. According to credible evidence, this integrated structure has enabled AT&T for many years to undermine the efforts of competitors seeking to enter the telecommunications market.

The key to the Bell System's power to impede competition has been its control of local telephone service. The local telephone network functions as the gateway to individual telephone subscribers. It must be used by long distance carriers seeking to connect one caller to another. Customers will only purchase equipment which can readily be connected to the local network through the telephone outlets in their homes and offices. The enormous cost of the wires, cables, switches, and other transmission facilities which comprise that network has completely insulated it from competition. Thus, access to AT&T's local network is crucial if long distance carriers and equipment manufacturers are to be viable competitors.

AT&T has allegedly used its control of this local monopoly to disadvantage these competitors in two principal ways. First, it has attempted to prevent competing long distance carriers and competing equipment manufacturers from gaining access to the local network, or to delay that access, thus placing them in an inferior position vis-à-vis AT&T's own services. Second, it has supposedly used profits earned from the monopoly local telephone operations to subsidize its long distance and equipment businesses in which it was competing with others.

The divestiture of the local Operating Companies from the Bell System will sever the relationship between this local monopoly and the other, competitive segments of AT&T, and it will thus ensure — certainly better than could any other type of relief — that the practices which allegedly have lain heavy on the telecommunications industry will not recur.

With the loss of control over the local network, AT&T will be unable to disadvantage its competitors, and the restrictions imposed on AT&T after the government's earlier antitrust suit — which limited AT&T to the provision of telecommunications services — will no longer be necessary.

The decree will thus allow AT&T to become a vigorous competitor in the growing computer, computer-related, and information markets. Other large and experienced firms are presently operating in these markets, and there is therefore no reason to believe that AT&T will be able to achieve monopoly dominance in these industries as it did in telecommunications. At the same time, by use of its formidable scientific, engineering, and management resources, including particularly the capabilities of Bell Laboratories, AT&T should be able to make significant contributions to these fields, which are at the forefront of innovation and technology, to the benefit of American consumers, national defense, and the position of American industry vis-à-vis foreign competition.[14]

---

14. [The court reiterated, however, its view that competitive and First Amendment concerns justified a seven-year ban on AT&T's entry into electronic publishing. Eds.]

After the divestiture, however, the Operating Companies will possess a monopoly over local telephone service. Therefore, the Operating Companies should be prohibited from providing long distance services and information services, and from manufacturing equipment used in the telecommunications industry. Participation in these fields carries with it a substantial risk that the Operating Companies would use the same anticompetitive techniques used by AT&T in order to thwart the growth of their own competitors. Moreover, contrary to the assumptions made by some, Operating Company involvement in these areas could not legitimately generate subsidies for local rates. Such involvement could produce substantial profits only if the local companies used their monopoly position to dislodge competitors or to provide subsidies for their competitive services or products — the very behavior the decree seeks to prevent.

Different considerations apply, however, to the marketing of customer premises equipment — the telephone and other devices used in subscribers' homes and offices — and the production of the Yellow Pages advertising directories. For a variety of reasons, there is little likelihood that these companies will be able to use their monopoly position to disadvantage competitors in these areas. In addition, their marketing of equipment will provide needed competition for AT&T, and the elimination of the restriction on their production of the Yellow Pages will generate a substantial subsidy for local telephone rates.[15]

§ 4.E.2. Discussion of the Government's Theory

The two main charges leveled against Bell were predatory cross-subsidization and discriminatory interconnection. To better understand these charges, consider two possible competitors to Bell: a firm that manufactures and sells interactive data processing telephones (let's call them computer phones), and an ordinary hot dog stand.

(1) *Predatory cross-subsidization.* In Judge Greene's opinion, the cross-subsidization claim is framed as follows: because Bell was not effectively controlled by price regulation, it was able to earn monopoly profits from its ownership of local exchange carriers; Bell could use, or threaten to use, those monopoly profits to subsidize below-cost pricing in other markets. In the context of our simple example, the argument would be that Bell could sell its computer phones below cost due to its monopoly profits from local exchange service, driving out any would-be competitor not on the merits of its computer phone but simply because Bell had such large cash reserves that it could subsidize this form of anticompetitive behavior.

15. The decree also provides for another method of subsidizing these rates. It permits the Operating Companies, under the supervision of state and federal regulators, to levy access charges upon long distance carriers and those companies that provide information services. These charges may, if the regulators desire, be set at levels which continue the present level of subsidy for local telephone rates.

That characterization of the cross-subsidization argument is problematic, however, in that it implies that Bell could use the same tactic in *any* market. That is, with the kind of cross-subsidization described above, why couldn't Bell use its monopoly profits to subsidize the costs not only of long-distance telephony but also of hot dog production, selling Bell hot dogs at prices below cost and driving Oscar Mayer out of the hot dog business? That, in fact, was not the government's theory, and so it is important to understand how the government's actual argument distinguished computer phones from hot dogs.

The key insight for understanding the government's theory of the case is this: the government's claim is not that Bell could monopolize computer phones because it had a lot of money. It does not ordinarily make sense for a company to sell its products below cost. Even cash-rich firms do not like to waste money. Rather, the government's claim was that Bell could sell computer phones below cost but nevertheless not lose money. Bell could, as an accounting matter, shift costs from the competitive computer phone market to its regulated local exchange business. If additional costs in the regulated business were simply factored into the rate base and thereby produced additional revenue in the regulated market (as ordinarily would be the case with rate-of-return regulation), then Bell could both recover its costs incurred in the competitive market and enjoy a competitive advantage in that market.

Here's how the scheme would work. If some of the costs of manufacturing computer phones could show up on Bell's books as costs of running the local exchange service, then the firm could underprice computer phones but recoup the difference by raising local telephone rates. Bell's captive local telephone customers would in essence subsidize prices for Bell's not-at-all-captive computer phone customers. Bell could get away with this cost shifting because the phony costs would be so similar to costs legitimately incurred in the provision of local telephone service that, to some extent at least, Bell's regulators would not notice. Charges related to the production of hot dog buns would be obvious to even the least competent regulator; but costs related to computer phones might be hard to distinguish from costs legitimately incurred in developing and maintaining the local telephone system. That is the subterfuge that makes "cross-subsidization" possible. Bell was in a special situation because it could use a regulated market to subsidize costs from a competitive one—something General Motors, McDonald's, and Oscar Mayer cannot do.

This wrinkle in the cross-subsidy theory is also the theory's Achilles heel: if cross-subsidy is a realistic fear only in cases where it may be difficult to sort out improper from proper cost accounting, then there is always a risk that legitimate cost accounting might be condemned (inadvertently) as predatory. To return to computer phones, suppose that there are economies of scope in making computer phones such that it is cheaper for a firm to make computer phones if the firm also runs a local exchange service. Perhaps, for example, expenditures to design and configure the local telephone network also help a firm to design and configure computer phones. If Bell were to allocate some of these joint costs to local service, is that a predatory act against competing computer phone makers? If not, how will regulators or antitrust authorities know which acts are predatory and which are not?

Has the regulated firm engaged in illegal predation every time it allocates costs in a manner that regulators subsequently deem inappropriate?

In any event, note that there are several preconditions that must be satisfied before a firm like Bell has an incentive to engage in predatory cross-subsidization. First, the firm has to have a dominant position in a market where demand is relatively inelastic. That is, the theory requires that the firm raise prices in its regulated market, something the firm would not want to do if those higher prices would cause its customers to leave in droves. Second, rate regulation has to be such that the regulator allows the regulated firm to increase its price only if the firm can show increased costs. Without that link between its asserted costs and the regulated price, the regulated firm would have had no reason to misallocate its costs because claiming higher costs in the regulated market would not accomplish anything for the firm. Third, there has to exist a competitive market with sufficiently overlapping costs such that the firm can incur costs in that competitive market but persuade regulators that those costs should be attributed to the regulated market instead. In Bell's case, for example, the market for hot dogs would not have sufficed. Arguably, however, the markets for computer equipment, CPE, and long-distance service did.

(2) *Discriminatory interconnection.* The second major charge leveled against Bell was that Bell used its monopoly over local exchange services to deny competitors in other markets (for example, computer phones) necessary access to the local exchange. The claim, in short, is that Bell raised its rivals' costs; or, in other words, that Bell was able to sell computer phones more cheaply because its costs of interconnection were lower. While subsidization claims focus on cost allocation as an accounting matter, discrimination claims focus on engineering and technology issues related to local exchange service itself.

Discriminatory interconnection is relevant only in instances where access to the monopolized telecommunications service (here, the local loop) is crucial to success in some otherwise-competitive market. Thus, if Bell said that only Bell computer phones could be connected to Bell-owned local exchanges, Bell might well gain a monopoly over computer phone sales. People would not want to buy computer phones that could not be connected to the phone system. But Bell could not plausibly threaten to obtain a monopoly in selling hot dogs by refusing to provide phone service to non-Bell hot dog stands. One can operate a hot dog stand without connecting it to the phone system.

An important question to ask when considering the discrimination theory is the question we briefly mentioned in the context of the market for CPE, namely: why would Bell try to expand its monopoly in local phone service provision into some related competitive market? Think, for example, about computer phones. Would Bell have been better off allowing for competitive provision of computer phones, since more competition would lead to better computer phones and hence more demand for local service? The problem for Bell was that it would not have been able to extract the value of efficiency gains by raising the prices it charged for local phone service because regulation constrained its ability to raise those prices.

Thus, again, it is the fact that Bell was regulated in one market that made anti-competitive behavior attractive in another. If Bell could have exercised its monopoly power unchecked in the local exchange market, it is very possible that Bell would not have engaged in discriminatory interconnection. Competition in computer phones would have led to increased demand for telephone service; and Bell would have adjusted its price and reaped rewards accordingly. Because Bell was constrained in the local exchange market, however, Bell had good reason to try to shift its market power from the regulated market to a competitive one where that power could be exercised more freely.

Notes and Questions

1. The Importance of Being Regulated. During all of its alleged bad acts, Bell was a regulated firm. Why was that not an absolute defense to the antitrust charge? That is, if Bell was doing something wrong, was it not the fault of the regulators for either not regulating correctly or not enforcing their regulations? Is it wrong to allow the government two bites at the apple: one through regulation and then a second through antitrust litigation? In its decisions denying Bell's motion to dismiss and motion for directed verdict, the District Court rejected that argument. In Chapter 6, we will see the Supreme Court give an answer under the Telecommunications Act of 1996 that is, at least potentially, in tension with that view.

2. New Entities. The divestiture gave rise to seven Regional Bell Operating Companies (RBOCs), also called Regional Holding Companies (RHCs) or simply Baby Bells. As the RBOC moniker suggests, these were regional combinations of BOCs. The Justice Department and AT&T discussed breaking Bell up into just two companies — one long-distance and manufacturing and one, nationwide local company. It was thought that having seven, separate regional companies would allow the companies to have appropriate scale but also allow regulators to begin to benchmark the companies against one another.

3. Equal Access. Part VIII of the MFJ is labeled "equal exchange access" and, in this section, Judge Greene considers the obligations to be imposed upon the BOCs with respect to their treatment of interexchange carriers (IXCs). Judge Greene points out that, prior to divestiture, significant "bias [had] been designed into the integrated telecommunications network" and thus, in Judge Greene's view, it was "imperative that any disparities in interconnection be eliminated so that all interexchange and information service providers will be able to compete on an equal basis." 552 F. Supp. at 195. Equal-access rules were the decree's means for accomplishing just that, ensuring that AT&T would not enjoy an artificial advantage in the long-distance market after divestiture. As the FCC later explained the rule:

> Equal access not only ensured that IXCs would receive equal transmission quality, but also that callers would have the opportunity to pre-subscribe their telephones to an IXC other than AT&T. Before the advent of equal access, all interstate calls dialed on a 1+ basis were routed to AT&T. A caller could reach an [alternative carrier] only by dialing a seven-digit phone number, as well as an often-lengthy identification code, prior to dialing the

> called number. Equal access enabled callers to select a carrier other than AT&T to provide them long-distance phone service on a simple "1+" dialing basis. Moreover, the balloting process through which equal access was implemented educated customers as to the availability of alternative suppliers of telecommunications services and encouraged them to make a choice among IXCs.

Competition in the Interstate Interexchange Marketplace, Notice of Proposed Rulemaking, 5 FCC Rcd. 2627, 2632, ¶ 41 (1990).

The BOCs were not the only local exchange carriers required to grant equal access to long-distance companies. In 1985, the FCC extended that obligation to all independent local exchange carriers, basing its decision in part on a 1983 consent decree between the government and a large independent LEC in which that LEC had agreed, like the BOCs in the MFJ, to provide equal access. MTS and WATS Market Structure Phase III, Report and Order, 100 F.C.C. 2d 860, 863–64, ¶ 9 (1985). The FCC's 1985 decision thus evened the playing field, applying the same equal-access requirement to all LECs whether they were subject to a particular consent decree or not.

4. Allocating Cellular. In its initial complaint, the Justice Department took the position that Bell was also using its control over the local exchange to injure the cellular telephony market. But when it came time to allocate cellular licenses, the Decree allocated them to the BOCs, defining such services as part of "exchange" communications and not allocating them to AT&T under the theory that they were potentially competitive services. *See* U.S. Department of Justice, Response to Public Comments on Proposed Modification of Final Judgment, 47 Fed. Reg. 23,320 (May 27, 1982). In 1982, cellular systems did use the local exchange significantly to complete calls and to provide internal connections between towers and switches in the cellular network. But allocating them to non-BOCs instead might have given a boost to the development of alternative infrastructures and would have anticipated the market that actually developed in which cellular telephony and landline telephony are at least partial competitors.

5. Administering the Decree. The MFJ might sound as if it was a document designed to end the Bell antitrust litigation. In reality, all parties to the case knew that the MFJ would need to be adjusted over time. Experience would teach which restrictions were too broad or too onerous, and changes in market conditions would make some once-reasonable restrictions unnecessary in later years. To handle all this, Judge Greene maintained significant flexibility both to eliminate decree provisions and to grant specific waivers, either in response to a request by one of the parties or completely of his own accord. The Bell System divestiture thus remained on Judge Greene's docket from 1982, the year he first approved the consent decree, until 1996, when the Telecommunications Act of 1996 explicitly took Judge Greene out of the telecommunications business. Indeed, those waiver requests and a related process called the Triennial Reviews of the consent decree guaranteed dozens of district court and D.C. Circuit opinions.

6. *Computer III* and FCC Line-of-Business Regulation. As we noted previously, in *Computer II* the FCC had imposed "structural separation" rules requiring Bell companies to provide "enhanced" services through separate subsidiaries. In a 1986 proceeding known as *Computer III*, the FCC returned to the issue post-divestiture and ruled that the divested BOCs should no longer be required to maintain corporate separation between their common carrier communications services and the unregulated provision of enhanced or data processing services over the telecommunications network. Amendment of Sections 64.702 of the FCC's Rules and Regulations (Third Computer Inquiry), Report and Order, 104 F.C.C. 2d 958 (1986) (*Computer III*). As the Ninth Circuit Court of Appeals described the FCC's rationale:

> The FCC decided that its structural separation regulations had imposed costs in terms of the unavailability of certain services, lost economies and efficiencies, and the inability of customers to obtain complete telecommunications and data processing solutions from a single vendor. The FCC also determined that the BOCs' ability to cross-subsidize had been restricted because of divestiture, the growth of competitive alternatives to the BOCs' ordinary telephone service, and political and regulatory pressures at the state level to keep local phone rates down. The BOCs' ability to discriminate by providing inferior network access had also diminished, according to the FCC, because of industry-wide coordination of network standards and the threat that enhanced services competitors could bypass the BOCs' local exchanges.

California v. FCC, 905 F.2d 1217, 1229 (9th Cir. 1990).

The Ninth Circuit reversed and remanded the decision to end structural separation as arbitrary and capricious on the record presented. The agency, in turn, reaffirmed its *Computer III* rules, albeit with further explanation specifically tailored to respond to the court's criticisms. *See* Computer III Remand Proceedings: Bell Operating Company Safeguards and Tier 1 Local Exchange Company Safeguards, Report and Order, 6 FCC Rcd. 7571 (1991). The Ninth Circuit again rejected as inadequate the FCC's cost-benefit analysis of ending structural separation requirements. California v. FCC, 39 F.3d 919 (9th Cir. 1994). The back-and-forth ended only in 1996, when the Telecommunications Act of 1996 established an entirely new set of restrictions and thus mooted these debates.

§ 4.F. The 1996 Act

Twelve years after the 1984 effective date of the AT&T Consent Decree, Congress passed the most significant revisions to the Communications Act ever. The Telecommunications Act of 1996, Pub. L. No. 104-104, 110 Stat. 56, sought to address fundamental changes in the market. Nevertheless, the 1996 Act was not a "clean sheet" attempt to determine the future of telecommunications or telecommunications regulation. Taking effect in February 1996, the 1996 Act includes very little on the internet, except for provisions in the so-called "Communications Decency Act," which was included as the last title in the 1996 Act (and was successfully attacked in Reno v. ACLU, 521 U.S. 844 (1997), excerpted in Chapter 11). Legislators are sometimes said to pass laws while looking in the rearview mirror, and from a current vantage point the 1996 Act certainly seems to embody that criticism. Our representatives might be somewhat forgiven, though, for the broadband internet, while expected, was still a relatively limited phenomenon at the time Congress acted. Moreover, the 1996 Act took as a given communications regulation by an expert administrative agency (specifically the FCC). Even though it weighed in at 110 pages, the 1996 Act consists almost entirely of amendments to the 1934 Act.

We will talk more about the 1996 Act's specific regulatory tools in subsequent chapters, but a brief overview is warranted.[16] The Act was motivated by the developments that we point to in Chapter 1: technological convergence and the pressures that it put on a siloed regulatory system, as well as the strong belief that competition would, in all circumstances, yield better results. As to telephony, the MFJ's view that local service remained a natural monopoly was harder to maintain as wireless, cable, and internet voice services increased—to say nothing of the political pressure brought by the Bell Operating Companies chafing under the line-of-business restrictions. The 1996 Act therefore created elaborate rights and procedures for companies to enter into local telephone markets, hoping to enhance competition and, when local competition developed, permit the BOCs into long-distance and other services. Direct Broadcast Satellite and other services made competition to cable television more possible. The 1996 Act reduced rate regulation and other limits on cable television services. Additionally, the importance of radio and television broadcast had particularly seemed to continue to wane, while the importance of other wireless services (especially wireless telephony and data) seemed to increase. The 1996 Act thus reduced limits on broadcast ownership and expanded spectrum auctions and flexible use possibilities, as we discuss in Chapters 9 and 10.

Thus, as a general matter, the 1996 Act sought to eliminate legal barriers to competition and to drive down to their narrowest scope any remaining natural monopoly services, while maintaining other Communications Act goals, such as universal service. As Dean Krattenmaker summarized:

> Think then, of the Telecommunications Act of 1996, as an effort to hit a legislative trifecta: (1) entry barriers will be torn down so that legal balkanization no longer stands in the path of technological convergence; (2) as crosscutting entry subsequently takes place all over the telecommunications field, the FCC will be charged with ferreting out predators and given special regulatory tools for this task; and (3) lest the new competition harm

16. The literature on the 1996 Act, its history, and its effects, is vast. Two pieces, written or co-written by authors of predecessors to this text that provide good overviews of the Act's motivations and main features are: Thomas G. Krattenmaker, The Telecommunications Act of 1996, 29 Conn. L. Rev. 123 (1996), and Jonathan E. Nuechterlein and Philip J. Weiser, Digital Crossroads: Telecommunications Law and Policy in the Internet Age (2d ed. 2013).

> the most vulnerable, pro-social cross-subsidies will be maintained and even added to the value produced by telecommunications firms and markets.[17]

This, of course, was the optimistic view (as Krattenmaker allows). For example, the Act did not eliminate spectrum licensing, and it did not "break up" the existing local telephony or cable television incumbents, even as it increased the possibilities of competition in and for those markets. As we turn to more detail, however, keep in mind these aspirations and ask both whether they were achieved and how they might have been better pursued.

17. Krattenmaker, *supra*, at 130–31 (footnotes omitted).

Chapter 5

Natural Monopoly Regulation

Introduction

Chapter 1 noted that one common justification for regulation is preventing the economic harms from monopoly, and Chapter 2 introduced the antitrust laws as a legal tool to do exactly that. But the antitrust laws are best suited to combat monopoly harm when a competitive market is preferred to a monopolized market. When monopoly is economically preferred, however, the antitrust laws are unhelpful.

Economists regularly debate when, if ever, a monopoly is preferred over competition, but one such instance might be when a market is characterized as a "natural monopoly." A natural monopoly is a situation when the total cost of supplying the output demanded in a market is lower if it is produced by only one firm rather than multiple firms. More simply, natural monopolies arise in industries where monopolies are more efficient than competition. Economists and policymakers have historically believed that natural monopolies arise in industries characterized by very high fixed costs and very low marginal costs, such as electricity, telephony, sewage, and other industries that are typically associated with utilities.

The presence of a natural monopoly might mean that competition is undesirable, and therefore the antitrust laws are inapt, but it also means that other kinds of regulations are required to constrain the monopolist from imposing economic harm. This chapter describes regulatory strategies that are commonly leveraged to oversee and curtail potential abuses from natural monopolies. Particular attention will be paid to the regulatory controls that have been imposed on telephone monopolies, but similar strategies can be, and have been, applied more generally to other utility monopolies. Note that policymakers have advocated using many of these same regulatory strategies for markets that are not natural monopolies but exhibit similar features, such as high fixed costs, entry barriers, and large network effects (the phenomenon in which the benefits of a service to a single user increase by the number of other users).

The chapter first discusses rate regulation: the attempt by government agencies to directly monitor the prices set by monopoly carriers. Rate regulation may seem to be the most direct response to a natural monopoly, and for a significant period of time telephone and cable television regulators did rely heavily on reviewing and limiting carriers' rates, but administering price regulation effectively is invariably more difficult than it sounds. Here, we consider the assorted techniques of rate regulation and their various shortcomings. Even though price regulation remains a standard tool for utility regulation and natural monopolies, it should be assessed soberly and compared to other alternatives.

The chapter then discusses assorted regulations that require monopolists to open their network (or provide their service) to others. These access regulations arise most typically in two settings: interconnection requirements, which require dominant networks to connect with other networks, and assorted rules that require providers to serve all those who request the service, including competitors. The all-access requirements discussed in this chapter are common carrier rules and nondiscrimination regulations. (Proposals for what is known as net neutrality, discussed in Chapter 6, are a particular kind of nondiscriminatory access regulation.) These regulatory strategies are designed to capitalize on the benefits of a monopoly or dominant network while limiting the dominant firm's ability to act as a bottleneck that could injure competitors or harm consumers. As is the case for price regulation, however, it is often hard to know when these access regulations are appropriate, whether they lead to genuine access, whether they undermine the value that the targeted company creates, and whether they enhance or impede competition.

A third regulatory strategy, which is closely aligned with the motivations that underlie and the doctrines that implement the antitrust laws, is to limit a monopolist's entry into either an upstream or downstream market. Such vertical prohibitions are motivated by the concern that a firm might leverage its monopoly power to stifle competition in an adjacent market.

The fourth regulatory strategy, closely related to the third, is unbundling, or forcing a dominant firm to provide services separately. In natural monopoly settings, unbundling regulations are generally used when the monopolist offers multiple and potentially complementary services together but policymakers want those ancillary services provided competitively. Unbundling is a strategy to limit the monopolist's dominance to the specific markets that are characterized as natural monopolies and to encourage competition where possible.

Finally, the chapter discusses universal access regulations, which require dominant firms to provide their service to an entire market. For example, a telephone utility might be required to supply telephony to everyone within a certain area, including households for whom service is costly to provide. These regulations are also designed to mitigate the economic harm of a monopolist—in particular, the monopolist's inclination to reduce output to monopolistic levels—but more generally they are instituted to pursue the noneconomic value of universality. Thus, the monopolist is required to provide universal access not so much to prevent economic harm, since providing service to some might cost more than the benefits such service generates (and thus, by definition, is not efficient), but instead as a political arrangement in which the regulated entity promises regulators it will serve remote areas in exchange for the regulator promising to preserve the entity's monopoly.

These regulatory strategies are often executed in tandem and are often tied to each other. For example, rate regulation of telephony was intimately connected with universal access requirements, so rates negotiated under rate regulation did not simply target the efficient marginal cost but instead considered the additional costs of providing widespread telephony. Thus, economic and non-economic motives unavoidably intersected. In addition, most of these utility-style regulations did not preempt the antitrust laws, and so regulated monopolists were also subject to the Sherman Act, although the intersection of antitrust and sector-specific regulations can be complicated (a topic covered in Chapter 8). And lastly, the regulation of natural monopolies becomes even more complex when, as was evident when policymakers passed the Telecommunications Act of 1996, markets that were previously deemed to be natural monopolies would be more efficient if offered competitively. Thus, the right policy requires not just instituting effective regulation but knowing how to remove it as well.

§ 5.A. Rate Regulation

Rate regulation is among the most common regulatory strategies and has been used, in the United States and elsewhere, for multiple industries and across many generations, and is probably the most frequent strategy in utility regulation. It also was the prevailing regulatory strategy for wired telephony for most of the 20th century, and both its merits and its shortcomings are evident from the history of the Bell monopoly.

Although the precise scope of the Bell monopoly was always a matter of dispute, there was never any doubt that the provision of local telephone service and, for several decades at least, the provision of long-distance service were both part of Bell's allowable monopoly franchise. The regulatory priority for these monopoly services, then, was simply to constrain their prices. But how?

Two primary strategies were used. The first, known as "cost of service" or "rate of return" regulation, is a regulatory approach under which rates are based on the costs incurred by the regulated party. If the regulated party can show higher costs, the regulator approves correspondingly higher rates. The second, "price cap" regulation, distances itself from cost estimates. This time, an initial maximum price is set with an eye toward likely costs, but after that the maximum price stays the same over a longer period than under rate of return regulation regardless of whether costs rise or fall.

Of these two kinds of price restraints, rate of return regulation is the older and more traditional method. In the past few decades, however, regulators have increasingly migrated to the price cap model, for reasons that will become apparent below.

§ 5.A.1. Rate of Return Regulation

Under rate of return regulation, prices in the regulated market are based on the costs incurred by the regulated party. Suppose, for instance, that the regulated party can prove that it spends $10 per customer on labor to provide the regulated service and that it had to invest another $5 million to build the relevant physical infrastructure. Under rate of return regulation, the regulator would allow a price that (a) let the regulated party recover in full its $10 marginal costs and (b) let the regulated party earn a return on its $5 million investment as well. The rate of return would in theory be set to match comparable market investments. That is, if investments in unregulated but comparable industries would typically yield a yearly 8% return on investment, regulators would attempt to approve prices that would generate an 8% return for the $5 million.

Note that the above discussion keeps referring to regulators "approving" rates rather than setting them. That is because the typical process under rate of return regulation is to have the regulated party propose a price and then have the regulator approve or disapprove that price. More specifically, the regulated party submits a document known as a tariff, a document that puts forward information about the service, the costs of providing that service, and the proposed pricing. Tariffs are then made available to the public and evaluated by the relevant regulator—for example, state public utilities commissions. Under the Communications Act of 1934 as amended and most state statutes, the carrier's proposed rates take effect a relatively short time after they are filed, unless the regulator affirmatively acts to suspend them pending investigation, or rejects them.

The fact that rate of return regulation is based on the regulated firm's costs raises an obvious problem: the critical information—information about costs—is hard for the regulator to verify, and thus the regulated party has a significant ability to manipulate the disclosure and influence the regulatory result. This was a particularly serious problem in the days when Bell was the only national telephone service provider. In those days, there were no "rival" firms against whose numbers Bell's numbers could be compared.

Even in cases where regulators can obtain accurate cost data, rate regulation raises several additional perplexing problems. Start with the difficulty of allocating costs. Regulators must divide a firm's costs into three categories: costs that may be passed on to consumers and on which the firm is allowed to earn a return; costs that may be passed through to consumers but on which regulators do not allow a return; and costs that the firm may not pass through at all to consumers. Typically, regulators allow firms a return on things like expenditures on physical capital and the costs of financing operations. Firms may pass through, but not earn a return on, expenditures like tax payments, labor wages, and energy costs. These are real costs but not capital costs. Firms generally may not pass through the costs of advertising, executive pay bonuses, or investments that regulators deem "imprudent."[1] Decisions

1. For example, the California Public Utilities Commission excluded from the rate base nearly 80 percent of the costs Pacific Gas & Electric incurred in building the Diablo Canyon Nuclear Power Plant because it believed that "unreasonable management was to blame for a large part of [the] cost overrun." State of California, Public Utilities Commission Annual Report 1986–1987, at 13 (1987).

to disallow "imprudent" costs often protect consumers from bearing costs that the monopoly could never pass through if it faced competition, but they also are vulnerable to hindsight bias. A regulator who knows that a given investment turned out poorly might punish the relevant firm even though, at the time, the decision to invest was honest, efficient, and well-reasoned.

Another problem with rate of return regulation is that it leaves the regulated party with little incentive to economize on its expenditures. After all, so long as the firm appears to be incurring reasonable costs—and realistically, how well can the regulator distinguish reasonable from unreasonable expenses?—under rate of return regulation the firm will be allowed to increase its prices and recoup those investments. Firms regulated under rate of return regulation are thus often accused of "gold-plating"—figuratively, using expensive gold wire when simple copper would do.

As the FCC noted in an order moving away from rate of return regulation,

> In a competitive environment, where prices are dictated by the market, a company's unit costs and profits generally are related inversely. If one goes up, the other goes down. Rate of return regulation stands this relationship on its head. Although carriers subject to such regulation are limited to earning a particular percentage return on investment during a fixed period, a carrier seeking to increase its dollar earnings often can do so merely by increasing its aggregate investment. In other words, under a rate of return regime, profits (i.e., dollar earnings) can go up when investment goes up. This creates a powerful incentive for carriers to "pad" their costs, regardless of whether additional investment is necessary or efficient.

Policy and Rules Concerning Rates for Dominant Carriers, Report and Order and Second Further Notice of Proposed Rulemaking, 4 FCC Rcd. 2873, 2889–90, ¶ 30 (1989).

Gold-plating is not as bad a problem as it might at first appear, however, and the reason is that there is often time between a change in costs and the corresponding change in the regulated price. For instance, if costs are at a certain level in January and, at that time, the regulator approves particular local telephone prices effective January through October, the telephone provider has some incentive to economize on its expenses. Any cost savings accomplished during that period translates into increased profits. Those profits will be lost once the government resets prices to reflect the new, presumably lower costs; but, during the time lag between changes in costs and changes in the approved schedule of prices, even a firm regulated under rate of return regulation can in theory have some incentive to spend wisely.

Firms regulated under rate of return principles not only have a dampened incentive to minimize costs; they also have strong incentives to pretend that costs incurred as part of other services were actually incurred as part of the regulated service. Suppose, for example, that a telephone provider must incur a significant expense in order to upgrade its infrastructure to provide unregulated internet service. If the firm can make the regulator think that this expense was incurred in order to provide a regulated service (say, local telephone service), the firm will be able to recoup this cost by raising local telephone prices and thus will have an unfair advantage when it comes to competing in the market for internet service provision. Note that, unlike the gold-plating example, expenses incurred in this example are not necessarily wasteful or inefficient; the problem here is that the regulation is being used to gain an unearned advantage in a related, unregulated market.

A final limitation of rate of return regulation derives from the fact that regulators tend to require long depreciation periods for physical plant investments. From the perspective of a state regulator, for example, a decision to allow a switch to be depreciated over ten years as opposed to, say, five years means that the regulated company's cost structure will be lower (because it will have to wait longer before buying a new switch). If, as is often the case, regulators are primarily concerned with keeping rates low, there is a very strong temptation to adopt artificially long depreciation schedules. That might be fine, but it does mean that out-of-date equipment will often remain in use much longer than it would in a competitive industry. In competitive sectors, after all, firms are not given the luxury of living by depreciation schedules. (For example, when MCI and Sprint invested in new long-haul facilities that used fiber optic technology — and advertised the ability to hear a pin drop when making calls on their networks — AT&T had no choice other than to write off its undepreciated investment in its antiquated microwave network.)

§ 5.A.2. Price Cap Regulation

Under price cap regulation, the government regulates by announcing the maximum price that will be allowed for a given service and, usually, by further specifying a formula under which that price will automatically adjust over time given, say, expected efficiency improvements and inflation. Price cap regulation can be accomplished in other ways as well. For instance, instead of specifying a cap for each regulated service, the government might announce a maximum average price for a group of services, in that way leaving the regulated party a little more flexibility in its price setting decisions.[2] The key intuition behind price cap regulation is that the government's maximum price does not vary closely with the regulated party's costs. If the regulated party can lower its costs, it can maintain its price and keep the extra profit for itself. The main allure of price cap regulation is thus that, like competition, price cap regulation creates a strong incentive for regulated firms to minimize their costs.

---

2. A helpful analogy here might be to think of the salary cap in professional football. The teams are to a large degree free to set salaries for individual players, but the National Football League constrains the maximum amount of money a team can pay its players in a given season. The league, in other words, sets a price cap on the group of salaries but not on any salary in particular.

That said, note that price cap works only if the government genuinely commits not to change the cap in light of changed circumstances. That commitment turns out to be hard to maintain. If costs drop precipitously, there is typically political pressure to lower the price cap accordingly and shift some of those savings (which become firm profits under a price cap) to customers. If costs skyrocket, the pressure goes in the other direction, as service providers pressure the government for relief from the cap. The more the price cap responds to these sorts of cost-based factors, the more price cap regulation begins to mimic rate of return regulation. Judicial review can potentially solve this problem, holding the regulator's feet to the fire despite these sorts of political pressures.

Another wrinkle to consider with respect to price caps is the worry that they might cause firms to skimp on quality—the opposite of gold-plating. After all, there are two ways to reduce costs: one is by identifying efficiency-enhancing improvements, but the other is by degrading the service. Strategic service degradation is a difficult strategy to thwart. Competition prevents this sort of thing in a normal market, but the markets at issue here are monopolies. In theory, the regulator can stop this response by defining and requiring a specific level of service. Indeed, many states that migrated to price cap regulation later developed retail quality of service standards that specified levels of expected performance. That said, this sort of regulatory oversight is imperfect, and some regulated firms may well profit from the strategy of "starving the network" even in the face of retail quality of service regulation.

§ 5.A.3. Rate Regulation as Markets Become Competitive

One of the major challenges that regulators face is managing rate regulation as markets make the transition from regulated monopolies to more competitive structures. Given that the lack of competition is generally the reason an industry is regulated to begin with, one might think that rate regulation should end with the arrival of competition. Generally, this presumption is correct; the problem for regulators, however, is that competition often is not immediately strong enough to discipline the dominant former monopolist. The FCC's approach therefore has been to conduct an ongoing examination to determine when a firm is no longer dominant before repealing or reducing rate regulation.

The effects of incorrectly regulated rates become particularly acute when a market is undergoing the transition to competition, especially in industries like telecommunications characterized by high fixed costs of production. Long-run prices for any good or service must be high enough for firms to recover their production costs. When firms must make large, fixed investments in infrastructure to provide service, prices must be above marginal cost if firms are to recover their initial capital outlays. No firm goes into business to lose money, although that is exactly what would happen if a high-fixed-cost industry had its prices driven down to the textbook competitive ideal of prices equal to marginal (or average variable) costs. *See, e.g.*, Hal R. Varian, Intermediate Microeconomics: A Modern Approach 410 (8th ed. 2009). Some margin above incremental, variable cost is necessary.[3] If regulators set prices so low that they do not provide an attractive rate of return on total costs, unregulated competitive entrants will not find the market attractive to enter. If regulators choose competitive pricing standards inappropriate to the economics of the industry and, in their efforts to restrain the dominant firm's perceived market power, force prices too close to marginal costs, regulators risk deterring the competitive entry that could obviate the need for regulation in the first place.

In a market moving toward competition, regulators walk a very fine line: regulated prices that are too high can act as focal points around which market prices cluster. That is, even if the regulated firm has downward pricing flexibility, prices may be higher than in an unregulated setting if the incumbent must file tariffs that give advance notice of its intention to lower prices. There is empirical evidence that AT&T acted as a price leader in the long-distance telephony market when it was required to file tariffs as a dominant firm. The principal competitors, MCI and Sprint, knew in advance what AT&T's prices would be and had incentive to follow just under the "umbrella" of AT&T's prices rather than aggressively cutting prices themselves. Paul W. MacAvoy, Testing for Competitiveness of Markets for Long Distance Telephone Services: Competition Finally?, 13 Rev. Indus. Org. 295, 298–305 (1998). Regulated prices that are too high thus accomplish nothing, except possibly to raise consumer prices in a market that would otherwise be naturally moving toward competition.

Prices that are too low also do harm. Entrants move into markets where they expect to earn a profit, and thus they need to be able to charge a high enough price to justify the necessary entry investments. If regulators allow or require the incumbent to set rates below that level, the result will be to deter competition and impede the benefits it would provide to consumers. Regulators thus face a tall order in markets in which competition is emerging: to set rates at exactly the level that will allow an efficient firm to attract the investment necessary to compete in the marketplace. Rates above that level will make consumers worse off than the unregulated market. Rates below that level will deter competition that would naturally lower prices and obviate the need for administratively costly regulation. Given the difficulties that regulators inevitably face in setting rates with such precision, regulators must be extremely cautious about extending rate regulation schemes from a monopoly setting into an emerging competitive environment.

Notes and Questions

1. Comparisons. How different are price caps from rate of return regulation in practice? After all, as we point out above, rate of return regulation begins to resemble

3. Economists sometimes refer to this idea as "workable" competition to distinguish it from the textbook ideal of "perfect" competition. *See* J.M. Clark, Toward a Concept of Workable Competition, 30 Am. Econ. Rev. 241 (1940).

price cap in instances where the relevant regulators are slow to adjust prices in response to changes in costs. Similarly, price cap regulation begins to resemble rate of return in instances where regulators respond to changes in cost.

2. Costs Shared by Multiple Products. The general theory behind rate of return regulation does not tell us very much about how common costs should be allocated among various intertwined products. For example, how should a regulator assign the capital costs of installing, and the operating costs of maintaining, a local switch that will be used to provide local, long-distance, and toll-free services? This is a particularly important question in instances where one of those services is subject to competition but the others are not. In such a case, after all, the regulated firm has an incentive to allocate the bulk of the common cost to the monopolized service, thereby enhancing its ability to underprice rivals in the competitive market while simultaneously tricking the regulator into thinking that higher prices in the regulated market would be appropriate. This is a variant of the now familiar predatory cross-subsidization argument.

The allure of price cap regulation is partly the standard attraction that price caps give firms an incentive to economize on costs, and partly a more tailored advantage: under price caps, a firm has less of an incentive to cross-subsidize by unfairly allocating common costs to monopolized markets. This is true because, in theory, price cap regulation is not tied to costs. That is not strictly true in practice, however, insofar as price caps do respond over time to changes in cost. Indeed, if a regulated firm thinks that there is some probability that the government will respond to cost changes, that firm will again have an incentive to allocate a disproportionate share of its common costs to the regulated market. In essence it will continue to behave as if rate of return regulation were still in place. Unless Congress and the relevant agencies can credibly commit not to react to unexpected profits, this strategic interaction will be at play and price cap regulation will not completely eliminate the incentive to engage in predatory cross-subsidization.

3. Regulating Bell. In light of the discussion above, should the FCC have adopted price cap regulation for Bell back before divestiture? Would that have obviated the need for the Bell divestiture?

§ 5.A.4. Price Regulation Strategies

We noted in the introduction to this chapter that price regulation and universal service requirements often go hand-in-hand. At the same time, the economic objectives of price regulation are often undermined by the social motivations that underlie universal access requirements. In short, universal service policies distort prices since they keep some prices artificially high in order to keep other prices artificially low. This raises the concern that universal service policies cause firms and individuals to make inefficient decisions—consuming too much of the goods priced below cost while consuming too little of the goods priced above cost. For example, if long-distance rates overstate the actual costs of providing long-distance service, consumers will see those higher rates and react by making fewer long-distance calls. Conversely, if residential rates are subsidized by business rates, residential users will underestimate the burden their calls impose on the telephone network and thus residential users will make inefficiently many calls. Equity and efficiency are thus in tension when it comes to setting prices in the telephone system; policies that manipulate rates on pure policy grounds often inadvertently lead to inefficient use of the telephone network.

The tension between equity and efficiency is actually a much broader problem in the telephone network. To see why, consider the following simple example.

Suppose that, in order to offer two services — say, local service and long-distance service — a telephone company must incur a significant fixed cost of $20,000. This figure represents the costs of laying the necessary telephone lines, purchasing and deploying routers, and so on. Suppose, further, that having made that initial infrastructure investment, the firm can offer local service to its customers at a cost of $20 per month and long-distance service at a cost of $25 per month. What price should the firm set for these two services in a purely efficiency-driven world?

Our initial inclination might be to suggest marginal cost, in this case $20 for local service and $25 for long-distance service. Were that feasible, that would of course be the right answer. By charging marginal cost, the firm would ensure that every consumer who values either service above its cost would buy that service, and, conversely, the firm would also ensure that service would be declined by any consumer for whom the benefits did not exceed the costs. This would be efficient, but, again, this is not practical. Marginal cost pricing would not allow the firm to in any way recoup its upfront fixed cost investment of $20,000.

It is clear, then, that the prices of one or both of these services must be set above marginal cost. But by how much? One possibility would be to price local service at its marginal cost ($20) but raise the price of long distance until the revenues there covered both long-distance costs and the fixed cost investment. Another possibility would be to price long distance at its marginal cost ($25) but raise the price of local service until those revenues covered both the costs of local service and the fixed cost investment. But there are an infinite number of other possibilities between these two extremes, and the puzzle here is to identify the most efficient choice.

British economist and mathematician Frank Ramsey considered this sort of problem back in 1927.[4] Ramsey found that the best approach is to raise the prices of both products such that each experiences the same percent reduction in demand. In other words, if marginal cost pricing would have led 4,000 consumers to purchase local service and 5,000 consumers to purchase long-distance service, then the most efficient prices that nevertheless allow the firm to recoup its fixed cost investment

4. Frank Ramsey, A Contribution to the Theory of Taxation, 37 Econ. J. 47 (1927). An accessible and helpful explanation of Ramsey pricing can be found in Kenneth Train, Optimal Regulation 117–40 (1991).

will result in the same 4:5 ratio in the consumption of the two goods. So, if the firm found that it could recover its fixed costs by raising prices such that, in the end, 3,600 people purchased local service and 4,500 purchased long distance, we would know that it had raised prices in the most efficient way possible because the ratio of the quantities demanded is the same before and after the price increase.

The intuition here is as follows. Marginal cost pricing would be the most efficient option were it plausible but, because of the fixed cost expenditure, it is not. We thus have to raise prices and, in turn, reduce consumption. Ramsey pricing suggests that, in raising prices, we should at least maintain the desirable relative output level as between the two services. That is, if a 4:5 ratio was the ratio of local service demanded versus long-distance service demanded under marginal cost pricing, the 4:5 ratio is still the best outcome in a world where prices must exceed marginal cost. The absolute levels of demand unavoidably must change; given that, the best option is to avoid skewing the relative consumption levels.

Ramsey's insight has an important policy implication, one that significantly sharpens the tension between equity and efficiency in this setting: under Ramsey pricing, price is raised more for the product that has the less "elastic" demand. Elasticity measures how sensitive consumers are to price. It is defined to be the percent change in quantity demanded that results from a 1 percent change in price. The more elastic the demand, the more output changes for a given price change. What this means is that, because Ramsey pricing requires that both services experience the same percent decrease in quantity demanded, the most efficient price pair will raise the price more on the good for which consumers are less sensitive to price. If consumers have a strong desire for local telephone service no matter what its price but are more sensitive to price when it comes to long-distance calling, Ramsey pricing would suggest that the fixed costs of the telephone system be recovered mainly by increasing the price of local phone service. Long-distance prices should stay near marginal cost—at least according to Ramsey's theory.

On other policy grounds, this outcome is distinctly unappealing. Indeed, it runs in the exact opposite direction of the relevant universal service subsidy. Remember, universal service keeps local service inexpensive by raising the price of long-distance service. But local service was considered the most "necessary" service, and as such, it would have the most inelastic demand. Hence, efficiency and equity really are in sharp tension in the telephone setting. Not only do universal service cross-subsidies cause inefficient overuse and underuse of particular telephone services, but more broadly, universal service policies tend to push prices in one direction whereas efficiency concerns would move them in the exact opposite direction.

This sort of tension between efficiency and public policy is not unique to telephone pricing: Ramsey pricing is often unattractive on policy grounds. For example, demand for clean drinking water is not very sensitive to price, yet it is unlikely that policymakers would be willing to raise the costs of drinking water as a way to fund the sewage and water treatment infrastructure. Similarly, people without cars likely have relatively inelastic demand for public transportation, yet few policymakers would be willing to pay for highway maintenance by raising the prices charged for public transportation. The question here is whether local phone service is so like drinking water (and public transportation) that equity concerns should trump Ramsey's efficiency-based logic.

Notes and Questions

1. **How Broad a Principle?** Above we consider increasing the prices of various telephone services as a way of paying for the telephone infrastructure. But would anything change if, instead of trying to pay for the telephone infrastructure, we were trying to pay for something completely unrelated to telephone service? Suppose, for instance, that a local politician wants to subsidize school lunches and has decided to do so by taxing telephone usage. Does Ramsey pricing tell us anything about how that tax should be collected, or is Ramsey irrelevant because school lunches are not logically related to telephone service?

2. **Cross-Subsidies and Ramsey.** How would Ramsey suggest that policymakers resolve the tension between universal service policies and economic efficiency? Can equity and efficiency goals both be satisfied simultaneously? Can the tension at least be mitigated?

3. **Test Your Understanding.** In order to raise money for new computers, the law school dean has decided to increase the prices charged for law textbooks at the bookstore, food at the law school cafeteria, and candy at a vending machine located in the law school basement. What do the economics behind Ramsey pricing suggest about which of these prices should be increased most significantly? Should the dean instead just charge for computer access?

4. **Paying the Fixed Costs.** We could avoid the difficult tradeoffs inherent in Ramsey pricing by having the government pay the fixed costs of telephone service. Would this be a better approach? If the fixed costs were paid in this manner, would there still be an argument in favor of cross-subsidies in telephone pricing? Would those cross-subsidies still raise efficiency concerns?

§ 5.B. Access

In the early days of the telephone system, Bell strategically refused to connect its telephone network to networks developed and owned by rivals. Denying interconnection was for Bell an effective tool: rivals could not realistically compete with the Bell network if their customers could not call Bell customers. However, allowing Bell to deny access to its network both hurt consumers and denied to the market the benefits of network efficiencies.

The harm caused by Bell's denials—and the broader concern that dominant networks might wield enormous economic and political power if they preserved the right to determine who can and who cannot obtain access—provided ready justifications for access requirements. Put another way, a number of regulations limit the ability of a dominant network to deny service, or otherwise shut off network access, to others, including to competitors. We discuss a number of common strategies to preserve access: interconnection requirements, common carriage, vertical foreclosure prohibitions, nondiscrimination requirements, and net neutrality. Several of these regulatory strategies were incorporated into the 1996 Telecommunications Act, but several also have roots in constitutional law, common law, and other statutes.

§ 5.B.1. Interconnection Under the Telecommunications Act of 1996

The lessons from Bell's access denials were not lost on the architects of the 1996 Act, who worried that incumbent local exchange carriers (ILECs) would similarly deny interconnection to competitive local exchange carriers (CLECs) which aimed to enter the market. Without interconnection, those new entrants could not match the appeal of the incumbents' established network and would be unable to seriously challenge the incumbents' dominant positions. Therefore, Congress required rival LECs to interconnect with one another and to exchange network traffic. Under §§ 251 and 252 of the 1996 Act, all telecommunications carriers are required to accept telephone traffic bound for their customers even if that traffic originated on a rival firm's telephone network and, conversely, to originate all of their customers' calls even when that traffic is bound for a customer of a rival network.

The FCC has defined interconnection as "the physical linking of two networks for the mutual exchange of traffic." 1996 Local Competition First Report and Order, 11 FCC Rcd. at 15,514, ¶ 26. Unlike the Act's unbundling provisions, which apply only to ILECs, the basic interconnection provisions of §§ 251 and 252 apply to all telecommunications carriers, whether established incumbents or new entrants. Section 251(a) sets forth the basic interconnection mandate: carriers must (1) interconnect directly or indirectly with the facilities and equipment of other carriers, and (2) refrain from installing any network facilities or functions that interfere with such interconnection. Section 251(c)(2) imposes some further obligations on the ILECs. In the FCC's words, "§ 251(c)(2) requires incumbent LECs to provide interconnection to any requesting telecommunications carrier at any technically feasible point. The interconnection must be at least equal in quality to that provided by the incumbent LEC to itself or its affiliates, and must be provided on rates, terms, and conditions that are just, reasonable, and nondiscriminatory." *Id.*

The 1996 Act not only mandated interconnection but also set out some general guidelines for the terms on which such "mutual exchange of traffic" should proceed. Most generally, § 251(b)(5) provides that all telecommunications carriers must "establish reciprocal compensation for the transport and termination of telecommunications." And § 252(d)(2) adds that, to qualify as "just and reasonable," reciprocal recovery by each carrier of the costs of transporting and terminating other carriers' traffic must be limited to "a reasonable approximation of the additional costs of terminating such calls." The Huber treatise usefully summarizes the Act's reciprocal compensation scheme as follows:

> When a customer of carrier A places a local call to a customer of carrier B, Carrier A must pay Carrier B for terminating the call. Conversely, when a customer of Carrier B places a call to a customer of Carrier A, Carrier B must pay. The Act provides that state commissions shall not consider reciprocal compensation arrangements to be just and reasonable unless they provide for the mutual and reciprocal recovery by each carrier of the costs associated with the transport and termination on each carrier's network of calls that originate on the other's network; such costs are to be determined on the basis of a reasonable approximation of the additional costs of terminating such calls. In other words, the Act looks to the marginal cost of carrying the additional traffic, not the fully distributed costs of the network.

Peter W. Huber et al., Federal Telecommunications Law 476 (2d ed. 1999). This standard is obviously different from the "total element long-run incremental cost" (TELRIC) standard that we discuss in greater detail in part § 5.D.2. With interconnection, the focus is on the marginal costs imposed; with unbundling, the TELRIC standard in addition to marginal costs considers asset depreciation, capital costs, and other network costs.

While the 1996 Act requires reciprocal agreements for the transport and termination of traffic, note that it does leave open the possibility that carriers would elect not to charge each other for such services. Section 252(d)(2)(B)(i) makes clear that nothing in the Act precludes "arrangements that waive mutual recovery (such as bill-and-keep arrangements)." Under bill-and-keep, Carriers A and B do not pay each other to terminate calls moving from the network of one to the network of the other. Instead, the carriers assume that these numbers will cancel out in the end and so each agrees to simply charge its own subscribers for local service and then originate and terminate whatever calls happen to pass through the system.

Interconnection in general, and reciprocal compensation in particular, raise a number of hard questions in practice. For one, exactly what telecommunications traffic is subject to reciprocal compensation agreements? Does § 251(b)(5) apply to all traffic, or to local calls only? The question is an important one. Elsewhere in the 1996 Act—and a topic we deal with more fully in § 5.E—long-distance carriers are obligated to pay local carriers something called an "access charge" which is a traditionally above-cost fee through which long-distance carriers subsidize local providers. If long-distance traffic were interpreted to fall within the reciprocal compensation regime, what would happen to this form of subsidy? In ¶ 1034 of its 1996 Local Competition, First Report and Order, 11 FCC Rcd. at 16,014, the FCC resolved this issue by distinguishing access charges from reciprocal compensation, ruling that reciprocal compensation applies only "to traffic that originates and terminates within a local area." Traffic that originates in one local area but terminates in another is therefore long-distance traffic, and hence subject to the access charge regime.

A second interconnection issue involves the question of which local service providers are eligible for reciprocal compensation. The 1996 Act makes clear that the provisions apply to "telecommunications carriers," but the Act left it to the FCC to decide what kind of entity qualifies under that designation. For example, must conventional, wireline telephone companies enter into reciprocal compensation agreements with wireless communications providers? The FCC also addressed this issue in its 1996 Local Competition, First Report and Order, ruling in ¶¶ 999–1015, 11 FCC Rcd. at 15,992–16,000, that wireline carriers and Commercial Mobile Radio Service providers (a technical designation for all the firms that sell mobile telecommunications for profit directly to the public) did have to interconnect with each other and also were on the hook for reciprocal compensation.

Although the basic rules of interconnection and compensation for telephony are well settled, specialized scraps continue — particularly when one party or another is perceived as taking advantage of the system. In the era of the dial-up internet, some ISPs established affiliated CLECs and sought reciprocal compensation payments from the ILECs. Given the technology, all of the traffic, and hence all of the money, flowed in one direction (to the CLEC) because people only called the ISP connection number, and no traffic flowed out. After a series of proceedings, including several proceedings in the D.C. Circuit, the FCC eventually put an end to that practice. *See generally* Core Commc'ns, Inc. v. FCC, 592 F.3d 139 (D.C. Cir. 2010).

An even more pointed dispute came to light when, in April 2007, several large carriers, notably large wireless carriers like AT&T/Cingular, acknowledged that they were blocking calls to certain free (to end-user consumers) conference calling services. FCC Chair Kevin Martin responded to this admission by warning the blocking carriers that unless they stopped blocking the calls, the FCC "would end up taking action as we saw necessary." The carriers at issue quickly agreed to stop blocking calls to the services at issue, but they have continued to pursue actions against such services. Why? Because, according to the blocking carriers, such services make their money by taking improper advantage of the current intercarrier compensation regime. Some free conferencing services work by routing their calls through small, local telephone exchanges in Iowa, hence the 712 area codes for those calls. The local, rural carriers through which the conference call services work charge termination fees (which include a number of subsidies) to the networks carrying the incoming calls. The terminating rural carriers then share these fees with the conference-call service provider. In this way consumers pay nothing, but the networks that originate calls to the "free" services pay substantial fees (which they typically do not or cannot pass through to consumers) that generate profits both for the conference-call service provider and the rural network that terminates its incoming calls.

AT&T and other carriers, while apparently no longer blocking calls to the services at issue, filed lawsuits and complaints to the FCC against the rural carriers in Iowa alleging that their deals with the conference-call services were scams that violate FCC rules and other laws. The FCC made clear that while it would entertain those petitions, the allegedly injured carriers could not block consumers' ability to reach the conference-call services in the interim.

Another difficult issue that arose involved the extent to which providers of local exchange service had to interconnect with carriers that were not themselves providing retail telecommunications services, and therefore were not seeking interconnection for the purpose of connecting their customers to the customers of other networks. The question came up in the context of efforts by Time Warner Cable (TWC) to connect its Voice over IP (VoIP) subscribers to the public switched telephone network (PSTN). To do so, TWC contracted with MCI and Sprint for wholesale transport and connection to the PSTN. Certain state commissions (South Carolina and Nebraska) ruled that the 1996 Act did not require rural ILECs to interconnect with MCI and Sprint where the interconnection was for those carriers' wholesale customers rather than for those carriers' retail subscribers. The rationale for the distinction was ostensibly that wholesale services were not qualifying "telecommunications" for purposes of the 1996 Act's interconnection requirements. The FCC's Wireline Competition Bureau issued a declaratory ruling stating that the states' interpretations of §§ 251(a) and (b) were incorrect and that local exchange carriers must interconnect with providers of wholesale telecommunications. Time Warner Cable Request for Declaratory Ruling that Competitive Local Exchange Carriers May Obtain Interconnection Under § 251 of the Communications Act of 1934, as Amended, to Provide Wholesale Telecommunications Services to VoIP Providers, Memorandum Opinion and Order, 22 FCC Rcd. 3513 (2007).

Notes and Questions

1. **The Ghost of Intercarrier Compensation.** The TWC decision and the call blocking issue discussed above both purported to be about interconnection. In fact, concerns about intercarrier compensation — or lack thereof — underpinned the disputes in both cases. In the Time Warner case, the rural telephone companies were concerned that, to the extent calls were traveling to and from VoIP, those providers would not pay the same amount as traditional providers. In the call blocking case, the traditional providers resented delivering calls to rural carriers who were serving the conferencing service. In both cases, denial of interconnection was a self-help remedy. Should this remedy have been permitted? If it had been permitted, what would have been the consequence?

2. **Wholesale versus Retail.** In most cases, VoIP providers have contracted with established firms to provide transport connectivity and interconnection. (In many cases, they also have contracted for numbers, emergency 911 support, and other services.) From a legal perspective, VoIP providers have taken the position that they are not telecommunications carriers, but rather customers of telecommunications carriers. If VoIP providers are only customers and have no legal standing to request interconnection on their own right, should they be entitled to obtain

interconnection derivatively through other telecommunications carriers? How about phone numbers?

§ 5.B.2. Common Carriage

As we discussed in the previous chapter, Congress has designated certain networks that were deemed to be natural monopolies as common carriers. In 1887, the Interstate Commerce Act required common carriage obligations on railroads, and the federal government during Progressive and New Deal eras imposed common carrier regulation on other forms of transportation, electricity transmission, natural gas transportation, and other industries. And in the Telecommunications Act of 1934, Congress—largely copying provisions from the Interstate Commerce Act of 1887—designated telephony networks as common carriers.

The motivations behind common carrier regulations resemble those behind interconnection requirements, namely, network monopolies might be tempted to use their power to exclude to extract exploitive and anticompetitive benefits; and meanwhile, broader interconnection enhances welfare for all. But tellingly, the Supreme Court ruled that common carriers are not obligated to interconnect with other networks (recall from the previous chapter that, in the Court's words, there was no obligation to be a "common carrier of common carriers." St. Louis, I.M. & S. Ry Co. v. S. Express, 117 U.S. 1, 21 (1886)), yet common carrier obligations can also fall upon entities that are not natural monopolies. One reason for this independent definition is that common carriage is a concept rooted in the common law and predated the industry regulations developed in the Progressive and New Deal eras. Under current law, it remains both a common law doctrine and a statutory designation that shapes regulatory policy.

One present-day policy question is whether, and how, to apply common carriage requirements to dominant internet platforms. The largest of the internet platforms seem to occupy a space similar to that occupied by the traditional telephone and television networks and providers. On these platforms, individuals may send messages, receive news and entertainment, engage in business, and interact with advertising. In Chapter 1, we summarized the economic motivations for regulation, which include the challenges presented by monopoly, network effects, and public goods, but we have also seen demands for access and the need for universal service as grounds for regulation. Most internet platforms make their services available to all, and some of them have grown quite large and powerful. Do their access decisions compare to Bell's denial of interconnections to competitors? Should these dominant platforms be regulated as common carriers or public utilities? Or would any such regulation be a mistake? Consider the case below, in which a plaintiff uses the Constitution, the Sherman Act, and the 1996 Act to argue for imposing access requirements onto a dominant search engine.

Kinderstart.com LLC v. Google, Inc.

No. C06-2057 JF (RS), 2006 WL 3246596 (N.D. Cal. July 13, 2006)

FOGEL, District Judge:

I. Background

Kinderstart alleges the following facts. Kinderstart operates a website, www.kinderstart.com, which is a directory and search engine for links to information and resources on subjects related to young children. At one point, Kinderstart was "one of the choicest Internet destinations for thousands of parents, caregivers, educators, nonprofit and advocacy representatives, and federal, state and local organizations and officials in the United States and worldwide to access vital information about infants and toddlers." First Amended Complaint (FAC) ¶ 19. It launched in May 2000 and at its peak was "presenting in excess of 10,000 page views to visitors on a monthly basis." *Id.* ¶ 20.

Google is the world's most widely used search engine. Google "actively invites to 'anyone with an Internet connection' worldwide to perform searches for Websites and Webpages" and presents results of its searches on a "Search Engine Results Page" or "Results Page." *Id.* ¶ 2. According to the FAC, Google "induces users, the public, and the cyberspace community at large to expect and believe that Results Pages generated from a search every single time will be objective and neutral, untrammeled by human intervention or preference and free of any arbitrariness." *Id.* ¶ 31. Google states on its "Technology Overview" page: "'There is no human involvement or manipulation of results, which is why users have come to trust Google as a source of objective information untainted by paid placement.'" *Id.* ¶ 27. Google states on its "Information for Webmasters" page: "'We're committed to providing thorough and unbiased search results for our users. We stop indexing pages of a site *only at the request of the webmaster who's responsible for those pages*, when it's spamming our index, or as required by law.'" FAC ¶ 38 (emphasis in original).

Google also "has ownership and control over a computer process known as 'PageRank™', an automated, computer algorithm that generates a score as a whole number up to '10'. PageRank reflects the extent and nature of hyperlinking within the Internet to a particular Website and its web pages." *Id.* ¶ 32. Kinderstart alleges that "PageRank is not a mere statement of opinion of the innate value or human appeal of a given Website and its web pages," but instead is "a mathematically-generated product of measuring and assessing the quantity and depth of all the hyperlinks on the Web that tie into PageRanked Website, under programmatic determination by Defendant Google." *Id.* ¶ 33. "On information and belief, PageRank as promulgated and propagated by Defendant Google throughout the Internet, has become the most widely accepted relative measure of the appeal, popularity and relevance of a Website on the Internet. As such, Defendant Google has created and now manages and controls the de facto and prevailing standard of PageRank for rating Websites throughout the United States." *Id.* ¶ 56.

Kinderstart alleges that Google "is a common carrier that makes a public offer to provide communications facilities for subscribers to freely use its facilities to link to and connect with one or more Websites that are hosted on the Internet." *Id.* ¶ 41. Kinderstart provides the following quotation from Google's Form 10-K for the fiscal year ending December 31, 2005:

> We maintain the largest, most comprehensive index of web sites and other content, and we make this information *freely available to anyone with an Internet connection.*

Id. ¶ 22 (emphasis in FAC).

Kinderstart claims that Google has engaged in "pervasive monopolistic practices," which have led to the denial of free speech rights, prevention and destruction of competition, and predatory pricing. *Id.* ¶ 18. Kinderstart further claims that "[a]ny Website seeking to gain visibility, site traffic and page views must rely upon Defendant Google's Google Engine as an essential facility for receiving search query hits." *Id.* ¶ 49. Although MSN and Yahoo also operate in the search engine market, they "are not focused principally on search technology and search-driven advertising." *Id.* ¶ 54.

According to Kinderstart, Google "does in fact monitor, manipulate and censor the output and content on Results Pages, whether programmatically through a computer or individually through the intervention and discretion of one or more human decision-makers under the employ, direction, supervision and/or oversight of Defendant Google." *Id.* ¶ 70. Google engages in the practice of "Blockage" of websites by "delisting, de-indexing and censoring" websites, including the unacknowledged practice of isolating a website from search queries, either permanently or for an unspecified probationary period. *Id.* ¶¶ 3, 60, 63. Blockage also includes "penalization," by which a site's PageRank is reduced or set to zero "presumably based on either stated or unstated 'quality guidelines.'" *Id.* ¶ 61. Websites may experience "Blockage" at any time and may be unable to receive an explanation from Google as to why it occurred. *Id.* ¶¶ 62, 63. Kinderstart alleges that although Google denies engaging in "Blockage," it has admitted engaging in the "euphemistically" named practices of "'search quality improvement' or anti-Webspamming." *Id.* ¶¶ 64, 65. Kinderstart alleges that the practice of "Blockage" is positively correlated with "the failure and/or the reduction in AdWords advertising." *Id.* ¶ 69.

In 2003, Kinderstart enrolled in Google's AdSense Program and paid for a series of sponsored links from Google. *Id.* ¶ 21. In or about August 2003, Kinderstart began placing advertisements from the Google Network onto its site and receiving payments from Google for these placements. *Id.* On March 19, 2005, Kinderstart's website "suffered a cataclysmic fall of 70% or more in its monthly page views and traffic." *Id.* ¶ 74. Kinderstart eventually "realized that common key word searches on Defendant Google's search engine no longer listed KSC.com as a result with any of its past visibility." *Id.* With this drop in search engine referrals, Kinderstart's "monthly AdSense revenue suffered an equally precipitous fall by over 80%." *Id.* ¶ 75. Kinderstart concludes that its website "was officially, practically and illegally Blocked by Defendant Google." *Id.* ¶ 76. Its website has been assigned a PageRank of "0" by the Google Toolbar. *Id.* ¶ 87. Kinderstart was not notified in advance that this would occur and has not been instructed as to how it can cause Google to cease the "Blockage." *Id.* ¶ 78. Kinderstart is not aware of any way in which it has violated Google's guidelines. *Id.* ¶ 85.

III. Discussion

1. Violation of Right to Free Speech

Kinderstart first claims that Google's practices violate Kinderstart's right to free speech under both the United States Constitution and the California Constitution.

A. U.S. Constitution

The Free Speech Clause of the First Amendment to the United States Constitution provides that "Congress shall make no law . . . abridging the freedom of speech." U.S. Const. amend. I. Google argues that Kinderstart's claim pursuant to the First Amendment must be dismissed because the First Amendment governs state actors, not private parties. The Ninth Circuit has recognized "at least four different criteria, or tests, used to identify state action: (1) public function; (2) joint action; (3) governmental compulsion or coercion; and (4) governmental nexus. Satisfaction of any one test is sufficient to find state action, so long as no countervailing factor exists." Kirtley v. Rainey, 326 F.3d 1088, 1092 (9th Cir. 2003). Kinderstart argues that First Amendment protections apply because Google has dedicated its search engine to "public use." For the reasons discussed below, the Court concludes that Kinderstart's allegations are insufficient under any of these tests.

1. Public Function

"Under the public function test, 'when private individuals or groups are endowed by the State with powers or functions governmental in nature, they become agencies or instrumentalities of the State and subject to its constitutional limitations.' To satisfy the public function test, the function at issue must be both traditionally and exclusively governmental." Lee v. Katz, 276 F.3d 550, 555 (9th Cir. 2002). Kinderstart alleges that "Defendant Google actively performs . . . state-like functions, including . . . the creation, management and stewardship of universal, public, Internet-accessible index, archive and repository of the world's Internet content and information that cover all essential topics and subject matter for use by the general public." FAC ¶ 105. However, these functions, made possible by new technology, are neither traditionally nor exclusively governmental. Kinderstart's assertion that Google's digital archive "has the *potential* to be the functional equivalent . . . of the U.S. Library of Congress," *id.* ¶ 24 (emphasis added), is no more than speculation that Google may perform a state function at some time in the future, not a viable claim that it does so today. Nor has Kinderstart alleged that the government has "endowed" Google with the powers or functions in question.

6. Private Space Dedicated for Public Use

Kinderstart next argues that "[s]tate action is present when open space is free, open and dedicated to public use where free speech can and should thrive." Opposition, p. 3. Kinderstart alleges that Google's search engine is "freely available to anyone with an Internet connection." FAC ¶ 22. The Ninth Circuit held in Venetian Casino Resort, LLC v. Local Joint Executive Bd., 257 F.3d 937, 943 (9th Cir. 2001), that a casino owner who had formally dedicated property for use as public sidewalk could not exclude union demonstrators from the property. However, the Supreme Court has made clear that merely opening a space to the public does not dedicate the space to public use. *See* PruneYard Shopping Center v. Robins, 447 U.S. 74, 81 (1980) ("[P]roperty does not 'lose its private character merely because the public is generally invited to use it for designated purposes.'"). Kinderstart has not alleged facts tending to show that Google has dedicated the operations of its search engine to public use. Kinderstart's argument that "[t]he sole function and purpose of the [Google] search engine is to promote and realize 24-7 speech and communication, openly and freely," Opposition, p. 4, is inconsistent with its allegation that "Defendant Google derives at least 98% of its total company revenues from [] *search-driven* advertising, which exceeded $3.1 billion for the year ended December 31, 2004." FAC ¶ 57 (emphasis added).

2. Attempted Monopolization Under Section 2 of the Sherman Act

Kinderstart next alleges a claim for attempted monopolization under Section 2 of the Sherman Act, 15 U.S.C. § 2, the elements of which are: (1) specific intent to control prices or destroy competition, (2) predatory or anticompetitive conduct directed toward accomplishing that purpose, (3) a dangerous probability of success and (4) causal antitrust injury. In order to make out a claim of attempted monopolization, the plaintiff first must define the relevant market. The relevant market is "the field in which meaningful competition is said to exist. . . ." Image Technical Services, Inc. v. Eastman Kodak Co., 125 F.3d 1195, 1202 (9th Cir. 1997). A private party has standing to sue only if "'adversely affected by an *anticompetitive* aspect of the defendant's conduct.'" Datagate, Inc. v. Hewlett-Packard Co., 941 F.2d 864, 868 (9th Cir. 1991) (quoting Atlantic Richfield Co. v. USA Petroleum Co., 495 U.S. 328, 339 (1990)).

Kinderstart alleges that it and Google are competitors in the "Search Engine Market" and the "Search Ad Market," but that Google has a dominant position in a third market, the "Website Ranking Market." Kinderstart claims that through its "statements, behavior, conduct, acts and omissions, . . . [Google] harbors and evinces specific intent to destroy competition in the Search Engine Market and the Search Ad Market," and to "control prices in the Search Ad Market." FAC ¶¶ 113–18. Kinderstart further claims that "Google has sufficient intent, power, and resources to create a dangerous probability" of success. FAC ¶ 119. Kinderstart alleges injury in the form of lost revenue, loss of returning and new web traffic, and loss of goodwill. FAC ¶¶ 121–22.

The Court concludes that Kinderstart has failed to allege facts sufficient to support a claim of anti-competitive conduct, such as denial of access to an essential facility or refusal-to-deal. Kinderstart does not identify any specific acts by Google that would evince an intent either to control prices in the Search Ad Market or to destroy competition in the Search Engine Market, nor has Kinderstart made clear what prices Google allegedly is attempting to control. Additionally, Kinderstart does not explain how the alleged conduct demonstrates the requisite intent. Although Kinderstart alleges that Blockage and PageRank devaluation have caused injury to Kinderstart in the form of lost traffic and revenue, the facts alleged are insufficient to show that Kinderstart has suffered an antitrust injury — the result of anti-competitive conduct. FAC ¶¶ 121, 122.

Moreover, Kinderstart's allegations that Google removed Kinderstart from search results and lowered its PageRank do not suffice to allege predatory conduct as opposed to legitimate competitive actions. "[A]s a general matter 'there is no duty to aid competitors.'" MetroNet Services Corp. v. Qwest Corp., 383 F.3d 1124, 1131 (9th Cir. 2004). Finally, Kinderstart alleged no facts sufficient to support its claim that Google has a dangerous probability of success in attempting to monopolize the Search Engine Market and Search Ad Market, or to show a causal antitrust injury.

3. Monopolization under Section 2 of the Sherman Act

Kinderstart argues that Google is an "essential facility" within the market, and that by manipulating its Results Pages, Google excludes competitors from this facility. Kinderstart concludes that Google is an "essential facility or essential medium" because "the indexing, linking and referrals to such content afforded by Kinderstart over the Internet are essential to the operations, Web traffic, commerce, communications, and expression of speech by Class members." FAC ¶ 125. However, the threshold for finding a facility "essential" in the Ninth Circuit is high: "A facility that is controlled by a single firm will be considered 'essential' only if control of the facility carries with it the power to eliminate competition in the downstream market." Alaska Airlines, Inc. v. United Airlines, Inc., 948 F.2d 536, 544 (9th Cir. 1991).

While Kinderstart alleges that its Web traffic dropped 70%, and its ad revenue dropped 80%, it does not allege that it or similarly situated class members face elimination as a result of Google's conduct. Instead it alleges that "in spite of Defendant Google's wrongful conduct as alleged above, [Kinderstart] maintains extensive Website Content and links within its directory and index that are fully and remain actively hyperlinked throughout the Internet, and continues to generate *sustainable* level of traffic and PageViews from visitors." FAC ¶ 168 (emphasis added). Additionally, Kinderstart alleges that class members "consistently receive significantly and relatively high rankings and referrals from other search engines such as MSN and Yahoo." FAC ¶ 80. Accordingly, Kinderstart has not alleged adequately that Google, or its search engine, is an "essential facility" within the Search Engine Market.

Kinderstart argues that by refusing to remedy the alleged "Blockage" of Kinderstart's website, Google has violated Section 2 under the "refusal to deal" doctrine as set forth in Aspen Skiing Co. v. Aspen Highlands Skiing Corp., 472 U.S. 585 (1985). In *Aspen*, the larger of two ski resorts with a long-standing, bilateral, cooperative and profitable arrangement to market joint ski passes later refused to deal with the smaller resort—not even allowing it to buy tickets at listed retail prices. *Id.* However, as the Supreme Court has noted, "*Aspen* is at or near the outer boundary of § 2 liability." Verizon Communications Inc. v. Law Offices of Curtis V. Trinko, LLP, 540 U.S. 398, 399 (2004). Moreover, the facts alleged by Kinderstart are distinguishable from those in *Aspen*. Kinderstart has alleged neither that Google sold PageRanks or Results Page listings to Kinderstart or others nor that Google refused to sell these at listed prices. In fact, Kinderstart itself notes that Google denies ever selling PageRanks or listings at all. Additionally, there is no allegation that the only written agreement between the parties, the AdSense agreement, is no longer in place.

4. Violations of the Communications Act (47 U.S.C. §§ 201)

Kinderstart claims that Google is a common carrier and, as such, has violated the Communications Act, 47 U.S.C. §§ 201, *et seq.* A common carrier "makes a public offering to provide communications facilities whereby all members of the public who choose to employ such facilities may communicate or transmit intelligence of their own design and choosing." FCC v. Midwest Video Corp., 440 U.S. 689, 701 (1979). As discussed above, while Kinderstart has alleged that Google invites the public to *search* using its search engine, it has not alleged facts that would show Google invites the public to *speak* using its search engine. Thus, Kinderstart has not alleged that Google provides facilities of the type covered by the Communications Act.

The Ninth Circuit's holding in Howard v. America Online, Inc., 208 F.3d 741, 753 (9th Cir. 2000) is instructive. In that case, the court held that America Online (AOL), an Internet Service Provider, "is not a common carrier under the Communications Act," noting that the plaintiff in that case had failed to show that AOL provided discrete "basic services" rather than "enhanced services" as defined by the Federal Communications Commission. Kinderstart alleges that Google's search results are generated using computer algorithms based on user input, that sites are listed on Results Pages based on Google's index and that PageRank is generated by a computer algorithm. In short, Kinderstart alleges that Google's search engine acts based on the content of user's queries and provides the user with additional, different, restructured search results—thus meeting the definition of "enhanced services."

Accordingly, Kinderstart's claim under the Communications Act will be dismissed with leave to amend.

Notes and Questions

1. "Common Carrier." The court concluded that Google is not a common carrier under the Communications Act because Google does not provide "communications facilities." That decision applies only to the Communications Act and does not address whether Google should be considered a common carrier more generally. Even before statutes, the common law imposed certain heightened standards of liability on common carriers. But, more relevantly, legislatures have imposed common carrier duties (or equivalent public utility obligations) on a wide variety of industries, ranging from grain elevators, to railroads, to buses and taxis, to stockyards, and innkeepers. *See, e.g.*, James B. Speta, A Common Carrier Approach to Internet Interconnection, 54 Fed. Comm. L.J. 225 (2002) (discussing the history).

2. "Common" Search Engine. In the common law and in the early statutes, a "common" calling was simply any service that was, in fact, provided to the public on an indiscriminate basis, or to a substantial segment of the public. Some cases added the notion that the user substantially directed the service, as in deciding where he or she was traveling or calling or shipping. *See, e.g.*, Speta, *supra*; Southwestern Bell Tel. Co. v. FCC, 19 F.3d 1475, 1480 (D.C. Cir. 1994). Google — or any other search engine — seems to meet those two criteria. The search engines are made available to anyone with an internet connection, and the search engines themselves attempt to index all content on the internet (or, in the case of a specialized search engine such as a hotels search engine, a substantial category of content). Most other internet platforms are also open to anyone who joins. Is this enough?

3. Economics. What about monopoly and network effects? Kinderstart made little progress in its Sherman Act claim. The European Commission, however, ruled under its competition laws that Google had illegally injured competition by discriminating against unaffiliated content (we discuss this ruling in Chapter 8.A.3). The European Commission ruled that "[d]ominant undertakings have a special responsibility not to impair, by conduct falling outside the scope of competition on the merits, genuine undistorted competition in the internal market. A system of undistorted competition can be guaranteed only if equality of opportunity is secured as between the various economic operators." Google Search (Shopping), Commission Decision ¶ 331, Case AT.39740 (European Commission, June 27, 2017) https://ec.europa.eu/competition/antitrust/cases/dec_docs/39740/39740_14996_3.pdf. Do you think Google owes a "special responsibility" to Kinderstart? How would you characterize that obligation, and would it lead to a result different from the one issued by the *Kinderstart* court?

4. One Justice's View. The rise of the dominant internet platforms, and their uncertain role in facilitating political mobilization, has sparked a slew of legislative and legal activities. The Supreme Court has not weighed in meaningfully into these efforts, but the opinion below confirms the obvious: these debates are of keen interest to the Justices. Although any Court action will likely involve the First Amendment and other constitutional doctrines, it is interesting that the common law and statutory frameworks of common carriers might also shape the Court's thinking.

Joseph R. Biden v. Knight First Amendment Institute

141 S. Ct. 1220 (2021)

The petition for a writ of certiorari is granted. The judgment is vacated, and the case is remanded to the United States Court of Appeals for the Second Circuit with instructions to dismiss the case as moot.

JUSTICE THOMAS, concurring.

When a person publishes a message on the social media platform Twitter, the platform by default enables others to republish (retweet) the message or respond (reply) to it or other replies in a designated comment thread. The user who generates the original message can manually "block" others from republishing or responding.

Donald Trump, then President of the United States, blocked several users from interacting with his Twitter account. They sued. The Second Circuit held that the comment threads were a "public forum" and that then-President Trump violated the First Amendment by using his control of the Twitter account to block the plaintiffs from accessing the comment threads. But Mr. Trump, it turned out, had only limited control of the account; Twitter has permanently removed the account from the platform.

Because of the change in Presidential administration, the Court correctly vacates the Second Circuit's decision. I write separately to note that this petition highlights the principal legal difficulty that surrounds digital platforms — namely, that applying old doctrines to new digital platforms is rarely straightforward. Respondents have a point, for example, that some aspects of Mr. Trump's account resemble a constitutionally protected public forum. But it seems rather odd to say that something is a government forum when a private company has unrestricted authority to do away with it.

The disparity between Twitter's control and Mr. Trump's control is stark, to say the least. Mr. Trump blocked several people from interacting with his messages. Twitter barred Mr. Trump not only from interacting with a few users, but removed him from the entire platform, thus barring *all* Twitter users from interacting with his messages. Under its terms of service, Twitter can remove any person from the platform — including the President of the United States — "at any time for any or no reason." Twitter Inc., User Agreement (effective June 18, 2020).

This is not the first or only case to raise issues about digital platforms. While this case involves a suit against a public official, the Court properly rejects today a separate petition alleging that digital platforms, not individuals on those platforms, violated public accommodations laws, the First Amendment, and antitrust laws. The petitions highlight two important facts. Today's digital platforms provide avenues for historically unprecedented amounts of speech, including speech by government actors. Also unprecedented, however, is the concentrated control of so much speech in the hands of a few private parties. We will soon have no choice but to address how our legal doctrines apply to highly concentrated, privately owned information infrastructure such as digital platforms.

I

A

If part of the problem is private, concentrated control over online content and platforms available to the public, then part of the solution may be found in doctrines that limit the right of a private company to exclude. Historically, at least two legal doctrines limited a company's right to exclude.

First, our legal system and its British predecessor have long subjected certain businesses, known as common carriers, to special regulations, including a general requirement to serve all comers. Justifications for these regulations have varied. Some scholars have argued that common-carrier regulations are justified only when a carrier possesses substantial market power. Others have said that no substantial market power is needed so long as the company holds itself out as open to the public. Ingate v. Christie, 3 Car. & K. 61, 63, 175 Eng. Rep. 463, 464 (N. P. 1850) ("[A] person [who] holds himself out to carry goods for everyone as a business ... is a common carrier."). And this Court long ago suggested that regulations like those placed on common carriers may be justified, even for industries not historically recognized as common carriers, when "a business, by circumstances and its nature, ... rise[s] from private to be of public concern." See German Alliance Ins. Co. v. Lewis, 233 U. S. 389, 411 (1914) (affirming state regulation of fire insurance rates). At that point, a company's "property is but its instrument, the means of rendering the service which has become of public interest." *Id.*

This latter definition of course is hardly helpful, for most things can be described as "of public interest." But whatever may be said of other industries, there is clear historical precedent for regulating transportation and communications networks in a similar manner as traditional common carriers. Telegraphs, for example, because they resembled railroad companies and other common carriers were bound to serve all customers alike, without discrimination.

In exchange for regulating transportation and communication industries, governments—both State and Federal—have sometimes given common carriers special government favors. For example, governments have tied restrictions on a carrier's ability to reject clients to immunity from certain types of suits or to regulations that make it more difficult for other companies to compete with the carrier (such as franchise licenses). By giving these companies special privileges, governments place them into a category distinct from other companies and closer to some functions, like the postal service, that the State has traditionally undertaken.

Second, governments have limited a company's right to exclude when that company is a public accommodation. This concept—related to common-carrier law—applies to companies that hold themselves out to the public but do not "carry" freight, passengers, or communications. It also applies regardless of the company's market power.

B

Internet platforms of course have their own First Amendment interests, but regulations that might affect speech are valid if they would have been permissible at the time of the founding. The long history in this country and in England of restricting the exclusion right of common carriers and places of public accommodation may save similar regulations today from triggering heightened scrutiny — especially where a restriction would not prohibit the company from speaking or force the company to endorse the speech. There is a fair argument that some digital platforms are sufficiently akin to common carriers or places of accommodation to be regulated in this manner.

1

In many ways, digital platforms that hold themselves out to the public resemble traditional common carriers. Though digital instead of physical, they are at bottom communications networks, and they "carry" information from one user to another. A traditional telephone company laid physical wires to create a network connecting people. Digital platforms lay information infrastructure that can be controlled in much the same way. And unlike newspapers, digital platforms hold themselves out as organizations that focus on distributing the speech of the broader public. Federal law dictates that companies cannot "be treated as the publisher or speaker" of information that they merely distribute. 47 U.S.C. § 230(c).

The analogy to common carriers is even clearer for digital platforms that have dominant market share. Similar to utilities, today's dominant digital platforms derive much of their value from network size. The Internet, of course, is a network. But these digital platforms are networks within that network. The Facebook suite of apps is valuable largely because 3 billion people use it. Google search — at 90% of the market share — is valuable relative to other search engines because more people use it, creating data that Google's algorithm uses to refine and improve search results. These network effects entrench these companies. Ordinarily, the astronomical profit margins of these platforms — last year, Google brought in $182.5 billion total, $40.3 billion in net income — would induce new entrants into the market. That these companies have no comparable competitors highlights that the industries may have substantial barriers to entry.

To be sure, much activity on the Internet derives value from network effects. But dominant digital platforms are different. Unlike decentralized digital spheres, such as the e-mail protocol, control of these networks is highly concentrated. Although both companies are public, one person controls Facebook (Mark Zuckerberg), and just two control Google (Larry Page and Sergey Brin). No small group of people controls e-mail.

Much like with a communications utility, this concentration gives some digital platforms enormous control over speech. When a user does not already know exactly where to find something on the Internet — and users rarely do — Google is the gatekeeper between that user and the speech of others 90% of the time. It can suppress content by deindexing or downlisting a search result or by steering users away from certain content by manually altering autocomplete results. Facebook and Twitter can greatly narrow a person's information flow through similar means. And, as the distributor of the clear majority of e-books and about half of all physical books, Amazon can impose cataclysmic consequences on authors by, among other things, blocking a listing.

It changes nothing that these platforms are not the sole means for distributing speech or information. A person always could choose to avoid the toll bridge or train and instead swim the Charles River or hike the Oregon Trail. But in assessing whether a company exercises substantial market power, what matters is whether the alternatives are comparable. For many of today's digital platforms, nothing is.

If the analogy between common carriers and digital platforms is correct, then an answer may arise for dissatisfied platform users who would appreciate not being blocked: laws that restrict the platform's right to exclude. When a platform's unilateral control is reduced, a government official's account begins to better resemble a government-controlled space.

2

Even if digital platforms are not close enough to common carriers, legislatures might still be able to treat digital platforms like places of public accommodation. Although definitions between jurisdictions vary, a company ordinarily is a place of public accommodation if it provides "lodging, food, entertainment, or other services to the public . . . in general." Black's Law Dictionary 20 (11th ed. 2019) (defining "public accommodation"). Twitter and other digital platforms bear resemblance to that definition. This, too, may explain the Second Circuit's intuition. Courts are split, however, about whether federal accommodations laws apply to anything other than physical locations.

Once again, a doctrine, such as public accommodation, that reduces the power of a platform to unilaterally remove a government account might strengthen the argument that an account is truly government controlled and creates a public forum. But no party has identified any public accommodation restriction that applies here.

II

The similarities between some digital platforms and common carriers or places of public accommodation may give legislators strong arguments for similarly regulating digital platforms. It stands to reason that if Congress may demand that telephone companies operate as common carriers, it can ask the same of digital platforms. That is especially true because the space constraints on digital platforms are practically nonexistent (unlike on cable companies), so a regulation restricting a digital platform's right to exclude might not appreciably impede the platform from speaking. Yet Congress does not appear to have passed these kinds of regulations. To the contrary, it has given digital platforms immunity from certain types of suits, with respect to content they distribute, 47 U.S.C. § 230, but it has not imposed corresponding responsibilities, like nondiscrimination, that would matter here.

None of this analysis means, however, that the First Amendment is irrelevant until a legislature imposes common carrier or public accommodation restrictions — only that the principal means for regulating digital platforms is through those methods. Some speech doctrines might still apply in limited circumstances, as this Court has recognized in the past. For example, although a private entity is not ordinarily constrained by the First Amendment, it is if the government coerces or induces it to take action the government itself would not be permitted to do, such as censor expression of a lawful viewpoint.

[But] no party has sued Twitter. The question facing the courts below involved only whether a government actor violated the First Amendment by blocking another Twitter user. That issue turns, at least to some degree, on ownership and the right to exclude.

* * *

The Second Circuit feared that then-President Trump cut off speech by using the features that Twitter made available to him. But if the aim is to ensure that speech is not smothered, then the more glaring concern must perforce be the dominant digital platforms themselves. As Twitter made clear, the right to cut off speech lies most powerfully in the hands of private digital platforms. The extent to which that power matters for purposes of the First Amendment and the extent to which that power could lawfully be modified raise interesting and important questions. This petition, unfortunately, affords us no opportunity to confront them.

Notes and Questions

1. Why Concur to a Cert. Denial? Concurrences to and dissents from orders like this have no precedential value, and Justice Thomas wrote only for himself. Whom do you think Justice Thomas intended as the primary audience? What kind of case do you think he wanted the Court to hear?

2. "Common Carrier." Justice Thomas noted that under the common law, designating an entity a "common carrier" limits its right to exclude. How might this common law doctrine differ from the statutory designation, under the Telecommunications Act, that was invoked by Kinderstart? The two arguments surely apply to different entities — the common law doctrine, for example, traditionally applied to innkeepers — but do they also rely on different economic or philosophical principles?

3. Common Carrier, Public Accommodation, and Monopoly. Justice Thomas wrote that governments can limit the right to exclude when an entity is found to be either a common carrier or a public accommodation, and that these are similar concepts. He also stated that entities can fall under either of these categories "regardless of a company's market power." At the same time, he seemed most concerned with the market power that certain digital platforms have amassed. What role is market power playing in his analysis? And if market power is his primary concern, is he suggesting that the antitrust laws are inadequate?

4. The Relevance of Market Power and the First Amendment. Justice Thomas noted that the First Amendment might prohibit the government from limiting Twitter's control of its platform, and that the First Amendment might also require Twitter, or Twitter users who are also public officials, to cede control of its platform. Does Twitter's market dominance — or a Twitter user's prominence — factor into the First Amendment analysis?

§ 5.B.3. Nondiscrimination Obligations

Cable television emerged in the 1980s mostly as franchise monopolies, and content producers and regulators were concerned that cable providers might exploit their position as the gateway to viewers. Thus, in the 1992 Cable Act, § 616, Congress said that the FCC must adopt regulations

> designed to prevent a multichannel video programming distributor from engaging in conduct the effect of which is to unreasonably restrain the ability of an unaffiliated video programming vender to compete fairly by discriminating in video programming distribution on the basis of affiliation or nonaffiliation of vendors in the selection, terms, or conditions for carriage of video programming by such vendors.

47 U.S.C. § 536(a)(3). The FCC's regulations mirrored this language and created a complaint mechanism for programmers who believed they had been the subject of such discrimination. In the FCC's nomenclature, these are the "program carriage rules" designed to ensure the carriage of content. 47 C.F.R. § 76.1302.

In 2011, the FCC described the prima facie case that a programmer must make. Revision of the Commission's Program Carriage Rules, Second Report and Order and Notice of Proposed Rulemaking, 26 FCC Rcd. 11,494 (2011). In brief, the FCC said that a complainant must show that it was treated differently from the way in which a multichannel video programming distributor (MVPD) treats similarly situated, affiliated programming and that this different treatment had the effect of "unreasonably restraining" its ability "to compete fairly." *Id.* ¶ 15. The D.C. Circuit's most important decision interpreting the FCC's regulations and discussing the programmer's burden of proof is excerpted below.

Comcast Cable Communications v. FCC

717 F.3d 982 (D.C. Cir. 2013)

Opinion for the Court filed by Senior Circuit Judge WILLIAMS, in which Circuit Judge KAVANAUGH and Senior Circuit Judge EDWARDS concur.

WILLIAMS, Senior Circuit Judge.

Regulations of the Federal Communications Commission, adopted under the mandate of § 616 of the Communications Act of 1934 and virtually duplicating its language, bar a multichannel video programming distributor (MVPD) such as a cable company from discriminating against unaffiliated programming networks in decisions about content distribution. More specifically, the regulations bar such conduct when the effect of the discrimination is to "unreasonably restrain the ability of an unaffiliated video programming vendor to compete fairly." 47 C.F.R. § 76.1301(c); *see also* 47 U.S.C. § 536(a)(3). Tennis Channel, a sports programming network and intervenor in this suit, filed a complaint against petitioner Comcast Cable, an MVPD, alleging that Comcast violated § 616 and the Commission's regulations by refusing to broadcast Tennis as widely (i.e., via the same relatively low-priced "tier") as it did its own affiliated sports programming networks, Golf Channel and Versus. An administrative law judge ruled against Comcast, ordering that it provide Tennis carriage equal to what it affords Golf and Versus, and the Commission affirmed. *See* Tennis Channel, Inc. v. Comcast Cable Commc'ns, LLC, Memorandum Opinion and Order, 27 FCC Rcd. 8508 (2012) (Order).

Comcast's arguments on appeal are, broadly speaking, threefold. First, it contends that Tennis's complaint was untimely filed. Second, Comcast poses a number of issues as to the meaning of § 616, including an argument that the Commission reads it so broadly as to violate Comcast's free speech rights under the First Amendment. We need not reach those issues, as Comcast prevails with its third set of arguments — that even under the Commission's interpretation of § 616 (the correctness of which we assume for purposes of this decision), the Commission has failed to identify adequate evidence of unlawful discrimination.

Many arguments within this third set involve complex and at least potentially sophisticated disputes. But Comcast also argued that the Commission could not lawfully find discrimination because Tennis offered no evidence that its rejected proposal would have afforded Comcast any benefit. If this is correct, as we conclude below, the Commission has nothing to refute Comcast's contention that its rejection of Tennis's proposal was simply "a straight up financial analysis," as one of its executives put it.

* * *

Comcast, the largest MVPD in the United States, offers cable television programming to its subscribers in several different distribution "tiers," or packages of programming services, at different prices. Since Versus's and Golf's launches in 1995, Comcast—which originally had a minority interest in the two networks, and now has 100% ownership—has generally carried the networks on its most broadly distributed tiers, Expanded Basic or the digital counterpart Digital Starter.

Tennis Channel, launched in 2003, initially sought distribution of its content on Comcast's less broadly distributed sports tier, a package of 10 to 15 sports networks that Comcast's subscribers can access for an extra $5 to $8 per month. In 2005, Tennis entered a carriage contract that gave Comcast the "right to carry" Tennis "on any . . . tier of service," subject to exclusions irrelevant here. Comcast in fact placed Tennis on the sports tier.

In 2009, however, Tennis approached Comcast with proposals that Comcast reposition Tennis onto a tier with broader distribution. Tennis's proposed agreement called for Comcast to pay Tennis for distribution on a per-subscriber basis. [E]ven with the discounts that Tennis offered, the amounts are substantial. Neither the analysis provided at the time, nor testimony received in this litigation, made (much less substantiated) projections of any resulting increase in revenue for Comcast, let alone revenue sufficient to offset the increased fees.

Comcast entertained the proposal, checking with "division and system employees to gauge local and subscriber interest." After those consultations, and based on previous analyses of interest in Tennis, Comcast rejected the proposal in June 2009. Tennis then filed its complaint with the Commission in January 2010, which led to the order now under review. By way of remedy, the ALJ ordered, and the Commission affirmed, that Comcast must "carry [Tennis] on the same distribution tier, reaching the same number of subscribers, as it does [Golf] and Versus." Order, 27 FCC Rcd. at 8543, ¶ 92.

The parties agree that Comcast distributes the content of affiliates Golf and Versus more broadly than it does that of Tennis. The question is whether that difference violates § 616 and the implementing regulations. There is also no dispute that the statute prohibits only discrimination based on affiliation. Thus, if the MVPD treats vendors differently based on a reasonable business purpose (obviously excluding any purpose to illegitimately hobble the competition from Tennis), there is no violation. The Commission has so interpreted the statute, and the Commission's attorney conceded as much at oral argument.

In contrast with the detailed, concrete explanation of Comcast's additional costs under the proposed tier change, Tennis showed no corresponding benefits that would accrue to Comcast by its accepting the change. Testimony from one of Comcast's executives identifies some of the factors it considers when deciding whether to move a channel to broader distribution:

> In deciding whether to carry a network and at what cost, Comcast Cable must balance the costs and benefits associated with a wide range of factors,

> including: the amount of the licensing fees (which is generally the most important factor); the nature of the programming content involved; the intensity and size of the fan base for that content; the level of service sought by the network; the network's carriage on other MVPDs; the extent of [most favored nation] protection provided; the term of the contract sought; and a variety of other operational issues.

Of course the record is very strong on the proposed increment in licensing fees, in itself a clear negative. The question is whether the other factors, and perhaps ones unmentioned by Comcast, establish reason to expect a net benefit.

But neither Tennis nor the Commission offers such an analysis on either a qualitative or a quantitative basis. Instead, the best the Commission offers, both in the Order and at oral argument, is that Tennis charges less per "rating point" than does either Golf or Versus. But those differentials are not affirmative evidence that acceptance of Tennis's 2009 proposal could have offered Comcast any net gain.

In the absence of evidence that the lower cost per ratings point is correlated with changes in revenues to offset the proposed cost increase for Tennis's broader distribution, the discussion of cost per ratings point is mere handwaving.

A rather obvious type of proof would have been expert evidence to the effect that X number of subscribers would switch to Comcast if it carried Tennis more broadly, or that Y number would leave Comcast in the absence of broader carriage, or a combination of the two, such that Comcast would recoup the proposed increment in cost. There is no such evidence. (Conceivably Tennis could have shown that the incremental losses from carrying Tennis in a broad tier would be the same as or less than the incremental losses Comcast was incurring from carrying Golf and Versus in such tiers. The parties do not even hint at this possibility, nor analyze its implications.)

Not only does the record lack affirmative evidence along these lines, there is evidence that no such benefits exist. After Tennis proposed the broader distribution of its content on Comcast's network, Comcast executives surveyed employees in various geographic divisions to gauge interest in the proposal. The executive in charge of the northern division reported that there was "[n]o interest whatsoever" in moving Tennis to a broader distribution, because there had never been "a request or a complaint to move Tennis Channel to a more available tier." Perhaps more telling is the natural experiment conducted in Comcast's southern division. There Comcast had in 2007 or 2008 acquired a distribution network from another MVPD that had distributed Tennis more broadly than did Comcast. When Comcast repositioned Tennis to the sports tier (a "negative repo" in MVPD lingo), thereby making it available to Comcast's general subscribers only for an additional fee, not one customer complained about the change.

Neither Tennis nor the Commission has invoked the concept that an otherwise valid business consideration is here merely pretextual cover for some deeper discriminatory purpose. Without showing any benefit for Comcast from incurring the additional fees for assigning Tennis a more advantageous tier, the Commission has not provided evidence that Comcast discriminated against Tennis on the basis of affiliation.

The petition is therefore Granted.

KAVANAUGH, Circuit Judge, concurring:

As the Court's opinion explains, the FCC erred in concluding that Comcast discriminated against the Tennis Channel on the basis of affiliation. I join the Court's opinion in full. I write separately to point out that the FCC also erred in a more fundamental way. Section 616's use of the phrase "unreasonably restrain"— an antitrust term of art— establishes that the statute applies only to discrimination that amounts to an unreasonable restraint under antitrust law. Vertical integration and vertical contracts— for example, between a video programming distributor and a video programming network— become potentially problematic under antitrust law only when a company has market power in the relevant market. It follows that Section 616 applies only when a video programming distributor possesses market power. But Comcast does not have market power in the national video programming distribution market, the relevant market analyzed by the FCC in this case. Therefore, as I will explain in Part I of this opinion, Section 616 does not apply here.

Applying Section 616 to a video programming distributor that lacks market power not only contravenes the terms of the statute, but also violates the First Amendment as it has been interpreted by the Supreme Court. As I will explain in Part II of this opinion, the canon of constitutional avoidance thus strongly reinforces the conclusion that Section 616 applies only when a video programming distributor possesses market power.

I

Congress enacted Section 616 (over the veto of President George H.W. Bush) as part of the Cable Television Consumer Protection and Competition Act of 1992, known as the Cable Act. The Cable Act included numerous provisions designed to curb abuses of cable operators' bottleneck monopoly power and to promote competition in the cable television industry. When the Act was passed, however, the video programming market looked quite different than it looks today. At the time, most households subscribed to cable in order to view television programming. And as Congress noted, "most cable television subscribers [had] no opportunity to select between competing cable systems." Cable Television Consumer Protection and Competition Act of 1992, Pub. L. No. 102-385, § 2(a)(2), 106 Stat. 1460, 1460 (1992). Congress decided to proactively counteract the bottleneck monopoly power that cable operators possessed in many local markets.

The Cable Act employs a variety of tools to advance competition. Some provisions directly prohibit practices that Congress viewed as anticompetitive in the market at the time. For example, the Act prohibits local franchising authorities from granting exclusive franchises to cable operators. *See id.* § 7(a), 106 Stat. at 1483. Similarly, the Act's "must-carry" provisions require cable operators to carry a specified number of local broadcast stations. *See id.* § 4, 106 Stat. at 1471.

In other parts of the Act, Congress borrowed from antitrust law, authorizing the FCC to regulate cable operators' conduct in accordance with antitrust principles. For example, the Act requires the FCC, when prescribing limits on the number of cable subscribers or affiliated channels, to take account of "the nature and market power of the local franchise." *See id.* § 11(c), 106 Stat. at 1488. Similarly, the Act allows rate regulation only of those cable systems that are not subject to effective competition. *See id.* § 3, 106 Stat. at 1464.

The provision at issue in this case, Section 616, incorporates traditional antitrust principles. Section 616 does not categorically forbid a video programming distributor from extending preferential treatment to affiliated video programming networks or lesser treatment to unaffiliated video programming networks. Rather, to violate Section 616, a video programming distributor must discriminate among video programming networks on the basis of affiliation, and the discrimination must "unreasonably restrain" an unaffiliated network's ability to compete fairly. 47 U.S.C. § 536(a)(3).

The phrase "unreasonably restrain" is of course a longstanding term of art in antitrust law. *See, e.g.*, Leegin Creative Leather Products, Inc. v. PSKS, Inc., 551 U.S. 877, 885 (2007) ("[T]he Court has repeated time and again that § 1 outlaws only unreasonable restraints."). When a statute uses a term of art from a specific field of law, we presume that Congress adopted "the cluster of ideas that were attached to each borrowed word in the body of learning from which it was taken." FAA v. Cooper, 566 U.S. 284, 292 (2012). From the "term of art" canon and Section 616's use of the antitrust term of art "unreasonably restrain," it follows that Section 616 incorporates antitrust principles governing unreasonable restraints.

So what does antitrust law tell us? In antitrust law, certain activities are considered per se anticompetitive. Otherwise, however, conduct generally can be considered unreasonable only if a firm, or multiple firms acting in concert, have market power.

This case involves vertical integration and vertical contracts. Beginning in the 1970s (well before the 1992 Cable Act), the Supreme Court has recognized the legitimacy of vertical integration and vertical contracts by firms without market power. Vertical integration and vertical contracts become potentially problematic only when a firm has market power in the relevant market. That's because, absent market power, vertical integration and vertical contracts are procompetitive. Vertical integration and vertical contracts in a competitive market encourage product innovation, lower costs for businesses, and create efficiencies—and thus reduce prices and lead to better goods and services for consumers.

Now back to Section 616: Because Section 616 incorporates antitrust principles and because antitrust law holds that vertical integration and vertical contracts are potentially problematic only when a firm has market power in the relevant market, it follows that Section 616 applies only when a video programming distributor has market power in the relevant market.

How, then, did the FCC reach the opposite conclusion in this case? The short answer is that the FCC badly misread the statute. Contrary to the plain language of

Section 616, the FCC stated that the term "unreasonably" modified "discriminating" not "restrain"—even though Section 616 says it applies only to discriminatory conduct that "unreasonably restrain[s]" the ability of a competitor to compete fairly. Because the FCC did not read Section 616 as written, it did not recognize the antitrust term of art "unreasonably restrain" that is apparent on the face of the statute. That erroneous reading of the text, in turn, led the FCC to mistakenly focus on the effects of Comcast's conduct on a competitor (the Tennis Channel) rather than on overall competition. That was a mistake because the goal of antitrust law (and thus of Section 616) is to promote consumer welfare by protecting competition, not by protecting individual competitors.

It is true that Section 616 references discrimination against competitors. But again, the statute does not ban such discrimination outright. It bans discrimination that unreasonably restrains a competitor from competing fairly. By using the phrase "unreasonably restrain," the statute incorporates an antitrust term of art, and that term of art requires that the discrimination in question hinder overall competition, not just competitors.

In sum, Section 616 targets instances of preferential program carriage that are anticompetitive under the antitrust laws. Section 616 thus may apply only when a video programming distributor possesses market power in the relevant market. Comcast has only about a 24% market share in the national video programming distribution market; it does not possess market power in the market considered by the FCC in this case. Therefore, the FCC erred in finding that Comcast violated Section 616.

II

To the extent there is uncertainty about whether the phrase "unreasonably restrain" in Section 616 means that the statute applies only in cases of market power or instead may have a broader reach, we must construe the statute to avoid "serious constitutional concerns." Edward J. DeBartolo Corp. v. Florida Gulf Coast Building & Construction Trades Council, 485 U.S. 568, 577 (1988). That canon strongly supports limiting Section 616 to cases of market power. Applying Section 616 to a video programming distributor that lacks market power would raise serious First Amendment questions under the Supreme Court's case law. Indeed, applying Section 616 to a video programming distributor that lacks market power would violate the First Amendment as it has been interpreted by the Supreme Court.

To begin with, the Supreme Court has squarely held that a video programming distributor such as Comcast both engages in and transmits speech, and is therefore protected by the First Amendment. *See* Turner Broadcasting System, Inc. v. FCC, 512 U.S. 622, 636 (1994). Just as a newspaper exercises editorial discretion over which articles to run, a video programming distributor exercises editorial discretion over which video programming networks to carry and at what level of carriage.

In its 1994 decision in *Turner Broadcasting*, the Supreme Court ruled that the Cable Act's must-carry provisions might satisfy intermediate First Amendment scrutiny, but the Court rested that conclusion on "special characteristics of the cable medium: the bottleneck monopoly power exercised by cable operators and the dangers this power poses to the viability of broadcast television." *Id.* at 661. When a cable operator has bottleneck power, the Court explained, it can "silence the voice of competing speakers with a mere flick of the switch." *Id.* at 656. In subsequently upholding the must-carry provisions, the Court reiterated that cable's bottleneck monopoly power was critical to the First Amendment calculus. *See* Turner Broadcasting System, Inc. v. FCC, 520 U.S. 180, 197–207 (1997) (controlling opinion of Kennedy, J.). The Court stated that "cable operators possess[ed] a local monopoly over cable households," with only one percent of communities being served by more than one cable operator. *Id.* at 197.

In 1996, when this Court upheld the Cable Act's exclusive-contract provisions against a First Amendment challenge, we likewise pointed to the "special characteristics" of the cable industry. *See* Time Warner Entertainment Co. v. FCC, 93 F.3d 957 (D.C. Cir. 1996). Essential to our decision were "both the bottleneck monopoly power exercised by cable operators and the unique power that vertically integrated companies have in the cable market." *Id.* at 978.

But in the 16 years since the last of those cases was decided, the video programming distribution market has changed dramatically, especially with the rapid growth of satellite and Internet providers. This Court has previously described the massive transformation, explaining that cable operators "no longer have the bottleneck power over programming that concerned the Congress in 1992." Comcast Corp. v. FCC, 579 F.3d 1, 8 (D.C. Cir. 2009).

In today's highly competitive market, neither Comcast nor any other video programming distributor possesses market power in the national video programming distribution market. To be sure, beyond an interest in policing anticompetitive behavior, the FCC may think it preferable simply as a communications policy matter to equalize or enhance the voices of various entertainment and sports networks such as the Tennis Channel. But as the Supreme Court stated in one of the most important sentences in First Amendment history, "the concept that government may restrict the speech of some elements of our society in order to enhance the relative voice of others is wholly foreign to the First Amendment." Buckley v. Valeo, 424 U.S. 1, 48–49 (1976).

The Supreme Court's precedents amply demonstrate that the FCC's interpretation of Section 616 violates the First Amendment. At a minimum, the Supreme Court's precedents raise serious First Amendment questions about the FCC's interpretation of Section 616. Under the constitutional avoidance canon, those serious constitutional questions require that we construe Section 616 to apply only when a video programming distributor possesses market power.

* * *

The FCC erred in concluding that Section 616 may apply to a video programming distributor without market power. For that reason, in addition to the reasons given by the Court, the FCC's Order cannot stand.

[Concurring opinion by Senior Circuit Judge EDWARDS omitted.]

Notes and Questions

1. **The First Amendment.** In 2013, the Second Circuit rejected a facial constitutional challenge to the FCC's 2011 regulations. That court stated, in some tension with Judge Kavanaugh, that, "[w]hile rapidly increasing competition in the video programming industry may undermine [the conclusion that the FCC's rules are constitutional] in the not-too-distant future, that time has not yet come." Time Warner Cable Inc. v. FCC, 729 F.3d 137, 155 (2d Cir. 2013). Does the First Amendment really require that the courts determine the level of competition in video distribution markets, instead of the legislature or the FCC?

2. **Regulation and Antitrust.** The opinions above raise the recurring theme of how a court should interpret an industry-specific statute and any subsequent agency rules when the antitrust laws and economic principles lie in the backdrop. Then-Judge Kavanaugh interpreted the Cable Act through the lens of antitrust principles. Does § 616 merely reinforce the application of longstanding antitrust principles (for of course antitrust law as it existed at the time of the 1992 Cable Act)? If so, then why did Congress enact § 616? Note that his opinion heavily rested on Comcast's market share and its exposure to national competition, and that in 1992 most television markets were dominated by a single cable television provider. Should the Cable Act and other similar statutes be read contextually? (Side question: did Kavanaugh define the market correctly?) Does your answer to these questions influence how one should understand what amounts to a "reasonable business purpose," the language Judge Williams relied upon for the majority opinion?

3. **Regulation or Antitrust.** How a court interprets a statute would presumably influence how Congress passes statutes. Are you convinced that the FCC could not interpret the statute as permitting a more prophylactic approach than antitrust? Might Congress want to introduce prophylactic prohibitions, or even introduce rules that deviate entirely from economic reasoning?

4. **Practical Effects.** The practical effect of the D.C. Circuit's decision has been to make a complaint very difficult to bring. How could an unaffiliated programmer practically show that its programming will benefit the cable operator, when most of the relevant information will be in the cable operator's hands? Could the FCC address this issue by revising its regulations? Consistently with the First Amendment?

§ 5.C. Vertical Prohibitions

Regulators of natural monopolies are typically concerned that the monopolist might leverage its advantage in one market to stifle competition in an adjacent market. For example, a railroad monopolist might enter into the oil refining market and limit its oil refinery competitors from shipping their product; thus, a monopoly in railroad transport might translate into an advantage, and perhaps another monopoly, in oil refining. An ancillary concern is that allowing a monopolist (though not a natural monopolist—can you see why?) to leverage its market power into an advantage in an adjacent market would also allow it to entrench its current monopoly. For example, a railroad monopolist might use its market power for an advantage in oil refining, and by harming others in the oil refinery market, it might deter oil refiners from entering the railroad market.

These concerns are commonly described as vertical foreclosure, that competition is harmed or entry is stifled if a dominant firm integrates into an adjacent market. One common regulatory response in telecommunications has been to prohibit or limit vertical arrangements, such as vertical entry (e.g., the railroad builds a refinery market), acquisitions (the railroad purchases a refinery), or exclusive arrangements (the railroad convinces certain refineries to make it their exclusive mode of transport).

A stylized set of economic assumptions underlies both the anticipated harm from vertical arrangements and the logic justifying their regulatory prohibition. It is also critical to remember that most vertical arrangements introduce efficiencies, so their prohibition must (presumably) rest on a confidence that their economic costs outweigh their benefits. In the materials that follow, consider both the economic rationale and legal basis behind the particular vertical prohibition. Note also the frequent references to the antitrust laws (which we discuss in Chapter 8). Since the antitrust laws are ostensibly designed to combat abuses and extensions of market power, a persistent question within these materials is why Congress decided to pursue its competition objectives though statutes and regulations that are specific to the telecommunications sector. Relatedly, it would be wise to consider noneconomic rationales—political incentives, distributional concerns, or others—that might also motivate regulators to issue and judges to support particular prohibitions.

We consider two categories of vertical prohibitions that the FCC has promulgated, over several decades, designed to preserve competition in broadcast markets. The first was designed to constrain the power of the dominant broadcast television networks (ABC, CBS, and NBC) from threatening the viability of unaffiliated broadcast licensees and independent content producers. The second was designed to constrain the power of dominant cable television companies.

§ 5.C.1. Regulation of Vertical Foreclosure by Television Networks

Until the late 1980s there were only three major broadcast television networks (ABC, CBS, and NBC), in part because of FCC allotment decisions we discuss in Chapter 9.C.1. Having only three networks gave rise to concerns about competition.

Broadcast television — or any other good — could be provided by a single integrated entity that both creates the products (television shows) and then delivers them to consumers (viewers) via a network of integrated distributors (wholly owned local affiliates). FCC regulations, however, did not allow for such complete vertical integration, and broadcast television therefore developed differently. Broadcast television networks were permitted to own some local television licensees, but the majority had to be owned by separate entities. The networks could produce some of their own programming, but much had to come from independent producers. The results were that networks bought many of their programs from unaffiliated producers and produced other programming in-house; and they owned some local television stations and entered into affiliation contracts with other, separately owned local stations under which the network agreed to provide programming and the local stations agreed to air it.

The restrictions on television networks' relationships with affiliates grew out of similar rules for radio and were originally promulgated in 1941 as the "chain broadcasting regulations" (upheld in NBC v. United States, 319 U.S. 190 (1943)). Like most FCC rules, they rely on the FCC's power over licensees (i.e., the local stations themselves). Many of these rules have been repealed.[5] Others have been modified and weakened over the years but remain in effect. Under the rules, licensees may not enter into agreements, express or implied, with networks that prohibit them from acquiring programs from another network; that hinder other local stations from airing programs offered by the network that the licensee has declined to air; that allow a network to control when a program is aired; that prevent the licensee from rejecting a network program "which the station reasonably believes to be unsatisfactory or unsuitable or contrary to the public interest" or from replacing a network program with one of greater local interest; or that bar the licensee from fixing or altering its rates for the sale of non-network broadcast time.[6]

The FCC opted in the early 1970s to regulate the relationship between program suppliers and television networks on the ground that the television networks could use their leverage as distributors to distort competition in the program supply market. In particular, the FCC adopted two types of rules. First, the prime time access

5. In 1995 the FCC repealed the network station ownership rule, which prohibited the major television networks (then ABC, CBS, and NBC) from owning TV stations in markets with "so few stations, or stations of such unequal desirability (in terms of coverage, power, frequency, or other related matters), that 'competition would be substantially restrained' by permitting network ownership." Review of the Commission's Regulations Governing Television Broadcasting, Report and Order, 10 FCC Rcd. 4538, 4538, ¶ 1 (1995). It also repealed the secondary affiliation rule, which had prevented the major networks from establishing a secondary affiliation in markets where two stations had network affiliations and there was at least one independent unaffiliated station. The FCC "conclude[d] that changes in the marketplace have made both rules obsolete." *Id.*

6. 47 C.F.R. §73.658. Other rules limit dual network operations, networks' representation of local stations, and territorial exclusivity in non-network arrangements. *Id.*

rule (PTAR) limited ABC, CBS, and NBC to supplying their affiliates with only three hours of programming for use during the four-hour "primetime" block. *See* Amendment of Part 73 of the Commission's Rules and Regulations with Respect to Competition and Responsibility in Network Television Broadcasting, Report and Order, 23 F.C.C. 2d 382 (1970). This rule meant that, for one primetime hour each night, even network affiliates had to turn to third-party suppliers or in-house talent for program content. The PTAR was defended largely on the grounds that (1) it carved out a market for independent producers to sell their programs directly to network affiliates and (2) it increased the profits of unaffiliated stations since, during that one primetime hour, affiliates and independents were on equal footing. In 1995, the FCC repealed the PTAR, summarizing its reasoning as follows:

> The three major networks do not dominate the markets relevant to PTAR. There are large numbers of sellers and buyers of video programming. Entry, even by small businesses, is relatively easy. There are a substantially greater number of broadcast programming outlets today than when PTAR was adopted in 1970 due to the growth in numbers of independent stations. In addition, nonbroadcast media have proliferated. Viewers can choose from program offerings on cable, so-called "wireless" cable, satellite television systems, and VCRs. Under these market conditions, PTAR is no longer needed to promote the development of non-network sources of television programming. We also find, given these market conditions, and the record before us, that the rule is not warranted as a means of promoting the growth of independent stations and new networks, or of safeguarding affiliate autonomy. Indeed, the rule generates costs and inefficiencies that are not now offset by substantial, if any, benefits.

Review of the Prime Time Access Rule, Section 73.658(k) of the Commission's Rules, Report and Order, 11 FCC Rcd. 546, 547–48, ¶ 3 (1995).

The second type of rule, and the focus of this section, were the so-called financial interest and syndication rules (sometimes called "fin-syn" for short). These rules and their subsequent evolution are described in more detail in Schurz Comm's, Inc. v. FCC, 982 F.2d 1043 (7th Cir. 1992), below. For simplicity, however, we can summarize the rules as follows: the fin-syn rules prohibited ABC, CBS, and NBC from (1) acquiring profit-sharing positions in network programs produced by independent companies and (2) licensing to independent stations the rights to show reruns of program series that had concluded their network runs. The rules respond to two fears. First, the FCC worried that networks would employ their power to extract excessively low fees or excessively generous grants of subsidiary rights from program suppliers. Second, the FCC thought that networks might seek to control the off-network syndication market in order to prevent competition from reruns (especially since these programs are typically telecast, in competition with network affiliates, by independent stations and cable networks).

Schurz Communications, Inc. v. FCC

982 F.2d 1043 (7th Cir. 1992)

Opinion for the court filed by Circuit Judge POSNER, in which BAUER, Chief Judge, and FAIRCHILD, Senior Circuit Judge, concur.

POSNER, Circuit Judge:

In 1970 the Federal Communications Commission adopted "financial interest and syndication" rules designed to limit the power of the then three television networks — CBS, NBC, and ABC — over television programming. 47 C.F.R. §73.658(j) (1990); *see* Network Television Broadcasting, Report and Order, 23 F.C.C. 2d 382, 387 (1970), *aff'd* under the name of Mt. Mansfield Television, Inc. v. FCC, 442 F.2d 470 (2d Cir. 1971). Each of the three networks consisted (as they still do) of several television stations, in key markets, owned and operated by the network itself, plus about two hundred independently owned stations electronically connected to the network by cable or satellite. In exchange for a fee paid them by the network, these affiliated stations broadcast programs that the network transmits to them, as well as to its owned and operated stations. The networking of programs intended for the early evening hours that are the "prime time" for adult television viewing gives advertisers access to a huge number of American households simultaneously, which in turn enables the networks to charge the high prices for advertising time that are necessary to defray the cost of obtaining the programming most desired by television viewers.

The financial interest and syndication rules adopted in 1970 forbade a network to syndicate (license) programs produced by the network for rebroadcast by independent television stations — that is, stations that were not owned by or affiliated with the network — or to purchase syndication rights to programs that it obtained from outside producers, or otherwise to obtain a financial stake in such programs. If the network itself had produced the program it could sell syndication rights to an independent syndicator but it could not retain an interest in the syndicator's revenues or profits.

Many syndicated programs are reruns, broadcast by independent stations, of successful comedy or dramatic series first shown on network television. Very few series are sufficiently successful in their initial run to be candidates for syndication. Independent stations like to air five episodes each week of a rerun series that originally had aired only once a week or less, so unless a series has a first run of several years — which few series do — it will not generate enough episodes to sustain a rerun of reasonable length. The financial interest and syndication rules thus severely limited the networks' involvement in supplying television programs other than for their own or their affiliated stations.

The concern behind the rules was that the networks, controlling as they did through their owned and operated stations and their affiliates a large part of the system for distributing television programs to American households, would unless restrained use this control to seize a dominating position in the production of television programs. That is, they would lever their distribution "monopoly" into a production "monopoly." They would, for example, refuse to buy programs for network distribution unless the producers agreed to surrender their syndication rights to the network. For once the networks controlled those rights, the access of independent television stations, that is, stations not owned by or affiliated with one of the networks, to reruns would be at the sufferance of the networks, owners of a competing system of distribution.

The Commission hoped the rules would strengthen an alternative source of supply (to the networks) for independent stations — the alternative consisting of television producers not owned by networks. The rules would do this by curtailing the ability of the networks to supply the program market represented by the independent stations, and by protecting the producers for that market against being pressured into giving up potentially valuable syndication rights. And the rules would strengthen the independent stations (and so derivatively the outside producers, for whom the independent stations were an important market along with the networks themselves) by securing them against having to purchase reruns from their competitors the networks.

The basis for this concern was never very clear. If the networks insisted on buying syndication rights along with the right to exhibit a program on the network itself, they would be paying more for their programming. (So one is not surprised that in the decade before the rules were adopted, the networks had acquired syndication rights to no more than 35 percent of their prime-time series, although they had acquired a stake in the syndicator's profits in a considerably higher percentage of cases.) If the networks then turned around and refused to syndicate independent stations, they would be getting nothing in return for the money they had laid out for syndication rights except a long-shot chance — incidentally, illegal under the antitrust laws — to weaken the already weak competitors of network stations. Nor was it clear just how the financial interest and syndication rules would scotch the networks' nefarious schemes. If forbidden to buy syndication rights, networks would pay less for programs, so the outside producers would not come out clear winners — indeed many would be losers. Production for television is a highly risky undertaking, like wildcat drilling for gas and oil. Most television entertainment programs are money losers. The losses are offset by the occasional hit that makes it into syndication after completing a long first run. The sale of syndication rights to a network would enable a producer to shift risk to a larger, more diversified entity presumptively better able to bear it. The resulting reduction in the risks of production would encourage new entry into production and thus give the independent stations a more competitive supply of programs. Evidence introduced in this proceeding showed that, consistent with this speculation, networks in the pre-1970 era were more likely to purchase syndication rights from small producers than from large ones.

Whatever the pros and cons of the original financial interest and syndication rules, in the years since they were promulgated the structure of the television industry has changed profoundly. The three networks have lost ground, primarily as a result of the expansion of cable television, which now reaches 60 percent of American homes, and videocassette recorders, now found in 70 percent of American homes. Today each of the three networks buys only 7 percent of the total video and film programming sold each year, which is roughly a third of the percentage in 1970. (The inclusion of films in the relevant market is appropriate because videocassettes enable home viewers to substitute a film for a television program.) And each commands only about 12 percent of total television advertising revenues. Where in 1970 the networks had 90 percent of the prime-time audience, today they have 62 percent, and competition among as well as with the three networks is fierce. They are, moreover, challenged today by a fourth network, the Fox Broadcasting Corporation, which emerged in the late 1980s.

Notwithstanding the fourth network, which might have been expected to reduce the number of independent stations by converting many of them to Fox network stations, the number of independent stations has increased fivefold since 1970. At the same time, contrary to the intention behind the rules yet an expectable result of them because they made television production a riskier business, the production of prime-time programming has become more concentrated. There are 40 percent fewer producers of prime-time programming today than there were two decades ago. And the share of that programming accounted for directly or indirectly by the eight largest producers, primarily Hollywood studios — companies large enough to bear the increased risk resulting from the Commission's prohibition against the sale of syndication rights to networks — has risen from 50 percent to 70 percent.

The evolution of the television industry, sketched above, suggested that the rules, if they were having any effect at all, were working perversely from a competitive standpoint. An extensive staff study ordered by the Commission concluded that the rules were obsolete and recommended that they be abandoned. Final Report of Network Inquiry Special Staff, FCC (1980). In 1983 the Commission issued a tentative decision agreeing with the staff, proposing radical revisions in the rules leading to their eventual repeal, but inviting further public comments on the details of its proposals. Tentative Decision and Request for Further Comments in Docket 82-345, 94 F.C.C. 2d 1019 (1983). The networks, the Commission found in the tentative decision, had lost any significant monopoly or market power that they may once have had. The financial interest and syndication rules were hampering the entry of new firms into production by blocking an important mechanism (the sale of syndication rights) by which new firms might have shifted the extraordinary risks of their undertaking to the networks.

Mainly as a result of congressional pressure, Hearings before the Subcomm. on Communications of the S. Comm. on Commerce, Science & Transportation on S. 1707, 98th Cong., 1st Sess. 6, 9 (1984), there was no follow-up to the tentative decision. The question what to do about the rules remained in limbo until 1990, when the Commission at the request of the Fox network initiated a fresh notice-and-comment rulemaking proceeding. After receiving voluminous submissions from the various segments of the television industry, the Commission held a one-day hearing, after which it issued an opinion, over dissents by two of the five commissioners, including the chairman, promulgating a revised set of financial interest and syndication rules. Evaluation of the Syndication and Financial Interest Rules, 56 Fed. Reg. 26,242 (1991), on reconsideration, 56 Fed. Reg. 64,207 (1991). The new rules (published at 47 C.F.R. §§ 73.658(k), 73.659–73.662, 73.3526(a)(11) (1991)) are different from the old and also more complicated. They define "network" as an entity that supplies at least 15 hours [per week] of prime-time programming to interconnected affiliates. They take off all restrictions on non-entertainment programming (that is, news and sports), and most restrictions on non-prime-time programming and on syndication for the foreign as distinct from the domestic market. But in a provision that has no counterpart in the old rules, the new ones provide that no more than 40 percent of a network's own prime-time entertainment schedule may consist of programs produced by the network itself. The new rules unlike the old permit a network to buy domestic syndication rights from outside producers of prime-time entertainment programming—provided, however, that the network does so pursuant to separate negotiations begun at least 30 days after the network and the producer have agreed on the fee for licensing the network to exhibit the program on the network itself. Even then the network may not arrange for the distribution of the programming to the independent stations; it must hire an independent syndicator for that. And it may acquire syndication rights only in reruns, not in first-run programs, and thus it may not distribute first-run programming other than to its network stations.

Although the Commission conceded that the networks may already have lost so much of their market power as no longer to pose a threat to competition as it is understood in antitrust law, it concluded that some restrictions remain necessary to assure adequate diversity of television programming.

The networks have petitioned this court to invalidate [the new rules] as arbitrary and capricious. 5 U.S.C. § 706(2)(A). They argue that the only administrative order supportable by the record compiled by the Commission would be a total repeal of the 1970 rules.

The difficult question presented by the petitions to review is not whether the Commission is authorized to restrict the networks' participation in program production and distribution. It is whether the Commission has said enough to justify, in the face of the objections lodged with it, the particular restrictions that it imposed in the order here challenged. It is not enough that a rule might be rational; the statement accompanying its promulgation must show that it is rational—must demonstrate that a reasonable person upon consideration of all the points urged pro and con the rule would conclude that it was a reasonable response to a problem that the agency was charged with solving.

The new rules flunk this test. The Commission's articulation of its grounds is not adequately reasoned. Key concepts are left unexplained, key evidence is overlooked, arguments that formerly persuaded the Commission and that time has only strengthened are ignored, contradictions within and among Commission decisions are passed over in silence. The impression created is of unprincipled compromises of Rube Goldberg complexity among contending interest groups viewed merely as clamoring suppliants who have somehow to be conciliated. The Commission said that it had been "confronted by alternative views of the television programming world so starkly and fundamentally at odds with each other that they virtually defy reconciliation." The possibility of resolving a conflict in favor of the party with the stronger case, as distinct from throwing up one's hands and splitting the difference, was overlooked. The opinion contains much talk but no demonstration of expertise, and a good deal of hand-wringing over the need for prudence and the desirability of avoiding "convulsive" regulatory reform, yet these unquestioned goods are never related to the particulars of the rules — rules that could have a substantial impact on an industry that permeates the daily life of this nation and helps shape, for good or ill, our culture and our politics.

Stripped of verbiage, the Commission's majority opinion, like a Persian cat with its fur shaved, is alarmingly pale and thin. It can be paraphrased as follows. The television industry has changed since 1970. There is more competition — cable television, the new network, etc. No longer is it clear that the networks have market power in an antitrust sense, which they could use to whipsaw the independent producers and strangle the independent stations. So there should be some "deregulation" of programming — some movement away from the 1970 rules. But not too much, because even in their decline the networks may retain some power to extort programs or program rights from producers. The networks offer advertisers access to 98 percent of American households; no competing system for the distribution of television programming can offer as much. Anyway the Commission's concern, acknowledged to be legitimate, is not just with market power in an antitrust sense but with diversity, and diversity is promoted by measures to assure a critical mass of outside producers and independent stations. So the networks must continue to be restricted — but less so than by the 1970 rules. The new rules will give the networks a greater opportunity to participate in programming than the old ones did, while protecting outside producers and independent stations from too much network competition.

All this is, on its face, plausible enough, but it is plausible only because the Commission, ostrich fashion, did not discuss the most substantial objections to its approach, though the objections were argued vigorously to it, by its own chairman among others. To begin with, the networks object that the new rules do not in fact increase their access to the programming market and may decrease it, in the face of the Commission's stated objective. The 40 percent limitation on the amount of prime-time entertainment that a network can supply from its in-house production is a new restriction on the networks, having no counterpart in the original rules. The carving out of nonentertainment programming from the restrictions imposed by the new rules is a throwaway, because there is no syndication market for news and sports programs. Also illusory, the networks argue, is the newly granted right to acquire syndication rights from outside producers, given the restrictions with which the new right is hedged about. A producer cannot wait until 30 days after negotiating the network license fee to sell off syndication rights, because the sale of those rights, the networks contend, is critical to obtaining the financing necessary to produce the program in the first place. These arguments may be right or wrong; our point is only that the Commission did not mention them. We are left in the dark about the grounds for its belief that the new rules will give the networks real, not imaginary, new opportunities in programming.

The new rules, like their predecessors, appear to harm rather than to help outside producers as a whole (a vital qualification) by reducing their bargaining options. It is difficult to see how taking away a part of a seller's market could help the seller. One of the rights in the bundle of rights that constitutes the ownership of a television program is the right to syndicate the program to nonnetwork stations. The new rules restrict—perhaps, as a practical matter, prevent—the sale of that right to networks. How could it help a producer to be forbidden to sell his wares to a class of buyers that may be the high bidders for them? Since syndication is the riskiest component of a producer's property right—for its value depends on the distinctly low-probability event that the program will be a smash hit on network television—restricting its sale bears most heavily on the smallest, the weakest, the newest, the most experimental producers, for they are likely to be the ones least able to bear risk. It becomes understandable why the existing producers support the financial interest and syndication rules: the rules protect these producers against new competition both from the networks (because of the 40 percent cap) and from new producers. The ranks of the outside producers of prime-time programming have been thinned under the regime of financial interest and syndication rules. The survivors are the beneficiaries of the thinning. They consent to have their own right to sell syndication rights curtailed as the price of a like restriction on their potential competitors, on whom it is likely to bear more heavily.

This analysis of risk and its bearing on competition in the program industry is speculative, theoretical, and may for all we know be all wet—though it is corroborated by the increasing concentration of the production industry since the rules restricting the sale of syndication rights were first imposed in 1970. The Commission was not required to buy the analysis. But as the analysis was more than plausible and had been pressed upon it by a number of participants in the rulemaking proceeding, the Commission majority was not entitled to ignore it. Not even to consider the possibility that the unrestricted sale of syndication rights to networks would strengthen the production industry (the industry—not necessarily its present occupants) and thereby increase programming diversity by enabling a sharing between fledgling producers and the networks of the risks of new production was irresponsible. For if the argument about risk sharing is correct, the rules are perverse; by discouraging the entry of new producers into the high-risk prime-time entertainment market, they are likely to reduce the supply of programs to the independent stations and so reduce diversity both of program sources and of program outlets. The Commission's stated desiderata are competition and diversity. The rules adopted by the Commission in order to achieve these desiderata have the remarkable property — if the risk-sharing argument that the Commission did not deign to address is correct — of disserving them both.

If the networks do have market power, the new rules (in this respect like the old) do not seem rationally designed to prevent its exercise. A rule telling a person he may not do business with some firm believed to have market power is unlikely to make the person better off. Suppose that in a competitive market a network would pay $2 million for first-run rights to some program and $1 million for syndication rights, for a total of $3 million, but that because of the lack of perfect substitutes for using this network to distribute his program the producer is willing to sell each of these rights to the network for half their competitive market value (i.e., for $1 million and $500,000 respectively). The producer is made no better off by being forbidden to sell the syndication rights to the network. He gets the same meager first-run license fee ($1 million) and now must cast about for another buyer for the syndication rights. That other buyer is unlikely to pay more than the network would ($500,000); otherwise the producer would have sold the syndication rights to him in the first place. It is no answer that the network would not have given the producer the option of selling it only first-run rights, that it would have insisted on the whole package so that it could control the program supply of the independent stations, which are heavily dependent on reruns and hence on syndication. The producer might indeed be desperate for network distribution, but that desperation would be reflected in the low price at which he was willing to sell the network whatever rights the network wanted. He cannot do better by being forbidden to make such a deal. If he could do better by selling syndication rights to someone else he would not accede to such unfavorable terms as the network offered.

If this is right, the new rules, at least insofar as they restrict network syndication, cannot increase the prices that producers receive. All they can do is increase the costs of production by denying producers the right to share risks with networks.

Finally, while the word diversity appears with incantatory frequency in the Commission's opinion, it is never defined. At argument one of the counsel helpfully distinguished between source diversity and outlet diversity. The former refers to programming sources, that is, producers, and the latter to distribution outlets, that is, television stations. The two forms of diversity are related because the station decides what programs to air and therefore affects producers' decisions about what to produce. A third, and one might suppose the critical, form of diversity is diversity in the programming itself; here "diversity" refers to the variety or heterogeneity of programs. The Commission neither distinguished among the types of diversity nor explained the interrelation among them. As it is very difficult to see how sheer number of producers or outlets could be thought a good thing — and anyway the rules seem calculated, however unwittingly, to decrease, or at least to freeze, but certainly not to increase, the number of producers — we assume that the Commission thinks of source diversity and outlet diversity as means to the end of programming diversity.

Are they? It has long been understood that monopoly in broadcasting could actually promote rather than retard programming diversity. If all the television channels in a particular market were owned by a single firm, its optimal programming strategy would be to put on a sufficiently varied menu of programs in each time slot to appeal to every substantial group of potential television viewers in the market, not just the largest group. For that would be the strategy that maximized the size of the station's audience. Suppose, as a simple example, that there were only two television broadcast frequencies (and no cable television), and that 90 percent of the viewers in the market wanted to watch comedy from 7 to 8 p.m. and 10 percent wanted to watch ballet. The monopolist would broadcast comedy over one frequency and ballet over the other, and thus gain 100 percent of the potential audience. If the frequencies were licensed to two competing firms, each firm would broadcast comedy in the 7 to 8 p.m. time slot, because its expected audience share would be 45 percent (one half of 90 percent), which is greater than 10 percent. Each prime-time slot would be filled with "popular" programming targeted on the median viewer, and minority tastes would go unserved. Some critics of television believe that this is a fair description of prime-time network television. Each network vies to put on the most popular programs and as a result minority tastes are ill served.

Well, so what? Almost everyone in this country either now has or soon will have cable television with 50 or 100 or even 200 different channels to choose among. With that many channels, programming for small audiences with specialized tastes becomes entirely feasible. It would not have been surprising, therefore, if the Commission had taken the position that diversity in prime-time television programming, or indeed in over-the-air broadcasting generally, was no longer a value worth promoting. It did not take that position. Instead it defended its restrictions on network participation in programming on the ground that they promote diversity. But it made no attempt to explain how they do this. It could have said, but did not, that independent television stations depend on reruns, which they would prefer to get from sources other than the networks with which they compete, and—since reruns are the antithesis of diversity—they use their revenue from reruns to support programming that enhances programming diversity. It could have said that programs produced by networks' in-house facilities are somehow more uniform than programs produced by Hollywood studios. It didn't say that either. It never drew the link between the rules, which on their face impede the production of television programs and the interest in diverse programming. The Commission may have thought the link obvious, but it is not. The rules appear to handicap the networks and by handicapping them to retard new entry into production; how all this promotes programming diversity is mysterious, and was left unexplained in the Commission's opinion.

That opinion, despite its length, is unreasoned and unreasonable, and therefore, in the jargon of judicial review of administrative action, arbitrary and capricious. The Commission's order is therefore vacated and the matter is returned to the Commission for further proceedings.

Notes and Questions

1. Subsequent Events. On remand, the FCC essentially repealed the financial interest and syndication rules as well as its newer limitation on networks producing their own programming. *See* Evaluation of the Syndication and Financial Interest Rules, Second Report and Order, 8 FCC Rcd. 3282 (1993). The FCC removed all restrictions on network acquisition of financial interests and syndication rights and eliminated entirely the cap on in-house production. Retained were the prohibitions on active network domestic syndication, whether in first-run or off-network syndication, but only as to primetime entertainment programming, only for a limited period, and only as to ABC, CBS, and NBC. The Seventh Circuit affirmed in Capital Cities/ABC, Inc. v. FCC, 29 F.3d 309 (7th Cir. 1994).

2. Promoting Competition. The 1991 rules were to some extent justified on the grounds that they would promote competition. The court, however, opined that "a rule telling a person he may not do business with some firm believed to have market power is unlikely to make the person better off." Of course, the 1991 rules did not tell program suppliers that they could not do business with the networks, only that they could not sell certain rights to them absent certain protections. Didn't the FCC adequately explain why producers might be harmed if, as a consequence of selling syndication rights to the networks, they eventually confronted a syndication market that was dominated by those networks? Precisely what flaw(s) in this argument did the court identify?

3. The First Amendment. Can you imagine any conceivable public interest rationale for the 1991 limit on the number of programs networks could produce for themselves? A rationale that would survive First Amendment objections? Might this aspect of the new rules have been a prime source of the court's "impression . . . of unprincipled compromises . . . among contending interest groups"?

4. Understanding Monopoly Incentives. Is it really true that "monopoly in broadcasting [can] actually promote rather than retard programming diversity?" Posner's simple example seems to work, but are important complexities left out of his discussion that undermine this claim? What assumptions about viewer tastes drive the model? Does the point still have force when we consider viewers who have first, second, and third choices in terms of their viewing preferences? What other refinements help us to evaluate this claim and its implications?

5. More Networks, Less Cash? Consider one more economic wrinkle relevant to understanding the market for program supply. One might suspect that, by increasing the number of networks or supporting the continued development of cable and satellite as distribution technologies, the FCC could increase profits in the program supply industry. The argument would be that the added competition would yield higher bids for any particular program. This is not necessarily true, however, since, as the number of outlets increases, the average audience per outlet likely decreases. Each outlet therefore attracts less advertising revenue and quite possibly ends up bidding less on content. Does this mean that increasing competition among outlets decreases competition among program suppliers? If so, now what?

§ 5.C.2. Regulation of Vertical Foreclosure by Cable Companies

As was noted in Section 5.B.3, cable television emerged in the 1980s mostly as franchise monopolies, and a principal purpose of the 1992 Cable Act was to encourage the continued deployment of multichannel technologies (such as digital broadcast satellite, or "DBS") that might ultimately compete with cable television. One barrier facing those rival technologies was the possibility that cable operators might make it difficult for them to obtain high-quality programming, either through exclusive contracts with content providers or through vertical integration into cable programming. Congress thus forbade cable operators, their affiliates, and their vendors from "engag[ing] in unfair methods of competition or unfair or deceptive acts or practices, the purpose or effect of which is to hinder significantly or to prevent any multichannel video programming distributor from providing satellite cable programming or satellite broadcast programming to subscribers or consumers." 47 U.S.C. § 548(b) (§ 628 of the Communications Act).[7] Note that this language—forbidding "unfair methods of competition" and "unfair or deceptive acts or practices"—mirrors the general language of § 5 of the Federal Trade Commission Act. 15 U.S.C. § 45(a)(1) ("Unfair methods of competition in or affecting commerce, and unfair or deceptive acts or practices in or affecting commerce, are hereby declared unlawful.").

In § 548(c)(2), Congress directed the FCC to develop regulations that more specifically proscribed the kinds of vertical restraints that the major networks were prohibited from engaging in with content providers (discussed in the previous section), and the FCC shortly thereafter interpreted these instructions to:

> (1) establish safeguards to prevent undue influence by cable operators upon actions by affiliated program vendors related to the sale of programming to unaffiliated distributors;
>
> (2) prohibit price discrimination by vertically integrated satellite cable programming vendors and satellite broadcast programming vendors; and
>
> (3) prohibit exclusive contracts between a cable operator and a vertically integrated programming vendor in areas that are not served by a cable

7. The statute's use of the terms "satellite cable programming or satellite broadcast programming," in § 548(b), meant that the statute applied only to that content distributed by cable companies to their individual systems using satellites. The initial effect of this provision was to limit the § 628 requirement to national cable programming (in effect exempting locally generated programming). But as cable companies began to distribute programming to their local systems by fiber optic cables, this limiting language rendered the provision underinclusive, as we will see.

> operator and any such exclusive arrangements in areas served by cable that are not found in the public interest by the Commission.

Implementation of Sections 12 and 19 of the Cable Television Consumer Protection and Competition Act of 1992: Development of Competition and Diversity in Video Programming Distribution and Carriage, First Report and Order, 8 FCC Rcd. 3359, 3361, ¶ 3 (1993).

§ 5.C.2.a. *The FCC's Program Access Rules*

The 1992 Act also required the program access rules to sunset in 2002 unless the FCC found that the rules "continue[d] to be necessary to preserve and protect competition and diversity in the distribution of video programming." 47 U.S.C. § 548(c)(5). In 2002, the FCC found exactly that and extended the rules through 2007, finding that "vertically integrated programmers retain the incentive to favor their affiliated cable operators over competitive MVPDs such that competition and diversity in the distribution of video programming would not be preserved and protected" — especially as there remains "'must have' vertically integrated programming for which there are no good substitutes." Implementation of the Cable Television Consumer Protection and Competition Act of 1992, Report and Order, 17 FCC Rcd. 12,124, 12,125, ¶ 4 (2002). Commissioner Kathleen Q. Abernathy dissented, arguing that increased competition in both the programming and distribution markets rendered the rules unnecessary: "In enacting the 1992 Cable Act, Congress stated that it was its policy to 'rely on the marketplace, to the maximum extent feasible[,] to achieve' the 'availability to the public of a diversity of views and information through cable television and other video distribution media.'" *Id.* at 12,175 (Abernathy, Comm'r, dissenting) (quoting 1992 Cable Act § 2(b)(1)–(2)).

The FCC similarly extended the rules in 2007 for an additional five years, noting that seventy percent of MVPD subscribers were still cable subscribers, an increase in horizontal concentration in the industry and clustering of cable systems, and the emergence of new entrants in the video marketplace, such as telephone companies. Implementation of the Cable Television Consumer Protection and Competition Act of 1992, Report and Order and Notice of Proposed Rulemaking, 22 FCC Rcd. 17,791, 17,829, ¶ 53 (2007). The D.C. Circuit upheld this extension. Cablevision Systems Corp. v. FCC, 597 F.3d 1306 (D.C. Cir. 2010). Judge Kavanaugh dissented on the ground that the regulation failed intermediate scrutiny under the First Amendment. *Id.* at 1315–16 (Kavanaugh, J., dissenting).

In 2012, the FCC issued an order in which it "decline[d] to extend the exclusive contract prohibition section of the program access rules beyond its October 5, 2012 sunset date." Revision of the Commission's Program Access Rules, Report and Order, Further Notice of Proposed Rulemaking, and Order on Reconsideration, 27 FCC Rcd. 12,605, 12,607, ¶ 1 (2012). The FCC summarized its decision and approach for the future as follows:

> 2. We find that a preemptive prohibition on exclusive contracts is no longer "necessary to preserve and protect competition and diversity in the distribution of video programming" considering that a case-by-case process will remain in place after the prohibition expires to assess the impact of individual exclusive contracts. 47 U.S.C. § 548(c)(5). [B]ecause the current market presents a mixed picture (with the cable industry now less dominant at the national level than it was when the exclusive contract prohibition was enacted, but prevailing concerns about cable dominance and concentration in various individual markets), we find that extending a preemptive ban on exclusive contracts sweeps too broadly. Rather, this mixed picture justifies a case-by-case approach in applying our program access rules.
>
> 3. We recognize that the potential for anticompetitive conduct resulting from vertical integration between cable operators and programmers remains a concern. For example, in some markets, vertical integration may result in exclusive contracts between cable operators and their affiliated programmers that preclude competitors in the video distribution market from accessing critical programming needed to attract and retain subscribers and thus harm competition. While the amount of satellite-delivered, cable-affiliated programming among the most popular cable networks has declined since 2007, some of that programming may still be critical for MVPDs to compete in the video distribution market. Congress has provided the Commission with the authority to address exclusive contracts on a case-by-case basis. We thus conclude that, in the context of present market conditions, such an individualized assessment of exclusive contracts in response to complaints is a more appropriate regulatory approach than the blunt tool of a prohibition that preemptively bans all exclusive contracts between satellite-delivered, cable-affiliated programmers and cable operators.

Id. at 12,608–10.

§ 5.C.2.b. MVPD Access to Buildings

The FCC's program access rules and the FCC's underlying theory of competition have expanded in several dimensions since 2007. Through merger review, the FCC extended them to an integrated satellite provider, and then, by rule, to programming distributed by MVPDs through terrestrial means. Chapter 8's examination of antitrust law includes the FCC's scrutiny of vertical mergers engineered by MVPDs and a discussion of the foreclosure dangers such mergers introduce. The FCC also used its § 628 authority to forbid exclusive contracts between MVPDs and the owners of apartment buildings and other multitenant dwellings. This of course had nothing to do with program exclusivity, but it operated on a similar theory: that exclusive contracts between MVPDs and a condominium or apartment complex (known generically as a multiple-dwelling unit) foreclosed an important area of competition between MVPDs and thus injured consumers.

National Cable & Telecommunications Ass'n v. FCC

567 F.3d 659 (D.C. Cir. 2009)

Opinion of the Court issued by Circuit Judge TATEL, in which Circuit Judge GARLAND and Senior Circuit Judge SILBERMAN concur.

TATEL, Circuit Judge.

Finding that exclusivity agreements between cable companies and owners of apartment buildings and other multi-unit developments have an anti-competitive effect on the cable market, the Federal Communications Commission banned such contracts. The Commission believes that these deals — which involve a cable company exchanging a valuable service like wiring a building for the exclusive right to provide service to the residents — may be regulated under section 628 of the Communications Act as cable company practices that significantly impair the ability of their competitors to deliver programming to consumers. The Commission thus forbade cable operators not only from entering into new exclusivity contracts, but also from enforcing old ones. Petitioners, associations representing cable operators and apartment building owners, argue that the Commission exceeded its statutory authority, arbitrarily departed from precedent, and otherwise violated the Administrative Procedure Act. Having carefully considered the parties' excellent submissions, we disagree and conclude that the Commission acted well within the bounds of both section 628 and general administrative law.

I

Understanding this controversy requires that we begin by explaining a few unintuitive statutory terms. The provision at issue here, section 628(b) of the Communications Act, makes it unlawful "for a cable operator . . . to engage in unfair methods of competition or unfair or deceptive acts or practices, the purpose or effect of which is to hinder significantly or to prevent any multichannel video programming distributor from providing satellite cable programming or satellite broadcast programming to subscribers or consumers." 47 U.S.C. § 548(b). "Cable operators" are just companies that deliver video programming by cable, like Comcast and Time-Warner. *See* 47 U.S.C. § 522(5)–(7). "Multichannel video programming distributors" (MVPDs) are a broader set of companies that provide video programming to subscribers. MVPDs include not only cable operators like Comcast but also direct broadcast satellite companies like DirecTV. *See* § 522(13). Although "satellite cable programming" and "satellite broadcast programming" differ somewhat — they originate from slightly different kinds of entities, *compare* § 548(i)(1), *and* 47 U.S.C. § 605(d)(1), *with* § 548(i)(3) — both terms essentially refer to programming (i.e., television shows) transmitted to MVPDs via satellite for retransmission to subscribers. For our purposes, the important point about them is this: petitioners nowhere dispute the Commission's finding that "most programming is delivered via satellite" and so falls within one of these two categories. Exclusive Service Contracts for Provision of Video Services in Multiple Dwelling Units and Other Real Estate Developments, Report and Order and Further Notice of Proposed Rulemaking, 22 FCC Rcd. 20,235, 20,255, ¶ 43 n.132 (2007) (Order). Section 628(b)'s plain terms thus prohibit cable company practices with the purpose or effect of preventing competing MVPDs, including other cable companies, from providing the two predominant types of programming to consumers.

The Commission first considered exclusivity contracts between cable operators and so-called multiple dwelling units (MDUs) as an ancillary part of its 2003 Inside Wiring Order. *See* Telecommunications Services Inside Wiring, First Order on Reconsideration and Section Report and Order, 18 FCC Rcd. 1342, 1366–70, ¶¶ 63–71 (2003). That proceeding primarily concerned the ownership status of certain wiring inside MDUs and the Commission's order considered some thirteen different issues presented by its new wiring rules. But the Commission also addressed a related issue raised in a separate notice of proposed rulemaking, namely "whether it would be appropriate to cap exclusive contracts to open up MDUs to potential competition on a building-wide or unit-to-unit basis, and, if so, what would represent a reasonable cap." *Id.* ¶ 63. Reviewing the evidence then available, the Commission found that there was no "sufficient basis in this record to ban or cap the term of exclusive contracts." *Id.* ¶ 68; *see also* ¶¶ 69–71.

Four years later, the Commission returned to exclusivity contracts in a rulemaking devoted solely to that question. Analyzing the competitive harms and benefits of exclusivity clauses, the Commission this time concluded that "exclusivity clauses cause significant harm to competition and consumers that the record did not reflect at the time of our 2003 Inside Wiring Order." Order, 22 FCC Rcd. at 20,247–51, ¶¶ 26–29. And because the Commission found that the record now supports regulation, this time it extensively analyzed its authority to ban such contracts, concluding that both section 628 and its "ancillary authority" empower it to act. The Commission accordingly prohibited cable companies from "enforcing existing exclusivity clauses and executing contracts containing new ones," *id.* at 20,251, ¶ 30, rejecting more limited remedial options.

II

Conceding that on a literal reading of the statute exclusivity contracts do have the "effect" of preventing competing MVPDs from "providing satellite cable programming or satellite broadcast programming to subscribers or consumers," § 548(b), petitioners nonetheless argue that section 628's text, structure, and history demonstrate that it was addressed to a different evil altogether. Congress, they argue, was concerned not with barriers to *service* but with practices that prevent cable competitors from obtaining certain kinds of *programming* that the American public wants to watch. Textually, they emphasize Congress's identification of "satellite cable programming" and "satellite broadcast programming" in particular, arguing that the Commission has read these well-defined terms out of the statute. Structurally, they emphasize section 628(c), which directs the Commission to implement subsection (b) with rules and procedures focused on fair dealing between programming vendors and MVPDs, not on anti-competitive barriers to service generally. Petitioners thus argue that in enacting section 628(b), Congress intended to prevent the cable industry from starving its competition of programming—nothing more, nothing less.

For its part, the Commission concedes that Congress's primary purpose in enacting section 628 was indeed to expand competition for programming, not service. But this primary purpose is hardly dispositive, it argues, because "statutory prohibitions often go beyond the principal evil to cover reasonably comparable evils, and it is ultimately the provisions of our laws rather than the principal concerns of our legislators by which we are governed." Oncale v. Sundowner Offshore Servs., Inc., 523 U.S. 75, 79, (1998). Reviewing the same text, structure, and legislative history, the Commission interprets section 628 to permit regulation of exclusive service agreements as an evil that easily falls within the literal terms of the statute and is reasonably comparable to the paradigmatic anti-competitive practices that section 628 specifically targets. We agree.

Beginning, "as always, with the plain language of the statute," Citizens Coal Council v. Norton, 330 F.3d 478, 482 (D.C. Cir. 2003), we find nothing in section 628 that unambiguously forecloses the Commission's interpretation. What the Commission forbade lies within the literal terms of section 628(b)'s proscription. Indeed, exclusivity agreements have both the proscribed "purpose" and the proscribed "effect"—cable operators execute them precisely so that they can be the sole company serving a building, and as petitioners themselves put it, "if you can't serve a building then you can't deliver satellite cable programming and satellite broadcast programming." Oral Arg. 3:29–3:34.

In the end, petitioners are unable to satisfy their heavy burden. To prevail at *Chevron* step one, they must show that section 628(b) is unambiguously limited to Congress's principal concern with unfair program hoarding. Because section 628's actual words reach the behavior the Commission prohibited, petitioners are left to argue "that the Commission relies almost entirely on a literal reading of the statutory language—not the most damning criticism when it comes to statutory interpretation." Consumer Elecs. Ass'n v. FCC, 347 F.3d 291, 297 (D.C. Cir. 2003). And while the statute's text, structure, and history do support the proposition that Congress was, in fact, principally concerned with program hoarding, none suggests that Congress chose its language to limit the Commission to regulating that evil alone. Indeed, having employed all available tools of statutory construction, we find little that suggests any congressional intent to limit section 628(b) to competition for programming, and so are unable to conclude that a reading literally permitted is nonetheless unambiguously foreclosed. At the very best, petitioners have demonstrated some ambiguity as to whether Congress intended to allow regulation of exclusivity contracts along with unfair dealing over programming—ambiguity the Commission reasonably resolved in favor of its own interpretation. Thus, concluding that section 628(b) authorizes the Commission's action, we need not consider the Commission's ancillary authority.

Real estate petitioners' separate attack on the Commission's authority has little merit. They argue that the exclusivity ban impermissibly regulates the real estate industry, which lies outside the Commission's jurisdiction. The terms of the challenged prohibition apply only to cable companies, however, and they neither require nor prohibit any action by MDUs. We decline to put issues relating to their cable service outside the Commission's authority simply because those issues also matter to their landlords.

V

In sum, we see the challenged order as fully authorized by section 628 and the product of careful agency reconsideration. The petitions for review are denied.

[Concurring opinion by Senior Circuit Judge SILBERMAN omitted.]

Notes and Questions

1. Regulatory Flexibility. In a portion of the opinion we did not excerpt, the D.C. Circuit noted that "Congress had a particular manifestation of a problem in mind, but in no way expressed an unambiguous intent to limit the FCC's power solely to that version of the problem." Nat'l Cable & Telecomm. Ass'n, 567 F.3d at 665. When should courts read statutes as embodying greater flexibility for agency action? What in § 628 connotes that such flexibility is appropriate?

2. The "Terrestrial Loophole." The program access rules applied, in the first instance, only to satellite-delivered programming, which meant that cable operators could avoid their application if the programming were delivered terrestrially (by fiber optic cable or otherwise). Section 628(b), as the D.C. Circuit noted in the case above, was written fairly broadly. In 2010, the FCC—addressing what was called the "terrestrial loophole"—relied on § 628 to "adopt rules permitting complainants to pursue program access claims involving terrestrially delivered, cable-affiliated programming similar to the claims that they may pursue with respect to satellite-delivered, cable-affiliated programming, where the purpose or effect of the challenged act is to significantly hinder or prevent the complainant from providing satellite cable programming or satellite broadcast programming." Consistent with its previous actions, the FCC targeted exclusive contracts, price discrimination, and other vertical restraints between cable operators and cable-affiliated programmers. Review of the Commission's Program Access Rules and Examination of Programming Tying Arrangements, First Report and Order, 25 FCC Rcd. 746 (2010).

§ 5.D. Unbundling

One strategy to limit the power of monopolists — one that was employed in the 1996 Act — is to require the monopolist to sell its separate services individually. This "unbundling" requirement rests on a theory that is similar to vertical restrictions: both strategies aim to prevent a monopolist from leveraging its monopoly power either to harm competition in an adjacent market or to entrench its current monopoly power. There also is a conceptual symmetry to both rules: vertical restrictions aim to prevent a monopolist from integrating its monopolized market with an upstream or downstream market, and unbundling requirements aim to prevent a monopolist from tying a monopolized product with an accompanying product.

Also like vertical integration, bundling complementary services often creates efficiencies, and perhaps for this reason, telephony networks typically own many separate elements and offer many combined services that constitute phone service (note in the first paragraph of AT&T Corp. v. Iowa Utilities Board, 525 U.S. 366 (1999), below, the many separate components that comprised a local telephone network in the 1990s). This tendency to bundle and charge a single price for potentially separable services makes unbundling a difficult policy to implement.

This section documents the FCC's efforts to implement the 1996 Act's policy to require ILECs to unbundle elements of their network for individual sale. It shows, first, that the FCC had trouble identifying the individual elements that ILECs had to make available for purchase, and second, that the FCC had trouble specifying the appropriate price for those unbundled elements.

§ 5.D.1. Identifying Unbundled Elements

AT&T Corp. v. Iowa Utilities Board

525 U.S. 366 (1999)

SCALIA, J., delivered the opinion of the Court, Parts I, III-A, III-C, III-D, and IV of which were joined by REHNQUIST, C.J., and STEVENS, KENNEDY, SOUTER, THOMAS, GINSBURG, and BREYER, JJ., Part II of which was joined by STEVENS, KENNEDY, SOUTER, and GINSBURG, JJ., and Part III-B of which was joined by REHNQUIST, C.J., and STEVENS, KENNEDY, THOMAS, GINSBURG, and BREYER, JJ. SOUTER, J., filed an opinion concurring in part and dissenting in part. THOMAS, J., filed an opinion concurring in part and dissenting in part, in which REHNQUIST, C.J., and BREYER, J., joined. BREYER, J., filed an opinion concurring in part and dissenting in part. O'CONNOR, J., took no part in the consideration or decision of these cases.

JUSTICE SCALIA delivered the opinion of the Court.

Until the 1990s, local phone service was thought to be a natural monopoly. States typically granted an exclusive franchise in each local service area to a local exchange carrier (LEC), which owned, among other things, the local loops (wires connecting telephones to switches), the switches (equipment directing calls to their destinations), and the transport trunks (wires carrying calls between switches) that constitute a local exchange network. Technological advances, however, have made competition among multiple providers of local service seem possible, and Congress recently ended the longstanding regime of state-sanctioned monopolies.

The Telecommunications Act of 1996 (1996 Act or Act) fundamentally restructures local telephone markets. States may no longer enforce laws that impede competition, and incumbent LECs are subject to a host of duties intended to facilitate market entry. Foremost among these duties is the LEC's obligation under 47 U.S.C. § 251(c) to share its network with competitors. Under this provision, a requesting carrier can obtain access to an incumbent's network in three ways: It can purchase local telephone services at wholesale rates for resale to end users; it can lease elements of the incumbent's network "on an unbundled basis"; and it can interconnect its own facilities with the incumbent's network. When an entrant seeks access through any of these routes, the incumbent can negotiate an agreement without regard to the duties it would otherwise have under §§ 251(b) or (c). *See* § 252(a)(1). But if private negotiation fails, either party can petition the state commission that regulates local phone service to arbitrate open issues, which arbitration is subject to § 251 and the FCC regulations promulgated thereunder.

Six months after the 1996 Act was passed, the FCC issued its First Report and Order implementing the local-competition provisions. Implementation of the Local Competition Provisions in the Telecommunications Act of 1996, First Report and Order, 11 FCC Rcd. 15,499 (1996). The numerous challenges to this rulemaking, filed across the country by incumbent LECs and state utility commissions, were consolidated in the United States Court of Appeals for the Eighth Circuit.

Incumbent LECs also made several challenges, only some of which are relevant here, to the rules implementing the 1996 Act's requirement of unbundled access. *See* 47 U.S.C. § 251(c)(3). Rule 319, the primary unbundling rule, sets forth a minimum number of network elements that incumbents must make available to requesting carriers. The LECs complained that, in compiling this list, the FCC had virtually ignored the 1996 Act's requirement that it consider whether access to proprietary elements was "necessary" and whether lack of access to nonproprietary elements would "impair" an entrant's ability to provide local service. *See* § 251(d)(2). In addition, the LECs thought that the list included items (like directory assistance and caller I.D.) that did not meet the statutory definition of "network element." *See* § 153(29). The Eighth Circuit rebuffed both arguments, holding that the Commission's interpretations of the "necessary and impair" standard and the definition of "network element" were reasonable and hence lawful thanks to *Chevron* deference. Chevron U.S.A. Inc. v. Natural Res. Def. Council, Inc., 467 U.S. 837 (1984).

II

B

We are of the view that the FCC did not adequately consider the "necessary and impair" standards when it gave blanket access to these network elements, and others, in Rule 319. That rule requires an incumbent to provide requesting carriers with access to a minimum of seven network elements: the local loop, the network interface device, switching capability, interoffice transmission facilities, signaling networks and call-related databases, operations support systems functions, and operator services and directory assistance. 47 C.F.R. § 51.319 (1997). If a requesting carrier wants access to additional elements, it may petition the state commission, which can make other elements available on a case-by-case basis.

Section 251(d)(2) of the Act provides:

> In determining what network elements should be made available for purposes of subsection (c)(3) of this section, the Commission shall consider, at a minimum, whether
>
> (A) access to such network elements as are proprietary in nature is necessary; and
>
> (B) the failure to provide access to such network elements would impair the ability of the telecommunications carrier seeking access to provide the services that it seeks to offer.

We agree with the incumbents that the Act requires the FCC to apply *some* limiting standard, rationally related to the goals of the Act, which it has simply failed to do. In the general statement of its methodology set forth in the First Report and Order, the Commission announced that it would regard the "necessary" standard as having been met regardless of whether "requesting carriers can obtain the requested proprietary element from a source other than the incumbent," since "requiring new entrants to duplicate unnecessarily even a part of the incumbent's network could generate delay and higher costs for new entrants, and thereby impede entry by competing local providers and delay competition, contrary to the goals of the 1996 Act." First Report and Order, 11 FCC Rcd. at 15,642, ¶ 283. And it announced that it would regard the "impairment" standard as having been met if "the failure of an incumbent to provide access to a network element would decrease the quality, or increase the financial or administrative cost of the service a requesting carrier seeks to offer, compared with providing that service *over other unbundled elements in the incumbent LEC's network*," *Id.* at 15,643, ¶ 285 (emphasis added) — which means that comparison with self-provision, or with purchasing from another provider, is excluded. Since any entrant will request the most efficient network element that the incumbent has to offer, it is hard to imagine when the incumbent's failure to give access to the element would not constitute an "impairment" under this standard.

The Commission asserts that it deliberately limited its inquiry to the incumbent's own network because no rational entrant would seek access to network elements from an incumbent if it could get better service or prices elsewhere. That may be. But that judgment allows entrants, rather than the Commission, to determine whether access to proprietary elements is necessary, and whether the failure to obtain access to nonproprietary elements would impair the ability to provide services. The Commission cannot, consistent with the statute, blind itself to the availability of elements outside the incumbent's network. That failing alone would require the Commission's rule to be set aside. In addition, however, the Commission's assumption that any increase in cost (or decrease in quality) imposed by denial of a network element renders access to that element "necessary," and causes the failure to provide that element to "impair" the entrant's ability to furnish its desired services is simply not in accord with the ordinary and fair meaning of those terms. An entrant whose anticipated annual profits from the proposed service are reduced from 100% of investment to 99% of investment has perhaps been "impaired" in its ability to amass earnings, but has not ipso facto been impaired "in its ability to provide the services it seeks to offer"; and it cannot realistically be said that the network element enabling it to raise its profits to 100% is "necessary."

The Commission began with the premise that an incumbent was obliged to turn over as much of its network as was "technically feasible," and viewed (d)(2) as merely permitting it to soften that obligation by regulatory grace:

> To give effect to both §§ 251(c)(3) and 251(d)(2), we conclude that the proprietary and impairment standards in § 251(d)(2) grant us the authority to refrain from requiring incumbent LECs to provide all network elements for which it is technically feasible to provide access on an unbundled basis.

First Report and Order, 11 FCC Rcd. at 15,641, ¶ 279.

The Commission's premise was wrong. Section 251(d)(2) does not authorize the Commission to create isolated exemptions from some underlying duty to make all network elements available. It requires the Commission to determine on a rational basis which network elements must be made available, taking into account the objectives of the Act and giving some substance to the "necessary" and "impair" requirements. The latter is not achieved by disregarding entirely the availability of elements outside the network, and by regarding any "increased cost or decreased service quality" as establishing a "necessity" and an "impair[ment]" of the ability to provide services.

C

It would be gross understatement to say that the Telecommunications Act of 1996 is not a model of clarity. It is in many important respects a model of ambiguity or indeed even self-contradiction. But Congress is well aware that the ambiguities it chooses to produce in a statute will be resolved by the implementing agency, *see Chevron*. We can only enforce the clear limits that the 1996 Act contains, which in the present case invalidate only Rule 319.

For the reasons stated, the judgment of the Court of Appeals is reversed in part and affirmed in part and is remanded for proceedings consistent with this opinion.

[Opinions of Justices SOUTER, THOMAS, and BREYER concurring in part and dissenting in part are omitted.]

Notes and Questions

1. The Statutory Design. The majority opinion held that the FCC erred in interpreting the 1996 Act's provisions on unbundled network elements (UNEs). What were the FCC's errors and what does the Court's decision require the agency to do on remand? What factors should determine whether an ILEC must make a particular network element available to competitors? According to the Court, what does the statute say? In your opinion, what *should* the statute say?

2. What Should Be Unbundled? The question of what should constitute a UNE is one that we will further consider in the materials that follow. Even at this early stage, consider what touchstones you might suggest to the FCC as a way of determining which items should be unbundled. Why should the local switch be unbundled but not, say, access to the ILEC's fleet of service trucks? What about historical information about customer calling habits? Access to the ILEC's administrative staff? What policies are motivating your intuitive responses to these suggestions? Can you formulate those into a coherent set of principles for unbundling?

3. Resale versus Unbundling. One issue along these lines is the question of whether CLECs should have to own some of their own facilities before using the unbundling provision to get access to the ILEC's infrastructure. That is, could a CLEC build its network by buying *all* of the necessary components as UNEs, or are the unbundling provisions open only to CLECs who have built some, but not all, of their own network? What did the FCC say on this issue? The Court? Does the result even matter given that CLECs have always had the option to purchase the service in question under the resale provisions? (Yes — but do you see why?)

4. New Infrastructure. Why aren't the unbundling and resale provisions limited to services and infrastructure that were deployed as of the enactment of the 1996 Act? Would not such a limitation level the playing field as of 1996 but also leave ILECs with substantial incentives to innovate? If the FCC had adopted such an interpretation, would the Court have allowed it to stand?

5. Facilities-Based Competition. Overall, what is the logic of having unbundling and resale as entry options? Don't these options discourage facilities-based competition? Isn't that contrary to the real goal of the 1996 Act? But wait: if facilities-based competition were the real goal of the 1996 Act, wouldn't the resale and unbundling provisions sunset after, say, ten years?

United States Telecom Ass'n v. FCC *[USTA II]*

359 F.3d 554 (D.C. Cir. 2004)

Opinion for the court filed by Senior Circuit Judge WILLIAMS, in which Circuit Judges EDWARDS and RANDOLPH concur.

WILLIAMS, Senior Circuit Judge:

I. Legal Background

In its first effort to interpret the "impairment" standard of § 251(d)(2) of the Telecommunications Act of 1996, the Commission held that lack of unbundled access to an element would "impair" a CLEC's ability to provide telecommunications service "if the quality of the service the entrant can offer, absent access to the requested element, declines and/or the cost of providing the service rises." Implementation of the Local Competition Provisions in the Telecommunications Act of 1996, 11 FCC Rcd. 15,499, 15,643 ¶ 285 (1996) (First Report and Order).

The Supreme Court found this reading of "impair" unreasonable in two respects. First, the Commission had irrationally refused to consider whether a CLEC could self-provision or acquire the requested element from a third party. AT&T Corp. v. Iowa Utilities Bd., 525 U.S. 366, 389 (1999) (*AT&T*). Second, the Commission had considered *any* increase in cost or decrease in quality, no matter how small, sufficient to establish impairment—a result the Court concluded could not be squared with the "ordinary and fair meaning" of the word "impair." *Id.* at 389–90 & n.11. The Court admonished the FCC that in assessing which cost differentials would "impair" a new entrant's competition within the meaning of the statute, it must "apply *some* limiting standard, rationally related to the goals of the Act." *Id.* at 388.

Responding to the *AT&T* decision, the Commission adopted a new interpretation under which a would-be entrant is "impaired" if, "taking into consideration the availability of alternative elements outside the incumbent's network, including self-provisioning by a requesting carrier or acquiring an alternative from a third-party supplier, lack of access to that element *materially diminishes* a requesting carrier's ability to provide the services it seeks to offer." Implementation of the Local Competition Provisions of the Telecommunications Act of 1996, 15 FCC Rcd. 3696, 3725, ¶ 51 (1999) (Third Report and Order) (emphasis added). But in United States Telecom Association v. FCC, 290 F.3d 415 (D.C. Cir. 2002) (*USTA I*), we held that this new interpretation of "impairment," while an improvement, was still unreasonable in light of the Act's underlying purposes.

The fundamental problem, we held, was that the Commission did not differentiate between those cost disparities that a new entrant in *any* market would be likely to face and those that arise from market characteristics "linked (in some degree) to natural monopoly . . . that would make genuinely competitive provision of an element's function wasteful." *USTA I*, 290 F.3d at 427. This distinction between different kinds of incumbent/entrant cost differentials is qualitative, not merely quantitative, which is why the Commission's addition of a requirement that the cost disparity be "material" was inadequate. *Id.* at 427–28.

We also made clear that the Commission's broad and analytically insubstantial concept of impairment failed to pursue the "balance" between the advantages of unbundling (in terms of fostering competition by different firms, even if they use the very same facilities) and its costs (in terms both of "spreading the disincentive to invest in innovation and creating complex issues of managing shared facilities," *id.* at 427), a balance that we found implicit in the *AT&T* Court's insistence on an unbundling standard "rationally related to the goals of the Act," *id.* at 428 (quoting *AT&T*).

We also objected to the Commission's decision to issue, with respect to most elements, broad unbundling requirements that would apply "in every geographic market and customer class, without regard to the state of competitive impairment in any particular market." *USTA I*, 290 F.3d at 422. Though the Act does not necessarily require the Commission to determine "on a localized state-by-state or market-by-market basis which unbundled elements are to be made available," *id.* at 425 (quoting Third Report and Order, 15 FCC Rcd. at 3753, ¶ 122), it does require "a more nuanced concept of impairment than is reflected in findings . . . detached from any specific markets or market categories." *USTA I*, 290 F.3d at 426. Thus, the Commission is obligated to establish unbundling criteria that are at least aimed at tracking relevant market characteristics and capturing significant variation.

Finally, we vacated the Commission's decision to require ILECs to unbundle the high-frequency portion of their copper loops to requesting CLECs—a practice known as "line sharing" and used by CLECs to provide broadband DSL service—because the Commission had failed to consider adequately whether intermodal competition from cable providers tilted the balance against this form of unbundling in the broadband market.

In response to *USTA I* the Commission again revised its definition of impairment. This time around, the Commission determined that a CLEC would "be impaired when lack of access to an incumbent LEC network element poses a *barrier or barriers to entry*, including operational and economic barriers, that are *likely to make entry into a market uneconomic*. That is, we ask whether all potential revenues from entering a market exceed the costs of entry, taking into consideration any countervailing advantages that a new entrant may have." Review of the Section 251 Unbundling Obligations of Incumbent Local Exchange Carriers, 18 FCC Rcd. 16,978, 17,035, ¶ 84 (2003) (Order) (emphasis added). The Commission clarified that the impairment assessment would take intermodal competition into account. *Id.* at 17,044–45, ¶¶ 97–98.

The Commission responded to our demand for a more "nuanced" application of the impairment standard by purporting to adopt a "granular" approach that would consider "such factors as specific services, specific geographic locations, the different types and capacities of facilities, and customer and business considerations." *Id.* at 17,058–59, ¶ 118. Where the Commission believed that the record could not support an absolute national impairment finding but at the same time contained too little information to make "granular" determinations, it adopted a provisional nationwide rule, subject to the possibility of specific exclusions, to be created by state regulatory commissions under a purported delegation of the Commission's own authority.

The Commission also resolved to use the "at a minimum" language in § 251(d)(2) to "inform [its] consideration of unbundling in contexts where some level of impairment may exist, but unbundling appeared likely to undermine important goals of the 1996 Act." *Id.* at 17,087, ¶ 173. Specifically, in connection with two broadband elements, "fiber-to-the-home" (FTTH) and hybrid loops (see below), it brought into the balance the risk that an unbundling order might deter investment in such facilities—contrary, as it saw the matter, to the statutory goal of encouraging prompt deployment of "advanced telecommunications capability." *Id.* at, 17,086–87, ¶¶ 172–73 (quoting § 706 of the Act). Additional issues also emerged in the rulemaking and will be addressed below.

3. The Commission's Definition of "Impairment"

As a general matter the ILECs argue the Commission's impairment standard is so open-ended that it imposes no meaningful constraints on unbundling, and would be unlawful even if applied by the FCC itself. More specifically, the ILECs claim that the Commission's unbundling test unlawfully permits states to consider as a potential source of impairment retail rates that are held below cost by state regulation against the ILECs' will, and unlawfully precludes consideration of intermodal competition when determining whether a market is suitable for competitive supply.

On the general point about the open-endedness of the Commission's standard, we observe that the Order's interpretation of impairment is an improvement over the Commission's past efforts in that, for the most part, the Commission explicitly and plausibly connects factors to consider in the impairment inquiry to natural monopoly characteristics (declining average costs throughout the range of the relevant market), or at least connects them (in logic that the ILECs do not seem to contest) to other structural impediments to competitive supply. These barriers include sunk costs, ILEC absolute cost advantages, first-mover advantages, and operational barriers to entry within the sole or primary control of the ILEC. In contrast to the First Report and Order and the Third Report and Order, the Commission has clarified that only costs related to structural impediments to competition are relevant to the impairment analysis.

Relation of "impairment" to the "at a minimum" clause. We note that there are at least two ways in which the Commission could have accommodated our ruling in *USTA I* that its impairment rule take into account not only the benefits but also the costs of unbundling, in order that its standard be "rationally related to the goals of the Act." *See USTA I*, 290 F.3d at 428. One way would be to craft a standard of impairment that built in such a balance, as for example by hewing rather closely to natural monopoly features. The other is to use a looser concept of impairment, with the costs of unbundling brought into the analysis under § 251(d)(2)'s "at a minimum" language. The Commission has chosen the latter, and we cannot fault it for doing so. This is especially true as the statutory structure suggests that "impair" must reach a bit beyond natural monopoly. While for "proprietary" network elements the statute mandates a decision whether they are "necessary," § 251(d)(1)(A), for nonproprietary ones it requires a decision whether their absence would "impair" the requester's provision of telecommunications service, § 251(d)(1)(B). Thus, in principle, there is no statutory offense in the Commission's decision to adopt a standard that treats impairment as a continuous rather than as a dichotomous variable, and potentially reaches beyond natural monopoly, but then to examine the full context before ordering unbundling.

That said, we do note that in at least one important respect the Commission's definition of impairment is vague almost to the point of being empty. The touchstone of the Commission's impairment analysis is whether the enumerated operational and entry barriers "make entry into a market uneconomic." Order, 18 FCC Rcd. at 17,020, ¶ 84. Uneconomic by whom? By *any* CLEC, no matter how inefficient? By an "average" or "representative" CLEC? By the most efficient existing CLEC? By a hypothetical CLEC that used "the most efficient telecommunications technology currently available," the standard that is built into TELRIC? We need not resolve the significance of this uncertainty, but we highlight it because we suspect that the issue of whether the standard is too open-ended is likely to arise again.

Intermodal alternatives. As for the ILECs' claim that the Commission's impairment standard unlawfully excludes consideration of intermodal alternatives, we observe that the Commission expressly stated that such alternatives are to be considered when evaluating impairment. Order, 18 FCC Rcd. at 17,044–46, 17,252–53, ¶¶ 97–98, 443. Whether the weight the FCC assigns to this factor is reasonable in a given context is a question that we need not decide, except insofar as we reaffirm *USTA I*'s holding that the Commission cannot ignore intermodal alternatives.

Impairment in markets where state regulation holds rates below historic costs. In the name of "universal service," state regulators have commonly employed cross-subsidies, tilting rate ceilings so that revenues from business and urban customers subsidize residential and rural ones. On remand from our decision in *USTA I*, the Commission decided to consider regulated below-cost retail rates as a factor that may "impair" CLECs in competing for mass market customers. *See* Order ¶ 518. The ILECs object strenuously, and it appears virtually certain that the issue will recur on remand.

The interesting case is the one where TELRIC rates are so low that unbundling *does* elicit CLEC entry, enabling CLECs to cut further into ILEC revenues in areas where the ILECs' service is mandated by state law—and mandated to be offered at artificially low rates funded by ILECs' supracompetitive profits in other areas. If the scheme of the Act is successful, of course, the very premise of these below-cost rate ceilings will be undermined, as those supracompetitive profits will be eroded by

Act-induced competition. In competitive markets, an ILEC can't be used as a piñata. The Commission has said nothing to address these obvious implications, or otherwise to locate its treatment of the issue in any purposeful reading of the Act.

B. Unbundling of High-Capacity Dedicated Transport Facilities

2. Remaining Dedicated Transport Issues

a. Route-Specific Analysis of Dedicated Transport

In *USTA I* we expressed skepticism regarding whether there could be impairment in markets "where the element in question—though not literally ubiquitous—is significantly deployed on a competitive basis," giving as a specific example interoffice dedicated transport. *USTA I*, 290 F.3d at 422. We do not see how the Commission can simply ignore facilities deployment along similar routes when assessing impairment. Suppose points A, B, and C are all in the same geographic market and are similarly situated with regard to the "barriers to entry" that the Commission says are controlling. Suppose further that multiple competitors supply DS1 transport between points A and B, but only the ILEC and one other CLEC have deployed DS1 transport between A and C. The Commission cannot ignore the A–B facilities deployment when deciding whether CLECs are impaired with respect to A–C deployment without a good reason. The Commission does explain why competition on the A–B route should not be *sufficient* to establish competition is possible on the A–C route, Order, 18 FCC Rcd. at 17,227–28, ¶ 401, but this cannot explain the Commission's implicit decision to treat competition on one route as *irrelevant* to the existence of impairment on the other.

b. Wireless Providers' Access to Unbundled Dedicated Transport

[T]he ILEC petitioners also attack the Commission's conclusion that providers of wireless service (also known as commercial mobile radio services, or CMRS) qualify for unbundled access to these facilities. According to the ILECs, the Commission not only failed to conduct the requisite impairment analysis for wireless providers, but in fact found that wireless growth has been "remarkable": 90% of the U.S. population lives in areas served by at least three wireless providers, 40% of Americans and 61% of American households own a wireless phone, wireless prices have been steadily declining, and 3–5% of wireless customers use wireless as their only phone, treating it as a full substitute for traditional land line service. Order, 18 FCC Rcd. at 17,017, ¶ 53. Although the ILECs implicitly concede that wireless providers would be impaired if they were denied any access to ILEC dedicated interoffice transport facilities, they point out that wireless providers have traditionally purchased such access from ILECs at wholesale rates (a transaction classified, since adoption of the Act, under § 251(c)(4)). And the data above clearly show that wireless carriers' reliance on special access has not posed a barrier that makes entry uneconomic. Indeed, the multi-million dollar sums that the Commission regularly collects in its auctions of such spectrum, and that firms pay to buy already-issued licenses, seem to indicate that wireless firms currently expect that net revenues will, by a large margin, more than recover all their non-spectrum costs (including return on capital).

The FCC and the wireless intervenors do not challenge the assertion that the current regime has witnessed a rapidly expanding and prosperous market for wireless service. Rather, they rely on the principle that "evidence that requesting carriers are using incumbent LEC tariffed services" is not "relevant to [the] unbundling determination." Order, 18 FCC Rcd. at 17,047–48, ¶ 102.

[T]he purpose of the Act is not to provide the widest possible unbundling, or to guarantee competitors access to ILEC network elements at the lowest price that government may lawfully mandate. Rather, its purpose is to stimulate competition—preferably genuine, facilities-based competition. Where competitors have access to necessary inputs at rates that allow competition not only to survive but to flourish, it is hard to see any need for the Commission to impose the costs of mandatory unbundling.

We therefore hold that the Commission's impairment analysis must consider the availability of tariffed ILEC special access services when determining whether would-be entrants are impaired, and vacate paragraphs 102–03 of the Order. This of course still leaves the Commission free to take into account such factors as administrability, risk of ILEC abuse, and the like. What the Commission may not do is compare unbundling only to self-provisioning or third-party provisioning, arbitrarily excluding alternatives offered by the ILECs.

III. CLEC Objections

A. Unbundling of Broadband Loops

3. Line sharing

In *USTA I*, we vacated the Commission's decision to provide CLECs with unbundled access to the high frequency portion of copper loops, primarily because the Commission had failed to consider the relevance of intermodal competition in the broadband market. On remand, the Commission decided to reverse its earlier position and eliminated this unbundling mandate. [W]e find that even if the CLECs are right that there is some impairment with respect to the elimination of mandatory line sharing, the Commission reasonably found that other considerations outweighed any impairment. We therefore uphold the Commission's rules concerning line sharing on the grounds that the decision not to unbundle this element was reasonable, even in the face of some CLEC impairment, in light of evidence that unbundling would skew investment incentives in undesirable ways and that intermodal competition from cable ensures the persistence of substantial competition in broadband.

VI. Conclusion

To summarize: We vacate the Commission's subdelegation to state commissions of decision-making authority over impairment determinations, and we also vacate and remand the Commission's nationwide impairment determinations [that formerly relied on the safety valve of state subdelegation].

We vacate the Commission's decision not to take into account availability of tariffed special access services when conducting the impairment analysis, and we therefore vacate and remand the decision that wireless carriers are impaired without unbundled access to ILEC dedicated transport.

Notes and Questions

1. **Impairment.** What was the court's concern about the substance of the FCC's impairment determinations? Did the court object to the general formulation of the impairment test or to the application of that test to specific network elements?

2. **The Economics of Natural Monopolies.** The D.C. Circuit appears to scrutinize the FCC's rules through the lens of economic theory, such that elements should be unbundled so as to curtail the monopolist's natural advantage but to curtail no more than that. The theory is to develop rules so that entrants and incumbents can compete fairly, and the D.C. Circuit fears that the FCC's plan would unfairly help entrants. Is that an accurate reading of the 1996 Act? And if it is, do you think that the court's framing is the path to an efficient outcome?

3. **Alternatives to Unbundling.** Notice that the court rejected the FCC's attempt to extend ILEC unbundling obligations to wireless telephone carriers. What was the basis for the FCC's determination that these carriers suffered any impairment? What was the basis of the court's rejection of that determination — that there was no evidence of impairment, that there were alternatives to unbundling, or both? The case took an important step in deciding that tariffed access to network elements could defeat a finding of impairment where the evidence shows that competitors were able to enter and prosper using tariffed access instead of TELRIC-priced UNEs. Does that make sense, or does it give too much power to the ILECs, who might have strategically started offering access at plausible, but above-TELRIC, prices?

4. **An Unusual Vacation.** In most of the cases we have seen thus far, when the D.C. Circuit finds the legal justification for a regulation wanting, it remands to the FCC for further proceedings. Vacatur is typically reserved for those rare situations where the court doubts that the agency will be able to justify retaining its rule and further believes that vacatur will cause only minimal disruption. In *USTA II*, however, the court ordered that the rejected rules be vacated within 60 days "in light of the FCC's failure, after eight years, to develop lawful unbundling rules, and its apparent unwillingness to adhere to prior judicial rulings." 359 F.3d at 595. Was it appropriate for the D.C. Circuit to give the FCC a mere sixty days to redo the regulations? Which way does the eight-year gestation of these rules cut? Does it indicate that the issue was too complex for resolution in sixty days, or that the FCC was wasting time? What information would you need in order to answer that question? Do you think the D.C. Circuit had that information? Is perhaps the D.C. Circuit itself to blame for the long delays in implementing the 1996 Act, given its persistent unwillingness to accept the FCC's rules?

5. **Fourth Time's the Charm.** After the D.C. Circuit in *USTA II* sent the FCC back to the drawing board once more, the FCC responded by adopting a new order in 2005 that applied the § 251 unbundling authority "in a more targeted manner" that

imposed "unbundling obligations only in those situations where we find that carriers genuinely are impaired without access to particular network elements and where unbundling does not frustrate sustainable, facilities-based competition." In reviewing this latest rule, the D.C. Circuit wrote that "[b]ecause we conclude the FCC's fourth try is a charm, we deny all petitions for review." Covad Commc'n Co. v. FCC, 450 F.3d 528, 531 (D.C. Cir. 2006). The D.C. Circuit's decision thus ended—almost 10 years after it began—a game of litigation ping pong over the proper scope of the 1996 Act's unbundling obligations. In so doing, it turned away the incumbents' arguments that the FCC's triggers for deregulation were too low and that the availability of special access services (a retail offering) should be relevant to whether unbundled access is required. Similarly, the court turned away the arguments made by competitors that the limitations on high-capacity circuits and unbundled switching were too stringent.

§ 5.D.2. Pricing Network Elements

In its opinion in *Iowa Utilities Board*, the Supreme Court did not reach the validity of the FCC's pricing rules for unbundled network elements. It instead remanded the challenge to the pricing rules for further consideration by the United States Court of Appeals for the Eighth Circuit. We excerpt the Supreme Court's subsequent decision below. Before turning to that document, however, it might be helpful to think through a simple example and in that way clarify exactly why this pricing issue has turned out to be such a difficult one. (Unfortunately, and significantly, the 1996 Act itself offers little guidance, with § 252 stipulating only that the prices for access to network elements must be based on "cost.")

Suppose that, in 1995, an ILEC invested $2 million to develop and install an advanced telecommunications device called the HyperSwitch. The HyperSwitch is a fictional component we invented just for this example, but, to be concrete, let us imagine that the HyperSwitch is a switch that is particularly efficient in networks where the amount of data traffic greatly exceeds the amount of voice traffic. Further suppose that, having built the HyperSwitch, the ILEC incurs an additional expense of two cents per call for each call routed through the switch. This marginal cost might represent any number of real-world costs, for example the cost of the electricity required to run the HyperSwitch, or the maintenance costs associated with switch use. The point is that, wholly apart from fixed costs (here, $2 million), there are marginal costs incurred on a per call basis, which is to say that it costs the ILEC something (two cents) every time anyone uses its switch.

Now, thinking about the HyperSwitch as a possible unbundled network element, our question is a deceptively simple one: what price should the ILEC be required to charge a CLEC for use of the HyperSwitch?

Let's state at the outset exactly what is at stake here. First, there is a distributional/fairness issue to keep in mind. The ILEC, at least, will argue that the regulated price must be high enough so as to allow the recovery of not just its marginal costs but also some fair proportion of its fixed costs. Set too low a price and the ILEC will complain that the regulation imposes an unfair burden — perhaps a burden so substantial as to amount to an unconstitutional "taking" of the ILEC's property. Note that this distributional issue affects other parties in addition to the ILECs. For example, if a potential new entrant were to determine that the government is treating ILECs unfairly, that new entrant might decide to enter instead an unregulated industry, not wanting to take the chance that the government will someday similarly mistreat it. ILEC distributional issues, then, are important to more than just the ILECs.

Second and relatedly, there is the question of the ILEC's future incentives to innovate. If the ILEC knows that its facilities will be offered to rivals at regulated rates and, worse, thinks that those rates will be too low, the ILEC might be reluctant to invest in new technologies like the HyperSwitch in the future. This is particularly troubling if we think that, thanks to their years of experience and considerable resources, incumbents are particularly well-suited to engage in innovation.

Third, there is a short-term efficiency worry to grapple with. Any price above marginal cost threatens to create a state of affairs where the HyperSwitch will be underused. After all, if the regulated price exceeds marginal cost, firms willing to pay more than marginal cost but less than the regulated price will not purchase access. Conversely, prices below marginal cost might lead to overuse.

Fourth and finally, we have to worry about the CLEC's incentive to invest in new technologies. If ILEC equipment is available at bargain basement prices, CLECs will be less likely to venture into the business of developing new equipment. This might not matter if we believe that ILECs will handle all necessary innovation; but, to whatever extent we want CLECs to innovate, this is a significant concern. Conversely, if ILEC equipment is priced too high, CLECs might build their own infrastructure even in cases where society would prefer that the CLEC just share the existing equipment. CLECs would be building not because the new infrastructure was cost-justified, but instead because the regulated price was so artificially high that the CLEC would rather build than pay the regulated rate. (Of course, in this situation the ILEC might voluntarily lower its asking price and in that way avoid the inefficient build-around.)

As even this deeply oversimplified example suggests, the reason it is so difficult to price unbundled network elements is that it is difficult to write a rule that simultaneously responds to all of the relevant concerns. Allow the incumbent to recover some of its up-front investment by charging more than marginal cost, and not only will the network element be underused, but also the CLEC might end up building new infrastructure even when, from a societal perspective, that redundant infrastructure is unnecessary. Force the incumbent to charge marginal cost, by contrast, and not only must the incumbent absorb a significant loss, but in the future incumbent firms will hesitate to invest in new technologies. Efficiently pricing our hypothetical HyperSwitch, in short, is a Herculean task.

Faced with these competing considerations, the FCC chose TELRIC, which at first looks like a rule that sacrifices some degree of efficiency in order to treat the ILECs well. Under TELRIC, the price an entrant pays for access to an incumbent's network element reflects the ILEC's marginal costs plus (a) a proportional share of most other, nonmarginal costs associated with the relevant network element and (b) a reasonable profit. To be more specific, under TELRIC an incumbent is allowed to charge CLECs a price for access that includes (1) any costs directly attributable to the CLECs' use (marginal costs); (2) a proportional share of the depreciation in the element's value over time; (3) a proportional share of overhead costs associated with the element's use (personnel costs, billing costs, and so on); and (4) a share of the cost of the capital invested in the element (either interest paid or the foregone returns on alternative investments). TELRIC thus seems to establish prices that are above marginal cost—indeed, prices that allow ILECs to recover nearly all of the costs associated with any particular network element.

A wrinkle, however, undermined this simple logic. The FCC decided that, when calculating rates under TELRIC, it would not consider what insiders call the "embedded costs" of facilities put in place before the 1996 Act. These embedded costs include any portion of the fixed costs of building the network that the incumbent has not yet recovered through its service prices. Instead, the FCC decided that, at any point in time, "the total element long-run incremental cost of an element should be measured based on the use of the most efficient telecommunications technology currently available and the lowest cost network configuration, given the existing location of the incumbent LEC's wire centers." 47 C.F.R. § 51.505(b)(1). The FCC's policy has therefore been the rule explained above, except that the costs are based not on the costs associated with the incumbent LEC's actual network, but on the costs associated with a hypothetically efficient network.

Unsurprisingly, ILECs challenged the FCC rules. First, the incumbents argued that a rule barring them from recovering the embedded costs of their networks constituted a taking of their property in violation of the Fifth Amendment. Second, the incumbents contended that, even if TELRIC did not represent an unconstitutional taking, the rule violated the plain language and express purpose of the 1996 Act. Section 252 did not say much, but it did say that prices for access to network elements had to be based on "cost"—and the incumbents argued that "cost" meant real costs and could not reasonably be interpreted to mean costs associated with some hypothetical telephone network that might never even be built. The Eighth Circuit reviewed these claims and struck down the FCC's pricing rules in 2000. Iowa Utils. Bd. v. FCC, 219 F.3d 744 (8th Cir. 2000). Both sides of the case appealed to the U.S. Supreme Court. The Court issued its decision in 2002, upholding the FCC's TELRIC approach as a reasonable exercise of agency discretion and as not presenting a facial violation of the Takings Clause. Excerpts of the majority opinion and of Justice Breyer's dissenting opinion follow.

VERIZON COMMUNICATIONS INC. v. FCC

535 U.S. 467 (2002)

SOUTER, J., delivered the opinion of the Court, in which REHNQUIST, C.J., and STEVENS, KENNEDY, and GINSBURG, JJ., joined, in which SCALIA and THOMAS, JJ., joined as to Part III, and in which THOMAS, J., also joined as to Part IV. BREYER, J., filed an opinion concurring in part and dissenting in part, in which SCALIA, J., joined as to Part VI. O'CONNOR, J., took no part in the consideration or decision of the cases.

Justice SOUTER delivered the opinion of the Court.

I

Two sets of related provisions for opening local markets concern us here. First, Congress required incumbent local-exchange carriers to share their own facilities and services on terms to be agreed upon with new entrants in their markets. 47 U.S.C. § 251(c). Second, knowing that incumbents and prospective entrants would sometimes disagree on prices for facilities or services, Congress directed the FCC to prescribe methods for state commissions to use in setting rates that would subject both incumbents and entrants to the risks and incentives that a competitive market would produce. § 252(d).

A

Under the local-competition provisions of the Act, Congress called for ratemaking different from any historical practice, to achieve the entirely new objective of uprooting the monopolies that traditional rate-based methods had perpetuated.

II

As to pricing, the Act provides that when incumbent and requesting carriers fail to agree, state commissions will set a "just and reasonable" and "nondiscriminatory" rate for interconnection or the lease of network elements based on "the cost of providing the . . . network element," which "may include a reasonable profit." § 252(d)(1). In setting these rates, the state commissions are, however, subject to that important limitation previously unknown to utility regulation: the rate must be "determined without reference to a rate-of-return or other rate-based proceeding." In AT&T Corp. v. Iowa Utilities Board, 525 U.S. 366 (1999), this Court upheld the FCC's jurisdiction to impose a new methodology on the States when setting these rates. The attack today is on the legality and logic of the particular methodology the Commission chose.

As for the method to derive a "nondiscriminatory," "just and reasonable rate for network elements," the Act requires the FCC to decide how to value "the cost . . . of providing the . . . network element [which] may include a reasonable profit," although the FCC is (as already seen) forbidden to allow any "reference to a rate-of-return or other rate-based proceeding," § 252(d)(1). Within the discretion left to it after eliminating any dependence on a "rate-of-return or other rate-based proceeding," the Commission chose a way of treating "cost" as "forward-looking economic cost," 47 C.F.R. § 51.505 (1997), something distinct from the kind of historically based cost generally relied upon in valuing a rate base. The FCC defined the "forward-looking economic cost of an element [as] the sum of (1) the total element long-run incremental cost of the element [TELRIC]; [and] (2) a reasonable allocation of forward-looking common costs," § 51.505(a), common costs being "costs incurred in providing a group of elements that cannot be attributed directly to individual elements," § 51.505(c)(1). Most important of all, the FCC decided that the TELRIC "should be measured based on the use of the most efficient telecommunications technology currently available and the lowest cost network configuration, given the existing location of the incumbent['s] wire centers." § 51.505(b)(1).

"The TELRIC of an element has three components, the operating expenses, the depreciation cost, and the appropriate risk-adjusted cost of capital." Implementation of Local Competition in Telecommunications Act of 1996, First Report and Order, 11 FCC Rcd. 15,499, 15,856, ¶ 703 (1996) (First Report and Order). *See also* 47 C.F.R. §§ 51.505(b)(2)–(3) (1997). A concrete example may help. Assume that it would cost $1 a year to operate a most-efficient loop element; that it would take $10 for interest payments on the capital a carrier would have to invest to build the lowest cost loop centered upon an incumbent carrier's existing wire centers (say $100, at 10 percent per annum); and that $9 would be reasonable for depreciation on that loop (an 11-year useful life); then the annual TELRIC for the loop element would be $20.

[T]he Eighth Circuit held that § 252(d)(1) foreclosed the use of the TELRIC methodology. In other words, the court read the Act as plainly requiring rates based on the "actual" not "hypothetical" "cost . . . of providing the . . . network element," and reasoned that TELRIC was clearly the latter. Iowa Utils. Bd. v. FCC, 219 F.3d 744, 750–751 (8th Cir. 2000). The Eighth Circuit added, however, that if it were wrong and TELRIC were permitted, the claim that in prescribing TELRIC the FCC had effected an unconstitutional taking would not be "ripe" until "resulting rates have been determined and applied." *Id.* at 753–754.

Before us, the incumbent local-exchange carriers claim error in the Eighth Circuit's holding that a "forward-looking cost" methodology (as opposed to the use of "historical" cost) is consistent with § 252(d)(1), and its conclusion that the use of the TELRIC forward-looking cost methodology presents no "ripe" takings claim. The FCC and the entrants, on the other side, seek review of the Eighth Circuit's invalidation of the TELRIC methodology and the additional combination rules. We granted certiorari, 531 U.S. 1124 (2001), and now affirm on the issues raised by the incumbents, and reverse on those raised by the FCC and the entrants.

III

A

The incumbent carriers' first attack charges the FCC with ignoring the plain meaning of the word "cost" as it occurs in the provision of § 252(d)(1) that "the just and reasonable rate for network elements . . . shall be . . . based on the cost (determined without reference to a rate-of-return or other rate-based proceeding) of providing the . . . network element. . . ." The incumbents do not argue that in theory the statute precludes any forward-looking methodology, but they do claim that the cost of providing a competitor with a network element in the future must be calculated using the incumbent's past investment in the element and the means of providing it. They contend that "cost" in the statute refers to "historical" cost, which they define as "what was in fact paid" for a capital asset, as distinct from "value," or "the price that would be paid on the open market." The argument boils down to the proposition that "the cost of providing the network element" can only mean, in plain language and in this particular technical context, the past cost to an incumbent of furnishing the specific network element actually, physically, to be provided.

The incumbents have picked an uphill battle. At the most basic level of common usage, "cost" has no such clear implication. A merchant who is asked about "the cost of providing the goods" he sells may reasonably quote their current wholesale market price, not the cost of the particular items he happens to have on his shelves, which may have been bought at higher or lower prices.

When the reference shifts from common speech into the technical realm, the incumbents still have to attack uphill. To begin with, even when we have dealt with historical costs as a ratesetting basis, the cases have never assumed a sense of "cost" as generous as the incumbents seem to claim. "Cost" as used in calculating the rate base under the traditional cost-of-service method did not stand for all past capital expenditures, but at most for those that were prudent, while prudent investment itself could be denied recovery when unexpected events rendered investment useless. And even when investment was wholly includable in the rate base, ratemakers often rejected the utilities' "embedded costs," their own book-value estimates, which typically were geared to maximize the rate base with high statements of past expenditures and working capital, combined with unduly low rates of depreciation. *See, e.g.*, FPC v. Hope Natural Gas Co., 320 U.S. 591, 597–598 (1944). It would also be a mistake to forget that "cost" was a term in value-based ratemaking and has figured in contemporary state and federal ratemaking untethered to historical valuation.

What is equally important is that the incumbents' plain-meaning argument ignores the statutory setting in which the mandate to use "cost" in valuing network elements occurs. First, the Act uses "cost" as an intermediate term in the calculation of "just and reasonable rates," 47 U.S.C. § 252(d)(1), and it was the very point of *Hope Natural Gas* that regulatory bodies required to set rates expressed in these terms have ample discretion to choose methodology, 320 U.S. at 602. Second, it would have been passing strange to think Congress tied "cost" to historical cost without a more specific indication, when the very same sentence that requires "cost" pricing also prohibits any reference to a "rate-of-return or other rate-based proceeding," § 252(d)(1), each of which has been identified with historical cost ever since *Hope Natural Gas* was decided.

The fact is that without any better indication of meaning than the unadorned term, the word "cost" in § 252(d)(1), as in accounting generally, is "a chameleon," Strickland v. Comm'r, Maine Dept. of Human Servs., 96 F.3d 542, 546 (1st Cir. 1996), a "virtually meaningless" term, R. Estes, Dictionary of Accounting 32 (2d ed. 1985). As Justice Breyer put it in *Iowa Utilities Bd.*, words like "cost" "give ratesetting commissions broad methodological leeway; they say little about the 'method employed' to determine a particular rate." 525 U.S. at 423 (opinion concurring in part and dissenting in part). We accordingly reach the conclusion adopted by the Court of Appeals, that nothing in § 252(d)(1) plainly requires reference to historical investment when pegging rates to forward-looking "cost."

B

The incumbents' alternative argument is that even without a stern anchor in calculating "the cost . . . of providing the . . . network element," the particular forward-looking methodology the FCC chose is neither consistent with the plain language of § 252(d)(1) nor within the zone of reasonable interpretation subject to deference under Chevron U.S.A. Inc. v. Natural Resources Defense Council, Inc., 467 U.S. 837, 843–845 (1984). This is so, they say, because TELRIC calculates the forward-looking cost by reference to a hypothetical, most efficient element at existing wire-centers, not the actual network element being provided.

a. [Undermining Competition]

The incumbents' (and Justice Breyer's) basic critique of TELRIC is that by setting rates for leased network elements on the assumption of perfect competition, TELRIC perversely creates incentives against competition in fact. The incumbents say that in purporting to set incumbents' wholesale prices at the level that would exist in a perfectly competitive market (in order to make retail prices similarly competitive), TELRIC sets rates so low that entrants will always lease and never build network elements. And even if an entrant would otherwise consider building a network element more efficient than the best one then on the market (the one assumed in setting the TELRIC rate), it would likewise be deterred by the prospect that its lower cost in building and operating this new element would be immediately available to its competitors; under TELRIC, the incumbents assert, the lease rate for an incumbent's existing element would instantly drop to match the marginal cost of the entrant's new element once built. According to the incumbents, the result will be, not competition, but a sort of parasitic free-riding, leaving TELRIC incapable of stimulating the facilities-based competition intended by Congress.

At the end of the day, theory aside, the claim that TELRIC is unreasonable as a matter of law because it simulates but does not produce facilities-based competition founders on fact. The entrants have presented figures showing that they have invested in new facilities to the tune of $55 billion since the passage of the Act (through 2000). The FCC's statistics indicate substantial resort to pure and partial facilities-based competition among the three entry strategies: as of June 30, 2001, 33 percent of entrants were using their own facilities; 23 percent were reselling services; and 44 percent were leasing network elements (26 percent of entrants leasing loops with switching; 18 percent without switching). The incumbents do not contradict these figures, but merely speculate that the investment has not been as much as it could have been under other ratemaking approaches, and they note that investment has more recently shifted to nonfacilities entry options. We, of course, have no idea whether a different forward-looking pricing scheme would have generated even greater competitive investment than the $55 billion that the entrants claim, but it suffices to say that a regulatory scheme that can boast such substantial competitive capital spending over a 4-year period is not easily described as an unreasonable way to promote competitive investment in facilities.

C

The incumbents' claim of TELRIC's inherent inadequacy to deal with depreciation or capital costs has its counterpart in a further argument. They seek to apply the rule of constitutional avoidance in saying that "cost" ought to be construed by reference to historical investment in order to avoid a serious constitutional question, whether a methodology so divorced from investment actually made will lead to a taking of property in violation of the Fifth (or Fourteenth) Amendment. The Eighth Circuit did not think any such serious question was in the offing, 219 F.3d at 753–754, and neither do we.

At the outset, it is well to understand that the incumbent carriers do not present the portent of a constitutional taking claim in the way that is usual in ratemaking cases. They do not argue that any particular, actual TELRIC rate is "so unjust as to be confiscatory," that is, as threatening an incumbent's "financial integrity." Duquesne Light Co., 488 U.S. at 307, 312. Indeed, the incumbent carriers have not even presented us with an instance of TELRIC rates, which are to be set or approved by state commissions and reviewed in the first instance in the federal district courts, 47 U.S.C. §§ 252(e)(4) and (e)(6). And this, despite the fact that some States apparently have put rates in place already using TELRIC.

The 1996 Act sought to bring competition to local-exchange markets, in part by requiring incumbent local-exchange carriers to lease elements of their networks at rates that would attract new entrants when it would be more efficient to lease than to build or resell. Whether the FCC picked the best way to set these rates is the stuff of debate for economists and regulators versed in the technology of telecommunications and microeconomic pricing theory. The job of judges is to ask whether the Commission made choices reasonably within the pale of statutory possibility in deciding what and how items must be leased and the way to set rates for leasing them. The FCC's pricing and additional combination rules survive that scrutiny.

The judgment of the Court of Appeals is reversed in part and affirmed in part, and the cases are remanded for further proceedings consistent with this opinion.

Justice BREYER, concurring in part and dissenting in part.

I agree with the majority that the Telecommunications Act of 1996 does not require a historical cost pricing system. I also agree that, at the present time, no taking of the incumbent firms' property in violation of the Fifth Amendment has occurred. I disagree, however, with the Court's conclusion that the specific pricing and unbundling rules at issue here are authorized by the Act.

II

The Telecommunications Act is not a ratemaking statute seeking better regulation. It is a deregulatory statute seeking competition. It assumes that, given modern technology, local telecommunications markets may now prove large enough for several firms to compete in the provision of some services — but not necessarily all services — without serious economic waste. It finds the competitive process an indirect but more effective way to bring about the common objectives of competition and regulation alike, namely low prices, better products, and more efficient production methods. But it authorizes the Commission to promulgate rules that will help achieve that procedural goal — the substitution of competition for regulation in local markets — where that transformation is economically feasible. The Act does not authorize the Commission to promulgate rules that would hinder the transition from a regulated to a competitive marketplace — whether or not those rules directly mandate lower "element" prices along the way.

The statute, then, seeks new local market competition insofar as local markets can support that competition without serious waste. And we must read the relevant rate setting provision — including the critical word "cost" — with that goal in mind.

III

The Commission's critics — Verizon, other incumbents, and experts whose published articles Verizon has lodged with the Court — concede that the statute grants the Commission broad authority to define "costs." They also concede that every rate-setting system has flaws.

Nonetheless, the critics argue, the Commission cannot lawfully choose a system that thwarts a basic statutory purpose without offering any significant compensating advantage. They take the relevant purpose as furthering local competition where feasible. They add that rates will further that purpose (1) if they discourage new firms from using the incumbent's facilities or "elements" when it is significantly less expensive, economically speaking, for the entrant to build or to buy elsewhere, and (2) if they encourage new firms to use the incumbent's facilities when it is significantly less expensive, economically speaking, for the entrant to do so. They point out that prices that approximately reflect an actual incumbent's actual additional costs of supplying the services (or "element") demanded will come close to doing both these things. But prices like the Commission's, based on the costs that a hypothetical "most efficient" firm would incur if hypothetically building largely from scratch, would do neither. Indeed, they would do exactly the opposite, creating incentives that hinder rather than further the statute's basic objective.

First, the critics ask, why, given such a system, would a new entrant ever build or buy a new element? After all, the Commission's rate-setting system sets the incumbent's compulsory leasing rate at a level that would rarely exceed the price of building or buying elsewhere. Second, what incentive would the Commission's rules leave the incumbents either to innovate or to invest in a new "element?" The rules seem to say that the incumbent will share with competitors the cost-reducing benefits of a successful innovation, while leaving the incumbent to bear the costs of most unsuccessful investments on its own. Why would investment not then stagnate?

Nor, in the critics' view, do the regulations possess any offsetting advantages. The hypothetical nature of the Commission's system means that experts must estimate how imaginary firms would rebuild their systems from scratch—whether, for example, they (hypothetically) would receive permission to dig up streets, to maintain unsightly telephone poles, or to share their pole costs with other users, say, cable operators—and they must then estimate what would turn out to be most "efficient" in such (hypothetical) future circumstances.

IV

The criticisms described in Part III are serious, potentially severing any rational relation between the Commission's regulations and the statutory provision's basic purposes. Hence, the Commission's responses are important. Do those responses reduce the force of the criticisms, blunt their edges, or suggest offsetting virtues? I have found six major responses. But none of them is convincing.

First, the FCC points out that rates will include not only a charge reflecting hypothetical "most-efficient-firm" costs but also a depreciation charge—a charge that can reconcile a firm's initial historic investment, say, in equipment, and the equipment's current value, which diminishes over time. If, for example, an incumbent's reasonable investment, measured actually and historically, came to \$50 million, but FCC experts predict a "most-efficient-firm-building-from-scratch" future replication cost of \$30 million, a depreciation charge could permit the incumbent to recoup the otherwise missing \$20 million. And, in theory, a state commission might structure a potentially complex depreciation charge so as both to permit recovery of historic investment and also to offset many of the improper investment incentives described in Part II.

This response, however, does not reflect what the Commission's regulations actually say. Those regulations say nothing about permitting recovery of reasonable historic investment nor about varying the charge to offset perverse investment incentives. Rather, they strongly indicate the opposite. They clearly require state commissions to use current depreciation rates right alongside the Commission's new and different "most-efficient-firm-building-from-scratch" charges. *See* First Report and Order, 11 FCC Rcd. at 15,856, ¶ 702. They do create an exception from "current" rates. But to take advantage of that exception "incumbent LECs" have to bear the "burden of demonstrating with specificity that the business risks that they face in providing unbundled network elements and interconnection services would justify a different . . . depreciation rate." *Id.*

Second, the FCC points out that a state commission can adjust permissible profit rates. In theory, such an adjustment could offset many of the improper investment incentives described in Part II. But, like the depreciation regulations, the profit regulations say nothing about the matter. Indeed, like the depreciation regulations, they suggest the opposite. The relevant FCC regulations say that "the currently authorized rate of return at the federal or state level is a reasonable starting point." *Id.* They, too, add an exception, available to "incumbent LEC's" that successfully "bear the burden of demonstrating with specificity that the business risks that they face in providing unbundled network elements and interconnection services would justify a different risk-adjusted cost of capital." *Id.* But this exception, like the depreciation exception, cannot respond to the critics' claims in the ordinary case for similar reasons.

Third, the Commission supports the reasonableness and practicality of its system with the claim that "a number of states" have used it successfully, as have several European nations. As to domestic experience, I can find no evidence that, prior to the promulgation of the rules at issue here, any State had successfully implemented the FCC's version of TELRIC. It is hardly surprising that since then several States have tried to apply it. Nor is it surprising that their implementation has produced criticisms similar to those made here.

Fourth, the FCC adds that its system seeks to base rates on the costs a hypothetical "most efficient firm" hypothetically would incur were it "building from scratch." And such a system, in its view, will "simulate" or "best replicate, to the extent possible, the conditions of a competitive market." This response, however, does not do more than describe that very feature of the system upon which the critics focus their attack.

Fifth, the Commission says that its regulations are simply suggestive, leaving States free to depart. The short but conclusive answer to this response is that the Commission considered a "suggestive" approach and rejected it.

Sixth, the majority (but not the Commission) points out that local commissions are likely to leave any given set of rates in effect for some period of time. And this "regulatory lag" will solve the problem. I do not understand how it could solve the main problem — that of leading new entrants to lease a more costly incumbent "element" where building or buying independently could prove less costly. Nor, given any new entrant's legal right to obtain a regulator's decision, am I certain that lags will prove significant. But, in any event, lags will differ, depending upon regulator, time, and circumstance, thereby introducing a near random element that might, or might not, ameliorate the system's otherwise adverse effects.

In sum, neither the Commission's nor the majority's responses are convincing.

Notes and Questions

1. Basis for Majority Opinion. What was the basis for the majority's decision? Was it that TELRIC represents a reasonable interpretation of the text of the 1996 Act, as a matter of administrative law? Or was it that TELRIC in fact achieves the Act's goals, as an empirical matter? Was the majority opinion's discussion of empirical evidence of competitive entry necessary to its decision, or was it dicta?

2. Key Difference Between Majority and Dissent. Justice Breyer dissented on the ground that TELRIC did not, as a matter of accepted economic theory, foster the 1996 Act's goal of creating genuine local exchange competition. What is the essence of his argument? How did he respond to the majority's claim that, theory aside, facilities-based local competition was developing?

3. Relationship to Impairment Test. Recall that the Supreme Court rejected the FCC's initial list of unbundled network elements on grounds that the FCC had applied the wrong standard for unbundling. What does the empirical evidence cited by the majority in support of TELRIC tell us about impairment, and about the relationship between TELRIC pricing and impairment? On one hand, the fact that facilities-based entry is occurring simultaneously with unbundling could mean that there is no impairment, but that TELRIC prices are so low that some entrants use UNEs rather than building their own facilities. On the other hand, the data could mean that there is impairment, but that TELRIC prices are so high that firms nonetheless build their own facilities instead of always entering through unbundling. Which of these possibilities is more likely? Which opinion, the majority or the dissent, does that possibility support?

4. Takings. The Supreme Court was not particularly sympathetic to the incumbents' assertion that the FCC's pricing methodology, if deemed permissible under the statute, would result in regulated prices so low as to constitute a taking of the incumbents' property without just compensation in violation of the Fifth Amendment, which states "Nor shall private property be taken for public use, without just compensation." U.S. Const., Amend. V. Two commentators explained the Takings issue in the TELRIC context as follows:

> The sweeping deregulation of public utilities being proposed and implemented at the state and federal levels promises to bring the benefits of competition to markets for electric power and telecommunications. Those benefits include improvements in operating efficiencies, competitive prices, efficient investment decisions, technological innovation, and product variety. The benefits of competition, however, do not include forced transfers of income from utility shareholders to their customers and competitors. As regulators dismantle barriers to entry and other regulatory restrictions, they must honor their past commitments and avoid actions that threaten to confiscate or destroy the property of utility investors on an unprecedented scale.

J. Gregory Sidak & Daniel F. Spulber, Deregulatory Takings and the Regulatory Contract 1–2 (1997). The crux of the Court's response was that the issue was not yet ripe; the incumbents should wait and raise their objection once they had specific

TELRIC rates in hand. But is that a sensible response? Delay might bring a reviewing court the benefit of having real numbers to work with. But delay also comes at a cost: without the promise of an eventual takings claim, incumbents have no choice but to fight tooth and nail to recover their historic costs through TELRIC. Had the Court evaluated and embraced the takings logic, by contrast, incumbents would have had less incentive to resist TELRIC pricing.

5. The Devil Is in the Details. In practice, TELRIC as a methodology turned out not to significantly constrain state regulators in their pricing outcomes. In the wake of the 1996 Act's passage, for example, the price of local loops in Chicago was under $3 whereas in New York City local loops were priced around $10. Reflecting the considerable opportunity for state regulators to reach vastly different results in applying the TELRIC standard, Raymond Gifford (former Chairman of the Colorado Public Utilities Commission) called TELRIC just a malleable means of inviting entry into selected markets by "creating a margin between wholesale and retail rates." Raymond L. Gifford, Regulatory Impressionism: What State Regulators Can and Cannot Do, 4 Rev. Network Econ. 466, 474 (2003).

6. TELRIC in the Aftermath. The Supreme Court upheld the FCC's TELRIC approach. But that does not mean the pricing of network elements ceased to be an issue. Within TELRIC there were still many administrative details to be argued: What was the correct cost of capital? How flexible should depreciation rates be and who should set them? Which elements should be priced on a usage-sensitive basis and which at a flat rate? How often should TELRIC be readjusted? In 2003, the FCC initiated an Notice of Proposed Rulemaking (NPRM) in which it proposed modifications to how it would measure forward-looking economic costs of unbundled network elements. Review of the Commission's Rules Regarding the Pricing of Unbundled Network Elements and the Resale of Service by Incumbent Local Exchange Carriers, Notice of Proposed Rulemaking, 18 FCC Rcd. 18,945 (2003). Most importantly, the FCC "tentatively conclude[d] that our TELRIC rules should more closely account for the real-world attributes of the routing and topography of an incumbent's network in the development of forward looking costs." *Id.* at 18,965, ¶ 52. The FCC never actually concluded this rulemaking proceeding, leaving the matter to the state commissions as they implemented further agreements between incumbents and new entrants. As unbundling has become much less of an issue, so too has TELRIC. But the discussion in this section is important for understanding regulation of rates for telecommunications inputs, an issue that is likely to remain important as smaller wireless carriers continue to seek regulated special access and roaming from the large, nationwide wireless networks.

§ 5.E. Universal Service

The regulatory strategies described in this chapter thus far primarily describe efforts to mitigate the economic harm of a monopolist. Though regulations that require universal access also generate economic benefits, they are mostly justified by the noneconomic value of universality. This value is deeply embedded within communications policy. The earliest visions for telephony included a commitment to universal access, and the centerpiece of the Kingsbury Commitment in 1914 was Bell's pledge to provide universal service in exchange for the government's abandonment of an antitrust action (in fact, the desirability of achieving universal access has often been a justification for allowing a telephony monopoly, not just something seen to mitigate the costs of monopoly).

Appropriately, the first section of the Communications Act of 1934 declares its purpose to be "to make available, so far as possible, to all the people of the United States, . . . a rapid, efficient, Nation-wide, and world-wide wire and radio communication service with adequate facilities at reasonable charges." 47 U.S.C. § 151. One interesting feature of that opening section is the inescapable connection between achieving universal service and the difficult challenges of doing so at reasonable prices. We noted at the top of this chapter that price regulation and universal service requirements often go hand-in-hand, and yet these twin objectives are often the source of tension between pursuing equity and pursuing efficiency. Thus, we see that rate regulation and universal access requirements are not only foundations to communications policy but also shape each other.

The two practical questions involving a universal access policy are (1) which services should be universal, and (2) how any such universality should be financed. This section examines how regulation has been used to pursue universal service first for telephony and then for internet service, and how the specific techniques to achieve universal service have changed over time.

§ 5.E.1. Achieving Universal Service Through Cross-Subsidies

Universal service was relatively easy to achieve when Bell ran a unified national phone system. When telephony was provided by a single integrated monopoly, the price for any one service did not have to reflect the costs of providing that service, and the only constraint was that the integrated provider needed to make a profit overall. An integrated provider could therefore be told to price its services such that some were priced below their actual costs while others were priced above cost, and the latter would in essence "cross-subsidize" the former.

Regulators took advantage of this easy price manipulation and built a large number of implicit cross-subsidies to make certain services affordable for all. For instance, Bell charged business customers higher rates than it charged residential customers for the same services, and those extra profits in the business sector were used to keep prices low for residential customers. Similarly, equal monthly subscriber fees were charged for both urban and rural users even though it was costlier to service sparsely populated regions, thus urban residents subsidized rural customers. And third, regulators increased long-distance rates to subsidize local service by allocating much of the fixed costs of local networks to revenue from above-cost long-distance prices. Because the Communications Act of 1934 vested jurisdiction over interstate rates in the FCC but left intrastate telephone rates to state regulation, this lattermost subsidy required federal and state regulators to collaborate in allocating costs to interstate and intrastate services, and a process of "separations and settlements" gave government officials significant discretion in making basic (local) telephone service affordable to low-income households.

Universal service was thus an implicit policy goal, implemented on an ad-hoc basis through the rate approval process, and was easily attainable because of—and perhaps in exchange for preserving—a unified monopoly provider. In 1970, however, the FCC made universal service more explicit by implementing the so-called "Ozark Plan" for federal universal service support. Prescriptions of Procedures for Separating and Allocating Plant Investment, Operating Expenses, Taxes and Reserves Between the Intrastate and Interstate Operations of Telephone Companies, Report and Order, 26 F.C.C. 2d 247 (1970). The Ozark Plan disproportionately allocated the fixed costs of the local telephone network to long-distance traffic. In particular, for every 1 percent of traffic consisting of long-distance calls, the plan required that 3.3 percent of local network costs be covered through long-distance prices. So, if there were 1000 total calls on a network, 900 of which were local and 100 of which were long distance, the costs of the network would be recovered 33 percent through long-distance rates and only 67 percent through local rates. It was in this way that the Ozark Plan expressly subsidized local rates; the Plan was implemented in 1971 and, by 1980, long-distance calls paid for approximately 25 percent of the common local line infrastructure even though those calls made up only 8 percent of traffic on the local networks. *See* Peter W. Huber et al., Federal Telecommunications Law 133 (2d ed. 1999).

Using cross subsidies to pursue universal service became much more difficult, however, after the 1984 breakup separated Bell into separate constituent parts. In the post-divestiture world, raising the price on long-distance service to subsidize local service would not work without a mechanism by which AT&T and the other long-distance carriers could be forced to transfer funds to the Bell Operating Companies and other local exchange carriers. At the same time, and in obvious tension with the Ozark Plan, the FCC was aiming to reduce long-distance rates and allocate costs more accurately since inflated long-distance rates were causing inefficient underutilization of long-distance service.

The FCC pursued universal service post-divestiture in two parts. The first was to create "access charges" paid by long-distance companies to local carriers for originating and terminating long-distance calls. *See* MTS and WATS Market Structure, Phase I, Third Report and Order, 93 F.C.C. 2d 241 (1983). The second was to allocate more of the fixed costs of the local network to local rates through a subscriber line charge (SLC) that would be paid by local phone service customers. The original plan was to peg the SLC at a fixed $6 per month, which would be offset by an immediate decrease in long-distance rates of five to ten cents a minute. However, in the face of virulent opposition from Congress, consumer advocates, and state regulators—all of whom liked the idea of keeping local rates low and who either did not factor long-distance spending into their assessment of consumer welfare or did not believe long-distance prices would actually fall—the FCC backed off. In the end, the FCC left the $6 SLC in place only for business users and capped the residential SLC at $3.50 per month. The FCC did not alter those charges until 2000, when it raised the residential SLC to $4.35 with conditional provision for increases up to $6.50 over the following three years. Access Charge Reform, Sixth Report and Order, 15 FCC Rcd. 12,962 (2000).

The important post-divestiture changes in universal service policies were thus (1) the shifting of a greater proportion of the costs of local service onto the charges for those services through the creation of the subscriber line charge; and (2) the creation of interstate access charges through which revenues from interexchange service could be transferred to local exchange carriers. The policy was not without opposition, as long-distance companies complained that access charges were significantly in excess of the local exchange companies' costs of originating and terminating traffic, thereby improperly inflating the local companies' profits while raising long-distance prices for consumers. Access charge reform therefore remained a contentious policy issue, one that would ultimately take center stage in the Telecommunications Act of 1996.

Notes and Questions

1. Other Cross-Subsidies. While the cross-subsidies outlined in the text were the ones with the strongest political appeal, a variety of other implicit cross-subsidies were long built into telephone rates. For example, long-distance calls tended to be more costly the longer they traveled and the longer they lasted because, in both cases, more system capacity is occupied by the call. Rates were and are set on both of these bases. But, time and distance being equal, frequency of infrastructure use also affected the cost of a call. If the line from, say, St. Louis to Chicago was used more frequently than another line of about the same length (say, Quincy, Illinois, to South Bend, Indiana) then the cost per call on the heavily used route was lower. Due to a policy of "nationwide rate averaging" in effect throughout the early history of telephone regulation, these cost differences were not reflected in long-distance prices and, hence, St. Louis/Chicago callers subsidized their Quincy/South Bend peers.

2. An Explicit Tax Alternative. Why was the desire to subsidize certain services by raising the rates on other services a good reason to favor an integrated telephone service provider? Couldn't these same policies have been achieved in a world with multiple carriers simply by implementing a targeted system of telecommunications taxes? Suppose, for example, that it is good policy to have business users subsidize residential ones. Why not just impose a tax on all business telephone service, no matter which firm provides it, and then use that money to subsidize the purchase of residential service? Phrased another way, are there reasons why an implicit subsidy scheme (the cross-subsidies) would be more desirable than an explicit equivalent (taxation)? Is it because implicit subsidies are easier for politicians to slip into legislation? What do you make of the fact that the implicit subsidy scheme hurt constituencies like business and urban users but helped constituencies like residential and rural users? Should cross-subsidies be understood as a means by which elected officials pandered to powerful special interests?

3. Entry Problems. As we noted in discussing the Bell Divestiture in Chapter 4, this universal service scheme affected the development of competition. How did these implicit cross-subsidies affect entry? Which markets would competitors seek to enter? What is the effect on the incumbent if new companies engage in selective entry? Should the incumbent be able to resist that selective entry? How could the system have been reformed to meet both universal service and competition goals?

§ 5.E.2. Universal Telephony Service After the 1996 Act

The central purpose of the 1996 Act was to introduce competition into all communications markets, most notably the local exchange markets that had been left as monopolies after divestiture. Since competitive markets, by definition, are designed to bring prices close to marginal costs, the cross-subsidies that became difficult after divestiture in 1984 became even more so as the potential for multiple local carriers was introduced in 1996. The central provision of the Act, 47 U.S.C. § 254, maintained a commitment to universal service but made two substantial changes to the status quo. The first was to broaden the definition of services that might be supported under a universal service regime both to include additional providers and to include advanced telecommunications services, a topic addressed in the next subsection. The second was to require that universal service support mechanisms be made explicit. As the Fifth Circuit said in a case reviewing important FCC first steps to implement § 254: "To attain the goal of local competition while preserving universal service, Congress directed the FCC to replace the patchwork of explicit and implicit subsidies with 'specific, predictable and sufficient Federal and State mechanisms to preserve and advance universal service.' 47 U.S.C. § 254(b)(5)." Texas Office of Public Utilities Counsel v. FCC, 183 F.3d 393, 406 (5th Cir. 1999). Similarly, § 254(e) provides that any universal service support received by a carrier "should be explicit and sufficient to achieve the purposes of this section." 47 U.S.C. § 254(e).[8]

Under § 254, access charge reform became the primary instrument to preserve the policy of universal access even as the telephony market changed dramatically. Access charges continued to overcompensate the ILECs such that they covered both the real expenses associated with origination and termination and represented a

8. The courts, however, have given the FCC significant leeway in implementing the "goal" of explicit support mechanisms, saying that "there is no timetable on *realization* of the reform." Competitive Telecomm. Ass'n v. FCC, 309 F.3d 8, 15 (D.C. Cir. 2002).

contribution by the long-distance carriers to the universal service infrastructure provided by the ILECs. In 1997, the FCC began the process of changing access charges by first noting that the "patchwork of implicit and explicit subsidies [inherent in the traditional system] generates inefficient and undesirable economic behavior." Access Charge Reform, First Report and Order, 12 FCC Rcd. 15,982 at 15,995–96, ¶ 30 (1997). For example, the access charge regime results in significantly higher long-distance rates, distorting demand, and may even induce some customers to bypass traditional telephone carriers, even if those carriers were the most efficient. *Id.* The FCC took important steps to take implicit subsidies out of access charges and, eventually, move access charges to competitive rates. *Id.* Litigation over the details of this transition were substantial, and in 2000, the FCC sought a more comprehensive solution by adopting a combined access charge reform and universal service proposal filed by the Coalition for Affordable Local and Long Distance Service (CALLS). *See* Access Charge Reform, Sixth Report and Order, 15 FCC Rcd. 12,962 (2000). The principal goals of the CALLS proposal were to (1) reduce access charges and thereby reduce long-distance calling rates; (2) require local exchange companies to recover more of the universal service subsidy directly from end users rather than indirectly through charges imposed on long-distance calling; and (3) make the universal service subsidy previously received implicitly through interstate access charges explicit and "portable" to different local carriers. The proposal gradually raised the subscriber line charge (SLC) on primary lines above the longtime level of $3.50, something the FCC had previously refused to do. Because telephone network costs are substantial while variable costs are low, an efficient pricing system (recall Ramsey pricing, discussed above in § 5.A.4) would include a substantial fixed fee for simply having a connection to the network. But such a pricing structure is politically controversial because then customers who make few calls may still be required to pay a monthly fee simply to remain connected.

The FCC's universal service and access charge reforms were subject to continued judicial review, causing the FCC to address access charge reform and universal service together with other issues of carrier-to-carrier compensation (e.g., reciprocal compensation payments between local carriers), under the more comprehensive heading of "intercarrier compensation" reform. In February 2011, the FCC released a Notice of Proposed Rulemaking designed to address both universal service and intercarrier compensation, promising fast action. Connect America Fund, Notice of Proposed Rulemaking and Further Notice of Proposed Rulemaking, 26 FCC Rcd. 4554 (2011). And the FCC did act quickly, issuing a comprehensive order in November that same year. Connect America Fund, Report and Order and Further Notice of Proposed Rulemaking, 26 FCC Rcd. 17,663 (2011). This order addressed both issues of intercarrier compensation and of universal service. On appeal, the Tenth Circuit issued two opinions, one on the intercarrier compensation issues and one on the universal service issues—both affirming the FCC's action. We excerpt here the Tenth Circuit's decision on the intercarrier compensation parts of the order.

FCC 11-161

753 F.3d 1015 (10th Cir. 2014)

Opinion for the court filed by Circuit Judge BACHARACH, in which BRISCOE, Chief Judge, and HOLMES, Circuit Judge, concur.

BACHARACH, Circuit Judge:

Issues Involving Intercarrier Compensation

Exercising its rulemaking authority under the Communications Act of 1934 and the Telecommunications Act of 1996, the FCC overhauled the intercarrier compensation regime and adopted a "uniform national bill-and-keep framework . . . for all telecommunications traffic exchanged with a [local exchange carrier]." Connect America Fund, Report and Order and Further Notice of Proposed Rulemaking, 26 FCC Rcd. 17,663, ¶ 34 (2011) (Order). To ease the transition to a new regime of bill-and-keep, the FCC also adopted a comprehensive plan to phase out the old intercarrier compensation system. The Petitioners challenge the plan on grounds that it exceeded the FCC's authority, was arbitrary and capricious, and resulted in a denial of due process. These challenges are rejected.

I. The FCC's Restructuring of the Telecommunications Market

A. The Old Regime

The FCC adopted the plan against the backdrop of two types of arrangements. One provided reciprocal compensation for local calls, and the other involved charges for long-distance carriers to connect to a local carrier's network. In the Order, the FCC revamped this regime, exercising authority over all traffic exchanged with a local exchange carrier (LEC), including intrastate calls.

Before 1996, regulation of telecommunications was generally divided between the FCC and state commissions. The FCC regulated interstate service, and state commissions regulated intrastate service. Under this division of authority, states granted exclusive franchises to LECs within their designated service areas. Through these franchises, the LECs owned the local telecommunications networks.

In 1996, Congress set out to restructure the market to enhance competition. These efforts led to enactment of the Telecommunications Act of 1996. In this statute, Congress empowered the FCC and created a new breed of competitors (called Competitive LECs or CLECs).

Under the new statute, all LECs would assume certain duties. One of these duties involved the establishment of arrangements for "reciprocal compensation" in the "transport and termination of telecommunications." 47 U.S.C. § 251(b)(5). This statutory duty includes two key terms underlying the present litigation: "reciprocal compensation" and "telecommunications." In the Order, the FCC recently interpreted these terms to cover all traffic, including intrastate service and use of local networks by long-distance carriers.

This interpretation reflects a departure from the FCC's previous reading of the 1996 Act. In the past, for example, the FCC had narrowly read the phrase "reciprocal compensation" as limited to local traffic. *See* Bell Atlantic Telephone Companies v. FCC, 206 F.3d 1, 4 (D.C. Cir. 2000). Under the FCC's previous interpretation, the parties or state commissions set the charges for intrastate traffic between two LECs.

The charges were called "access charges" because long-distance carriers (called IXCs) paid LECs for the opportunity to use their networks at the start- and end-points of the calls. This system is known as "exchange access." 47 U.S.C. § 153(20).

In exchange access, long-distance calls start (or "originate") on an LEC's network, continue on the IXC's network to another local telephone exchange, and end (or "terminate") on the network of another LEC.

The three different combinations led to three different types of access charges, each with its own mode of regulation:

- Interstate IXC–LEC Traffic: For this kind of traffic, the IXC paid an access charge to the originating LEC and a terminating interstate access charge to the terminating LEC. The access charges were regulated by the FCC.
- Intrastate IXC–LEC Traffic: For traffic within a single state by an IXC and LEC, the IXC paid an access charge to the originating LEC and an access charge to the terminating LEC. The access charge was governed by state law and was typically set above interstate rates.
- Local LEC–LEC Traffic: For local traffic between two LECs, the LECs paid each other consistently with their reciprocal compensation arrangement. The arrangement was either negotiated by the parties or set by the states using a methodology prescribed by the FCC under 47 §§ 201(b) and 251(b)(5).

Each arrangement assumed that the calling party should pay for the call. This assumption was based on the view that the callers were the only persons that benefited from the call and that they should bear all of the costs. Thus, callers paid their own carriers, which in turn paid other carriers for access to their networks to reach the person being called.

B. The New Regime

In the Order, the FCC restructured this system in three ways. First, the FCC reinterpreted the 1996 law to cover all traffic, including traffic subject to charges for access to a network. Second, the FCC claimed that it could prevent state commissions from approving access charges for intrastate calls in the absence of an agreement between the parties. Third, the FCC rejected the idea that a caller should bear the full cost of the call; thus, the FCC prescribed a new system, known as "bill-and-keep," for all traffic.

"Bill-and-keep" anticipates that carriers will recover their costs from their end-user customers rather than from other carriers. In moving to "bill-and-keep," the FCC reasoned that the parties to a call should split the costs because both enjoy the benefits. Once bill-and-keep is fully implemented for all traffic exchanged with an LEC, the calling party and the called party will divide the costs.

C. The Transition from the Old Regime to the New Regime

Recognizing that the change would disrupt the market, the FCC opted to gradually transition to bill-and-keep. In the transition period, incumbent LECs (ILECs) could recover some, but not all, of their lost intercarrier compensation revenue through the FCC's funding mechanisms.

D. The Types of Challenges

The Petitioners challenge four aspects of the reforms: (1) implementation of bill-and-keep for all traffic; (2) limitations on funding mechanisms during the transitional period; (3) irregularities in the rule-making process; and (4) application of the reforms to particular circumstances. We reject all of the challenges.

II. Challenges to the FCC's Authority to Implement a National Bill-and-Keep Framework for All Traffic

In the Order, the FCC concluded that 47 U.S.C. § 251(b)(5) applied to all telecommunications traffic exchanged with an LEC. Based on this conclusion, the FCC prescribed bill-and-keep as the default methodology for that traffic. The Petitioners challenge not only the FCC's authority to regulate the traffic, but also the way in which the FCC chose to exercise this authority. Thus, we must address both challenges: the FCC's authority and the content of the new regulations.

The FCC claims authority under 47 U.S.C. §§ 251(b)(5) and 201(b) to implement bill-and-keep as the default intercarrier compensation framework for all traffic exchanged with an LEC. For traffic between LECs and wireless providers, the FCC also invokes authority under 47 U.S.C. § 332. And for interstate traffic, the FCC relies on 47 U.S.C. § 201.

A. Standard of Review

Congress has unambiguously authorized the FCC to administer the Communications Act through rulemaking and adjudication. Thus, we apply *Chevron* deference to the FCC's interpretation of the statute and its own authority. *Chevron* involves a two-step inquiry. Chevron U.S.A., Inc. v. Natural Res. Def. Council, Inc., 467 U.S. 837, 842–43 (1984).

In the first step, we ask whether Congress has spoken on the issue. When the statute is unambiguous, we look no further. "[I]f the statute is silent or ambiguous with respect to the specific issue," we must decide "whether the agency's answer is based on a permissible construction of the statute." *Chevron*, 467 U.S. at 843.

B. The FCC's Authority Over Access Charges on All Traffic

The FCC interprets 47 U.S.C. § 201(b) and § 251(b)(5) to apply to all traffic, including access given to long-distance carriers, intrastate traffic, and origination. This interpretation is reasonable.

1. Traffic Between LECs and Long-Distance Carriers

In adopting the new regulations, the FCC concluded that it had jurisdiction over all traffic between LECs and long-distance carriers.

a. The FCC's Rationale

This interpretation flows in part from the language in § 251(b)(5). This section provides that each LEC must "establish reciprocal compensation arrangements for the transport and termination of telecommunications." 47 U.S.C. § 251(b)(5). The term "telecommunications" is defined in the statute and "encompasses communications traffic of any geographic scope . . . or regulatory classification." 47 U.S.C. § 153(50). Because the term is untethered to geographic or regulatory limits, the FCC regards its authority under § 251(b)(5) to cover all traffic regardless of geography or regulatory classification. In addition, the FCC relies on 47 U.S.C. § 201(b), which authorizes the adoption of regulations as necessary to carry out §§ 251 and 252.

Based on the broad definition of "telecommunications" and the text of § 201, the FCC recently concluded that § 251(b)(5) covers all traffic between IXCs and LECs. In doing so, the FCC recognized that it had changed its interpretation of § 251(b)(5). But the FCC reasoned that its earlier reading of the law had been "inconsistent" with the text.

c. Traffic Between LECs and IXCs as "Reciprocal Compensation"

The FCC broadly interprets the phrase "reciprocal compensation" to encompass any intercarrier compensation agreements between carriers. The Petitioners raise two challenges to this conclusion under the first step of *Chevron*: (1) Congress used the term "reciprocal compensation" as a technical term of art to denote local traffic between two LECs; and (2) the plain meaning of "reciprocal compensation" cannot include traffic between IXCs and LECs because the payments go only one way (to the LECs).

i. "Reciprocal Compensation" as a Term of Art

Under step one of *Chevron*, we start with the statutory text to determine whether the phrase "reciprocal compensation" is a term of art. At this step, we give technical terms of art their established meaning absent a contrary indication in the statute.

The Petitioners rely on two pieces of evidence: (1) an FCC website description of the term "reciprocal compensation," which limited its application to local calls; and (2) accounts in the trade press, which discussed state-imposed reciprocal compensation requirements for local traffic. The two pieces of evidence do not eliminate ambiguity in the phrase.

ii. Plain Meaning of the Term "Reciprocal Compensation"

The Petitioners also argue that the FCC has distorted the plain meaning of the term "reciprocal compensation." Joint Intercarrier Compensation Principal Br. of Pet'rs at 25–26. According to the Petitioners, traffic between an LEC and IXC is not "reciprocal" because the charges and traffic go only one way. For this position, the Petitioners contend that for compensation to be "reciprocal," both carriers must pay each other. Relying on this definition, the Petitioners argue that access charges "are never reciprocal" because the IXC pays the LECs on both ends to originate and terminate the traffic. *Id.*

Section 251(b)(5) requires LECs to establish arrangements for "reciprocal compensation." 47 U.S.C. § 251(b)(5). Thus, we could adopt the Petitioners' interpretation only if the statute requires traffic and compensation to "actually flow to and from both carriers ... to be a 'reciprocal compensation arrangement.'" Pac. Bell v. Cook Telecom, Inc., 197 F.3d 1236, 1244 (9th Cir. 1999). This is a reasonable reading of the statute. But the statute can also be read to simply require the existence of reciprocal obligations. A carrier can have a reciprocal entitlement to compensation for transporting and terminating traffic even if it does not ultimately transport or terminate a call.

The statutory term "reciprocal compensation" is ambiguous; thus, we reach the second step of *Chevron*. At step two, we conclude that the FCC reasonably interpreted the term "reciprocal compensation" for "telecommunications" to include the traffic between IXCs and LECs.

d. The Petitioners' Reliance on §§ 252(d)(2)(A) and 251(c)(2)(A)

The Petitioners argue that two other statutory sections (§§ 252(d)(2)(A) and 251(c)(2)(A)) would prevent application of § 251(b)(5) to access traffic. We disagree.

i. Section 252(d)(2)(A)

The Petitioners invoke § 252(d)(2)(A), arguing that it precludes an expansive reading of § 251(b)(5) because traffic never originates on an IXC's network. This argument is invalid.

Section 252(d)(2)(A) applies to state commission arbitrations of interconnection agreements between an ILEC and another telecommunications carrier. *See* 47 U.S.C. § 252. Under this section, state commissions can consider reciprocal compensation terms just and reasonable only if they "provide for the mutual and reciprocal recovery by each carrier of costs associated with the transport and termination on each carrier's network facilities of calls that originate on the network facilities of the other carrier." *Id.* at § 252(d)(2)(A). Because IXCs do not originate calls, the Petitioners contend that reciprocal compensation arrangements cannot apply to traffic between LECs and IXCs.

The FCC rejected this argument, reasoning that § 252(d)(2)(A) does not limit § 251(b)(5). In rejecting the argument, the FCC found that § 252(d)(2)(A) "'deals with the mechanics of who owes what to whom,'" but "'does not define the scope of traffic to which § 251(b)(5) applies.'" Order ¶ 768 (quoting High-Cost Universal Service Support, Order on Remand and Report and Order and Further Notice of Proposed Rulemaking, 24 FCC Rcd. 6475, 6481, ¶ 12 (2008) (High-Cost Universal Service Support). With this finding, the FCC reiterated that Congress did not intend "'the pricing standards in section 252(d)(2) to limit the otherwise broad scope of section 251(b)(5).'" *Id.* (quoting High-Cost Universal Service Support, 24 FCC Rcd. at 6480, ¶ 11). Instead, the FCC concluded that § 252(d)(2)'s pricing rules do "not address what happens when carriers exchange traffic that originates or terminates on a third carrier's network." High-Cost Universal Service Support, 24 FCC Rcd. at 6481, ¶ 12.

The FCC's interpretation is reasonable. Section 251(b)(5) broadly refers to "the transport and termination of telecommunications." 47 U.S.C. § 251(b)(5). This section is incorporated into § 252(d)(2), but not the other way around. Consequently, there is nothing in § 252(d)(2) to suggest that it limits the scope of § 251(b)(5). In these circumstances, the FCC reasonably relied on the breadth of § 251(b)(5) to conclude that it is not narrowed by § 252(d)(2).

ii. Section 251(c)(2)(A)

The Petitioners also rely on § 251(c)(2)(A), which distinguishes between "exchange access" and "exchange service." This section requires ILECs to provide telecommunications carriers with interconnection to their networks "for the transmission and routing of telephone exchange service [local calls] and exchange access [long-distance calls]." 47 U.S.C. § 251(c)(2)(A). Because the section distinguishes between "exchange service" and "exchange access," the Petitioners argue that "reciprocal compensation" must refer to something other than "exchange access." Joint Intercarrier Compensation Principal Br. of Pet'rs at 11–12. We reject this argument.

The Petitioners' argument does not render § 251(b)(5) unambiguous or vitiate the reasonableness of the FCC's interpretation. For this argument, the Petitioners incorrectly conflate "exchange service" and "reciprocal compensation." Section 251(c)(2)(A) refers to an ILEC's duty to allow others to interconnect for local- and long-distance calls. This duty is distinct from the duty in § 251(b)(5) to establish arrangements for reciprocal compensation. Thus, § 251(c)(2)(A) does not unambiguously shed light on how the FCC should interpret § 251(b)(5).

2. Preemption of State Regulatory Authority Over Intrastate Access Charges

The Petitioners argue that even if the FCC can regulate IXC–LEC traffic, this authority would include calls that were interstate, but not intrastate. [T]he Petitioners argue that § 152(b) and § 601(c)(1) require the FCC to narrowly interpret § 251(b)(5) to avoid interference with state regulation of intrastate traffic. We disagree. Otherwise, we would be interpreting §§ 152(b) and 601(c)(1) in a way that would upset the regulatory scheme envisioned in the 1996 Act.

Section 152(b) simply limits the FCC's ancillary jurisdiction. *See* AT&T Corp. v. Iowa Utilities Bd., 525 U.S. 366, 380–81 & n.7 (1999) (stating that § 152(b) serves only to limit the FCC's ancillary authority). And, § 601(c)(1) does not limit Congress's actual delegation of authority to the FCC. Because §§ 152(b) and 601(c)(1) do not unambiguously narrow the scope of § 251(b)(5), we proceed to *Chevron*'s second step.

At that step, we defer to the FCC's interpretation of a statutory ambiguity that concerns the scope of its regulatory authority. Administrative deference is suitable here. Congress appears to grant plenary authority to the FCC through § 251, and §§ 152(b) and 601(c)(1) do not preclude the FCC from interpreting § 251(b)(5) to allow preemption of state regulation over intrastate access charges.

The Petitioners further rely on 47 U.S.C. § 251(d)(3) to rebut the FCC's interpretation that § 251(b)(5) includes intrastate traffic between IXCs and LECs. Section 251(d)(3), entitled "Preservation of State access regulations," prevents the FCC from preempting state commissions' regulations, orders, or policies that: (1) establish LEC access and interconnection obligations, (2) are consistent with the requirements of § 251, and (3) do not substantially prevent implementation of the requirements of § 251 and the purposes of the Communications Act of 1934. 47 U.S.C. § 251(d)(3). According to the Petitioners, § 251(d)(3) prevents the FCC from preempting state access charges.

This argument is unpersuasive. The FCC reasonably concluded that § 251(d)(3) does not speak to the preemptive effect of § 251(b)(5) or limit the permissible interpretations of the statute or the FCC's rulemaking authority. The FCC has interpreted intrastate traffic as subject to § 251(b)(5); and, in exercising the grant of power under § 251(b)(5), the FCC is establishing a national bill-and-keep policy for all access traffic.

C. Bill-and-Keep as a Default Methodology

The FCC not only extended its regulations to all access traffic, but also began a transition to bill-and-keep as the default standard for reciprocal compensation. According to the FCC's interpretation of its authority, § 201(b) allows the adoption of rules and regulations to implement § 251(b)(5). In implementing § 251(b)(5), the FCC considers bill-and-keep to be "just and reasonable" under § 201(b); thus, the FCC concluded it has statutory authority to implement bill-and-keep as the default reciprocal compensation standard for all traffic subject to § 251(b)(5).

In arriving at this conclusion, the FCC addressed opposition based on §§ 252(c) and 252(d)(2). Section 252 does two things: (1) It preserves state rate-setting authority in state commission arbitrations involving ILECs and other carriers; and (2) it defines "just and reasonable" rates. 47 U.S.C. § 252.

For two reasons, the FCC concluded that these provisions did not prevent adoption of a bill-and-keep methodology. First, the FCC pointed to *AT&T*, 525 U.S. at 384, which authorizes the FCC to establish a pricing methodology for state commissions to apply in these arbitrations. In choosing among pricing methodologies, the FCC found specific approval of bill-and-keep in 47 U.S.C. § 252(d)(2)(B). Second, the FCC found that bill-and-keep is just and reasonable under § 252(d)(2) because it allows carriers to recover their transport and termination costs from their end-users.

Both conclusions are criticized by the Petitioners. They argue that: (1) bill-and-keep effectively sets a zero rate that infringes on state rate-setting authority under

§ 252(d), and (2) bill-and-keep does not lead to just and reasonable intercarrier compensation rates under §§ 252(d)(2)(A) and 201(b).

Because the statute expressly authorizes bill-and-keep arrangements along with state rate-setting authority, we believe the FCC's interpretation of § 252(d)(2) is reasonable and entitled to deference under *Chevron*.

Under section 252(d)(2), states continue to enjoy authority to arbitrate "terms and conditions" in reciprocal compensation. *See* 47 U.S.C. § 252(d)(2). For example, even under bill-and-keep arrangements, states must arbitrate the "edge" of carrier's networks. This reservoir of state authority can be significant.

The "edge" of a carrier's network consists of the points "at which a carrier must deliver terminating traffic to avail itself of bill-and-keep." *Id.* The location of the "edge" of a carrier's network determines the transport and termination costs for the carrier.

The FCC reasonably determined that by continuing to set the network "edge," states retain their role under § 252(d) in "determin[ing] the concrete result in particular circumstances." Order ¶ 776.

In *AT&T*, the Supreme Court upheld the FCC's rule-making authority over §§ 251 and 252. *AT&T*, 525 U.S. at 378. Interpreting § 252(c)(2)'s reservation of rate-setting authority to state commissions, the Court upheld the FCC's requirement that state commissions use a particular methodology for prices involving interconnection and unbundled access. *See id.* at 384–85. In doing so, the Supreme Court concluded that the FCC has rulemaking authority to implement a pricing methodology for the states to implement, "determining the concrete result in particular circumstances. That is enough to constitute the establishment of rates." *Id.* at 384.

The Petitioners [also] point to 47 U.S.C. §§ 201(b) and 252(d)(2), arguing that they require rates to be "just and reasonable." Joint Intercarrier Compensation Principal Br. of Pet'rs at 39–40. Invoking these sections, the Petitioners argue that the FCC's bill-and-keep methodology is not "just and reasonable." Joint Intercarrier Compensation Principal Br. of Pet'rs at 39–42. This argument is invalid under *Chevron*.

According to the FCC, bill-and-keep allows for just and reasonable rates by providing for the "mutual and reciprocal recovery of costs through the offsetting of reciprocal obligations." Federal Resp'ts' Final Resp. to the Joint Intercarrier Compensation Principal Br. of Pet'rs at 33–34. Under a bill-and-keep arrangement, each carrier obtains an "in kind" exchange.

The FCC reasoned that under this methodology, a carrier that terminates a call that originates with another carrier performs a service for its end-user, the call's recipient. Because both end-users benefit from the call, the end-users should split the cost and pay their respective carriers for the call. Through this in-kind exchange of services, bill-and-keep allows carriers to obtain compensation for the call from their own customers.

III. Challenges to Cost Recovery as Arbitrary and Capricious

The Petitioners have challenged not only the ultimate goal of the reforms, but also the way in which the FCC chose to transition toward a national bill-and-keep methodology.

A. The Transitional Plan

Perceiving that an immediate change would unduly disrupt the market, the FCC elected to gradually move toward a bill-and-keep methodology. The FCC decided to transition terminating access charges to bill-and-keep over a six-year period for price cap carriers and over a nine-year period for rate-of-return carriers. The FCC limited interstate originating access charges to existing levels, but has not yet decided how to transition these charges to bill-and-keep.

The FCC created a federal recovery mechanism to ease the transition to bill-and-keep for incumbent LECs. This recovery mechanism is not revenue neutral, for the FCC helps incumbent LECs recover only part of their lost revenues. The amount of the recovery will be based on existing trends that show declining revenues. For price-cap carriers, the recovery generally starts at 90% of 2011 revenues and declines 10% per year. For rate-of-return carriers, the recovery starts at 2011 revenues for switched access and net reciprocal compensation. When the FCC acted, rate-of-return carriers were experiencing yearly drops in revenue of: (1) 3% for interstate switched access, and (2) 10% for intrastate intercarrier compensation. Choosing a benchmark between 3% and 10%, the FCC chose to reduce the eligible recovery for rate-of-return carriers by 5% each year.

Under the FCC's recovery mechanism, carriers can recover part of their lost revenues through: (1) a federally tariffed Access Recovery Charge on end-users, and (2) supplemental support from the Connect America Fund. The Access Recovery Charge is limited to prevent individual end-users from paying excessive rates and is allocated at a carrier's holding-company level. To obtain supplemental support from the Connect America Fund, carriers must meet certain broadband obligations.

[The Court rejected these challenges, as well as challenges to the FCC's procedures and many, more limited challenges brought by various industry segments.]

VI. Conclusion

We deny all of the petitions for review involving the FCC's regulations regarding intercarrier compensation.

Notes and Questions

1. The End of the End? The FCC's clear direction was to eliminate access charges and other vestiges of the intercarrier compensation regime that traditionally supported universal service. What were the forces that drove the FCC in this direction? Local competition? Regulatory arbitrage? Better economics?

2. A New Beginning. Although we have separated the issues of intercarrier compensation reform and the funding of broadband universal service, keep in mind that they are intimately related — indeed, they are two parts of the very same order.

The FCC placed a high priority on broadband networks, and even said that plain old telephone services would be provided over broadband networks. That may have been correct generally, but deploying new broadband networks was more expensive than sustaining plain old telephone service, which may have done the job just fine (depending of course on what the "job" is). Was the FCC being paternalistic? Is there an appropriate way to gauge what the market wants?

3. Legal Authority and the States. Recall that in *Iowa Utilities Board* the Supreme Court held that the FCC, and not the states, had primary authority to implement the local competition provisions of the 1996 Telecommunications Act (47 U.S.C. §§ 251 & 252). But this order was an important further step. The FCC's scheme of intercarrier compensation applied to intrastate traffic, and this was a significant change from the traditional scheme in which the FCC regulated interstate access charges and left the matter of intrastate access charges to the States. What role was left for the States after this order? Should the States have had any continuing role?

4. Bill-and-Keep. The court approved the FCC's move to bill-and-keep for all intercarrier compensation, after a transition period. Under bill-and-keep, carriers do not pay one another for the termination of traffic, even if traffic flows are imbalanced. Rather, to the extent that a carrier needs capital to increase capacity due to traffic flowing into it — traffic that it must terminate for its customers — the carrier must increase its charges to its own customers who, as the FCC says, benefit from receiving calls.

5. Phantom Traffic and Access Stimulation. Two of the FCC's motivations (although by no means its only motivations) for moving to a single, unified bill-and-keep scheme for intercarrier compensation were phantom traffic and access stimulation. Phantom traffic was traffic in which the sending network masked its true origination in order to take advantage of a lower-priced termination fee, for example masking long-distance traffic as local. The problem of access stimulation arose where a LEC made an arrangement with an entity that received many calls but made few (such as a "free" conference call service) and then raised its terminating access fees significantly. Long-distance carriers did not raise their rates on a call-by-call basis to their subscribers, and so they unhappily absorbed the very-high termination fees. In an earlier phase of the Connect America Fund proceeding, the FCC adopted rules designed to limit both of these practices. Connect America Fund, Report and Order and Further Notice of Proposed Rulemaking, 26 FCC Rcd. 17,663 (2011). The move to universal bill-and-keep eliminated the incentive to engage in either practice.

§ 5.E.3. Broadband Universal Service

As discussed above, the 1996 Act required a transition from implicit cross-subsidies to explicit charges that could be distributed to meet the traditional goals of telephone universal service. But although the Act did not, in general, address the internet, its universal service reforms were somewhat more forward-looking. Thus, § 254(b)(3) expressly stated the policy that "[c]onsumers in all regions of the Nation, including low-income consumers and those in rural, insular, and high cost areas, should have access to telecommunications and information services, including interexchange and advanced telecommunications and information services, that are reasonably comparable to those services provided in urban areas and that are available at rates that are reasonably comparable to rates charged for similar services in urban areas." This broad policy of access to advanced telecommunications and information services was made more specific for schools, libraries, and health care providers. In § 254(h), the 1996 Act required the FCC to create a specific universal service policy to ensure that each of these would have "access to advanced telecommunications and information services." § 254(h)(2).

The 1996 Act amendments also allowed the FCC to expand the base of providers to which universal service payments were made (such as allowing it to make universal service payments to wireless companies) and to expand the base of companies that would contribute to universal service funds. In Vonage Holdings Corp. v. FCC, 489 F.3d 1232 (D.C. Cir. 2007), the D.C. Circuit held that § 254(d) authorized the FCC to require "interconnected VoIP" providers to contribute to the universal service fund. Interconnected VoIP providers are those companies offering Voice-over-Internet-Protocol telephony whose services allow customers to receive calls from and make calls to traditional telephone lines.[9] The FCC therefore was able to execute access charges to pursue a policy of expanded broadband access.

In recognition of the need to modernize its universal service policies for a broadband world, the FCC crafted a National Broadband Plan in 2010, which called for expanding support for such connections beyond the realm of schools, libraries, and rural health care providers. FCC, National Broadband Plan, § 8.3 (2010), https://www.fcc.gov/general/national-broadband-plan. In arguing that "the current regulatory framework will not close the broadband availability gap," the FCC charted out a comprehensive reform program to shift from primarily supporting voice communications to supporting a broadband platform. *Id.* Noting that "[t]his reform must be staged over time to realign these systems to support broadband and minimize regulatory uncertainty for investment," it laid out the following blueprint.

> Stage One of this comprehensive reform program starts with building the institutional foundation for reform, identifying funding that can be shifted immediately to jump start broadband deployment in unserved areas, creating the framework for a new Connect America Fund and a Mobility Fund,

9. Section 254(d) has two layers concerning contributions. Its "mandatory" provision states that "[e]very telecommunications carrier that provides interstate telecommunications services shall contribute" to the universal service fund. The section also has a permissive component, that provides that "[a]ny other provider of interstate telecommunications may be required to contribute to the preservation and advancement of universal service in the public interest." The FCC was required to utilize its permissive authority because it had previously characterized VoIP as an "information service." VoIP providers therefore used (and offered) telecommunications, but they did not offer "telecommunications services."

> establishing a long-term vision for ICC [intercarrier compensation], and examining middle-mile costs and pricing. In Stage Two, the FCC will begin disbursements from the CAF [Connect American Fund] and Mobility Fund, while implementing the first step in reducing intercarrier compensation rates and reforming USF [Universal Service Fund] contribution methodology. Stage Three completes the transformation of the legacy High-Cost program, ends support for voice-only networks and completes reforms of ICC.

Id.

In 2011, the FCC issued an order implementing the goals of the National Broadband Plan. The excerpt below is from the Tenth Circuit's opinion discussing and affirming the FCC's broadband universal service program, the Connect America Fund.

FCC 11-161

753 F.3d 1015 (10th Cir. 2014)

Opinion for the court filed by Chief Judge BRISCOE, in which HOLMES, Circuit Judge, concurs. BACHARACH, Circuit Judge, concurring in part and dissenting in part.

BRISCOE, Chief Judge:

In late 2011, the Federal Communications Commission issued an order comprehensively reforming and modernizing its universal service and intercarrier compensation systems. Connect America Fund, Report and Order and Further Notice of Proposed Rulemaking, 26 FCC Rcd. 17,663 (2011) (Order). Petitioners, each of whom were parties to the FCC's rulemaking proceeding below, filed petitions for judicial review of the FCC's Order. [P]etitioners assert a host of challenges to the portions of the Order revising how universal service funds are to be allocated to and employed by recipients. After carefully considering those claims, we find them either unpersuasive or barred from judicial review. Consequently, we deny the petitions to the extent they are based upon those claims.

II. Background

G. The FCC's Report and Order of November 18, 2011

On November 18, 2011, the FCC released its 752-page Order. The Order stated that "[t]he universal service challenge of our time is to ensure that all Americans are served by networks that support high-speed Internet access—in addition to basic voice service—where they live, work, and travel." Order ¶ 5. In turn, the Order stated that the "existing universal service and intercarrier compensation systems [we]re based on decades-old assumptions that fail[ed] to reflect today's networks, the evolving nature of communications services, or the current competitive landscape." Order ¶ 6. In light of these factors, the Order purported to "comprehensively reform[] and modernize[] the universal service and intercarrier compensation systems to ensure that robust, affordable voice and broadband service, both fixed and mobile, [we]re available to Americans throughout the nation." Order ¶ 1.

The Order summarized the key components of the universal service reform the FCC would be implementing. Because the vast majority of Americans "that lack access to residential fixed broadband at or above the [FCC]'s broadband speed benchmark live in areas served by price cap carriers," i.e., "Bell Operating Companies and other large and mid-sized carriers," the FCC stated that it "w[ould] introduce targeted, efficient support for broadband in two phases" for these areas. Order ¶ 21. Phase I of this plan, intended "[t]o spur immediate broadband buildout," would freeze "all existing high-cost support to price cap carriers" and make "an additional $300 million in CAF funding . . . available." Order ¶ 22. "Frozen support w[ould] be immediately subject to the goal of achieving universal availability of voice and broadband, and subject to obligations to build and operate broadband-capable networks in areas unserved by an unsubsidized competitor over time." *Id.* Phase II of the plan "w[ould] use a combination of a forward-looking broadband cost model and competitive bidding to efficiently support deployment of networks providing both voice and broadband service for five years." Order ¶ 23.

With respect to rate-of-return carriers, which "serve[d] less than five percent of access lines in the U.S.," but received "total support from the high-cost fund . . . approaching $2 billion annually," the Order imposed substantial reforms. Order ¶ 26. In particular, any such carriers "receiving legacy universal service support, or CAF support to offset lost ICC revenues," were required to "offer broadband service meeting initial CAF requirements . . . upon their customers' reasonable requests." *Id.* The Order noted that, because of "the economic challenges of extending service in the high-cost areas of the country served by rate-of-return carriers, this flexible approach [would] not require rate-of-return companies to extend service to customers absent such a request." *Id.*

The Order indicated that a CAF Mobility Fund would be created to "promot[e] the universal availability" of "mobile voice and broadband services." Order ¶ 28. Phase I of the CAF Mobility Fund would "provide up to $300 million in one-time support to immediately accelerate deployment of networks for mobile voice and broadband services in unserved areas." *Id.* This support, the Order indicated, would "be awarded through a nationwide reverse auction." *Id.* Phase II of the Mobility Fund would "provide up to $500 million per year in ongoing support" in order to "expand and sustain mobile voice and broadband services in communities in which service would be unavailable absent federal support." *Id.* Included in this $500 million annual budget was "ongoing support for Tribal areas of up to $100 million per year." *Id.* Phase II also anticipated "eliminat[ing] the identical support rule that determines the amount of support for mobile, as well as wireline, competitive ETCs [(eligible telecommunications carriers)]," Order ¶ 29, and the creation of a "Remote Areas Fund" designed "to ensure that Americans living in the most remote areas in the nation, where the cost of deploying traditional terrestrial broadband networks is extremely high, can obtain affordable access through alternative technology platforms, including satellite and unlicensed wireless services," Order ¶ 30.

IV. Universal Service Fund Issues

A. Joint Universal Service Fund Principal Brief

1. Did the FCC's Broadband Requirement Exceed Its Authority under 47 U.S.C. § 254?

[T]he resolution of this issue hinges, in substantial part, on the interpretation of two subsections of § 254: subsection (c)(1) and subsection (e). Addressing these subsections in order, it is beyond dispute that subsection (c)(1) expressly authorizes the FCC to define "periodically" the types of telecommunications services that are encompassed by "universal service" and thus "supported by Federal universal service support mechanisms." Further, there is no question that the FCC, to date, has interpreted the term "telecommunications services" to include only telephone services and not VoIP or other broadband internet services. All that said, however, nothing in the language of subsection (c)(1) serves as an express or implicit limitation on the FCC's authority to determine what a USF recipient may or must do with those funds. More specifically, nothing in subsection (c)(1) expressly or implicitly deprives the FCC of authority to direct that a USF recipient, which necessarily provides some form of "universal service" and has been deemed by a state commission or the FCC to be an eligible telecommunications carrier under 47 U.S.C. § 214(e), use some of its USF funds to provide services or build facilities related to services that fall outside of the FCC's current definition of "universal service." In other words, nothing in the statute limits the FCC's authority to place conditions, such as the broadband requirement, on the use of USF funds.

That leaves § 254(e), the second sentence of which the FCC asserts authorizes it to direct that USF recipients provide broadband Internet access to customers upon reasonable request. The threshold question we must address, under *Chevron*, is whether Congress in § 254(e) "has directly spoken to the precise question at issue," Chevron U.S.A., Inc. v. Natural Res. Def. Council, Inc., 467 U.S. 837, 842 (1984), i.e., did Congress in the second sentence of § 254(e) delegate authority to the FCC to identify precisely what a recipient of USF funds must do with those funds, *id.* at 844.

As noted above, the second sentence of subsection (e) provides that "[an eligible telecommunications] carrier [designated under 47 U.S.C. § 214(e)] that receives [Federal universal service] support shall use that support only for the provision, maintenance, and upgrading of facilities and services for which the support is intended." 47 U.S.C. § 254(e). Quite clearly, this language does not explicitly delegate any authority to the FCC. But the question remains whether this language can reasonably be construed, as the FCC suggests, as an implicit grant of authority to specify what a USF recipient may or must do with the funds?

Upon careful examination, we conclude that the FCC's interpretation of § 254(e) is not "arbitrary, capricious, or manifestly contrary to the statute." *Chevron*, 467 U.S.

at 844. Congress clearly intended, by way of the second sentence of § 254(e), to mandate that USF funds be used by recipients "only for the provision, maintenance, and upgrading of facilities and services for which the support is intended." And it seems highly unlikely that Congress would leave it to USF recipients to determine what "the support is intended" for. Instead, as the FCC suggests, it is reasonable to conclude that Congress left a gap to be filled by the FCC, i.e., for the FCC to determine and specify precisely how USF funds may or must be used.

The FCC also, in our view, reasonably concluded that Congress's use of the terms "facilities" and "service" in the second sentence of § 254(e) afforded the FCC "the flexibility not only to designate the types of telecommunications services for which support would be provided, but also to encourage the deployment of the types of facilities that will best achieve the principles set forth in section 254(b)." Order ¶ 64.

(d) Does Section 706 of the Act, 47 U.S.C. § 1302, Serve as an Independent Grant of Authority to the FCC to Impose the Broadband Requirement?

In a related attack on the FCC's broadband requirement, petitioners argue that section 706 of the Communications Act of 1934 (the Act), 47 U.S.C. § 1302, does not, contrary to the conclusion reached by the FCC in the Order, serve as an independent grant of authority to the FCC.

We reject petitioners' arguments. To be sure, both section 706(a) and section 706(b) focus on "the deployment . . . of advanced telecommunications capability to all Americans." Further, both sections make reference, in terms of achieving such deployment, to the removal of "barriers to infrastructure investment." But that is where the similarities end. As noted, section 706(a) is a general directive stating that the FCC "shall encourage the deployment . . . of advanced telecommunications capability to all Americans . . . by utilizing . . . price cap regulation, regulatory forbearance, measures that promote competition in the local telecommunications market, or other regulating methods that remove barriers to infrastructure investment." The FCC has concluded "that section 706(a) gives [it] an affirmative obligation to encourage the deployment of advanced services, relying on [its] authority established elsewhere in the [1996] Act." In re Deployment of Wireline Services Offering Advanced Telecommunications Capability, Memorandum Opinion and Order, and Notice of Proposed Rulemaking, 13 FCC Rcd. 24,012, 24,046, ¶ 74 (1998). In other words, the FCC has concluded that section 706(a) is "not . . . an independent grant of authority, but rather, . . . a direction to the [FCC] to use the forbearance [and other] authority granted elsewhere in the Act." *Id.* at 24,047 (¶ 76).

In contrast, section 706(b) requires the FCC to perform two related tasks. First, the FCC must conduct an annual inquiry to "determine whether advanced telecommunications capability is being deployed to all Americans in a reasonable and timely fashion." Second, and most importantly for purposes of this appeal, if the FCC's annual "determination is negative," it is required to "take immediate action to accelerate deployment of such capability by removing barriers to infrastructure investment and by promoting competition in the telecommunications market." Unlike section 706(a), section 706(b) does not specify how the FCC is to accomplish this latter task, or otherwise refer to forms of regulatory authority that are afforded to the FCC in other parts of the Act. As the FCC concluded in the Order, section 706(b) thus appears to operate as an independent grant of authority to the FCC "to take steps necessary to fulfill Congress's broadband deployment objectives," and "it is hard to see what additional work section 706(b) does if it is not an independent source of authority." Order ¶ 70.

2. Did the FCC Act Arbitrarily in Simultaneously Imposing the Broadband Requirement and Reducing USF Support?

Petitioners next complain that the FCC's broadband requirement was "impose [d] . . . in the face of a *net reduction* to USF and related intercarrier compensation revenues for rural carriers." Pet'r Br. 3 at 29 (emphasis in original). They argue, in turn, that "[t]his 'do more with less' directive flies in the face of Congress's interrelated requirements under section 254(b) that the FCC use USF to keep quality service 'affordable,' that consumers in high cost areas receive services comparable to those available to their urban counterparts at 'reasonably comparable' rates, that USF support mechanisms be 'predictable and sufficient' to preserve and advance universal service, and that telecommunications service providers contribute equitably to achieve that objective." *Id.* (citing 47 U.S.C. §§ 254(b)(1), (3), (5)). And, they argue, the FCC "made no attempt to measure whether reduced support, coupled with the added costs of the broadband obligation, will allow carriers to meet the universal service objectives of section 254(b)." *Id.* at 30.

This is not the first time we have analyzed § 254(b). In *Qwest Corp.,* we noted that "[t]he plain text of the statute . . . indicates a mandatory duty on the FCC" to "base its universal policies on the principles listed in § 254(b)." Qwest Corp. v. FCC, 258 F.3d 1191, 1200 (10th Cir. 2001). "However," we emphasized, "each of the principles in § 254(b) internally is phrased in terms of 'should,'" which "indicates a recommended course of action, but does not itself imply the obligation associated with 'shall.'" *Id.* Consequently, we held, "the FCC must base its policies on the principles, but any particular principle can be trumped in the appropriate case." *Id.* In other words, "the FCC may exercise its discretion to balance the principles against one another when they conflict, but may not depart from them altogether to achieve some goal." *Id.*

a) Does the Order Fail to Ensure that USF Support for Rural Carriers is Sufficient to Preserve and Advance Universal Service?

Petitioners argue that the FCC failed to ensure that USF support for rural carriers is "'sufficient' . . . to achieve Congress's goals." Pet'r Br. 3 at 30. "The overarching problem," petitioners assert, "is that the [FCC] improperly limited its analysis to whether, without reform [i.e., a fixed budget], USF support would be *excessive.*"

Id. at 31 (emphasis in original). As a result, petitioners assert, "[t]he Order leaves unanalyzed whether reduced USF support will be sufficient to preserve and enhance traditional voice services." *Id.*

The term "sufficient" is mentioned in both § 254(b)(5) ("There should be specific, predictable and sufficient Federal and State mechanisms to preserve and advance universal service.") and § 254(e) ("Any such support should be . . . sufficient to achieve the purposes of this section."). The Fifth Circuit has concluded, however, that "§ 254(b) [simply] identifies a set of principles and does not lay out any specific commands for the FCC," and that "[e]ven § 254(e), which is framed as a direct, statutory command, is ambiguous as to what constitutes 'sufficient' support." Texas Office of Public Util. Counsel v. FCC, 183 F.3d 393, 425 (5th Cir. 1999). Consequently, the Fifth Circuit concluded, a reviewing court need "not consider the language an expression of Congress's 'unambiguous intent' allowing *Chevron* step-one review," and instead need only "review [the FCC's] interpretation for reasonability under *Chevron* step-two." *Id.* at 425–26. Because we agree with the Fifth Circuit, we need determine in this case only that the FCC's "sufficiency" analysis was not arbitrary, capricious, or manifestly contrary to the statute.

In setting the overall budget for the Connect America Fund (CAF), the FCC expressed a "commitment to controlling the size of the universal service fund," and, consequently, it "sought comment on setting an overall budget for the CAF such that the sum of the CAF and any existing legacy high-cost support mechanisms . . . in a given year would remain equal to current funding levels." Order ¶ 121. "[A] broad cross-section of interested stakeholders . . . agreed" with this proposal, "with many urging the [FCC] to set that budget at $4.5 billion per year, the estimated size of the program in fiscal year (FY) 2011." Order ¶ 122. After considering these comments, the FCC concluded that the "establish[ment] [of] a defined budget for the high-cost component of the universal service fund" would "best ensure that [it] ha[d] in place 'specific, predictable, and sufficient' funding mechanisms to ensure [its] universal service objectives." Order ¶ 123. In reaching this conclusion, the FCC expressed concern that, "were the CAF to significantly raise the end-user cost of services, it could undermine [the FCC's] broader policy objectives to promote broadband and mobile deployment and adoption." Order ¶ 124. And, consistent with many of the comments it received, the FCC "establish[ed] an annual funding target, set at the same level as [its] current estimate for the size of the high-cost program for FY 2011, of no more than $4.5 billion." Order ¶ 125. The FCC found "that amount [was not] excessive given" its decision to "expand the high-cost program in important ways to promote broadband and mobility; facilitate intercarrier compensation reform; and preserve universal voice connectivity." *Id.* "At the same time," the FCC found that "a higher budget [was not] warranted, given the substantial reforms [it was] adopt[ing] to modernize [its] legacy funding mechanisms to address long-standing inefficiencies and wasteful spending." *Id.* The FCC also noted that it would need "to evaluate the effect of these reforms before adjusting [its] budget," *id.*, and it specifically stated that it "anticipate[d] . . . revisit[ing] and adjust[ing] accordingly the appropriate size of each of [its] programs by the end of the six-year period, based on market developments," Order ¶ 18.

In sum, the FCC determined that budgetary "sufficiency" for price cap and rate-of-return carriers could be achieved through a combination of measures, including, but not limited to: (1) maintaining current USF funding levels while reducing or eliminating waste and inefficiencies that existed in the prior USF funding scheme; (2) affording carriers the authority to determine which requests for broadband service are reasonable; (3) allowing carriers, when necessary, to use the waiver process; and (4) conducting a budgetary review by the end of six years. And, relatedly, the FCC quite clearly rejected any notion that budgetary "sufficiency" is equivalent to "complete" or "full" funding for carrying out the broadband and other obligations imposed upon carriers who are voluntary recipients of USF funds. In our view, these determinations were not arbitrary, capricious, or manifestly contrary to the directives outlined in § 254. To contrary, the FCC's determinations, particularly when considered in light of the other statutory directives the FCC was charged with achieving, were reasonable and sufficient to survive scrutiny under *Chevron* step-two analysis.

c) Does the Order's Establishment of a Budget Cap, Without Widening the Contribution Base, Fail to Protect Affordability or Ensure Equitable Fund Contributions?

Petitioners argue that the Order's imposition of a USF budget cap, "[w]ithout widening the contribution base, . . . will do nothing to ensure affordability." Pet'r Br. 3 at 34. "The problem," according to petitioners, "is that telecommunications voice revenues are declining." *Id.* As a result, they argue, "[e]ven a fixed budget will have to be recovered from fewer customers, whose individual charges will *go up* (become *less* affordable), unless the contribution base is widened." *Id.* at 34–35 (emphasis in original). In turn, petitioners argue that, even assuming that the FCC acted within its authority in imposing the broadband mandate, "it is inequitable to exempt telecommunications providers who also offer broadband from being required to contribute to universal service from the revenues they receive for such services, particularly since rural carriers assuming a broadband obligation will incur added costs." *Id.* at 35. And, they argue, it is not enough for the FCC to "decide at some unspecified future date . . . whether to expand its contribution base." *Id.*

Two points are clear from the Order and the parties' briefs. First, the Order concluded that the existing contribution framework (which is comprised of assessments paid by interstate telecommunications service providers) was sufficient to satisfy the annual USF budget established in the Order. Second, the FCC chose to address potential changes to the contribution framework in a separate proceeding. More specifically, the FCC in a separate rulemaking docket has sought comment on proposals to reform and modernize how USF contributions are assessed and recovered.

See Universal Service Contribution Methodology; A National Broadband Plan for Our Future, Further Notice of Proposed Rulemaking, 27 FCC Rcd. 5357, 5358 (2012).

As the FCC correctly notes in its appellate response brief, 47 U.S.C. § 154(j) affords it the discretion to "conduct its proceedings in such manner as will best conduce to the proper dispatch of business and to the ends of justice." FCC Br. 3 at 68. And we agree with the FCC that its decision to address USF contributions not in the Order, but rather in a separate proceeding, falls well within that discretion.

3. Does the FCC's Use of Auctions to Distribute USF Violate § 214(e)?

Petitioners contend that the FCC's use of auctions to distribute USF violates 47 U.S.C. § 214(e). According to petitioners, "Congress," by way of § 214(e), "expressly gave State commissions the job of deciding *who* would receive universal service support and *where* supported services would be advertised and provided by the carrier." Pet'r Br. 3 at 40 (emphasis in original). More specifically, petitioners assert, § 214(e) "provides that only ETCs may receive USF support and that, with narrow exceptions, only states may designate ETCs and their service areas." *Id.* at 39. And, they assert, "[o]nce an ETC is designated by a state commission to serve a particular service area under section 214(e)(2), it is eligible to receive funding and must offer and advertise the supported services throughout its service area." *Id.*

Petitioners complain that "[t]he Order contravenes this statutory scheme in two respects." *Id.* "First," petitioners assert, the Order "adopted various competitive bidding mechanisms to distribute USF support, and provided that the [FCC] will define the geographic areas to be auctioned off." *Id.* at 39–40. "Second," petitioners assert, "the FCC created an entirely new 'conditional designation,' nowhere mentioned in the statute, that will require state commissions to conditionally designate 'ETCs' before auctions to distribute Mobility Fund support are concluded." *Id.* at 40.

The key flaw in petitioners' argument, as the FCC correctly notes in its response brief, is that "it conflates eligibility for subsidies with the right to receive subsidies." FCC Br. 3 at 62. To be sure, § 214(e) authorizes state commissions to decide which entities will be designated as ETCs and, relatedly, to determine the service areas served by those ETCs. But nothing in § 214(e) gives authority to the state commissions to allocate USF funds, nor does § 214(e) give a designated ETC the absolute right to receive USF funds. Rather, as the language of § 214(e)(1) makes clear, "[a] common carrier designated as an eligible telecommunications carrier under paragraph (2), (3), or (6) shall be *eligible* to receive universal service support in accordance with section 254 [47 USCS § 254]." 47 U.S.C. § 214(e) (emphasis added). Had Congress intended designated ETCs to automatically receive USF funds, it could and should have omitted the phrase "be eligible to" from the language of § 214(e)(1).

4. Was the FCC's Decision to Reduce USF Support in Areas with "artificially low" End User Rates Unlawful or Arbitrary?

Petitioners contend that the FCC's decision to reduce USF support in areas with "artificially low" end user rates was both unlawful and arbitrary.

The portion of the Order being challenged by petitioners is a section entitled "Reducing High Cost Loop Support for Artificially Low End-User Rates." Therein, the Order "adopt[ed] a rule," applicable "to both rate-of-return carriers and price cap companies," "to limit high-cost support where end-user rates do not meet a specified local floor." Order ¶ 235. In doing so, the Order noted there was "evidence in the record" indicating that "there [were] a number of carriers with local rates that [we]re significantly lower than rates that urban consumers pay." Order ¶ 235. "For example," the Order noted, there were "two carriers in Iowa and one carrier in Minnesota [that] offer[ed] local residential rates below $5 per month." *Id.* The Order concluded that Congress did not "intend[] to create a regime in which universal service subsidizes artificially low local rates in rural areas when it adopted the reasonably comparable principle in section 254(b); rather, [the Order concluded], it [wa]s clear from the overall context and structure of the statute that its purpose [wa]s to ensure that rates in rural areas not be significantly higher than in urban areas." *Id.*

Petitioners argue that "the de facto effect of the Order "is that the FCC is setting local rates." Pet'r Br. 3 at 41. "And," they argue, "since local rate setting is exclusively the province of state commissions under the Act, 47 U.S.C. § 152(b), the Order unlawfully usurps a power reserved to the states." *Id.* "The perverse result of this portion of the Order, petitioners argue, is that to avoid depriving local carriers of needed USF support, states must raise some local rates above levels they would have deemed reasonable." *Id.* at 41–42.

The FCC asserts, however, and we agree, that we are not bound to examine the "practical effect" of an agency order. As the District of Columbia Circuit has noted, "no canon of administrative law requires [a reviewing court] to view the regulatory scope of agency actions in terms of their practical or even foreseeable effects." *Id.* As the District of Columbia Circuit noted, "[o]therwise, [a reviewing court] would have to conclude, for example, that the Environmental Protection Agency regulates the automobile industry when it requires states and localities to comply with national ambient air quality standards, or that the Department of Commerce regulates foreign manufacturers when it collects tariffs on foreign-made goods." *Id.* Thus, we summarily reject the petitioners' argument regarding the practical effect of the Order's new rate floors.

In any event, to the extent the Order encourages states to adjust local rates to ensure that they are not excessively low in comparison to urban rates, that appears to be permissible under, and indeed is consistent with, the universal service principles outlined in the Act. As we noted in *Qwest Corp.*, "the FCC may not simply assume that the states will act on their own to preserve and advance universal service." 258 F.3d at 1204. Rather, the FCC "remains obligated to create some inducement . . . for the states to assist in implementing the goals of universal service," i.e., in this case to ensure that rural rates are not artificially low. *Id.* The portion of the Order at issue appears to serve that purpose by encouraging states to set rural rates that are least comparable to urban rates.

5. Does the Order Unlawfully Deprive Rural Carriers of a Reasonable Opportunity to Recover Their Prudently-Incurred Costs?

Petitioners argue that the Order unlawfully deprives rural carriers of a reasonable opportunity to recover their prudently-incurred costs. In support, petitioners assert that "they are required to continue to provide current services and, at considerable additional expense, to provide broadband service as well." Pet'r Br. 3 at 43. "At the same time," they assert, "their ICC revenue streams are being narrowed and their USF support will be capped, reduced or eliminated outright (depending on their regulatory status)." *Id.* In turn, petitioners argue that "[i]t would be one thing if the [FCC] had tied the reductions in USF support to a determination that the individual carriers had imprudently incurred costs, or that they were recovering the costs of investments not 'used and useful' in delivering regulated services, or that these costs could somehow be recovered from end users without violating the statutory universal service principle calling for rural service rates to be reasonably comparable with those in urban areas." *Id.* at 44. "But," they assert, "the FCC made none of these findings." *Id.* at 45. Lastly, petitioners acknowledge that the Order contains a waiver provision, but they argue that that provision applies only in narrow circumstances and does not reflect "[t]he constitutional test," which they assert "is whether the carrier has been afforded a reasonable opportunity to recover its costs." *Id.*

The FCC asserts, in response, that all of this amounts to an "unsubstantiated takings claim" that "is not ripe." FCC Br. 3 at 39. The FCC notes that the Order made clear that if "any rate-of-return carrier can effectively demonstrate that it needs additional support to avoid constitutionally confiscatory rates, the [FCC] will consider a waiver request for additional support." Order ¶ 294. The FCC thus argues that "[n]o takings claim is ripe until a party has invoked that process and been denied." FCC Br. 3 at 39.

In any event, however, it is clear to us that the FCC did not act arbitrarily in implementing changes to the USF mechanisms. Notably, the Order includes a section expressly discussing the "Impact of These Reforms on Rate-of-Return Carriers and the Communities They Serve." In that section, the FCC concluded that its "intercarrier compensation reforms" would provide rate-of-return carriers with "greater certainty and a more predictable flow of revenues than the status quo." Order ¶ 286. The FCC further noted that the Order's "package of universal service reforms [wa]s targeted at eliminating inefficiencies and closing gaps in [the] system, not at making indiscriminate industry-wide reductions." Order ¶ 287. Relatedly, the FCC noted that its "reforms w[ould] not affect all carriers in the same manner or in the same magnitude," but it expressed confidence "that carriers that invest and operate in a prudent manner will be minimally affected." Order ¶ 289. In support, the FCC stated that its "analysis show[ed] that nearly 9 out of 10 rate-of-return carriers w[ould] see reductions in high-cost universal service receipts of less than 20 percent annually, . . . approximately 7 out of 10 w[ould] see reductions of less than 10 percent, . . . almost 34 percent . . . w[ould] see no reductions whatsoever, and more than 12 percent . . . w[ould] see an increase in high-cost universal service receipts." Order ¶ 290. The FCC also "reject[ed] the sweeping argument that the rule changes . . . would unlawfully necessarily affect a taking." Order ¶ 293. And it emphasized "that carriers have no vested property interest in USF." *Id.* More specifically, it noted "there [wa]s no statutory provision or Commission rule that provides companies with a vested right to continued receipt of support at current levels, and we are not aware of any other, independent source of law that gives particular companies an entitlement to ongoing USF support." Order ¶ 293. Lastly, the FCC concluded that "carriers ha[d] not shown that elimination of USF support w[ould] result in confiscatory end-user rates." Order ¶ 294. In reaching this conclusion, the FCC noted that, "[t]o the extent that any rate-of-return carriers can effectively demonstrate that it needs additional support to avoid constitutionally confiscatory rates, the Commission will consider a waiver request for additional support." *Id.*

Nothing about this analysis is remotely arbitrary or capricious. Rather, we conclude the FCC's analysis is both reasoned and reasonable. Further, the FCC's analysis is entirely consistent with the overarching universal service principles outlined in 47 U.S.C. § 254(b), including the principle that "[t]here should be specific, predictable and sufficient Federal and State mechanisms to preserve and advance universal service." 47 U.S.C. § 254(b)(5).

8. Does Eliminating USF Support for the Highest-Cost Areas Defeat the Very Purpose of Universal Service?

Petitioners complain that the Order delays indefinitely, and thereby effectively eliminates, support for remote, so-called "extremely high-cost areas," and thus defeats the very purpose of universal service. Pet'r Br. 3 at 52.

We begin our analysis of this claim by outlining the Order's treatment of universal funding for "extremely high-cost" service areas. The Order, in pertinent part, "adopt[s] Phase II of the Connect America Fund: a framework for extending broadband to millions of unserved locations over a five-year period, including households, businesses, and community anchor institutions, while sustaining existing voice and broadband services." Order ¶ 156. The primary focus of CAF Phase II is to provide "increased support to areas served by price cap carriers." Order ¶ 159. Those areas, the Order noted, accounted for "more than 83 percent of the unserved locations in the nation" in 2010, but only "receive[d] approximately 25 percent of high-cost support." Order ¶ 158.

"CAF Phase II will have an annual budget of no more than $1.8 billion," which will be distributed "us[ing] a combination of competitive bidding and a new forward-looking model of the cost of constructing modern multi-purpose networks." *Id.* "Using th[is] [forward-looking] model," the FCC "will estimate the support necessary to serve areas where costs are above a specified benchmark, but below a second 'extremely high-cost' benchmark." *Id.* The FCC "delegate[d] to the Wireline

Competition Bureau the responsibility for setting the extremely high-cost threshold in conjunction with adoption of a final-cost model." Order ¶ 169.

Relatedly, the Order created a "Remote Areas Fund" intended "to ensure that the less than one percent of Americans living in remote areas where the cost of deploying traditional terrestrial broadband networks is extremely high can obtain affordable broadband." Order ¶ 1224. The Remote Areas Fund, the Order indicated, will receive "$100 million in annual CAF funding to maximize the availability of affordable broadband in such areas." Order ¶ 168. In the FNPRM portion of the Order, the FCC "s[ought] comment on how best to utilize" the Remote Areas Fund. *Id.* The Order proposed that the "universal service goals [could be fulfilled in extremely high-cost areas] by taking advantage of services such as next-generation broadband satellite service or wireless internet service provider (WISP)." *Id.* The Order also sought "comment on how to structure the Remote Areas Fund." Order ¶ 1225. In doing so, the Order proposed several alternative structures, including "a portable consumer subsidy," *id.*, "a competitive bidding process," Order ¶ 1226, and "a competitive proposal evaluation process," Order ¶ 1227.

As the FCC notes in its response brief, until the Remote Areas Fund distribution rules "are in place, extremely high-cost areas will continue to receive support under existing mechanisms for price cap and rate-of-return carriers." FCC Br. 3 at 64 (citing Order ¶¶ 133 (freezing support for price-cap carriers), 195 (maintaining support for rate-of-return carriers)).

In light of these undisputed facts, it is readily apparent that the Order neither "indefinitely" delays distribution of the Remote Areas Fund, nor effectively denies USF funding to extremely high-cost areas. Further, any specific challenges that petitioners may seek to assert against the manner in which the Remote Areas Fund is distributed are not yet ripe.

V. Conclusion

We deny the petitions for review.

BACHARACH, Circuit Judge, concurring in part and dissenting in part.

I join virtually all of Chief Judge Briscoe's thorough, persuasive opinion. But, I respectfully dissent on Part IV(A)(2). There, the majority rejects the Petitioners' challenge to the sufficiency of the budget for the Universal Service Fund. On this limited issue, I respectfully dissent. In my view, the FCC failed to supply a rational basis for its conclusion that an annual budget of $4.5 billion would suffice with the new requirements for broadband capability. In this respect, I believe the FCC acted arbitrarily in violation of the Administrative Procedure Act.

Notes and Questions

1. Other Challenges. The Tenth Circuit rejected a number of other challenges that we have not excerpted here, including specific and vigorous challenges brought by wireless carriers, rural LECs, and tribal entities.

2. Public Interest Obligations. Note that the FCC required that carriers, as a condition of receiving support, commit to providing both voice service and broadband service (under specific metrics). The FCC ensured the maintenance of voice service, but noted that such service would be provided over broadband network infrastructure. Is that a sensible approach? On what basis would you argue for a different one?

3. Section 706. Did the FCC need to rely on § 706 in addition to § 254 for authority to reorient universal service to support broadband deployment? Note that the FCC's authority under § 706 is also controversial in the net neutrality context, as is discussed in Chapter 6. There, the argument is parallel — whether the section gives the FCC general authority to regulate and promote internet services, or whether the FCC is limited to the specific (deregulatory) tools identified in § 706(a).

4. Even Less for the States. Recall the significant shrinking of the states' role under the intercarrier compensation part of the order, discussed above. Here, the court affirmed the FCC's decision to impose service requirements and limit funding through the auction mechanism. The states still had a role (the court says) by designating eligible telecommunications carriers, but now not all ETCs will receive universal service funds. Could Congress, in the 1996 Act, really have intended such a diminished role for the states? Does that mean the FCC is wrong?

5. Why Not a Broad-Based Tax? The obvious alternative to USF payments is to collect funds for broadband universal service via a broad-based tax. (After all, assuming that we want to subsidize internet or telecommunications for particular groups, there is no requirement that the funds come from those services.) Broad-based taxes exist of course — notably, taxes on all income, from whatever source derived. Why not raise the broadband universal service funds through such a tax, thereby ending the regulatory arbitrage opportunities created by a more narrowly focused tax?

Is the answer that money to fund a service should come from users of that service? After all, governments often fund highway construction from highway tolls. But, if that is so, is it consistent with the goals of expanding the network? The answer might be yes, if we assume that the number of net givers who will abandon the network because of higher fees will be smaller than the number of net receivers who will join the network because of the subsidies they will receive. But that takes us back to the question of evaluating the effect of the universal service program, which might be difficult to do. And, in any event, wouldn't we achieve greater expansion of telecommunications service if the fee were not levied on that service?

Is the answer instead that voters would not support an increase in income taxes to fund these programs, but they will not complain as loudly about fees on broadband services because they are not as aware of the taxes they effectively pay on such services? On this reasoning, a program that might be politically untenable if funded via a broad-based tax becomes politically viable if funded via a fee on telecommunications services. If that is not the explanation, why not move to a broad-based tax? If it is the explanation, does it cast doubt on the wisdom of the program? To put the point differently, if a program would be unpopular if voters were aware of it and thus is viable only because voters are unaware of it, should that tell members of Congress who support the programs that maybe they have a faulty sense of what is in the public interest? Or would continuation of the program be an example of legislators appropriately acting in the public's best interest, even if the public (or a majority of it, anyway) does not believe that it is in their interest?

6. How Much to Spend? The National Broadband Plan noted that bringing service to the 250,000 housing units with the highest gaps (less than 0.2% of houses in America) cost an average of $56,000 per house. Should the government tell some Americans that it is just too expensive for the government to pay to give them broadband service? If so, where should it draw the line?

7. Further Expansion of Broadband Universal Service. In 1985, the FCC established two programs, known as Lifeline and Link-Up, that were designed to reduce initial connection (Link-Up) and monthly charges (Lifeline) for low-income consumers. MTS and WATS Market Structure, Amendment of Part 67 of the Commission's Rules and Establishment of a Joint Board, 50 Fed. Reg. 939 (1985). The FCC stated that it needed to create these programs "to prevent degradation of universal service and the division of our society into information 'haves' and 'have nots.'" *Id.* at 941, ¶ 9. In 2016, the FCC made good on its promises to transition traditional universal service programs to support broadband access by modifying these programs. Lifeline and Link Up Reform and Modernization, Third Report and Order, Further Report and Order, and Order on Reconsideration, 31 FCC Rcd. 3962 (2016). In this order, the FCC made Lifeline funding available for standalone broadband services and mixed voice and broadband services, while setting minimum standards for such services and attempting to streamline processes by which carriers can qualify as eligible providers. Indeed, the FCC decided that, following a transition period, funding would not be allowed for standalone voice services.

In a companion order, the FCC also set specific broadband buildout requirements for rate-of-return carriers still receiving high-cost support. Connect America Fund, Report and Order, Order and Order on Reconsideration, and Further Notice of Proposed Rulemaking, 31 FCC Rcd. 3087 (2016). The FCC allowed rate-of-return carriers to select quicker targets in exchange for greater funding, but it made clear that it would "adopt specific broadband deployment obligations for all rate-of-return carriers, and not just for those that elect the voluntary path to the [increased funding] model." *Id.* at 3092, ¶ 7. To respond to competitive concerns, the FCC also adopted what it called a "robust challenge process" to ensure that subsidized carriers would buildout only to those areas not currently being served by "a qualifying unsubsidized competitor." *Id.* at 3092, ¶ 8.

8. Wireless Broadband Support. In a 2017 order, the FCC adopted a framework to ensure broadband wireless coverage throughout the United States. Connect America Fund: Universal Service Reform — Mobility Fund, Report and Order and Further Notice of Proposed Rulemaking, 32 FCC Rcd. 2152 (2017). Shifting more than $4.5 billion from existing programs, the new framework had three key elements. First, the FCC committed to subsidize the deployment of 4G LTE service, the then-most-current deployed technology for wireless broadband, to ensure equivalent coverage of uncovered areas. Second, the FCC established a process to ensure that funds would only be used to subsidized buildouts in uncovered areas. If an area had an unsubsidized commercial provider, the FCC stated that buildout subsidies in that area constitute unfair competition. And, third, the FCC provided that it would adopt a "reverse auction" framework for new buildouts, to ensure than new construction occurs at the lowest cost. Estimating that uncovered areas included three million Americans, the FCC reaffirmed its commitment to wireless broadband universal service.

Chapter 6

Regulating Internet Access

Introduction

The previous chapter discussed assorted regulatory strategies to restrain the dominance of telecommunications monopolies, including preventing networks from offering favorable treatment to some customers while discriminating against others. This chapter discusses one particular but especially important policy debate regarding access: network neutrality for broadband internet access service.[1] This debate arises within a broader question of how (and whether) to regulate broadband internet access service, and documenting the debate illustrates central legal and policy challenges in internet and telecommunications policy.

Net neutrality involves three intertwined questions that arise throughout this chapter. First, what, if any, authority does the FCC have to regulate broadband providers? Congress has not given the FCC explicit authority to regulate internet access (or much of anything else about the internet, with the notable exception of its failed attempts at regulating sexual content, discussed in Chapter 11). So the FCC (and the courts) have had to look to more general statutory provisions. At one extreme is the view that the FCC has authority to regulate all "interstate . . . communication by wire or radio" so long as its regulations fit within the general purposes of the Act, 47 U.S.C. §151. At the other extreme is the view that the FCC has authority only to regulate the types of services specifically described in the main titles of the Act (i.e., common carrier, broadcast, and cable services). Under the broader view, the FCC has regulatory authority over broadband transmission because broadband is undoubtedly communications. Under the narrower view, the FCC does not have authority over broadband transmission unless the service provided via broadband is itself a common carrier, broadcast, or cable service over which Congress has expressly granted the FCC authority. In between these views is the position finally

1. The particular focus of regulatory concern in the net neutrality proceeding, and thus a major focus of this chapter, is broadband internet access service, which the FCC defines as "[a] mass-market retail service by wire or radio that provides the capability to transmit data to and receive data from all or substantially all Internet endpoints, including any capabilities that are incidental to and enable the operation of the communications service, but excluding dial-up Internet access service." Preserving the Open Internet, Report and Order, 25 FCC Rcd. 17,905, ¶ 44 (2010); Protecting and Promoting the Open Internet, Report and Order on Remand, Declaratory Ruling, and Order, 30 FCC Rcd. 5601, 5610, ¶ 25 (2015); Restoring Internet Freedom, Declaratory Ruling, Report and Order, and Order, 33 FCC Rcd. 311, 318–19, ¶ 21 (2018).

adopted by the FCC and partially endorsed by the D.C. Circuit, that Congress did grant the FCC at least some specific authority over internet communications.

The second question is closely related: What kind of communications service is broadband internet access service? Under the narrow view of the FCC's regulatory authority, classification means a great deal because it ties broadband service into the specific regulatory scheme created by Congress in one of the titles of the Act. Even under the broader view, classification is important, because the constraints on the FCC's authority may depend on whether a service falls within an established category or within the FCC's residual authority over all interstate communications.

Third, what regulation of broadband networks is appropriate? That is, once we have answered the questions about regulatory authority, what forms of regulation make the most sense? These three inquiries interact with one another: for instance, classification decisions (question two) may be affected by one's view of the appropriate regulation to be applied (question three). Indeed, that has been the story of broadband internet access regulation—the regulatory goals of the FCC have had a great influence on the regulatory classification of internet access.

§ 6.A. Regulatory Characterization of Broadband Services

One of the linchpin requirements of common carrier regulation is that the carrier provide service on a nondiscriminatory basis. 47 U.S.C. § 202(a). Although the matter was in some doubt early on, U.S. regulators and courts long ago established that federal common carrier law requires carriers to treat their competitors the same as other customers—that is, to sell to competitors any service made generally available, even if the competitor would turn around and use that service as part of an offering that competed with the carrier itself. In the *Computer II* inquiry discussed in Chapter 4, the FCC adopted rules that confirmed these general principles in the context of "information services" (then called "enhanced services") offered by facilities-based common carriers. That is, these incumbent common carriers were required to provide nondiscriminatory access to any underlying transport services ("telecommunications services") that the carriers used to provide their own information services, so that the information services market could develop in a competitive fashion. This requirement ensured that rival, unaffiliated information service providers could gain equal access to essential inputs.

When dial-up internet access services began sprouting up in the early to mid 1990s, internet service providers (ISPs) took advantage of the right to gain access to telecommunications infrastructure on the same terms that incumbents applied to other services, including the incumbents' own. That form of "open access," among other things, enabled over 3,000 providers to provide dial-up internet access. And when incumbent telephone companies started offering broadband digital subscriber line service (DSL) internet access, the FCC applied the same regime. Broadband transmission was a telecommunications service that the telephone companies had to offer to ISPs on an unbundled basis (i.e., as a stand-alone service the competitors could purchase and use to offer competing internet access service). The incumbents could offer their own internet access, but they had to make their transmission capacity available to competing ISPs. Deployment of Wireline Services Offering Advanced Telecommunications Capability, Memorandum Opinion and Order, and Notice of Proposed Rulemaking, 13 FCC Rcd. 24,012, 24,030–31, ¶¶ 36–37, (1998).

Cable companies had never been regulated as traditional common carriers and so were not subject to this regime. When cable companies began to offer cable broadband internet services, they argued that they should not be subject to the regime applicable to DSL service, and thus should not be required to unbundle access to their underlying infrastructure and provide it to would-be competitors. Needless to say, ISPs complained, calling on the FCC to make clear that the Communications Act required cable companies to provide such access.

In Inquiry Concerning High-Speed Access to the Internet Over Cable and Other Facilities, Declaratory Ruling and Notice of Proposed Rulemaking, 17 FCC Rcd. 4798 (2002), the FCC concluded that cable modem service was an information service, not a telecommunications service, under the Communications Act:

> As currently provisioned, cable modem service supports such functions as email, newsgroups, maintenance of the user's World Wide Web presence, and the DNS [domain name system]. Accordingly, we find that cable modem service, an Internet access service, is an information service. This is so regardless of whether subscribers use all of the functions provided as part of the service, such as email or web-hosting, and regardless of whether every cable modem service provider offers each function that could be included in the service. As currently provisioned, cable modem service is a single, integrated service that enables the subscriber to utilize Internet access service through a cable provider's facilities and to realize the benefits of a comprehensive service offering.

Id. at 4822–23, ¶ 38 (footnotes omitted). Several parties challenged the FCC's order (which we do not excerpt because it is discussed in the following opinion), and the Supreme Court rejected that challenge in the case excerpted below.

National Cable & Telecommunications Ass'n v. Brand X Internet Services

545 U.S. 967 (2005)

THOMAS, J., delivered the opinion of the Court, in which REHNQUIST, C.J., and STEVENS, O'CONNOR, KENNEDY, and BREYER, JJ., joined. STEVENS, J., and BREYER, J., filed concurring opinions. SCALIA, J., filed a dissenting opinion, in which SOUTER and GINSBURG, JJ., joined as to Part I.

JUSTICE THOMAS delivered the opinion of the Court.

Title II of the Communications Act of 1934 subjects all providers of "telecommunications servic[e]" to mandatory common-carrier regulation, § 153(44). In the order under review, the Federal Communications Commission concluded that cable companies that sell broadband Internet service do not provide "telecommunications servic[e]" as the Communications Act defines that term, and hence are exempt from mandatory common-carrier regulation under Title II. We must decide whether that conclusion is a lawful construction of the Communications Act under Chevron U.S.A., Inc. v. Natural Resources Defense Council, Inc., 467 U. S. 837 (1984), and the Administrative Procedure Act, 5 U.S.C. § 555 et seq. We hold that it is.

II

At issue in these cases is the proper regulatory classification under the Communications Act of broadband cable Internet service. The Act, as amended by the Telecommunications Act of 1996, defines two categories of regulated entities relevant to these cases: telecommunications carriers and information-service providers. The Act regulates telecommunications carriers, but not information-service providers, as common carriers. Telecommunications carriers, for example, must charge just and reasonable, nondiscriminatory rates to their customers, 47 U.S.C. §§ 201–09, design their systems so that other carriers can interconnect with their communications networks, § 251(a)(1), and contribute to the federal "universal service" fund, § 254(d). These provisions are mandatory, but the Commission must forbear from applying them if it determines that the public interest requires it. §§ 160(a), (b). Information-service providers, by contrast, are not subject to mandatory common-carrier regulation under Title II, though the Commission has jurisdiction to impose additional regulatory obligations under its Title I ancillary jurisdiction to regulate interstate and foreign communications, *see* §§ 151–61.

These two statutory classifications originated in the late 1970s, as the Commission developed rules to regulate data-processing services offered over telephone wires. That regime, the "Computer II" rules, distinguished between "basic" service (like telephone service) and "enhanced" service (computer-processing service offered over telephone lines). Amendment of Section 64.702 of the Commission's Rules and Regulations (Second Computer Inquiry), 77 F.C.C. 2d 384, 417–23, ¶¶ 86–101 (1980) (hereinafter Computer II). The Computer II rules defined both basic and enhanced services by reference to how the consumer perceives the service being offered.

In particular, the Commission defined "basic service" as "a pure transmission capability over a communications path that is virtually transparent in terms of its interaction with customer supplied information." *Id.* at 420, ¶ 96. By "pure" or "transparent" transmission, the Commission meant a communications path that enabled the consumer to transmit an ordinary-language message to another point, with no computer processing or storage of the information, other than the processing or storage needed to convert the message into electronic form and then back into ordinary language for purposes of transmitting it over the network—such as via a telephone or a facsimile. Basic service was subject to common-carrier regulation.

"[E]nhanced service," however, was service in which "computer processing applications [were] used to act on the content, code, protocol, and other aspects of the subscriber's information," such as voice and data storage services, *id.* at 420–21, ¶ 97, as well as "protocol conversion" (i.e., ability to communicate between networks that employ different data-transmission formats), *id.* at 421–22, ¶ 99. By contrast to basic service, the Commission decided not to subject providers of enhanced service, even enhanced service offered via transmission wires, to Title II common-carrier regulation. The Commission explained that it was unwise to subject enhanced service to common-carrier regulation given the "fast-moving, competitive market" in which they were offered. *Id.* at 434, ¶ 129.

The definitions of the terms "telecommunications service" and "information service" established by the 1996 Act are similar to the Computer II basic- and enhanced-service classifications. "Telecommunications service"—the analog to basic service—is "the offering of telecommunications for a fee directly to the public . . . regardless of the facilities used." 47 U.S.C. § 153(46). "Telecommunications" is "the transmission, between or among points specified by the user, of information of the user's choosing, without change in the form or content of the information as sent and received." § 153(43). "Telecommunications carrier[s]"—those subjected to mandatory Title II common-carrier regulation—are defined as "provider[s] of telecommunications services." § 153(44). And "information service"—the analog to enhanced service—is "the offering of a capability for generating, acquiring, storing, transforming, processing, retrieving, utilizing, or making available information via telecommunications . . ." § 153(20).

In September 2000, the Commission initiated a rulemaking proceeding to, among other things, apply these classifications to cable companies that offer broadband Internet service directly to consumers. In March 2002, that rulemaking culminated in the Declaratory Ruling under review in these cases. Inquiry Concerning High-Speed Access to the Internet Over Cable and Other Facilities, Declaratory Ruling and Notice of Proposed Rulemaking, 17 FCC Rcd. 4798 (2002) (hereinafter Declaratory Ruling). In the Declaratory Ruling, the Commission concluded that broadband Internet service provided by cable companies is an "information service" but not a "telecommunications service" under the Act, and therefore not subject to mandatory Title II common-carrier regulation. In support of this conclusion, the Commission relied heavily on its Universal Service Report. *See* Declaratory Ruling at 4821–22, ¶¶ 36–37 (citing Federal-State Joint Board on Universal Service, 13 FCC Rcd. 11,501 (1998) (hereinafter Universal Service Report or Report)). The Universal Service Report classified "non-facilities-based" ISPs—those that do not own the transmission facilities they use to connect the end user to the Internet—solely as information-service providers. *See* Universal Service Report at 11,533, ¶ 67. Unlike those ISPs, cable companies own the cable lines they use to provide Internet access. Nevertheless, in the Declaratory Ruling, the Commission found no basis in the statutory definitions for treating cable companies differently from non-facilities-based ISPs: Both offer "a single, integrated service that enables the subscriber to utilize Internet access service ... and to realize the benefits of a comprehensive service offering." Declaratory Ruling at 4823, ¶ 38. Because Internet access provides a capability for manipulating and storing information, the Commission concluded that it was an information service. *Id.*

The integrated nature of Internet access and the high-speed wire used to provide Internet access led the Commission to conclude that cable companies providing Internet access are not telecommunications providers. This conclusion, the Commission reasoned, followed from the logic of the Universal Service Report. The Report had concluded that, though Internet service "involves data transport elements" because "an Internet access provider must enable the movement of information between customers' own computers and distant computers with which those customers seek to interact," it also "offers end users information-service capabilities inextricably intertwined with data transport." Universal Service Report at 11,539–40, ¶ 80. ISPs, therefore, were not "offering ... telecommunications ... directly to the public," §153(46), and so were not properly classified as telecommunications carriers, *see id.* at 11,540, ¶ 81. In other words, the Commission reasoned that consumers use their cable modems not to transmit information "transparently," such as by using a telephone, but instead to obtain Internet access.

The Commission applied this same reasoning to cable companies offering broadband Internet access. Its logic was that, like non-facilities-based ISPs, cable companies do not "offe[r] telecommunications service to the end user, but rather ... merely us[e] telecommunications to provide end users with cable modem service." Declaratory Ruling at 4824, ¶ 41. Though the Commission declined to apply mandatory Title II common-carrier regulation to cable companies, it invited comment on whether under its Title I jurisdiction it should require cable companies to offer other ISPs access to their facilities on common-carrier terms. *Id.* at 4839, ¶ 72.

IV

[*Chevron*'s framework applies to the Commission's interpretation of "telecommunications service."] We next address whether the Commission's construction of the definition of "telecommunications service," 47 U.S.C. §153(46), is a permissible reading of the Communications Act under the *Chevron* framework. *Chevron* established a familiar two-step procedure for evaluating whether an agency's interpretation of a statute is lawful. At the first step, we ask whether the statute's plain terms "directly addres[s] the precise question at issue." 467 U.S. at 843. If the statute is ambiguous on the point, we defer at step two to the agency's interpretation so long as the construction is "a reasonable policy choice for the agency to make." *Id.* at 845. The Commission's interpretation is permissible at both steps.

A

We first set forth our understanding of the interpretation of the Communications Act that the Commission embraced. The issue before the Commission was whether cable companies providing cable modem service are providing a "telecommunications service" in addition to an "information service."

The Commission first concluded that cable modem service is an "information service," a conclusion unchallenged here. The Act defines "information service" as "the offering of a capability for generating, acquiring, storing, transforming, processing, retrieving, utilizing, or making available information via telecommunications. . . ." § 153(20). Cable modem service is an information service, the Commission reasoned, because it provides consumers with a comprehensive capability for manipulating information using the Internet via high-speed telecommunications. That service enables users, for example, to browse the World Wide Web, to transfer files from file archives available on the Internet via the "File Transfer Protocol," and to access e-mail and Usenet newsgroups. Like other forms of Internet service, cable modem service also gives users access to the Domain Name System (DNS). DNS, among other things, matches the Web page addresses that end users type into their browsers (or "click" on) with the Internet Protocol (IP) addresses of the servers containing the Web pages the users wish to access. All of these features, the Commission concluded, were part of the information service that cable companies provide consumers. Declaratory Ruling ¶¶ 36–38.

At the same time, the Commission concluded that cable modem service was not "telecommunications service." "Telecommunications service" is "the offering of telecommunications for a fee directly to the public." 47 U.S.C. § 153(46). "Telecommunications," in turn, is defined as "the transmission, between or among points specified by the user, of information of the user's choosing, without change in the form or content of the information as sent and received." § 153(43). The Commission conceded that, like all information-service providers, cable companies use "telecommunications" to provide consumers with Internet service; cable companies provide such service via the high-speed wire that transmits signals to and from an end user's computer. Declaratory Ruling ¶ 40. For the Commission, however, the question whether cable broadband Internet providers "offer" telecommunications involved more than whether telecommunications was one necessary component of cable modem service. Instead, whether that service also includes a telecommunications "offering" "tur[ned] on the nature of the functions the *end user* is offered," *id.* at 4822, ¶ 38 (emphasis added), for the statutory definition of "telecommunications service" does not "res[t] on the particular types of facilities used," *id.* at 4821, ¶ 35; *see* § 153(46) (definition of "telecommunications service" applies "regardless of the facilities used").

Seen from the consumer's point of view, the Commission concluded, cable modem service is not a telecommunications offering because the consumer uses the high-speed wire always in connection with the information-processing capabilities provided by Internet access, and because the transmission is a necessary component of Internet access: "As provided to the end user the telecommunications is part and parcel of cable modem service and is integral to its other capabilities." Declaratory Ruling at 4823, ¶ 39. The wire is used, in other words, to access the World Wide Web, newsgroups, and so forth, rather than "transparently" to transmit and receive ordinary-language messages without computer processing or storage of the message. The integrated character of this offering led the Commission to conclude that cable modem service is not a "stand-alone," transparent offering of telecommunications. *Id.* at 4823–25, ¶¶ 41–43.

B

This construction passes *Chevron*'s first step. Respondents argue that it does not, on the ground that cable companies providing Internet service necessarily "offe[r]" the underlying telecommunications used to transmit that service. The word "offering" as used in § 153(46), however, does not unambiguously require that result. Instead, "offering" can reasonably be read to mean a "stand-alone" offering of telecommunications, i.e., an offered service that, from the user's perspective, transmits messages unadulterated by computer processing. That conclusion follows not only from the ordinary meaning of the word "offering," but also from the regulatory history of the Communications Act.

1

In the telecommunications context, it is at least reasonable to describe companies as not "offering" to consumers each discrete input that is necessary to providing, and is always used in connection with, a finished service. We think it no misuse of language, for example, to say that cable companies providing Internet service do not "offer" consumers DNS, even though DNS is essential to providing Internet access. Declaratory Ruling at 4810, n.74, 4822–23, ¶ 38. Likewise, a telephone company "offers" consumers a transparent transmission path that conveys an ordinary-language message, not necessarily the data transmission facilities that also "transmi[t] . . . information of the user's choosing," § 153(43), or other physical elements of the facilities used to provide telephone service, like the trunks and switches, or the copper in the wires. What cable companies providing cable modem service and telephone companies providing telephone service "offer" is Internet service and telephone service respectively—the finished services, though they do so using (or "via") the discrete components composing the end product, including data transmission. Such functionally integrated components need not be described as distinct "offerings."

In response, the dissent argues that the high-speed transmission component necessary to providing cable modem service is necessarily "offered" with Internet service because cable modem service is like the offering of pizza delivery service together with pizza, and the offering of puppies together with dog leashes. *Post* (opinion of SCALIA, J.). The dissent's appeal to these analogies only underscores that the term "offer" is ambiguous in the way that we have described. The entire question is whether the products here are functionally integrated (like the components of a car) or functionally separate (like pets and leashes). That question turns not on the language of the Act, but on the factual particulars of how Internet technology works and how it is provided, questions *Chevron* leaves to the Commission to resolve in the first instance. As the Commission has candidly recognized, "the question may not always be straightforward whether, on the one hand, an entity is providing a single information service with communications and computing components, or, on the other hand, is providing two distinct services, one of which is a telecommunications service." Universal Service Report at 11,530, ¶ 60. Because the term "offer" can sometimes refer to a single, finished product and sometimes to the "individual components in a package being offered" (depending on whether the components "still possess sufficient identity to be described as separate objects," *post*), the statute fails unambiguously to classify the telecommunications component of cable modem service as a distinct offering. This leaves federal telecommunications policy in this technical and complex area to be set by the Commission, not by warring analogies.

We also do not share the dissent's certainty that cable modem service is so obviously like pizza delivery service and the combination of dog leashes and dogs that the Commission could not reasonably have thought otherwise. For example, unlike the transmission component of Internet service, delivery service and dog leashes are not integral components of the finished products (pizzas and pet dogs). One can pick up a pizza rather than having it delivered, and one can own a dog without buying a leash. By contrast, the Commission reasonably concluded, a consumer cannot purchase Internet service without also purchasing a connection to the Internet and the transmission always occurs in connection with information processing. In any event, we doubt that a statute that, for example, subjected offerors of "delivery" service (such as Federal Express and United Parcel Service) to common-carrier regulation would unambiguously require pizza-delivery companies to offer their delivery services on a common-carrier basis.

C

We also conclude that the Commission's construction was "a reasonable policy choice for the [Commission] to make" at *Chevron*'s second step. 467 U.S. at 845.

As we understand the Declaratory Ruling, the Commission did not say that any telecommunications service that is priced or bundled with an information service is automatically unregulated under Title II. The Commission said that a telecommunications input used to provide an information service that is not "separable from the data-processing capabilities of the service" and is instead "part and parcel of [the information service] and is integral to [the information service's] other capabilities" is not a telecommunications offering. Declaratory Ruling at 4823, ¶ 39.

This construction does not leave all information service offerings exempt from mandatory Title II regulation. "It is plain," for example, that a local telephone company "cannot escape Title II regulation of its residential local exchange service simply by packaging that service with voice mail." Universal Service Report at 11,530, ¶ 60. That is because a telephone company that packages voice mail with telephone service offers a transparent transmission path—telephone service—that transmits information independent of the information-storage capabilities provided by voice mail. For instance, when a person makes a telephone call, his ability to convey and receive information using the call is only trivially affected by the additional voice-mail capability. By contrast, the high-speed transmission used to provide cable modem service is a functionally integrated component of that service because it transmits data only in connection with the further processing of information and is necessary to provide Internet service. The Commission's construction therefore was more limited than respondents assume.

Respondents answer that cable modem service does, in fact, provide "transparent" transmission from the consumer's perspective, but this argument, too, is mistaken. Respondents characterize the "information-service" offering of Internet access as consisting only of access to a cable company's e-mail service, its Web page, and the ability it provides consumers to create a personal Web page. When a consumer goes beyond those offerings and accesses content provided by parties other than the cable company, respondents argue, the consumer uses "pure transmission" no less than a consumer who purchases phone service together with voice mail.

This argument, we believe, conflicts with the Commission's understanding of the nature of cable modem service, an understanding we find to be reasonable. When an end user accesses a third-party's Web site, the Commission concluded, he is equally using the information service provided by the cable company that offers him Internet access as when he accesses the company's own Web site, its e-mail service, or his personal Web page. For example, as the Commission found below, part of the information service cable companies provide is access to DNS service. A user cannot reach a third-party's Web site without DNS, which (among other things) matches the Web site address the end user types into his browser (or "clicks" on with his mouse) with the IP address of the Web page's host server. It is at least reasonable to think of DNS as a "capability for ... acquiring ... retrieving, utilizing, or making available" Web site addresses and therefore part of the information service cable companies provide. 47 U.S.C. § 153(20). Similarly, the Internet service provided by cable companies facilitates access to third-party Web pages by offering consumers the ability to store, or "cache," popular content on local computer servers. *See* Declaratory Ruling at 4810, ¶ 17, and n.76. Cacheing obviates the need for the end user to download anew information from third-party Web sites each time the consumer attempts to access them, thereby increasing the speed of information retrieval. In other words, subscribers can reach third-party Web sites via "the World Wide Web, and browse their contents, [only] because their service provider offers the 'capability for ... acquiring, [storing,] ... retrieving [and] utilizing ...

information.'" Universal Service Report at 11,538, ¶ 76 (quoting 47 U.S.C. § 153(20)). "The service that Internet access providers offer to members of the public is Internet access," Universal Service Report at 11,539, ¶ 79, not a transparent ability (from the end user's perspective) to transmit information. We therefore conclude that the Commission's construction was reasonable.

V

The questions the Commission resolved in the order under review involve a "subject matter [that] is technical, complex, and dynamic." Nat'l Cable & Telecomms. Ass'n v. Gulf Power Co., 534 U.S. 327, 339 (2002). The Commission is in a far better position to address these questions than we are. Nothing in the Communications Act or the Administrative Procedure Act makes unlawful the Commission's use of its expert policy judgment to resolve these difficult questions.

[Concurring opinions of JUSTICE STEVENS and JUSTICE BREYER are omitted.]

JUSTICE SCALIA, with whom JUSTICE SOUTER and JUSTICE GINSBURG join as to Part I, dissenting.

I

The Court concludes that the word "offer" is ambiguous. It seems to me, however, that the analytic problem pertains not really to the meaning of "offer," but to the identity of what is offered. The relevant question is whether the individual components in a package being offered still possess sufficient identity to be described as separate objects of the offer, or whether they have been so changed by their combination with the other components that it is no longer reasonable to describe them in that way.

If, for example, I call up a pizzeria and ask whether they offer delivery, both common sense and common "usage," *ante*, would prevent them from answering: "No, we do not offer delivery — but if you order a pizza from us, we'll bake it for you and then bring it to your house." The logical response to this would be something on the order of, "so, you *do* offer delivery." But our pizzaman may continue to deny the obvious and explain, paraphrasing the FCC and the Court: "No, even though we bring the pizza to your house, we are not actually 'offering' you delivery, because the delivery that we provide to our end users is 'part and parcel' of our pizzeria-pizza-at-home service and is 'integral to its other capabilities.'" *Cf.* Declaratory Ruling at 4823, ¶ 39; *ante*. Any reasonable customer would conclude at that point that his interlocutor was either crazy or following some too-clever-by-half legal advice.

Despite the Court's mighty labors to prove otherwise, the telecommunications component of cable-modem service retains such ample independent identity that it must be regarded as being on offer — especially when seen from the perspective of the consumer or the end user, which the Court purports to find determinative. The Commission's ruling began by noting that cable-modem service provides *both* "high-speed access to the Internet" *and* other "applications and functions,"

Declaratory Ruling at 4799, ¶ 1, because that is exactly how any reasonable consumer would perceive it: as consisting of two separate things.

Since the delivery service provided by cable (the broadband connection between the customer's computer and the cable company's computer-processing facilities) is downstream from the computer-processing facilities, there is no question that it merely serves as a conduit for the information services that have already been "assembled" by the cable company in its capacity as ISP. This is relevant because of the statutory distinction between an "information service" and "telecommunications." The former involves the capability of getting, processing, and manipulating information. § 153(20). The latter, by contrast, involves no "change in the form or content of the information as sent and received." § 153(43). When cable-company-assembled information enters the cable for delivery to the subscriber, the information service is already complete. The information has been (as the statute requires) generated, acquired, stored, transformed, processed, retrieved, utilized, or made available. All that remains is for the information in its final, unaltered form, to be delivered (via telecommunications) to the subscriber.

Notes and Questions

1. Substance and Semantics. As the majority noted, the common carrier provisions of Title II "are mandatory, but the Commission must forbear from applying them if it determines that the public interest requires it." Could the FCC have avoided all the definitional wrangling over "telecommunications service" and "information service" by saying that, whatever cable modem service is, in the FCC's opinion the public interest requires forbearance from common carrier regulation? Had *Brand X* come out the other way, could the FCC have forborne from applying Title II and create the same substantive policy result of nonregulation?

2. Telecommunications versus Telecommunications Service. One of the most confusing aspects of the *Brand X* case and the regulatory battles that preceded it is the difference between "telecommunications" and a "telecommunications service." As Justice Thomas explained, a firm offers a "telecommunications service" if that is the product sold to the public. By contrast, a firm can sell an "information service" that relies on and even includes a "telecommunications" component. The essential regulatory question—and what Justices Thomas and Scalia argue over—is whether a product that provides telecommunications along with some additional functionality should be characterized as a "telecommunications service" or an "information service."

3. The Consumer Perspective. The majority and dissent part ways over what the consumer is buying under the label of "cable modem service." Justice Thomas, writing for the majority, defines the product as "Internet access" with the emphasis on *internet.* The transport aspect of such internet service is merely an integral component. Justice Scalia, in dissent, also defines the service as "Internet access" but puts the emphasis on high-speed *access.* To him consumers are not buying the internet, so to speak, but high-speed transport *to* the internet. Who is right? Should it matter that the internet exists independently of cable systems and that it is neither owned by nor dependent on them? If that is the case, what are the cable operators selling other than transport? What exactly are the cable operators selling to which transport is (as the majority finds) a mere component?

4. The End of Unbundling Requirements. Shortly after *Brand X*, the FCC revisited its 1998 order on DSL service noted above and concluded that DSL, like cable modem service, should be treated as an information service. Appropriate Framework for Broadband Access to the Internet Over Wireline Facilities, Report and Order and Notice of Proposed Rulemaking, 20 FCC Rcd. 14,853, 14,864, ¶ 15 (2005). These rules also eliminated the requirement that incumbents offer unbundled (stand-alone) transmission DSL service to unaffiliated companies. *Id.* at 14,865, ¶¶ 18–19.

This order, in combination with the 2002 rules upheld in *Brand X*, marked the end of any requirements that companies providing broadband internet service offer unbundled access to competitors. The demise of these access requirements meant that any entity that wanted to operate as an ISP would have to invest in its own means of transmission or persuade an incumbent to agree to a contract guaranteeing transmission.[2] Some companies with their own transmission wires or spectrum might have been happy to enter into such contracts, but because they were not treated as common carriers, they could refuse to do so.

§ 6.B. Net Neutrality

The demise of requirements that broadband internet access providers share their capacity with other ISPs did not mean the end of any regulation of such providers. The policy debate shifted to arguments about what has become known as net neutrality. In the words of two economists studying the debate, "[n]et neutrality has no widely accepted precise definition, but usually means that broadband service providers charge consumers only once for Internet access, do not favor one content provider over another, and do not charge content providers for sending information over broadband lines to end users." Robert W. Hahn & Scott Wallsten, The Economics of Net Neutrality, 3 The Economists' Voice 1 (2006), http://dx.doi.org/10.2202/1553-3832.1194. Net neutrality rules thus seek to prevent broadband internet access service providers from imposing fees on or discriminating against content, applications, and services that ride on their networks. A particular flashpoint in the debate is whether broadband internet access providers should be allowed to charge a content, applications, or services provider different prices for different levels of

2. A competitor could still access an incumbent's local loop (the loop unbundling requirement survived this order) and invest in its own electronics (which could be collocated at the incumbent's facilities) to provide high-speed access services over those wires. But the competitive ISP could not simply buy high-speed access services from the incumbent.

transmission quality. For example, consider a provider of video programming or telemedicine over the internet that wishes to avoid any disruption in service. Can that provider purchase such assured quality from the company that owns the underlying network and provides internet access? Advocates of net neutrality say no: such tiering of service quality would force companies to "pay to play" and in that way effectively relegate entities with less money to spend to lower quality connections. The long-run concern is that the public internet will become a repository of second-rate service while high-quality transmission will become the province of increasingly private, pay-to-play networks.

Opponents argue that the ability of network owners to charge content providers simply requires that those services imposing costs on the network bear those costs; the charges, in turn, allow content providers to get the quality they need to launch successful new services that require particular levels of transmission quality. Charging for tiers of service thereby fosters innovation in applications and ensures efficient use of the internet infrastructure. It also provides additional revenue that might encourage further deployment of high-speed networks.

The FCC's initial foray into net neutrality regulation was modest: in 2005, it issued a five-paragraph non-binding policy statement in which it articulated four fairly minimal principles. Appropriate Framework for Broadband Access to the Internet over Wireline Facilities, Policy Statement, 20 FCC Rcd. 14,986 (2005).[3] The next important development squarely raised the question of FCC jurisdiction to regulate broadband internet service. In 2007, some Comcast subscribers alleged that the company was secretly degrading peer-to-peer traffic. The FCC investigated the claims. Comcast initially denied the allegations, but it eventually admitted to degrading the traffic. This led to an FCC order (the culmination of an adjudication). Formal Complaint of Free Press & Public Knowledge Against Comcast Corp. for Secretly Degrading Peer-to-Peer Applications, Memorandum Opinion and Order, 23 FCC Rcd. 13,028 (2008). In its order, the FCC found that Comcast had violated the principles embodied in the FCC's 2005 internet policy statement, and it ordered Comcast to cease and desist certain practices (which Comcast agreed to do). Comcast challenged the FCC's authority to issue this order, leading to the following opinion.

---

3. The four principles were that consumers are entitled "to access the lawful Internet content of their choice," "to run applications and use services of their choice, subject to the needs of law enforcement," "to connect their choice of legal devices that do not harm the network," and "to competition among network providers, application and service providers, and content providers." *Id.*

Comcast Corp. v. FCC

600 F.3d 642 (D.C. Cir. 2010)

Opinion for the Court filed by Circuit Judge TATEL, in which Circuit Judge SENTELLE and Senior Circuit Judge RANDOLPH concur.

TATEL, Circuit Judge:

I

In 2007 several subscribers to Comcast's high-speed Internet service discovered that the company was interfering with their use of peer-to-peer networking applications. Peer-to-peer programs allow users to share large files directly with one another without going through a central server. Such programs also consume significant amounts of bandwidth.

Challenging Comcast's action, two non-profit advocacy organizations, Free Press and Public Knowledge, filed a complaint with the Federal Communications Commission and, together with a coalition of public interest groups and law professors, a petition for declaratory ruling. Both filings argued that Comcast's actions "violat[ed] the FCC's Internet Policy Statement." Issued two years earlier, that statement "adopt[ed] the ... principles" that "consumers are entitled to access the lawful Internet content of their choice ... [and] to run applications and use services of their choice." Appropriate Framework for Broadband Access to the Internet Over Wireline Facilities, Policy Statement, 20 FCC Rcd. 14,986, 14,988, ¶ 4 (2005). Comcast defended its interference with peer-to-peer programs as necessary to manage scarce network capacity.

Following a period of public comment, the Commission issued the order challenged here. Formal Compl. of Free Press & Public Knowledge Against Comcast Corp. for Secretly Degrading Peer-to-Peer Applications, Memorandum Opinion and Order, 23 FCC Rcd. 13,028 (2008) (Order). The Commission began by concluding not only that it had jurisdiction over Comcast's network management practices, but also that it could resolve the dispute through adjudication rather than through rulemaking. On the merits, the Commission ruled that Comcast had "significantly impeded consumers' ability to access the content and use the applications of their choice," and that because Comcast "ha[d] several available options it could use to manage network traffic without discriminating" against peer-to-peer communications, its method of bandwidth management "contravene[d] ... federal policy." Because by then Comcast had agreed to adopt a new system for managing bandwidth demand, the Commission simply ordered it to make a set of disclosures describing the details of its new approach and the company's progress toward implementing it. The Commission added that an injunction would automatically issue should Comcast either fail to make the required disclosures or renege on its commitment.

II

Through the Communications Act of 1934, as amended over the decades, 47 U.S.C. §151 et seq., Congress has given the Commission express and expansive authority to regulate common carrier services, including landline telephony, *id.* § 201 et seq. (Title II of the Act); radio transmissions, including broadcast television, radio, and cellular telephony, *id.* § 301 et seq. (Title III); and "cable services," including cable television, *id.* § 521 et seq. (Title VI). In this case, the Commission does not claim that Congress has given it express authority to regulate Comcast's Internet service. Indeed, in its still-binding 2002 Cable Modem Order, the Commission ruled that cable Internet service is neither a "telecommunications service" covered by Title II of the Communications Act nor a "cable service" covered by Title VI. High-Speed Access to the Internet Over Cable and Other Facilities, Declaratory Ruling and Notice of Proposed Rulemaking, 17 FCC Rcd. 4798, 4802, ¶ 7 (2002), *aff'd,* Nat'l Cable & Telecomms. Ass'n v. Brand X Internet Servs., 545 U.S. 967 (2005). The Commission therefore rests its assertion of authority over Comcast's network management practices on the broad language of section 4(i) of the Act: "The Commission may perform any and all acts, make such rules and regulations, and issue such orders, not inconsistent with this chapter, as may be necessary in the execution of its functions," 47 U.S.C. § 154(i).

Courts have come to call the Commission's section 4(i) power its "ancillary" authority, a label that derives from three foundational Supreme Court decisions: United States v. Southwestern Cable Co., 392 U.S. 157 (1968), United States v. Midwest Video Corp., 406 U.S. 649 (1972) (*Midwest Video I*), and FCC v. Midwest Video Corp., 440 U.S. 689 (1979) (*Midwest Video II*). All three cases dealt with Commission jurisdiction over early cable systems at a time when, as with the Internet today, the Communications Act gave the Commission no express authority to regulate such systems. (Title VI, which gives the Commission jurisdiction over "cable services," was not added to the statute until 1984.)

In the first case, *Southwestern Cable*, the Supreme Court considered a challenge to a Commission order restricting the geographic area in which a cable company could operate. The Supreme Court sustained that order, explaining that even though the then-existing Communications Act gave the Commission no express authority over cable television, the Commission could nonetheless regulate cable television to the extent "reasonably ancillary to the effective performance of the Commission's various responsibilities for the regulation of television broadcasting." 392 U.S. at 178. Four years later, in *Midwest Video I*, the Court again sustained the Commission's use of its ancillary authority, this time to support issuance of a regulation that required cable operators to facilitate the creation of new programs and to transmit them alongside broadcast programs they captured from the air. In *Midwest Video II*, the Court rejected the Commission's assertion of ancillary authority, setting aside regulations that required cable systems to make certain channels available for public use.

We recently distilled the holdings of these three cases into a two-part test. In American Library Ass'n v. FCC, 406 F.3d 689 (D.C. Cir. 2005), we wrote: "The Commission ... may exercise ancillary jurisdiction only when two conditions are satisfied: (1) the Commission's general jurisdictional grant under Title I [of the Communications Act] covers the regulated subject and (2) the regulations are reasonably ancillary to the Commission's effective performance of its statutorily mandated responsibilities." 406 F.3d at 691–92. Comcast concedes that the Commission's action here satisfies the first requirement because the company's Internet service qualifies as "interstate and foreign communication by wire" within the meaning of Title I of the Communications Act. 47 U.S.C. § 152(a). Whether the Commission's action satisfies *American Library*'s second requirement is the central issue in this case.

IV A

The Commission relies principally on section 230(b), part of a provision entitled "Protection for private blocking and screening of offensive material," 47 U.S.C. § 230, that grants civil immunity for such blocking to providers of interactive computer services, *id.* § 230(c)(2). Setting forth the policies underlying this protection, section 230(b) states, in relevant part, that "[i]t is the policy of the United States ... to promote the continued development of the Internet and other interactive computer services" and "to encourage the development of technologies which maximize user control over what information is received by individuals, families, and schools who use the Internet." In this case the Commission found that Comcast's network management practices frustrated both objectives.

In addition to section 230(b), the Commission relies on section 1, in which Congress set forth its reasons for creating the Commission in 1934: "For the purpose of regulating interstate and foreign commerce in communication by wire and radio so as to make available, so far as possible, to all the people of the United States ... a rapid, efficient, Nation-wide, and world-wide wire and radio communication service ... at reasonable charges, ... there is created a commission to be known as the 'Federal Communications Commission' ..." 47 U.S.C. § 151. The Commission found that "prohibiting unreasonable network discrimination directly furthers the goal of making broadband Internet access service both 'rapid' and 'efficient.'"

The Commission acknowledges that section 230(b) and section 1 are statements of policy that themselves delegate no regulatory authority. Still, the Commission maintains that the two provisions, like all provisions of the Communications Act, set forth "statutorily mandated responsibilities" that can anchor the exercise of ancillary authority. "The operative provisions of statutes are those which *declare the legislative will*," the Commission asserts. "Here, the legislative will has been declared by Congress in the form of a policy, along with an express grant of authority to the FCC to perform all actions necessary to execute and enforce all the provisions of the Communications Act."

In support of its reliance on congressional statements of policy, the Commission points out that in both *Southwestern Cable* and *Midwest Video I* the Supreme Court linked the challenged Commission actions to the furtherance of various congressional "goals," "objectives," and "policies." In particular, the Commission notes that in *Midwest Video I*, the plurality accepted its argument that the Commission's "concern with CATV carriage of broadcast signals . . . extends . . . to requiring CATV affirmatively to further statutory *policies*." According to the Commission, since congressional statements of policy were sufficient to support ancillary authority over cable television, it may likewise rely on such statements — section 230(b) and section 1 — to exercise ancillary authority over the network management practices of Internet providers.

We read *Southwestern Cable* and *Midwest Video I* quite differently. In those cases, the Supreme Court relied on policy statements not because, standing alone, they set out "statutorily mandated responsibilities," but rather because they did so in conjunction with an express delegation of authority to the Commission, i.e., Title III's authority to regulate broadcasting.

The teaching of *Southwestern Cable*, *Midwest Video I*, [and] *Midwest Video II* — that policy statements alone cannot provide the basis for the Commission's exercise of ancillary authority — derives from the "axiomatic" principle that "administrative agencies may [act] only pursuant to authority delegated to them by Congress." Policy statements are just that — statements of policy. They are not delegations of regulatory authority. To be sure, statements of congressional policy can help delineate the contours of statutory authority. Consider, for example, the various services over which the Commission enjoys express statutory authority. When exercising its Title II authority to set "just and reasonable" rates for phone service, 47 U.S.C. § 201(b), or its Title III authority to grant broadcasting licenses in the "public convenience, interest, or necessity," *id.* § 307(a), or its Title VI authority to prohibit "unfair methods of competition" by cable operators that limit consumer access to certain types of television programming, *id.* § 548(b), the Commission must bear in mind section 1's objective of "Nation-wide . . . wire and radio communication service . . . at reasonable charges," *id.* § 151. In all three examples, section 1's policy goal undoubtedly illuminates the scope of the "authority delegated to [the Commission] by Congress," — though it is Titles II, III, and VI that do the delegating. So too with respect to the Commission's section 4(i) ancillary authority. Although policy statements may illuminate that authority, it is Title II, III, or VI to which the authority must ultimately be ancillary.

In this case the Commission cites neither section 230(b) nor section 1 to shed light on any express statutory delegation of authority found in Title II, III, VI, or, for that matter, anywhere else. That is, unlike the way it successfully employed policy statements in *Southwestern Cable* and *Midwest Video I*, the Commission does not rely on section 230(b) or section 1 to argue that its regulation of an activity over which it concededly has no express statutory authority (here Comcast's Internet management practices) is necessary to further its regulation of activities over which it does have express statutory authority (here, for example, Comcast's management of its Title VI cable services).

Instead, the Commission maintains that congressional policy by itself creates "statutorily mandated responsibilities" sufficient to support the exercise of section 4(i) ancillary authority. Not only is this argument flatly inconsistent with

Southwestern Cable, *Midwest Video I*, [and] *Midwest Video II*, but if accepted it would virtually free the Commission from its congressional tether. As the Court explained in *Midwest Video II*, "without reference to the provisions of the Act" expressly granting regulatory authority, "the Commission's [ancillary] jurisdiction . . . would be unbounded." Indeed, Commission counsel told us at oral argument that just as the Order seeks to make Comcast's Internet service more "rapid" and "efficient," the Commission could someday subject Comcast's Internet service to pervasive rate regulation to ensure that the company provides the service at "reasonable charges," 47 U.S.C. §151. Were we to accept that theory of ancillary authority, we see no reason why the Commission would have to stop there, for we can think of few examples of regulations that apply to Title II common carrier services, Title III broadcast services, or Title VI cable services that the Commission, relying on the broad policies articulated in section 230(b) and section 1, would be unable to impose upon Internet service providers.

Because the Commission has failed to tie its assertion of ancillary authority over Comcast's Internet service to any "statutorily mandated responsibility," we grant the petition for review and vacate the Order.

Notes and Questions

1. What Is the Difference? How different was the FCC's losing argument in *Comcast* from its winning arguments in the cases the court discusses? Was the court trying to rein in ancillary jurisdiction? If so, is that because the FCC's power would otherwise seem unlimited, and unlimitable? What remains of ancillary jurisdiction, and in particular, the FCC's authority under Title I?

2. Deference? The FCC is usually entitled to deference for its interpretations of the Communications Act, under the *Chevron* doctrine discussed in *Brand X* and elsewhere. Why didn't the court discuss *Chevron* deference?

3. More Than a Bump in the Road. The impact of this decision was not limited to net neutrality. The FCC (in the Broadband Plan and other initiatives) had articulated a wide range of possible actions with respect to broadband, for all of which it planned to rely on ancillary jurisdiction. This included changes to universal service, consumer protection, privacy, cyber security, and access for people with disabilities. As we saw in Chapter 5.E, the Tenth Circuit found that the FCC's universal service rules were authorized. In re FCC 11-161, 753 F.3d 1015 (10th Cir. 2014). Is the Tenth Circuit's reasoning in tension with the opinion above?

4. The FCC's Policy Reasoning. In its decision against Comcast, the FCC concluded that Comcast blocked peer-to-peer traffic because it was acting to protect revenues that it earned through its video services (traditional channels and especially video-on-demand). Assuming that the FCC is correct that Comcast would have such an incentive, is that only because Comcast (by virtue of net neutrality norms or otherwise) is not permitted to apply a premium charge to other video providers using the internet platform (e.g., YouTube or Netflix)? Such premium charges are common in traditional video markets.

5. Next Steps. As a result of the court's decision, the FCC was faced with a choice (unless and until Congress passed new legislation): leave broadband internet access service unregulated, attempt to revive its theory of ancillary jurisdiction, or revisit its classification of internet access service as an information service regulated under Title I rather than a common carrier service regulated under Title II. In the wake of the D.C. Circuit's decision, the FCC proceeded to adopt a more comprehensive regime without classifying internet access service under Title II. Preserving the Open Internet, Report and Order, 25 FCC Rcd. 17,905 (2010). The rules stated that internet openness "enables a virtuous circle of innovation in which new uses of the network—including new content, applications, services, and devices—lead to increased end-user demand for broadband, which drives network improvements, which in turn lead to further innovative network uses." *Id.* at 17,910, ¶ 14. The specific rules imposed disclosure, anti-discrimination, and anti-blocking requirements on fixed broadband providers (generally those providing broadband internet access via wire).[4] The disclosure rule merely required the disclosure of information regarding network management practices, performance, and terms of service, but the anti-discrimination and anti-blocking rules had more bite: fixed broadband providers could not "unreasonably discriminate in transmitting lawful network traffic" and could not "block lawful content, applications, services, or non-harmful devices." *Id.* at 17,942, ¶ 63, 17,944, ¶ 68. These limits were subject to "reasonable network management"—practices "ensuring network security and integrity," "addressing traffic that is unwanted by end users," "and reducing or mitigating the effects of congestion on the network." *Id.* at 17,952, ¶ 82.

When the rules were challenged in the D.C. Circuit, the good news for the FCC was that the court found that it had authority to regulate broadband internet access as a Title I information service (that is, without classifying it as a Title II common carrier service). Verizon v. FCC, 740 F.3d 623 (D.C. Cir. 2014). The court found such authority under §§706(a) and (b) of the 1996 Telecommunications Act (which is part of Title I). Section 706(a) directs the FCC to "encourage the deployment ... of advanced telecommunications capability ... by utilizing ... price cap regulation, regulatory forbearance, measures that promote competition in the local telecommunications market, or other regulating methods that remove barriers to infrastructure investment." 47 U.S.C. §1302(a). Section 706(b) provides that if the FCC find that "advanced telecommunications capability is [not] being deployed to all Americans in a reasonable and timely fashion," it "shall take immediate action to accelerate deployment of such capability by removing barriers to infrastructure investment

4. The order applied weaker rules on mobile broadband providers, stating that compared to the fixed broadband market the mobile broadband market was more competitive and rapidly evolving, network speeds and penetration were lower, and operational constraints were higher. *See id.* at 17,956–57, ¶¶ 94–95.

and by promoting competition in the telecommunications market." *Id.* § 1302(b). And § 706(d) defines "advanced telecommunications capability" to include "broadband telecommunications capability." *Id.* § 1302(d)(1). The court held that the FCC's interpretation of these provisions as providing regulatory authority was reasonable under *Chevron.* (Does this mean that in the proceeding against Comcast the FCC erred in failing to rely on § 706?)

The bad news for the FCC in the D.C. Circuit's opinion is in the excerpt below.

Verizon v. FCC

740 F.3d 623 (D.C. Cir. 2014)

Opinion for the Court filed by Circuit Judge TATEL. Opinion concurring in part and dissenting in part filed by Senior Circuit Judge SILBERMAN.

TATEL, Circuit Judge.

III

Even though section 706 grants the Commission authority to promote broadband deployment by regulating how broadband providers treat edge providers, the Commission may not, as it recognizes, utilize that power in a manner that contravenes any specific prohibition contained in the Communications Act.

We think it obvious that the Commission would violate the Communications Act were it to regulate broadband providers as common carriers. Given the Commission's still-binding decision to classify broadband providers not as providers of "telecommunications services" but instead as providers of "information services," such treatment would run afoul of section 153(51): "A telecommunications carrier shall be treated as a common carrier under this [Act] only to the extent that it is engaged in providing telecommunications services." 47 U.S.C. § 153(51). Likewise, because the Commission has classified mobile broadband service as a "private" mobile service, and not a "commercial" mobile service, treatment of mobile broadband providers as common carriers would violate section 332: "A person engaged in the provision of a service that is a private mobile service shall not, insofar as such person is so engaged, be treated as a common carrier for any purpose under this [Act]." 47 U.S.C. § 332(c)(2).

Thus, we must determine whether the requirements imposed by the [challenged] order subject broadband providers to common carrier treatment. Preserving the Open Internet, Report and Order, 25 FCC Rcd. 17,905 (2010) (Open Internet Order). If they do, then given the manner in which the Commission has chosen to classify broadband providers, the regulations cannot stand.

A

Offering little guidance as to the meaning of the term "common carrier," the Communications Act defines that phrase, somewhat circularly, as "any person engaged as a common carrier for hire." 47 U.S.C. § 153(11). Courts and the

Commission have therefore resorted to the common law to come up with a satisfactory definition.

Although the nature and scope of the duties imposed on common carriers have evolved over the last century, the core of the common law concept of common carriage has remained intact. In National Association of Regulatory Utility Commissioners v. FCC, 525 F.2d 630, 642 (D.C. Cir. 1976) (*NARUC I*), we identified the basic characteristic that distinguishes common carriers from "private" carriers — i.e., entities that are not common carriers — as "[t]he common law requirement of holding oneself out to serve the public indiscriminately." "[A] carrier will not be a common carrier," we further explained, "where its practice is to make individualized decisions, in particular cases, whether and on what terms to deal." *Id.* at 641. Similarly, in National Association of Regulatory Utility Commissioners v. FCC, 533 F.2d 601, 608 (1976) (*NARUC II*), we concluded that "the primary sine qua non of common carrier status is a quasi-public character, which arises out of the undertaking to carry for all people indifferently." (Internal quotation marks omitted).

For our purposes, perhaps the seminal case applying this notion of common carriage is FCC v. Midwest Video Corp., 440 U.S. 689 (1979) (*Midwest Video II*). At issue in *Midwest Video II* was a set of regulations compelling cable television systems to operate a minimum number of channels and to hold certain channels open for specific users. 440 U.S. at 692–93. Cable operators were barred from exercising any discretion over who could use those latter channels and what those users could transmit. They were also forbidden from charging users any fee for some of the channels and limited to charging an "appropriate" fee for the remaining channels. *Id.* at 693–94. Because at that time the Commission had no express statutory authority over cable systems, it sought to justify these rules as ancillary to its authority to regulate broadcasting. *Id.* at 696–99.

Rejecting this argument, the Supreme Court held that the Commission had no power to regulate cable operators in this fashion. The Court reasoned that if the Commission sought to exercise such ancillary jurisdiction over cable operators on the basis of its authority over broadcasters, it must also respect the specific statutory limits of that authority, as "without reference to the provisions of the Act directly governing broadcasting, the Commission's jurisdiction . . . would be unbounded." *Midwest Video II*, 440 U.S. at 706. Congress had expressly prohibited the Commission from regulating broadcasters as common carriers, a limitation that must then, according to the Court, also extend to cable operators. *Id.* at 707. And the challenged regulations, the Court held, "plainly impose common-carrier obligations on cable operators." *Id.* at 701. In explaining this conclusion, the Court largely reiterated the nature of the obligations themselves: "Under the rules, cable systems are required to hold out dedicated channels on a first-come, nondiscriminatory basis. Operators are prohibited from determining or influencing the content of access programming. And the rules delimit what operators may charge for access and use of equipment." *Id.* at 701–02.

C

We have little hesitation in concluding that the anti-discrimination obligation imposed on fixed broadband providers has "relegated [those providers], pro tanto, to common carrier status." *Midwest Video II*, 440 U.S. at 700–01. In requiring broadband providers to serve all edge providers without "unreasonable discrimination," this rule by its very terms compels those providers to hold themselves out "to serve the public indiscriminately." *NARUC I*, 525 F.2d at 642.

The Commission has provided no basis for concluding that in permitting "reasonable" network management, and in prohibiting merely "unreasonable" discrimination, the Order's standard of "reasonableness" might be more permissive than the quintessential common carrier standard. [T]he language of the Open Internet Order's anti-discrimination rule mirrors, almost precisely, section 202's language establishing the basic common carrier obligation not to "make any unjust or unreasonable discrimination." 47 U.S.C. § 202. Indeed, confirming that the two standards are equivalent, the Commission responded to commenters who argued that the "no unreasonable discrimination" requirement was too vague by quoting another commenter who observed that "[s]eventy-five years of experience have shown [the 'unreasonable' qualifier in Section 202] to be both administrable and indispensable to the sound administration of the nation's telecommunications laws." Open Internet Order, 25 FCC Rcd. at 17,949, ¶ 77 n.240.

[The Commission, in the Open Internet Order and its briefs,] makes no distinction at all between the anti-discrimination and anti-blocking rules, seeking to justify both types of rules with explanations that, as we have explained, are patently insufficient.

The disclosure rules are another matter. Verizon does not contend that these rules, on their own, constitute per se common carrier obligations, nor do we see any way in which they would.

IV

For the forgoing reasons, although we reject Verizon's challenge to the Open Internet Order's disclosure rules, we vacate both the anti-discrimination and the anti-blocking rules.

[Concurring and dissenting opinion of Senior Circuit Judge SILBERMAN is omitted.]

Notes and Questions

1. Obvious? Is it obvious that the imposition of this nondiscrimination requirement is to treat a broadband internet access provider as a common carrier? One of us has written that it is not. James B. Speta, Unintentional Antitrust: The FCC's Only (and Better) Way Forward after the Mess of Verizon v. FCC, 66 Fed. Comm. L.J. 491, 497 (2014) ("The history of common carriage and the history of the Communications Act support an argument that common carriage involves more than just nondiscrimination requirements."). The FCC did not impose rate regulation, tariff-filing, universal service, and many of the other obligations that have always come with "treat[ing]" a company or a service as a "common carrier." Interestingly, the internet service providers' biggest concern, and principal argument for reversing the FCC's open internet approach, was that its classification decision would lead to rate regulation of internet access service.

2. Another Leveraging Example. Although broadband infrastructure and, therefore, the net neutrality debate are "new," we have seen this concern arise throughout the history and across the breadth of communications regulation: from the concerns over broadcaster and cable company control over content to the Bell System's control over manufacturing and long distance. What is different about this debate? What is the same?

3. Net Neutrality via Common Carriage. After *Verizon*, the FCC was basically left with the choice of reclassifying broadband service as a common carrier service, adopting much weaker net neutrality rules, or abandoning net neutrality regulation altogether. In 2015, the FCC chose the first option and reclassified broadband internet access service as a common carrier service, and it imposed net neutrality regulations. The FCC's order and accompanying statements are more than 400 pages. Below we excerpt the FCC's summary of its rules and its discussion of their desirability. We leave the discussion of the central legal issues to the D.C. Circuit case upholding the rules.

Protecting and Promoting the Open Internet

Report and Order on Remand, Declaratory Ruling, and Order, 30 FCC Rcd. 5601 (2015)

I. Introduction

1. The open Internet drives the American economy and serves, every day, as a critical tool for America's citizens to conduct commerce, communicate, educate, entertain, and engage in the world around them. The benefits of an open Internet are undisputed. But it must remain open: open for commerce, innovation, and speech; open for consumers and for the innovation created by applications developers and content companies; and open for expansion and investment by America's broadband providers. For over a decade, the Commission has been committed to protecting and promoting an open Internet.

2. Four years ago, the Commission adopted open Internet rules to protect and promote the "virtuous cycle" that drives innovation and investment on the Internet—both at the "edges" of the network, as well as in the network itself. In the years that those rules were in place, significant investment and groundbreaking innovation continued to define the broadband marketplace. Preserving the Open Internet, Report and Order, 25 FCC Rcd. 17,905, 17,910, 17,906, ¶¶ 14, 1 (2010) (2010 Open Internet Order).

3. Likewise, innovation at the edge moves forward unabated.

4. The lesson of this period, and the overwhelming consensus on the record, is that carefully-tailored rules to protect Internet openness will allow investment and innovation to continue to flourish.

II. A Strong Rules That Protect Consumers from Past and Future Tactics that Threaten the Open Internet

1. Clear, Bright-Line Rules

14. Because the record overwhelmingly supports adopting rules and demonstrates that three specific practices invariably harm the open Internet—Blocking, Throttling, and Paid Prioritization—this Order bans each of them, applying the same rules to both fixed and mobile broadband Internet access service.

15. *No Blocking.* Consumers who subscribe to a retail broadband Internet access service must get what they have paid for—access to all (lawful) destinations on the Internet. This essential and well-accepted principle has long been a tenet of Commission policy, stretching back to its landmark decision in *Carterfone*, which protected a customer's right to connect a telephone to the monopoly telephone network. Use of the Carterfone Device in Message Toll Telephone Service, 13 F.C.C. 2d 420 (1968), *recon. denied*, 14 F.C.C. 2d 571 (1968). Thus, this Order adopts a straightforward ban:

> *A person engaged in the provision of broadband Internet access service, insofar as such person is so engaged, shall not block lawful content, applications, services, or non-harmful devices, subject to reasonable network management.*

16. *No Throttling.* The 2010 open Internet rule against blocking contained an ancillary prohibition against the degradation of lawful content, applications, services, and devices, on the ground that such degradation would be tantamount to blocking. This Order creates a separate rule to guard against degradation targeted at specific uses of a customer's broadband connection:

> *A person engaged in the provision of broadband Internet access service, insofar as such person is so engaged, shall not impair or degrade lawful Internet traffic on the basis of Internet content, application, or service, or use of a non-harmful device, subject to reasonable network management.*

17. The ban on throttling is necessary both to fulfill the reasonable expectations of a customer who signs up for a broadband service that promises access to all of the lawful Internet, and to avoid gamesmanship designed to avoid the no-blocking rule by, for example, rendering an application effectively, but not technically, unusable. It prohibits the degrading of Internet traffic based on source, destination, or content. It also specifically prohibits conduct that singles out content competing with a broadband provider's business model.

18. *No Paid Prioritization.* Paid prioritization occurs when a broadband provider accepts payment (monetary or otherwise) to manage its network in a way that benefits particular content, applications, services, or devices. To protect against "fast lanes," this Order adopts a rule that establishes that:

A person engaged in the provision of broadband Internet access service, insofar as such person is so engaged, shall not engage in paid prioritization.

"Paid prioritization" refers to the management of a broadband provider's network to directly or indirectly favor some traffic over other traffic, including through use of techniques such as traffic shaping, prioritization, resource reservation, or other forms of preferential traffic management, either (a) in exchange for consideration (monetary or otherwise) from a third party, or (b) to benefit an affiliated entity.

2. No Unreasonable Interference or Unreasonable Disadvantage to Consumers or Edge Providers

20. The key insight of the virtuous cycle is that broadband providers have both the incentive and the ability to act as gatekeepers standing between edge providers and consumers.[5] As gatekeepers, they can block access altogether; they can target competitors, including competitors to their own video services; and they can extract unfair tolls. Such conduct would, as the Commission concluded in 2010, "reduce the rate of innovation at the edge and, in turn, the likely rate of improvements to network infrastructure." 2010 Open Internet Order, 25 FCC Rcd. at 17,911, ¶ 14. In other words, when a broadband provider acts as a gatekeeper, it actually chokes consumer demand for the very broadband product it can supply.

21. The bright-line bans on blocking, throttling, and paid prioritization will go a long way to preserve the virtuous cycle. But not all the way. Gatekeeper power can be exercised through a variety of technical and economic means, and without a catch-all standard, it would be that, as Benjamin Franklin said, "a little neglect may breed great mischief." Benjamin Franklin, Poor Richard's Almanac (1757). Thus, the Order adopts the following standard:

Any person engaged in the provision of broadband Internet access service, insofar as such person is so engaged, shall not unreasonably interfere with or unreasonably disadvantage (i) end users' ability to select, access, and use broadband Internet access service or the lawful Internet content, applications, services, or devices of their choice, or (ii) edge providers' ability to make lawful content, applications, services, or devices available to end users. Reasonable network management shall not be considered a violation of this rule.

22. This "no unreasonable interference/disadvantage" standard protects free expression, thus fulfilling the congressional policy that "the Internet offer[s] a forum for a true diversity of political discourse, unique opportunities for cultural development, and myriad avenues for intellectual activity." 47 U.S.C. § 230(a)(3). And the standard will permit considerations of asserted benefits of innovation as well as threatened harm to end users and edge providers.

---

5. [In an earlier paragraph, the order invokes "a 'virtuous cycle' in which innovations at the edges of the network enhance consumer demand, leading to expanded investments in broadband infrastructure that, in turn, spark new innovations at the edge." ¶ 7. Eds.]

4. Scope of the Rules

25. The open Internet rules described above apply to both fixed and mobile broadband Internet access service. Consistent with the 2010 Order, today's Order applies its rules to the consumer-facing service that broadband networks provide, which is known as "broadband Internet access service" (BIAS) and is defined to be:

> *A mass-market retail service by wire or radio that provides the capability to transmit data to and receive data from all or substantially all Internet endpoints, including any capabilities that are incidental to and enable the operation of the communications service, but excluding dial-up Internet access service. This term also encompasses any service that the Commission finds to be providing a functional equivalent of the service described in the previous sentence, or that is used to evade the protections set forth in this Part.*

26. As in 2010, BIAS does not include enterprise services, virtual private network services, hosting, or data storage services. Further, we decline to apply the open Internet rules to premises operators to the extent they may be offering broadband Internet access service as we define it today.

III. B. The Continuing Need for Open Internet Protections

75. In *Verizon*, the D.C. Circuit affirmed the underlying basis for the Commission's open Internet rules, holding that "the Commission [had] more than adequately supported and explained its conclusion that edge provider innovation leads to the expansion and improvement of broadband infrastructure." 740 F.3d at 644. The court also found "reasonable and grounded in substantial evidence" the Commission's finding that Internet openness fosters the edge provider innovation that drives the virtuous cycle. *Id.* The record on remand continues to convince us that broadband providers—including mobile broadband providers—have the incentives and ability to engage in practices that pose a threat to Internet openness, and as such, rules to protect the open nature of the Internet remain necessary. Today we take steps to ensure that the substantial benefits of Internet openness continue to be realized.

1. An Open Internet Promotes Innovation, Competition, Free Expression, and Infrastructure Deployment

76. In the [Notice of Proposed Rulemaking in this proceeding], we sought comment on and expressed our continued commitment to an important principle underlying the Commission's prior policies—that the Internet's openness promotes innovation, investment, competition, free expression, and other national broadband goals. The record before us convinces us that these findings, made by the Commission in 2010 and upheld by the D.C. Circuit, remain valid. If anything, the remarkable increases in investment and innovation seen in recent years—while the rules were in place—bear out the Commission's view. For example, in addition to broadband infrastructure investment, there has been substantial growth in the digital app economy, video over broadband, and VoIP, as well as a rise in mobile e-commerce. Overall Internet adoption has also increased since 2010. Both within the network

and at its edges, investment and innovation have flourished while the open Internet rules were in force.

77. The record before us also overwhelmingly supports the proposition that the Internet's openness is critical to its ability to serve as a platform for speech and civic engagement, and that it can help close the digital divide by facilitating the development of diverse content, applications, and services. The record also supports the proposition that the Internet's openness continues to enable a "virtuous [cycle] of innovation in which new uses of the network — including new content, applications, services, and devices — lead to increased end-user demand for broadband, which drives network improvements, which in turn lead to further innovative network uses." 2010 Open Internet Order, 25 FCC Rcd. at 17,910–11, ¶ 14. End users experienced the benefits of Internet openness that stemmed from the Commission's 2010 open Internet rules — increased consumer choice, freedom of expression, and innovation.

2. Broadband Providers Have the Incentive and Ability to Limit Openness

78. Broadband providers function as gatekeepers for both their end user customers who access the Internet, and for various transit providers, CDNs [content delivery networks], and edge providers attempting to reach the broadband provider's end-user subscribers. As discussed in more detail below, broadband providers (including mobile broadband providers) have the economic incentives and technical ability to engage in practices that pose a threat to Internet openness by harming other network providers, edge providers, and end users.

a. Economic Incentives and Ability

79. As explained in detail in the 2010 Open Internet Order, broadband providers not only have the incentive and ability to limit openness, but they had done so in the past. The D.C. Circuit found that the Commission "adequately supported and explained" that, absent open Internet rules, "broadband providers represent a threat to Internet openness and could act in ways that would ultimately inhibit the speed and extent of future broadband deployment." *Verizon*, 740 F.3d at 645. The record generated in this proceeding convinces us that the Commission's conclusion in the 2010 Open Internet Order — that providers of broadband have a variety of strong incentives to limit Internet openness — remains valid today.

80. Broadband providers' networks serve as platforms for Internet ecosystem participants to communicate, enabling broadband providers to impose barriers to end-user access to the Internet on one hand, and to edge provider access to broadband subscribers on the other. This applies to both fixed and mobile broadband providers. Although there is some disagreement among commenters, the record provides substantial evidence that broadband providers have significant bargaining power in negotiations with edge providers and intermediaries that depend on access to their networks because of their ability to control the flow of traffic into and on their networks. Another way to describe this significant bargaining power is in terms of

a broadband provider's position as gatekeeper — that is, regardless of the competition in the local market for broadband Internet access, once a consumer chooses a broadband provider, that provider has a monopoly on access to the subscriber. Many parties demonstrated that both mobile and fixed broadband providers are in a position to function as a gatekeeper with respect to edge providers. Once the broadband provider is the sole provider of access to an end user, this can influence that network's interactions with edge providers, end users, and others. As the Commission and the court have recognized, broadband providers are in a position to act as a "gatekeeper" between end users' access to edge providers' applications, services, and devices and reciprocally for edge providers' access to end users. *Verizon*, 740 F.3d at 646 (quoting 2010 Open Internet Order, 25 FCC Rcd. at 17,919, 17,935, ¶¶ 24, 50). Broadband providers can exploit this role by acting in ways that may harm the open Internet, such as preferring their own or affiliated content, demanding fees from edge providers, or placing technical barriers to reaching end users. Without multiple, substitutable paths to the consumer, and the ability to select the most cost-effective route, edge providers will be subject to the broadband provider's gatekeeper position. The D.C. Circuit noted that the Commission "convincingly detailed" broadband providers' market position, which gives them "the economic power to restrict edge-provider traffic and charge for the services they furnish edge providers," and further stated that the Commission reasonably explained that "this ability to act as a 'gatekeeper' distinguishes broadband providers from other participants in the Internet marketplace who have no similar 'control [[over] access to the Internet for their subscribers and for anyone wishing to reach those subscribers.'" *Id.* The ability of broadband providers to exploit this gatekeeper role could be mitigated if consumers multi-homed (i.e., bought broadband service from multiple networks). However, multi-homing is not widely practiced and imposes significant additional costs on consumers. The gatekeeper role could also be mitigated if a consumer could easily switch broadband providers. But, as discussed further below, the evidence suggests otherwise.

81. The broadband provider's position as gatekeeper is strengthened by the high switching costs consumers face when seeking a new service. Among the costs that consumers may experience are: high upfront device installation fees; long-term contracts and early termination fees; the activation fee when changing service providers; and compatibility costs of owned equipment not working with the new service. These costs may limit consumers' willingness and ability to switch carriers, if such a choice is indeed available. Commenters also point to an information problem, whereby consumers are unsure about the causes of problems or limitations with their services — for example, whether a slow speed on an application is caused by the broadband provider or the edge provider — and as such consumers may not feel that switching providers will resolve their Internet access issues. Additionally, consumers on unlimited data plans may be confused by slowed data speeds because broadband providers have not adequately communicated contractually-imposed data management practices and usage thresholds. Switching costs are also a critical

factor that negatively impacts mobile broadband consumers, in particular due to the informational uncertainties mentioned below, among other reasons. Ultimately, when consumers face this kind of friction in switching to meaningful competitive alternatives, it decreases broadband provider's responsiveness to consumer demands and limits the provider's incentives to improve their networks. Additionally, 45 percent of households have only a single provider option for 25 Mbps/3 Mbps broadband service, indicating that 45 percent of households do not have any choices to switch to at this critical level of service.

82. Broadband providers may seek to gain economic advantages by favoring their own or affiliated content over other third-party sources. Technological advances have given broadband providers the ability to block content in real time, which allows them to act on their financial incentives to do so in order to cut costs or prefer certain types of content. Data caps or allowances, which limit the amount and type of content users access online, can have a role in providing consumers options and differentiating services in the marketplace, but they also can negatively influence customer behavior and the development of new applications. Similarly, broadband providers have incentives to charge for prioritized access to end users or degrade the level of service provided to non-prioritized content. When bandwidth is limited during peak hours, its scarcity can cause reliability and quality concerns, which increases broadband providers' ability to charge for prioritization. Such practices could result in so-called "tolls" for edge providers seeking to reach a broadband provider's subscribers, leading to reduced innovation at the edge, as well as increased rates for end users, reducing consumer demand, and further disrupting the virtuous cycle. Commenters expressed considerable concern regarding the harmful effects of paid prioritization on Internet openness. Further, as discussed above, a broadband provider's incentive to favor affiliated content or the content of unaffiliated firms that pay for it to do so, to block or degrade traffic, to charge edge providers for access to end users, and to disadvantage non-prioritized transmission all increase when end users are less able to respond by switching to rival broadband providers.

83. In addition to the harms outlined above, broadband providers' behavior has the potential to cause a variety of other negative externalities that hurt the open nature of the Internet. Broadband providers have incentives to engage in practices that will provide them short term gains but will not adequately take into account the effects on the virtuous cycle. In the Open Internet Order, the Commission found that the unaccounted-for harms to innovation are negative externalities, and are likely to be particularly large because of the rapid pace of Internet innovation, and wide-ranging because of the role of the Internet as a general purpose technology. Further, the Commission noted that a broadband provider may hesitate to impose costs on its own subscribers, but it will typically not take into account the effect that reduced edge provider investment and innovation has on the attractiveness of the Internet to end users that rely on other broadband providers—and will therefore ignore a significant fraction of the cost of forgone innovation. The record supports our view

that these negative externality problems have not disappeared, and in some cases, may be more prevalent. In order to mitigate these negative results, the Commission needs to act to promote Internet openness.

84. A final point on this question of economic incentives and ability is worth noting. Broadband providers have the ability to act as gatekeepers even in the absence of "the sort of market concentration that would enable them to impose substantial price increases on end users." *Verizon*, 740 F.3d at 648 (citing 2010 Open Internet Order, 25 FCC Rcd. at 17,923, ¶ 32). We therefore need not consider whether market concentration gives broadband providers the ability to raise prices. The Commission came to this conclusion in the Open Internet Order, and we conclude the same here. As the Commission noted in the Open Internet Order, threats to Internet-enabled innovation, growth, and competition do not depend on broadband providers having market power with respect to their end users. In *Verizon*, the court agreed, explaining that "broadband providers' ability to impose restrictions on edge providers simply depends on end users not being fully responsive to the imposition of such restrictions." 740 F.3d at 648. As we have concluded in this section, this remains true today.

Notes and Questions

1. Market Power. Note that the rules disavow any reliance on broadband providers' market power with respect to possible price increases, emphasizing their ability to act as gatekeepers. But is market power with respect to end users relevant to the argument for net neutrality more generally? In a world with many competitors offering broadband internet access, presumably companies would compete on whatever axes consumers value. If end users value net neutrality, then in a competitive market wouldn't we expect one of the companies to promise net neutrality? Note the order's reference to end users not being fully responsive to violations of net neutrality. Is that more likely to be because end users don't know or don't care? If the latter, does that undercut the argument for net neutrality? Or does it merely highlight that there are costs to non-neutrality (for instance, to innovation) that end users don't fully bear?

2. What About Allowing Paid Prioritization Offered to All? These rules prohibited paid prioritization. An alternative would have been to allow broadband providers to charge for higher levels of service but require them to make the menu of levels available to all on an equal basis, so that everyone who wanted priority would pay the same price for the privilege. Many common carriers have offered tiered pricing (again, with the same prices available to all). Why not allow that here? Is it because of the fear that the free level of service would be very low quality, thus effectively forcing all the content, applications, and services providers to pay? Is it because of the fear that smaller companies do not have the same ability to pay for prioritization as their larger competitors do? Of course, smaller companies may not be as able to pay for lots of things that would increase the speed of their service (e.g., better servers and data centers that are geographically distributed near users). Is the disparity in ability to pay for internet access service different, as a matter of substantive policy, from the disparity in ability to pay for servers and data centers? Or does the disparity for all of them raise similar policy concerns, but internet access service is an area where the FCC can reduce the advantages provided by ability to pay, whereas the FCC cannot do so with respect to servers and data centers?

3. **"Permissionless Innovation."** Some net neutrality opponents (and the FCC in its 2018 order repealing the net neutrality rules) have argued net neutrality replaces an open internet ecosystem with one where a significant number of innovations could be implemented only with advance permission. Is that a fair characterization? In a portion of the rules that we did not excerpt, the FCC provided for waivers of its prohibition on paid prioritization (while also noting that such waivers would be disfavored). Would those emphasizing permissionless innovation prefer that no such waivers be allowed?

More generally, what potentially valuable innovations might be affected by the FCC's rules? What metric enables the striking of a balance between the innovations the FCC argues would be helped by the order and those that might be hindered?

4. **Affirmed.** In the opinion excerpted below, the D.C. Circuit upheld the FCC's 2015 Open Internet Order against all the challenges presented.

United States Telecom Ass'n v. FCC

825 F.3d 674 (D.C. Cir. 2016)

Opinion for the Court filed by Circuit Judges TATEL and SRINIVASAN. Opinion concurring in part and dissenting in part filed by Senior Circuit Judge WILLIAMS.

TATEL and SRINIVASAN, Circuit Judges:

I. D

A few months after our decision in Verizon v. FCC, 740 F.3d 623 (D.C. Cir. 2014), the Federal Communications Commission issued a notice of proposed rulemaking to "find the best approach to protecting and promoting Internet openness." Protecting and Promoting the Open Internet, Notice of Proposed Rulemaking, 29 FCC Rcd. 5561, 5563, ¶ 4 (2014). After receiving nearly four million comments, the Commission promulgated the order at issue in this case, Protecting and Promoting the Open Internet, Report and Order on Remand, Declaratory Ruling, and Order, 30 FCC Rcd. 5601 (2015) ("2015 Open Internet Order" or "the Order").

The Order consists of three components. First, the Commission reclassified both fixed and mobile "broadband Internet access service" as telecommunications services. 2015 Open Internet Order, 30 FCC Rcd. at 5743–44, ¶ 331. Because the Commission concluded that the telecommunications service offered to end users necessarily includes the arrangements that broadband providers make with other networks to exchange traffic—commonly referred to as "interconnection arrangements"—the Commission determined that Title II would apply to those arrangements as well. The Commission also reclassified mobile broadband service, which it had previously deemed a "private mobile service," exempt from common carrier regulation, as a "commercial mobile service," subject to such regulation.

In the Order's second component, the Commission carried out its statutory mandate to forbear "from applying any regulation or any provision" of the Communications Act if it determines that the provision is unnecessary to ensure just and reasonable service or protect consumers and determines that forbearance is "consistent with the public interest." 47 U.S.C. § 160(a). Specifically, the Commission forbore from applying certain Title II provisions to broadband service, including section 251's mandatory unbundling requirements.

In the third portion of the Order, the Commission promulgated five open internet rules, which it applied to both fixed and mobile broadband service. The first three of the Commission's rules, which it called "bright-line rules," ban blocking, throttling, and paid prioritization. The anti-blocking and anti-throttling rules prohibit broadband providers from blocking "lawful content, applications, services, or non-harmful devices" or throttling—degrading or impairing—access to the same. *Id.* at 5648, ¶ 112, 5651, ¶ 119. The anti-paid-prioritization rule bars broadband providers from "favor[ing] some traffic over other traffic ... either (a) in exchange for consideration (monetary or otherwise) from a third party, or (b) to benefit an affiliated entity." *Id.* at 5653, ¶ 125. The fourth rule, known as the "General Conduct Rule," prohibits broadband providers from "unreasonably interfer[ing] with or unreasonably disadvantag[ing] (i) end users' ability to select, access, and use broadband Internet access service or the lawful Internet content, applications, services, or devices of their choice, or (ii) edge providers' ability to make lawful content, applications, services, or devices available to end users." *Id.* at 5660, ¶ 136. The Commission set forth a nonexhaustive list of factors to guide its application of the General Conduct Rule, which we discuss at greater length below. Finally, the Commission adopted an enhanced transparency rule, which builds upon the transparency rule that it promulgated in its 2010 Open Internet Order and that we sustained in *Verizon*.

II

In the 2015 Open Internet Order, the Commission determined that broadband service satisfies the statutory definition of a telecommunications service: "the offering of telecommunications for a fee directly to the public." 47 U.S.C. § 153(53). In accordance with Nat'l Cable & Telecomm. Ass'n v. Brand X Internet Servs., 545 U.S. 967 (2005), the Commission arrived at this conclusion by examining consumer perception of what broadband providers offer. In *Brand X*, the Supreme Court held that it was "consistent with the statute's terms" for the Commission to take into account "the end user's perspective" in classifying a service as "information" or "telecommunications." 545 U.S. at 993. Specifically, the Court held that the Commission had reasonably concluded that a provider supplies a telecommunications service when it makes a "'stand-alone' offering of telecommunications, i.e., an offered service that, from the user's perspective, transmits messages unadulterated by computer processing." *Id.* at 989. In the Order, the Commission concluded that consumers perceive broadband service both as a standalone offering and as providing telecommunications. These conclusions about consumer perception find extensive support in the record and together justify the Commission's decision to reclassify broadband as a telecommunications service.

With respect to its first conclusion—that consumers perceive broadband as a standalone offering—the Commission explained that broadband providers offer two separate types of services: "a broadband Internet access service," 30 FCC Rcd. at 5750, ¶ 341, which provides "the ability to transmit data to and from Internet endpoints," *id.* at 5755, ¶ 350; and "'add-on' applications, content, and services that are generally information services," *id.* at 5750, ¶ 341, such as email and cloud-based storage programs. It found that from the consumer's perspective, "broadband Internet access service is today sufficiently independent of these information services that it is a separate offering." *Id.* at 5757–58, ¶ 356.

In support of its conclusion, the Commission pointed to record evidence demonstrating that consumers use broadband principally to access third-party content, not email and other add-on applications. "As more American households have gained access to broadband Internet access service," the Commission explained, "the market for Internet-based services provided by parties other than broadband Internet access providers has flourished." *Id.* at 5753, ¶ 347. Indeed, from 2003 to 2015, the number of websites increased from "approximately 36 million" to "an estimated 900 million." *Id.* By one estimate, two edge providers, Netflix and YouTube, "account for 50 percent of peak Internet download traffic in North America." *Id.* at 5754, ¶ 349.

That consumers focus on transmission to the exclusion of add-on applications is hardly controversial. Even the most limited examination of contemporary broadband usage reveals that consumers rely on the service primarily to access third-party content.

The Commission found, moreover, that broadband consumers not only focus on the offering of transmission but often avoid using the broadband providers' add-on services altogether, choosing instead "to use their high-speed Internet connections to take advantage of competing services offered by third parties." 2015 Open Internet Order, 30 FCC Rcd. at 5753, ¶ 347. For instance, two third-party email services, Gmail and Yahoo! Mail, were "among the ten Internet sites most frequently visited during the week of January 17, 2015, with approximately 400 million and 350 million visits respectively." *Id.* at 5753, ¶ 348. Some "even advise consumers specifically *not* to use a broadband provider-based email address[] because a consumer cannot take that email address with them if he or she switches providers." *Id.*

In support of its second conclusion—that from the user's point of view, the standalone offering of broadband service provides telecommunications—the Commission explained that "[u]sers rely on broadband Internet access service to transmit 'information of the user's choosing,' 'between or among points specified by the user,'" without changing the form or content of that information. 2015 Open Internet Order, 30 FCC Rcd. at 5761, ¶ 361 (quoting 47 U.S.C. § 153(50)); *see also id.* at 5762–63, ¶ 362. The Commission grounded that determination in record evidence that "broadband Internet access service is marketed today primarily as a conduit for the transmission of data across the Internet." *Id.* at 5757, ¶ 354.

[Broadband providers'] advertisements, moreover, "link higher transmission speeds and service reliability with enhanced access to the Internet at large — to any 'points' a user may wish to reach." *Id.* at 5756, ¶ 352. For example, RCN brags that its service is "ideal for watching Netflix," and Verizon touts its service as "work[ing] well for uploading and sharing videos on YouTube." *Id.* Based on the providers' emphasis on how useful their services are for accessing third-party content, the Commission found that end users view broadband service as a mechanism to transmit data of their own choosing to their desired destination — i.e., as a telecommunications service.

Petitioners assert numerous challenges to the Commission's decision to reclassify broadband. Finding that none has merit, we uphold the classification. Significantly, although our colleague believes that the Commission acted arbitrarily and capriciously when it reclassified broadband, he agrees that the Commission has statutory authority to classify broadband as a telecommunications service.

B

This brings us to petitioners' substantive challenges to reclassification. Specifically, they argue that the Commission lacks statutory authority to reclassify broadband as a telecommunications service. They also argue that, even if it has such authority, the Commission failed to adequately explain why it reclassified broadband from an information service to a telecommunications service. Finally, they contend that the Commission had to determine that broadband providers were common carriers under this court's [established] test in order to reclassify.

1

In addressing petitioners' first argument, we follow the Supreme Court's decision in *Brand X* and apply *Chevron*'s two-step analysis. At *Chevron* step one, we ask "whether Congress has directly spoken to the precise question at issue." *Chevron*, 467 U.S. at 842. Where "the intent of Congress is clear, that is the end of the matter; for [we], as well as the agency, must give effect to the unambiguously expressed intent of Congress." *Id.* at 842–43. But if "the statute is silent or ambiguous with respect to the specific issue," we proceed to *Chevron* step two, where "the question for the court is whether the agency's answer is based on a permissible construction of the statute." *Id.* at 843.

As part of its challenge to the Commission's reclassification, US Telecom argues that broadband is unambiguously an information service, which would bar the Commission from classifying it as a telecommunications service. The Commission maintains, however, that *Brand X* established that the Communications Act is ambiguous with respect to the proper classification of broadband. As the Commission points out, the Court explained that whether a carrier provides a "telecommunications service" depends on whether it makes an "offering" of telecommunications. *Brand X*, 545 U.S. at 989; *see also* 47 U.S.C. § 153(53) ("The term 'telecommunications service' means the *offering* of telecommunications for a fee directly to the public. . . ." (emphasis added)). The term "offering," the Court held, is ambiguous. *Brand X*, 545 U.S. at 989.

Seeking to escape *Brand X*, US Telecom argues that the Court held only that the Commission could classify as a telecommunications service the "last mile" of transmission, which US Telecom defines as the span between the end user's computer and the broadband provider's computer. Here, however, the Commission classified "the *entire* broadband service from the end user all the way to edge providers" as a telecommunications service. US Telecom Pet'rs' Br. 44. According to US Telecom, "[t]he ambiguity addressed in *Brand X* thus has no bearing here because the Order goes beyond the scope of whatever ambiguity [the statute] contains."

We have no need to resolve this dispute because, even if the *Brand X* decision was only about the last mile, the Court focused on the nature of the functions broadband providers offered to end users, not the length of the transmission pathway, in holding that the "offering" was ambiguous. As discussed earlier, the Commission adopted that approach in the Order in concluding that the term was ambiguous as to the classification question presented here: whether the "offering" of broadband internet access service can be considered a telecommunications service. In doing so, the Commission acted in accordance with the Court's instruction in *Brand X* that the proper classification of broadband turns "on the factual particulars of how Internet technology works and how it is provided, questions *Chevron* leaves to the Commission to resolve in the first instance." 545 U.S. at 991.

Amici Members of Congress in Support of Petitioners advance an additional argument that post-Telecommunications Act legislative history "demonstrates that Congress never delegated to the Commission" authority to regulate broadband service as a telecommunications service. In support, they point out that Congress has repeatedly tried and failed to enact open internet legislation, confirming, in their view, that the Commission lacks authority to issue open internet rules. But as the Supreme Court has made clear, courts do not regard Congress's "attention" to a matter subsequently resolved by an agency pursuant to statutory authority as "legislative history demonstrating a congressional construction of the meaning of the statute." American Trucking Ass'ns v. Atchison, Topeka, & Santa Fe Railway Co., 387 U.S. 397, 416–17 (1967).

This brings us, then, to petitioners' and intervenors' *Chevron* step two challenges.

First, US Telecom argues that the Commission's classification is unreasonable because many broadband providers offer information services, such as email, alongside internet access. According to US Telecom, because broadband providers still offer such services, consumers must perceive that those providers offer an information service. For its part, the Commission agreed that broadband providers offer email and other services, but simply concluded that "broadband Internet access service is today sufficiently independent of these information services that it is a separate offering." 2015 Open Internet Order, 30 FCC Rcd. at 5758, ¶ 356. US Telecom nowhere challenges that conclusion, and for good reason: the record contains extensive evidence that consumers perceive a standalone offering of transmission, separate from the offering of information services like email and cloud storage.

US Telecom next contends that the Commission's reclassification of broadband was unreasonable because DNS and caching do not fall within the Communications Act's telecommunications management exception. As noted above, that exception excludes from the definition of an information service "any [service] for the management, control, or operation of a telecommunications system or the management of a telecommunications service." 47 U.S.C. § 153(24). The Commission found that "[w]hen offered as part of a broadband Internet access service, caching [and] DNS [are] simply used to facilitate the transmission of information so that users can access other services." 2015 Open Internet Order, 30 FCC Rcd. at 5770, ¶ 372. Challenging this interpretation, US Telecom argues that DNS and caching fall outside the exception because neither "manage[s] a telecommunications system or service," but are instead examples of the "many core information-service functions associated with Internet access." US Telecom claims that the Commission's use of the telecommunications management exception was also unreasonable because the Commission "contends that the *same functions*—DNS and caching—are used for telecommunications management when offered as part of Internet access, but are an *information service* when third-party content providers similarly offer them." US Telecom Pet'rs' Br. 40. We are unpersuaded.

First, the Commission explained that the Communications Act's telecommunications management exception encompasses those services that would have qualified as "adjunct-to-basic" under the Computer II regime.[6] To qualify as an adjunct-to-basic service, a service had to be "'basic in purpose and use' in the sense that [it] facilitate[d] use of the network, and ... [it] could 'not alter the fundamental character of the [telecommunications service].'" *Id.* at 5767, ¶ 367 (last alteration in original) (quoting North American Telecommunications Ass'n, Memorandum Opinion and Order, 101 F.C.C. 2d 349, 359, 360, ¶¶ 24, 27 (1985)). The Commission concluded that DNS and caching satisfy this test because both services facilitate use of the network without altering the fundamental character of the telecommunications service. DNS does so by "allow[ing] more efficient use of the telecommunications network by facilitating accurate and efficient routing from the end user to the receiving party." *Id.* at 5768, ¶ 368. Caching qualifies because it "enabl[es] the user to obtain more rapid retrieval of information through the network." *Id.* at 5770, ¶ 372 (internal quotation marks omitted). US Telecom does not challenge the applicability of the adjunct-to-basic standard, nor does it give us any reason to believe that the Commission's application of that standard was unreasonable.

As to US Telecom's second point, the Commission justified treating third-party DNS and caching services differently on the ground that when such services are

6. [Computer II is discussed in Part II of *Brand X*, excerpted above. Eds.]

"provided on a stand-alone basis by entities other than the provider of Internet access service[,] . . . there would be no telecommunications service to which [the services are] adjunct." 2015 Open Internet Order, 30 FCC Rcd. at 5769, ¶ 370 n.1046. Again, US Telecom has given us no basis for questioning the reasonableness of this conclusion. Once a carrier uses a service that would ordinarily be an information service—such as DNS or caching—to manage a telecommunications service, that service no longer qualifies as an information service under the Communications Act. The same service, though, when unconnected to a telecommunications service, remains an information service.

2

We next consider US Telecom's argument that the Commission failed to adequately explain why, having long classified broadband as an information service, it chose to reclassify it as a telecommunications service.

As relevant here, "[t]he APA's requirement of reasoned decision-making ordinarily demands that an agency acknowledge and explain the reasons for a changed interpretation." *Verizon*, 740 F.3d at 636.

US Telecom contends that the Commission lacked good reasons for reclassifying broadband because "as *Verizon* made clear, and as the [Commission] originally recognized, it could have adopted appropriate Open Internet rules based upon § 706 *without* reclassifying broadband." But the Commission did not believe it could do so. Specifically, the Commission found it necessary to establish three bright-line rules, the anti-blocking, anti-throttling, and anti-paid-prioritization rules, all of which impose per se common carrier obligations by requiring broadband providers to offer indiscriminate service to edge providers, *see Verizon*, 740 F.3d at 651–52. "[I]n light of *Verizon*," the Commission explained, "absent a classification of broadband providers as providing a 'telecommunications service,' the Commission could only rely on section 706 to put in place open Internet protections that steered clear of regulating broadband providers as common carriers per se." 2015 Open Internet Order, 30 FCC Rcd. at 5614, ¶ 42. This, in our view, represents a perfectly "good reason" for the Commission's change in position.

Raising an additional argument, US Telecom asserts that reclassification "will undermine" investment in broadband. The partial dissent agrees, pointing specifically to 47 U.S.C. § 207, which subjects Title II common carriers to private complaints. The Commission, however, reached a different conclusion with respect to reclassification's impact on broadband investment. It found that "Internet traffic is expected to grow substantially in the coming years," driving investment, 2015 Open Internet Order, 30 FCC Rcd. at 5792, ¶ 412; that Title II regulation had not stifled investment when applied in other circumstances; and that "major infrastructure providers have indicated that they will in fact continue to invest under the [Title II] framework," *id.* at 5795, ¶ 416. In any event, the Commission found that the virtuous cycle—spurred by the open internet rules—provides an ample counterweight, in that any harmful effects on broadband investment "are far outweighed by positive effects on innovation and investment in other areas of the ecosystem that [its] core broadband polices will promote." *Id.* at 5791, ¶ 410. In reviewing these conclusions, we ask not whether they "are correct or are the ones that we would reach on our own, but only whether they are reasonable." EarthLink, Inc. v. FCC, 462 F.3d 1, 12 (D.C. Cir. 2006).

Finally, the partial dissent disagrees with our conclusion that the Commission had "good reasons" to reclassify because, according to the partial dissent, it failed to make "a finding of market power or at least a consideration of competitive conditions." Concurring & Dissenting Op. But nothing in the statute requires the Commission to make such a finding. Under the Act, a service qualifies as a "telecommunications service" as long as it constitutes an "offering of telecommunications for a fee directly to the public." 47 U.S.C. § 153(53).

US Telecom next argues that the Commission "could not rationally abandon its prior policy without account[ing] for reliance interests that its prior policy engendered." The Commission, however, did not fail to "account" for reliance interests. FCC v. Fox Televisions Stations, Inc., 556 U.S. 502, 515 (2009). Quite to the contrary, it expressly considered the claims of reliance and found that "the regulatory status of broadband Internet access service appears to have, at most, an indirect effect (along with many other factors) on investment." 2015 Open Internet Order, 30 FCC Rcd. at 5760, ¶ 360. The Commission explained that "the key drivers of investment are demand and competition," not the form of regulation. *Id.* at 5792, ¶ 412. Additionally, the Commission noted that its past regulatory treatment of broadband likely had a particularly small effect on investment because the regulatory status of broadband service was settled for only a short period of time. *Id.* at 5760–61, ¶ 360. As the Commission pointed out, just five years after *Brand X* upheld the Commission's classification of broadband as an information service, the Commission asked in a notice of inquiry whether it should reclassify broadband as a telecommunications service. *Id.* at 5760, ¶ 360.

III

Having thus rejected petitioners' arguments against reclassification, we turn to US Telecom's challenges to the Commission's regulation of interconnection arrangements — arrangements that broadband providers make with other networks to exchange traffic in order to ensure that their end users can access edge provider content anywhere on the internet. Broadband providers have such arrangements with backbone networks, as well as with certain edge providers, such as Netflix, that connect directly to broadband provider networks. In the Order, the Commission found that regulation of interconnection arrangements was necessary to ensure broadband providers do not "use terms of interconnection to disadvantage edge providers" or "prevent[] consumers from reaching the services and applications of their choosing." 2015 Open Internet Order, 30 FCC Rcd. at 5694, ¶ 205.

As authority for regulating interconnection arrangements, the Commission relied on Title II. "Broadband Internet access service," it explained, "involves the exchange of traffic between a . . . broadband provider and connecting networks," since "[t]he representation to retail customers that they will be able to reach 'all or substantially all Internet endpoints' necessarily includes the promise to make the interconnection arrangements necessary to allow that access." *Id.* at 5693–94, ¶ 204. Because the "same data is flowing between the end user and edge consumer," the end user necessarily experiences any discriminatory treatment of the edge provider, the Commission reasoned, making interconnection "simply derivative of" the service offered to end users. *Id.* at 5748–49, ¶ 339.

As a result, the Commission concluded that it could regulate interconnection arrangements under Title II as a component of broadband service. It refrained, however, from applying the General Conduct Rule or any of the bright-line rules to interconnection arrangements because, given that it "lack[ed] [a] background in practices addressing Internet traffic exchange," it would be "premature to adopt prescriptive rules to address any problems that have arisen or may arise." *Id.* at 5692–93, ¶ 202. Rather, it explained that interconnection disputes would be evaluated on a case-by-case basis under sections 201, 202, and 208 of the Communications Act.

US Telecom argues that our decision in *Verizon* prevents the Commission from regulating interconnection arrangements under Title II without first classifying the arrangements as an offering of telecommunications to edge providers and backbone networks. As US Telecom points out, *Verizon* recognized that broadband, and thus interconnection arrangements, provides a service not only to end users but also to edge providers and backbone networks, namely, the ability to reach the broadband provider's users. According to US Telecom, *Verizon* therefore requires the Commission to classify this service to edge providers and backbone networks as a telecommunications service before it regulates interconnection arrangements under Title II.

US Telecom misreads *Verizon*. Although *Verizon* does recognize that broadband providers' delivery of broadband to end users also provides a service to edge providers, it does not hold that the Commission must classify broadband as a telecommunications service in both directions before it can regulate the interconnection arrangements under Title II. The problem in *Verizon* was not that the Commission had misclassified the service between carriers and edge providers but that the Commission had failed to classify broadband service as a Title II service at all. The Commission overcame this problem in the Order by reclassifying broadband service—and the interconnection arrangements necessary to provide it—as a telecommunications service.

VI

We turn next to petitioners' challenges to the particular rules adopted by the Commission. As noted earlier, the Commission promulgated five rules in the Order: rules banning (i) blocking, (ii) throttling, and (iii) paid prioritization; (iv) a General Conduct Rule; and (v) an enhanced transparency rule. Petitioners Alamo and Berninger (together, Alamo) challenge the anti-paid-prioritization rule as beyond the Commission's authority.

A

In its challenge to the anti-paid-prioritization rule, petitioner Alamo contends that, even with reclassification of broadband as a telecommunications service, the Commission lacks authority to promulgate such a rule under section 201(b) of Title II and section 303(b) of Title III. The Commission, however, grounded the rules in "multiple, complementary sources of legal authority"—not only Titles II and III, but also section 706 of the Telecommunications Act of 1996 (now codified at 47 U.S.C. § 1302). *Id.* at 5720–21, ¶¶ 273–74. As to section 706, this court concluded in *Verizon* that it grants the Commission independent rulemaking authority. Alamo nonetheless argues that the Commission lacks authority to promulgate rules under section 706.

As we held in *Verizon* and reaffirm today, the Commission's section 706 authority extends to rules "governing broadband providers' treatment of internet traffic"—including the anti-paid-prioritization rule—in reliance on the virtuous cycle theory. *Verizon*, 740 F.3d at 628. Even if there were any lingering uncertainty about the import of our decision in *Verizon*, we fully adopt here our findings and analysis in *Verizon* concerning the existence and permissible scope of the Commission's section 706 authority, including our conclusion that the Commission's virtuous cycle theory provides reasonable grounds for the exercise of that authority.

That brings us to our colleague's suggestion that the Order embodies a "central paradox[]" in that the Commission relied on the Telecommunications Act to "increase regulation" even though the Act was "intended to 'reduce regulation.'" Concurring & Dissenting Op. We are unmoved. The Act, by its terms, aimed to "encourage the rapid deployment of new telecommunications technologies." Telecommunications Act of 1996, Pub. L. 104-104, 110 Stat 56. If, as we reiterate here (and as the partial dissent agrees), section 706 grants the Commission rulemaking authority, it is unsurprising that the grant of rulemaking authority might occasion the promulgation of additional regulation. And if, as is true here (and was true in *Verizon*), the new regulation is geared to promoting the effective deployment of new telecommunications technologies such as broadband, the regulation is entirely consistent with the Act's objectives.

VII

We finally turn to Alamo and Berninger's First Amendment challenge to the open internet rules. Having upheld the FCC's reclassification of broadband service as common carriage, we conclude that the First Amendment poses no bar to the rules.

B

Alamo argues that the open internet rules violate the First Amendment by forcing broadband providers to transmit speech with which they might disagree. We are unpersuaded. We have concluded that the Commission's reclassification of broadband service as common carriage is a permissible exercise of its Title II authority, and Alamo does not challenge that determination. Common carriers have long been subject to nondiscrimination and equal access obligations akin to those imposed by the rules without raising any First Amendment question. Those obligations affect a common carrier's neutral transmission of *others'* speech, not a carrier's communication of its own message.

Because the constitutionality of each of the rules ultimately rests on the same analysis, we consider the rules together. The rules generally bar broadband providers from denying or downgrading end-user access to content and from favoring certain content by speeding access to it. In effect, they require broadband providers to offer a standardized service that transmits data on a nondiscriminatory basis. Such a constraint falls squarely within the bounds of traditional common carriage regulation.

The "basic characteristic" of common carriage is the "requirement [to] hold[] oneself out to serve the public indiscriminately." *Verizon*, 740 F.3d at 651 (internal quotation marks omitted). That requirement prevents common carriers from "mak[ing] individualized decisions, in particular cases, whether and on what terms to deal." FCC v. Midwest Video Corp., 440 U.S. 689, 701 (1979). In the communications context, common carriers "make[] a public offering to provide communications facilities whereby all members of the public who choose to employ such facilities may communicate or transmit intelligence of their own design and choosing." *Id.* That is precisely what the rules obligate broadband providers to do.

Equal access obligations of that kind have long been imposed on telephone companies, railroads, and postal services, without raising any First Amendment issue. *See* Denver Area Educational Telecommunications Consortium, Inc. v. FCC, 518 U.S. 727, 739 (1996) (plurality opinion) (noting that the "speech interests" in leased channels are "relatively weak because [the companies] act less like editors, such as newspapers or television broadcasters, than like common carriers, such as telephone companies"); FCC v. League of Women Voters of California, 468 U.S. 364, 378 (1984) ("Unlike common carriers, broadcasters are entitled under the First Amendment to exercise the widest journalistic freedom consistent with their public duties."). The Supreme Court has explained that the First Amendment comes "into play" only where "particular conduct possesses sufficient communicative elements," Texas v. Johnson, 491 U.S. 397, 404 (1989), that is, when an "intent to convey a particularized message [is] present, and in the surrounding circumstances the likelihood [is] great that the message would be understood by those who viewed it," Spence v. Washington, 418 U.S. 405, 410–11 (1974). The absence of any First Amendment concern in the context of common carriers rests on the understanding that such entities, insofar as they are subject to equal access mandates, merely facilitate the transmission of the speech of others rather than engage in speech in their own right.

As the Commission found, that understanding fully applies to broadband providers. In the Order, the Commission concluded that broadband providers "exercise little control over the content which users access on the Internet" and "allow Internet end users to access all or substantially all content on the Internet, without alteration, blocking, or editorial intervention," thus "display[ing] no such intent to convey a message in their provision of broadband Internet access services." 2015 Open Internet Order, 30 FCC Rcd. at 5869, ¶ 549. In turn, the Commission found, end users "expect that they can obtain access to all content available on the Internet, without the editorial intervention of their broadband provider." *Id.* Because "the accessed speech is not edited or controlled by the broadband provider but is directed by the end user," *id.* at 5869–70, ¶ 549, the Commission concluded that broadband providers act as "mere conduits for the messages of others, not as agents exercising editorial discretion subject to First Amendment protections," *id.* at 5870, ¶ 549. Petitioners provide us with no reason to question those findings.

Because the rules impose on broadband providers the kind of nondiscrimination and equal access obligations that courts have never considered to raise a First Amendment concern—*i.e.*, the rules require broadband providers to allow "all members of the public who choose to employ such facilities [to] communicate or transmit intelligence of their own design and choosing," *Midwest Video*, 440 U.S. at 701 (internal quotation marks omitted)—they are permissible. Of course, insofar as a broadband provider might offer its own *content*—such as a news or weather site—separate from its internet access service, the provider would receive the same protection under the First Amendment as other producers of internet content. But the challenged rules apply only to the provision of internet access as common carriage, as to which equal access and nondiscrimination mandates present no First Amendment problem.

VIII

For the foregoing reasons, we deny the petitions for review.

WILLIAMS, Senior Circuit Judge, concurring in part and dissenting in part:

I agree with much of the majority opinion but am constrained to dissent. In my view the Commission's Order must be vacated for three reasons:

I. The Commission's justification of its switch in classification of broadband from a Title I information service to a Title II telecommunications service fails for want of reasoned decisionmaking. (a) Its assessment of broadband providers' reliance on the now-abandoned classification disregards the record. Furthermore, the Commission relied on explanations contrary to the record before it and failed to consider issues critical to its conclusion. (b) To the extent that the Commission relied on changed factual circumstances, its assertions of change are weak at best and linked to the Commission's change of policy by only the barest of threads. (c) To the extent that the Commission justified the switch on the basis of new policy perceptions, its explanation of the policy is watery thin and self-contradictory.

II. The Commission has erected its regulatory scheme on two statutory sections that would be brought into play by reclassification (if reclassification were supported by reasoned decisionmaking), but the two statutes do not justify the rules the Commission has adopted.

Application of Title II gives the Commission authority to apply § 201(b) of the Communications Act, 47 U.S.C. § 201(b). The Commission invokes a new interpretation of § 201 to sustain its ban on paid prioritization. But it has failed to offer a reasonable basis for that interpretation. Absent such a basis, the ban is not in accordance with law.

Application of Title II also removes an obstacle to most of the Commission's reliance on § 706 of the Telecommunications Act of 1996, 47 U.S.C. § 1302, namely any rules that have the effect of treating the subject firms as common carriers. *See* Verizon v. FCC, 740 F.3d 623, 650 (D.C. Cir. 2014). But the limits of § 706 itself render it inadequate to justify the ban on paid prioritization and kindred rules.

III. The Commission's decision to forbear from enforcing a wide array of Title II's provisions is based on premises inconsistent with its reclassification of broadband. Its explicit refusal to take a stand on whether broadband providers (either as a group or in particular instances) may have market power manifests not only its doubt as to whether it could sustain any such finding but also its pursuit of a "Now you see it, now you don't" strategy. The Commission invokes something very like market power to justify its broad imposition of regulatory burdens, but then finesses the issue of market power in justifying forbearance.

[T]he Commission chose to regulate under a Title designed to temper the effects of market power by close agency supervision of firm conduct, but forbore from provisions aimed at constraining market power by compelling firms to share their facilities, all with no effort to perform a market power analysis. The Order's combined reclassification-forbearance decision is arbitrary and capricious.

The ultimate irony of the Commission's unreasoned patchwork is that, refusing to inquire into competitive conditions, it shunts broadband service onto the legal track suited to natural monopolies. Because that track provides little economic space for new firms seeking market entry or relatively small firms seeking expansion through innovations in business models or in technology, the Commission's decision has a decent chance of bringing about the conditions under which some (but by no means all) of its actions could be grounded — the prevalence of incurable monopoly.

Notes and Questions

1. Following a Roadmap? The D.C. Circuit majority characterized the FCC as having followed a roadmap set out for it by the Supreme Court in *Brand X* and by the Court of Appeals itself in *Comcast* and *Verizon*. Do you think that is a fair characterization of what the FCC did?

2. Is the Provision of Internet Access "Speech" under the First Amendment? The full D.C. Circuit declined to review the opinion en banc, but that denial yielded opinions that addressed at greater length the First Amendment arguments discussed in part VII of the opinion above.

United States Telecom Ass'n v. FCC

855 F.3d 381 (D.C. Cir. 2017) (on petition for rehearing en banc)

Before: GARLAND, Chief Circuit Judge, HENDERSON, ROGERS, TATEL, BROWN, GRIFFITH, KAVANAUGH, SRINIVASAN, MILLETT, PILLARD, and WILKINS, Circuit Judges.

ORDER

Per Curiam

ORDERED that the petitions be denied.

SRINIVASAN, Circuit Judge, joined by TATEL, Circuit Judge, concurring in the denial of rehearing en banc:

Our dissenting colleague argues that the First Amendment poses an independent bar to the FCC's Order, Protecting and Promoting the Open Internet, Report and Order on Remand, Declaratory Ruling, and Order, 30 FCC Rcd. 5601 (2015) (Order). The Order, he submits, infringes the First Amendment rights of broadband ISPs. Specifically, he understands Supreme Court precedent to recognize a First Amendment entitlement on the part of an ISP to block its subscribers from accessing certain internet content based on the ISP's own preferences, even if the ISP has held itself out as offering its customers an indiscriminate pathway to internet content of their own — not the ISP's — choosing.

[T]he net neutrality rule raises no issue under the First Amendment. The key to understanding why lies in perceiving when a broadband provider falls within the rule's coverage. As the Order explains, broadband ISPs that are subject to the rule "sell retail customers the ability to go anywhere (lawful) on the Internet" — they "represent[] that they will transport and deliver traffic to and from all or substantially all Internet endpoints." Order ¶ 27; *see id.* ¶¶ 15, 350. They "display no . . . intent to convey a message in their provision" of internet access, *id.* ¶ 549, as would be necessary "to bring the First Amendment into play," Texas v. Johnson, 491 U.S. 397, 404 (1989).

In particular, "[b]roadband providers" subject to the rule "represent that their services allow Internet end users to access all or substantially all content on the Internet, *without alteration, blocking, or editorial intervention.*" Order ¶ 549 (emphasis added). Customers, "in turn, expect that they can obtain access to all content available on the Internet, *without the editorial intervention of their broadband provider.*" *Id.* (emphasis added). Therefore, as the panel decision held and the agency has confirmed, the net neutrality rule applies only to "those broadband providers that hold themselves out as neutral, indiscriminate conduits" to any internet content of a subscriber's own choosing. *U.S. Telecom Ass'n*, 825 F.3d at 743.

While the net neutrality rule applies to those ISPs that hold themselves out as neutral, indiscriminate conduits to internet content, the converse is also true: the rule does not apply to an ISP holding itself out as providing something other than a neutral, indiscriminate pathway—i.e., an ISP making sufficiently clear to potential customers that it provides a filtered service involving the ISP's exercise of "editorial intervention." Order ¶ 549. For instance, Alamo Broadband, the lone broadband provider that raises a First Amendment challenge to the rule, posits the example of an ISP wishing to provide access solely to "family friendly websites." Such an ISP, as long as it represents itself as engaging in editorial intervention of that kind, would fall outside the rule. The Order thus specifies that an ISP remains "free to offer 'edited' services" without becoming subject to the rule's requirements. Order ¶ 556.

There is no need in this case to scrutinize the exact manner in which a broadband provider could render the FCC's Order inapplicable by advertising to consumers that it offers an edited service rather than an unfiltered pathway. No party disputes that an ISP could do so if it wished, and no ISP has suggested an interest in doing so in this court. That may be for an understandable reason: a broadband provider representing that it will filter its customers' access to web content based on its own priorities might have serious concerns about its ability to attract subscribers. Additionally, such a provider, by offering filtered rather than indiscriminate access, might fear relinquishing statutory protections against copyright liability afforded to ISPs that act strictly as conduits to internet content. *See* 17 U.S.C. § 512.

In the event that an ISP nonetheless were to choose to hold itself out to consumers as offering them an edited service rather than indiscriminate internet access—despite the potential effect on its subscriber base—it could then bring itself outside the rule. In that sense, the rule could be characterized as "voluntary," *infra* at footnote 7 (Kavanaugh, J., dissenting), but in much the same way that just about any regulation could be considered voluntary, insofar as a regulated entity could always transform its business to such an extent that it is no longer in the line of business covered by the regulation.

Contrary to our dissenting colleague's argument, the Supreme Court's *Turner Broadcasting* decisions do not grant ISPs a First Amendment shield against the net neutrality rule's obligations. Those decisions arose in a markedly different context. They addressed the validity under the First Amendment of statutory "must-carry" requirements calling for cable television operators to "devote a portion of their channels to the transmission of local broadcast television stations." Turner Broad. Sys., Inc. v. FCC, 512 U.S. 622, 626, 630 (1994).

The Supreme Court ultimately upheld the must-carry obligations. In the process of doing so, however, the Court recognized that a cable operator's choices about which programming to carry on its channels implicate the First Amendment's protections. That is because a cable operator engages in protected First Amendment activity when it "exercis[es] editorial discretion over which stations or programs to include in its repertoire." *Turner*, 512 U.S. at 636.

The same cannot be said of broadband providers subject to the FCC's Order. Whereas a cable operator draws the protections of the First Amendment when it exercises editorial discretion about which programming to carry, an ISP falling within the net neutrality rule represents that it gives subscribers indiscriminate access to internet content without any editorial intervention. Cable operators, that is, engage in editorial discretion; ISPs subject to the net neutrality rule represent that they do not. The very practice bringing cable operators within the fold of the First Amendment's protections is inapplicable in the case of broadband providers subject to the net neutrality rule.

Our dissenting colleague likewise errs in fearing a slippery slope under which the government could require widely used web platforms such as Facebook, Google, Twitter, and YouTube, or a widely used commercial marketplace such as Amazon, to accept or promote all relevant content on nondiscriminatory terms. Those companies evidently do not share our colleague's concern — all but one is a member of a group that supports the rule in this court. That may be in part because those companies, in contrast with broadband ISPs, are not considered common carriers that hold themselves out as affording neutral, indiscriminate access to their platform without any editorial filtering. If an agency sought to impose such a characterization on them, they would presumably disagree. Here, by contrast, the rule applies only to ISPs that represent themselves as neutral, indiscriminate conduits to internet content, and no ISP subject to the rule — including Alamo Broadband — has disclaimed that characterization in this court.

The real slippery-slope concerns run in the reverse direction. Under our dissenting colleague's approach, broadband ISPs would have a First Amendment entitlement to block and throttle content based on their own commercial preferences even if they had led customers to anticipate neutral and indiscriminate access to all internet content. There is no apparent reason the same conclusion would not also obtain in the case of telephone service, which, like broadband service, is classified as common carriage.

For all of those reasons, broadband ISPs have no First Amendment entitlement to hold themselves out as indiscriminate conduits but then to act as something different. The net neutrality rule assures that broadband ISPs live up to their promise to consumers of affording them neutral access to internet content of their own choosing. The rule, in doing so, does not infringe the First Amendment.

KAVANAUGH, Circuit Judge, dissenting from the denial of rehearing en banc:

Under the Supreme Court's landmark decisions in Turner Broadcasting System, Inc. v. FCC, 512 U.S. 622 (1994), and Turner Broadcasting System, Inc. v. FCC, 520 U.S. 180 (1997), the First Amendment bars the Government from restricting the editorial discretion of Internet service providers, absent a showing that an Internet service provider possesses market power in a relevant geographic market. Here, however, the FCC has not even tried to make a market power showing. Therefore, under the Supreme Court's precedents applying the First Amendment, the net neutrality rule violates the First Amendment.

Here, of course, we deal with Internet service providers, not cable television operators. But Internet service providers and cable operators perform the same kinds of functions in their respective networks. Just like cable operators, Internet service providers deliver content to consumers. Internet service providers may not necessarily generate much content of their own, but they may decide what content they will transmit, just as cable operators decide what content they will transmit. Deciding whether and how to transmit ESPN and deciding whether and how to transmit ESPN.com are not meaningfully different for First Amendment purposes.

Indeed, some of the same entities that provide cable television service — colloquially known as cable companies — provide Internet access over the very same wires. If those entities receive First Amendment protection when they transmit television stations and networks, they likewise receive First Amendment protection when they transmit Internet content. It would be entirely illogical to conclude otherwise. In short, Internet service providers enjoy First Amendment protection of their rights to speak and exercise editorial discretion, just as cable operators do.

The FCC's theory is circular, in essence saying: "They have no First Amendment rights because they have not been regularly exercising any First Amendment rights and therefore they have no First Amendment rights." It may be true that some, many, or even most Internet service providers have chosen not to exercise much editorial discretion, and instead have decided to allow most or all Internet content to be transmitted on an equal basis. But that "carry all comers" decision itself is an exercise of editorial discretion. Moreover, the fact that the Internet service providers have not been aggressively exercising their editorial discretion does not mean that they have no *right* to exercise their editorial discretion.

[T]he FCC claims that, under the net neutrality rule, an Internet service provider supposedly may opt out of the rule by choosing to carry only *some* Internet content. But even under the FCC's description of the rule, an Internet service provider that chooses to carry most or all content still is not allowed to *favor* some content over other content when it comes to price, speed, and availability. That half-baked regulatory approach is just as foreign to the First Amendment. If a bookstore (or Amazon) decides to carry all books, may the Government then force the bookstore (or Amazon) to feature and promote all books in the same manner? If a newsstand carries all newspapers, may the Government force the newsstand to display all newspapers in the same way? May the Government force the newsstand to price them all equally? Of course not. There is no such theory of the First Amendment. Here, either Internet service providers have a right to exercise editorial discretion, or they do not. If they have a right to exercise editorial discretion, the choice of whether and how to exercise that editorial discretion is up to them, not up to the Government.

Think about what the FCC is saying: Under the rule, you supposedly can exercise your editorial discretion to refuse to carry some Internet content. But if you choose to carry most or all Internet content, you cannot exercise your editorial discretion to favor some content over other content. What First Amendment case or principle supports that theory? Crickets.[7] In light of the *Turner Broadcasting* decisions, Internet service providers have First Amendment rights. Of course, under the Supreme Court's case law, First Amendment rights are not always absolute: The Government may sometimes infringe on First Amendment rights if the Government shows a sufficient justification for doing so.

Turner Broadcasting establishes that, to impose content-neutral regulations on Internet service providers, the Government must satisfy the intermediate scrutiny test. To satisfy the intermediate scrutiny test, the Government's regulation must promote a "substantial governmental interest," be "unrelated to the suppression of free expression," and impose a restriction on First Amendment rights that "is no greater than is essential to the furtherance of that interest." *Turner Broadcasting*, 512 U.S. at 662.

Does the FCC's net neutrality rule satisfy intermediate scrutiny? The answer is no.

Applying intermediate scrutiny, the *Turner Broadcasting* Court held that content-neutral restrictions on a communications service provider's speech and editorial rights may be justified if the service provider possesses "bottleneck monopoly power" in the relevant geographic market. *Id.* at 661. But absent a demonstration of a company's market power in the relevant geographic market, the Government may not interfere with a cable operator's or an Internet service provider's First Amendment right to exercise editorial discretion over the content it carries.

At the time of the *Turner Broadcasting* decisions, cable operators exercised monopoly power in the local cable television markets. The problem for the FCC in this case is that here, unlike in *Turner Broadcasting*, the FCC has not shown that Internet service providers possess market power in a relevant geographic market. Indeed, the FCC freely acknowledges that it has not even tried to demonstrate market power. The FCC's Order states that "these rules do not address, and are not designed to deal with, the acquisition or maintenance of market power or its abuse, real or potential." Order ¶ 11 n.12 (2015).

Rather than addressing any problem of market power, the net neutrality rule instead compels private Internet service providers to supply an open platform for all

7. The concurrence in the denial of rehearing en banc seems to suggest that the net neutrality rule is voluntary. According to the concurrence, Internet service providers may comply with the net neutrality rule if they want to comply, but can choose not to comply if they do not want to comply. To the concurring judges, net neutrality merely means "if you say it, do it." If that description were really true, the net neutrality rule would be a simple prohibition against false advertising. But that does not appear to be an accurate description of the rule. *See* Protecting and Promoting the Open Internet, Report and Order on Remand, Declaratory Ruling, and Order, 30 FCC Rcd. 5601, 5682, ¶ 187 (2015) (Order) (imposing various net neutrality requirements on an Internet service provider that "provides the capability" to access "all or substantially all" content on the Internet) (italics omitted). It would be strange indeed if all of the controversy were over a "rule" that is in fact entirely voluntary and merely proscribes false advertising.

would-be Internet speakers, and thereby diversify and increase the number of voices available on the Internet. The rule forcibly reduces the relative voices of some Internet service and content providers and enhances the relative voices of other Internet content providers.

To be sure, the interests in diversifying and increasing content are important governmental interests in the abstract, according to the Supreme Court. But absent some market dysfunction, Government regulation of the content carriage decisions of communications service providers is not *essential* to furthering those interests, as is required to satisfy intermediate scrutiny. If the relevant communications marketplace is a competitive market, the theory is that the marketplace itself will both generate and provide room for a diversity and multiplicity of voices, without a need or justification for Government interference with private editorial choices. That is the lesson of *Turner Broadcasting*; and indeed, it is the lesson of the entire history of First Amendment and competition law.

Consider the implications if the law were otherwise. If market power need not be shown, the Government could regulate the editorial decisions of Facebook and Google, of MSNBC and Fox, of NYTimes.com and WSJ.com, of YouTube and Twitter. Can the Government really force Facebook and Google and all of those other entities to operate as common carriers? Can the Government really impose forced-carriage or equal-access obligations on YouTube and Twitter? If the Government's theory in this case were accepted, then the answers would be yes. After all, if the Government could force Internet service providers to carry unwanted content even absent a showing of market power, then it could do the same to all those other entities as well. There is no *principled* distinction between this case and those hypothetical cases.

In short, under *Turner Broadcasting*, the net neutrality rule flunks intermediate scrutiny because the FCC has not shown that Internet service providers possess market power in a relevant geographic market.

[Dissenting opinion of Judge BROWN is omitted.]

Notes and Questions

1. Which Comes First? The dissent argued that the First Amendment limits the FCC's ability to impose common carrier rules on internet providers, and requires the FCC to find a monopoly problem or other market failure before imposing such regulation. The concurring opinion responded that the FCC's rules apply only to those companies that "hold themselves out as neutral, indiscriminate conduits to internet content," so the editorial discretion that the First Amendment would protect is missing. As you will see below, the 2015 FCC and the 2018 FCC disagreed about whether broadband access providers are best understood as common carriers. But neither the 2015 nor the 2018 FCC treated monopoly as a statutory prerequisite to Title II classification.

2. Editorial Discretion. As Judges Srinivasan and Tatel noted, ISPs can avoid net neutrality regulations by offering an edited internet experience to customers, and they would then clearly be speakers for First Amendment purposes. Why don't ISPs do that? Are you expecting an edited experience when you buy internet service (as opposed to what you expect when you buy a book or a newspaper, or watch a channel)? If not, and if your ISP never expresses an interest in substantively editing your internet experience, is that relevant to the question whether your ISP is engaged in speech for First Amendment purposes?

3. What About Telephony and FedEx? The dissent suggested that transmission of bits is speech so long as the transmitter could exercise editorial discretion over what it transmitted, whether it chose to edit or not. To what other activities might this apply? Consider the following:

> Imagine that FedEx decided to speed up the delivery of documents addressed to companies with which it had a financial relationship. A congressional decision to ban such a practice would not seem to raise First Amendment issues. Yes, FedEx would be moving First Amendment-protected materials — documents — from one user to another, but it is hard to see how transporting documents turns a company into a speaker for First Amendment purposes. More precisely, the freedom of speech would not seem to encompass FedEx's business model. A company devoted to transporting messages with which it agreed — imagine a courier service that limited itself to communications between Republican- or Democratic-affiliated groups — would be a different matter. In that situation, the act of transmission would entail a communication: "We, the Republican [or Democratic] delivery service, are bringing you a document from a kindred spirit." But for a company like FedEx that does not so limit itself, there is no similar communication. The arrival of a FedEx truck gives no one any information about the content of the relevant document.
>
> Importantly, the argument that transmission equals speech would apply not only to ordinary carriers like FedEx but also to common carriers that carry speech. The obvious example is local telephone companies. They carry central forms of speech — conversations. If regulation of speech transmitters really does implicate the Free Speech Clause, then most (if not all) regulations of common carriers would trigger First Amendment scrutiny that would likely invalidate many of them.

Stuart Minor Benjamin, Transmitting, Editing, and Communicating: Determining What "The Freedom Of Speech" Encompasses, 60 Duke L.J. 1673, 1685–86 (2011). Local telephone companies have the technological ability to exercise some kinds of editorial discretion over what is transmitted over their lines. Under the dissent's reasoning are regulations of local telephone companies subject to First Amendment scrutiny? In the previous century did the Bell Telephone Company, with some of the best lawyers money could buy, fail to make a winning First Amendment argument against the regulations applied to it?

4. Congress. Would the dissent's limitation also apply to an Act of Congress, or does it apply only to an agency like the FCC? The First Amendment applies just as much to Congress as to other governmental actors, of course. But should the courts give greater deference to Congress's factfinding? If so, is that because Congress is better at factfinding than the FCC is (or the courts are)? If courts should defer to Congress (lest the First Amendment enable a new form of judicial second-guessing of economic regulation), then why can't Congress create a statute that delegates the factfinding to the agency?

5. Re-reclassifying and Eliminating the 2015 Rules.[8] 2017 brought a new Chair for the FCC (who as a commissioner dissented from the FCC's 2015 Open Internet Order) and a shift in the FCC's majority. The FCC quickly moved to undo the net neutrality regulatory regime (quickly in the world of administrative law, anyway). First, in February 2017, the Wireless Telecommunications Bureau announced that it was withdrawing a previous report on so-called "zero rating" practices by several wireless companies and terminating its investigations into those practices. Policy Review of Mobile Broadband Operators' Sponsored Data Offerings for Zero Rated Content and Services, Order, 2017 WL 483678 (Wireless Telecomm. Bureau). Second, and more significantly, in 2018 the FCC reclassified broadband internet access service as a Title I information service and rejected the rules that the 2015 rules had imposed. Below we excerpt the FCC's discussion of its policy rationale, and we leave the discussion of the legal issues to the court opinion.

Restoring Internet Freedom

Declaratory Ruling, Report and Order, and Order, 33 FCC Rcd. 311 (2018)

C. Public Policy Supports Classifying Broadband Internet Access Service As An Information Service

86. While our legal analysis concluding that broadband Internet access service is best classified as an information service under the Act is sufficient grounds alone on which to base our classification decision, the public policy arguments advanced in the record and economic analysis reinforce that conclusion. We find that reinstating the information service classification for broadband Internet access service is more likely to encourage broadband investment and innovation, furthering our goal of making broadband available to all Americans and benefitting the entire Internet ecosystem.

---

8. Actually, the 2018 rules were a re-re-reclassification for DSL: as we noted above, in 2005, DSL (which had been classified as a telecommunications service under Title II) was reclassified as an information service under Title I. In 2015, it was re-reclassified back to Title II as a telecommunications service. In 2018, it was re-re-reclassified back to Title I as an information service.

87. Based on the record in this proceeding, we conclude that economic theory, empirical studies, and observational evidence support reclassification of broadband Internet access service as an information service rather than the application of public-utility style regulation on ISPs. We find the Title II classification likely has resulted, and will result, in considerable social cost, in terms of foregone investment and innovation. At the same time, classification of broadband Internet access service under Title II has had no discernable incremental benefit relative to Title I classification. The regulations promulgated under the Title II regime appear to have been a solution in search of a problem. Close examination of the examples of harm cited by proponents of Title II to justify heavy-handed regulation reveal that they are sparse and often exaggerated. Moreover, economic incentives, including competitive pressures, support Internet openness. We find that the gatekeeper theory, the bedrock of the Title II Order's overall argument justifying its approach, is a poor fit for the broadband Internet access service market. Protecting and Promoting the Open Internet, Report and Order on Remand, Declaratory Ruling, and Order, 30 FCC Rcd. 5601 (2015) (Title II Order).[9] Further, even if there may be potential harms, we find that pre-existing legal remedies, particularly antitrust and consumer protection laws, sufficiently address such harms so that they are outweighed by the well-recognized disadvantages of public utility regulation. As such, we find that public policy considerations support our legal finding that broadband Internet access service is an information service under the Act.

1. Title II Regulation Imposes Substantial Costs on the Internet Ecosystem

88. The Commission has long recognized that regulatory burdens and uncertainty, such as those inherent in Title II, can deter investment by regulated entities. This concern is well-documented in the economics literature on regulatory theory, and the record also supports the theory that the regulation imposed by Title II will negatively impact investment. The balance of the evidence in the record suggests that Title II classification has reduced ISP investment in broadband networks, as well as hampered innovation, because of regulatory uncertainty. The record also demonstrates that small ISPs, many of which serve rural consumers, have been particularly harmed by Title II. And there is no convincing evidence of increased investment in the edge that would compensate for the reduction in network investment.

89. *Investment by ISPs.* The owners of network infrastructure make long-term, irreversible investments. In theory, public utility regulation is intended to curb monopoly pricing just enough that the firm earns a rate of return on its investments equivalent to what it would earn in a competitive market. In practice, public utility

9. [The "Title II Order" is the same as the "2015 Open Internet Order" excerpted above and discussed in USTA v. FCC, 825 F.3d 674 (D.C. Cir. 2016). The 2018 FCC order's use of the shorthand "Title II Order" reflects the policy orientation of the 2018 FCC majority and its desire to contrast what it refers to as the "public-utility style regulation" of the 2015 order with its preferred light-touch regime. Eds.]

regulation can depress profits below the competitive rate of return for a variety of reasons. This reduction in the expected return reduces the incentive to invest. Importantly, the risk that regulation might push returns below the competitive level also creates a disincentive for investment.

90. We first look to broadband investment in the aggregate and find that it has decreased since the adoption of the Title II Order. ISP capital investment increased each year from the end of the recession in 2009 until 2014, when it peaked. In 2015, capital investment by broadband providers appears to have declined for the first time since the end of the recession in 2009. And investment levels fell again in 2016—down more than 3 percent from 2014 levels. Although declines in broadband capital investments have occurred in the past with changes in the business cycle, the most recent decline is particularly curious given that the economy has not experienced a recession in recent years but rather has been growing. While observing trends in the data by itself cannot establish the cause of directional movements, the stark trend reversal that has developed in recent years suggests that changes to the regulatory environment created by the Title II Order have stifled investment.

91. Comparisons of ISP investment before and after the Title II Order suggest that reclassification has discouraged investment.

98. [W]e conclude that reclassification of broadband Internet access service from Title II to Title I is likely to increase ISP investment and output. The studies in the record that control the most carefully for other factors that may affect investment support this conclusion. Consequently, we disagree with commenters who assert that Title II has increased or had no effect on ISP investment, given the failure of other studies to account for complexity of corporate decision-making and the macroeconomic effects that can play a role in investment cycles. We also disagree with commenters who assert that it may be too soon to meaningfully assess the economic effects that Title II has had on broadband infrastructure investment.

99. *Regulatory Uncertainty.* The evidence that Title II has depressed broadband investment is bolstered by other record evidence showing that Title II stifled network innovation. Among the unseen social costs of regulation are those broadband innovations and developments that never see the light of day. ISP investment does not simply take the form of greater deployment, but can also be directed toward new and more advanced services for consumers. Research and development is an inherently risky part of any business, and the Commission's actions should not introduce greater uncertainty and risk into the process without a clear need to do so. Numerous commenters have stated that the uncertainty regarding what is allowed and what is not allowed under the new Title II broadband regime has caused them to shelve projects that were in development, pursue fewer innovative business models and arrangements, or delay rolling out new features or services. Even large ISPs with significant resources have not been immune to the dampening effect that uncertainty can have on a firm's incentive to innovate.

100. Utility-style regulation is particularly inapt for a dynamic industry built on technological development and disruption. Within the communications industry, it is apparent that the most regulated sectors, such as basic telephone service, have experienced the least innovation, whereas those sectors that have been traditionally free to innovate, such as Internet service, have greatly evolved. Incumbents have often used Commission regulation under the direction of the "public interest" to thwart innovation and competitive entry into the sector and protect existing market structures. Given the unknown needs of the networks of the future, it is our determination that the utility-style regulations potentially imposed by Title II run contrary to the public interest.

101. The record confirms that concern about "regulatory creep"—whereby a regulator slowly increases its reach and the scope of its regulations—has exacerbated the regulatory uncertainty created by the Title II Order. Even at the time of adoption, the Commission itself did not seem to know how the Title II Order would be interpreted. As then-Chairman Wheeler stated in February 2015, "we don't really know. No blocking, no throttling, no fast lanes. Those can be bright-line rules because we know about those issues. But we don't know where things go next." Statement of Tom Wheeler, Former Chairman, FCC, Press Conference (Feb. 26, 2015), https://www.c-span.org/video/?c4534447/wheeler-general-conduct-standard. With future regulations open to such uncertainties, Title II regulation adds a risk premium on each investment decision, which reduces the expected profitability of potential investments and deters investment. Further, providers have asserted that although the Commission forbore from the full weight of Title II in the Title II Order, they were less willing to invest due to concerns that the Commission could reverse course in the future and impose a variety of costly regulations on the broadband industry—such as rate regulation and unbundling/open access requirements—placing any present investments in broadband infrastructure at risk. These concerns were compounded by the fact that while the Title II Order itself announced forbearance from ex ante price regulation, at the same time it imposed price regulation with its ban on paid prioritization arrangements, which mandated that ISPs charge edge providers a zero price. These threats to the ISP business model have been felt throughout financial markets.

102. We conclude that this ever-present threat of regulatory creep is substantially likely to affect the risk calculus taken by ISPs when deciding how to invest their shareholders' capital, potentially deterring them from investing in broadband, and to encourage them to direct capital toward less inherently-risky business operations.

107. *Investment at the Edge*. Finally, to more fully discern the impact of Title II, we must look at investment throughout the broadband ecosystem, including investment and innovation at the edge, as well as with other ecosystem participants (manufacturers, etc.). We agree with commenters who assert that looking only at ISP investment ignores investment that is occurring at the edge. While there is tremendous investment occurring at the edge, the record does not suggest a correlation

between edge provider investment and Title II regulation, nor does it suggest a causal relationship that edge providers have increased their investments as a result of the Title II Order.

108. In fact, one could argue that in the absence of Title II regulation, edge providers would have made even higher levels of investment than they undertook. In many cases, the strongest growth for a firm or industry predates the Title II Order.

2. Utility-Style Regulation of Broadband Is a Solution in Search of a Problem

109. *The Internet was open before Title II, and many economic factors support openness.* The Internet thrived for decades under the light-touch regulatory regime in place before the Title II Order, as ISPs built networks and edge services were born. [T]he incremental benefits of Title II over light-touch regulation are inconsequential, and pale in comparison to the significant costs of public-utility regulation.

110. The Internet as we know it developed and flourished under light-touch regulation. It is self-evident that the hypothetical harms against which the Title II Order purported to protect did not thwart the development of the Internet ecosystem. Edge providers have been able to disrupt a multitude of markets—finance, transportation, education, music, video distribution, social media, health and fitness, and many more—through innovation, all without subjecting the networks that carried them to onerous utility regulation. It is telling that the Title II Order and its proponents in this proceeding can point only to a handful of incidents that purportedly affected Internet openness, while ignoring the two decades of flourishing innovation that preceded the Title II Order.

116. Because of the paucity of concrete evidence of harms to the openness of the Internet, the Title II Order and its proponents have heavily relied on purely speculative threats. We do not believe hypothetical harms, unsupported by empirical data, economic theory, or even recent anecdotes, provide a basis for public-utility regulation of ISPs. Indeed, economic theory demonstrates that many of the practices prohibited by the Title II Order can sometimes harm consumers and sometimes benefit consumers; therefore, it is not accurate to presume that all hypothetical effects are harmful. Intrusive, investment-inhibiting Title II regulation requires a showing of actual harms, and after roughly fifteen years of searching, proponents of Title II have found "astonishing[ly]" few. *See USTA*, 825 F.3d at 761–62 (Williams, J., dissenting); Verizon v. FCC, 740 F.3d 623, 664–65 (D.C. Cir. 2014) (Silberman, J., dissenting). Further, the transparency rule we adopt today will require ISPs to clearly disclose such practices and this, coupled with existing consumer protection and antitrust laws, will significantly reduce the likelihood that ISPs will engage in actions that would harm consumers or competition. To the extent that our approach relying on transparency requirements, consumer protection laws, and antitrust laws does not address all concerns, we find that any remaining unaddressed harms are small relative to the costs of implementing more heavy-handed regulation.

117. *Incentives.* We find, based on the record before us, that ISPs have strong incentives to preserve Internet openness, and these interests typically outweigh any

countervailing incentives an ISP might have. Consequently, Title II regulation is an unduly heavy-handed approach to what, at worst, are relatively minor problems. Although the Title II Order argued that ISPs were incentivized to harm edge innovation, it also conceded that ISPs benefit from the openness of the Internet. The Title II Order found that "when a broadband provider acts as a gatekeeper, it actually chokes consumer demand for the very broadband product it can supply." 30 FCC Rcd. at 5608, ¶ 20. We agree. The content and applications produced by edge providers often complement the broadband Internet access service sold by ISPs, and ISPs themselves recognize that their businesses depend on their customers' demand for edge content. It is therefore no surprise that many ISPs have committed to refrain from blocking or throttling lawful Internet conduct notwithstanding any Title II regulation. Finally, to the extent these economic forces fail in any particular situation, existing consumer protection and antitrust laws additionally protect consumers.

118. The Open Internet and Title II Orders claimed to base their actions on a theory that broadband adoption is driven by a "virtuous cycle," whereby edge provider development "increase[s] end-user demand for [Internet access services], which [drive] network improvements, which in turn lead to further innovative network uses." Preserving the Open Internet, Report and Order, 25 FCC Rcd. 17,905, 17,910–11, ¶ 14 (2010) (Open Internet Order); Title II Order, 30 FCC Rcd. at 5603, 5604, 5608–09, ¶¶ 2, 7, 20–21. The Title II Order concluded that Commission action was necessary to protect this virtuous cycle because "gatekeeper" power on the part of ISPs might otherwise thwart it, Title II Order, 30 FCC Rcd at 5608–09, 5628, ¶¶ 20–21, 78, as ISPs "are unlikely to fully account for the detrimental impact on edge providers' ability and incentive to innovate and invest." Open Internet Order, 25 FCC Rcd at 17,918–21, ¶¶ 23–25. However, the economic analysis in the Open Internet Order and Title II Order was at best only loosely based on the existing economics literature, in some cases contradicted peer-reviewed economics literature, and included virtually no empirical evidence.

119. The underlying economic model of the virtuous cycle is that of a two-sided market. In a two-sided market, intermediaries — ISPs in our case — act as platforms facilitating interactions between two different customer groups, or sides of the market — edge providers and end users. The Open Internet Order takes the position that edge provider innovation drives consumer adoption of Internet access and platform upgrades. The key characteristic of a two-sided market, however, is that participants on each side of the market value a platform service more as the number and/or quality of participants on the platform's other side increases. (The benefits subscribers on one side of the market bring to the subscribers on the other, and vice versa, are called positive externalities.) Thus, rather than a single side driving the market, both sides generate network externalities, and the platform provider profits by inducing both sides of the market to use its platform. In maximizing profit, a platform provider sets prices and invests in network extension and innovation, subject to costs and competitive conditions, to maximize the gain both sides of the market obtain from interacting across the platform. The more competitive the market, the larger

the net gains to subscribers and edge providers. Any analysis of such a market must account for each side of the market and the platform provider.

120. Innovation by ISPs may take the form of reduced costs, network extension, increased reliability, responsiveness, throughput, ease of installation, and portability. These types of innovations are as likely to drive additional broadband adoption as are services of edge providers. In 2016, nearly 80 percent of Americans used fixed Internet access at home. There is no evidence that the remaining nearly one-fifth of the population are all waiting for the development of applications that would make Internet access useful to them. Rather, the cost of broadband Internet access service is a central reason for non-adoption. ISP innovation that lowers the relative cost of Internet access service is as likely as edge innovation, if not more so, to positively impact consumer adoption rates. Indeed, ISPs likely play a crucial role by offering, for example, low-margin or loss-leading offers designed to induce skeptical Internet users to discover the benefits of access. In response to a larger base of potential customers, the returns to innovation by edge providers would be expected to rise, thereby spurring additional innovative activity in that segment of the market.

121. Accordingly, arguments that ISPs have other incentives to take actions that might harm the virtuous cycle, and hence might require costly Title II regulation, need to be explained and evaluated empirically. In a two-sided market, three potential reasons for Title II regulation arise: the extent to which ISPs have market power in selling Internet access to end users; the extent to which ISPs have market power in selling to edge providers access to the ISP's subscribers (end users), which seems to primarily be to what the Commission and others appear to be referring when using the term "gatekeeper"; and the extent to which the positive externalities present in a two-sided market might lead to market failure even in the absence (or because of that absence) of ISP market power. In considering each of these, we find that, where there are problems, they have been overestimated, and can be substantially eliminated or reduced by the more light-handed approach this order implements.

122. Our approach recognizes our limits as regulators, and is appropriately focused on the long-lasting effects of regulatory decisions. Thus, we seek to balance the harms that arise in the absence of regulation against the harms of regulation, accounting for, in particular, the effects of our actions on investment decisions that could increase competition three to five or more years from now. We note that our reclassification of broadband Internet access service as an information service leaves the usual recourse of antitrust and consumer protection action available to all parties. That is, heavy-handed Title II regulation is unnecessary to enforce antitrust and consumer protection laws.

123. *Fixed ISPs Often Face Material Competitive Constraints.* The premise of Title II and other public utility regulation is that ISPs can exercise market power sufficient to substantially distort economic efficiency and harm end users. However, analysis of broadband deployment data, coupled with an understanding of ISPs' underlying cost structure, indicates fixed broadband Internet access providers frequently face

competitive pressures that mitigate their ability to exert market power. Therefore, the primary market failure rationale for classifying broadband Internet access service under Title II is absent. Furthermore, the presence of competitive pressures in itself protects the openness of the Internet. The theory that competition is the best way to protect consumers is the "heart of our national economic policy" and the premise of the 1996 Act.[10] We therefore find that the competition that exists in the broadband market, combined with the protections of our consumer protection and antitrust laws against anticompetitive behaviors, will constrain the actions of an ISP that attempts to undermine the openness of the Internet in ways that harm consumers, and to the extent they do not, any resulting harms are outweighed by the harms of Title II regulation.

129. *There is even greater competition in mobile wireless.* Mobile wireless ISPs face competition in most markets, with widespread and ever extending head-to-head competition between four major carriers. As of January 2017, at least four wireless broadband service providers covered approximately 92 percent of the U.S. population with 3G technology or better. Even in rural areas at least four service providers covered approximately 69 percent of the population.

130. Both the Title II Order and its supporters in the current proceeding fail to properly account for the pressure mobile Internet access exerts on fixed, including fixed wireline, Internet access supply. While we recognize that fixed and mobile Internet access have different characteristics and capabilities, for example, typically trading off speed and data caps limits against mobility, increasing numbers of Internet access subscribers are relying on mobile services only.

131. *ISP Competition in Supplying Edge Providers Access to End Users.* On the other side of the market, to the extent ISPs have market power in supplying edge providers, ISP prices to edge providers could distort economic efficiency (a potential harm that is distinct from anticompetitive behavior or because of a failure to internalize a relevant externality). Loosely speaking, such power over an edge provider can arise under one of two conditions: the ISP has conventional market power over the edge provider because it controls a substantial share of (perhaps a specific subset of) end-user subscribers that are of interest to the edge provider, or that edge provider's customers only subscribe to one ISP (a practice known as single homing).

132. Narrowly focusing on fixed ISPs, Comcast, the largest wireline ISP, has approximately one quarter of all residential subscribers in the US, while at speeds of at least 25 Mbps down and 3 Mbps up, the Herfindahl-Hirschman Index measure of concentration for the supply of access to residential fixed broadband Internet access

10. Hon. Maureen K. Ohlhausen, Antitrust Over Net Neutrality, 15 Colo. Tech. L.J. 119, 122 (2016) (quoting Standard Oil Co. v. FTC, 340 U.S. 231, 249 (1951)) (Ohlhausen, Antitrust Over Net Neutrality); Preamble, Telecommunications Act of 1996, Pub. L. No. 104-104, 110 Stat. 56 (1996). [At the time of this order, Ohlhausen was the Acting Chairman of the FTC. Eds.]

service subscribers meets the Department of Justice (DOJ) designation of "moderately concentrated."

133. Large shares of end-user subscribers, and/or market concentration, however, do not seem a likely source or indicator of conventional market power capable of significantly distorting efficient choices, with the possible exception of edge providers whose services require characteristics currently only available on high-speed fixed networks (such as video, which requires both high speeds and substantial monthly data allowances, and gaming and certain other applications, which require high speeds and low latency). Given Comcast's market share, even a fledgling edge provider that can only be viable in the long term if it offers service to three quarters of broadband subscribers, may not depend on gaining access to any single provider. And calculating market shares for wireline ISPs based on their end users may be too simplistic if edge providers can reach end users at locations other than their homes, such as at work, or through a mobile ISP. In addition, ISPs have good incentives to encourage new entrants that bring value to end users, both because such new entrants directly increase the value of the platform's service, and because they place competitive pressure on other edge providers, forcing lower prices, again increasing the value of the platform's service. Moreover, those smaller edge providers may benefit from tiered pricing, such as paid prioritization, as a means of gaining entry. In fact, some edge providers might consider reaching end users on mobile devices to be roughly as valuable as, or more valuable than, reaching end users on wireline networks.

134. In addition, larger edge providers, such as Amazon, Facebook, Google and Microsoft, likely have significant advantages that would reduce the prospect of inefficient outcomes due to ISP market power. For example, the market capitalization of the smallest of these five companies, Amazon, is more than twice that of the largest ISP, Comcast, and the market capitalization of Google alone is greater than every cable company in America combined. Action by these larger edge providers preventing or reducing the use of ISP market power could spill over to smaller edge providers, and in any case, is unlikely to anticompetitively harm them given existing antitrust protections. Consequently, any market power even the largest ISPs have over access to end users is limited in the extent it can distort edge provider decisions (or those of their end users).

135. Despite the preceding analysis, a second claim is made that relies solely on the second factor, single homing: "regardless of the competition in the local market for broadband Internet access, once a consumer chooses a broadband provider, that provider has a monopoly on access to the subscriber . . . Once the broadband provider is the sole provider of access to an end user, this can influence that network's interactions with edge providers, end users, and others." Title II Order, 30 FCC Rcd. at 5629–30, ¶ 80. Commenters have echoed this "terminating access monopoly" concern. The Title II Order contended that these forces applied to all ISPs, whether large or small, fixed or mobile, fiber or satellite, and "therefore [it] need not consider whether market concentration gives broadband providers the ability to raise prices." *Id.* at 5633, ¶ 84.

136. As a blanket statement, this position is not credible. It is unlikely that any ISP, except the very largest, could exercise substantial market power in negotiations with Google or Netflix, but almost certainly no small wireless ISP, or a larger but still small rural cable company or incumbent LEC, could do so. Further, from the perspective of many edge providers, end users do not single home, but subscribe to more than one platform (e.g., one fixed and one mobile) capable of granting the end user effective access to the edge provider's content (i.e., they multi-home). As the Title II Order acknowledges, to the extent multihoming occurs in the use of an application, there is no terminating monopoly.

137. Moreover, to the extent a terminating monopoly exists for some edge providers, and it is not offset or more than offset by significant advantages, there is the question of the extent to which the resulting prices are economically inefficient. A terminating (access) monopoly arises when customers on one side of the market, roughly speaking end users in our case, single home with little prospect of switching to another platform in the short run, while customers on the other side, roughly speaking edge providers in our case, find it worthwhile to multi-home. The terminating monopoly differs from conventional market power because it can arise despite effective competition between platforms. In that case, platforms must vigorously compete for single-homing end users, but have less need to compete for edge providers, who subscribe to all platforms. This means each ISP faces strong pressures to cut prices to end users, but does not face similar pressures in pricing to edge providers. However, ISPs are unlikely to earn supranormal profits, so any markups earned from edge providers in excess of total costs are generally passed through to end users. While such an outcome generally will not be efficient, there is no general presumption about the extent of that inefficiency, or even if prices to the multi-homers ideally should be lower than would emerge in the absence of a termination monopoly. In the present case, there is no substantive evidence in the record that demonstrates how different efficient prices to edge providers would be from the prices that would emerge without rules banning paid prioritization or prohibiting ISPs from charging providers at all.

138. Lastly, we find the record presents no compelling evidence that any inefficiencies, to the extent they exist, justify Title II regulation. There is no empirical evidence that the likely effects from conventional market power or the terminating monopoly, to the extent they exist, are likely to be significant, let alone outweigh the harmful effects of Title II regulation. For all these reasons, we find no case for supporting Title II regulation of ISP prices to edge providers.

139. *Externalities Associated with General-Purpose Technologies Are Not a Convincing Rationale for Title II Regulation.* Some commenters make somewhat inchoate arguments that ISPs should not be permitted to treat different edge providers' content differently or charge more than a zero price because the Internet is a "general purpose technology" and/or the services of some edge providers create positive externalities that the edge providers cannot appropriate. Unfortunately, these commentators fail to define or substantiate the extent of the problem, if any; fail

to demonstrate how much the situation would be improved by requiring nondiscriminatory treatment of all edge providers; do not explain why, if nondiscriminatory treatment is required, it should be at a zero price; do not assess whether the costs of such an intervention would be offset by the benefits; and do not consider whether other less regulatory measures would be more appropriate. Instead, these commenters seek to apply Title II regulation to all ISPs, and consider the solution to their concern that certain services or the Internet itself might be inefficiently undersupplied (for reasons well beyond the control of ISPs) to be a ban on ISPs only (and not other input suppliers of edge providers) charging edge providers *any* price. We reject this approach as unreasonable and unreasoned.

3. Pre-Existing Consumer Protection and Competition Laws Protect the Openness of the Internet

140. In the unlikely event that ISPs engage in conduct that harms Internet openness, despite the paucity of evidence of such incidents, we find that utility-style regulation is unnecessary to address such conduct. Other legal regimes — particularly antitrust law and the FTC's authority under Section 5 of the FTC Act to prohibit unfair and deceptive practices — provide protection for consumers. These long-established and well-understood antitrust and consumer protection laws are well-suited to addressing any openness concerns, because they apply to the whole of the Internet ecosystem, including edge providers, thereby avoiding tilting the playing field against ISPs and causing economic distortions by regulating only one side of business transactions on the Internet.

141. *Consumer Protection.* The FTC has broad authority to protect consumers from "unfair or deceptive acts or practices." 15 U.S.C. § 45(a)(1). As the nation's premier consumer protection agency, the FTC has exercised its authority, which arises from Section 5 of the FTC Act, to protect consumers in all sectors of the economy. The FTC has used its Section 5 authority to enjoin some of the practices at issue in this proceeding, such as throttling. The FTC is prohibited under the FTC Act from regulating common carriers. As a result, the Commission's classification of broadband Internet access service as a common carriage telecommunications service stripped the FTC of its authority over ISPs. Therefore, the return to Title I will increase the FTC's effectiveness in protecting consumers. Today's reclassification of broadband Internet access service restores the FTC's authority to enforce any commitments made by ISPs regarding their network management practices that are included in their advertising or terms and conditions. The FTC's unfair-and-deceptive-practices authority "prohibits companies from selling consumers one product or service but providing them something different," which makes voluntary commitments enforceable. Acting [FTC] Chairman Ohlhausen Comments at 10–11. The FTC also requires the "disclos[ur]e [of] material information if not disclosing it would mislead the consumer," so if an ISP "failed to disclose blocking, throttling, or other practices that would matter to a reasonable consumer, the FTC's deception authority would apply." *Id.* at 11. Today's reclassification also restores the FTC's authority to take enforcement action against unfair acts or practices. An unfair act or practice

is one that creates substantial consumer harm, is not outweighed by countervailing benefits to consumers, and that consumers could not reasonably have avoided. A unilateral change in a material term of a contract can be an unfair practice.

142. Many of the largest ISPs have committed in this proceeding not to block or throttle legal content. These commitments can be enforced by the FTC under Section 5, protecting consumers without imposing public-utility regulation on ISPs.

143. *Antitrust.* The antitrust laws, particularly Sections 1 and 2 of the Sherman Act, as well as Section 5 of the FTC Act, protect competition in all sectors of the economy where the antitrust agencies have jurisdiction. When challenged as anticompetitive under the antitrust laws, the types of conduct and practices prohibited under the Title II Order would likely be evaluated under the "rule of reason," which amounts to a consumer welfare test. The Communications Act includes an antitrust savings clause, so the antitrust laws apply with equal vigor to entities regulated by the Commission. Should the hypothetical anticompetitive harms that proponents of Title II imagine eventually come to pass, application of the antitrust laws would address those harms.

144. Section 1 of the Sherman Act bars contracts, combinations, or conspiracies in restraint of trade, making anticompetitive arrangements illegal. If ISPs reached horizontal agreements to unfairly block, throttle, or discriminate against Internet conduct or applications, these agreements likely would be per se illegal under the antitrust laws. Section 2 of the Sherman Act, which applies if a firm possesses or has a dangerous probability of achieving monopoly power, prohibits exclusionary conduct, which can include refusals to deal and exclusive dealing, tying arrangements, and vertical restraints. Section 2 makes it unlawful for a vertically integrated ISP to anticompetitively favor its content or services over unaffiliated edge providers' content or services.

146. Among the benefits of the antitrust laws over public utility regulation are (1) the rule of reason allows a balancing of pro-competitive benefits and anti-competitive harms; (2) the case-by-case nature of antitrust allows for the regulatory humility needed when dealing with the dynamic Internet; (3) the antitrust laws focus on protecting competition; and (4) the same long-practiced and well-understood laws apply to all Internet actors.

147. *Reasonableness.* The unilateral conduct that is covered by Section 2 of the Sherman Act would be evaluated under a standard similar to the rule of reason applicable to conduct governed by Section 1, "an all-encompassing inquiry, paying close attention to the consumer benefits and downsides of the challenged practice based on the facts at hand." Ohlhausen, Antitrust Over Net Neutrality, 15 Colo. Tech. L.J. at 142. We believe that such an inquiry will strike a better balance in protecting the openness of the Internet and continuing to allow the "permissionless innovation" that made the Internet such an important part of the modern U.S. economy, as antitrust uses a welfare standard defined by economic analysis shaped by a significant body of precedent. R Street Comments at 26–27.

149. We reject commenters' assertions that the case-by-case nature of antitrust enforcement makes it inherently flawed. A case-by-case approach minimizes the costs of overregulation, including tarring all ISPs with the same brush, and reduces the risk of false positives when regulation is necessary. We believe the Commission's bright-line and Internet conduct rules are more likely to inhibit innovation before it occurs, whereas antitrust enforcement can adequately remedy harms should they occur. As such, we reject the argument that innovation is best protected by ex ante rules and command-and-control government regulation. Further, while a handful of ISPs are large and vertically integrated with content producers, most ISPs are small companies that have no leverage in negotiations with large edge providers, which include some of the most valuable companies in the world. Regulating these companies is unnecessarily harmful. The antitrust laws can be tailored to the ISP's circumstances.

150. Moreover, the case-by-case analysis, coupled with the rule of reason, allows for innovative arrangements to be evaluated based on their real-world effects, rather than a regulator's ex ante predictions. Such an approach better fits the dynamic Internet economy than the top-down mandates imposed by Title II. Further, the antitrust laws recognize the importance of protecting innovation. Indeed, the FTC has pursued several cases in recent years where its theory of harm was decreased innovation. Accordingly, we believe that antitrust law can sufficiently protect innovation, which is a matter of particular importance for the continued development of the Internet. We also find that the combination of the transparency rule, ISP commitments, and their enforcement by the FTC sufficiently address the argument made by several commenters that antitrust moves too slowly and is too expensive for many supposed beneficiaries of regulation.

151. Additionally, the existence of antitrust law deters much potential anticompetitive conduct before it occurs, and where it occurs offers recoupment through damages to harmed competitors. Some commenters have cast doubt on the effectiveness of ex post enforcement, preferring ex ante rules. Yet as the FTC staff noted in its comments, this is a false dichotomy. "Effective rule of law requires both appropriate standards — whether established by common law court, Congress in statute, or by an agency in rules — and active enforcement of those standards." FTC Staff Comments at 21. Even the "bright line" rules in the Title II Order contain an exception for "reasonable network management." *See, e.g.*, 47 C.F.R. § 8.5. An ISP accused of violating those rules would be the subject of an ex post FCC enforcement action. The FCC would have to determine ex post whether a challenged practice constituted technical network management or not.

152. Moreover, economic research has demonstrated that the threat of antitrust enforcement deters anticompetitive actions.

153. *Focus on protecting competition*. One of the benefits of antitrust law is its strong focus on protecting competition and consumers. If a particular practice benefits consumers, antitrust law will not condemn it. The fact that antitrust law protects

competition means that it also protects other qualities that consumers value. "[The] assumption that competition is the best method of allocating resources in a free market recognizes that all elements of a bargain—quality, service, safety, and durability—and not just the immediate cost, are favorably affected by the free opportunity to select among alternative offers." Nat'l Soc'y of Pro. Eng'rs v. United States, 435 U.S. 679, 695 (1978). The market competition that antitrust law preserves will protect values such as free expression, to the extent that consumers value free expression as a service attribute and are aware of how their ISPs' actions affect free expression. The lack of evidence of harms to free expression on the Internet also bolsters our belief that Title II is unnecessary to protect social values that are not the focus of antitrust.

154. Finally, applying antitrust principles to ISP conduct is consistent with longstanding economic and legal principles that cover all sectors of the economy, including the entire Internet ecosystem. Applying the same body of law to ISPs, edge providers, and all Internet actors avoids the regulatory distortions of Title II, which "impos[ed] asymmetric behavioral regulations ... on broadband ISPs under the banner of protecting Internet openness, but le[ft] Internet edge providers free to threaten or engage in the same types of behavior prohibited to ISPs free of any ex ante constraints." ACA Comments at 67. Our decision today to return to light-touch Title I regulation and the backstop of generally-applicable antitrust and consumer protection law "help[s] to ensure a level, technology-neutral playing field" for the whole Internet. NCTA Comments at 56.

Notes and Questions

1. Compare and Contrast. What are the most foundational disagreements between the 2015 and 2018 orders? What, if any, significant areas of agreement exist between them?

2. Market Power. The 2018 order's emphasis on the importance of market power stands in stark contrast to the 2015 order's rejection of any reliance on market power. On what basis should policymakers and judges (and you) determine the relevance of market power in justifying net neutrality regulations? And what sorts of market power are the strongest justifications for net neutrality regulations?

3. Incentives. The 2018 order suggests that broadband access providers have strong incentives not to block or impede valuable content for consumers. On what basis would you agree or disagree with that assertion?

4. Who Needs Whom? Who needs whom more, as between broadband internet access providers and Google? Google wants as much access as possible to customers, but broadband providers know their customers want access to Google. Does your answer change if broadband internet access providers have enough competitors to lack market power?

5. Other Agencies and Laws. Note the order's emphasis on other agencies (notably the FTC) and other laws (notably the Sherman Act). That implicates one of the central foci on this casebook (the different laws and entities that might regulate the internet). Does the order fail to consider some of the disadvantages of those other agencies and regimes? If so, which of those disadvantages are most important, and what difference should they make?

6. Public Comments. This proceeding "prompted more comments than any other rulemaking in the Commission's history"—more than 22 million comments during the comment period. Restoring Internet Freedom ¶ 19 (not excerpted above). The 2018 order's response to the public comments was contained in the following two paragraphs:

> 344. In reviewing the record in this rulemaking, the Commission complied with its obligations under the Administrative Procedure Act (APA), 5 U.S.C. § 553, including the obligation to consider all "relevant matter" received, In re FCC 11-161, 753 F.3d 1015 (10th Cir. 2014), *quoting* Vermont Public Service Board v. FCC, 661 F.3d 54, 63 (D.C. Cir. 2011), to adequately consider "important aspect[s] of the problem," Motor Veh. Mfrs. Ass'n v. State Farm Ins., 463 U.S. 29, 43 (1983), and to "reasonably respond to those comments that raise significant problems," North Carolina v. FAA, 957 F.2d 1125, 1135 (4th Cir. 1992). Consistent with these obligations, the Commission focused its review of the record on the submitted comments that bear substantively on the legal and public policy consequences of the actions we take today.[11] Thus, our decision to restore Internet freedom did not rely on comments devoid of substance, or the thousands of identical or nearly-identical non-substantive comments that simply convey support or opposition to the proposals in the [NPRM in this proceeding].
>
> 345. Because we have complied with our obligations under the APA, we reject calls to delay adoption of this Order out of concerns that certain non-substantive comments (on which the Commission did not rely) may have been submitted under multiple different names or allegedly "fake" names.[12] The Commission is under no legal obligation to adopt any "procedural devices" beyond what the APA requires, such as identity-verification procedures. In addition, the Commission has previously decided not to apply its internal rules regarding false statements in the rulemaking context because we do not want "to hinder full and robust public participation in such policymaking proceedings by encouraging collateral wrangling over the truthfulness of the parties' statements." Amendment of Section 1.17 of

---

11. We note, for example, that it appears that 7.5 million identical one-sentence comments were submitted from about 45,000 unique e-mail addresses, all generated by a single fake e-mail generator website. Moreover, we received over 400,000 comments supporting Internet regulation that purported to be from the same mailing address in Russia.

12. *See, e.g.*, Brian Fung, FCC Net Neutrality Process 'Corrupted' by Fake Comments and Vanishing Consumer Complaints, Officials Say, Washington Post (Nov. 24, 2017), https://www.washingtonpost.com/news/the-switch/wp/2017/11/24/fcc-net-neutrality-process-corrupted-by-fake-comments-and-vanishing-consumer-complaints-officials-say/.

> the Commission's Rules Concerning Truthful Statements to Commission, Report and Order, 18 FCC Rcd. 4016, 4021–22, ¶ 13 (2003). To the extent that members of the public are concerned about the presence in the record of identical or nearly-identical non-substantive comments that simply convey support or opposition to the proposals in the [NPRM in this proceeding], those comments in no way impeded the Commission's ability to identify or respond to material issues in the record. Indeed, the Order demonstrates the Commission's deep engagement with the substantive legal and public policy questions presented in this proceeding.

Many of the comments indeed appear to have been fraudulent, although most of the non-fraudulent comments appear to have favored net neutrality rules. *See, e.g.*, Paul Hitlin, Kenneth Olmstead & Skye Toor, Public Comments to the Federal Communications Commission About Net Neutrality Contain Many Inaccuracies and Duplicates, Pew Research Center (Nov. 29, 2017), http://www.pewinternet.org/2017/11/29/public-comments-to-the-federal-communications-commission-about-net-neutrality-contain-many-inaccuracies-and-duplicates; Stanford Center for Internet and Society, Filtering Out the Bots: What Americans Actually Told the FCC about Net Neutrality Repeal (Oct. 2018), https://cyberlaw.stanford.edu/files/blogs/FilteringOutTheBotsUniqueNetNeutralityComments.pdf.

Commissioner Clyburn, dissenting from the 2018 order, complained about the order's lack of engagement with the comments: "I hold in my hand letters that plead with the FCC to keep our net neutrality rules in place but what is striking and in keeping with the new norm, despite the millions of comments, letters, and calls received, this Order cites, not even one consumer comment." Restoring Internet Freedom, 33 FCC Rcd. at 533 (dissenting statement of Commissioner Mignon L. Clyburn).

Should the 2018 order have said more about the public comments? More fundamentally, multi-member bipartisan agencies with fixed terms (like the FCC) were designed to have great insulation from political considerations and popular pressure. Should the FCC be influenced by comments from the citizenry, assuming it can separate real from fake comments? If so, what category of individuals should be counted—should it be the public as a whole, or only those who really care about the issue? If the answer is the former, then broad-based polls would seem to better reflect the relevant constituency than would the comments by those who took the time and trouble to submit their views. Assuming that the focus was on those who cared about the issue, it is still not clear that individual commenters are a good proxy, because a large percentage of individual comments are prompted (if not scripted) by campaigns launched by interest groups, and it would be quite surprising if the ability and energy required to organize such campaigns was distributed among interest groups in such a way as to reflect the proportions of concerned individuals who are on each side of an issue. *See* Stuart Minor Benjamin, Evaluating E-Rulemaking: Public Participation and Political Institutions, 55 Duke L.J. 893, 903–08, 933–35 (2006).

7. **Back to the D.C. Circuit.** Net neutrality supporters challenged the 2018 order, so it was back to the D.C. Circuit for the FCC and net neutrality. In the opinion below, the D.C. Circuit largely upheld the order.

Mozilla Corp. v. FCC

940 F.3d 1 (D.C. Cir. 2019)

Opinion for the court per curiam. Concurring opinions filed by Circuit Judges MILLETT and WILKINS. Opinion concurring in part and dissenting in part filed by Senior Circuit Judge WILLIAMS.

PER CURIAM:

In 2018, the Federal Communications Commission adopted an order classifying broadband Internet access service as an information service under Title I of the Communications Act of 1934, as amended by the Telecommunications Act of 1996. *See* Restoring Internet Freedom, Declaratory Ruling, Report and Order, and Order, 33 FCC Rcd. 311 (2018) (2018 Order). In so doing, the agency pursued a market-based, "light-touch" policy for governing the Internet and departed from its 2015 order that had imposed utility-style regulation under Title II of the Act. *See* Protecting and Promoting the Open Internet, Report and Order on Remand, Declaratory Ruling, and Order, 30 FCC Rcd. 5601 (2015) (Title II Order).

The 2018 Order accomplishes a number of objectives. First, and most importantly, it classifies broadband Internet as an "information service," and mobile broadband as a "private mobile service." Second, relying on Section 257 of the Act (located in Title II but written so as to apply to Titles I through VI), the Commission adopts transparency rules intended to ensure that consumers have adequate data about Internet Service Providers' network practices. Third, the Commission undertakes a cost-benefit analysis, concluding that the benefits of a market-based, "light-touch" regime for Internet governance outweigh those of common carrier regulation under Title II, resting heavily on the combination of the transparency requirements imposed by the Commission under Section 257 with enforcement of existing antitrust and consumer protection laws. The Commission likewise finds that the burdens of the Title II Order's conduct rules exceed their benefits.

I. Broadband Internet Classification

The central issue before us is whether the Commission lawfully applied the statute in classifying broadband Internet access service as an "information service." We approach the issue through the lens of the Supreme Court's decision in *Brand X*, which upheld the Commission's 2002 refusal to classify cable broadband as a "telecommunications service." Nat'l Cable & Telecomm. Ass'n v. Brand X Internet Servs., 545 U.S. 967, 974 (2005). The Commission's classification of cable modem as an "information service" was not challenged in *Brand X*, but, given that "telecommunications service" and "information service" have been treated as mutually exclusive by the Commission since the late 1990s, a premise Petitioners do not challenge, we view *Brand X* as binding precedent in this case.

We start, of course, with the statutory definition. Section 47 U.S.C. § 153(24) reads:

> The term "information service" means the offering of a capability for generating, acquiring, storing, transforming, processing, retrieving, utilizing, or making available information via telecommunications . . . but does not include any use of any such capability for the management, control, or operation of a telecommunications system or the management of a telecommunications service.

The final clause is known as the "telecommunications management" exception. The Act defines "telecommunications service" as follows:

> The term "telecommunications service" means the offering of telecommunications for a fee directly to the public, or to such classes of users as to be effectively available directly to the public, regardless of the facilities used.

Id. § 153(53).

The Commission appears to make two arguments for its classification. It states first that "broadband Internet access service necessarily has the capacity or potential ability to be used to engage in the activities within the information service definition — 'generating, acquiring, storing, transforming, processing, retrieving, utilizing, or making available information via telecommunications,'" 2018 Order ¶ 30 (quoting 47 U.S.C. § 153(24)), and on that basis alone merits an "information service" classification. The Commission then goes on to say: "But even if 'capability' were understood as requiring more of the information processing to be performed by the classified service itself, we find that broadband Internet access service meets that standard." 2018 Order ¶ 33.

[W]e hold that classifying broadband Internet access as an "information service" based on the functionalities of DNS and caching is "'a reasonable policy choice for the [Commission] to make' at *Chevron*'s second step." *Brand X*, 545 U.S. at 997 (alteration in original) (quoting Chevron U.S.A. Inc. v. Natural Res. Def. Cncl., 467 U.S. 837, 845 (1984)).

A. The Supreme Court's Decision in *Brand X*

Brand X held that, by virtue of the ambiguity of the word "offering," the FCC could permissibly choose not to classify cable modem service as a "telecommunications service." *Brand X*, 545 U.S. at 973–74, 989–92. As to DNS and caching, the *Brand X* Court endorsed the Commission's argument that those functionalities can be relied on to classify cable modem service as an "information service." Challengers opposing the FCC had argued that when consumers "go[] beyond" certain Internet services offered by cable modem companies themselves — for example, beyond access to proprietary email and Web pages (commonly referred to as the cable modem companies' "walled gardens") — the companies were "offering" a "telecommunications service" rather than an "information service." *Id.* at 998. The Court rejected this claim. It found that such a view "conflicts with the Commission's understanding of the nature of cable modem service," which the Court deemed "reasonable."

Id.; *cf.* 2018 Order ¶ 51. The Court explained that—when a user accesses purely third-party content online—"he is *equally using* the information service provided by the cable company that offers him Internet access as when he accesses the company's own Web site, its email service, or his personal Web page," *Brand X*, 545 U.S. at 999 (emphasis added), i.e., "walled garden" services. Why so?

Brand X's answer, as relevant here, lay in DNS and caching. The argument proceeded in two steps—first, showing that DNS and caching themselves can properly fall under the "information service" rubric; second, showing that these "information services" are sufficiently integrated with the transmission element of broadband that it is reasonable to classify cable modem service as an "information service." *See Brand X*, 545 U.S. at 999–1000.

B. DNS and Caching in the 2018 Order

The reasoning in the 2018 Order tallies with the line of argument in *Brand X* described above. The Commission's principal claim is that "ISPs offer end users the capability to interact with information online . . . through a variety of functionally integrated information processing components that are part and parcel of the broadband Internet access service offering itself"—including DNS and caching. 2018 Order ¶ 33. The Commission describes DNS and caching as "integrated information processing capabilities offered as part of broadband Internet access service to consumers today." *Id.* We hold that under *Brand X* this conclusion is reasonable.

C. Objections to the Classification

Petitioners raise numerous objections aimed to show that the Commission's reliance on DNS and caching for classifying broadband as an "information service" is unreasonable at *Chevron*'s second step. We find them unconvincing.

1. "Walled Garden" Reading of Brand X

First, to short-circuit the Commission's reliance on *Brand X*, Petitioners try to characterize the Court's reasoning in that case as dependent on a vision of Internet providers as offering mainly access to their "walled gardens." They assert that in *Brand X* "the Court was focused on the [broadband Internet access service (BIAS)] providers' add-on information services, such as ISP-provided email," and that "the Court had no occasion to consider the proper classification of a service combining telecommunications with nothing more than DNS and caching." This reading is unpersuasive because it airbrushes out the lengthy discussion summarized above in which the Court finds "reasonable" the Commission's "information-service" classification even where "a consumer goes beyond [walled garden] offerings and accesses content provided by parties other than the cable company," *Brand X*, 545 U.S. at 998—by virtue of the functionalities of DNS and caching. We thus reject Petitioners' attempt to discredit the Commission's sensible reliance on *Brand X*'s treatment of DNS and caching.

2. "Telecommunications Management" Exception

Petitioners assert that DNS and caching fall under the "telecommunications management" exception (TME) and so cannot be relied on to justify an "information service" classification. We find that Petitioners' arguments do not hold up, either because they rest on a misreading of *Brand X* and United States Telecom Ass'n v. FCC, 825 F.3d 674 (D.C. Cir. 2016) (*USTA*) or do not adequately grapple with the Commission's reasonable explanation as to why DNS and caching fall outside that exception. Our discussion here will be quite involved in part because *Brand X* did not directly confront whether DNS and caching may fall within the TME.

a. The Commission's Interpretation

To begin with, Petitioners misconstrue *USTA*. As they do persistently, they gloss passages that find parts of the Title II Order to be *permissible* readings of the statute as *mandating* those readings — when the passages plainly do not do so. A case in point is the treatment of the TME. Petitioners say that "[t]his Court has *already agreed* that DNS and caching fall within the terms of the telecommunications management exception." Mozilla Br. 43 (emphasis added) (citing *USTA*). Yet all we said in *USTA* was that we were "unpersuaded" that the FCC's "use of the telecommunications management exception was . . . unreasonable." *USTA*, 825 F.3d at 705. The Title II Order, in other words, adopted a permissible reading, though not a required one. This holding in no way bars the Commission from adopting a contrary view now — so long as it adequately justifies that view, as we find it has.

If a service is "directed at . . . customers or end users," 2018 Order ¶ 36 (quoting United States v. Western Elec. Co., No. 82-0192, 1989 WL 119060, at *1 (D.D.C. Sept. 11, 1989)), or benefits users "in significant part," *id.* ¶ 38, or "predominantly," *id.* ¶ 42, it does not call for TME classification. We view this construction as an adequately justified departure from the Title II Order's understanding of the TME in the face of a dauntingly ambiguous provision with inevitably fuzzy borderline cases and complex and possibly inconsistent (or at least orthogonal) policy implications.

Given the Commission's approach, it need not — and does not — deny that even those services properly classed under the TME benefit end users *in some respect*.

But a rule involving a spectrum or continuum commonly requires a decider to select a point where both ends are in play. Night and day are distinguishable, however difficult classification may be at dawn and dusk. The Commission notes that its "focus remains on the purpose or use of the specific function in question and not merely whether the resulting service, as a whole, is useful to end-users." 2018 Order ¶ 38 n.135. While DNS might play a role in managing a network, the Commission reasonably concluded that DNS "is a function that is useful and essential to providing Internet access for the ordinary consumer," *id.* ¶ 36, and that these benefits to the end user predominate over any management function DNS might serve. The Commission says that caching "benefits" users through "rapid retrieval of information from a local cache," *id.* ¶ 42, and can also be used "as part of a service, such as DNS, which is *predominantly* to the benefit of the user (DNS caching)," *id.* (emphasis added). "Although confronted with claims that DNS is, *in significant part*, designed to be useful to end-users rather than providers, the Title II Order nonetheless decided that it fell within the [TME]." *Id.* ¶ 38 (emphasis added). The Commission reasonably declined to follow this route. It chose a different, and reasonable, alternative.

b. Modification of Final Judgment Precedent

In adopting its approach to the TME, the Commission rested on precedent from a line of judicial decisions interpreting the Modification of Final Judgment (MFJ), a consent decree entered into between the Department of Justice and AT&T in 1982 as part of the breakup of the AT&T monopoly to create a set of independent regional Bell Operating Companies (BOCs).

The Commission makes a good case for the persuasiveness of this precedent. First, the definition of "information service" in the 1996 Act—including the TME—is lifted nearly verbatim from the 1982 consent decree. Second, in the case on which the Commission principally relies, the court was interpreting the MFJ's TME equivalent and adopted a reading in keeping with its understanding of Department of Justice policy at the time.

In *Western Electric,* Judge Greene addressed the question whether the consent decree permitted the BOCs to offer relay services for customers who use "telecommunications devices for the deaf" (TDDs). 1989 WL 119060 at *1. The court held that, because TDD services involve "transformation of information"—"the very crux and purpose of the TDD relay services"—they "f[e]ll squarely" within the definition of "information services," which covers the capability to "transform[] . . . information." *Id.* [T]he court explained that the TME "was *directed at* internal operations, not at services for customers or end users." *Id.* (emphasis added) (citation omitted).

[T]he Commission rightly acknowledges that being "directed at" one end of a spectrum does not rule out embodying certain aspects from the other end. The agency was within its rights to treat [the *Western Electric*] analysis—which in essence interpreted the statutory provision at issue and squared with the government's position supporting enforcement of the antitrust decree—as support for its construction of the TME.

The Commission offers an added reason to put stock in the MFJ precedent: It believed that Petitioners' approach risked causing the TME exception to swallow the "information services" category. It said, plausibly, that such an "expansive view" of the TME assigns it an outsized role, thereby "narrowing . . . the scope of information services" in a way that clashes with the Commission's pre-1996 Act approach to cabining the "basic services" category, *see* 2018 Order ¶ 38 & n.135, and the 1996 Act's imperative to "preserve the vibrant and competitive free market . . . for the

Internet . . . unfettered by Federal or State regulation," *id.* ¶ 39 (quoting 47 U.S.C. § 230(b)(2)), which the Commission permissibly uses as a rationale to interpret a vague provision in a way that limits regulatory burdens. In sum, the Commission lawfully construed an ambiguous statutory phrase in a way that tallies with its policy judgment, as is its prerogative.

The Commission extends the same logic to caching, though matters here are less obvious. It explains that caching "does not merely 'manage' an ISP's broadband Internet access service and underlying network," but "enables and enhances consumers' access to and use of information online." 2018 Order ¶ 42. Granted, some ISPs describe caching in terms indicating that it is a network management practice, and caching can help reduce ISPs' costs. But these facts are not determinative. The Commission is entitled to draw its own conclusions based on its (permissible) interpretation of the TME, so long as consistent with the record. Here it has done that.

4. Functional Integration

Petitioners then open a new — and final — line of attack: *Even if* DNS and caching are "information services," the Commission's reliance on them to classify broadband as an "information service" was still unreasonable. As a threshold matter, we note that *Brand X* already held it reasonable for the Commission to conclude that DNS and caching are information services functionally integrated with the offering of "Internet access [service]" "to members of the public." *Brand X*, 545 U.S. at 1000.

Petitioners first play up the facts that users may obtain DNS from providers other than their ISPs and that caching is not utterly indispensable. We find the objection misguided. As the Commission explained, "[T]he fact that some consumers obtain [DNS and caching] from third-party alternatives is not a basis for ignoring the capabilities that a broadband provider actually 'offers.'" 2018 Order ¶ 50. The agency reasonably concluded that, notwithstanding the availability of alternative sources of DNS, a market where "the vast majority of ordinary consumers" — "[a]pproximately 97 percent" — "rely upon the DNS functionality provided by their ISP," 2018 Order ¶ 34 & n.109 (citation omitted in second quotation), as "part and parcel of the broadband Internet access service," *id.* ¶ 42, meets *Brand X*'s requirements for functional integration. *Chevron* licenses these interpretive steps.

Second, Petitioners focus on what they dub the "relative importance" of the "inextricably intertwined" components at play — DNS/caching and high-speed transmission. Yet that did not keep the Court from finding reasonable the FCC's position that DNS and caching were functionally integrated with high-speed transmission.

Finally, Petitioners contend that even if DNS and caching *were* functionally integrated with transmission, that "does not automatically lead to an information service classification." But the Supreme Court has never imposed or even hinted at such a quantitative standard to determine whether inextricably intertwined functionalities can justify an "information service" classification. We see no basis for launching such a notion on our own. We conclude, under the guidance of *Brand X*, that the Commission permissibly classified broadband Internet access as an "information service" by virtue of the functionalities afforded by DNS and caching.

II. Mobile Broadband Classification

In keeping with its classification of broadband Internet as an "information service" not subject to Title II, the Commission classified mobile broadband as a "private mobile service" — a classification that under the statute automatically exempted it from common carriage treatment — just as the sole alternative classification available under the statute would have automatically *required* common carriage treatment. *See* 47 U.S.C. § 332(c)(1)–(2). We uphold this classification as reasonable under *Chevron*. As we said in *USTA* (and as the Title II Order and Petitioners recognize), the Commission has compelling policy grounds to ensure consistent treatment of the two varieties of broadband Internet access, fixed and mobile, subjecting both, or neither, to Title II.

III. Section 706 Authority

Petitioners additionally argue that the Commission could have addressed the harms of blocking and throttling and issued open Internet rules under Section 706 of the Telecommunications Act. In Verizon v. FCC, 740 F.3d 623 (D.C. Cir. 2014) we noted that the language of Section 706 is ambiguous. Thus, we proceed to Step Two of the analysis and ask whether the Commission's understanding of Section 706 as hortatory represents a reasonable interpretation of the statute. We find that it does. Indeed, we have previously held that the language of Section 706(a) could "certainly be read as simply setting forth a statement of congressional policy" and "just as easily be read to vest the Commission with actual authority. *Id.* at 637. We have also understood Section 706(b) to be similarly permissive. Furthermore, in support of its interpretation, the Commission notes that Section 706 lacks details "identify[ing] the providers or entities whose conduct could be regulated," whereas other provisions of the Act that unambiguously grant regulatory authority do specify such details. 2018 Order ¶ 271. We find the Commission's rationales in favor of its reading of Section 706 to be reasonable.

V. Arbitrary and Capricious Challenges

The Commission claims that we can uphold its entire rulemaking on the weight of its statutory interpretation alone. In the Commission's view, the reasonableness of its interpretation necessarily insulates the 2018 Order from arbitrary and capricious challenge. That argument misunderstands the law. To be sure, the analysis of an agency's statutory interpretation at *Chevron* Step Two has some overlap with arbitrary and capricious review. [But e]ach test must be independently satisfied.

This is a case in point. The Commission has advanced what is, under controlling precedent, a reasonable interpretation of the statute for purposes of *Chevron*. But aspects of the Commission's decision are still arbitrary and capricious under the Administrative Procedure Act because of the Commission's failure to address an important and statutorily mandated consideration.

A. Effects on Investment and Innovation

Petitioners challenge the Commission's conclusion that reclassification of broadband as an information service is "likely to increase ISP investment and output," 2018 Order ¶ 98, focusing almost entirely on the Commission's suggestion that the Title II Order may well have led to reduced investment in broadband. They object to particular studies on which the agency relies, the explanations it offers for its conclusions, and its failure to credit certain data. We find that the agency's position as to the economic benefits of reclassification away from "public-utility style regulation," *id.* ¶ 90, which the Commission sees as "particularly inapt for a dynamic industry built on technological development and disruption," *id.* ¶ 100, is supported by substantial evidence, and so reject Petitioners' objections.

B. Harms to Edge Providers and Consumers

Petitioners emphasize that, historically, the "FCC has repeatedly found that [broadband providers] have the ability and incentive to harm edge providers and consumers." According to Petitioners, the Commission ignored these prior findings when it issued the 2018 Order. Under FCC v. Fox Television Stations, Inc., when an agency changes its policy "a reasoned explanation is needed for disregarding facts and circumstances that underlay or were engendered by the prior policy." 556 U.S. 502, 515–16 (2009). While "[a]n agency cannot simply disregard contrary or inconvenient factual determinations that it made in the past, any more than it can ignore inconvenient facts when it writes on a blank slate," *Id.* at 537 (Kennedy, J., concurring), such is not the case here.

The Commission reasonably concluded that the harms the Title II Order was designed to prevent did not require the prior Order's regulatory measures but could instead be mitigated—at a lower cost—with transparency requirements, consumer protection, and antitrust enforcement measures. Even if the conduct rules lead to marginal deterrence, the Commission determined that the "substantial costs" are "not worth the possible benefits." 2018 Order ¶ 245; *see also id.* ¶¶ 240–66. In arriving at this conclusion, the Commission "scrutinize[ed] closely each prior conduct rule." 2018 Order ¶ 239. Rather than ignoring its prior findings, the Commission changed its balancing of the relevant incentives. The Commission employed a different method to address its previous concerns regarding broadband providers' behavior and incentives. In so doing, the Commission provided a "reasoned explanation" for its changed view as required by *Fox*.

1. Reliance on the Transparency Rule

The Commission, in large part, undergirds its light-touch regime with its finding that the transparency rule's disclosure requirements will discourage broadband providers from engaging in harmful practices. Specifically, the Commission reasoned that public disclosure requirements would encourage broadband providers to abide by open Internet principles and "incentivize[] quick corrective measures by providers if problematic conduct is identified." *Id.* Disclosure could help ensure that "those affected by such conduct will be in a position to make informed competitive choices or seek available remedies for anticompetitive, unfair, or deceptive practices." *Id.* ¶ 217. But Petitioners contend that the Commission's reliance on the transparency rule was unreasonable because "[d]isclosure does little for consumers with no practical alternatives." We disagree and find that the Commission offered a reasonable justification for the transparency rules. Since the Commission first adopted a transparency rule in 2010, "almost no incidents of harm to Internet openness have arisen." 2018 Order ¶ 242; *see also id.* ¶ 241. Based on this record, the Commission concluded that "public scrutiny and market pressure" is an effective "disinfectant" and leads to "increasingly fast [broadband provider]-driven resolution[s]" when issues do arise. *Id.* ¶ 243. Beyond its claim that the transparency rule does not go far enough to protect some consumers, Petitioners offer no more elaborate reason for explaining how the Commission's reliance on disclosure was impermissible. Seeing none, we reject Petitioners' arbitrary-and-capricious challenge.

2. Reliance on Competition

Petitioners contend that the Commission acted arbitrarily and capriciously in changing its view about the magnitude of competitive pressures in the fixed broadband market. Recall, the "premise of Title II and other public utility regulation is that [broadband providers] can exercise market power sufficient to substantially distort economic efficiency and harm end users." 2018 Order ¶ 123. But in the most recent order, the Commission concluded that "fixed broadband Internet access providers frequently face competitive pressures that mitigate their ability to exert market power." 2018 Order ¶ 217. Petitioners responded with three arguments, none of which we find surmount the highly deferential standard of review.

First, Petitioners claim that the Commission arbitrarily accepted a lack of competition in the fixed broadband market. For example, Petitioners lament that almost half of Americans have either one or no choice for residential high-speed wireline broadband providers. Another 45 percent have only two high-speed wireline options. Despite this information, the Commission concludes that competition is "widespread." 2018 Order ¶ 125.

We are satisfied by the Commission's reasons for believing that competition exists in the broadband market. The Commission turns to empirical research that supports the claim that the presence of two wireline providers is enough to ensure that meaningful competition exists. Consumers in areas with fewer than two providers may also reap the benefits of competition; a provider in this area "will tend to treat customers that do not have a competitive choice as if they do" because competitive pressures elsewhere "often have spillover effects across a given corporation." *Id.* ¶ 127. Additionally, these providers could face hefty operational and reputational cost from acting badly in uncompetitive areas. Based on these reasonable findings and our highly deferential standard of review, it was not arbitrary for the Commission to conclude that fixed broadband providers face competitive pressures.

Second, Petitioners worry that even if there is competition in the local market for broadband, once a consumer chooses a broadband provider, that provider has a monopoly on access to her. In turn, the provider can use that access to control the interaction between edge providers, end users, and others. The Title II Order took this "terminating access monopoly" concern seriously and found that it enabled broadband providers of all types and sizes to raise prices. Petitioners claim that the Commission's 2018 Order shifts from this previous position without explanation. This is not so.

The Commission offered several reasons for rejecting its prior finding of a terminating monopoly. For example, it notes that many customers can access edge provider's content from multiple sources (i.e., fixed and mobile). *See* 2018 Order ¶ 136. In this way, there is no terminating monopoly. *Id.* Additionally, the Commission argued that even if a terminating monopoly exists for some edge providers the commenters did not offer sufficient evidence in the record to demonstrate that the resulting prices will be inefficient. *Id.* ¶ 137. Given these reasons, we reject Petitioners' claim that the Commission's conclusion on terminating monopolies is without explanation.

Third, Petitioners argue that the Commission disregards its previous determination that broadband provider market power is strengthened by the high costs of switching broadband providers. The Title II Order found that, when switching providers, "consumers may experience []: high upfront device installation fees; long-term contracts and early termination fees; the activation fee when changing service providers; and compatibility costs of owned equipment not working with the new service." Title II Order ¶ 81. However, the Commission's most recent order was skeptical of whether the rate of consumers changing providers — the "churn" rate — is as low as it previously found. *See* 2018 Order ¶ 128. More importantly, the Commission contends that low churn rates do not per se indicate market power. *See id.* Instead, they could be a function of competitive actions taken by broadband providers to attract and retain customers. *See id.* And such action to convince customers to switch providers, the Commission argues, is indicia of material competition for new customers. *See id.* This rationale provides a reasoned explanation for departing from prior findings on churn rates and broadband provider market power.

3. Reliance on Antitrust and Consumer Protection Laws

The Commission found that "[i]n the unlikely event that ISPs engage in conduct that harms Internet openness," legal regimes like "antitrust law and the FTC's authority under Section 5 of the FTC Act to prohibit unfair and deceptive practice" will provide protection for consumers. *See* 2018 Order ¶ 140. The Commission reasoned that antitrust and consumer protection laws are particularly well-suited to addressing openness concerns because "they apply to the whole of the Internet ecosystem, including edge providers, thereby avoiding tilting the playing field against ISPs and causing economic distortions by regulating only one side of business transactions on the Internet." *Id.* Petitioners argue that reliance on antitrust and consumer protection law was an improper delegation of authority. We disagree.

To be sure, the Commission's discussion of antitrust and consumer protection law is no model of agency decisionmaking. The Commission theorized why antitrust and consumer protection law is preferred to ex ante regulations but failed to provide any meaningful analysis of whether these laws would, in practice, prevent blocking and throttling. For example, the Commission opines that "[m]ost of the examples of net neutrality violations discussed in the Title II Order could have been investigated as antitrust violations," *see* 2018 Order ¶ 145, but fails to explain what, if any, concrete remedies might address these antitrust violations. It is concerning that the Commission provides such an anemic analysis of the safety valve that it insists will limit anticompetitive behavior among broadband providers. Nonetheless, we cannot go so far as to say that this failure is so profound that the agency "entirely failed to consider an important aspect of the problem," Motor Vehicle Mfrs. Ass'n v. State Farm Mut. Auto. Ins. Co., 463 U.S. 29, 43 (1983), or otherwise engaged in unreasoned decisionmaking. That is especially true because the Commission viewed those laws as only one part of a larger regulatory and economic framework that it believes will limit broadband providers' engagement in undesirable practices. The Commission barely survives arbitrary and capricious review on this issue.

D. Reliance Interests

Petitioners argue[s] that the Commission paid too little heed to the reliance that various parties—particularly edge providers and state and local governments—allegedly placed on the Title II Order in making investments that Petitioners see as jeopardized by the Commission's action here. The Commission acknowledged, as it must, the significance of reliance interests as a potential weight against its decision, but found the submissions wanting.

[A]ssuming the change in agency position implicated serious reliance interests, we agree with the Commission that such reliance would have been unreasonable on the facts before us. Insofar as the regulation on which reliance is asserted is simply the Title II Order's package of rules and policies, we think this is a fair response. [I]n light of the Commission's approach to classifying cable modem service and Internet access since the late 1990s, the Title II Order could reasonably have been viewed as a regulatory step that might soon be reversed.

[Thus, w]e conclude that the agency's treatment of reliance interests is not arbitrary or capricious.

G. Cost-Benefit Analysis

Petitioners next take exception to the Commission's cost-benefit analysis. We review cost-benefit analyses with deference, and here find nothing arbitrary in the Commission's choice of methodology or explanation of its conclusions.

First, Petitioners claim that the agency did not account for harms to "innovation and democratic discourse" that the 2018 Order would supposedly bring about. Second, they assert that the Commission failed to factor in the "cost to consumers of decreased innovation and other consumer harms," citing a comment about Comcast's interference with file sharing, and news stories from 2007–2008 describing how "Comcast had blocked users' ability to share copies of the King James Bible," *Id.* at 73–74.

As an initial matter, Petitioners do not explain how the 2018 Order would harm "innovation and democratic discourse" beyond quoting an assertion by a commentator that "ex post enforcement would hamstring nascent industries." *Id.* at 73. [T]he Commission's cost-benefit analysis makes a reasonable case that its "light-touch" approach is more conducive to innovation and openness than the Title II Order. We do note that antitrust enforcement by the Commission's sister agencies (the Department of Justice and the FTC, the latter being released by the 2018 Order from the statutory exclusion effected by application of Title II) aims at generating and protecting competition, *see* Part V.B.3; at least as a general matter, it seems reasonable to expect that competition would tend to multiply the voices in the public square. The agency says as much, noting that "the transparency rule and the ISP commitments backed up by FTC enforcement are targeted to preserving free expression, particularly the no-blocking commitment," and that "[t]he market competition that antitrust law preserves will protect values such as free expression." 2018 Order ¶ 153. At the same time, the Commission frankly acknowledges that "[t]he competitive process and antitrust would not protect free expression in cases where consumers have decided that they are willing to tolerate some blocking or throttling in order to obtain other things of value." *Id.* n.558.

In weighing the costs and benefits of Title II regulation against those of a deregulatory strategy, the agency finds that, on almost every point, the latter approach is preferable. Title II regulation would "discourage[] investment in the network," which, in turn, may cause "society . . . to lose some spillover benefits," 2018 Order ¶ 310, including forgone "improvements in productivity and innovation that occur because broadband is a general-purpose technology," *id.* Conduct rules mandated by the Title II Order, the Commission said, have "large [negative] effects on consumers obtaining innovative services," such as zero-rating. *Id.* ¶ 318. Following up its prior observation that "smaller edge providers may benefit from tiered pricing, such as paid prioritization, as a means of gaining entry," *id.* ¶ 133, it reasoned that removal of the Title II Order's ban could yield "innovative services and business models," *id.* ¶ 321. Whatever harms might occur absent a ban on paid prioritization, the agency estimated them to be "small" and "infrequent," *id.* ¶ 320, and thus outweighed by the costs of the Title II Order. As for rules against blocking and throttling, the agency states that their costs are "likely small," though they could grow if compliance becomes more onerous. *Id.* ¶ 322. The benefits of such rules, however, are "approximately zero," *id.* ¶ 323—a point Petitioners do not grapple with. That is so, in the agency's view, because the 2018 Order's transparency rules—combined with the deterrent effects of "market forces, public opprobrium, and enforcement of the consumer protection laws"—can "mitigate potential harms." 2018 Order ¶ 323; *cf.* ¶ 315 (explaining that the Title II Order's transparency rules would "impose significant additional costs" without "additional benefits"). In sum, a "light-touch" approach can in the Commission's judgment secure Internet openness and encourage innovation at lower cost than the Title II Order, while yielding unique benefits.

The Commission's reasoning rehearsed above is not plagued by "serious flaw[s]" that so "undermin[e]" its cost-benefit analysis as to render the rule "unreasonable."

Nat'l Ass'n of Home Builders v. EPA, 682 F.3d 1032, 1040 (D.C. Cir. 2012). We therefore reject Petitioners' objections on this front.

VI. Preemption

We vacate the portion of the 2018 Order that expressly preempts "any state or local requirements that are inconsistent with [its] deregulatory approach." 2018 Order ¶ 194; *see id.* ¶¶ 194–204 (Preemption Directive). The Commission ignored binding precedent by failing to ground its sweeping Preemption Directive — which goes far beyond conflict preemption — in a lawful source of statutory authority. That failure is fatal.

The relevant portion of the Order provides that "regulation of broadband Internet access service should be governed principally by a uniform set of federal regulations," and not "by a patchwork that includes separate state and local requirements." 2018 Order ¶ 194. In service of that goal, the 2018 Order expressly "preempt[s] any state or local measures that would effectively impose rules or requirements that we have repealed or decided to refrain from imposing in this order or that would impose more stringent requirements for any aspect of broadband service that we address in this order." *Id.* ¶ 195. In other words, the Preemption Directive invalidates all state and local laws that the Commission deems to "interfere with federal regulatory objectives" or that involve "any aspect of broadband service . . . address[ed]" in the Order. *Id.* ¶¶ 195–96.

The Preemption Directive conveys more than a mere intent for the agency to preempt state laws in the future if they conflict with the 2018 Order. The Order was meant to have independent and far-reaching preemptive effect from the moment it issued. And the Commission meant for that preemptive effect to wipe out a broader array of state and local laws than traditional conflict preemption principles would allow.

The Governmental Petitioners challenge the Preemption Directive on the ground that it exceeds the Commission's statutory authority. They are right.

A. Express and Ancillary Authority

"The [Commission], like other federal agencies, literally has no power to act unless and until Congress confers power upon it." American Library Ass'n v. FCC., 406 F.3d 689, 698 (D.C. Cir. 2005) (formatting modified). For the Preemption Directive to stand, then, the Commission must have had express or ancillary authority to issue it. It had neither.

The Preemption Directive could not possibly be an exercise of the Commission's express statutory authority. By reclassifying broadband as an information service, the Commission placed broadband *outside* of its Title II jurisdiction. And broadband is not a "radio transmission" under Title III or a "cable service" under Title VI. So the Commission's express authority under Titles III or VI does not come into play either. Nor did Congress statutorily grant the Commission freestanding preemption authority to displace state laws even in areas in which it does not otherwise have regulatory power.

Neither can the Commission house the Preemption Directive in its ancillary authority under Title I. "Title I is not an independent source of regulatory authority." People of the State of California v. FCC, 905 F.2d 1217, 1240 n.35 (9th Cir. 1990) (citing United States v. Southwestern Cable Co., 392 U.S. 157, 178 (1968)). As a result, ancillary jurisdiction exists only when "(1) the Commission's general jurisdictional grant under Title I of the Communications Act covers the regulated subject and (2) the regulations are reasonably ancillary to the Commission's effective performance of its statutorily mandated responsibilities." *American Library*, 406 F.3d at 691–92 (formatting modified).

Under binding circuit precedent, those "statutorily mandated responsibilities" must themselves be dictated by Title II, III, or VI of the Act — none of which apply since the Commission took broadband out of Title II. *See* Comcast Corp. v. FCC, 600 F.3d 642, 654 (D.C. Cir. 2010) ("[I]t is Title II, III, or VI to which the authority must ultimately be ancillary.").

The Commission seemingly agrees because nowhere in the 2018 Order or its briefing does it claim ancillary authority for the Preemption Directive.

B. The Commission's Asserted Sources of Authority

With express and ancillary preemption authority off the table, the Commission was explicit that it was grounding its Preemption Directive in (i) the "impossibility exception" to state jurisdiction, and (ii) the "federal policy of nonregulation for information services." 2018 Order ¶¶ 198, 202. Neither theory holds up.

1. Impossibility Exception

All the impossibility exception does is help police the line between those communications matters falling under the Commission's authority (Section 152(a)) and those remaining within the States' wheelhouse (Section 152(b)). Specifically, if the matter involves interstate communications or a mix of state and federal matters *and* it falls within the impossibility exception, then the Commission may regulate to the extent of its statutory authority. If not, the matter falls within the States' jurisdiction. In other words, the impossibility exception presupposes the existence of statutory authority to regulate; it does not serve as a substitute for that necessary delegation of power from Congress.

2. Federal Policy of Nonregulation

What the Commission calls the "federal policy of nonregulation for information services," Commission Br. 123, cannot sustain the Preemption Directive either.

First, as a matter of both basic agency law and federalism, the power to preempt the States' laws must be conferred by Congress. It cannot be a mere byproduct of self-made agency policy. Doubly so here where preemption treads into an area—State regulation of intrastate communications—over which Congress expressly "deni[ed]" the Commission regulatory authority, Louisiana Public Service Comm'n v. FCC, 476 U.S. 355, 374 (1986) (*Louisiana PSC*).

Presumably recognizing as much, the Commission attempts to house its preemption authority in 47 U.S.C. § 230(b)(2). That provision says that "the policy of the United States [is] . . . to preserve the vibrant and competitive free market that presently exists for the Internet and other interactive computer services, unfettered by Federal or State regulation." *Id.* No dice. As the Commission has itself acknowledged, "[p]olicy statements are just that—statements of policy. They are not delegations of regulatory authority." *Comcast*, 600 F.3d at 654. Second, the Commission points to 47 U.S.C. § 153(51), which defines "telecommunications carrier," and provides that "[a] telecommunications carrier shall be treated as a common carrier under this chapter only to the extent that it is engaged in providing telecommunications services."

That does not work either. Section 153(51) is a definitional provision in Title I, and so is "not an independent source of regulatory authority." *People of State of Cal.*, 905 F.2d at 1240 n.35. Quite the opposite. As the parties agree, that provision is a *limitation* on the Commission's authority.

It also would make no sense for Congress to bury the enormously far-reaching and consequential authority to override every single State's *statutorily conferred* power to regulate intrastate communications deep within a list of fifty-nine definitions in a non-regulatory portion of the statute, and then articulate the relevant definition as a *restriction* of the Commission's power.

Third, the Commission points to 47 U.S.C. § 160(e). That provision says that "[a] State commission may not continue to apply or enforce any provision of [the Act] that the Commission has determined to forbear from applying under subsection (a)." Subsection (a), in turn, gives the Commission some flexibility to forbear from regulating technologies classified under Title II.

That Title II provision has no work to do here because the 2018 Order took broadband out of Title II. So the Commission is not "forbear[ing] from applying any provision" of the Act to a Title-II technology. 47 U.S.C. § 160(e). On top of that, Section 160(e)—as a part of Title I—does not itself delegate any preemption authority to the Commission.

3. Case Precedent

Governing precedent nails the coffin shut on the Preemption Directive.

In *Louisiana PSC*, the Supreme Court squarely rejected the Commission's argument that it "is entitled to pre-empt inconsistent state regulation" just because it "frustrates federal policy." 476 U.S. at 368. In doing so, the Court was explicit that, if the Commission cannot tether a rule of preemption to a relevant source of statutory authority, courts "simply cannot accept [the] argument that the [Commission] may nevertheless take action which it thinks will best effectuate a federal policy." *Id.* at 374. That fits this case to a T.

Likewise, in City of New York v. FCC, on which the Commission and their amici heavily rely, the Supreme Court repeated that "an agency literally has no power to act, let alone pre-empt the validly enacted legislation of a sovereign State, unless and until Congress confers power upon it." 486 U.S. 57, 66 (1988). The Court then added that "the best way of determining whether Congress intended the regulations of an administrative agency to displace state law is to examine the nature and scope of the authority granted by Congress to the agency." *Id.* (quoting *Louisiana PSC*, 476 U.S. at 374). Needless to say, no such examination can occur if there is no legislative grant of authority against which to evaluate the preemptive rule, and certainly not when, as here, Congress expressly *withheld* regulatory authority over the matter.

Not only is the Commission lacking in its own statutory authority to preempt, but its effort to kick the States out of intrastate broadband regulation also overlooks the Communications Act's vision of dual federal-state authority and cooperation in this area specifically. Even the 2018 Order itself acknowledges the States' central role in "policing such matters as fraud, taxation, and general commercial dealings," 2018 Order ¶ 196, "remedying violations of a wide variety of general state laws," *id.* ¶ 196 n.732, and "enforcing fair business practices," *id.* ¶ 196—categories to which broadband regulation is inextricably connected.

C. Conflict Preemption

Finally, the Commission argues that we should leave the Preemption Directive undisturbed because principles of conflict preemption would lead to the same result.

Any intuitive appeal this argument might have offered evaporated at oral argument when the Commission confirmed what the Preemption Directive's plain language bespeaks: It sweeps "broader than ordinary conflict preemption." Oral Arg. Tr. 171; *see* 2018 Order ¶ 195 (preempting "any state or local measures that would effectively impose rules or requirements that we have repealed or decided to refrain from imposing in this order or that would impose more stringent requirements for any aspect of broadband service that we address in this order"). The necessary consequence of this position is that ordinary conflict preemption principles cannot salvage the Preemption Directive.

Beyond that, the Commission's conflict-preemption argument tries to force a square peg into a round hole. Conflict preemption applies to "state law that *under the circumstances of the particular case* stands as an obstacle to the accomplishment and execution of the full purposes and objectives of Congress—whether that 'obstacle' goes by the name of conflicting; contrary to; repugnance; difference; irreconcilability; inconsistency; violation; curtailment; interference, or the like." Geier v. American Honda Motor Co., Inc., 529 U.S. 861, 873 (2000) (formatting modified).

Because a conflict-preemption analysis "involves fact-intensive inquiries," it "mandates deferral of review until an actual preemption of a specific state regulation occurs." Alascom, Inc. v. FCC, 727 F.2d 1212, 1220 (D.C. Cir. 1984). Without the facts of any alleged conflict before us, we cannot begin to make a conflict-preemption assessment in this case, let alone a categorical determination that any and all forms of state regulation of intrastate broadband would inevitably conflict with the 2018 Order.

To be sure, *Chevron* and *Brand X* together confirm that the Commission has interpretive "discretion" to classify broadband as either an information service or a telecommunications service. Congress, in other words, created an interpretive statutory fork in the road and gave the Commission the authority to choose the path.

But the Commission's power to choose one regulatory destination or another does not carry with it the option to mix and match its favorite parts of both. The dissenting opinion's defense of the Preemption Directive makes the mistake of collapsing the distinction between (i) the Commission's authority to make a threshold classification decision, and (ii) the authority to issue affirmative and State-displacing legal commands within the bounds of the classification scheme the Commission has selected (here, Title I). The agency's power to do the former says nothing about its authority to do the latter. *Chevron*, after all, is not a magic wand that invests agencies with regulatory power beyond what their authorizing statutes provide. Instead, the point of *Chevron* was simply to draw lines between the courts' and administrative agencies' respective roles in interpreting ambiguous statutes.

The dissenting opinion's theory of *Chevron* preemption, in other words, takes the discretion to decide which definition best fits a real-world communications service and attempts to turn that subsidiary judgment into a license to reorder the entire statutory scheme to enforce an overarching "nationwide regime" that enforces the policy preference underlying the definitional choice. Nothing in *Chevron* goes that far. And doing so here would turn every exercise of *Chevron* Step-Two interpretation into a bureaucratic blunderbuss capable of demolishing state laws across the Nation any time the agency fears that state regulation might intrude on its regulatory or deregulatory ethos.

At bottom, the Commission lacked the legal authority to categorically abolish all fifty States' statutorily conferred authority to regulate intrastate communications. For that reason, we vacate the Preemption Directive. And because no particular state law is at issue in this case and the Commission makes no provision-specific arguments, it would be wholly premature to pass on the preemptive effect, under conflict or other recognized preemption principles, of the remaining portions of the 2018 Order.

VII. Conclusion

For the foregoing reasons, the petitions for review are granted in part and denied in part.

MILLETT, Circuit Judge, concurring:

I join the Court's opinion in full, but not without substantial reservation. The Supreme Court's decision in *Brand X* compels us to affirm as a reasonable option the agency's reclassification of broadband as an information service based on its provision of Domain Name System (DNS) and caching. But I am deeply concerned that the result is unhinged from the realities of modern broadband service.

As our opinion today recognizes, auxiliary services like DNS and caching remain in the broadband bundle. But their salience has waned significantly since *Brand X* was decided. DNS is readily available, free of charge, and at a remarkably high quality, from upwards of twenty different third-party providers. And caching has been fundamentally stymied by the explosion of Internet encryption. For these accessories to singlehandedly drive the Commission's classification decision is to confuse the leash for the dog. In 2005, the Commission's classification decision was "just barely" permissible. *Brand X*, 545 U.S. at 1003 (Breyer, J., concurring). Almost fifteen years later, hanging the legal status of Internet broadband services on DNS and caching blinks technological reality.

In an area so fraught with political contest and technical complexity, we ordinarily grant the administering agency the widest possible berth in interpreting and administering a technical statutory scheme. But that discretion is not unlimited, and it cannot be invoked to sustain rules fundamentally disconnected from the factual landscape the agency is tasked with regulating. By putting singular and dispositive regulatory weight on broadband's incidental offering of DNS and caching, the Commission misses the technological forest for a twig.

Yet, as a lower court, we are bound to "the [Supreme Court] case which directly controls," and so we must follow *Brand X*, as the court's opinion does. Agostini v. Felton, 521 U.S. 203 (1997). It is the Supreme Court's sole "prerogative" to read *Brand X* in light of the facts of its day, *id.*, and to require the Commission to bring the law into harmony with the realities of the modern broadband marketplace. Until it does — or until Congress steps up to the legislative plate — I am bound to concur in sustaining the Commission's action.

WILKINS, Circuit Judge, concurring:

I too join the Court's opinion in full. As Judge Millett's concurring opinion persuasively explains, we are bound by the Supreme Court's decision in *Brand X* even though critical aspects of broadband Internet technology and marketing underpinning the Court's decision have drastically changed since 2005. But revisiting *Brand X* is a task for the Court — in its wisdom — not us.

WILLIAMS, Senior Circuit Judge, concurring in part and dissenting in part:

And be these juggling fiends no more believed,

That palter with us in a double sense;

That keep the word of promise to our ear,

And break it to our hope.

So says Macbeth, finding that the witches' assurances were sheer artifice and that his life is collapsing around him. The enactors of the 2018 Order, though surely no Macbeths, might nonetheless feel a certain kinship, being told that they acted lawfully in *rejecting* the heavy hand of Title II for the Internet, but that each of the 50 states is free to impose just that. (Many have already enacted such legislation. *See, e.g.*, Cal. S. Comm. on Judiciary, SB 822 Analysis 1 (2018) (explaining that California has expressly "codif[ied] portions of the recently-rescinded ... rules"). If Internet communications were tidily divided into federal markets and readily severable state markets, this might be no problem. But no modern user of the Internet can believe for a second in such tidy isolation; indeed, the Commission here made an uncontested finding that it would be "impossible" to maintain the regime it had adopted under Title I in the face of inconsistent state regulation. On my colleagues' view, state policy trumps federal; or, more precisely, the most draconian state policy trumps all else. "The Commission may lawfully decide to free the Internet from Title II," we say, "It just can't give its decision any effect in the real world."

The Commission has invoked the "impossibility exception," a well-established ground of FCC preemption. As formulated by our circuit, the exception permits the Commission to preempt state regulation "when (1) the matter to be regulated has both interstate and intrastate aspects ...; (2) FCC preemption is necessary to protect a valid federal regulatory objective ...; and (3) state regulation would 'negate[] the exercise by the FCC of its own lawful authority' because regulation of the interstate aspects of the matter cannot be 'unbundled' from regulation of the intrastate aspects." Public Service Comm'n of Maryland v. FCC, 909 F.2d 1510, 1515 (D.C. Cir. 1990).

Supreme Court decisions make clear that a federal agency's authority to preempt state law *need not be expressly granted*. When a federal agency "promulgates regulations intended to pre-empt state law [i.e., with an express statement of agency intent], the court's inquiry is ... limited," Fidelity Federal Savings & Loan Ass'n v. de la Cuesta, 458 U.S. 141, 154 (1982):

> If [the agency's] choice represents a reasonable accommodation of conflicting policies that were committed to the agency's care by the statute, we should not disturb it unless it appears from the statute or its legislative history that the accommodation is not one that Congress would have sanctioned.

Id. (quoting United States v. Shimer, 367 U.S. 374, 383 (1961)).

Given the Commission's undisputed findings here, the only vulnerability of its position is the possibility suggested in the last clause—whether "it appears from the statute or its legislative history that the accommodation is not one that Congress would have sanctioned." Inquiry into that question proceeds in the usual way of discerning congressional intent.

It is hard to imagine a rational Congress providing for use of Title I, but requiring that any *national* deregulatory policy be implemented only to the degree that it might prove achievable under the internal constraints of Title II.

[T]he question turns on whether we see preemption as serving to protect the federal *regulations* from state frustration or to protect federal choice of a *regulatory regime* from state frustration. The majority staunchly believes that preemption serves solely to protect *affirmative* federal *regulations*. Responding to the Commission's reliance on the preemption that automatically follows forbearance under Title II, it says, "the Commission [has] broad authority over services classified under Title II, unlike those classified under Title I." True enough. But the lesson it draws is a complete non sequitur: The broad authority under Title II, says the majority, is "why the Act carves out more space for federal objectives to displace those of the States in the Title II context." This explanation assumes an *asymmetry* in preemption implications between (i) heavy-handed regulation and (ii) light-touch regulation. If an agency decides that a robust regulatory scheme is apt in a given sector (say, under Title II), the majority is ready to infer authority to preempt. But, the majority insists, if the agency determines that an industry will flourish best under competitive market norms and accordingly adopts a "light-touch" path, preemption is suddenly superfluous *because* the agency now has less "power to regulate services." A clearer insistence on the unsupported notion that preemption protects *only regulation* itself, *not* a regime of lawful regulatory choices, is hard to imagine.

Dirigiste state regulation in a sector that an agency thinks works best under market norms would undercut the agency's aims, *no more, no less*, than state rules undermining the agency's affirmative regulations.

In the majority's view, when the Commission adopts a deregulatory regime under Title I, there's no there there. Of course no one wants the majority to decide a case not before it; but if the handwaving toward conflict preemption is to mean anything, it requires a vision of a Commission exercise of power with which some state regulation could actually conflict. This the majority denies absolutely. Rather, the majority insists that power to preempt depends either on the Commission's "express and expansive authority" "to regulate certain technologies," or on "ancillary authority." The latter in turn requires that the Commission's action be "reasonably ancillary to the Commission's effective performance of its statutorily mandated responsibilities," which are *exclusively* its responsibilities under Title II, III, and VI of the Act. There is no room in this concept for authority to establish a regulatory regime for broadband as an information service—meaning, given the extreme paucity of affirmative regulatory authority under Title I, a highly deregulatory regime.

My colleagues and I agree that the 1996 Act affords the Commission authority to apply Title II to broadband, or not. Despite the ample and uncontested findings of the Commission that the absence of preemption will gut the order by leaving all broadband subject to state regulation in which the most intrusive will prevail, and despite Supreme Court authority inferring preemptive power to protect an agency's regulatory choices, they vacate the preemption directive. Thus, the Commission can choose to apply Title I and not Title II—but if it does, its choice will be meaningless. I respectfully dissent.

Notes and Questions

1. Deference. Many petitioners pressed the point that the FCC has changed its mind almost completely, now a few times, in the span of a relatively small number of years—and they argued these changes did not seem to be the exercise of reasoned policymaking judgment. The D.C. Circuit followed Supreme Court precedent that an agency is entitled to change its mind, and that the standard of review does not change simply because the agency has changed its mind. Is it a problem that net neutrality is largely up to the FCC?

2. Where Was Congress? Relatedly, every dispute in this chapter (with the exception of the First Amendment arguments) could have been avoided if Congress had enacted legislation. The debates about regulatory authority arose because the Communications Act does not specify (or create) the regulatory category applicable to internet access. And the back-and-forth about the substance of the net neutrality rules arose because Congress did not specify the substance of the laws applicable to internet access. Put differently, with a single piece of legislation, the disputes in this chapter would not have arisen, and the FCC would not have had the major role it has played.

Throughout this entire saga, congressional committees and individual senators and representatives were quite vocal. But no legislation was enacted. Do you think Congress should have acted? If so, exactly what should the legislation have said?

3. Preemption and the Role of States. What is the significance of the majority's decision on preemption? The dissent treated it as undermining the rest of the FCC's order. But the majority makes clear that, if a conflict arises, conflict preemption is available. If you were a state legislator, what, exactly, would you propose as a form of internet access regulation that would not give to a successful preemption challenge (if the FCC decided to argue for preemption)? Note that in ACA Connects v. Bonta, 24 F.4th 1233 (9th Cir. 2022), the Ninth Circuit rejected a preemption challenge to a California statute that essentially codified the FCC's 2015 net neutrality rules for California customers. We excerpt that opinion in Chapter 7.E.

4. Section 706. Recall the D.C. Circuit's holding in *Verizon* with respect to the FCC's regulatory authority under § 706. Would the FCC have better achieved its intended policy results—of no "public utility regulation," transparency rules, and preemption of state net neutrality laws—if it had agreed that § 706 did in fact give it some new authority? Did the FCC commissioners in the majority not want to rely on broad FCC authority that they believed it should not invoke and/or did not have under a correct reading of the statute? If not, what else might explain the FCC's failure to rely on § 706? If so, is that a persuasive reason not to rely on § 706?

Chapter 7

Federal or State Regulation?

Introduction

In the United States' federal system, any given regulation can frequently be promulgated either at the federal or state level—or at both. Regulation can and does also occur at the municipal level, and in the communications field much of cable television's regulation began and continues at the local level. As in other fields, federal regulation often has the benefit of greater uniformity (and hence simplicity for national businesses), while state or local regulation can respond to differing local conditions and more easily allow comparisons among different regulatory models. Regulatory systems that combine federal and state actions seek to enjoy benefits of both, sometimes more or less successfully. The decision of *where* to regulate can be quite consequential, both in balancing uniformity and local sensitivity and in practical effectiveness of any given policy.

Over its history, internet and telecommunications law has used (or at least included) all of these options. The original 1934 Act itself was of two minds: the Act treated all spectrum as federal property and exclusively used federal regulation, but the Act carved out significant state regulatory authority over common carrier telecommunications. The federal statutory cable provisions, enacted beginning in the 1980s, started from a baseline of local regulation. And the Telecommunications Act of 1996 significantly altered the balance between federal and state authority, increasing federal authority while also specifically identifying state agencies as important implementing agencies.

As we discussed in much more detail in Chapter 6, neither the FCC nor the courts (nor Congress, perhaps most notably) has fully resolved the extent to which the FCC, under the Communications Act or otherwise, has jurisdiction to regulate internet services. After reviewing the way regulatory authority over traditional communications services has been allocated, this chapter turns to a few areas of internet policy—from infrastructure to services—in which the question over federal or state power is hotly contested.

§ 7.A. The 1934 Act: Spectrum and Telephony

The federal government has asserted nearly complete authority over spectrum regulation. As we discuss in more detail in Chapter 9, the 1934 Act absorbed provisions that had declared federal ownership of all spectrum and that gave federal agencies exclusive jurisdiction over spectrum allocation and most aspects of spectrum policy. State and local governments retained some authority that affects wireless services, principally around tower siting and infrastructure, but even there (as this chapter will discuss), federal authorities have increasingly set the parameters in which states and localities act.

As to telephony, from its creation in 1934, the FCC has always shared jurisdiction with state regulators. The 1934 Act's limitation of federal authority is clearly stated, if not always so easily implemented in practice: the Act is not to be construed "to give the Commission jurisdiction with respect to . . . practices, services, facilities, or regulations for or in connection with *intra*state communication service by wire or radio of any carrier." 47 U.S.C. § 152(b) (emphasis added). Indeed, the 1934 Act on its face restricts FCC jurisdiction to "*inter*state and foreign communication by wire or radio." 47 U.S.C. § 152(a) (emphasis added). The Act thus appears to keep the FCC out of the business of regulating what, in 1934, accounted for the vast bulk of telephone usage: local telephony.

The 1934 Act in this way marked an important departure from earlier telephone regulation. Before the Act, telephone service had been regulated by the Interstate Commerce Commission (ICC), an agency charged with the task by the Mann-Elkins Act of 1910, Pub. L. No. 61-281, 36 Stat. 539. The ICC had enjoyed broad power to preempt any state regulation with which it disagreed. In fact, in *The Shreveport Rate Case* of 1914, the Supreme Court affirmed that the ICC had preemption authority whenever an intrastate rate would frustrate the achievement of a federal statutory goal. Houston, East & West Texas Railway Co. v. United States, 234 U.S. 342 (1914) (*The Shreveport Rate Case* or *Shreveport*). Although that case involved railroad rates, not telephony, the Court was interpreting the ICC's authority under a statute that applied equally to both.

The scope of federal authority in telephony had received a further, though less direct, boost from the Supreme Court in 1930 as well. In Smith v. Illinois Bell Telephone Co., 282 U.S. 133 (1930), the Court ruled that state regulations must be strictly limited to intrastate facilities and services. Rates for local service could not incorporate the full costs of local network facilities so long as even a tiny fraction of the traffic on those facilities was interstate. The costs imposed on the local network by interstate calls had to be "separated" from the intrastate costs for the purposes of setting local rates. While this case did not directly broaden federal authority, it did narrow state authority.

The Communications Act of 1934 effectively nullified *The Shreveport Rate Case*'s applicability to telecommunications. The rule of construction contained in § 152(b) of the 1934 Act is sweeping: "*nothing* in this chapter shall be construed" to preempt state jurisdiction over intrastate services or facilities. *Id.* (emphasis added). The implication is that, even if state regulation of intrastate service might make implementation of some telephony provision of the 1934 Act more difficult, federal regulators could not, as they could under *Shreveport*, preempt the inconvenient state law. Section 152(b) thus appears to give clear primacy to state regulators where intrastate telephony is involved. One limitation on that primary state role is that § 410(c) of the

Act gives the FCC ultimate authority, after consultation with a joint board of state and federal regulators, to decide the respective degrees to which network facilities are used for interstate and intrastate service. Section 410 thus gives the Commission some discretion to decide where to draw the line between interstate and intrastate telecommunications and, within reason, to adjust its jurisdiction accordingly.

The practical complications of § 410 aside, the 1934 Act quite consciously tried to reserve substantial authority to the states. But the actual operation and judicial interpretation of § 152(b) turned out, for a time at least, to be somewhat different from what might have been expected given the text of the provision. After several decades during which there was little conflict between state and federal goals — and correspondingly few jurisdictional squabbles — some disagreement began to arise, notably as the FCC began to promote competition in certain areas of telecommunications. One particular set of conflicts resulted in a series of court decisions that greatly expanded federal regulatory power at the expense of the states. The first such decision was in N.C. Util. Comm'n v. FCC, 537 F.2d 787 (4th Cir. 1976) (*NCUC I*). There, the Fourth Circuit ruled that the FCC could preempt a state law regulating certain types of basic telephone equipment so long as the equipment affected by the regulation would be used for interstate, as well as intrastate, telephone communication. The FCC had been trying to promote competition in the market for telephone equipment and found the state law at issue to be antithetical to that policy. Notable about the Fourth Circuit's decision was that it allowed preemption even though the telephone equipment at issue was used almost exclusively for local calling.

A second case arising one year later out of the same regulatory proceeding even more radically expanded federal jurisdiction. In N.C. Util. Comm'n v. FCC, 552 F.2d 1036 (4th Cir. 1977) (*NCUC II*), the Fourth Circuit decided that it was a practical impossibility to separate the interstate and intrastate uses of most telephone equipment and thus granted the FCC even broader authority to preempt state law. In short, while under *NCUC I* the FCC could preempt a state law only if it could be shown to affect interstate telephone service, under *NCUC II* the FCC could preempt a state law in any case where the effects on interstate and intrastate service were inseparable. This in some ways turned § 152(b) on its head by shifting the presumption in favor of federal rather than state regulation. Moreover, it seemed to reinstate the pro-preemption doctrine of *The Shreveport Rate Case*, a doctrine that was well known when Congress decided to adopt a contrary rule of construction in the 1934 Act.

The *NCUC* cases would not remain good law for long. A number of other federal courts had adopted the *NCUC* tests, *see, e.g.*, Cal. v. FCC, 567 F.2d 84 (D.C. Cir. 1977); N.Y. Tel. Co. v. FCC, 631 F.2d 1059 (2d Cir. 1980), when, in 1986, the question of federal authority in telecommunications finally reached the Supreme Court. The case was La. Pub. Serv. Comm'n v. FCC, 476 U.S. 355 (1986) (*Louisiana PSC*). At issue was the FCC's decision that its depreciation rules for the installation of wires on a customer's premises would preempt any state regulations prescribing different depreciation rates. The Supreme Court reversed the FCC's ruling, holding that, although 47 U.S.C. § 220 gave the agency broad authority to prescribe depreciation rates, it did not unambiguously provide for preemption of contrary state depreciation rules.

The Court further found that the rates at issue did not involve either costs that were incapable of separation between interstate and intrastate components or a conflict that would completely negate the federal rule. The Court therefore held that, where separation is not impossible and where application of a federal rule will not be nullified by contrary state provisions, preemption of state regulation of intrastate telecommunications can occur only where expressly and unambiguously provided for by statute. *Louisiana PSC,* 476 U.S. at 375–76.

The principle for allocation of jurisdiction between state authorities and the FCC has not changed much since *Louisiana PSC*. The 1996 Act in some instances gives the FCC the kind of express authority that, under *Louisiana PSC*, is necessary for preemption of state regulations governing intrastate communications.

§ 7.B. Jurisdiction to Implement the 1996 Act: Local Competition, National Regulation

The 1996 Act assailed the federal/state divide in telephony regulation, instituting a model of cooperative federalism. In particular, under the 1996 Act, states were no longer free to regulate intrastate services on their own, but rather were asked to work in partnership with the FCC to facilitate local competition.[1] Needless to say, the transition did not go smoothly, and the new jurisdictional arrangement gave rise to litigation and legal uncertainty.

Perhaps the most significant provision of the 1996 Act was one that simply forbade the states from issuing monopoly licenses for telecommunications services and undertaking other regulation that had the effect of monopolizing such services. Consistent with the Act's overall intent to increase competition in all markets, Congress added to the Act an explicit provision stating: "No State or local statute or regulation, or other State or local legal requirement, may prohibit or have the effect of prohibiting the ability of any entity to provide any interstate or intrastate telecommunications service." 47 U.S.C. § 253(a). Although the section preserved the states' authority to regulate, on a "competitively neutral basis," public rights-of-way (§ 253(c)) and to promote universal service (§ 253(b)), Congress also gave the FCC authority to preempt state or local laws if it found a violation of subsections (a) or (b). 47 U.S.C. § 253(d). Explicit state laws forbidding competition were not all that widespread, but Congress wanted to be clear that competition was the law of the land.

The 1996 Act also gave the FCC significant authority over implementation of its local competition provisions, while preserving some role for the states. The jurisdictional battle began shortly after the enactment of the 1996 Act. After the incumbent

1. As a technical matter, states were not required to implement the 1996 Act, as commandeering of this type is unconstitutional under the Tenth Amendment. *See* Printz v. United States, 521 U.S. 898 (1997). As a practical matter, and with very few exceptions, the states opted to maintain some authority (within a federal framework) rather than yield the entire field of facilitating local competition to the FCC.

local exchange carriers challenged the FCC's rules, the Eighth Circuit invalidated some of those rules on the ground that—under the preemption standard set forth in *Louisiana PSC*—the FCC lacked jurisdiction to promulgate those rules. The Eighth Circuit found that §§ 251 and 252 of the 1996 Act expressly refer to state commissions as the bodies responsible for setting rates for unbundled network elements (UNEs), and, further, that neither provision provides the necessary unambiguous authority for preemption by the FCC. The Supreme Court reviewed the Eighth Circuit's decision, starting its opinion by explaining the jurisdictional dispute at the heart of the case:

> The basic attack was jurisdictional. The LECs and state commissions insisted that primary authority to implement the local-competition provisions belonged to the States rather than to the FCC. They thus argued that many of the local-competition rules were invalid, most notably the one requiring that prices for interconnection and unbundled access be based on "Total Element Long Run Incremental Cost" (TELRIC)—a forward-looking rather than historic measure. The Court of Appeals agreed and vacated the pricing rules, as well as several other aspects of the Order, as reaching beyond the Commission's jurisdiction. It held that the general rulemaking authority conferred upon the Commission by the Communications Act of 1934 extended only to interstate matters, and that the Commission therefore needed specific congressional authorization before implementing provisions of the 1996 Act addressing intrastate telecommunications. It found no such authorization for the Commission's rules regarding pricing, dialing parity, exemptions for rural LECs, the proper procedure for resolving local-competition disputes, and state review of pre-1996 interconnection agreements. Indeed, with respect to some of these matters, the Eighth Circuit said that the 1996 Act had affirmatively given exclusive authority to the state commissions.
>
> The Court of Appeals found support for its holdings in 47 U.S.C. § 152(b) (§ 2(b) of the Communications Act of 1934), which, it said, creates a presumption in favor of preserving state authority over intrastate communications. It found nothing in the 1996 Act clear enough to overcome this presumption.

AT&T Corp. v. Iowa Utilities Board, 525 U.S. 366, 374–75 (1999).

The Supreme Court reversed the Eighth Circuit's holding with respect to jurisdiction:

> Section 201(b), a 1938 amendment to the Communications Act of 1934, provides that "the Commission may prescribe such rules and regulations as may be necessary in the public interest to carry out the provisions of this Act." Since Congress expressly directed that the 1996 Act, along with its local-competition provisions, be inserted into the Communications Act of 1934, the Commission's rulemaking authority would seem to extend to implementation of the local-competition provisions.

> The incumbent LECs and state commissions argue, however, that § 201(b) rulemaking authority is limited to those provisions dealing with purely interstate and foreign matters, because the first sentence of § 201(a) makes it "the duty of every common carrier engaged in interstate or foreign communication by wire or radio to furnish such communication service upon reasonable request therefor. . . ." It is impossible to understand how this use of the qualifier "interstate or foreign" in § 201(a), which limits the class of common carriers with the duty of providing communication service, reaches forward into the last sentence of § 201(b) to limit the class of provisions that the Commission has authority to implement. We think that the grant in § 201(b) means what it says: The FCC has rulemaking authority to carry out the "provisions of this Act," which include §§ 251 and 252, added by the Telecommunications Act of 1996.

Id. at 377–78.

Moreover, the Court found that § 152(b) did not constitute a bar to the FCC's pricing rules because the 1996 Act expressly applies to intrastate telecommunications and thus expressly gives the Commission authority to make rules on those intrastate matters covered by the 1996 Act:

> Our view is unaffected by 47 U.S.C. § 152(b), which reads: "Except as provided in §§ 223 through 227 . . . , inclusive, and § 332 . . . , and subject to the provisions of § 301 of this title . . . , nothing in this chapter shall be construed to apply or to give the Commission jurisdiction with respect to . . . charges, classifications, practices, services, facilities, or regulations for or in connection with intrastate communication service. . . ." The local-competition provisions are not identified in § 152(b)'s "except" clause. Seizing on this omission, respondents argue that the 1996 Act does nothing to displace the presumption that the States retain their traditional authority over local phone service. The fallacy in this reasoning is that it ignores the fact that § 201(b) explicitly gives the FCC jurisdiction to make rules governing matters to which the 1996 Act applies.

Id. at 379–80.

In reaching this decision, the Supreme Court seems to have limited the scope of *Louisiana PSC*. The Court interpreted that case to require express and unambiguous preemption authority only in situations where the FCC has not otherwise been given explicit rulemaking authority. *Id.* at 381. The Court's decision in *Iowa Utilities Board* thus empowered the FCC relative to state commissions.

The majority opinion on jurisdiction was met with vigorous dissent. Justice Thomas's partially dissenting opinion, *id.* at 402, in which Justice Breyer and Chief Justice Rehnquist joined, found nothing in § 201(b) to trump the overarching rule of construction established in § 152(b). Justice Thomas argued that, if anything, the local competition provisions of the 1996 Act were deliberately meant to "respect[] the States' historical role as the dominant authority with respect to intrastate communications." *Id.* at 411. In his own partial dissent, *id.* at 412, Justice Breyer further emphasized the role of state commissions in the statutory provisions at issue. He pointed to the express reference in § 252(c) to "State commission[s]" as the entities charged to set rates for unbundled network elements. Justice Breyer rejected both the argument that the 1996 Act in some way required the particular method prescribed by the Commission, *id.* at 424, as well as the alternative argument that the states retained sufficient discretion under the Commission rules to have meaningful independent jurisdiction over UNE rates, *id.* at 423.

Notes and Questions

1. Jurisdictional Policy. While the courtroom debate turns on technical detail, the policy issue underlying the 1996 Act's jurisdiction provisions is a simple one: are there convincing arguments as to why the federal commission should take the lead in implementing the resale and unbundling provisions? Are these issues of primarily local concern? Is the point here that these local regulations were expected to have a significant effect on the national telecommunications market? Or is it simply that, as an expert agency, the FCC is more likely to set appropriate rules? Does the statute allow the Court to adequately consider these core issues? If so, is that an appropriate task for judges? If not, is that wise, on the theory that this should be Congress's responsibility, or foolish, because it relegates the Justices to arguing over strained readings of ambiguous phrases?

2. Choosing Not to Regulate. In *Iowa Utilities Board*, the Supreme Court held that the FCC had authority to exercise jurisdiction over UNE rates. Several years later, a jurisdictional dispute again arose but this time over the FCC's decision *not* to exercise its authority under the Act. In its 2003 Triennial Review Order on unbundled network elements (discussed in greater detail in the next sections), the FCC declined to decide whether incumbent local telephone companies should have to unbundle switching to residential and other "mass-market" customers. The FCC instead stated that "the Commission sets out specific criteria that states shall apply to determine, on a granular basis, whether economic and operational impairment exists in a particular market. State Commissions must complete such proceedings within 9 months." Press Release, FCC, FCC Adopts New Rules for Networking Unbundling Obligations of Incumbent Local Phone Carriers (Feb. 20, 2003). The incumbents again challenged the FCC on jurisdictional grounds. This time, the argument was not that the FCC improperly preempted the states, but that the Commission improperly delegated authority to the states. The D.C. Circuit agreed and held that the FCC improperly handed off its responsibility to decide which network elements incumbents had to unbundle for the benefit of competitors that wanted to enter the market. The relevant excerpt from the D.C. Circuit's decision follows.

United States Telecom Ass'n v. FCC [*USTA II*]

359 F.3d 554 (D.C. Cir. 2004)

Opinion for the court filed by Senior Circuit Judge WILLIAMS, in which Circuit Judges EDWARDS and RANDOLPH concur.

WILLIAMS, Senior Circuit Judge:

The FCC acknowledges that § 251(d)(2) instructs "the Commission" to "determine[]" which network elements shall be made available to CLECs on an unbundled basis. But it claims that agencies have the presumptive power to subdelegate to state commissions, so long as the statute authorizing agency action refrains from foreclosing such a power. Given the absence of any express foreclosure, the Commission argues that its interpretation of the statute on the matter of subdelegation is entitled to deference under Chevron U.S.A. v. Natural Resources Defense Council, Inc., 467 U.S. 837 (1984). And it claims that its interpretation is reasonable given the state commissions' independent jurisdiction over the general subject matter, the magnitude of the regulatory task, and the need for close cooperation between state and federal regulators in this area.

The Commission's position is based on a fundamental misreading of the relevant case law. When a statute delegates authority to a federal officer or agency, subdelegation to a subordinate federal officer or agency is presumptively permissible absent affirmative evidence of a contrary congressional intent. But the cases recognize an important distinction between subdelegation to a *subordinate* and subdelegation to an *outside party*. The presumption that subdelegations are valid absent a showing of contrary congressional intent applies only to the former. There is no such presumption covering subdelegations to outside parties. Indeed, if anything, the case law strongly suggests that subdelegations to outside parties are assumed to be improper absent an affirmative showing of congressional authorization.

This distinction is entirely sensible. When an agency delegates authority to its subordinate, responsibility—and thus accountability—clearly remain with the federal agency. But when an agency delegates power to outside parties, lines of accountability may blur, undermining an important democratic check on government decision-making. Also, delegation to outside entities increases the risk that these parties will not share the agency's "national vision and perspective," Nat'l. Park and Conservation Ass'n v. Stanton, 54 F. Supp. 2d 7, 20 (D.D.C. 1999), and thus may pursue goals inconsistent with those of the agency and the underlying statutory scheme. In short, subdelegation to outside entities aggravates the risk of policy drift inherent in any principal-agent relationship.

The fact that the subdelegation in this case is to state commissions rather than private organizations does not alter the analysis. Although United States v. Mazurie, 419 U.S. 544 (1975), noted that "limits on the authority of *Congress* to delegate its legislative power ... are [] less stringent in cases where the entity exercising the delegated authority itself possesses independent authority over the subject matter," *id.*

at 556–57 (emphasis added), that decision has no application here: it involved a constitutional challenge to an express *congressional* delegation, rather than an administrative subdelegation, and the point of the discussion was to distinguish the still somewhat suspect case of congressional delegation to purely private organizations.

We therefore hold that, while federal agency officials may subdelegate their decision-making authority to subordinates absent evidence of contrary congressional intent, they may not subdelegate to outside entities—private or sovereign—absent affirmative evidence of authority to do so.

The Commission's plea for *Chevron* deference is unavailing. A general delegation of decision-making authority to a federal administrative agency does *not*, in the ordinary course of things, include the power to subdelegate that authority beyond federal subordinates. It is clear here that Congress has not delegated to the FCC the authority to subdelegate to outside parties. The statutory "silence" simply leaves that lack of authority untouched. In other words, the failure of Congress to use "Thou Shalt Not" language doesn't create a statutory ambiguity of the sort that triggers *Chevron* deference.

We therefore vacate, as an unlawful subdelegation of the Commission's § 251(d)(2) responsibilities, those portions of the Order that delegate to state commissions the authority to determine whether CLECs are impaired without access to network elements, and in particular we vacate the Commission's scheme for subdelegating mass market switching determinations.

Notes and Questions

1. Separating Law and Policy. In the decision excerpt above, the court held that the FCC could not, as a matter of law, delegate its rulemaking authority to the states. As a matter of policy, however, might such delegation sometimes be beneficial because of states' greater knowledge of their local market conditions? Are there reasons to give up these advantages and force the FCC to make the necessary decisions instead?

2. State Law, State Regulators, and the 1996 Act. In light of the two excerpts above, one might well wonder what states *could* do. The Supreme Court said they cannot have exclusive jurisdiction over UNE pricing, and the Court of Appeals said they cannot be given jurisdiction to establish which elements must be unbundled. What is left for the states to regulate? That is, under the 1996 Act as interpreted above, exactly how much authority do state regulators have left?

§ 7.C. Cable Television

As cable television grew in the 1960s and 1970s, the FCC found itself without a clear statutory mandate to regulate it. The FCC had Title II, which addressed common carrier telephony, and Title III, which addressed broadcasting. Cable—the delivery of video over wires—did not fit either scheme. At first, the FCC declined to regulate cable television, but it later decided that it could regulate because the exercise of such authority would be "ancillary" to its power over broadcasting.

Although the Supreme Court generally (but not uniformly) upheld the FCC's cable regulations, Congress finally stepped in. Almost twenty years after the FCC first began to regulate cable television under its Title I authority, Congress devised a statutory framework to govern the industry and provided the FCC with explicit jurisdiction over cable television. That framework, set out in the Cable Communications Policy Act of 1984, Pub. L. No. 98-549, 98 Stat. 2779, amended the 1934 Act by adding a Title VI that regulates cable television. It also amended § 152(a) of the Communications Act, 47 U.S.C. § 152, to clearly state that the "provisions of this [Act] shall apply with respect to cable service, to all persons engaged within the United States in providing such service, and to the facilities of cable operators which relate to such service."

The FCC is not the only regulatory authority that has shown interest in cable television over the years. Cable television developed as a service provided to local communities that was regulated by states and localities. Local governments insisted that cable providers apply to them for permission to be a local "cable franchisee" and local franchise authorities would often extract costly concessions from cable providers in exchange for granting those franchise rights. Many local franchise authorities granted exclusive franchises (i.e., a local monopoly). It was not clear that cable television was a natural monopoly and thus that competition among cable operators would not work. But these local franchise authorities chose not to allow competition.

At the same time that Congress stepped in to establish jurisdiction for the FCC, Congress stepped into this jurisdictional issue as well. Three statutes were passed between 1984 and 1996: the Cable Communications Policy Act of 1984, Pub. L. No. 98-549, 98 Stat. 2779 (1984); the Cable Television Consumer Protection and Competition Act of 1992, Pub. L. No. 102-385, 106 Stat. 1460; and the Telecommunications Act of 1996, Pub. L. No. 104-104, 110 Stat. 56. Taken together, the three significantly constrained local authority over cable service.

Four constraints turned out to be of practical importance. First, the 1984 Act limited local government's ability to use the threat of franchise nonrenewal as a means by which to discipline cable franchisees. The Act did so by creating a strong presumption that a cable franchisee will have its franchise renewed at the end of its term. Under the Act, local authorities can refuse to renew only by producing evidence of substantial noncompliance with franchise terms and, even then, the local authority must give the cable operator notice and an opportunity to cure any alleged failures. 47 U.S.C. § 546. Renewals cannot be denied on the basis of the mix or quality of the cable services provided by the system, at least if those services comply with franchise terms. Decisions not to renew are subject to judicial review.

Second, the 1984 Act capped the franchise fee that local government could charge, specifically prohibiting local authorities from charging a fee exceeding five percent of the cable system's gross revenues. 47 U.S.C. § 542(b).

Third, the 1992 Act prohibited local government from (1) granting exclusive franchises and (2) unreasonably refusing to award additional competitive franchises. 47 U.S.C. § 541. That is, local authorities could neither make a legally binding promise that a particular franchisee would be the exclusive cable provider nor credibly commit to accomplishing the same result de facto by refusing to award later franchises. This constrained local government's clout; after the 1992 Act, local governments were no longer in the business of granting lucrative, legally guaranteed monopolies. Instead, to whatever extent the market would bear, cable franchisees would be subject to competition.

Fourth, the three statutes together largely stripped local government of its power to regulate cable rates. The 1984 Act took the first step, forbidding local rate regulation in situations where the FCC determined that local cable providers faced "effective competition." The FCC interpreted that phrase quite broadly, announcing that a cable provider faces effective competition so long as its subscribers could receive three over-the-air television signals. Rate regulation thus largely disappeared. The 1992 Act called for the reinstitution of a stronger form of rate regulation. That Act required cable operators to (1) establish a "basic tier" of services consisting of all signals carried pursuant to must-carry obligations and retransmission consent and also all public, educational, or governmental channels; (2) price that basic tier separately; and (3) force subscribers to purchase the basic tier as a precondition to subscribing to other services. The statute then permitted local authorities to regulate rates for the basic tier, and again established an exception that would stop rate regulation in instances where the Commission determines that there is adequate competition. This time, the Commission's standards were more demanding. As a result, most providers were subject to rate regulation, at least until DBS providers rose to prominence and began to provide the competition contemplated by the statute. Meanwhile, the 1992 Act gave the Commission authority to entertain complaints regarding cable services that were outside the basic tier, but the Telecommunications Act of 1996 repealed that authority. The 1996 Act also set a series of tests that essentially eliminated all rate regulation when there is effective competition. Thus, as a result of these three Acts, there is limited rate regulation still in place—notably, only for the basic tier at the local level where other multichannel video programming distributors (MVPDs) have not yet been deemed to provide adequate competition. In virtually all of the country, then, the result is that cable prices are not subject to rate regulation.

Our commentary thus far focuses on the ways in which the 1984 and 1992 Cable Acts constrained local government. The Acts were not entirely bad news for local authorities, however. Indeed, even though the Acts constrained local government's ability to regulate price and limited the size of any franchise fee, the Acts at the same time combined to authorize local government to impose three significant obligations on cable franchisees. First, the 1984 Act added § 611 to the Communications Act of 1934, which provides that local franchise authorities "may ... require as part of a [cable] franchise ... [or] franchise renewal ... that channel capacity be designated for public, educational, or governmental use." 47 U.S.C. § 531(b). As the name implies, these "PEG" channels carry governmental and educational information that might be of interest to local subscribers but be undersupplied by market forces. These channels constitute an implicit tax imposed on franchisees; instead of taking a higher fee and then purchasing channel capacity, the local government is allowed to take a fee of no more than five percent of revenues but can then require the franchisee to provide a certain number of PEG channels.

Second, the 1984 and 1992 Acts combined to add § 612 to the Communications Act. This provision requires certain cable systems to lease some of their channel capacity to unaffiliated firms, and to do so at regulated rates. 47 U.S.C. § 532. These channels are typically referred to as "leased access" channels. Whether channels must be set aside and, if so, how many, is determined by the statute based on the size of the cable system at issue. The statute further allows cable operators who are required to provide leased access capacity to instead devote up to one third of that capacity to "programming from a qualified minority programming source or from any qualified educational programming source, whether or not such source is affiliated with the cable operator." 47 U.S.C. § 532(i).

Third, the Acts did leave local governments with the power to require that any would-be cable provider negotiate and sign a franchise agreement with local authorities. To be sure, the various constraints above limited the terms of that agreement; but still much was in play. For instance, under most franchise agreements, cable franchisees must commit to meet certain deployment goals ("build-out requirements") on specific deadlines. And franchise agreements can obligate would-be franchisees to provide cable infrastructure that the locality itself can use, such as through the PEG channels authorized (but not required) by federal law. Indeed, burdens along these lines can be so severe that there have been movements to strip local government of the franchising power entirely. The argument is that franchise agreements impose such burdens on entrants that they are chilling what would otherwise be significant MVPD entry—not only from traditional providers like cable companies, but also from newer entrants like telephone companies which are experimenting with the use of the telephone infrastructure as a delivery mechanism for video programming.

In terms of litigation, most of the changes we summarize here were put into place without triggering court review. The most notable exception: cable operators brought suit contending that the PEG and leased access provisions violated their First Amendment rights and therefore were unconstitutional on their face. The highest court to address those claims was the Court of Appeals for the D.C. Circuit in Time Warner Entertainment Co. v. FCC, 93 F.3d 957 (D.C. Cir. 1996).[2] With

2. The challenges to the PEG and leased access provisions were part of a larger facial challenge to many different portions of the 1984 and 1992 Cable Acts. All told, the plaintiff cable television system owners/operators and programmers argued that the following provisions infringed upon their First Amendment right to freedom of speech: §§ 611 (public, educational, and governmental

respect to leased access, the court found that the regulation was not content-based because "[programmers'] qualification to lease time on those channels depends not on the content of their speech, but on their lack of affiliation with the operator, a distinguishing characteristic stemming from considerations relating to the structure of cable television." *Id.* at 969. The court's application of the intermediate scrutiny applicable to content-neutral speech regulations is encapsulated in the following paragraph:

> Time Warner thinks it sufficient to allege in its brief that there is not now, nor will there be under new FCC regulations, any appreciable demand by unaffiliated programmers for access to cable systems because cable systems are already carrying a wide variety of programs from diverse sources and because leased access does not make economic sense in light of the costs of production. For the sake of argument, we shall accept this assertion as true. We will assume, in other words, that on remand Time Warner could prove the factual propositions contained in its brief. Would that render the leased access provisions unconstitutional? We think not. If unaffiliated programmers have not and will not lease time on the channels set aside for them—if, in other words, Time Warner made its best case—we fail to see how the company could establish that the provisions violate its First Amendment right to free speech. Under § 532(b)(4), a "cable operator may use any unused channel capacity" set aside for leased access "until the use of such channel capacity is obtained, pursuant to a written agreement, by a person unaffiliated with the operator." That is, if unaffiliated programmers have not and, as Time Warner predicts, will not exploit the leased access provisions, then the provisions will have no effect on the speech of the cable operators. None of their programming would have to be dropped. The channels set aside for leasing will either be vacant or they will be occupied according to the wishes of the cable operators. The operators' editorial control will remain unimpaired and so will their First Amendment right to determine what will appear on their cable systems.

---

programming) and 612 (leased access) of the 1984 Act, and §§ 3 (rate regulation), 10(d) (obscenity liability), 11(c) (subscriber limitation, channel occupancy, and program creation restrictions), 15 (premium channel preview notice), 19 (vertically integrated programming), 24 (municipal immunity), and 25 (direct broadcast satellite set-aside) of the 1992 Act. *See Time Warner*, 93 F.3d at 962. In addition, the suit originally included a constitutional challenge to the must-carry provisions (§§ 4 and 5) of the 1992 Cable Act. Pursuant to a special jurisdictional provision of the 1992 Cable Act that applied only to challenges to §§ 4 and 5, the must-carry challenge was severed, sent to a three-judge panel of the district court, and appealed directly to the Supreme Court, resulting in Turner Broadcasting Sys., Inc. v. FCC, 512 U.S. 622 (1994) (*Turner I*), and, after the *Time Warner* opinion was issued, Turner Broadcasting Sys., Inc. v. FCC, 520 U.S. 180 (1997) (*Turner II*). Both *Turner I* and *Turner II* are excerpted and discussed in Chapter 3.

Id. at 970–71. As to PEG channels, the court stated as follows:

> To prevail in its facial challenge, Time Warner must "establish that no set of circumstances exists under which the Act would be valid." United States v. Salerno, 481 U.S. 739, 745 (1987). Consideration of this standard is somewhat tricky here since rather than *requiring* PEG channel capacity, the statute merely *permits* local franchise authorities to require PEG programming as a franchise condition. In fact, prior to the passage of the 1984 Cable Act, and thus, in the absence of federal permission, many franchise agreements provided for PEG channels. In passing the PEG provision, Congress thus merely recognized and endorsed the preexisting practice of local franchise authorities conditioning their cable franchises on the granting of PEG channel access. All the statute does, then, is preempt states from prohibiting local PEG requirements (if any states were to choose to do so) and preclude federal preemption challenges to such requirements, challenges that cable operators might have brought in the absence of the provision. [A] statute that simply permits franchise authorities to regulate where they had previously done so raises no First Amendment problems unless the localities themselves infringe on cable operators' speech.
>
> Time Warner must therefore show that no franchise authority could ever exercise the statute's grant of authority in a constitutional manner. We can, of course, imagine PEG franchise conditions that would raise serious constitutional issues. For example, were a local authority to require as a franchise condition that a cable operator designate three-quarters of its channels for "educational" programming, defined in detail by the city council, such a requirement would certainly implicate First Amendment concerns. At the same time, we can just as easily imagine a franchise authority exercising its power without violating the First Amendment. For example, a local franchise authority might seek to ensure public "access to a multiplicity of information sources," Turner Broad. Sys., Inc. v. FCC, 512 U.S. 622, 663 (1994), by conditioning its grant of a franchise on the cable operator's willingness to provide access to a single channel for "public" use, defining "public" broadly enough to permit access to everyone on a nondiscriminatory, first-come, first-serve basis. Under *Turner*, such a scheme would be content-neutral, would serve an "important purpose unrelated to the suppression of free expression," *id.* at 662, and would be narrowly tailored to its goal. Time Warner's facial challenge therefore fails.

93 F.3d at 972–73.

Notes and Questions

1. PEG and Leased Access. Note the differing rationales behind PEG and leased access channels. The idea behind PEG channels is to expand the information provided to the public on crucial issues. In this way, the goal of increasing valuable programming via PEG channels is similar to the theory of Red Lion Broadcasting Co. v. FCC, 395 U.S. 367 (1969), which is excerpted in Chapter 11. Commercial leased access regulations, by contrast, are usually defended on the ground that they promote competition among program suppliers. The theory is that a cable network might seek to enter into a contract with a cable operator that effectively excludes other networks, but the leased access capacity will enable those other networks to get on the system nevertheless. Thus, the rationale behind leased access is to make sure that cable companies do not freeze out potentially popular channels with which the cable companies are not affiliated, similar to the rationale for vertical integration limits discussed in Chapter 10.

2. Rationale for Regulation. What programs would be shown on cable under a leased access regime that would not obtain carriage without leased access? Wouldn't cable operators, seeking to satisfy a wide range of viewers' desires, carry any available programming that is expected to be profitable? If a hypothetical XYZ pay cable network offering movies and sports could make more money for the cable system than, say, HBO, wouldn't the cable system carry XYZ?

3. Heads I Win, Tails You Lose? With regard to leased access, was Time Warner in a no-win position? If Time Warner argued (as it did) that it already carried a wide variety of programs from different sources so there was no demand (and thus no need) for leased access, the D.C. Circuit could respond (as it did) that the leased access regime did not harm Time Warner. If Time Warner argued instead that many unaffiliated programmers would be clamoring for leased access channels and filling up the leased access channels, then the court might well have responded that this demonstrated the need for leased access, and thus showed that leased access was responding to a real, nonconjectural harm. Could Time Warner have made an argument that would have avoided both of these responses?

4. Compelled Access. The general problem of compelled access to media platforms is one that we have seen and will continue to see throughout this casebook. The question is always the same: should we impose on owners of communication infrastructure "common carrier" obligations, in essence separating legal authority over the conduit from legal authority over the content? Despite the prevalence of the issue, courts have not settled on a single approach to the question of whether mandated access can be squared with the First Amendment principle of freedom of speech and the press. Meanwhile, the imposition of common carrier duties on telephone companies was never questioned on constitutional grounds, but—following the lead of Miami Herald Publishing Co. v. Tornillo, 418 U.S. 241 (1974) (discussed in Chapter 11)—it seems to be flatly unconstitutional to impose common carrier obligations on the print media. Is a single, coherent principle available for resolving questions about compelled access to the mass media?

5. Regulators as Bottleneck. The 1984 Act, the 1992 Act, and the 1996 Act all suggest, in various ways, that local government is an obstacle to entry in the cable market. If that is true, why did these statutes leave the local government with franchising authority at all? That is, why should would-be entrants have to apply to the relevant local government and negotiate franchise terms within the constraints of federal law, rather than more simply entering upon compliance with some statewide or federally mandated list of requirements? Those requirements could include default provisions requiring that a franchise fee be paid to the local government and that a certain number of PEG channels are provided. The point is that the rules could be set up such that there were established requirements, rather than requirements that must be negotiated each time. In short, given how little discretion they legitimately have anyway, why not put local governments out of the business of cable regulation entirely?

§ 7.D. Jurisdiction to Promote Competition in MVPD Markets

As telephone companies upgraded their infrastructures with more fiber optics to have the bandwidth to compete with cable companies' internet and video services, the telephone companies pushed not only to enter video markets but also to do so via statewide franchises. Telephone companies feared that obtaining local franchises would be burdensome and that local cable companies might be powerful in some local jurisdictions. This led to some states, including major ones such as California, Texas, and New Jersey, to pass legislation providing for statewide franchising. In addition, the FCC, after developing significant evidence that local franchising processes were delaying competitive video entry, adopted an order aimed at easing the path of telephone companies into video programming markets, by "adopt[ing] measures to address a variety of means by which local franchise authorities, i.e., county- or municipal-level franchising authorities, are unreasonably refusing to award competitive franchises." Implementation of Section 621(a)(1) of the Cable Communications Policy Act of 1984, Report and Order, 22 FCC Rcd. 5101, 5102, ¶ 1 (2007). The FCC's rules set time limits on local franchise authority processing of new applications for franchises. The rules also limited the use of "build out requirements" as franchise conditions, finding that such conditions limited competition by creating economic barriers to entry. Finally, the rules limited local franchise fees and requirements that new entrants provide PEG channels.

Local franchise authorities and incumbent cable television companies challenged the rules. To echo *Iowa Utilities Board*, "[t]he basic attack was jurisdictional." 525 U.S. at 374. In Alliance for Community Media v. FCC, 529 F.3d 763 (6th Cir. 2008), the Sixth Circuit relatively easily found that the FCC had rulemaking authority. The court conceded that the relevant provision of the Communications Act did not give the FCC any role but rather was stated as a limitation on local franchise authorities: "[A] franchising authority may not grant an exclusive franchise and may not unreasonably refuse to award an additional competitive franchise." 47 U.S.C. § 541(a)(1). The section gave a disappointed franchise applicant the right to judicial review, not an appeal to the FCC. *See* 47 U.S.C. § 555. The court nevertheless found that the 1996 Act gave the FCC rulemaking power:

> Petitioners are . . . correct in noting that, while the text expressly references franchising authorities, it is silent as to the agency's role in the process of

> awarding cable franchises. Where petitioners' argument falls short, however, is in equating the omission of the agency from section 621(a)(1) with an absence of rulemaking authority.
>
> In AT&T Corp. v. Iowa Utilities Board, 525 U.S. 366 (1999), the Supreme Court considered a challenge by state utility commissions and local exchange carriers to local competition rules issued by the FCC pursuant to the Telecommunications Act of 1996. In considering whether the FCC possessed the regulatory authority to interpret the provisions of the Telecommunications Act of 1996 at issue, the Court hinged its analysis on section 201(b), a 1938 amendment to the Communications Act of 1934. Section 201(b) provides, in relevant part, that "[t]he Commission may prescribe such rules and regulations as may be necessary in the public interest to carry out the provisions of this Act." 47 U.S.C. § 201(b). The Court reasoned that "[s]ince Congress expressly directed that the 1996 Act, along with its local-competition provisions, be inserted into the Communications Act of 1934 . . . the Commission's rulemaking authority would seem to extend to implementation of the local competition provisions." 525 U.S. at 377–78. In other words, *AT&T Corp.* espoused a plain reading of section 201(b): "We think that the grant in § 201(b) means what it says: The FCC has rulemaking authority to carry out the 'provisions of this Act,' which include §§ 251 and 252, added by the Telecommunications Act of 1996." *Id.* at 378.
>
> We find that the logic of *AT&T Corp.* controls the disposition of the jurisdictional argument petitioners raise here. Just as Congress ratified the Telecommunications Act of 1996 as an amendment to be incorporated into the original Communications Act of 1934, Congress likewise passed the Cable Television Consumer Protection and Competition Act of 1992, Pub. L. No. 102-385, 106 Stat. 1460, which revised section 621(a)(1) to include the bar on unreasonable refusals to award additional franchises, as an amendment to the original Communications Act of 1934. Through this process of amendment, Congress incorporated section 621(a)(1) into the Communications Act of 1934, and the statutory language at issue here thus qualifies as a "provision[] of this Act" within the meaning of section 201(b). Thus, because "the grant in § 201(b) means what it says[,]" we are bound by this plain meaning and thereby conclude that, pursuant to section 201(b), the FCC possesses clear jurisdictional authority to formulate rules and regulations interpreting the contours of section 621(a)(1). *See AT&T Corp.*, 525 U.S. at 378.

529 F.3d at 773–74. The Sixth Circuit then upheld the rules on the merits as well.

Notes and Questions

1. Video Competition. Although the FCC had substantial evidence that local governments were, in fact, slowing down entry, at the end of the day video competition came principally from satellite providers (which of course do not need local franchises) and from telephone companies, with relatively limited entry by new facilities-based competitors such as second cable television companies.

2. The Timing Issue. Two scholars have suggested that *Iowa Utilities Board* might be wrong in construing the breadth of the § 201(b) rulemaking grant, noting that the legislative history of a 1938 amendment to the Communications Act seems to suggest it only applies to very particular subject matter (furnishing of reports of ships at sea). Thomas W. Merrill & Kathryn Tongue Watts, Agency Rules with the Force of Law: The Original Convention, 116 Harv. L. Rev. 467, 519–20 & nn.263–64 (2002). But even if one prefers the broader, textualist outcome in *Iowa Utilities Board*, the Communications Act in 1938 did not include *any* cable provisions. It might be one thing to say, as the Court did, that Congress in the 1996 Act intentionally added the local competition provisions to Title II of the Act, thereby invoking section 201(b), and an entirely different matter to say that section 201(b) applies to titles of the Communications Act not at all in existence in 1938. But that may also depend on whether one thinks that the FCC should have similar authority to limit local authorities' implementation and interpretation of federal law.

§ 7.E. Internet Services

Regrettably, just as federal regulation of many important aspects of internet services remains unsettled, the question of which level of government has or should have authority to regulate remains open as well. At times, in the absence of more specific congressional action, the FCC has sought to use its Communications Act authority to address various internet issues. We looked closely at this as a general matter in Chapter 6. Here, we touch more briefly on a few specific developments, both at the infrastructure layer and at the higher services level.

One important area that, as a threshold matter, went in the direction of the states was their control over local government entry into internet services. Relying on § 253, municipalities across the country argued that their states could not forbid them from offering telecommunications services, including internet services. After all, the statute literally says that "[n]o State . . . may prohibit . . . *any entity* . . . to provide . . . telecommunication service." 47 U.S.C. § 253(a) (emphasis supplied). The FCC, however, refused to preempt such state laws, and in Nixon v. Missouri Municipal League, 541 U.S. 125 (2004), the Supreme Court held that § 253(a) did not require states to allow municipalities or municipally-owned utilities to enter telecommunications markets. Municipalities have generally been considered creatures of state law, and the Court held, consistent with many precedents, that Congress would have to (and did not in § 253) clearly show its intent to disrupt the states' authority over their own creations (the local governments). Later, the FCC tried to enhance the scope of municipal offerings where not completely forbidden by state law. In 2015, the FCC was faced with state laws that permitted municipalities and municipally-owned utilities to provide broadband, but restricted their provision to their utility service areas and imposed certain other conditions on their ability to offer broadband services. The FCC preempted the territorial restriction and most of the other conditions as creating barriers to broadband deployment, but the Sixth Circuit reversed. *See* City of Wilson, North Carolina, Petition for Preemption, Memorandum Opinion and Order, 30 FCC Rcd. 2408 (2015), *rev'd*, Tennessee v. FCC, 832 F.3d 597 (6th Cir. 2016). The Sixth Circuit, following *Nixon*, said that "[t]he FCC order essentially serves to re-allocate decision-making authority between the states and their municipalities." This preemption by the FCC of the allocation of power between a state and its subdivisions *requires* at least a clear statement in the authorizing federal legislation. The FCC relies upon § 706 of the Telecommunications Act of 1996 for the authority to preempt in this case, but that statute falls far short of such a clear statement." *Id.* at 600. (We discussed § 706 in the previous chapter.)

By contrast, the FCC has prevailed in its broad interpretation of federal authority to regulate pole access, an important infrastructure element. As noted in section D, the FCC, using authority under the Communications Act, has limited state and local authority over rights of way and other properties, in order to promote entry and competition in MVPD services. The FCC has also used its authority under the so-called "Pole Attachments Act," 47 U.S.C. § 224, to facilitate the deployment of wires that carry internet services. Initially added to the Communications Act in 1978, § 224 allowed cable television companies access to telephone poles (and similar facilities, such as ducts, conduits, and rights of way) at regulated rates, so that telephone companies and municipalities could not block their access to customers. In the 1996 Act, Congress expanded § 224 to give access rights to any provider of telecommunications services. This was, of course, necessary if the new telephone companies were to enter markets to provide facilities-based services. Both before and after the 1996 Act, the FCC took the position that cable television systems could demand access and other rights under § 224, even if the cable systems also used the wires to provide internet services. *See* Texas Util. Elec. Co. v. FCC, 97 F.2d 925, 927, 929 (D.C. Cir. 1993) (upholding the FCC's interpretation). After the 1996 Act, certain incumbents (pole owners) challenged the FCC's position again, and the Eleventh Circuit agreed with their narrower interpretation — that the "mixed" nature of the services provided meant that the facilities did not have rights under § 224. The Supreme Court reversed, adopting the FCC's interpretation in National Cable Television Association, Inc. v. Gulf Power Co., 534 U.S. 327 (2002). The Court held that § 224 gave access rights to providers — "cable television systems" and "provider[s] of telecommunications services" — and that those entities offering cable television or telecommunications services did not lose their status as such simply because they used the same facilities to provide additional services. The Court's decision not only empowers the FCC's vis-à-vis incumbents but also divests state governments from regulating infrastructure in this manner.

The clash between federal and state authority over internet services has also been manifest at the internet service provider level, as we discussed in Chapter 6. To the extent that internet access services are common carrier "telecommunications services," then the FCC has the very significant authority provided by Title II of the 1934 Act and the local competition provisions of the 1996 Act. But, if internet services are not telecommunications services, then the FCC's authority (including its authority to preempt state regulation) is much more modest, leaving the states in the drivers' seat, as the next case shows:

ACA Connects v. Bonta

24 F.4th 1233 (9th Cir. 2022)

Opinion for the court filed by Circuit Judge SCHROEDER, joined by Circuit Judges WALLACE and FORREST.

SCHROEDER, Circuit Judge:

For the broadband internet industry, the critical regulatory issues that have emerged so far in this century concern access to the internet: what entities have access, on what terms, and to what extent access should be regulated. The administrative enthusiasm of the Federal Communications Commission (FCC) has seemingly ebbed and flowed with the political tides, culminating most recently in its 2018 decision to stop treating broadband services as "telecommunications services" subject to relatively comprehensive, common-carrier regulation pursuant to Title II of the Communications Act, and to classify them instead under Title I as lightly regulated "information services." Restoring Internet Freedom, Declaratory Order, Report and Order, and Order, 33 FCC Rcd. 311 (2018) (2018 Order).

This 2018 Order had the significant result of terminating federal regulation intended to protect equal access to the internet, popularly known as "net neutrality" rules. This in turn has raised immediate questions about the extent of states' authority in the field. In this appeal, we consider the broadband industry's contention that, when the FCC reclassified broadband services under Title I, thereby abandoning its regulatory authority with respect to net neutrality, California was preempted from stepping into the breach to enact its own net neutrality protections.

Plaintiffs-Appellants are a group of industry trade associations representing communications service providers who sought an injunction to prevent the California Attorney General from enforcing the California Internet Consumer Protection and Net Neutrality Act of 2018 (SB-822). Cal. Stats. 2018, ch. 976. This state law, in essence, codified the rescinded federal net neutrality rules, but limits its application to broadband internet services provided to customers in California. The district court ruled in favor of California and denied the service providers' request for a preliminary injunction to block enforcement of the statute. The district court concluded there was no preemption because the FCC lacked the requisite regulatory authority.

The district court's decision was in line with the D.C. Circuit's recent holding in Mozilla Corp. v. FCC, 940 F.3d 1 (D.C. Cir. 2019). The court in *Mozilla* reviewed the validity of the FCC's 2018 reclassification decision and an accompanying order preempting state net neutrality rules. The court upheld the reclassification, but struck down the preemption order. The critical issue with respect to preemption was whether the FCC retained the statutory authority to adopt federal net neutrality rules after its decision to reclassify broadband internet services under Title I of the Communications Act. The D.C. Circuit held that, under Title I, the FCC did not have the authority to regulate broadband services in this manner, and because federal regulatory authority is a prerequisite to preemption, the FCC could not expressly preempt the states.

The service providers here nevertheless contend that the California statute is preempted on the basis of both conflict and field preemption. They argue first that SB-822 is preempted because it conflicts with the policy underlying the FCC's reclassification decision; that policy was to eliminate all net neutrality regulation of broadband services, not to replace federal regulations with what could become a checkerboard of state regulations. The service providers additionally contend that SB-822 is preempted because it conflicts with the Communications Act itself and its limitations on federal regulation. They argue as well that even if there is no preemption by virtue of any identifiable conflict, federal law occupies the field of interstate services and therefore preempts state laws regulating intrastate services that intrude upon the field of interstate services.

I. The California Statute Does Not Conflict With the FCC's Reclassification of Broadband Services Under Title I

Resolution of the question of conflict preemption in this case involves a straightforward application of federal preemption principles. The service providers argue that the FCC's 2018 reclassification of broadband services as Title I information services, which eliminated the federal net neutrality rules promulgated under Title II, preempts state net neutrality rules. They essentially contend that the state regulation conflicts with the absence of federal regulation. A fundamental principle of preemption, however, is that an absence of federal regulation may preempt state law only if the federal agency has the statutory authority to regulate in the first place. La. Pub. Serv. Comm'r v. FCC, 476 U.S. 355, 374 (1986). The D.C. Circuit applied this principle when it vacated the FCC's Preemption Directive, as it recognized that the FCC does not have the authority to adopt federal net neutrality rules and is therefore unable to preempt such state regulation. Neither party challenges the validity or finality of *Mozilla*, so we look to the D.C. Circuit's analysis to guide our own.

This is in accord with the D.C. Circuit's decision in *Mozilla*. It followed the principles articulated in Ray v. Atlantic Richfield Co., 435 U.S. 151 (1978), and *Louisiana* when it vacated the FCC's "Preemption Directive" that accompanied the "Reclassification Order." The Preemption Directive had declared as preempted "any state or local requirements that are inconsistent with [the Order's] deregulatory approach," 2018 Order, 33 FCC Rcd. at 427, ¶ 194, including "any state or local measures that would effectively impose rules or requirements that [the Reclassification Order] repealed," *id.* ¶ 195. But unlike the situation in *Ray* where the federal agency retained its regulatory authority and the state was preempted, the Preemption Directive did not rest on any regulatory authority. By reclassifying broadband as an information service, the FCC surrendered its authority to regulate with respect to net neutrality. And just as in *Louisiana*, where a federal agency was unable to preempt state law without the authority to regulate, the Preemption Directive exceeded the FCC's

Title I statutory authority to regulate broadband and, therefore, exceeded its authority to preempt state regulation.

The service providers try to avoid the effect of reclassification to Title I by arguing that the decision was not an abdication of authority but an exercise of discretion under the statute as to the appropriate classification of communications services. The service providers are correct that the 2018 decision was an exercise of statutory authority to make a classification decision, but they fail to acknowledge that the effect of that decision was to eliminate the agency's authority to impose net neutrality rules.

Indeed, the FCC itself has acknowledged that it did away with the statutory authority to adopt net neutrality rules when it reclassified broadband internet services as information services under Title I. It said as much in the Reclassification Order. *See, e.g.*, 2018 Order, 33 FCC Rcd. at 470, ¶ 267 (finding after reclassification no "source[] of statutory authority that individually or in the aggregate" supports net neutrality conduct rules). This conclusion had experience behind it. The FCC tried unsuccessfully to adopt net neutrality rules under Title I several times in the early 2000s and was unable to do so until broadband services were reclassified as a telecommunications service under Title II in 2015. The FCC knew that its reclassification decision in 2018 stripped the FCC of its authority to adopt federal net neutrality rules, and the D.C. Circuit held it also stripped it of its power to preempt. Accordingly, there can be no preemption of the California statute as a result of the Reclassification Order.

The service providers point instead to the reasons for the reclassification to contend that the FCC's policy goals underlying the reclassification decision have preemptive effect. They point out that the FCC made the reclassification decision in reliance on its policy judgment that a light-touch regulatory framework would be most effective. They contend that, because the D.C. Circuit upheld these policy-based grounds for the FCC's decision, the FCC's policy behind the decision forms a valid predicate for conflict preemption.

Yet the Supreme Court has expressly rejected the argument that an agency's policy preferences can preempt state action in the absence of federal statutory regulatory authority. The Supreme Court warned that to permit preemption on the basis of policy rather than legislation would allow a federal agency to confer power upon itself and override the power of Congress. As the Supreme Court said, "[t]his we are both unwilling and unable to do." *Louisiana*, 476 U.S. at 375.

In spite of the D.C. Circuit's conclusion, the service providers go on to contend that this court has already decided the preemption issue in its favor. They point to our decision in People of State of California v. FCC, 39 F.3d 919, 931–32 (9th Cir. 1994), where we recognized some limited preemptive authority under Title I when state regulation would make it impossible for federal regulatory measures to take effect. That principle is not applicable here, because the FCC has adopted no relevant regulatory measures.

California arose at a time of unusual regulatory activity that preceded the advent of the internet and followed the break-up of AT&T. The break-up resulted in the creation of Regional Bell Operating Companies (BOCs) that could participate in the growing industry providing information services over telephone lines. To prevent the BOCs from having a competitive advantage as a result of their control of these lines, the FCC had originally ordered the BOCs to structurally separate their telephone operations from the related services. In 1986, however, the FCC determined that actual structural separation was not necessary and that less stringent, and less costly, measures could serve the same purpose. When it eliminated the structural separation requirements and substituted less stringent measures, it also entered an order preempting any state from imposing more stringent measures, as, for example, structural separation.

States, not surprisingly, challenged the preemption order, contending that the FCC, per the Supreme Court's decision in *Louisiana*, had no preemptive authority when acting pursuant to Title I. We held that our own decisions had recognized an "impossibility" exception to allow the FCC to preempt state measures that would be inconsistent with lawful federal regulation. Since the federal regulation allowed the enhanced services to be provided on an integrated basis, but BOC's compliance with state regulations could result in structural separation, we upheld the limited preemptive order. The situation was very similar to that in *Ray*, where the exercise of federal regulatory authority preempted inconsistent state measures.

In this case, of course, the FCC has not adopted any regulatory measures. It has instead diminished its authority to regulate by its reclassification of the service providers to a relatively unregulated category under the Communications Act. There is thus no conflict between the state's enactment of SB-822 and the FCC's order. *California* is therefore in line with *Ray, Mozilla*, and our decision today. Without the underlying authority to regulate net neutrality under Title I, the FCC is without the authority to preempt California from doing so.

In a similar vein, we reject the service providers' argument about the FCC's disclosure requirements. The Reclassification Order was accompanied by disclosure requirements, known as a Transparency Rule. This Transparency Rule requires broadband providers to disclose practices that, for payment or to benefit an affiliate, block, throttle, or prioritize internet traffic. But the D.C. Circuit did not hold that the Transparency Rule had any effect on the states' ability to regulate net neutrality.

The legal effect of the reclassification, and the adoption of the Transparency Rule, was to diminish federal regulatory authority. As a result, despite the FCC's policy preference for a lightly-regulated broadband marketplace, the agency no longer had the requisite authority to adopt federal net neutrality rules and could not preempt states from adopting them.

The district court correctly decided that the service providers are unlikely to succeed on the merits of their claim that SB-822 conflicts with the FCC's 2018 Order.

II. There Is No Conflict Between the California Statute and the Communications Act

The service providers' alternative position relates to the Communications Act itself. They contend that the California statute conflicts with the text of two provisions of the Communications Act. 47 U.S.C. §§153(51), 332(c)(2). According to the service providers, these provisions limit the states' ability to regulate broadband services. The provisions, however, do not support this theory.

Section 153(51) is located in the Communication Act's lengthy list of definitions. This section defines a "telecommunications carrier" and it further provides that a "telecommunications carrier shall be treated as a common carrier *under this chapter* only to the extent that it is engaged in providing telecommunications services." 47 U.S.C. §153(51) (emphasis added).

Section 332 pertains to mobile broadband, which is the high-speed internet access delivered to cell phones and other mobile devices. For mobile broadband, there is a dual classification system that is similar to the classification system for telecommunications and information services. A "commercial mobile service" is subject to common carrier status and a "private mobile service" is not. 47 U.S.C. §§332(c)(1)–(2). Section 332(c)(2), defines "private mobile services," stating in relevant part that "[a] person engaged in the provision of a service that is a private mobile service shall not, insofar as that person is so engaged, be treated as a common carrier for any purpose *under this chapter*." 47 U.S.C. §332(c)(2) (emphasis added).

The text of each provision defines and limits only the FCC's regulatory authority and makes no mention of the states' authority to regulate. The provisions explicitly state that they are defining the extent of FCC regulation under "this chapter," meaning Chapter 5 of the Communications Act, and do not mention, let alone defend or displace, the regulatory authority of the states. The two provisions thus prevent the FCC itself, and not the states, from imposing common carrier regulations on either information services or private mobile services.

If there were any remaining doubt, the Savings Provision in Section 601(c)(1) of the Telecommunications Act provides even more evidence that Section 153(51) was not intended to limit the states' authority. *See* Telecommunications Act of 1996, Pub. L. No. 104-104, §601(c)(1), 101 Stat. 56, 143 (1996), *reprinted in* 47 U.S.C. §152 note. The Savings Provision says "[t]his Act and the amendments made by this Act shall not be construed to modify, impair, or supersede Federal, State, or local law unless *expressly* so provided in such Act or amendments." *Id.* (emphasis added). Because the 1996 Amendments added Section 153(51) to the Communications Act, and Section 153(51) contains no express statement of preemption, the Savings Provision precludes any inference of preemptive intent. Therefore, the service providers cannot successfully maintain that the California statute conflicts with the Communications Act.

III. The California Statute Does Not Impermissibly Touch on the Field of Interstate Communications

Even in the absence of an express or conflicting Congressional command, a state law may be preempted when federal law so thoroughly occupies a legislative field as to demonstrate Congressional intent to exclude all state law. In this appeal, the service providers argue that the field of interstate communications services is exclusively federal and that SB-822 therefore impermissibly regulates in that field.

SB-822 limits its application, however, to broadband internet access services "provided to customers in California" and to internet service providers that "provide[] broadband Internet access service to an individual, corporation, government, or other customer in California." Cal. Civ. Code § 3100(b), (k). In Greater Los Angeles Agency on Deafness, Inc. v. Cable News Network, Inc., 742 F.3d 414, 433 (9th Cir 2014), we reviewed an analogous California statute that regulated online content only when it was accessed by California viewers. We held that such state regulation of internet services does not have the practical effect of regulating wholly interstate conduct.

The service providers also point to a statement by the Supreme Court interpreting Section 152 as affording the FCC "plenary authority" over interstate communications. *Louisiana*, 476 U.S. at 360. They ask us to conclude that state regulations may not touch on interstate communications. Yet the division of regulatory authority is not so simple and *Louisiana* does not go so far. The *Louisiana* Court rejected any interpretation of the Communications Act that would neatly divide power between federal and state authority. The Supreme Court said in reference to Section 152:

> while the Act would seem to divide the world into two hemispheres—one comprised of interstate service, over which the FCC would have plenary authority, and the other made up of intrastate service, over which the States would retain exclusive jurisdiction—in practice, the realities of technology and economics belie such a clean parceling of responsibility. This is so because virtually all telephone plant that is used to provide intrastate service is also used to provide interstate service, and is thus conceivably within the jurisdiction of both state and federal authorities. Moreover, because the same carriers provide both interstate and intrastate service, actions taken by federal and state regulators within their respective domains necessarily affect the general financial health of those carriers, and hence their ability to provide service, in the other "hemisphere."

Id. Contrary to the service providers' contention, the *Louisiana* Court described the Communications Act as establishing dual state and federal regulatory authority.

Conclusion

The judgment of the United States District Court for the District of Eastern California denying a preliminary injunction that would bar enforcement of SB-822 is affirmed.

[Concurring opinion of Circuit Judge WALLACE is omitted.]

Notes and Questions

1. The Structure of Preemption. As the opinion demonstrates in its structure, legal doctrine provides several paths to find that state law has been preempted by federal law. The most direct is to find express preemption, which arises when Congress by statute provides that state law is preempted (and such law is within Congress's powers) or when Congress delegates authority to an administrative agency and the administrative agency by rule provides that state law is preempted (and, of course, as the case shows, the agency's action is within *its* authority). Federal preemption can also be implied. Where compliance with both federal law and state law is impossible, the state law is preempted. Where compliance with state law would frustrate the purpose of federal law, courts can hold that the state law provides an "obstacle" and is therefore preempted. And, finally, where federal law "occupies the field," courts will find that state law is preempted, even if the statute does not expressly say so. In each of these "implied preemption" doctrines, the question is ultimately one of congressional intent.

2. Mere Policy Preference? The Supreme Court's decision in National Cable & Telecommunications Association v. Brand X Internet Services, 545 U.S. 967 (2005), excerpted in Chapter 6, holds that the Communications Act is ambiguous in its classification of internet access services. Under the *Chevron* doctrine, as *Brand X* also holds, this means that Congress intended that the FCC resolve that question. If that is the case, are you persuaded by the Ninth Circuit's holding that the classification decision does not actually constitute regulation — regulation that goes beyond a mere policy preference?

3. Where Is Congress? Should there be so much uncertainty over whether federal law should preempt state law as to internet services? As a matter of policy, is this a realm in which extensive state experimentation would seem to be important and valuable? As we have seen repeatedly (and will see further), Congress has left the field very open when it comes to internet regulation. What do you think it should do (if anything)?

4. Other Internet Regulation. The states have also begun to regulate other aspects of internet services. As we will discuss in further detail in Chapter 13, no general federal privacy law exists. In that absence, several states (most notably California) have passed broad privacy statutes applicable to internet services, including platforms. The Communications Act (in § 222) does have some privacy regulation, but it too (as we will see) only applies to common carriers, and such arguments are even more tenuous as one moves above internet access services to web services and internet platforms. Similarly, a few states have passed laws directly regulating social media platforms, but those have generally fared poorly against First Amendment challenges (and arguments of federal preemption have not been necessary).

Chapter 8

Antitrust in Networked Industries

Introduction

Chapter 5, in opening a discussion of regulatory strategies to curtail the abuses of natural monopolies, noted that the antitrust laws, rather than industry-specific regulations, are the preferred instrument to combat monopoly harm when a competitive market is preferred to a monopolized market. This seminal observation leads to some important implications. First, in combatting monopoly power, policymakers must ask the first-order question of whether an industry is optimally organized as a regulated monopoly and whether welfare-enhancing competition is feasible. Second, courts that are asked to apply the antitrust laws against a monopolist might hesitate if the monopolist appears to offer greater efficiencies than a competitive market or if the monopolist is governed by sector-specific regulation. Recall from Chapter 2 that monopolies are not per se illegal, and there is nothing wrong under the antitrust laws with obtaining or maintaining a monopoly through "superior skill, foresight, and innovation." United States v. Aluminum Co. of America, 148 F.2d 416, 430 (2d Cir. 1945) (Hand, J.). For similar reasons, a monopolist that is governed by sector-specific regulation might have been deemed by Congress to be superior to a competitive market.

Antitrust law is especially important, and perhaps especially complicated, when applied to the internet and telecommunications sectors because both seminal questions above are almost necessarily implicated. First, much of the telecommunications sector is governed by the Communications Act, so a court adjudicating an antitrust claim must weigh the appropriate application of antitrust law within the shadow of the Act. And second, many major services in the telecommunications sector, from telephony to cable television to broadband access to internet platforms, tend towards monopoly. Throughout the past century of telecommunications policy and especially during the internet age, courts must routinely ask whether to curtail antitrust law in favor of an industry-specific statute, and whether using the antitrust laws to restrain the incumbent monopoly would favorably serve the public.

This chapter focuses on two central applications of the antitrust laws. It first discusses actions under Section 2 of the Sherman Act, 15 U.S.C. § 2, which targets anticompetitive conduct by monopolists. It then addresses actions under Section 7 of the Clayton Act, which prohibits acquisitions or mergers where "the effect of such acquisition may be substantially to lessen competition, or to tend to create a monopoly." 15 U.S.C. § 18. (The third leg of antitrust's three-legged stool involves prohibiting illegal cartels, which is less central to telecommunications policy.) In each of the cases below, a central question is how to apply the antitrust laws to a telecommunications sector characterized by the particular economic features (such as positive externalities, scale efficiencies, and large returns to innovation) and the particular political features (such as the centrality of communication in a democracy and a commitment to universal access) that make the field unique. In the background of each case lurks the underlying question of whether antitrust and sector-specific regulations are compliments, substitutes, or at odds with one another.

§ 8.A. Monopoly Leverage and Maintenance

Recall from Chapter 2 that a successful claim under § 2 of the Sherman Act requires a showing both that (a) the defendant possesses monopoly power, and (b) the defendant has engaged in anticompetitive conduct. Both of these legal tests confront particularly challenging questions in the telecommunications sector. Part 8.A.1 focuses on the first of these tests, the "power" element, and delves into difficult questions concerning how to define markets under the antitrust laws. Parts 8.A.2 and 8.A.3 then focus on the second test, the so-called "conduct" requirement, and examines common questions in determining whether a telecommunications monopolist has violated the antitrust laws.

§ 8.A.1. Market Definition in Digital Markets

The determination of market power is central under the antitrust laws, whether applying the Sherman Act, Clayton Act, or another antitrust statute. Under current law, determining market power typically involves a sequence of steps that first requires defining the relevant market. Market definition is usually a difficult, fact-intensive exercise that involves both rigorous empirical analysis and rough estimations, but it might be particularly difficult when applying the antitrust laws to internet platforms. Consider the two cases below, one against Facebook and the other against Apple, and try to identify the particular features of internet platforms that resist standard market analysis. Consider also what these difficulties might mean for competition policy in internet markets.

FTC v. Facebook, Inc.

560 F. Supp. 3d 1 (D.D.C. 2021)

BOASBERG, District Judge:

At the time of the last great antitrust battle in our courthouse—between the United States and Microsoft—Mark Zuckerberg was still in high school. Only after his arrival at Harvard did he launch "The Facebook" from his dorm room. Nearly twenty years later, both federal and state regulators contend, in two separate actions before this Court, that Facebook is now the one violating the antitrust laws. The company, they allege, has long had a monopoly in the market for what they call "Personal Social Networking Services." And it has allegedly maintained that monopoly, in violation of Section 2 of the Sherman Act, through two different kinds of actions: first, by acquiring firms that it believed were well positioned to erode its monopoly—most notably, Instagram and WhatsApp; and second, by adopting policies preventing interoperability between Facebook and certain other apps that it saw as threats, thereby impeding their growth into viable competitors.

Facebook now separately moves to dismiss both the State action and the FTC action. Although the Court does not agree with all of Facebook's contentions here, it ultimately concurs that the agency's Complaint is legally insufficient and must therefore be dismissed. The FTC has failed to plead enough facts to plausibly establish a necessary element of all of its Section 2 claims—namely, that Facebook has monopoly power in the market for Personal Social Networking (PSN) Services. The Complaint contains nothing on that score save the naked allegation that the company has had and still has a dominant share of that market (in excess of 60%). Such an unsupported assertion might (barely) suffice in a Section 2 case involving a more traditional goods market, in which the Court could reasonably infer that market share was measured by revenue, units sold, or some other typical metric. But this case involves no ordinary or intuitive market. Rather, PSN services are free to use, and the exact metes and bounds of what even constitutes a PSN service—i.e., which features of a company's mobile app or website are included in that definition and which are excluded—are hardly crystal clear. In this unusual context, the FTC's inability to offer any indication of the metric(s) or method(s) it used to calculate Facebook's market share renders its vague "60%-plus" assertion too speculative and conclusory to go forward.

I. Background

At the dawn of our century, in the much earlier days of the internet, a number of websites began to offer what came to be known as "social networking" services. Friendster and Myspace, both launched in 2002, were among the earliest. Although the precise definition of a "Personal Social Networking Service" is disputed (as that is the market in which Facebook has its alleged monopoly), it can be summarized here as one that enables users to virtually connect with others in their network and to digitally share their views and experiences by posting about them in a shared, virtual social space. For example, users might view and interact with a letter-to-the-editor-style post on politics by a neighbor, pictures from a friend's recent party, or a birth announcement for a newborn cousin. Perhaps because humans are naturally social, this new way of interacting became hugely popular. Although Myspace and Friendster had an early lead, by 2009 they had been surpassed by a new competitor. Created at Harvard in 2004, "The Facebook," as it was initially called, was a social-networking service initially limited to college students. Within a few years, it had expanded to the general public (and dropped "The" from its name). By at least 2011, it was the dominant player in personal social networking. Today, the FTC alleges, its flagship product, Facebook Blue, has hundreds of millions of users in the United States.

Facebook Blue is what its millions of users think of when they think of "Facebook." Generally speaking, using Facebook Blue entails interacting with user-created content—i.e., content created or shared by one's Facebook "friends,"—or creating content oneself by posting. That is not all that users see or do, however. They may also, for instance, encounter publisher-created content like news articles and advertisements in their "news feed." Such content can come in text, photo, or video form. In addition, Facebook users can play games or use other applications built either by Facebook or by third parties. Facebook also offers other services beyond Facebook Blue to its users, such as Facebook Messenger, a free mobile-messaging service.

Unlike most businesses, Facebook charges users no fee; instead, it makes money by selling advertising. By leveraging the vast quantity of user data it collects, the company allows advertisers to target different campaigns and messages to different groups of users. Under this business model, as the Complaint puts it, Facebook refrain[s] from charging a monetary price . . . to users, relying instead on monetizing user data and engagement through advertising." Put differently, users exchange their time, attention, and personal data, rather than money, for access to Facebook. That approach has been highly profitable: in 2019, for instance, global advertisers paid Facebook nearly $70 billion, and it made profits of more than $18 billion. To be clear, although Facebook's data-collection and -use practices have been subject to increasing scrutiny, they are not the subject of this action.

III. Analysis

The offense of monopoly maintenance under Section 2 of the Sherman Act has two elements: (1) the possession of monopoly power in the relevant market and (2) the willful maintenance of that power as distinguished from growth or development as a consequence of a superior product, business acumen, or historic accident. This second element is usually referred to by the shorthand of "anticompetitive" or "exclusionary conduct." Facebook, in seeking dismissal, contends that the Complaint does not allege facts establishing either element. The Court agrees that the first—the possession of monopoly power in the market for Personal Social

Networking Services (as defined by the agency)—is not adequately pleaded here. No more is needed to conclude that the Complaint must be dismissed.

A. Monopoly Power

Begin with the linchpin of this Opinion: whether the FTC has plausibly alleged, as it must, that Facebook exercises monopoly power. As explained by the Circuit in *Microsoft*, monopoly power is "the power to control prices or exclude competition," such that a firm is a monopolist "if it can profitably raise prices substantially above the competitive level." Where a plaintiff can provide direct proof that a "firm has in fact profitably done so, the existence of monopoly power is clear." *Id.* Because such proof is rare, however, plaintiffs and courts usually search for indirect or "circumstantial evidence" of monopoly power by inferring it from "a firm's possession of a dominant share of a relevant market." *Id.*

Although the FTC briefly suggests in its Opposition that it can offer direct proof of market power, it spends nearly its entire brief arguing why it has sufficiently pleaded indirect proof—viz., that Facebook has a dominant share of a relevant product and geographic market (the United States market for Personal Social Networking Services). Because the agency thus makes no real direct-proof argument, the Court will analyze the Complaint's market-power allegations using the indirect framework. Again, that framework first requires the plaintiff to establish the relevant market in which the defendant firm allegedly has monopoly power. It then demands that a plaintiff establish that the defendant has a dominant share of that market protected by entry barriers. As the Court explains below, it is the market-share step that trips up the FTC here.

1. Market Definition

The market-definition inquiry in this case is somewhat unusual because, unlike familiar consumer goods like tobacco or office supplies, there is no obvious or universally agreed-upon definition of just what a personal social networking service is. As a result, to discharge its burden to define the relevant market, the FTC must do two things here. First, it must provide a definition of PSN services (which, obviously, would include at least Facebook Blue). Second, it must further explain whether and why other, non-PSN services available to the public either are or are not reasonably interchangeable substitutes with PSN services. Ultimately, that analysis should demonstrate that Facebook holds a dominant share of a market that includes such substitutes, if any.

On the first point, the agency explains that PSN services are "online services that enable and are used by people to maintain personal relationships and share experiences with friends, family, and other personal connections in a shared social space." Such services are allegedly defined, and distinguished, by their having three key elements. First, they are built on a social graph that maps the connections between users and their friends, family, and other personal connections. Second, they include features that many users regularly employ to interact with personal connections and share their personal experiences in a shared virtual social space, including in a one-to-many 'broadcast' format. And third, they include features that allow users to find and connect with other users, to make it easier for each user to build and expand their set of personal connections. The social graph also supports this feature by informing the user which new connections might be available based on her existing network.

Having defined PSN services, Plaintiff then alleges that there are in fact no other types of internet services that are adequate substitutes. It buttresses that conclusion by explaining why four different kinds of arguably comparable online services are not reasonably interchangeable with PSN services. First, "specialized social networking services" that focus on professional connections (e.g., LinkedIn) are not substitutes because they are designed for and used primarily by professionals for sharing professional content. They therefore would not be used, as PSN services are, to maintain personal relationships and share experiences with friends, family, and other personal connections. The same is true, alleges the FTC, for "interest-based" social-networking services such as Strava (which relates to physical exercise). The agency also pleads that PSN services are not reasonably interchangeable with services that allow for consuming and sharing video or audio content, such as YouTube, Spotify, Netflix, or Hulu. That is because users of such services mostly consume such content passively or share content created by others (rather than content they have created), and such sharing, where it occurs, is not to the user's network of personal connections but rather to a general and wide audience of unknown users. *Id.* In such a setting, users do not usually communicate with friends, family, and other personal connections, which is the hallmark of a PSN service. Finally, Plaintiff explains that "mobile messaging services" cannot be substituted for PSN services because the former (i) lack a "shared social space" for interaction and (ii) do not employ a social graph to facilitate users' finding and "friending" other users they may know. Zuckerberg himself has colorfully explained one key difference in use that allegedly flows from these disparate features: a PSN service is "the digital equivalent of a town square," whereas a mobile messaging service is "the digital equivalent of [a] living room."

According to the FTC, then, the relevant market here thus includes PSN services — such as Facebook Blue, Instagram, and Path — and no other kinds of services.

On this issue, Facebook contends that, for a number of reasons, Plaintiff's allegations regarding market definition fall short of the pleading-stage requirement that such alleged product market be plausible. Defendant directly takes aim at the FTC's allegation that users of PSN services would not switch, if prodded by a price increase or quality decrease in a PSN service, to other means of communicating and sharing with their personal connections that lack a "connection-finder" built on the user's social graph (the third leg of the agency's definition of a PSN). That is implausible, Facebook contends, because it is obvious that people also know how to connect and share with family and friends via many other technologies, such as email, messaging, photo-sharing, and video-chats. This argument asks the Court to engage in the sort of deeply fact-intensive inquiry that is improper at this stage. Although open to dispute, the agency's allegation that users view services with and without a social-graph-based connection-finder as fundamentally different and non-interchangeable is at least theoretically rational, and thus hardly facially unsustainable. This is therefore not one of the relatively rare cases of a glaring deficiency in the market-definition pleadings that renders dismissal at the 12(b)(6) stage appropriate.

Facebook's final fruitless market-definition argument is that the Complaint impermissibly distinguishes PSN services from other possible substitutes based on their primary uses. The company asserts that the question is whether other services can perform the same functions as PSN services, not whether they are primarily used that way. That misstates the law. The analysis looks to both whether two products can be used for the same purpose, and, if so, whether and to what extent purchasers are willing to substitute one for the other. It is for this reason that pen-and-paper do-it-yourself tax prep and assisted tax prep could be outside the market for digital do-it-yourself tax-prep services despite both providing the same basic function, and that Medicare Advantage plans and Original Medicare plans could constitute distinct product markets despite both being capable of providing healthcare insurance to seniors. The fact that other services are not primarily used for the sort of personal sharing that is the hallmark of a PSN service seems a plausible reason why little switching would occur. Whether due to network effects or the norms around what sort of content is generally posted on different platforms, it is not a stretch to imagine that users are reluctant to share a highly personal milestone on LinkedIn or post a video of their child's first steps to YouTube.

2. Market Share

Although the Court therefore finds that the Complaint's allegations do enough to make out a plausible market for PSN services, that hardly ends the analysis. After all, while courts typically evaluate market definition and market share separately, the two inquiries ultimately come together to produce the conclusion that matters: the defendant's market power. That point can be lost if courts compartmentalize the two issues and examine the sufficiency of a plaintiff's market-share showings without looking back to how convincingly, or how tenuously, the market has been defined. Particularly where the market is idiosyncratically drawn, findings or allegations as to a particular market share carry much less meaning.

This case, at least as pleaded by the FTC, exemplifies that principle. Although the Court, as just explained, finds the contours of the asserted product market plausible, the Complaint is undoubtedly light on specific factual allegations regarding consumer-switching preferences. Given that thin showing, and the fact that the PSN-services product market is somewhat idiosyncratically drawn to begin with, the Court must demand something more robust from Plaintiff's market-share allegations. As it happens, however, those allegations are even more tentative: the FTC alleges only that Facebook has maintained a dominant share of the U.S. personal social networking market (in excess of 60%) since 2011, and that no other social network of comparable scale exists in the United States. That is it. These allegations—which do not even provide an estimated actual figure or range for Facebook's market share at any point over the past ten years—ultimately fall short of plausibly establishing that Facebook holds market power.

Even accepting that merely alleging market share "in excess of 60%" might sometimes be acceptable, it cannot suffice in this context, where Plaintiff does not even allege what it is measuring. Indeed, in its Opposition the FTC expressly contends that it need not specify which metrics or method it used to calculate Facebook's market share. In a case involving a more typical goods market, perhaps the Court might be able to reasonably infer how Plaintiff arrived at its calculations—e.g., by proportion of total revenue or of units sold. As the above market-definition analysis underscores, however, the market at issue here is unusual in a number of ways, including that the products therein are not sold for a price, meaning that PSN services earn no direct revenue from users. The Court is thus unable to understand exactly what the agency's "60%-plus" figure is even referring to, let alone able to infer the underlying facts that might substantiate it.

Rather than undergirding any inference of market power, Plaintiff's allegations make it even less clear what the agency might be measuring. The overall revenues earned by PSN services cannot be the right metric for measuring market share here, as those revenues are all earned in a separate market—viz., the market for advertising. Percent of daily users or monthly users of PSN services—metrics the Complaint mentions offhandedly—are not much better, as they might significantly overstate or understate any one firm's market share depending on the various proportions of users who have accounts on multiple services, not to mention how often users visit each service and for how long.

What about the share of total time spent by users on PSN services? Plaintiff says nothing about that metric in its Complaint. And although it seems tenable at first glance, that metric may also be of limited utility. That is because at least some of the features offered by a Facebook or Instagram or Path are not, seemingly, part of those firms' PSN-services offerings as defined by the FTC; time spent on those apps or websites, accordingly, is not necessarily time spent on a PSN service.

Nor do the difficulties stop there. Readers may well have noticed that the discussion to this point has consistently referred to Instagram and Facebook as examples of PSN services. That is because, outside of Path, Myspace, and Friendster, all of which seem to be long defunct or quite small, Plaintiff's Complaint does not identify any other providers of PSN services. Yet the FTC is apparently unwilling to allege that Facebook has ever (pre- or post-Instagram acquisition) had something like 85% or even 75% market share; instead it hedges by offering only that the number is somewhere north of 60%. The question naturally arises: which firms make up the remaining 30–40%? Although Plaintiff is correct that it is not required to identify every alleged competitor in its pleadings, its choice to identify essentially none is striking. Its complaint must therefore be dismissed.

The Court's decision here does not rest on some pleading technicality or arcane feature of antitrust law. Rather, the existence of market power is at the heart of any monopolization claim. The FTC's Complaint says almost nothing concrete on the key question of how much power Facebook actually had, and still has, in a properly defined antitrust product market. It is almost as if the agency expects the Court to simply nod to the conventional wisdom that Facebook is a monopolist. After all, no one who hears the title of the 2010 film "The Social Network" wonders which company it is about. Yet, whatever it may mean to the public, "monopoly power" is a term of art under federal law with a precise economic meaning: the power to profitably raise prices or exclude competition in a properly defined market. To merely allege that a defendant firm has somewhere over 60% share of an unusual, nonintuitive product market — the confines of which are only somewhat fleshed out and the players within which remain almost entirely unspecified — is not enough. The FTC has therefore fallen short of its pleading burden.

Notes and Questions

1. The Difficulty in Defining Markets. The court ultimately concluded that Facebook operated in a market of PSN services. Can you describe what that market includes and what it excludes? Should the FTC be obligated to define this market with precision? The court hinted at a disconnect between antitrust formalities and conventional wisdom when it concedes, "no one who hears the title of the 2010 film 'The Social Network' wonders which company it is about." Is antitrust law defying common sense in putting these preliminary burdens on regulators? Or is the greater danger that antitrust law might leap to conclusions (stoked by political whims) if it skips these disciplining legal formalities?

2. Defining Markets for Internet Platforms. One additional difficulty in defining markets for internet platforms is that they necessarily involve a bundle of distinct services, and the only commonality that many of these services share is that they are exchanged on platforms.

3. Direct versus Indirect Evidence of Market Power. The court noted that the "indirect" method of establishing market power requires first defining the relevant market and then calculating the defendant's market share in that market. This indirect and rather convoluted method is the prevailing approach in antitrust analysis, but it also has come under criticism by leading antitrust scholars. *See, e.g.*, Louis Kaplow, Why (Ever) Define Markets?, 124 Harv. L. Rev. 437 (2010). But the court also suggested that more direct methods of identifying market power are possible. What might those be? Evidence of monopolistic intent? Monopoly prices? Reduced output? How might those direct methods be applied to internet platforms?

4. Metrics for Market Share. The court suggested a number of metrics for market share: number of accounts, overall revenue, daily users, and total time spent. Which of these do you think best measures Facebook's power in the PSN services market? How would you advise the FTC to establish Facebook's monopoly power, using either direct or indirect approaches?

5. A Revised Complaint. The FTC submitted a revised complaint, in which it offered two metrics to measure market share: the size of the active user base and the length of time users spend on the service. Judge Boasberg ruled that the amended complaint "cleared the pleading bar and may proceed to discovery." FTC v. Facebook, Inc., 581 F. Supp. 3d 34 (2022).

* * *

Market definition questions are also difficult when digital platforms invite others to offer services atop the platforms but under restrictive rules. Such is the situation for Apple's "walled garden," which is Apple's software platform upon which software developers create and market their individual games. While Apple's iPhone competes with other phone manufacturers, and its iOS operating system therefore competes with Android-based systems, an important antitrust question is whether Apple's App Store constitutes an "aftermarket" — a distinct market of Apple services that have no substitute — that Apple monopolizes. Many software developers feel constrained by Apple's control of its iOS ecosystem and are frustrated by what they consider to be monopolistic pricing and conduct. Similar complaints (and lawsuits) have been directed at Google's control of the Google Play Store on Android systems.

Epic, a game and software development company whose flagship video game is the popular Fortnite, has been one of the most vocal critics of Apple's App Store policies. Before filing its lawsuit challenging Apple's App Store restrictions, Epic conceived and executed a plan, called "Project Liberty," to circumvent Apple's 30% commission on in-app purchases. Epic intentionally violated Apple's policies by secretly introducing a "hotfix" into an update to the Fortnite iOS app on August 3, 2020, that, when activated by Epic, would give users the option to directly pay Epic (at a cheaper rate than the in-app payment option) for in-game purchases through an alternative payment system. Epic activated the hotfix on the morning of August 13, 2020, and Apple removed the Fortnite iOS app from the App Store within hours. Apple also informed Epic Games that it would revoke all developer tools, which would preclude updates for its programs and software.

The hotfix was an intentional prelude to an antitrust lawsuit, and Epic filed a complaint against Apple later that day, alleging that Apple's App Store restrictions violated federal and California antitrust laws. A three-week bench trial was held in 2021, focused largely on how antitrust law should treat Apple's "aftermarket," and Judge Gonzalez Rogers issued the order below.

Epic Games, Inc. v. Apple, Inc.

559 F. Supp. 3d 898 (N.D. Cal., 2021)

ROGERS, District Judge:

Plaintiff Epic Games, Inc. sued Apple, Inc. alleging violations of federal and state antitrust laws and California's unfair competition law based upon Apple's operation of its App Store. Broadly speaking, Epic Games claimed that Apple is an antitrust monopolist over (i) Apple's own system of distributing apps on Apple's own devices in the App Store and (ii) Apple's own system of collecting payments and commissions of purchases made on Apple's own devices in the App Store. Said differently, plaintiff alleged an antitrust market of one, that is, Apple's "monopolistic" control over its own systems relative to the App Store. Apple obviously disputed the allegations.

Antitrust law protects competition and not competitors. Competition results in innovation and consumer satisfaction and is essential to the effective operation of a free market system. Antitrust jurisprudence also evaluates both market structure and behavior to determine whether an actor is using its place in the market to artificially restrain competition. Central to antitrust cases is the appropriate determination of the "relevant market." Epic Games structured its lawsuit to argue that Apple does not compete with anyone; it is a monopoly of one. Apple, by contrast, argues that the effective area of competition is the market for all digital video games in which it and Epic Games compete heavily. In the digital video game market, Apple argues that it does not enjoy monopoly power, and therefore does not violate federal and state law.

The Court disagrees with both parties' definition of the relevant market.

Ultimately, after evaluating the trial evidence, the Court finds that the relevant market here is *digital mobile gaming transactions*, not gaming generally and not Apple's own internal operating systems related to the App Store.

Having defined the relevant market as digital mobile gaming transactions, the Court cannot ultimately conclude that Apple is a monopolist under either federal or state antitrust laws. While the Court finds that Apple enjoys considerable market share of over 55% and extraordinarily high profit margins, these factors alone do not show antitrust conduct. Success is not illegal. Epic Games failed in its burden to demonstrate Apple is an illegal monopolist.

I. The Parties

In 2007, Apple developed the iPhone, creating a new and innovative ecosystem to break into the cellular device market with a multi-touch interface powered by advanced hardware and software architecture. The device offered users the ability to access email, browse the web, and perform certain software applications by simply tapping a square-ish icon on the screen called an "app," short for a software application. These apps operate from a foundational layer of software called an operating system which, in the iPhone ecosystem, is called the iOS.

Apple has maintained control of its own operating system for mobile devices, called iOS, since its inception. Apple's creation and cultivation of the iOS device (and its ecosystem) has been described as a walled garden. Said differently, it is a closed platform whereby Apple controls and supervises access to any software which accesses the iOS devices (defined as iPhones and iPads; also referred to collectively as iOS devices). Apple justifies this control primarily in the name of consumer privacy, security, as well as monetization of its intellectual property. Evidence supports the argument that consumers value these attributes.

Initially, when the iPhone was first launched, Apple developed and preinstalled the device with a few "native" apps. On October 17, 2007, Apple announced that it would allow third-party developers to create iOS apps by licensing them with the interfaces and technology to do so. In the beginning, the App Store's U.S. storefront offered 452 third-party apps (including 131 game apps) by 312 distinct developers. In fiscal year 2019, there were over 300,000 game apps available on the App Store.

Apple distributes its basic developer tools for free but charges an annual fee for membership in its developer program to distribute apps. Through the Developer Product Licensing Agreement (DPLA), Apple licenses, wholesale, its intellectual property. The DPLA [also] details programming requirements and establishes payment terms. [Among other obligations], developers are required to create apps for Apple products which could only be distributed through the App Store [and agree that] for all digital purchases, Apple charges a 30% commission.

Epic Games is a multi-billion dollar video game company. In 2010, Epic Games agreed to and signed a DPLA with Apple. Epic Games released three iOS games and Apple featured each of them at major events allowing Epic Games to make use of Apple's brand. In early 2018, Epic Games and Apple arranged for the release of *Fortnite*. The product generated an immensely profitable revenue stream for Epic Games.

However, Epic Games was also required by contract to pay Apple a 30% commission on every purchase made through the App Store, whether an initial download or an in-app purchase. Consequently, Fortnite generated a profitable revenue stream for Apple as well. Epic Games tried to use Fortnite as leverage to force Apple to reduce its commission fee and to open its closed platform. When Apple refused, Epic Games breached its contract, which it concedes, and filed this lawsuit. Apple countersued for breach of contract.

II. Parties' Proposed Relevant Product Market and Finding

Plaintiff focuses its challenge on Apple's control over the distribution of apps to its users and the requirement that developers of apps use Apple's in-app purchases or in-app payments (IAP) system if purchases are offered in the app. A threshold step in any antitrust case is to accurately define the relevant market, which refers to the area of effective competition. Epic Games constructs a framework to argue that there are three separate product markets at issue. In the foremarket, Epic Games identifies the product market as one for "Smartphone Operating Systems." Epic Games contends in turn that there are two derivative and relevant aftermarkets that flow from this initial foremarket, including the "iOS App Distribution" market and "iOS In-App Payment Solutions." Epic Games logic flows as follows: the iOS in-app payment solutions market is an aftermarket of the iOS app distribution market which is further an aftermarket of the smartphone operating systems foremarket.

In effect, plaintiff really urges a single-brand analysis because Apple's exclusionary conduct impacts Epic Games' ability to compete in that space, both with respect to gaming and non-gaming apps. [Epic argues] foremarket and aftermarket are related but two separate markets, the source of Apple's market power stems from its walled garden, and competition in the initial market does not discipline Apple's market in the proposed aftermarket.

Determining whether a single-brand market is proper requires a factual inquiry into the commercial realities faced by consumers. The Supreme Court [has] identified two factors that supported the aftermarket framework: the existence of significant (i) information costs and (ii) switching costs.

As to information costs, the Supreme Court noted that for the service-market price to affect equipment demand, consumers must inform themselves of the total cost of the 'package' at the time of purchase; that is, consumers must engage in accurate lifecycle pricing. Much of this information is difficult — some of it impossible — to acquire at the time of purchasing, and even if consumers were capable of acquiring and processing the complex body of information, they may choose not to do so as acquiring such information is expensive. Indeed, if the costs of service are small relative to the equipment price, or if consumers are more concerned about equipment capabilities than service costs, they may not find it cost efficient to compile the information.

As to switching costs, the Supreme Court stated that if the cost of switching is high, consumers who already have purchased the equipment, and are thus 'locked in,' will tolerate some level of service-price increases before changing equipment brands. Under this scenario, a seller profitably could maintain supracompetitive prices in the aftermarket if the switching costs were high relative to the increase in service prices, and the number of locked-in customers were high relative to the number of new purchasers. The Supreme Court further noted that this strategy was likely to prove profitable especially where a seller could simply charge new customers below-marginal cost on the equipment and recoup the charges in service, or offer specific packages including lifetime warranties or long-term service agreements that are not available to locked-in customers.

Since 1992, five circuit courts and numerous district courts refused to find a single-brand aftermarket where customers had knowledge of the alleged restrictive policies and were not subject to a post-purchase policy change. Big tech may ultimately convince the Supreme Court to change the calculus, but for now the state of antitrust law has that distinct parameter.

With these principles in mind, the Court analyzes the evidence presented. Issues of lock-in or switching costs, and notice or consumer knowledge, fall under the analysis of evaluating whether competition in the initial market suffices to discipline anticompetitive practices in the aftermarkets.

First, the evidence shows no material change in the conditions for accessing the App Store for either side of the platform. For consumers, iOS has always been a closed system, and the App Store has been a "walled garden" with respect to native apps from its inception; even prior to any time in which Apple was alleged to have become a monopolist. Indeed, it is undisputed by the parties that a key distinguishing feature of the iOS platform is its closed platform model, as compared to the open Android platform maintained by its main competitor Google. At the very least, previous consumers of iOS devices would have been familiar with the iOS platform and the App Store model when they repurchased a device prior to 2011.

Second, Epic Games failed to prove lock-in, even absent a policy shift. Given the weak showing, plaintiff either found itself with an unachievable task or insufficient time to address the issue. In short, there is no evidence in the record demonstrating that consumers are unaware that the App Store is the sole means of digital distribution on the iOS platform. Specifically, there is no evidence in the form of consumer survey data demonstrating the extent of consumers knowledge when purchasing of an iOS device, much less that they are unaware they are purchasing into a closed ecosystem that is tightly controlled by Apple.

Epic Games' sole focus on iOS devices simply ignores the market reality that is available to consumers. The Court's definition of the product as "digital mobile game transactions" takes into account that the App Store competes against other platforms for both consumers and developers. Indeed, several recent entrants into the mobile gaming submarket, from Nintendo, Microsoft, and Nvidia, show that this submarket is presently evolving and is dynamic. Moreover, the continued rise and popularity of cross-platform games like Fortnite and Minecraft offered on a variety of platforms, even beyond mobile gaming devices, are making switching between platforms seamless because a consumer can carry over rewards and progress between the diverse platforms. As a result, neither consumers nor developers are "locked-in" to the App Store for digital mobile game transactions—they can and do pursue game transactions on a variety of other mobile platforms and increasingly other game platforms. Although the state of the wider gaming market is not at a level where the entirety of these gaming platforms can truly be characterized as competing for purposes of antitrust law (e.g., substitutes), the continued rise of cross-platform games, technologies, and innovative ways in which to reach consumers only demonstrate that these differing platforms are converging and ever intertwining.

Apple, on the other hand, contends that there is only one relevant product: digital game transactions. This includes any and all digital gaming transactions made on any gaming platform. Having considered and reviewed the evidence, the Court concludes that the appropriate submarket to consider is the mobile gaming transactions market. This relevant product market would include mobile game transactions on both mobile phone and tablet devices, which have the competitive advantage of mobility or portability as compared to other platforms and devices.

Substantial evidence was presented showing that mobile gaming is a distinct submarket. As an initial matter, Apple's own documents recognize mobile gaming as a submarket. One industry report describes mobile gaming as a "$100 billion industry by itself" that accounts for 59% of global gaming revenue. While PC and console gaming has grown more slowly, mobile gaming has experienced double-digit growth driven by "the free-to-play model" with in-app purchases. Remarkably, this rapid growth has not significantly cannibalized revenues from the PC or console gaming markets, which suggests that consumers are not necessarily substituting among them.

Even without Apple documents, the experts largely agree that mobile and non-mobile platforms provide different types of games. Only 12% and 16% of the most popular App Store games are available on consoles, and console games are largely separate from mobile games. [And] the most popular games on mobile are only available on mobile, with a few games also available on PCs. The types of games are also different, with many more casual games on mobile and core games on PC and console platforms. For those games that are available on multiple platforms, such as Fortnite, playing and spending on different platforms is complementary, rather than substitution-focused, because playing on another device increases the playtime and spending on the previous devices.

Assessing Apple's Market Power in the Relevant Product Market

The Court has found Apple's market share in mobile gaming transactions appears to fluctuate anywhere from approximately 52% to 57% over the course of the three years in evidence. While the prior figures suggest that Apple's share in mobile gaming is increasing, the more recent year reflects some stability in the market between Apple and its main competitor, Google. That Apple has more than a majority in a mostly duopolistic, and otherwise highly concentrated, market indicates that Apple has considerable market power.

Apple's market share is below the general ranges of where courts found monopoly power under Section 2.

On the one hand, only a small number of platforms, and their attendant licenses on which to distribute mobile games, exist—namely iOS and Android. Moreover, economies of scale in the form of network effects favor these established digital gaming stores and platforms over new entrants. Finally, new entrants may face information barriers to entry, as users may not know that cheaper game distribution may be available on alternative platforms. Although these factors do not create "lock-in," they are evidence of some entry barriers for new companies providing mobile game transactions.

On the other hand, there are significant changes in both the wider gaming market and the mobile gaming market — both appear to be in flux. Indeed, the evidence reflects that the wider gaming market is both dynamic and evolving. Mobile gaming transactions do not appear to be immune to this dynamism. The introduction of the hybrid platform the Nintendo Switch in 2017 provides some evidence that the barriers of entry are not so high as to deter competitors in related markets from entering the mobile gaming transactions market.

Moreover, Microsoft and Nvidia's efforts into mobile game streaming are further evidence that these entry barriers are not so substantial to prevent new market entrants. Indeed, these competitors are moving into the same lucrative mobile gaming submarket without facing substantial market barriers to entry. In short, these competitors appear to be leveraging either existing intellectual property in the form of hardware and gaming content as well as existing established networks, including its own consumer and developer bases, to break into this market space. Given this recent movement by competitors, it is hard to characterize the entry barriers as oppressive or high on this record.

In sum, given the totality of the record, and its underdeveloped state, while the Court can conclude that Apple exercises market power in the mobile gaming market, the Court cannot conclude that Apple's market power reaches the status of monopoly power in the mobile gaming market. That said, the evidence does suggest that Apple is near the precipice of substantial market power, or monopoly power, with its considerable market share. Apple is only saved by the fact that its share is not higher, that competitors from related submarkets are making inroads into the mobile gaming submarket, and, perhaps, because plaintiff did not focus on this topic.

Notes and Questions

1. Aftermarkets and Antitrust Law. *Epic v. Apple* illustrates a difficult but seminal issue in how the Sherman Act is enforced against dominant platforms. Although different platforms clearly compete for new users, current users of platforms cannot easily change business strategies or transport data in response to a platform price hike (or quality reduction). The question is whether these "switching costs," and the difficulty to anticipate them in advance, gives platforms monopoly power in their "aftermarket." The seminal case involving aftermarkets is Eastman Kodak v. Image Tech. Servs., 504 U.S. 451 (1992), in which the Supreme Court found that Kodak copier replacement parts is an aftermarket over which Kodak enjoyed a monopoly. The legal question was whether purchasers of Kodak copiers (which at the time were durable goods of significant expense that required periodic repairs) would instead purchase rival copiers if Kodak raised the price of its replacement parts. Although the *Kodak* case was criticized at the time and (as was discussed by the *Epic v. Apple* court in an excerpt not included above) has not been attentively followed in subsequent years by courts of appeals, the theory seems to have found support by those seeking to apply the Sherman Act against dominant internet platforms. Do you think there are material differences between the facts of *Kodak* and those of *Epic v. Apple*? Might that make the theory more (or less) applicable to the platforms?

2. A Partial Victory. In addition to making claims under the Sherman Act, Epic also sued Apple under California's Unfair Competition Law. The court (in sections not included above) agreed that certain anti-steering provisions in Apple's DPLA violated California's Unfair Competition Law (UCL). To remedy that violation, the court issued a nationwide, permanent injunction preventing Apple from enforcing the anti-steering provisions, which extends to all app categories (not just gaming apps). In effect, the injunction gives app developers the ability to avoid Apple's 30% IAP commission by directing users to external websites for in-app purchases. If state law can stop what the Sherman Act cannot, is that a failure of the Sherman Act?

3. Multiple Suits. Epic also sued Google for similar restraints on its Google Play Store. And developers separately sued Apple for the same conduct, and the parties reached a comprehensive settlement. Indeed, these lawsuits were already pending before the Supreme Court well before the commencement of this action. The first, Apple iPhone Antitrust Litigation, 4:11-cv-6714-YGR (Pepper), was filed in 2011 on behalf of a class of iOS device consumers alleging harm from the commission rate. The second, filed in 2019 after Pepper returned from the Supreme Court, was Donald Cameron v. Apple Inc., 4:19-cv-3074-YGR (Cameron), which was filed on behalf of a class of iOS app developers also alleging violations of antitrust and competition laws. If these courts follow Judge Gonzalez's conclusion that Apple's App Store is not its own aftermarket, is the result of all of these cases — including those against Google — predetermined?

§ 8.A.2. Interconnection

We detailed in Chapter 5 the many regulatory strategies that aimed to prevent monopolists from denying access to their networks. The Bell monopoly strategically refused to connect its telephone network with its competitors, thereby preventing rivals from competing with Bell and denying consumers the benefits of complete coverage. Similar concerns motivated lawmakers to develop mechanisms in the 1992 Cable Act, the 1996 Telecommunications Act, and the common law (among others) that can limit a dominant network's ability to deny service.

Courts applying the antitrust laws have developed doctrines that similarly restrain a monopolist's discretion to transact with others. Doctrines that limit so-called "unilateral refusals to deal" are controversial and, as the cases below suggest, rely on poorly defined standards. Importantly, several of these antitrust cases arose within regulated industries, and a preliminary question is whether to apply the antitrust laws when a comprehensive, sector-specific regulatory scheme is at work. An even more fundamental question is whether to require interconnection or dealing under the antitrust laws without regard to any comprehensive regulation of a natural monopolist. As you'll see, these cases involve not just foundational questions but difficult questions of implementation and policy. One critical question is whether these doctrines adequately arm the Sherman Act to confront potential monopolistic harm from dominant platforms.

The two cases excerpted below address that question.

Otter Tail Power Company v. United States

410 U.S. 366 (1973)

DOUGLAS, J., delivered the opinion of the Court, in which BRENNAN, WHITE, and MARSHALL, JJ., joined. STEWART, J., filed an opinion concurring in part and dissenting in part, in which BURGER, C.J., and REHNQUIST, J., joined. BLACKMUN and POWELL, JJ., took no part in the consideration or decision of the case.

JUSTICE DOUGLAS delivered the opinion of the Court.

The District Court found that Otter Tail had attempted to monopolize and had monopolized the retail distribution of electric power in its service area in violation of § 2 of the Sherman Act. The District Court found that Otter Tail had attempted to prevent communities in which its retail distribution franchise had expired from replacing it with a municipal distribution system. The principal means employed were (1) refusals to sell power at wholesale to proposed municipal systems in the communities where it had been retailing power; (2) refusals to "wheel" power to such systems, that is to say, to transfer by direct transmission or displacement electric power from one utility to another over the facilities of an intermediate utility.

Otter Tail sells electric power at retail in 465 towns in Minnesota, North Dakota, and South Dakota. In towns where Otter Tail distributes at retail, it operates under municipally granted franchises which are limited from 10 to 20 years. Each town in Otter Tail's service area generally can accommodate only one distribution system, making each town a natural monopoly market for the distribution and sale of electric power at retail. The aggregate of towns in Otter Tail's service area is the geographic market in which Otter Tail competes for the right to serve the towns at retail. That competition is generally for the right to serve the entire retail market within the composite limits of a town, and that competition is generally between Otter Tail and a prospective or existing municipal system. These towns number 510 and of those Otter Tail serves 91%, or 465.

Between 1945 and 1970, there were contests in 12 towns served by Otter Tail over proposals to replace it with municipal systems. In only three ... municipal systems actually established. Proposed municipal systems have great obstacles; they must purchase the electric power at wholesale. To do so they must have access to existing transmission lines. The only ones available belong to Otter Tail. Otter Tail refused to sell the new systems energy at wholesale and refused to agree to wheel power from other suppliers of wholesale energy.

As respects Elbow Lake and Hankinson, Otter Tail simply refused to deal, although according to the findings it had the ability to do so. Elbow Lake, cut off from all sources of wholesale power, constructed its own generating plant. Both Elbow Lake and Hankinson requested the Bureau of Reclamation and various cooperatives to furnish them with wholesale power; they were willing to supply it if Otter Tail would wheel it. But Otter Tail refused, relying on provisions in its contracts which barred the use of its lines for wheeling power to towns which it had served at retail. Elbow Lake after completing its plant asked the Federal Power Commission, under § 202(b) of the Federal Power Act, to require Otter Tail to interconnect with the town and sell it power at wholesale.[1] The Federal Power Commission ordered first a temporary and then a permanent connection. Hankinson tried unsuccessfully to get relief from the North Dakota Commission and then filed a complaint with the federal commission seeking an order to compel Otter Tail to wheel. While the application was pending, the town council voted to withdraw it and subsequently renewed Otter Tail's franchise.

I

Otter Tail contends that by reason of the Federal Power Act it is not subject to antitrust regulation with respect to its refusal to deal. We disagree with that position. "Repeals of the antitrust laws by implication from a regulatory statute are strongly disfavored, and have only been found in cases of plain repugnancy between the antitrust and regulatory provisions." Activities which come under the jurisdiction of a regulatory' agency nevertheless may be subject to scrutiny under the antitrust laws.

The District Court determined that Otter Tail's consistent refusals to wholesale or wheel power to its municipal customers constituted illegal monopolization. Otter Tail maintains here that its refusals to deal should be immune from antitrust prosecution because the Federal Power Commission has the authority to compel involuntary interconnections of power pursuant to § 202(b) of the Federal Power Act. The essential thrust of § 202, however, is to encourage voluntary interconnections of power. Only if a power company refuses to interconnect voluntarily may the Federal Power Commission, subject to limitations unrelated to antitrust considerations, order the interconnection. The standard which governs its decision is whether such action is "necessary or appropriate in the public interest." Although antitrust considerations may be relevant, they are not determinative.

There is nothing in the legislative history which reveals a purpose to insulate electric power companies from the operation of the antitrust laws. To the contrary, the history of Part II of the Federal Power Act indicates an overriding policy of

---

1. This request was for standby power to supplement Elbow Lake's new generating plant. The Court below found that it was economically unfeasible for anyone to build new transmission facilities to wheel electricity to Elbow Lake or Hankinson. Further, the area's major generator of electricity, the Bureau of Reclamation, was forbidden to construct new transmission facilities to serve towns where wheeling arrangements could be negotiated.

maintaining competition to the maximum extent possible consistent with the public interest. As originally conceived, Part II would have included a "common carrier" provision making it "the duty of every public utility to transmit energy for any person upon reasonable request." In addition, it would have empowered the Federal Power Commission to order wheeling if it found such action to be "necessary or desirable in the public interest." These provisions were eliminated to preserve "the voluntary action of the utilities."

It is clear, then, that Congress rejected a pervasive regulatory scheme for controlling the interstate distribution of power in favor of voluntary commercial relationships.[2] When these relationships are governed in the first instance by business judgment and not regulatory coercion, courts must be hesitant to conclude that Congress intended to override the fundamental national policies embodied in the antitrust laws.

Thus, there is no basis for concluding that the limited authority of the Federal Power Commission to order interconnections was intended to be a substitute for, or to immunize Otter Tail from, antitrust regulation for refusing to deal with municipal corporations.

II

The decree of the District Court enjoins Otter Tail from "(r)efusing to sell electric power at wholesale to existing or proposed municipal electric power systems in cities and towns located in (its service area)" and from refusing to wheel electric power over its transmission lines from other electric power lines to such cities and towns. But the decree goes on to provide:

> The defendant shall not be compelled by the Judgment in this case to furnish wholesale electric service or wheeling service to a municipality except at rates which are compensatory and under terms and conditions which are filed with and subject to approval by the Federal Power Commission.

So far as wheeling is concerned, there is no authority granted the Commission under Part II of the Federal Power Act to order it, for the bills originally introduced contained common carrier provisions which were deleted. The Act as passed contained only the interconnection provision set forth in § 202(b). The common carrier provision in the original bill and the power to direct wheeling were left to the "voluntary coordination of electric facilities." Insofar as the District Court ordered wheeling to correct anticompetitive and monopolistic practices of Otter Tail, there is no conflict with the authority of the Federal Power Commission.

2. In addition to the powers noted in the text, the Federal Power Commission (FPC) had the power to regulate the rates charged for wheeling or for wholesale electricity. See Brief for the United States at 15–16. Retail rates were not subject to FPC regulation, and the states and municipalities in which Otter Tail operated tended not to regulate them either.

As respects the ordering of interconnections, there is no conflict on the present record. Elbow Lake applied to the Federal Power Commission for an interconnection with Otter Tail and, as we have said, obtained it. Hankinson renewed Otter Tail's franchise. So the decree of the District Court, as far as the present record is concerned, presents no actual conflict between the federal judicial decree and an order of the Federal Power Commission. It will be time enough to consider whether the antitrust remedy may override the power of the Commission under § 202(b) as, if, and when the Commission denies the interconnection and the District Court nevertheless undertakes to direct it. At present, there is only a potential conflict, not a present concrete case or controversy concerning it.

III

The record makes abundantly clear that Otter Tail used its monopoly power in the towns in its service area to foreclose competition or gain a competitive advantage, or to destroy a competitor, all in violation of the antitrust laws. The District Court determined that Otter Tail has "a strategic dominance in the transmission of power in most of its service area" and that it used this dominance to foreclose potential entrants into the retail area from obtaining electric power from outside sources of supply. Use of monopoly power "to destroy threatened competition" is a violation of the "attempt to monopolize" clause of § 2 of the Sherman Act.

When a community serviced by Otter Tail decides not to renew Otter Tail's retail franchise when it expires, it may generate, transmit, and distribute its own electric power. We recently described the difficulties and problems of those isolated electric power systems. Interconnection with other utilities is frequently the only solution. That is what Elbow Lake in the present case did. There were no engineering factors that prevented Otter Tail from selling power at wholesale to those towns that wanted municipal plants or wheeling the power. The District Court found—and its findings are supported—that Otter Tail's refusals to sell at wholesale or to wheel were solely to prevent municipal power systems from eroding its monopolistic position.

V

Otter Tail argues that, without the weapons which it used, more and more municipalities will turn to public power and Otter Tail will go downhill. "The promotion of self-interest alone does not invoke the rule of reason to immunize otherwise illegal conduct." The Sherman Act assumes that an enterprise will protect itself against loss by operating with superior service, lower costs, and improved efficiency. Otter Tail's theory collided with the Sherman Act as it sought to substitute for competition anticompetitive uses of its dominant economic power.

The fact that three municipalities which Otter Tail opposed finally got their municipal systems does not excuse Otter Tail's conduct. That fact does not condone the antitrust tactics which Otter Tail sought to impose. The proclivity for predatory practices has always been a consideration for the District Court in fashioning its antitrust decree.

We do not suggest, however, that the District Court, concluding that Otter Tail violated the antitrust laws, should be impervious to Otter Tail's assertion that compulsory interconnection or wheeling will erode its integrated system and threaten its capacity to serve adequately the public. As the dissent properly notes, the Commission may not order interconnection if to do so "would impair (the utility's) ability to render adequate service to its customers." The District Court in this case found that the "pessimistic view" advanced in Otter Tail's "erosion study" "is not supported by the record." Affirmed.

JUSTICE STEWART, with whom CHIEF JUSTICE BURGER and JUSTICE REHNQUIST join, concurring in part and dissenting in part.

In the face of natural monopolies at retail and similar economies of scale in the subtransmission of power, Congress was forced to address the very problem raised by this case—use of the lines of one company by another. One obvious solution would have been to impose the obligations of a common carrier upon power companies owning lines capable of the wholesale transmission of electricity. Such a provision was originally included in the bill. Yet, after substantial debate, the Congress declined to follow this path.

This legislative history, especially when viewed in the light of repeated subsequent congressional refusals to impose common carrier obligations in this area, indicates a clear congressional purpose to allow electric utilities to decide for themselves whether to wheel or sell at wholesale as they see fit. This freedom is qualified by a grant of authority to the Commission to order interconnection (but not wheeling) in certain circumstances. But the exercise of even that power is limited by a consideration of the ability of the regulated utility to function.

As the District Court found, Otter Tail is a vertically integrated power company. But the bulk of its business — some 90% of its income — derives from sales of power at retail. As a retailer of power, Otter Tail asserted a legitimate business interest in keeping its lines free for its own power sales and in refusing to lend a hand in its own demise by wheeling cheaper power from the Bureau of Reclamation to municipal consumers which might otherwise purchase power at retail from Otter Tail itself.

Here, a monopoly is sure to result either way. If the consumers of Elbow Lake receive their electric power from a municipally owned company or from Otter Tail, there will be a monopoly at the retail level, for there will in any event be only one supplier. The very reason for the regulation of private utility rates — by state bodies and by the Commission — is the inevitability of a monopoly that requires price control to take the place of price competition.

Verizon Communications Inc. v. Law Offices of Curtis V. Trinko, LLP

540 U.S. 398 (2004)

SCALIA, J., delivered the opinion of the Court, in which REHNQUIST, C.J., and O'CONNOR, KENNEDY, GINSBURG, and BREYER, JJ., joined. STEVENS, J., filed an opinion concurring in the judgment, in which SOUTER and THOMAS, JJ., joined.

JUSTICE SCALIA delivered the opinion of the Court.

The Telecommunications Act of 1996 imposes certain duties upon incumbent local telephone companies in order to facilitate market entry by competitors, and establishes a complex regime for monitoring and enforcement. In this case we consider whether a complaint alleging breach of the incumbent's duty under the 1996 Act to share its network with competitors states a claim under § 2 of the Sherman Act.

I

Petitioner Verizon Communications Inc. is the incumbent local exchange carrier (LEC) serving New York State. Before the 1996 Act, Verizon, like other incumbent LECs, enjoyed an exclusive franchise within its local service area. The 1996 Act sought to "uproo[t]" the incumbent LECs' monopoly and to introduce competition in its place. Central to the scheme of the Act is the incumbent LEC's obligation under 47 U.S.C. § 251(c) to share its network with competitors, including provision of access to individual elements of the network on an "unbundled" basis. New entrants, so-called competitive LECs, resell these unbundled network elements (UNEs), recombined with each other or with elements belonging to the LECs.

Verizon has signed interconnection agreements with rivals such as AT&T, as it is obliged to do under § 252, detailing the terms on which it will make its network elements available. (Because Verizon and AT&T could not agree upon terms, the open issues were subjected to compulsory arbitration under §§ 252(b) and (c).) Part of Verizon's UNE obligation under § 251(c)(3) is the provision of access to operations support systems (OSS), a set of systems used by incumbent LECs to provide services to customers and ensure quality. Verizon's interconnection agreement and long-distance authorization each specified the mechanics by which its OSS obligation would be met. As relevant here, a competitive LEC sends orders for service through an electronic interface with Verizon's ordering system, and as Verizon completes certain steps in filling the order, it sends confirmation back through the same interface. Without OSS access a rival cannot fill its customers' orders.

In late 1999, competitive LECs complained to regulators that many orders were going unfilled, in violation of Verizon's obligation to provide access to OSS functions. The [New York Public Service Commission (PSC)] and FCC opened parallel investigations, which led to a series of orders by the PSC and a consent decree with the FCC. Under the FCC consent decree, Verizon undertook to make a "voluntary contribution" to the U.S. Treasury in the amount of $3 million; under the PSC orders, Verizon incurred liability to the competitive LECs in the amount of $10 million. Under the consent decree and orders, Verizon was subjected to new performance measurements and new reporting requirements to the FCC and PSC, with additional penalties for continued noncompliance. In June 2000, the FCC terminated the consent decree. The next month the PSC relieved Verizon of the heightened reporting requirement.

Respondent Law Offices of Curtis V. Trinko, LLP, a New York City law firm, was a local telephone service customer of AT&T. The day after Verizon entered its consent decree with the FCC, respondent filed a complaint . . . on behalf of itself and a class of similarly situated customers. The complaint alleged that Verizon had filled rivals' orders on a discriminatory basis as part of an anticompetitive scheme to discourage customers from becoming or remaining customers of competitive LECs, thus impeding the competitive LECs' ability to enter and compete in the market for local telephone service. The complaint sought damages and injunctive relief for violation of § 2 of the Sherman Act. We granted certiorari, limited to the question whether the Court of Appeals erred in reversing the District Court's dismissal of respondent's antitrust claims.

II

To decide this case, we must first determine what effect (if any) the 1996 Act has upon the application of traditional antitrust principles. Under the sharing duties of § 251(c), incumbent LECs are required to offer three kinds of access. Perhaps most intrusive is the duty to offer access to UNEs on "just, reasonable, and nondiscriminatory" terms, a phrase that the FCC has interpreted to mean a price reflecting long-run incremental cost. A rival can interconnect its own facilities with those of the incumbent LEC, or it can simply purchase services at wholesale from the incumbent and resell them to consumers. The Act also imposes upon incumbents the duty to allow physical "collocation"—that is, to permit a competitor to locate and install its equipment on the incumbent's premises—which makes feasible interconnection and access to UNEs.

That Congress created these duties, however, does not automatically lead to the conclusion that they can be enforced by means of an antitrust claim. Indeed, a detailed regulatory scheme such as that created by the 1996 Act ordinarily raises the question whether the regulated entities are not shielded from antitrust scrutiny altogether by the doctrine of implied immunity. In some respects the enforcement scheme set up by the 1996 Act is a good candidate for implication of antitrust immunity, to avoid the real possibility of judgments conflicting with the agency's regulatory scheme "that might be voiced by courts exercising jurisdiction under the antitrust laws."

Congress, however, precluded that interpretation. Section 601(b)(1) of the 1996 Act is an antitrust-specific saving clause providing that "nothing in this Act or the amendments made by this Act shall be construed to modify, impair, or supersede the applicability of any of the antitrust laws." This bars a finding of implied immunity. As the FCC has put the point, the saving clause preserves those "claims that satisfy established antitrust standards."

But just as the 1996 Act preserves claims that satisfy existing antitrust standards, it does not create new claims that go beyond existing antitrust standards; that would be equally inconsistent with the saving clause's mandate that nothing in the Act "modify, impair, or supersede the applicability" of the antitrust laws. We turn, then, to whether the activity of which respondent complains violates pre-existing antitrust standards.

III

The complaint alleges that Verizon denied interconnection services to rivals in order to limit entry. If that allegation states an antitrust claim at all, it does so under § 2 of the Sherman Act, which declares that a firm shall not "monopolize" or "attempt to monopolize." It is settled law that this offense requires, in addition to the possession of monopoly power in the relevant market, "the willful acquisition or maintenance of that power as distinguished from growth or development as a consequence of a superior product, business acumen, or historic accident." The mere possession of monopoly power, and the concomitant charging of monopoly prices, is not only not unlawful; it is an important element of the free-market system. The opportunity to charge monopoly prices—at least for a short period—is what attracts "business acumen" in the first place; it induces risk taking that produces innovation and economic growth. To safeguard the incentive to innovate, the possession of monopoly power will not be found unlawful unless it is accompanied by an element of anticompetitive *conduct*.

Firms may acquire monopoly power by establishing an infrastructure that renders them uniquely suited to serve their customers. Compelling such firms to share the source of their advantage is in some tension with the underlying purpose of antitrust law, since it may lessen the incentive for the monopolist, the rival, or both to invest in those economically beneficial facilities. Enforced sharing also requires antitrust courts to act as central planners, identifying the proper price, quantity, and other terms of dealing—a role for which they are ill suited. Moreover, compelling negotiation between competitors may facilitate the supreme evil of antitrust: collusion. Thus, as a general matter, the Sherman Act "does not restrict the long recognized right of [a] trader or manufacturer engaged in an entirely private business, freely to exercise his own independent discretion as to parties with whom he will deal."

However, "[t]he high value that we have placed on the right to refuse to deal with other firms does not mean that the right is unqualified." Aspen Skiing Co. v. Aspen Highlands Skiing Corp., 472 U.S. 585, 601 (1985). Under certain circumstances, a refusal to cooperate with rivals can constitute anticompetitive conduct and violate § 2. We have been very cautious in recognizing such exceptions, because of the uncertain virtue of forced sharing and the difficulty of identifying and remedying anticompetitive conduct by a single firm. The question before us today is whether the allegations of respondent's complaint fit within existing exceptions or provide a basis, under traditional antitrust principles, for recognizing a new one.

The leading case for § 2 liability based on refusal to cooperate with a rival, and the case upon which respondent understandably places greatest reliance, is *Aspen Skiing*. *Aspen Skiing* is at or near the outer boundary of § 2 liability. The Court there found significance in the defendant's decision to cease participation in a cooperative venture. The unilateral termination of a voluntary *(and thus presumably profitable)* course of dealing suggested a willingness to forsake short-term profits to achieve an anticompetitive end. Similarly, the defendant's unwillingness to renew the ticket *even if compensated at retail price* revealed a distinctly anticompetitive bent.

The refusal to deal alleged in the present case does not fit within the limited exception recognized in *Aspen Skiing*. The complaint does not allege that Verizon voluntarily engaged in a course of dealing with its rivals, or would ever have done so absent statutory compulsion. Here, therefore, the defendant's prior conduct sheds no light upon the motivation of its refusal to deal — upon whether its regulatory lapses were prompted not by competitive zeal but by anticompetitive malice. The contrast between the cases is heightened by the difference in pricing behavior. In *Aspen Skiing*, the defendant turned down a proposal to sell at its own retail price, suggesting a calculation that its future monopoly retail price would be higher. Verizon's reluctance to interconnect at the cost-based rate of compensation available under § 251(c)(3) tells us nothing about dreams of monopoly.

The specific nature of what the 1996 Act compels makes this case different from *Aspen Skiing* in a more fundamental way. In *Aspen Skiing*, what the defendant refused to provide to its competitor was a product that it already sold at retail — to oversimplify slightly, lift tickets representing a bundle of services to skiers. Similarly, in *Otter Tail*, another case relied upon by respondent, the defendant was already in the business of providing a service to certain customers (power transmission over its network), and refused to provide the same service to certain other customers. In the present case, by contrast, the services allegedly withheld are not otherwise marketed or available to the public. The sharing obligation imposed by the 1996 Act created "something brand new" — "the wholesale market for leasing network elements." The unbundled elements offered pursuant to § 251(c)(3) exist only deep within the bowels of Verizon; they are brought out on compulsion of the 1996 Act and offered not to consumers but to rivals, and at considerable expense and effort. New systems must be designed and implemented simply to make that access possible — indeed, it is the failure of one of those systems that prompted the present complaint.

We conclude that Verizon's alleged insufficient assistance in the provision of service to rivals is not a recognized antitrust claim under this Court's existing refusal-to-deal precedents. This conclusion would be unchanged even if we considered to be established law the "essential facilities" doctrine crafted by some lower courts, under which the Court of Appeals concluded respondent's allegations might state a claim. We have never recognized such a doctrine, and we find no need either to recognize it or to repudiate it here. It suffices for present purposes to note that the indispensable requirement for invoking the doctrine is the unavailability of access to the "essential facilities"; where access exists, the doctrine serves no purpose. Thus, it is said that "essential facility claims should . . . be denied where a state or federal agency has effective power to compel sharing and to regulate its scope and terms." P. Areeda & H. Hovenkamp, Antitrust Law. Respondent believes that the existence of sharing duties under the 1996 Act supports its case. We think the opposite: The 1996 Act's extensive provision for access makes it unnecessary to impose a judicial doctrine of forced access. To the extent respondent's "essential facilities" argument is distinct from its general § 2 argument, we reject it.

IV

Finally, we do not believe that traditional antitrust principles justify adding the present case to the few existing exceptions from the proposition that there is no duty to aid competitors.

One factor of particular importance is the existence of a regulatory structure designed to deter and remedy anticompetitive harm. Where such a structure exists, the additional benefit to competition provided by antitrust enforcement will tend to be small, and it will be less plausible that the antitrust laws contemplate such additional scrutiny. The regulatory framework that exists in this case demonstrates how, in certain circumstances, "regulation significantly diminishes the likelihood of major antitrust harm." Consider, for example, the statutory restrictions upon Verizon's entry into the potentially lucrative market for long-distance service. To be allowed to enter the long-distance market in the first place, an incumbent LEC must be on good behavior in its local market. Authorization by the FCC requires state-by-state satisfaction of § 271's competitive checklist, which as we have noted includes the nondiscriminatory provision of access to UNEs. The FCC's § 271 authorization order for Verizon to provide long-distance service in New York discussed at great length Verizon's commitments to provide access to UNEs, including the provision of OSS. Those commitments are enforceable by the FCC through continuing oversight; a failure to meet an authorization condition can result in an order that the deficiency be corrected, in the imposition of penalties, or in the suspension or revocation of long-distance approval.

The regulatory response to the OSS failure complained of in respondent's suit provides a vivid example of how the regulatory regime operates. When several competitive LECs complained about deficiencies in Verizon's servicing of orders, the FCC and PSC responded. The FCC soon concluded that Verizon was in breach of its sharing duties under § 251(c), imposed a substantial fine, and set up sophisticated measurements to gauge remediation, with weekly reporting requirements and specific penalties for failure. The PSC found Verizon in violation of the [Performance Assurance Plan (PAP)] even earlier, and imposed additional financial penalties and measurements with *daily* reporting requirements. In short, the regime was an effective steward of the antitrust function.

Against the slight benefits of antitrust intervention here, we must weigh a realistic assessment of its costs. Under the best of circumstances, applying the requirements of § 2 "can be difficult" because "the means of illicit exclusion, like the means of legitimate competition, are myriad." United States v. Microsoft Corp., 253 F.3d 34, 58 (CADC 2001) (en banc) (per curiam). Mistaken inferences and the resulting false condemnations are especially costly, because they chill the very conduct the antitrust laws are designed to protect. The cost of false positives counsels against an undue expansion of § 2 liability. One false-positive risk is that an incumbent LEC's failure to provide a service with sufficient alacrity might have nothing to do with exclusion. Allegations of violations of § 251(c)(3) duties are difficult for antitrust courts to evaluate, not only because they are highly technical, but also because they are likely to be extremely numerous, given the incessant, complex, and constantly changing interaction of competitive and incumbent LECs implementing the sharing and interconnection obligations. Amici States have filed a brief asserting that competitive LECs are threatened with "death by a thousand cuts," the identification of which would surely be a daunting task for a generalist antitrust court. Judicial oversight under the Sherman Act would seem destined to distort investment and lead to a new layer of interminable litigation, atop the variety of litigation routes already available to and actively pursued by competitive LECs.

Even if the problem of false positives did not exist, conduct consisting of anticompetitive violations of § 251 may be, as we have concluded with respect to above-cost predatory pricing schemes, "beyond the practical ability of a judicial tribunal to control." Brooke Group Ltd. v. Brown & Williamson Tobacco Corp., 509 U.S. 209, 223 (1993). Effective remediation of violations of regulatory sharing requirements will ordinarily require continuing supervision of a highly detailed decree. We think that Professor Areeda got it exactly right: "No court should impose a duty to deal that it cannot explain or adequately and reasonably supervise. The problem should be deemed irremedia[ble] by antitrust law when compulsory access requires the court to assume the day-to-day controls characteristic of a regulatory agency." Areeda, 58 Antitrust L.J., at 853. In this case, respondent has requested an equitable decree to "preliminarily and permanently enjoin Verizon from providing access to the local loop market to rivals on terms and conditions that are not as favorable" as those that Verizon enjoys. An antitrust court is unlikely to be an effective day-to-day enforcer of these detailed sharing obligations.

The 1996 Act is in an important respect much more ambitious than the antitrust laws. It attempts "*to eliminate the monopolies* enjoyed by the inheritors of AT&T's local franchises." Verizon Communications Inc. v. FCC, 535 U.S. 467, 476 (2002) (emphasis added). Section 2 of the Sherman Act, by contrast, seeks merely to prevent unlawful monopolization. It would be a serious mistake to conflate the two goals. The Sherman Act is indeed the "Magna Carta of free enterprise," United States v. Topco Assocs., Inc., 405 U.S. 596, 610 (1972), but it does not give judges carte blanche to insist that a monopolist alter its way of doing business whenever some other approach might yield greater competition. We conclude that respondent's complaint fails to state a claim under the Sherman Act.

[Concurring opinion of JUSTICE STEVENS is omitted.]

Notes and Questions

1. When Does the Sherman Act Apply? Both the above cases confronted the question of whether the Sherman Act should apply when a comprehensive regulatory regime, using the many devices described in Chapter 5 (and perhaps others), is already in place to restrain the ills of monopoly power. The question in *Trinko* was easier to answer because § 601(b)(1) of the 1996 Telecommunications Act contains a "saving clause" that preserves the applicability of the antitrust laws. In *Otter Tail*, the court sustained the antitrust action because it concluded there was no conflict between the Sherman Act judgement and the Federal Power Act. How would you characterize the dissent's response? More recently, the Supreme Court ruled that when a statutory regime does not have a saving clause, the test is whether there is a "clear repugnancy" between the antitrust action and the background statutory regime. Credit Suisse Secs. v. Billing, 551 U.S. 264 (2007). Do you think *Otter Tail* would come out the same way under this updated standard?

2. Common Carriage and the Sherman Act. Recall that Kinderstart's suit against Google, discussed in Chapter 5, also contained a Sherman Act claim. Kinderstart argued that "Google violated Section 2 under the 'refusal to deal' doctrine as set forth in *Aspen Skiing*." In *Aspen Skiing*, discussed at length in *Trinko*, the larger of two co-located ski resorts was found to have violated the Sherman Act after it decided to discontinue a long-standing, mutually profitable arrangement to market joint ski passes with its smaller neighbor. As noted in *Trinko*, a violation was found in *Aspen Skiing* because the monopolist terminated a profitable course of dealing, thus bearing short-term losses while inflicting pain onto a rival (and onto consumers). Does this doctrine fit the common carriage doctrine described in Chapter 5? Might the Sherman Act and common carriage requirements stem from distinctly different motivations? If so, how might Kinderstart have made a stronger argument?

3. Interconnection under Intellectual Property and Digital Security Laws. Interconnection disputes involving internet platforms are also sometimes governed by other statutes. Consider the dispute between Power Ventures and Facebook. Power Ventures offered its users the ability to aggregate their assorted social networking accounts (including Facebook, LinkedIn, Twitter, and AOL or Yahoo instant messaging) in a single site. They did this by "scraping" content from the other sites. Facebook objected to Power Ventures' scraping (even though users authorized Power Ventures to obtain their account data) and sued under an assortment of intellectual property laws (the Lanham Act, the Digital Millennium Copyright Act, and copyright laws) and digital security laws (the Computer Fraud and Abuse Act, The Controlling the Assault of Non-Solicited Pornography and Marketing Act) to deny Power Ventures' access. Facebook ultimately prevailed, winning both injunctive relief and statutory damages. Facebook, Inc. v. Power Ventures, Inc., 844 F.3d 1058 (9th Cir. 2016).

It might be said that antitrust and intellectual property law are flip sides of the same coin since, roughly speaking, both are legal frameworks to empower successful commercial enterprise while limiting the excesses of monopoly power. Should intellectual property law, like the Sherman Act, impose limits on a monopolist's unilateral refusals to interconnect with others?

4. Institutional Competence. *Trinko* suggested that overseeing interconnection arrangements is beyond the purview of antitrust courts. Does such a view indicate that antitrust law is incapable of replacing regulation in a network industry in which interconnection issues are likely to be contested? If so, should the DOJ, FTC, and FCC reconceptualize their respective roles? Or should courts adapt to increase their capacity to enforce antitrust law? If so, how?

§ 8.A.3. Vertical Restraints

Chapter 5, and in particular part 5.C, detailed the many prohibitions imposed on telecommunications monopolies designed to prevent them from extending their market dominance into adjacent markets. The Sherman Act similarly restrains parties with monopoly power from engaging in restrictive vertical arrangements. Consider the cases below and assess how the Sherman Act scrutinizes monopolists' use of vertical restraints. Do these cases reveal similar or different policy motivations that underlie those described in Chapter 5? Are they operationalized differently?

United States v. Microsoft Corp.

253 F.3d 34 (D.C. Cir. 2001)

Before: EDWARDS, Chief Judge, WILLIAMS, GINSBURG, SENTELLE, RANDOLPH, ROGERS and TATEL, Circuit Judges.

PER CURIAM:

I. Introduction

A. Background

In July 1994, officials at the Department of Justice (DOJ), on behalf of the United States, filed suit against Microsoft, charging the company with, among other things, unlawfully maintaining a monopoly in the operating system market through anticompetitive terms in its licensing and software developer agreements. . . .

On May 18, 1998, the United States and a group of State plaintiffs filed separate (and soon thereafter consolidated) complaints, asserting antitrust violations by Microsoft and seeking preliminary and permanent injunctions against the company's allegedly unlawful conduct. Relying almost exclusively on Microsoft's varied efforts to unseat Netscape Navigator as the preeminent internet browser, plaintiffs charged four distinct violations of the Sherman Act: (1) unlawful exclusive dealing arrangements; (2) unlawful tying of IE to Windows 95 and Windows 98; (3) unlawful maintenance of a monopoly in the PC operating system market; and (4) unlawful attempted monopolization of the internet browser market. The States also brought pendent claims charging Microsoft with violations of various State antitrust laws.

B. Overview

Before turning to the merits of Microsoft's various arguments, we pause to reflect briefly on two matters of note, one practical and one theoretical.

The practical matter relates to the temporal dimension of this case. The litigation timeline in this case is hardly problematic. Indeed, it is noteworthy that a case of this magnitude and complexity has proceeded from the filing of complaints through trial to appellate decision in a mere three years.

What is somewhat problematic, however, is that just over six years have passed since Microsoft engaged in the first conduct plaintiffs allege to be anticompetitive. As the record in this case indicates, six years seems like an eternity in the computer industry. By the time a court can assess liability, firms, products, and the marketplace are likely to have changed dramatically. This, in turn, threatens enormous practical difficulties for courts considering the appropriate measure of relief in equitable enforcement actions, both in crafting injunctive remedies in the first instance and reviewing those remedies in the second. Conduct remedies may be unavailing in such cases, because innovation to a large degree has already rendered the anticompetitive conduct obsolete (although by no means harmless). And broader structural remedies present their own set of problems, including how a court goes about *restoring* competition to a dramatically changed, and constantly changing, marketplace. That is just one reason why we find the District Court's refusal in the present case to hold an evidentiary hearing on remedies—to update and flesh out the available information before seriously entertaining the possibility of dramatic structural relief—so problematic.

We do not mean to say that enforcement actions will no longer play an important role in curbing infringements of the antitrust laws in technologically dynamic markets, nor do we assume this in assessing the merits of this case. Even in those cases where forward-looking remedies appear limited, the Government will continue to have an interest in defining the contours of the antitrust laws so that law-abiding firms will have a clear sense of what is permissible and what is not. And the threat of private damage actions will remain to deter those firms inclined to test the limits of the law.

The second matter of note is more theoretical in nature. We decide this case against a backdrop of significant debate amongst academics and practitioners over the extent to which "old economy" § 2 monopolization doctrines should apply to firms competing in dynamic technological markets characterized by network effects. In markets characterized by network effects, one product or standard tends towards dominance, because the utility that a user derives from consumption of the good increases with the number of other agents consuming the good. For example, an individual consumer's demand to use (and hence her benefit from) the telephone network increases with the number of other users on the network whom she can call or from whom she can receive calls. Once a product or standard achieves wide acceptance, it becomes more or less entrenched. Competition in such industries is "for the field" rather than "within the field."

In technologically dynamic markets, however, such entrenchment may be temporary, because innovation may alter the field altogether. See Joseph A. Schumpeter, Capitalism, Socialism, and Democracy (1942). Rapid technological change leads to markets in which firms compete through innovation for temporary market dominance, from which they may be displaced by the next wave of product advancements. Microsoft argues that the operating system market is just such a market.

Whether or not Microsoft's characterization of the operating system market is correct does not appreciably alter our mission in assessing the alleged antitrust violations in the present case. Indeed, there is some suggestion that the economic consequences of network effects and technological dynamism act to offset one another, thereby making it difficult to formulate categorical antitrust rules absent a particularized analysis of a given market. Moreover, it should be clear that Microsoft makes no claim that anticompetitive conduct should be assessed differently in technologically dynamic markets.

With this backdrop in mind, we turn to the specific challenges raised in Microsoft's appeal.

II. Monopolization

Section 2 of the Sherman Act makes it unlawful for a firm to "monopolize." 15 U.S.C. § 2. The offense of monopolization has two elements: (1) the possession of monopoly power in the relevant market and (2) the willful acquisition or maintenance of that power as distinguished from growth or development as a consequence of a superior product, business acumen, or historic accident. The District Court applied this test and found that Microsoft possesses monopoly power in the market for Intel-compatible PC operating systems. Focusing primarily on Microsoft's efforts to suppress Netscape Navigator's threat to its operating system monopoly, the court also found that Microsoft maintained its power not through competition on the merits, but through unlawful means. Microsoft challenges both conclusions.

A. Monopoly Power

[The Court of Appeals affirmed the finding that Microsoft is a monopolist in the "Intel-compatible PC operating system market, with Windows accounting for more than a 95% market share. In response to Microsoft's argument that "because of the possibility of competition from new entrants, looking to current market share alone can be misleading," the court replied that an "applications barrier to entry" secures Windows' dominance.]

B. Anticompetitive Conduct

As discussed above, having a monopoly does not by itself violate § 2. A firm violates § 2 only when it acquires or maintains, or attempts to acquire or maintain, a monopoly by engaging in exclusionary conduct "as distinguished from growth or development as a consequence of a superior product, business acumen, or historic accident." (Hand, J.) ("The successful competitor, having been urged to compete, must not be turned upon when he wins.").

In this case, after concluding that Microsoft had monopoly power, the District Court held that Microsoft had violated § 2 by engaging in a variety of exclusionary acts (not including predatory pricing), to maintain its monopoly by preventing the effective distribution and use of products that might threaten that monopoly. Specifically, the District Court held Microsoft liable for: (1) the way in which it integrated IE into Windows; (2) its various dealings with Original Equipment Manufacturers (OEMs), Internet Access Providers (IAPs), Internet Content Providers (ICPs), Independent Software Vendors (ISVs), and Apple Computer; (3) its efforts to contain and to subvert Java technologies; and (4) its course of conduct as a whole. Upon appeal, Microsoft argues that it did not engage in any exclusionary conduct.

Whether any particular act of a monopolist is exclusionary, rather than merely a form of vigorous competition, can be difficult to discern: the means of illicit exclusion, like the means of legitimate competition, are myriad. The challenge for an antitrust court lies in stating a general rule for distinguishing between exclusionary acts, which reduce social welfare, and competitive acts, which increase it.

1. Licenses Issued to Original Equipment Manufacturers

The District Court condemned a number of provisions in Microsoft's agreements licensing Windows to OEMs, because it found that Microsoft's imposition of those provisions (like many of Microsoft's other actions at issue in this case) serves to reduce usage share of Netscape's browser and, hence, protect Microsoft's operating system monopoly. The reason market share in the browser market affects market power in the operating system market is complex, and warrants some explanation.

Browser usage share is important because a browser (or any middleware product, for that matter) must have a critical mass of users in order to attract software developers to write applications relying upon the APIs it exposes, and away from the APIs exposed by Windows. Applications written to a particular browser's APIs, however, would run on any computer with that browser, regardless of the underlying operating system. The overwhelming majority of consumers will only use a PC operating system for which there already exists a large and varied set of applications, and for which it seems relatively certain that new types of applications and new versions of existing applications will continue to be marketed. If a consumer could have access to the applications he desired — regardless of the operating system he uses — simply by installing a particular browser on his computer, then he would no longer feel compelled to select Windows in order to have access to those applications; he could select an operating system other than Windows based solely upon its quality and price. In other words, the market for operating systems would be competitive.

Therefore, Microsoft's efforts to gain market share in one market (browsers) served to meet the threat to Microsoft's monopoly in another market (operating systems) by keeping rival browsers from gaining the critical mass of users necessary to attract developer attention away from Windows as the platform for software development.

The restrictions Microsoft places upon Original Equipment Manufacturers are of particular importance in determining browser usage share because having an OEM pre-install a browser on a computer is one of the two most cost-effective methods by far of distributing browsing software. The District Court found that the restrictions Microsoft imposed in licensing Windows to OEMs prevented many OEMs from distributing browsers other than IE. In particular, the District Court condemned the license provisions prohibiting the OEMs from: (1) removing any desktop icons, folders, or "Start" menu entries; (2) altering the initial boot sequence; and (3) otherwise altering the appearance of the Windows desktop.

The District Court concluded that the first license restriction—the prohibition upon the removal of desktop icons, folders, and Start menu entries—thwarts the distribution of a rival browser by preventing OEMs from removing visible means of user access to IE. The OEMs cannot practically install a second browser in addition to IE, the court found, in part because "[p]re-installing more than one product in a given category . . . can significantly increase an OEM's support costs, for the redundancy can lead to confusion among novice users." That is, a certain number of novice computer users, seeing two browser icons, will wonder which to use when and will call the OEM's support line. Support calls are extremely expensive and, in the highly competitive original equipment market, firms have a strong incentive to minimize costs.

By preventing OEMs from removing visible means of user access to IE, the license restriction prevents many OEMs from pre-installing a rival browser and, therefore, protects Microsoft's monopoly from the competition that middleware might otherwise present. Therefore, we conclude that the license restriction at issue is anticompetitive.

The second license provision at issue prohibits OEMs from modifying the initial boot sequence—the process that occurs the first time a consumer turns on the computer. Prior to the imposition of that restriction, among the programs that many OEMs inserted into the boot sequence were Internet sign-up procedures that encouraged users to choose from a list of IAPs assembled by the OEM." Microsoft's prohibition on any alteration of the boot sequence thus prevents OEMs from using that process to promote the services of IAPs, many of which—at least at the time Microsoft imposed the restriction—used Navigator rather than IE in their internet access software. (Upon learning of OEM practices including boot sequence modification, Microsoft's Chairman, Bill Gates, wrote: "Apparently a lot of OEMs are bundling non-Microsoft browsers and coming up with offerings together with [IAPs] that get displayed on their machines in a FAR more prominent way than MSN or our Internet browser."). Microsoft does not deny that the prohibition on modifying the boot sequence has the effect of decreasing competition against IE by preventing OEMs from promoting rivals' browsers. Because this prohibition has a substantial effect in protecting Microsoft's market power, and does so through a means other than competition on the merits, it is anticompetitive. Again the question whether the provision is nonetheless justified awaits later treatment.

Finally, Microsoft imposes several additional provisions that, like the prohibition on removal of icons, prevent OEMs from making various alterations to the desktop: Microsoft prohibits OEMs from causing any user interface other than the Windows desktop to launch automatically, from adding icons or folders different in size or shape from those supplied by Microsoft, and from using the "Active Desktop" feature to promote third-party brands. These restrictions impose significant costs upon the OEMs; prior to Microsoft's prohibiting the practice, many OEMs would change the appearance of the desktop in ways they found beneficial.

The dissatisfaction of the OEM customers does not, of course, mean the restrictions are anticompetitive. The anticompetitive effect of the license restrictions is, as Microsoft itself recognizes, that OEMs are not able to promote rival browsers, which keeps developers focused upon the APIs in Windows. [Trial Court] Findings of Fact ¶ 212 (quoting Microsoft's Gates as writing, "[w]inning Internet browser share is a very very important goal for us," and emphasizing the need to prevent OEMs from promoting both rival browsers and IAPs that might use rivals' browsers). This kind of promotion is not a zero-sum game; but for the restrictions in their licenses to use Windows, OEMs could promote multiple IAPs and browsers. By preventing the OEMs from doing so, this type of license restriction, like the first two restrictions, is anticompetitive: Microsoft reduced rival browsers' usage share not by improving its own product but, rather, by preventing OEMs from taking actions that could increase rivals' share of usage.

2. Integration of IE and Windows

Although Microsoft's license restrictions have a significant effect in closing rival browsers out of one of the two primary channels of distribution, the District Court found that "Microsoft's executives believed . . . its contractual restrictions placed on OEMs would not be sufficient in themselves to reverse the direction of Navigator's usage share. Consequently, in late 1995 or early 1996, Microsoft set out to bind [IE] more tightly to Windows 95 as a technical matter."

Technologically binding IE to Windows, the District Court found, both prevented OEMs from pre-installing other browsers and deterred consumers from using them. In particular, having the IE software code as an irremovable part of Windows meant that pre-installing a second browser would "increase an OEM's product testing costs," because an OEM must test and train its support staff to answer calls related to every software product preinstalled on the machine; moreover, pre-installing a browser in addition to IE would to many OEMs be "a questionable use of the scarce and valuable space on a PC's hard drive."

Although the District Court, in its Conclusions of Law, broadly condemned Microsoft's decision to bind "Internet Explorer to Windows with technological shackles," its findings of fact in support of that conclusion center upon three specific actions Microsoft took to weld IE to Windows: excluding IE from the "Add/Remove Programs" utility; designing Windows so as in certain circumstances to override the user's choice of a default browser other than IE; and commingling code related to browsing and other code in the same files, so that any attempt to delete the files containing IE would, at the same time, cripple the operating system.

As a general rule, courts are properly very skeptical about claims that competition has been harmed by a dominant firm's product design changes. In a competitive market, firms routinely innovate in the hope of appealing to consumers, sometimes in the process making their products incompatible with those of rivals; the imposition of liability when a monopolist does the same thing will inevitably deter a certain amount of innovation. This is all the more true in a market, such as this one, in which the product itself is rapidly changing. Judicial deference to product innovation, however, does not mean that a monopolist's product design decisions are per se lawful.

The District Court first condemned as anticompetitive Microsoft's decision to exclude IE from the "Add/Remove Programs" utility in Windows 98. Microsoft had included IE in the Add/Remove Programs utility in Windows 95, but when it modified Windows 95 to produce Windows 98, it took IE out of the Add/Remove Programs utility. This change reduces the usage share of rival browsers not by making Microsoft's own browser more attractive to consumers but, rather, by discouraging OEMs from distributing rival products. Because Microsoft's conduct, through something other than competition on the merits, has the effect of significantly reducing usage of rivals' products and hence protecting its own operating system monopoly, it is anticompetitive; we defer for the moment the question whether it is nonetheless justified.

Second, the District Court found that Microsoft designed Windows 98 "so that using Navigator on Windows 98 would have unpleasant consequences for users" by, in some circumstances, overriding the user's choice of a browser other than IE as his or her default browser. Plaintiffs argue that this override harms the competitive process by deterring consumers from using a browser other than IE even though they might prefer to do so, thereby reducing rival browsers' usage share and, hence, the ability of rival browsers to draw developer attention away from the APIs exposed by Windows. Microsoft does not deny, of course, that overriding the user's preference prevents some people from using other browsers. Because the override reduces rivals' usage share and protects Microsoft's monopoly, it too is anticompetitive.

Finally, the District Court condemned Microsoft's decision to bind IE to Windows 98 "by placing code specific to Web browsing in the same files as code that provided operating system functions." Putting code supplying browsing functionality into a file with code supplying operating system functionality ensures that the deletion of any file containing browsing-specific routines would also delete vital operating system routines and thus cripple Windows. As noted above, preventing an OEM from removing IE deters it from installing a second browser because doing so increases the OEM's product testing and support costs; by contrast, had OEMs been able to remove IE, they might have chosen to pre-install Navigator alone.

Microsoft offers no justification for excluding IE from the Add/Remove Programs utility and comingling browser and operating system code. Accordingly, we hold that [this exclusion and commingling] constitute exclusionary conduct, in violation of § 2. Although Microsoft does make some general claims regarding the benefits of integrating the browser and the operating system, it neither specifies nor substantiates those claims. [Yet] the plaintiff bears the burden not only of rebutting a proffered justification but also of demonstrating that the anticompetitive effect of the challenged action outweighs it. In the District Court, plaintiffs appear to have done neither, [so] Microsoft may not be held liable for this aspect of its product design.

3. Agreements with Internet Access Providers

The District Court also condemned as exclusionary Microsoft's agreements with various IAPs The IAPs include both Internet Service Providers, which offer consumers internet access, and Online Services (OLSs) such as America Online (AOL), which offer proprietary content in addition to internet access and other services. The District Court deemed Microsoft's agreements with the IAPs unlawful because:

> Microsoft licensed [IE] and the [IE] Access Kit to hundreds of IAPs for no charge. Then, Microsoft extended valuable promotional treatment to the ten most important IAPs in exchange for their commitment to promote and distribute [IE] and to exile Navigator from the desktop. Finally, in exchange for efforts to upgrade existing subscribers to client software that came bundled with [IE] instead of Navigator, Microsoft granted rebates—and in some cases made outright payments—to those same IAPs.

The District Court condemned Microsoft's actions in (1) offering IE free of charge to IAPs and (2) offering IAPs a bounty for each customer the IAP signs up for service using the IE browser. In effect, the court concluded that Microsoft is acting to preserve its monopoly by offering IE to IAPs at an attractive price. Similarly, the District Court held Microsoft liable for (3) developing the IE Access Kit (IEAK), a software package that allows an IAP to "create a distinctive identity for its service in as little as a few hours by customizing the [IE] title bar, icon, start and search pages," and (4) offering the IEAK to IAPs free of charge, on the ground that those acts, too, helped Microsoft preserve its monopoly. Finally, the District Court found that (5) Microsoft agreed to provide easy access to IAPs' services from the Windows desktop in return for the IAPs' agreement to promote IE exclusively and to keep shipments of internet access software using Navigator under a specific percentage, typically 25%. We address the first four items—Microsoft's inducements—and then its exclusive agreements with IAPs.

Although offering a customer an attractive deal is the hallmark of competition, the Supreme Court has indicated that in very rare circumstances a price may be unlawfully low, or "predatory." Plaintiffs argued before the District Court that Microsoft's pricing was indeed predatory; but instead of making the usual predatory pricing argument—that the predator would drive out its rivals by pricing below cost on a particular product and then, sometime in the future, raise its prices on that product above the competitive level in order to recoup its earlier losses—plaintiffs argued that by pricing below cost on IE (indeed, even paying people to take it),

Microsoft was able simultaneously to preserve its stream of monopoly profits on Windows, thereby more than recouping its investment in below-cost pricing on IE. The District Court did not assign liability for predatory pricing, however, and plaintiffs do not press this theory on appeal.

The rare case of price predation aside, the antitrust laws do not condemn even a monopolist for offering its product at an attractive price, and we therefore have no warrant to condemn Microsoft for offering either IE or the IEAK free of charge or even at a negative price. Likewise, as we said above, a monopolist does not violate the Sherman Act simply by developing an attractive product. Therefore, Microsoft's development of the IEAK does not violate the Sherman Act.

We turn now to Microsoft's deals with IAPs concerning desktop placement. Microsoft concluded these exclusive agreements with all the leading IAPs, including the major OLSs. The most significant of the OLS deals is with AOL, which, when the deal was reached, accounted for a substantial portion of all existing Internet access subscriptions and attracted a very large percentage of new IAP subscribers. Under that agreement Microsoft puts the AOL icon in the OLS folder on the Windows desktop and AOL does not promote any non-Microsoft browser, nor provide software using any non-Microsoft browser except at the customer's request, and even then AOL will not supply more than 15% of its subscribers with a browser other than IE.

In this case, plaintiffs allege that, by closing to rivals a substantial percentage of the available opportunities for browser distribution, Microsoft managed to preserve its monopoly in the market for operating systems. The IAPs constitute one of the two major channels by which browsers can be distributed. Microsoft has exclusive deals with fourteen of the top fifteen access providers in North America which account for a large majority of all Internet access subscriptions in this part of the world. By ensuring that the "majority" of all IAP subscribers are offered IE either as the default browser or as the only browser, Microsoft's deals with the IAPs clearly have a significant effect in preserving its monopoly; they help keep usage of Navigator below the critical level necessary for Navigator or any other rival to pose a real threat to Microsoft's monopoly.

4. Dealings with Internet Content Providers, Independent Software Vendors, and Apple Computer

The District Court held that Microsoft engages in exclusionary conduct in its dealings with ISVs, which develop software; and Apple, which is both an OEM and a software developer. The District Court described Microsoft's deals with ISVs as follows:

> In dozens of "First Wave" agreements signed between the fall of 1997 and the spring of 1998, Microsoft has promised to give preferential support, in the form of early Windows 98 and Windows NT betas, other technical information, and the right to use certain Microsoft seals of approval, to important ISVs that agree to certain conditions. One of these conditions is that the ISVs use Internet Explorer as the default browsing software for

> any software they develop with a hypertext-based user interface. Another condition is that the ISVs use Microsoft's "HTML Help," which is accessible only with Internet Explorer, to implement their applications' help systems.

The District Court further found that the effect of these deals is to ensure that many of the most popular Web-centric applications will rely on browsing technologies found only in Windows, and that Microsoft's deals with ISVs therefore increase the likelihood that the millions of consumers using applications designed by ISVs that entered into agreements with Microsoft will use Internet Explorer rather than Navigator.

The District Court did not specifically identify what share of the market for browser distribution the exclusive deals with the ISVs foreclose. Although the ISVs are a relatively small channel for browser distribution, they take on greater significance because, as discussed above, Microsoft had largely foreclosed the two primary channels to its rivals. In that light, one can tell from the record that by affecting the applications used by "millions" of consumers, Microsoft's exclusive deals with the ISVs had a substantial effect in further foreclosing rival browsers from the market. Because, by keeping rival browsers from gaining widespread distribution (and potentially attracting the attention of developers away from the APIs in Windows), the deals have a substantial effect in preserving Microsoft's monopoly, we hold that plaintiffs have made a *prima facie* showing that the deals have an anticompetitive effect.

Of course, that Microsoft's exclusive deals have the anticompetitive effect of preserving Microsoft's monopoly does not, in itself, make them unlawful. A monopolist, like a competitive firm, may have a perfectly legitimate reason for wanting an exclusive arrangement with its distributors. Accordingly, Microsoft had an opportunity to, but did not, present the District Court with evidence demonstrating that the exclusivity provisions have some such procompetitive justification. On appeal Microsoft likewise does not claim that the exclusivity required by the deals serves any legitimate purpose; instead, it states only that its ISV agreements reflect an attempt to persuade ISVs to utilize Internet-related system services in Windows rather than Navigator. As we explained before, however, keeping developers focused upon Windows — that is, preserving the Windows monopoly — is a competitively neutral goal. Microsoft having offered no procompetitive justification for its exclusive dealing arrangements with the ISVs, we hold that these arrangements violate § 2 of the Sherman Act.

Finally, the District Court held that Microsoft's dealings with Apple violated the Sherman Act. Apple is vertically integrated: it makes both software (including an operating system, Mac OS), and hardware (the Macintosh line of computers). Microsoft primarily makes software, including, in addition to its operating system, a number of popular applications. One, called "Office," is a suite of business productivity applications that Microsoft has ported to Mac OS. The District Court found that ninety percent of Mac OS users running a suite of office productivity applications use Microsoft's Mac Office. Further, the District Court found that:

> In 1997, Apple's business was in steep decline, and many doubted that the company would survive much longer. Many ISVs questioned the wisdom of continuing to spend time and money developing applications for the Mac OS. Had Microsoft announced in the midst of this atmosphere that it was ceasing to develop new versions of Mac Office, a great number of ISVs, customers, developers, and investors would have interpreted the announcement as Apple's death notice.

Microsoft recognized the importance to Apple of its continued support of Mac Office. *See* internal Microsoft e-mail ("[We] need a way to push these guys[, *i.e.*, Apple] and [threatening to cancel Mac Office] is the only one that seems to make them move."); ("[Microsoft Chairman Bill] Gates asked whether Microsoft could conçeal from Apple in the coming month the fact that Microsoft was almost finished developing Mac Office 97."); ("I think . . . Apple should be using [IE] everywhere and if they don't do it, then we can use Office as a club.").

In June 1997 Microsoft Chairman Bill Gates determined that the company's negotiations with Apple "have not been going well at all. . . . Apple let us down on the browser by making Netscape the standard install." Gates then reported that he had already called Apple's CEO to ask "how we should announce the cancellation of Mac Office." The District Court further found that, within a month of Gates' call, Apple and Microsoft had reached an agreement pursuant to which Microsoft's primary obligation is to continue releasing up-to-date versions of Mac Office for at least five years and Apple has agreed to bundle the most current version of IE with Mac OS and to make IE the default browser. The agreement further provides that Navigator is not installed on the computer hard drive during the default installation, which is the type of installation most users elect to employ, and Apple may not position icons for non-Microsoft browsing software on the desktop of new Macintosh PC systems or Mac OS upgrades. The agreement also prohibits Apple from encouraging users to substitute another browser for IE, and states that Apple will encourage its employees to use IE.

This exclusive deal between Microsoft and Apple has a substantial effect upon the distribution of rival browsers. If a browser developer ports its product to a second operating system, such as the Mac OS, it can continue to display a common set of APIs. Thus, usage share, not the underlying operating system, is the primary determinant of the platform challenge a browser may pose. Pre-installation of a browser (which can be accomplished either by including the browser with the operating system or by the OEM installing the browser) is one of the two most important methods of browser distribution, and Apple had a not insignificant share of worldwide sales of operating systems. (Microsoft has 95% of the market not counting Apple and well above 80% with Apple included in the relevant market). Because

Microsoft's exclusive contract with Apple has a substantial effect in restricting distribution of rival browsers, and because (as we have described several times above) reducing usage share of rival browsers serves to protect Microsoft's monopoly, its deal with Apple must be regarded as anticompetitive.

Microsoft offers no procompetitive justification for the exclusive dealing arrangement. It makes only the irrelevant claim that the IE-for-Mac Office deal is part of a multifaceted set of agreements between itself and Apple; that does not mean it has any procompetitive justification. Accordingly, we hold that the exclusive deal with Apple is exclusionary, in violation of § 2 of the Sherman Act.

Notes and Questions

1. Antitrust and "Schumpeterian" Competition. The court cited Joseph Schumpeter in framing the market context for its analysis. Schumpeter is famous for popularizing the phrase "creative destruction" to describe innovation-sensitive markets in which innovators introduce new products that wholly replace legacy markets. How much of this opinion is dependent on a Schumpeterian framework? The court invested several pages describing the operating system market as one characterized by network externalities and rapid technological change. How central is that framing for the court's ruling? Does that framing apply to telecommunications markets, or specifically internet markets, in a way that either highlights or limits the opinion's significance?

2. Antitrust versus Natural Monopoly Regulation. The court was careful to recognize that vertically restrictive arrangements can generate useful efficiencies and therefore can be "perfectly legitimate," even for monopolists. Compare that statement, and the court's subsequent balancing assessment, with the regulatory approach towards vertical dealings described in Chapter 5.C, which were much more categorical and prophylactic. Should vertical arrangements be policed differently for natural versus other monopolists? For telecommunications versus internet monopolists?

3. Rulemaking versus Litigation. The court contrasts the dynamism of software and internet markets with the six-year lag between the targeted conduct and the conclusion of the plodding antitrust litigation. How does that inform the policy debate over using litigation versus rulemaking or other preemptive regulations? Can you find elements in the *Microsoft* decision that, although lamenting the time-consuming litigation, indicates that ex post review of anticompetitive conduct is nonetheless superior to ex ante injunctive tools?

4. A Chicago School or Post-Chicago School Success? Consider the different schools of antitrust thought described in Chapter 2.B (and in particular Questions 4 and 5). How would adherents to the alternative schools view the *Microsoft* ruling?

United States v. Google LLC

No. 1:20-cv-03010 (D.D.C. Jan. 15, 2021)
Amended Complaint

The United States of America, acting under the direction of the Acting Attorney General of the United States, and the States of Arkansas, California, Florida, Georgia, Indiana, Kentucky, Louisiana, Michigan, Mississippi, Missouri, Montana, South Carolina, Texas, and Wisconsin, acting through their respective Attorneys General, bring this action under Section 2 of the Sherman Act, 15 U.S.C. § 2, to restrain Google LLC (Google) from unlawfully maintaining monopolies in the markets for general search services, search advertising, and general search text advertising in the United States through anticompetitive and exclusionary practices, and to remedy the effects of this conduct.

1. Two decades ago, Google became the darling of Silicon Valley as a scrappy startup with an innovative way to search the emerging internet. That Google is long gone. The Google of today is a monopoly gatekeeper for the internet, and one of the wealthiest companies on the planet, with a market value of $1 trillion and annual revenue exceeding $160 billion. For many years, Google has used anticompetitive tactics to maintain and extend its monopolies in the markets for general search services, search advertising, and general search text advertising — the cornerstones of its empire.

2. As in many other businesses, a general search engine must find an effective path to consumers for it to be successful. Today, general search engines are distributed primarily on mobile devices (smartphones and tablets) and computers (desktops and laptops). These devices contain web browsers (software applications for accessing information on the internet) and other "search access points" that call on a general search engine to respond to a user's query. Over the last ten years, internet searches on mobile devices have grown rapidly, eclipsing searches on computers and making mobile devices the most important avenue for search distribution in the United States.

3. For a general search engine, by far the most effective means of distribution is to be the preset default general search engine for mobile and computer search access points. Even where users can change the default, they rarely do. This leaves the preset default general search engine with *de facto* exclusivity. As Google itself has recognized, this is particularly true on mobile devices, where defaults are especially sticky.

4. For years, Google has entered into exclusionary agreements, including tying arrangements, and engaged in anticompetitive conduct to lock up distribution channels and block rivals. Google pays *billions* of dollars each year to distributors — including popular-device manufacturers such as Apple, LG, Motorola, and Samsung; major U.S. wireless carriers such as AT&T, T-Mobile, and Verizon; and browser developers such as Mozilla, Opera, and UCWeb to secure default status for its general search engine and, in many cases, to specifically prohibit Google's counterparties from dealing with Google's competitors. Some of these agreements also

require distributors to take a bundle of Google apps, including its search apps, and feature them on devices in prime positions where consumers are most likely to start their internet searches.

5. Google's exclusionary agreements cover just under 60 percent of all general search queries. Nearly half the remaining queries are funneled through Google owned-and-operated properties (e.g., Google's browser, Chrome). Between its exclusionary contracts and owned-and-operated properties, Google effectively owns or controls search distribution channels accounting for roughly 80 percent of the general search queries in the United States. Largely as a result of Google's exclusionary agreements and anticompetitive conduct, Google in recent years has accounted for nearly 90 percent of all general-search-engine queries in the United States, and almost 95 percent of queries on mobile devices.

6. Google has thus foreclosed competition for internet search. General search engine competitors are denied vital distribution, scale, and product recognition—ensuring they have no real chance to challenge Google. Google is so dominant that "Google" is not only a noun to identify the company and the Google search engine but also a verb that means to search the internet.

7. Google monetizes this search monopoly in the markets for search advertising and general search text advertising, both of which Google has also monopolized for many years. Google uses consumer search queries and consumer information to sell advertising. In the United States, advertisers pay about $40 billion annually to place ads on Google's search engine results page (SERP). It is these search advertising monopoly revenues that Google "shares" with distributors in return for commitments to favor Google's search engine. These enormous payments create a strong disincentive for distributors to switch. The payments also raise barriers to entry for rivals—particularly for small, innovative search companies that cannot afford to pay a multi-billion-dollar entry fee. Through these exclusionary payoffs, and the other anticompetitive conduct described below, Google has created continuous and self-reinforcing monopolies in multiple markets.

8. Google's anticompetitive practices are especially pernicious because they deny rivals scale to compete effectively. General search services, search advertising, and general search text advertising require complex algorithms that are constantly learning which organic results and ads best respond to user queries; the volume, variety, and velocity of data accelerates the automated learning of search and search advertising algorithms. When asked to name Google's biggest strength in search, Google's former CEO explained: "Scale is the key. We just have so much scale in terms of the data we can bring to bear." By using distribution agreements to lock up scale for itself and deny it to others, Google unlawfully maintains its monopolies.

9. Google's grip over distribution also thwarts potential innovation. For example, one company recently started a subscription-based general search engine that does not rely on advertising profits derived from monetizing user information. Another, DuckDuckGo, differentiates itself from Google through its privacy-protective

policies. But Google's control of search access points means that these new search models are denied the tools to become true rivals: effective paths to market and access, at scale, to consumers, advertisers, or data.

10. Google's practices are anticompetitive under long-established antitrust law. Almost 20 years ago, the D.C. Circuit in *United States v. Microsoft* recognized that anticompetitive agreements by a high-tech monopolist shutting off effective distribution channels for rivals, such as by requiring preset default status (as Google does) and making software undeletable (as Google also does), were exclusionary and unlawful under Section 2 of the Sherman Act.

11. Back then, Google claimed Microsoft's practices were anticompetitive, and yet, now, Google deploys the same playbook to sustain its own monopolies. But Google did learn one thing from Microsoft—to choose its words carefully to avoid antitrust scrutiny. Referring to a notorious line from the *Microsoft* case, Google's Chief Economist wrote: "We should be careful about what we say in both public and private. 'Cutting off the air supply' and similar phrases should be avoided." Moreover, as has been publicly reported, Google's employees received specific instructions on what language to use (and not use) in emails because "Words matter. Especially in antitrust law." In particular, Google employees were instructed to avoid using terms such as "bundle," "tie," "crush," "kill," "hurt," or "block" competition, and to avoid observing that Google has "market power" in any market.

12. Google has refused to diverge from its anticompetitive path. Earlier this year, while the United States was investigating Google's anticompetitive conduct, Google entered into agreements with distributors that are *even more* exclusionary than the agreements they replaced. Also, Google has turned its sights to emerging search access points, such as voice assistants, ensuring that they too are covered by the same anticompetitive scheme. And Google is now positioning itself to dominate search access points on the next generation of search platforms: internet-enabled devices such as smart speakers, home appliances, and automobiles (so-called internet-of-things, or IoT, devices).

13. Absent a court order, Google will continue executing its anticompetitive strategy, crippling the competitive process, reducing consumer choice, and stifling innovation. Google is now the unchallenged gateway to the internet for billions of users worldwide. As a consequence, countless advertisers must pay a toll to Google's search advertising and general search text advertising monopolies; American consumers are forced to accept Google's policies, privacy practices, and use of personal data; and new companies with innovative business models cannot emerge from Google's long shadow. For the sake of American consumers, advertisers, and all companies now reliant on the internet economy, the time has come to stop Google's anticompetitive conduct and restore competition.

Notes and Questions

1. Six Years? This suit was filed in 2021, amidst a flurry of other antitrust suits filed against Google (and the other dominant internet platforms). In *Microsoft*, the court lamented, "What is somewhat problematic, however, is that just over six years have passed since Microsoft engaged in the first conduct plaintiffs allege to be anticompetitive. As the record in this case indicates, six years seems like an eternity in the computer industry." Does this suggest that the Sherman Act, at least in the way that it is currently enforced, has deep limitations to policing anticompetitive conduct in internet markets? Or in all markets? It likely is safe to assume that approximately six years will elapse before the Department of Justice obtains relief against Google (if any is obtained at all). What kind of remedy would be useful at that point?

2. *Microsoft*, Part II? Notice the complaint's heavy reliance on the *Microsoft* ruling. The Department of Justice couched this as a *Microsoft* case, where vertical arrangements with smartphone makers and browser developers lock in Google's leadership in the search market. How is the case against Google different from the one against Microsoft? What might be Google's best arguments to counter the application of *Microsoft*?

3. Shoe on the Other Foot? What do you think were Microsoft's leaders' views in 2021 of the *Microsoft* ruling? Might they have been enthusiastic about using it to open search and mobile platform markets?

4. A Presage? Google in Europe. In 2022, the European Union's General Court affirmed the European Commission's conclusion that Google abused its dominant position in internet search and smartphone software markets by entering into restrictive arrangements with mobile phone manufacturers that assured preinstallation of Google search products. Although European competition law differs from U.S. antitrust law in important ways, the specifics of this ruling embraced many theories that motivate the American suit against Google. *See* Judgment of the General Court (Sixth Chamber, Extended Composition) of 14 Sept. 2022, *Google and Alphabet v. Commission*, T-604/18, EU:T:2022:541, https://eur-lex.europa.eu/legal content/EN/TXT/?uri= CELEX:62018TJ0604.

5. Antitrust Enforcement, Big Tech, and Vertical Agreements. At around the time the Department of Justice brought this suit, other antitrust enforcers brought similarly conceived actions against other dominant internet platforms. In 2021, the District of Columbia sued Amazon, claiming the internet retail giant was illegally securing its monopoly through a "Fair Pricing Policy" that prohibited its vendors from selling goods on other platforms at prices lower than those on Amazon (the suit was dismissed in an oral ruling in 2022). Also in 2021, a group of state attorneys general accused Google of forcing restrictive terms on software developers that sell apps on the Google Play Store, the same theory used by Epic in its suit against

Apple. And multiple state and national authorities continued to scrutinize Apple's App Store restrictions even after its victory over Epic (see § 8.A.1). Note that all of these cases claimed that the monopolist-defendant violated the Sherman Act by implementing vertical restraints that secured its market power. Why do you think this is the prevailing theory behind these antitrust actions? Reciprocally, if this is the prevailing approach of enforcers, why do you think internet giants continue to rely so heavily on vertical restraints? Do these cases offer any additional insight to the materials discussed in Chapter 5, especially part 5.C, that detailed the many statutory and regulatory prohibitions preventing telecommunications networks from engaging in vertical agreements?

* * *

Google's conduct has also received scrutiny from the European Commission, which is Europe's antitrust authority. Europe's analog to § 2 of the Sherman Act is Article 102 of the Treaty on the Functioning of the European Union (formerly Article 82 of the Treaty establishing the European Community). Article 102 targets firms with "a dominant position" that engage in "abusive" conduct. Thus, the framework of Article 102 parallels that of § 2 of the Sherman Act, in that liability comes after establishing that a firm (a) has market power, and (b) engages in anticompetitive conduct. But the language differences — "dominant" instead of monopoly" and "abusive" instead of "anticompetitive" — might signal substantive differences between European and American competition law.

Consider the European Commission's ruling below that concluded that Google's presentation of search results violated Article 102. Do you see differences between American and European competition law? More specifically, what precisely was Google doing that the European Commission found objectionable? What harm to competition (if any) was Google causing and what efficiencies (if any) did the Commission consider?

Google Search (Shopping)

Commission Decision, Case AT.39740
(European Commission, June 27, 2017) https://ec.europa.eu
/competition/antitrust/cases/dec_docs/39740/39740_14996_3.pdf

(1) This Decision is addressed to Google Inc. (Google) and to Alphabet Inc. (Alphabet) [Google's parent company].

(2) The Decision establishes that the more favourable positioning and display by Google, in its general search results pages, of its own comparison shopping service compared to competing comparison shopping services (the Conduct) infringes Article 102 of the Treaty on the Functioning of the European Union (Treaty) and Article 54 of the Agreement on the European Economic Area (EEA Agreement).

(7) Google's business model is based on the interaction between the online products and services it offers free of charge and its online advertising services from which it generates the main source of its revenue.

(10) When a user enters a keyword or a string of keywords (a "query") in Google Search, Google's general search results pages return different categories of search results, including generic search results and specialised search results. In addition, Google Search may return a third category of results, namely online search advertisements.

(11) When a user enters a query, Google's programmes essentially run two sets of algorithms: generic search algorithms and specialised search algorithms.

(12) Google's generic search algorithms are designed to rank pages containing any possible content. Google applies these algorithms to all types of pages, including the web pages of competing specialised search services. By contrast, specialised search algorithms "*are specifically optimized for identifying relevant results for a particular type of information*" [citing Google's submission], such as news, local businesses or product information.

(13) The results of these two sets of algorithms — the generic search results and the specialised search results — appear together on Google's general search results pages.

(14) Generic search results typically appear on the left side of Google's general search results pages in the form of blue links with short excerpts ("snippets") in order of their "web rank". Generic search results can link to any page on the internet, including web pages of specialised search services competing with Google's specialised search services.

(17) Google does not charge websites ranked in generic search results on its general search results pages and does not accept any payment that would allow websites to rank higher in these results.

(23) In response to a user query, Google's general search results pages may also return specialised search results from Google's specialised search services. In most instances, specialised search results are displayed with attractive graphical features, such as large scale pictures and dynamic information. Specialised search results in a particular category are positioned within sets referred to by Google as "Universals" or "OneBoxes". They are in most instances positioned above generic search results, or among the first of them.

(26) Google's comparison shopping service is one of Google's specialised search services. In response to queries, it returns product offers from merchant websites, enabling users to compare them.

(27) Google launched the first version of its comparison shopping service in December 2002 in the US under the brand name "Froogle". Froogle operated as a standalone website. Merchants did not have to pay to be listed in Froogle as it was monetised by advertisements. Google launched Froogle in the United Kingdom in October 2004 and in Germany in November 2004.

(28) In April 2007, Google renamed Froogle as "Google Product Search" and subsequently launched along the standalone Google Product Search website a dedicated "Universal" or "OneBox" for Google Product Search, referred to as the "Product

Universal". Google did not, however, change the business model of its comparison shopping service: like Froogle, merchants did not have to pay to be listed in Google Product Search as it was monetised by advertisements.

(31) In May 2012, Google renamed Google Product Search as "Google Shopping" and revamped the Product Universal which was renamed first "Commercial Unit" and then "Shopping Unit". At the same time, Google also changed the business model of its comparison shopping service (both the standalone website and the Universal) to a "paid inclusion" model, in which merchants pay Google when their product is clicked on in Google Shopping, to more closely reflect the industry standard.

(264) The dominant position referred to in Article 102 of the Treaty relates to a position of economic strength enjoyed by an undertaking which enables it to prevent effective competition being maintained on the relevant market by affording it the power to behave to an appreciable extent independently of its competitors, its customers and ultimately of its consumers.

(265) The existence of a dominant position derives in general from a combination of several factors which, taken separately, are not necessarily determinative.

(266) One important factor is the existence of very large market shares, which are in themselves, save in exceptional circumstances, evidence of the existence of a dominant position. An undertaking which holds a very large market share for some time, without smaller competitors being able to meet rapidly the demand from those who would like to break away from that undertaking, is by virtue of that share in a position of strength which makes it an unavoidable trading partner and which, already because of this, secures for it, at the very least during relatively long periods, that freedom of action which is the special feature of a dominant position. That is the case where a company has a market share of 50% or above. Likewise, a share of between 70% and 80% is, in itself, a clear indication of the existence of a dominant position in a relevant market. The ratio between the market share held by the dominant undertaking and that of its nearest rivals is also a highly significant indicator.

(271) The Commission concludes that Google holds a dominant position in each national market for general search services since 2008, apart from in the Czech Republic, where Google holds a dominant position since 2011.

(277) 2010 data by Nielsen (based on page views) indicates that Google's share of the national markets for general search services in 2010 was 84.6% in France, 85.3% in Germany, 85.9% in Italy, 91.3% in Spain and 81.3% in the United Kingdom. None of Google's competitors had a market share exceeding 4.1% in any of these five countries.

(278) November 2014 data by AT Internet (based on site visits) similarly indicates that Google's share of the national markets for general search services in November 2014 was 93.5% in France, 94.1% in Germany, 96.6% in Spain and 92.6% in the United Kingdom. None of Google's competitors had a market share exceeding 3.9% in any of these four countries.

(280) The only European Economic Area (EEA) countries in which Google did not hold a market share above 90% in 2016 were [] the Czech Republic, the United Kingdom and Norway. It should be noted, however, that in those countries, Google was by far the market leader, having overtaken Seznam in the Czech Republic since at least January 2011.

(285) The Commission concludes that the national markets for general search services are characterised by the existence of a number of barriers to entry and expansion.

(286) First, the establishment of a fully-fledged general search engine requires significant investments in terms of time and resources. For example, each year since at least 2009, Microsoft has invested [a significant amount] in R&D and capital expenditure in the development and maintenance of the latest version of its general search engine launched in June 2009 under the brand name "Bing". Other companies indicate that the costs associated with the establishment of a fully-fledged general search engine constitute a barrier to entry. For example, [. . .] argues that it only operates its own general search technology for [. . .] language websites because "*investments are too large to develop such technology for [. . .] language websites*". [. . .] says that "*the incremental costs of converting [. . .] into a viable, competitive broad search service would [. . .] require years of development*". As for [. . .], a company that already has substantial server capacities in place [. . .], it says: "*Investment in equipment and personnel would likely be the primary costs, and they would be very high. In addition, obtaining the large quantity of data necessary to develop an effective [general] search engine (e.g., the information upon which relevancy algorithms can be built and improved) would be a significant barrier to entry*".[3]

(287) Second, because a general search service uses search data to refine the relevance of its general search results pages, it needs to receive a certain volume of queries in order to compete viably. The greater the number of queries a general search service receives, the quicker it is able to detect a change in user behaviour patterns and update and improve its relevance. This is supported by internal Google documents and by evidence from a number of other general search services.

(288) A general search service also needs to receive a certain volume of queries in order to improve the relevance of its results for uncommon ("tail") queries. Tail queries are important because users evaluate the relevance of a general search service on a holistic basis and expect to obtain relevant results for both common ("head") and uncommon tail queries. The greater the volume of data a general search service possesses for rare tail queries, the more users will perceive it as providing more relevant results for all types of queries.

(289) In that regard, there may be diminishing returns to scale in terms of improvements in relevance once the volume of queries a general search service

3. [. . .] reply to [. . .] the Commission's request for information [. . .]. [All ellipses were in the original, as the document redacted the names of the entities that provided these quotations. Eds.]

receives exceeds a certain volume. It may also be that the lower success and relevance of a general search service can be explained by other reasons, such as the fact that it does not localise its search results in different countries, that its web index is more limited in depth, or that it is slower in updating its index in order to deliver fresh content to users. Regardless of the veracity of such arguments, however, they remain of limited relevance for the assessment of barriers to entry and expansion on the national markets for general search services because of the underlying fact that a general search service has to receive at least a certain minimum volume of queries in order to compete viably.

(291) Third, general search services constantly invest to improve their product and a new entrant would have no choice but to attempt to match these investments. The following chart shows worldwide capital investments made by Google and Yahoo in their general search services between 2006 and 2015.

Table 4: Google's and Yahoo's worldwide capital investments (in millions of USD) in their general search services between 2006 and 2015

	2006	2007	2008	2009	2010
Google	1,903	2,403	2,360	809	4,018
Yahoo	689	602	674	433	714
	2011	**2012**	**2013**	**2014**	**2015**
Google	3,438	3,273	7,358	10,959	9,915
Yahoo	593	506	338	372	543

(292) Fourth, the existence of positive feedback effects on both sides of the two-sided platform formed by general search services and online search advertising creates an additional barrier to entry.

(293) The positive feedback effects on the online search advertising side are due to the link between the number of users of a general search service and the value of the online search advertisements shown by that general search engine. The higher the number of users of a general search service, the greater the likelihood that a given search advertisement is matched to a user and converted into a sale. This in turn increases the price that a general search engine can charge advertisers if their search advertisements are clicked on. The general search engine can then reinvest that revenue in seeking to attract new users of its general search service.

(300) Since 2007, there has been only one significant entrant in the national markets for general search services, Microsoft, which launched the latest version of its general search service, Bing, in 2009. Since 2009, however, Bing's market shares have never exceeded 10% in any EEA country.

(306) Contrary to what Google claims, the Commission concludes that notwithstanding the technical ability of users to switch between different general search

services, only a minority of users in the EEA that use Google's general search service as their main general search service use other general search services (a behaviour known as "multi-homing").

(331) Dominant undertakings have a special responsibility not to impair, by conduct falling outside the scope of competition on the merits, genuine undistorted competition in the internal market. A system of undistorted competition can be guaranteed only if equality of opportunity is secured as between the various economic operators. The scope of the special responsibility of the dominant undertaking has to be considered in light of the specific circumstances of the case.

(334) Article 102 of the Treaty and Article 54 of the EEA Agreement prohibit not only practices by an undertaking in a dominant position which tend to strengthen that position, but also the conduct of an undertaking with a dominant position in a given market that tends to extend that position to a neighbouring but separate market by distorting competition. Therefore, the fact that a dominant undertaking's abusive conduct has its adverse effects on a market distinct from the dominated one does not preclude the application of Article 102 of the Treaty or Article 54 of the EEA Agreement. It is not necessary that the dominance, the abuse and the effects of the abuse are all in the same market.

(341) The Commission concludes that the Conduct constitutes an abuse of Google's dominant position in each of the thirteen national markets for general search services where Google either launched the Product Universal or, if the Product Universal was never launched in that market, the Shopping Unit. The Conduct is abusive because it constitutes a practice falling outside the scope of competition on the merits as it: (i) diverts traffic in the sense that it decreases traffic from Google's general search results pages to competing comparison shopping services and increases traffic from Google's general search results pages to Google's own comparison shopping service; and (ii) is capable of having, or likely to have, anticompetitive effects in the national markets for comparison shopping services and general search services.

(344) The Commission concludes that notwithstanding Google's arguments to the contrary, Google positions and displays, in its general search results pages, its own comparison shopping service more favourably compared to competing comparison shopping services. While competing comparison shopping services can appear only as generic search results and are prone to the ranking of their web pages in generic search results on Google's general search results pages being reduced ("demoted") by certain algorithms, Google's own comparison shopping service is prominently positioned, displayed in rich format and is never demoted by those algorithms.

(697) Google and Alphabet should be required to bring the infringement established by this Decision effectively to an end and henceforth refrain from any measure that has the same or an equivalent object or effect.

(699) Any measure chosen by Google and Alphabet should, however, ensure that Google treats competing comparison shopping services no less favourably than

its own comparison shopping service within its general search results pages. The principles mentioned in recital (700) should apply irrespective of whether Google chooses to display a Shopping Unit or another equivalent form of grouping of links to or search results from comparison shopping services.

(700) In particular, any measure chosen by Google and Alphabet:

(a) should apply to all devices, irrespective of the type of device on which the search is performed;

(b) should apply to all users of Google situated in the thirteen EEA countries in which the Conduct takes place, irrespective of the Google domain that they use (including Google.com);

(c) should subject Google's own comparison shopping service to the same underlying processes and methods for the positioning and display in Google's general search results pages as those used for competing comparison shopping services. Such processes and methods should include all elements that have an impact on the visibility, triggering, ranking or graphical format of a search result in Google's general search results pages, including:

- processes and methods or relevance standards determining the triggering of comparison shopping services on the general search results pages in response to a query;
- processes and methods determining the positioning and display of comparison shopping services in response to a query, including relevance standards, ranking algorithms, adjustment or demotion mechanisms and their respective conditions, parameters and signals;
- type of landing pages for clicks on comparison shopping services;
- visual appearance on comparison shopping services and branding possibilities;
- type and granularity of information on the results of comparison shopping services available to users; and
- the possibility of interaction with users.

(d) should not lead to competing comparison shopping services being charged a fee or another form of consideration that has the same or an equivalent object or effect as the infringement established by this Decision.

Notes and Questions

1. Why Only Europe? The Federal Trade Commission considered a similar complaint into Google's self-preferencing search practices but, by a unanimous vote, declined to bring an enforcement action. One FTC Commissioner explained that "Google's display of its own content could plausibly be viewed as an improvement in the overall quality of Google's search product" and that "we have not found sufficient evidence that Google manipulates its search algorithms to unfairly disadvantage vertical websites that compete with Google-owned vertical properties." *See* Google Inc.: Statement of the Federal Trade Commission Regarding Google's Search Practices, FTC File No. 111-0163 (Jan. 3, 2013), https://www.ftc.gov/public-statements/2013/01/statement-commission-regarding-googles-search-practices What do the opposite decisions in the United States and Europe indicate about differences in U.S. and E.U. law? Based on the ruling above, do you think the E.U. rejects the FTC's acceptance that self-preferencing search results can be a quality improvement?

2. Monopoly. The European Commission's case rested upon its finding that Google has a dominant position in the market for "general search services" that exceeded 90%. Under U.S. antitrust law, a market share above 90% would be highly suggestive of monopoly position, *see Aluminum Co. of America*, 148 F.2d at 424 (90% of supply "is enough to constitute a monopoly"). But recall the observation in *Microsoft* that in technologically dynamic markets, competition is usually over sequential markets, not concurrent markets. How does the European Commission address the possibility that a 90% market share in internet search might not reflect monopoly power?

3. A "Special Responsibility." The European Commission stated that "[d]ominant undertakings have a special responsibility not to impair, by conduct falling outside the scope of competition on the merits, genuine undistorted competition in the internal market. A system of undistorted competition can be guaranteed only if equality of opportunity is secured as between the various economic operators." Does this comport with what is reflected in *Syufy Enterprises* (discussed in § 2.B) and Trinko (above in § 8.A.2)? If you think this approach differs from American antitrust law, what consequences would that have for Amazon and Facebook in Europe? Put another way, might Kinderstart.com's claim against Google, discussed in § 5.B.2, have been more successful in Europe?

4. Search Results and the First Amendment. When a search engine responds to a user's query, is it engaged in "speech" for First Amendment purposes under the prevailing jurisprudence, such that regulation of its responses would be subject to judicial scrutiny as a speech regulation? If brought in the United States, would the Google Search case implicate the First Amendment? See Chapter 12 for more.

§ 8.B. Mergers

Merger review is a central part of antitrust law and probably constitutes the lion's share of antitrust practice. The Clayton Act of 1914 prohibits mergers and acquisitions where the effect "may be to substantially lessen competition, or to tend to create a monopoly." 15 U.S.C. § 18. The Hart-Scott-Rodino Act amended the Clayton Act to require companies planning large mergers or acquisitions to notify the government of their plans in advance. So-called "pre-merger review" is now a significant part of antitrust law practice and policy.

Merger review is also an important part of telecommunications policy, and it always has been. Recall from Chapter 4 that the Justice Department filed an antitrust suit in 1913 against Bell to limit its mergers with local carriers, and that part of the "Kingsbury Commitment" (the agreement that settled that case) was an agreement to stop acquiring independent competitors. In an illustration of another facet of merger policy, the Department of Justice in later years approved most of Bell's special applications to acquire local companies, mostly on the grounds that those acquisitions helped resolve inefficient fragmentation of the phone system by non-interconnecting carriers, and in 1921, Congress permanently suspended the non-acquisition provisions of the Kingsbury Commitment and gave the Interstate Commerce Commission authority to exempt telephone company mergers from the antitrust laws. The resulting statute, the Willis-Graham Act, was expressly aimed at eliminating the inefficient fragmentation of the phone system caused by the lack of local interconnection. Willis-Graham Act, Pub. L. No. 67-15, 42 Stat. 27 (1921), *repealed by* Telecommunications Act of 1996, Pub. L. No. 104-104, §601(b)(2), 110 Stat. 56, 143. And of course, the Bell breakup in 1984 was one of the signature moments in U.S. telecommunications policy.

These historical snapshots illustrate why mergers, acquisitions, and general concerns about industry concentration have long been a priority for telecommunications policymakers. The network effects inherent in communications naturally move the market towards singular control (the efficient monopolist) and reveal the inefficiencies of a fragmented, albeit competitive, market. At the same time, those very efficiencies give dominant providers enormous economic and political control over the nation's information networks. Concerns over industry concentration may be of even greater importance as the digital age produces new and faster mechanisms for communication. And notably, today's internet platforms — the networks that currently generate the greatest angst over industrial power — are not readily susceptible to statutory restraints, as the Bell system was, so efforts to restrain their market power might rely on merger policy more than efforts to restrain their telecommunications predecessors.

In this subsection, we review the elements of merger policy in the telecommunications sector which, it must be emphasized, relies on both antitrust law and the Telecommunications Act; on both the FTC and the Justice Department's Antitrust Division as well as the FCC. It begins by describing the institutional framework that supports merger policy in the telecommunications sector, and it articulates the standards that the different agencies apply in scrutinizing acquisitions. It then examines the two prevailing categories of mergers: horizontal mergers, which are mergers of firms that compete in a common market, and vertical mergers, which involve mergers of companies that transact with each other between markets. Although the standard to determine a merger's legality is the same for all mergers, mergers are generally scrutinized as either horizontal or vertical because those merger types present distinct economic challenges. As you go through these materials, we encourage you to bear in mind the central questions we have asked throughout this casebook:

what advantages and disadvantages do ex ante, or prophylactic, policies like premerger review have over ex post remedial measures? How do general legal remedies, such as those expressed in antitrust law, compare to those born out of sector-specific regulation? And more specifically, how does the antitrust approach to consolidation in telecommunications markets compare to the FCC approach?

§ 8.B.1. Institutional and Statutory Landscape

Both the FTC and the Justice Department's Antitrust Division play central roles in merger policy. They review a proposed merger, estimate its likely impact on competition and consumers, and then decide whether to acquiesce, approve, challenge, or investigate further. The agencies also publish merger guidelines that convey how the agencies review mergers and which mergers are likely to be challenged. The guidelines are critical policy instruments and sometimes are even given the force of law in court opinions. Illustrative of how horizontal and vertical mergers present distinct problems, the agencies issue Horizontal Merger Guidelines and Vertical Merger Guidelines separately. Also illustrative of their differences and the economics that underlie each, the Vertical Merger Guidelines have been revised more frequently, usually following a change in party control of the White House, than the Horizontal Merger Guidelines. *See* U.S. Dept. of Justice & FTC, Horizontal Merger Guidelines, revised April 8, 1997, https://www.justice.gov/atr/horizontal-merger-guidelines-0; U.S. Dept. of Justice & FTC, Vertical Merger Guidelines, revised June 30, 2020, https://www.ftc.gov/system/files/documents/reports/us-department-justice-federal-trade-commission-vertical-merger-guidelines/vertical_ merger_guidelines_6-30-20.pdf.

The FCC also plays an important role in merger policy in the telecommunications sector. Historically, the FCC's primary merger-related role was its authority to exempt local telephone company mergers from antitrust scrutiny. Prior to the Telecommunications Act of 1996, the FTC could exempt mergers from standard antitrust review and thus could trump both the Department of Justice and the FTC. The 1996 Act removed that preemptive role but preserved the FCC's role in merger policy in §§ 214(a) and 310(d). Section 214(a) requires the FCC to certify that any acquisition of lines by a common carrier will serve the present and future "public convenience and necessity." Similarly, no transfer of a spectrum license can occur without a finding by the FCC that the transfer will serve the "public interest, convenience, and necessity." 47 U.S.C. § 310(d).[4] The FCC thus has the authority and indeed the obligation to review transfers of licenses that are part of a proposed merger or acquisition.

---

4. The FCC also retains merger authority under the Clayton Antitrust Act, which grants the FCC concurrent jurisdiction with the Justice Department to act on transactions among "common carriers engaged in wire or radio communications." 15 U.S.C. § 21. The FCC has not availed itself of this authority, however, because it instead reviews transactions under its § 310(d) public interest authority.

Therefore, both the antitrust agencies and the FCC have concurrent jurisdiction for most proposed acquisitions in the telecommunications sector, but they operate those authorities under different standards. As we shall see, the FCC's "public interest" standard and the antitrust "substantially lessen competition" standard can reflect both overlapping and conflicting policy values. We sampled the antitrust standard and its focus on economic welfare in Chapter 2, in *United States v. Syufy Enterprises*, 903 F.2d 659 (9th Cir. 1990) ("We make it clear today, if it was not before, that an efficient, vigorous, aggressive competitor is not the villain antitrust laws are aimed at eliminating. Fostering an environment where businesses fight it out using the weapon of efficiency and consumer goodwill is what the antitrust laws are meant to champion."). Consider how the FCC explained its review of mergers under the public interest standard.

Applications of Comcast Corp., General Electric Co., and NBC Universal, Inc. for Consent to Assign Licenses and Transfer Control of Licensees

Memorandum Opinion and Order, 26 FCC Rcd. 4238 (2011)

IV. Standard of Review and Public Interest Framework

22. Pursuant to Section 310(d) of the Act, we must determine whether the proposed assignment and transfer of control of certain licenses and authorizations held and controlled by Comcast and NBCU will serve "the public interest, convenience, and necessity." In making this determination, we must assess whether the proposed transaction complies with the specific provisions of the Act, other applicable statutes, and the Commission's Rules. If the transaction would not violate a statute or rule, the Commission considers whether a grant could result in public interest harms by substantially frustrating or impairing the objectives or implementation of the Act or related statutes. The Commission then employs a balancing test, weighing any potential public interest harms of the proposed transaction against any potential public interest benefits. The Applicants bear the burden of proving, by a preponderance of the evidence, that the proposed transaction, on balance, serves the public interest. If we are unable to find that the proposed transaction serves the public interest for any reason, or if the record presents a substantial and material question of fact, we must designate the Application for hearing.

23. Our public interest evaluation necessarily encompasses the "broad aims of the Communications Act," Michael Katz, Jonathan Orszag, & Theresa Sullivan, An Economic Analysis of Consumer Harm from the Current Retransmission Consent Regime, Nov. 12, 2009, at ¶¶ 30–36, which include, among other things, a deeply rooted preference for preserving and enhancing competition in relevant markets, accelerating private-sector deployment of advanced services, ensuring a diversity of information sources and services to the public, and generally managing spectrum in the public interest. Our public interest analysis may also entail assessing

whether the transaction will affect the quality of communications services or will result in the provision of new or additional services to consumers. In conducting this analysis, the Commission may consider technological and market changes as well as trends within the communications industry, including the nature and rate of change.

24. Our competitive analysis, which forms an important part of the public interest evaluation, is informed by but not limited to traditional antitrust principles. The DOJ reviews communications transactions pursuant to Section 7 of the Clayton Act, and if it wishes to block a transaction, it must demonstrate to a court that the transaction may substantially lessen competition or tend to create a monopoly. The Commission's competitive analysis under the public interest standard is somewhat broader. For example, the Commission considers whether a transaction will enhance, rather than merely preserve, existing competition, and often takes a more expansive view of potential and future competition in analyzing that issue.

25. Our analysis recognizes that a proposed transaction may have both beneficial and harmful consequences. Our public interest authority enables us, where appropriate, to impose and enforce transaction-related conditions targeted to ensure that the public interest is served by the transaction. Section 303(r) of the Act authorizes the Commission to prescribe restrictions or conditions, not inconsistent with the law, which may be necessary to carry out the provisions of the Act. Indeed, unlike the role of antitrust enforcement authorities, our public interest authority enables us to rely upon our extensive regulatory and enforcement experience to impose and enforce conditions to ensure that a transaction will yield overall public interest benefits. In exercising this broad authority, the Commission generally has imposed conditions to confirm specific benefits or remedy specific harms likely to arise from transactions and that are related to the Commission's responsibilities under the Act and related statutes.

Notes and Questions

1. A Flexible Standard. The FCC has elsewhere interpreted its public interest standard to be "a flexible one that encompasses the broad aims of the Communications Act." Applications of Teleport Commc'ns Grp. Inc., Transferor, & AT&T Corp., Transferee, for Consent to Transfer of Control of Corps. Holding Point-to-Point Microwave Licenses and Authorizations to Provide Int'l Facilities-Based and Resold Commc'ns Servs., Memorandum Opinion and Order, 13 FCC Rcd. 15,236, 15,242, ¶ 11 (1998) (internal quotation marks omitted). In judging common carrier mergers, the FCC has typically focused on competition issues and FCC goals regarding the equitable build-out of new services. Meanwhile, in transactions involving broadcast licenses, the FCC has typically focused on issues related to diversity (which has been defined in different ways, see Chapter 10.C). Importantly, however, under the public interest standard as interpreted by the FCC, the FCC need not show that a transaction is likely to reduce competition in order to challenge that transaction. Under the "broad aims" of the Act, the FCC could instead decide that a merger might affect any of the Act's goals (as the FCC interprets them) and, for any of those reasons, block, condition, or approve a transaction regardless of its competitive effects.

2. Different from Antitrust Review? The most obvious difference between the FCC's review of proposed transactions and those by the antitrust agencies is the flexible standard. Whereas antitrust review ostensibly involves only an assessment of the transaction's economic impact, the FCC's "in the public interest" standard clearly invites non-economic considerations.

Other differences should be appreciated as well. One might think from the excerpt above that the FCC would impose more demanding scrutiny to proposed transactions than the antitrust agencies. First, it stated that the petitioners have the burden of proof that the transaction is in the public interest, whereas the antitrust agencies have the burden to prove that a particular transaction harms competition. And second, the excerpt indicated that petitioners before the FCC must prove that the transaction will enhance competition, whereas antitrust agencies must prove that the transaction will harm competition.

In reality, however, it is not clear that these standards are in effect. Here is how one former FCC Commissioner, who previously had worked in the DOJ Antitrust Division, contrasted the two agencies' merger review procedures:

> Here's how things work at the Department of Justice. Parties submit pre-merger notification documents pursuant to the Hart-Scott-Rodino (HSR) Act. Of particular importance, they submit what are known in the antitrust world as "4(c)" and "4(d)" documents—materials that shed light on how the merging parties themselves see the effects of the proposed deal. The Division staff review the HSR documents, especially the 4(c) and 4(d) documents, and determine whether more searching scrutiny is required. If it is, the Division issues what is known as a "second request," a more detailed request for documents. Ultimately, the Division staff analyze all the evidence and soberly detail the aspects of a transaction. What is the product or service market? What is the geographic market? Who are the competitors? What are their market shares? What effect would consummation of the transaction have on competition? What are the competitive harms? Are there efficiencies that might be recognized? Could the combined entity engage in vertical restraints of trade? Are any divestitures necessary in instances of horizontal overlap? And so on. The career staff determine what the resolution should be and make a recommendation to the Assistant Attorney General of the Antitrust Division. Based on that recommendation, the Assistant Attorney General then decides upon the Justice Department's approach to the deal. And the Justice Department is accountable to the courts should it seek to block a merger or impose conditions. This professional process has been well-established for decades.

> Here's how things work at the Federal Communications Commission. Parties file the requisite notification papers. Then, they wait for the FCC to start the 180-day "shot clock," which kicks off the agency's review and sets the aspirational deadline for decision. (Sometimes, the parties feel compelled to hire a politically connected insider to help get that clock started.) Once the shot clock starts, the staff's review begins. Unlike at the Department of Justice, the process is politicized from the beginning; the FCC staff report to the Chairman's Office and are often overseen directly by someone loyal to the Chairman's Office. Separately, and more significantly, the parties are required to negotiate behind closed doors with the Chairman's Office or Office of General Counsel (which, again, reports directly to the Chairman's Office) on conditions to be attached to the deal. Months can go by without any transparency, internal or external, regarding the ornaments that the Chairman's Office is seeking to place on the Christmas tree. Even Commissioners have no insight as a matter of right, and parties have told me that they are explicitly warned not to tell anyone else at the Commission about the conditions the Chairman's Office is seeking. And when it comes to those conditions, there is no need for them to be relevant to the merger ("merger-specific," in antitrust parlance). Indeed, that's often why the Commission blows so far past the ill-named "shot clock"; it takes time to get the parties to "voluntarily" submit to the forced extraction of every ounce of extraneous "value." Once the Chairman's Office agrees with the parties on what the resolution will be, FCC staff write an order implementing the Chairman's deal. That order is then sent to other Commissioners' offices, with the Chairman's favorable vote sending the unmistakable message that the order is a fait accompli—take it or leave it, with perhaps a little latitude to accommodate a few more goodies requested by a member of the majority.

Dissenting Statement of Commissioner Ajit Pai, 31 FCC Rcd. 6,327, 6,666–70 (2016) Applications of Charter Communications Inc., TWC, and Advance/Newhouse Partnership for Consent to Assign or Transfer Control of Licenses and Authorizations.

Is what Commissioner Pai (later in his statement) called "fact-free, dilatory, politically motivated, non-transparent decision-making" inevitable under a flexible standard? Recall similar debates, discussed in Chapter 2 and highlighted in part 2.B, over whether the Sherman Act should advance non-economic values.

§ 8.B.2. Horizontal Mergers

As was discussed above, the FTC and the DOJ's Antitrust Division review mergers based on whether the proposed transactions may, in the language of the Clayton Act, "substantially lessen competition, or tend to create a monopoly." 15 U.S.C. § 18. And, also discussed above, to offer guidance to would-be merging parties and to make transparent their internal review process, the agencies disseminate merger guidelines that specify how they evaluate acquisitions and outline their enforcement policies.

The Horizontal Merger Guidelines are used for any acquisition with horizontal elements, that is, any combination of firms that compete within the same market at the time of the proposed merger. The guidelines describe the agencies' analytical process in determining whether to challenge a horizontal merger as follows:

> First, the Agency assesses whether the merger would significantly increase concentration and result in a concentrated market, properly defined and measured. Second, the Agency assesses whether the merger, in light of market concentration and other factors that characterize the market, raises concern about potential adverse competitive effects. Third, the Agency assesses whether entry would be timely, likely, and sufficient either to deter or to counteract the competitive effects of concern. Fourth, the Agency assesses any efficiency gains that reasonably cannot be achieved by the parties through other means. Finally the Agency assesses whether, but for the merger, either party to the transaction would be likely to fail, causing its assets to exit the market. The process of assessing market concentration, potential adverse competitive effects, entry, efficiency and failure is a tool that allows the Agency to answer the ultimate inquiry in merger analysis: whether the merger is likely to create or enhance market power or to facilitate its exercise.

Horizontal Merger Guidelines, revised April 8, 1997, https://www.justice.gov/atr/horizontal-merger-guidelines-0.

The meat of this five-step process lies in the first two steps: defining the relevant market and then assessing post-merger market concentration. As we observed in *FTC v. Facebook* and *Epic v. Apple*, *see* § 9.A.1, defining the proper market is both complicated and critical in properly assessing the economic consequences of a merger. It can also be deceptively difficult, as the proposed merger between Sirius Satellite Radio and XM Satellite Radio — discussed below — illustrated. We first offer a popular description of the merger analysis and then share the Antitrust Division's conclusion after its review.

Satellite Sisters: XM and Sirius Satellite Radio Merger

James Surowiecki, The New Yorker (March 12, 2007)

When the satellite-radio companies XM and Sirius announced, last month, that they were planning to merge, it looked like a futile attempt to flout antitrust regulations. The merger would benefit Sirius and XM — which, despite signing high-profile figures like Howard Stern and Bob Dylan, have cumulatively lost close to seven billion dollars — but it would confront radio listeners with a satellite-radio monopoly. Not surprisingly, then, when Sirius's C.E.O., Mel Karmazin, appeared before Congress to defend his plans, he was grilled by legislators convinced that regulators would block the merger.

The XM-Sirius deal looks sketchy, since monopolies created by merger are usually bad for consumers. So why does the deal have any chance at all? It comes down to the question of what market XM and Sirius are in. If it's just satellite radio, then they are competing only with each other and the deal would be sure to send prices soaring. But it makes more sense to see XM and Sirius as part of the bigger radio and digital audio markets and thus in competition with AM/FM, HD, and Internet radio. In that case, even a merged company would have only a small percentage of radio listeners, and competition would limit its ability to raise prices.

Consumers, then, have little to fear from a merged satellite company in the radio market, and they may actually have a lot to gain. Dominated by chains like Clear Channel, AM/FM radio has become a catalogue of bland choices, pre-programmed playlists, and syndicated talk. A recent study by the Future of Music Coalition found that four companies received fifty per cent of all radio advertising revenue and had nearly fifty per cent of all listeners. Even among competitors, there is often tremendous overlap in music playlists; in this environment, XM and Sirius, which offer real diversity across three hundred channels, are a gain for consumer choice. And there's no reason to think that this diversity would ebb after a merger; no one wants to pay thirteen dollars a month to hear the same songs he could have got free from his local KISS-FM.

The National Association of Broadcasters, which represents commercial radio stations, has lobbied hard against the deal, arguing that XM and Sirius compete only with each other. But the very fact that broadcasters are fighting the merger demonstrates that they view Sirius and XM as a threat. Similarly, for fifteen years AM/FM stations have done everything they could to cripple satellite radio, lobbying the F.C.C. to stop its roll-out in the nineteen-nineties and persistently trying to limit the types of programming XM and Sirius can carry. Just last month, a bill was introduced in Congress — for the third time in as many years — that would bar satellite stations from providing local traffic and weather.

Broadcasters understand that a merger between Sirius and XM would help extend satellite radio's reach, making it a more formidable competitor. Many consumers have hesitated to subscribe to satellite because they didn't know which company would survive. And desirable content is split between the companies: if you want major-league baseball and Bob Edwards, you need XM, but if you want N.F.L. games and Howard Stern, you need Sirius. Allowing Sirius and XM to merge would eliminate this problem in one stroke. And that would significantly increase the competitive pressure on traditional radio stations, perhaps forcing them to abandon their cookie-cutter model. Paradoxically, by reducing choice you could stimulate more diversity. Sometimes, it seems, you can have fewer competitors but more competition.

Statement of the Department of Justice Antitrust Division on Its Decision to Close Its Investigation of XM Satellite Radio Holdings Inc.'s Merger with Sirius Satellite Radio Inc.

Press Release, DOJ (Mar. 24, 2008)
http://www.usdoj.gov/opa/pr/2008/March/08_at_226.html

After a careful and thorough review of the proposed transaction, the Division concluded that the evidence does not demonstrate that the proposed merger of XM and Sirius is likely to substantially lessen competition, and that the transaction therefore is not likely to harm consumers.

Analysis

Extent of Likely Future Competition between XM and Sirius

The Division's analysis considered the extent to which the two satellite radio providers compete with one another. Although the firms in the past competed to attract new subscribers, there has never been significant competition between them for customers who have already subscribed to one or the other service and purchased the requisite equipment. Also, competition for new subscribers is likely to be substantially more limited in the future than it was in the past.

As to existing subscribers, the Division found that satellite radio equipment sold by each company is customized to each network and will not function with the other service. XM and Sirius made some efforts to develop an interoperable radio capable of receiving both sets of satellite signals. Depending on how such a radio would be configured, it could enable consumers to switch between providers without incurring the costs of new equipment. The Division's investigation revealed, however, that no such interoperable radio is on the market and that such a radio likely would not be introduced in the near term. Data analyzed by the Division confirmed that subscribers rarely switch between XM and Sirius.

As to new subscribers, XM and Sirius sell satellite radios and service primarily through two distribution channels: (1) car manufacturers that install the equipment in new cars and (2) mass-market retailers that sell automobile aftermarket equipment and other stand-alone equipment. Car manufacturers account for an increasingly large portion of XM and Sirius sales, and the parties have focused more and more of their resources on attracting subscribers through the car manufacturer channel. However, XM and Sirius have entered into sole-source contracts with all the major automobile manufacturers that fix the amount of these subsidies and other pertinent terms through 2012 or beyond. Moreover, there was no evidence that competition between XM or Sirius beyond the terms of these contracts would affect customers' choices of which car to buy. As a result, there is not likely to be significant competition between XM and Sirius for satellite radio equipment and service sold through the car manufacturer channel for many years.

The Division's investigation identified the mass-market retail channel as an arena in which XM and Sirius would compete with one another for the foreseeable future. Both XM and Sirius devote substantial effort and expense to attracting subscribers in this arena, with both companies offering discounts, most commonly in the form of equipment rebates, to attract consumers. Retail channel sales have dropped significantly since 2005, and the parties contended that the decline was accelerating. However, retail outlets still account for a large portion of the firms' sales, and the Division was unable to determine with any certainty that this channel would not continue to be important in the future.

Effect on Competition in the Retail Channel

Because XM and Sirius would no longer compete with one another in the retail channel following the merger, the Division examined what alternatives, if any, were available to consumers interested in purchasing satellite radio service, and specifically whether the relevant market was limited to the two satellite radio providers, such that their combination would create a monopoly. The parties contended that they compete with a variety of other sources of audio entertainment, including traditional AM/FM radio, HD Radio, MP3 players (e.g., iPods®), and audio offerings delivered through wireless telephones.

The Division found that evidence developed in the investigation did not support defining a market limited to the two satellite radio firms, and similarly did not establish that the combined firm could profitably sustain an increased price to satellite radio consumers. XM and Sirius seek to attract subscribers in a wide variety of ways, including by offering commercial-free music (with digital sound quality), exclusive programming (such as Howard Stern on Sirius and "Oprah & Friends" on XM), niche music formats, out-of-market sporting events, and a variety of news and talk formats in a service that is accessible nationwide. The variety of these offerings reflects an effort to attract consumers with highly differentiated interests and tastes. Thus, while the satellite radio offerings of XM and Sirius likely are the closest substitutes for some current or potential customers, the two offerings do not appear to be the closest substitutes for other current or potential customers. For example, a potential customer considering purchasing XM service primarily to listen to Major League Baseball games or one considering purchasing Sirius service primarily to listen to Howard Stern may not view the other satellite radio service, which lacks the desired content, as a particularly close substitute. Similarly, many customers buying radios in the retail channel are acquiring an additional receiver to add to an existing XM or Sirius subscription for their car radio, and these customers likely would not respond to a price increase by choosing a radio linked to the other satellite radio provider. The evidence did not demonstrate that the number of current or potential customers that view XM and Sirius as the closest alternatives is large enough to make a price increase profitable. Importantly in this regard, the parties do not appear to have the ability to identify and price discriminate against those actual or potential customers that view XM and Sirius as the closest substitutes.

Likely Efficiencies

To the extent there were some concerns that the combined firm might be able profitably to increase prices in the mass-market retail channel, efficiencies flowing from the transaction likely would undermine any such concern. The Division's investigation confirmed that the parties are likely to realize significant variable and fixed cost savings through the merger. It was not possible to estimate the magnitude of the efficiencies with precision due to the lack of evidentiary support provided by XM and Sirius, [but] the merger is likely to allow the parties to consolidate development, production and distribution efforts on a single line of radios and thereby eliminate duplicative costs and realize economies of scale. These efficiencies alone likely would be sufficient to undermine an inference of competitive harm.

Effect of Technological Change

Any inference of a competitive concern was further limited by the fact that a number of technology platforms are under development that are likely to offer new or improved alternatives to satellite radio. Most notable is the expected introduction within several years of next-generation wireless networks capable of streaming Internet radio to mobile devices. [C]onsumers are likely to have access to new alternatives, including mobile broadband Internet devices, by the time the current long-term contracts between the parties and car manufacturers expire.

Notes and Questions

1. Internal Contradictions? The DOJ stated in the introduction that it found no evidence that the merger will substantially lessen competition. The DOJ later stated that XM and Sirius devoted "substantial effort" to competing with each other in the mass-market retail channel, a channel whose future importance the DOJ could not discount. Did the Antitrust Division reconcile its overall conclusion of no harm to competition with the harm to competition in the mass-market retail channel? If so, how?

2. Intermodal Competition. The DOJ concluded, and the Surowiecki column suggested, that "satellite radio" was not a market in and of itself because it competed with AM/FM radio, HD radio, MP3 players, and audio offerings delivered through wireless telephones. What else might be in this expansive market? Audiobooks? Podcasts? Personal recordings? At what point does the market become so expansive that no merger could ever be found to have attained market power?

3. Betting on Innovation. The DOJ's conclusion relied, in part, on future technological events that it believed would transform the marketplace in which satellite radio operated. On what technologies did the DOJ rely, and upon what evidence did it do so? And if the new technologies are attractive, why did they rely on this merger to develop? Should the DOJ decide mergers based on the prospects of technologies it finds attractive?

4. Hard to Assess. As the DOJ noted, closing statements like the one above are short on factual specifics, often due to confidentiality concerns for both the merging parties and third-party witnesses. This makes closing statements hard to assess, although one can wonder whether, on key points like market definition and innovation, the DOJ could have provided more public facts to make their analysis more convincing. Do you think the merger review process, despite confidentiality concerns, should be more transparent? Or should these closing statements, or other merger settlements, be subject to additional review? What would be the costs and benefits of introducing more transparency or scrutiny to mergers that the agencies decide not to challenge?

5. Merger of Monopolies? Recall from Chapter 4 that antitrust litigation led to the breakup of AT&T and the creation of seven regional Baby Bells. In the late 1990s, those Baby Bells started to merge with each other, first with the merger of Texas-based SBC and California-based Pacific Telesis (the combination included five other southwestern states) and then a merger of New York-based NYNEX and Pennsylvania-based Bell Atlantic (which included eleven other states). In both cases, the Antitrust Division offered little scrutiny and issued prompt approvals. How could antitrust law allow these mergers, especially when each of the LECs involved enjoyed regional monopolies?

* * *

After the DOJ concluded its investigation, the FCC approved the XM/Sirius merger later in 2008. The FCC approval came with several conditions: that the merged company cap prices for three years, that it set aside 8% of its channel capacity for minority and noncommercial programming, and that it pay nearly $20 million in fines for past violations of FCC rules. Applications for Consent to the Transfer of Control of Licenses: XM Satellite Radio Holdings Inc., Transferor, to Sirius Satellite Radio Inc., Transferee, Memorandum Opinion and Order and Report and Order, 23 FCC Rcd. 12,348 (2008). Examine the statement below and contrast the FCC's approach with the DOJ's Antitrust Division.

Commission Approves Transaction between Sirius Satellite Radio Holdings Inc. and XM Satellite Radio Holdings, Inc. Subject to Conditions

Press Release, FCC (July 28, 2008), 2008 WL 2902112

On July 25, 2008, the Commission voted to approve the application of Sirius Satellite Radio Inc. (Sirius) and XM Satellite Radio Holdings Inc. (XM; jointly, the Applicants) to transfer control of the licenses and authorizations held by Sirius and XM and their subsidiaries for the provision of satellite digital audio radio service (or SDARS) in the United States. The Commission found that grant of the application, with the voluntary commitments made by the Applicants and other conditions, is in the public interest. The transaction will benefit consumers by making available to them a wider array of programming choices at various price points and by affording them greater choice and control over the programming to which they subscribe.

Highlights of the Commission's action are noted below:

- After reviewing the empirical data available as part of its competitive analysis, the Commission determined there was insufficient evidence in the record to predict the likelihood of anticompetitive harms. It therefore evaluated the application under "worst-case" assumptions, i.e., that the relevant market is limited to SDARS. This approach permitted the Commission to protect consumers from potential adverse effects of the transaction while also allowing the Commission to balance potential harms against potential public interest benefits. The Commission concluded that the merger, absent the Applicants' voluntary commitments and other conditions, would result in potential harms. With those commitments and conditions to mitigate the harms, however, the Commission found the transaction to be in the public interest. All of the voluntary commitments must continue in effect at least three years after consummation of the merger.
- The Commission accepted the Applicants' voluntary commitments to:
    - Cap prices for 36 months after consummation of the transaction, subject to certain cost pass-throughs after one year. In addition, six months prior to the end of commitment period, the Commission will seek public comment on whether the cap continues to be necessary in the public interest and will determine whether it should be extended, removed, or modified. The merger approval is conditioned on the Commission's ability to modify or extend the price cap beyond the three-year commitment period.
    - Offer to consumers, within three months of consummation of the transaction, the ability to receive a number of new programming packages, including the ability to select programming on an a la carte basis.
    - Make available 4 percent of its capacity for use by certain Qualified Entities, and an additional 4 percent of capacity for the delivery of noncommercial educational or informational (NCE) programming, which will enhance the diversity of programming available to consumers.
    - Offer interoperable receivers in the "retail after-market," i.e., receivers available at retail outlets for installation in consumers' automobiles or homes, within nine months of consummation of the merger.
    - Refrain from entering into any agreement that would grant an equipment manufacturer an exclusive right to manufacture, market, and sell SDARS receivers. Applicants also commit to refrain from barring any manufacturer from including in any receiver non-interfering hybrid digital terrestrial radio functionality, iPod compatibility, or other audio technology. In addition, Applicants commit to make available the intellectual property needed to allow any device manufacturer to develop equipment that can deliver SDARS.
    - File the applications needed to provide Sirius satellite service to Puerto Rico via terrestrial repeaters within three months of the consummation of the merger.

- Although the Commission found it unnecessary to impose a condition requiring the inclusion of hybrid digital radio technology in SDARS receivers, it recognized that important questions have been raised about hybrid digital radio that warrant further examination in a separate proceeding. The Commission therefore committed to initiating a notice of inquiry within 30 days after adoption of the merger order to gather additional information on the issues.
- The Commission reiterated that SDARS licensees are already prohibited, independent of the merger, from using terrestrial repeaters to distribute local content—including both programming and advertising—that is distinct from that provided to subscribers nationwide via satellite.
- The Commission prohibited the merged entity from entering into agreements that would bar any terrestrial radio station from broadcasting live local sporting events.

Notes and Questions

1. "Worst-Case" Assumptions. The FCC agreed with the DOJ that there was insufficient evidence to show a likelihood of harmful effects. The agency then said it would therefore review the merger under "worst-case" assumptions. In some ways this is startling: Was the FCC saying that even absent likelihood of harm, it would challenge or condition a merger to address the worst possible outcome of the transaction? If so, by what standard will this "worst-case" assumption be judged? Must it be reasonably supported by the evidence? Merely plausible? It is unimaginable that in a trial, even a civil one, legal liability would be explicitly determined by the worst possible interpretation of the facts as opposed to the interpretation supported by the preponderance of the evidence. Under what authority or logic was the FCC allowing itself to proceed under an assumption of harm from the merger even while acknowledging that the evidence did not support the likelihood of harm?

2. The Pricing Condition. One might argue that the FCC's worst-case assumption was just a reasonable way to protect consumers in the face of an uncertain prediction about the effects of the merger. In that light, the three-year pricing cap might not look so bad even if imposed under a worst-case assumption. Although the evidence did not allow the agencies to predict that the merger would *likely* lead to price increases, neither did it rule out the possibility that such effects *could* occur. So perhaps the FCC was just using its ability to obtain a pricing commitment from the parties to protect the public interest. What do you think of that interpretation and its implications for the FCC's role in merger review?

3. What Interests Is the FCC Advancing? If the motivation behind the pricing condition is to find a backstop to the market analysis (i.e., safeguarding the FCC in case of a miscalculation), what is the motivation behind the channel set-aside condition? Is this condition motivated by a market failure justification? Or by any of the justifications for regulation we discuss in Chapter 1?

§ 8.B.3. Vertical Mergers

Whereas the Horizontal Merger Guidelines are used for any acquisition with horizontal elements, the Vertical Merger Guidelines are used for those without any horizontal elements, i.e., elements of merging firms that are not within the same market and do not directly compete with each other.

Many antitrust scholars, particularly those in the Chicago School, believe that strictly vertical mergers should receive minimal, if any, scrutiny. One reason is precisely because they do not contain any horizontal elements and thus do not increase the concentration of any particular market. Other reasons are that vertical integration generates efficiencies that are hard to measure, and that alleged fears of vertical foreclosure — the primary harm that motivated many of the regulations discussed in Chapter 5 — are overstated. Recent scholarship has questioned the Chicago School's assurances that vertical mergers require little policing, but so long as both scholarly and political consensus remains elusive, the Vertical Merger Guidelines find themselves revised whenever party control of the White House changes.

The Vertical Merger Guidelines identify potential harms to competition that might arise from the combination of non-horizontal firms. They do not map out a systematic analytical process like their horizontal counterparts do, nor do they offer similarly detailed guidance. Perhaps that is because the impact of vertical mergers is highly contextual and can present an assortment of competitive benefits as well as competitive harms. It is revealing, therefore, that many of the most prominent challenges to vertical mergers have taken place in the telecommunications sector. It is also striking that even though vertical mergers provoke limited alarm in most antitrust regulators, telecommunications law includes a variety of prohibitions on vertical acquisitions and vertical restraints (see Chapter 5).

This subsection details agency scrutiny of three vertical mergers: Comcast's acquisition of NBC Universal, AT&T's acquisition of Time Warner, and News Corp.'s acquisition of DirecTV. Echoing many of the themes in Chapter 5, the concern the agencies expressed regarding these mergers involved a fear that a vertically integrated distributor would use content to harm competition with other distributors. Consider the economic arguments regarding each merger, the view of emerging technologies that shape those views, and what might be the ideal regulatory framework to examine them.

Comcast/NBCU Acquisition

Much of the debate over the FCC's approach to mergers came to a head in the Comcast/NBCU merger, a merger between a large cable and telecommunications distributor with a large provider of viewing content. The merger implicated terrestrial television, cable television, video content, broadband internet, and emerging business possibilities combining these assets.

The Department of Justice cleared the merger after the merging parties agreed to significant conditions through a consent decree, wherein the Department sues to block the transaction but simultaneously enters with the court a settlement with the merging parties that embodies a final judgment (under the Tunney Act, 15 U.S.C. § 16, a judge must deem a consent decree to be in the public interest and offer outside parties opportunities to issue objections before granting approval and putting it into effect). Like many mergers in the telecommunications sector, this merger also required FCC approval, and the FCC and DOJ coordinated their reviews and issued coordinated conditions for approval.

Here, we set out an excerpt of the DOJ's "competitive impact statement" which both justifies the Department's intervention in the proposed merger and argues why agreed-upon remedies adequately address concerns to competition.

United States v. Comcast Corp.

Civil Action No. 1:11CV00106 (D.D.C. Jan. 18, 2011)
(competitive impact statement)
https://www.justice.gov/atr/case-document/file/492251/download

I. Description of Events Giving Rise to the Alleged Violation

A. Defendants, the Proposed Transaction, and the Department's Investigation

On December 3, 2009, Comcast Corporation (Comcast), General Electric Company (GE), NBC Universal, Inc. (NBCU), and Navy, LLC (Newco), announced plans to form a new Joint Venture (JV) to which Comcast and GE will contribute broadcast and cable network assets. As a result of the transaction, Comcast — the nation's largest cable company — will have majority control of a JV holding highly valued video programming needed by Comcast's video distribution rivals to compete effectively.

Comcast is the largest cable company in the nation, with approximately 23 million video subscribers. NBCU wholly owns the NBC and Telemundo broadcast networks, as well as ten local NBC owned and operated television stations (O&Os), 16 Telemundo O&Os, and one independent Spanish language television station. NBCU and Comcast are participants in the video programming industry, in which content is produced and distributed to viewers through their television sets or, increasingly, through Internet-connected devices. Historically, the video programming industry has had three different levels: content production, content aggregation or networks, and distribution.

Content Production

Television production studios produce television shows and coordinate how, when, and where their content is licensed in order to maximize revenues.

Programming Networks

Networks aggregate content to provide a 24-hour service that is attractive to consumers. The most popular networks, by far, are the four broadcast networks. However, cable networks have grown in popularity and number, and at the end of 2009 there were an estimated 600 national, plus another 100 regional, cable programming networks.

Video Programming Distribution

Video programming distributors acquire the rights to transmit cable programming networks or individual programs or movies, aggregate the content, and distribute it to their subscribers or users. Traditional video programming distributors, referred to as multichannel video programming distributors (MVPDs), typically offer hundreds of channels of professional video programming to residential customers for a fee. Online Video Programming Distributors (OVDs) are relatively recent entrants into the video programming distribution market. They deliver a variety of on-demand professional, full-length video programming over the Internet, whether streamed to Internet-connected televisions or other devices, or downloaded for later viewing.

B. Competition from OVDs

OVDs are relatively recent entrants into the video programming distribution market. Their services are available to any consumer with high-speed Internet service sufficient to receive video of an acceptable quality. OVDs have increased substantially the amount of full-length professional content they distribute online. Some of these OVD products and services undoubtedly will be viewed by consumers as closer substitutes for MVPD services than others.

Unlike MVPDs, OVDs do not own distribution facilities and are dependent upon ISPs for the delivery of their content to viewers. Therefore, the future growth of OVDs depends, in part, on how quickly ISPs expand and upgrade their broadband facilities and the preservation of their incentives to innovate and invest. OVDs would be harmed competitively if ISPs that are also MVPDs (e.g., cable companies, telcos) were to impair or delay the delivery of video because OVDs pose a threat to those MVPDs' traditional video programming distribution businesses. Growth of OVDs also will depend, in part, on their ability to acquire programming from content producers. Some cable companies, such as Comcast and Cablevision Corp., have purchased or launched their own cable networks.

Comcast and other MVPDs recognize the threat posed to their video distribution business from the growth of OVDs. Many internal documents reflect Comcast's assessment that OVDs are growing quickly and pose a competitive threat to traditional forms of video programming distribution. Comcast's and other MVPDs' reactions to the emergence of OVDs demonstrate that they view OVDs as a future competitive threat and are adjusting their investment decisions today in response to that threat.

D. The Anticompetitive Effects of the Proposed Transaction

Vertical mergers have the potential to harm competition by changing the merged firm's ability or incentives to deal with upstream or downstream rivals. For example, the merger may give the vertically integrated entity the ability to establish or protect market power in a downstream market by denying or raising the price of an input to downstream rivals that a stand-alone upstream firm otherwise would sell to those downstream firms. The merged firm may find it profitable to forego the benefits of dealing with its rivals in order to hobble them as competitors to its own downstream operations.

A merged firm can more readily harm competition when its rivals offer new products or technologies whose competitive potential is evolving. Nascent competitors may be relatively easy to quash. Even if a vertical merger only delays nascent competition, an increase in the duration of a firm's market power can result in significant competitive harm.

Ability and Incentive to Harm Rival MVPDs

If the proposed transaction is approved, Comcast through the JV will gain control of NBCU's content, including a substantial amount of valuable broadcast and cable programming. Competing MVPDs will be forced to obtain licenses for NBCU content from their rival, Comcast. Unlike a stand-alone programmer, Comcast's pricing and distribution decisions will take into account the impact of those decisions on the competitiveness of rival MVPDs. As a result, Comcast will have a strong incentive to disadvantage its competitors by denying them access to valuable programming or raising their licensing fees above what a stand-alone NBCU would have found it profitable to charge.

By disadvantaging competitors in this manner, Comcast through the JV will cause some of its rivals' customers to seek an alternative MVPD provider. Many of these dissatisfied customers likely will become Comcast subscribers, making it profitable for Comcast and the JV to increase licensing fees above the stand-alone NBCU levels. Those increased fees likely will lead to higher prices for subscribers of other MVPDs and perhaps further migration by those subscribers to Comcast.

Comcast has engaged in such strategies in the past. For example, Comcast has withheld its RSN in Philadelphia in order to discriminate against, and thereby disadvantage, DBS providers against which Comcast competes in that city. The DBS providers' market shares are lower and Comcast's subscription fees are higher in Philadelphia than in comparable markets. This appears to have been a profitable strategy for Comcast because the overall benefit to its cable business of retaining subscribers seems to have outweighed the substantial losses associated with failing to earn licensing fees for the withheld RSN from DBS companies.

Incentive and Ability to Harm OVDs

Comcast, through the JV, also could discriminate against competing OVDs in similar ways, thereby diminishing the competitive threat posed by individual OVDs and impeding the development of OVDs, generally. The JV could charge OVDs higher content fees than the stand-alone NBCU would have charged, or impose different terms for NBCU content than Comcast negotiates for itself. The JV also could withhold NBCU content completely, thereby diminishing OVDs' ability to compete for video programming distribution customers, again to Comcast's benefit. Either situation could delay significantly the development of OVDs as a competitive alternative to traditional video programming distribution services.

Over the last several years, NBCU has been one of the content providers most willing to experiment with different methods of online distribution. It was a driving force behind the creation and success of Hulu, and is now a partner in, and major content contributor to, the recently launched Hulu Plus, a subscription version of Hulu. Prior to the JV announcement, NBCU entered into several contracts with OVDs to distribute its content online through Apple iTunes and Amazon, and on a subscription basis through Netflix. Allowing the JV to proceed removes NBCU content from the control of a company that supported the development of OVDs and places it in the control of a company that views OVDs as a serious competitive threat. Comcast's acquisition of NBCU's interest in Hulu would give it the ability to hamper Hulu's strategic and competitive development by refusing to agree to major actions by Hulu, or by blocking Hulu's access to NBCU content.

II. Explanation of the Proposed Final Judgment

The proposed Final Judgment ensures that Comcast, through the JV, will not impede the development of emerging online video distribution competition by denying access to the JV's content to such competitors. The proposed Final Judgment also contains provisions that protect Comcast's traditional video distribution competitors. The proposed Final Judgment thereby protects consumers by eliminating the likely anticompetitive effects of the proposed transaction.

A. The Proposed Final Judgment Protects Emerging Online Video Competition

1. The Proposed Final Judgment requires the JV to license its broadcast, cable, and film content to OVDs on terms comparable to those in similar licensing arrangements with MVPDs or OVDs. The JV must license linear feeds of video programming to any requesting OVD on terms that are economically equivalent to the terms on which the JV licenses that programming to MVPDs, so the JV will not be able to use its control of content to impede competitive pressure exerted on traditional forms of video programming distribution from OVDs that choose to offer linear channels and associated VOD content.

   The JV [must alternatively] license to an OVD, broadcast, cable, or film content comparable in scope and quality to the content the OVD receives from one of the JV's programming peers.

2. The Proposed Final Judgment Prevents Comcast, through the JV, from Adversely Affecting Hulu. Defendants [must] relinquish their voting and other governance rights in Hulu, and [not receive] confidential or competitively sensitive information concerning Hulu one of the most successful

OVDs to date. Comcast has an incentive to prevent Hulu from becoming an even more attractive avenue for viewing video programming because Hulu would then exert increased competitive pressure on Comcast's cable business. The JV [must] continue to supply Hulu with content commensurate with the supply of content provided to Hulu by its other media owners.

3. The Proposed Final Judgment Prohibits Defendants from Discriminating Against, Retaliating Against, or Punishing Video Programmers and OVDs for invoking any provisions of the proposed Final Judgment or any FCC rule or order, or for furnishing information to the Department concerning Defendants' compliance with the proposed Final Judgment.
4. The Proposed Final Judgment Prohibits Defendants from Limiting Distribution to OVDs through Restrictive Licensing Practices. These provisions ensure that Comcast cannot use restrictive contract terms to harm the development of OVDs and, at the same time, preserve the JV's incentives to produce and exploit quality programming. The proposed Final Judgment strikes a balance by allowing reasonable and customary exclusivity provisions that enhance competition while prohibiting those provisions that, without any offsetting procompetitive benefits, hinder the development of effective competition from OVDs.
5. The Proposed Final Judgment Prohibits Unreasonable Discrimination in Internet Broadband Access. OVDs are dependent upon ISPs' access networks to deliver video content to their subscribers. Without the protections secured in the proposed Final Judgment, Comcast would have the ability, for instance, to give priority to non-OVD traffic on its network, thus adversely affecting the quality of OVD services that compete with Comcast's own MVPD or OVD services. Comcast also would be able to favor its own services by not subjecting them to the network management practices imposed on other services.

B. The Proposed Final Judgment Preserves Traditional Video Competition

The FCC Order approving this transaction requires the JV to license all of its programming to MVPDs, including its cable networks, and includes an arbitration mechanism that contains several enhancements to its existing commercial arbitration process when licensing disputes between Defendants and other MVPDs arise. The proposed Final Judgment prohibits Defendants from discriminating against, retaliating against, or punishing any MVPD for obtaining video programming, for furnishing any information to the United States about any noncompliance with the proposed Final Judgment, or for invoking the arbitration provisions of the FCC Order.

Notes and Questions

1. Why Approve? Given its concerns, why did the DOJ and FCC approve the merger? The agencies' bottom line was that the negotiated conditions eliminated most of the possibility for anticompetitive behavior. Are you persuaded?

2. Vertical Foreclosure. Most of the predicted harms appear premised on what antitrust calls vertical foreclosure—that the vertically-integrated Comcast and NBCU will use its content assets to harm its competitors in distribution. On what assumptions does vertical foreclosure rest? What market features would allow anticompetitive foreclosure and what market features would not make it possible? Additionally, are there assumptions of how the integrated firm will behave? Contrast the DOJ's analysis in Comcast-NBCU with the district court's analysis in the AT&T-Time Warner merger, below.

3. What Innovation? Can you see any online video products or services that the combined company could offer without making the identical content available to competitors? If not, why did the parties agree to the merger under the imposed conditions? The most skeptical observers of the merger expressed concern that the conditions sunset in seven years, which was not a long time, and that Comcast could simply bide its time until then. The somewhat less skeptical observers posited that the merger closed simply because it was better than failure.

4. Nascent Competition. The DOJ appeared to be especially concerned that a vertically-integrated Comcast-NBCU might harm nascent markets ("Nascent competitors may be relatively easy to quash.") and it focuses particular attention on the emerging market for OVDs. Is this concern warranted, or is it wiser to assume that valuable technologies will emerge without regulatory assistance? Is the DOJ engaging in some selective industrial policy?

AT&T/Time Warner Acquisition

In 2017, AT&T proposed to acquire through merger Time Warner Inc. (the content company, not the cable television company), thus revisiting the combination of distribution and content that was a big part of the Comcast/NBCU merger. This time, the parties ensured that there were no license transfers attendant to the merger, so the FCC did not have jurisdiction to review it. Nevertheless, based on similar concerns about the competitive impact of this vertical combination, the Department of Justice sought to block the merger under the antitrust laws. The United States District Court for the District of Columbia, following a trial, ruled against the government.

UNITED STATES v. AT&T

310 F. Supp. 3d 161 (D.D.C. 2018)

RICHARD J. LEON, United States District Judge

If there ever were an antitrust case where the parties had a dramatically different assessment of the current state of the relevant market and a fundamentally different vision of its future development, this is the one. Small wonder it had to go to trial!

The U.S. Department of Justice's Antitrust Division brought this suit, on behalf of the United States of America (the Government or the plaintiff), to block the merger of AT&T Inc. (AT&T) and Time Warner Inc. (Time Warner) as a violation of Section 7 of the Clayton Act, 15 U.S.C. § 18. The Government claims, in essence, that permitting AT&T to acquire Time Warner is likely to substantially lessen competition in the video programming and distribution market nationwide by enabling AT&T to use Time Warner's "must have" television content to either raise its rivals' video programming costs or, by way of a "blackout," drive those same rivals' customers to its subsidiary, DirecTV. Thus, according to the Government, consumers nationwide will be harmed by increased prices for access to Turner networks, notwithstanding the Government's concession that this vertical merger would result in hundreds of millions of dollars in annual cost savings to AT&T's customers and notwithstanding the fact that (unlike in "horizontal" mergers) no competitor will be eliminated by the merger's proposed vertical integration.

Not surprisingly, the defendants, AT&T, Time Warner, and DirecTV, strongly disagree. Their vision couldn't be more different. The video programming and distribution market, they point out, has been, and is, in the middle of a revolution where high-speed internet access has facilitated a "veritable explosion" of new, innovative video content and advertising offerings over the past five years. Trial Tr. (Tr.) 1397:1–4 (Montemagno (Charter)). Vertically integrated entities like Netflix, Hulu, and Amazon have achieved remarkable success in creating and providing affordable, on-demand video content directly to viewers over the internet. Meanwhile, web giants Facebook and Google have developed new ways to use data to create effective — and lucrative — digital advertisements tailored to the individual consumer.

As a result of these "tectonic changes" brought on by the proliferation of high-speed internet access, video programmers such as Time Warner and video distributors such as AT&T find themselves facing two stark realities: declining video subscriptions and flatlining television advertising revenues. Indeed, cost-conscious consumers increasingly choose to "cut" or "shave" the cord, abandoning their traditional cable- or satellite-TV packages for cheaper content alternatives available over the internet. At the same time, Facebook's and Google's dominant digital advertising platforms have surpassed television advertising in revenue. Watching vertically integrated, data-informed entities thrive as television subscriptions and advertising revenues declined, AT&T and Time Warner concluded that each had a problem that the other could solve: Time Warner could provide AT&T with the ability to experiment with and develop innovative video content and advertising offerings for AT&T's many video and wireless customers, and AT&T could afford Time Warner access to customer relationships and valuable data about its programming. Together, AT&T and Time Warner concluded that both companies could stop "chasing taillights" and catch up with the competition. Those were the circumstances that drove AT&T, a distributor of content, and Time Warner, a content creator and programmer, to announce their historic $108 billion merger in October 2016 (the "proposed merger" or "challenged merger"). Those are the circumstances that cause them to claim today that their merger will increase not only innovation, but competition in this marketplace for years to come.

Section 7 of the Clayton Act assigns this Court the "uncertain task" of weighing the parties' competing visions of the future of the relevant market and the challenged merger's place within it. Nothing less than a comprehensive inquiry into future competitive conditions in that market is expected. And the Government has the burden of proof to demonstrate that the merger is likely to lessen competition substantially in that uncertain future.

Analysis

The challenged vertical merger here would unite Time Warner, a creator and supplier of popular video content, with AT&T, a large downstream purchaser and distributor of video content. The Government concedes that the challenged merger, like most vertical mergers, will result in significant benefits to customers of the merged company. Specifically, the Government's lead expert, Professor Carl Shapiro, estimates that the merger will cause AT&T to lower the price of DirecTV, resulting in $352 million in annual savings for DirecTV's customers.

Notwithstanding those conceded consumer benefits, the Government contends that the challenged merger is likely to lessen competition substantially and thus should be enjoined under Section 7. The challenged merger would likely result in a substantial lessening of competition, according to the Government, in three "mutually reinforcing" ways.

The Government's primary theory of harm to competition focuses on the challenged merger's integration of Turner's important video content—content that includes, among other things, the networks CNN, TNT, and TBS—with AT&T's video distributors, U-verse and DirecTV. Specifically, the Government contends that, should the challenged merger proceed, Turner's relationship with AT&T will enable Turner to extract greater prices from AT&T's rival distributors for its "must-have" content than it could without the merger. The Government argues that distributors would then pass on those price increases to their subscribers, resulting in an increase of hundreds of millions of dollars in annual consumer payments.

Having heard and considered the evidence adduced at trial, I conclude that the Government has failed to clear the first hurdle of showing that the proposed merger is likely to increase Turner's bargaining leverage in affiliate negotiations;

I thus need not consider the separate legal question of whether any effects associated with the Government's increased-leverage theory would result in a substantial lessening of competition for purposes of the Clayton Act's prohibitions. The Government's proof at trial falls *far* short of establishing the validity of its increased-leverage theory.

A. Background of Increased-Leverage Theory of Harm

The terms under which distributors may license and display programmers' content are set through a "very tough" series of affiliate negotiations. Tr. 1023:2 (Breland (Turner)). As with any type of bargaining, each party to an affiliate negotiation attempts to take advantage of its points of leverage, and "reaching a deal in the end can come down to a battle of the competing bargaining leverages." Tr. 1025:20–22 (Breland (Turner)). In the event an affiliate negotiation is unsuccessful, the distributor will lose the rights to display the programmer's content to its customers. Such a situation is known in the industry as a programming "blackout," or "going dark." Tr. 129:4–9 (Fenwick (Cox)).

Blackouts have significant, if not "catastrophic," negative consequences for programmers — in the form of lost advertising and affiliate fee revenues. *Id.* at 1128:7–12 (Breland (Turner)). Distributors, for their part, may lose subscribers. In "almost every negotiation," therefore, programmers and distributors threaten blackouts in an attempt to gain concessions. Tr. at 1026:17–1027:3 (Breland (Turner)). Given that blackouts are negative events for both programmers and distributors, however, deals between programmers and distributors are invariably struck in order to avoid long-term blackouts. Indeed, when it comes to Turner, the record shows that there has *never* been a long-term blackout of the Turner networks. That fact is by no means lost on either side.

That background brings us to the Government's increased-leverage theory. Notably, under that theory, the Government does *not* allege that a post-merger Turner would be incentivized to start *actually* engaging in long-term blackouts with distributors. That is so, as Professor Shapiro concedes, because withholding Turner content would not be "profitable" to the merged entity given the attendant losses in significant advertising and affiliate fee revenues. In other words, and in contrast to a prevalent theory of vertical merger antitrust harm, Turner will not "foreclose" downstream distributors from accessing Turner content.

Instead, the Government's increased-leverage theory of harm posits that Turner's bargaining position in affiliate negotiations would improve after the merger due to its relationship with AT&T. That is so, the Government argues, because Turner and its distributor counterparties would recognize that, should Turner fail to strike a deal and engage in a long-term blackout with a distributor, Turner would no longer face the mere downside of losing affiliate fees and advertising revenues. Rather, some of those losses would be offset, according to the Government, by new benefits to AT&T's video distribution companies via the following chain of events: 1) some of the rival distributor's customers would depart or fail to join the distributor due to the missing Turner content; 2) some portion of those lost customers would choose to sign up with AT&T's video distributors (which would have Turner); and 3) AT&T would profit from those gained subscribers. As a result, the Government predicts that Turner's downside position in the event of a blackout would improve as a result of the proposed merger. That improved downside position, according to the Government, would in turn enable Turner to demand higher prices for its content in post-merger affiliate fee negotiations with distributors — price increases that would ultimately be passed on to consumers.

At trial, the Government relied on two primary categories of evidence to support its increased-leverage theory of harm. First, it offered so-called "real-world objective evidence" — namely, statements contained within defendants' prior regulatory filings and internal business documents as well as testimony from third-party competitor witnesses. Second, the Government called an expert, Professor Carl Shapiro, to testify about its increased-leverage theory, which is based on an economic theory of bargaining known as the Nash bargaining theory, and to estimate the consumer harm associated with the increased-leverage theory. For the following reasons, neither category of evidence was effective in proving the Government's increased-leverage theory. Accordingly, as to this theory, the Government has failed to meet its burden of proof to show that the merger is likely to result in a substantial lessening of competition.

B. The Government's So-Called "Real-World Objective Evidence" Is Insufficient to Support Its Increased-Leverage Theory of Harm

To support its increased-leverage theory of harm, the Government first points to various pieces of the so-called "real-world objective evidence" it offered at trial. Proposed Conclusions of Law of the United States (Gov't PCOL) ¶ 21. That evidence primarily consisted of defendants' ordinary course-of-business documents and excerpts of regulatory filings submitted by defendants in prior administrative proceedings, as well as the testimony of third-party witnesses from AT&T's rival distribution companies. Of particular importance here, the Government's so-called real-world evidence was directed at explaining and establishing two main concepts. First, the Government sought to establish the importance of Turner content to distributors and the resulting leverage Turner enjoys in affiliate fee negotiations. Second, the Government relied on this so-called "real-world objective evidence" to substantiate its prediction that Turner's leverage with distributors would *increase* as a result of Turner's post-merger relationship with AT&T. Neither, however, provided persuasive support for the Government's increased-leverage theory of harm. How so?

1. Evidence Regarding the Popularity of Turner Content Is of Limited Probative Value in Evaluating the Contention that Turner Will Gain Increased Leverage Due to the Proposed Merger

At trial, much time was spent debating the "must-have" status of Turner's programming content. According to the Government, distributors literally "'must have'" Turner's content in order "to compete effectively" in the video distribution industry. Gov't Post-Tr. Br. 4. Defendants countered that the term "must have" is simply a marketing phrase used to mean "popular" and, similarly, that Turner content is not actually necessary to allow distributors to operate their businesses successfully.

Based on the evidence, I agree with defendants that Turner's content is not *literally* "must have" in the sense that distributors cannot effectively compete without it. The evidence showed that distributors have successfully operated, and continue to operate, without the Turner networks or similar programming.

I accept the Government's contention that Turner has popular content — especially live sporting events and live news — and, as a result, enjoys bargaining leverage with distributors. Importantly, however, accepting that straightforward proposition — *i.e.*, that popular programmers such as Turner are able to demand more for their content than less popular programmers — does not prove that the challenged *merger* would harm competition pursuant to the Government's increased-leverage theory of harm. To prove its increased-leverage theory, in other words, it is not sufficient for the Government to put forward evidence that Turner has important content and thus bargaining leverage — that fact is true today, pre-merger. Rather, the Government's increased-leverage theory posits that Turner's pre-merger bargaining leverage would materially increase as a result of its post-merger relationship with AT&T and that, as a result, distributors would cede greater affiliate fees than they would absent the merger.

2. Defendants' Own Statements and Documents Provide Little Support for the Contention that Turner Will Gain Increased Leverage Due to the Proposed Merger

[D]espite the Government's efforts to paint a contrary picture, this is not a case containing direct, probative evidence of anticompetitive intent on the part of high-level executives within the merging company. [AT&T Chairman and CEO] Stephenson's statements and the Government's other proffered documentary evidence instead suggest, at the very most, that AT&T (or its third-party consultants) recognized that one *possibility* of uniting content and distribution would be to withhold or otherwise limit content from other distributors in an attempt to benefit AT&T's distribution platforms. But evidence indicating defendants' recognition that it could be possible to act in accordance with the Government's theories of harm is a far cry from evidence that the merged company is likely to do so (much less succeed in generating anticompetitive harms as a result). That is especially true when the Government's documentary evidence is weighed against the considerable contrary evidence — including other evidence related to the motivation for the challenged merger — that came out at trial. *See, e.g.*, Defs.' PFOF ¶¶ 49–62 (collecting evidence regarding the proposed merger's ability to "enable the combined company to respond to the challenges posed by the current transformation of the video marketplace and, in so doing, bring better products and better value to consumers"). Thus, taking such documentary evidence for all it's worth, that evidence is only marginally probative of the viability of the Government's increased-leverage theory of harm.

3. Third-Party Competitor Witness Testimony Provides Little Support for the Contention that Turner Will Gain Increased Leverage Due to the Proposed Merger

[T]he bulk of the third-party competitor testimony proffered by the Government was speculative, based on unproven assumptions, or unsupported — or even contradicted — by the Government's own evidence. Especially in view of the fact that the third-party competitor witnesses have an incentive to oppose a merger that would allow AT&T to increase innovation while lowering costs, such testimony falls far short of persuasively "show[ing] that this merger threatens" to harm competition by allowing Turner to wield increased bargaining leverage. Gov't Post-Tr. Br. 8.

C. The Government's Expert Testimony Is Also Insufficient to Support Its Increased-Leverage Theory of Harm

In addition to offering the so-called "real-world objective evidence" set out above, the Government called noted antitrust economist, Professor Carl Shapiro, to testify in support of its increased-leverage theory. Professor Shapiro first discussed the academic underpinnings of the theory, explaining that it was grounded in an economic concept known as the Nash bargaining theory. Thereafter, Professor Shapiro opined that Turner's post-merger leverage would increase pursuant to those economic principles. In order to predict the increased distributor costs and consumer harms that would result from Turner's increased post-merger leverage, Professor Shapiro constructed economic models. Acknowledging that proper antitrust analysis of a proposed vertical merger requires balancing the merger's proconsumer benefits with its harms, Professor Shapiro testified that the challenged merger would result in annual consumer cost increases that would far outweigh the $350 million in annual elimination of double marginalization (EDM) savings he conceded the merger would generate. He thus concluded, based on his economic modeling, that the merger was likely to cause a substantial lessening of competition by increasing consumer costs as a result of Turner's increased bargaining leverage.

The Court accepts Professor Shapiro's (and the Government's) argument that, generally, "a firm with multiple divisions will act to maximize profits across them." Gov't Post-Tr. Br. 19. That profit-maximization premise is *not* inconsistent, however, with the witness testimony that the identity of a programmer's owner has not affected affiliate negotiations in real-world instances of vertical integration. Rather, as those witnesses indicated, vertically integrated corporations have previously determined that the best way to increase company-wide profits is for the programming and distribution components to separately maximize their respective revenues. *See, e.g.*, Tr. 2015:16–19 (Bond (NBCU)) ("Q: And, in fact, what you were doing is trying to maximize the revenue of NBC as a programmer in those negotiations, correct? A: Yes, sir."). In the case of programmers, that means pursuing deals "to be on all the platforms," rather than undertaking a "series of risks" to threaten a long-term blackout. *Id.* at 1129:17–22 (Breland (Turner)). So understood, the consistent and, in this Court's judgment, credible, trial testimony is not in fact in "serious tension" with "economic logic" — just with Professor Shapiro's opinion that the identity of a programmer's owner influences negotiations!

Next, Professor Shapiro's opinion that Turner's post-merger relationship with AT&T will enable Turner to more credibly threaten a distributor with a long-term blackout in order to extract greater affiliate fees was severely undermined by defendants' evidence that such a blackout would be infeasible. *See id.* at 2195:4–7 (Shapiro) ("Q: Explain to His Honor why blackouts are relevant here for this discussion today. A: Well, even though they don't happen very much, that's the key to leverage, okay?"). Indeed, the evidence showed that there has never been, and is likely never going to be, an actual long-term blackout of Turner content. Numerous witnesses explained, and Professor Shapiro acknowledged, that a long-term blackout of Turner content, even post-merger, would cause Turner to lose more in affiliate fee and advertising revenues than the merged entity would gain. Given that, there is an insufficient evidentiary basis to support Professor Shapiro's contention that a post-merger Turner would, or even could, drive up prices by *threatening* distributors with long-term blackouts.

It is worth emphasizing again that Professor Shapiro does *not* contend that Turner's economics are going to somehow flip after the merger — he acknowledged, for example, that Turner would lose over $100 million per month during a post-merger blackout with a large distributor. As a result, Professor Shapiro testified that Turner would not be incentivized to *actually* engage in a long-term blackout with a distributor.

In view of that evidence on the prospects of a long-term blackout, the lynchpin of Professor Shapiro's testimony (and, accordingly the Government's increased-leverage theory) is the *assumption* that a post-merger Turner would gain increased leverage by wielding a blackout threat that will only be somewhat less incredible. That does not make sense as a matter of logic and, more importantly, that has not been supported by sufficient real-world evidence.

IV. The Government Has Failed to Meet Its Burden to Show that the Proposed Merger Is Likely to Substantially Lessen Competition on the Theory that AT&T Will Act to Harm Virtual MVPDS through Its Ownership of Time Warner Content

The Government's second theory of competitive harm relates to virtual MVPDs. Virtual MVPDs, like traditional MVPDs, offer consumers linear (or "live") television programming in exchange for a subscription fee. Unlike traditional MVPDs, however, virtual MVPDs transmit their video content over the internet. Compared to traditional MVPDs, virtual MVPDs generally offer lower-cost programming packages to consumers; those packages, known in the industry as "skinny bundles," contain fewer networks than do the larger bundles offered by MVPDs. Although virtual MVPDs are of recent vintage, they are quickly gaining market share in the video programming and distribution industry. Examples of virtual MVPDs include AT&T's DirecTV Now, DISH's Sling TV, Sony's Playstation Vue, Hulu Live, Google's YouTube TV, FuboTV, and Philo.

Unilateral Theory. The Government first claims that AT&T has an incentive to harm innovative virtual MVPDs and could act unilaterally on that incentive by foreclosing or restricting virtual MVPDs' access to "must-have" Turner content. That is a curious claim, to say the least, in light of Professor Shapiro's testimony that, in his view, "standing alone, acting unilaterally, the — AT&T *will* still want to license the Turner content to virtual MVPDs." Tr. 2260:19–21 (Shapiro) (emphasis added). That is so, according to Professor Shapiro, because as with traditional MVPDs, it would be "profitable" for the merged entity to continue to license Time Warner content to virtual MVPDs. *Id.* at 2293:14–17.

[D]efendants put forward additional evidence that AT&T would have incentive to *license* Time Warner content to virtual MVPDs after the merger. For starters, given Turner's imperative of broad distribution, Turner executives testified that it is important for Turner's content to be included on virtual MVPDs as they continue to grow in relevance. With consumers choosing to cut or shave the cord, Turner has "embrac[ed] virtual MVPDs," Turner CEO John Martin testified, "because, again, we need to be distributed to as full distribution as possible." *Id.* at 607:13–16 (Martin (Turner)).

The entire premise of the proposed merger — allowing AT&T to go mobile with video content — provides yet another reason to reject the Government's unilateral merger theory. AT&T's largest business is its wireless business, where it has more than 100 million subscribers. On its own, if separated from the rest of the corporation, AT&T's wireless business would be "number 37 on the Fortune 500" — approximately the size of Proctor & Gamble. *Id.* at 3379:20–3380:1 (Stephenson (AT&T)).

Industry trend-lines point toward increased video consumption in the future — and AT&T aims to ride these tailwinds. AT&T views mobile consumption of video, including through virtual MVPDs, as a critical part of its post-merger future. Notably, the benefits associated with AT&T customers accessing virtual MVPD content continue to accrue even when they use DirecTV Now's competitors like Sling and YouTube TV. All of this gives the combined entity even more reason to distribute Time Warner content as broadly as possible in order to encourage the proliferation of virtual MVPDs.

Second, from the other direction, the Government advances an alternative unilateral claim: that AT&T would have the ability to break the "skinny bundle" models of virtual MVPDs by forcing those distributors to take *too many* Turner networks. Citing the testimony of Sling's President, Warren Schlichting, the Government argues that a post-merger requirement that Sling "take eight Turner networks instead of four would 'break [Sling's] model'" and, indeed, would have a snowball effect with other programmers. Gov't PFOF ¶ 288 (quoting Tr. 265:17–266:8, 268:9–23 (Schlichting (DISH)).

That argument, however, ignores that Turner has less of an imperative to risk a deal with Sling (or other virtual MVPDs) by insisting on carriage of all of its networks. That is so, the evidence indicates, because Turner has a highly "concentrated portfolio of networks," Tr. 558:1 (Martin (Turner)), with 85 to 90% of Turner's revenues deriving from only four networks. That fact, as Time Warner CEO Jeff Bewkes noted—means Turner is "better placed" to succeed in the skinny bundle model. Tr. 3126:22. The Government's skinny bundle point also overlooks the fact that Turner—like other programmers—already fights tooth and nail to get all of its networks into all of the packages of every distributor. Simply put, the Government has not produced sufficient evidence to show that the challenged merger is likely to make a meaningful difference to that dynamic. For all of the above reasons, I conclude that the Government has failed to meet its burden on its claims arising from AT&T's asserted potential to unilaterally harm virtual MVPDs through its post-merger control of Turner content.

Coordination Theory. The Government posits that the challenged merger would also create a likelihood that AT&T would coordinate with Comcast-NBCU to harm virtual MVPDs. In contrast to the unilateral withholding claim just discussed, the Government did at least attempt to provide some expert support for this coordination claim. Unfortunately for the Government, however, neither that expert testimony nor its other evidence is even close to sufficient to support its coordination claim. How so?

As it does for its other claims, the Government relies on a key assumption when pressing its theory of coordinated effects. Here, the Government assumes that, "[a]s the only two vertically integrated traditional MVPDs, Comcast and AT&T would share an incentive to slow the entry and growth of virtual MVPDs." Gov't PFOF ¶ 299. To act on that incentive, the Government further asserts, the companies could "'mutually forbear'" from licensing their programming content "'without any communication between them.'" *Id.* (quoting Tr. 2265:5–2265:6 (Shapiro)). Not only is that theory overly speculative, it ignores key differences between AT&T and Comcast that undermine the Government's argument.

First, the Government has failed to put forward sufficient evidence to show more than a theoretical "possibility" of coordination.

Second, the Government's argument regarding the incentive of AT&T and Comcast to coordinate to harm virtual MVPDs ignores that both stand to lose large amounts of affiliate fee and advertising revenues by withholding their content from virtual MVPDs. Unsurprisingly, NBCU has licensed its content to each virtual MVPD. The Government has not explained why either company would be willing to forgo those affiliate fees and advertising revenues from virtual MVPDs. Nor has the Government proffered any expert analysis, for example, of how those economics could, or would, change assuming a coordinated blackout of both Turner and NBCU.

Third, and critically, the Government's argument also ignores key differences between the two companies — differences that AT&T executives believe give AT&T a competitive advantage over Comcast moving forward in this new era of rising virtual MVPD prevalence. AT&T's John Stankey, who will be responsible for running Time Warner should the challenged merger proceed, emphatically (and credibly) stated at trial that he could not "even imagine" aligning with Comcast given the companies' history of dealings, adding, "I'm not going to cooperate with somebody I don't like." Tr. at 3255:2–3256:2 (Stankey (AT&T)).

The most obvious "advantage" AT&T has over Comcast when it comes to virtual MVPDs is that, unlike Comcast, AT&T has a vast wireless business with over 100 million customers. The reasons to encourage, not quash, virtual MVPDs unilaterally become even more compelling in the context of a coordination claim with Comcast — a competitor that is much more beholden to legacy cable infrastructure and the traditional MVPD business model.

The Government does not dispute that AT&T's wireless business confers strong incentives to maximize distribution to virtual MVPDs. Nor can it be questioned that AT&T's strong positioning in the world of mobile content distribution gives it a powerful disincentive to work with Comcast to stifle those mobile providers of video. AT&T has plainly positioned itself to ride industry tailwinds in support of mobile consumption of video. As John Stankey explained, AT&T acquired DirecTV in 2015 not in order to double down on the satellite business, a concededly mature and declining asset, but to "pick up a lot of new customers that we could work on migrating" to new products. *Id.* at 3207:18–20 (Stankey (AT&T)). Indeed, as soon as the merger closed, AT&T began renegotiating DirecTV's contracts to allow for a mobile, direct-to-consumer option, DirecTV Now. Nowhere does the Government explain why AT&T would deploy valuable Time Warner content to prop up a rival's business model, while harming its own. Go figure!

This fundamental problem of incentives and profitability buries the Government's claim. It is beyond dispute that neither the proffered concentration in the MVPD market (which, by the way, will be the same post-merger), nor the importance of Turner and NBCU content, nor some transparency in "key information," nor any other of the Government's evidence on the coordination theory (alone or in combination), can establish a "risk of coordination" unless the parties have an incentive or interest to collude in the first place.

Even assuming, contrary to the evidence, that AT&T would want to coordinate with Comcast under the Government's theory, the staggered, lengthy industry contracts would make that coordination strategy extremely risky. *See id.* at 643:20–644:2 (Martin (Turner)) (testifying that "because of the length of these contracts, because they're typically years in length," a strategy set "in 2013" would "begin to show up in '15, '16 and '17"); *id.* at 87:9–11 (Fenwick (Cox)) (testifying that affiliate agreements run "between five and eight years on average"). Under the Government's coordination theory, one party—AT&T or Comcast—would have to "jump first," giving up valuable programming rights on the hope that the other, in some years' time, would elect to do the same. Indeed, this barrier to coordination is so great as to put to rest the notion not only that AT&T and Comcast would have the *incentive* to coordinate, but that the post-merger marketplace would afford them the *ability* to do so. Whether by way of tacit coordination or an illegal agreement, putting such blind faith in one's chief competitor strikes this Court as exceedingly implausible! The Government puts forward no persuasive reason why AT&T and Comcast would engage in such conduct.

V. The Government Has Failed to Meet Its Burden to Show that the Proposed Merger Is Likely to Substantially Lessen Competition on the Theory that AT&T Will Restrict Distributors' Use of HBO as a Promotional Tool

The Government's final theory centers on HBO. On this score, the Government alleges that the combined entity will have the "incentive and ability" to prevent rival distributors from using HBO as a promotional tool to attract and retain customers. Under this theory, the combined entity would "foreclos[e] competitors of the purchasing firm in the merger from access to a potential source of supply, *or from access on competitive terms.*" Gov't PCOL ¶ 61 [internal citation omitted]. The basic idea, the Government tells us, is that rival distributors' use of HBO in promotions will tend to draw potential customers to those MVPDs and away from AT&T, thereby giving AT&T reason to withhold or restrict its consent to use HBO in marketing, discounts, and bundles. At the risk of stating the obvious, this is a gossamer thin claim.

The Government has failed to meet its burden of proof on this theory for two independent reasons. *First*, the Government has failed to show that the merged entity would have *any* incentive to foreclose rivals' access to HBO-based promotions. This is because the Government's promotion-withholding theory conflicts with HBO's business model, which remains "heavily dependent" on promotion by distributors. Tr. 3074:5–6 (Bewkes (Time Warner)).

Second, the Government fails to establish that HBO promotions are so valuable that withholding or restricting them will drive customers to AT&T. Put differently, the Government has failed to show that the marketplace substitutes for HBO are "inferior, inadequate, or more costly." Gov't PCOL ¶ 62 (internal quotation marks omitted).

For these two, independent reasons, the Government has failed to provide sufficient evidence to support its final theory in this case. Accordingly, I reject outright the assertion that the combined entity would likely restrict HBO as a promotional tool in order to harm AT&T's distribution rivals and thereby lessen competition in the marketplace.

* * *

Thus, for all of the foregoing reasons, the Government's request to enjoin the proposed merger is DENIED.

Notes and Questions

1. Competing Visions. The opinion began by laying out the two sides' very different framing of competition and the market, and these companies' place within the market. What factual assertions, or assumptions, distinguished these visions from each other? How important was the choice between those understandings of the state of the markets and competition? How important should it have been? On what basis should a judge (or an ordinary citizen) choose between those understandings?

2. Carry That Weight. The opinion placed significant weight on the testimony of executives from the companies that were seeking to merge. Was that appropriate, or a mistake? If the latter, what should the court have looked to? Pay particular attention to the disagreement over the significance of "blackouts," the temporary removal of "must have" content when negotiations between producers and distributors hit an impasse. The executives said blackouts rarely happen and that they would never institute them because they would injure commercial interests. The government's expert agreed that blackouts are rare but stated that the mere threat of imposing a blackout could have significant pricing consequences. Should the executive's narrative or the game theorist's estimations hold more sway?

3. AT&T-Time Warner versus Comcast-NBCU. This casebook section began with the assertion that these two vertical mergers introduced similar issues. However, Judge Leon's analysis was substantially different from the DOJ's analysis in Comcast-NBCU, above. Did the judge simply fail to understand the government's argument and the anticompetitive harms from the vertical merger? Or were the government's fears of vertical foreclosure unsubstantiated in both cases, and it simply was inadequately vetted in Comcast-NBCU? Note the DOJ's observation in Comcast-NBCU that Comcast had, in the Philadelphia market, discriminated against rival DBSs. Is that immaterial for these mergers, or is it specific to Comcast?

4. Vertical Mergers. What does the reasoning of this case indicate for the law of vertical mergers? Had it preceded the Comcast-NBCU proposed merger, would that merger agreement have been different? Under the opinion's reasoning and treatment of the government's burdens, what sorts of vertical mergers would be blocked? To put the point differently, does the opinion suggest that antitrust law poses no major obstacles to vertical mergers in the world of telecommunications and the internet?

News Corp./DirecTV Acquisition

In 2003, News Corp. announced its intention to purchase DirecTV (a subsidiary of Hughes Electronics), thereby creating the first vertically integrated Direct Broadcast Satellite (DBS) provider. That December, the DOJ tersely announced that it would not challenge News Corp.'s acquisition. It noted that "[t]he Department's decision was based in part on the recent announcement by the FCC that it will approve the transaction subject to certain conditions" and that "[i]n light of the FCC's decision, which addresses the Department's most significant concerns with the proposed transaction, the Department has decided to close its investigation." Justice Department Will Not Challenge News Corp.'s Acquisition of Hughes Electronics Corp., Department of Justice, Dec. 19, 2003, https://www.justice.gov/archive/atr/public/press_releases/2003/201918.htm.

The FCC had a more robust response, including a divided vote and a dissenting opinion. Consistent with the fears of foreclosure reflected in the vertical merger challenges discussed above, its concerns focused on reducing News Corp.'s ability to withhold its programming content from cable television and DBS providers that compete with DirecTV. News Corp. later spun off DirecTV, selling it to Liberty Media Corporation (as it happens, Liberty also owns programming interests, and the FCC went on to impose a similar set of requirements as a condition of approving that merger), but we nonetheless include the order approving the original acquisition because it clearly describes the FCC's underlying competition concerns from vertical mergers. Note that the FCC largely premises its concerns and its authority to demand concessions on the program access requirements, provided in § 628 of the Communications Act (47 U.S.C. § 548(b)), which we discuss in Chapter 5.

General Motors Corp. and Hughes Electronics Corp., Transferors, and the News Corp. Ltd, Transferee, for Authority to Transfer Control

Memorandum Opinion and Order, 19 FCC Rcd. 473 (2004)

V. Introduction to the Video Programming and Mvpd Markets

A. Background

39. The proposed transaction involves the acquisition by News Corp., a major owner of both broadcast and cable video programming content and programming-related technologies, of a 34% interest in Hughes Electronics, owner of DirecTV, a DBS provider that is the second largest MVPD in the United States and the largest MVPD that has a national service footprint. News Corp. presently has no MVPD assets in the United States; its primary domestic business is the provision of video programming to MVPDs in every area of the country. Similarly, Hughes currently does not participate in the video programming market as a programming supplier; rather, its DirecTV subsidiary functions as a purchaser and distributor of multichannel video programming to subscribing customers. By acquiring DirecTV, News Corp. immediately transforms itself from a supplier of video programming MVPDs to a vertically integrated MVPD competitor. News Corp. thus becomes a vertically integrated supplier of broadcast and cable video programming to all of its MVPD competitors in every region of the country.

B. Applicable Regulatory Framework

41. The program access provisions, contained in section 628 of the Communications Act, were adopted as part of the Cable Television Consumer Protection and Competition Act of 1992. At the time, Congress was concerned that most cable operators enjoyed a monopoly in program distribution at the local level. Congress found that vertically integrated program suppliers had the incentive and ability to favor their affiliated cable operators over nonaffiliated cable operators and programming distributors using other technologies. Section 628 is intended to foster the development of competition to traditional cable systems by governing the access of competing MVPDs to cable programming services. DBS was among the technologies that Congress intended to foster through the program access provisions.

42. The program access rules specifically prohibit cable operators, a satellite cable programming vendor in which a cable operator has an attributable interest, or a satellite cable programming vendor from:

- Engaging in unfair acts or practices which hinder significantly or prohibit an MVPD from providing satellite cable programming to subscribers or consumers.
- Discriminating in the prices, terms and conditions of sale or delivery of satellite cable programming.
- Entering into exclusive contracts with cable operators unless the Commission finds the exclusivity to be in the public interest.

43. Aggrieved entities can file a complaint with the Commission. Remedies for violations of the rules may include the imposition of damages and the establishment of reasonable prices, terms and conditions for the sale of programming. Broadcast programming is not subject to the program access rules.

44. The Commission's 2002 examination of whether the exclusivity prohibition should sunset placed substantial weight on whether, in the absence of the exclusivity prohibition, vertically integrated programmers would currently have the incentive and ability to favor their affiliated cable operators over nonaffiliated cable operators and program distributors using other technologies and, if they would, whether such behavior would result in a failure to protect and preserve competition and diversity in the distribution of video programming. The Commission held that access to all vertically integrated satellite cable programming continues to be necessary in order for competitive MVPDs to remain viable in the marketplace. The Commission further found that an MVPD's ability to provide service that is competitive with an incumbent cable operator is significantly harmed if denied access to "must have" vertically integrated programming for which there are no good substitutes, such as regional news and sports networks. The Commission also found that vertically integrated programmers retain the incentive to favor their affiliated cable operators over competing MVPDs. In that regard, the Commission found that cable operators continue to dominate the MVPD marketplace and that horizontal consolidation

and clustering combined with affiliation with regional programming, have contributed to cable's overall market dominance. In addition, the Commission determined that an economic basis for denial of access to vertically integrated programming to competitive MVPDs continues, and that such denial would harm such competitors' ability to compete for subscribers. The prohibition on exclusive contracts for satellite-delivered cable or satellite-delivered broadcast programming was therefore extended for five years, until October 5, 2007.

VI. Analysis of Potential Harms in the Relevant Markets

71. Vertical transactions have the potential for anticompetitive effects. In particular, a vertically integrated firm that competes both in an upstream input market and a downstream output market, such as post-transaction News Corp., may have the incentive and ability to: (1) discriminate against particular rivals in either the upstream or downstream markets (e.g., by foreclosing rivals from inputs or customers); or (2) raise the costs to rivals generally in either of the markets.

80. There is an additional reason why temporary foreclosure may be profitable. Specifically, by temporarily foreclosing supply of the input to a downstream competitor or by threatening to engage in temporary foreclosure, the integrated firm may improve its bargaining position so as to be able to extract a higher input price from the downstream competitor than it could have negotiated if it were a non-integrated input supplier. In order for an integrated firm successfully to employ temporary foreclosure or the threat of temporary foreclosure as a strategy to increase its bargaining position, the foreclosure strategy must be credible. This means that competitors must believe that temporary foreclosure is profitable (whether or not it actually is) in order to extract a higher input price. For example, if the vertically integrated firm, by temporarily withholding an input from a competitor, can cause the competitor to lose sufficient revenue or suffer other competitive harms, the competitor might agree to pay a higher price for the input, which could lead to higher prices for the output, thus injuring consumers. Even if the vertically integrated firm suffered a loss in profits from engaging in a specific instance of temporary foreclosure, it might nevertheless find it to be a profitable strategy over the longer run. Specifically, if by temporarily foreclosing certain competitors, the vertically integrated firm may signal to other downstream competitors its willingness to foreclose, which may cause other downstream competitors to agree to a higher price without the vertically integrated firm's having to actually engage in repeated foreclosures.

107. Applicants have offered that "neither News Corp. nor DirecTV will discriminate against unaffiliated programming services in the selection, price, terms or conditions of carriage." Consolidated Application of Gen. Motors Corp. and Hughes Elecs. Corp., Transferors, and the News Corp. Ltd., Transferee, for Auth. to Transfer Control, 53, Attachment G, MB Dkt. No. 03-124 (May 2003) (May 2003 Filing). We conclude that Applicants' proposed commitment to allow unaffiliated programmers access to the DirecTV platform on nondiscriminatory terms and conditions

adequately addresses concerns raised regarding unaffiliated video programmers' access to the DirecTV platform. We will therefore condition our grant of the Application on compliance with this access commitment.

114. In addition, Applicants commit to not entering into exclusive arrangements for the distribution of an affiliated programming rights holder's satellite cable programming.

132. In conclusion, we believe as a general matter that the Commission's program access rules are satisfactory to address any imbalance of power between News Corp. and competing MVPDs with respect to national and non-sports regional cable programming networks. Likewise, our acceptance of the offered conditions ensures that any imbalance that may exist between DirecTV and some of its competitors in the MVPD market is remedied in the same manner as with vertically integrated MVPDs that use cable technology to deliver their product to consumers, regardless of the effect of any post-closing changes in the corporate relationships between News Corp. and its various cable programming affiliates. In contrast, as described below, the record indicates that News Corp. has considerable market power with respect to its regional sports networks and its local broadcast station signals, that the transaction is likely to increase its incentive and ability to use that market power to obtain substantially greater fee increases and other carriage concessions for such programming than it can today, and that additional remedial actions are therefore warranted for such video programming.

147. We conclude that News Corp. currently possesses significant market power with respect to its regional sports networks (RSNs) within each of their specific geographic regions, and that the proposed transaction will enhance News Corp.'s incentive and ability to temporarily withhold or threaten to withhold access to its RSN programming to increase the fees it receives for the programming, over and above what it could negotiate absent the transaction, to the ultimate detriment of the public. Moreover, we find that in contrast to the situation with respect to access to national and non-sports regional programming, neither our program access rules nor Applicants' proposed program access commitments are sufficient to protect against these likely transaction-specific harms.

173. We [believe] that a neutral dispute resolution forum would provide a useful backstop to prevent News Corp. from exercising its increased market power to force rival MVPDs to either accept inordinate affiliate fee increases for access to RSN programming and/or other unwanted programming concessions or potentially to cede critical content to their most powerful DBS competitor, DirecTV. We therefore create a mechanism whereby an aggrieved MVPD may choose to submit a dispute with News Corp. over the terms and conditions of carriage of RSNs to commercial arbitration to constrain News Corp.'s increased incentive to use temporary foreclosure strategies during carriage negotiations for RSN programming in each region in which News Corp. owns or holds a controlling interest or manages any

non-broadcast RSN, and require News Corp. to permit the MVPD to continue to carry the RSN while the dispute is being resolved.

175. Thus, our remedy is to allow MVPDs to demand commercial arbitration when they are unable to come to a negotiated "fair" price for the programming. The staff analysis has found that the allure of temporary withholding to News Corp. is substantial, even after the ability invariably to obtain supracompetitive affiliate fee increases is eliminated. Accordingly we do not allow News Corp. to deauthorize carriage of the RSN after an MVPD has chosen to avail itself of the arbitration condition. We also specify that expedited arbitration procedures be used and that the final offers submitted to the arbitrator by each side may not include any compensation for RSN carriage in the form of the MVPD's agreement to carry any video programming networks or any other service other than the RSN.

Dissenting Statement of Commissioner Jonathan S. Adelstein

Deciding whether a fox should guard a hen house is a far more serious exercise than this Order reflects. Granted, the birds in this case are not hens but valuable satellites with a national footprint from which nearly 12 million people receive video programming through DirecTV. And the Fox in this case is already one of the world's largest media conglomerates, with a vast array of global content and distribution assets. The acquisition of Hughes Electronics Corporation by News Corporation (News Corp.) will result in unprecedented control over local and national media properties in one global media empire. Its shockwaves will undoubtedly recast our entire media landscape.

Never before has a single corporation been armed with a national video distribution platform; a major broadcast network; television stations in nearly every major media market — reaching more than 44 percent of the country — with guaranteed carriage rights on other distribution platforms; multiple cable networks (11 national and 22 regional, including sports networks with exclusive rights); a major film and television studio; newspaper, magazine and book publishing operations; significant video programming and broadcasting satellite backhaul capacity; and the leading program guide and programming-related technologies to facilitate a consumer's viewing experience. With this unprecedented combination, News Corp. could be in a position to raise programming prices for consumers, harm competition in video programming and distribution markets nationwide, and decrease the diversity of media voices. I wish the full dangers of this combination would have been more thoroughly examined and confronted.

News Corp. is now in a position to distribute programs or sporting events either on its broadcast network, cable networks, regional networks, television stations, or even over pay-per-view. Imagine the increased bargaining power of News Corp. as it sits at various negotiating tables in these interconnected industries, finding itself on all sides at once, and with an increased arsenal of weapons against rival programmers or distributors. News Corp. will be in a position to demand higher programming fees or demand concessions without fear of losing distribution.

This merger also threatens disruptive effects for competing programmers, particularly independent programmers and producers. Even without the merger, through the use of retransmission consent, News Corp. has been able to expand its cable networks faster than any other cable programmer. I will continue to monitor closely whether News Corp. provides opportunities for both established and new networks, particularly new entrants, to negotiate carriage on fair and reasonable terms on DirecTV. New Spanish-language networks, for example, have reached agreement with cable providers and are attempting to negotiate carriage on DirecTV. Given DirecTV's history of promoting a diversity of programming, I would be concerned if its acquisition by News Corp. resulted in a loss of diverse, independent or minority-owned programming to an eager public in order to favor networks it owns.

These many concerns call for a more serious examination of the concentration resulting from the merger, or other more comprehensive structural or behavioral conditions. While this Order does contain some important protections, not all the effects on consumers and competition have been fully analyzed or remedied to assure fair competition and protection of consumer interests. I dissent.

Notes and Questions

1. **Vertical Integration Redux.** How does the FCC's review of News Corp.'s acquisition of DirecTV compare to the analyses in Comcast/NBCU and AT&T/Time Warner, above? We note at the top of this casebook section that the FCC applies a different standard than the antitrust agencies. Was that different standard reflected in the FCC's review?

2. **Fox in the Henhouse.** For Commissioner Adelstein, the prospect of greater vertical integration created heartburn. In the FCC's order, however, vertical integration was cited as a source of valuable economic efficiencies. Was Commissioner Adelstein discounting the merger's efficiencies? Would greater efficiencies have convinced him that the vertical merger is in the public interest?

3. **Competition in Video Programming Distribution.** The three vertical mergers discussed in this section revealed what was a growing market for programming distribution (including MVPD and OVD). In News Corp./DirecTV, the competitive concern was that vertical integration might advantage a DBS over MVPDs. In Comcast/NBCU, the concern was that vertical integration might advantage an MVPD over OVDs. What motivated these competitive concerns? Were there technological reasons why one distribution form might have had an advantage over another? Was it only a matter of which distributor had exclusive access to content? Is there a point at which distribution markets become sufficiently competitive that vertical acquisitions of these kinds are entirely unproblematic? Or might there always be a

competitive threat when those with access to content, which by definition is unique, own a distribution method?

§ 8.B.4. Acquisition of Nascent Competitors

One vexing, but critically important, question for antitrust law is whether to halt mergers that neither exacerbate any existing market power nor cause any immediate harm to competition but have a reasonably high potential of harming competition in the future. So-called "potential competition" cases usually present the possibility that a merger would prevent a new, emerging, or unrealized market from ever being realized (thus, the merger does not harm competition, but instead harms potential competition).

The doctrine is both imprecise and controversial. Although much of merger law involves predictions of the future, regulators arguing that a merger would eliminate potential competition are engaging in deep speculation. At the same time, much of the venture capital and start-up economy is premised on the hope that emerging companies will be purchased by incumbent companies, and economic theory posits that firms defending monopolies would pay more than any other established firm to acquire a nascent competitor that might challenge their market leadership.

Perhaps the danger of allowing nascent competitors to be acquired, and thereby eliminating potential competition, is greatest when the acquiring firm is a dominant digital platform. For the many reasons discussed throughout this casebook, dominant platforms enjoy scale and scope economies that would allow them to incorporate new products and enjoy continued comparative advantages over rivals. To be sure, many efficiencies can take place when dominant platforms acquire new firms and expand their offerings. But this process also blocks the possibility that any purchased firm would become the possible replacement of, or improvement upon, the incumbent platform. Some commentators have described tech markets as having "kill-zones" where dominant tech incumbent firms suppress competition through acquisitions of nascent competitors.

Current Antitrust Thinking on Nascent Competitors: The But-For World

Potential and nascent competition have seen renewed interest from academics and antitrust practitioners in recent years.[5] Both the FTC and the OECD have held hearings focusing on potential competition, and the DOJ's Antitrust Division and the FTC in early 2022 signaled they will pursue a more aggressive approach to acquisitions of

5. *See, e.g.*, Cunningham, Colleen, Florian Ederer, and Song Ma, Killer Acquisitions, 129 J. Political Economy, 649 (2021) (finding that 5–7 percent of the acquisitions undertaken in life sciences may have resulted in the termination of a target firm's drug development project because of the acquiring firm's interest in reducing competition for its own products).

nascent competitors.[6] But proving that these acquisitions are illegal requires assessing several potential scenarios in what is best described as the *but-for world.*

Specifically, in evaluating whether an acquisition of a nascent competitor will harm competition, a regulator must consider:

1. Would the nascent competitor survive and prosper, *but for* the acquisition of the incumbent? Note that firms in many technology markets exhibit high failure rates, and many of those that succeed rely on financing by or collaboration with incumbent firms.
2. Would the nascent competitor, *but for* the acquisition, operate in the same antitrust market as the incumbent, such that the entrant would indeed compete with the incumbent? Such an evaluation becomes more complex if the nascent competitor is not in the same market as the acquirer at the time of the acquisition, or if the market in which competition is anticipated does not currently exist.
3. Would the nascent competitor, *but for* the acquisition, meaningfully — and within a reasonably foreseeable period of time — offer a competitive threat to the incumbent? Are we sure just how much competition was lost because of the acquisition, and are we even sure technology would not have moved on by the time the nascent competitor hits the market?[7]

The more a market and its surrounding technologies are in flux, the harder it is to answer these questions. Consider the FTC's pains to scrutinize Google's acquisition of Double Click in 2007.

Google/Double Click

FTC File 071-0170, 2007 WL 4624893
Statement of the Federal Trade Commission

The Federal Trade Commission has voted 4–1 to close its investigation of Google's proposed acquisition of DoubleClick after a thorough examination of the evidence bearing on the transaction.

The Commission dedicated extensive resources to this investigation because of the importance of the Internet and the role advertising has come to play in the development and maintenance of this rapidly evolving medium of communication. Online advertising fuels the diversity and wealth of free information available on

6. "Request for Information on Merger Enforcement," U.S. Department of Justice and U.S. Federal Trade Commission, January 18, 2022, https://www.ftc.gov/news-events/news/press-releases/2022/01/federal-trade-commission-justice-department-seek-strengthen-enforcement-against-illegal-mergers.

7. *See* Vivek Mani, Economic Issues in Assessing Potential and Nascent Competition, National Law Review (June 8, 2022).

the Internet today. Our investigation focused on the impact of this transaction on competition in the online advertising marketplace.

I. Background

The evidence in this case shows that advertisers buy online advertising space from both search engine providers, like Google, and content providers (referred to as publishers in the online advertising business). However, the evidence in this case shows that the advertising space sold by search engines is not a substitute for space sold directly or indirectly by publishers or vice versa. Or, to put it in terms of merger analysis, the evidence shows that the sale of search advertising does not operate as a significant constraint on the prices or quality of other online advertising sold directly or indirectly by publishers or vice versa.

Search engines allow users to find specific information on the Internet by typing a query into a search query box. In addition to providing the user with results, search engines serve advertisements that are keyed off the search terms typed in by the user. Advertisers view online content providers differently. A user's visit to a particular content page may reveal some insight into that user's interests. However, users visiting a content page do not declare their interests in the same way they do when they type in a keyword on a search engine.

Google, through its AdWords business, is the dominant provider of sponsored search advertising, and most of its online advertising revenue is generated by the sale of advertising space on its search engine results pages. DoubleClick does not sell sponsored search advertising. In fact, it does not currently sell any form of advertising.

The sale of advertising space is publishers' primary source of revenue. The evidence shows that today large publishers use two channels to sell their inventory of available advertising space. The first channel is direct sales, with publishers using their own sales forces. The second channel large publishers use to sell their advertising inventory is indirect sales, with publishers and advertisers using the services of ad intermediation firms to place advertisements.

Google is an ad intermediary. Google's ad intermediation product, AdSense, is a leading provider of contextual advertising. The evidence shows that contextually targeted advertising is part of the broader ad intermediation market that includes all ads sold by intermediaries. DoubleClick does not provide contextual advertising, and it does not currently act as an intermediary.

Third party ad servers play an important role in the delivery and tracking of online advertisements. On the publisher side, third party ad servers manage the flow of advertising on publishers' websites by selecting the advertisements that generate the greatest revenue consistent with a publisher's contractual obligations with its advertisers. Ad server products are also used on the advertiser side to ensure that the ads selected by the publishers' tools are transmitted to the publishers' sites and served. When a publisher side ad server makes a call to retrieve an advertisement, the advertiser side ad server determines the optimal advertisements, pulls that ad from its inventory, and serves it into the designated place on the publisher's web page.

DoubleClick is the leading firm in the third party ad serving markets. It faces competition from several significant competitors in the United States, such as 24/7 Real Media, aQuantive, and ValueClick. A number of smaller recent entrants also compete head-to-head with these better established competitors. Further, the competitive dynamics of these markets have been altered by recent transactions, such as Microsoft's acquisition of aQuantive, WPP's acquisition of 24/7 Real Media, and AOL's acquisition of AdTech. To date, Google has not released or sold a commercially viable ad serving product in the United States.

II. Competitive Effects Analysis

After carefully reviewing the evidence, we have concluded that Google's proposed acquisition of DoubleClick is unlikely to substantially lessen competition. We analyzed three principal theories of potential competitive harm in the course of this investigation.

First, we assessed whether the evidence supported a challenge to this merger based on the theory that it threatened to eliminate direct and substantial competition between Google and DoubleClick. We concluded that it did not. As discussed above, Google sells advertising on its search engine and through its ad intermediation product, AdSense. It had been developing a third party ad serving solution prior to its agreement to purchase DoubleClick, but it had not released a commercially viable product. DoubleClick sells two third party ad serving products — DART for Advertisers (DFA) and DART for Publishers (DFP). It does not buy or sell advertisements or advertising inventory.

Second, we assessed whether the evidence supported a challenge based on the theory that the transaction threatened to eliminate potential competition in any relevant market. We have concluded that it does not. Google had been attempting to develop a third party ad serving solution at the time of the transaction, and therefore is a potential future competitor of DoubleClick and other third party ad serving firms. For the elimination of this potential competition to be a competitive concern, Google must be uniquely positioned to have a substantial competition-enhancing effect on the third party ad serving markets.

A pivotal consideration in any potential competition case is the current market dynamic. In this case, Google's entry is unlikely to have a significant procompetitive effect because the evidence shows that the third party ad serving markets are competitive despite relatively high levels of concentration in both markets. Although DoubleClick enjoys a significant share of today's third party ad serving markets, it does not appear that DoubleClick has market power in these markets. More specifically, prices and margins in the third party ad serving markets have eroded substantially over the past few years. The evidence shows that this decline in prices and margins is largely attributable to aggressive competition. Further, the evidence indicates that ad serving has become a commodity good, as competition from small third party ad serving competitors has forced larger competitors to slash prices. The recent acquisitions of existing third party ad servers by firms with significant financial resources are likely to increase further the competitiveness of this market.

In addition, there is no evidence that Google's developmental product is unique relative to existing third party ad servers, nor is the evidence clear that Google is certain to be successful in winning customers for these products. For these reasons, we have concluded that it is unlikely that the elimination of Google as a potential competitor in the third party ad serving markets would have a significant impact on competition.

Finally, we assessed whether the evidence supported a challenge based on any non-horizontal theory of harm, such as the possibility that Google could leverage DoubleClick's leading position in third party ad serving to its advantage in the ad intermediation market. A number of potential leveraging theories were proffered that could, in principle, raise competitive concerns. We have concluded, however, that these theories are not supported by the record evidence in this matter.

For each of these concerns, the threshold issue is whether DoubleClick (as the putative acquired party) enjoys significant market power in third party ad serving. A leveraging strategy cannot be effective, and thus anticompetitive, unless the merged firm has market power in one of the complementary products. As discussed above, the evidence suggests that DoubleClick does not have market power despite its high market share. The third party ad serving markets are competitive and are likely to become even more so in the future.

The markets within the online advertising space continue to quickly evolve, and predicting their future course is not a simple task. Accounting for the dynamic nature of an industry requires solid grounding in facts and the careful application of tested antitrust analysis. Because the evidence did not support the theories of potential competitive harm, there was no basis on which to seek to impose conditions on this merger. We want to be clear, however, that we will closely watch these markets and, should Google engage in unlawful tying or other anticompetitive conduct, the Commission intends to act quickly.

Notes and Questions

1. Three Theories of Harm. The FTC reported that, for this single transaction, it considered three possible theories of harm: horizontal concentration, vertical foreclosure, and the elimination of potential competition. It is unusual for the FTC to explore all three theories for a single transaction (can you say why?), but it is illustrative of antitrust law that a plaintiff must articulate a plausible theory of harm to competition.

2. The Dissent. Commissioner Pamela Jones Harbour dissented. She thought that DoubleClick was offering new services that would more directly compete with Google, and vice-versa, and that it was too early in the internet's development to allow the combination of two of the largest advertising services. She also argued that there were significant network effects in advertising, particularly the sort of behavioral advertising that both companies were enabling. Does this reflect a philosophical (or ideological) dispute with the other commissioners or a different factual understanding of the relevant markets?

3. The Limits of Merger Analysis? The details of the online advertising market are not just hard to follow for the layman. The FTC statement described multiple products in overlapping but distinct markets and a rapidly changing technological landscape. What must a plaintiff do to prove that an acquisition will harm competition? The prevailing strategy is to argue that the participating firms compete in a common market, but that is hard when markets and products are so fluidly defined (on this point, consider the question raised regarding the dissenting vote). An alternative approach is to find how specific markets might be leveraged or stifled. But what about the most intuitive argument when dominant platforms are involved: the more these firms acquire, the less likely any new entity will challenge their dominance. This is why many critics want to prevent dominant platforms from acquiring any firms: even if a particular acquisition is justified on efficiency grounds, the platform's enduring dominance causes long-term competitive harm. Is this argument impossibly vague and ill-defined? Or does it identify a weakness in current merger analysis?

4. Winning on a Potential Competition Theory. As noted above, successfully arguing that an acquisition will harm potential competition requires an articulation of a *but-for* world. The FTC suggests that one way to win would be to show that the purchasing firm had a superior product that it would have developed absent the acquisition. Another way to win is to prove that the purchasing firm is "uniquely positioned to have a substantial competition-enhancing effect on the third party ad serving markets." Why would these be successful arguments?

5. Lessons for FTC v. Facebook? Recall our discussion of the FTC's suit against Facebook in part §8.A.1. There, the FTC argued that Facebook's acquisition of then-nascent Instagram and WhatsApp harmed potential competition by preventing those upstarts from challenging Facebook's dominance. How can this claim be characterized as a *but-for* argument, and what must the FTC prove to win?

Chapter 9

Regulating the Spectrum

Introduction

In Chapter 7 we considered federal, state, and local regulation of various aspects of internet and telecommunications services, including regulations central to the physical rollout of wired and wireless networks. But in that chapter we did not focus on private ownership versus government control of the means of communication themselves — the wires and wireless frequencies used to provide service.

With respect to wires, the reason for not including this discussion is fairly obvious: the government has never prohibited private ownership of wires and has never claimed pervasive control over all wires. Some local governments have chosen to provide service over their own wires, rather than solely rely on private companies, but no government has passed legislation that prevents private ownership of wires or private provision of services over wires. It is conceivable that the government could attempt to nationalize all the existing wires used for internet and telecommunications and deny any private company the ability to create its own wired networks, but that possibility seems sufficiently remote that it is useful only as an unrealistic hypothetical.

By contrast, government control, and a denial of private ownership, is the longstanding state of affairs with respect to wireless frequencies. Section 301 of the Communications Act of 1934 announced that the federal government controls the spectrum and that it may grant licenses but not property rights:

> It is the purpose of this chapter, among other things, to maintain the control of the United States over all the channels of radio transmission; and to provide for the use of such channels, but not the ownership thereof, by persons for limited periods of time, under licenses granted by Federal authority, and no such license shall be construed to create any right, beyond the terms, conditions, and periods of the license. No person shall use or operate any apparatus for the transmission of energy or communications or signals by radio . . . except under and in accordance with this chapter and with a license in that behalf granted under the provisions of this chapter.

The government uses this authority to permit, but significantly regulate, private use of the airwaves. This chapter focuses on that regime. The absence of any equivalent regime for wires is always in the background. Because there is no equivalent regime for wires, there are no comparable statutes, regulations, and cases to discuss. But a question to consider as you read these materials is whether this divergence between wired and wireless regulatory regimes is justified, and, if not, how that should inform regulatory policy.

This chapter addresses three key questions that flow from the government's control of wireless frequencies: the relative merits of granting licenses to private companies versus allowing unlicensed use (like a commons), the rights the government confers on spectrum users, and, insofar as the government grants licenses, how it chooses to assign them.

§ 9.A. Characteristics of Electromagnetic Waves

As we noted earlier, the term telecommunications refers to the transmission of electronic communications over long distances. There are many ways to communicate at a distance. Smoke signals, semaphore flags, and automobile turn signals communicate modest amounts of information over relatively short distances. Modern telecommunications via electromagnetic waves, by contrast, permit almost instantaneous transmission of large quantities of information between a transmitter and a receiver across vast distances by encoding information in the wave.

There are two main channels across which these electromagnetic waves can travel: over wires or through the air.[1] Technologies like the telegraph, landline telephone, and cable television use large networks of wires to bring a signal directly to the receiver's device. By contrast, wireless technologies like mobile phones and broadcast television allow individuals to communicate at a distance using electromagnetic waves that travel through the air. This is no small trick; the information transmitted through broadcast technology must travel with no carrying case, no dedicated path, and no container. Broadcasting and other wireless technologies make use of radio waves, a subset of the much greater electromagnetic spectrum.

For the purposes of understanding telecommunications regulation, readers do not need detailed knowledge of exactly how wireless communication works. Nonetheless, it is helpful to know a few details about how electromagnetic waves carry information from place to place before engaging in a larger discussion about spectrum regulation.

One important characteristic of an electromagnetic wave is its frequency. In normal usage, the word "frequency" refers to the number of times a given event repeats during a specific period. In telecommunications, the word has a similar meaning. Electromagnetic waves typically look a lot like any other wave — they start at zero, then move up and down in the pattern of a sine wave before returning to zero. Each movement from zero up to the crest, back through zero and down to the trough, and back up to zero again is a cycle. The unit of measurement of frequency is called the

1. Technically speaking, electromagnetic waves can travel in free space where there is no air. Most popular accounts, however, refer to electromagnetic waves as using "airwaves," and we will use this convention as well.

hertz. A one-hertz (Hz) wave completes one cycle every second, and a one-kilohertz (kHz) wave accomplishes one thousand cycles in that same amount of time. The physical distance between the crests of each wave constitutes the wavelength, and this distance decreases as the frequency increases. Very long waves thus have very low frequencies because they repeat infrequently. Short waves have high frequencies because they recur more often.

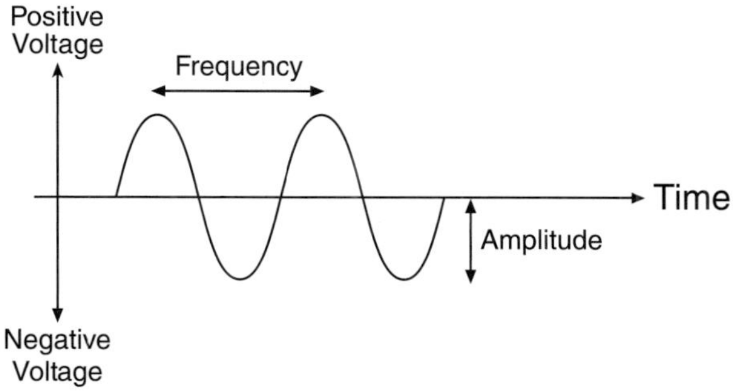

Electromagnetic Waves. Electromagnetic waves are typically transmitted as sine waves. Two important attributes of the wave are its frequency and its amplitude.

For our purposes, we will use the term spectrum to refer to the range of electromagnetic wavelengths (i.e., frequencies) currently suitable for wireless transmission.[2] Unsurprisingly, the amount of usable spectrum has expanded substantially during the past 100 years. For example, when the FCC was first established in 1934, the usable spectrum spanned less than 300 megahertz (MHz), which is to say less than 300 million hertz. That increased by more than a factor of 100 by the end of World War II, to 40 gigahertz (GHz), or 40 billion hertz, and by a factor of 1000 by the 21st century (to above 300 GHz).[3]

Different frequencies of electromagnetic waves have somewhat different characteristics. All else equal, lower frequency waves (with longer wavelengths) can travel further than waves at higher frequencies, because they are less susceptible to interference from physical obstacles or the sun's radiation. However, because lower frequency waves complete fewer cycles in a second, they can communicate less information. Thus, services with higher frequency waves can transmit more data but will require more antennas in a given service area.[4]

The different characteristics of the various frequencies are important to note, but there is no invariable requirement that a particular service use only an exact set of

2. The radio spectrum is a subset of the larger electromagnetic spectrum, which includes gamma rays, visible light, ultraviolet waves, and other forms of electromagnetic radiation.

3. To minimize reader confusion, in this chapter we will generally refer to bandwidth by the long form (e.g., megahertz) and specific frequencies by the abbreviated form (e.g., MHz).

4. Transmissions at the very lowest frequencies require very large antennas because exceedingly long waves must be propagated. In the highest frequencies, the wavelengths are so small that they can be packed into narrow focused beams of electromagnetic radiation, like those employed in microwave and radar.

frequencies. Every service can operate on more than one set of frequencies, and every frequency is suitable for more than one service. Old-fashioned radio broadcasting, for example, takes place all the way from 535 kHz to 108 MHz (108,000 kHz). That said, to generate a high-quality signal for a given service, some bands are likely to be more desirable than others. Propagation characteristics, for instance, make certain frequency ranges more suitable for particular purposes than others. The presence of other services on nearby (or the same) frequencies also might matter. For example, a service within one set of frequencies can create spillover effects that would render neighboring frequencies unsuitable for some services (say, broadcast television) but satisfactory for another service (say, mobile broadband).

Separate from its location in the spectrum (frequency), the amount of spectrum that a given service uses (its bandwidth) is also often very important. More bandwidth means more capacity for data transmission. The preferred amount of bandwidth for a particular use depends on the amount and types of information that must be impressed on the electromagnetic waves. For example, much more bandwidth is required to carry a video signal than to carry the human voice. The preferred amount of bandwidth also depends on the type of technology being employed. Some technologies can compress information into a smaller bandwidth, but at the expense of eliminating some information.

All else equal, the more bandwidth available for a given transmission, the more capacity and thus the more data that can be transmitted. A broader range of frequencies for a given service (say, 20 megahertz versus 10 megahertz blocks for mobile broadband), or for a given signal within that service (say, 6 megahertz versus 2 megahertz for a given television channel), allows for more data to be sent. This is true for wireless and wired communications. Using the same technology, a wire with greater capacity can transmit many more video streams than can a wire with less capacity. And a 20 megahertz block of frequency can carry more data than a 5 megahertz block can carry.

In discussing signal propagation thus far, we have held constant one critical part of the equation: the sophistication of the transmitter and receiver. In reality, however, the capability of these technologies makes a huge difference. We discuss the impact of equipment sophistication on signal propagation at greater depth in Section 9.A.2.

§ 9.A.1. Wires versus Airwaves as a Means of Propagation

Electromagnetic waves can travel from transmitter to receiver over either the airwaves or over wires (or both). Each medium is suitable for telecommunications and each is used by telecommunications technologies.

When waves are transmitted along a wire, the wire guides the signal. Today, transmitting information by wire at higher bandwidth usually employs one of two technologies. Coaxial cable is a braided metallic cylinder surrounding a wire. The wire carries the electromagnetic waves while the cylinder prevents signals from other wires, or outside radiation, from interfering with the signals on the wire. Optical fiber (or fiber optic) cable, a technology that entered widespread use in the 1980s, uses laser light traveling through optical fiber made of very thin glass to transmit information. It has even greater bandwidth than coaxial cable. Optical fiber is particularly well suited for information transmitted at high bandwidth, for transmission over very long distances, and for carrying many signals within one cable.

In contrast, when transmitting through the air, electromagnetic waves can be radiated in all directions (as conventional broadcasting does). Wireless waves can also be directed to a single direction, as with a wire going from point A to point B. A series of microwave transmitters linked together into a 2000-mile hookup, for example, each transmit only to a given area. The direction and characteristics of the signal are determined by the size, shape, and direction of the transmitting antenna. Transmitters for broadcasting, for instance, are designed to allow their signals to travel in all directions because their viewers are typically scattered throughout a geographic region.

In almost every case, more than one telecommunications technology can accomplish a given end. Voice and video can be transmitted by wire or over the air. Transoceanic cables can substitute for geostationary orbiting satellites. Multichannel packages of television signals can be sent to the home by cable or satellite. Choosing a telecommunications technology is therefore like choosing virtually any other good. One compares price and quality. For a specific task, some are cheaper, some are faster, and some are more reliable. The distinct advantage of spectrum, for instance, is mobility and the absence of the large infrastructure investment associated with wired systems. Wireline communication, in turn, offers enhanced privacy. Perhaps more importantly, signals carried via wire do not typically interfere with each other (the wire is designed to avoid such interference). By contrast, as we will discuss below, wireless transmissions may interfere with each other, and concerns about interference have played a major role in spectrum policy.

As new use cases arise, new configurations of telecommunications technology are developed to create cost-effective ways of satisfying these desires. Cable television wedded the use of wires and radio technology to serve the desires of viewers for more signals of greater clarity. Mobile telephony combined the same technologies to increase accessibility at some cost in clarity and in the ability to exclude unwanted listeners. Still, some telecommunications technologies like mobile phones require access to the spectrum in order to function (although it is amusing to imagine the knots that would be created by pedestrians or drivers using wired phones).

Given the technological substitutability of wired and wireless transmissions, the relative regulation of the two technologies can also impact the choices of telecommunications companies. Regulation can be a powerful tool for the government to maximize the value of information transmitted through wireless and wired channels. Regulation can also have a distorting impact. For example, if the FCC places far more onerous restrictions on wireless channels than on wired, telecommunications providers may shift their attention towards wired technologies. Throughout the rest of this chapter, which focuses on regulation of the spectrum, keep the availability of wired alternatives in the back of your mind.

§ 9.A.2. The Spectrum as a Resource

The government's regulation of spectrum treats it as if it were a natural resource, one to be allocated for specific uses and assigned to specific users. This approach is helpful in reminding us that spectrum shares many basic properties with other natural resources:

Spectrum can help to create both wealth and value. People are often willing to pay substantial sums for the ability to send or receive large quantities of data quickly and from far away.

Spectrum can be used in varying amounts for the same purpose. To get a television signal from a New York stage to a Los Angeles nightclub, one could use no spectrum (send it via wire, door to door), some spectrum (wire from New York to Los Angeles, but wireless to the nightclub), or nothing but spectrum (transmit directly from stage to satellite, which transmits, in turn, directly to the nightclub).

Spectrum use is costly in that devoting frequencies to one use increases the costs of (and possibly prohibits) employing those frequencies for a different desired use. If one person operates a high-power television broadcasting transmitter on a given frequency, it will be difficult if not impossible for someone else to use that frequency for mobile telephony, FM radio, or dispatching ambulances in the same location at the same time.

The amount and value of usable spectrum can be increased with appropriate investments in technology. Not only has the range of *usable* frequencies increased over time, but so, too, has the range of *high-value* frequencies. Historically, the most valuable spectrum bands have been low-band frequencies (below 1 GHz) because of their suitability for transmission over long distances. Indeed, the FCC sometimes referred to these frequencies as "beachfront" spectrum. Implementation of Section 6002(b) of the Omnibus Budget Reconciliation Act of 1993, Fourteenth Report, 25 FCC Rcd. 11,407, 11,572 ¶ 269 (2010). But with the rise of 5G services, mid-band spectrum (frequencies between 1 and 6 GHz, which are well-suited to 5G) became highly valuable.

Relatedly, within any existing range of usable frequencies spectrum capacity (and thus value to users) can be increased by advances in the sophistication of the devices used. In a world of unsophisticated equipment, signals in the same frequency band at the same time and in the same location are very likely to cancel each other out because the receiver cannot focus on particular types of signals. But more advanced transmitters and receivers permit more efficient use of limited spectrum. For example, greater complexity in network algorithms can reduce interference problems by allowing equipment to use the algorithms to detect the desired signal. Multiple-input, multiple-output (MIMO) systems can combine data streams arriving from different paths and at different times, permitting the transmission of multiple messages at the same frequency without interference. Another possibility is that transmitters can use ultra-wideband technology, which sends messages through quick, short pulses across a wide bandwidth to avoid interference. More simply, digital compression allows a broadcaster to send much more information over the same amount of spectrum that would otherwise be occupied by an uncompressed analog signal.

This highlights the ways in which wireless frequencies are more flexible than land. A rough land analogy would exist if we could simply make beaches much longer, or add hundreds of stories to existing buildings.

In short, "[w]ith airwaves, as with other media, the more you spend, the more you can send; it all comes down to engineering and smart management." Peter Huber, Law and Disorder in Cyberspace: Abolish the FCC and Let Common Law Rule the Telecosm 75 (1997).

§ 9.B. Rationales for Regulation: Scarcity/Interference

Some of the regulations discussed in this casebook have applied equally to spectrum licensees and the owners of wires.

But there is a particularly important regulatory difference between wires and spectrum, involving ownership and control. In contrast to the government's denial of private ownership of wireless frequencies (embodied in 47 U.S.C. § 301), the government has allowed private ownership of wires that provide telecommunications and internet services. Some localities and other government units have bought and thus owned wires they have used to provide service, but that does not entail the government prohibiting private ownership of wires, which it has never done. And common carrier regulation is quite significant, but such regulation is quite different from government control of the allocation and use of wires.

What remains to be explained is why the federal government is so involved in the allocation of frequencies given that it does not allocate wires (or printing presses, or most other resources). It may seem tempting to say that the federal government controls the spectrum because it does not allow private ownership of spectrum. But that just begs the question why the government does not allow private ownership of wireless frequencies. The government once owned huge chunks of land that it sold (or gave) to settlers. Why shouldn't it have done the same thing with spectrum? The government can assume ownership of any property for public use via eminent domain (so long as it pays just compensation). Why does it make sense for the government to own the airwaves but not assume ownership of other resources?

Separate from the more general justifications for regulation discussed in Chapter 1, one argument historically has been central to the justification of government regulation of spectrum: that the spectrum is scarce. This argument arose principally in the broadcast context—as that was the main use of spectrum for much of the 20th century—but it applies to spectrum regulation more generally. As you consider this argument, see if it helps you to answer the following questions: Why did the federal government decide to seize the spectrum and give an administrative agency, rather than producers, ultimate control over how producers would deliver information products over the air to consumers? Why did the government likewise give that same federal agency influence over the content of the information transmitted instead of simply allowing consumers to determine content through their viewing and purchasing decisions? Are there good reasons that we allocate spectrum through an administrative agency but leave the distribution of their other equipment—like wires—to conventional markets?

As we noted above, signals over modern wires do not interfere with each other, but interference has long been a major concern with respect to wireless transmissions. Two parties cannot broadcast on the same frequency, at the same time, in the same place, in the same direction without causing one another at least some interference. If two parents with similarly pitched voices simultaneously call for their respective children from the same porch in the same direction, the two messages will likely become garbled. Similarly, if one person starts tapping his finger in a pond, the ripples will travel cleanly until someone else starts tapping in that same water, at which time both patterns will likely be lost. One goal of telecommunications policy is to ensure that wireless transmitters do not interfere with one another in comparable ways, rendering each other's communications incomprehensible.

Low levels of interference with wireless transmissions are ubiquitous. Even a small electric appliance like a light fixture creates an electromagnetic field that can introduce a tiny amount of interference for nearby users of adjacent frequencies. In some cases, the emitted radio frequency energy is so small that it does not create a noticeable loss of signal quality. The real fear is of more significant interference—harmful interference, as it were—such that one set of electromagnetic waves overlaps with another set to a sufficient degree that a receiver can hear neither clearly. This concept, however, is to some extent in the eye of the beholder, because interference is a function of what the receiver can hear. As we noted above, more sophisticated transmitters and/or receivers are better able to communicate the intended signal and thus avoid interference.

The case of managing interference disputes, and the analogy to disputes over land, lends itself to an application of the Coase Theorem. Most law students (and professors) don't realize that this most famous of law and economics principles actually emerged from eventual Nobel Laureate Ronald Coase's study of spectrum.[5]

5. The first footnote of Coase's The Problem of Social Cost states: "This article, although concerned with a technical problem of economic analysis, arose out of the study of the Political Economy of Broadcasting which I am now conducting. The argument of the present article was implicit in a previous article dealing with the problem of allocating radio and television frequencies (The

What Coase realized about the spectrum is that a dispute about interference did not lend itself to a judgment that one user created a nuisance for the other — say, a TV station next to a wireless dispatch system. Rather, the relevant benefit (freedom from interference) and harm (harmful interference) were reciprocal. As such, neither the party creating the interference (the high-powered TV station) nor the party experiencing the interference (the low-powered dispatch system) could claim an a priori right against the other. In Coase's view, then, the critical role of government was not to determine who had a prevailing moral right against another — which is exactly how the FCC traditionally thought of spectrum management — but rather who had what property right (e.g., the right to broadcast at a certain frequency at a certain power in a certain area).

With property rights well defined and enforced, Coase explained, parties to a dispute could bargain as to how to allocate the right. In our TV station-dispatch system hypothetical, Coase would suggest that the FCC needed merely to specify the nature of the property rights of each party and, assuming no transaction costs, the two parties should reach an efficient outcome. This efficient outcome can include a maze of possibilities that command-and-control regulation might overlook, including the higher power system paying for the lower power system to upgrade its receivers to protect that system against interference.

Even if the FCC were to define property rights along the lines discussed above, the FCC would need to adopt both ex ante and ex post oversight of interference management. Most users value certainty of transmission very highly. Identifying the source of interference so that it does not recur in the future will provide little solace to the user whose very important message was not successfully transmitted. As a result, a system that relies solely on ex post solutions is not one that most service providers would favor. And the points previously noted highlight the complexities of reaching private agreements among all the parties who could contribute to interference. Most commentators thus conclude that the most efficient response to the possibilities of interference includes some role for the government — a regulatory regime that has some ex ante rules that the government can impose on everyone. But that does not necessarily justify any role for the government beyond policing interference.

A bigger government role in spectrum regulation has often been justified based on a concern related to interference: scarcity. If two radio stations cannot both broadcast on the same frequency at the same time, and if there are a limited number of frequencies at which radio communication can take place, then at some point demand might exceed supply. How soon that constraint is reached depends heavily on government policy. If the government sets a low price for spectrum use, demand may reach unsustainable levels. If prices for access to spectrum rise, private parties

Federal Communications Commission, 2 J.L. & Econ. (1959))." Ronald H. Coase, The Problem of Social Cost, 3 J.L. & Econ. 1 n.1 (1960).

will search both for wired alternatives and for ways to use their spectrum more efficiently (e.g., more sophisticated transmitters and receivers).

The idea that spectrum is subject to interference and thus scarce has long been the most common argument put forward in favor of government regulation of spectrum. The Supreme Court itself adopted this rationale in its earliest case addressing the government's control over the spectrum, NBC v. United States, 319 U.S. 190 (1943). The Court stated that:

> [There are] certain basic facts about radio as a means of communication—its facilities are limited; they are not available to all who may wish to use them; the radio spectrum simply is not large enough to accommodate everybody. There is a fixed natural limitation upon the number of stations that can operate without interfering with one another. Regulation of radio was therefore as vital to its development as traffic control was to the development of the automobile. In enacting the Radio Act of 1927, the first comprehensive scheme of control over radio communication, Congress acted upon the knowledge that if the potentialities of radio were not to be wasted, regulation was essential.

Id. at 213. As we will see in Chapter 11, the Supreme Court adopted similar reasoning in Red Lion Broadcasting Co. v. FCC, 395 U.S. 367, 399 (1969).

The Court was understandably concerned that interference would destroy the utility of the spectrum as a resource. As we have noted, if two transmitters broadcast at the same time, on the same frequency, from the same location, in the same direction, and at the same power, neither of them is likely to be heard. But every rivalrous resource is subject to interference. If two people try to sit in the same desk chair at the same time, they will interfere with each other. That's why we call such goods rivalrous. Saying that wireless frequencies are scarce because of interference does not distinguish them from virtually any other good. The Supreme Court in *NBC* and *Red Lion* emphasized that there was excess demand for the free broadcasting licenses provided by the government and suggested that this highlighted the scarcity of spectrum. But almost all resources—e.g., wires, labor, steel, land, and investment capital—are scarce in that (a) if given away at no charge people would request more of them than is available and (b) if we could create more of them, that additional increment could also be put to productive use. Again, the way in which wireless frequencies are scarce fails to distinguish them from virtually every other good, most of which are not allocated by the government.

One might want to argue that wireless frequencies are different from other resources in that the frequencies are finite, and most other resources are not. But, as we noted previously, the throughput of spectrum has increased dramatically over the years. Improvements in technology have greatly increased the range of usable spectrum, as higher and higher frequencies can be used to send data. And technology has also enabled us to send more and more data over the same block of frequencies (through, for example, digital compression). Besides, at any given point there are only so many trees in the world, so many pounds of steel, and so on. Just as we could expend more resources to get more throughput through existing wires and to produce more wires, we could expend more resources to increase the communications capacity of the spectrum.

The foregoing addresses the question whether spectrum is unusually scarce. The argument does not stop there, of course; the key assertion is that scarcity justifies government control. But to say that spectrum is scarce is only to say that the use of spectrum must be allocated among those who desire it. Use of any scarce resource must be allocated. In the U.S. economy, this allocation usually is accomplished by prices set in open markets. It is unsatisfying, then, to say that administrative allocation of spectrum is necessary because of spectrum scarcity. The real issue seems to be whether spectrum is scarce in some special way (unlike, say, wires or land) that peculiarly requires a nonmarket allocation mechanism.

To return to the chair example above, two people cannot comfortably sit at the same time in the same desk chair, yet that fact has not led government to regulate chair use. Rather, ownership of the chair is taken to confer the authority to exclude others from sitting in it, and, with that property right in place, government regulation is deemed unnecessary. Thomas Hazlett puts the point this way: "The interference problem is [rightly understood to be] one of defining separate frequency 'properties,' but it is logically unconnected to the issue of who is to harvest those frequencies. To confuse the *definition* of spectrum rights with the *assignment* of spectrum rights is to believe that, to keep intruders out of (private) backyards, the government must own (or allocate) all the houses. It is a public policy non sequitur." Thomas W. Hazlett, The Rationality of Broadcast Regulation, 33 J.L. & Econ. 133, 138 (1990).

Coase elaborated on these arguments and criticized government control of spectrum in testimony before the FCC excerpted below.

Why Not Use the Pricing System in the Broadcast Industry?

Ronald Coase, Testimony before the FCC, December 1959, *reprinted in* 4·Study of Radio & Television Network Broadcasting (No. 12,782) (1959)

I appear before you with a strong conviction and a bold proposal. My conviction is that the principles under which the American economic system generally operates are fundamentally sound. My proposal is that the American broadcasting industry adopt those principles.

In presenting my case, I suffer from the disadvantage that, at the outset, I must attack a position which, although I am convinced it is erroneous, is nonetheless firmly held by many of those most knowledgeable about the broadcasting industry. Most authorities argue that the administrative assignment of radio and television frequencies by the Commission is called for by the technology of the industry. The number of frequencies, we are told, is limited, and people want to use more of them than are available.

But the situation so described is in no sense peculiar to the broadcasting industry. All resources used in the economic system are limited in amount and are scarce in that people want to use more of them than exists. This is so whether we think of labor, land, or capital. However, we do not ordinarily consider that this situation calls for government regulation. It is true that some mechanism has to be employed to decide who, out of the many claimants, should be allowed to use the scarce resources. But the usual way of handling this problem in the American economic system is to employ the pricing mechanism, and this allocates resources to users without the need for government regulation.

This is the system under which broadcasting concerns obtain the labor, land, and capital equipment they require. There is no reason why the same system could not be adopted for radio and television frequencies. If these were disposed of by selling or leasing them to the highest bidder, there would be no need to use such criteria as proposed or past programming as a basis for the selection of broadcast station operators. Such a system would require a delimitation of the property rights acquired, and there would almost certainly also have to be some general regulation of a technical character. But such regulation would not preclude the existence of private rights in frequencies, just as zoning and other regulations do not preclude the existence of private property in houses.

Such a use of the pricing mechanisms would bring the same advantages to the radio and television industry as its use confers on the rest of the American economy. It would avoid the need for much of the costly and time-consuming procedures involved in the assignment of frequencies by the Commission. It would rule out inefficient use of frequencies by bringing any proposal for the use of such frequencies up against the test of the market, with its precise monetary measure of cost and benefit. It would avoid the threat to freedom of the press in its widest sense which is inherent in present procedures, weak though that threat may be at the moment. And it would avoid that arbitrary enrichment of private operators of radio and television stations which inevitably follows from the present system. A station operator who is granted a license to use a particular frequency in a particular place may be granted a very valuable right, one for which he would be willing to pay millions of dollars and which he would be forced to pay if others could bid for the frequency. We sometimes hear denunciations of giveaways and their corrupting influence. You, gentlemen, are administering what must be one of the biggest giveaways of all.

It has been my experience that such a suggestion as I have made horrifies my listeners. I am told that it is necessary to choose those who should operate radio and television stations to make sure that the public interest is served and that programs of the right kind are transmitted. But, put this way, the case for governmental selection of broadcast station operators represents a significant shift of position from that which justifies it on technological grounds. It is, of course, a tenable position. But if the object of the selection is, in part, directly or indirectly, to influence programming, we have to face squarely the issue of freedom of the press so far as broadcasting is concerned.

But in any case it may be doubted whether an indirect attempt to influence programming through the selection of broadcast station operators could ever be very effective. For over 30 years, the federal government has been selecting broadcast station operators on the basis, among other things, of their good character and their devotion to the public interest. By now one would expect the broadcasting industry to be a beacon of virtue, shining out in a wicked world. Such, I am afraid, is not the case.

Notes and Questions

1. A Road Not Taken. A state court adopted a property rights approach before Congress legislated otherwise. In Tribune Co. v. Oak Leaves Broadcasting Station, (Ill. Cir. Ct. 1926), *reprinted in* 68 Cong. Rec. 215, 215–19 (1926), the Chicago Tribune Company alleged that WGN (a radio station it owned and named for itself, the "World's Greatest Newspaper") had been broadcasting daily for two years, had expended substantial money on equipment, and had a large and regular audience; and that the defendant, Oak Leaves, after jumping frequencies twice, had landed at a frequency quite close to WGN's. WGN asserted that Oak Leaves had moved in so close because it was an unpopular station. According to WGN, Oak Leaves' hope was that some of WGN's listeners would tune to the wrong station by accident. Oak Leaves essentially responded that the separation was ample, and therefore it had not harmed WGN.

The trial judge received "thousands of affidavits" filed by the parties, providing him with a considerable amount of information about a new and complex industry. *Id.* at 218. His opinion noted the local mores whereby all the Chicago stations went silent on a specific night so that their listeners could tune in to distant stations. It also noted that the public had become educated in the use of radio and knew how to obtain the type of programming it desired. This would prove difficult, the judge concluded, unless a greater separation was maintained within a 100-mile radius.

The trial judge thus resolved the issue by defining property rights. Drawing analogies to the law of unfair competition and also the law of water rights, the judge concluded that, by reason of use and expenditure of money and effort, the plaintiff had under the common law acquired something "generally recognized" as property. *Id.* at 219.

2. Reactions to Property Rights. Congress rejected the property rights approach, prohibiting such rights in the Radio Act of 1927 (and continuing that prohibition in the Communications Act of 1934). Why do you think Congress made that decision? Thomas Hazlett argues that the 1927 policy debate in Congress over the creation of the Federal Radio Commission was "led by men who clearly understood—and articulated—that interference was not the problem, interference was the opportunity." Hazlett, *supra*, at 162. That is, according to Hazlett, those leading the debate saw concerns about interference as enabling them to justify government control of the airwaves. Does that argument ignore more public-regarding rationales for

Congress's decision? What groups might have effectively resisted government control, and why do you think that didn't happen?

By 1959, when Coase gave his testimony, private spectrum rights were politically unimaginable. Perhaps the most striking evidence is that, right after Coase delivered the talk excerpted above, the floor was opened for questions, and then-FCC Commissioner Philip Cross began the question period by asking Coase, in all seriousness, "Are you spoofing us? Is this all a big joke?" Ronald Coase, Comment on Thomas W. Hazlett: Assigning Property Rights to Radio Spectrum Users: Why Did FCC License Auctions Take 67 Years?, 41 J.L. & Econ. 577, 579 (1998). When Coase expressed those same ideas in a paper for the Rand Corporation, one referee who reviewed the document advised Rand to kill the project entirely, and another "stated that, by definition, the spectrum was a public good and consequently a market solution was not appropriate and that the project represented a waste of Rand's resources." *Id.* at 580. Consider the following statement from the memorandum rejecting Coase's paper for Rand: "I am afraid that to issue [Coase's paper] ... is asking for trouble in the Washington/Big Business maelstrom because we haven't in the first place measured up to the intellectual requirements of the problem selected for study." *Id.*

3. Defining Property Rights. In order for a market system to work, the government would need to delimit specific bundles of rights that could then be recognized in particular users. Just as land ownership includes, among other things, the right to exclude others under certain circumstances and rights with respect to the use of natural resources above and below ground level, spectrum ownership, too, would have to be articulated in terms of specific rights to use and exclude. How difficult would that articulation be? More difficult than it is in other settings? Enough to explain why we regulate spectrum but not wires or wood pulp?

Think specifically about how you would define property rights in spectrum. Perhaps in terms of inputs, with the government recognizing in a particular party the (transferable?) right to build a tower of a certain height, at a particular location, transmitting a signal at a particular frequency and power level, during particular times, and in a particular direction? Indeed, a group of scholars in 1969 proposed just such a definition of spectrum property rights based on parameters of time, geographic area, power, and wave frequency. Arthur S. De Vany et al., A Property System for Market Allocation of the Electromagnetic Spectrum: A Legal-Economic-Engineering Study, 21 Stan. L. Rev. 1499 (1969). The FCC has shied away from a more precise effort to define interference rights.

4. The Coase Theorem. Coase is perhaps most famous for his work on the importance of transaction costs. Yet, might it be argued that, in his remarks before the FCC, Coase neglected the important role transaction costs play in the market for telecommunications services? Think about how many parties use spectrum on both the national and international level, both as suppliers of telecommunications services and as consumers of those services, or how even a single radio signal at a relatively low energy level can still interfere with dozens of signals hundreds of miles away. Did Coase jump over this point too quickly? Are transaction costs a good reason for government regulation of the spectrum? Does Coase's argument apply more strongly to some services, such as those with a limited number of spectrum licensees (e.g., mobile telephony), than to others (e.g., radio broadcasting)?

5. Zoning. Thus far, the theme of this section has been to point out that scarcity/interference is a common problem to which the typical response is not to regulate but instead to define property rights and then defer to market interactions. With respect to land ownership, however, government does regulate, in particular via zoning laws. Does Coase's attack call zoning laws into question? Or is Coase's argument consistent with a methodological framework that would call for a zoning of the spectrum? How would such a system work?

Looked at another way, is there something special about both land and spectrum that distinguishes them from other goods? For example, the government uses land for public purposes (say, government buildings and public parks) and the government also has significant demand for spectrum (for example, military use and police radio). Does this fact help to explain why, for spectrum and land use, scarcity/interference has led to government regulation whereas for wires and other resources it has led to more market-based solutions?

6. Markets and Regulation. What is lost by the use of an administrative agency instead of market forces? Are there corresponding gains? Are traditional worries about markets — say, the fear of monopoly or concerns about distributional effects — more salient in the spectrum context? Can a market work in spectrum given that, for services like broadcasting, the equipment that transmits signals is typically owned by one group (broadcasters), whereas the equipment that receives those signals is typically owned by another, independent group (consumers)? Is this why we regulate? If we ask advertising-based broadcasters to bid for spectrum, would they bid less than subscription services would, on the theory that the revenues from commercial advertisements are likely less than what viewers would directly pay for content? (If that is the case, is it an argument against free broadcast and in favor of subscription television instead?) Does regulation perhaps preserve more flexibility for the government than a market regime would?

§ 9.C. Managing the Spectrum

As we have noted, Congress never controlled the distribution of wires, but it did decide to control the spectrum (while allowing private uses of much of it). By statute, the National Telecommunications and Information Administration (NTIA) regulates federal government use of the spectrum, and the FCC regulates all other uses. *See* Telecommunications Authorization Act, Pub. L. No. 102-538, 106 Stat. 3533 (1992), (codified as amended at 47 U.S.C. § 303). This book focuses on the regulation of private activity and so does not focus on the NTIA. But it bears noting that the relationship between government and private uses of spectrum (and thus between the NTIA and the FCC) has taken on particular significance as demand for ever-higher frequencies for private use have conflicted with federal government usage of spectrum.[6]

So the FCC is in charge of regulating the private use of spectrum, but what does that entail? There are many possible variations (the most prominent of which are discussed in the following sections), but we start with the basic model the FCC has historically applied.

Its first step is to determine which services it will allow on which frequencies, and how many users it will allow to provide those services. This process (generally called allocation) entails the FCC deciding what services it is going to permit and the quantity and wavelengths of frequencies at which it will allow those services. As an example, the FCC decided to authorize FM radio broadcasting on the 20 megahertz span between 88 MHz and 108 MHz. In any given allocation, the FCC can permit one type of service, several types of services, or any type of service, and can make its rules accordingly. And it can choose to grant licenses to one entity, a number of designated entities, or to leave a set of frequencies completely open for unlicensed use.

In addition to determining the quantity and particular set of frequencies to allocate for a given service or services, the FCC determines how (if at all) to allot licenses for the service, and what sort of service rules it will impose. That is, the FCC decides how big a range of frequencies each license will cover (e.g., 100 licenses covering 2 megahertz each, which totals 200 megahertz, or 5 licenses covering 40 megahertz each, also totaling 200 megahertz); how much area each license is authorized to cover (e.g., Indiana alone, Indiana plus Ohio, or the entire United States); what the limits are on the power levels of the transmitters; and whether and how it will create buffers between users or between services to avoid interference. Taken together, these decisions are sometimes called the band plan.

The FCC also creates rules for the assignment, transfer, and renewal of spectrum licenses. Over time, the FCC has dramatically changed its approach with respect to this task. In the beginning, the FCC assigned licenses through comparative hearings in which each licensee was evaluated in terms of its ability to provide the service in question. Licenses lasted for a few years, after which time a licensee had to petition the FCC for renewal, and there were restrictions on transfer. As we discuss in § 9.F below, the FCC now assigns licenses using an auction mechanism, transfers usually are not questioned, and licenses are almost always renewed.

Notes and Questions

1. Analogies. What is the best analogy to spectrum regulation? Probably the most common analogy is to the regulation of land use. Is that an apt analogy? If so, what does it tell us? Are zoning regulations the equivalent of the band plan? More

6. The Citizens Broadband Radio Service proceeding noted below is one example of an attempt at accommodation of government and private uses of wireless frequencies.

generally, what are the land equivalents of the various decisions that the FCC makes? What are the greatest similarities and the sharpest divergences between spectrum regulation and land regulation? What, if anything, should spectrum regulators learn from land use regulators, and vice-versa? How would you compare the externalities involved in spectrum regulation with those involved in land regulation? How would you compare the desirability of requirements that spectrum licensees and landholders take specific actions deemed to be in the public interest?

Or maybe the analogy to land is inapt. If so, why? And, more to the point, are there any good analogies to spectrum regulation? If not, what should that tell us, and what should it tell FCC commissioners?

2. Political Responsiveness versus Insulation. Are the sorts of decisions the FCC makes technocratic ones that should be left to experts? Are they political ones that should be made by elected officials representing the popular will? Something else? Note that FCC commissioners are nominated by the President and confirmed by the Senate, but (unlike the heads of executive agencies like the departments of State, Treasury, Justice, and Defense) they are insulated to some degree from the political process by having fixed terms. So they are chosen by elected officials but have some insulation from political control. Is that the right balance? On what basis, and using what metrics, would you answer that question?

§ 9.C.1. A Note on Tradeoffs: Allotment

Every decision the government makes with respect to spectrum (or anything else) involves tradeoffs. Allocating more bandwidth to one service, for example, will often require reducing the bandwidth devoted to another service, and assigning a license to one user will often entail rejecting a license application from another user.

Allotment of television broadcasting stations provides a nice example of similar tradeoffs. The FCC has often articulated the goals of broadcast regulation to be competition and diversity.[7] *See, e.g.*, 1998 Biennial Regulatory Review, Notice of Inquiry, 13 FCC Rcd. 11,276, 11,277 ¶ 4 (1998) ("For more than a half century, the Commission's regulation of broadcast service has been guided by the goals of promoting competition and diversity."). A third goal that the FCC often includes with competition and diversity is localism. *See, e.g.*, Broadcast Localism, Notice of Inquiry, 19 FCC Rcd. 12,425 ¶ 1 (2004) ("As with competition and diversity, localism has been a cornerstone of broadcast regulation for decades.").

These three goals are in tension with one another. For instance, treating diversity as a goal separate and distinct from competition must mean that, in some cases, competition should be sacrificed, at least to some extent, to achieve diversity.

7. As we discuss in Chapter 10.C, it has identified five different types of diversity: viewpoint, program, outlet, source, and minority and female ownership, with viewpoint diversity as its most common focus.

Otherwise, the goal of diversity is doing no work. The conflict between localism and the other goals has been particularly sharp in the broadcasting context. The FCC chose to place at least one television station in as many communities as possible.[8] The FCC could have designated single nationwide licenses as opposed to ones based in local communities. By so doing, a single firm could broadcast on channel 2 in a more effective fashion and without the need for as many empty stations that ensue when one firm broadcasts on channel 2 from, say, New York City and another firm broadcasts on channel 3 from Philadelphia. Because of interference concerns where these channels might overlap (say, in Princeton, New Jersey), the result of this policy is that large swaths of territory will not be within range of a channel 2 signal (New York City) or a channel 3 signal (Philadelphia). Creating nationwide licenses would have given individuals access to more stations (by avoiding interference problems created through assigning stations to each city).

The FCC's decision not to maximize the number of stations but instead to focus on ensuring local stations in each community thus meant that individuals would be able to see local news and weather, but it also reduced the number of national broadcast networks that could be created — helping ensure that, for decades, there would be only three commercial broadcast television networks. Even as of 1980, an FCC study found that although 92% of U.S. households could receive at least three commercial television channels (ABC, CBS, and NBC), only 64% could receive a fourth channel, making it hard for a fourth network to compete.[9] The irony is that the existence of only three national broadcast networks led the FCC to regulate the networks' behavior. The FCC, concerned that the existence of only three networks did not ensure adequate competition, imposed a series of restraints on the networks' relationships with their affiliates and their program suppliers (discussed in Chapter 5.C.1).

This is not to say that the FCC necessarily made a mistake in focusing on localism. That said, some decisions on how to design the scope of spectrum licenses are widely understood, in retrospect, to have been mistakes. There is broad agreement, for example, that regulators erred when they followed a local model for mobile telephone providers. The decision to create a large number of locally based licenses proved highly inefficient because users wanted national service, and negotiating roaming agreements between local carriers entailed large transaction costs. The FCC's initial emphasis on localism for mobile phone service was eventually overcome through market consolidation, but that emphasis resulted in early network infrastructure that was less advanced and efficient.

---

8. Sometimes Congress has made the allotment choices itself. Notably, a 1928 amendment to the Radio Act mandated an equalization of radio stations across five geographical zones. Pub. L. No. 70-195, 45 Stat. 373 (1928). Offered by a Tennessee member of Congress, it sought to replace stations in the more populous East with newcomers in the South and West.

9. *See* FCC Network Inquiry Special Staff, New Television Networks: Entry, Jurisdiction, Ownership, and Regulation 68 (1980); Christopher S. Yoo, The Rise and Demise of the Technology-Specific Approach to the First Amendment, 91 Geo. L.J. 245, 275–79, 279 n.155 (2003).

Notes and Questions

1. **Broader Applications.** The FCC has not emphasized localism or diversity in its regulation of internet access. Is that a mistake? How might they apply in the context of internet access regulation?

2. **Principles.** Is there any metric for the FCC to use in trading off among competition, diversity, and localism? And why those three goals? Should it add other goals to those three, or subtract one or two? On what basis should it decide whether to do so?

§ 9.D. Allocating the Spectrum

We know that the government decided not to confer property rights in spectrum but to allow private uses of much of it. The government could simply grant everyone, or a select number of private licensees, the right to transmit as they see fit over the entire range of usable frequencies, without bothering to allocate users into specific frequency bands. The FCC has opted against this approach, which would severely limit the number of users in a given area due to a higher likelihood of interference. Instead, the FCC has divided the spectrum into different frequency bands, as discussed above. In addition to managing interference, this approach also allows the government to choose bands that are well-suited to particular uses. For example, broadcast television has historically occupied lower frequency bands that permit transmission across long distances with fewer transmitters.

Once the FCC divides the spectrum into different frequency bands, it must decide exactly what rights to confer on users. Should the FCC grant licenses requiring particular services and technologies, with no ability on the part of the licensee to change services or subdivide its spectrum rights? Should it grant licenses providing the licensee with complete flexibility? Should it allow unlicensed uses, either in addition to or instead of licensed uses?

Over time, the FCC's answers have changed. In the early days, the FCC was heavy-handed: through its band plan, the FCC would decide not only exactly what services would be offered at what frequencies but also how many licensees would be allowed to offer those services. The FCC has moved toward allowing spectrum flexibility, both by granting more rights to licensees and by opening more bands to unlicensed uses.

This section addresses spectrum allocation and provides an overview of the various ways the FCC has broadened the rights of spectrum users. We begin in § 9.D.1 by considering different models of spectrum control, looking at the FCC's own study of the tradeoffs. In § 9.D.2 we provide an overview of potential ways of implementing flexibility against the backdrop of existing allocations and incumbents. Sections 9.D.3 and 9.D.4 examine dedicating spectrum to unlicensed uses and allowing unlicensed uses on a more opportunistic basis.

§ 9.D.1. Models of Spectrum Control

Traditionally, the FCC would identify one or two services as permissible on a block of frequencies and choose a licensee who would then be allowed to operate one or both services on the relevant frequencies. For example, the FCC's practice for most of the 20th century was to determine which frequencies each broadcast television channel would occupy, and a given licensee could offer only a single broadcast television stream on the channel it occupied. The FCC made clear that its licensees were under no circumstances allowed to use their frequencies for unapproved services, even if those other uses would not cause interference problems. Relatedly, although licensees could transfer their licenses to third parties, they could not subdivide their spectrum usage rights and transfer some of them to a third party (say, the right for a third party to engage in a low-power noninterfering use) while keeping the rest. As a matter of engineering, usage rights are readily divisible across many dimensions (frequency, space, power, and time), but under the FCC rules that prevailed for many years, licensees' only option was to transfer all their rights en masse. Thus legal rules limited what science would otherwise have allowed and market forces might otherwise have demanded.

This traditional command-and-control approach has some obvious drawbacks. First, it produces underused, and in some cases unused, spectrum. Because licensees will not benefit from using less of their assigned spectrum (via, for example, digital compression), they have no incentive under command-and-control regulation to expend any resources to economize on spectrum. Indeed, licensees may have an incentive *not* to use spectrum efficiently. If a spectrum licensee opts for more effective technology and frees up spectrum as a result, that spectrum might well give the government the opportunity to increase competition by letting someone else use the newly free spectrum to compete against that licensee.

Command-and-control regulation produces unused spectrum in cases where there is a single authorized service but that service is not profitable in a given area. For instance, in many less-populated areas of the United States, UHF (ultra high frequency) television was allocated by the FCC but not sufficiently attractive to entice any broadcasters, leaving UHF spectrum idle in those communities.[10]

Second, allowing only one service on a given block of spectrum prevents licensees from introducing new services. Innovative services will not have the opportunity to prove their value if they are not allowed on the spectrum in the first place. Flexibility would both give licensees the incentive to optimize their use of spectrum and provide the FCC with new information about how spectrum can be used and how valuable particular services are.

10. *See* Stuart Minor Benjamin, The Logic of Scarcity: Idle Spectrum as a First Amendment Violation, 52 Duke L.J. 1, 18 (2002).

The FCC has recognized the benefits of moving away from command and control toward more flexibility and market forces. The 2010 National Broadband Plan said:

> The current spectrum policy framework sometimes impedes the free flow of spectrum to its most highly valued uses. The federal government, on behalf of the American people and under the auspices of the FCC and NTIA, retains all property rights to spectrum. In several instances, both agencies assign large quantities of spectrum to specific uses, sometimes tied to specific technologies. In some cases, this approach is appropriate to serve particular public interests that flexible use licenses and market-based allocations alone would not otherwise support. However, because mission needs and technologies evolve, there must be a public review process to ensure that decisions about federal and non-federal use that may have worked in the past can be revisited over time. In general, where there is no overriding public interest in maintaining a specific use, flexibility should be the norm.
>
> In the case of commercial spectrum, the failure to revisit historical allocations can leave spectrum handcuffed to particular use cases and outmoded services, and less valuable and less transferable to innovators who seek to use it for new services. The market for commercial, licensed spectrum does not always behave like a typical commodities market. Commercially licensed spectrum does not always move efficiently to the use valued most highly by markets and consumers. For example, a megahertz-pop may be worth a penny in one industry context and a dollar in another.[11] Legacy "command and control" rules, high transaction costs and highly fragmented license regimes sometimes preserve outmoded band plans and prevent the aggregation (or disaggregation) of spectrum into more valuable license configurations.

FCC, National Broadband Plan § 5.1 (2010), https://www.fcc.gov/general/national-broadband-plan.

The FCC's most sustained discussion of different possible models of spectrum regulation was an FCC task force whose mission was to "[p]rovide specific recommendations to the Commission for ways in which to evolve the current 'command and control' approach to spectrum policy into a more integrated, market-oriented approach that provides greater regulatory certainty while minimizing regulatory intervention" and also protecting against interference. FCC, Spectrum Policy Task Force Report, ET Docket No. 02-135 at 1 (Nov. 2002). That task force issued a report in 2002 that reviewed spectrum policy and recommended significant changes designed to meet these stated goals.

11. Dollars per megahertz of spectrum, per person reached ($ per megahertz-pop) is the convention used to estimate the market value of spectrum.

Spectrum Policy Task Force Report

FCC, ET Docket No. 02-135 (Nov. 2002),
https://www.fcc.gov/document/spectrum-policy-task-force

V. Key Elements of New Spectrum Policy

A. Maximizing Flexibility of Spectrum Use

As a general proposition, flexibility in spectrum regulation is critical to improving access to spectrum. In this context, "flexibility" means granting both licensed users and unlicensed device operators the maximum possible autonomy to determine the highest valued use of their spectrum, subject only to those rules that are necessary to afford reasonable opportunities for access by other spectrum users and to prevent or limit interference among multiple spectrum uses. Flexibility enables spectrum users to make fundamental choices about how they will use spectrum (including whether to use it or transfer their usage rights to others), taking into account market factors such as consumer demand, availability of technology, and competition. By leaving these choices to the spectrum user, this approach tends to lead to efficient and highly-valued spectrum uses. In most instances, a flexible use approach is preferable to the Commission's traditional "command-and-control" approach to spectrum regulation, in which allowable spectrum uses are limited based on regulatory judgments.

The Commission should seek to avoid rules that restrict spectrum use to particular services or applications, so long as the user operates within the technical parameters applicable to the particular band in question. Furthermore, these technical parameters should themselves be limited to those that are necessary to define the user's RF [radio frequency] environment in terms of maximum allowable output and required tolerance of interference.

Such flexibility can be implemented under more than one regulatory model for defining spectrum usage rights. As discussed further below, the Task Force advocates expanding the future use of two alternative regulatory models — one based on awarding exclusive spectrum usage rights and the other on creating unlicensed spectrum "commons" — both of which are premised on the concept of flexible use. Under either model, the Commission should give spectrum users maximum possible autonomy in the following areas:

> *Choice of uses or services that are provided on spectrum.* Spectrum users should have the maximum possible flexibility to decide how spectrum will be used, e.g., whether to provide commercial services or to use spectrum for private, internal needs, so long as they comply with the general parameters applicable to the band (including any applicable power limits or interference limits).
>
> *Choice of technology that is most appropriate to the spectrum environment.* Spectrum users should be allowed to choose the technology that is best-suited to their proposed use or service. They should be allowed to

adapt their technology to their particular spectrum environment, e.g., to use lower power in spectrum-congested areas and higher power in less-congested (e.g., rural) areas.

Right to transfer, lease, or subdivide spectrum rights. An efficient secondary markets regime should be in place to facilitate the negotiated movement of spectrum rights from one party to another. In more narrowly-defined services (e.g., public safety), spectrum users should have the ability to lease excess capacity for other uses through time sharing of spectrum or other mechanisms.

B. Clear and Exhaustive Definition of Spectrum Rights and Responsibilities

While commenters and workshop participants were vocal about their desire for more flexible rights, they were equally interested in firmness and clarity in the rules they are required to follow. Most commenters and workshop participants also agreed with the proposition that spectrum users' rights and obligations are often not defined with sufficient clarity under the FCC's current rules. An overarching principle eventually emerged: all spectrum users require clear rules governing their interactions with the Commission and other spectrum users. Regardless of how or to whom particular rights are assigned, ensuring that all rights are clearly delineated is important to avoiding disputes, and provides a clear common framework from which spectrum users can negotiate alternative arrangements.

VII. Spectrum Usage Models

A. Comparison of Alternative Spectrum Usage Models

The Task Force examined the Commission's spectrum policies and rules in relation to three general models for assigning spectrum usage rights:

"Command-and-control" model. The traditional process of spectrum management in the United States, currently used for most spectrum within the Commission's jurisdiction, allocates and assigns frequencies to limited categories of spectrum users for specific government-defined uses. Service rules for the band specify eligibility and service restrictions, power limits, build-out requirements, and other rules.

"Exclusive use" model. A licensing model in which a licensee has exclusive and transferable rights to the use of specified spectrum within a defined geographic area, with flexible use rights that are governed primarily by technical rules to protect spectrum users against interference. Under this model, exclusive rights resemble property rights in spectrum, but this model does not imply or require creation of "full" private property rights in spectrum.

"Commons" or "open access" model. Allows unlimited numbers of unlicensed users to share frequencies, with usage rights that are governed by technical standards or etiquettes but with no right to protection from

> interference. Spectrum is available to all users that comply with established technical "etiquettes" or standards that set power limits and other criteria for operation of unlicensed devices to mitigate potential interference.

There is, of course, some overlap among these models as well as variations that combine elements of each. For example, spectrum users that are regulated on a command-and-control basis may have some of the same rights as spectrum users who are subject to the exclusive use model (e.g., exclusive and transferable rights, interference protection). Moreover, spectrum that is subject to the exclusive use or commons model may nonetheless be subject to some degree of command-and-control restriction (e.g., limiting usage based on international allocation restrictions). Nonetheless, the key distinction between the command-and-control approach and the other two models is that the former typically imposes significantly greater usage restrictions on spectrum (and sometimes on the eligibility of spectrum users), thereby restricting flexibility of spectrum use to a far greater degree than either of the other two models.

The Task Force recommends that the Commission base its spectrum policy on a balance of the three basic spectrum rights models outlined above: an exclusive use approach, a commons approach, and (to a more limited degree) a command-and-control approach. It is further recommended that the Commission fundamentally alter the existing balance among these models—which is dominated by legacy command-and-control regulation—by expanding the use of both the exclusive use and commons models throughout the radio spectrum, and limiting the use of the command-and-control model to those instances where there are compelling public policy reasons. Thus, to the extent feasible, the Commission should identify more spectrum for both licensed and unlicensed uses under flexible rules, and should transition existing spectrum that is subject to more restrictive command-and-control regulation to these models to the greatest extent possible.

In proposing to reshape the balance among the three models, the Task Force recognizes that the models themselves are not pure and mutually exclusive approaches to spectrum management, but rather are representative approaches on a broader continuum that may be subject to variation in particular instances. Thus, for any given spectrum band or proposed use, the Commission may find it beneficial to incorporate elements from more than one model. For example, as discussed further below, spectrum that is licensed under an exclusive use approach could also be subject to an "underlay" easement that is available to low-power unlicensed devices using a commons approach. Similarly, services that require some dedication of spectrum on a command-and-control basis (e.g., public safety) may benefit from partial application of the exclusive-use model to enable them to lease spectrum capacity to others when it is not otherwise needed. As a general matter, however, the Task Force believes that there is considerable room to move from the largely ad hoc regulation of particular bands that has evolved historically to a more consistent and comprehensive application of these models across the radio spectrum as a whole. If these models are consistently applied in all Commission spectrum policy decisions, it has the potential to significantly reduce the artificial scarcity of spectrum that currently exists as a result of barriers to access. This approach will have the beneficial effect of reducing the cost of obtaining exclusive spectrum rights in the market and will also help to alleviate congestion of spectrum that is made available on a commons basis, thus mitigating the risk of the "tragedy of the commons" — oversaturation resulting in inefficient use.

B. Application of Exclusive Use and Commons Models

The recommendation to move towards greater reliance on exclusive use and commons models requires that the Commission determine the appropriate balance between these two models. Ultimately, wherever there are competing uses for a resource — that is, wherever there is scarcity — some mechanism must exist for allocating that resource. A mechanism based on markets, such as an exclusive use model, will be most efficient in most cases. However, government may also wish to promote the important efficiency and innovation benefits of a spectrum commons by allocating spectrum bands for shared use, much as it allocates land to public parks.

There are a number of variables that may be relevant to this determination with respect to any particular band, but the Task Force believes that the key factors to be considered are (1) spectrum scarcity, and (2) transaction costs associated with moving spectrum from less efficient to more efficient use. In this context, "spectrum scarcity" means the degree to which particular spectrum is subject to competing demands for use so that the demand exceeds the current supply; and "transaction costs" means the expenditure of time and resources required for a potential spectrum user to obtain the spectrum access rights from one or many parties necessary to its proposed spectrum use.

1. Factors Favoring Exclusive Use Model

The exclusive use model should be applied to most spectrum, particularly in bands where scarcity is relatively high and transaction costs associated with market-based negotiation of access rights are relatively low. The exclusive use model is appropriate because where spectrum is subject to competing demands, and therefore more likely to have a high market value, this approach creates the strongest incentives for parties to put spectrum to its highest valued use. In addition, where rights and responsibilities are clearly defined and effectively enforced, the characteristics of this model — e.g., exclusivity, flexibility, and transferability — generally provide a clear framework for market-based assignment and negotiation of access rights among spectrum users, thereby limiting transaction costs.

These variables suggest that in the lower portion of the radio spectrum, particularly bands below 5 GHz, the Commission should focus primarily, though not exclusively, on using the exclusive use model. The propagation characteristics in this portion of the spectrum (which can support a wide variety of high- and low-power, fixed and mobile uses), combined with the high level of incumbent use (including government as well as nongovernment uses), result in a large number of competing demands for a relatively small amount of available spectrum. These factors tend to weigh in favor of an exclusive use approach with flexible rules because it provides a mechanism for spectrum users to choose among the full range of technically feasible spectrum use options based on market forces. Moreover, the typical transaction costs associated with negotiation of access rights tend to be relatively low in relation to the value of this spectrum.

Even in situations where usable spectrum is scarce but transaction costs are potentially high, the exclusive use model still may be most appropriate, though other variables may also come into play. The presence of high transaction costs means that some transfers of spectrum will not occur, and some valuable uses therefore will not appear in the market. However, wherever scarcity exists, there will be competing claims to the resource, and the exclusive use model is most effective at balancing these competing claims. Moreover, the greater the scarcity, the greater will be the incentive for parties to find ways to overcome these high transaction costs. In contrast, as discussed below, a commons approach may be less effective in cases of high scarcity, despite its advantages in addressing high transaction costs.

Finally, while these factors weigh in favor of applying the exclusive use model under the above-described circumstances, it should be emphasized that they do not preclude the introduction of unlicensed "underlays" into exclusive use bands. As discussed below, the criteria that favor use of the commons model apply to potential underlay uses of spectrum below the interference temperature threshold, and may apply in some cases to opportunistic uses above the threshold, depending on the nature of the proposed use.

2. Factors Favoring Commons Model

The commons model should be applied to significant portions of the spectrum, particularly in bands where scarcity is low and transaction costs associated with market mechanisms are high. The commons approach makes increased access possible by replacing the negotiation of spectrum access rights among rights holders and prospective users with a commons model governed by user protocols and etiquette. These protocols promote efficiency through spectrum sharing, typically by requiring commons to operate at low power for a short time in limited areas, which allows multiple users to operate on the same spectrum. This approach also promotes technological innovation by providing a spectrum environment in which to develop new technologies. Users do not pay for access to the spectrum, so they will channel their investment exclusively into developing robust technology that can function in this environment and continue to function as the environment grows more congested.

Where both spectrum scarcity and transaction costs are low, the commons model again may be the most appropriate, though this situation is less clear. Under these circumstances, the presence of low transaction costs would add to the efficiency-creating characteristics of the commons. On the other hand, it also is possible that the exclusive use model would provide comparable benefits, as the price will be close to zero if spectrum is abundant. With low transaction costs as well as low price, interested users should have unrestricted access to the spectrum they need.

The variables described above tend to tilt in favor of expanded use of the commons model in higher spectrum bands, particularly above 50 GHz, based on the physical characteristics of the spectrum itself. In these bands, the propagation characteristics of spectrum preclude many of the applications that are possible in lower bands (e.g., mobile service, broadcasting), and instead favor short-distance line-of-sight operation using narrow transmission beams. Thus, these bands are well-suited to accommodate multiple devices operating within a small area without interference. Moreover, administering these uses on an individualized licensed basis would involve very high transaction costs.

The Task Force does not advocate the wholesale conversion of all spectrum to a commons approach as some commenters appear to advocate. Although the commons model is in many ways a highly deregulatory "Darwinian" approach, as its proponents point out, productive use of spectrum commons by unlicensed devices, particularly in lower spectrum bands, typically requires significant regulatory limitations on device transmitter power that preclude many other technically and economically feasible spectrum uses that rely on higher-power signal propagation over longer distances, or that require greater protection from interference. In addition, some commons proponents themselves state that setting aside additional spectrum for use on a commons basis is not essential to the continued success of unlicensed technology because the technological capability exists to prevent congestion from occurring in existing unlicensed bands.

This does not, however, mean that only higher band spectrum should be subject to a commons approach. The record shows that the Commission's dedication of some lower band spectrum to unlicensed uses, e.g., 2.4 GHz, is yielding significant technological and economic benefits in the form of low-power short-distance communications and emerging mesh network technologies that should be further encouraged. The Task Force therefore recommends that the commons model continue to be applied selectively to other lower spectrum bands.

In addition, the commons approach has potential applicability in the creation of underlay rights across the entire range of spectrum for low-power, low-impact devices. To the extent that the Commission establishes "interference temperature" rules for particular bands,[12] the spectrum environment that is created below the temperature threshold has the characteristics that weigh most heavily in favor of the commons approach: low scarcity due to technical restrictions on the power and operating range of devices and high transaction costs associated with negotiating access. Therefore, the commons approach should presumptively be used for

12. [An omitted section of the report explains that "The interference temperature metric would establish maximum permissible levels of interference, thus characterizing the 'worst case' environment in which a receiver would be expected to operate. Different threshold levels could be set for each band, geographic region or service." Eds.]

operations below the interference temperature threshold. In addition, the commons model may be appropriate for some opportunistic, non-interfering uses of exclusively licensed spectrum above the interference temperature threshold, although this approach raises more significant challenges.

An important caveat must accompany any recommendation for a commons model: although there are indications that technology can go a long way to forestall scarcity concerns, if scarcity eventually does arise in particular spectrum bands in the future, then the commons model may need to evolve to address the problem. Because there is no price mechanism in the commons model to use as a tool for allocating scarce resources among competing users, there is always the risk that free access will eventually lead to interference and over-saturation, i.e., the "tragedy of the commons." These problems can be overcome to some extent through regulatory guidance, requirements such as power and emission limits, and sharing etiquettes. But if actual spectrum scarcity still occurs, rights may need to be redefined and market mechanisms (e.g., band managers) introduced because without them there are insufficient incentives to avoid overuse.

C. Limited Use of Command and Control

The command-and-control model should be applied only in situations where prescribing spectrum use by regulation is necessary to accomplish important public interest objectives or to conform to treaty obligations. With respect to the command-and-control model, as noted above, the Task Force recognizes that continued use of this approach may be required in situations where prescribing spectrum use by regulation is necessary to accomplish compelling public interest objectives. However, such objectives should be carefully defined, and the amount of spectrum subject to a command-and-control regime should be limited to that which ensures that those objectives are achieved. Many spectrum users will claim that they warrant special consideration and thus deserve exemption from any reform of their service allocation rules. It is therefore critical to distinguish between special interest and the public interest, establishing a high bar for any service to clear prior to receiving an exemption.

In general, command-and-control regulation should be reserved only for spectrum uses that provide clear, non-market public interest benefits or that require regulatory prescription to avoid market failure. For example, radioastronomy may need to have dedicated, protected spectrum bands for the foreseeable future, due to its highly sensitive applications and the fact that its benefits accrue to society as a whole and only over the long run. Public safety and critical infrastructure may also require dedicated spectrum at particular times to ensure priority access for emergency communications. Other areas where limited use of command-and-control may be justified include international/satellite, public safety, and broadcasting.

Subject to these exceptions, the Commission should eschew command-and-control regulation, and legacy command-and-control bands should be transitioned to more flexible rules and uses to the maximum extent possible (whether under the exclusive rights or the commons model).

Notes and Questions

1. Why Flexibility? At the time this report was written, the FCC had a long history of command-and-control regulation. Yet the report makes it seem almost obvious that flexible approaches are better. Is it possible that the FCC was simply being short-sighted all these years? Is the report slighting the reasons why the FCC has for so many years limited licensees' choice of services?

2. Models of Spectrum Control. The report lists two main alternatives to "command and control": exclusive use and commons. Are there other models that might be worth considering? The report states that exclusive use "does not imply or require creation of 'full' private property rights in spectrum." Should the report have advocated the creation of such property rights? Is the explanation that 47 U.S.C. § 301 prohibits any private party from obtaining such rights, so that the FCC cannot, on its own, grant them? Or is there some other reason to want "exclusive use" that does not encompass full private property rights?

3. Subtle Constraints. The report casts a commons as a flexible approach, but then concedes that "productive use of spectrum commons . . . typically requires significant regulatory limitations on device transmitter power that preclude many other technically and economically feasible spectrum uses that rely on higher-power signal propagation over longer distances, or that require greater protection from interference." What does this sentence mean? Is the point that even the seemingly uber-flexible commons necessarily excludes certain uses and users? Are there distributional effects to requiring spectrum users to operate more sophisticated (and expensive) equipment?

4. Scarcity. One factor emphasized throughout the report is the relative scarcity of the spectrum under consideration. What claim is made about scarcity under a commons approach? Will scarcity disappear, such that an unlimited number of users can step forward to use the commons without any shortage of supply? If so, how exactly would that work? If not, then what is the claim? That scarcity is less likely to occur? That scarcity can be more equitably addressed? Something else?

§ 9.D.2. Transitioning to Flexibility and Dealing with Incumbents

One of the prominent themes of the report is moving from command-and-control to spectrum flexibility. Importantly, the government does not operate on a clean slate. Virtually all the frequencies suitable for new, flexible licenses are already licensed (or are utilized by the federal government for its own activities). So a big question is how the FCC should deal with existing licensees.

One possibility is to allow existing licensees to offer new services. Such an approach has the virtue of simplicity, but it also has some potential drawbacks. It would entail an enormous windfall for most existing licensees, who generally paid relatively small sums for their licenses—prices that were low precisely because the licenses narrowly constrained the services that could be offered. Instead of the government receiving revenues from auctioning licenses, all the value from the newly broadened rights would go to existing licensees.[13] Giving rights to existing licensees also might be inefficient. It might give rise to high transaction costs, especially if licenses for the existing service were allotted in relatively small geographic regions (as most were) and new services would be most valuable on a broader geographic basis. Finally, giving new flexible rights to existing licensees could create holdout costs: a licensee whose license was necessary for the creation of a nationwide band in a particular frequency would seek to extract huge sums from the entity that had gathered all the other frequencies in that band.

At the other extreme, a quite different approach also has the virtue of simplicity: the government could reclaim all the existing licenses for a given set of frequencies. But depending on how the licenses were structured, the government might have to wait until a given license expired (as we discuss below, licenses are for a set number of years). And reclaiming spectrum might reduce investment and upset investment-backed expectations due to the abruptness of the revocation. Avoiding abrupt changes allows for greater investment—more expected years of operation should translate into more investment.

Middle ground approaches also exist. The FCC proposed, and Congress adopted, one such possibility we discuss at the end of this chapter—"incentive auctions"—under which auction revenue is shared with incumbent licensees who agreed to relinquish some of their spectrum usage rights.

A different possible middle ground is to authorize new services to be provided by new licensees who operate alongside the existing incumbents providing their original service. Note that this approach still leaves the original licensee with no incentive to economize on its use of spectrum. Allowing a new licensee to offer the new service introduces another wrinkle as well: if two or more licensees are licensed to use the same frequency but as part of different services, the FCC will have to articulate and enforce rules that determine which service has priority in the event that there turns out to be interference.

As it happens, the FCC has never simply decided to end a service—it has always given licensees time and some opportunity to recoup their costs. Beyond that, the FCC usually presumes the status quo, putting the burden on a new service to justify changing the existing arrangement. And it often treats as a relevant consideration

13. Auctions have generated more than $200 billion in revenue for the federal government. *See* Question 5 on page 505.

the preservation of the existing service, even if that service has not proven valuable to users.

This may reflect not only concerns about investment but also a basic rule of political economy: incumbents standing to lose their licenses face a certain loss and will organize effectively to keep that license; potential entrants lose an opportunity to buy a license, which is less certain (because they may not win the auction) and less beneficial (because they will pay market prices at auction) than keeping the license is for the incumbent. The result is that incumbents who fear losing their licenses usually lobby more effectively than potential entrants.

Notes and Questions

1. Flexibility Wins. The FCC had been moving toward flexibility even before the report was written. The report cemented what was already becoming the dominant approach to new allocations. For example, back in 1992 the FCC allowed new flexible broadband services on spectrum that had been allocated to lower-valued uses. Redevelopment of Spectrum to Encourage Innovation in the Use of New Telecommunications Technologies, First Report and Order and Third Notice of Proposed Rulemaking, 7 FCC Rcd. 6886 (1992). The FCC specified that the licenses could be used to provide "any mobile communications service" as well as "fixed services" provided in combination with mobile ones — as long as the license is not used to provide a broadcasting service. 47 C.F.R. § 24.3. And in Service Rules for the 746–764 and 776–794 MHz Bands, and Revisions to Part 27 of the Commission's Rules, First Report and Order, 15 FCC Rcd. 476 (2000), the FCC issued an order reallocating spectrum that had been dedicated to broadcasting. Instead of picking a particular service that licensees could offer, the FCC authorized licensees to choose among a wide range of wireless services. Similarly, in Service Rules for Advanced Wireless Services in the 1.7 GHz and 2.1 GHz Bands, Report and Order, 18 FCC Rcd. 25,162 ¶ 13 (2003), the FCC issued an order announcing that "[i]n order to promote innovative services and encourage the flexible and efficient use of the 1710–1755 and 2110–2155 MHz bands, we permit licensees to use this spectrum for any use permitted by the United States Table of Frequency Allocations contained in Part 2 of our rules (i.e., fixed or mobile services)." That flexibility has continued in new allocations since then, and Congress has explicitly endorsed it. The 2012 legislation authorizing the incentive auctions noted above granted the FCC authority "to permit the assignment of new initial licenses subject to flexible-use service rules." Middle Class Tax Relief and Job Creation Act of 2012, Pub. L. No. 112-96, § 6402, 126 Stat. 156, 224 Spectrum Act § 6402 (2012).

2. Adding New Licensees Alongside Existing Ones. As suggested above, sometimes the FCC has provided for new licensees to operate on spectrum already used by other services. Indeed, in the FCC's first major proceeding allowing for flexible broadband licenses (the 1992 proceeding mentioned in the note above), the FCC allowed existing licensees to continue operating alongside the new services. It also allowed those incumbents to move to higher frequencies and allowed the new licensees to pay the incumbents to leave the frequencies (thus allowing the new licensees to operate without having to concern themselves with creating or receiving interference). In allowing for such payments, the FCC stated: "Our principal desire is to compensate existing [licensees] for the costs of relocation [to higher frequencies]. We recognize, however, that such market-based negotiations could possibly result in windfalls for the incumbent licensees." Redevelopment of Spectrum To Encourage Innovation in the Use of New Telecommunications Technologies, Notice of Proposed Rulemaking, 7 FCC Rcd. 1542, 1545 n.20 (1992). One can imagine the amused reaction of the incumbents to this statement. (And the FCC later modified the transition plan to mitigate potential windfalls. *See* Amendment to the Commission's Rules Regarding a Plan for Sharing the Costs of Microwave Relocation, Second Report and Order, 12 FCC Rcd. 2705 (1997).)

One other element of this proceeding bears note. The FCC noted that the incumbents provided fixed (as opposed to mobile) service (in this case, fixed microwave) and stated:

> We also will encourage fixed microwave operators to consider other non-radio alternative media to meet their telecommunication needs, particularly fiber optic circuits. In allocating spectrum, one of the primary considerations is whether there is a technological dependence of the service on radio rather than wire lines. Mobile communications necessarily will always require use of radio spectrum, and in the past the Commission provided large amounts of spectrum for fixed microwave because wireline alternatives often were economically prohibitive. However, in the last five years technological advancements in optical communications have resulted in fiber being very competitive with fixed microwave.

7 FCC Rcd. at 1545 n.17. The incumbents' incentive to move to wire was blunted, however, by the fact that they were not paying anything for their frequencies but would have to pay for wires. Indeed, the FCC recognized this and proposed tax incentives for the incumbents to move to wires, *see id.*—an incentive that would not be necessary if incumbents paid for both frequencies and wires (or, conversely, if both were provided gratis).

3. Allowing Incumbents to Provide New Services. In 2016 the FCC issued rules for wireless broadband services at 28 GHz, 37–39 GHz, and 64–71 GHz. Use of Spectrum Bands Above 24 GHz for Mobile Radio Services, Report and Order and Further Notice of Proposed Rulemaking, 31 FCC Rcd. 8014 (2016).[14]

The order followed the dominant approach of allowing a wide range of services on these frequencies. As for the licensing regime, the order provided for licensed spectrum in the 28 GHz and 37–39 GHz bands and unlicensed spectrum in the

14. Such frequencies, often called millimeter wave (mmW) bands, are much higher than those that historically have been used for cellular services. At such high frequencies, signals do not travel very far and require a line of sight, but they can contain a lot of data.

64–71 GHz band. Many bands above 24 GHz, including the 37–39 GHz bands, have allocations to the federal government (usually for military purposes). The order concluded that sharing between government and private operations is possible in these bands, and it mandated such sharing.

The 28 GHz and 39 GHz bands also had allocations, and licenses, for fixed commercial services. The order noted two possibilities for those existing services: allowing the incumbent licensees to offer mobile services (which would make their licenses much more valuable) or having an overlay auction that would separately license mobile rights to winning bidders (while maintaining incumbents' licenses and prohibiting interference with incumbents' services). The order chose the former option but acknowledged that this "could be viewed as a windfall to those licensees." *Id.* ¶ 42. It concluded that "the benefits of expediting service and ease of coordinating fixed and mobile service outweigh any foreseeable disadvantages of granting mobile rights to incumbents." What is the best argument for an overlay auction, or some other method for assignment of mobile licenses that would avoid a windfall for the incumbents? Is it the importance of avoiding a windfall? If so, how strong an argument is that?

§ 9.D.3. Dedicating Spectrum to Unlicensed Uses

In addition to flexibility, the other major element of the Spectrum Policy Task Force Report was the model of usage that might be desirable on any given set of frequencies. The report suggested that in some circumstances a spectrum commons might be preferable to exclusive use. The 2010 National Broadband Plan recommended the following with respect to unlicensed devices:

> As the FCC seeks to free up additional spectrum for broadband, it should make a sufficient portion available for use exclusively or predominantly by unlicensed devices. This would enable innovators to try new ideas to increase spectrum access and efficiency through unlicensed means, and should enable new unlicensed providers to serve rural and unserved communities. Such an approach would represent a departure from the way the FCC has treated most unlicensed operations in the past. Unlicensed operations are typically overlays to licensed bands, with intensive unlicensed use emerging in some bands (e.g., the 2.4 GHz band) over a long period of time. However, targeting bands for unlicensed use could yield important benefits.

FCC, National Broadband Plan § 5.6 (2010), https://www.fcc.gov/general/national-broadband-plan.

As both the Spectrum Policy Task Force Report and National Broadband Plan indicate, the FCC dedicated frequencies at 2.4 GHz for unlicensed operation, enabling, inter alia, unlicensed devices using Wi-Fi and Bluetooth. The blocks of lower band spectrum devoted to unlicensed uses are a small fraction of the total bandwidth, however, and both propose licensing most of the lower band frequencies (which are most suitable not only to Wi-Fi but also to mobile internet access). By contrast, some commentators have advocated dedicating large blocks of lower band frequencies exclusively to unlicensed uses. One of the most prominent is Yochai Benkler. Below, we excerpt Benkler's most complete articulation of his views on an unlicensed commons.

Some Economics of Wireless Communications

Yochai Benkler, 16 Harv. J.L. & Tech. 25 (2002)

In the first half of the 20th century there was roughly universal agreement that "spectrum" was scarce, and that if it was to be used efficiently, it had to be regulated by an expert agency. A little over forty years ago, Coase wrote a seminal critique of this system, explaining why spectrum scarcity was no more reason for regulation than is wheat scarcity. "Scarcity" was the normal condition of all economic goods, and markets, not regulation, were the preferred mode of allocating scarce resources. In the 1960s and 1970s, a number of academic studies of property rights in spectrum elaborated on Coase's work, but these remained largely outside the pale of actual likely policy options. It was only in the 1980s that a chairman of the Federal Communications Commission voiced support for a system of market-based allocation, and only in the 1990s did Congress permit the FCC to use auctions instead of comparative hearings to assign spectrum. But auctions in and of themselves, without flexible use rights, are but a pale shadow of real market-based allocation. Indeed, they might better be understood as a type of fee for government licenses than as a species of market allocation. Since the mid-1980s, and with increasing acceptance into the 1990s, arguments emerged within the FCC in favor of introducing a much more serious implementation of market-based allocation. This would call for the definition and auctioning of perpetual, exclusive property rights akin to those we have in real estate, which could be divided, aggregated, resold, and reallocated in any form their owners chose to use.

Just as this call for more perfect markets in spectrum allocations began to emerge as a real policy option, a very different kind of voice began to be heard on spectrum policy. This position was every bit as radically different from the traditional approach as the perfected property rights approach, but in a radically different way. The argument was that technology had rendered the old dichotomy between government licensing of frequencies and property rights in frequencies obsolete. It was now possible to change our approach, and instead of creating and enforcing a market in property rights in spectrum blocks, we could rely on a market in smart radio equipment that would allow people to communicate without *anyone* having to control "the spectrum." Just as no one "owns the Internet," but intelligent computers communicate with each other using widely accepted sharing protocols, so too could computationally intensive radios. In the computer hardware and software markets and the Internet communications market, competition in the *equipment market*, not competition in the infrastructure market (say, between Verizon and AOL Time Warner), was the driving engine of innovation, growth, and welfare. This approach has been called a "spectrum commons" approach, because it regards bandwidth as a common resource that all equipment can call on, subject to sharing protocols, rather than as a controlled resource that is always under the control of someone, be it a property owner, a government agency, or both. It is important to understand, however, that this metaphor has its limitations. Like its predecessor positions on spectrum management, it uses the term "spectrum" as though it describes a discrete resource whose utilization is the object of analysis. In fact, as this Article explains, "spectrum" is not a discrete resource whose optimal utilization is the correct object of policy. The correct object of optimization is wireless network communications capacity. Like trade with India, which is only one parameter of welfare in Britain, bandwidth is only one parameter in determining the capacity of a wireless network. Focusing *solely* on it usually distorts the analysis. I will therefore mostly refer in this Article to "open wireless networks" rather than to spectrum commons. Like "the open road" or the "open architecture" of the Internet, it describes a network that treats some resources as open to all equipment to use, leaving it to the equipment manufacturers—cars or computers, respectively, in those open networks—to optimize the functionality they provide using that resource.

Most of the initial responses to this critique were largely similar to the responses that greeted the economists' critique forty years ago—incomprehension, disbelief, and mockery leading Noam to call the standard economists' view "the new orthodoxy." *See* Eli Noam, Spectrum Auctions: Yesterday's Heresy, Today's Orthodoxy, Tomorrow's Anachronism. Taking the Next Step to Open Spectrum Access, 41 J.L. & Econ. 765, 768 (1998). But reality has a way of forcing debates. The most immediate debate-forcing fact is the breathtaking growth of the equipment market in high-speed wireless communications devices, in particular the rapidly proliferating 802.11x family of standards (best known for the 802.11b or "Wi-Fi" standard), all of which rely on utilizing frequencies that no one controls. Particularly when compared to the anemic performance of licensed wireless services in delivering high-speed wireless data services, and the poor performance of other sectors of the telecommunications and computer markets, the success of Wi-Fi forces a more serious debate. It now appears that serious conversation between the two radical critiques of the licensing regime is indeed beginning to emerge.

To provide the economic analysis, I offer a general, though informal, model for describing the social cost of wireless communications, aggregating the equipment and servicing costs involved, the displacement of communications not cleared, and the institutional and organizational overhead in the form of transaction costs and administrative costs. In comparing these, I suggest that while investment patterns in equipment will likely differ greatly, it is not clear that we can say, a priori, whether equipment costs involved in open wireless networks will be higher or lower than equipment costs involved in spectrum property-based networks. Investment in the former will be widely decentralized, and much of it will be embedded in end-user owned equipment that will capitalize ex ante the cost and value of free communications over the lifetime of the equipment. Investment in the latter will be more centrally capitalized because consumers will not both invest ex ante in capitalization of the value of free communication and pay usage fees ex post. Since the value added by spectrum property is in pricing usage to improve the efficiency of allocation over time, it will need lower ex ante investment levels at the end user terminal and higher investment levels at the core of the network. Which of the two will have higher total costs over the lifetime of the network is not clear.

The most complicated problem is defining the relative advantages and disadvantages of spectrum property-based networks and open wireless networks insofar as they displace some communications in order to clear others. Backing out of contemporary multi-user information theory, I propose a general description of the displacement effect of wireless communications. Then, I suggest reasons to think that open wireless networks will systematically have higher capacity, that is, that each communication cleared through an open network will displace fewer communications in total. This, in turn, leaves the range in which spectrum property-based systems can improve on open wireless systems in terms of efficiency as those cases where the discriminating power of pricing is sufficiently valuable to overcome the fact that open wireless systems have cleared more communications but without regard to the willingness and ability of the displaced communications to pay. As a spectrum property-based network diverges from locally and dynamically efficient pricing, the likelihood that it will improve efficiency declines.

As for overhead, or transaction and administrative costs, I suggest reasons to think that both direct transaction costs associated with negotiating transactions for spectrum and clearing transmission rights, and administrative costs associated with a property-type regime rather than with an administrative framework for recognizing and generalizing privately set equipment standards, will be lower for open wireless networks. In particular, I emphasize how the transaction costs of a property system will systematically prevent efficient pricing, and therefore systematically undermine the one potential advantage of a spectrum property-based system.

My conclusion is that the present state of our technological knowledge, and the relevant empirical experience we have with the precursors of open wireless networks and with pricing in wired networks, lean toward a prediction that open wireless networks will be more efficient in the foreseeable future. This qualitative prediction, however, is not sufficiently robust to permit us to make a decisive policy choice between the two approaches given our present limited practical experience with either. We can, however, quite confidently state the following propositions:

1. Creating and exhaustively auctioning perfect property rights to all spectrum frequencies is an unfounded policy. None of our technical, theoretical, or empirical data provides sufficient basis for believing that an exhaustive system that assigns property rights to all bands of frequencies will be systematically better than a system that largely relies on equipment-embedded communications protocols that are permitted to use bandwidth on a dynamic, unregulated basis.

2. Creating such a property system will burden the development of computationally intensive, user equipment-based approaches to wireless communications,

potentially locking us into a lower development trajectory for wireless communications systems. This is particularly so for the dominant position that advocates creating perfect property rights in spectrum blocks, but is true even with modified systems, such as the proposal to include an easement for non-interfering transmissions or the proposal of dynamic market clearance on the basis of spot-market transactions and forward contracts.

3. It is theoretically possible that pricing will sometimes improve the performance of wireless communications networks. The geographically local nature of wireless communications network capacity, the high variability in the pattern of human communications, and the experience of wired networks suggest, however, that if pricing will prove to be useful at all:

3a. It will be useful only occasionally, at peak utilization moments, and the cost-benefit analysis of setting up a system to provide for pricing must consider the value of occasional allocation efficiency versus the cost of the drag on communications capacity at all other times.

3b. It will be more useful if there are no property rights to specific bands, but rather all bandwidth will be available for dynamic contracting through an exchange system on the Noam model.

3c. At most, the possibility of implementing pricing models suggests the creation of some spectrum for a real-time exchange alongside a commons. It does not support the proposal of a Big Bang auction of perfect property rights in all usable frequencies.

As a policy recommendation, it is too early to adopt a Big Bang approach to spectrum policy—either in favor of property or in favor of a commons. From a purely economic perspective, it would be sensible for current policy to experiment with both.

Notes and Questions

1. Dedicated Spectrum versus Underlay Rights. In a portion of his article we did not excerpt, Benkler lists a number of possible forms of spectrum rights. Most notably, he refers to both dedicated commons bands and underlay rights to already-assigned bands. The latter is what has been proposed as an easement creating an underlay commons, and what the Spectrum Policy Task Force Report conceptualizes as an underlay commons below an interference temperature. The underlay approach is thus not inconsistent with having property rights in spectrum.[15] Dedicating spec-

15. As one of us put it, "This is purely a question of how the rights in the license are constructed and construed. If a license to broadcast television were construed as giving the licensee complete control over a given range of frequencies, then any potential user would have to obtain the existing licensee's agreement before it could offer a new service. If, on the other hand, a license to broadcast were construed as conferring only the right to broadcast on that range of frequencies without interference, and as not including a broader property right in that range of frequencies, then a potential

trum to a commons, however, is inconsistent with property rights. The whole point is that no one would have the right to exclude; the sole use of the spectrum would be as a commons. Benkler's disagreement with an easement or underlay commons is that he advocates such a devotion of large blocks of frequencies solely to commons, and his article focuses on that proposal.

2. Open Access? One can imagine a regime of truly open access to the spectrum, a regime in which anyone could transmit over a given set of frequencies however she sees fit. The concern about such freedom is interference: any given user has an interest in ensuring that her message gets through, even if that means increasing power and/or the number of messages sent (to create redundancy) such that others' messages cannot be heard. Recognizing this danger, the FCC has never allowed truly open access. For unlicensed uses, the FCC sets out the protocols that acceptable devices must use and then certifies equipment that meets that standard.

Benkler does not deny that interference can occur with truly open access. Rather, in the remainder of the paper he argues that new network designs can eliminate the dangers posed by interference, with the result that a commons is an efficient—indeed, possibly the most efficient—option. Specifically, he envisions abundant networks comprising devices that operate at low-power, send computationally complex transmissions, and not only send the owner's messages but also repeat others' messages, so that each additional user also represents additional capacity. Benkler's proposal would have the FCC or a private entity certify that user devices meet these standards. The envisioned networks will thus have some controls. In order to avoid the interference that would arise from truly open access, some entity—whether public or private—will determine what sort of devices can operate.

3. Policing the Spectrum Commons. Advocates of spectrum commons sometimes downplay the considerable challenges of ensuring that users of unlicensed spectrum cooperate with one another. In the worst of all worlds, users of unlicensed spectrum will interfere with one another and continually adjust their equipment to overpower one another. Such a "tragedy of the commons" scenario may be able to be overcome through some combination of government regulation, market forces, and self-regulatory efforts (say, by enforcing a limit on power levels or enforcing the use of cooperative protocols that require users to "listen before talking").

4. Why Won't a Private Entity Create These Networks? Just as the FCC could design transmission standards and certify devices, so too could an owner of spectrum in fee simple. If the envisioned abundant networks are so capacious, why wouldn't private owners with full property rights create them? Benkler responded to this question in another paper, arguing that the transaction costs of privately creating these networks are high, because at the time the FCC usually allocated spectrum in small slices (e.g., six megahertz for each broadcaster), but an abundant network might

new user would not have to gain the agreement of the licensee." Stuart Minor Benjamin, The Logic of Scarcity: Idle Spectrum as a First Amendment Violation, 52 Duke L.J. 1, 85 n.259 (2002).

occupy 50 or 100 megahertz. *See* Yochai Benkler, Overcoming Agoraphobia: Building the Commons of the Digitally Networked Environment, 11 Harv. J.L. & Tech. 287, 364–65 (1998). One response would be for the FCC to start licensing spectrum in larger blocks and thus eliminate these costs, and the FCC in fact moved to larger allocations.

A very different argument is that owners won't create these networks even if the spectrum is allotted in big blocks, because abundant networks will be less remunerative for the owners. But why would that be? Owners would have lots of pricing options — for example, per message, per minute, per month, and/or bundled in the price of the user device. Is the problem that owners would not be able to capture the value of these networks? The question, though, is a comparative one — whether it is more difficult to capture the value of these networks than of other kinds of wireless services — and it is not at all clear that capturing the value of the envisioned networks is any more difficult. Finally, maybe the problem is that these abundant networks will not be as remunerative because people will simply pay more money for other services. But if that is so, isn't the entire case for those networks undermined?

This assumes that licensees are legally permitted to create private commons. That was not clear when Benkler wrote, but in 2004 the FCC authorized private commons, as we discuss below.

5. Should We Prefer Government-Created Networks? Assuming that private owners would create these networks, that still does not mean that private ownership is preferable. What are the tradeoffs? To oversimplify dramatically, the main advantage of private ownership is flexibility. The profit motive gives private owners a greater incentive to choose the best system and to make changes as new possibilities arise. And private companies' decisions are not subject to the exhaustive procedures that are imposed on government actors. The main disadvantage of private ownership is the danger of monopoly. But can't the danger of monopoly be minimized by the FCC auctioning off enough spectrum to support five or ten of these envisioned networks? More generally, are there other ways the government could avoid monopolization (spectrum ownership limits; requiring that bidders act only as band managers; mandating interoperability)?[16]

Does the foregoing miss the real advantage of government-created networks, namely that the government would let users access the spectrum free of charge? But why is that desirable? Everyone who creates a network (whether mobile broadband, broadcast television, or car dealerships) wants the government to contribute, free of charge, some otherwise expensive element of that network. Why subsidize these networks? Is it because government control will in fact be more responsive to users' desires than private control will be? Does that position understate the government's incentives and/or the possibility that the market will provide citizens with the networks that they want?

16. We consider spectrum ownership limits in Chapter 10.B.

6. Uncertainty. One obvious difference between the government creating these abundant networks and leaving it to the private market is that the latter option does not guarantee that they will be created. But is that a bug or a feature? These networks may not develop as hoped, either because they do not work as planned or do work but people do not flock to them. Is it better for the risk of failure to fall on private owners rather than on taxpayers?

7. Further Reading. Many of the issues raised here are covered in greater detail in Stuart Minor Benjamin, Spectrum Abundance and the Choice Between Private and Public Control, 78 N.Y.U. L. Rev. 2007 (2003).

§ 9.D.4. Unlicensed Usage Without Dedicated Spectrum

Dedicating frequencies to an unlicensed commons is one way to provide for unlicensed uses, but the FCC can permit unlicensed uses without dedicating frequencies to them. The FCC can allow unlicensed services to operate on licensed spectrum bands that have available capacity such that the unlicensed use will not significantly interfere with the primary, authorized service. In allowing such unlicensed uses, the FCC has imposed restrictions on unlicensed devices designed to avoid harmful interference with incumbents (as well as services on adjacent bands). Indeed, the rules applicable to most unlicensed devices mandate not only that such devices not cause harmful interference with other users (generally by operating at very low power over short distances and using dynamic spectrum sharing) but also that they accept whatever interference they receive. *See* Revision of Part 15 of the Commission's Rules to Permit Unlicensed National Information Infrastructure (U-NII) Devices in the 5 GHz Band, First Report and Order, 29 FCC Rcd. 4127 ¶ 3 (2014).

§ 9.D.4.a. Unlicensed Devices on Vacant Frequencies

There are many ways to allow unlicensed devices to operate on bands with existing uses. The underlay commons noted above and in the Spectrum Policy Task Force Report is one. Prominent among the other ways of accommodating unlicensed uses is allowing them in unutilized frequencies. That is the idea behind allowing unlicensed uses in broadcast television frequencies that are not used by television stations or other authorized services, often called white spaces. These white spaces are generally vacant frequency bands between occupied (licensed) broadcast channels — the vacant frequencies could not accommodate a broadcaster or other high-power service but can accommodate low-power devices.

The possibility of white space devices produced debate on two questions. First, should such devices be permitted? Broadcasters said no, contending that the risk of interference is too great and highlighting that such spaces serve to protect them against the possibility of interference. Google, Intel, Microsoft and others argued in favor, saying that the devices can avoid interference and provide for the possibility of wireless broadband networks with considerable download speeds (because of the favorable propagation characteristics of the spectrum devoted to broadcasting). The second question is whether the spectrum white spaces should be licensed or unlicensed (with most of the companies supporting white space devices arguing for unlicensed).

In the order excerpted below, the FCC addressed both questions.

Unlicensed Operation in the TV Broadcast Bands and Additional Spectrum for Unlicensed Devices below 900 MHz and in the 3 GHz Band

Second Report and Order and Memorandum Opinion and Order, 23 FCC Rcd. 16,807 (2008)

32. [W]e conclude that low power devices can and should be allowed to operate in the TV bands on frequencies that are not being used by authorized services. This decision will provide significant benefits for the public by enabling the development and operation of a wide range of new unlicensed wireless communications devices and systems in spectrum where signals are less subject to propagation losses than they are in the bands currently available for such devices. The propagation characteristics of these bands will allow the development of devices that can provide service at greater ranges than existing unlicensed devices. Proponents of broadband devices and services in particular indicate that there is need for new broadband devices that will take advantage of the more desirable propagation characteristics of the TV bands. [W]e believe that the propagation advantages of this spectrum will make it possible for wireless ISPs (WISPs) and others to improve or extend their reach to customers in rural and other less densely populated areas. We also anticipate that these new devices will have economic benefits for consumers and businesses by facilitating the development of additional competition in the broadband market.

33. It is, of course, most important that we ensure that new unlicensed devices do not interfere with the incumbent licensed services in the TV bands. We now conclude that, with appropriate requirements and conditions on their operation, it is possible for both fixed and personal/portable low power devices to use the TV white spaces without disrupting the important television, public safety, and other services that use these frequencies. Because unlicensed broadband devices will share spectrum with broadcast TV and other licensed services, they will need the capability to avoid causing harmful interference to licensed services in the TV band. Specifically, an unlicensed device will need to be able to determine whether a TV channel or portion of a TV channel is unused before it transmits. Additionally, an unlicensed device will need features that enable it to avoid occupying a frequency band or to cease operation on a frequency when a licensed user commences transmission on a channel that was previously unused by a television band licensed service. The rules we are adopting will require that unlicensed TVBDs include these capabilities.

A. Licensed vs. Unlicensed Operation

36. A number of commenters submit that vacant spectrum in the TV bands should be licensed and that this regimen is necessary in order to enable the use of that spectrum for providing wireless broadband and mobile data services. These parties argue that companies need the assurance that they will be entitled to protection from harmful interference before they will make the investments necessary to provide these services. They claim that licensing would encourage innovation because a licensee would receive all of the benefits of its innovation instead of having to share those benefits with others. Other parties continue to argue that this spectrum would be more effectively used on an unlicensed basis. For example, the New America Foundation responds that the existing unlicensed bands have been used for a large number of innovative products, that innovation is encouraged by the low barriers to entry in an unlicensed regime, and that the TV bands have better propagation properties than currently available unlicensed bands, which would cause innovation to flourish. It further states that many unlicensed uses such as community networks and rural service do not require a large infrastructure investment, so licensing is not needed to ensure the provision of service. Tropos Networks adds that the expense of acquiring licenses can make providing wireless broadband services prohibitive in rural and Native American tribal areas. Those supporting the licensed and unlicensed approaches argue a number of additional points and counter points as described below.

37. Charles Jackson and Dorothy Robyn argue that the TV bands are not well suited to the low-power uses planned by unlicensed advocates. They contend that under an unlicensed approach, devices would likely have to operate in 6 megahertz channels—which are far smaller than the available bandwidth in the 2.4 GHz or 5.0 GHz unlicensed bands—because the TV band white spaces occur in 6 megahertz increments. Jackson/Robyn further argue that the use of this spectrum for low-power unlicensed devices would fail to take advantage of the better propagation properties of the TV bands compared to those of higher frequencies and to exploit the capability that it is easier to manufacture equipment that generates significant power in the TV bands than at higher frequencies. The White Space Coalition disputes these views, arguing that Jackson/Robyn's claim that the TV band is not suited to unlicensed uses is premised on the assumption that future unlicensed uses will be identical to the current uses of those unlicensed bands. It contends that the better propagation properties of the TV bands would make it likely that new unlicensed applications would be developed in the future that would not be possible in other bands.

38. Supporters of a licensed approach also hold that there is no need for additional spectrum for unlicensed devices. In this regard, Qualcomm submits that there is no evidence that consumers have had to return unlicensed devices because the unlicensed spectrum is too crowded. The Association for Maximum Service Television and the National Association of Broadcasters (MSTV/NAB) add there is over 100 megahertz of unlicensed spectrum below 2 GHz and that 255 MHz of spectrum in

the 5 GHz band was made available for unlicensed use in 2003 and so there is plenty of spectrum available for unlicensed use. The White Space Coalition counters these arguments, stating that the propagation characteristics of the TV band are superior to the other unlicensed bands for many applications and that none of the other unlicensed spectrum is below 900 MHz.

44. *Discussion*: [O]ur goal in this proceeding is to allow new uses of radio on unused television channels at locations where such operations will not result in harmful interference to, or disrupt, TV and other authorized services. For the reasons discussed below, we conclude that it is in the public interest to allow TV band devices to operate in these bands on an unlicensed basis pursuant to restrictions carefully designed to protect users of incumbent licensed services. This approach permits us to introduce new innovative uses while protecting the continued operation and growth of the TV broadcast and other authorized services in these bands. Because unlicensed operations are not allowed to cause interference to authorized services, the interference protection status of existing services operating in these bands will not be affected, consistent with the Commission's goals in this proceeding.

45. The record developed in response to [earlier proceedings on this issue] indicates that there is a need for additional spectrum for unlicensed broadband devices, particularly in the lower frequency bands. A number of WISPs have noted that the TV frequencies would provide improved signal coverage over other unlicensed bands, including improved in-building penetration properties which other unlicensed bands lack. We disagree with Jackson/Robyn that the 6 megahertz size of TV channels and propagation characteristics of these bands make them inappropriate for unlicensed use. Unlicensed devices will not be limited to 6 megahertz bandwidth, as they will be allowed to operate across multiple channels in locations where the bandwidth is available. The signal coverage afforded by the propagation characteristics of this spectrum is also desired by proponents of unlicensed devices in that it will facilitate the provision of improved and/or more economical wireless Internet service to consumers, particularly in rural areas where transaction costs may be higher than elsewhere. Further, as argued by comments filed by the White Space Coalition and other parties who have expressed interest in developing or operating low power devices in these bands, other innovative uses for this spectrum may emerge once it is made available for unlicensed use.

46. While we recognize the arguments in the record in support of a licensed approach for making the TV white space spectrum available for new uses, we conclude that such an approach is not practicable for many kinds of devices that could use these bands, and thus would reduce the benefits available. [A] licensed model tends to work best when spectrum rights are clearly defined, exclusive, flexible and transferable. When spectrum rights lack these attributes, potential licensees face uncertainty and may lack incentives to invest in a license or offer service. We conclude that attributes supporting the successful use of licensing would be difficult to accomplish here, particularly if we want to maintain our stated goal of not affecting

the interference protection status of existing services. The frequencies and amount of unused TV band spectrum will vary from location to location and could change over time as additional television stations and other primary and secondary operations are licensed or as existing operations change frequency.

47. [W]e are adopting a number of requirements for TV band devices that will significantly reduce the potential for these devices to cause harmful interference to authorized services and will make it possible to identify the source of any interference that might occur. In particular, TV band devices will be allowed to operate only after they have identified which channels in their area are available for their use. To ensure that devices adhere to this requirement, we are requiring that fixed and personal/portable TV band devices that do not operate in client mode to access a central database system and that fixed devices register with the database system. Registration of fixed TV band devices will facilitate locating the source of an interference problem should it occur from these higher power devices. We are not requiring registration of personal/portable devices, as the lower operating power and non-directional antennas of personal/portable devices will limit the potential interference range of those devices to the immediate vicinity of a device. We are also concerned that a registration requirement for personal/portable devices could significantly limit the types of devices that could operate by necessitating that a device includes the capability to input alphanumeric data.

48. With regard to the argument that a licensing regime would encourage investment in the provision of services using wireless spectrum, we observe the stability normally provided by exclusive licensing would be difficult to achieve for TV band device operation. To avoid affecting the interference protection status of incumbent services, the licenses here would afford no right to interference-free operation. Instead, the licensee would merely have the right to operate on those television channels that are not currently in use by other higher-priority users. The specific channels and amount of available spectrum available at a given location could change over time as additional television channels are allocated, as low power auxiliary devices make use of the channels, and the other services that use these bands similarly initiate new or modify existing operations. Hence, we do not believe that the issuance of licenses would necessarily provide the benefits that the proponents of licensing claim because of the tenuous nature of the rights that would actually be granted by the license. Furthermore, there has been tremendous growth in the development of new technologies and the introduction of new services that rely on unlicensed devices, which belies the assertion that a licensing regime is needed to encourage investment in spectrum development.

49. [A] number of parties draw attention to the potential revenue that could be raised by auctioning the unused television bands under a licensing regime. We believe that these arguments are misplaced and do not address our goal in this proceeding, which is to allow new uses on unused television channels in locations where such operations will not result in harmful interference to or disrupt TV and other authorized services. Thus, the regulatory model used here must be appropriate to

facilitate new uses while protecting the various types of incumbent uses, not chosen merely because it could provide revenue from auctioning licenses.

Notes and Questions

1. Minimizing Interference. Consider the restrictions on white spaces devices in ¶ 47. Is this too protective of incumbents, or insufficiently protective? On what basis would you so conclude?

2. Idle Hands. Beyond the specifics of the services envisioned, or the choice between licensed and unlicensed, there is the simple fact that government restrictions — here preventing non-television users from this valuable spectrum — have left some transmission capacity idle. The idea with these new services is that they can be added even though there is no room for more of the previously authorized services. These new services use unutilized spectrum, in that way increasing the total capacity of information carried over the air. Is there an argument that the First Amendment obliges Congress and the FCC to allow such services? After all, the idea behind these services is that there is idle spectrum out there — spectrum that could be used to support communication but is currently unused because of the regulations in place. If that is right, is there any defense, or are regulations that bar white spaces or underlay service unlawful restrictions on speech? *See* Stuart Minor Benjamin, The Logic of Scarcity: Idle Spectrum as a First Amendment Violation, 52 Duke L.J. 1 (2002).

3. Substitutes. There are other frequencies on which unlicensed devices can operate, such as the 5 GHz band where they do operate. The appeal of lower frequencies (such as those in the 600 MHz range that were the subject of the incentive auctions noted above and discussed at the end of this chapter) for unlicensed devices is that these lower frequencies have different, and in many ways more attractive, propagation characteristics. As the FCC stated in a 2014 order, "spectrum in the 600 MHz frequency range has excellent propagation characteristics that allow signals to reach farther and penetrate walls and other structures, thus making it well suited for a variety of unlicensed applications." Expanding the Economic and Innovation Opportunities of Spectrum Through Incentive Auctions, Report and Order, 29 FCC Rcd. 6567, 6685 ¶ 271 (2014). But, of course, that also makes them more valuable for licensed devices — and more valuable for the federal treasury, via the auction proceeds they generate. Which way do these points cut, in terms of the desirability of devoting more of this spectrum to unlicensed uses?

§ 9.D.4.b. Spectrum Sharing and Government Spectrum

The options for a given spectrum band are by no means limited to use by a single licensed service, a commons, and a combination of the two. There are many other possibilities, most of which are forms of spectrum sharing. Broadly defined, shared spectrum is the norm — most frequencies have more than one licensed use. Sometimes more than one use is co-primary (so they have equal status with respect to each other) and one or more is secondary, and sometimes there is one primary use and the other(s) operates on a secondary basis. Similar to the Part 15 rules discussed above, secondary users must avoid harmful interference to primary users and must accept harmful interference from primary users. *See, e.g.*, Redesignation of 17.7–19.7 GHz Frequency Band, Report and Order, 15 FCC Rcd. 13,430, 13,481 n.115 (2000).

But the term spectrum sharing is often used specifically to refer to the avoidance of interference among different services via automated techniques, allowing for nearly instantaneous adjustments to avoid interference. *See* Amendment of the Commission's Rules with Regard to Commercial Operations in the 3550–3650 MHz Band, Notice of Proposed Rulemaking and Order, 27 FCC Rcd. 15,594 ¶ 5 (2012). A given spectrum band can be shared between licensed services or between licensed and unlicensed services.[17] Allowing white spaces devices in the bands allocated for television broadcasting is a form of spectrum sharing. But there are many other varieties of sharing. *See* John Leibovitz & Ruth Milkman, Taking Stock of Spectrum Sharing (2021), https://ssrn.com/abstract=3916386.

Below we consider spectrum sharing in the context of an aspect of spectrum that we have not yet focused on: federal government spectrum usage. In 2012 the President's Council of Advisors on Science and Technology (PCAST) issued the report below focusing on the sharing of spectrum allocated to the federal government. The report responded to a widespread belief that spectrum used by the federal government presents a particularly promising opportunity as a source of new spectrum capacity for non-governmental users. Those seeking frequencies have focused on the federal government because much of the government's spectrum is less intensively utilized than is commercial spectrum. To put the point differently, in terms of underutilized spectrum, some of the blocks of spectrum used by the federal government are particularly attractive candidates.

Realizing the Full Potential of Government-Held Spectrum to Spur Economic Growth

President's Council of Advisors on Science and Technology (2012)
Executive Summary, https://obamawhitehouse.archives.gov/sites/default/files/microsites/ostp/pcast_spectrum_report_final_july_20_2012.pdf

[C]learing and reallocation of Federal spectrum is not a sustainable basis for spectrum policy due to the high cost, lengthy time to implement, and disruption to the Federal mission. Further, although some have proclaimed that clearing and reallocation will result in significant net revenue to the government, we do not anticipate that will be the case for Federal spectrum.

This study finds that today's apparent shortage of spectrum is in fact an illusion brought about because of the way spectrum is managed. If the Nation instead expands its options for managing Federal spectrum, we can transform the availability of a precious national resource—spectrum—from scarcity to abundance.

17. Spectrum dedicated to an unlicensed commons also involves sharing, but by convention most references to "spectrum sharing" do not include such commons.

This expansion can be done in such a way that it will not result in a loss of revenue to the Federal Government and may result in new revenue either from enhanced economic growth and innovation or from modest leasing fees. But in either case, the value to the Federal Government will be greater if the spectrum is available for reuse or relicensing more often than it is today. The new system for Federal spectrum management that this report calls for—a new spectrum architecture and a corresponding shift in the architecture of future radio systems that use it—can multiply the effective capacity of spectrum by a factor of 1,000.

The essential element of this new Federal spectrum architecture is that the norm for spectrum use should be sharing, not exclusivity. Technology innovations of recent years make this transformation eminently achievable. Two trends are especially important. First, instead of just the tall cell towers that provide coverage for very large geographic areas, many wireless services are already moving to "small cell" operations that provide services for very small geographic areas, reducing the potential for interference so that other services may operate much closer to them. The huge explosion of Wi-Fi services is one example of this evolution. Second, improvements in performance make it possible for devices to deliver services seamlessly even in the presence of signals from other systems, so that they do not need exclusive frequency assignments, only an assurance that potentially interfering signals will not rise above a certain level.

Taking these and other developments into account, this report argues that spectrum should be managed not by fragmenting it into ever more finely divided exclusive frequency assignments, but by specifying large frequency bands that can accommodate a wide variety of compatible uses and new technologies that are more efficient with larger blocks of spectrum.

To make an analogy, today's spectrum use resembles road transportation at the beginning of the automotive revolution when we created our highways and interconnection and commerce flowed. The mid-1980s innovation of "unlicensed" spectrum use, which makes spectrum available at no cost to any user willing to abide by technical conditions of use, has been essential to the rise of Wi-Fi and represents a wireless analogy to the early shared roadways. The rest of the spectrum system, however, still looks like a series of narrow roads. What PCAST proposes is creating the spectrum equivalent of wide multi-lane superhighways, where the lanes are continuously shared by many cars, trucks, and other vehicles. Spectrum superhighways would be large stretches of spectrum that can be shared by many different types of wireless services, just as vehicles share a superhighway by moving from one lane to another. In contrast to the way we have allocated spectrum, the road system has always let Federal and commercial vehicles share the same highways, with the proviso that government use was allowed to preempt commercial users' rights for reasons of public safety, emergency medical rescue, or national security. There is no reason that the same principles cannot apply to spectrum management. Users of spectrum can make use of the wireless equivalents of signals, sensors, and stop lights to avoid "collisions" with other users.

Federal spectrum, instead of being divided into small, dedicated frequency blocks as it is at present, should be divided into substantial frequency blocks spanning several hundred megahertz. Establishing these wide bands will make it easier for spectrum sharing to be the norm, a transformation in which all Federal agencies would be required to cooperate. Making spectrum access available to a wide range of services and applications will also require provision of a framework that establishes minimum technical standards for the coexistence of transmitters and receivers, in contrast to the present system that focuses on transmitters. Finally, simple measures that assess individual spectrum uses solely by their need for megahertz must be replaced by more sophisticated metrics that reveal how effectively a stretch of spectrum can accommodate a variety of complementary services within a given area.

Federal users currently have no incentives to improve the efficiency with which they use their own spectrum allocation, nor does the Federal system as a whole have incentives to improve its overall efficiency. This report therefore proposes an accounting, allocation, and incentive system (nominally called "Spectrum Currency") that would reward agencies that move quickly to promote more effective spectrum use by making some of their spectrum available for sharing with other Federal and non-Federal users.

One of the other important directions that spectrum policy must take is to create a marketplace that can accommodate the widest range of commercial users, from initial venture-funded startups to established service providers. Today's spectrum ecosystem offers only the choice between unlicensed and long term, renewable licensed spectrum. The number of business entities that can participate in auctions for nationwide, long term spectrum licenses is limited. Experimenting with shorter-term, lower cost, spectrum license options for commercial users sharing Federal spectrum, will foster new innovative ideas, increase the number of participants in this market, contribute to economic growth, and also provide a way to collect an ongoing stream of revenue, if that is desired.

Notes and Questions

1. Sharing. The fact that spectrum is lightly used does not necessarily mean that clearing it of those uses will be easy, and in fact PCAST finds that it will not be easy. Thus PCAST suggests sharing. Is the case for sharing a compelling one? Should PCAST have pushed harder to have the government simply vacate the spectrum? Or, by contrast, is imposing sharing a mistake, given the importance of the government uses?

2. Government Incentives. As the PCAST report acknowledges, federal users lack an incentive to vacate, or efficiently use, spectrum, because they cannot monetize it. This is analogous to the command-and-control approach to spectrum. Indeed, in some ways the problem is worse than the command-and-control regime that applied to many commercial uses, because federal government users cannot confidently transfer their spectrum usage in return for something else they value. PCAST suggests overcoming this problem by creating a shadow currency that would value spectrum and that could be used by agencies insofar as they freed up spectrum capacity. The problem is that such a shadow currency has not been implemented, and agencies may fear that it will never actually materialize (e.g., even if they receive such currency, it will be used as a justification to reduce other spending, mitigating its value). Is there any credible commitment that the President, or Congress, could make that would come close to approximating the value of the spectrum and thus provide government users with a significant incentive to give up some of their spectrum?

3. FCC Response. In 2010, the NTIA (which controls federal government spectrum) proposed making the 3.5 GHz band available for shared use. Like almost all other frequencies, that band had incumbents — in this case, Department of Defense radars and non-federal satellite stations. In response to the NTIA proposal and the PCAST report, and to the possibility of spectrum sharing more generally, the FCC adopted three-tiered shared access for this band. Incumbents were in the highest tier, the key element of which was protection from interference by those in the other tiers. The other two tiers (which the FCC called Citizens Broadband Radio Service) were "Priority Access" for users with stringent quality-of-service needs (such as hospitals, utilities, and public safety entities), and "General Authorized Access" (GAA), which was designed to provide low-cost entry to innovative new devices. Akin to most unlicensed services, GAA licensees are required to accept interference from, and not cause harmful interference to, higher-tiered licensees. On the questioning of licensing these two lower tiers, the FCC "adopt[ed] a hybrid framework that selects, automatically, the best approach based on local supply and demand. Where competitive rivalry for spectrum access is low, the GAA tier provides a low-cost entry point to the band, similar to unlicensed access. Where rivalry is high, an auction resolves mutually exclusive applications in specific geographic areas for [Priority Access Licenses]." Amendment of the Commission's Rules with Regard to Commercial Operations in the 3550–3650 MHz Band, Report and Order and Second Further Notice of Proposed Rulemaking, 30 FCC Rcd. 3959 ¶ 5 (2015).

4. How to Evaluate Success? On what basis should the FCC determine whether its regime is working well? Should it focus on interference? Should it focus on the services offered and used by GAA users? Should it value some kinds of uses more highly than others (e.g., uses that allow ordinary people to communicate on matters of importance to them)? How should it define, and how should it defend, such metrics?

5. Evaluation of Different Options. The examples discussed above are among the most prominent ways of allowing unlicensed wireless uses, but of course there are many other options. How would you identify and evaluate the various options? Your evaluation will depend in part on what goals you prioritize. How would you articulate those goals and argue for their primacy? Your evaluation also will likely depend on what technology currently allows, or may allow in the near future. How would you determine that?

6. Analogies. Are there analogues to licensed versus unlicensed use with respect to internet platforms? For instance, are individuals on social media the equivalent of unlicensed devices? Or are internet platforms disanalogous, because channels of communication are fundamentally different from the content that those channels carry?

Return to the argument for dedicated spectrum for unlicensed uses. Is there an equivalent with respect to wires? Is it government provision of wires and internet service? But part of the appeal of unlicensed is being free of gatekeepers, and government provision of wired service replaces one gatekeeper (a company) with another (a local government).

More broadly, what are the best analogies to the various options for allowing licensed uses, unlicensed uses, and the various combinations of licensed and unlicensed? Do they shed any light on the optimal approach to licensed and unlicensed uses?

§ 9.E. Moving Licenses Closer to Property Rights

Giving flexibility to those providing services (over spectrum or otherwise) has enormous value to them. So does preventing those who might interfere with one's service (and the FCC does police interference). Also valuable are rights of disposition — the ability to subdivide, lease, transfer, and indefinitely retain spectrum rights. In this section, we address those issues.

§ 9.E.1. Spectrum Subdivision and Leasing (and the Possibility of a Private Commons)

If a licensee can divide and lease its spectrum rights in any way that it chooses, and the lessor and lessee can utilize those rights in any way that they choose, then effectively there is complete spectrum flexibility. The FCC has not, in fact, allowed lessees to offer any service they please (in significant part because of concerns about interference), nor has it given licensees the right to subdivide and lease as they see fit. But in 2003 it issued an order allowing licensees to enter into leases (of any duration) under which the lessee exercises working (de facto) control, so long as the licensee retains legal (de jure) control. *See* Promoting Efficient Use of Spectrum Through Elimination of Barriers to the Development of Secondary Markets, Report and Order and Further Notice of Proposed Rulemaking, 18 FCC Rcd. 20,604 (2003). This does not go as far as Coase might like (because it obviously falls short of full divisibility and transferability), but it enhanced the development of secondary markets in spectrum.

Building on this order, the FCC shortly thereafter authorized licensees and lessees to create "private commons" of the sort noted in Question 4 after the Benkler excerpt above. *See* Promoting Efficient Use of Spectrum Through Elimination of Barriers to the Development of Secondary Markets, Second Report and Order, Order on Reconsideration, and Second Further Notice of Proposed Rulemaking, 19 FCC Rcd. 17,503 ¶ 91 (2004).

Notes and Questions

1. What Does Experience Reveal? No private commons were created in response to this order. What should that tell us? That not enough people would use a commons to make it economically attractive? That more than enough people would use a commons to make it economically attractive, but licensees are too short-sighted, intransigent, or ideologically opposed to commons to create them, despite the money they would make? That more than enough people would use a true commons to make it economically viable, but not enough would use a private commons because of differences between government-created commons and private commons? What differences would those be?

§ 9.E.2. License Transfer

With two significant exceptions, licensees have always been free to transfer their licenses to other entities, and licenses have routinely changed hands from the earliest days of licensing to the present. The first exception was that, in the days when the FCC assigned licenses via comparative hearings, there was a waiting period during which the party originally awarded a license was not allowed to sell it.[18]

The reason for having any waiting period at all was that waiting periods gave the FCC's initial assignment hearings meaning. The FCC's assignment hearings took the agency, and the applicants, a significant amount of time (and money) and were designed to find the entity that would provide the best service. Allowing immediate transfer would render the FCC's careful weighing meaningless — or, more precisely, would simply determine which private party would obtain the right to turn around and auction that license to the highest bidder.

The FCC put forward the argument against having a waiting period in its notice proposing shortening the waiting period (for licenses awarded via comparative hearing) from three years to one:

> [T]he "three year rule" artificially restricts a station from going to its "higher valued use." A buyer ready and willing to utilize its resources to pay the required price for a given property is more likely to provide the service most desired in a community than an unwilling owner restricted from selling a property it no longer desires only by Commission fiat. Further, the

18. *See* Amendment of Part I of the Commission's Rules Adding Section 1.365 Concerning Applications for Voluntary Assignments or Transfers of Control, Report and Order, 32 F.C.C. 689 (1962) (imposing a three-year waiting period); Amendment of the Commission's Rules Regarding Applications for Voluntary Assignments or Transfers of Control, 47 Fed. Reg. 55,924 (Dec. 14, 1982) (shortening the waiting period to one year).

> rule's restrictions impose an undesirable cost upon both the present owner, who may be forced to suffer financial loss or forego more appropriate investment opportunities, and upon the public, which may suffer reduced service from a failing operation or lose the opportunity to receive better service which an influx of new capital or a more willing operator might provide.

Applications for Voluntary Assignments or Transfers of Control, 47 Fed. Reg. 985, 986 (Jan. 8, 1982).

The argument for a waiting period became much weaker (if not nonexistent) when the FCC abandoned hearings and began to make initial assignments by auction. Once licenses are auctioned to the highest bidder, there would seem to be little reason not to allow a private auction soon thereafter. Today licensees are free to transfer their licenses subject only to 47 U.S.C. § 310(d), which provides in relevant part:

> No construction permit or station license, or any rights thereunder, shall be transferred, assigned, or disposed of in any manner . . . to any person except upon application to the Commission and upon finding by the Commission that the public interest, convenience, and necessity will be served thereby. . . . [B]ut in acting thereon the Commission may not consider whether the public interest, convenience, and necessity might be served by the transfer, assignment, or disposal of the permit or license to a person other than the proposed transferee or assignee.

On the one hand, this provision enables transfers by preventing the FCC from considering whether another transferee would be preferable and subjecting transfers only to the public interest, convenience, and necessity standard. On the other hand—and this is the second significant exception—transfers require FCC approval, and the public interest, convenience, and necessity standard gives the FCC a lot of discretion. In applying this provision, the FCC has routinely approved garden-variety transfers but has engaged in much more rigorous review of some transfers—primarily in the context of mergers that may have anticompetitive effects.[19] Section 310(d) is thus often a significant element of the FCC's merger review process: the most common jurisdictional hook for the FCC's merger review is the fact that one of the companies needs FCC approval to transfer its various licenses to the other. Moreover, as Chapter 8.B indicates, in contrast to the arguable narrowness of the antitrust standards applicable to DOJ and FTC merger review, the public interest standard of § 310(d) gives the FCC broad authority to reject transfers (pursuant to a merger or otherwise). The result is that § 310(d) broadly empowers the FCC and it sometimes uses that power to implement competition policy, but ordinary

19. *See, e.g.*, Jon Sallet, FCC Transaction Review: Competition and the Public Interest, FCC (Aug. 12, 2014), https://perma.cc/R8T7-HWQ3; Aaron V. Yuratovich, You'll Know it When You See it: The FCC's Elusive Public Interest Standard, 73 Admin. L. Rev. 713 (2021).

transfers are routinely approved. We consider the debate over FCC merger review and this jurisdictional hook in Chapter 8.B.

Notes and Questions

1. Elephants in the Room. Under current law, the FCC is not allowed to consider whether transfer to some other party—someone other than the willing transferor and the willing transferee—would better serve the public interest. Why? Can you structure a rule that would allow the FCC to consider outsiders? What problems might arise under that approach?

2. If Transfers Are a Good Idea . . . Do the arguments against limits on transfer suggest treating licenses like any other commodity? If so, does that suggest that there should be no limits on subdividing and leasing, and that licenses should be perpetual (i.e., no need for renewal)? Or are the arguments for those other limits different?

§ 9.E.3. License Renewal

Spectrum licenses are of limited duration. For example, commercial television and radio licenses are awarded under current law for eight-year periods. 47 U.S.C. § 307(c)(1). Every licensee must therefore periodically appear before the FCC and petition that its license be renewed. This gives the FCC the power to influence licensee behavior; every decision a licensee makes throughout its tenure is made in the shadow of an implicit threat of an FCC response come renewal time. This form of implicit regulation—regulation through the threat of license nonrenewal or some lesser ramification such as renewal for a shorter-than-normal period—is a prime example of what is sometime referred to as regulation by raised eyebrow.

Indeed, the threat of nonrenewal is the primary means that the FCC has used in attempting to influence licensees' behavior. When the government has wanted a licensee to offer more programming that the government deems valuable (such as children's television), or to offer less programming that the government deems unworthy (such as commercials), or to adopt certain business practices (such as an affirmative action program), the main lever it has used to influence licensees in the desired direction has been the specter of license nonrenewal.[20] Licenses are sufficiently valuable to licensees that they generally fall into line and obey the government's directives in order to keep their licenses at renewal time.

---

20. *See, e.g.*, Action For Children's Television v. FCC, 564 F.2d 458, 467–68 (D.C. Cir. 1977) (finding that the FCC's collection of data on children's programming and threat to include it as a factor in renewal decisions inspired industry self-regulation); Action for Children's Television v. FCC, 821 F.2d 741 (D.C. Cir. 1987) (considering the impact of mandatory logs of advertising during children's programming, available to FCC in license renewal determinations, on licensee behavior); Lutheran Church-Missouri Synod v. FCC, 141 F.3d 344, 349 (D.C. Cir. 1998) (recognizing that failure to comply with FCC affirmative action regulations could affect license renewal).

The big policy debate regarding license renewal has been over how much discretion the FCC should enjoy with respect to its renewal decisions. One possibility is to give the FCC broad discretion, the logic being that the FCC is supposed to select the most promising licensees and greater discretion to analyze an incumbent's record would maximize the FCC's ability to do just that. True, this might be a little unfair to incumbents; the FCC really would have nothing to compare the incumbent's record to, except perhaps a challenger's promises. But the FCC could account for this imbalance, for example by holding challengers to the promises they make. There are two possible advantages to empowering the FCC in this way: first, if subject to broad review, poor and even average incumbents could be identified and replaced as their licenses expire; and second, during their terms, licensees hoping ultimately to renew their licenses would be very responsive to regulation by raised eyebrow, thus empowering the FCC to adjust its policies from time to time to respond to changing conditions.

Another possibility would be to constrain the FCC via a strong presumption of renewal that would be satisfied so long as the licensee complied with clear and objective requirements. Such an approach would allow the FCC to deny renewal to licenses that failed to meet minimum standards but would deprive it of the power to regulate implicitly. Regulation by raised eyebrow works, after all, only to the extent that the FCC has discretion in its renewal decisions. The prime advantage of this approach is that licensees would likely have stronger incentives to make long-term investments related to their licenses. A licensee would seem more likely to invest in expensive equipment and marketing if it knew that, so long as it followed clear rules laid down by the FCC, it would be allowed to keep its license and thus reap long-term benefits from those investments. Indeed, a further possibility is that the government could guarantee renewal for incumbents, which would, of course, render the time limits on licenses meaningless and deprive the FCC of any leverage flowing from renewal.

The government's policies on license duration and renewal expectancies have changed over the years. License duration has generally become longer (e.g., the 1996 Telecommunications Act extended the length of broadcast licenses from five years to eight years).[21] More importantly, renewal expectancies have become stronger. Section 204 of the 1996 Telecommunications Act amended the Communications Act to provide that, when an incumbent broadcaster seeks renewal of its license, the FCC must grant the application if the licensee has served the public interest, has committed no "serious violations" of the Communications Act or the FCC's rules, and has not committed any other violations "which, taken together, would constitute a pattern of abuse," 47 U.S.C. § 309(k). Even then, the FCC can impose a smaller sanction than nonrenewal, such as renewal for a shorter-than-normal duration, *see id.* § 309(k)(2), or renewal plus a fine under 47 U.S.C. § 503. If and only if

21. Telecommunications Act of 1996, Pub. L. No. 104-104, § 203, 110 Stat. 56, 112 (codified at 47 U.S.C. § 307(c)(1)).

the incumbent flunks one of the tests mentioned above and "no mitigating factors justify the imposition of lesser sanctions," the FCC must deny the incumbent's renewal application and consider other applicants for the license. *Id.* § 309(k)(3). Importantly, this renewal presumption precludes the FCC from considering other licensees. Section 309(k)(4) explicitly states that "the Commission shall not consider whether the public interest, convenience, and necessity might be served by the grant of a license to a person other than the renewal applicant."

Nonbroadcast spectrum licensees have not received similar attention from the courts or Congress, but they, too, have a strong presumption of renewal. Build-out requirements sometimes obligate licensees for new services to deploy those new services within specific time limits,[22] but, beyond that, most nonbroadcast licensees can expect renewal if they have "substantially complied" with statutory and regulatory requirements and provided "service which is sound, favorable, and substantially above a level of mediocre service which just might minimally warrant renewal."[23]

Notes and Questions

1. Empirical Evidence. Denials of license renewals have been few and far between. During the 1970s, for example, the FCC revoked or denied only 64 radio and television station licenses. Moreover, a study of those denials and revocations reveals that, even before deregulation, factors mentioned in the Policy Statement on Comparative Broadcast Hearings, Public Notice, 1 F.C.C. 2d 393 (1965) (excerpted below), rarely accounted for license revocations or refusals to renew. Instead, the most frequent reasons given by the agency were: misrepresentations to the FCC (18); abandonment of license or failure to prosecute renewal (16); departure from promised programming (11); fraudulent billing practices (11); and unauthorized transfer of control (10). In most cases, more than one reason was given. Over-commercialization was cited once, violation of the personal-attack rules twice, and fairness violations three times. Further, the study's authors note that, even when used, programming-related rationales "were usually part of a longer litany of charges against the licensee." Frederic A. Weiss et al., Station License Revocations and Denials of Renewal, 1970–78, 24 J. Broad. 69, 77 (1980). The FCC, in short, was reluctant to rely on subjective factors alone when denying a renewal application.

In more recent years, denials of renewals have been even rarer, and even then have generally been based only on objective factors.[24] One notorious but perhaps

22. *See, e.g.*, 47 C.F.R. § 25.144(b) (requiring that digital satellite radio licensees must have one space station in orbit within four years and full operation within six years).

23. *See, e.g.*, 47 C.F.R. § 90.743 (using this language with respect to renewal of licenses for private land mobile services), § 27.14 (miscellaneous wireless services), § 24.203 (personal communications services), and § 101.1011 (local multipoint distribution services).

24. For instance, among the handful of denials or revocations, one was a revocation of a direct broadcast satellite license because the licensee failed to commence operations within the specified time limit, *see* Advanced Commc'ns Corp. Application for Extension of Time to Construct, Launch, and Operate a Direct Broadcast Satellite System, Memorandum Opinion and Order,

revealing case not involving objective factors involved a radio station (KDND, owned by a company called Entercom) that in 2007 held a "Hold Your Wee for a Wii" contest, despite many warnings of possible harms to contestants, that in fact led to the death of one of the contestants. When the station's license came up for renewal, the FCC declined to deny renewal and instead referred the question of renewal to the FCC's administrative law judge. Entercom License, Hearing Designation Order and Notice of Opportunity for Hearing, 31 FCC Rcd. 12,196 (2016). Before the hearing, Entercom announced both its intent to acquire CBS radio and that it would surrender its license because it had "determined it is in the company's best interests to voluntarily turn in the KDND license to facilitate the timely FCC approvals for the planned combination with CBS Radio." Victor A. Patton, Media Watchdog Expresses Interest in 107.9 FM's Future, Sacramento Bus. J. (Feb. 9, 2017). The then-chief of the FCC's enforcement division agreed with this characterization, stating that Entercom's motive was the pending merger with CBS Radio. Dan Morain, Sue from Fiddletown Took a Stand in the Public Interest, Sacramento Bee (April 4, 2017). This highlights the power that flows from the FCC's ability to deny license transfers that we mentioned above: the acquisition of CBS Radio required the transfer of its stations, and Entercom determined that smoothing its path toward those transfers was worth surrendering the license (which it valued at $13.5 million, but that pales in comparison to the $1.6 billion value of the merger).

2. Odd Regulatory Strategy? Why did (and does) the FCC have broadcast regulations that it enforces only through the threat of nonrenewal and yet weaken the force of that threat by very rarely denying a renewal application? Is the answer that the FCC wants to exercise significant control over licensees? If so, then it would presumably regularly reject incumbents who do the worst job (relative to the other incumbents) of following the agency's wishes. Is the answer, instead, that the FCC is captured by incumbents and wants to let them operate as they see fit? If so, then why have the regulations in the first place? Is the answer that the FCC wants to give the appearance of regulating behavior without actually exercising much influence? If so, whom is the FCC trying to fool? Or is the answer that even a very small chance of losing valuable licenses will cause licensees to follow the FCC's regulatory "suggestions?"

3. Alternatives. Congress could have granted a renewal expectancy and yet still have the FCC seriously review incumbents' records — requiring that an incumbent satisfy a set of stringent objective criteria in order to receive a strong renewal presumption. So long as those criteria are well articulated ex ante, the FCC's discretion would be

---

11 FCC Rcd. 3399 (1995), *aff'd sub. nom.* Advanced Commc'ns Corp. v. FCC, 376 F.3d 1153 (D.C. Cir. 2004), and another was a denial of renewal of an amateur radio license to a licensee based on his fraud conviction and his misrepresentations about that conviction to the FCC, *see* Application of Herbert L. Schoenbohm for Amateur Station and Operator License, Order, 13 FCC Rcd. 23,774 (1998), *aff'd sub. nom.* Schoenbohm v. FCC, 2004 F.3d 243 (D.C. Cir. 2000).

minimized, and licensees would therefore still have a strong incentive to make long-term investments, right? Did Congress let incumbents off too easily, then?

4. How Much Further to Full Property Rights? As the materials above indicate, licenses do not have complete freedom to subdivide, lease, and transfer their licenses to other entities and do not have a guaranteed renewal expectancy: the limits imposed by the FCC are modest but still exist. But if there were no such limits, would we have something akin to fee-simple property rights in spectrum as a practical matter (47 U.S.C. § 301 of course prevents formal property rights)? The answer is that this is necessary but not sufficient. Among the most important sticks in the bundle of rights is the right to exclude, and the FCC sometimes adds users to a given set of frequencies over the opposition of the existing licensee. That said, this is a question of license definition. Just as we would not treat an airplane's flight over a parcel as interfering with the landowner's right to exclude, a spectrum license might be defined to exclude protection of the licensee against noninterfering uses. And, as we have seen, the FCC has generally protected licensees against interference.

On the other hand, flexible licenses give licensees more leeway than fee simple generally does. Because of zoning, landowners in cities are restricted in the size and use of buildings on their land beyond what can reasonably be deemed interference with their neighbors. Flexible spectrum licenses, by contrast, allow for most non-interfering uses, and aesthetic ugliness does not count as interference.

The current system is not akin to property rights for spectrum — the limits on the rights of disposition alone defeat such a claim. But we are also far from pervasive government control. That once existed but no longer does.

Do any of the regulations considered in this chapter make particular (or particularly little) sense? And are any of these regulations models (or anti-models) for regulations of wires?

§ 9.F. Assignment Mechanisms

When new frequencies become available under the band plan or when a new service is approved for use as part of the band plan, the FCC has to decide whether the service will be a licensed or unlicensed service. If unlicensed, the FCC must promulgate the various technical standards discussed in the previous section. If licensed, the FCC must not only define the details of those licenses — how much spectrum will be allocated per license, what uses will be permitted, and so on — but also how the licenses will be distributed. The FCC has used three primary mechanisms for the initial assignment of spectrum licenses over time: merit, as measured by the FCC (comparative hearings); random selection (lotteries); and willingness to pay (auctions).

For most of the 20th century, the FCC assigned licenses via comparative hearing. This flowed from 47 U.S.C. § 309(a), which directed the FCC to choose licensees based on "public interest, convenience, and necessity," and Ashbacker Radio Corp. v. FCC, 326 U.S. 327, 333 (1945), which held that this provision required that the FCC conduct a comparative hearing whenever there were two or more applications for a given license. And given that the only cost of obtaining a license was the application process itself, routinely there were multiple applicants for a given license.

The "public interest, convenience, and necessity" language gave the FCC very broad discretion. Indeed, the D.C. Circuit flatly stated in Johnston Broad. Co. v. FCC, 175 F.2d 351, 357 (D.C. Cir. 1949), that, in comparative hearings, "there are no established criteria by which a choice between the applicants must be made." This opened the door to political considerations. Licenses given out in Franklin D. Roosevelt's and Harry Truman's administrations (mainly radio) tended to go to Democrats who supported the New Deal, including Lyndon Johnson's wife, Lady Bird, who received licenses despite no prior industry experience.[25] Licenses given out in Dwight Eisenhower's administration (mainly television) tended to go to Republican supporters.[26]

Despite (or partially because of?) the enormous discretion the FCC had in choosing among applicants, for most of the 20th century comparative hearings seemed entrenched. Recall that Coase's testimony excerpted above argued both for property rights in spectrum and for transferring those rights to the highest bidder—and also recall the negative reaction to his views. And in 1977 two FCC commissioners said that the odds of Congress abandoning comparative hearings "are about the same as those on the Easter Bunny in the Preakness." Formulation of Policies Relating to the Broadcast Renewal Applicant, Stemming from the Comparative Hearing Process, Report and Order, 66 F.C.C. 2d 419, 434 n.18 (1977) (separate statement of Hooks & Fogarty, Comm'rs).

But it turns out that the Easter Bunny did win the Preakness.

In response to concerns about the fairness of comparative hearings, Congress in 1982 authorized the FCC to assign licenses via random selection among all the applicants (i.e., lottery). 47 U.S.C. § 309(i)(1). This avoided favoritism, but it did not alter a dynamic applicable to both hearings and lotteries: the transferability of licenses and the presumption of renewal meant that licenses were routinely sold by the initial licensee. Thus the FCC's assignment of licenses effectively determined who would be allowed to auction off the license that the government would for some reason not sell itself. Policymakers came to realize that any method of assignment is an auction mechanism; all that changes is the identity of the auctioneer. In 1985 the FCC Chair called for auctions, and Congress authorized them in 1993 and mandated them in

25. *See* Robert Caro, Means of Ascent 89–105 (1990).

26. *See* William B. Ray, FCC: The Ups and Downs of Radio-TV Regulation 45 (1990); Bernard Schwartz, Comparative Television and the Chancellor's Foot, 47 Geo. L.J. 655, 690–94 (1959).

1997.[27] Whether that strikes you as a speedy or slow process of change, it was certainly a major transformation in the method of assignment approach. The idea that licenses should be auctioned went from unrealistic to conventional wisdom in the space of twenty years, and auctions became a settled aspect of spectrum policy—as settled as the preference for hearings had once seemed to be.

In the influential paper excerpted below, two FCC economists broke down the merits and demerits of hearings, lotteries, and auctions.

Using Auctions to Select FCC Licensees

Evan Kwerel & Alex D. Felker, FCC Office of Plans & Policy, Working Paper No. 16 (1985), http://transition.fcc.gov/Bureaus/OPP/working_papers/oppwp16.pdf

I. Introduction

As part of its duties under the Communications Act of 1934, the Federal Communications Commission is charged with managing the radio frequency spectrum. Traditionally, the Commission has performed this duty by first *allocating* a portion of spectrum in a given area to a particular purpose. Then the Commission *assigns* channels within an allocation to individual licensees. Both allocations and assignments have important implications for consumer welfare and have been the subject of many public policy analyses. This paper examines only the assignment process and assumes no changes are made in either the current eligibility criteria for holding a license or the terms, conditions or rights of a license. We conclude that in most cases auctioning previously unassigned channels is likely to result in the same ultimate assignment as present mechanisms. But because they require winning bidders to make substantial payments in return for being licensed, auctions are an efficient way of reducing the number of applicants. Thus, auctions are likely to impose lower costs on the Commission and society than the other methods considered.

II. Description of Alternative Procedures for Selecting FCC Licensees

A radio channel that is assigned to only one party is said to be *exclusive*. If more than one party applies for a given exclusive channel, these applications are said to be *mutually exclusive*.

There are three methods that could be used to select among mutually exclusive applications: comparative hearings, lotteries, and a system of competitive bids (auctions).

A. Comparative Hearings

In practice, comparative hearings have proven to be a costly and generally ineffective means of selection. There are two main problems with this process. First, there

27. *See* Omnibus Budget Reconciliation Act of 1993, Pub. L. No. 103-66, § 6002, 107 Stat. 312, 387–97 (codified as amended at 47 U.S.C. § 309) (authorizing auctions); 47 U.S.C. § 309(i)–(j) (requiring auctions).

is substantial disagreement about what the comparative criteria should be and how they should be weighted, and it is not unusual for disagreement to exist as to which applicant is, in fact, the most socially worthy. There is considerable doubt, therefore, as to how effective comparative hearings are in furthering social goals.

A second problem concerns the cost of these hearings (including delay). It is not uncommon for litigation to drag on for years, with participants incurring huge legal bills. These long litigation periods harm both the applicant ultimately selected and the public. The new licensee loses an income stream; the public is without an additional service. But because delay favors existing licensees, they have strong incentives to file petitions to deny or otherwise utilize the administrative process as a means of retarding competitors' entry.

B. Lotteries

In recognition of these and other problems, the Congress in 1982 gave the Commission permissive authority to award licenses by random selection. The FCC's initial experience with lotteries suggests that this method has its own significant difficulties. Once it became known that the lottery entry requirements were reasonably low, many individuals elected to participate. In the Low Power Television Service alone there are about 20,000 applications awaiting lottery.

The Commission has attempted to reduce its administrative burden by creating narrow filing "windows" and encouraging settlements among applicants. But applicants have, in turn, adjusted their filing strategies. Hence, with each new call for lottery applications, larger numbers of applications are received.

C. Auctions

A third possible selection method is a competitive bidding system where licenses are awarded to those users willing to pay the most for them. Although they have never been used to award radio licenses, federal government experience with auctions is longstanding and extensive.

The U.S. Department of the Interior (DOI), for example, has been successfully auctioning leases on tracts in the Outer Continental Shelf (OCS) for 31 years. The OCS is a major source of domestic oil and gas production, and between 1954 and 1983 total revenues from the auctions program were approximately $68 billion. Under the OCS Lands Act of 1953, private parties submit sealed bids for the right to explore and develop a specified tract on the OCS. The DOI has used a number of different systems for auctioning leases. Currently, a tract is leased to the party offering the highest up front "cash bonus" provided there are at least three bids. If there are fewer than three bids, the high bid is not accepted unless it exceeds the U.S. Geological Survey's estimate of the tract's value. In addition to paying a cash bonus for a tract, the lessee must also pay the government a fixed share of the revenues produced on the tract. The "royalty rate" is typically 16? percent of the market price of the oil and gas at the wellhead. About 30 percent of the total government revenues from OCS leasing have come from royalty payments. The primary economic reason for relying on a royalty system in addition to cash bonus bids is that oil exploration is an extremely risky enterprise and royalties provide for a sharing of this risk between the government and private parties. Discussions with DOI officials indicate that the sealed bid auctions have been relatively simple to administer and free of any charges of corruption.

Other examples of federal auctions are: Treasury Bill auctions; leases of geothermal steam land; auctions of seized and unclaimed property; disposing of surplus equipment by the General Services Administration; and disposing of dead seamen's effects.

III. Comparison of Selection Procedures

In this section comparative hearings, lotteries, and auctions are compared with respect to their ownership effects, processing speeds, private costs, and government costs. Other considerations in choosing among selection methods are also discussed.

A. Effect on Ownership

The initial method of selecting a license may have little effect on who ultimately holds it because FCC licensees have considerable freedom to trade their authorizations. For example, in 1983 sixty-five percent of commercial television licenses [and seventy-five percent of commercial radio licenses] were held by someone other than the initial licensee. Thus, the qualifications of most present-day broadcasters were never considered in a comparative context.

In the cellular service many applicants have elected to reach settlements amongst themselves rather than face the uncertainties of either comparative hearings or lotteries. The Commission has generally honored these agreements and in those cases where all mutually exclusive applicants have settled, the agency has issued an authorization without utilizing any selection procedure.

Since the assignment method has little effect on who holds a license in the long run, we conclude that ownership distributions would not be significantly changed if initial authorizations were awarded by auction. But, as will be argued in the following section, auctions would reduce the delays and transactions costs involved in initial assignments and avoid the need for resale.

This conclusion about the ultimate ownership distribution should lay to rest any concerns that under an auction large firms would monopolize spectrum. We believe that this is unlikely for at least four reasons. If such firms were willing and able to monopolize spectrum under auctions, they could also do so under the current selection schemes by purchasing licenses from parties that won the initial assignment. Yet monopolization has not been observed in spectrum, nor has it been observed for other resources such as land that are also fixed in supply. Moreover, apparently no firm has sufficient wealth to buy up all the spectrum. Thirdly, since much of the usable radio spectrum has already been assigned, monopolizing the spectrum is unlikely to be a profitable strategy unless it could be accomplished without alerting the present holders of licenses. Otherwise existing licensees would hold out for high prices so as to reap much of the potential gains from monopolizing the market. Finally, any move to "corner the spectrum market" would presumably violate existing antitrust laws.

B. Delay in Making Assignments

Each assignment mechanism imposes a delay cost upon both the licensee and the public. The public's cost due to loss of service is difficult to estimate. But the cost imposed upon the successful applicant can be estimated by calculating the difference between the present value of the assignment under both delayed and non-delayed scenarios. With a nominal annual interest rate of 10%, a one year delay imposes a cost equal to 9% of the assignment's value, a two year delay imposes a 17% penalty, and a three year delay a 25% penalty.

Comparative hearings are generally lengthy proceedings. Broadcast cases often go on for two years or longer. Even the especially streamlined hearings used to grant cellular licenses in the top 30 markets averaged 18 months in length.

Lotteries have proven to be slower than expected. Most of the delay is created by huge numbers of applications, each of which must be logged, filed and prescreened prior to selection. Over 5000 applications were filed for cellular markets 91–120, and it is our best guess that the processing delay in these cases will average at least 12 months.

Auctioned assignments will probably attract far fewer applicants than lotteries because under an auction the winner must pay for the license. Thus, administrative delays will likewise be much shorter.

C. Private Application Costs

Comparative hearings and lotteries use up a great deal of real resources (primarily the time of legal, engineering, and economic consultants).[28] Auctions, however, involve primarily a transfer of resources (to the government in the form of the winning bid). Hence the use of auctions to award licenses could substantially reduce the total private and public resources expended in the process.

D. Cost of Administering Selections

There are two components to the cost incurred by the FCC in selecting among mutually exclusive applicants. One is "professional" cost. This includes the money spent on salary and support for professionals to review and analyze applicant documentation, and select a licensee. For example, professional costs are the major component of the FCC expenditures for a comparative hearing before an administrative law judge. We refer to the other cost category as "administrative." It includes money

28. Note that much of these resources are not "wasted" for successful applicants, because presumably the contribution of these consultants would be valuable in formulating a business. For unsuccessful applicants, however, all these expenditures are truly wasted, and represent a waste to society as well.

spent on space to house applications, as well as salary and support for the staff who records applicant information and maintains the documents. For lotteries and auctions, FCC costs are primarily administrative. Auctions would have lower administrative costs than lotteries because they would attract fewer applicants.

E. Other Considerations in Choosing Among Selection Methods

Auctions could prove attractive to taxpayers not just because they would reduce FCC costs but because they would provide a return for the valuable consideration granted licensees. The revenues raised through auctions would also help reduce the budget deficit.

Auctions could also provide the Commission with useful information on the value of spectrum in alternative uses. The amount bidders are willing to pay for a license reflects their estimates of the value customers place on the service they propose to provide. The Commission should consider reallocating spectrum to the higher valued use if it were to find that the bids on licenses for one use greatly exceeded the bids on licenses for similar spectrum allocated to another use.[29]

These findings of efficiency gains from auctions only apply in the case of selecting licensees for *unassigned* channels. Auctioning licenses at renewal appears to be analogous to having the government own all the land in a city and auction off parcels for five year terms. Licensees would tend to be discouraged from investing in equipment, training, and marketing that would have little value without a license.

Notes and Questions

1. Governmental Costs. Are you persuaded by Kwerel and Felker's discussion of the governmental costs of the different approaches? Hearings, of course, can be expensive to conduct, especially given the many possible layers of review. Auctions and lotteries seem likely to be less expensive, the main costs of each being paperwork-related — for example the costs of confirming that applicants meet some basic financial qualifications. Lotteries are likely to be more expensive on this score than auctions, however, since (assuming that lotteries are inexpensive for applicants to enter) there would likely be more applications to process in a lottery than in a comparable auction or hearing.

2. Private Costs. Similarly, which approach likely minimizes private costs for applicants? Hearings are expensive for applicants because they must pay for representation (perhaps at several formal interactions) and submit to a possibly expensive fact-finding process. Some of those expenses have value, of course; the ascertainment procedure, for example, is expensive for an applicant but also generates information

29. It is important to understand the limited nature of the proposal discussed here. We are proposing that auctions be used only to choose among potential *users*. The *use* of the spectrum would continue to be determined by an administrative process. Even greater public benefits could be achieved, however, by allowing winning bidders increased flexibility in what they do with their assignments.

that may be useful to the applicant should he be awarded the license at issue. Lotteries are probably the least expensive for applicants, the only real cost being the time to fill out a lottery application. And the primary expense involved in auctions would be the cost of developing a good bidding strategy, a cost that surely varies considerably party to party and auction to auction.

3. Rewards to the Government. Would one approach better inform the FCC as to how it should design the band plan? Does one approach give the government greater revenues? Does one approach give the government greater influence over licensee behavior? Auctions surely get a plus on the first two counts here. First, auctions help the government see how much a given slice of spectrum is worth, which might help the FCC in its spectrum-management duties. Note that this information is available under hearings and lotteries, too, but only some time after the initial assignment, when licensees start to sell their licenses on the open market. Second, auctions obviously fill the government's coffers rather effectively; it is hard to imagine those same revenues being generated by hearings or lotteries. As for the third factor — the extent of the government's influence over licensee behavior — it seems that hearings would earn the nod on this criterion because, while auctions largely defer to the marketplace and lotteries defer to chance, hearings (as we have seen) to some degree force licensees to defer to the FCC and its ever-powerful eyebrow. Whether that's good or bad as a policy matter, of course, depends on your perspective.

4. Empirical Data. The FCC's actual experience with hearings and lotteries confirmed many of Kwerel and Felker's hypotheses about their costs. For instance, when the FCC held hearings for cellular telephone licenses, there were more than ten applicants for each available license, and many of those applications contained more than 1000 pages of argument and documentation. The result was that the selection of licensees took almost two years on average. The FCC's switch to lotteries entailed its own complications, as the FCC itself noted:

> Initially, the Commission screened applicants and allowed only qualified providers to participate in the lottery. Even this minimal degree of screening proved to be extremely burdensome on the Commission's resources. For example, it took twenty months for the first set of cellular applications to be screened before the lottery.
>
> By 1987, the FCC was forced to abandon pre-lottery screening and open the process to all potential applicants. "Application mills" sprang up to assist almost 400,000 different firms claiming to be spectrum "providers" in their efforts to win a cellular license, and a broad range of spectrum speculators participated in and won lotteries in cellular and other services. Many license winners, with no intention of providing service to the public, were now eager to trade their license rights for windfall profits, and a secondary market in FCC licenses emerged. Even when lotteries themselves could be conducted

> quickly, it took years for secondary markets to reassign licenses to the parties that valued them the most and to aggregate these licenses efficiently.

FCC Report to Congress on Spectrum Auctions, 1997 WL 629251, at *6 (1997). The report noted that there were almost 400,000 cellular license lottery applications. *Id.* The sheer weight of the lottery applications was so great that the shelving collapsed in an FCC facility holding the applications. Nicholas W. Allard, The New Spectrum Auction Law, 18 Seton Hall Legis. J. 13, 26 n.46 (1993).

5. Auction Revenues. Auctions have been a financial windfall for the government. The FCC has conducted dozens of auctions for spectrum licenses, producing more than $200 billion in net winning bids. The prices paid for different kinds of licenses have varied greatly, depending on such factors as the frequencies involved, the amount of bandwidth allotted to each license, and the services authorized. For instance, the 2001 auction of 422 broadband licenses at frequencies (1.8–2.0 GHz) well suited for mobile broadband technology that was newly developed as of 2001 yielded $16.9 billion in net winning bids and the 2021 auction of 5,684 broadband licenses at frequencies (3.7–4.0 GHz) well suited for mobile broadband technology that was newly developed as of 2021 yielded $81.1 billion. By contrast, the 2001 auction of 317 narrowband mobile telephony licenses at 900 MHz yielded $8.3 million in net winning bids and the 2005 auction of 22 licenses for a television and internet delivery service yielded $133 thousand. *See* Auctions Summary, FCC, https://www.fcc.gov/wireless/auctions/auctions-summary.

The difference in the prices paid reflects in part the role of technology in enabling services that users highly value (mainly mobile broadband for access to mobile networks) at ever-higher frequencies. In the early 21st century, spectrum below 1 GHz was ideal for then-current mobile telephone technology. As time went on, the range of ideal spectrum expanded, encompassing frequencies well above 1 GHz.

That takes us back to some of the fundamental questions in this chapter: Should spectrum policy be guided by the prices paid for spectrum? What other considerations should influence the allocation, allotment, and assignment of spectrum?

6. The Logic of Auction Revenues. The positive political dynamic engendered by the adoption of auctions is that the government has an incentive to ensure that unused or vastly underused spectrum is vacated so that it can be auctioned to a buyer that will put it to a more socially valuable use. The negative political dynamic of spectrum auctions is that politicians sometimes view spectrum policy as a subset of budgetary policy—i.e., asking how spectrum policy can be engineered to deliver the most revenue to the government. This mindset might lead the government to withhold spectrum in order to create more demand and, consequently, higher prices. This mindset might also lead the government to be more skeptical of leaving spectrum unlicensed because, regardless of the merits of that policy, it will not produce auction revenue. Is the logic of auction revenues, on balance, a positive or negative force in spectrum policy?

7. Incentive Auctions. The order excerpted above reflects the FCC's embrace of auctions. Embrace of auctions is reflected in the incentive auctions proposed by the FCC's National Broadband Plan and legislated by Congress. The Plan proposed that

> Congress should grant the FCC authority to conduct incentive auctions to accelerate productive use of encumbered spectrum. Incentive auctions can provide a practical, market-based way to reassign spectrum, shifting a contentious process to a cooperative one. In an incentive auction, incumbents receive a portion of the proceeds realized by the auction of their spectrum licenses. This sharing of proceeds creates appropriate incentives for incumbents to cooperate with the FCC in reallocating their licensed spectrum to services that the market values more highly. A market-based mechanism—an auction—determines the value of the spectrum; market-based incentives, such as a share of the revenue received, encourage existing licensees to participate, accelerating the repurposing of spectrum and reducing the cost. Incentive auctions can be especially useful where fragmentation of spectrum licenses makes it difficult for private parties to aggregate spectrum in marketable quantities.

FCC, National Broadband Plan, § 5.3 (2010), http://www.fcc.gov/national-broadband-plan.

In 2012, Congress passed legislation that implements these auctions. Middle Class Tax Relief and Job Creation Act of 2012, Pub. L. No. 112-96, 126 Stat. 156. Title VI of that legislation creates a new statutory section entitled "Incentive Auctions" that authorizes the FCC to share auction revenue with a licensee that "relinquish[es] voluntarily some or all of its licensed spectrum usage rights in order to permit the assignment of new initial licenses subject to flexible-use service rules." *Id.* § 6402 (creating a new provision, 47 U.S.C. § 309(j)(8)(G)). The FCC has always had the ability to reclaim spectrum from existing licensees, authorize new services for that spectrum, and assign it to licensees for those new services. What the FCC lacked was the ability to share auction revenues with those who relinquished spectrum usage rights. This legislation permitted such sharing.

There was no debate over the assignment mechanism that would be used: auctions were the clear choice. The debate over the legislation, and the legislation itself, focused particularly on spectrum devoted to broadcasting, as data indicated that the gap between the value of spectrum to broadcasters (particularly those with low viewership) and the value to providers of services like wireless broadband was extremely large. Indeed, the size of that gap helps to explain why incentive auctions were included in a broader budget-related bill: Incentive auctions offset the cost of other measures in the legislation because they were projected to raise billions of dollars for the federal government, in light of the difference in value between the old and new uses. As the title of the legislation indicates, incentive auctions were part of a legislative package designed to fund programs and reduce taxes. Inclusion of incentive auctions helped make the legislation revenue-neutral.

But how could the government gain those revenues? Why wouldn't existing licensees hold out for valuations that captured for themselves all the difference in value between the old and new uses? The answer, in particular with respect to broadcasters, turns in significant part on the fact that the revenue projections, and a successful auction, did not depend on all broadcast licensees giving up all their spectrum usage rights. If a significant portion of licensees agreed to relinquish all their spectrum usage, or a portion of those rights (in which case they would share channels with another broadcaster, something that digital compression allows), the government could have a successful auction. And that, in turn, meant that the government could ask existing licensees to submit their reservation price (the price at which they would be willing to sell their license), knowing that it did not need to pay the reservation price for a broadcaster who submitted an exorbitant one.

The incentive auctions for broadcast television spectrum entail two auctions — a "reverse auction" in which broadcasters submit their prices to relinquish spectrum, and a "forward auction" of flexible-use licenses for the newly available spectrum in which new users would submit their prices to license spectrum. *See id.* §§ 6403(a) & (c). This arrangement allows the FCC to construct supply and demand curves and then determine the optimal amount of spectrum to shift from existing to new users and uses. A third major element of the incentive auction process involves the FCC reorganizing the broadcast television spectrum, by reassigning some licensees to different frequencies and setting up channel-sharing for those who give up some but not all of their frequencies. Such moves are essential to creating blocks of spectrum for new licensees. The legislation provided for such consolidation (often called repacking), with some limitations — notably that broadcast licensees cannot be involuntarily relocated from UHF to VHF channels. *See id.* § 6403(b)(3).[30] As the FCC noted in its 2012 notice of proposed rulemaking on incentive auctions in discussing reverse auctions, forward auctions, and repacking,

> [e]ach of the three pieces presents distinct policy, auction design, implementation and other issues, and the statute in a number of cases imposes specific requirements for each piece. At the same time, all three pieces are interdependent: the amount of spectrum available in the forward auction will depend on reverse auction bids and repacking, winning reverse auction bidders will be paid from the forward auction proceeds, and our repacking

30. There is some irony here, as in the early decades of television broadcasting VHF (channels 2 to 13) were the prime channels, and UHF (channels 14 and above) were less desirable and less valuable. Indeed, early FCC policy regarding cable television was heavily influenced by the Commission's desire to help UHF gain a foothold in its competition against the dominant VHF broadcasters. UHF is now more valuable because VHF's advantage of being lower on the television dial is overwhelmed by UHF frequencies' better propagation characteristics for new wireless services.

> methodology will help to determine which reverse auction bids we accept and what channels we assign the broadcast stations that remain on the air. For the incentive auction to succeed, all three pieces must work together.

Expanding the Economic and Innovation Opportunities of Spectrum Through Incentive Auctions, Notice of Proposed Rulemaking, 27 FCC Rcd. 12,357 ¶ 5 (2012).

The result was perhaps the most complex auction plan in human history. The FCC brought in economists who specialize in auctions and created an incentive auctions task force, and the resulting order implementing auctions (promulgated two years after the notice of proposed rulemaking quoted above) contained more than 800 paragraphs plus a technical appendix. Expanding the Economic and Innovation Opportunities of Spectrum Through Incentive Auctions, Report and Order, 29 FCC Rcd. 6567 (2014). As we noted above, this complexity could have been avoided by simply allowing existing licensees to provide new services, but at a cost in efficiency (and in revenue for the government). Another way of simplifying would have been for the government simply to have reclaimed the relevant spectrum and then auctioned it, but that would have raised fairness concerns for the licensees removed from the spectrum and would have been politically impossible.

Chapter 10

Ownership Limits

Introduction

Policymakers rightly worry about the harms from monopoly, or more generally from the concentration of ownership in a particular market. In most industries, the harms from concentrated ownership are policed by the generally-applicable antitrust laws. But in some telecommunications markets, policymakers have instituted industry-specific rules to limit concentrated ownership.

Policymakers might prefer sector-specific regulations to antitrust laws for a number of reasons. Perhaps lawmakers have goals that are not encompassed by the antitrust statutes, or they are not confident that antitrust enforcers will be as aggressive with respect to a particular industry as the lawmakers want them to be, or they want to create clear rules applicable to particular arrangements rather than rely on more flexible antitrust standards. On this last point, sector-specific statutes usually do not create bright-line rules, but they often direct an agency to develop clear rules.

Industry-specific laws focused on competition can take many forms. For example, the regime at issue in the *Turner* cases excerpted in Chapter 3.A (which obliged cable operators to carry local television broadcasters) was justified as promoting competition. 47 U.S.C. § 548, which prohibits cable operators from preventing content suppliers' contracting with rival distributors (like DBS operators), was similarly framed as preserving competition. And net neutrality rules prevent broadband internet access providers from discriminating against unaffiliated content, applications, and service providers (though, as Chapter 6 discusses, many supporters of net neutrality regulation see it as far more than a competition law).

But the most common form of industry-specific competition rules are ownership limits. Most frequently they limit horizontal concentration (a given company's or stakeholder's share of a particular type of service in a geographic area), vertical integration (arising when a company produces consecutive inputs for a product), or cross-ownership (arising when the owner of a company in one market cannot control a company in a related market). Note that promoting competition may not be the sole focus of these rules. Indeed, in the regulation of broadcasters, the FCC explicitly states that its focus is on competition, localism, and viewpoint diversity.

In this chapter we focus on ownership limits. Specifically, we address the three main areas of telecommunications that have been the focus of regulations limiting ownership — cable television, wireless frequencies, and broadcasting. As you read these materials, consider the similarities and differences among the rules and their application to the relevant industries. Do some make more sense than others? Should the legal constraints on these rules differ? And consider the point made at the end of the previous paragraph: to what extent should, and does, the government take into account considerations beyond competition? As we noted in Chapter 9.C.1, if factor X does any work, that entails not maximizing factor Y.[1] What, if any, goals beyond competition should ownership limits serve? Exactly what role should those goals play? Indeed, should a goal other than competition be the prime goal of ownership limits?

§ 10.A. Cable Television Ownership Limits

Many firms create and produce informational, educational, and entertainment programming that they then supply to cable operators — as well as to streaming services, broadcasters, operators of direct broadcast satellite (DBS), and so on. Among these production firms are the major Hollywood movie studios, smaller independent producers, and the major professional sports leagues. There were two worries about cable operators' power vis-à-vis these firms: First, that a given cable operator (or several colluding with each other) might grow large enough to have monopsony power and thereby be able to make unreasonable demands that the programmers might be effectively compelled to accept (because a refusal to accept would deprive them of vital access); and, second, that cable providers would start to produce and favor their own content, effectively blocking independent program suppliers from their wires.[2]

These concerns could be addressed at least in part by antitrust law, as we discuss in Chapter 8. But they have also been addressed by horizontal and vertical ownership limits that Congress mandated in 1992 and the FCC implemented. The horizontal limits responded to the first concern and vertical limits responded to the second. The materials that follow address the judicial response to those limits.

---

1. If including factor X always produces the same result as ignoring it, it is not doing any work.

2. Other structural regulations of cable operators focus less on possible harms to program suppliers than on possible harms to competing program distribution technologies. The must-carry provisions discussed in Chapter 3.A fit into this category, protecting as they do conventional broadcasters. So, too, does 47 U.S.C. § 548 (mentioned above), an umbrella provision designed to increase "competition and diversity in the multichannel video programming market." 47 U.S.C. § 548(a). It requires the FCC to issue regulations that, among other things, prohibit cable operators from causing affiliated content providers to discriminate against other players in the multichannel video programming market. *Id.* § 548(c)(2)(B). These regulations are often referred to as the "program access rules" because they ensure that multichannel video program distributor (MVPD) rivals to the cable incumbents have access to programming affiliated with established cable providers.

Time Warner Entertainment Co. v. FCC [*Time Warner II*]

240 F.3d 1126 (D.C. Cir. 2001)

Opinion for the Court filed by Circuit Judge WILLIAMS, in which Circuit Judges RANDOLPH and TATEL concur.

WILLIAMS, Circuit Judge:

Section 11(c) of the Cable Television Consumer Protection and Competition Act of 1992, Pub. L. No. 102-385, 106 Stat. 1460 (1992 Cable Act), amends 47 U.S.C. § 533 to direct the Federal Communications Commission to set two types of limits on cable operators. The first type is horizontal, addressing operators' scale: "limits on the number of cable subscribers a person is authorized to reach through cable systems owned by such person, or in which such person has an attributable interest." 47 U.S.C. § 533(f)(1)(A). The second type is vertical, addressing operators' integration with "programmers" (suppliers of programs to be carried over cable systems): "limits on the number of channels on a cable system that can be occupied by a video programmer in which a cable operator has an attributable interest." 47 U.S.C. § 533(f)(1)(B). The FCC has duly promulgated regulations. Petitioners Time Warner and AT&T challenge the horizontal limit as in excess of statutory authority, as unconstitutional infringements of their freedom of speech, and as products of arbitrary and capricious decision making which violate the Administrative Procedure Act. Time Warner similarly challenges the vertical limit. Together with AT&T, Time Warner also challenges as arbitrary and capricious the rules for determining what counts as an "attributable interest." Concluding that the FCC has not met its burden under the First Amendment and, in part, lacks statutory authority for its actions, we remand for further consideration of both limits. In addition we vacate specific portions of the attribution rules as lacking rational justification.

* * *

The horizontal rule imposes a 30% limit on the number of subscribers that may be served by a multiple cable system operator (MSO). *See* 47 C.F.R. § 76.503; Implementation of Section 11(c) of the Cable Television Consumer Protection and Competition Act of 1992, Horizontal Ownership Limits, Third Report and Order, 14 FCC Rcd. 19,098, 19,119, ¶ 55 (1999) (Third Report). Both the numerator and denominator of this fraction include only current subscribers to multichannel video program distributor (MVPD) services. Subscribers include not only users of traditional cable services but also subscribers to non-cable MVPD services such as Direct Broadcast Satellite (DBS), a rapidly growing segment of the MVPD market. The Commission pointed out that under this provision the nominal 30% limit would allow a cable operator to serve 36.7% of the nation's cable subscribers if it served none by DBS. In an express effort to encourage competition through new provision of cable, the Commission excluded from any MSO's numerator all new subscribers signed up by virtue of "overbuilding," the industry's term for cable laid in competition with a preexisting cable operator. Further, subscribers to a service franchised after the rule's adoption do not go into an MSO's numerator, even if not the result of an overbuild.

As a result, the rule's main bite is on firms obtaining subscribers through merger or acquisition.

The vertical limit is currently set at 40% of channel capacity, reserving 60% for programming by non-affiliated firms. *See* 47 C.F.R. § 76.504; Implementation of Sections 12 and 19 of the Cable Television Consumer Protection and Competition Act of 1992, Horizontal and Vertical Ownership Limits, Second Report and Order, 8 FCC Rcd. 8565, 8593 ¶ 68 (1993) (Second Report). Channels assigned to broadcast stations, leased access, and for public, educational, or governmental uses are included in the calculation of channel capacity. Capacity over 75 channels is not subject to the limit, so a cable operator is never required to reserve more than 45 channels for others (.60 × 75 = 45).

As cable operators, Time Warner and AT&T "exercise[] editorial discretion in selecting the programming [they] will make available to [their] subscribers," Time Warner Entm't Co. v. United States, 211 F.3d 1313, 1316 (D.C. Cir. 2000) (*Time Warner I*), and are "entitled to the protection of the speech and press provisions of the First Amendment," Turner Broad. Sys., Inc. v. FCC, 512 U.S. 622, 636 (1994) (*Turner I*). The horizontal limit interferes with petitioners' speech rights by restricting the number of viewers to whom they can speak. The vertical limit restricts their ability to exercise their editorial control over a portion of the content they transmit.

In *Time Warner I* we upheld the statutory provisions against a facial attack, after finding them subject to intermediate rather than, as the cable firms argued, strict scrutiny. The regulations here present a related but independent set of questions. Constitutional authority to impose some limit is not authority to impose any limit imaginable.

Under the formula set forth in United States v. O'Brien, 391 U.S. 367, 377 (1968), and reaffirmed by Turner Broadcasting System, Inc. v. Federal Communications Commission, 520 U.S. 180, 189 (1997) (*Turner II*), a governmental regulation subject to intermediate scrutiny will be upheld if it "advances important governmental interests unrelated to the suppression of free speech and does not burden substantially more speech than necessary to further those interests." *Id.* (quoting *O'Brien*, 391 U.S. at 377).

The interests asserted in support of the horizontal and vertical limits are the same interrelated interests that we found sufficient to support the statutory scheme in *Time Warner I*: "the promotion of diversity in ideas and speech" and "the preservation of competition." *Time Warner I*, 211 F.3d at 1319; *see also Turner I*, 512 U.S. at 662–64 (concluding that both qualify as important governmental interests).

* * *

The FCC asserts that a 30% horizontal limit satisfies its statutory obligation to ensure that no single "cable operator or group of cable operators can unfairly impede . . . the flow of video programming from the video programmer to the consumer," 47 U.S.C. § 533(f)(2)(A), while adequately respecting the benefits of clustering [i.e., the strategy under which MSOs concentrate their operations within a particular geographic region] and the economies of scale that are thought to come with larger size. *See* Third Report ¶ 61. In setting the limit at 30%, it assumed there was a serious risk of collusion. But while collusion is a form of anti-competitive behavior that implicates an important government interest, the FCC has not presented the "substantial evidence" required by *Turner I* and *Turner II* that such collusion has in fact occurred or is likely to occur; so its assumptions are mere conjecture.

Part VI of the Third Report lays out the calculations that lead the FCC to the 30% limit. First the FCC determines that the average cable network needs to reach 15 million subscribers to be economically viable. This is 18.56% of the roughly 80 million MVPD subscribers, and the FCC rounds it up to 20% of such subscribers. The FCC then divines that the average cable programmer will succeed in reaching only about 50% of the subscribers linked to cable companies that *agree* to carry its programming, because of channel capacity, "programming tastes of particular cable operators," or other factors. Third Report, 14 FCC Rcd. at 19,117, ¶ 49. The average programmer therefore requires an "open field" of 40% of the market to be viable (.20/.50 = .40).

Finally, to support the 30% limit that it says is necessary to assure this minimum, the Commission reasons as follows: With a 30% limit, a programmer has an "open field" of 40% of the market even if the two largest cable companies deny carriage, acting "individually or collusively." *Id.* at 19,119, ¶ 53. A 50% rule is inadequate because, if a duopoly were to result, "[t]he probability of tacit collusion is higher with 2 competitors than 3 competitors." *Id.* at 19,118, ¶ 51. Even if collusion were not to occur, *independent* rejections by two MSOs could doom a new programmer, thwarting congressional intent as the Commission saw it. See *id.* A 40% limit is insufficient for the same reason: "two MSOs, . . . representing a total of 80% of the market, might decline to carry the new network" and leave only 20% "open," which by hypothesis is not enough (because of the 50% success rate). *Id.* at 19,119, ¶ 52. Although the Commission doesn't spell out the intellectual process, it is necessarily defining the requisite "open field" as the residue of the market after a programmer is turned down either (1) by one cable company acting alone, or (2) by a set of companies acting either (a) collusively or (b) independently but nonetheless in some way that, because of the combined effect of their choices, threatens fulfillment of the statutory purposes. We address the FCC's authority to regulate each of these scenarios in turn.

The Commission is on solid ground in asserting authority to be sure that no single company could be in a position single-handedly to deal a programmer a death blow. Statutory authority flows plainly from the instruction that the Commission's regulations "ensure that no cable operator or group of cable operators can unfairly impede, either because of *the size of any individual operator* or because of joint actions of operators of sufficient size, the flow of video programming from the video programmer to the consumer." 47 U.S.C. § 533(f)(2)(A) (emphasis added). Constitutional authority is equally plain. As the Supreme Court said in *Turner II*: "We have identified a corresponding 'governmental purpose of the highest order' in ensuring public access to 'a multiplicity of information sources.'" 520 U.S. at 190 (quoting *Turner I*, 512 U.S. at 663). If this interest in diversity is to mean anything in this context, the government must be able to ensure that a programmer have at least two conduits through which it can reach the number of viewers needed for viability—independent of concerns over anticompetitive conduct.

Assuming the validity of the premises supporting the FCC's conclusion that a 40% "open field" is necessary (a question that we need not answer here), the statute's express concern for the act of "any individual operator" would justify a horizontal limit of 60%. To reach the 30% limit, the FCC's action necessarily involves one or the other of two additional propositions: Either there is a material risk of collusive denial of carriage by two or more companies, or the statute authorizes the Commission to protect programmers against the risk of completely *independent* rejections by two or more companies leaving less than 40% of the MVPD audience potentially accessible. Neither proposition is sound.

First, we consider whether there is record support for inferring a non-conjectural risk of collusive rejection. Either Congress or the Commission could supply that record, and we take them in that order. We give deference to the predictive judgments of Congress, *see Turner II*, 520 U.S. at 195–96, but Congress appears to have made no judgment regarding collusion. The statute plainly alludes to the *possibility* of collusion when it authorizes regulations to protect against "*joint* actions by a group of operators of sufficient size." 47 U.S.C. § 533(f)(2)(A) (emphasis added). But this phrase, while granting the Commission authority to take action in the event that it finds collusion extant or likely, is not itself a congressional finding of actual or probable collusion. Such findings have not been made. No reference to collusion appears in the Act's findings or policy, nor in the legislative history discussing the horizontal or vertical limits. *See* H.R. Rep. No. 102-628, at 40–43 (1992) (House Report); S. Rep. No. 102-92, at 24–29, 32–34, *reprinted in* 1992 U.S.C.C.A.N. 1133, at 1156–62, 1165–67. It was thus appropriate for the FCC to describe Congress's reference to "joint" action as merely a "legislative *assumption*." Third Report, 14 FCC Rcd. at 19,116, ¶ 43 (emphasis added).

The Commission's own findings amount to precious little. It says only:

> The legislative assumption [about joint action] is not unreasonable given an environment in which all the larger operators in the industry are vertically integrated so that all are both buyers and sellers of programming and have mutual incentives to reach carriage decisions beneficial to each other. Operators have incentives to agree to buy their programming from one another. Moreover, they have incentives to encourage one another to carry the same non-vertically integrated programming in order to share the costs of such programming.

Id. None of these assertions is supported in the record. The Commission never explains why the vertical integration of MSOs gives them "mutual incentive to reach carriage decisions beneficial to each other," what may be the firms' "incentives to buy . . . from one another," or what the probabilities are that firms would engage in reciprocal buying (presumably to reduce each other's average programming costs). After all, the economy is filled with firms that, like MSOs, display partial upstream vertical integration. If that phenomenon implies the sort of collusion the Commission infers, one would expect the Commission to be able to point to examples. Yet it names none. Further, even if one accepts the proposition that an MSO could benefit from sharing the services of specific programmers, programming is not more attractive for this purpose merely because it originates with another MSO's affiliate rather than with an independent.

The only justification that the FCC offers in support of its collusion hypothesis is the economic commonplace that, all other things being equal, collusion is less likely when there are more firms. This observation will always be true, although marginally less so for each additional firm; but by itself it lends no insight into the question of what the appropriate horizontal limit is. *Turner I* demands that the FCC do more than "simply 'posit the existence of the disease sought to be cured.'" *Turner I*, 512 U.S. at 664. It requires that the FCC draw "reasonable inferences based on substantial evidence." *Turner I*, 512 U.S. at 666. Substantial evidence does not require a complete factual record—we must give appropriate deference to predictive judgments that necessarily involve the expertise and experience of the agency. *See Turner II*, 520 U.S. at 196. But the FCC has put forth no evidence at all that indicates the prospects for collusion.

That having been said, we do not foreclose the possibility that there are theories of anti-competitive behavior other than collusion that may be relevant to the horizontal limit and on which the FCC may be able to rely on remand. *See* 47 U.S.C. § 533(f)(1). Indeed, Congress considered, among other things, the ability of MSOs dominant in specific cable markets to extort equity from programmers or force exclusive contracts on them. A single MSO, acting alone rather than "jointly," might perhaps be able to do so while serving somewhat less than the 60% of the market (i.e., less than the fraction that would allow it unilaterally to lock out a new cable programmer) despite the existence of antitrust laws and specific behavioral prohibitions enacted as part of the 1992 Cable Act, *see* 47 U.S.C. § 536, and the risk might justify a prophylactic limit under the statute. *See Time Warner I*, 211 F.3d at 1322–23. So the absence of any showing of a serious risk of collusion does not *necessarily* preclude a finding of a sufficient governmental interest in preventing unfair competition. (We express no opinion on whether exploitation of a monopoly position in a specific cable market to extract rents that would otherwise flow to programmers alone gives rise to an "important governmental interest" justifying a burden on speech.) But the FCC made no attempt to justify its regulation on these grounds.

With the risk of collusion inadequately substantiated to support the 30% limit and no attempt to find other anticompetitive behavior, there remains the Commission's alternative ground—that programming choices made "unilaterally" by multiple cable companies, Third Report, 18 FCC Rcd. at 19,118, ¶ 51, might reduce a programmer's "open field" below the 40% benchmark. The only support the Commission offered for regulation based on this possibility was the idea that every additional chance for a programmer to secure access would enhance diversity:

> [T]he 30% limit serves the salutary purpose of ensuring that there will be at least 4 MSOs in the marketplace. The rule thus maximizes the potential number of MSOs that will purchase programming. With more MSOs making purchasing decisions, this increases the likelihood that the MSOs will make different programming choices and a greater variety of media voices will therefore be available to the public.

Id. at 19,119, ¶ 54. Petitioners challenge the FCC's authority to regulate for this purpose on both constitutional and statutory grounds.

We have some concern how far such a theory may be pressed against First Amendment norms. Everything else being equal, each additional "voice" may be said to enhance diversity. And in this special context, every additional splintering of the cable industry increases the number of *combinations* of companies whose acceptance would in the aggregate lay the foundations for a programmer's viability. But at some point, surely, the marginal value of such an increment in "diversity" would not qualify as an "important" governmental interest. Is moving from 100 possible combinations to 101 "important"? It is not clear to us how a court could determine the point where gaining such an increment is no longer important. And it would be odd to discover that although a newspaper that is the only general daily in a metropolitan area cannot be subjected to a right of reply, *see* Miami Herald Publishing Co. v. Tornillo, 418 U.S. 241 (1974), it could in the name of diversity be forced to self-divide. Certainly the Supreme Court has not gone so far.

We need not face that issue, however, because we conclude that Congress has not given the Commission authority to impose, solely on the basis of the "diversity" precept, a limit that does more than guarantee a programmer two possible outlets (each of them a market adequate for viability). We analyze the agency action under the familiar framework of Chevron USA, Inc. v. Natural Resources Defense Council, Inc., 467 U.S. 837 (1984). If we find (using traditional tools of statutory interpretation) that Congress has resolved the question, that is the end of the matter.

We begin with the statutory language. The relevant section requires the FCC to

> ensure that no cable operator or group of cable operators can unfairly impede, either because of the size of any individual operator or because of joint actions by a group of operators of sufficient size, the flow of video programming from the video programmer to the consumer.

47 U.S.C. § 533(f)(2)(A).

The language addresses only "unfair[]" impediments to the flow of programming. The word "unfair" is of course extremely vague. Certainly, the action of several firms that is "joint," in the sense of collusive, may often entail unfairness of a conventional sort. The statute goes further, plainly treating exercise of editorial discretion by a single cable operator as "unfair" simply because that operator is the only game in town. (And *Time Warner I* authoritatively determines that the government may constitutionally impose limits solely on that ground.) But we cannot see how the word unfair could plausibly apply to the legitimate, independent editorial choices of multiple MSOs. A broad interpretation is plausible *only* for actions that impinge at least to some degree on the interest in competition that lay at the heart of Congress's concern. The Commission's reading of the clause effectively deletes the word "joint" and opens the door to illimitable restrictions in the name of diversity.

On the record before us, we conclude that the 30% horizontal limit is in excess of statutory authority. While a 60% limit might be appropriate as necessary to ensure that programmers had an adequate "open field" even in the face of rejection by the largest company, the present record supports no more. In addition, the statute allows the Commission to act prophylactically against the risk of "unfair" conduct by cable operators that might unduly impede the flow of programming, either by the "joint" actions of two or more companies or the independent action of a single company of sufficient size. But the Commission has pointed to nothing in the record supporting a non-conjectural risk of anticompetitive behavior, either by collusion or other means. Accordingly, we reverse and remand with respect to the 30% rule.

* * *

The FCC presents its 40% vertical limit as advancing the same interests invoked in support of its statutory authority to adopt the rule: diversity in programming and fair competition. As with the horizontal rules the FCC must defend the rules themselves under intermediate scrutiny and justify its chosen limit as not burdening substantially more speech than necessary. Far from satisfying this test, the FCC seems to have plucked the 40% limit out of thin air.

The FCC relies almost exclusively on the congressional findings that vertical integration in the cable industry could "make it difficult for non-cable affiliated . . . programmers to secure carriage on vertically integrated cables systems" and that "vertically integrated program suppliers have the incentive and the ability to favor their affiliated cable operators . . . and program distributors." Second Report, 8 FCC Rcd. at 8583, ¶ 41 (citing 1992 Cable Act § 2(a)(5)). Regulatory limits in response to these consequences would "increase the diversity of voices available to the public." Second Report, *Id.* ¶ 42 (citing Senate Report at 80).

We recognize that in drawing a numerical line an agency will ultimately indulge in some inescapable residue of arbitrariness; even if 40% is a highly justifiable pick, no one could expect the Commission to show why it was materially better than 39% or 41%. But to pass even the arbitrary and capricious standard, the agency must at least reveal "'a rational connection between the facts found and the choice made.'" Dickson v. Sec'y of Def., 68 F.3d 1396, 1404–05 (D.C. Cir. 1995) (quoting Motor Vehicle Mfrs. Ass'n v. State Farm Mut. Auto. Ins. Co., 463 U.S. 29, 43 (1983)). Here the FCC must also meet First Amendment intermediate scrutiny. Yet it appears to provide nothing but the conclusion that "we believe that a 40% limit is appropriate to balance the goals." *See* Second Report, 8 FCC Rcd. at 8594, ¶ 68. What are the conditions that make 50% too high and 30% too low? How great is the risk presented by current market conditions? These questions are left unanswered by the Commission's discussion.

In fairness, the FCC does make an attempt to review some relevant conditions. The FCC cites the House Report's conclusion that "some" vertically integrated MSOs favor their affiliates and "may" discriminate against others. *Id.* at 8584, ¶ 42 (citing House Report at 43). But it also notes a report that none of the top five MSOs "showed a pattern" of favoring their affiliates. *Id.* ¶ 43. Indeed, the FCC concludes that "vertical relationships had increased both the quality and quantity of cable programming services." *Id.* at 8584, ¶ 44. But still it settled on a limit of 40%. There is no effort to link the numerical limits to the benefits and detriments depicted. Further, given the pursuit of diversity, one might expect some inquiry into whether innovative independent originators of programming find greater success selling to affiliated or to unaffiliated programming firms, but there is none.

We find that the FCC has failed to justify its vertical limit as not burdening substantially more speech than necessary. Accordingly, we reverse and remand to the FCC for further consideration.

Notes and Questions

1. Why Horizontal and Vertical Restrictions? As the opinion noted, Congress mandated both horizontal and vertical restrictions. Why both? Once effective horizontal restrictions exist, what public purpose is achieved by the rules limiting vertical integration? How, for example, could an MSO that accounted for, say, ten percent of cable subscribers nationwide hope to benefit by favoring programming in which it has an "attributable interest" over programming that the market prefers? Conversely, once effective vertical restrictions exist, what purpose is served by horizontal restrictions?

2. Market Power. As the opinion also noted, market power can be exercised either unilaterally or collectively (i.e., collusion). The opinion suggested, however, that arguments based on prophylactic concerns must be developed with considerable care — i.e., the FCC is not entitled to presume that a limited number of providers will collude. Was the court too harsh on the FCC's "open field" analysis? Antitrust today generally draws a very sharp distinction between a cartel, in which the members of a market agree to act together, and the kind of tacit coordination that frequently happens in a concentrated market. But the consumer harm of high prices can be quite similar. Regulation could seek to limit concentration for the purpose of limiting implicit coordination.

3. Application of the First Amendment. *Time Warner II* (and *Time Warner I* before it) concluded that the horizontal and vertical limits trigger First Amendment scrutiny, finding the issue so easy that its reasoning occupied a single paragraph (and we did not delete any discussion in that paragraph). *Turner I*, as we saw in Chapter 3.A, concluded that a regulation requiring cable operators to carry local broadcasters implicates the First Amendment, but does that mean that *every* regulation of cable operators is subject to First Amendment scrutiny? What about, for instance, regulation of the rates that cable companies charge their subscribers? As it happens, the D.C. Circuit addressed such regulation (which had been mandated by Congress), and it concluded that the First Amendment did apply. Indeed, it found the question easy, too. Below is the entirety of the court's discussion of whether the First Amendment applied:

> The First Amendment forbids some but not all economic regulations affecting speech. Some laws survive so long as they have a rational basis. Other laws will fall unless they rest on some extraordinary justification. Still other laws need to satisfy a standard somewhere between these two extremes. As to the Commission's cable rate regulations, we know from Turner Broadcasting v. FCC, 512 U.S. 622 (1994), that rational basis cannot be the test. *Turner Broadcasting* holds that cable operators are entitled to the protection of the First Amendment's command that Congress shall not abridge the freedom of speech, or of the press; and that laws of less than general application aimed at the press or elements of it are "always subject to at least some degree of heightened First Amendment scrutiny." *Id.* at 640–41.

Time Warner Entertainment Co. v. FCC, 56 F.3d 151, 181 (D.C. Cir. 1995). The court upheld the rate regulation against First Amendment challenge, but it is notable that it applied First Amendment scrutiny in the first place. As one of us noted,

> The nexus between rate regulation and cable operators' exercise of editorial discretion is not obvious. One could argue that rate regulation reduces revenues, which limits the ability of a cable operator to produce the content it wants and to exercise editorial discretion as it sees fit. But this argument would suggest that virtually every regulation that specifically applies to a company engaged in speech will be subject to First Amendment scrutiny, because almost any regulation can have the effect of reducing revenue.

Stuart Minor Benjamin, Algorithms and Speech, 161 U. Penn. L. Rev. 1445, 1490–91 (2013).

Was the D.C. Circuit correct in all these cases that the First Amendment applied? If so, does that have impact on your assessment of *Turner I*'s application of First Amendment scrutiny to the must-carry regime?

4. Diversity. The court attached little weight to the FCC's claim that diversity concerns supported the imposition of the ownership restrictions. Why? Was it based on a concern that the FCC invoked diversity as an ad hoc and manipulable consideration? Something else?

5. Other Goals? What about goals beyond diversity and competition? One obvious possibility would be a focus on content—that ownership limits will lead to the provision of better programming. But, as *Turner I* and the cases in Chapter 11 highlight, regulations aimed at content are subject to strict First Amendment scrutiny (and such scrutiny is nearly always fatal). Is there something else that the government should have articulated as a goal of these ownership limits?

6. Limits on Creating Programming. Section 11(c)(2) of the 1992 Cable Act not only required the FCC to promulgate rules regarding vertical integration and horizontal concentration but also required the FCC to "consider the necessity and appropriateness of imposing limitations on the degree to which multichannel video programming distributors may engage in the creation or production of video programming." 1992 Cable Act §§ 11(c)(2), 613(f)(1)(C). Interestingly, in just a few short paragraphs of its first order on vertical integration limits, the FCC determined that no restrictions were necessary. The FCC's key reasoning was that

> [i]n view of the structural and behavioral restrictions already required under the 1992 Act, we do not believe that additional restrictions on the ability of multichannel distributors to engage in the creation or production of video programming are warranted at the present time. We conclude that at the present time the objectives of such a restriction are fully addressed by the other provisions of the 1992 Cable Act.

Implementation of Sections 11 and 13 of the Cable Television Consumer Protection and Competition Act of 1992: Horizontal and Vertical Ownership Limits, Second Report and Order, 8 FCC Rcd. 8565, 8608, ¶ 106 (1993). This category of regulations was the only one for which the FCC had the discretion to decide not to regulate. Given its decision, do you think the FCC would also have chosen not to promulgate vertical or horizontal restraints, were those options available? If so, what, if anything, should that tell Congress?

7. As Applied Challenge versus Facial Challenge. *Time Warner II* ended an almost decade-long litigation. Immediately after the 1992 Cable Act was passed, cable providers challenged the ownership restriction provision on First Amendment grounds, claiming that, on its face, the statute was unconstitutional. After a series of decisions, the D.C. Circuit ultimately concluded, in *Time Warner I*, that neither the subscriber limits provision nor the channel occupancy provision facially violated the First Amendment. Then, in *Time Warner II*, the D.C. Circuit concluded that the regulations could not survive an as applied challenge.

8. Abandonment of Vertical Limits. After *Time Warner II*, the FCC engaged in a lengthy process to reconsider the horizontal and vertical limits, culminating (seven years after *Time Warner II*) in a 2008 order. In that order, the FCC did not reinstate vertical limits, concluding that it did not have sufficient evidence to support them. Cable Horizontal and Vertical Ownership Limits, Fourth Report & Order and Further Notice of Proposed Rulemaking, 23 FCC Rcd. 2134, 2192 ¶ 135 (2008). Indeed, in the many years since *Time Warner II*, through FCC chairs from both political parties, the FCC has never again imposed vertical limits on cable operators (which, remember, Congress mandated). The hurdles posed by First Amendment scrutiny have apparently been sufficient to dissuade the FCC from investing the time and energy to promulgate new vertical limits. Does that suggest that the application of the First Amendment to ownership limits is a bad idea? That the evidence supporting vertical limits was flimsy, and First Amendment scrutiny helped reveal that?

9. A Second Try on Horizontal Limits (with the Same Result). In the 2008 order, the FCC did impose new horizontal limits. Cable operators challenged them, and the D.C. Circuit rejected them in the opinion below.

Comcast Corp. v. FCC

579 F.3d 1 (D.C. Cir. 2009)

Opinion for the Court filed by Circuit Judge GINSBURG, in which Circuit Judge KAVANAUGH and Senior Circuit Judge RANDOLPH concur.

GINSBURG, Circuit Judge:

Comcast Corporation and several intervenors involved in the cable television industry petition for review of a rule in which the Federal Communications Commission capped at 30% of all subscribers the market share any single cable television operator may serve. We agree with Comcast that the 30% subscriber limit is arbitrary and capricious. We therefore grant the petition and vacate the Rule.

In 2001 we considered a petition for review of a then newly revised version of the 30% subscriber limit. Time Warner Entertainment Co. v. FCC (*Time Warner II*), 240 F.3d 1126 (D.C. Cir. 2001).

On remand [after *Time Warner II*], the Commission adopted the current version of the 30% subscriber limit. The Rule here under review was designed to ensure that no single cable operator "can, by simply refusing to carry a programming network, cause it to fail." The Commission's Cable Horizontal and Vertical Ownership Limits, Fourth Report and Order and Further Notice of Proposed Rulemaking, 23 FCC Rcd. 2134, 2154, ¶ 40 (2008) (Fourth Report). Based upon the record before the court in *Time Warner II*, the subscriber limit under this standard could not have been lower than 60%. Based upon the present record, however, the Commission concluded no cable operator could safely be allowed to serve—*mirabile dictu*—more than 30% of all subscribers. *Plus ça change, plus c'est la même chose?*

In re-calculating the minimum viable scale, the Commission relied upon a study's finding regarding the number of viewers a cable network needed to reach in order to have a 70% chance of survival after five years, using data on the survival of cable networks between 1984 and 2001. Based upon the study, the FCC found the minimum viable scale was 19.03 million subscribers, about four million more than the agency had found were necessary in 1999.

To determine the total number of subscribers, the FCC counted all cable subscribers and DBS customers, totaling approximately 96 million (up from 80 million in 1999). In re-calculating the penetration rate, the Commission observed, "many, if not most, new cable networks are placed on a digital tier. A consequence of being placed on a digital tier versus one of the basic levels of service . . . is a much lower penetration rate." *Id.* at 2163, ¶ 60. Using an in-house study of the tiering and subscribership data for a sample of cable operators and a linear regression model, the Commission determined the penetration rate of the average network was 27.42%, or slightly more than half the 50% penetration rate it found in 1999. *Id.* at 2164, ¶ 61.

From these data, the Commission calculated that a video programming network, to be viable, required an open field of 70% (up from 40% in 1999). Therefore, no cable operator could serve more than 30% of all subscribers.

Although the Commission recognized "that competition in the downstream market [especially from DBS companies] may affect the ability of a large cable operator to prevent successful entry by a programming network, and that [the] open field analysis does not directly measure this," it decided not to adjust the subscriber limit to account for such competition because doing so would be "quite difficult." The FCC then gave four reasons it did not regard competition from DBS companies as significant: Customers are reluctant to switch from cable service to DBS because (1) switching is costly; and (2) cable operators offer non-video services, such as telephone and internet access, that are not available with DBS; and (3) "video programming is a product, the quality of which cannot be known with certainty until it is consumed." *Id.* at 2168, ¶ 70. Additionally, (4) "[c]ompetitive pressures from DBS will not provide any assistance to networks that," not having a contract with the largest cable operator, are unable to "launch due to a lack of financing." *Id.* at 2169, ¶ 71.

We may set aside the Commission's decision "only if [it] was 'arbitrary, capricious, an abuse of discretion, or otherwise not in accordance with law.'" Mission Broad. Corp. v. FCC, 113 F.3d 254, 259–60 (D.C. Cir. 1997) (quoting 5 U.S.C. § 706(2)(A)).

Whether a cable operator serving more than 30% of subscribers can exercise "bottleneck monopoly power," depends "not only on its share of the market, but also on the elasticities of supply and demand, which in turn are determined by the *availability* of competition." *Time Warner II*, 240 F.3d at 1134. A cable operator faces competition primarily from non-cable companies, such as those providing DBS service and, increasingly, telephone companies providing fiber optic service. As Comcast points out, DBS companies alone now serve approximately 33% of all subscribers. Recognizing the growing importance particularly of DBS, in *Time Warner II* we said in no uncertain terms that "in revisiting the horizontal rules the Commission will have to take account of the impact of DBS on [cable operators'] market power." *Id.*

Of the three aspects of the Commission's open field model—minimum viable scale, total number of subscribers, and penetration rate—only the total subscribers measure fully takes account of the competition from DBS companies and companies offering fiber optic services. As Comcast points out, the measure of minimum viable scale relies upon data from 1984–2001 and, as a result, fails to consider the impact of DBS companies' growing market share (from 18% to 33%) over the six years immediately preceding issuance of the Rule, as well as the growth of fiber optic companies. The penetration rate calculation, by the Commission's own admission, leaves out data regarding DBS penetration — an omission the FCC attempts to justify with the question-begging assertion that such data would not have materially changed the penetration rate.

Comcast argues the Commission has offered no plausible reason for its failure to heed our explicit direction in *Time Warner II* to consider the competitive impact of DBS companies. Instead the Commission made the four non-empirical observations we enumerated above. As for the first, transaction costs undoubtedly do deter some cable customers from switching to satellite services, but Comcast points to record evidence that almost 50% of all DBS customers formerly subscribed to cable; in the face of that evidence, the Commission's observation that cost may deter some customers from switching to DBS is feeble indeed. With regard to the second — that some cable consumers may be reluctant to switch to a satellite television service because, unlike cable companies, DBS companies do not offer internet and telephone services — the Commission does not point to any evidence tending to show these inframarginal customers are numerous enough to confer upon cable operators their supposed bottleneck power over programming. Moreover, as Comcast points out, both DirecTV and Dish Network have partnered with telephone companies to offer bundled DBS and telephone services.

The Commission's third justification — that consumers will not switch providers to access new programming because they cannot know the quality of the programming before consuming it — warrants little discussion. As Comcast points out, there is no record support for this conjecture. In any event, it is common knowledge that new video programming is advertised on other television stations and in other media, and can be previewed over the Internet, thus providing consumers with information about the quality of competing services. The FCC's fourth reason — that without its subscriber cap an upstart network will have trouble securing financing unless it has a contract with a cable company serving more than 30% of the market — is no more convincing than the other three when one recalls DBS companies already serve more than 30% of the market.

Finally, we note the Commission's observation that assessing competition from DBS companies is difficult — possibly true even if unexplained — does not justify the agency's failure to consider competition from DBS companies in important aspects of its model. That a problem is difficult may indicate a need to make some simplifying assumptions, but it does not justify ignoring altogether a variable so clearly relevant and likely to affect the calculation of a subscriber limit — not to mention one the court had directed the agency to consider.

Comcast, on the other hand, points beyond DBS companies' growing market share to their exclusive arrangements with certain highly sought after programmers as evidence that competition has led and will likely continue to lead subscribers to switch services. Indeed, Commissioner McDowell pointed out in dissent that, as of the date of the Fourth Report, DirecTV and Dish Network each served more customers than any cable company save Comcast itself. Comcast also points to evidence that the number of cable networks has increased by almost 500% since 1992 and has grown at an ever faster rate since 2000, and that a much lower percentage of cable networks are vertically integrated with cable operators than was the case when the Congress passed the 1992 Act. There can be no doubt that consumers are now able to receive far more channels than they could in 1999, let alone 1992.

In sum, the Commission has failed to demonstrate that allowing a cable operator to serve more than 30% of all cable subscribers would threaten to reduce either competition or diversity in programming. First, the record is replete with evidence of ever increasing competition among video providers: Satellite and fiber optic video providers have entered the market and grown in market share since the Congress passed the 1992 Act, and particularly in recent years. Cable operators, therefore, no longer have the bottleneck power over programming that concerned the Congress in 1992. Second, over the same period there has been a dramatic increase both in the number of cable networks and in the programming available to subscribers.

In view of the overwhelming evidence concerning "the dynamic nature of the communications marketplace," 47 U.S.C § 533(f)(2)(E), and the entry of new competitors at both the programming and the distribution levels, it was arbitrary and capricious for the Commission to conclude that a cable operator serving more than 30% of the market poses a threat either to competition or to diversity in programming. Considering the marketplace as it is today and the many significant changes that have occurred since 1992, the FCC has not identified a sufficient basis for imposing upon cable operators the "special obligations," *Turner I*, 512 U.S. at 641, represented by the 30% subscriber limit. We conclude the Commission has failed to "examine[] the relevant data and articulate[] a satisfactory explanation for its action," Fresno Mobile Radio, Inc. v. FCC, 165 F.3d 965, 968 (D.C. Cir. 1999), and hold the 30% subscriber cap is arbitrary and capricious.

[The Court vacated the FCC's rule, instead of remanding the matter to the agency for further proceedings.]

[Concurring opinion of Judge RANDOLPH omitted.]

Notes and Questions

1. Switching Costs. The court rejected the FCC's conclusion that subscribers unhappy with their cable service would face switching costs sufficiently high to impede their migration from cable to DBS. On what basis did the court reject that conclusion? Is the evidence the court relies upon persuasive? Is this approach consistent with the idea (embedded in the statute) of having an expert administrative agency that makes predictions in uncertain circumstances?

2. The Road Not Taken. What did the court think the FCC should have done that it didn't do? Why do you think the FCC didn't do those things? Is the problem that the court had unreasonable expectations of what the FCC should show? That the FCC had no good basis for imposing any horizontal limit but was required to do so by Congress? (But if so, why didn't the FCC decline to impose horizontal limits the same way it decided not to impose vertical limits?) More generally, what should an agency, and a court, do if Congress requires an agency to impose an ownership (or any other) limit but there is no strong evidence to support any meaningful limit?

3. Do We Need a Cap? Putting aside questions about administrative law and standard of review, was the court right that the changing video marketplace rendered the FCC's proposed cap unnecessary? Was there really a need for a cable subscriber cap at all?

4. Bright-Line Rules versus Antitrust. As to numerical limits on concentration: Congress or an agency like the FCC can establish bright-line rules that make case-by-case antitrust oversight unnecessary. But one question is whether, in practice, such rules operate effectively. Does the experience with the horizontal and vertical limits cast doubt on relying on bright-line rules? On sector-specific rules?

As to antitrust: whatever the FCC did or does with respect to any ownership limits, antitrust laws still restrain an entity's ability to buy most of its competitors. Even if the FCC blesses a single company's purchase of most of the players in a given market, the Department of Justice would likely step in to prevent it. Antitrust laws are, of course, laws of general applicability. They apply to all products and markets—whether widgets or bits. In light of the presence of antitrust laws, are communications-specific ownership rules appropriate? Does the FCC's expertise about communications companies make such sector-specific rules more attractive? Does its relative lack of expertise about antitrust law make them less attractive?

5. Giving Up. The FCC has not promulgated horizontal limits on cable ownership in the years since this opinion. So, decades after Congress mandated horizontal and vertical cable limits, no such limits have ever gone into effect. The FCC tried once with vertical limits and twice with horizontal limits, and each time the D.C. Circuit rejected them. The D.C. Circuit found the First Amendment applicable to both limits, but it squarely relied on the First Amendment only with respect to vertical limits, as it found the horizontal limits insufficiently justified on administrative law grounds. But the bottom line is that, in the wake of the two opinions excerpted above, no horizontal or vertical limits have been implemented.

§ 10.B. Spectrum Ownership Limits

The FCC has also used regulation to affect market structure in mobile markets. Initially, the FCC made choices concerning eligibility for licenses in order to promote and maintain competition in mobile services, much as it did in setting licensing policy in television. Later, the FCC turned to limits on the amount of spectrum that mobile carriers could acquire, initially by setting absolute limits and later by setting "screens" that entail heightened FCC review of transactions that raise aggregation concerns. These spectrum ownership regulations directly affect the number and viability of competitors in local markets. In the order below, the FCC imposed spectrum screens as a means of policing ownership levels and discussed the theory behind them.

Policies Regarding Mobile Spectrum Holdings: Expanding the Economic and Innovation Opportunities of Spectrum Through Incentive Auctions

Report and Order, 29 FCC Rcd. 6133 (2014)

II. Background

A. Statutory Authority

6. The Communications Act requires the Commission to examine closely the impact of spectrum aggregation on competition, innovation, and the efficient use of spectrum to ensure that spectrum is assigned in a manner that serves the public interest, convenience, and necessity. In particular, Section 309(j)(3) of the Communications Act provides that, in designing systems of competitive bidding, the Commission must (1) "include safeguards to protect the public interest in the use of the spectrum," and must seek to promote various objectives, including (2) "promoting economic opportunity and competition and ensuring that new and innovative technologies are readily accessible to the American people by avoiding excessive concentration of licenses and by disseminating licenses among a wide variety of applicants," (3) encouraging rapid deployment "including . . . in rural areas," and (4) promoting "efficient and intensive use" of spectrum. 47 U.S.C. § 309(j)(3). Additionally, under the Communications Act, when reviewing a proposed license assignment or transfer application, the Commission must determine whether the applicant has demonstrated that the proposed assignment or transfer of control of licenses will serve the public interest, convenience, and necessity. Section 309(j)(3)(B) is forward-looking, and requires the Commission to rely upon its predictive judgment to proactively guard against potential harms. In Section 6404 of the Spectrum Act, Pub. L. 112-96, tit. VI, § 6404, Congress reaffirmed the extent of the Commission's existing (and well established) authority in future auctions and under future market conditions "to adopt and enforce rules of general applicability, including rules concerning spectrum aggregation that promote competition." 47 U.S.C. § 309(j)(17)(b).

B. History of Spectrum Aggregation Limits

7. Title III of the Communications Act requires the Commission to assign frequencies for radio stations "as public convenience, interest, or necessity requires," to "generally encourage the larger and more effective use of radio in the public interest," and to "[m]ake such rules and regulations and prescribe such restrictions, not inconsistent with law, as may be necessary to carry out the provisions of this chapter." 47 U.S.C. §§ 303(c), 303(g), 303(r). Our competitive analysis, "which has always formed a vital part of this public interest mandate, is informed by, but not limited to, traditional antitrust principles." Applications of Cellco Partnership d/b/a Verizon Wireless and SpectrumCo LLC and Cox TMI, LLC for Consent to Assign AWS-1 Licenses, Memorandum Opinion and Order, 27 FCC Rcd. 10,698, 10,710, ¶ 29 (2012). As the courts have made clear, ". . . the competitive consequences of proposals before the FCC 'must be read in the light of the special considerations that have influenced

Congress to make specific provision for the particular industry.'" United States v. FCC, 652 F.2d 72, 86, 88 (D.C. Cir. 1980) (en banc) (quoting FCC v. RCA Communs., Inc., 346 U.S. 86 (1953)). As noted above, those specific provisions include Section 309(j)(3) of the Communications Act in designing systems of competitive bidding, and Section 310(d)'s public interest mandate with respect to secondary market transactions.

9. *Cellular Service.* In 1981, the Commission established the rules for the licensing of 800 MHz cellular radiotelephone ("cellular") service. In doing so, it acknowledged the D.C. Circuit's concern that the Commission's 40 megahertz allocation plan, which had initially provided for only one licensee per market, led to assertions with "significant plausibility" that "AT&T will operate most, if not all, of the cellular systems eventually put in operation." Use of the Bands 825–845 MHz and 870–890 MHz for Cellular Communications Systems; and Amendment of Parts 2 and 22 of the Commission's Rules Relative to Cellular Communications Systems, Report and Order, 86 F.C.C. 2d 469, 472, ¶ 6 (1981) (quoting NARUC v. FCC, 525 F.2d 630, 636 (D.C. Cir. 1976)). The court had upheld that allocation five years earlier, "strongly influenced by the position of the Justice Department," while also upholding the allocation only "at this time" and imposing on the Commission a "duty of continual supervision" that "includes being on the lookout for possible anticompetitive effects." *NARUC v. FCC,* 525 F.2d at 638. Consistent with that mandate, the Commission changed its policy, and instead sought to create head-to-head competition by licensing cellular spectrum to two service providers, one of which was the incumbent wireline provider, in each geographic area.

12. *CMRS Spectrum Cap.* In 1994, the Commission instituted a new spectrum limit that prohibited a provider of commercial mobile radio service from holding attributable interests in Commercial Mobile Radio Service (CMRS) licenses exceeding 45 megahertz in any licensed geographic service area. In 2001, in response to the growth of competition in the provision of mobile wireless services in the 1990s, the Commission initiated a transition away from the CMRS spectrum cap in favor of case-by-case review by scheduling the cap for elimination as of January 1, 2003.

13. *Case-by-Case Review.* [In] 2004, the Commission for the first time articulated its framework for a case-by-case review of spectrum aggregation (and market share concentration, if appropriate). [T]he Commission applied an initial screen to help identify for case-by-case review local markets where changes in spectrum holdings resulting from the transaction may be of particular concern.

14. [T]he Commission has placed a significant emphasis on increased below-1-GHz spectrum concentration as a factor in its case-by-case review because below-1 GHz spectrum possesses favorable propagation characteristics and is relatively scarce as compared to higher band spectrum

21. Consistent with the evolution of the marketplace and the Commission's statutory directives and policy goals, and in light of the evolution of wireless services demanded by consumers, we must ensure that multiple service providers have access

to spectrum in the foreseeable future. Existing marketplace conditions, including concerns about the potential for anticompetitive behavior, inform our predictive judgment but are not determinative as to whether we need to act. [T]he mobile spectrum holdings policies we adopt today are necessary to preserve and promote consumer choice and competition among multiple service providers, promote the efficient and intensive use of spectrum, maximize economic opportunity, and foster the deployment of innovative technologies.

C. Ensuring that All Americans Benefit from Mobile Wireless Competition

28. [W]e recognize the important tradeoffs in the policy decision at hand. Policies that would limit the ability of major providers to acquire additional spectrum licenses may limit their ability to provide new services or serve new customers. At the same time, policies that would allow these service providers to acquire all or substantially all of the spectrum licenses to be auctioned in the near future, particularly spectrum licenses being auctioned in the Incentive Auction,[3] or that would allow further concentration in below-1-GHz spectrum in secondary market transactions without enhanced scrutiny, would raise significant competitive issues.

29. The Commission has examined these tradeoffs as part of its wholesale review of its spectrum aggregation policies. In the course of our current review, several parties, including the Antitrust Division of the Department of Justice (DOJ), have expressed specific concerns about potential threats to competition in the mobile wireless marketplace, and in particular, the need for access to spectrum as a critical factor to ensure competition in the future. Based upon current marketplace conditions, DOJ concludes that mobile wireless providers possess "the ability and, in some cases, the incentive to exercise at least some degree of market power, particularly given that there is already significant nationwide concentration in the wireless industry." DOJ Apr. 11, 2013 Ex Parte Submission at 8. DOJ therefore recommends that "the Commission should consider the potential that the acquisition of specific blocks of spectrum may have to foreclose or raise the costs of competitors in its policies on spectrum acquisition." *Id.* at 11.

31. *Advantages of Different Types of Spectrum Holdings.* Commenters in this proceeding consistently recognize that different frequencies possess different characteristics for the provision of mobile wireless services. Their agreement on the fundamentals of spectrum notwithstanding, commenters draw highly divergent policy conclusions from these differences [with some arguing that the technical differences require accounting for different spectrum bands differently, and others arguing that the differences in technical characteristics are irrelevant to a competition analysis].

41. *Raising Rivals' Costs and Foreclosure.* In 2001, while not observing specific evidence of foreclosure by wireless providers of their competitors' access to spectrum,

3. [The incentive auction to which the order refers is discussed on pages 506–08. Eds.]

the Commission nonetheless recognized that "it is at least a threshold possibility that because the supply of suitable spectrum is limited, firms in CMRS markets might choose to overinvest in spectrum in order to deter entry, depending on the costs of doing so." CMRS Cap Sunset Order, Report and Order, 16 FCC Rcd. 22,668, 22,691–92, ¶ 44 (2001). Various commenters in this proceeding address the potential for harm to consumers as a result of anticompetitive actions by the largest providers in the market, in particular actions related to raising rivals' costs and foreclosure. In certain situations, a dominant firm may raise rivals' costs by a variety of means, including input monopolization. As rivals' costs are raised, the competitiveness of the marketplace is likely to diminish. Foreclosure can occur when competitors have an incentive and ability to acquire an input not only to put it to their own use, but also to withhold it from their rivals. While there is general consensus among commenters that increased concentration of an essential input, in this case, spectrum, could in theory lead to anti-competitive effects in downstream markets, commenters disagree about the relative risk that such strategies would be utilized in today's wireless marketplace, the costs associated with such a strategy, and whether low-band spectrum is sufficiently distinct from high-band spectrum to form the basis for a successful strategy to raise rivals' costs or foreclose competition.

42. AT&T and Verizon Wireless argue that while anticompetitive behavior to raise rivals' cost or foreclose competition is theoretically possible, the risk of such action is virtually nonexistent, as marketplace conditions will make it irrational for any firm to pursue such strategies. Specifically, AT&T and Verizon Wireless argue that a firm would have to ensure that no other existing spectrum holder sells or leases spectrum to a potential entrant. Further, they claim that while the costs of such anticompetitive strategies would be borne by a few, the benefits would be enjoyed by all existing providers, thus reducing the pay-off and effectively precluding such strategies from occurring. Finally, AT&T and Verizon Wireless argue that the Commission's build-out requirements would impose additional, preclusive costs on such strategies without requiring as much intervention in the market.

43. In contrast, DOJ expresses concern that larger service providers may possess the incentive and ability to foreclose or raise the costs of smaller service providers by obtaining the spectrum that their smaller rivals or potential rivals need to compete. DOJ remarks that "[i]n a highly concentrated industry with large margins between the price and incremental cost of existing wireless broadband services, the value of keeping spectrum out of competitors' hands could be very high." DOJ Apr. 11, 2013 Ex Parte Submission at 11. DOJ explains that "when market power is *not* an issue," it would normally expect the highest use value for new spectrum to come from the highest bidders. *Id.* at 10. Absent compelling evidence that the largest incumbent providers are already using their existing spectrum licenses efficiently and their networks are still capacity-constrained, the highest bidder may be relying on the profits from foreclosure strategy and is not necessarily the bidder that will "generate the greatest benefits to consumers." *Id.* DOJ concludes that the Commission should "consider the potential that the acquisition of specific blocks of spectrum may have

to foreclose or raise the costs of competitors in its policies on spectrum acquisition" and advises that "[t]he Commission's policies, particularly regarding auction of new low-frequency spectrum, can potentially improve the competitive landscape by preventing the leading carriers from foreclosing their rivals from access to low-frequency spectrum." *Id.* at 11, 14.

44. *Discussion.* Section 309(j) requires the Commission to balance a number of specific statutory objectives including competition, diversity and the avoidance of excessive concentration in designing its rules regarding spectrum licenses and the competitive bidding assignment process. Bearing this in mind, we find that, under the totality of circumstances, the public interest will be advanced by the decisions we make today, namely: reaffirming the current case-by-case review of proposed transactions, with continued use of a spectrum screen triggered at aggregations of approximately one third or more of the spectrum suitable and available for mobile telephony/broadband; updating the spectrum screen to include spectrum currently suitable and available for mobile telephony/broadband; treating certain levels of increased aggregations of below-1-GHz spectrum as an enhanced factor during case-by-case review of secondary market transactions involving below-1-GHz spectrum; and establishing a market-based spectrum reserve in the upcoming 600 MHz auction.

45. There are three independent bases for our conclusion, each of which we find warrants the policies we adopt today: (1) the importance of access to low-band spectrum to promote variety in licensees and the advancement of rural deployment as directed by Section 309(j), (2) the benefits to consumers associated with robust competition among multiple providers having access to low-band spectrum, and (3) the potential for competitive harm if we do not provide safeguards to mitigate against the possibility of providers raising rivals' costs or foreclosing competition by denying competitors access to low-band spectrum.

46. Our findings are compelled by the changing circumstances posed by the marketplace today: increased consolidation, the growth in demand for mobile broadband, and the significance of the upcoming 600 MHz auction. First, we recognize that the mobile wireless marketplace has undergone considerable consolidation, both in terms of number of firms and relative market shares, as well as increased concentration of low-band spectrum. While limited amounts of low-band spectrum might theoretically be acquired in secondary market transactions, as noted below the vast bulk of that spectrum has already been acquired. In considering secondary-market acquisitions, the Commission is barred by the Communications Act from considering "whether the public interest, convenience, and necessity might be served by the transfer" to any other party outside the application presented. 47 U.S.C. § 310(d). There is also significantly less low-band spectrum than there is high-band spectrum.

47. Second, our findings are informed by the skyrocketing consumer demand for mobile broadband. Today, consumers are demanding more data at higher speeds, while at home, at work, and in transit. We find that to provide this level of service

in the marketplace to the benefit of consumers, providers will need to deploy more spectrum that can provide both coverage and in-building penetration, as well as spectrum that can provide the increased throughput for mobile broadband applications. In the next few decades, the demands on wireless networks and the need for access to spectrum will continue to increase.

48. Third, our findings are based on the recognition that the 600 MHz spectrum that will be made available in the Incentive Auction will be the last offering of a significant amount of nationwide greenfield low-band spectrum for the foreseeable future. This is particularly important because of the very different characteristics of low-band spectrum. Low-band spectrum possesses distinct propagation advantages for network deployment, particularly in rural areas and indoors. As a result, the auction of spectrum below 1 GHz presents a once-in-a-generation opportunity to promote competition as specifically required by Section 309(j).

58. *Benefits to Consumers from Promotion of Competition in Mobile Wireless Markets.*

59. [W]e believe that holding a mix of spectrum bands is advantageous to providers and that consumers benefit when multiple providers have access to a mix of spectrum bands. The continually evolving marketplace makes having a mix of low- and high-band spectrum more important for the deployment of robust high quality networks by multiple service providers, which in turn can increase competition, drive down prices, and ensure continued innovation and investment. We find that a service provider holding a mix of low- and high-band spectrum licenses would have greater flexibility and would be better able to optimize its network costs for a given quality level, thus promoting the efficient and intensive use of spectrum. Consumers of wireless services benefit from multiple providers having access to a mix of spectrum bands.

60. *Potential for Competitive Harm from Increased Aggregation of Spectrum.* We also find that in the absence of additional below-1-GHz spectrum on a nationwide basis, there is a substantial likelihood of competitive harm if providers that currently lack sufficient access to such spectrum cannot acquire it. The leading providers have most of the low-band spectrum available today. If they were to acquire all or substantially all of the remaining low-band spectrum, they would benefit independently of any deployment of this newly acquired spectrum to the extent that their rivals are denied its use. Without access to this low-band spectrum, their rivals would be less able to provide a competitive alternative. Deploying high-band spectrum is more costly, more time-consuming, and more subject to variation given the increased number of cell sites required for deployment to achieve similar service quality and the accompanying need for cell tower siting authorizations and zoning approvals. Although alternative methods to increase rural and in-building coverage to serve additional customers are available, such as adding towers, splitting cells, or acquiring roaming rights on other networks, these substitute inputs are not nearly as cost effective and likely would increase costs.

61. Along with an attenuated ability to increase output or service quality in response to price increases, providers that lack access to low-band spectrum may lack the ability quickly to expand coverage or provide new or innovative services, which would have a significant impact on competition in the mobile wireless marketplace. The consumer harms from the raising of rivals' costs from increased concentration of low-band spectrum outweigh the potential benefits of unlimited spectrum aggregation. Accordingly, we find that the limited restrictions we adopt today will reasonably balance our goals of promoting competition, ensuring the efficient use of spectrum, and avoiding an excessive concentration of licenses in accord with Section 309(j).

62. *Foreclosure.* We agree with the Antitrust Division of the DOJ, one of our nation's expert antitrust agencies: there is a risk of foreclosure in downstream wireless markets. Today's mobile wireless marketplace is characterized by factors that, according to DOJ, increase the potential for anticompetitive conduct, including high market concentration, highly concentrated holdings of low-band spectrum, high margins, and high barriers to entry. These risk factors increase the incentive and ability for a provider with low-band spectrum to bid for the spectrum in an attempt to stifle competition that may arise if multiple licensees were to hold low frequency spectrum. As a result, such a provider might be the highest bidder in a spectrum auction, not because it will put the spectrum to its highest use, but because it is motivated to engage in a foreclosure strategy.

63. We find unpersuasive various arguments by AT&T and Verizon Wireless that the possibility of future limits on the ability of providers to compete should not be considered in our evaluation of whether to limit their acquisition of low-band spectrum given current market conditions. This is a forward-looking rulemaking that must consider the potential for competitive harms in the future.

64. We also disagree with AT&T's argument that any potential for competitive harm from concentrated spectrum holdings will be addressed by market prices reflecting the total cost of deploying with different bands, such that the greater costs associated with high-band spectrum will result in lower prices for it. Initially, these arguments, as presented, are theoretical and speculative, and not necessarily predictive of actual pricing in spectrum markets in the future. In fact, there is substantial evidence in the record that AT&T's equilibrium pricing model does not apply in the marketplace for acquiring wireless spectrum. As a threshold matter, the model ignores the likelihood of foreclosure. But it also ignores that this particular market is very illiquid. Unlike a fluid and active commodities market, spectrum is made available for initial licensing at irregular times and in irregular amounts. The secondary market for spectrum licenses in any geographic area has very few buyers and sellers. Providers often hold onto spectrum for decades for a number of reasons, including the value they may assign to keeping spectrum out of the hands of potential competitors. This lack of liquidity necessarily limits the accuracy of spectrum pricing.

65. We also note that spectrum transactions occur with imperfect information regarding the costs and timing of deployment, neither of which is entirely within a

provider's control. Thus, while providers that value high-band spectrum less than low-band spectrum will offer to pay relatively less for high-band spectrum, this does not mean that spectrum markets will accurately price spectrum to fully reflect deployment costs, particularly low-band spectrum that is relatively scarce. [W]e acknowledge that there are many factors that may determine the price of spectrum, and we find that we cannot rely on price differentials alone to address competitive concerns.

D. Conclusion

69. [W]e find that the burden that some providers may experience by limits on their ability to acquire increasing amounts of below-1-GHz spectrum, when tailored to the minimum we believe necessary to promote competition as described below, will be outweighed by the public interest benefits that will flow from the preservation and promotion of robust and sustainable competition. By adopting clear and transparent spectrum aggregation limits, we aim to ensure that American consumers have meaningful choices among multiple service providers in the future.

Notes and Questions

1. Antitrust? The FCC's screens simply set a threshold at which the agency will scrutinize a transaction more closely to ascertain competitive effects. What is the value of these screens, above and beyond the case-by-case inquiry the FCC (and the antitrust authorities) could apply to any transaction? Is it that the screens effectively provide safe harbors, creating some market certainty? But the FCC did not describe the screens as safe harbors. So why have screens?

2. Protecting Applications Providers. Recall that the horizontal concentration limits for cable companies were intended to protect programmers from the monopsony power of cable companies. Does that same concern arise here, given that the vast majority of mobile phones use applications and services offered by third-party providers?

3. A Theory of Market Structure? Does the FCC put forward a clear theory of what a competitive market structure would look like? Is it the FCC's expectation that mobile carriers need to be roughly equal in size in order to compete? Do they need to have nationwide footprints? Usual competition theory asks the economic question (whether two services exert pricing constraint on each other), not the functional question (whether the services operate in the same manner). If regional carriers, or smaller national carriers, constrain the pricing power of the larger national carriers, then the market is competitive despite perhaps being lopsided. Similarly, the FCC suggests that carriers are "warehousing" spectrum to keep it out of competitors' hands. Given what the FCC itself has said about the explosive growth of mobile data demand, how did the FCC know that the carriers don't simply have different projections of future need? These are empirical questions, and both the AT&T/T-Mobile merger (which the authorities successfully sought to block) and the T-Mobile/Sprint merger (which several states unsuccessfully sought to block, *see* New York v.

Deutsche Telekom AG, 439 F. Supp. 3d 179 (S.D.N.Y. 2020)) were pursued on the carriers' theory that size and network scale were very important to competition.

4. Foreclosing the Possibility of Foreclosure. In the 600 MHz incentive auction that was the focus of this order, the two companies with the most below-1-GHz spectrum (Verizon and AT&T) ultimately either did not bid (Verizon) or bid relatively little (AT&T). *See* https://www.fcc.gov/auction/1002. Does this mean that the spectrum limits had no impact or were otherwise useless? Not necessarily. The spectrum limits eliminated the possibility of foreclosure on the part of Verizon and AT&T, so it is impossible to know whether foreclosure would have been attractive to those companies had it been available.

5. No Judges. Verizon and AT&T, as the main objects of the spectrum screens, were the most obvious potential plaintiffs in a lawsuit against this order, but neither they nor any of the other players challenged this order. This may have reflected any of a variety of considerations, including a desire not to delay auctions, an assessment that a challenge would likely lose, or Verizon and AT&T's relative disinterest in the 600 MHz spectrum that was the focus of the order.

6. First Amendment? Would *Turner I* provide any support for a potential First Amendment argument against spectrum ownership limits? Recall the argument with respect to cable was that horizontal limits on cable ownership restricted the number of people with whom speakers (cable operators) could communicate. For that argument to have traction with respect to spectrum limits, mobile phone companies would have to be speakers, so under *Turner I* they would have to exercise editorial discretion in choosing what to communicate and seek to communicate messages in doing so. Does that describe mobile phone service providers?

§ 10.C. Broadcast Ownership Limits

As Chapter 5.C.1 discusses, for much of the 20th century, broadcasters (particularly in television as opposed to radio) were subject to a range of structural regulations. Another method the FCC has employed to foster competition in broadcasting is limiting the number of communications platforms any single entity can own or control. There are two main categories of such limitations. First, there have been "multiple ownership" rules that restrict ownership within the same service or closely connected services. So, for example, the Local Television Ownership Rule and the Local Radio Ownership Rule limit the number of television and radio stations, respectively, that a single entity can hold in a given market, and the National Television Ownership Rule limits the percent of the national audience that a single television broadcaster can reach through stations it owns or controls. And the Dual Network Rule prohibits combinations among the ABC, CBS, Fox, and NBC television networks.

Second, the FCC promulgated various "cross ownership" rules that restrict ownership across different communications services. For example, the Newspaper/

Broadcast Cross-Ownership (NBCO) Rule prohibited common ownership of a daily print newspaper and a full-power radio or television broadcast station in the same community. Similarly, the Radio/Television Cross-Ownership Rule limited shared ownership of radio and television stations in the same market.[4]

In the Telecommunications Act of 1996, Congress reduced the FCC's power to control the market structure of broadcasting, particularly of radio broadcasting, by raising the number of stations a single licensee could own in a given geographic market. Pub. L. No. 104-104, § 202(b), 110 Stat. 56 (1996). It similarly raised the ceiling on the percent of viewing households that a single owner of television stations could serve nationwide. *Id.* §§ 202(c)(1), 202(e). Significantly, the 1996 Act also contained a provision—§ 202(h)—that ordered the FCC to undertake biennial (now quadrennial) reviews of its media ownership regulations and to "repeal or modify any regulation it determines to be no longer in the public interest."[5]

The FCC issued an order in 2003 relaxing many of these rules. 2002 Biennial Regulatory Review—Review of the Commission's Broadcast Ownership Rules and Other Rules Adopted Pursuant to Section 202 of the Telecommunications Act of 1996, Report and Order and Notice of Proposed Rulemaking, 18 FCC Rcd. 13,620 (2003). The new rules met a storm of opposition. During the rulemaking proceeding, the FCC received more than 1,000,000 comments, nearly all of which opposed changes that would have allowed for greater media consolidation. After the rules were issued, Congress passed legislation overriding one of the rule changes (the FCC had raised the national television ownership cap from 35% to 45%, and by legislation Congress set the cap at 39%). Consolidated Appropriations Act, 2004, Pub. L. No. 108-199, tit. VI, § 629, 118 Stat. 3 (2004).

In its 2003 order, the FCC evaluated the various ownership restrictions based on the goals of competition, diversity, and localism that it had long articulated (*see* Chapter 9.C.1). It identified five types of diversity that it said were relevant to media ownership rules: (1) viewpoint diversity ("the availability of media content reflecting a variety of perspectives"); (2) program diversity (a variety of program formats); (3) outlet diversity ("in a given market, there are multiple independently-owned firms"); (4) source diversity ("the availability of media content from a variety of content producers"); and (5) minority and female ownership diversity. 18 FCC Rcd. 13,620 ¶¶ 19, 36, 38, 42 & 46. In its discussions of diversity in the 2003 order, the FCC primarily focused on viewpoint diversity.

This is particularly relevant in light of the litigation that followed the 2003 order (involving four separate opinions by the Third Circuit rejecting FCC orders on ownership rules). The Third Circuit's main objection to the FCC's orders was that they did not take sufficient account of female and minority ownership. *See*

4. Our use of the past tense in this paragraph is not a mistake: as you will see shortly, these rules have been repealed.

5. Congress modified this provision in 2004 to call for quadrennial as opposed to biennial reviews. *See* Consolidated Appropriations Act, Pub. L. No. 108-199, § 629, 118 Stat. 3, 99–100 (2004).

Prometheus Radio Project v. FCC, 373 F.3d 372, 420–21 (3d Cir. 2004) ("By failing to mention anything about the effect this change would have on potential minority station owners, the Commission has not provided a reasoned analysis") (internal quotation marks omitted); Prometheus Radio Project v. FCC, 652 F.3d 431, 470 (3d Cir. 2011) (the challenged order "does not explain how the eligible entity definition adopted would increase broadcast ownership by minorities and women").

In response to the Third Circuit's third rejection, the FCC in 2016 issued an order largely retaining its ownership rules but not adopting any race- or gender-specific provisions. As to the latter decision, the FCC stated:

> 297. [W]e have studied this issue repeatedly and find that there is no evidence in the record that is sufficient to satisfy the constitutional standards to adopt race- or gender-conscious measures. And no commenter has proposed actionable study designs that would likely provide the evidence necessary to support race- and/or gender-conscious measures. While we find that a reviewing court could find the Commission's interest in promoting a diversity of viewpoints over broadcast media compelling, we do not believe that the record evidence sufficiently demonstrates that adoption of race-conscious measures would be narrowly tailored to further that interest. In particular, we find that the evidence in the record, including the numerous studies that have been conducted or submitted, does not demonstrate a connection between minority ownership and viewpoint diversity that is direct and substantial enough to satisfy strict scrutiny. The two recent studies that directly address the impact of minority ownership on viewpoint diversity find almost no statistically significant relationship between such ownership and their measure of viewpoint diversity.
>
> 298. In addition, we do not believe that the record evidence establishes a sufficiently strong relationship between diversity of viewpoint and female ownership of broadcast stations that would satisfy the constitutional standards for gender-based classifications. We find that the evidence in the record does not reveal that the content provided via women-owned broadcast stations substantially contributes to viewpoint diversity in a manner different from other stations or otherwise varies significantly from that provided by other stations. Because the studies in the record do not indicate that increased female ownership will increase viewpoint diversity, we believe that they do not provide a rationale for adopting gender-based diversity measures.

Quadrennial Regulatory Review, Second Report and Order, 31 FCC Rcd. 9864 ¶¶ 297, 298 (2016).

Media companies disappointed in the FCC's decision to keep its ownership rules petitioned the FCC for reconsideration, and in 2017 (under a new chair), the FCC eliminated some of the ownership rules. Our excerpt below focuses on the FCC's discussion of the impact of its decisions on minority and female ownership, in light of the fact that that was the basis of the Third Circuit's objections.

2014 Quadrennial Regulatory Review

Order on Reconsideration and Notice of Proposed Rulemaking
32 FCC Rcd. 9802 (2017)

A. Newspaper/Broadcast Cross-Ownership Rule

15. We find that the NBCO Rule must be repealed because it is not necessary to promote the Commission's policy goals of viewpoint diversity, localism, and competition, and therefore does not serve the public interest. We affirm the Commission's longstanding determination that the rule does not advance localism and competition goals, and find today that it is no longer necessary to promote viewpoint diversity, the rule's only remaining policy justification. Although elimination of the rule could theoretically diminish viewpoint diversity to a limited extent due to the loss of an independent voice as a result of any newspaper/broadcast combination, we find that this impact will be mitigated by the multiplicity of alternative sources of local news and information available in the marketplace and the overall financial decline of newspapers. In addition, we find that this concern is outweighed by the countervailing benefits to consumers that can result from newspaper/broadcast combinations. Finally, based on our review of the record, we find that eliminating the rule will have no material effect on minority and female broadcast ownership.

Minority and Female Ownership

44. We find that repealing the NBCO Rule will not have a material impact on minority and female ownership. After seeking public comment on this topic a number of times, the Commission expressed its view that the rule does not promote or protect minority and female ownership. Not only have past debates on this issue not persuaded the Commission that the ban on newspaper/broadcast combinations is necessary to protect or promote minority and female ownership, no arguments were made in this reconsideration proceeding that would lead us to conclude otherwise. On the contrary, two organizations representing minority media owners seek relief from the rule's restrictions. The National Newspaper Publishers Association (NNPA), a trade organization representing more than 200 Black-owned media companies, claims that the NBCO Rule should be eliminated because it impedes its members, which are "trusted community voices," from competing with large, unregulated rivals. NNPA Feb. 13, 2017 Ex Parte Letter at 1. NNPA decries the rule's disincentive for its newspaper members to maximize their publication schedules given that the rule applies to daily newspapers. It argues that the rule "prevents diverse local voices with strong community ties from identifying and investing in new ways to serve their readers, listeners and viewers." *Id.* at 2. In addition, NABOB has reversed its long-held opposition to the elimination of the ban on newspaper/radio cross-ownership, arguing that the broadcast industry — particularly NABOB's minority-owned member stations — should not be constrained from competing for audience share and advertising revenue. According to NABOB, the ban on newspaper/radio cross-ownership has "outlived its usefulness," and we agree. NABOB Feb. 24, 2017 Ex Parte Letter at 3.

45. These comments directly refute arguments in the record that repealing the rule will harm small broadcasters, including minority and women broadcasters, because they are at a competitive disadvantage compared to large media outlets. [M]erging with a newspaper could boost the ability of a small broadcaster to compete more effectively in the market and to improve its local news offerings. NNPA and NABOB seek—and our action today will provide—the flexibility to do just that.

46. [L]ifting the ban on newspaper/radio combinations is unlikely to have a significant effect on minority and female ownership in the radio market given that the thousands of radio stations across the country offer plenty of purchasing opportunities for minorities and women and at lower cost than most other forms of traditional media. In addition, we do not anticipate that lifting the ban on newspaper/television combinations will lead to a meaningful decrease in the number of minority-owned television stations. Some groups previously expressed concern that minority-owned television stations would be targeted for acquisition if the ban were relaxed to favor waiver requests for certain newspaper/television combinations with stations ranked below the top four television stations in a market—a category that includes many minority-owned stations. Removing the ban across-the-board will ensure that no artificial incentives are created, and the record provides no evidence that minority- and female-owned stations will be singled out for acquisition, as some commenters have speculated. To the contrary, record evidence demonstrates that previous relaxations of other ownership rules have not resulted in an overall decline in minority and female ownership of broadcast stations, and we see no evidence to suggest that eliminating the NBCO Rule will produce a different result and precipitate such a decline. Ultimately, given the state of the newspaper industry, we expect that broadcasters may be better positioned to be the buyer, rather than the seller, in most transactions that flow from the rule's repeal. Furthermore, NNPA's submission suggests that some minority media owners may be poised to pursue cross-ownership acquisition and investment opportunities. Therefore, eliminating the rule potentially could increase minority ownership of newspapers and broadcast stations.

B. Radio/Television Cross-Ownership Rule

49. [W]e eliminate the Radio/Television Cross-Ownership Rule, concluding that the Commission erred in finding the rule necessary to promote viewpoint diversity in local markets. Specifically, we find that we can no longer justify retention of the rule in light of broadcast radio's diminished contributions to viewpoint diversity and the variety of other media outlets that contribute to viewpoint diversity in local markets. In addition, given that the current rule already permits a significant degree of common ownership, we conclude that its elimination will have a negligible effect in most markets, particularly as ownership will continue to be limited by the Local Television and Local Radio Ownership Rules.

Minority and Female Ownership

64. [W]e find that the record fails to demonstrate that eliminating the Radio/Television Cross-Ownership Rule is likely to harm minority and female ownership.

While broadcast radio remains an important entry point into media ownership, eliminating this rule will not result in significant additional consolidation because of the constraints of the Local Radio Ownership Rule. Furthermore, there is no evidence that any additional common ownership that would be permitted as a result of eliminating the Radio/Television Cross-Ownership Rule would disproportionately or negatively impact minority- and female-owned stations. Indeed, the analyses within the contexts of the Local Television Ownership Rule and the Local Radio Ownership Rule suggest that previous relaxations of those rules have not resulted in reduced levels of minority and female ownership. We find that the record provides no information to suggest that eliminating the Radio/Television Cross-Ownership Rule will have a different impact on minority and female ownership.

65. In the [2016 Second Report and Order that this order reconsiders], the Commission found that although the rule could help promote opportunities for diversity in broadcast television and radio ownership, it was not being retained for "the purpose of preserving or creating specific amounts of minority and female ownership." 2014 Quadrennial Regulatory Review, Second Report and Order, 31 FCC Rcd. 9864, 9951–52, ¶ 215 (2016) (Second Report and Order). The Commission's comment, however, did not indicate a belief that the rule would promote minority and female ownership specifically, but rather that the rule would promote ownership diversity generally by requiring the separation of radio and television broadcasters. We cannot justify retaining the rule under Section 202(h) [of the Telecommunications Act of 1996] based on the unsubstantiated hope that the rule will promote minority and female ownership.

C. Local Television Ownership Rule

66. Upon reconsideration, we find that the Local Television Ownership Rule adopted in the Second Report and Order is not supported by the record and must be modified. Specifically, we eliminate the requirement that at least eight independently owned television stations must remain in the market after combining ownership of two stations in a market, as the Commission's rationale for retaining the test was unsupported by the record and we conclude that it is no longer necessary in the public interest.

Minority and Female Ownership

83. We find that the modifications we adopt to the Local Television Ownership Rule are not likely to harm minority and female ownership. As noted in the Second Report and Order, data in the record demonstrate that relaxation of the Local Television Ownership Rule in 1999 did not have a negative impact on overall minority ownership levels. In this lengthy proceeding, no party has presented contrary evidence or a compelling argument demonstrating why relaxing this rule will have a different impact. Indeed, consistent with the Second Report and Order, we find that the record does not support a causal connection between modifications to the Local Television Ownership Rule and minority and female ownership levels.

84. In the Second Report and Order, the Commission stated that ensuring the presence of independently owned broadcast television stations in the local market indirectly increases the likelihood of a variety of viewpoints and preserving ownership opportunities for new entrants. The Commission's comment, however, did not indicate a belief that the rule would promote minority and female ownership specifically, but rather that the rule would promote ownership diversity generally by limiting common ownership of broadcast television stations. This statement will continue to be true with respect to the revised rule that we adopt today. Under Section 202(h), however, we cannot continue to subject broadcast television licensees to aspects of the Local Television Ownership Rule that can no longer be justified based on the unsubstantiated hope that these restrictions will promote minority and female ownership.

Notes and Questions

1. Saying More? The excerpt above does not include the data the FCC presented and relied on, but it does include almost the entirety of its substantive discussions of the effects of its rule changes on minority and female ownership. Should it have been required to say more in order to demonstrate that it reasonably explained its actions? If so, what? Or should it have said more as a matter of good governance? If so, what?

2. The Third Circuit Responds. The Third Circuit invalidated this order, holding that "the Commission did not adequately consider the effect its sweeping rule changes will have on ownership of broadcast media by women and racial minorities. Although it did ostensibly comply with our prior requirement to consider this issue on remand, its analysis is so insubstantial that we cannot say it provides a reliable foundation for the Commission's conclusions." Prometheus Radio Project v. FCC, 939 F.3d 567, 573 (3d Cir. 2019). The Supreme Court reversed in the opinion below.

FCC v. Prometheus Radio Project

141 S. Ct. 1150 (2021)

KAVANAUGH, J., delivered the opinion for a unanimous Court. THOMAS, J., filed a concurring opinion.

JUSTICE KAVANAUGH delivered the opinion of the Court.

The Federal Communications Commission possesses broad statutory authority to regulate broadcast media "as public convenience, interest, or necessity requires." 47 U.S.C. § 303; *see also* § 309(a). Exercising that authority, the FCC has historically maintained several strict ownership rules. The rules limit the number of radio stations, television stations, and newspapers that a single entity may own in a given market. The FCC has long explained that the ownership rules seek to promote competition, localism, and viewpoint diversity by ensuring that a small number of entities do not dominate a particular media market.

This case concerns three of the FCC's current ownership rules. The first is the Newspaper/Broadcast Cross-Ownership Rule. Initially adopted in 1975, that rule prohibits a single entity from owning a radio or television broadcast station and a daily print newspaper in the same media market. The second is the Radio/Television Cross-Ownership Rule. Initially adopted in 1970, that rule limits the number of combined radio stations and television stations that an entity may own in a single market. And the third is the Local Television Ownership Rule. Initially adopted in 1964, that rule restricts the number of local television stations that an entity may own in a single market.

The FCC adopted those rules in an early-cable and pre-Internet age when media sources were more limited. By the 1990s, however, the market for news and entertainment had changed dramatically. Technological advances led to a massive increase in alternative media options, such as cable television and the Internet. Those technological advances challenged the traditional dominance of daily print newspapers, local radio stations, and local television stations.

To ensure that the FCC's ownership rules do not remain in place simply through inertia, Section 202(h) of the Telecommunications Act of 1996 directs the FCC to review its ownership rules every four years to determine whether those rules remain "necessary in the public interest as the result of competition." § 202(h). After conducting each quadrennial Section 202(h) review, the FCC "shall repeal or modify" any rules that it determines are "no longer in the public interest." *Id.* Section 202(h) establishes an iterative process that requires the FCC to keep pace with industry developments and to regularly reassess how its rules function in the marketplace.

Soon after Section 202(h) was enacted, the FCC stated that the agency's traditional public interest goals of promoting competition, localism, and viewpoint diversity would inform its Section 202(h) analyses. The FCC has also said that, as part of its public interest analysis under Section 202(h), it would assess the effects of the ownership rules on minority and female ownership.

Since 2002, the Commission has repeatedly sought to change several of its ownership rules—including the three rules at issue here—as part of its Section 202(h) reviews. *See* 2002 Biennial Regulatory Review, Report and Order and Notice of Proposed Rulemaking, 18 FCC Rcd. 13,620 (2003) (2002 Review) (eliminating strict caps on newspaper/broadcast and radio/television cross-ownership and modifying the Local Television Ownership Rule); 2006 Quadrennial Regulatory Review, Report and Order and Order on Reconsideration, 23 FCC Rcd. 2010, 2021 (2008) (relaxing the Newspaper/Broadcast Cross-Ownership Rule). But for the last 17 years, the Third Circuit has rejected the FCC's efforts as unlawful under the APA. *See* Prometheus

Radio Project v. FCC, 373 F.3d 372 (3d Cir. 2004); Prometheus Radio Project v. FCC, 652 F.3d 431 (3d Cir. 2011); *see also* Prometheus Radio Project v. FCC, 824 F.3d 33 (3d Cir. 2016). As a result, those three ownership rules exist in substantially the same form today as they did in 2002.[6]

The current dispute arises out of the FCC's most recent attempt to change its ownership rules. In its quadrennial Section 202(h) order issued in 2016, the FCC concluded that the Newspaper/Broadcast Cross-Ownership, Radio/Television Cross-Ownership, and Local Television Ownership Rules remained necessary to serve the agency's public interest goals of promoting "competition and a diversity of viewpoints in local markets." 2014 Quadrennial Regulatory Review, Second Report and Order, 31 FCC Rcd. 9864, 9865 (2016) (2016 Order). The FCC therefore chose to retain the existing rules with only "minor modifications." *Id.*

A number of groups sought reconsideration of the 2016 Order. In 2017, the Commission (with a new Chair) granted reconsideration. 2014 Quadrennial Regulatory Review, Order on Reconsideration and Notice of Proposed Rulemaking, 32 FCC Rcd. 9802 (2017) (2017 Reconsideration Order). On reconsideration, the FCC performed a new public interest analysis. The agency explained that rapidly evolving technology and the rise of new media outlets—particularly cable and Internet—had transformed how Americans obtain news and entertainment, rendering some of the ownership rules obsolete. As a result of those market changes, the FCC concluded that the three ownership rules no longer served the agency's public interest goals of fostering competition, localism, and viewpoint diversity. The FCC explained that permitting efficient combinations among radio stations, television stations, and newspapers would benefit consumers.

The Commission also considered the likely impact of any changes to its ownership rules on minority and female ownership. The FCC concluded that repealing or modifying the three ownership rules was not likely to harm minority and female ownership.

Based on its analysis of the relevant factors, the FCC decided to repeal the Newspaper/Broadcast and Radio/Television Cross-Ownership Rules, and to modify the Local Television Ownership Rule.

The Third Circuit vacated the 2017 Reconsideration Order. The court did not dispute the FCC's conclusion that those three ownership rules no longer promoted the agency's public interest goals of competition, localism, and viewpoint diversity. But the court held that the record did not support the FCC's conclusion that the

---

6. The FCC currently has two other ownership rules that are subject to its quadrennial Section 202(h) review: (1) the Local Radio Ownership Rule, which limits the number of radio stations that an entity may own in a single market, and (2) the Dual Network Rule, which prohibits mergers among the top four television broadcast networks (ABC, CBS, Fox, and NBC). The FCC has one additional ownership rule, the National Television Ownership Rule, which is not subject to review under Section 202(h). That rule limits the number of television stations that a single entity may own nationwide. Those other rules are not at issue in this case.

rule changes would "have minimal effect" on minority and female ownership. Prometheus Radio Project v. FCC, 939 F.3d 567, 584 (3d Cir. 2019). The court directed the Commission, on remand, to "ascertain on record evidence" the effect that any rule changes were likely to have on minority and female ownership, "whether through new empirical research or an in-depth theoretical analysis." *Id.* at 587.

In the 2017 Reconsideration Order, the FCC changed three of its ownership rules because it concluded that the rules were no longer in the public interest. In particular, the FCC concluded that the rules no longer served the agency's goals of fostering competition, localism, and viewpoint diversity, and further concluded that repealing or modifying the rules was not likely to harm minority and female ownership.

Prometheus argues that the FCC's predictive judgment regarding minority and female ownership was arbitrary and capricious under the APA. *See* 5 U.S.C. §706(2)(A). We disagree.

The APA's arbitrary-and-capricious standard requires that agency action be reasonable and reasonably explained. Judicial review under that standard is deferential, and a court may not substitute its own policy judgment for that of the agency. A court simply ensures that the agency has acted within a zone of reasonableness and, in particular, has reasonably considered the relevant issues and reasonably explained the decision

In its 2017 Reconsideration Order, the FCC analyzed the significant record evidence of dramatic changes in the media market over the past several decades. After thoroughly examining that record evidence, the Commission determined that the Newspaper/Broadcast Cross-Ownership, Radio/Television Cross-Ownership, and Local Television Ownership Rules were no longer necessary to serve the agency's public interest goals of promoting competition, localism, and viewpoint diversity. The FCC therefore concluded that repealing the two cross-ownership rules and modifying the Local Television Ownership Rule would fulfill "the mandates of Section 202(h)" and "deliver on the Commission's promise to adopt broadcast ownership rules that reflect the present, not the past." 32 FCC Rcd. at 9803.

In analyzing whether to repeal or modify those rules, the FCC also addressed the possible impact on minority and female ownership. The Commission explained that it had sought public comment on the issue of minority and female ownership during multiple Section 202(h) reviews, but "no arguments were made" that would lead the FCC to conclude that the existing rules were "necessary to protect or promote minority and female ownership." *Id.* at 9822. Indeed, the FCC stated that it had received several comments suggesting the opposite—namely, comments suggesting that eliminating the Newspaper/Broadcast Cross-Ownership Rule "potentially could *increase* minority ownership of newspapers and broadcast stations." *Id.* at 9823 (emphasis added). Based on the record, the Commission concluded that repealing or modifying the three rules was not likely to harm minority and female ownership.

In challenging the 2017 Reconsideration Order in this Court, Prometheus does not seriously dispute the FCC's conclusion that the existing rules no longer serve the agency's public interest goals of competition, localism, and viewpoint diversity. Rather, Prometheus targets the FCC's assessment that altering the ownership rules was not likely to harm minority and female ownership.

Prometheus asserts that the FCC relied on flawed data in assessing the likely impact of changing the rules on minority and female ownership. Prometheus further argues that the FCC ignored superior data available in the record.

Prometheus initially points to two data sets on which the FCC relied in the 2016 Order and the 2017 Reconsideration Order. Those data sets measured the number of minority-owned media outlets before and after the Local Television Ownership Rule and the Local Radio Ownership Rule were relaxed in the 1990s. Together, the data sets showed a slight decrease in the number of minority-owned media outlets immediately after the rules were relaxed, followed by an eventual increase in later years. The 2016 Order cited those data sets and explained that the number of minority-owned media outlets had increased over time. But the FCC added that there was no record evidence suggesting that past changes to the ownership rules had caused minority ownership levels to increase.

In the 2017 Reconsideration Order, the FCC referred to the 2016 Order's analysis of those data sets. The FCC stated that data in the record suggested that the previous relaxations of the Local Television Ownership and Local Radio Ownership Rules "have not resulted in reduced levels of minority and female ownership." 2017 Reconsideration Order, 32 FCC Rcd. at 9831. The FCC further explained that "no party" had "presented contrary evidence or a compelling argument demonstrating why" altering the rules would have a different impact today. *Id.* at 9839. The FCC therefore concluded that "the record provides no information to suggest" that eliminating or modifying the existing rules would harm minority and female ownership. *Id.* at 9831.

Prometheus insists that the FCC's numerical comparison was overly simplistic and that the data sets were materially incomplete. But the FCC acknowledged the gaps in the data. And despite repeatedly asking for data on the issue, the Commission received no other data on minority ownership and no data at all on female ownership levels. The FCC therefore relied on the data it had (and the absence of any countervailing evidence) to predict that changing the rules was not likely to harm minority and female ownership.

Prometheus also asserts that countervailing—and superior—evidence was in fact in the record, and that the FCC ignored that evidence. Prometheus identifies two studies submitted to the FCC by Free Press, a media reform group. Those studies purported to show that past relaxations of the ownership rules and increases in media market concentration had led to decreases in minority and female ownership levels. According to Prometheus, the Free Press studies undercut the FCC's prediction that its rule changes were unlikely to harm minority and female ownership.

The FCC did not ignore the Free Press studies. The FCC simply interpreted them differently. In particular, in the 2016 Order, the Commission explained that its data sets and the Free Press studies showed the same long-term increase in minority ownership after the Local Television Ownership and Local Radio Ownership Rules were relaxed. Moreover, as counsel for Prometheus forthrightly acknowledged at oral argument, the Free Press studies were purely backward-looking, and offered no statistical analysis of the likely future effects of the FCC's proposed rule changes on minority and female ownership.

In short, the FCC's analysis was reasonable and reasonably explained for purposes of the APA's deferential arbitrary-and-capricious standard. The FCC considered the record evidence on competition, localism, viewpoint diversity, and minority and female ownership, and reasonably concluded that the three ownership rules no longer serve the public interest. The FCC reasoned that the historical justifications for those ownership rules no longer apply in today's media market, and that permitting efficient combinations among radio stations, television stations, and newspapers would benefit consumers. The Commission further explained that its best estimate, based on the sparse record evidence, was that repealing or modifying the three rules at issue here was not likely to harm minority and female ownership. The APA requires no more.[7]

To be sure, in assessing the effects on minority and female ownership, the FCC did not have perfect empirical or statistical data. Far from it. But that is not unusual in day-to-day agency decisionmaking within the Executive Branch. The APA imposes no general obligation on agencies to conduct or commission their own empirical or statistical studies. And nothing in the Telecommunications Act (or any other statute) requires the FCC to conduct its own empirical or statistical studies before exercising its discretion under Section 202(h). Here, the FCC repeatedly asked commenters to submit empirical or statistical studies on the relationship between the ownership rules and minority and female ownership. Despite those requests, no commenter produced such evidence indicating that changing the rules was likely to harm minority and female ownership. In the absence of additional data from commenters, the FCC made a reasonable predictive judgment based on the evidence it had.

In light of the sparse record on minority and female ownership and the FCC's findings with respect to competition, localism, and viewpoint diversity, we cannot

7. Because we hold that the Third Circuit's judgment must be reversed under ordinary principles of arbitrary-and-capricious review, we need not reach the industry petitioners' alternative argument that the text of Section 202(h) does not authorize (or at least does not require) the FCC to consider minority and female ownership when the Commission conducts its quadrennial reviews. We also need not consider the industry petitioners' related argument that the FCC, in its Section 202(h) review of an ownership rule, may not consider minority and female ownership unless promoting minority and female ownership was part of the FCC's original basis for that ownership rule.

say that the agency's decision to repeal or modify the ownership rules fell outside the zone of reasonableness for purposes of the APA.

We reverse the judgment of the U. S. Court of Appeals for the Third Circuit.

JUSTICE THOMAS, concurring.

The FCC had no obligation to consider minority and female ownership. Nothing in § 202(h) of the Telecommunications Act of 1996 directs the FCC to consider rates of minority and female ownership.

From its infancy, the FCC has generally focused on consumers, not producers. The year after it was established, the agency that would later become the FCC made clear that "'emphasis must be first and foremost on the interest, the convenience, and the necessity of the listening public, and not on the interest, convenience, or necessity of the individual broadcaster.'" FCC v. Pottsville Broadcasting Co., 309 U.S. 134, 139 n.2 (1940) (quoting a 1928 agency document).

The FCC kept true to that design when promulgating ownership rules. For example, when it created the Newspaper/Broadcast Cross-Ownership Rule at issue here, the agency explained that its "ownership rules rest on two foundations: the twin goals of diversity of viewpoints and economic competition," and that viewpoint diversity is the "higher" policy. Amendment of Sections 73.34, 73.240, And 73.636 of the Commission's Rules, 50 F.C.C. 2d 1046, 1074 (1975). To these two consumer-focused goals, the FCC has also added a third: localism. 2002 Biennial Regulatory Review, Report and Order and Notice of Proposed Rulemaking, 18 FCC Rcd. 13,620, 13,624 ¶ 8, 13,645 ¶ 81 (2003). None of these objectives advances demographic diversity of owners for the sake of owners.

To be sure, the FCC has sometimes considered minority and female ownership of broadcast media when discussing ownership rules. Time after time, however, it has viewed those forms of diversity not "as policy goals in and of themselves, but as proxies for viewpoint diversity." 2002 Biennial Regulatory Review, Notice of Proposed Rulemaking, 17 FCC Rcd. 18,503, 18,519 ¶ 41& n.116, 18,521 ¶ 50 (2002); Policies and Rules Regarding Minority and Female Ownership of Mass Media Facilities, 10 FCC Rcd. 2788, 2788 ¶¶ 1–2 (1995) ("promoting minority ownership of broadcasting and cable television facilities serves to enhance the diversity of viewpoints presented"). The FCC has also said that ownership diversity "promote[s] competition." *Id.* at 2789 ¶ 6.

Even while trying to abide by the Third Circuit's improper mandate, the FCC clarified in this proceeding that it considered ownership diversity a potential means to pursue viewpoint diversity, not a freestanding goal of its ownership rules. To cite just a few examples, in its 2016 order the FCC explained that it "has a long history of promulgating rules and regulations intended to promote diversity of ownership among broadcast licensees, and *thereby* foster a diversity of voices." 2016

Order ¶ 237 (emphasis added). It afforded certain companies waivers from various rules to "serve our broader goal of diversity of ownership, and *thus* viewpoint diversity." *Id.* ¶ 238 (emphasis added). And it noted that it could not promulgate a race-conscious regulation without first "demonstrat[ing] a connection between minority ownership and viewpoint diversity" that would "satisfy strict scrutiny." *Id.* ¶ 297.

The Third Circuit had no authority to require the FCC to consider minority and female ownership. So in future reviews, the FCC is under no obligation to do so.

Notes and Questions

1. Predictions. The majority opinion noted that the FCC asked commenters to submit empirical or statistical evidence on the likelihood that new ownership rules would reduce minority and female ownership, and none were forthcoming. Forward-looking studies are particularly difficult to generate in rapidly changing fields. In the absence of reasonably reliable data, should courts defer to agencies? What else should courts do? What else should agencies do?

2. That Was Quick. After 17 years of back-and-forth between the FCC and the Third Circuit, encompassing four FCC quadrennial reviews that bled into each other, the Supreme Court unanimously made short work of the Third Circuit's objections and ended the *Prometheus* litigation. And during that 17-year period, the competitive landscape for the relevant media entities changed dramatically. Is there a lesson to be learned in this extensive process? That a court should be hesitant to interfere with agencies' decisions in fast-moving fields, even if the court thinks the agency may have erred? That an agency should be more responsive to courts, even if the agency does not believe it can gather the data the court requests? That the Supreme Court should have granted certiorari in one of the earlier petitions and thus weighed in earlier?

3. Section 202(h) and Minority/Female Ownership. Consider Justice Thomas's contention that § 202(h) does not require consideration of minority and female ownership. Should the FCC treat ownership diversity as a proxy for viewpoint diversity? Should it treat ownership diversity as an important goal in its own right? Should it ignore ownership diversity? What are the relevant considerations in answering those questions?

Part Three

Noneconomic Regulation of Internet and Telecommunications

Chapter 11

Content-Based Regulations

Introduction

Chapter 3 focused on the sorts of laws that trigger any First Amendment judicial scrutiny, but it also addressed aspects of the application of that scrutiny. Notably, Turner Broadcasting System, Inc. v. FCC, 512 U.S. 622 (1994) (*Turner I*), applies the distinction between content-neutral and content-based regulations of speech. In this chapter we focus more directly on the application of First Amendment scrutiny to speech regulations. Every application of the First Amendment entails a judgment that the First Amendment applies at all. But in this chapter's cases the Court treated the answer to the latter question as obvious and focused instead on exactly how to apply the First Amendment to the regulation at issue.

All the cases in this chapter involve content-based regulations. Governments can enact content-neutral speech regulations, of course. As we saw in Chapters 3 and 10, courts have held that the cable must-carry regulations as well as horizontal and vertical limits on cable ownership are content-neutral regulations subject to intermediate scrutiny. But most regulation aimed at speech conducted over the internet or telecommunications has focused on content, and thus is content based. The reason is fairly straightforward: elected officials have been motivated by a desire to mandate content they deem valuable or to limit content they deem harmful, so they have enacted content-based laws. If an elected official wants to ensure that contrasting opinions are presented, or that indecency is not presented, the surest way to do so is through laws directly so providing.

The direct regulation of speech falls into two categories—obliging providers to provide content the government deems to be valuable or restricting content it deems harmful. The former is a form of access regulation, the key element of which is that the regulated entities are required to carry content the government has determined to be valuable. The apparent concern underlying these regulations is that an unregulated market might underproduce such content, because this content is not as remunerative as what it would replace and/or because the programmers' views might otherwise lead them to deny access to some people or viewpoints. Restrictions on harmful speech, by contrast, are aimed at suppressing speech that regulated entities might want to carry but that give rise to cognizable harms (in the case of indecency and violence, particularly to children). The fear is that an unregulated market will produce too much of such harmful speech.

§ 11.A. Mandating Carriage of Speech Deemed Valuable

We begin with regulations requiring the presentation of speech deemed valuable. There are two major Supreme Court opinions on such regulations, both giving a right of reply to those who are criticized. The central difference is that one applies to broadcasters and the other to newspapers. And, as we shall see, the regulation applicable to broadcasters was permitted and the one applicable to newspapers was invalidated.

Red Lion Broadcasting Co. v. FCC

395 U.S. 367 (1969)

WHITE, J., delivered the opinion of the Court, in which WARREN, C.J., BLACK, HARLAN, BRENNAN, STEWART, and MARSHALL JJ., joined. DOUGLAS, J., took no part in the Court's decision.

JUSTICE WHITE delivered the opinion of the Court.

The Federal Communications Commission has for many years imposed on radio and television broadcasters the requirement that discussion of public issues be presented on broadcast stations, and that each side of those issues must be given fair coverage. This is known as the fairness doctrine. Two aspects of the fairness doctrine, relating to personal attacks in the context of controversial public issues and to political editorializing, were codified more precisely in the form of FCC regulations in 1967. The two cases before us now, which were decided separately below, challenge the constitutional and statutory bases of the doctrine and component rules. *Red Lion* involves the application of the fairness doctrine to a particular broadcast, and *RTNDA* [the companion case] arises as an action to review the FCC's 1967 promulgation of the personal attack and political editorializing regulations, which were laid down after the *Red Lion* litigation had begun.

I

The Red Lion Broadcasting Company is licensed to operate a Pennsylvania radio station, WGCB. On November 27, 1964, WGCB carried a 15-minute broadcast by the Reverend Billy James Hargis as part of a 'Christian Crusade' series. A book by Fred J. Cook entitled "Goldwater — Extremist on the Right" was discussed by Hargis, who said that Cook had been fired by a newspaper for making false charges against city officials; that Cook had then worked for a Communist-affiliated publication; that he had defended Alger Hiss and attacked J. Edgar Hoover and the Central Intelligence Agency; and that he had now written a "book to smear and destroy Barry Goldwater." When Cook heard of the broadcast he concluded that he had been personally attacked and demanded free reply time, which the station refused. After an exchange of letters among Cook, Red Lion, and the FCC, the FCC declared that the Hargis broadcast constituted a personal attack on Cook; that Red Lion had failed to meet its obligation under the fairness doctrine to send a tape, transcript, or summary of the broadcast to Cook and offer him reply time; and that the station must provide reply time whether or not Cook would pay for it. On review in the Court of Appeals for the District of Columbia Circuit, the FCC's position was upheld as constitutional and otherwise proper.

Not long after the *Red Lion* litigation was begun, the FCC [adopted rules] making the personal attack aspect of the fairness doctrine more precise and more readily enforceable, and specifying its rules relating to political editorials. [T]he rules were held unconstitutional in the *RTNDA* litigation by the Court of Appeals for the Seventh Circuit, on review of the rule-making proceeding, as abridging the freedoms of speech and press.

As they now stand amended, the regulations read as follows:

> Personal attacks; political editorials.
>
> (a) When, during the presentation of views on a controversial issue of public importance, an attack is made upon the honesty, character, integrity or like personal qualities of an identified person or group, the licensee shall, no later than 1 week after the attack, transmit to the person or group attacked (1) notification of the date, time and identification of the broadcast; (2) a script or tape (or an accurate summary if a script or tape is not available) of the attack; and (3) an offer of a reasonable opportunity to respond over the licensee's facilities.
>
> (b) The provisions of paragraph (a) shall not be applicable (1) to attacks on foreign groups or foreign public figures; (2) to personal attacks which are made by legally qualified candidates on other such candidates and (3) to bona fide newscasts....
>
> (c) Where a licensee, in an editorial, (i) endorses or (ii) opposes a legally qualified candidate or candidates, the licensee shall, within 24 hours after the editorial, transmit to respectively (i) the other qualified candidate or candidates for the same office or (ii) the candidate opposed in the editorial (1) notification of the date and the time of the editorial; (2) a script or tape of the editorial; and (3) an offer of a reasonable opportunity for a candidate or a spokesman of the candidate to respond over the licensee's facilities.

II

Before 1927, the allocation of frequencies was left entirely to the private sector, and the result was chaos. It quickly became apparent that broadcast frequencies constituted a scarce resource whose use could be regulated and rationalized only by the Government. Without government control, the medium would be of little use because of the cacophony of competing voices, none of which could be clearly and predictably heard. Consequently, the Federal Radio Commission was established to allocate frequencies among competing applicants in a manner responsive to the public "convenience, interest, or necessity."

Very shortly thereafter the Commission expressed its view that the "public interest requires ample play for the free and fair competition of opposing views, and the commission believes that the principle applies to all discussions of issues of importance to the public." Great Lakes Broadcasting Co., 3 F.R.C. Ann. Rep. 32, 33 (1929). This doctrine was applied through denial of license renewals or construction permits, both by the FRC and its successor FCC. After an extended period during which the licensee was obliged not only to cover and to cover fairly the views of others, but also to refrain from expressing his own personal views, Mayflower Broadcasting Corp., 8 F.C.C. 333 (1940), the latter limitation on the licensee was abandoned and the doctrine developed into its present form.

There is a twofold duty laid down by the FCC's decisions and described by the 1949 Report on Editorializing by Broadcast Licensees, 13 F.C.C. 1246 (1949). The broadcaster must give adequate coverage to public issues, and coverage must be fair in that it accurately reflects the opposing views. This must be done at the broadcaster's own expense if sponsorship is unavailable.

III

The broadcasters challenge the fairness doctrine and its specific manifestations in the personal attack and political editorial rules on conventional First Amendment grounds, alleging that the rules abridge their freedom of speech and press. Their contention is that the First Amendment protects their desire to use their allotted frequencies continuously to broadcast whatever they choose, and to exclude whomever they choose from ever using that frequency. No man may be prevented from saying or publishing what he thinks, or from refusing in his speech or other utterances to give equal weight to the views of his opponents. This right, they say, applies equally to broadcasters.

A

Although broadcasting is clearly a medium affected by a First Amendment interest, differences in the characteristics of new media justify differences in the First Amendment standards applied to them.

Just as the Government may limit the use of sound-amplifying equipment potentially so noisy that it drowns out civilized private speech, so may the Government limit the use of broadcast equipment. The right of free speech of a broadcaster, the user of a sound truck, or any other individual does not embrace a right to snuff out the free speech of others.

The lack of know-how and equipment may keep many from the air, but only a tiny fraction of those with resources and intelligence can hope to communicate by radio at the same time if intelligible communication is to be had, even if the entire radio spectrum is utilized in the present state of commercially acceptable technology.

Where there are substantially more individuals who want to broadcast than there are frequencies to allocate, it is idle to posit an unabridgeable First Amendment right to broadcast comparable to the right of every individual to speak, write, or publish. If 100 persons want broadcast licenses but there are only 10 frequencies to allocate, all of them may have the same "right" to a license; but if there is to be any effective communication by radio, only a few can be licensed and the rest must be barred from the airwaves. It would be strange if the First Amendment, aimed at protecting and furthering communications, prevented the Government from making radio communication possible by requiring licenses to broadcast and by limiting the number of licenses so as not to overcrowd the spectrum.

By the same token, as far as the First Amendment is concerned those who are licensed stand no better than those to whom licenses are refused. A license permits broadcasting, but the licensee has no constitutional right to be the one who holds the license or to monopolize a radio frequency to the exclusion of his fellow citizens. There is nothing in the First Amendment which prevents the Government from requiring a licensee to share his frequency with others and to conduct himself as a proxy or fiduciary with obligations to present those views and voices which are representative of his community and which would otherwise, by necessity, be barred from the airwaves.

[T]he people as a whole retain their interest in free speech by radio and their collective right to have the medium function consistently with the ends and purposes of the First Amendment. It is the right of the viewers and listeners, not the right of the broadcasters, which is paramount. It is the purpose of the First Amendment to preserve an uninhibited marketplace of ideas in which truth will ultimately prevail, rather than to countenance monopolization of that market, whether it be by the Government itself or a private licensee. It is the right of the public to receive suitable access to social, political, esthetic, moral, and other ideas and experiences which is crucial here. That right may not constitutionally be abridged either by Congress or by the FCC.

B

Rather than confer frequency monopolies on a relatively small number of licensees, in a Nation of 200,000,000, the Government could surely have decreed that each frequency should be shared among all or some of those who wish to use it, each being assigned a portion of the broadcast day or the broadcast week. The ruling and regulations at issue here do not go quite so far. They assert that under specified circumstances, a licensee must offer to make available a reasonable amount of broadcast time to those who have a view different from that which has already been expressed on his station. The expression of a political endorsement, or of a personal attack while dealing with a controversial public issue, simply triggers this time sharing. As we have said, the First Amendment confers no right on licensees to prevent others from broadcasting on "their" frequencies and no right to an unconditional monopoly of a scarce resource which the Government has denied others the right to use.

Otherwise, station owners and a few networks would have unfettered power to make time available only to the highest bidders, to communicate only their own views on public issues, people and candidates, and to permit on the air only those with whom they agreed. There is no sanctuary in the First Amendment for unlimited private censorship operating in a medium not open to all.

C

It is strenuously argued, however, that if political editorials or personal attacks will trigger an obligation in broadcasters to afford the opportunity for expression to speakers who need not pay for time and whose views are unpalatable to the licensees, then broadcasters will be irresistibly forced to self-censorship and their coverage of controversial public issues will be eliminated or at least rendered wholly ineffective. Such a result would indeed be a very serious matter, for should licensees actually eliminate their coverage of controversial issues, the purposes of the doctrine would be stifled.

At this point, however, that possibility is at best speculative. The communications industry, and in particular the networks, have taken pains to present controversial issues in the past, and even now they do not assert that they intend to abandon their efforts in this regard. And if experience with the administration of those doctrines indicates that they have the net effect of reducing rather than enhancing the volume and quality of coverage, there will be time enough to reconsider the constitutional implications. The fairness doctrine in the past has had no such overall effect.

That this will now occur seems unlikely, however, since if present licensees should suddenly prove timorous, the Commission is not powerless to insist that they give adequate and fair attention to public issues. It does not violate the First Amendment to treat licensees given the privilege of using scarce radio frequencies as proxies for the entire community, obligated to give suitable time and attention to matters of great public concern. Congress need not stand idly by and permit those with licenses to ignore the problems which beset the people or to exclude from the airways anything but their own views of fundamental questions.

The statute mandates the issuance of licenses if the "public convenience, interest, or necessity will be served thereby." 47 U.S.C. § 307(a). In applying this standard the Commission for 40 years has been choosing licensees based in part on their program proposals. The Court [has previously recognized] that the Commission was more than a traffic policeman concerned with the technical aspects of broadcasting and that it neither exceeded its powers under the statute nor transgressed the First Amendment in interesting itself in general program format and the kinds of programs broadcast by licensees. NBC v. United States, 319 U.S. 190 (1943).

D

There is no question here of the Commission's refusal to permit the broadcaster to carry a particular program or to publish his own views; of a discriminatory refusal to require the licensee to broadcast certain views which have been denied access to the airwaves; of government censorship of a particular program contrary to § 326; or of the official government view dominating public broadcasting. Such questions would raise more serious First Amendment issues.

E

It is argued that even if at one time the lack of available frequencies for all who wished to use them justified the [fairness doctrine], this condition no longer prevails so that continuing control is not justified. To this there are several answers.

Scarcity is not entirely a thing of the past. Advances in technology, such as microwave transmission, have led to more efficient utilization of the frequency spectrum, but uses for that spectrum have also grown apace. Among the various uses for radio frequency space, including marine, aviation, amateur, military, and common carrier users, there are easily enough claimants to permit use of the whole with an even smaller allocation to broadcast radio and television uses than now exists.

Comparative hearings between competing applicants for broadcast spectrum space are by no means a thing of the past.

Nothing in this record, or in our own researches, convinces us that the resource is no longer one for which there are more immediate and potential uses than can be accommodated, and for which wise planning is essential.

In view of the scarcity of broadcast frequencies, the Government's role in allocating those frequencies, and the legitimate claims of those unable without governmental assistance to gain access to those frequencies for expression of their views, we hold the regulations and ruling at issue here are both authorized by statute and constitutional.

Miami Herald Publishing Co. v. Tornillo

418 U.S. 241 (1974)

BURGER, C.J., delivered the opinion of the Court, in which DOUGLAS, BRENNAN, STEWART, WHITE, MARSHALL, BLACKMUN, POWELL, and REHNQUIST JJ., joined. BRENNAN, J., filed a concurring opinion in which REHNQUIST, J., joined. WHITE, J., filed a concurring opinion.

CHIEF JUSTICE BURGER delivered the opinion of the Court.

In the fall of 1972, Tornillo, Executive Director of the Classroom Teachers Association, was a candidate for the Florida House of Representatives. On September 20, 1972, and again on September 29, 1972, the Miami Herald printed editorials critical of Tornillo's candidacy. In response to these editorials Tornillo demanded that the Herald print verbatim his replies. The Herald declined to print Tornillo's replies, and Tornillo brought suit. The action was premised on [a] Florida "right of reply" statute which provides that if a candidate for nomination or election is assailed regarding his personal character or official record by any newspaper, the candidate has the right to demand that the newspaper print, free of cost to the candidate, any reply the candidate may make to the newspaper's charges. The reply must appear in as conspicuous a place and in the same kind of type as the charges which prompted the reply, provided it does not take up more space than the charges. Failure to comply with the statute constitutes a first-degree misdemeanor. The Herald contends the statute is void on its face because it purports to regulate the content of a newspaper in violation of the First Amendment.

Tornillo and supporting advocates of an enforceable right of access to the press vigorously argue that government has an obligation to ensure that a wide variety of views reach the public. Newspapers have become big business and there are far fewer of them to serve a larger literate population. Chains of newspapers, national newspapers, national wire and news services, and one-newspaper towns are the dominant features of a press that has become noncompetitive and enormously powerful and influential in its capacity to manipulate popular opinion and change the course of events. The result of these vast changes has been to place in a few hands the power to inform the American people and shape public opinion. In effect, it is claimed, the public has lost any ability to respond or to contribute in a meaningful way to the debate on issues.

The obvious solution, which was available to dissidents at an earlier time when entry into publishing was relatively inexpensive, today would be to have additional newspapers. But the same economic factors which have caused the disappearance of vast numbers of metropolitan newspapers have made entry into the marketplace of ideas served by the print media almost impossible. It is urged that the claim of newspapers to be "surrogates for the public" carries with it a concomitant fiduciary obligation to account for that stewardship. From this premise it is reasoned that the only effective way to insure fairness and accuracy and to provide for some accountability is for government to take affirmative action. The First Amendment interest of the public in being informed is said to be in peril because the "marketplace of ideas" is today a monopoly controlled by the owners of the market.

However much validity may be found in these arguments, at each point the implementation of a remedy such as an enforceable right of access necessarily calls for some mechanism, either governmental or consensual. If it is governmental coercion, this at once brings about a confrontation with the express provisions of the First Amendment and the judicial gloss on that Amendment developed over the years.

The clear implication [of our previous cases] has been that any such compulsion to publish that which reason tells them should not be published is unconstitutional. A responsible press is an undoubtedly desirable goal, but press responsibility is not mandated by the Constitution and like many other virtues it cannot be legislated.

Tornillo's argument that the Florida statute does not amount to a restriction of the Herald's right to speak because "the statute in question here has not prevented the Miami Herald from saying anything it wished" begs the core question. The Florida statute operates as a command in the same sense as a statute or regulation forbidding the Herald to publish specified matter. The Florida statute exacts a penalty on the basis of the content of a newspaper. The first phase of the penalty resulting from the compelled printing of a reply is exacted in terms of the cost in printing and composing time and materials and in taking up space that could be devoted to other material the newspaper may have preferred to print. It is correct, as Tornillo contends, that a newspaper is not subject to the finite technological limitations of time that confront a broadcaster but it is not correct to say that, as an economic reality, a newspaper can proceed to infinite expansion of its column space to accommodate the replies that a government agency determines or a statute commands the readers should have available.

Faced with the penalties that would accrue to any newspaper that published news or commentary arguably within the reach of the right-of-access statute, editors might well conclude that the safe course is to avoid controversy. Therefore, under the operation of the Florida statute, political and electoral coverage would be blunted or reduced. Government-enforced right of access inescapably "dampens the vigor and limits the variety of public debate," New York Times Co. v. Sullivan, 376 U.S. 254, 279 (1964).

Even if a newspaper would face no additional costs to comply with a compulsory access law and would not be forced to forgo publication of news or opinion by the inclusion of a reply, the Florida statute fails to clear the barriers of the First Amendment because of its intrusion into the function of editors. A newspaper is more than a passive receptacle or conduit for news, comment, and advertising. The choice of material to go into a newspaper, and the decisions made as to limitations on the size and content of the paper, and treatment of public issues and public officials—whether fair or unfair—constitute the exercise of editorial control and judgment. It has yet to be demonstrated how governmental regulation of this crucial process can be exercised consistent with First Amendment guarantees of a free press as they have evolved to this time.

[Concurring opinions of JUSTICE BRENNAN and of JUSTICE WHITE are omitted.]

Notes and Questions

1. A Precursor. *Red Lion* cites an important precursor on scarcity—NBC v. United States, 319 U.S. 190 (1943), in which the Court faced its first serious challenge to the regulation of broadcasting. At issue were the chain broadcasting rules, which limited the ability of radio networks to control the programming of their broadcast affiliates. NBC's arguments to the Court focused on the First Amendment. NBC contended that "[r]adio is no less entitled to the protection of the guaranties of the First Amendment than is the press." Brief for Appellant NBC at 38, *NBC*. Concerns about interference, NBC argued, could not justify the government's regulatory regime. The Supreme Court rejected NBC's arguments. As we noted on page 450 in Chapter 9, the Court concluded that government control of the spectrum, and the rules it implemented pursuant to that control, were justified by the scarcity of the spectrum. The Court stated that:

> [There are] certain basic facts about radio as a means of communication—its facilities are limited; they are not available to all who may wish to use

> them; the radio spectrum simply is not large enough to accommodate everybody. There is a fixed natural limitation upon the number of stations that can operate without interfering with one another. Regulation of radio was therefore as vital to its development as traffic control was to the development of the automobile.

319 U.S. at 213. Its direct discussion of the First Amendment argument likewise occupied a single paragraph, the bulk of which follows:

> We come, finally, to an appeal to the First Amendment. The Regulations, even if valid in all other respects, must fall because they abridge, say the appellants, their right of free speech. If that be so, it would follow that every person whose application for a license to operate a station is denied by the Commission is thereby denied his constitutional right of free speech. Freedom of utterance is abridged to many who wish to use the limited facilities of radio. Unlike other modes of expression, radio inherently is not available to all. That is its unique characteristic, and that is why, unlike other modes of expression, it is subject to governmental regulation. Because it cannot be used by all, some who wish to use it must be denied. But Congress did not authorize the Commission to choose among applicants upon the basis of their political, economic or social views, or upon any other capricious basis. If it did, or if the Commission by these Regulations proposed a choice among applicants upon some such basis, the issue before us would be wholly different. The question here is simply whether the Commission, by announcing that it will refuse licenses to persons who engage in specified network practices (a basis for choice which we hold is comprehended within the statutory criterion of "public interest"), is thereby denying such persons the constitutional right of free speech. The right of free speech does not include, however, the right to use the facilities of radio without a license.

Id. at 226–27. *NBC* treated the chain broadcasting rules at issue as content neutral. The regulation at issue in *Red Lion* was content based and thus presented a different constitutional question. Still, *NBC*'s focus on scarcity laid some of the groundwork for *Red Lion*.

2. Missing Citation. The Court's decision in *Tornillo* is strong and sweeping, written as if the result flows inexorably from deeply established precedent under the First Amendment. Interestingly, the opinion contains no discussion of—or even citations to—*Red Lion*, which had been decided five years before (and was invoked repeatedly in the *Tornillo* briefs). Is this because the two cases cannot be reconciled? Because a case about broadcast has no bearing on a case about print media?

3. Similar Arguments. At first blush, at least, all the arguments rejected in *Red Lion* seem to be the very ones accepted in *Tornillo*. More specifically, the *Tornillo* Court overturned the Florida statute for two reasons. First, a "compulsion to publish that which reason tells them should not be published is unconstitutional." Second, "under the operation of the Florida statute, political and electoral coverage would be blunted or reduced." These arguments seem to reflect precisely the issues addressed by the *Red Lion* Court. As *Red Lion* noted, the broadcasters in that case contended "that the First Amendment protects their desire to use their allotted frequencies continuously to broadcast whatever they choose, and to exclude whomever they choose from ever using that frequency," and "that if political editorials or personal attacks will trigger an obligation in broadcasters to afford the opportunity for expression to speakers who need not pay for time and whose views are unpalatable to the licensees, then broadcasters will be irresistibly forced to self-censorship and their coverage of controversial public issues will be eliminated or at least rendered wholly ineffective."

4. Assumptions Underlying the Fairness Doctrine. What does the requirement to air opposing views assume about viewers' preferences and behaviors? Presumably viewers who want to see opposing views can find them, and viewers who do not want to see opposing views can change the channel when the opposing view is aired. The beneficiaries would be viewers who would not have sought opposing views but do not change the channel when presented with them and then benefit from the exposure. These benefits seem more likely in a world in which there are few channels (so it might not be easy to find opposing views or change the channel when opposing views were presented). How does a proliferation of information sources change the calculus?

5. Scarcity. Relatedly, *Red Lion* suggested that the basis for special First Amendment treatment of broadcasters is the scarcity of the broadcast spectrum. Chapter 9.B considers the general question of spectrum scarcity in some detail, so that discussion need not be repeated here. But consider the specific reasoning offered by *Red Lion* in the last two paragraphs of the opinion as edited above. Can you think of any "resource" (including paper and ink) for which there are *not* "more immediate and potential uses than can be accommodated, and for which wise planning is [not] essential"? Moreover, similar arguments were raised and rejected in *Tornillo*. Indeed, as the *Tornillo* Court itself reported, there are only a few owners of newspapers; entry into the newspaper market is "almost impossible"; and, just like broadcasts, newspapers are subject to limits on how much information they can transmit. Interestingly, the petitioners in *Red Lion* emphasized that viable daily newspapers were scarcer than broadcasters. Brief for Petitioners at 35, *Red Lion* (reporting census findings that as of 1967, there were "6253 commercial radio and television stations in the United States, compared to only 1754 daily newspapers, a ratio of better than 3½ to 1"). Does any of this undermine the difference in the Court's treatment of Red Lion's and Tornillo's arguments?

6. Print versus Broadcast. Are there other bases for distinguishing broadcast from print that would justify the lesser First Amendment protection afforded to broadcasters? One commonly noted rationale is that the government licenses the spectrum, and for many years distributed licenses without charge, so public interest obligations like a mandated right of reply were perhaps permissible conditions on the use of government resources. But, given our discussion of scarcity and interference in

Chapter 9.B, is that argument convincing? And how does the argument change now that licenses are distributed by auction, not hearing? Are there other bases for distinguishing broadcasting from print? That broadcasting is an unusually powerful medium? That it is ubiquitous? That it greatly influences our culture? But none of these attributes fits only broadcasting, does it? And if broadcasting is unique in one or more of these manners, why would that suggest that broadcasters should receive less rather than more First Amendment protection?

7. Choosing an Approach. Arguably, then, one must choose between the First Amendment jurisprudence of *Tornillo* and that of *Red Lion.* Which makes more sense? Does *Tornillo* overstate the dangers of government regulation and the extent to which editors will be chilled by it? Why did the *Tornillo* Court fail to conclude that "it is the right of the [readers], not the right of the [publishers], which is paramount"? Does *Red Lion* fail to appreciate that the fairness doctrine gives significant discretion to government actors to determine which speech triggers a mandated opportunity to respond? Does it fail to appreciate the fact that even a minor threat against a very valuable broadcasting license can be weighty? Is *Red Lion* flawed by its failure to subject a content-specific speech regulation to strict scrutiny, or is *Tornillo* flawed because it uses such a high standard of review that a beneficial regulation was needlessly found unconstitutional?

8. Multiple First Amendment Constituencies. Consider *Red Lion*'s suggestion that the First Amendment rights of broadcast licensees are counterbalanced by the First Amendment rights of viewers and listeners. In particular, consider the Court's reference to "the right of the public to receive suitable access to social, political, esthetic, moral, and other ideas and experiences." Is such a reading of the First Amendment persuasive? Is it necessary to accept this reading in order to uphold a right-of-reply statute? And what are the implications of the quoted language? For example, does this language suggest that the fairness doctrine is not merely permissible but is in fact constitutionally *required*? That is, does it indicate that, by creating a licensing regime but not creating any explicit fairness obligation, the 1934 Act itself violated the First Amendment? Similarly, does the public's right to suitable access mean that television networks are acting unconstitutionally when they imitate each other's most popular programming and thereby fail to provide a wide range of programming alternatives? Does the First Amendment thus justify a rule forbidding a radio station to switch from a unique, financially viable format to another format already employed by several stations in the same market? This issue arose in FCC v. WNCN Listeners Guild, 450 U.S. 582 (1981). The Court's opinion (by Justice White, who also wrote the majority opinion in *Red Lion*) addressed the point as follows:

> [The Listeners Guild contends that] the Policy Statement conflicts with the First Amendment rights of listeners "to receive suitable access to social, political, esthetic, moral, and other ideas and experiences." Red Lion Broadcasting Co. v. FCC, 395 U.S. 367, 390 (1969). Although observing that the interests of the people as a whole were promoted by debate of public issues on the radio, we did not imply [in *Red Lion*] that the First Amendment

> grants individual listeners the right to have the Commission review the abandonment of their favorite entertainment programs. The Commission seeks to further the interests of the listening public as a whole by relying on market forces to promote diversity in radio entertainment formats and to satisfy the entertainment preferences of radio listeners. This policy does not conflict with the First Amendment.

450 U.S. at 603–04. Are you persuaded?

9. Factual Speech Compulsions. *Tornillo* (and *Turner I*) applied the same scrutiny to their speech compulsions that the Court applies to speech restrictions. Other Supreme Court cases have similarly held. Notable in this regard is Riley v. National Federation of the Blind, 487 U.S. 781 (1988), invalidating on First Amendment grounds a requirement that fundraisers disclose to potential donors the percentage of charitable contributions that were actually given to the charity. The Court applied strict scrutiny, stating that the factual nature of the required disclosures made no difference:

> The constitutional equivalence of compelled speech and compelled silence in the context of fully protected expression was established in *Tornillo*. [*Tornillo*] cannot be distinguished simply because [it] involved compelled statements of opinion while here we deal with compelled statements of "fact": either form of compulsion burdens protected speech. Thus, we would not immunize a law requiring a speaker favoring a particular government project to state at the outset of every address the average cost overruns in similar projects, or a law requiring a speaker favoring an incumbent candidate to state during every solicitation that candidate's recent travel budget. Although the foregoing factual information might be relevant to the listener, and, in the latter case, could encourage or discourage the listener from making a political donation, a law compelling its disclosure would clearly and substantially burden the protected speech.

Id. at 797–798.

The most important precedential aspect of *Riley* is its holding with respect to factual compulsions. Also noteworthy is its conclusion that the requirement flunked the narrow tailoring component of strict scrutiny because there were less speech restrictive alternatives available to achieve the government's interest in reducing donor misperception, in that the state could publish the information on its own or more vigorously enforce antifraud laws. *Id.* at 800–801. Neither of these alternatives seems as effective in advancing the government's interest as mandated disclosure would be, but *Riley* held that they were sufficient to doom the statute. This highlights how difficult it is for the government to satisfy strict scrutiny, a theme that arises in other cases in this chapter.

10. Application to Must-Carry. Recall from Chapter 3.A that Congress required that cable operators carry local broadcast television stations, and that in *Turner I* the Supreme Court applied First Amendment scrutiny and found that this mandatory access was content neutral. The government argued for lenient scrutiny under *Red Lion*, and the cable operators argued for strict scrutiny under *Tornillo*. Below is an excerpt of the Court's rejection of both arguments, leading to its application of the intermediate scrutiny ordinarily applied to content-neutral speech regulations. We begin with its dismissal of the analogy to broadcasting:

> We address first the Government's contention that regulation of cable television should be analyzed under the same First Amendment standard that applies to regulation of broadcast television. It is true that our cases have permitted more intrusive regulation of broadcast speakers than of speakers in other media. *Compare* Red Lion Broadcasting Co. v. FCC (television), and National Broadcasting Co. v. United States (radio), *with* Miami Herald Publishing Co. v. Tornillo (print), and Riley v. National Federation of Blind of N.C. (personal solicitation). But the rationale for applying a less rigorous standard of First Amendment scrutiny to broadcast regulation, whatever its validity in the cases elaborating it, does not apply in the context of cable regulation.
>
> The justification for our distinct approach to broadcast regulation rests upon the unique physical limitations of the broadcast medium.
>
> The broadcast cases are inapposite in the present context because cable television does not suffer from the inherent limitations that characterize the broadcast medium. Indeed, given the rapid advances in fiber optics and digital compression technology, soon there may be no practical limitation on the number of speakers who may use the cable medium. Nor is there any danger of physical interference between two cable speakers attempting to share the same channel. In light of these fundamental technological differences between broadcast and cable transmission, application of the more relaxed standard of scrutiny adopted in *Red Lion* and the other broadcast cases is inapt when determining the First Amendment validity of cable regulation.

512 U.S. at 637–39. And below is *Turner I*'s discussion later in the opinion why *Tornillo* did not apply:

> Appellants maintain that the must-carry provisions trigger strict scrutiny because they compel cable operators to transmit speech not of their choosing. Relying principally on *Tornillo*, appellants say this intrusion on the editorial control of cable operators amounts to forced speech which, if not *per se* invalid, can be justified only if narrowly tailored to a compelling government interest.
>
> *Tornillo* [does] not control this case for the following reasons. First, the must-carry rules are content neutral in application.
>
> Second, appellants do not suggest, nor do we think it the case, that must-carry will force cable operators to alter their own messages to respond to

> the broadcast programming they are required to carry. Given cable's long history of serving as a conduit for broadcast signals, there appears little risk that cable viewers would assume that the broadcast stations carried on a cable system convey ideas or messages endorsed by the cable operator.
>
> Finally, the asserted analogy to *Tornillo* ignores an important technological difference between newspapers and cable television. Although a daily newspaper and a cable operator both may enjoy monopoly status in a given locale, the cable operator exercises far greater control over access to the relevant medium. A daily newspaper, no matter how secure its local monopoly, does not possess the power to obstruct readers' access to other competing publications—whether they be weekly local newspapers, or daily newspapers published in other cities. Thus, when a newspaper asserts exclusive control over its own news copy, it does not thereby prevent other newspapers from being distributed to willing recipients in the same locale.
>
> The same is not true of cable. When an individual subscribes to cable, the physical connection between the television set and the cable network gives the cable operator bottleneck, or gatekeeper, control over most (if not all) of the television programming that is channeled into the subscriber's home. Hence, simply by virtue of its ownership of the essential pathway for cable speech, a cable operator can prevent its subscribers from obtaining access to programming it chooses to exclude. A cable operator, unlike speakers in other media, can thus silence the voice of competing speakers with a mere flick of the switch.
>
> The potential for abuse of this private power over a central avenue of communication cannot be overlooked. The First Amendment's command that government not impede the freedom of speech does not disable the government from taking steps to ensure that private interests not restrict, through physical control of a critical pathway of communication, the free flow of information and ideas.

Id. at 653–57.

As to the broadcasting analogy, *Turner I* followed a pattern that is reflected in other cases in this chapter of limiting application of the broadcasting cases. With respect to *Tornillo*, *Turner I* relied on content neutrality but also on the bottleneck control arising from the fact that cable operators controlled the one source of video programming for most customers. Do any providers of services over the internet or telecommunications currently have such bottleneck control, and if so, over what, exactly, do they have that control?

11. The FCC Abandons the Fairness Doctrine. Although the Supreme Court has not abandoned *Red Lion*, the FCC did abandon the fairness doctrine. In 1986, the D.C. Circuit held that Congress had not codified the doctrine, finding it to be "an administrative construction, not a binding statutory directive," Telecommunications Research & Action Center v. FCC, 801 F.2d 501, 517 (D.C. Cir. 1986), and in 1987, the

D.C. Circuit remanded a case to the FCC for it either to abandon the fairness doctrine as against the public interest, or to defend the doctrine's constitutionality, and thus retain and enforce it. Meredith Corp. v. FCC, 809 F.2d 863 (D.C. Cir. 1987). In 1987, the FCC repealed the fairness doctrine in Complaint of Syracuse Peace Council against Television Station WTVH Syracuse, New York, Memorandum Opinion and Order, 2 FCC Rcd. 5043 (1987) (*Syracuse Peace Council*). In this Order, the FCC first "evaluate[d] the constitutionality of the fairness doctrine under the standard enunciated in *Red Lion* and its progeny," *id.* ¶ 36, concluding that:

> the fairness doctrine in operation disserves both the public's right to diverse sources of information and the broadcaster's interest in free expression. Its chilling effect thwarts its intended purpose, and it results in excessive and unnecessary government intervention into the editorial processes of broadcast journalists. We hold, therefore, that under the constitutional standard established by *Red Lion* and its progeny, the fairness doctrine contravenes the First Amendment and its enforcement is no longer in the public interest.

Id. ¶ 61. The order then went on to articulate its preferred constitutional approach, stating in part:

> We believe that the role of the electronic press in our society is the same as that of the printed press. Both are sources of information and viewpoint. Accordingly, the reasons for proscribing government intrusion into the editorial discretion of print journalists provide the same basis for proscribing such interference into the editorial discretion of broadcast journalists. The First Amendment was adopted to protect the people *not from journalists, but from government.* It gives the people the right to receive ideas that are unfettered by government interference. We fail to see how that right changes when individuals choose to receive ideas from the electronic media instead of the print media.

Id. ¶ 97. The D.C. Circuit affirmed the FCC's repeal of the fairness doctrine without reaching the constitutional grounds, instead finding the FCC's public interest determination to be sufficient. Syracuse Peace Council v. FCC, 867 F.2d 654 (D.C. Cir. 1989). Shortly after the FCC repealed the fairness doctrine, both houses of Congress voted in favor of a bill that would have reinstated the doctrine by congressional mandate. President Reagan vetoed the bill, explaining in a statement to the press that, in his view, the fairness doctrine was unconstitutional. Veto of the Fairness in Broadcasting Act of 1987, 23 Weekly Comp. Pres. Doc. 715 (June 19, 1987) (vetoing S. 742–100 (1987), *reprinted in* 133 Cong. Rec. H4160 (daily ed. June 3, 1987)).

12. Repeal of the Personal Attack and Political Editorial Rules. The FCC's decision in *Syracuse Peace Council* repealed the fairness doctrine. The focus of *Red Lion*, however, was not the fairness doctrine generally but instead the specific rules mandating that broadcasters provide airtime for responses to any "personal attacks" or "political editorials" that are broadcast. Broadcasters filed a petition at the FCC in 1980 requesting repeal of the personal attack and political editorial rules. After years of inaction at the FCC (despite broadcasters' prodding), in 1996 broadcasters filed a petition in the D.C. Circuit for a writ of mandamus to order the FCC to act on the petition to eliminate the rules. The D.C. Circuit so ordered, but the FCC deadlocked, and then with a new set of commissioners deadlocked again (the first deadlock arose because the FCC had an open seat and the second because the FCC chair had represented the broadcasters in their challenge to the rules). After another D.C. Circuit order to resolve the matter, the chair unrecused himself and a majority of Commissioners voted to suspend but not eliminate the rules. The D.C. Circuit rebuffed the FCC's planned suspension and issued a writ of mandamus directing it to immediately repeal the personal attack and political editorial rules. The court did not reach the question of whether the rules were consistent with the First Amendment, instead basing its decision on the FCC's response (or lack thereof) to the court's orders. Radio-Television News Directors Ass'n v. FCC, 229 F.3d 269 (D.C. Cir. 2000). Thus, 20 years after the initial petition, the personal attack and political editorials were repealed.

13. What Content Mandates Remain? With the demise of the fairness doctrine and the personal attack and political editorial rules, what regulations requiring the carriage of desired content remain? The main categories are regulations regarding children's television and candidates for election.

Children's Television

In 1990 Congress enacted legislation applicable to each television broadcast station requiring the FCC to prescribe standards "limit[ing] the duration of advertising in children's television programming to not more than 10.5 minutes per hour on weekends and not more than 12 minutes per hour on weekdays." Children's Television Act of 1990, Pub. L. No. 101-437, 104 Stat. 996; 47 U.S.C. §§ 303a & 303b. The FCC's regulations implementing the statute have not been particularly onerous. In 2019 the FCC kept a requirement from earlier regulations that broadcasters air at least 26 hours per quarter of weekly children's television programs but provided that only a majority of the programming be regularly scheduled and permitted broadcasters to air up to 13 hours per quarter of programming on a multicast stream rather than on their primary stream (or channel). Children's Television Programming Rules, Report and Order and Further Notice of Proposed Rulemaking, 34 FCC Rcd. 5822 (2019). As a dissenting commissioner noted, "our new rules will allow broadcasters to air less than one hour of regularly scheduled children's programming per month on their most widely viewed primary stream. One third of a broadcaster's annual hours can be moved to an unpopular multicast stream, and an additional third will not need to be regularly scheduled." *Id.* at 5895 (dissenting statement of Commissioner Geoffrey Starks).

Candidate Access

The two central laws regarding candidate access are the reasonable access requirements of 47 U.S.C. § 312(a)(7) and the equal time rule, 47 U.S.C. § 315. Section 312(a)(7) grants candidates for federal office the right to purchase broadcast time for their advertisements at the broadcaster's lowest unit charge for the particular class of advertisement. Congress extended the reasonable access requirement to advertisements on programming that DBS providers directly control (thus excluding the vast majority of the channels they offer, which they transmit but do not directly program) but not to cable providers. *See* 47 U.S.C. § 335; 47 C.F.R. § 25.701(b); Codification of the Commission's Political Programming Policies, Report and Order, 7 FCC Rcd. 678, 680 n.11 (1991). The apparent rationale for the distinction is that broadcast and DBS use spectrum and cable does not, and *Red Lion* provides a basis only for regulating spectrum usage.

Section 315 provides that if a television programmer allows "a legally qualified candidate for any public office" (city, state or federal) to gain air time, the station must allow the candidate's opponent(s) a like opportunity. Thus, if candidate *A* is given free air time, *A*'s opponent(s) must be given free air time; and if *A* bought air time, *A*'s opponent(s) must be allowed to buy an equal amount at the same rate.[1] This requirement applies to broadcasters as well as cable and DBS operators, but for the latter two only to the small amount of programming they directly control. *See* 47 U.S.C. §§ 315, 335; 47 C.F.R. § 25.701(b). Importantly, the equal time rule exempts from this requirement any "bona fide newscast, bona fide news interview, bona fide news documentary, or on-the-spot coverage of bona fide news events (including but not limited to political conventions and activities incidental thereto)." These exceptions have been interpreted fairly broadly, such that a talk show ("Donahue") and "Politically Incorrect with Bill Maher" were granted exemptions from the equal time requirement as bona fide news interview programs. Multimedia Entertainment, Inc., 56 Rad. Reg. (P & F) 143, 146 (1984); Request of ABC, Inc. for Declaratory Ruling, Staff Ruling, 15 FCC Rcd. 1355 (1999). And the bona fide news events exception applies to televised political debates, thereby allowing debates that do not include every candidate for a given office. Petitions of Henry Geller and National Association of Broadcasters and the Radio-Television News Directors Association to Change Commission Interpretation of Subsections 315(a)(3) and (4) of the Communications Act, Report and Order, 54 Rad. Reg. 2d (P & F) 1246 (1983), *aff'd*, League of Women Voters Educ. Fund v. FCC, 731 F.2d 995 (D.C. Cir. 1984).

The Supreme Court, relying on *Red Lion*, upheld § 312(a)(7) against a First Amendment challenge in CBS v. FCC, 453 U.S. 367 (1981), and the D.C. Circuit concluded that *Red Lion* foreclosed any First Amendment challenges to § 315. Branch v. FCC, 824 F.2d 37, 49–50 (D.C. Cir. 1987). And, in light of their status as statutory

1. So, for example, in 2015, Republican presidential candidate Donald Trump hosted "Saturday Night Live," after which NBC filed a notice with the FCC that the equal time rule had been triggered. Other Republican candidates then requested free airtime, and NBC agreed to provide them with a similar amount of airtime (Trump had been on the air for 12 minutes) in the three states where significant presidential campaigning had occurred (Iowa, New Hampshire, and South Carolina). *See* Ted Johnson, NBC Reaches Agreement on Equal Time After Trump's 'SNL' Gig, Variety (Nov. 23, 2015)

commands, the FCC has enforced these rules. This stands in contrast to rules that the FCC created on its own. Not only did the FCC reject the fairness doctrine, but it also rejected an election rule known as the Zapple doctrine that had relied on the fairness doctrine. The Zapple doctrine applied the fairness doctrine to situations in which supporters of a political candidate purchased broadcast air time to support the candidate — the doctrine required the broadcaster to sell comparable air time to supporters of opposing candidates. Request by Nicholas Zapple, Communications Counsel, Committee on Commerce for Interpretative Ruling Concerning Section 315 Fairness Doctrine, 23 F.C.C. 2d 707 (1970). In 2014, in response to a complaint, the FCC (through the chief of its Media Bureau, to whom the commissioners delegated such responses) stated in relevant part that "we have no basis to enforce the Zapple doctrine. The doctrine was based on an interpretation of the fairness doctrine, which the FCC abrogated in *Syracuse Peace Council*. Given the fact that the Zapple doctrine was based on an interpretation of the fairness doctrine, which has no current legal effect, we conclude that the Zapple doctrine similarly has no current legal effect." WISN(AM), Milwaukee, WI, Letter (Media Bureau), 29 FCC Rcd. 5010 (2014).

14. Is That All? These remaining mandated content regulations may seem fairly meager. In this regard, note that neither the children's television nor candidate access rules (nor any other mandatory access rules) apply to websites or social media platforms. The rationales for broadcast regulation do not seem to apply to the internet, and Reno v. ACLU, 521 U.S. 844 (1997), so holds, specifically distinguishing *Red Lion* and FCC v. Pacifica Foundation (discussed immediately below). Is there a persuasive argument for compelling some websites and social media platforms to include some forms of speech? How would you identify and define those forms of speech?

§ 11.B. Restrictions on Speech Deemed Harmful

We now turn to regulations limiting content deemed harmful. Such laws have focused on indecency, violence, and false statements. Among these three, indecency has received the most legislative attention. Congress has enacted legislation regulating indecency on broadcast, cable television, telephony, and the internet, and each category has produced at least one major Supreme Court opinion. Indecency thus has the distinction of being the only content that Congress has seen fit to regulate, and the Supreme Court has seen fit to address, with respect to all four of the basic forms of communication that make up internet and telecommunications. And with respect to internet indecency, Congress enacted new legislation after the Supreme Court invalidated its first foray.

We begin with regulation of indecency. We then turn to the other forms of harmful content that has been the subject of regulatory focus (though much less than indecency) — violent content and false statements.

§ 11.B.1. Indecency

§ 11.B.1.a. Regulation of Broadcast Indecency

FCC v. Pacifica Foundation

438 U.S. 726 (1978)

STEVENS, J., delivered the opinion of the Court (Parts I, II, III, and IV-C) and an opinion in which BURGER, C.J., and REHNQUIST, J., joined (Parts IV-A and IV-B). POWELL, J., filed an opinion concurring in part and concurring in the judgment, in which BLACKMUN, J., joined. BRENNAN, J., filed a dissenting opinion, in which MARSHALL, J., joined. STEWART, J., filed a dissenting opinion in which BRENNAN, WHITE, and MARSHALL, JJ., joined.

JUSTICE STEVENS delivered the opinion of the Court (Parts I, II, III and IV-C) and an opinion in which CHIEF JUSTICE BURGER and JUSTICE REHNQUIST joined (Parts IV-A and IV-B).

A satiric humorist named George Carlin recorded a 12-minute monologue entitled "Filthy Words" before a live audience in a California theater. He began by referring to his thoughts about "the words you couldn't say on the public, ah, airwaves, um, the ones you definitely wouldn't say, ever." He proceeded to list those words and repeat them over and over again in a variety of colloquialisms.[2] The transcript of the recording indicates frequent laughter from the audience.

At about 2 o'clock in the afternoon on Tuesday, October 30, 1973, a New York radio station, owned by respondent Pacifica Foundation, broadcast the "Filthy Words" monologue. A few weeks later a man, who stated that he had heard the broadcast while driving with his young son, wrote a letter complaining to the Commission. He stated that, although he could perhaps understand the "record's being sold for private use, I certainly cannot understand the broadcast of same over the air that, supposedly, you control."

The complaint was forwarded to the station for comment. In its response, Pacifica explained that the monologue had been played during a program about contemporary society's attitude toward language and that, immediately before its broadcast, listeners had been advised that it included "sensitive language which might be regarded as offensive to some." Pacifica characterized George Carlin as "a significant social satirist" who "like Twain and Sahl before him, examines the language of ordinary people. . . . Carlin is not mouthing obscenities, he is merely using words to satirize as harmless and essentially silly our attitudes towards those words." Pacifica stated that it was not aware of any other complaints about the broadcast.

---

2. [Carlin identified the seven words as shit, piss, fuck, cunt, cocksucker, motherfucker, and tits. At the time, the FCC had seven commissioners. An industry joke in the aftermath of *Pacifica* was that, for future enforcement efforts, each commissioner was assigned one word. Eds.]

On February 21, 1975, the Commission issued a declaratory order granting the complaint. [The Commission concluded that certain words depicted sexual and excretory activities in a patently offensive manner, noted that they "were broadcast at a time when children were undoubtedly in the audience (i. e., in the early afternoon)," and that the prerecorded language, with these offensive words "repeated over and over," was "deliberately broadcast." Citizen's Complaint Against Pacifica Found. Station WBAI (FM), Memorandum Opinion & Order, 56 F.C.C. 2d 94, 99 (1975). In summary, the Commission stated: "We therefore hold that the language as broadcast was indecent and prohibited by 18 U.S.C. [§] 1464." *Id.*

II

[Here, the Court concluded that § 326 of the Communications Act, which forbids the Commission to engage in censorship, "does not limit the Commission's authority to impose sanctions on licensees who engage in obscene, indecent, or profane broadcasting." The Court found that the section forbids censorship in advance of broadcast. And, "[e]ntirely apart from the fact that the subsequent review of program content is not the sort of censorship at which the statute was directed, its history makes it perfectly clear that it was not intended to limit the Commission's power to regulate the broadcast of obscene, indecent, or profane language."]

III

The only other statutory question presented by this case is whether the afternoon broadcast of the "Filthy Words" monologue was indecent within the meaning of 18 U.S.C. § 1464. [The section forbids "any obscene, indecent, or profane language by means of radio communications." The Court held that "obscene" and "indecent," as those words are employed in § 1464, have different meanings. To be obscene, language must appeal to the prurient interest and lack serious value.] Prurient appeal is an element of the obscene, but the normal definition of "indecent" merely refers to nonconformance with accepted standards of morality.

IV

Pacifica makes two constitutional attacks on the Commission's order. First, it argues that the Commission's construction of the statutory language broadly encompasses so much constitutionally protected speech that reversal is required even if Pacifica's broadcast of the "Filthy Words" monologue is not itself protected by the First Amendment. Second, Pacifica argues that inasmuch as the recording is not obscene, the Constitution forbids any abridgment of the right to broadcast it on the radio.

A

The first argument fails because our review is limited to the question whether the Commission has the authority to proscribe this particular broadcast.

It is true that the Commission's order may lead some broadcasters to censor themselves. At most, however, the Commission's definition of indecency will deter only the broadcasting of patently offensive references to excretory and sexual organs and activities.[3] While some of these references may be protected, they surely lie at the periphery of First Amendment concern.

B

When the issue is narrowed to the facts of this case, the question is whether the First Amendment denies government any power to restrict the public broadcast of indecent language in any circumstances. For if the government has any such power, this was an appropriate occasion for its exercise.

[T]he fact that society may find speech offensive is not a sufficient reason for suppressing it. If there were any reason to believe that the Commission's characterization of the Carlin monologue as offensive could be traced to its political content—or even to the fact that it satirized contemporary attitudes about four-letter words—First Amendment protection might be required. But that is simply not this case. These words offend for the same reasons that obscenity offends.

Although these words ordinarily lack literary, political, or scientific value, they are not entirely outside the protection of the First Amendment. Some uses of even the most offensive words are unquestionably protected. Indeed, we may assume, *arguendo*, that this monologue would be protected in other contexts. Nonetheless, the constitutional protection accorded to a communication containing such patently offensive sexual and excretory language need not be the same in every context. Words that are commonplace in one setting are shocking in another. To paraphrase Mr. Justice Harlan, one occasion's lyric is another's vulgarity. *Cf.* Cohen v. California, 403 U.S. 15, 25 (1971).[4]

In this case it is undisputed that the content of Pacifica's broadcast was "vulgar," "offensive," and "shocking." Because content of that character is not entitled to absolute constitutional protection under all circumstances, we must consider its context in order to determine whether the Commission's action was constitutionally permissible.

C

We have long recognized that each medium of expression presents special First Amendment problems. And of all forms of communication, it is broadcasting that has received the most limited First Amendment protection. Thus, although other speakers cannot be licensed except under laws that carefully define and narrow official discretion, a broadcaster may be deprived of his license and his forum if the Commission decides that such an action would serve "the public interest, convenience, and necessity." 47 U.S.C. §§ 309(a), 312(a)(2). Similarly, although the First Amendment protects newspaper publishers from being required to print the replies of those whom they criticize, Miami Herald Publishing Co. v. Tornillo, 418 U.S. 241

---

3. A requirement that indecent language be avoided will have its primary effect on the form, rather than the content, of serious communication. There are few, if any, thoughts that cannot be expressed by the use of less offensive language.

4. [The Court's opinion in *Cohen* said that "one man's vulgarity is another's lyric." Eds.]

(1974), it affords no such protection to broadcasters; on the contrary, they must give free time to the victims of their criticism. Red Lion Broadcasting Co. v. FCC, 395 U.S. 367 (1969).

The reasons for these distinctions are complex, but two have relevance to the present case. First, the broadcast media have established a uniquely pervasive presence in the lives of all Americans. Patently offensive, indecent material presented over the airwaves confronts the citizen, not only in public, but also in the privacy of the home, where the individual's right to be left alone plainly outweighs the First Amendment rights of an intruder. Because the broadcast audience is constantly tuning in and out, prior warnings cannot completely protect the listener or viewer from unexpected program content. To say that one may avoid further offense by turning off the radio when he hears indecent language is like saying that the remedy for an assault is to run away after the first blow. One may hang up on an indecent phone call, but that option does not give the caller a constitutional immunity or avoid a harm that has already taken place.

Second, broadcasting is uniquely accessible to children, even those too young to read. Although Cohen's written message [a jacket with the words "Fuck the Draft"] might have been incomprehensible to a first grader, Pacifica's broadcast could have enlarged a child's vocabulary in an instant. Other forms of offensive expression may be withheld from the young without restricting the expression at its source. Bookstores and motion picture theaters, for example, may be prohibited from making indecent material available to children. We held in Ginsberg v. New York, 390 U.S. 629 (1968), that the government's interest in the "well-being of its youth" and in supporting "parents' claim to authority in their own household" justified the regulation of otherwise protected expression.[5] The ease with which children may obtain access to broadcast material, coupled with the concerns recognized in *Ginsberg*, amply justify special treatment of indecent broadcasting.

It is appropriate, in conclusion, to emphasize the narrowness of our holding. This case does not involve a two-way radio conversation between a cab driver and a dispatcher, or a telecast of an Elizabethan comedy. We have not decided that an occasional expletive in either setting would justify any sanction or, indeed, that this broadcast would justify a criminal prosecution. The Commission's decision rested entirely on a nuisance rationale under which context is all-important. The concept requires consideration of a host of variables. The time of day was emphasized by the Commission. The content of the program in which the language is used will

5. The Commission's action does not by any means reduce adults to hearing only what is fit for children. *Cf.* Butler v. Michigan, 352 U.S. 380, 383 (1957). Adults who feel the need may purchase tapes and records or go to theaters and nightclubs to hear these words. In fact, the Commission has not unequivocally closed even broadcasting to speech of this sort; whether broadcast audiences in the late evening contain so few children that playing this monologue would be permissible is an issue neither the Commission nor this Court has decided.

also affect the composition of the audience,[6] and differences between radio, television, and perhaps closed-circuit transmissions, may also be relevant. As Mr. Justice Sutherland wrote, a "nuisance may be merely a right thing in the wrong place—like a pig in the parlor instead of the barnyard." Euclid v. Ambler Realty Co., 272 U.S. 365, 388 (1926). We simply hold that when the Commission finds that a pig has entered the parlor, the exercise of its regulatory power does not depend on proof that the pig is obscene.

Appendix to Opinion of the Court

The following is a verbatim transcript of "Filthy Words" prepared by the Federal Communications Commission.

Aruba-du, ruba-tu, ruba-tu. I was thinking about the curse words and the swear words, the cuss words and the words that you can't say, that you're not supposed to say all the time, [']cause words or people into words want to hear your words. Some guys like to record your words and sell them back to you if they can, (laughter) listen in on the telephone, write down what words you say. A guy who used to be in Washington, knew that his phone was tapped, used to answer, Fuck Hoover, yes, go ahead. (laughter) Okay, I was thinking one night about the words you couldn't say on the public, ah, airwaves, um, the ones you definitely wouldn't say, ever, [']cause I heard a lady say bitch one night on television, and it was cool like she was talking about, you know, ah, well, the bitch is the first one to notice that in the litter Johnie right (murmur) Right. And, uh, bastard you can say, and hell and damn so I have to figure out which ones you couldn't and ever and it came down to seven but the list is open to amendment, and in fact, has been changed, uh, by now, ha, a lot of people pointed things out to me, and I noticed some myself. The original seven words were, shit, piss, fuck, cunt, cocksucker, motherfucker, and tits. Those are the ones that will curve your spine, grow hair on your hands and (laughter) maybe, even bring us, God help us, peace without honor (laughter) um, and a bourbon. (laughter) And now the first thing that we noticed was that word fuck was really repeated in there because the word motherfucker is a compound word and it's another form of the word fuck. (laughter) You want to be a purist it doesn't really—it can't be on the list of basic words. Also, cocksucker is a compound word and neither half of that is really dirty. The word—the half sucker that's merely suggestive (laughter) and the word cock is a half-way dirty word, 50% dirty—dirty half the time, depending on what you mean by it. (laughter) Uh, remember when you first heard it, like in 6th grade, you used to giggle. And the cock crowed three times, heh (laughter) the cock—three times. It's in the Bible, cock in the Bible. (laughter) And the first time you heard about a cock-fight, remember—What? Huh? naw. It ain't that, are you stupid? man. (laughter, clapping) It's chickens, you know, (laughter) Then you

6. Even a prime-time recitation of Geoffrey Chaucer's Miller's Tale would not be likely to command the attention of many children who are both old enough to understand and young enough to be adversely affected by passages such as: "And prively he caughte hire by the queynte." The Canterbury Tales, Chaucer's Complete Works (Cambridge ed. 1933), p. 58.

have the four letter words from the old Angle-Saxon fame. Uh, shit and fuck. The word shit, uh, is an interesting kind of word in that the middle class has never really accepted it and approved it. They use it like, crazy but it's not really okay. It's still a rude, dirty, old kind of gushy word. (laughter) They don't like that, but they say it, like, they say it like, a lady now in a middle-class home, you'll hear most of the time she says it as an expletive, you know, it's out of her mouth before she knows. She says, Oh shit oh shit, (laughter) oh shit. If she drops something, Oh, the shit hurt the broccoli. Shit. Thank you. (footsteps fading away) (papers ruffling)

Read it! (from audience)

Shit! (laughter) I won the Grammy, man, for the comedy album. Isn't that groovy? (clapping, whistling) (murmur) That's true. Thank you. Thank you man. Yeah. (murmur) (continuous clapping) Thank you man. Thank you. Thank you very much, man. Thank, no, (end of continuous clapping) for that and for the Grammy, man, [']cause (laughter) that's based on people liking it man, yeh, that's ah, that's okay man. (laughter) Let's let that go, man. I got my Grammy. I can let my hair hang down now, shit. (laughter) Ha! So! Now the word shit is okay for the man. At work you can say it like crazy. Mostly figuratively, Get that shit out of here, will ya? I don't want to see that shit anymore. I can't *cut* that shit, buddy. I've had that shit up to here. I think you're full of shit myself. (laughter) He don't know shit from Shinola. (laughter) you know that? (laughter) Always wondered how the Shinola people felt about that (laughter) Hi, I'm the new man from Shinola, (laughter) Hi, how are ya? Nice to see ya. (laughter) How are ya? (laughter) Boy, I don't know whether to shit or wind my watch. (laughter) Guess, I'll shit on my watch. (laughter) Oh, *the* shit is going to hit *de* fan. (laughter). Built like a brick shit-house. (laughter) Up, he's up shit's creek. (laughter) He's had it. (laughter) He hit me, I'm sorry. (laughter) Hot shit, holy shit, tough shit, eat shit. (laughter) shit-eating grin. Uh, whoever thought of that was ill. (murmur laughter) He had a shit-eating grin! He had a what? (laughter) Shit on a stick. (laughter) Shit in a handbag. I always like that. He ain't worth shit in a handbag. (laughter) Shitty. He acted real shitty. (laughter) You know what I mean? (laughter) I got the money back, but a real shitty attitude. Heh, he had a shit-fit. (laughter) Wow! Shit-fit. Whew! Glad I wasn't there. (murmur, laughter) All the animals—Bull shit, horseshit, cow shit, rat shit, bat shit. (laughter) First time I heard bat shit, I really came apart. A guy in Oklahoma, Boggs, said it, man. Aw! Bat shit. (laughter) Vera reminded me of that last night, ah (murmur). Snake shit, slicker than owl shit. (laughter) Get your shit together. Shit or get off the pot. (laughter) I got a shit-load full of them. (laughter) I got a shit-pot full, all right. Shit-head, shit-heel, shit in your heart, shit for brains, (laughter) shit-face, heh (laughter) I always try to think how that could have originated; the first guy that said that. Somebody got drunk and fell in some shit, you know. (laughter) Hey, I'm shit-face. (laughter) Shit-face, *today.* (laughter) Anyway, enough of that shit. (laughter) The big one, the word fuck that's the one that hangs them up the most. [']Cause in a lot of cases that's the very act that hangs them up the most. So, it's natural that the word would, uh, have the same effect. It's a great word, fuck, nice word, easy word, cute word, kind of. Easy word to say. One syllable, short u. (laughter) Fuck. (murmur) You know, it's easy. Starts with a nice soft sound fuh ends with a *kuh*. Right? (laughter) A little something for everyone. Fuck (laughter) Good word. Kind of a proud word, too. Who are you? I am *FUCK*, (laughter) *FUCK OF THE MOUNTAIN*. (laughter) Tune in again next week to FUCK OF THE MOUNTAIN. (laughter) It's an interesting word too, [']cause it's got a double kind of a life—personality—dual, you know, whatever the right phrase is. It leads a double life, the word fuck. First of all, it means, sometimes, most of the time, fuck. What does it mean? It means to make love. Right? We're going to make love, yeh, we're going to fuck, yeh, we're going to fuck, yeh, we're going to make love. (laughter) we're really going to fuck, yeh, we're going to make love. Right? And it also means the beginning of life, it's the act that begins life, so there's the word hanging around with words like love, and life, and yet on the other hand, it's also a word that we really use to hurt each other with, man. It's a heavy. It's one that you have toward the end of the argument. (laughter) Right? (laughter) You finally can't make out. Oh, fuck you man. I said, fuck you. (laughter, murmur) Stupid fuck. (laughter) Fuck you and everybody that looks like you. (laughter) man. It would be nice to change the movies that we already have and substitute the word fuck for the word kill, wherever we could, and some of those movie cliches would change a little bit. Madfuckers still on the loose. Stop me before I fuck again. Fuck the ump, fuck the ump, fuck the ump, fuck the ump, fuck the ump. Easy on the clutch Bill, you'll fuck that engine again. (laughter) The other shit one was, I don't give a shit. Like it's worth something, you know? (laughter) I don't give a shit. Hey, well, I don't take no shit, (laughter) you know what I mean? You know why I don't take no shit? (laughter) [']Cause I don't give a shit. (laughter) If I give a shit, I would have to pack shit. (laughter) But I don't pack no shit cause I don't give a shit. (laughter) You wouldn't shit me, would you? (laughter) That's a joke when you're a kid with a worm looking out the bird's ass. You wouldn't shit me, would you? (laughter) It's an eight-year-old joke but a good one. (laughter) The additions to the list. I found three more words that had to be put on the list of words you could never say on television, and they were fart, turd and twat, those three. (laughter) Fart, we talked about, it's harmless. It's like tits, it's a cutie word, no problem. Turd, you can't say but who wants to, you know? (laughter) The subject never comes up on the panel so I'm not worried about that one. Now the word twat is an interesting word. Twat! Yeh, right in the twat. (laughter) Twat is an interesting word because it's the only one I know of, the only slang word applying to the, a part of the sexual anatomy that doesn't have another meaning to it. Like, ah, snatch, box and pussy all have other meanings, man. Even in a Walt Disney movie, you can say, We're going to snatch that pussy and put him in a box and bring him on the airplane. (murmur, laughter) Everybody loves it. The twat stands alone, man, as it should. And two-way words. Ah, ass is okay providing you're riding into town on a religious feast day. (laughter) You can't say, up your *ass*. (laughter) You can say, stuff it! (murmur) There are certain things you can say its weird but you can just come so close. Before I cut, I, uh, want to, ah, thank you for listening to my words, man, fellow, uh space travelers. Thank you man for tonight and thank you also. (clapping whistling)

JUSTICE POWELL, with whom JUSTICE BLACKMUN joins, concurring in part and concurring in the judgment.

I join Parts I, II, III, and IV-C of Justice Stevens' opinion.

I do not subscribe to the theory that the Justices of this Court are free generally to decide on the basis of its content which speech protected by the First Amendment is most "valuable" and hence deserving of the most protection, and which is less "valuable" and hence deserving of less protection. In my view, the result in this case does not turn on whether Carlin's monologue, viewed as a whole, or the words that constitute it, have more or less "value" than a candidate's campaign speech. This is a judgment for each person to make, not one for the judges to impose upon him.

The result turns instead on the unique characteristics of the broadcast media, combined with society's right to protect its children from speech generally agreed to be inappropriate for their years, and with the interest of unwilling adults in not being assaulted by such offensive speech in their homes.

JUSTICE BRENNAN, with whom JUSTICE MARSHALL joins, dissenting.

Without question, the privacy interests of an individual in his home are substantial and deserving of significant protection. In finding these interests sufficient to justify the content regulation of protected speech, however, the Court commits two errors. First, it misconceives the nature of the privacy interests involved where an individual voluntarily chooses to admit radio communications into his home. Second, it ignores the constitutionally protected interests of both those who wish to transmit and those who desire to receive broadcasts that many — including the FCC and this Court — might find offensive.

I believe that an individual's actions in switching on and listening to communications transmitted over the public airways and directed to the public at large do not implicate fundamental privacy interests, even when engaged in within the home. Instead, because the radio is undeniably a public medium, these actions are more properly viewed as a decision to take part, if only as a listener, in an ongoing public discourse.

[U]nlike other intrusive modes of communication, such as sound trucks, "[t]he radio can be turned off," Lehman v. Shaker Heights, 418 U.S. 298, 302 (1974) — and with a minimum of effort. Whatever the minimal discomfort suffered by a listener who inadvertently tunes into a program he finds offensive during the brief interval before he can simply extend his arm and switch stations or flick the "off" button, it is surely worth the candle to preserve the broadcaster's right to send, and the right of those interested to receive, a message entitled to full First Amendment protection.

The Court's balance, of necessity, fails to accord proper weight to the interests of listeners who wish to hear broadcasts the FCC deems offensive. It permits majoritarian tastes completely to preclude a protected message from entering the homes of a receptive, unoffended minority.

[P]arents, *not* the government, have the right to make certain decisions regarding the upbringing of their children. As surprising as it may be to individual Members of this Court, some parents may actually find Mr. Carlin's unabashed attitude towards the seven "dirty words" healthy, and deem it desirable to expose their children to the manner in which Mr. Carlin defuses the taboo surrounding the words.[7]

I would place the responsibility and the right to weed worthless and offensive communications from the public airways where it belongs and where, until today, it resided: in a public free to choose those communications worthy of its attention from a marketplace unsullied by the censor's hand.

II

The idea that the content of a message and its potential impact on any who might receive it can be divorced from the words that are the vehicle for its expression is transparently fallacious. A given word may have a unique capacity to capsule an idea, evoke an emotion, or conjure up an image. Indeed, for those of us who place an appropriately high value on our cherished First Amendment rights, the word "censor" is such a word.

My Brother Stevens finds relevant to his First Amendment analysis the fact that "[a]dults who feel the need may purchase tapes and records or go to theaters and nightclubs to hear [the tabooed] words." My Brother Powell agrees: "The Commission's holding does not prevent willing adults from purchasing Carlin's record, from attending his performances, or, indeed, from reading the transcript reprinted as an appendix to the Court's opinion." The opinions of my Brethren display both a sad insensitivity to the fact that these alternatives involve the expenditure of money, time, and effort that many of those wishing to hear Mr. Carlin's message may not be able to afford, and a naive innocence of the reality that in many cases, the medium may well be the message.

The airways are capable not only of carrying a message, but also of transforming it. A satirist's monologue may be most potent when delivered to a live audience; yet the choice whether this will in fact be the manner in which the message is delivered and received is one the First Amendment prohibits the government from making.

III

[I]n our land of cultural pluralism, there are many who think, act, and talk differently from the Members of this Court, and who do not share their fragile sensibilities. It is only an acute ethnocentric myopia that enables the Court to approve the censorship of communications solely because of the words they contain. The words that the Court and the Commission find so unpalatable may be the stuff of

7. The opinions of my Brothers Powell and Stevens rightly refrain from relying on the notion of "spectrum scarcity" to support their result. As Chief Judge Bazelon noted below, "although scarcity has justified *increasing* the diversity of speakers and speech, it has never been held to justify censorship." Pacifica Foundation v. FCC, 556 F.2d 9, 29 (1977).

everyday conversations in some, if not many, of the innumerable subcultures that compose this Nation. As one researcher concluded, "[w]ords generally considered obscene like 'bullshit' and 'fuck' are considered neither obscene nor derogatory in the [black] vernacular except in particular contextual situations and when used with certain intonations." C. Bins, Toward an Ethnography of Contemporary African American Oral Poetry, Language and Linguistics Working Papers No. 5, p. 82 (Georgetown Univ. Press 1972).

Today's decision will thus have its greatest impact on broadcasters desiring to reach, and listening audiences composed of, persons who do not share the Court's view as to which words or expressions are acceptable and who, for a variety of reasons, including a conscious desire to flout majoritarian conventions, express themselves using words that may be regarded as offensive by those from different socio-economic backgrounds. In this context, the Court's decision may be seen for what, in the broader perspective, it really is: another of the dominant culture's inevitable efforts to force those groups who do not share its mores to conform to its way of thinking, acting, and speaking.

[Dissenting opinion of JUSTICE STEWART is omitted.]

Notes and Questions

1. Uniquely Pervasive, Accessible Speech? In previous cases, the Supreme Court had rejected punishment for using these words in print. *Pacifica* relied on the uniqueness of broadcasting in upholding the constitutionality of the FCC's order. (Our edit of *Pacifica* deletes only a few citations and one footnote from Part IV-C of the Court's opinion.) Is *Pacifica* convincing in asserting that broadcasting is uniquely pervasive and uniquely accessible to children? That such uniqueness justifies the FCC penalizing indecency? That it justifies penalizing this broadcast?

Are these claims more persuasive than the claim in *Red Lion* that broadcasting is unique because it employs scarce resources?

2. Scarcity. Neither Justice Stevens' opinion nor Justice Powell's concurrence placed any weight on the scarcity rationale, and Justice Brennan's dissent stated flatly that scarcity cannot support censorship. The argument for this position is fairly straightforward: the theory of scarcity seeks to justify regulations that expand voices, not those that contract them. But could the scarcity argument apply more broadly? If scarcity justifies requirements that broadcasters provide favored programming, why wouldn't it also justify prohibiting them from wasting that scarce resource on disfavored programming, especially because such a prohibition would then make room for more valuable programming? After all, if the government prohibited all low-value programming, it would not be replaced with silence but with other programs that presumably would be of greater value.

In this regard, consider the statement in *Red Lion* regarding the "right of the public to receive suitable access to social, political, esthetic, moral, and other ideas and experiences." *Red Lion*, 395 U.S. at 390. If indecency has little value, would the right of the public suggested in *Red Lion* be vindicated by the replacement of indecency with speech that is more valuable?

3. The Unique Status of Broadcasting. Notice that two of the five Justices in the majority (Powell and Blackmun) relied exclusively on the unique status of broadcasting. For the others (Stevens, Burger, and Rehnquist), it was also important that indecent speech was being regulated. (*See* Part IV-B of the Stevens opinion, which Powell and Blackmun declined to join.) What, if any, limits do you suppose the Powell-Blackmun view would place on the ability of the FCC to censor? If broadcasting is unique, is it possible that other media are similarly unique? If other media are similarly unique, does this suggest that broadcasting is not unique after all?

4. Children. The FCC's briefs emphasized that its indecency regulation was aimed at protecting children under the age of twelve from indecent material. Does *Pacifica* suggest that its lenient review applies only to protections of "children . . . too young to read"? Conversely, would its reasoning apply if the FCC defined "children" as everyone under the age of eighteen?

5. Subsequent History. Through press announcements shortly after *Pacifica*, the FCC stated that it believed the decision applied only to the repeated use, solely for shock value, of the words Carlin employed, when broadcast before 10:00 p.m. The FCC brought no further indecency cases until, on a single day in 1987, it issued three indecency opinions and announced that it was broadening its interpretation of indecency.[8] The definition of indecent broadcast material was no longer limited to "the seven specific words at issue." Pacifica Foundation, Memorandum Opinion and Order, 2 FCC Rcd. 2698 ¶ 12. The FCC then said that "speech involving the description or depiction of sexual or excretory functions must be examined in context to determine whether it is patently offensive under contemporary community standards applicable to the broadcast medium." *Id.* ¶ 13. On reconsideration, the FCC noted that 12:00 midnight was its "current thinking" as to when the risk of children in the broadcast audience could reasonably be thought minimized. Infinity Broadcasting Corp. of Pennsylvania, 3 FCC Rcd. 930, 937 n.47 (1987).

Pacifica appealed these decisions, setting in motion a legal back-and-forth between Congress, the FCC, and the courts. In Action for Children's Television v. FCC, 852 F.2d 1332, 1335, 1342 (D.C. Cir. 1988) (*ACT I*), the D.C. Circuit rejected vagueness and overbroad challenges to the broader definition of indecency but found that the midnight time channeling advice "was not adequately thought

---

8. Pacifica Foundation, Memorandum Opinion and Order, 2 FCC Rcd. 2698 (1987); Infinity Broadcasting Corp. of Pa., Memorandum Opinion and Order, 2 FCC Rcd. 2705 (1987); Regents of the University of California, Memorandum Opinion and Order, 2 FCC Rcd. 2703 (1987). To avoid any doubt on this score, the FCC also issued a public notice summarizing the three orders released that day and "put[ting] all broadcast and amateur radio licensees on notice as to new standards that the Commission will apply in enforcing the prohibition against obscene and indecent transmissions." New Indecency Enforcement Standards to be Applied to All Broadcast and Amateur Radio Licensees, Public Notice, 2 FCC Rcd. 2726 (1987); *see ACT I*, 852 F.2d at 1336.

through." The court instructed the FCC, on remand, to "afford broadcasters clear notice of reasonably determined times at which indecent material safely may be aired." *Id.* at 1343. Before the FCC could follow this instruction, Congress intervened and required the FCC to ban indecent broadcasts altogether. Department of Commerce Appropriations Act, 1989, Pub. L. No. 100-459, § 608, 102 Stat. 2186, 2228 (1988). The FCC complied. Enforcement of Prohibitions Against Broadcast Obscenity and Indecency in 18 U.S.C. § 1464, Order, 4 FCC Rcd. 457 ¶ 2 (1988). In Action for Children's Television v. FCC, 932 F.2d 1504, 1509 (D.C. Cir. 1991) (*ACT II*), the D.C. Circuit struck down the total ban, concluding that neither the FCC's action nor the Congressional mandate that prompted it could pass constitutional muster. Shortly after the Supreme Court denied certiorari in *ACT II*, Congress intervened again, passing the Public Telecommunications Act of 1992, Pub. L. No. 102-356, 106 Stat. 949. Section 16(a) of the Act required the FCC to promulgate regulations to prohibit the broadcasting of indecent programming between 6:00 a.m. and midnight. 47 U.S.C. § 303 note. The FCC complied again. Enforcement of Prohibitions Against Broadcast Indecency in 18 U.S.C. § 1464, Report and Order, 8 FCC Rcd. 704, 711 (1993). Sitting en banc, the D.C. Circuit upheld section 16(c). Action for Children's Television v. FCC (*ACT III*), 58 F. 3d 654, 669 (D.C. Cir. 1995). The court held that the midnight to 6:00 a.m. safe harbor was narrowly tailored to serve the compelling government interests of protecting children from indecent material and facilitating parental supervision, and thus survived First Amendment scrutiny. The court stated that "the Supreme Court has never suggested that a scientific demonstration of psychological harm is required in order to establish the constitutionality of measures protecting minors from exposure to indecent speech." *Id.* at 661–62. And as to tailoring, the court concluded that the statute reduced children's exposure to indecency and "does not unnecessarily interfere with the ability of adults to watch or listen to such materials both because substantial numbers of them are active after midnight and because adults have so many alternative ways of satisfying their tastes at other times." *Id.* at 667.

In 2001, the FCC issued a policy statement that was designed to "provide guidance to the broadcast industry" on the FCC's indecency enforcement policies. Industry Guidance on the Commission's Case Law Interpreting 18 U.S.C. § 1464 and Enforcement Policies Regarding Broadcast Indecency, Policy Statement, 16 FCC Rcd. 7999 ¶ 1 (2001). It restated the FCC's existing position, emphasizing explicitness, repetition, and whether the material was designed to titillate or for its shock value. *Id.* ¶ 10. Insofar as this policy statement was designed to offer clarity, that was undermined by the FCC issuing and then reversing two indecency fines.[9]

---

9. *See* KBOO Foundation, Notice of Apparent Liability for Forfeiture, 16 FCC Rcd. 10,731 ¶ 8 (2001) (concluding in a single paragraph that broadcast of the song "Your Revolution" by Sarah Jones was indecent, even though its most graphic phrase was "A six foot blow job machine."); KBOO Foundation, Memorandum Opinion and Order, 18 FCC Rcd. 2472 ¶ 9 (2003) (rescinding the previous order without suggesting that any new facts had come to light, stating that "we now conclude that the broadcast was not indecent because, on balance and in context, the sexual descriptions in

In 2004, in the course of another reversal, the FCC issued an order declaring that "While prior Commission and staff action have indicated that isolated or fleeting broadcasts of the 'F-Word' such as that here are not indecent or would not be acted upon, . . . we conclude that any such interpretation is no longer good law." Complaints Against Various Broadcast Licensees Regarding Their Airing of the "Golden Globe Awards" Program, Memorandum Opinion and Order, 19 FCC Rcd. 4975, 4890 ¶ 12 (2004) (reversing an order finding Bono's utterance "This is really, really fucking brilliant" upon receiving a Golden Globe Award not indecent, and instead finding the utterance actionably indecent). But shortly thereafter, the FCC found repeated use of the word "fuck" to show "the horrors of war" in a Veterans' Day context not indecent. Complaints Against Various Television Licensees Regarding Their Broadcast on November 11, 2004, of the ABC Television Network's Presentation of the Film "Saving Private Ryan," Memorandum Opinion and Order, 20 FCC Rcd. 4507 ¶¶ 13, 16 (2005) (noting that "in context, the dialogue, including the complained-of material, is neither gratuitous nor in any way intended or used to pander, titillate or shock").

In 2003, the FCC began issuing fines 30 times the previous average in high profile cases.[10] In 2006, Congress raised the stakes further by passing legislation raising the FCC's maximum authority to fine broadcast licensees from $32,500 per violation to $325,000 per violation, with a $3 million cap for a multiday continuing violation. Broadcast Decency Enforcement Act of 2005, Pub. L. No. 109-235, 120 Stat. 491. Also in 2006, Fox brought a challenge to the FCC's imposition of fines for the iterations of "fuck" by Cher and Nicole Richie at the 2002 and 2003 Billboard Music Awards. The Second Circuit rejected the FCC's shift in policy as violating the Administrative Procedure Act and declined to address the First Amendment challenge. Fox Television Stations, Inc. v. FCC, 489 F.3d 444, 462 (2d Cir. 2007). The Supreme Court reversed and remanded, finding no violation of the Administrative Procedure Act

---

the song are not sufficiently graphic to warrant sanction."); Citadel Broadcasting Company, Notice of Apparent Liability for Forfeiture, 16 FCC Rcd. 11,839 (2001) (imposing a fine for the airing of the "radio edit" version of Eminem's song "The Real Slim Shady," even though the radio edit omitted the most offensive language); Citadel Broadcasting Company, Memorandum Opinion and Order, 17 FCC Rcd. 483 (2002) (reversing that fine, despite the absence of any new facts).

10. Until 2003, FCC fines for indecency (called "Notices of Apparent Liability") were fairly rare and relatively small. From November 1999 through September 2003, for example, the FCC issued a total of twenty-two Notices of Apparent Liability totaling $265,900, for an average of $12,086 per fine. *See* FCC Enforcement Bureau, Obscene, Profane & Indecent Broadcasts: Notices of Apparent Liability, https://www.fcc.gov/general/obscene-profane-indecent-broadcasts-notices-apparent-liability. Beginning in October 2003, however, the Commission started issuing big fines in some high-profile cases. For instance, the Commission issued a $3.6 million for CBS broadcasters' airing an episode of "Without a Trace" featuring a teenage orgy, $1.1 million for Fox broadcasters' airing of contestants cavorting with strippers on "Married with America," $550,000 against Viacom for the 2004 Super Bowl halftime show, and $495,000 against Clear Channel for a Howard Stern episode featuring "dialogue between cast members regarding the sexual practices of certain program cast members and a discussion with a guest regarding 'Sphincterine,' a purported personal hygiene product designed for use prior to sexual activity." Clear Channel Broadcasting Licenses, Inc., Notice of Apparent Liability for Forfeiture, 19 FCC Rcd. 6773 ¶ 2 (2004).

and declining to reach the First Amendment issue, given that the Second Circuit had not reached that issue. FCC v. Fox Television Stations, Inc. 556 U.S. 502, 529 (2009) (*Fox I*). On remand, the Second Circuit confronted the First Amendment issues that it had avoided in its original opinion and held that the FCC's flexible standard for determining patent offensiveness was unconstitutionally vague. Fox Television Stations, Inc. v. FCC, 613 F.3d 317, 330 (2d Cir. 2010). The Supreme Court granted certiorari and vacated the Second Circuit's opinion on fair notice grounds under the Due Process Clause and for that reason declining to address the First Amendment arguments. FCC v. Fox Television Stations, Inc., 567 U.S. 239, 258 (2012) (*Fox II*). Thus the FCC's handling of Cher's and Nicole Richie's language resulted in two Supreme Court opinions that had no holding on, or even substantive discussion of, *Pacifica* and the First Amendment issues raised by the FCC's imposition of these penalties.

In light of this history, what advice would you give to: (a) a member of Congress who wanted to regulate broadcast indecency as much as the First Amendment allows, (b) an FCC Commissioner who wanted to have some enforceable and meaningful limits on broadcast indecency, and (c) a television broadcaster who wanted to air as much indecency as possible without being subject to huge fines?

6. Empirical Data on Indecency. In *Fox I*, the majority held that the applicable law (the Administrative Procedure Act) did not require empirical evidence of harms from exposure to expletives:

> There are some propositions for which scant empirical evidence can be marshaled, and the harmful effect of broadcast profanity on children is one of them. One cannot demand a multiyear controlled study, in which some children are intentionally exposed to indecent broadcasts (and insulated from all other indecency), and others are shielded from all indecency. It is one thing to set aside agency action under the Administrative Procedure Act because of failure to adduce empirical data that can readily be obtained. It is something else to insist upon obtaining the unobtainable.

556 U.S. at 519. Justice Breyer, in response, stated:

> Like the majority, I do not believe that an agency must always conduct full empirical studies of such matters. But the FCC could have referred to, and explained, relevant empirical studies that suggest the contrary. One review of the empirical evidence, for example, reports that "[i]t is doubtful that children under the age of 12 understand sexual language and innuendo; therefore it is unlikely that vulgarities have any negative effect." Barbara K. Kaye & Barry S. Sapolsky, Watch Your Mouth! An Analysis of Profanity Uttered by Children on Prime-Time Television, 7 J. Mass Comm'n & Soc'y 429, 433 (2004) (citing two studies).

Id. at 564 (Breyer, J., dissenting).

Fox I focused on expletives. There is more empirical evidence on the possible harms associated with consumption of visual indecency, most notably pornography.

Some research has found a positive relationship between exposure to some forms of pornography and sexism.[11] Other studies have found that pornography use is associated with either no effect or a decrease in sex crimes and sexism.[12]

What, if any, role should such studies play in considering the First Amendment issues raised by indecency regulation?

§ 11.B.1.b. Regulation of Cable Indecency

18 U.S.C. § 1464 prohibits "any obscene, indecent, profane language by means of radio communication," and so does not apply outside the "radio communication" context. 18 U.S.C. § 1468 is the companion statute that specifically applies to "cable television [and] subscription services on television," but it prohibits only obscenity.[13] Congress has, though, enacted legislation aimed at channeling (though not banning) cable indecency.

As *Pacifica* and its aftermath showed, the federal government has long sought to reduce the amount of indecent programming available on broadcast television. The federal government's efforts at regulating cable indecency, by contrast, are both of somewhat more recent vintage and narrower scope. It was not until the 1992 Cable Act that Congress made any serious effort to regulate cable indecency. The regulation involved the only channels (apart from those subject to must-carry, addressed in the *Turner* cases in Chapter 3.A) that cable operators are mandated to carry and thus do not choose: the commercial leased access and public, educational, or governmental (PEG) channels. The Supreme Court's splintered response follows.

---

11. *See, e.g.,* Malvina N. Skorska et al., Experimental Effects of Degrading Versus Erotic Pornography Exposure in Men on Reactions Toward Women (Objectification, Sexism, Discrimination), 27 Canadian J. Hum. Sexuality 1 (2018); Gert Martin Hald et al., Pornography and Attitudes Supporting Violence Against Women: Revisiting the Relationship in Nonexperimental Studies, 36 Aggressive Behavior 14 (2010).

12. *See, e.g.,* Milton Diamond, Pornography, Public Acceptance and Sex Related Crime: A Review, 32 Int'l J.L. & Psychiatry 304 (2009); Taylor Kohut et al., Is Pornography Really About "Making Hate to Women"? Pornography Users Hold More Gender Egalitarian Attitudes Than Nonusers in a Representative American Sample, 53 J. Sex Research 1 (2016); Dan J. Miller et al., Pornography Use and Sexism Among Heterosexual Men, 37 Communication Res. Reports 110 (2020); David Speed et al., Pornography Consumption and Attitudes Towards Pornography Legality Predict Attitudes of Sexual Equality, 58 J. Sex. Research 396 (2021); Crystal A. Jackson et al., Exposing Men's Gender Role Attitudes as Porn Superfans, 34 Sociological Forum 483 (2019); Sheila Garos et al., Sexism and Pornography Use: Toward Explaining Past (Null) Results, 16 J. Psychology & Hum. Sexuality 69 (2008).

13. More broadly, the FCC's longstanding position has been that "subscription-based services do not call into play the issue of indecency," Litigation Recovery Trust, Memorandum Opinion and Order, 17 FCC Rcd. 21,852, 21,856 (2002), and that "[c]onsistent with existing case law, the Commission does not impose regulations regarding indecency on services lacking the indiscriminate access to children that characterizes broadcasting." Harriscope of Chicago, Inc., Memorandum Opinion and Order, 3 FCC Rcd. 757, 760 n.2 (1988).

Denver Area Educational Telecommunications Consortium, Inc. v. FCC

518 U.S. 727 (1996)

BREYER, J., announced the judgment of the Court and delivered the opinion of the Court with respect to Part III, in which STEVENS, O'CONNOR, KENNEDY, SOUTER, and GINSBURG, JJ., joined, an opinion with respect to Parts I, II, and V, in which STEVENS, O'CONNOR and SOUTER, JJ., joined, and an opinion with respect to Parts IV and VI, in which STEVENS and SOUTER, JJ., joined. STEVENS, J., and SOUTER, J., filed concurring opinions. O'CONNOR, J., filed an opinion concurring in part and dissenting in part. KENNEDY, J., filed an opinion concurring in part, concurring in the judgment in part, and dissenting in part, in which GINSBURG, J., joined. THOMAS, J., filed an opinion concurring in the judgment in part and dissenting in part, in which REHNQUIST, C.J., and SCALIA, J., joined.

JUSTICE BREYER announced the judgment of the Court.

I

A "leased channel" is a channel that federal law requires a cable system operator to reserve for commercial lease by unaffiliated third parties. About 10 to 15 percent of a cable system's channels would typically fall into this category. "Public, educational, or governmental channels" (which we shall call "public access" channels) are channels that, over the years, local governments have required cable system operators to set aside for public, educational, or governmental purposes as part of the consideration an operator gives in return for permission to install cables under city streets and to use public rights-of-way. Between 1984 and 1992, federal law (as had much pre-1984 state law, in respect to public access channels) prohibited cable system operators from exercising *any* editorial control over the content of any program broadcast over either leased or public access channels.

In 1992, in an effort to control sexually explicit programming conveyed over access channels, Congress enacted the three provisions before us. The first two provisions relate to leased channels. The first says:

> This subsection shall permit a cable operator to enforce prospectively a written and published policy of prohibiting programming that the cable operator reasonably believes describes or depicts sexual or excretory activities or organs in a patently offensive manner as measured by contemporary community standards.

Cable Television Consumer Protection and Competition Act of 1992 (1992 Act or Act), Pub. L. No. 102-385, § 10(a)(2), 106 Stat. 1460, 1486 (1992).

The second provision, applicable only to leased channels, requires cable operators to segregate and to block similar programming if they decide to permit, rather than to prohibit, its broadcast. The provision tells the Federal Communications Commission (FCC or Commission) to promulgate regulations that will (a) require "programmers to inform cable operators if the program[ming] would be indecent as defined by Commission regulations"; (b) require "cable operators to place" such material "on a single channel"; and (c) require "cable operators to block such single channel unless the subscriber requests access to such channel in writing." 1992 Act, § 10(b)(1).

The third provision is similar to the first provision, but applies only to public access channels. The relevant statutory section instructs the FCC to promulgate regulations that will

> enable a cable operator of a cable system to prohibit the use, on such system, of any channel capacity of any public, educational, or governmental access facility for any programming which contains obscene material, sexually explicit conduct, or material soliciting or promoting unlawful conduct.

1992 Act, § 10(c).

The FCC, carrying out this statutory instruction, promulgated regulations defining "sexually explicit" in language almost identical to that in the statute's leased channel provision, namely as descriptions or depictions of "sexual or excretory activities or organs in a patently offensive manner" as measured by the cable viewing community.

The upshot is that the federal law before us (the statute as implemented through regulations) now *permits* cable operators either to allow or to forbid the transmission of "patently offensive" sex-related materials over both leased and public access channels, and *requires* those operators, at a minimum, to segregate and to block transmission of that same material on leased channels.

II

We turn initially to the provision that *permits* cable system operators to prohibit "patently offensive" (or "indecent") programming transmitted over leased access channels. 1992 Act, § 10(a). [The Court of Appeals] viewed this statute's "permissive" provisions as not themselves restricting speech, but, rather, as simply reaffirming the authority to pick and choose programming that a private entity, say, a private broadcaster, would have had in the absence of intervention by any federal, or local, governmental entity.

Nonetheless, petitioners point to circumstances that, in their view, make the analogy with private broadcasters inapposite and make this case a special one, warranting a different constitutional result. As a practical matter, they say, cable system operators have considerably more power to "censor" program viewing than do broadcasters, for individual communities typically have only one cable system, linking broadcasters and other program providers with each community's many subscribers. Moreover, concern about system operators' exercise of this considerable power originally led government — local and federal — to insist that operators provide leased and public access channels free of operator editorial control. To permit system operators to supervise programming on leased access channels will create the very private-censorship risk that this anticensorship effort sought to avoid.

Under these circumstances, petitioners conclude, Congress' "permissive" law, *in actuality*, will "abridge" their free speech. And this Court should treat that law as a congressionally imposed, content-based, restriction unredeemed as a properly tailored effort to serve a "compelling interest."

Like petitioners, Justices Kennedy and Thomas would have us decide these cases simply by transferring and applying literally categorical standards this Court has developed in other contexts. For Justice Kennedy, leased access channels are like a common carrier, cablecast is a protected medium, strict scrutiny applies, § 10(a) fails this test, and, therefore, § 10(a) is invalid. For Justice Thomas, the case is simple because the cable operator who owns the system over which access channels are broadcast, like a bookstore owner with respect to what it displays on the shelves, has a predominant First Amendment interest. Both categorical approaches suffer from the same flaws: They import law developed in very different contexts into a new and changing environment, and they lack the flexibility necessary to allow government to respond to very serious practical problems without sacrificing the free exchange of ideas the First Amendment is designed to protect.

The history of this Court's First Amendment jurisprudence, however, is one of continual development, as the Constitution's general command that "Congress shall make no law ... abridging the freedom of speech, or of the press," has been applied to new circumstances requiring different adaptations of prior principles and precedents.

This tradition teaches that the First Amendment embodies an overarching commitment to protect speech from government regulation through close judicial scrutiny, thereby enforcing the Constitution's constraints, but without imposing judicial formulas so rigid that they become a straitjacket that disables government from responding to serious problems. This Court, in different contexts, has consistently held that government may directly regulate speech to address extraordinary problems, where its regulations are appropriately tailored to resolve those problems without imposing an unnecessarily great restriction on speech. Justices Kennedy and Thomas would have us further declare which, among the many applications of the general approach that this Court has developed over the years, we are applying here. But no definitive choice among competing analogies (broadcast, common carrier, bookstore) allows us to declare a rigid single standard, good for now and for all future media and purposes. That is not to say that we reject all the more specific formulations of the standard — they appropriately cover the vast majority of cases involving government regulation of speech. Rather, aware as we are of the changes taking place in the law, the technology, and the industrial structure related to telecommunications, we believe it unwise and unnecessary definitively to pick one analogy or one specific set of words now. We therefore think it premature to answer the broad questions that Justices Kennedy and Thomas raise in their efforts to find a definitive analogy, deciding, for example, the extent to which private property can be designated a public forum; whether public access channels are a public forum; whether the Government's viewpoint neutral decision to limit a public forum is subject to the same scrutiny as a selective exclusion from a pre-existing public forum; whether exclusion from common carriage must for all purposes be treated like exclusion from a public forum; and whether the interests of the owners of communications media always subordinate the interests of all other users of a medium.

Rather than decide these issues, we can decide these cases more narrowly, by closely scrutinizing § 10(a) to assure that it properly addresses an extremely important problem, without imposing, in light of the relevant interests, an unnecessarily great restriction on speech.

First, the provision before us comes accompanied with an extremely important justification, one that this Court has often found compelling — the need to protect children from exposure to patently offensive sex-related material.

Second, the provision arises in a very particular context — congressional *permission* for cable operators to regulate programming that, but for a previous Act of Congress, would have had no path of access to cable channels free of an operator's control. The First Amendment interests involved are therefore complex, and require a balance between those interests served by the access requirements themselves (increasing the availability of avenues of expression to programmers who otherwise would not have them) and the disadvantage to the First Amendment interests of cable operators and other programmers (those to whom the cable operator would have assigned the channels devoted to access).

Third, the problem Congress addressed here is remarkably similar to the problem addressed by the FCC in *Pacifica*, and the balance Congress struck is commensurate with the balance we approved there. In *Pacifica* this Court considered a governmental ban of a radio broadcast of "indecent" materials.

The Court found this ban constitutionally permissible primarily because "broadcasting is uniquely accessible to children" and children were likely listeners to the program there at issue — an afternoon radio broadcast. *Id.* at 749–50. In addition, the Court wrote, "the broadcast media have established a uniquely pervasive presence in the lives of all Americans," *id.* at 748, "[p]atently offensive, indecent material . . . confronts the citizen, not only in public, but also in the privacy of the home," generally without sufficient prior warning to allow the recipient to avert his or her eyes or ears, *id.*; and "[a]dults who feel the need may purchase tapes and records or go to theaters and nightclubs" to hear similar performances. *Id.* at 750 n.28.

All these factors are present here. Cable television broadcasting, including access channel broadcasting, is as "accessible to children" as over-the-air broadcasting, if not more so. Cable television systems, including access channels, "have established a uniquely pervasive presence in the lives of all Americans." *Pacifica, supra*, at 748. "Patently offensive" material from these stations can "confront[] the citizen" in the "privacy of the home," *Pacifica, supra*, at 748, with little or no prior warning. There is nothing to stop "adults who feel the need" from finding similar programming elsewhere, say, on tape or in theaters.

Fourth, the permissive nature of § 10(a) means that it likely restricts speech less than, not more than, the ban at issue in *Pacifica*. [A]lthough the provision does create a risk that a program will not appear, that risk is not the same as the certainty that accompanies a governmental ban.

The existence of this complex balance of interests persuades us that the permissive nature of the provision, coupled with its viewpoint-neutral application, is a constitutionally permissible way to protect children from the type of sexual material that concerned Congress, while accommodating both the First Amendment interests served by the access requirements and those served in restoring to cable operators a degree of the editorial control that Congress removed in 1984.

III

The statute's second provision significantly differs from the first, for it does not simply permit, but rather requires, cable system operators to restrict speech — by segregating and blocking "patently offensive" sex-related material appearing on leased channels (but not on other channels). 1992 Act, § 10(b). In particular, this provision and its implementing regulations require cable system operators to place "patently offensive" leased channel programming on a separate channel; to block that channel; to unblock the channel within 30 days of a subscriber's written request for access; and to reblock the channel within 30 days of a subscriber's request for reblocking. Also, leased channel programmers must notify cable operators of an intended "patently offensive" broadcast up to 30 days before its scheduled broadcast date.

These requirements have obvious restrictive effects. The Government argues that, despite these adverse consequences, the "segregate and block" requirements are lawful because they are "the least restrictive means of realizing" a "compelling interest," namely "protecting the physical and psychological well-being of minors." *See* Brief for Federal Respondents 11.

We agree with the Government that protection of children is a "compelling interest." But we do not agree that the "segregate and block" requirements properly accommodate the speech restrictions they impose and the legitimate objective they seek to attain. Nor need we here determine whether, or the extent to which, *Pacifica* does, or does not, impose some lesser standard of review where indecent speech is at issue, *compare* 438 U.S. at 745–48 (opinion of Stevens, J.) (indecent materials enjoy lesser First Amendment protection), *with id.* at 761–62 (Powell, J., concurring in part and concurring in judgment) (refusing to accept a lesser standard for nonobscene, indecent material). That is because once one examines this governmental restriction, it becomes apparent that, not only is it not a "least restrictive alternative" and is not "narrowly tailored" to meet its legitimate objective, it also seems considerably "more extensive than necessary." That is to say, it fails to satisfy this Court's formulations of the First Amendment's "strictest," as well as its somewhat less "strict," requirements.

Several circumstances lead us to this conclusion. For one thing, the law, as recently amended, uses other means to protect children from similar "patently offensive" material broadcast on *un*leased cable channels, i.e., broadcast over any of a system's numerous ordinary, or public access, channels. The law, as recently amended, requires cable operators to "scramble or . . . block" such programming on any (unleased) channel "*primarily dedicated* to sexually-oriented programming." Telecommunications Act of 1996, § 505, 110 Stat. 136 (emphasis added). In addition, cable operators must honor a subscriber's request to block any, or all, programs on any channel to which he or she does not wish to subscribe. § 504. And manufacturers, in the future, will have to make television sets with a so-called "V-chip" — a device that will be able automatically to identify and block sexually explicit or violent programs. § 551.

Although we cannot, and do not, decide whether the new provisions are themselves lawful (a matter not before us), we note that they are significantly less restrictive than the provision here at issue. They do not force the viewer to receive (for days or weeks at a time) all "patently offensive" programming or none; they will not lead the viewer automatically to judge the few by the reputation of the many; and they will not automatically place the occasional viewer's name on a special list. They therefore inevitably lead us to ask why, if they adequately protect children from "patently offensive" material broadcast on ordinary channels, they would not offer adequate protection from similar leased channel broadcasts as well? Alternatively, if these provisions do not adequately protect children from "patently offensive" material broadcast on ordinary channels, how could one justify more severe leased channel restrictions when (given ordinary channel programming) they would yield so little additional protection for children?

The record does not answer these questions. It does not explain why, under the new Act, blocking alone — without written access-requests — adequately protects children from exposure to regular sex-dedicated channels, but cannot adequately protect those children from programming on similarly sex-dedicated channels that are leased. It does not explain why a simple subscriber blocking request system, perhaps a phone-call based system, would adequately protect children from "patently offensive" material broadcast on ordinary non-sex-dedicated channels (i.e., almost all channels) but a far more restrictive segregate/block/written-access system is needed to protect children from similar broadcasts on what (in the absence of the segregation requirement) would be non-sex-dedicated channels that are leased. Nor is there any indication Congress thought the new ordinary channel protections less than adequate.

Consequently, we cannot find that the "segregate and block" restrictions on speech are a narrowly, or reasonably, tailored effort to protect children. For that reason they are not consistent with the First Amendment.

IV

The statute's third provision, as implemented by FCC regulation, is similar to its first provision, in that it too *permits* a cable operator to prevent transmission of "patently offensive" programming, in this case on public access channels. 1992 Act § 10(c). But there are four important differences.

The first is the historical background. [C]able operators have traditionally agreed to reserve channel capacity for public, governmental, and educational channels as part of the consideration they give municipalities that award them cable franchises. Significantly, these are channels over which cable operators have not historically exercised editorial control. Unlike § 10(a) therefore, § 10(c) does not restore to cable operators editorial rights that they once had.

The second difference is the institutional background that has developed as a result of the historical difference. When a "leased channel" is made available by the operator to a private lessee, the lessee has total control of programming during the leased time slot. Public access channels, on the other hand, are normally subject to complex supervisory systems of various sorts, often with both public and private elements. *See* § 531(b) (franchising authorities "may require rules and procedures for the use of the [public access] channel capacity"). Municipalities generally provide in their cable franchising agreements for an access channel manager, who is most commonly a nonprofit organization, but may also be the municipality, or, in some instances, the cable system owner. Access channel activity and management are partly financed with public funds—through franchise fees or other payments pursuant to the franchise agreement, or from general municipal funds and are commonly subject to supervision by a local supervisory board.

This system of public, private, and mixed nonprofit elements, through its supervising boards and nonprofit or governmental access managers, can set programming policy and approve or disapprove particular programming services. Whether these locally accountable bodies prescreen programming, promulgate rules for the use of public access channels, or are merely available to respond when problems arise, the upshot is the same: There is a locally accountable body capable of addressing the problem, should it arise, of patently offensive programming broadcast to children, making it unlikely that many children will in fact be exposed to programming considered patently offensive in that community.

Third, the existence of a system aimed at encouraging and securing programming that the community considers valuable strongly suggests that a "cable operator's veto" is less likely necessary to achieve the statute's basic objective, protecting children, than a similar veto in the context of leased channels.

Finally, our examination of the legislative history and the record before us is consistent with what common sense suggests, namely that the public/nonprofit programming control systems now in place would normally avoid, minimize, or eliminate any child-related problems concerning "patently offensive" programming. The Commission itself did not report *any* examples of "indecent" programs on public access channels.

The upshot, in respect to the public access channels, is a law that could radically change present programming-related relationships among local community and nonprofit supervising boards and access managers, which relationships are established through municipal law, regulation, and contract. In doing so, it would not significantly restore editorial rights of cable operators, but would greatly increase the risk that certain categories of programming (say, borderline offensive programs) will not appear. At the same time, given present supervisory mechanisms, the need for this particular provision, aimed directly at public access channels, is not obvious. [W]e conclude that the Government cannot sustain its burden of showing that § 10(c) is necessary to protect children or that it is appropriately tailored to secure that end. Consequently, we find that this third provision violates the First Amendment.

VI

For these reasons, the judgment of the Court of Appeals is affirmed insofar as it upheld § 10(a); the judgment of the Court of Appeals is reversed insofar as it upheld § 10(b) and § 10(c).

[Concurring opinions of JUSTICE STEVENS and of JUSTICE SOUTER are omitted.]

JUSTICE O'CONNOR, concurring in part and dissenting in part.

I am not persuaded that the difference in the origin of the access channels is sufficient to justify upholding § 10(a) and striking down § 10(c). The interest in protecting children remains the same, whether on a leased access channel or a public access channel, and allowing the cable operator the option of prohibiting the transmission of indecent speech seems a constitutionally permissible means of addressing that interest. Nor is the fact that public access programming may be subject to supervisory systems in addition to the cable operator, sufficient in my mind to render § 10(c) so ill-tailored to its goal as to be unconstitutional.

JUSTICE KENNEDY, with whom JUSTICE GINSBURG joins, concurring in part, concurring in the judgment in part, and dissenting in part.

Though I join Part III of the opinion (there for the Court) striking down § 10(b) of the Act, and concur in the judgment that § 10(c) is unconstitutional, with respect I dissent from the remainder.

I

Two provisions of the 1992 Act, §§ 10(a) and (c), authorize the operator of a cable system to exclude certain programming from two different kinds of channels. Section 10(a) concerns leased access channels. Section 10(c) involves public, educational, and governmental access channels (or PEG access channels, as they are known).

Though the two provisions differ in significant respects, they have common flaws. In both instances, Congress singles out one sort of speech for vulnerability to private censorship in a context where content-based discrimination is not otherwise permitted. Sections 10(a) and (c) disadvantage nonobscene, indecent programming, a protected category of expression on the basis of its content. The Constitution in general does not tolerate content-based restriction of, or discrimination against, speech. In the realm of speech and expression, the First Amendment envisions the citizen shaping the government, not the reverse.

Sections 10(a) and (c) are unusual. They do not require direct action against speech, but do authorize a cable operator to deny the use of its property to certain forms of speech. As a general matter, a private person may exclude certain speakers from his or her property without violating the First Amendment, and if §§ 10(a) and (c) were no more than affirmations of this principle they might be unremarkable. Access channels, however, are property of the cable operator, dedicated or otherwise reserved for programming of other speakers or the government. A public access channel is a public forum, and laws requiring leased access channels create common-carrier obligations. When the government identifies certain speech on the basis of its content as vulnerable to exclusion from a common carrier or public forum, strict scrutiny applies. These laws cannot survive this exacting review. However compelling Congress' interest in shielding children from indecent programming, the provisions in this case are not drawn with enough care to withstand scrutiny under our precedents.

III B

In providing public access channels under their franchise agreements, cable operators are not exercising their own First Amendment rights. They serve as conduits for the speech of others. Section 10(c) thus restores no power of editorial discretion over public access channels that the cable operator once had; the discretion never existed. It vests the cable operator with a power under federal law, defined by reference to the content of speech, to override the franchise agreement and undercut the public forum the agreement creates. By enacting a law in 1992 excluding indecent programming from protection but retaining the prohibition on cable operators' editorial control over all other protected speech, the Federal Government at the same time ratified the public-forum character of public access channels but discriminated against certain speech based on its content.

[I]t seems to me clear that when a local government contracts to use private property for public expressive activity, it creates a public forum. Regulations of speech content in a designated public forum, whether of limited or unlimited character, are "subject to the highest scrutiny" and "survive only if they are narrowly drawn to achieve a compelling state interest." International Soc. for Krishna Consciousness, Inc. v. Lee, 505 U.S. 672, 678 (1992).

C

The constitutionality under Turner Broadcasting System, Inc. v. FCC, 512 U.S. 622 (1994), of requiring a cable operator to set aside leased access channels is not before us. For purposes of this case, we should treat the cable operator's rights in these channels as extinguished, and address the issue these petitioners present: namely, whether the Government can discriminate on the basis of content in affording protection to certain programmers.

Laws requiring cable operators to provide leased access are the practical equivalent of making them common carriers, analogous in this respect to telephone companies: They are obliged to provide a conduit for the speech of others.

Laws removing common-carriage protection from a single form of speech based on its content should be reviewed under the same standard as content-based restrictions on speech in a public forum. Making a cable operator a common carrier does not create a public forum in the sense of taking property from private control and dedicating it to public use; rather, regulations of a common carrier dictate the manner in which private control is exercised. A common-carriage mandate, nonetheless, serves the same function as a public forum. It ensures open, nondiscriminatory access to the means of communication. This purpose is evident in the statute itself and in the committee findings supporting it.

Giving government free rein to exclude speech it dislikes by delimiting public fora (or common-carriage provisions) would have pernicious effects in the modern age. Minds are not changed in streets and parks as they once were. To an increasing degree, the more significant interchanges of ideas and shaping of public consciousness occur in mass and electronic media. The extent of public entitlement to participate in those means of communication may be changed as technologies change; and in expanding those entitlements the Government has no greater right to discriminate on suspect grounds than it does when it effects a ban on speech against the backdrop of the entitlements to which we have been more accustomed. It contravenes the First Amendment to give Government a general license to single out some categories of speech for lesser protection so long as it stops short of viewpoint discrimination.

IV

At a minimum, the proper standard for reviewing §§10(a) and (c) is strict scrutiny. The plurality gives no reason why it should be otherwise. I would hold these enactments unconstitutional because they are not narrowly tailored to serve a compelling interest.

The Government has no compelling interest in restoring a cable operator's First Amendment right of editorial discretion. As to §10(c), Congress has no interest at all, since under most franchises operators had no rights of editorial discretion over PEG access channels in the first place. As to §10(a), any governmental interest in restoring operator discretion over indecent programming on leased access channels is too minimal to justify the law. First, the transmission of indecent programming over leased access channels is not forced speech of the operator. *Turner, supra*, at 655–56. Second, the discretion conferred by the law is slight. The operator is not authorized to place programs of its own liking on the leased access channels, nor to remove other speech (racist or violent, for example) that might be offensive to it or to viewers. The operator is just given a veto over the one kind of lawful speech Congress disdains.

Congress does have, however, a compelling interest in protecting children from indecent speech. Sections 10(a) and (c) nonetheless are not narrowly tailored to protect children from indecent programs on access channels. First, to the extent some operators may allow indecent programming, children in localities those operators serve will be left unprotected. [T]he interest in protecting children from indecency only at the caprice of the cable operator is not compelling.

Second, to the extent cable operators prohibit indecent programming on access channels, not only children but adults will be deprived of it. A block-and-segregate requirement similar to § 10(b), but without its constitutional infirmity of requiring persons to place themselves on a list to receive programming, protects children with far less intrusion on the liberties of programmers and adult viewers than allowing cable operators to ban indecent programming from access channels altogether.

Sections 10(a) and (c) present a classic case of discrimination against speech based on its content. There are legitimate reasons why the Government might wish to regulate or even restrict the speech at issue here, but §§ 10(a) and 10(c) are not drawn to address those reasons with the precision the First Amendment requires.

VI

In agreement with the plurality's analysis of § 10(b) of the Act, insofar as it applies strict scrutiny, I join Part III of its opinion. Its position there, however, cannot be reconciled with upholding § 10(a). In the plurality's view, § 10(b), which standing alone would guarantee an indecent programmer some access to a cable audience, violates the First Amendment, but § 10(a), which authorizes exclusion of indecent programming from access channels altogether, does not. There is little to commend this logic or result. I dissent from the judgment of the Court insofar as it upholds the constitutionality of § 10(a).

JUSTICE THOMAS, joined by CHIEF JUSTICE REHNQUIST and JUSTICE SCALIA, concurring in the judgment in part and dissenting in part.

I agree with the principal opinion's conclusion that § 10(a) is constitutionally permissible, but I disagree with its conclusion that §§ 10(b) and (c) violate the First Amendment.

II A

As I read [the provisions on leased access and PEG channels], they provide leased and public access programmers with an expansive and federally enforced statutory right to transmit virtually any programming over access channels, limited only by the bounds of decency.

Petitioners must concede that cable access is not a constitutionally required entitlement and that the right they claim to leased and public access has, by definition, been governmentally created at the expense of cable operators' editorial discretion. Just because the Court has apparently accepted, for now, the proposition that the Constitution permits some degree of forced speech in the cable context does not mean that the beneficiaries of a government-imposed forced speech program enjoy additional First Amendment protections beyond those normally afforded to purely private speakers.

The question petitioners pose is whether §§ 10(a) and (c) are improper restrictions on their free speech rights, but *Turner* strongly suggests that the proper question is whether the leased and public access requirements (with §§10(a) and (c)) are improper restrictions on the *operators'* free speech rights. In my view, the constitutional presumption properly runs in favor of the operators' editorial discretion, and that discretion may not be burdened without a compelling reason for doing so.

It is one thing to compel an operator to carry leased and public access speech, in apparent violation of Miami Herald Publishing Co. v. Tornillo, 418 U.S. 241 (1974), but it is another thing altogether to say that the First Amendment forbids Congress to give back part of the operators' editorial discretion, which all recognize as fundamentally protected, in favor of a broader access right. It is no answer to say that leased and public access are content neutral and that §§10(a) and (c) are not, for that does not change the fundamental fact, which petitioners never address, that it is the operators' journalistic freedom that is infringed, whether the challenged restrictions be content neutral or content based.

Sections 10(a) and (c) do not burden a programmer's right to seek access for its indecent programming on an operator's system. Rather, they merely restore part of the editorial discretion an operator would have absent Government regulation without burdening the programmer's underlying speech rights.

B

That the leased access provisions may be described in common carrier terms does not demonstrate that access programmers have obtained a First Amendment right to transmit programming over leased access channels. Labeling leased access a common carrier scheme has no real First Amendment consequences. It simply does not follow from common carrier status that cable operators may not, with Congress' blessing, decline to carry indecent speech on their leased access channels. Common carriers are private entities and may, consistent with the First Amendment, exercise editorial discretion in the absence of a specific statutory prohibition.

C

Petitioners argue that public access channels are public forums in which they have First Amendment rights to speak and that §10(c) is invalid because it imposes content-based burdens on those rights.

Cable systems are not public property. Cable systems are privately owned and privately managed, and petitioners point to no case in which we have held that government may designate private property as a public forum. The public forum doctrine is a rule governing claims of "a right of access to public property," Perry Ed. Ass'n v. Perry Local Educators' Ass'n, 460 U.S. 37, 44 (1983), and has never been thought to extend beyond property generally understood to belong to the government.

Government control over its own property or private property in which it has taken a cognizable property interest is consistent with designation of a public forum. But we have never even hinted that regulatory control, and particularly direct regulatory control over a private entity's First Amendment speech rights, could justify creation of a public forum.

[E]ven were I inclined to view public access channels as public property, which I am not, the numerous additional obligations imposed on the cable operator in managing and operating the public access channels convince me that these channels share few, if any, of the basic characteristics of a public forum. For this reason, and the other reasons articulated earlier, I would sustain both § 10(a) and § 10(c).

III

Most sexually oriented programming appears on premium or pay-per-view channels that are naturally blocked from nonpaying customers by market forces, and it is only governmental intervention in the first instance that requires access channels, on which indecent programming may appear, to be made part of the basic cable package. Section 10(b) does nothing more than adjust the nature of government-imposed leased access requirements in order to emulate the market forces that keep indecent programming primarily on premium channels (without permitting the operator to charge subscribers for that programming).

Unlike §§ 10(a) and (c), § 10(b) clearly implicates petitioners' free speech rights. Though § 10(b) by no means bans indecent speech, it clearly places content-based restrictions on the transmission of private speech by requiring cable operators to block and segregate indecent programming that the operator has agreed to carry. Consequently, § 10(b) must be subjected to strict scrutiny and can be upheld only if it furthers a compelling governmental interest by the least restrictive means available. The parties agree that Congress has a "compelling interest in protecting the physical and psychological well-being of minors" and that its interest "extends to shielding minors from the influence of [indecent speech] that is not obscene by adult standards." *See* Sable Communications of California, Inc. v. FCC, 492 U.S. 115, 126 (1989). Because § 10(b) is narrowly tailored to achieve that well-established compelling interest, I would uphold it.

The Court strikes down § 10(b) by pointing to alternatives, such as reverse blocking and lockboxes, that it says are less restrictive than segregation and blocking. Though these methods attempt to place in parents' hands the ability to permit their children to watch as little, or as much, indecent programming as the parents think proper, they do not effectively support parents' authority to direct the moral upbringing of their children. The FCC recognized that leased-access programming comes "from a wide variety of independent sources, with no single editor controlling [its] selection and presentation." Implementation of Section 10 of the Cable Consumer Protection and Competition Act of 1992: Indecent Programming and Other Types of Materials on Cable Access Channels, First Report and Order, 8 FCC Rcd. 998, 1000 (1993). Thus, indecent programming on leased access channels is "especially likely to be shown randomly or intermittently between non-indecent programs." *Id.* Rather than being able to simply block out certain channels at certain times, a subscriber armed with only a lockbox must carefully monitor all leased-access programming and constantly reprogram the lockbox to keep out undesired programming. Thus, even assuming that cable subscribers generally have the technical proficiency to properly operate a lockbox, by no means a given, this distinguishing characteristic of leased access channels makes lockboxes and reverse-blocking largely ineffective.

The United States has carried its burden of demonstrating that § 10(b) and its implementing regulations are narrowly tailored to satisfy a compelling governmental interest. Accordingly, I would affirm the judgment of the Court of Appeals in its entirety. I therefore concur in the judgment upholding § 10(a) and respectfully dissent from that portion of the judgment striking down §§ 10(b) and (c).

Notes and Questions

1. What Is the Correct Framing? Note the different ways the opinions frame the channels and the provisions involved. Is the leased access regime a form of common carriage? Should leased access instead be understood as a restriction on cable operators' speech? Could it be both? Neither? And should §§ 10(a) & (c) be understood as restoring cable operators' editorial discretion? As government restrictions on indecency? On what considerations should a court rely in answering those questions? What turns on the answers to these questions beyond the provisions at issue in this case? That is, what is the larger significance of the legal characterization of the leased access and PEG channels?

2. Different Foci. Here is one oversimplified characterization of the opinions' foci with respect to §§ 10(a) & (c): Thomas focused on the rights of cable operators and argued for no regulation; Kennedy focused on the power of television in a democracy and argued for unfettered discussion; and Breyer focused on the power of cable in the home and argued for content controls. Is that accurate? Useful?

3. Flexibility. Justice Breyer did not adopt either of the "categorical approaches" that Justices Kennedy and Thomas preferred and explicitly refused to pick "a rigid single standard, good for now and for all future media and purposes." Justices Kennedy and Thomas (in portions of their opinions that we largely deleted for space reasons) criticized him for refusing to do so. This clash invokes the longstanding dispute over whether clear rules or fluid standards are preferable. One added element in this instance is that everyone expects continued technological change, and everyone thinks that the uncertainty produced by such change supports their position. Who is right? Does the likelihood of continued technological development indicate that courts should lay down clear rules so that people can rely on them in choosing a course of action, or that courts should allow themselves the flexibility to craft new approaches when they seem appropriate?

4. Do No Harm. Justice Souter's concurring opinion in *Denver Area* (which we deleted for space reasons) expressed agreement with Justice Breyer's unwillingness to choose a doctrinal category in analyzing the First Amendment issues, and Souter closed by invoking a "rule familiar to every doctor of medicine: 'First, do no harm.'" 518 U.S. at 778. Justice Kennedy, in his partial concurrence and partial dissent, quoted this statement but added: "The question, though, is whether the harm is in sustaining the law or striking it down." *Id.* at 787. What *is* the "do no harm" position in this case? Is there an answer to that question that does not assume its conclusion?

5. Less Speech Restrictive Alternatives. Section 504 of the Telecommunications Act of 1996 provides that "[u]pon request by a cable service subscriber, a cable operator shall, without charge, fully scramble or otherwise fully block" any channel the subscriber does not wish to receive, and § 505 requires cable television operators who provide channels "primarily dedicated to sexually-oriented programming" either to "fully scramble or otherwise fully block" those channels. 47 U.S.C. §§ 560 & 561. Note that in *Denver Area* Justice Breyer's opinion rejected § 10(b) based in part on the existence of these provisions, because they demonstrated that there was an equally effective less speech restrictive alternative to § 10(b). Breyer's opinion also noted that "we cannot, and do not, decide whether the new provisions are themselves lawful (a matter not before us)." This is consistent with the Court's practice in First Amendment cases of invalidating provisions based on less restrictive alternatives that may not themselves be constitutional. As it turned out, the Court did not have very long to wait until it considered §§ 504 and 505. In United States v. Playboy Entertainment Group, Inc., 529 U.S. 803 (2000), the Court invalidated § 505 on First Amendment grounds because § 504 was an equally effective less speech restrictive alternative to § 505. So the existence of §§ 504 and 505 helped to invalidate § 10(b), and then the existence of § 504 helped to invalidate § 505.

6. The Broadcasting Analogy. The Court has limited *Red Lion* to the broadcasting context and has similarly limited *Pacifica*, with the exception of Justice Breyer's plurality opinion in *Denver Area*. Breyer emphasized that the statute permitted cable operators to block indecency (unlike *Pacifica*'s mandated restrictions on indecency) but also stated that the unique elements of broadcasting that *Pacifica* invoked applied to cable television (and thus are not unique). Does the reasoning of the plurality opinion suggest that *Pacifica* should apply to other forms of communication? That question arose with respect to telephony and the internet, as the following materials indicate.

7. Regulation of Indecency via Telephone. In the 1980s Congress became concerned about children's ability to use "dial-a-porn" services and passed legislation criminalizing obscene or indecent telephone communications to minors (or to any non-consenting person). Pub. L. No. 98-214, § 8(a), 97 Stat. 1467, 1469–70 (1983) (amending 47 U.S.C. § 223(b)). The Second Circuit invalidated § 223(b) insofar as it applied to nonobscene speech, Carlin Communications, Inc. v. FCC, 837 F.2d 546 (2d Cir. 1988), and Congress responded by amending § 223(b) to prohibit obscene or indecent commercial telephone messages directed to any person regardless of age. Pub. L. No. 100-297, § 6101, 102 Stat. 130, 424 (1988). The Supreme Court held that the statute flunked the strict scrutiny applicable to content-based regulations of speech. Sable Communications of California, Inc. v. FCC, 492 U.S. 115 (1989). The government unsurprisingly sought to rely on *Pacifica*. *Sable* characterized *Pacifica* as "an emphatically narrow holding," *id.* at 127, and then distinguished *Pacifica* by noting that it did not involve a total ban on indecency and stating that, in contrast to the pervasiveness and accessibility of broadcasting,

> the dial-it medium requires the listener to take affirmative steps to receive the communication. There is no "captive audience" problem here; callers will generally not be unwilling listeners. The context of dial-in services, where a caller seeks and is willing to pay for the communication, is manifestly different from a situation in which a listener does not want the received message. Placing a telephone call is not the same as turning on a radio and being taken by surprise by an indecent message. Unlike an unexpected outburst on a radio broadcast, the message received by one who places a call to a dial-a-porn service is not so invasive or surprising that it prevents an unwilling listener from avoiding exposure to it.

Id. at 128.

Sable did state (in language quoted in other cases in this chapter) that "there is a compelling interest in protecting the physical and psychological well-being of minors. This interest extends to shielding minors from the influence of literature that is not obscene by adult standards." *Id.* at 126. But it found that the statute did not satisfy strict scrutiny's narrow tailoring requirement. The Court held that requiring (as FCC regulations did before the statutory amendment was enacted) a credit card, access code, or scrambling would likely be effective in allowing adult access to dial-a-porn, with "only a few of the most enterprising and disobedient young people" gaining access, such that a total ban on adult access "exceeds that which is necessary to limit the access of minors." *Id.* at 131.

Less than six months after the Supreme Court issued its opinion in *Sable*, Congress amended § 223(b) again, to bring it into conformity with the Court's opinion. Pub. L. No. 101-166, Title V, § 521(1), 103 Stat. 1159, 1192–93 (1989). The amendment retained the ban on obscene communications but regulated (rather than banning) minors' access to indecent telephone communications. And it provided an affirmative defense to prosecution for providers that comply with FCC regulations. Those regulations (like earlier regulations) provided that an affirmative defense required that providers use credit cards, access codes, or scrambling. Regulations Concerning Indecent Communications by Telephone, Report and Order, 5 FCC Rcd. 4926 ¶ 27 (1990). The FCC further provided that, because none of those protections is foolproof, that an affirmative defense would also require "reverse blocking"—that is, blocking connections to dial-a-porn providers unless the customer requested access. *Id.* n.16. The FCC concluded "voluntary blocking" (allowing connections unless the customer requests blocking) would be less effective and thus that voluntary blocking was not an equally effective alternative that would cause reverse blocking to flunk the narrow tailoring requirement of the First Amendment. *Id.* ¶ 18.

Litigants unsuccessfully challenged both the federal dial-a-porn statute (i.e., § 223, as amended in 1989) and the 1990 FCC Report and Order as inconsistent with the First Amendment. Information Providers' Coalition for Defense of the First Amendment v. FCC, 928 F.2d 866 (1991); Dial Information Services Corp. of New York v. Thornburgh, 938 F.2d 1535 (1991).

§ 11.B.1.c. Regulation of Internet Indecency

There are myriad laws that affect internet content. Almost every category of law that applies to offline activity can apply to online activity as well. In many cases, the law is one of general application and questions arise regarding exactly how it will apply to the online world. For instance, a number of lawsuits have involved questions over the online contacts sufficient to establish personal jurisdiction. *See, e.g.*, Cybersell, Inc. v. Cybersell, Inc., 130 F.3d 414 (9th Cir. 1997). Congress has also enacted some statutes with the internet specifically in mind.[14] An example is the Twenty-First Century Communications and Video Accessibility Act, Pub. L. No. 111-260, 124 Stat. 2751 (2010), which directs the FCC to ensure access for people with disabilities to communications technologies including the internet.

But Congress and the FCC have generally shied away from direct regulation of internet content.[15] That is, the government by and large has not promulgated regulations aimed specifically at the content traveling via the internet. There is one major exception, however: Congress has attempted to limit the availability of indecent content.

As the internet became more popular in the mid-1990s, Congress became concerned about the ability of children to gain access to sexual material via the internet. Congress passed the Communications Decency Act (CDA) as part of the Telecommunications Act of 1996. It was challenged immediately, resulting in the opinion below.

---

14. States have also passed legislation regulating aspects of online activity, but those statutes face the hurdle posed by the negative implications of the Commerce Clause of the Constitution (often called the "dormant commerce clause"). *See, e.g.*, ACLU v. Johnson, 194 F.3d 1149 (10th Cir. 1999).

15. Copyright laws affect content (although the Supreme Court has ruled copyright regulation does not trigger rigorous First Amendment scrutiny, *see* Eldred v. Reno, 537 U.S. 186, 218–221 (2003)), but they do not involve the government favoring or disfavoring specific content.

Reno v. ACLU

521 U.S. 844 (1997)

STEVENS, J., delivered the opinion of the Court, in which SCALIA, KENNEDY, SOUTER, THOMAS, GINSBURG, and BREYER, JJ., joined. O'CONNOR, J., filed an opinion concurring in the judgment in part and dissenting in part, in which REHNQUIST, C.J., joined.

JUSTICE STEVENS delivered the opinion of the Court.

At issue is the constitutionality of two statutory provisions enacted to protect minors from "indecent" and "patently offensive" communications on the Internet. Notwithstanding the legitimacy and importance of the congressional goal of protecting children from harmful materials, we agree with the three-judge District Court that the statute abridges "the freedom of speech" protected by the First Amendment.

II

The Telecommunications Act of 1996, Pub. L. No. 104-104, 110 Stat. 56 (1996), was an unusually important legislative enactment. As stated on the first of its 103 pages, its primary purpose was to reduce regulation and encourage "the rapid deployment of new telecommunications technologies." The major components of the statute have nothing to do with the Internet; they were designed to promote competition in the local telephone service market, the multichannel video market, and the market for over-the-air broadcasting. The Act includes seven Titles, six of which are the product of extensive committee hearings and the subject of discussion in Reports prepared by Committees of the Senate and the House of Representatives. By contrast, Title V—known as the "Communications Decency Act of 1996" (CDA)—contains provisions that were either added in executive committee after the hearings were concluded or as amendments offered during floor debate on the legislation. An amendment offered in the Senate was the source of the two statutory provisions challenged in this case. They are informally described as the "indecent transmission" provision and the "patently offensive display" provision.

The first, 47 U.S.C. § 223(a) (Supp. 1997), prohibits the knowing transmission of obscene or indecent messages to any recipient under 18 years of age. It provides in pertinent part:

> (a) Whoever—
>
> (1) in interstate or foreign communications—
>
> * * *
>
> (B) by means of a telecommunications device knowingly—
>
> (i) makes, creates, or solicits, and
>
> (ii) initiates the transmission of,
>
> any comment, request, suggestion, proposal, image, or other communication which is obscene or indecent, knowing that the recipient of the

communication is under 18 years of age, regardless of whether the maker of such communication placed the call or initiated the communication;

* * *

(2) knowingly permits any telecommunications facility under his control to be used for any activity prohibited by paragraph (1) with the intent that it be used for such activity,

shall be fined under Title 18, or imprisoned not more than two years, or both.

The second provision, § 223(d), prohibits the knowing sending or displaying of patently offensive messages in a manner that is available to a person under 18 years of age. It provides:

(d) Whoever—

(1) in interstate or foreign communications knowingly—

(A) uses an interactive computer service to send to a specific person or persons under 18 years of age, or

(B) uses any interactive computer service to display in a manner available to a person under 18 years of age,

any comment, request, suggestion, proposal, image, or other communication that, in context, depicts or describes, in terms patently offensive as measured by contemporary community standards, sexual or excretory activities or organs, regardless of whether the user of such service placed the call or initiated the communication; or

(2) knowingly permits any telecommunications facility under such person's control to be used for an activity prohibited by paragraph (1) with the intent that it be used for such activity,

shall be fined under Title 18, or imprisoned not more than two years, or both.

The breadth of these prohibitions is qualified by two affirmative defenses. One covers those who take "good faith, reasonable, effective, and appropriate actions" to restrict access by minors to the prohibited communications. § 223(e)(5)(A). The other covers those who restrict access to covered material by requiring certain designated forms of age proof, such as a verified credit card or an adult identification number or code. § 223(e)(5)(B).

IV

In arguing for reversal, the Government contends that the CDA is plainly constitutional under Ginsberg v. New York, 390 U.S. 629 (1968) [and] FCC v. Pacifica Foundation, 438 U.S. 726 (1978). A close look at these cases, however, raises—rather than relieves—doubts concerning the constitutionality of the CDA.

In *Ginsberg*, we upheld the constitutionality of a New York statute that prohibited selling to minors under 17 years of age material that was considered obscene as to them even if not obscene as to adults. We relied not only on the State's independent interest in the well-being of its youth, but also on our consistent recognition of the principle that "the parents' claim to authority in their own household to direct the rearing of their children is basic in the structure of our society." 390 U.S. at 639.

In four important respects, the statute upheld in *Ginsberg* was narrower than the CDA. First, we noted in *Ginsberg* that "the prohibition against sales to minors does not bar parents who so desire from purchasing the magazines for their children." *Id.* at 639. Under the CDA, by contrast, neither the parents' consent—nor even their participation—in the communication would avoid the application of the statute. Second, the New York statute applied only to commercial transactions, *id.* at 647, whereas the CDA contains no such limitation. Third, the New York statute cabined its definition of material that is harmful to minors with the requirement that it be "utterly without redeeming social importance for minors." *Id.* at 646. The CDA fails to provide us with any definition of the term "indecent" as used in § 223(a)(1) and, importantly, omits any requirement that the "patently offensive" material covered by § 223(d) lack serious literary, artistic, political, or scientific value. Fourth, the New York statute defined a minor as a person under the age of 17, whereas the CDA, in applying to all those under 18 years, includes an additional year of those nearest majority.

In *Pacifica*, we upheld a declaratory order of the Federal Communications Commission, holding that the broadcast of a recording of a 12-minute monologue entitled "Filthy Words" that had previously been delivered to a live audience "could have been the subject of administrative sanctions." 438 U.S. at 730.

As with the New York statute at issue in *Ginsberg*, there are significant differences between the order upheld in *Pacifica* and the CDA. First, the order in *Pacifica*, issued by an agency that had been regulating radio stations for decades, targeted a specific broadcast that represented a rather dramatic departure from traditional program content in order to designate when—rather than whether—it would be permissible to air such a program in that particular medium. The CDA's broad categorical prohibitions are not limited to particular times and are not dependent on any evaluation by an agency familiar with the unique characteristics of the Internet. Second, unlike the CDA, the Commission's declaratory order was not punitive; we expressly refused to decide whether the indecent broadcast "would justify a criminal prosecution." *Id.* at 750. Finally, the Commission's order applied to a medium which as a matter of history had "received the most limited First Amendment protection," *id.* at 748, in large part because warnings could not adequately protect the listener from unexpected program content. The Internet, however, has no comparable history. Moreover, the District Court found that the risk of encountering indecent material by accident is remote because a series of affirmative steps is required to access specific material.

These precedents, then, surely do not require us to uphold the CDA and are fully consistent with the application of the most stringent review of its provisions.

V

[S]ome of our cases have recognized special justifications for regulation of the broadcast media that are not applicable to other speakers, *see* Red Lion Broadcasting Co. v. FCC, 395 U.S. 367 (1969); FCC v. Pacifica Foundation, 438 U.S. 726 (1978). In these cases, the Court relied on the history of extensive government regulation of the broadcast medium; the scarcity of available frequencies at its inception; and its "invasive" nature.

Those factors are not present in cyberspace. Neither before nor after the enactment of the CDA have the vast democratic forums of the Internet been subject to the type of government supervision and regulation that has attended the broadcast industry. Moreover, the Internet is not as "invasive" as radio or television. The District Court specifically found that "[c]ommunications over the Internet do not 'invade' an individual's home or appear on one's computer screen unbidden. Users seldom encounter content 'by accident.'" 929 F. Supp. at 844 (finding 88). It also found that "almost all sexually explicit images are preceded by warnings as to the content," and cited testimony that "'odds are slim' that a user would come across a sexually explicit sight by accident." *Id.*

We distinguished *Pacifica* in Sable Communications of California, Inc. v. FCC, 492 U.S. 115 (1989), on just this basis. In *Sable,* a company engaged in the business of offering sexually oriented prerecorded telephone messages (popularly known as "dial-a-porn") challenged the constitutionality of an amendment to the Communications Act of 1934 that imposed a blanket prohibition on indecent as well as obscene interstate commercial telephone messages. We held that the statute was constitutional insofar as it applied to obscene messages but invalid as applied to indecent messages. We explained that "the dial-it medium requires the listener to take affirmative steps to receive the communication." *Id.* at 127–28. "Placing a telephone call," we continued, "is not the same as turning on a radio and being taken by surprise by an indecent message." *Id.* at 128.

Finally, unlike the conditions that prevailed when Congress first authorized regulation of the broadcast spectrum, the Internet can hardly be considered a "scarce" expressive commodity. It provides relatively unlimited, low-cost capacity for communication of all kinds. This dynamic, multifaceted category of communication includes not only traditional print and news services, but also audio, video, and still images, as well as interactive, real-time dialogue. Through the use of chat rooms, any person with a phone line can become a town crier with a voice that resonates farther than it could from any soapbox. Through the use of Web pages, mail exploders, and newsgroups, the same individual can become a pamphleteer. As the District Court found, "the content on the Internet is as diverse as human thought." 929 F. Supp. at 842 (finding 74). We agree with its conclusion that our cases provide no basis for qualifying the level of First Amendment scrutiny that should be applied to this medium.

VII

We are persuaded that the CDA lacks the precision that the First Amendment requires when a statute regulates the content of speech. In order to deny minors access to potentially harmful speech, the CDA effectively suppresses a large amount of speech that adults have a constitutional right to receive and to address to one another. That burden on adult speech is unacceptable if less restrictive alternatives would be at least as effective in achieving the legitimate purpose that the statute was enacted to serve.

The District Court was correct to conclude that the CDA effectively resembles the ban on "dial-a-porn" invalidated in *Sable*. In *Sable*, this Court rejected the argument that we should defer to the congressional judgment that nothing less than a total ban would be effective in preventing enterprising youngsters from gaining access to indecent communications.

In arguing that the CDA does not so diminish adult communication, the Government relies on the incorrect factual premise that prohibiting a transmission whenever it is known that one of its recipients is a minor would not interfere with adult-to-adult communication. The findings of the District Court make clear that this premise is untenable.

The District Court found that at the time of trial existing technology did not include any effective method for a sender to prevent minors from obtaining access to its communications on the Internet without also denying access to adults. By contrast, the District Court found that "[d]espite its limitations, currently available *user-based* software suggests that a reasonably effective method by which *parents* can prevent their children from accessing sexually explicit and other material which *parents* may believe is inappropriate for their children will soon be widely available." *Id.* at 842 (finding 73) (emphases added).

The breadth of the CDA's coverage is wholly unprecedented. Unlike the regulations upheld in *Ginsberg* and *Pacifica*, the scope of the CDA is not limited to commercial speech or commercial entities. Its open-ended prohibitions embrace all nonprofit entities and individuals posting indecent messages or displaying them on their own computers in the presence of minors. The general, undefined terms "indecent" and "patently offensive" cover large amounts of nonpornographic material with serious educational or other value. Moreover, the "community standards" criterion as applied to the Internet means that any communication available to a nationwide audience will be judged by the standards of the community most likely to be offended by the message.

The breadth of this content-based restriction of speech imposes an especially heavy burden on the Government to explain why a less restrictive provision would not be as effective as the CDA. It has not done so. The arguments in this Court have referred to possible alternatives such as requiring that indecent material be "tagged" in a way that facilitates parental control of material coming into their homes, making exceptions for messages with artistic or educational value, providing some tolerance for parental choice, and regulating some portions of the Internet — such as commercial web sites — differently than others, such as chat rooms. Particularly in the light of the absence of any detailed findings by the Congress, or even hearings addressing the special problems of the CDA, we are persuaded that the CDA is not narrowly tailored if that requirement has any meaning at all.

XI

In this Court, though not in the District Court, the Government asserts that — in addition to its interest in protecting children — its "equally significant" interest in fostering the growth of the Internet provides an independent basis for upholding the constitutionality of the CDA. The Government apparently assumes that the unregulated availability of "indecent" and "patently offensive" material on the Internet is driving countless citizens away from the medium because of the risk of exposing themselves or their children to harmful material.

We find this argument singularly unpersuasive. The dramatic expansion of this new marketplace of ideas contradicts the factual basis of this contention. The record demonstrates that the growth of the Internet has been and continues to be phenomenal. As a matter of constitutional tradition, in the absence of evidence to the contrary, we presume that governmental regulation of the content of speech is more likely to interfere with the free exchange of ideas than to encourage it. The interest in encouraging freedom of expression in a democratic society outweighs any theoretical but unproven benefit of censorship.

For the foregoing reasons, the judgment of the District Court is affirmed.

[Concurring and dissenting opinion of JUSTICE O'CONNOR is omitted.]

Notes and Questions

1. *Pacifica*. After *Reno v. ACLU*, what is left of the rationale articulated in *Pacifica*? Is the point that *Pacifica* protects children "too young to read" who might be harmed by hearing or learning a dirty word over the radio, but who are unable to access internet indecency?

Is *Pacifica* now explicable only by the history of extensive government regulation of broadcast? Does the Court's reliance on the absence of existing internet regulation mean that Congress's choice was to regulate the internet at its inception or lose the opportunity to regulate? In other words, by waiting for the internet to develop, did Congress forego its chance to regulate at all? Is that an appropriate message to send to Congress? Does it create the right incentives?

2. Outdated Findings. Appellate courts rely on factual findings made by trial courts, and this case is no exception. The district court made extensive factual findings, and the Supreme Court quoted them at length (we deleted most from our excerpt above) and relied on them. Some of those findings were outdated by the time the Supreme Court ruled and became more obviously so as time progressed. Consider, for example, the findings on which the Supreme Court relied that "[u]sers seldom encounter content 'by accident'" and that "[a]lmost all sexually explicit images are preceded by warnings as to the content." Does that ring true? Interestingly, the district court itself recognized the possibility of stale findings, saying (in a statement the Supreme Court did not quote): "Because of the rapidity of developments in this field, some of the technological facts we have found may become partially obsolete by the time of publication of these Findings." ACLU v. Reno, 929 F. Supp. 824, 838 n.12 (E.D. Pa. 1996). Is a focus on currently existing technology appropriate? Is it necessary, given the Court's task of determining whether the CDA is constitutional? Does this mean that technological change may have undermined the Court's invalidation of the CDA? What does this mean for the staying power of Supreme Court decisions in rapidly changing spheres like the internet? *See* Stuart Minor Benjamin, Stepping into the Same River Twice: Rapidly Changing Facts and the Appellate Process, 78 Tex. L. Rev. 269, 290–96, 369–373 (1999).

3. The Child Online Protection Act. Is it possible to draft a statute that would pass constitutional muster but nonetheless restrict indecency on the internet? Congress, in an apparent attempt at doing so, responded to *Reno v. ACLU* by enacting the Child Online Protection Act, Pub. L. No. 105-277, 112 Stat. 2681 (1998) (COPA). Like the Communications Decency Act, COPA criminalizes certain disfavored online speech, and like the CDA it has affirmative defenses for those who restrict minors' access to covered material via credit card authorization, adult identification numbers, or other reasonable measures. COPA, however, is narrower than the CDA in several ways, including: (a) COPA's restrictions apply only to communications on the World Wide Web; content distributed through other internet-based services (such as email) is not covered; (b) whereas the CDA applied to commercial and noncommercial speakers alike, COPA applies only to communications made "for commercial purposes"; and (c) COPA applies only to "material that is harmful to minors," a term of art that is arguably narrower than "indecent" or "patently offensive" speech.

Shortly after COPA was enacted, the ACLU challenged its constitutionality, and a U.S. District Court granted the ACLU's motion for a preliminary injunction. The Third Circuit affirmed the injunction, finding that COPA was likely overbroad because its definition of "harmful to minors" relied on "contemporary community standards." *See* 47 U.S.C. § 231(e)(6); ACLU v. Reno, 31 F. Supp. 2d 473 (E.D. Pa. 1999), *aff'd*, 217 F.3d 162 (3d Cir. 2000).

The Supreme Court granted certiorari in that case and, in 2002, a splintered Court reversed. Ashcroft v. ACLU, 535 U.S. 564 (2002) (*Ashcroft I*). There was no majority for a rationale, but a majority of the Court did agree on the conclusion:

> We hold only that COPA's reliance on community standards to identify "material that is harmful to minors" does not *by itself* render the statute substantially overbroad for purposes of the First Amendment. We do not express any view as to whether COPA suffers from substantial overbreadth for other reasons, whether the statute is unconstitutionally vague, or whether the District Court correctly concluded that the statute likely will

> not survive strict scrutiny analysis once adjudication of the case is completed below. While respondents urge us to resolve these questions at this time, prudence dictates allowing the Court of Appeals to first examine these difficult issues.
>
> Petitioner does not ask us to vacate the preliminary injunction entered by the District Court, and in any event, we could not do so without addressing matters yet to be considered by the Court of Appeals. As a result, the Government remains enjoined from enforcing COPA absent further action by the Court of Appeals or the District Court.

Id. at 585–86.

So the case was remanded for consideration of the many arguments that the challengers to the statute actually put forward, as opposed to the community standards argument that the Third Circuit had seized on. In the meantime, the injunction remained in effect. On remand, the Third Circuit turned to the questions left open by *Ashcroft I.* Once again it affirmed the district court's grant of a preliminary injunction against the enforcement of COPA, albeit on different grounds—indeed, on multiple grounds. The Third Circuit concluded as follows:

> In sum, the District Court did not abuse its discretion in granting the plaintiffs a preliminary injunction on the grounds that COPA, in failing to satisfy strict scrutiny, had no probability of success on the merits. COPA is clearly a content-based restriction on speech. Although it does purport to serve a compelling governmental interest, it is not narrowly tailored, and thus fails strict scrutiny. COPA also fails strict scrutiny because it does not use the least restrictive means to achieve its ends. The breadth of the "harmful to minors" and "commercial purpose" text of COPA, especially in light of applying community standards to a global medium and the burdens on speech created by the statute's affirmative defenses, as well as the fact that Congress could have, but failed to, employ the least restrictive means to accomplish its legitimate goal, persuade us that the District Court did not abuse its discretion in preliminarily enjoining the enforcement of COPA....
>
> Our analysis of whether COPA is overbroad is akin to the portion of the strict scrutiny analysis we have conducted in which we concluded that COPA is not narrowly tailored. We conclude that the statute is substantially overbroad in that it places significant burdens on Web publishers' communication of speech that is constitutionally protected as to adults and adults' ability to access such speech. In so doing, COPA encroaches upon a significant amount of protected speech beyond that which the Government may target constitutionally in preventing children's exposure to material that is obscene for minors.

ACLU v. Ashcroft, 322 F.3d 240, 265–66, 266–67 (3d Cir. 2003). The Supreme Court affirmed and remanded in the opinion excerpted below.

Ashcroft v. ACLU [*Ashcroft II*]

542 U.S. 656 (2004)

KENNEDY, J., delivered the opinion of the Court, in which STEVENS, SOUTER, THOMAS, and GINSBURG, JJ., joined. STEVENS, J., filed a concurring opinion, in which GINSBURG, J., joined. SCALIA, J., filed a dissenting opinion. BREYER, J., filed a dissenting opinion, in which REHNQUIST, C.J., and O'CONNOR, J., joined.

JUSTICE KENNEDY delivered the opinion of the Court.

I

In response to the Court's decision in Reno v. ACLU, 521 U.S. 844 (1997), Congress passed the Child Online Protection Act (COPA), Pub. L. No. 105-277, Title XIV § 1403, 112 Stat. 2681, 736–37 (1998) (codified and amended as 47 U.S.C. § 231). COPA imposes criminal penalties of a $50,000 fine and six months in prison for the knowing posting, for "commercial purposes," of World Wide Web content that is "harmful to minors." § 231(a)(1). Material that is "harmful to minors" is defined as:

> any communication, picture, image, graphic image file, article, recording, writing, or other matter of any kind that is obscene or that—
>
> (A) the average person, applying contemporary community standards, would find, taking the material as a whole and with respect to minors, is designed to appeal to, or is designed to pander to, the prurient interest;
>
> (B) depicts, describes, or represents, in a manner patently offensive with respect to minors, an actual or simulated sexual act or sexual contact, an actual or simulated normal or perverted sexual act, or a lewd exhibition of the genitals or post-pubescent female breast; and
>
> (C) taken as a whole, lacks serious literary, artistic, political, or scientific value for minors.

§ 231(e)(6).

"Minors" are defined as "any person under 17 years of age." § 231(e)(7). A person acts for "commercial purposes only if such person is engaged in the business of making such communications." "Engaged in the business," in turn,

> means that the person who makes a communication, or offers to make a communication, by means of the World Wide Web, that includes any material that is harmful to minors, devotes time, attention, or labor to such activities, as a regular course of such person's trade or business, with the objective of earning a profit as a result of such activities (although it is not necessary that the person make a profit or that the making or offering to make such communications be the person's sole or principal business or source of income).

§ 231(e)(2).

While the statute labels all speech that falls within these definitions as criminal speech, it also provides an affirmative defense to those who employ specified means to prevent minors from gaining access to the prohibited materials on their Web site. A person may escape conviction under the statute by demonstrating that he

> has restricted access by minors to material that is harmful to minors—
>
> (A) by requiring use of a credit card, debit account, adult access code, or adult personal identification number[,]
>
> (B) by accepting a digital certificate that verifies age, or
>
> (C) by any other reasonable measures that are feasible under available technology.

§ 231(c)(1).

Since the passage of COPA, Congress has enacted additional laws regulating the Internet in an attempt to protect minors. For example, it has enacted a prohibition on misleading Internet domain names, 18 U.S.C. § 2252B, in order to prevent Web site owners from disguising pornographic Web sites in a way likely to cause uninterested persons to visit them. It has also passed a statute creating a "Dot Kids" second-level Internet domain, the content of which is restricted to that which is fit for minors under the age of 13. 47 U.S.C. § 941.

II A

"This Court, like other appellate courts, has always applied the abuse of discretion standard on the review of a preliminary injunction." Walters v. National Ass'n of Radiation Survivors, 473 U.S. 305, 336 (1985) (O'Connor, J., concurring). If the underlying constitutional question is close, therefore, we should uphold the injunction and remand for trial on the merits. Applying this mode of inquiry, we agree with the Court of Appeals that the District Court did not abuse its discretion in entering the preliminary injunction.

The District Court, in deciding to grant the preliminary injunction, concentrated primarily on the argument that there are plausible, less restrictive alternatives to COPA. A statute that "effectively suppresses a large amount of speech that adults have a constitutional right to receive and to address to one another . . . is unacceptable if less restrictive alternatives would be at least as effective in achieving the legitimate purpose that the statute was enacted to serve." *Reno*, 521 U.S. at 874. When plaintiffs challenge a content-based speech restriction, the burden is on the Government to prove that the proposed alternatives will not be as effective as the challenged statute. *Id.*

In considering this question, a court assumes that certain protected speech may be regulated, and then asks what is the least restrictive alternative that can be used to achieve that goal. The purpose of the test is not to consider whether the challenged restriction has some effect in achieving Congress' goal, regardless of the restriction it imposes. The purpose of the test is to ensure that speech is restricted no further than necessary to achieve the goal, for it is important to assure that legitimate speech is not chilled or punished. For that reason, the test does not begin with the status quo of existing regulations, then ask whether the challenged restriction has some additional ability to achieve Congress' legitimate interest. Any restriction on speech could be justified under that analysis. Instead, the court should ask whether the challenged regulation is the least restrictive means among available, effective alternatives.

[O]n this record there are a number of plausible, less restrictive alternatives to the statute. The primary alternative considered by the District Court was blocking and filtering software. Blocking and filtering software is an alternative that is less restrictive than COPA, and, in addition, likely more effective as a means of restricting children's access to materials harmful to them.

Filters are less restrictive than COPA. They impose selective restrictions on speech at the receiving end, not universal restrictions at the source. Under a filtering regime, adults without children may gain access to speech they have a right to see without having to identify themselves or provide their credit card information. Even adults with children may obtain access to the same speech on the same terms simply by turning off the filter on their home computers. Above all, promoting the use of filters does not condemn as criminal any category of speech, and so the potential chilling effect is eliminated, or at least much diminished. All of these things are true, moreover, regardless of how broadly or narrowly the definitions in COPA are construed.

Filters also may well be more effective than COPA. First, a filter can prevent minors from seeing all pornography, not just pornography posted to the Web from America. The District Court noted in its factfindings that one witness estimated that 40% of harmful-to-minors content comes from overseas. COPA does not prevent minors from having access to those foreign harmful materials. That alone makes it possible that filtering software might be more effective in serving Congress' goals. Effectiveness is likely to diminish even further if COPA is upheld, because the providers of the materials that would be covered by the statute simply can move their operations overseas. It is not an answer to say that COPA reaches some amount of materials that are harmful to minors; the question is whether it would reach more of them than less restrictive alternatives. In addition, the District Court found that verification systems may be subject to evasion and circumvention, for example by minors who have their own credit cards. Finally, filters also may be more effective because they can be applied to all forms of Internet communication, including e-mail, not just communications available via the World Wide Web.

That filtering software may well be more effective than COPA is confirmed by the findings of the Commission on Child Online Protection, a blue-ribbon commission created by Congress in COPA itself. It unambiguously found that filters are more effective than age-verification requirements. *See* Commission on Child Online Protection, Report to Congress, at 19–21, 23–25, 27 (Oct. 20, 2000).

Filtering software, of course, is not a perfect solution to the problem of children gaining access to harmful-to-minors materials. It may block some materials that are not harmful to minors and fail to catch some that are. Whatever the deficiencies of filters, however, the Government failed to introduce specific evidence proving that existing technologies are less effective than the restrictions in COPA. The District Court made a specific factfinding that "[n]o evidence was presented to the Court as to the percentage of time that blocking and filtering technology is over- or under-inclusive." ACLU v. Reno, 31 F. Supp. 2d at 492 (E.D. Pa. 1999). In the absence of a showing as to the relative effectiveness of COPA and the alternatives proposed by respondents, it was not an abuse of discretion for the District Court to grant the preliminary injunction. The Government's burden is not merely to show that a proposed less restrictive alternative has some flaws; its burden is to show that it is less effective. *Reno*, 521 U.S. at 874. It is not enough for the Government to show that COPA has some effect. Nor do respondents bear a burden to introduce, or offer to introduce, evidence that their proposed alternatives are more effective. The Government has the burden to show they are less so. The Government having failed to carry its burden, it was not an abuse of discretion for the District Court to grant the preliminary injunction.

One argument to the contrary is worth mentioning—the argument that filtering software is not an available alternative because Congress may not require it to be used. That argument carries little weight, because Congress undoubtedly may act to encourage the use of filters. We have held that Congress can give strong incentives to schools and libraries to use them. United States v. American Library Ass'n., Inc, 539 U.S. 194 (2003). It could also take steps to promote their development by industry, and their use by parents. It is incorrect, for that reason, to say that filters are part of the current regulatory status quo. The need for parental cooperation does not automatically disqualify a proposed less restrictive alternative. United States v. Playboy Entertainment Group, Inc., 529 U.S. 803, 824 (2000) ("A court should not assume a plausible, less restrictive alternative would be ineffective; and a court should not presume parents, given full information, will fail to act.").

B

There are also important practical reasons to let the injunction stand pending a full trial on the merits. First, the potential harms from reversing the injunction outweigh those of leaving it in place by mistake.

Second, there are substantial factual disputes remaining in the case. As mentioned above, there is a serious gap in the evidence as to the effectiveness of filtering software.

Third, and on a related point, the factual record does not reflect current technological reality—a serious flaw in any case involving the Internet. The technology of the Internet evolves at a rapid pace. Yet the factfindings of the District Court were entered in February 1999, over five years ago. Since then, certain facts about the Internet are known to have changed. *Compare, e.g.*, 31 F. Supp. 2d at 481 (36.7 million Internet hosts as of July 1998) *with* Internet Systems Consortium, Internet Domain Survey (Jan. 2004), http://ftp.isc.org/www/survey/reports/2004/01/ (233.1 million hosts as of Jan. 2004). It is reasonable to assume that other technological developments important to the First Amendment analysis have also occurred during that time. More and better filtering alternatives may exist than when the District Court entered its findings. Indeed, we know that after the District Court entered its factfindings, a congressionally appointed commission issued a report that found that filters are more effective than verification screens.

Delay between the time that a district court makes factfindings and the time that a case reaches this Court is inevitable, with the necessary consequence that there will be some discrepancy between the facts as found and the facts at the time the appellate court takes up the question. *See, e.g.*, Benjamin, Stepping into the Same River Twice: Rapidly Changing Facts and the Appellate Process, 78 Texas L. Rev. 269, 290–296 (1999) (noting the problems presented for appellate courts by changing facts in the context of cases involving the Internet, and giving as a specific example the Court's decision in *Reno*). We do not mean, therefore, to set up an insuperable obstacle to fair review. Here, however, the usual gap has doubled because the case has been through the Court of Appeals twice. The additional two years might make a difference. By affirming the preliminary injunction and remanding for trial, we allow the parties to update and supplement the factual record to reflect current technological realities.

Remand will also permit the District Court to take account of a changed legal landscape. Since the District Court made its factfindings, Congress has passed at least two further statutes that might qualify as less restrictive alternatives to COPA — a prohibition on misleading domain names, and a statute creating a minors-safe "Dot Kids" domain. Remanding for trial will allow the District Court to take into account those additional potential alternatives.

On this record, the Government has not shown that the less restrictive alternatives proposed by respondents should be disregarded. Those alternatives, indeed, may be more effective than the provisions of COPA. The District Court did not abuse its discretion when it entered the preliminary injunction. The judgment of the Court of Appeals is affirmed, and the case is remanded for proceedings consistent with this opinion.

[Concurring opinion of JUSTICE STEVENS and dissenting opinion of JUSTICE SCALIA are omitted.]

JUSTICE BREYER, with whom CHIEF JUSTICE REHNQUIST and JUSTICE O'CONNOR join, dissenting.

Like the Court, I would subject the Act to "the most exacting scrutiny," Turner Broadcasting System, Inc. v. FCC, 512 U.S. 622, 642 (1994), requiring the Government to show that any restriction of nonobscene expression is "narrowly drawn" to further a "compelling interest" and that the restriction amounts to the "least restrictive means" available to further that interest, Sable Commc'ns of Cal., Inc. v. FCC, 492 U.S. 115, 126 (1989). *See also* Denver Area Ed. Telecommunications Consortium, Inc. v. FCC, 518 U.S. 727, 755–56 (1996).

Nonetheless, my examination of (1) the burdens the Act imposes on protected expression, (2) the Act's ability to further a compelling interest, and (3) the proposed "less restrictive alternatives" convinces me that the Court is wrong. I cannot accept its conclusion that Congress could have accomplished its statutory objective—protecting children from commercial pornography on the Internet—in other, less restrictive ways.

I

[T]he Act, properly interpreted, imposes a burden on protected speech that is no more than modest.

A

The Act's definitions limit the material it regulates to material that does not enjoy First Amendment protection, namely legally obscene material, and very little more. [T]he Act's definitions limit the statute's scope to commercial pornography. It affects unprotected obscene material. Given the inevitable uncertainty about how to characterize close-to-obscene material, it could apply to (or chill the production of) a limited class of borderline material that courts might ultimately find is protected.

B

The Act does not censor the material it covers. Rather, it requires providers of the "harmful to minors" material to restrict minors' access to it by verifying age. They can do so by inserting screens that verify age using a credit card, adult personal identification number, or other similar technology. *See* § 231(c)(1). In this way, the Act requires creation of an Internet screen that minors, but not adults, will find difficult to bypass.

II

I turn next to the question of "compelling interest," that of protecting minors from exposure to commercial pornography. No one denies that such an interest is "compelling." *See Denver Area*, 518 U.S. at 743 (interest in protecting minors is "compelling"); *Sable*, 492 U.S. at 126 (same). Rather, the question here is whether the Act, given its restrictions on adult access, significantly advances that interest. In other words, is the game worth the candle?

The majority argues that it is not, because of the existence of "blocking and filtering software." *Ante*. The majority refers to the presence of that software as a "less restrictive alternative." But that is a misnomer—a misnomer that may lead the reader to believe that all we need do is look to see if the blocking and filtering software is less restrictive; and to believe that, because in one sense it is (one can turn off the software), that is the end of the constitutional matter.

But such reasoning has no place here. Conceptually speaking, the presence of filtering software is not an *alternative* legislative approach to the problem of protecting children from exposure to commercial pornography. Rather, it is part of the status quo, i.e., the backdrop against which Congress enacted the present statute. It is always true, by definition, that the status quo is less restrictive than a new regulatory law. It is always less restrictive to do *nothing* than to do *something*. But "doing nothing" does not address the problem Congress sought to address—namely that, despite the availability of filtering software, children were still being exposed to harmful material on the Internet.

Thus, the relevant constitutional question is not the question the Court asks: Would it be less restrictive to do nothing? Of course it would be. Rather, the relevant question posits a comparison of (a) a status quo that includes filtering software with (b) a change in that status quo that adds to it an age-verification screen requirement. Given the existence of filtering software, does the problem Congress identified remain significant? Does the Act help to address it? These are questions about the relation of the Act to the compelling interest. Does the Act, compared to the status quo, significantly advance the ball? (An affirmative answer to these questions will not justify "[a]ny restriction on speech," as the Court claims, for a final answer in respect to constitutionality must take account of burdens and alternatives as well.)

The answers to these intermediate questions are clear: Filtering software, as presently available, does not solve the "child protection" problem. It suffers from four serious inadequacies that prompted Congress to pass legislation instead of relying on its voluntary use. First, its filtering is faulty, allowing some pornographic material to pass through without hindrance. Just last year, in *American Library Ass'n*, Justice Stevens described "fundamental defects in the filtering software that is now available or that will be available in the foreseeable future." 539 U.S. at 221 (dissenting opinion). He pointed to the problem of underblocking: "Because the software relies on key words or phrases to block undesirable sites, it does not have the capacity to exclude a precisely defined category of images." *Id.* That is to say, in the absence of words, the software alone cannot distinguish between the most obscene pictorial image and the Venus de Milo. No Member of this Court disagreed.

Second, filtering software costs money. Not every family has the $40 or so necessary to install it. By way of contrast, age screening costs less.

Third, filtering software depends upon parents willing to decide where their children will surf the Web and able to enforce that decision. As to millions of American families, that is not a reasonable possibility. More than 28 million school age children have both parents or their sole parent in the work force, at least 5 million children are left alone at home without supervision each week, and many of those children will spend afternoons and evenings with friends who may well have access to computers and more lenient parents.

Fourth, software blocking lacks precision, with the result that those who wish to use it to screen out pornography find that it blocks a great deal of material that is valuable. As Justice Stevens pointed out, "the software's reliance on words to identify undesirable sites necessarily results in the blocking of thousands of pages that contain content that is completely innocuous for both adults and minors, and that no rational person could conclude matches the filtering companies' category definitions, such as pornography or sex." *Id.* at 222 (internal quotation marks and citations omitted).

Nothing in the District Court record suggests the contrary.

In sum, a "filtering software status quo" means filtering that underblocks, imposes a cost upon each family that uses it, fails to screen outside the home, and lacks precision. Thus, Congress could reasonably conclude that a system that relies entirely upon the use of such software is not an effective system. And a law that adds to that system an age-verification screen requirement significantly increases the system's efficacy. That is to say, at a modest additional cost to those adults who wish to obtain access to a screened program, that law will bring about better, more precise blocking, both inside and outside the home.

The Court's response—that 40% of all pornographic material may be of foreign origin—is beside the point. Even assuming (I believe unrealistically) that *all* foreign originators will refuse to use screening, the Act would make a difference in respect to 60% of the Internet's commercial pornography. I cannot call that difference insignificant.

The upshot is that Congress could reasonably conclude that, despite the current availability of filtering software, a child protection problem exists. It also could conclude that a precisely targeted regulatory statute, adding an age-verification requirement for a narrow range of material, would more effectively shield children from commercial pornography.

IV

My conclusion is that the Act, as properly interpreted, risks imposition of minor burdens on some protected material—burdens that adults wishing to view the material may overcome at modest cost. At the same time, it significantly helps to achieve a compelling congressional goal, protecting children from exposure to commercial pornography. There is no serious, practically available "less restrictive" way similarly to further this compelling interest. Hence the Act is constitutional.

Notes and Questions

1. Battle Lines. What is the nature of the disagreement between the majority and Justice Breyer's dissent? Did they interpret the law differently, or was their dispute mainly over the underlying facts? Did the majority agree with Justice Breyer that COPA regulated "legally obscene material, and very little more"? Was the dispute between the majority and Justice Breyer mainly over the effectiveness of filtering?

2. Why Remand? In Part II-B, the Court emphasized that "the factual record does not reflect current technological reality." The Court acknowledged that some delay was inevitable, but said that the delay in this case was particularly long because of the many trips to appellate courts. (Whose fault is that?) But should the Court remand yet again? Or should the Court have updated the record and determined the degree to which filtering is an effective alternative to COPA? Is that the appropriate role for an appellate court?

3. The Final Chapter on COPA. The Supreme Court's opinion in *Ashcroft II* upheld the injunction and remanded the case for yet further proceedings. The district court then invalidated COPA as violating the First Amendment, holding that it was overinclusive (because it prohibited more speech than necessary to further the compelling interest in protecting minors), did not employ the least speech restrictive alternative (because it found that filters were such an alternative), and was vague and overbroad for multiple reasons. ACLU v. Gonzales, 478 F. Supp. 2d 775, 821 (E.D. Pa. 2007). The Third Circuit affirmed. ACLU v. Mukasey, 534 F.3d 181 (3d Cir. 2008). The United States petitioned for Supreme Court review, but in 2009 the Court denied certiorari, leaving the Third Circuit opinion as the last word. What, if anything, should this decade-long litigation process tell us about the ability of courts to respond to the fast-changing world of the internet?

4. Now What? If you were a supporter of internet indecency legislation, what would you do? Would you push for new legislation? Would you instead pursue other avenues to protect children from indecent online material? What avenues would those be, and how much confidence would you have in their efficacy?

5. Social Media, the Cyber Age, and Caution. In Packingham v. North Carolina, 137 S. Ct. 1730, 1731 (2017), the Supreme Court voted unanimously to invalidate a North Carolina statute making it a felony for a registered sex offender "to access a commercial social networking Web site where the sex offender knows that the site permits minor children to become members or to create or maintain personal Web pages." But Justice Alito, joined by Roberts and Thomas, concurred only in the judgment. All the Justices agreed that the statute was not sufficiently tailored. Both opinions emphasized the possible application of the statute to the same specific websites (amazon.com, washingtonpost.com, and webmd.com).

So where did the opinions differ? The central disagreement between the two opinions was how judges applying the First Amendment should respond to the changing nature of cyberspace. From the majority:

> The nature of a revolution in thought can be that, in its early stages, even its participants may be unaware of it. And when awareness comes, they still may be unable to know or foresee where its changes lead. So too here. While we now may be coming to the realization that the Cyber Age is a revolution of historic proportions, we cannot appreciate yet its full dimensions and vast potential to alter how we think, express ourselves, and define who we want to be. The forces and directions of the Internet are so new, so protean, and so far reaching that courts must be conscious that what they say today might be obsolete tomorrow.
>
> This case is one of the first this Court has taken to address the relationship between the First Amendment and the modern Internet. As a result, the Court must exercise extreme caution before suggesting that the First

> Amendment provides scant protection for access to vast networks in that medium

Id. at 1736.

And from the concurrence:

> The Court is correct that we should be cautious in applying our free speech precedents to the internet. Cyberspace is different from the physical world, and if it is true, as the Court believes, that "we cannot appreciate yet" the "full dimensions and vast potential" of "the Cyber Age," we should proceed circumspectly, taking one step at a time. It is regrettable that the Court has not heeded its own admonition of caution.

Id. at 1744 (Alito, J., concurring).

These dueling opinions pick up on two themes that arose in other cases excerpted above. The first is the majority's point that "what [courts] say today might be obsolete tomorrow." This has long been a major consideration in cases involving changing technologies like the internet, and the Court invoked rapidly changing facts in its remand in *Ashcroft II*.

The second is the question of the best default position with respect to the First Amendment when applied to changing phenomena (like cyberspace). Should judges err on the side of starchy application of free speech tests, or a more flexible approach? In *Packingham*, Justice Kennedy's majority opinion, consistent with his First Amendment jurisprudence more generally, treated broad and rigorous application of First Amendment tests as the default position in the ever-changing world of cyberspace. Justice Alito's concurrence wanted a default that took smaller steps and gave judges (and thus legislatures) more flexibility.

6. Libraries, Filtering, and Federal Assistance. While the federal government has lost in its efforts under COPA, it has found other ways to encourage the use of internet filters. As *Ashcroft II* noted, in 2003 a fractured Supreme Court upheld the Children's Internet Protection Act, 114 Stat. 2763A-335 (2000) (CIPA), against a facial First Amendment challenge. CIPA places conditions on the government program that allows libraries to buy internet access at a discount. Specifically, CIPA provides that a library may not receive federal assistance for internet access unless it has "a policy of internet safety for minors that includes the operation of a technology protection measure . . . that protects against access" by all persons to visual depictions that constitute "obscen[ity]" or "child pornography," and that protects against access by minors to visual depictions that are "harmful to minors." 20 U.S.C. §§ 9134(f)(1)(A)(i) and (B)(i); 47 U.S.C. §§ 254(h)(6)(B)(i) and (C)(i). Public libraries, library associations, library patrons, and website publishers brought a facial constitutional challenge to CIPA, and a three-judge district court held that it unconstitutionally induced libraries to violate the First Amendment. American Library Ass'n, Inc. v. United States, 201 F. Supp. 2d 401 (E.D. Pa. 2002).

The Supreme Court reversed, although no opinion commanded a majority of the Court. United States v. American Library Ass'n, Inc., 539 U.S. 194 (2003). The opinions did not focus on the internet as a special category, nor did they purport to alter the approach to internet indecency laid out in *Reno v. ACLU.* Rather, the analysis centered on the status of libraries. Indeed, Chief Justice Rehnquist's plurality opinion relied on its finding that libraries were not a public forum. The opinion also emphasized that libraries had the same authority over internet access that they had over their print collections:

> A library's need to exercise judgment in making collection decisions depends on its traditional role in identifying suitable and worthwhile material; it is no less entitled to play that role when it collects material from the Internet than when it collects material from any other source. Most libraries already exclude pornography from their print collections because they deem it inappropriate for inclusion. We do not subject these decisions to heightened scrutiny; it would make little sense to treat libraries' judgments to block online pornography any differently, when these judgments are made for just the same reason.

American Library Ass'n, 539 U.S. at 208.

There was some discussion of an issue specific to the internet — the significance of the district court's finding that the use of the filters would result in the blocking of "content that is completely innocuous for both adults and minors, and that no rational person could conclude matches the filtering companies' category definitions, such as 'pornography' or 'sex.'" *Id.* at 208–09 (quoting *American Library Ass'n*, 201 F. Supp. 2d at 449). Justice Stevens emphasized such "overblocking" in his dissent, and argued that CIPA did not clearly provide adults with a ready means of avoiding those filters. The other Justices did not dispute the existence of overblocking, but instead argued that adults could easily have sites unblocked, or filters removed, at their request, and that this allowed the statute to pass muster as against a facial challenge. Indeed, Justices Kennedy and Breyer (who concurred only in the judgment, providing the fifth and sixth votes to reverse) relied on these points. *See American Library Ass'n*, 539 U.S. at 219 (Breyer, J., concurring) (emphasizing that this was a facial challenge, and that, "As the plurality points out, the Act allows libraries to permit any adult patron access to an 'overblocked' Web site; the adult patron need only ask a librarian to unblock the specific Web site or, alternatively, ask the librarian, 'Please disable the entire filter.'"); *id.* at 215 (Kennedy, J., concurring) (noting the same points and adding that, "If some libraries do not have the capacity to unblock specific Web sites or to disable the filter or if it is shown that an adult user's election to view constitutionally protected internet material is burdened in some other substantial way, that would be the subject for an as-applied challenge, not the facial challenge made in this case.").

§ 11.B.2. Violence

In contrast to the many enactments aimed at indecency, there have been fewer laws regulating violent content. Congress has never enacted legislation directly regulating violent content.[16] The closest it came was § 551 of the Telecommunications Act of 1996, Pub. L. No. 104-104, 110 Stat. 56, 139–42 (1996). Entitled "Parental Choice in Television Programming," it provides that unless distributors of video programming established "voluntary rules for rating video programming that contains sexual, violent, or other indecent material" and, further, agreed "voluntarily to broadcast signals that contain ratings of such programming," the FCC was to create an advisory committee, develop such a regime, and impose it upon broadcasters through regulation. § 551(e) (codified as a note to 47 U.S.C. § 303). The provision also requires that television manufacturers include in all television sets (13-inch diagonal or greater) a feature that enables viewers to block the display of programs based on their ratings. § 551(c) (codified at 47 U.S.C. § 303(x)). Section 551 thus does not directly limit (much less ban) violence on television. Instead, it creates a mechanism to create ratings that allow viewers to block categories of programming (not limited to violence) that they find objectionable. Once § 551 was enacted, the television industry was not about to permit a group picked by the FCC to rate its programs, so the industry devised a ratings system on its own, and the FCC found these ratings acceptable. Implementation of Section 551 of the Telecommunications Act of 1996: Video Programming Ratings, Report and Order, 13 FCC Rcd. 8232 (1998).[17]

California, in contrast to Congress, chose to directly regulate violent content. Specifically, it enacted legislation regulating violent video games, by restricting their sale or rental to minors. In the case excerpted below, the Supreme Court held that California's statute violates the First Amendment.

---

16. In case you were wondering, the Motion Picture Association rating system is a voluntary scheme that is not legally required.

17. Most cable and DBS channels put ratings on their programming in the same way that broadcasters do, and the FCC has required that cable and satellite operators include that information in their transmissions. *See* Implementation of the Satellite Home Viewer Improvement Act of 1999: Broadcast Signal Carriage Issues & Retransmission Consent Issues, Report and Order, 16 FCC Rcd. 1918 ¶ 103 (2000). Beyond that, as we noted in Question 5 after *Denver Area*, cable operators must block any channel that a subscriber does not wish to receive. 47 U.S.C. § 560.

Brown v. Entertainment Merchants Association et al.

564 U.S. 786 (2011)

SCALIA, J., delivered the opinion of the Court, in which KENNEDY, GINSBURG, SOTOMAYOR, and KAGAN, JJ., joined. ALITO, J., filed an opinion concurring in the judgment, in which ROBERTS, C.J., joined. THOMAS, J., and BREYER, J., filed dissenting opinions.

JUSTICE SCALIA delivered the opinion of the Court.

I

Cal. Civ.Code Ann. §§1746–1746.5 (Act), prohibits the sale or rental of "violent video games" to minors, and requires their packaging to be labeled "18." The Act covers games "in which the range of options available to a player includes killing, maiming, dismembering, or sexually assaulting an image of a human being, if those acts are depicted" in a manner that "[a] reasonable person, considering the game as a whole, would find appeals to a deviant or morbid interest of minors," that is "patently offensive to prevailing standards in the community as to what is suitable for minors," and that "causes the game, as a whole, to lack serious literary, artistic, political, or scientific value for minors." §1746(d)(1)(A). Violation of the Act is punishable by a civil fine of up to $1,000.

II

California correctly acknowledges that video games qualify for First Amendment protection. The Free Speech Clause exists principally to protect discourse on public matters, but we have long recognized that it is difficult to distinguish politics from entertainment, and dangerous to try. "Everyone is familiar with instances of propaganda through fiction. What is one man's amusement, teaches another's doctrine." Winters v. New York, 333 U.S. 507, 510 (1948). Like the protected books, plays, and movies that preceded them, video games communicate ideas — and even social messages — through many familiar literary devices (such as characters, dialogue, plot, and music) and through features distinctive to the medium (such as the player's interaction with the virtual world). That suffices to confer First Amendment protection. Under our Constitution, "esthetic and moral judgments about art and literature . . . are for the individual to make, not for the Government to decree, even with the mandate or approval of a majority." United States v. Playboy Entertainment Group, Inc., 529 U.S. 803, 818 (2000). And whatever the challenges of applying the Constitution to ever-advancing technology, "the basic principles of freedom of speech and the press, like the First Amendment's command, do not vary" when a new and different medium for communication appears. Joseph Burstyn, Inc. v. Wilson, 343 U.S. 495, 503 (1952).

The most basic of those principles is this: "[A]s a general matter, . . . government has no power to restrict expression because of its message, its ideas, its subject matter, or its content." Ashcroft v. American Civil Liberties Union, 535 U.S. 564, 573 (2002) (internal quotation marks omitted).

[The case would be different] if there were a longstanding tradition in this country of specially restricting children's access to depictions of violence, but there is none. Certainly the *books* we give children to read—or read to them when they are younger—contain no shortage of gore. Grimm's Fairy Tales, for example, are grim indeed. As her just deserts for trying to poison Snow White, the wicked queen is made to dance in red hot slippers "till she fell dead on the floor, a sad example of envy and jealousy." The Complete Brothers Grimm Fairy Tales 198 (2006 ed.). Cinderella's evil stepsisters have their eyes pecked out by doves. *Id.* at 95. And Hansel and Gretel (children!) kill their captor by baking her in an oven. *Id.* at 54.

High-school reading lists are full of similar fare. Homer's Odysseus blinds Polyphemus the Cyclops by grinding out his eye with a heated stake. In the Inferno, Dante and Virgil watch corrupt politicians struggle to stay submerged beneath a lake of boiling pitch, lest they be skewered by devils above the surface. And Golding's Lord of the Flies recounts how a schoolboy called Piggy is savagely murdered *by other children* while marooned on an island.[18] This is not to say that minors' consumption of violent entertainment has never encountered resistance. In the 1800's, dime novels depicting crime and "penny dreadfuls" (named for their price and content) were blamed in some quarters for juvenile delinquency. When motion pictures came along, they became the villains instead. For a time, our Court did permit broad censorship of movies because of their capacity to be "used for evil," *see* Mutual Film Corp. v. Industrial Comm'n of Ohio, 236 U.S. 230, 242 (1915), but we eventually reversed course, *Joseph Burstyn, Inc.*, 343 U.S., at 502. Radio dramas were next, and then came comic books. Many in the late 1940's and early 1950's blamed comic books for fostering a "preoccupation with violence and horror" among the young, leading to a rising juvenile crime rate. But efforts to convince Congress to restrict comic books failed. And, of course, after comic books came television and music lyrics.

California claims that video games present special problems because they are "interactive," in that the player participates in the violent action on screen and determines its outcome. The latter feature is nothing new: [Y]oung readers of choose-your-own-adventure stories have been able to make decisions that determine the plot by following instructions about which page to turn to. As for the argument that video games enable participation in the violent action, that seems to us more a

18. Justice Alito accuses us of pronouncing that playing violent video games "is not different in 'kind'" from reading violent literature. Well of course it is different in kind, but not in a way that causes the provision and viewing of violent video games, unlike the provision and reading of books, not to be expressive activity and hence not to enjoy First Amendment protection. Reading Dante is unquestionably more cultured and intellectually edifying than playing Mortal Kombat. But these cultural and intellectual differences are not *constitutional* ones. Crudely violent video games, tawdry TV shows, and cheap novels and magazines are no less forms of speech than The Divine Comedy, and restrictions upon them must survive strict scrutiny. Even if we can see in them "nothing of any possible value to society . . . , they are as much entitled to the protection of free speech as the best of literature." Winters v. New York, 333 U.S. 507, 510 (1948).

matter of degree than of kind. As Judge Posner has observed, all literature is interactive. "[T]he better it is, the more interactive. Literature when it is successful draws the reader into the story, makes him identify with the characters, invites him to judge them and quarrel with them, to experience their joys and sufferings as the reader's own." American Amusement Machine Ass'n. v. Kendrick, 244 F.3d 572, 577 (C.A.7 2001) (striking down a similar restriction on violent video games).

Justice Alito has done considerable independent research to identify video games in which "the violence is astounding." "Victims are dismembered, decapitated, disemboweled, set on fire, and chopped into little pieces.... Blood gushes, splatters, and pools." Justice Alito recounts all these disgusting video games in order to disgust us—but disgust is not a valid basis for restricting expression. And the same is true of Justice Alito's description of those video games he has discovered that have a racial or ethnic motive for their violence—"'ethnic cleansing' [of]... African-Americans, Latinos, or Jews." To what end does he relate this? Does it somehow increase the "aggressiveness" that California wishes to suppress? Who knows? But it does arouse the reader's ire, and the reader's desire to put an end to this horrible message. Thus, ironically, Justice Alito's argument highlights the precise danger posed by the California Act: that the *ideas* expressed by speech—whether it be violence, or gore, or racism—and not its objective effects, may be the real reason for governmental proscription.

III

Because the Act imposes a restriction on the content of protected speech, it is invalid unless California can demonstrate that it passes strict scrutiny—that is, unless it is justified by a compelling government interest and is narrowly drawn to serve that interest.

The State's evidence is not compelling. California relies primarily on the research of Dr. Craig Anderson and a few other research psychologists whose studies purport to show a connection between exposure to violent video games and harmful effects on children. These studies have been rejected by every court to consider them, and with good reason: They do not prove that violent video games *cause* minors to *act* aggressively (which would at least be a beginning). Instead, "[n]early all of the research is based on correlation, not evidence of causation, and most of the studies suffer from significant, admitted flaws in methodology." 556 F.3d 950, 964 (9th Cir. 2009) [case below]. They show at best some correlation between exposure to violent entertainment and minuscule real-world effects, such as children's feeling more aggressive or making louder noises in the few minutes after playing a violent game than after playing a nonviolent game.[19] Even taking for granted Dr. Anderson's conclusions that violent video games produce some effect on children's feelings

19. One study, for example, found that children who had just finished playing violent video games were more likely to fill in the blank letter in "explo_e" with a "d" (so that it reads "explode") than with an "r" ("explore"). App. 496, 506. The prevention of this phenomenon, which might have been anticipated with common sense, is not a compelling state interest.

of aggression, those effects are both small and indistinguishable from effects produced by other media. In his testimony in a similar lawsuit, Dr. Anderson admitted that the "effect sizes" of children's exposure to violent video games are "about the same" as that produced by their exposure to violence on television. App. 1263. And he admits that the *same* effects have been found when children watch cartoons starring Bugs Bunny or the Road Runner, *id.* at 1304, or when they play video games like Sonic the Hedgehog that are rated "E" (appropriate for all ages), *id.* at 1270, or even when they "vie[w] a picture of a gun," *id.* at 1315–16.[20]

Of course, California has (wisely) declined to restrict Saturday morning cartoons, the sale of games rated for young children, or the distribution of pictures of guns. The consequence is that its regulation is wildly underinclusive when judged against its asserted justification, which in our view is alone enough to defeat it. Underinclusiveness raises serious doubts about whether the government is in fact pursuing the interest it invokes, rather than disfavoring a particular speaker or viewpoint. Here, California has singled out the purveyors of video games for disfavored treatment—at least when compared to booksellers, cartoonists, and movie producers—and has given no persuasive reason why.

California claims that the Act is justified in aid of parental authority: By requiring that the purchase of violent video games can be made only by adults, the Act ensures that parents can decide what games are appropriate. At the outset, we note our doubts that punishing third parties for conveying protected speech to children *just in case* their parents disapprove of that speech is a proper governmental means of aiding parental authority. Accepting that position would largely vitiate the rule that "only in relatively narrow and well-defined circumstances may government bar public dissemination of protected materials to [minors]." Erznoznik v. City of Jacksonville, 422 U.S. 205, 212–13 (1975).

But leaving that aside, California cannot show that the Act's restrictions meet a substantial need of parents who wish to restrict their children's access to violent

20. Justice Alito is mistaken in thinking that we fail to take account of "new and rapidly evolving technology." The studies in question pertain to that new and rapidly evolving technology, and fail to show, with the degree of certitude that strict scrutiny requires, that this subject-matter restriction on speech is justified. Nor is Justice Alito correct in attributing to us the view that "violent video games really present no serious problem." Perhaps they do present a problem, and perhaps none of us would allow our own children to play them. But there are all sorts of "problems"—some of them surely more serious than this one—that cannot be addressed by governmental restriction of free expression: for example, the problem of encouraging anti-Semitism (National Socialist Party of America v. Skokie, 432 U.S. 43 (1977) (per curiam)), the problem of spreading a political philosophy hostile to the Constitution (Noto v. United States, 367 U.S. 290 (1961)), or the problem of encouraging disrespect for the Nation's flag (Texas v. Johnson, 491 U.S. 397 (1989)).

Justice Breyer would hold that California has satisfied strict scrutiny based upon his own research into the issue of the harmfulness of violent video games. [W]e do not see how [this research] could lead to Justice Breyer's conclusion, since he admits he cannot say whether the studies on his side are right or wrong. Similarly, Justice Alito says he is not "sure" whether there are any constitutionally dispositive differences between video games and other media. If that is so, then strict scrutiny plainly has not been satisfied.

video games but cannot do so. The video-game industry has in place a voluntary rating system designed to inform consumers about the content of games. The system, implemented by the Entertainment Software Rating Board (ESRB), assigns age-specific ratings to each video game submitted: EC (Early Childhood); E (Everyone); E10+ (Everyone 10 and older); T (Teens); M (17 and older); and AO (Adults Only — 18 and older). The Video Software Dealers Association encourages retailers to prominently display information about the ESRB system in their stores; to refrain from renting or selling adults-only games to minors; and to rent or sell "M" rated games to minors only with parental consent. This system does much to ensure that minors cannot purchase seriously violent games on their own, and that parents who care about the matter can readily evaluate the games their children bring home. Filling the remaining modest gap in concerned parents' control can hardly be a compelling state interest.

And finally, the Act's purported aid to parental authority is vastly overinclusive. Not all of the children who are forbidden to purchase violent video games on their own have parents who *care* whether they purchase violent video games. While some of the legislation's effect may indeed be in support of what some parents of the restricted children actually want, its entire effect is only in support of what the State thinks parents *ought* to want. This is not the narrow tailoring to "assisting parents" that restriction of First Amendment rights requires.

JUSTICE ALITO, with whom CHIEF JUSTICE ROBERTS joins, concurring in the judgment.

The California statute that is before us in this case represents a pioneering effort to address what the state legislature and others regard as a potentially serious social problem: the effect of exceptionally violent video games on impressionable minors, who often spend countless hours immersed in the alternative worlds that these games create. Although the California statute is well intentioned, its terms are not framed with the precision that the Constitution demands, and I therefore agree with the Court that this particular law cannot be sustained.

I disagree, however, with the approach taken in the Court's opinion. In considering the application of unchanging constitutional principles to new and rapidly evolving technology, this Court should proceed with caution. We should make every effort to understand the new technology. We should take into account the possibility that developing technology may have important societal implications that will become apparent only with time. We should not jump to the conclusion that new technology is fundamentally the same as some older thing with which we are familiar. And we should not hastily dismiss the judgment of legislators, who may be in a better position than we are to assess the implications of new technology. The opinion of the Court exhibits none of this caution.

In the view of the Court, all those concerned about the effects of violent video games — federal and state legislators, educators, social scientists, and parents — are unduly fearful, for violent video games really present no serious problem. Spending hour upon hour controlling the actions of a character who guns down scores of innocent victims is not different in "kind" from reading a description of violence in a work of literature.

The Court is sure of this; I am not. There are reasons to suspect that the experience of playing violent video games just might be very different from reading a book, listening to the radio, or watching a movie or a television show.

I

Respondents in this case, representing the video game industry, ask us to strike down the California law on two grounds: The broad ground adopted by the Court and the narrower ground that the law's definition of "violent video game," *see* Cal. Civ.Code Ann. § 1746(d)(1)(A) (West 2009), is impermissibly vague. Because I agree with the latter argument, I see no need to reach the broader First Amendment issues addressed by the Court. Here, the California law does not define "violent video games" with the "narrow specificity" that the Constitution demands.

II C

[T]he Court is far too quick to dismiss the possibility that the experience of playing video games (and the effects on minors of playing violent video games) may be very different from anything that we have seen before. Any assessment of the experience of playing video games must take into account certain characteristics of the video games that are now on the market and those that are likely to be available in the near future.

Today's most advanced video games create realistic alternative worlds in which millions of players immerse themselves for hours on end. These games feature visual imagery and sounds that are strikingly realistic, and in the near future video-game graphics may be virtually indistinguishable from actual video footage. Many of the games already on the market can produce high definition images, and it is predicted that it will not be long before video-game images will be seen in three dimensions. It is also forecast that video games will soon provide sensory feedback. By wearing a special vest or other device, a player will be able to experience physical sensations supposedly felt by a character on the screen.

Persons who play video games also have an unprecedented ability to participate in the events that take place in the virtual worlds that these games create. Players can create their own video-game characters and can use photos to produce characters that closely resemble actual people. A person playing a sophisticated game can make a multitude of choices and can thereby alter the course of the action in the game.

In some of these games, the violence is astounding. Victims by the dozens are killed with every imaginable implement, including machineguns, shotguns, clubs, hammers, axes, swords, and chainsaws. Victims are dismembered, decapitated, disemboweled, set on fire, and chopped into little pieces. They cry out in agony and beg for mercy. Blood gushes, splatters, and pools. Severed body parts and gobs of human remains are graphically shown. In some games, points are awarded based, not only on the number of victims killed, but on the killing technique employed.

It also appears that there is no antisocial theme too base for some in the video-game industry to exploit. There are games in which a player can take on the identity and reenact the killings carried out by the perpetrators of the murders at Columbine High School and Virginia Tech. The objective of one game is to rape a mother and her daughters; in another, the goal is to rape Native American women. There is a game in which players engage in "ethnic cleansing" and can choose to gun down African-Americans, Latinos, or Jews. In still another game, players attempt to fire a rifle shot into the head of President Kennedy as his motorcade passes by the Texas School Book Depository.

If the technological characteristics of the sophisticated games that are likely to be available in the near future are combined with the characteristics of the most violent games already marketed, the result will be games that allow troubled teens to experience in an extraordinarily personal and vivid way what it would be like to carry out unspeakable acts of violence.

It is certainly true, as the Court notes, that "'[l]iterature when it is successful draws the reader into the story, makes him identify with the characters, invites him to judge them and quarrel with them, to experience their joys and sufferings as the reader's own.'" But only an extraordinarily imaginative reader who reads a description of a killing in a literary work will experience that event as vividly as he might if he played the role of the killer in a video game.

When all of the characteristics of video games are taken into account, there is certainly a reasonable basis for thinking that the experience of playing a video game may be quite different from the experience of reading a book, listening to a radio broadcast, or viewing a movie. And if this is so, then for at least some minors, the effects of playing violent video games may also be quite different. The Court acts prematurely in dismissing this possibility out of hand.

JUSTICE BREYER, dissenting.

The interest that California advances in support of the statute is compelling. As this Court has previously described that interest, it consists of both (1) the "basic" parental claim "to authority in their own household to direct the rearing of their children," which makes it proper to enact "laws designed to aid discharge of [parental] responsibility," and (2) the State's "independent interest in the well-being of its youth." Ginsberg v. New York, 390 U.S. 629, 639–40 (1968).

Both interests are present here. As to the need to help parents guide their children, the Court noted in 1968 that "'parental control or guidance cannot always be provided.'" *Id.* at 640. Today, 5.3 million grade-school-age children of working parents are routinely home alone. Thus, it has, if anything, become more important to supplement parents' authority to guide their children's development.

As to the State's independent interest, we have recognized "a compelling interest in protecting the physical and psychological well-being of minors." Sable Communications of California, Inc. v. FCC, 492 U.S. 115, 126 (1989).

[E]xtremely violent games can harm children by rewarding them for being violently aggressive in play, and thereby often teaching them to be violently aggressive in life. And video games can cause more harm in this respect than can typically passive media, such as books or films or television programs.

There are many scientific studies that support California's views. Social scientists, for example, have found *causal* evidence that playing these games results in harm. Longitudinal studies, which measure changes over time, have found that increased exposure to violent video games causes an increase in aggression over the same period.

Experimental studies in laboratories have found that subjects randomly assigned to play a violent video game subsequently displayed more characteristics of aggression than those who played nonviolent games.

Surveys of eighth and ninth grade students have found a correlation between playing violent video games and aggression.

And "meta-analyses," *i.e.,* studies of all the studies, have concluded that exposure to violent video games "was positively associated with aggressive behavior, aggressive cognition, and aggressive affect," and that "playing violent video games is a *causal* risk factor for long-term harmful outcomes." Anderson et al., Violent Video Game Effects on Aggression, Empathy, and Prosocial Behavior in Eastern and Western Countries: A Meta-Analytic Review, 136 Psychological Bull. 151, 167, 169 (2010) (emphasis added).

Some of these studies take care to explain in a commonsense way why video games are potentially more harmful than, say, films or books or television. In essence, they say that the closer a child's behavior comes, not to watching, but to *acting* out horrific violence, the greater the potential psychological harm.

Experts debate the conclusions of all these studies. Like many, perhaps most, studies of human behavior, each study has its critics, and some of those critics have produced studies of their own in which they reach different conclusions. I, like most judges, lack the social science expertise to say definitively who is right. But associations of public health professionals who do possess that expertise have reviewed many of these studies and found a significant risk that violent video games, when compared with more passive media, are particularly likely to cause children harm.

Unlike the majority, I would find sufficient grounds in these studies and expert opinions for this Court to defer to an elected legislature's conclusion that the video games in question are particularly likely to harm children. This Court has always thought it owed an elected legislature some degree of deference in respect to legislative facts of this kind, particularly when they involve technical matters that are beyond our competence, and even in First Amendment cases. The majority, in reaching its own, opposite conclusion about the validity of the relevant studies, grants the legislature no deference at all.

[Dissenting opinion of JUSTICE THOMAS is omitted.]

Notes and Questions

1. Is It Speech? Before *Entertainment Merchants* was decided, there was some disagreement among scholars as to whether video games are speech for First Amendment purposes. The majority treated the question as an easy one. Under the majority's approach, are there any interactive or immersive online experiences that would not be speech?

2. Constitutionally Relevant Differences. In a portion of his concurrence that we omitted, Justice Alito argued that the statute was impermissibly vague, relying on First Amendment vagueness cases (including *Reno v. ACLU*). But (in the portion we included) he also argued that the speech entailed in violent video games might be different in kind from other forms of speech. Are the differences between the experience of playing a violent video game and watching a violent movie of constitutional significance? On what basis would you draw such a distinction? What are its elements? If violent video games are not constitutionally different from, say, movies, are there other interactive games that you think should be constitutionally different? Would you draw the same constitutional lines for interactive sexual experiences? Why or why not?

3. What Role for Empirical Data? Justice Breyer discussed and cited many studies (our excerpt is a representative sample) and found them sufficient. The majority found the studies insufficient. What studies could satisfy the majority's standards (note that the majority requires studies "prov[ing] that violent video games *cause* minors to *act* aggressively")? Are such studies realistically obtainable, given the many confounding variables that any such studies have to deal with? If not, what, if anything, should that tell us?

4. How Could a Legislature Respond? After *Reno v. ACLU*, *Ashcroft II*, and *Entertainment Merchants*, what legislation would you propose to a legislator who wanted to regulate violence or indecency on the internet or in video games? If the answer is that Congress cannot place any restrictions on violence or indecency, is that an indictment of the Court and/or the First Amendment? A tribute to them?

§ 11.B.3. False Statements

Defamation is the central legal regulation of false factual statements. Defamation (libel for written words, slander for spoken words) applies to false statements of fact, not mere opinion. Unlike other legal regimes we consider in the casebook, libel and slander are torts that predate the Constitution and have a long history in the common law (though now many states have defamation statutes). This raises questions about hurdles to the application of the First Amendment to the defamation regime, given that the First Amendment prohibits the government from abridging speech.[21] It might seem both that defamation law does not involve the government and that in any event the First Amendment does not impinge on a longstanding common law tort that was long assumed to be unaffected by the passage of the First Amendment. Indeed, that was the prevailing view until the Supreme Court decided *New York Times v. Sullivan*. In *Sullivan*, the Court held that a state court enforcing a tort judgment was sufficient government involvement to trigger the application of the First Amendment, and that the First Amendment imposes significant limits on defamation. *Sullivan* not only transformed defamation law but also treated it as, in effect, a form of regulation. We include it in this casebook because of the significant limits it imposes on the regulation of false factual statements.

Defamation addresses false factual statements that damage a person's or organization's reputation. Some other kinds of false statements are not protected by the First Amendment—notably perjury, impersonating a government official, and fraud aimed at getting money. But what about more generic knowing falsehoods (a.k.a. lies) that might mislead listeners, and in particular voters? *United States v. Alvarez* addresses such falsehoods, applying First Amendment scrutiny and invalidating the statute. *Alvarez* thus imposes significant limits on the ability of the government to regulate lies.

New York Times Co. v. Sullivan

376 U.S. 254 (1964)

BRENNAN, J., delivered the opinion of the Court, in which WARREN, C.J., BLACK, DOUGLAS, CLARK, HARLAN, STEWART, and WHITE, JJ., joined. BLACK, J., filed a concurring opinion, in which DOUGLAS, J., joined. GOLDBERG, J., filed an opinion concurring in the result, in which DOUGLAS, J., joined.

JUSTICE BRENNAN delivered the opinion of the Court.

We are required in this case to determine for the first time the extent to which the constitutional protections for speech and press limit a State's power to award damages in a libel action brought by a public official against critics of his official conduct.

Respondent L. B. Sullivan is "Commissioner of Public Affairs and [his] duties are supervision of the Police Department, Fire Department, Department of Cemetery and Department of Scales" [of Montgomery, Alabama]. A jury [in a libel suit] awarded him damages of $500,000, the full amount claimed, against all the petitioners, and the Supreme Court of Alabama affirmed. Respondent's complaint alleged

21. The First Amendment's text refers only to *Congress* abridging the freedom of speech, but the Supreme Court has long interpreted "Congress" to refer to any government actor. Indeed, *New York Times v. Sullivan* was one of the cases that helped to establish this interpretation.

that he had been libeled by statements in a full-page advertisement that was carried in the New York Times.

It is uncontroverted that some of the statements contained in the [advertisement] were not accurate.

The manager of the [Times'] Advertising Acceptability Department testified that he had approved the advertisement for publication because he knew nothing to cause him to believe that anything in it was false, and because it bore the endorsement of "a number of people who are well known and whose reputation" he "had no reason to question." Neither he nor anyone else at the Times made an effort to confirm the accuracy of the advertisement, either by checking it against recent Times news stories relating to some of the described events or by any other means.

[W]e consider this case against the background of a profound national commitment to the principle that debate on public issues should be uninhibited, robust, and wide-open, and that it may well include vehement, caustic, and sometimes unpleasantly sharp attacks on government and public officials. The present advertisement, as an expression of grievance and protest on one of the major public issues of our time, would seem clearly to qualify for the constitutional protection. The question is whether it forfeits that protection by the falsity of some of its factual statements and by its alleged defamation of respondent.

[C]onstitutional protection does not turn upon "the truth, popularity, or social utility of the ideas and beliefs which are offered." N.A.A.C.P. v. Button, 371 U.S. 415, 445 (1963). As Madison said, "Some degree of abuse is inseparable from the proper use of every thing; and in no instance is this more true than in that of the press." 4 Elliot's Debates on the Federal Constitution (1876), p. 571. [E]rroneous statement is inevitable in free debate, and . . . must be protected if the freedoms of expression are to have the "breathing space" that they "need . . . to survive." N.A.A.C.P. v. Button, 371 U.S. at 433.

> Cases which impose liability for erroneous reports of the political conduct of officials reflect the obsolete doctrine that the governed must not criticize their governors. . . . The interest of the public here outweighs the interest of appellant or any other individual. The protection of the public requires not merely discussion, but information. . . . Errors of fact, particularly in regard to a man's mental states and processes, are inevitable. . . . Whatever is added to the field of libel is taken from the field of free debate.

Sweeney v. Patterson, 128 F.2d 457, 458 (D.C. Cir. 1942).

Injury to official reputation affords no more warrant for repressing speech that would otherwise be free than does factual error. [Government officials] are to be treated as "men of fortitude, able to thrive in a hardy climate." Craig v. Harney, 331 U.S. 367, 376 (1947). Criticism of their official conduct does not lose its constitutional protection merely because it is effective criticism and hence diminishes their official reputations.

If neither factual error nor defamatory content suffices to remove the constitutional shield from criticism of official conduct, the combination of the two elements is no less inadequate.

The state rule of law is not saved by its allowance of the defense of truth. A rule compelling the critic of official conduct to guarantee the truth of all his factual assertions—and to do so on pain of libel judgments virtually unlimited in amount—leads to "self-censorship." Allowance of the defense of truth, with the burden of proving it on the defendant, does not mean that only false speech will be deterred.[22]

Under such a rule, would-be critics of official conduct may be deterred from voicing their criticism, even though it is believed to be true and even though it is in fact true, because of doubt whether it can be proved in court or fear of the expense of having to do so. They tend to make only statements which "steer far wider of the unlawful zone." Speiser v. Randall, 357 U.S. 513, 526 (1958). The rule thus dampens the vigor and limits the variety of public debate.

The constitutional guarantees require, we think, a federal rule that prohibits a public official from recovering damages for a defamatory falsehood relating to his official conduct unless he proves that the statement was made with "actual malice"—that is, with knowledge that it was false or with reckless disregard of whether it was false or not.

JUSTICE BLACK, with whom JUSTICE DOUGLAS joins, concurring:

This Nation, I suspect, can live in peace without libel suits based on public discussions of public affairs and public officials. But I doubt that a country can live in freedom where its people can be made to suffer physically or financially for criticizing their government, its actions, or its officials. An unconditional right to say what one pleases about public affairs is what I consider to be the minimum guarantee of the First Amendment.

I regret that the Court has stopped short of this holding indispensable to preserve our free press from destruction.

[Concurring opinion of JUSTICE GOLDBERG is omitted.]

Notes and Questions

1. Later Cases. *Sullivan* arose out of a specific historical context involving attempts to reduce national media coverage of the civil rights movement. In the many years since then, the Supreme Court has had many opportunities to curtail or overrule *Sullivan* and has never done so. It has held that the constitutional minima for defamation of private figures on matters of public concern and on matters of private concern are lower, but it has also construed "private figure" and "private concern"

22. Even a false statement may be deemed to make a valuable contribution to public debate, since it brings about "the clearer perception and livelier impression of truth, produced by its collision with error." Mill, On Liberty (Oxford: Blackwell, 1947), at 15.

fairly narrowly, with the result that most people who participate in public debates are construed as public figures addressing matters of public concern. *See* Gertz v. Robert Welch, Inc., 418 U.S. 323 (1974); Dun & Bradstreet v. Greenmoss Builders, 472 U.S. 749 (1985).

2. Other Countries. In the years since *Sullivan*, many other countries (including Australia, New Zealand, Canada, and the United Kingdom) have explicitly considered following *Sullivan*, and none has chosen to do so.[23] Should that tell us anything?

3. Too Far or Not Far Enough? Note Justice Black's view that the First Amendment is an absolute bar to liability for criticism of government officials. On the other hand, Justice White (who joined the majority in *Sullivan*) later became a forceful critic of the regime. *See* Dun & Bradstreet v. Greenmoss Builders, 472 U.S. 749 (1985) (White, J., concurring in the judgment); *Gertz* (White, J., dissenting). More recently, Justices Thomas and Gorsuch criticized *Sullivan* and its progeny in dissents from denial of certiorari. *See, e.g.,* Berisha v. Lawson, 141 S. Ct. 2424, 2424 (2021) (Thomas, J. dissenting from the denial of certiorari); *id.* at 2425 (Gorsuch, J., dissenting from the denial of certiorari); McKee v. Cosby, 139 S. Ct. 675, 675 (2019) (Thomas, J., concurring in denial of certiorari). Denials of certiorari have no precedential value, much less dissents from such denials, so we excerpt below Justice Gorsuch's dissent from the denial of certiorari in *Berisha v. Lawson* simply to highlight a more recent argument for limiting (if not overruling) *Sullivan* that is relevant to some of the themes of this casebook:

> Since 1964, our Nation's media landscape has shifted in ways few could have foreseen. Back then, building printing presses and amassing newspaper distribution networks demanded significant investment and expertise. Broadcasting required licenses for limited airwaves and access to highly specialized equipment. Comparatively large companies dominated the press, often employing legions of investigative reporters, editors, and fact-checkers. [T]hanks to revolutions in technology, today virtually anyone in this country can publish virtually anything for immediate consumption virtually anywhere in the world.
>
> The effect of these technological changes on our Nation's media may be hard to overstate. Large numbers of newspapers and periodicals have failed. Network news has lost most of its viewers. With their fall has come the rise of 24-hour cable news and online media platforms that "monetize anything that garners clicks." Logan, Rescuing Our Democracy by Rethinking New York Times Co. v. Sullivan, 81 Ohio St. L.J. 759, 800 (2020). No doubt, this new media world has many virtues — not least the access it affords those who seek information about and the opportunity to debate public affairs.

---

23. *See* Lange v. Australian Broadcasting Corporation, (1997) 189 C.L.R. 520 (H.C.) (Austl.); Lange v. Atkinson [1998] 3 NZLR 424 (Ct. App.) (N.Z.); Hill v. Church of Scientology, [1995] 2 S.C.R. 1130 (Can.); Reynolds v. Times Newspapers Limited, 4 All E.R. 609 (1999) (H.L.) (U.K.).

> At the same time, some reports suggest that our new media environment also facilitates the spread of disinformation. A study of one social network reportedly found that "falsehood and rumor dominated truth by every metric, reaching more people, penetrating deeper . . . and doing so more quickly than accurate statements." *Id.* at 804. All of which means that "the distribution of disinformation" — which "costs almost nothing to generate" — has become a "profitable" business while "the economic model that supported reporters, fact-checking, and editorial oversight" has "deeply erod[ed]." *Id.* at 800.
>
> What started in 1964 with a decision to tolerate the occasional falsehood to ensure robust reporting by a comparative handful of print and broadcast outlets has evolved into an ironclad subsidy for the publication of falsehoods by means and on a scale previously unimaginable. If ensuring an informed democratic debate is the goal, how well do we serve that interest with rules that no longer merely tolerate but encourage falsehoods in quantities no one could have envisioned almost 60 years ago?
>
> [P]rivate citizens can become "public figures" on social media overnight. Individuals can be deemed "famous" because of their notoriety in certain channels of our now-highly segmented media even as they remain unknown in most. *See, e.g.*, Hibdon v. Grabowski, 195 S.W.3d 48, 59, 62 (Tenn. App. 2005) (holding that an individual was a limited-purpose public figure in part because he "entered into the jet ski business and voluntarily advertised on the news group rec.sport.jetski, an internet site that is accessible worldwide"). Lower courts have even said that an individual can become a limited purpose public figure simply by *defending* himself from a defamatory statement. Other persons, such as victims of sexual assault seeking to confront their assailants, might choose to enter the public square only reluctantly and yet wind up treated as limited purpose public figures too.
>
> Not only has the doctrine evolved into a subsidy for published falsehoods on a scale no one could have foreseen, it has come to leave far more people without redress than anyone could have predicted. Rules intended to ensure a robust debate over actions taken by high public officials carrying out the public's business increasingly seem to leave even ordinary Americans without recourse for grievous defamation.

Berisha v. Lawson, 141 S. Ct. at 2427–29 (Gorsuch, J., dissenting from the denial of certiorari).

On what basis should we assess whether *Sullivan* should be retained? Does the internet, and social media in particular, affect the considerations in constitutionally relevant ways? If so, how, exactly? If not, why not?

4. **The Benefits of False Statements?** The majority said that even false statements can make a valuable contribution to public debate. Is that true? Might false statements'

harms so outweigh their benefits that they should not be protected? That question arose in litigation after Congress enacted the Stolen Valor Act, 18 U.S.C. § 704, which punished a category of false statements that Congress found particularly troubling—lying about military medals. In the following opinion, the Supreme Court held that the Stolen Valor Act violated the First Amendment.

United States v. Alvarez

567 U.S. 709 (2012)

KENNEDY, J., announced the judgment of the Court and delivered an opinion, in which ROBERTS, C.J., and GINSBURG and SOTOMAYOR, JJ., joined. BREYER, J., filed an opinion concurring in the judgment, in which KAGAN, J., joined. ALITO, J., filed a dissenting opinion, in which SCALIA and THOMAS, JJ., joined.

JUSTICE KENNEDY announced the judgment of the Court.

Lying was his habit. Xavier Alvarez, the respondent here, lied when he said that he played hockey for the Detroit Red Wings and that he once married a starlet from Mexico. But when he lied in announcing he held the Congressional Medal of Honor (Medal), respondent ventured onto new ground; for that lie violates a federal criminal statute, the Stolen Valor Act of 2005, 18 U.S.C. § 704.

In 2007, respondent attended his first public meeting as a board member of the Three Valley Water District Board. The board is a governmental entity with headquarters in Claremont, California. He introduced himself as follows: "'I'm a retired marine of 25 years. I retired in the year 2001. Back in 1987, I was awarded the Congressional Medal of Honor. I got wounded many times by the same guy.'" United States v. Alvarez, 617 F.3d 1198, 1201–02 (9th Cir. 2010). None of this was true.

Respondent's claim to hold the Congressional Medal of Honor (Medal) was false. There is no room to argue about interpretation or shades of meaning. On this premise, respondent violated § 704(b):

> Whoever falsely represents himself or herself, verbally or in writing, to have been awarded any decoration or medal authorized by Congress for the Armed Forces of the United States . . . shall be fined under this title, imprisoned not more than six months, or both.

Respondent challenges the statute as a content-based suppression of pure speech, speech not falling within any of the few categories of expression where content-based regulation is permissible. The Government defends the statute as necessary to preserve the integrity and purpose of the Medal, an integrity and purpose it contends are compromised and frustrated by the false statements the statute prohibits. It argues that false statements "have no First Amendment value in themselves," and thus "are protected only to the extent needed to avoid chilling fully protected speech." Brief for United States 18, 20. Although the statute covers respondent's speech, the Government argues that it leaves breathing room for protected speech, for example speech which might criticize the idea of the Medal or the importance of the military. The Government's arguments cannot suffice to save the statute.

"[A]s a general matter, the First Amendment means that government has no power to restrict expression because of its message, its ideas, its subject matter, or its content." Ashcroft v. American Civil Liberties Union, 535 U.S. 564, 573 (2002) (internal quotation marks omitted). As a result, the Constitution "demands that content-based restrictions on speech be presumed invalid . . . and that the Government bear the burden of showing their constitutionality." Ashcroft v. American Civil Liberties Union, 542 U.S. 656, 660 (2004).

In light of the substantial and expansive threats to free expression posed by content-based restrictions, this Court has rejected as "startling and dangerous" a "free-floating test for First Amendment coverage . . . [based on] an ad hoc balancing of relative social costs and benefits." United States v. Stevens, 559 U.S. 460, 470 (2010). Instead, content-based restrictions on speech have been permitted, as a general matter, only when confined to the few "historic and traditional categories [of expression] long familiar to the bar." *Id.* at 468 [internal quotation omitted]). Among these categories are advocacy intended, and likely, to incite imminent lawless action, obscenity, defamation, speech integral to criminal conduct, so-called "fighting words," child pornography, fraud, true threats, and speech presenting some grave and imminent threat the government has the power to prevent, although a restriction under the last category is most difficult to sustain.

Absent from those few categories where the law allows content-based regulation of speech is any general exception to the First Amendment for false statements. This comports with the common understanding that some false statements are inevitable if there is to be an open and vigorous expression of views in public and private conversation, expression the First Amendment seeks to guarantee. *See* New York Times Co. v. Sullivan, 376 U.S. 254, 271 (1964) ("Th[e] erroneous statement is inevitable in free debate").

The Government disagrees with this proposition. It cites language from some of this Court's precedents to support its contention that false statements have no value and hence no First Amendment protection. These isolated statements in some earlier decisions do not support the Government's submission that false statements, as a general rule, are beyond constitutional protection. That conclusion would take the quoted language far from its proper context. For instance, the Court has stated "[f]alse statements of fact are particularly valueless [because] they interfere with the truth-seeking function of the marketplace of ideas," Hustler Magazine, Inc. v. Falwell, 485 U.S. 46, 52 (1988), and that false statements "are not protected by the First Amendment in the same manner as truthful statements," Brown v. Hartlage, 456 U.S. 45, 60–61 (1982).

These quotations all derive from cases discussing defamation, fraud, or some other legally cognizable harm associated with a false statement, such as an invasion of privacy or the costs of vexatious litigation. In those decisions the falsity of the speech at issue was not irrelevant to our analysis, but neither was it determinative. The Court has never endorsed the categorical rule the Government advances: that false statements receive no First Amendment protection. Our prior decisions have not confronted a measure, like the Stolen Valor Act, that targets falsity and nothing more.

Even when considering some instances of defamation and fraud, the Court has been careful to instruct that falsity alone may not suffice to bring the speech outside the First Amendment. The statement must be a knowing or reckless falsehood. *See Sullivan* at 280 (prohibiting recovery of damages for a defamatory falsehood made about a public official unless the statement was made "with knowledge that it was false or with reckless disregard of whether it was false or not").

The Government thus seeks to use this principle for a new purpose. It seeks to convert a rule that limits liability even in defamation cases where the law permits recovery for tortious wrongs into a rule that expands liability in a different, far greater realm of discourse and expression. That inverts the rationale for the exception. The requirements of a knowing falsehood or reckless disregard for the truth as the condition for recovery in certain defamation cases exists to allow more speech, not less. A rule designed to tolerate certain speech ought not blossom to become a rationale for a rule restricting it.

18 U.S.C. § 1001's prohibition on false statements made to Government officials, in communications concerning official matters, does not lead to the broader proposition that false statements are unprotected when made to any person, at any time, in any context.

The same point can be made about what the Court has confirmed is the "unquestioned constitutionality of perjury statutes." United States v. Grayson, 438 U.S. 41, 54 (1978). It is not simply because perjured statements are false that they lack First Amendment protection. Perjury undermines the function and province of the law and threatens the integrity of judgments that are the basis of the legal system. Unlike speech in other contexts, testimony under oath has the formality and gravity necessary to remind the witness that his or her statements will be the basis for official governmental action, action that often affects the rights and liberties of others. Sworn testimony is quite distinct from lies not spoken under oath and simply intended to puff up oneself.

As our law and tradition show, then, there are instances in which the falsity of speech bears upon whether it is protected. Some false speech may be prohibited even if analogous true speech could not be. This opinion does not imply that any of these targeted prohibitions are somehow vulnerable. But it also rejects the notion that false speech should be in a general category that is presumptively unprotected.

The probable, and adverse, effect of the Act on freedom of expression illustrates, in a fundamental way, the reasons for the law's distrust of content-based speech prohibitions.

Permitting the government to decree this speech to be a criminal offense, whether shouted from the rooftops or made in a barely audible whisper, would endorse government authority to compile a list of subjects about which false statements are punishable. That governmental power has no clear limiting principle. Our constitutional tradition stands against the idea that we need Oceania's Ministry of Truth. *See* G. Orwell, Nineteen Eighty-Four (1949). Were this law to be sustained, there could be an endless list of subjects the National Government or the States could single out. Where false claims are made to effect a fraud or secure moneys or other valuable considerations, say offers of employment, it is well established that the Government may restrict speech without affronting the First Amendment. But the Stolen Valor Act is not so limited in its reach. Were the Court to hold that the interest in truthful discourse alone is sufficient to sustain a ban on speech, absent any evidence that the speech was used to gain a material advantage, it would give government a broad censorial power unprecedented in this Court's cases or in our constitutional tradition. The mere potential for the exercise of that power casts a chill, a chill the First Amendment cannot permit if free speech, thought, and discourse are to remain a foundation of our freedom.

The previous discussion suffices to show that the Act conflicts with free speech principles. But even when examined within its own narrow sphere of operation, the Act cannot survive. In assessing content-based restrictions on protected speech, the Court has not adopted a free-wheeling approach, but rather has applied the "most exacting scrutiny." Turner Broadcasting System, Inc. v. FCC, 512 U.S. 622, 642 (1994). Although the objectives the Government seeks to further by the statute are not without significance, the Court must, and now does, find the Act does not satisfy exacting scrutiny.

The Government is correct when it states military medals "serve the important public function of recognizing and expressing gratitude for acts of heroism and sacrifice in military service," and also "'foste[r] morale, mission accomplishment and esprit de corps' among service members." Brief for United States 37, 38.

But to recite the Government's compelling interests is not to end the matter. The First Amendment requires that the Government's chosen restriction on the speech at issue be "actually necessary" to achieve its interest. *Entertainment Merchants Ass'n.*, 564 U.S. at 799. There must be a direct causal link between the restriction imposed and the injury to be prevented. The link between the Government's interest in protecting the integrity of the military honors system and the Act's restriction on the false claims of liars like respondent has not been shown.

The Government points to no evidence to support its claim that the public's general perception of military awards is diluted by false claims such as those made by Alvarez.

The lack of a causal link between the Government's stated interest and the Act is not the only way in which the Act is not actually necessary to achieve the Government's stated interest. The Government has not shown, and cannot show, why counterspeech would not suffice to achieve its interest. The facts of this case indicate that the dynamics of free speech, of counterspeech, of refutation, can overcome the lie. Respondent lied at a public meeting. Even before the FBI began investigating him for his false statements "Alvarez was perceived as a phony," 617 F.3d, at 1211. Once the lie was made public, he was ridiculed online, his actions were reported in the press, and a fellow board member called for his resignation.

The remedy for speech that is false is speech that is true. This is the ordinary course in a free society. The response to the unreasoned is the rational; to the uninformed, the enlightened; to the straightout lie, the simple truth. The theory of our Constitution is "that the best test of truth is the power of the thought to get itself accepted in the competition of the market," Abrams v. United States, 250 U.S. 616, 630 (1919) (Holmes, J., dissenting). The First Amendment itself ensures the right to respond to speech we do not like, and for good reason. Freedom of speech and thought flows not from the beneficence of the state but from the inalienable rights of the person. And suppression of speech by the government can make exposure of falsity more difficult, not less so. Society has the right and civic duty to engage in open, dynamic, rational discourse. These ends are not well served when the government seeks to orchestrate public discussion through content-based mandates.

JUSTICE BREYER, with whom JUSTICE KAGAN joins, concurring in the judgment.

As the dissent points out, "there are broad areas in which any attempt by the state to penalize purportedly false speech would present a grave and unacceptable danger of suppressing truthful speech." Laws restricting false statements about philosophy, religion, history, the social sciences, the arts, and the like raise such concerns, and in many contexts have called for strict scrutiny. But this case does not involve such a law. The dangers of suppressing valuable ideas are lower where, as here, the regulations concern false statements about easily verifiable facts that do not concern such subject matter. Such false factual statements are less likely than are true factual statements to make a valuable contribution to the marketplace of ideas. And the government often has good reasons to prohibit such false speech. But its regulation can nonetheless threaten speech-related harms.

False factual statements can serve useful human objectives, for example: in social contexts, where they may prevent embarrassment, protect privacy, shield a person from prejudice, provide the sick with comfort, or preserve a child's innocence; in public contexts, where they may stop a panic or otherwise preserve calm in the face of danger; and even in technical, philosophical, and scientific contexts, where (as Socrates' methods suggest) examination of a false statement (even if made deliberately to mislead) can promote a form of thought that ultimately helps realize the truth.

Moreover, as the Court has often said, the threat of criminal prosecution for making a false statement can inhibit the speaker from making true statements, thereby "chilling" a kind of speech that lies at the First Amendment's heart. *See, e.g.*, Gertz v. Welch, 418 U.S. 323, 340–41 (1974). Hence, the Court emphasizes mens rea requirements that provide "breathing room" for more valuable speech by reducing an honest speaker's fear that he may accidentally incur liability for speaking.

Further, the pervasiveness of false statements, made for better or for worse motives, made thoughtlessly or deliberately, made with or without accompanying harm, provides a weapon to a government broadly empowered to prosecute falsity without more. And those who are unpopular may fear that the government will use that weapon selectively, say, by prosecuting a pacifist who supports his cause by (falsely) claiming to have been a war hero, while ignoring members of other political groups who might make similar false claims.

I also must concede that many statutes and common-law doctrines make the utterance of certain kinds of false statements unlawful. Those prohibitions, however, tend to be narrower than the statute before us, in that they limit the scope of their application, sometimes by requiring proof of specific harm to identifiable victims; sometimes by specifying that the lies be made in contexts in which a tangible harm to others is especially likely to occur; and sometimes by limiting the prohibited lies to those that are particularly likely to produce harm.

Statutes prohibiting trademark infringement present, perhaps, the closest analogy to the present statute. Trademarks identify the source of a good; and infringement causes harm by causing confusion among potential customers (about the source) and thereby diluting the value of the mark to its owner, to consumers, and to the economy. Similarly, a false claim of possession of a medal or other honor creates confusion about who is entitled to wear it, thus diluting its value to those who have earned it, to their families, and to their country. But trademark statutes are focused upon commercial and promotional activities that are likely to dilute the value of a mark. Indeed, they typically require a showing of likely confusion, a showing that tends to ensure that the feared harm will in fact take place.

[The Stolen Valor Act] ranges very broadly. And that breadth means that it creates a significant risk of First Amendment harm. As written, it applies in family, social, or other private contexts, where lies will often cause little harm. It also applies in political contexts, where although such lies are more likely to cause harm, the risk of censorious selectivity by prosecutors is also high.

Like both the plurality and the dissent, I believe the statute nonetheless has substantial justification. It seeks to protect the interests of those who have sacrificed their health and life for their country. The statute serves this interest by seeking to preserve intact the country's recognition of that sacrifice in the form of military honors. To permit those who have not earned those honors to claim otherwise dilutes the value of the awards.

We must therefore ask whether it is possible substantially to achieve the Government's objective in less burdensome ways. In my view, the answer to this question is "yes." As is indicated by the limitations on the scope of the many other kinds of statutes regulating false factual speech, it should be possible significantly to diminish or eliminate these remaining risks by enacting a similar but more finely tailored statute. For example, not all military awards are alike. Congress might determine that some warrant greater protection than others. And a more finely tailored statute might, as other kinds of statutes prohibiting false factual statements have done, insist upon a showing that the false statement caused specific harm or at least was material, or focus its coverage on lies most likely to be harmful or on contexts where such lies are most likely to cause harm.

I recognize that in some contexts, particularly political contexts, such a narrowing will not always be easy to achieve. In the political arena a false statement is more likely to make a behavioral difference (say, by leading the listeners to vote for the speaker) but at the same time criminal prosecution is particularly dangerous (say, by radically changing a potential election result) and consequently can more easily result in censorship of speakers and their ideas. Thus, the statute may have to be significantly narrowed in its applications.

The Government has provided no convincing explanation as to why a more finely tailored statute would not work. In my own view, such a statute could significantly reduce the threat of First Amendment harm while permitting the statute to achieve its important protective objective. That being so, I find the statute as presently drafted works disproportionate constitutional harm. It consequently fails intermediate scrutiny, and so violates the First Amendment.

JUSTICE ALITO, with whom JUSTICE SCALIA and JUSTICE THOMAS join, dissenting.

Only the bravest of the brave are awarded the Congressional Medal of Honor, but the Court today holds that every American has a constitutional right to claim to have received this singular award. The Court strikes down the Stolen Valor Act of 2005, which was enacted to stem an epidemic of false claims about military decorations. These lies, Congress reasonably concluded, were undermining our country's system of military honors and inflicting real harm on actual medal recipients and their families.

Building on earlier efforts to protect the military awards system, Congress responded to this problem by crafting a narrow statute that presents no threat to the freedom of speech. The statute reaches only knowingly false statements about hard facts directly within a speaker's personal knowledge. These lies have no value in and of themselves, and proscribing them does not chill any valuable speech.

By holding that the First Amendment nevertheless shields these lies, the Court breaks sharply from a long line of cases recognizing that the right to free speech does not protect false factual statements that inflict real harm and serve no legitimate interest. I would adhere to that principle and would thus uphold the constitutionality of this valuable law.

Time and again, this Court has recognized that as a general matter false factual statements possess no intrinsic First Amendment value.

Consistent with this recognition, many kinds of false factual statements have long been proscribed without "'rais[ing] any Constitutional problem.'" United States v. Stevens, 559 U.S. 460, 469 (2010) (quoting Chaplinsky v. New Hampshire, 315 U.S. 568, 571–72 (1942)). Laws prohibiting fraud, perjury, and defamation, for example, were in existence when the First Amendment was adopted, and their constitutionality is now beyond question.

[F]alse statements of fact merit no First Amendment protection in their own right. It is true, as Justice Breyer notes, that many in our society either approve or condone certain discrete categories of false statements, including false statements made to prevent harm to innocent victims and so-called "white lies." But respondent's false claim to have received the Medal of Honor did not fall into any of these categories.

While we have repeatedly endorsed the principle that false statements of fact do not merit First Amendment protection for their own sake, we have recognized that it is sometimes necessary to "exten[d] a measure of strategic protection" to these statements in order to ensure sufficient "'breathing space'" for protected speech. *Gertz,* 418 U.S., at 342 (quoting *NAACP v. Button,* 371 U.S. 415, 433 (1963)). Thus, in order to prevent the chilling of truthful speech on matters of public concern, we have held that liability for the defamation of a public official or figure requires proof that defamatory statements were made with knowledge or reckless disregard of their falsity. *See* New York Times Co. v. Sullivan, 376 U.S. 254, 279–280 (1964) (civil liability). This same requirement applies when public officials and figures seek to recover for the tort of intentional infliction of emotional distress. And we have imposed "[e]xacting proof requirements" in other contexts as well when necessary to ensure that truthful speech is not chilled. *Madigan,* 538 U.S., at 620 (complainant in a fraud action must show that the defendant made a knowingly false statement of material fact with the intent to mislead the listener and that he succeeded in doing so). All of these proof requirements inevitably have the effect of bringing some false factual statements within the protection of the First Amendment, but this is justified in order to prevent the chilling of other, valuable speech.

These examples by no means exhaust the circumstances in which false factual statements enjoy a degree of instrumental constitutional protection. On the contrary, there are broad areas in which any attempt by the state to penalize purportedly false speech would present a grave and unacceptable danger of suppressing truthful speech. Laws restricting false statements about philosophy, religion, history, the social sciences, the arts, and other matters of public concern would present such a threat. The point is not that there is no such thing as truth or falsity in these areas or that the truth is always impossible to ascertain, but rather that it is perilous to permit the state to be the arbiter of truth.

Even where there is a wide scholarly consensus concerning a particular matter, the truth is served by allowing that consensus to be challenged without fear of reprisal. Today's accepted wisdom sometimes turns out to be mistaken. And in these contexts, "[e]ven a false statement may be deemed to make a valuable contribution to public debate, since it brings about 'the clearer perception and livelier impression of truth, produced by its collision with error.'" *Sullivan,* 376 U.S. at 279 n. 19 (quoting J. Mill, On Liberty 15 (R. McCallum ed. 1947)).

Allowing the state to proscribe false statements in these areas also opens the door for the state to use its power for political ends. Statements about history illustrate this point. If some false statements about historical events may be banned, how certain must it be that a statement is false before the ban may be upheld? And who should make that calculation? While our cases prohibiting viewpoint discrimination would fetter the state's power to some degree, the potential for abuse of power in these areas is simply too great.

In stark contrast to hypothetical laws prohibiting false statements about history, science, and similar matters, the Stolen Valor Act presents no risk at all that valuable speech will be suppressed. The speech punished by the Act is not only verifiably false and entirely lacking in intrinsic value, but it also fails to serve any instrumental purpose that the First Amendment might protect. Tellingly, when asked at oral argument what truthful speech the Stolen Valor Act might chill, even respondent's counsel conceded that the answer is none.

Notes and Questions

1. **Agreement**. The various opinions disagreed about the breadth and application of protections for false statements, but all nine Justices agreed that some false statements are constitutionally protected. Is it surprising that none agreed with the government's position that false statements are categorically unprotected?

2. **Philosophy**. Justice Alito's dissent suggested that "[l]aws restricting false statements about philosophy, religion, history, the social sciences, the arts, and other matters of public concern" would be unconstitutional and Justice Breyer's concurrence made a similar point about "[l]aws restricting false statements about philosophy, religion, history, the social sciences, the arts, and the like." The plurality, which of course adopted a broader view of First Amendment protection of false statements than the concurrence or dissent did, presumably would protect more false statements. What metric should the Court use to determine the categories of speech in which false statements are constitutionally protected?

3. **Politics**. Alvarez made his false statement as a government official in a public meeting. He thus lied in a context in which the lie might have benefited his political stature. Justice Breyer's concurrence discussed the tradeoffs arising from application of a ban on false statements in political contexts. What considerations should predominate? Should lies in the political context be more or less protected than lies in other contexts?

4. **Counterspeech**. Are you persuaded by the plurality's discussion of counterspeech? Note its conclusion that the government not only did not but also could not show

why counterspeech would not achieve its goals, indicating that there is no showing the government could have made. Is there a set of facts that you think should be sufficient to demonstrate the inadequacy of counterspeech? More generally, is there a set of facts that should justify the Stolen Valor Act?

5. **Empirical Data on False Statements**. Because of the many topics that are subject to false statements, measuring the generalized harm of falsity is difficult. There have been studies of the effects of false statements on specific topics (e.g., voting, climate change, and vaccines). They have mixed results, with some studies finding small but statistically significant effects and some studies finding no statistically significant effects.[24] There is some evidence that false news spreads faster than the truth and that people tend to believe false information after repeated exposure to the falsehood.[25]

As with regulation of indecency and violent content, on what basis should courts decide how much weight to place on empirical data when considering First Amendment challenges to regulation of falsehoods? Should empirical data play the same role in the First Amendment analysis of regulation of indecency, violent content, and false statements?

6. **Scope**. The online and offline worlds are awash with false statements. What sorts of regulations of false statements do *Sullivan* and *Alvarez* allow? What meaningful regulation of false statements might be permissible beyond the categories noted in the opinions above (like fraud and defamation)?

Relatedly there is widespread concern about false or misleading speech in the public sphere, often termed disinformation, misinformation, or fake news. There are varying definitions of each of these terms, but the underlying concern is that public discourse and understanding can be harmed by false or misleading statements. What room does *Alvarez* leave for regulation of such speech?

---

24. *See, e.g.*, Kenneth Michael White et al., Information, Misinformation, and Political Participation, 27 Amer. Rev. Pol. 71 (2006); Aaron M. McCright, Meghan Charters, Katherine Dentzman & Thomas Dietz, Examining the Effectiveness of Climate Change Frames in the Face of a Climate Change Denial Counter-Frame, 8 Topics Cognitive Sci. 76 (2016); Piotr Rzymski et al., The Strategies to Support the COVID-19 Vaccination with Evidence-Based Communication and Tackling Misinformation, 9 Vaccines 109 (2021).

25. *See, e.g.*, Soroush Vosoughi et al., The Spread of True and False News Online, 359 Sci. 1146 (2018); Lisa K. Fazio et al., Knowledge Does Not Protect Against Illusory Truth, 144 J. Experim. Psych. 993 (2015); Danielle C. Polage, Making up History: False Memories of Fake News Stories, 8 Europe's J. Psych. 245 (2012).

Chapter 12

Regulating Algorithms

Introduction

Chapters 3 and 11 address when any First Amendment judicial scrutiny applies and the treatment of content-based regulations in a broad range of contexts. In this chapter, we focus on the possible application of the First Amendment to the regulation of the algorithms that internet platforms rely on. Turner Broadcasting System, Inc. v. FCC, 512 U.S. 622 (1994) (*Turner I*) indicates that the regulation of humans' decisions about what content to include on an internet platform would implicate the First Amendment as a regulation of editorial discretion. But what about the regulation of algorithms that internet platforms use to develop and curate their content? Would such regulations trigger First Amendment scrutiny?

This question is particularly important because many advocates and policymakers have proposed regulations of platforms' algorithms as a means of mitigating perceived harms or increasing perceived benefits of those platforms. For instance, some have proposed regulating the algorithms used to prioritize posts, or to recommend or autoplay content.[1] Relatedly, some have proposed regulating the degree to which platforms are allowed to prioritize the goods and services they offer.[2] Other possibilities include requiring that algorithms deprioritize, or block, false information or content that disparages or encourages hostility toward people based on characteristics like ethnicity and religion.[3]

1. *See, e.g.*, Interim Report: Review into Online Targeting § 8.4 (Center for Data Ethics and Innovation, July 25, 2019) (UK), https://www.gov.uk/government/publications/interim-reports-from-the-centre-for-data-ethics-and-innovation/interim-report-review-into-online-targeting (exploring "mechanisms to restrict the types of inferences that can be made and used in targeting processes, or the types and narrowness of targeting that can be undertaken"); Jason A. Gallo & Clare Y. Cho, Cong. Rsch. Serv., R46662, Social Media: Misinformation and Content Moderation Issues for Congress 23 (2021) (asserting that federal regulations could set standards for content moderation in counteracting misinformation).

2. *See, e.g.*, Australian Competition & Consumer Comm'n, Discussion Paper for Interim Report No. 5: Updating Competition and Consumer Law for Digital Platform Services § 8.1.1 (Feb. 2022) (calling for regulation against self-preferencing by key digital platforms).

3. *See, e.g.*, the proposed Health Misinformation Act of 2021 (limiting liability protection if a platform promotes health misinformation during a declared public health emergency) and the proposed Algorithmic Justice and Online Platform Transparency Act of 2021 (requiring platforms to affirmatively eliminate discriminatory results from their algorithms).

Other proposals would require allowing users to opt out of a platform's default algorithm and choose different prioritization.[4] One of us has called for regulation that forces major platforms to allow consumers to choose among third-party filters to curate and order the content they see on the platforms.[5]

First Amendment scrutiny would be a serious impediment to such regulation of algorithms. The question we address in this chapter is whether regulations of algorithms would in fact trigger First Amendment scrutiny. Should regulation of algorithms be treated differently from similar decisions made by humans?

Note that this is different from the question whether computer code itself is speech for First Amendment purposes, such that regulations on the distribution of code implicated the First Amendment.[6] Such regulations of the distribution of code have treated the code itself as a national security concern. The regulatory focus with respect to internet platforms has not been on the distribution of code but instead on the outputs of that code—the decisions created by algorithms. The question whether the First Amendment applies to regulation of the outputs of algorithms (like search engine results) is different from the question whether the algorithms used by those search engines are speech. Even if the algorithms are not speech, their products may be.

We begin with excerpts of two law review articles taking contrasting positions and then excerpt a judicial opinion addressing the issue.

---

4. *See, e.g.*, the proposed Filter Bubble Transparency Act of 2021 (requiring large platforms to explain their algorithms to consumers and offer alternative feeds).

5. *See* Francis Fukuyama, Barak Richman, Ashish Goel, Roberta R. Katz, A. Douglas Melamed & Marietje Schaake, Middleware for Dominant Digital Platforms: A Technological Solution to a Threat to Democracy, https://fsi-live.s3.us-west-1.amazonaws.com/s3fs-public/cpc-middleware_ff_v2.pdf.

6. For what it is worth, the few courts that considered the issue found by and large that regulations of computer code were regulations of speech. *See* Universal City Studios, Inc. v. Corley, 273 F.3d 429, 447 (2d Cir. 2001) (holding that the First Amendment covers computer programs, and stating that "[a] recipe is no less 'speech' because it calls for the use of an oven, and a musical score is no less 'speech' because it specifies performance on an electric guitar"); Bernstein v. Dep't of Justice, 176 F.3d 1132, 1141 (9th Cir. 1999) (concluding that "encryption software, in its source code form and as employed by those in the field of cryptography, must be viewed as expressive for First Amendment purposes"), *reh'g en banc granted and opinion withdrawn*, 192 F.3d 1308 (9th Cir. 1999).

Stuart Minor Benjamin, Algorithms and Speech

161 U. Penn. L. Rev. 1445 (2013)

II. The Centrality and Expansion of Supreme Court Jurisprudence

The central broadly accepted form of legal authority with respect to the Free Speech Clause is Supreme Court jurisprudence. Free Speech Clause cases have been a significant part of the Supreme Court's docket for almost a century. The number of cases, combined with the broadly accepted common law approach to interpreting the Court's cases, makes for a fairly rich jurisprudence. Indeed, what is striking for my purposes is how broadly the Court has interpreted the scope of the Free Speech Clause, particularly in recent years, with the result that one can fairly answer most of the questions about algorithms without relying on any particular theories of the First Amendment. The ordinary lawyerly tools of case interpretation take us a fair distance.

III. Supreme Court Jurisprudence and Algorithm-Based Decisions

In Turner Broadcasting System, Inc. v. FCC (*Turner I*), confronting a First Amendment challenge to a statute that required cable operators to air local broadcast television stations, the Court flatly rejected the suggestion that this was ordinary economic regulation, and more specifically that cable operators were not engaged in speech for First Amendment purposes:

> There can be no disagreement on an initial premise: Cable programmers and cable operators engage in and transmit speech, and they are entitled to the protection of the speech and press provisions of the First Amendment. Through "original programming or by exercising editorial discretion over which stations or programs to include in its repertoire," cable programmers and operators "see[k] to communicate messages on a wide variety of topics and in a wide variety of formats."[7]

Turner I's focus on seeking to communicate messages is consistent with Supreme Court jurisprudence that has always treated substantive communication or self-expression as a necessary condition for the application of the First Amendment. In every case in which the Court has applied the First Amendment, abridgement of substantive communication has been the issue. Some of those abridgements are content-neutral, but the key is that they interfere with a person's or entity's ability to communicate content. The touchstone of the Court's First Amendment cases has always been that the underlying activity entails an expression of ideas. Communication thus seems to require, at a minimum, a speaker who seeks to transmit some substantive message or messages to a listener who can recognize that message. Thus,

---

7. 512 U.S. 622, 636 (1994) (alteration in original) (citation omitted) (quoting City of Los Angeles v. Preferred Commc'ns, Inc., 476 U.S. 488, 494 (1986)). As the internal quotation indicates, the Court put forward the same test in *Preferred Communications*.

in order to communicate, one must have a message that is sendable and receivable and that one actually chooses to send.

The Court's reasoning indicates that the First Amendment encompasses many algorithm-based manipulations. Consider a person who creates a billboard or webpage entitled "Our National Debt" that presents a running (and thus increasing) tally of the U.S. national debt.[8] The central feature of this billboard or webpage is simply a dollar figure generated by a computer running a program designed to measure the national debt. There need be no human involvement beyond creating the billboard or webpage and the program measuring the debt. Yet I don't think there is any real doubt that such a billboard or webpage would constitute speech in light of the Supreme Court's jurisprudence. It conveys a substantive message. Its running total of the national debt reflects a focus on and interest in the size of the national debt. It may not be clear to viewers exactly what the creator is trying to say about the national debt, but if nothing else the billboard or webpage communicates that the national debt is sufficiently important to merit this focus.[9]

Significantly, many communications that the Supreme Court treats as speech do not express a clear viewpoint, from a banner stating "BONG HiTS 4 JESUS"[10] to almost every form of art.

Imagine that a person sets up a bulletin board (an old-fashioned, physical bulletin board) on which she posts every article she finds that uses some specific words (say, "God is dead"). She is not creating the articles; she is merely collecting articles written by others. And she is not editing beyond looking for the words; she is indiscriminately amassing all articles that use these words. But I think we would regard the bulletin board as speech for First Amendment purposes. The bulletin board would be communicating a substantive message to those who viewed it. Her viewpoint might not be clear (does she agree or disagree that God is dead?) but, if nothing else, the bulletin board tells her viewers that she thinks this topic is important enough to merit special attention, in the form of her bulletin board. Presenting all articles containing the words "God is dead" (or "Boston St. Patrick's Day Parade," for that matter) would not present a single clear message; rather, as in *Turner I*, it would constitute an exercise of editorial discretion through which the bulletin board editor

---

8. This is not a product of my imagination, of course. There is a well-known, billboard-sized "National Debt Clock" in Manhattan. Its central features are tallies of the national debt and the debt per American family. (The only text reads "Our National Debt," "Your Family Share," and "The National Debt Clock.") The clock simply follows an algorithm to calculate the national debt and then displays the result. There are also websites that perform similar functions.

9. Note that the fact that the person or entity claiming to be engaged in speech does not create the underlying content is irrelevant for purposes of First Amendment coverage.

10. *See* Morse v. Frederick, 551 U.S. 393, 397 (2007). The Court treated the banner as speech under the First Amendment even though "the message on Frederick's banner is cryptic. It is no doubt offensive to some, perhaps amusing to others. To still others, it probably means nothing at all." *Id.* at 401.

sought to communicate a message about the importance of articles containing the words "God is dead."

Now imagine that the bulletin board editor discovers the Internet, and she transmogrifies her physical bulletin board into a virtual one. She performs computer searches for "God is dead" and posts links to all the articles that incorporate this phrase. Then she realizes that she can largely automate this process, so she creates a macro that lets her hit a single key to search the Web for the words "God is dead," and another macro that lets her hit a second key to upload onto her bulletin board any link that is not already posted. She begins to tire of performing these searches and realizes that a trained monkey could perform this task. Fortunately for her, she has a trained monkey, so she decides to let the monkey hit the two keys. The bulletin board editor then combines the operation into a single key for the monkey. Finally, after the monkey tires of all this typing, the bulletin board editor realizes that she can create a program that will automatically perform the search and post the relevant links without needing the monkey. Once the program starts, it continually searches the Web. In these steps from a physical bulletin board to an automated process, nothing relevant to free speech coverage under the Supreme Court's jurisprudence has changed. When it was physical, the editor's bulletin board communicated the importance to her of articles containing the words "God is dead." The same thing is communicated when the process is automated.

Similarly, consider the following progression: a time-pressed reporter realizes that she can write more articles if she uses some standard boilerplate to communicate information that arises repeatedly. She starts with cutting and pasting but finds that too laborious. So she creates macros for standard descriptions (e.g., "Team *A* scored seven runs in the third inning, and team *B* then scored nine runs in the third inning"). The macros become more complex, and utilize fancier language (e.g., "in one inning the visitors notched an impressive 7 runs in the top half of the third inning, but the home team responded with a whopping nine runs in the bottom of the third"). The macros become so sophisticated that the reporter can create a template for virtually every outcome, and by adding some facts can stitch together blocks of text that produce a coherent article. Eventually, the reporter's computer skills become so advanced that she can input some basic data from a spreadsheet (e.g., the box score from a baseball game) and run a macro that creates an entire article based on those facts. Finally she creates a macro that gathers those facts and writes the article, leaving her creative input entirely in the creation of the programs.

This is not a fanciful example. A company called Narrative Science "produce[s] content by way of algorithm, no human reporting necessary," for publications such as *Forbes*. Narrative Science employs "meta-writers" and engineers who work with its clients to determine what facts and angles are of interest to them, compile a relevant vocabulary, and create algorithms to construct the articles. As with the example of the "God is dead" bulletin board, it is hard to see how any step in this progression crosses a line between speech and nonspeech that arises from the Court's jurisprudence. The reporter/programmer is producing a substantive communication via editorial decisions. She designs the boilerplate and the mechanisms to put it together, and she does so in order to convey substantive information. Note that in all the steps of the progression, the reporter/programmer is relying to some degree on boilerplate that she did not create specially for the occasion. With each step she pushes more of her input to the front end (the creation of the boilerplate and the macros to input them), and leaves more implementation for the programs she has created.[11]

Most of the examples above involve webpages that focus on one particular area of interest. Does the analysis change without that focus? No. Suppose someone decides to create a website with the most important news of the moment, and the creator's substantive judgment is that importance is a function of popularity: the more popular an item is, the more important it is. So she creates an algorithm to identify news-oriented websites and to measure the popularity of items appearing on those websites, and the product of those algorithms yields an ever-changing set of links (in order of popularity) on her webpage. Above the links, her webpage says, "Here is the most important news, and by 'most important' I mean most popular." Her page would just be an automated collection of links, but under *Turner I* it would be speech. Similarly, a search engine that tells users "We prioritize websites that are family friendly" is communicating a substantive message in its deletion of adult-oriented links. Or, in a different vein, an aggregator or search engine that promises "We prioritize links that have the most outrageous porn on the Web" is sending a substantive message that its users will receive, and that the Supreme Court's jurisprudence would treat as speech.

That brings me to a search engine called blekko. It presents itself on its main page as "the spam-free search engine," and beyond that states flatly: "blekko biases towards quality sites. We do not attempt to gather all of the world's information. We purposefully bias our index away from sites with low quality content." Not much translation is needed here: blekko is making editorial decisions based on quality. Blekko is not generating the linked-to content on its own, but the same is true of most of the examples above (and of the Drudge Report and other link aggregators).[12]

That said, there are two distinctions between blekko and most of the examples above that might seem relevant for First Amendment purposes. First, whereas one might surmise that the creators of the National Debt webpage and the "God is dead" link page are motivated by a particular viewpoint (even if one might guess incorrectly what that viewpoint was), one cannot plausibly ascribe any viewpoint to blekko, as it is a general interest tool. Second, rather than collect items of interest in advance, it searches for them based on the user's preferences. These two points are closely related. Search engines respond to users' queries and present information in light of those queries, and they do not screen for or focus on particular viewpoints.

---

11. We have not yet, to my knowledge, reached that point with law review articles. Beep.

12. A search engine called DuckDuckGo adopts a strategy that is in some ways between blekko and Google, in that it focuses on blocking spam as a proxy for relevance.

As to the first point, under the prevailing jurisprudence, First Amendment coverage is not limited to speakers with a specific viewpoint, or even to speech of particular value. Magazines that publish articles on politics from every political perspective engage in what everyone would agree is speech, even if the editors themselves have no identifiable political views of their own. Regarding the second point, this seems to be a distinction without a difference for First Amendment purposes. Consider two platforms. The first compiles in advance a list of all the information sources that it judges to be of high quality, and it lets users search among and select those sources in a variety of ways. The second platform does not compile anything in advance, but instead selects the information sources it judges to be of high quality in response to users' queries. We can call the first platform "digital cable television that emphasizes quality" and the second platform "blekko." They are making the same judgments (well, assuming a digital cable television operator that in fact emphasizes quality). The only difference is the users' browsing experience, for users who choose to browse rather than simply search. It is difficult to see how anything of constitutional significance could turn on this distinction. Even if it did, it is not clear which way the distinction would cut. Having an installed library of choices allows users to passively graze (or channel surf, in the digital cable context), whereas giving only the choice of search requires more active participation on the part of the user. The result is that the product of that search may be less reflective of the decisions of the platform and more reflective of the decisions of the user, but it is not clear whether that makes this product more or less clearly "speech." In any event, nothing seems to turn on the level of user participation, because both platforms are best understood as engaging in speech under the Court's First Amendment jurisprudence.

Is Google different from blekko under the Supreme Court's jurisprudence? I think not. Google often articulates its goals in terms of quality. For instance, it presented its 2011 changes to its algorithms (known as Panda) as a means of returning more high-quality websites.[13] Google also articulates its goals in terms of relevance and usefulness for its users.

What if we assume that Google (or another algorithm-based provider) does not care about "quality," but instead only about relevance and usefulness for the user? Are Google's algorithm-based outputs based on its understanding of relevance and usefulness speech under the Supreme Court's jurisprudence? Yes. Google disclaims any adoption of the expression in the sites it finds, but it is making all sorts of judgments in determining what its customers want. There is a reasonable argument against this conclusion, flowing from the position that editing and transmitting information

---

13. *See* Matt Cutts, *Another Step to Reward High-Quality Sites*, Google Webmaster Central Blog (Apr. 24, 2012, 2:45 PM), http://googlewebmastercentral.blogspot.com/2012/04/another-step-to-reward-high-quality.html ("The goal of many of our ranking changes is to help searchers find sites that provide a great user experience and fulfill their information needs. We also want the 'good guys' making great sites for users, not just algorithms, to see their effort rewarded. To that end we've launched Panda changes that successfully returned higher-quality sites in search results.").

based on what users want is not an expression of the speaker's own desires and thus is not real speech. As I discuss in the next Part, however, the Supreme Court has not adopted that position and its jurisprudence is not consistent with it.

Many algorithm-based outputs will not constitute speech under this jurisprudence because they are not sending a substantive message. Transmission Control Protocol and Internet Protocol (often referred to as TCP/IP) route information through the Internet, but its creators are not communicating a substantive message in doing so. But when people create algorithms in order to selectively present information based on its perceived importance or value or relevance, *Turner I* indicates that they are speakers for purposes of the First Amendment (or the Supreme Court's jurisprudence, at any rate). Nothing in the Court's jurisprudence supports the proposition that reliance on algorithms transforms speech into nonspeech. The touchstone is sending a substantive message, and such a message can be sent with or without relying on algorithms.[14]

IV. Producing a Different Result

[T]here are a host of competing conceptions of free speech, none of which has been widely accepted as explaining or driving First Amendment doctrine. But let me now ask whether adopting one of the competing theories of the First Amendment would produce a different result without upending existing case law. More broadly, how easy or hard would it be to craft a coherent exception to the prevailing First Amendment jurisprudence such that algorithm-based decisions, or search results more specifically, would not be encompassed by the First Amendment but most of the remaining First Amendment jurisprudence would remain? This is

14. In his article [below], Tim Wu argues that under the prevailing jurisprudence, the key inquiry is whether the alleged speaker adopts the information it provides as its own. *See* Wu ("Neither the newspaper nor cable operator cases support the idea that the First Amendment protects something like an index, as opposed to content adopted or selected by the speaker as its own. It is that step—the adoption of information, as a publisher, as opposed to merely pointing the user to it—that marks the difference."). I agree with Wu that the Supreme Court's jurisprudence does not support treating an unedited index as speech, but I do not think the line he articulates arises from, or is consistent with, that jurisprudence. The Court in *Turner I* held that cable operators engage in speech because of their editing, without any suggestion that cable operators do, or need to, adopt as their own the communications of the channels they carry. *See* 512 U.S. 622, 636 (1994) ("Through . . . 'exercising editorial discretion over which stations . . . to include in its repertoire,' cable . . . operators 'see[k] to communicate messages . . .'"); *see also* Hurley v. Irish-Am. Gay, Lesbian & Bisexual Grp. of Bos., Inc., 515 U.S. 557, 570 (1995) (noting that "even the simple selection of a paid noncommercial advertisement for inclusion in a daily paper" "fall[s] squarely within the core of First Amendment security"). Under *Turner I*, engaging in substantive editing sends a message and thus triggers application of the First Amendment—no adoption or endorsement of the carried programming is needed. To use Wu's example, no one who watches Fox News, MSNBC, or any other cable channel addressing topic X says, "Look what my cable operator said about X yesterday," or, "It was interesting what my cable operator had to say about *X*." Nonetheless, the First Amendment encompasses the cable operator's selection of channels. *See* Wu, *infra* at page 666 (using the quoted language to illustrate the line he sees between speech and nonspeech in the jurisprudence relevant to search engines); *see also infra* note 15 (discussing the implications of Wu's line).

different from asking whether, in the first instance, any theory of the First Amendment would exclude algorithm-based decisions from coverage. The answer to that question is yes. That is, we could rely on a particular conception of the First Amendment that would radically rethink the Supreme Court's existing approach in ways that would exclude search engine results and much else. We could, for example, limit "the freedom of speech" in the First Amendment to core political speech, or speech that directly promotes a meaningfully constrained notion of democratic deliberation or self-government, and thereby exclude search engine results, as a category, from the ambit of the First Amendment. We would also exclude most forms of art, however. My question in this Part is, without radically changing our First Amendment jurisprudence, how easy would it be to exclude algorithm- based decisions, or search engine results more specifically?

A. Relying on Particular Theories of the First Amendment

The most obvious possibility would be to focus the First Amendment analysis on individuals. This could lead to a suggestion that communications by corporations do not constitute speech. But newspapers and magazines are owned by corporations, and a revamping of the First Amendment to exclude those publications as speech would be a radical departure from our existing jurisprudence.

One might instead try to exclude from First Amendment coverage speech that a corporation makes purely for its own benefit. The problem is that it is difficult to come up with any articulation of speech in a corporation's interest that would exclude algorithm-based decisions, or more specifically search engine results, without also excluding newspapers and magazines. A distinction based on speech that is in a corporation's interest fails to distinguish newspapers and magazines. Same for excluding speech that is aimed solely at increasing a corporation's value. Indeed, for a newspaper or magazine owner who is a faithful agent, with shareholders who want the highest possible return on their investment, presumably all the owner's actions would be undertaken in order to maximize shareholder value. Simply stated, search results are in the search engine's interests in the same way that compelling content is in the interest of any conveyor of content, whether newspaper, political website, or porn website.

A more conventional line would distinguish commercial speech. A number of theorists have argued for the exclusion of commercial speech from First Amendment coverage. This would be a fairly significant reworking of First Amendment jurisprudence. Excluding commercial speech also would not affect most algorithm-based decisions. It would apply to search engines' (and newspapers') advertisements, but most search engine results are not paid advertisements.

A different way of emphasizing individuals would focus on their expression. Theories focused on self-expression, for example, emphasize that it is an individual's self-expression that matters, and autonomy-based theories similarly emphasize individual autonomy. The problem is that many algorithm-based decisions similarly involve the creator's self-expression and autonomy. Depending on the algorithm,

algorithm-based decisions may well constitute self-expression, enhance autonomy, and contain meaningful thought. The algorithm is simply a means to gather relevant information, but the creator chooses what to gather. The person who creates the National Debt webpage, or the "God is dead" linkpage, is expressing a view about the importance of those topics. Or consider a webpage that uses an algorithm to amass links to articles with the words "Obama sucks" or "Romney sucks." These webpages require less curating than does the Drudge Report, but all of them reflect autonomous expression.

Search engines are a closer question, but a definition of self-expression that excludes them would be a fairly crabbed one. Start with a search engine that focuses on family-friendly material (or, if you prefer, porn). This seems to encode autonomous expression — "We value family-friendly material/porn, and we want to make it easier for you to find it." Of course, the creators' actual motivation might be more base — most obviously, "We just want to make money." But that may well be the true motivation for many newspapers and magazines, and many artists, for that matter (I'm looking at you, Jeff Koons). And because theories of self-expression and individual autonomy treat art as squarely within their understanding of speech, those who emphasize self-expression or autonomy usually do not focus on the speaker's subjective motivation, but instead on the apparent expression reflected in the message. In this case there is an apparent expression, as I noted above.

It is a very small step from that expression to blekko's expression. Instead of "We value family-friendly material/porn, and we want to make it easier for you to find it," the expression would be "We value quality websites, and we want to make it easier for you to find them." And it is then another small step to Google's expression. As I noted above, Google, too, articulates quality as its goal. But even if we credit only its focus on relevance, substituting "relevant" for "quality" in the expression does not make it any less of an expression. In all cases, the algorithm creators are expressing their views about what they value.

Perhaps Google in particular (and maybe blekko, too) is different, insofar as its message is not so much "We value relevant websites" but more like "We select for you what you want." In the latter formulation, Google arguably is not expressing its own preferences so much as it is indicating that it wants to satisfy ours.

Differentiating Google for purposes of First Amendment coverage based on its catering to users' interests would be a significant shift in First Amendment jurisprudence, as publications and editors that frankly focus on their viewers' or readers' interests would be unprotected. It has not mattered in the past whether a magazine owner (or cable operator) was merely responding to a market opportunity or was expressing its own subjective preferences, but now that difference would be dispositive. If we define unprotected speech to include speech that responds to public demand, only the few publications that push their ideas regardless of public interest would be speakers, and that would upend most First Amendment law.

Beyond that, this would be a mighty thin reed on which to rest a distinction. We can recharacterize Google's position as "Our preference is to select for you what we believe you find valuable." If we substitute "is" for "you find," or change the locution to "we believe you should find valuable," there is clearly expression. So we would be putting an enormous amount of weight on the creators' articulation as focused on what others want.

Articulating one's goal in terms of serving others is still an exercise of autonomy and a form of self-expression. "What makes you happy makes me happy" is an expression of self—one that looks to another for one's happiness, but an expression of personal motivation nonetheless. In the same way, the artist who proclaims that she is guided by what her viewers want has still made a self-defining and art-defining statement.

It also bears noting that decisions about what users want are analogous to the decisions of cable operators that the Court found to be speech in *Turner I*. In their briefs, the cable operators stressed that a key consideration in choosing what channels to include was what they thought their customers wanted. Indeed, a major element of the cable operators' argument that there was no sufficient justification for the statute was their assertion that cable operators would be guided by viewer interest and thus would air the most popular channels whether or not they had an ownership interest in them. The cable operators, in choosing what channels to air, were engaged in editing, on whatever substantive basis they chose, and those editorial decisions constituted speech. The cable operators claimed they were editing in light of their sense of their customers' wishes, and Google is doing the exact same thing.[15]

A different tack would entail a focus on the audience. Some Supreme Court opinions and some commentators have emphasized the importance of listeners and

15. Tim Wu contends [below] that under the Supreme Court's jurisprudence the crucial question is whether the alleged speaker adopts the information provided as its own. As I noted above, this distinction is inconsistent with the prevailing Supreme Court jurisprudence. Beyond that, it would not exclude all algorithm-based outputs from First Amendment coverage. The National Debt billboard, the "God is Dead" webpage, and the articles written by the journalist using boilerplate and by Narrative Science all entail adoption by their creators. Wu's focus on functionality would exclude certain categories of substantive editing, whether they were produced by humans or algorithms. His emphasis on search engines "merely pointing the user to [information]" applies with equal strength to human and nonhuman pointers. So a human who manually performs the functions of a search engine or an automated concierge would not be engaged in speech. By hypothesis, such a human would not adopt the information provided but instead would search for and retrieve it exactly as an algorithm would. Algorithms make such nonadoptive retrieval more common, but in Wu's formulation the line between algorithms and non-algorithms is not central to First Amendment coverage. This is an important area of agreement between Wu and me: algorithm-based outputs underscore the breadth of the test that the Supreme Court has developed, but do not provide a useful line at which to limit that breadth.

viewers having access to a wide range of views. But a "right to receive information" is articulated as an addition to the rights of speakers, as opposed to a substitute for them, and so would not limit the treatment of algorithm-based decisions as speech. It does bear noting, though, that a focus on the rights of the audience might buttress the position of some algorithm-based outputs — in particular, search engines. One way of conceptualizing the rights of listeners and viewers is as a right to unencumbered access to information. Such a conceptualization would lend support to the treatment of an individual's search results as part of the information that is encompassed by the Free Speech Clause. A different conceptualization would interpret the rights of listeners and viewers as justifying government regulation of information providers, but application of such arguments to exclude information providers from coverage by the Free Speech Clause would be a radical change in First Amendment jurisprudence. For better or worse, the Supreme Court's jurisprudence has decisively rejected this vision.[16]

Yet another direction would focus on the government's purpose or motive in enacting a particular regulation. Some commentators (including then-professor Elena Kagan) have suggested that First Amendment coverage should turn on the government's purpose or motive, such that an economic motive should not trigger First Amendment coverage but a censorious motive should. Whatever the merits of this approach, and whatever its application to algorithm-based outputs, it is inconsistent with a significant number of Supreme Court cases that applied the First Amendment despite the fact that the underlying regulation had an economic motive.[17]

There are of course other theories of the First Amendment, but all would either draw arbitrary lines or exclude much that we currently consider to be speech.

---

16. *See, e.g.*, Miami Herald Publ'g Co. v. Tornillo, 418 U.S. 241, 258 (1974) (holding unconstitutional a state statute guaranteeing political candidates media access to respond to criticism). Indeed, the Supreme Court has largely abandoned its intimation in Red Lion Broad. Co. v. FCC that the First Amendment empowers the government to give access rights to listeners and viewers. 395 U.S. 367 (1969). As it turns out, broadcasting is the only area that the Court has treated as justifying a right of access — and even there, the Court has held that broadcasters have First Amendment rights (just diminished ones).

17. *See* Sorrell v. IMS Health Inc., 564 U.S. 552, 567 (applying First Amendment scrutiny to a regulation motivated by economic considerations and stating that, "[w]hile the burdened speech results from an economic motive, so too does a great deal of vital expression"); *Turner I*, 512 U.S. 622, 638 (1994) (applying First Amendment scrutiny to legislation while also finding that "Congress' overriding objective in enacting [a law requiring cable carriage of local television broadcasters] was . . . to preserve access to free television programming for the 40 percent of Americans without cable").

Tim Wu, Machine Speech

161 U. Penn. L. Rev. 1495 (2013)

Introduction

Computers are making an increasing number of important decisions in our lives. They fly airplanes, navigate traffic, and even recommend books. In the process, computers reason through automated algorithms and constantly send and receive information, sometimes in ways that mimic human expression. When can such communications, called here "algorithmic outputs," claim First Amendment protection?

The question of "rights for robots," if once limited to science fiction, has now entered the public debate. In recent years, firms like Verizon and Google have relied on First Amendment defenses against common-law and regulatory claims by arguing that some aspect of an automated process is speech protected by the Constitution. *See, e.g.*, Search King, Inc. v. Google Tech., Inc., No. 02-1457, 2003 WL 21464568, at *4 (W.D. Okla. May 27, 2003) (finding that Google PageRanks are entitled to "full" First Amendment protection). These questions will only grow in importance as computers become involved in more areas of human decisionmaking.

A simple approach, favored by some commentators, says that the First Amendment presumptively covers algorithmic output so long as the program seeks to communicate some message or opinion to its audience. But while simplicity is attractive, so is being right. In practice, the approach yields results both absurd and disruptive; the example of the car alarm shows why. The modern car alarm is a sophisticated computer program that uses an algorithm to decide when to communicate its opinions, and when it does it seeks to send a particularized message well understood by its audience. It meets all the qualifications stated: yet clearly something is wrong with a standard that grants Constitutional protection to an electronic annoyance device. Something is missing.

The big missing piece is functionality. More specifically, what's being overlooked is the differential treatment courts should accord communications closely tied to some functional task. A close reading of the relevant cases suggests that courts, in fact, limit coverage in a way that reserves the power of the state to regulate the functional aspects of the communication process, while protecting its expressive aspects. Here, I go further and suggest that the law contains a de facto functionality doctrine that must be central to any consideration of machine speech.

The doctrine operates in two distinct ways. First, courts tend to withhold protection from carrier/conduits—actors who handle, transform, or process information, but whose relationship with speech or information is ultimately functional. Definitive examples are Federal Express or the telephone company, common carriers to whom the law does not grant speech rights. Those who merely carry information from place to place (courier services) generally don't enjoy First Amendment protection, while those who select a distinct repertoire, like a newspaper or cable operator, do. Similarly, those who provide the facilities for job interviews are not recognized as speakers, nor are the manufacturers of technologies that record or transform information from one form into another—like a typewriter, photocopier, or loudspeaker.

Second, courts do not normally protect tools—works whose use of information is purely functional, such as navigational charts, court filings, or contracts. The reasons are complex, and related to a broader nonprotection of information that by its very communication performs some task. In the words of language philosophers these are "speech acts," "illocutionary acts," or "situation-altering utterances." The broader category includes the communications embodied in criminal commands, commercial paper, nutritional information, and price-fixing conspiracies.

Combined, these two tendencies form a de facto functionality doctrine, which, as we shall see, is central to understanding the First Amendment in the context of algorithmic output (and, thankfully, excludes car alarms from the protections of the Constitution). For one thing, in many cases the fact that an algorithm makes the decisions in software cases is in tension with the requirement of knowing selection or intimate identification. Other times, algorithmic output falls into the category of communication that acts by its very appearance. Warnings, status indications, directions, and similar signals are common outputs for computer software in this category. These outputs act to warn or instruct and are therefore similar analytically to something like a criminal command or conspiracy.

In an area as complex as this, a rule of thumb might be useful. Generally, we can distinguish software that serves as a "speech product" from that which is a "communication tool." Communication tools fall into the categories just described: they primarily facilitate the communications of another person, or perform some task for the user. In contrast, speech products are technologies like blog posts, tweets, video games, newspapers, and so on, that are viewed as vessels for the ideas of a speaker, or whose content has been consciously curated.

The boundary between one and the other may be imperfect, but it must be drawn somewhere if the First Amendment is to be confined to its primary goal of protecting the expression of ideas, and if we are to prevent its abuse. If a software designer is primarily interested in facilitating some task for the user, he will be unlikely to have the space to communicate his own ideas. At a minimum, his ideas must bend to operations. Thus, the intent is not to communicate ideas, or, as the Supreme Court puts it, "affect public attitudes and behavior in a variety of ways, ranging from direct espousal of a political or social doctrine to the subtle shaping of thought which characterizes all artistic expression." Joseph Burstyn, Inc. v. Wilson, 343 U.S. 495, 501 (1952) (footnote omitted).

In what follows, I introduce these ideas more thoroughly and, along the way, consider the speech status of blogging and microblogging software like Twitter, GPS navigation software, search engines, and automated concierges. The importance of these matters cannot be overstated. Too little protection would disserve speakers who have evolved beyond the printed pamphlet. Too much protection would threaten to constitutionalize many areas of commerce and private concern without promoting the values of the First Amendment.

III. The First Amendment's de Facto Functionality Doctrine

Here is my thesis: Functionality will usually be the line that divides speech and communications in this area, in the absence of suspicious censorial motives. Doctrinally, this takes courts into an area of the First Amendment that is among the least well understood. But a careful look at the cases suggests that courts already maintain an informal exclusion based on functional considerations.

A. Functionality Generally

Functionality as a legal concept is employed mainly in copyright, patent, and trademark law, each of which has distinctive doctrinal versions. Sometimes described as the "nonfunctionality requirement," this doctrine denies the benefits of the law to some otherwise qualifying expressive work, based on the argument that the work is primarily designed or intended to perform some task unrelated to the goals of the law in question. As such, it acts to prevent a party from using the law to achieve objectives completely unrelated to the goals of that law. It is a limit on opportunism.

This might be easier to understand using an example. If viewed as a work of sculpture, a car engine might be indistinguishable from any other detailed metal sculpture and thus qualify for the legal protection that copyright, trademarks, or design patents give to expressive work. But the functionality doctrine denies protection because the car engine is designed for another purpose: powering a vehicle.

The functionality doctrine is a typical common law invention in the sense that it responds, on a case-by-case basis, to overreaching parties and untenable consequences.

[A] nearly identical problem confronts judges facing a First Amendment plaintiff pressing claims that cover highly functional elements, namely, rich opportunities for lawyerly opportunism. As in the intellectual property area, protecting functionality may yield consequences unrelated to the goals of the Constitution.

B. The First Amendment's Functionality Doctrine

Courts considering these matters should be aware that the First Amendment already contains a de facto functionality doctrine (or, stated differently, it has a nonfunctionality requirement), though it is not as explicit as in intellectual property law. Long before the development of advanced software, courts declined to extend First Amendment protection, based on the potential for gamesmanship or on concerns about the disruption of some other system or legal regime.

There are two different ways in which the functionality doctrine operates. First is the carrier/conduits category. Here, the actor's *relationship* to the information in question is too mechanical to make it a speaker. The claimant does handle or transform information, but its relationship is characterized by a lack of identification with the information it handles, along with a lack of specific knowledge and usually a lack of legal responsibility. Sometimes courts call the actions "conduct" instead of speech. In any event, this is where we find telephone companies, courier services, law schools hosting job interviews, and manufacturers of typewriters and television sets. All of these firms handle or transform speech, but none is a speaker (not even a loudspeaker). As I will suggest, many software products will fall into this category as well.

In a second category are communicative tools. In this category, the information conveyed, in context, is functional: it performs some task other than the communication of ideas. Navigational charts are the definitive example, but the rationale is closely related to the academically well-studied topic of "speech acts" or "situation-altering utterances."

1. Carrier/Conduits

The first version of the functionality doctrine excludes from First Amendment protection actors whose involvement with information is too distant or mechanical to be speech. This covers those that handle or transform information in a manner usually lacking specific choices as to content, lack specific knowledge as to what they are handling, or do not identify as the publisher of that information.

Several prominent Supreme Court cases help clarify this. In *Turner Broadcasting System*, the Court explained that a cable operator obtains First Amendment protection only because it "exercis[es] editorial discretion over which stations or programs to include in its repertoire." Turner Broad. Sys., Inc. v. FCC, 512 U.S. 622, 636 (1994) (quoting City of Los Angeles v. Preferred Commc'ns, Inc., 476 U.S. 488, 494 (1986)). The knowing selection of that repertoire distinguishes cable operators from carriers that merely move information without identifying or selecting the content they carry. The same inference applies to a newspaper: a newspaper knowingly selects and identifies with the content it presents. In contrast, a telephone company, which merely carries information from place to place, has never been able to claim First Amendment rights.

The category is also well illustrated by Rumsfeld v. Forum for Academic & Institutional Rights, Inc., 547 U.S. 47 (2006). Even though law schools refused to allow military recruiters on campus in opposition to "don't ask, don't tell," the schools weren't considered speakers. As the Court explained, "accommodating the military's message does not affect the law schools' speech, because the schools are not speaking when they host interviews and recruiting receptions." *Id.* at 64. In particular, the Court stressed the unlikelihood that the law schools would be identified with the military recruiters' speech merely on account of their hosting them.

The cable, newspaper, and interview-hosting cases all suggest the same conclusion. They describe a difference between a publisher, who actively curates the sum total of the information presented and is identified with it, and those entities that have a more mechanical relationship to the information they carry, process, or otherwise handle. A court might say the latter are engaged in "conduct;" we can also say that, by operation of the de facto functionality doctrine, these companies are not protected by the First Amendment.

2. Communicative Tools

Sometimes courts decline to protect communications as speech based on an assessment that the information in question acts as a tool. The paradigmatic examples are maps and navigational charts.[18] As the Ninth Circuit explained:

> Aeronautical charts are highly technical tools. They are graphic depictions of technical, mechanical data. The best analogy to an aeronautical chart is a compass. Both may be used to guide an individual who is engaged in an activity requiring certain knowledge of natural features. Computer software that fails to yield the result for which it was designed may be another.

Winter v. G.P. Putnam's Sons, 938 F.2d 1033, 1035–36 (9th Cir. 1991). Courts decline to protect tools for reasons that overlap with its treatment of what philosophers of language call "speech acts." Some communications by their very issuance or utterance perform some action, such as "[s]aying 'kill' to a trained attack dog." Catharine A. MacKinnon, Only Words 12 (1993) (emphasis omitted). That is to say, some communications don't simply express a view, or even cause some effect, but accomplish something by their very utterance. Expressing a verbal acceptance of an offer not only tells people something, but also creates a legally binding agreement.

Hence, the same rationale that claims tools are not speech says that legal documents like contracts, wills, commercial paper, and the like are not subject to First Amendment protection as against the law of contracts, trusts and estates, or financial regulation.

Between these two strands of doctrine, I think we can safely say that, like other areas of the law, the First Amendment usually denies protection to carrier/conduits and mere communicative tools. The reasons, while rarely given, seem to be similar to those found in intellectual property cases: judges fear the consequences of allowing a law intended to protect expression to venture into areas where other motivations are paramount. They may also fear opportunism on the part of lawyers — an effort to use the Constitution for goals quite unrelated to speech. Beyond this, and the caveat that a censorial motive would probably trump the functionality doctrine, it is hard to say more.

---

18. *See* Brocklesby v. United States, 767 F.2d 1288, 1295 n.9 (9th Cir. 1985) (refusing to address whether "the First Amendment renders the theory of strict liability for a defective product inapplicable to . . . charts," because the argument was not raised in the court below).

IV. Easy and Hard Cases: Search Engines and Concierges

A. Easy Cases

As indicated by Brown v. Entertainment Merchants Ass'n the courts will recognize as speech a wide range of communications that are made using a computer program. 564 U.S. 786, 790 (2011) (holding that the First Amendment protects video games). While not strictly specified by *Brown*, I predict that this will include blog posts, tweets, online photo streams, and probably slightly shorter or more symbolic expressions such as Yelp or Amazon reviews written by humans. These forms of expression are sometimes heavily shaped by computer programs, but in the same way that the choice of charcoal or paintbrush shapes an artist's output.

At the other extreme, some of the output of computer programs will fall into the heart of the functionality exclusion. Car alarms and antilock braking systems are clear examples of communicative tools. Alarms act on the user as a warning. This doesn't mean it is impossible that the sound of a car alarm could form a part of protected speech (say, as part of a song or art installation). But more generally, an alarm functions to warn that a car may be in the process of being stolen.

Software navigation and map programs offer harder cases. Based on my description of the functionality doctrine, I believe that these technologies are still unprotected tools, because their communications perform a function unrelated to the communication of ideas, namely, telling someone how to get from A to B. Consider, for example, Rosenberg v. Harwood, No. 100916536, 2011 WL 3153314 (D. Utah May 27, 2011). A woman claimed that, relying on Google Maps' walking directions, she stepped onto a freeway and was hit by a car. Google answered the complaint with, among other defenses, an argument that its directions are protected speech. While the court wisely avoided the constitutional question, its analysis suggests that the First Amendment argument should be rejected under the functionality doctrine. The map was meant to assist the user with a task, not to express to him any ideas or to influence his worldview. Directions are much like commands, more speech acts than anything else. For that reason the First Amendment ordinarily ought not to be triggered.

B. Hard Cases

1. Search Engines

Search engines are programs that use an algorithm to guess, within some enormous body of text, items that represent the best match for the user's search. Search engines were once mainly used for searching specialized databases, but they have become ubiquitous over the last decade. The well-known Westlaw program uses various sophisticated algorithms to retrieve documents based on keywords or search codes that the user composes. More important to nonlawyers is the Google search engine, which returns the links to webpages it deems most likely relevant to a user's keywords (or, in search engine parlance, most likely to provide answers). A sophisticated search engine like Google's also creates an index with a consistent and constant ranking of all of the potential results for a given search.

Given the functional nature of search engines (as the word "engine" suggests), it might seem easy to conclude that search results do not trigger the First Amendment. In a 2008 paper, Oren Bracha and Frank Pasquale reached that conclusion with relative ease. *See* Oren Bracha & Frank Pasquale, Federal Search Commission? Access, Fairness, and Accountability in the Law of Search, 93 Cornell L. Rev. 1149, 1193–1201 (2008). However, several matters make the claim worth further discussion.

First, Google has repeatedly claimed in court that its selection of search results is protected speech and has won such claims in federal district court. *See* Langdon v. Google, Inc., 474 F. Supp. 2d 622, 629–30 (D. Del. 2007); *Search King*, 2003 WL 21464568, at *4. Second, by the mid-2000s, online search was a dominant method for finding information. Search engines like Google and Microsoft's Bing function like a switchboard for the Internet—a means of connecting users, websites, and advertisements in one place. Indeed, so powerful are search engines as an information gateway that it is typical for governments to focus regulations on them as a means of trying to regulate speech. Many countries, including the United States, censor search results to some extent for various reasons, ranging from political control of citizens to copyright protection.

The most prominent case discussing a search engine's First Amendment rights is *Search King*. Search King, a search optimization firm, promised to elevate its clients' results in a Google search. Google caught wind of the scheme and actively demoted Search King's clients. Unhappy with the demotions, Search King sued Google in Oklahoma for tortious interference with contract. Google raised the First Amendment among its defenses. The district court held that Google's rankings of webpages are protected speech, and on that basis refused to grant Search King a preliminary injunction.

Under the doctrine of constitutional avoidance, the district court erred in reaching the First Amendment issue. The tort claim was frivolous and easily dismissed, based on the court's own finding that the acts were not wrongful. Constitutional avoidance was designed for exactly this kind of case, where a complex constitutional issue of first impression might be addressed unnecessarily.

Nor is the district court's reasoning particularly helpful (other than as an example of oversimplification). It construed Google's search results as protected speech because search results are a form of "opinion." As the court wrote: "PageRanks are opinions—opinions of the significance of particular web sites as they correspond to a search query.... Accordingly, the Court concludes that Google's PageRanks are entitled to 'full constitutional protection.'" *Search King*, 2003 WL 21464568, at *4.

Holding that any communication is protected speech if it can be called an "opinion" is hopelessly overbroad. For example, a person's written will is, by its nature, something of a ranking of his relatives and friends, and thus an opinion, yet not one that gains First Amendment protection. The approach is particularly useless in the software context, for nearly any automated function could in some sense be called an "opinion." Car alarms express the alarm's opinion that a car is in danger of being stolen, and an automatic transmission that shifts from third to fourth gear might be said to be expressing either its (or the manufacturer's) opinion as to when to switch gears. It isn't that the opinionated selection of information can never be enough to make someone a speaker, a point to which I return in the consideration of concierge services. But calling something an "opinion" cannot be conclusive.

In defense of the district court, its opinion was an unpublished dismissal with limited precedential value. More elaborate arguments appear in Eugene Volokh and Donald Falk's white paper for Google, Eugene Volokh & Donald Falk, First Amendment Protection for Search Engine Search Results 6–7 (2012), and in Stuart Benjamin's article in this issue. Volokh and Falk's argument depends on the claim that Google is akin to a newspaper or other publisher. A newspaper selects the most important stories of the day and presents them on the front page. Google's search engine, similarly, ranks the world's webpages with respect to their relevance to various criteria, and hence, according to Volokh and Falk, gains the same protections.

Volokh and Falk's paper, however, misapplies the relevant law. Newspapers and other publishers, unlike mere functional carriers of information, gain protection because their work product reflects a knowing selection and arrangement of the entirety of the articles that make up the final newspaper. The newspaper selects and endorses its articles, and it also usually commissions their authorship in the first place. The articles, in some sense, *are* the newspaper, and thus it makes sense to say something like, "Look what The Washington Post said about X yesterday."

In contrast, Google comes to a mass of information and indexes it. It does not endorse the sites it ranks—the millions of websites accessible through Google's search engine cannot be said to be Google's speech product. If a Google search turns up website Y about topic X, no one says, "It was interesting what Google had to say about X." Google's sorting of results and generation of an index might therefore be best characterized as "conduct" under *Rumsfeld*. Google helps its users find websites, but it does not sponsor or publish those websites.

Nor, as a legal matter, is Google responsible for the sites it links, as Google has repeatedly asserted to gain statutory immunities. *See, e.g.*, Parker v. Google, Inc., 242 F. App'x 833, 836–39 (3d Cir. 2007) (rejecting petitioner's claims of copyright infringement and defamation against Google because, among other reasons, Google was not the information content provider). As Bracha and Pasquale point out, "Dogged by complaints related to the content of listed websites, search engines ... claim merely to be the infrastructure or platform that delivers content." Bracha & Pasquale at 1192. In short, as neither a conscious curator nor a legally responsible publisher of content, a Google search is a far cry from a newspaper.

Unlike Volokh and Falk, Stuart Benjamin relies not on a metaphor, but rather his restatement of the *Spence* test to conclude that search engine output counts as "speech" for the First Amendment. While Benjamin's "sending a message" standard accurately describes what the Court *says*, it doesn't come close to describing what courts *do*. As applied to software, it misses the importance of functionality. Taken more generally, the standard is overbroad: everything from nonpolitical vandalism through political assassination "sends a message," but not all of that can reasonably be speech.

In any event, even by Benjamin's own standard, the argument that the operation of a search engine "entails transmission of ideas" is a stretch; it demands a conception of "idea" that widens the category beyond recognition. According to Benjamin, Google hopes to convey ideas like "quality" or "usefulness," but then so too did the designers of my coffeemaker. A theory that turns the design of home appliances into a form of constitutional speech is probably overbroad. The point is that there necessarily must be some line between actual speech products and mere tools in order to avoid ridiculous results, and the *Spence* standard ain't it.

If Google isn't a vessel for ideas, what then, is it? While useful, Google's main search, in particular, is probably best akin to a highly advanced and powerful index. Neither the newspaper nor cable operator cases support the idea that the First Amendment protects something like an index, as opposed to content adopted or selected by the speaker as its own. It is that step—the adoption of information, as a publisher, as opposed to merely pointing the user to it—that marks the difference.

Examining the respective purposes of the search engine creator and the newspaper editor is also illustrative. A newspaper's purpose is to communicate ideas, stories, impressions, and viewpoints to its audience. It is a definitional part of "the press" named in the First Amendment itself, with distinctive and unusual organizational goals. The search engine's primary purpose is, variously, to locate information or, more recently, provide answers, but in any event, its first objective is to serve as a tool for helping its users locate desired information within a giant collection of information. While searching "who was Walter Pater" produces Google's best guess of what the user wants, it does not produce a series of choices that represent the "direct espousal of a political or social doctrine" on behalf of the designer. Joseph Burstyn, Inc. v. Wilson, 343 U.S. 495, 501 (1952). Rather, Google is just trying to find what the user wants. That is the difference, in some fundamental way, between a tool and speech—the first directly serves the user, while the second attempts to persuade him.

This analysis is subject to two caveats. First, over the last five years, both Google and Bing have begun to offer more of their own content in many searches, and these communications, produced and endorsed by the company itself, will sometimes be protected speech. Second, some of Google's specific searches are more carefully curated than its general search. Third, as stated earlier, a censorial motive on the part of the Government is a trump card that would change everything. Were Congress to pass a law asking Google to manually demote sites critical of "the World's Greatest Deliberative Body," it is not hard to predict immediate judicial scrutiny.

The fact that a search engine is functional does not mean the First Amendment has no role in search-related cases. Rather, as suggested by the discussion of Twitter and microblogging, the important First Amendment issues in search will often come from the perspective of users. Consider were a state to order all search engines to block results linking to information it deemed treasonous or a threat to national security (as the Chinese government does). Laws based on the censorial motive would demand First Amendment scrutiny, though such scrutiny would mainly be based on the speakers' and users' rights. The reason is that the burden in such a case falls directly on the speaker and the listener, even though it is the search engine, the intermediary, that is being used as the enforcer.

This may seem a superficial or technical difference, but it is not, for it changes the kind of cases that can be brought. The law in question must somehow burden a search engine's users. It is not enough that it is an annoyance to the owner of the search engine.

2. Automated Concierges and Other Services

A trend in the personal technology industries is for computers to take on the role of personalized assistants, or curators of sorts. This is an area where Apple and Amazon are leaders. Apple's iTunes offers, for example, a "Genius" function that creates a playlist based on its user's musical preferences. Amazon makes book recommendations based on what it thinks its customers will like, and so on.

When, if at all, do laws affecting such recommenders or concierges trigger First Amendment scrutiny? Imagine, for example, that a concierge gave advice that led to some injury. Would a product liability lawsuit be subject to First Amendment scrutiny?

We might first consider what the law has done with the human equivalents. On the one hand, private advice, especially communications in the course of professional services, is treated as a form of functional communication and doesn't usually trigger First Amendment protection.[19] This is why a doctor may be liable for malpractice if he gives a very bad or grossly erroneous diagnosis. On the other hand, if a doctor writes a book that happens to be wrong about medical facts, his efforts are likely nonetheless to be protected by the First Amendment against product liability law.[20]

We are back, then, to the question that has been the center of this Article, but seen from a different angle. Is the output of a concierge program merely providing some function for its user like the doctor's diagnosis? Or does such advice fall closer

---

19. *See, e.g.,* Togstad v. Vesely, Otto, Miller & Keefe, 291 N.W.2d 686, 695 (Minn. 1980) (per curiam) (affirming a lower court decision to hold a lawyer liable for negligent advice given to a client without any consideration of First Amendment implications).

20. *See, e.g.,* Winter v. G.P. Putnam's Sons, 938 F.2d 1033, 1036 (9th Cir. 1991) (declining to "extend liability . . . to the ideas and expressions contained in a book" because of the First Amendment, even though the book was a "reference guide" with information on "the habitat, collection, and cooking of mushrooms").

to a recognized medium, the generalized book or instruction manual that happens to be communicating one-on-one simply as a matter of technological form?

To answer the question we must distinguish between two types of recommendation tools. Some concierge or recommendation programs rely on nothing more than data already provided by the user to deliver a "recommendation," which is really nothing more than reminding the user what she already wants. These are tools unlikely to be protected. In contrast, it is also possible to imagine an intelligent concierge program that would be more distinctly opinionated and therefore protected. Imagine a program that embodied the programmer's deeply held views as to the best restaurants in New York. The program might reflect snobbish disregard of "New American" cooking and a celebration of French Cuisine above all else. Asked for recommendations, this program would return not simply a mechanical projection based on the user's previous choices, but rather a true recommendation based on the opinions, and indeed the prejudices, of the programmer.

This kind of concierge, I predict, is far more likely to qualify for First Amendment coverage, based on the idea that it can be called a speech product. The rule of thumb is this: the more the concierge merely tells the user about himself, the more like a tool and less like protected speech the program is. The more the programmer puts in place his opinion, and tries to influence the user, the more likely there will be First Amendment coverage. These are the kinds of considerations that ultimately should drive every algorithmic output case that courts could encounter.

Conclusion

The questions considered in this Article seem likely to grow in importance, and courts will be asked to answer important category-defining questions in the coming years. Perhaps it might be helpful if the somewhat hidden functionality doctrine of the First Amendment were less mysterious. This Article has made an effort to bring to light that obscure area of the law.

Notes and Questions

1. Agreement and Disagreement. On what do Benjamin and Wu agree? On what, precisely, do they disagree? Are there areas where they are talking past each other?

2. What Is at Stake? Benjamin and Wu focus on the question whether or not the First Amendment applies. This is different, of course, from the question whether the First Amendment, once applied, would invalidate a given regulation.

But note that most of the proposals for regulation of algorithms focus on the content that algorithms prioritize (or deprioritize), and thus would ordinarily be subject to strict scrutiny if First Amendment scrutiny applies. And, as we saw in Chapter 11, such scrutiny is almost always fatal. It might seem tempting to suggest that laws requiring disclosures to consumers are subject to less rigorous scrutiny, but Riley v. National Federation of the Blind, 487 U.S. 781 (1988), noted on page 563, holds otherwise. Indeed, *Riley* applied strict scrutiny to required disclosures that were purely factual.

Proposals aimed at platforms' advertising would be subject to the intermediate scrutiny applicable to commercial speech, but as Sorrell v. IMS Health Inc., excerpted in Chapter 3.A, demonstrates, such scrutiny, while less daunting than strict scrutiny, is still fairly rigorous. Content-neutral proposals not aimed at commercial speech would be subject to intermediate scrutiny, which like the scrutiny applied to commercial speech is heightened but not as rigorous as strict scrutiny. But the Supreme Court has held that a speech regulation is content based (and thus not content neutral) if it "applies to particular speech because of the topic discussed or the idea or message expressed." Reed v. Gilbert, 576 U.S. 155, 163 (2015). Which, if any, proposals for algorithm regulation would be content neutral? What would they achieve?

This highlights the stakes involved in the question whether the First Amendment applies in the first place. If it does, the hurdles for meaningful regulation will be fairly high, and possibly insuperable.

3. What Is to Be Done? If the rejection of algorithm regulations seems problematic, should we make a constitutional distinction between algorithm-based and human-based decisions, or make some other distinction? On what basis would you choose your preferred constitutional distinction?

In this regard, note Wu's distinction between recommendation algorithms that rely on data provided by the user and algorithms that reflect the programmer's views. Is that an attractive constitutional line to draw? What if the programmer's deeply held view is that most people want more of what they have already seen but do not realize that (or do not admit it to themselves)? In those circumstances, would a program relying on data provided by the user also reflect the programmer's views? Or is that example so absurd that it supports the distinction Wu draws?

4. Search Engines versus Other Algorithms. The articles pay particular attention to algorithms used in search engines. Is there a constitutional distinction between algorithms used to generate search results and those used to prioritize, recommend, or automatically play content on social media? If so, what is the basis for that distinction? And which would be subject to more protection, and why?

5. Antitrust. In a portion of his article that we deleted for space reasons, Benjamin argues (invoking FTC v. Superior Court Trial Lawyers Association, 493 U.S. 411 (1990), excerpted in Chapter 3.B) that antitrust claims arising out of an entity's use of algorithmic speech could be brought without triggering First Amendment scrutiny. But that is cold comfort to regulators who cannot, or do not want to, rely on antitrust law to regulate the use of algorithms.

6. Cases. One of the few cases that addressed the issues raised in the articles above is the *Search King* case that Wu discussed, which held that search results are protected speech. Another is the case excerpted below.

Jian Zhang et al. v. Baidu.Com Inc.

10 F. Supp. 3d 433 (S.D.N.Y. 2014)

FURMAN, District Judge:

Background

The following facts, which are taken from the Complaint unless otherwise noted, are assumed to be true for purposes of this motion. Baidu operates a Chinese search engine service called Baidu.com, through which it "offers multiple services to locate information, products and services using Chinese-language search terms, such as, search by Chinese phonetics, advanced search, snapshots, spell checker, stock quotes, news, images, video, weather, train and flight schedules and other local information." (Compl. ¶ 13).

Plaintiffs, self-described "promoters of democracy in China through their writings, publications and reporting of pro-democracy events," allege that Baidu

> censor[s] and block[s] from search engine results any article, publication, video, audio and any information in whatever format if its content deals with the Democracy movement in China or any of the following topics that are related to the Chinese Democracy movement: The June 4th Movement, The Jasmine Revolution, The Jasmine Movement; The China Democracy Party National Committee and the Tiananmen Square Incident or movement.

(Compl. ¶ 22). Plaintiffs claim that Baidu engages in this "censorship" at the behest of the People's Republic of China, which was named as a defendant in the Complaint but was never served and is no longer a party to the case.

Each Plaintiff has published — on the Internet — articles, video recordings, audio recordings, or other publications regarding the democracy movement in China. Although such publications appear in results returned by other search engines, such as Google and Bing, they do not appear in Baidu's search results because Baidu deliberately blocks them. On these bases, Plaintiffs bring eight claims: (1) conspiracy to violate their civil rights, pursuant to 42 U.S.C. § 1985; (2) violation of their civil rights on the basis of race, pursuant to 42 U.S.C. § 1981; (3) violation of their civil rights under color of state law, pursuant to 42 U.S.C. § 1983; (4–7) denial of their right to equal public accommodations, in violation of New York Civil Rights Law §§ 40 and 40-c, New York Executive Law § 296(2), and New York City Administrative Code § 8-107(4)(a); and (8) denial of the equal protection of the laws guaranteed by New York Constitution Article 1, § 11.

Discussion

First, as a general matter, the Government may not interfere with the editorial judgments of private speakers on issues of public concern — that is, it may not tell a private speaker what to include or not to include in speech about matters of public concern. Second, that rule is not "restricted to the press, being enjoyed by business corporations generally and by ordinary people engaged in unsophisticated expression as well as by professional publishers." Hurley v. Irish-American Gay, Lesbian, & Bisexual Group of Boston, 515 U.S. 557, 574 (1995). Third, the First Amendment's protections apply whether or not a speaker articulates, or even has, a coherent or precise message, and whether or not the speaker generated the underlying content in the first place. And finally, it does not matter if the Government's intentions are noble—for example, to promote "press responsibility," Miami Herald Publishing Co. v. Tornillo, 418 U.S. 241, 256 (1974), or to prevent expression that is "misguided, or even hurtful," *Hurley,* 515 U.S. at 574; *see also* Turner Broad. Sys., Inc. v. FCC, 512 U.S. 622, 640 (1994) ("[T]he mere assertion of dysfunction or failure in a speech market, without more, is not sufficient to shield a speech regulation from the First Amendment standards. . . ."). Put simply, "[d]isapproval of a private speaker's statement"—no matter how justified disapproval may be—"does not legitimize use of the [Government's] power to compel the speaker to alter the message by including one more acceptable to others." *Hurley,* 515 U.S. at 581.

In light of those principles, there is a strong argument to be made that the First Amendment fully immunizes search-engine results from most, if not all, kinds of civil liability and government regulation. *See, e.g.,* Stuart Minor Benjamin, Algorithms and Speech, 161 U. Pa. L. Rev. 1445, 1458–72 (2013); Eugene Volokh & Donald M. Falk, Google First Amendment Protection for Search Engine Search Results, 8 J.L. Econ. & Pol'y 883, 884–92 (2012). The central purpose of a search engine is to retrieve relevant information from the vast universe of data on the Internet and to organize it in a way that would be most helpful to the searcher. In doing so, search engines inevitably make editorial judgments about what information (or kinds of information) to include in the results and how and where to display that information (for example, on the first page of the search results or later). In these respects, a "search engine's editorial judgment is much like many other familiar editorial judgments," such as the newspaper editor's judgment of which wire-service stories to run and where to place them in the newspaper, the guidebook writer's judgments about which attractions to mention and how to display them, and Matt Drudge's judgments about which stories to link and how prominently to feature them. Volokh & Falk; *accord* Benjamin.

On that theory of the First Amendment's protection of search-engine results, the fact that search engines often collect and communicate facts, as opposed to opinions, does not alter the analysis. As the Supreme Court has held, "the creation and dissemination of information are speech within the meaning of the First Amendment. Facts, after all, are the beginning point for much of the speech that is most essential to advance human knowledge and to conduct human affairs." Sorrell v. IMS Health Inc., 564 U.S. 552, 570 (2011). Nor does the fact that search-engine results may be produced algorithmically matter for the analysis. After all, the algorithms themselves were written by human beings, and they "inherently incorporate the search engine company engineers' judgments about what material users are most likely to find responsive to their queries." Volokh & Falk; Benjamin. In short, one could forcefully argue that "what is true for parades and newspaper op-ed pages is at least as true for search engine output. When search engines select and arrange others' materials, and add the all-important ordering that causes some materials to be displayed first and others last, they are engaging in fully protected First Amendment expression — '[t]he presentation of an edited compilation of speech generated by other persons.'" Volokh & Falk (quoting *Hurley,* 515 U.S. at 570).

In contrast to that robust theory of the First Amendment in this context, some scholars have relied on the Supreme Court's decision in *Turner* — which Plaintiffs here do not cite — to advocate for a lower level of protection of search-engine results. *See, e.g.,* Oren Bracha & Frank Pasquale, Federal Search Commission? Access, Fairness, and Accountability in the Law of Search, 93 Cornell L. Rev. 1149, 1191–94 (2008).

This Court, however, need not resolve the scholarly debate in order to decide the present motion because, whether or not the First Amendment shields all search engines from lawsuits based on the content of their search results, it plainly shields Baidu from Plaintiffs' claims in this lawsuit.[21] Here, the very theory of Plaintiffs' claims is that Baidu exercises editorial control over its search results on certain political topics — namely, by disfavoring expression concerning "the Democracy movement in China" and related subjects. (Compl. ¶ 22). In other words, Plaintiffs do not — and, in light of their own allegations, cannot — make any argument that Baidu is merely an "infrastructure or platform that delivers content" in a neutral way. Bracha & Pasquale (arguing that because "search engines do not function as publishers or editors of the content to which they channel users," their results should not be treated as speech covered by the First Amendment). Instead, they seek to hold Baidu liable for, and thus punish Baidu for, a conscious decision to design its search-engine algorithms to favor certain expression on core political subjects over other expression on those same political subjects. To allow such a suit to proceed would plainly "violate[] the fundamental rule of protection under the First Amendment, that a speaker has the autonomy to choose the content of his own message." *Hurley,* 515 U.S. at 573.

That conclusion is compelled as much by *Turner* as it is by *Tornillo* and *Hurley.* First, in light of *Turner,* "[t]here can be no disagreement" that Baidu is "engage[d] in and transmit[s] speech" and is thus "entitled to the protection of the speech and press provisions of the First Amendment" because Plaintiffs' own theory is that the company "exercise[s] editorial discretion" over its search results and thereby "seek[s] to communicate messages on a wide variety of topics and in a wide variety of formats." 512 U.S. at 636 (internal quotation marks and alterations omitted). Second, *Turner*'s three principal rationales for applying a lower level of scrutiny to the

21. Given the allegations in this case, there is also no need to address whether laws of general applicability, such as antitrust laws, can be applied to search engines without implicating the First Amendment. *Compare* Benjamin *with* Volokh & Falk.

must-carry cable regulations — namely, that cable companies were mere conduits for the speech of others, that they had the physical ability to silence other speakers, and that the regulations at issue were content-neutral — are inapplicable here. With respect to the first rationale, it is debatable whether any search engine is a mere "conduit" given the judgments involved in designing algorithms to choose, rank, and sort search results. But whether or not that proposition is true as a general matter, it is plainly "not apt here," as Plaintiffs' own allegations of censorship make clear that Baidu is "'more than a passive receptacle or conduit for news, comment, and advertising.'" *Hurley,* 515 U.S. at 575. As Plaintiffs themselves allege, for example, Baidu "purposely designs its search engine algorithms to exclude any pro-democracy topics, articles, publications, and multimedia coverage." (Compl. ¶ 20).

The second rationale, too, has no application here, as search engine operators (at least in the United States and given today's technology) lack the physical power to silence anyone's voices, no matter what their alleged market shares may be. As Plaintiffs' own publications make clear, Baidu does not have the ability to block "pro-democracy" writings from appearing on the Internet in this country altogether; it can only control whether it will help users find them. And if a user is dissatisfied with Baidu's search results, he or she "has access, with just a click of the mouse, to Google, Microsoft's Bing, Yahoo! Search, and other general-purpose search engines, as well as to almost limitless other means of finding content on the Internet, including specialized search engines, social networks, and mobile apps." Volokh & Falk.

It is, however, *Turner*'s third rationale for applying intermediate scrutiny that puts the final nail in the coffin for Plaintiffs' claims in this case. In *Turner,* the Court concluded that the regulations at issue were content-neutral, as they did not "impose[] a restriction, penalty, or burden by reason of the views, programs, or stations the cable operator has selected or will select." 512 U.S. at 644. By contrast, although the present case does not involve government regulation per se, Plaintiffs call upon the Court to impose a penalty on Baidu precisely because of what it does and does not choose to say. [T]o allow Plaintiffs' suit to proceed, let alone to hold Baidu liable for its editorial judgments, would contravene the principle upon which "[o]ur political system and cultural life rest": "that each person should decide for himself or herself the ideas and beliefs deserving of expression, consideration, and adherence." *Id.* at 641.

In short, Plaintiffs' efforts to hold Baidu accountable in a court of law for its editorial judgments about what political ideas to promote cannot be squared with the First Amendment.

Notes and Questions

1. A "Federal Search Commission." Wu and Judge Furman refer to an article calling for a "Federal Search Commission" based on the authors' "claim that search engines constitute one of the most important gatekeepers on the Internet [and] the problems caused by search engines' bias." Oren Bracha & Frank Pasquale, Federal

Search Commission? Access, Fairness, and Accountability in the Law of Search, 93 Cornell L. Rev. 1149, 1152 (2008). But how does a regulator choose the benchmarks it will use to identify what fair or unbiased search engine results look like? What would neutral benchmarks look like? Should a regulator focus on whether the search engine gives the answers that users want and value? But, if so, why wouldn't the search engine have sufficient incentives to provide users what they want and value?

2. What Is Safe? If you were advising a member of Congress, what regulations of algorithms would you identify as *clearly* avoiding any First Amendment problems? What would you identify as *likely* avoiding any First Amendment problems?

Chapter 13

Privacy Regulation

Introduction

One of the principal calls for regulation of internet services and platforms concerns privacy. Individuals not only conduct significant business over internet platforms, they reveal some of their most intimate details — from what they search for, to whom they "friend," to where they are, and to what they like and don't like. This data is valuable to the platform providers and to others who may be able to track it, such as ISPs, websites, browsers, and advertising networks. Indeed, collecting this data is the basis for the advertising model on which much of the internet as we know it depends. When the individual receives a service free of monetary charge — whether it is broadcast television or internet search — the individual is not the customer, the individual is the thing being sold. The internet takes the "mass eyeballs" market for broadcasting advertisers and, by aggregating and analyzing incredible amounts of data, allows very targeted advertising to individuals, as well as the creation of data profiles that may be combined and sold on their own.

Notwithstanding our chapter title, the United States has no "internet privacy regulation." Generalized privacy statutes or digital privacy statutes do exist in some other countries and in some U.S. states, but the United States federal government has taken an industry-specific and a practice-specific approach. Some industries, such as health care and financial services, have important privacy laws and regulation, and these regulations apply to internet services that touch on them, such as online health and online banking. Moreover, occasionally, a practice will give rise to specific privacy regulation in the communications or internet space, such as the Videotape Privacy Protection Act, 18 U.S.C. § 2710, which was prompted by an attempt to find Supreme Court nominee Robert Bork's rental history and now makes illegal the "wrongful disclosure of video tape rental or sales records" or similar audiovisual use records, or the Children's Online Privacy Protection Act (COPPA), 15 U.S.C. §§ 6501–6506, which covers much of what online providers must do with respect to users under 13. The most significant statutes address the government's attempts to secure electronic data, as through wiretapping, other forms of interception, or requests to private companies that hold electronic communications. These laws generally touch on criminal investigations or other government actions, and we treat them as beyond the scope of this book. Here, we principally address privacy regulation as it pertains generally to the development of telecommunications and internet business models.

What might generalized privacy regulation or at least general internet privacy regulation include? The starting point is a definition of information subject to protection, which is generally termed "personally identifiable information." One definition, from the rules of the White House Office of Management and Budget, reflects a common approach.

> Personally Identifiable Information (PII) means information that can be used to distinguish or trace an individual's identity, either alone or when combined with other personal or identifying information that is linked or linkable to a specific individual. Some information that is considered to be PII is available in public sources such as telephone books, public Web sites, and university listings. This type of information is considered to be Public PII and includes, for example, first and last name, address, work telephone number, email address, home telephone number, and general educational credentials. The definition of PII is not anchored to any single category of information or technology. Rather, it requires a case-by-case assessment of the specific risk that an individual can be identified. Non-PII can become PII whenever additional information is made publicly available, in any medium and from any source, that, when combined with other available information, could be used to identify an individual.

2 C.F.R. § 200.1.

Second, the law must define what entities are covered, although the notion of general regulation is that virtually all parties that might collect or handle PII would be covered, so long as they are within the jurisdictional reach of the regulation. Third, privacy regulation generally includes transparency rules, so that those who collect or handle information state clearly their practices. Fourth, regulation must specify when (if ever) and how persons may give their consent for the collection and use of their PII. Many privacy practices today are "opt out," meaning that a company discloses (somewhere in its terms and conditions) its data and privacy practices and that consent is implied if the consumer uses the offered services. An "opt in" regime, for all PII or for especially sensitive PII, requires affirmative consent, usually combined with the clear specific disclosure of the relevant practice or practices. Somewhere in the middle would be regulation that requires providers to offer options or tools by which users could choose the level of privacy protection. Fifth, privacy regulation usually imposes data security requirements on those who collect or use PII, including limitations on sharing the data with others. Last, a privacy regime needs an enforcement apparatus, whether public, private, or both. Of course, we might be content with no general privacy regime if we think that markets will sort this all out. To the extent that individuals actually value privacy (an open question[1]), they will value doing business with companies that respect their privacy.

---

1. The so-called "privacy paradox" arises because many more individuals say that they care about privacy than act in ways that protect their privacy. For an article that discusses this phenomenon and provides an entry into the research, as well as a critique of it, see Daniel J. Solove, The

We start with some background on common law protections for privacy using a few cases that have sought to apply these concepts to platforms. We then address the Federal Trade Commission's efforts. Using its § 5 authority to prohibit "[u]nfair methods of competition [and] unfair or deceptive acts or practices in or affecting commerce," 15 U.S.C. § 45(a)(1), the FTC has taken significant actions to promote privacy and has called for Congress to consider generalized internet privacy regulation. We then briefly look to the Communications Act, because it protects "customer proprietary network information" and that protection could provide the basis for regulating some internet services, either directly or as a model to be extended. Finally, we address European and state privacy regulation, which, both because of the global nature of the internet and the absence of U.S. federal regulation, have a significant impact on internet services.

§ 13.A. Common Law Tort Protections

In the United States, the common law can provide some limited protection for privacy, and we start here as background to the more regulatory efforts. Since the early 1900s, most states' tort law has evolved to recognize individual privacy as a legally protected interest. Usually traced back to a law review article coauthored by future Supreme Court Justice Louis Brandeis, invasions of privacy can arise from (1) an intrusion upon an individual's seclusion; (2) the public disclosure of embarrassing private facts; (3) the portrayal of an individual in a "false light"; and (4) the commercial appropriation of a person's likeness (often referred to as the right of publicity, which has itself evolved into its own tort). Samuel D. Warren & Louis D. Brandeis, The Right to Privacy, 4 Harv. L. Rev. 193 (1890).

The following two cases summarize California law, which is largely typical, in the context of two internet disputes.

Myth of the Privacy Paradox, 68 Geo. Wash. L.J. 1 (2021). For a survey of the research, see Spyros Kokolakis, Privacy Attitudes and Privacy Behaviour: A Review of Current Research on the Privacy Paradox Phenomenon, 64 Computers & Security 122 (2017). For one particularly telling experiment that concludes that stated consumer valuations of privacy are not terribly informative, see Angela G. Winegar & Cass R. Sunstein, How Much Is Data Privacy Worth? A Preliminary Investigation, 42 J. Consumer Policy 425, 425 (2019) ("Do consumers value data privacy? How much? In a survey of 2,416 Americans, we find that the median consumer is willing to pay just $5 per month to maintain data privacy (along specified dimensions), but would demand $80 to allow access to personal data.").

Jackson v. Mayweather

217 Cal. Rptr. 3d 234 (Cal. App. 2 Dist. 2017)

Opinion for the Court filed by Presiding Judge PERLUSS, in which Appellate Judges ZELON and SEGAL concurred.

Following the final breakup of what she has described as a physically and verbally abusive relationship with former boxing champion Floyd Mayweather, Jr., Shantel Jackson sued Mayweather for, among other claims, invasion of privacy (both public disclosure of private facts and false light portrayal), defamation and intentional and negligent infliction of emotional distress. Those five causes of action were based, either entirely or in substantial part, on Mayweather's social media postings about the termination of Jackson's pregnancy and its relationship to the couple's separation and his comments during a radio interview concerning the extent to which Jackson had undergone cosmetic surgery procedures. Mayweather filed a special motion to strike those causes of action. The trial court denied the motion. We reverse that ruling with respect to Jackson's claims for defamation and false light portrayal, as well as her cause of action for public disclosure of private facts based on Mayweather's statements that Jackson had an abortion and his comments about her cosmetic surgery.

Factual And Procedural Background

1. Jackson's Complaint

Jackson and Mayweather were a highly publicized celebrity couple for a number of years and were at one point engaged to be married. However, the relationship frayed. In November 2013 Jackson became pregnant by Mayweather. Jackson alleged she told Mayweather and one friend of her pregnancy, but no one else. A December 2013 sonogram revealed Jackson was carrying twins. At Mayweather's request Jackson gave him a copy of the sonogram. According to the complaint, "In January of 2014, Ms. Jackson's pregnancy terminated and Mr. Mayweather was so informed."

On April 12, 2014 Jackson attended a basketball game with the rapper Nelly and posted a photograph of the two of them on her social media pages. Mayweather threatened to post photographs he had taken of Jackson sleeping naked if she did not take down the Nelly photograph. Jackson rejected the demand and also refused to reconcile with Mayweather. In response, on May 1, 2014 Mayweather posted on his Facebook and Instagram accounts, "the real reason me and Shantel Christine Jackson @MissJackson broke up was because she got an abortion, and I'm totally against killing babies. She killed our twin babies. #ShantelJackson #Floyd Mayweather #TheMoneyTeam #TMT." Mayweather also posted a copy of the sonogram of the twin fetuses and a summary medical report regarding the pregnancy. Media outlets, including TMZ, republished the sonogram and medical report. The following day Mayweather again discussed Jackson's abortion during a radio interview and also stated she had undergone extensive cosmetic surgery procedures.

Based on the allegations regarding Mayweather's posting of information about Jackson's pregnancy and its termination, including the sonogram and medical report, and the broadcast of the statement she had cosmetic surgery on her face and body, Jackson's complaint asserted causes of action for invasion of privacy (public disclosure of private facts), invasion of privacy (false light portrayal) and defamation.

2. The Special Motion To Strike

Contending there was no merit to Jackson's claims, Mayweather argued Jackson had surrendered her right to privacy when she made herself newsworthy by virtue of her relationship with Mayweather. She had willingly participated in publication of private details about that relationship. Accordingly, the reason for the relationship's demise was equally newsworthy.

With respect to Mayweather's May 1, 2014 post that he had ended their relationship because of the abortion, Jackson declared, "He knew that the real reason I would not come back to him was because he wouldn't change his ways" — that is, Mayweather would not alter his abusive behavior toward her. She further declared she considered her pregnancy, the termination of the pregnancy and her medical reports to be private information, something that Mayweather knew.

With respect to the radio broadcast on May 2, 2014, Jackson declared that any cosmetic surgery procedures she had undergone were confidential. Moreover, during that broadcast Mayweather had falsely said she had cosmetic surgery to change her nose, chin and cheeks. In addition, during the same broadcast Mayweather had falsely claimed she terminated the pregnancy because she was concerned about her looks and "didn't want to mess my body up." According to Jackson the postings and false statements by Mayweather caused a massive negative public reaction, which included death threats and offensive comments describing her as a "baby killer" and a "whore."

Jackson argued Mayweather's conduct giving rise to her claims — his disregard for her medical privacy — was entirely unrelated to the public debate over abortion.

3. The Trial Court's Order Denying the Motion

The trial court denied Mayweather's motion [to strike]. The court explained abortion is an issue of widespread interest, Jackson was a person in the public eye, and Jackson's relationship with Mayweather was a matter of public interest and media attention. However, the court concluded Jackson had established a likelihood of prevailing on each of her claims. Citing case law, the court reasoned that whether Mayweather's statements were subject to a newsworthy privilege or were otherwise protected by the First Amendment depended on contemporary standards and thus was largely a question of fact for a jury to decide. The court also ruled that Jackson's evidence was sufficient to establish a prima facie case that Mayweather knowingly disseminated false information concerning the reasons for the couple's breakup and the extent of Jackson's cosmetic surgery.

Discussion

3. Jackson Failed To Demonstrate a Probability of Prevailing on Her Cause of Action for Defamation and Most Aspects of Her Causes of Action for Invasion of Privacy

Jackson's causes of action for public disclosure of private facts, false light portrayal and defamation are based on Mayweather's May 1, 2014 social media postings regarding the termination of her pregnancy and his reaction to it and on his subsequent statements regarding her cosmetic surgery.

a. Invasion of privacy: public disclosure of private facts

"[U]nder California common law the dissemination of truthful, newsworthy material is not actionable as a publication of private facts." Shulman v. Group W Productions, Inc., 955 P.2d 469, 479 (Cal. 1998). To establish tort liability for this type of invasion of privacy, the plaintiff must plead and prove (1) public disclosure (2) of a private fact (3) that would be offensive and objectionable to the reasonable person and (4) is not of legitimate public concern. With respect to the fourth element, the Supreme Court held in *Shulman*, that "newsworthiness" is a complete bar to liability for publication of truthful information. In analyzing the element of newsworthiness, appellate decisions "balance the public's right to know against the plaintiff's privacy interest by drawing a protective line at the point the material revealed ceases to have any substantial connection to the subject matter of the newsworthy report." *Id.* at 485.

Although "legitimate public interest does not include a morbid and sensational prying into private lives for its own sake," *id.* at 485, the protection accorded the right to disseminate truthful information by both the common law and the constitutional guarantee of freedom of expression "'appl[ies] with equal force to the publication whether it be a news report or an entertainment feature. . . .' Thus, newsworthiness is not limited to 'news' in the narrow sense of reports of current events. 'It extends also to the use of names, likenesses or facts in giving information to the public for purposes of education, amusement or enlightenment, when the public may reasonably be expected to have a legitimate interest in what is published.'" *Id.* at 486.

The question whether a publication was newsworthy is different, in both a legal and practical sense, from whether it was offensive within the meaning of the private facts tort. Jackson's pregnancy, the subsequent termination of that pregnancy—whether by abortion (which she has neither admitted nor denied) or otherwise—and her use of cosmetic surgery to enhance her appearance would, under many circumstances, be considered intensely private information; and its unwanted disclosure might well be offensive to a reasonable person. Nonetheless, at a time when entertainment news and celebrity gossip often seem to matter more than serious policy discussions, given Jackson's high profile and voluntary disclosure on social media of many aspects of her personal life, the publication of those otherwise intimate facts must necessarily be considered newsworthy under the broad definition of that term developed and applied by the Supreme Court and courts of appeal.

Although Jackson cannot base her private facts cause of action on Mayweather's disclosures that she had an abortion and had undergone cosmetic surgery, Mayweather's posting of the sonogram of the twins Jackson had been carrying before her pregnancy terminated and the summary medical report regarding her pregnancy falls outside the protection accorded a newsworthy report. On this record at least, publishing those images served no legitimate public purpose, even when one includes entertainment news within the zone of protection.

Jackson has made a prima facie showing that Mayweather's publication of the sonogram and summary medical report involved a "morbid and sensational" prying into her private life and thus constituted a cognizable basis for her invasion of privacy claim. Accordingly, Jackson adequately demonstrated a probability of prevailing on her cause of action for public disclosure of private facts based on the posting of these two items. To that limited extent only, we affirm the trial court's ruling denying the special motion to strike as directed to Jackson's first cause of action for invasion of privacy.

c. Invasion of privacy: false light portrayal

"False light is a species of invasion of privacy, based on publicity that places a plaintiff before the public in a false light that would be highly offensive to a reasonable person, and where the defendant knew or acted in reckless disregard as to the falsity of the publicized matter and the false light in which the plaintiff would be placed." Price v. Operating Engineers Local Union No. 3 125 Cal. Rptr. 3d 220, 225 (Cal. App. 4th Dist. 2011). "A 'false light' claim, like libel, exposes a person to hatred, contempt, ridicule, or obloquy and assumes the audience will recognize it as such." M.G. v. Time Warner, Inc., 107 Cal. Rptr. 2d 504, 514 (Cal. App. 4th Dist. 2001). "'A "false light" cause of action is in substance equivalent to a libel claim, and should meet the same requirements of the libel claim, including proof of malice [where malice is required for the libel claim].'" Medical Marijuana, Inc. v. ProjectCBD.com, 212 Cal. Rptr. 3d 45, 55 (Cal. App. 4th Dist. 2016).

Jackson acknowledges her false light claim is based on the same statements as the cause of action for disclosure of private facts—that is, Mayweather's assertion that he broke off the couple's relationship because Jackson had an abortion and his comments that she had cosmetic surgery on her face, as well as other parts of her body. Those claims suffer from the same fatal defects as Jackson's defamation claim: Mayweather's allegedly false explanation for the couple's breakup did not expose Jackson to "hatred, contempt, ridicule, or obloquy"; his exaggerated description of the extent of Jackson's cosmetic surgery was, in substance, truthful. Neither statement is sufficient to establish a prima facie case for false light portrayal.

Disposition

The order denying the special motion to strike is reversed with respect to Jackson's causes of action for defamation and false light portrayal and her cause of action for public disclosure of private facts based on Mayweather's statements that she had an abortion and his comments about cosmetic surgery. In all other respects the order is affirmed.

Notes and Questions

1. *Disclosure* of Private Facts. The "disclosure of private facts" branch of the privacy tort has some salience for the internet era, but the tort also has some limitations. The disclosure required is public disclosure, and internet data collectors will frequently not disclose the data publicly at all—using it instead for targeted advertising or other internal or limited purposes. From one perspective, this might mean that the collection and use is not harmful. But it also means that the tort does not prevent the development of data profiles where the advertising (or other use) brings embarrassment.

2. Disclosure of *Private* Facts. This branch of the tort also requires that the facts be private, which raises the possibility of consent through contract or behavior. Much of the information that platforms and other entities accumulate is given to the platform through affirmative behavior (posts, comments, data entry, etc.). Additionally, websites and platforms describe, albeit at reasonably high levels of generality, the information that is being collected and how it might be used. Do users read these statements? Unsurprisingly, most research says that users do not. *See, e.g.*, Jonathan A. Ober & Anne Oeldorf-Hirsch, The Biggest Lie on the Internet: Ignoring the Privacy Policies and Terms of Service Policies of Social Networking Services, 23 Information, Comm., & Soc'y 128 (2020).

3. False Light. The decision describes false light as essentially the same as defamation, given that the plaintiff and defendant are public figures. Accordingly, the platform must falsely portray the user. As already noted, platforms and internet services might not publicly portray the user at all. Moreover, what are platforms' incentives to portraying the user in a false light? The platforms and other internet services collect user information in order to sell advertising or sell the data itself to companies who will use it for other purposes (from political campaigns to marketers). In other words, isn't there an economic incentive to be accurate?

4. Intrusion upon Seclusion. The third branch of privacy tort, intrusion upon seclusion, does not require that the information be false or, necessarily, that it be publicly disclosed (although there is usually a damages requirement). In this next case, we see how it might apply in the context of platforms.

McDonald v. Kiloo ApS

385 F. Supp. 3d 1022 (N.D. Cal. 2019)

DONATO, District Judge:

These cases are related actions brought by parents over gaming apps for kids. All of the cases are putative class actions and allege that the apps were used to track online behavior on a device and user-specific level, and that defendants exploited the data, without disclosure or consent, for profit. In effect, the complaints allege that the apps were covert collectors of behavioral data for delivery of targeted advertising to users, namely the kids who played the games.

Plaintiffs have sued a number of "developer defendants" and "SDK defendants." The developer defendants, which include Disney, Viacom, Kiloo and Sybo, are the companies that created the games and made them available for download. The SDK defendants are mobile advertising and app monetization companies that provide "software development kits" containing code to collect user data. These defendants include AdColony, Chartboost, Tapjoy, Flurry and other entities. Plaintiffs allege that the developer defendants embedded the SDK defendants' code into the games to gather and transmit to the SDK defendants "persistent identifiers" and personal data for tracking, profiling and ad targeting.

All the cases assert privacy claims under the California Constitution and for intrusion upon seclusion under California law.

Discussion

I. State Law Privacy Claims

A. California Intrusion Upon Seclusion

A California tort claim for intrusion upon seclusion is alleged for all named plaintiffs and putative class members. While plaintiffs pursue the tort on behalf of a proposed 34-state class in all three cases, the named plaintiffs themselves are from California, New York, and Massachusetts.

For the elements of the tort, plaintiffs say that (1) they and their children had "reasonable expectations of privacy in their mobile devices and their online behavior"; (2) defendants "intentionally intruded on and into plaintiffs' and class members' solitude, seclusion, or private affairs by intentionally designing" the games and SDKs to "surreptitiously obtain, improperly gain knowledge of, review, and/or retain plaintiffs' and class members' activities through the monitoring technologies and activities" described in the complaints; and (3) these intrusions were "highly offensive to a reasonable person." Plaintiffs contend that "California law on intrusion upon seclusion is applicable for all members of the Intrusion Upon Seclusion Class because there is no conflict of law between the law in California and any of the states in which the Class members reside. The jurisprudence in California and each of the relevant states adheres to Restatement (Second) of Torts, § 652B with no material variation." Defendants do not disagree on the choice-of-law issue and focus on California law for their joint arguments to dismiss this claim. The Court is sitting in diversity jurisdiction and is guided principally by decisions of the California Supreme Court. In Hill v. National Collegiate Athletic Association, 865 P.2d 633 (Cal. 1994), the California Supreme Court discussed state privacy law in the context of a claim under the "Privacy Initiative," a voter initiative which added the phrase "and privacy" to the California Constitution, article I, section 1 in November 1972. As amended, the section states: "All people are by nature free and independent and have inalienable rights. Among these are enjoying and defending life and liberty, acquiring, possessing, and protecting property, and pursuing and obtaining safety, happiness, and privacy."

Examining a claim brought by student athletes who were required to provide urine samples under closely monitored conditions, the *Hill* court held that "a plaintiff alleging an invasion of privacy in violation of the state constitutional right to privacy must establish each of the following: (1) a legally protected privacy interest; (2) a reasonable expectation of privacy in the circumstances; and (3) conduct by defendant constituting a serious invasion of privacy." 865 P.2d at 657. For the last element, the court stated that "[a]ctionable invasions of privacy must be sufficiently serious in their nature, scope, and actual or potential impact to constitute an egregious breach of the social norms underlying the privacy right." *Id.* at 655. The court also observed, more than once, that "privacy interests and accompanying legal standards are best viewed flexibly and in context," and "[w]hatever their common denominator, privacy interests are best assessed separately and in context." *Id.* at 654. The court ultimately concluded there was no constitutional privacy violation and reversed the permanent injunction against the NCAA's drug testing program, both because student athletes had diminished expectations of privacy in that context and the NCAA had competing interests that were "reasonably calculated to further its legitimate interest in maintaining the integrity of intercollegiate athletic competition." *Id.* at 660. On the seriousness of the privacy invasion, the court held that the "NCAA's use of a particularly intrusive monitored urination procedure justifies further inquiry, even under conditions of decreased expectations of privacy." *Id.* at 659.

[T]he Court is mindful of the importance of having an adequate factual record before dismissing a privacy case. With this guidance in mind, the Court finds that plaintiffs have adequately alleged an intrusion upon seclusion claim and the offensiveness element in particular, which is the only element of the intrusion claim that defendants squarely challenge. Plaintiffs state in detail what data was secretly collected, how the collection was done, and how the harvested data was used. They also present detailed and specific allegations about why these intrusions would have been highly offensive to the reasonable person on the basis of multiple sources, including reports, studies, surveys, case law and secondary legal materials.

Current privacy expectations are developing, to say the least, with respect to a key issue raised in these cases — whether the data subject owns and controls his or her personal information, and whether a commercial entity that secretly harvests it commits a highly offensive or egregious act. The Court cannot say that the answers are so patently obvious that plaintiffs' allegations are implausible or inadequate as a matter of law.

In re Nickelodeon Consumer Privacy Litigation, 827 F.3d 262 (3d Cir. 2016), does not carry the day for defendants. The court addressed an intrusion upon seclusion claim under New Jersey law, which, like California law, looks to the Second Restatements of Torts. This Court agrees with *Nickelodeon* that the status of game users as minors is not a main driver of the privacy analysis, but the case is otherwise not germane. *Nickelodeon* affirmed the dismissal of Google because "courts have long understood that tracking cookies can serve legitimate commercial purposes." *Id.* at 294 & n.203. Even if that debatable principle were embraced, it does not necessarily fit the scope of behavioral tracking that the mobile applications here are alleged to have practiced. As the United States Supreme Court has observed on several occasions, a mobile phone has become "almost a 'feature of human anatomy'" that provides a wealth of personal information about its user. Carpenter v. United States, 138 S. Ct. 2206, 2218 (2018) (quoting Riley v. California, 573 U.S. 373, 385 (2014)). Cell phones and mobile devices are "compulsively" carried and used by most people, *see, e.g., Carpenter*, 138 S. Ct. at 2218, including kids. The persistent identifiers and other data harvested to track users on these ubiquitous mobile devices involve collection practices that exceed those of the cookies in *Nickelodeon*, and without a "long" understanding suggesting that that is okay to do.

This is enough to let the complaints go forward. The parties devoted considerable attention to a few other issues that do not need to be addressed at this stage of the case. One is deceit. The presence of an affirmative misrepresentation has been found significant by other courts. While courts have found this kind of "plus" factor to be significant in establishing an expectation of privacy or making a privacy intrusion especially offensive, no court has held deceit to be a requirement of an intrusion claim. The parties do not suggest otherwise, and for the reasons discussed above, the Court concludes that plaintiffs here have sufficiently stated a claim even without that factor. The Court also notes that defendants have not challenged plaintiffs' expectation of privacy in any event, but only the gravity of the alleged invasion.

Both sides also discuss the contracts that existed between the developer defendants and the SDK defendants, as well as the defendants' respective privacy policies. These documents will likely be pertinent to issues of notice and consent, and the ultimate resolution of plaintiffs' intrusion claims. As framed, however, they are not appropriate for resolution as a part of this analysis of whether or not plaintiffs have sufficiently stated an intrusion claim to go forward.

[The Court treated the claim under the California Constitution as identical to the tort claim.]

Notes and Questions

1. Settlement. The litigation was eventually settled, with the defendants promising to make certain changes to their privacy practices.

2. Offensive? Do you agree with the court that the collection of the information and its use for advertising is highly offensive? The plaintiffs do not assert that the children were offended by the collection of the digital information when it was collected (as the plaintiff athletes might have been in *Hill*). And the plaintiffs also do not assert offense from the advertising that was allegedly generated from the data collection. What is the offensive practice, and why is it offensive?

3. Injury? Apart from offensiveness, do the plaintiffs assert any other injury from the collection and use of the information? In a portion of the opinion that we have omitted, the court holds that plaintiffs have not alleged any economic injury. Should such injury be required? Any injury?

§ 13.B. Protection by Contract

Tort protections will often be limited by the parties' agreement (or manifestation of agreement) to terms of service that include privacy policies. Similarly, some platforms might promise privacy protections or at least certain practices that do protect privacy. When they do, contract law can vindicate privacy rights.

The case below involves a breach of contract claim against Facebook. In federal courts, plaintiffs must establish standing in order to satisfy the jurisdictional requirements of Article III, and the opinion below focuses on that issue.

In re: Facebook Privacy Litigation

192 F. Supp. 3d 1053 (N.D. Cal. 2016)

WHYTE, District Judge:

Plaintiffs Katherine Pohl and Wendy Marfeo bring this putative class action against Facebook, Inc. for breach of contract and fraud. Facebook moves to dismiss for lack of Article III standing. [T]he court grants Facebook's motion to dismiss for lack of standing as to Ms. Pohl and denies Facebook's motion to dismiss for lack of standing as to Ms. Marfeo.

I. Background

Facebook provides social networking services to its users free of charge. Facebook users must register on the website using their real names. After registering, users may then post other personal information to a Facebook profile page. Facebook generates revenue through advertising. Facebook is able to target ads to particular demographics using the personal information provided by its registered users. Targeted advertising is valuable to Facebook's advertisers. According to Facebook, the "ad targeting is done entirely anonymously. If advertisers select demographic targeting for their ads, Facebook automatically matches those ads to the appropriate audience. Advertisers only receive anonymous data reports." Third Amended Complaint ¶ 28 (quoting Facebook's Privacy Guide). Plaintiffs allege that Facebook has "consistently and adamantly promised" not to share any user's specific identity or personally identifiable information (PII) with its advertising partners.

Ms. Pohl and Ms. Marfeo claim that Facebook violated its own policies and promises by disclosing their "sensitive personally identifiable information" to advertisers. Specifically, plaintiffs allege that when they clicked on Facebook ads, Facebook sent "referer headers" to the advertisers that would allow the advertiser to identify the user who clicked the ad.

When an Internet user navigates to a website by clicking a link, the user's browser may send a "referer header" to the destination website's server. A "referer header" typically contains the URL of the website the user was visiting when he or she clicked the link. Each Facebook user account is tied to a unique user ID number or username. Before July 2010, "if a Facebook user navigated the Facebook website in a particular way and clicked on a third-party advertisement linked to an external page, the resulting referer header may have included a user's Facebook username or user ID." A referer header containing a user ID or username from a referring Facebook profile page is not enough to identify the Facebook user who clicked on the ad; the same referer header would be generated for any user visiting that particular profile page, not just a user visiting his or her own profile page.

During the same timeframe, however, Facebook may have "included a particular string of characters in users' profile page URLs ('ref=profile')" if a "user took certain steps to navigate *to his or her own profile page*." As a result, some referer headers sent to external advertisers included "both the 'ref=profile' string and the user ID or username of the user who clicked the ad." Facebook acknowledges that "in theory," a recipient of both the "ref=profile" string and a user ID or username would be able to identify the Facebook user who clicked on the ad. Plaintiffs assert two causes of action based on the transmission of these referer headers — breach of contract and fraud.

II. Analysis

Plaintiffs have the burden to establish standing. "To establish standing, a plaintiff must show that (1) he or she has suffered an injury in fact that is concrete and particularized, and actual or imminent; (2) the injury is fairly traceable to the challenged conduct; and (3) the injury is likely to be redressed by a favorable court decision." WildEarth Guardians v. US Dep't of Agric., 795 F.3d 1148, 1154 (9th Cir. 2015). Facebook argues that neither Ms. Pohl nor Ms. Marfeo can establish the first of these requirements — injury in fact.

To establish injury in fact, a plaintiff must show that he or she suffered "an invasion of a legally protected interest" that is "concrete and particularized" and "actual or imminent, not conjectural or hypothetical." Lujan v. Defenders of Wildlife, 504 U.S. 555, 560 (1992).

A. Plaintiff Katherine Pohl

Ms. Pohl's claims are dismissed for lack of standing. Plaintiffs' breach of contract and fraud claims both rely on allegations that Facebook disclosed plaintiffs' personal information to third party advertisers. Facebook's ad-click data shows that Ms. Pohl's only ad click during the class period directed Ms. Pohl to the advertiser's Facebook page, rather than the advertiser's external website. Therefore, the referer header associated with Ms. Pohl's ad click would have been sent to a Facebook server, rather than any third party advertiser's server. Plaintiffs concede that "the information Facebook has produced to date indicates that Pohl's personal information was not transmitted to an advertiser's external website." Ms. Pohl, therefore, lacks standing and cannot represent the putative class in this case.

B. Plaintiff Wendy Marfeo

Plaintiffs submit three theories for Ms. Marfeo's injury in fact: 1) there is a credible threat that Ms. Marfeo will be harmed in the future by the release of her personal information, 2) Ms. Marfeo was denied the benefit of the bargain she made with Facebook, and 3) Ms. Marfeo is entitled to seek nominal damages for breach of contract.

1. Threat of Future Harm

Plaintiffs have not established injury in fact through threat of future harm. At the hearing, plaintiffs alleged injury via a "credible threat of future harm by releasing this information and making it available." Allegations of "possible future injury" are not sufficient to establish injury in fact. Plaintiffs do not identify any evidence to show that a release of Ms. Marfeo's personal information is impending. Plaintiffs' evidence of disclosure is limited to Ms. Marfeo's ad clicks in 2009 and 2010 and the resulting referer headers. Evidence from more than five years ago, with no suggestion of disclosure since then, cannot establish that a release of Ms. Marfeo's personal information is certainly impending.

2. Benefit of the Bargain

Plaintiffs allege that Ms. Marfeo suffered injury in fact because she did not receive the promised confidentiality for which she bargained. Facebook challenges plaintiffs' benefit of the bargain theory on three grounds: 1) Facebook never agreed to pay users in exchange for consent to disclose information, 2) plaintiffs cannot establish harm without evidence of receipt or use by a third party, and 3) plaintiffs cannot establish breach without evidence of receipt by a third party. The court is not persuaded by Facebook's arguments. Although Ms. Marfeo may have significant difficulty proving damages under the benefit of the bargain theory, she has established standing.

The court is not persuaded that plaintiffs' benefit of the bargain is premised on any promise by Facebook to pay users for disclosure on per-transaction basis. Plaintiffs confirmed at the hearing that plaintiffs are not alleging a promise to pay on a per-transaction basis, emphasizing that any discussion of what Ms. Marfeo might have received from advertisers in exchange for her consent is relevant only to ascertaining the value of the benefit of bargain that Ms. Marfeo was allegedly denied. Plaintiffs' representations at the hearing echo the benefit of the bargain theory set forth in the TAC: "Plaintiffs and each class member gave up something of value, PII, in exchange *for access to Facebook and Facebook's privacy promises.* Facebook materially breached the contracts by violating its privacy terms, thus depriving Plaintiffs and Class members the benefit of the bargain." The court is skeptical about plaintiffs' ability to establish the value of the benefit allegedly denied to Ms. Marfeo, but the court is satisfied that plaintiffs have alleged Ms. Marfeo received less than she bargained for from Facebook.

Nor is the court is persuaded that plaintiffs must establish third party receipt or use under a benefit of the bargain theory. While plaintiff must establish that Ms. Marfeo was denied a "benefit" of the bargain, there is no requirement that the benefit relate to third party receipt or use. Plaintiffs allege that Ms. Marfeo did not receive the full benefit of her bargain because Facebook transmitted her personal information to advertisers and that the value of the benefit she was denied can be ascertained by measuring the value of her personal information.

3. Nominal Damages for Breach of Contract

The injury alleged is "concrete" in that plaintiffs specify the contractual terms to which Ms. Marfeo agreed and the manner of breach by Facebook. The breach is "particularized" in that it involves disclosure of Ms. Marfeo's own personal information and "actual" in that plaintiffs claim the breach has already occurred. Facebook does not challenge plaintiffs' evidence that Facebook had a contractual duty not to share plaintiffs' personal information, at least for purposes of this motion. Nor does Facebook challenge plaintiffs' evidence that Ms. Marfeo's personal information was transmitted to third parties. Therefore, plaintiffs have established injury in fact through Ms. Marfeo's breach of contract claim for nominal damages.

III. Conclusion

For these reasons, Facebook's motion to dismiss for lack of standing as to Ms. Pohl is granted. Facebook's motion to dismiss for lack of standing as to Ms. Marfeo is denied.

Notes and Questions

1. Thresholds. Establishing standing is the first step in bringing a case in federal court, but it is one that knocks out many claimants who cannot establish they have suffered a concrete injury. The court permitted the case to go forward for a determination of breach of contract without a showing of damages. This is significant because compensatory damages may be difficult to establish.

2. Effectiveness. What would be the effect of a successful breach of contract case against Facebook in the real world? Could Facebook be required to cease the referer practices described here? Or would Facebook simply change its terms of services to state that such practices might be undertaken? If it did, would consumers stop using

Facebook? Under contract law, those terms would usually be binding, even if users did not read them and did not anticipate the practice.

3. Causation. An additional limitation on common law remedies, both contract and tort, is the doctrine of causation. In general, private remedies require that the plaintiff show that the defendant's action is the cause of the plaintiff's injury. Even if a plaintiff can show that the defendant collected or shared personally identifiable information and that the plaintiff suffered some injury such as identity theft or harassment, the plaintiff may not be able to link a particular collection and disclosure to the injury. Government action does not have either a specific injury requirement or the causation difficulties, because governments can simply act to enforce the law.

§ 13.C. FTC Privacy Supervision

As already noted, the FTC has authority to take action against companies under its "unfair and deceptive trade practices" authority. The easiest FTC cases are similar to contract actions, arising when a company does not follow its own privacy policies, for then the FTC can (and does) simply say that the company has engaged in a "deceptive" practice in violation of the Act. The more difficult cases arise when the FTC attempts to define a practice as "unfair," as the baseline for fairness is always contested.

A quintessential example of the first type of FTC case arose when it became clear that pictures sent through the Snapchat application did not really disappear as advertised. But the FTC also stated other claims that straddled the boundary between deceptive and unfair.

Snapchat, Inc.

2015-1 Trade Cas. ¶ 17,115 (F.T.C.) (2014), 2014 WL 7495798

Complaint

The Federal Trade Commission, having reason to believe that Snapchat, Inc. (respondent) has violated the provisions of the Federal Trade Commission Act, and it appearing to the Commission that this proceeding is in the public interest, alleges:

Respondent's Business Practices

3. Snapchat provides a mobile application that allows consumers to send and receive photo and video messages known as "snaps." Before sending a snap, the application requires the sender to designate a period of time that the recipient will be allowed to view the snap. Snapchat markets the application as an "ephemeral" messaging application, having claimed that once the timer expires, the snap "disappears forever."

5. Both the iTunes App Store and the Google Play store list Snapchat among the top 15 free applications. As of September 2013, users transmit more than 350 million snaps daily.

Snapchat's "Disappearing" Messages
(Counts 1 and 2)

6. Snapchat marketed its application as a service for sending "disappearing" photo and video messages, declaring that the message sender "control[s] how long your friends can view your message." Before sending a snap, the application requires the sender to designate a period of time—with the default set to a maximum of 10 seconds—that the recipient will be allowed to view the snap.

7. Since the application's launch on iOS until May 2013, and since the application's launch on Android until June 2013, Snapchat disseminated, or caused to be disseminated, to consumers the following statements on its product description page on the iTunes App Store and Google Play: "You control how long your friends can view your message—simply set the time up to ten seconds and send. They'll have that long to view your message and then it disappears forever."

8. From October 2012 to October 2013, Snapchat disseminated, or caused to be disseminated, to consumers the following statement on the "FAQ" page on its website:

> Is there any way to view an image after the time has expired?
>
> No, snaps disappear after the timer runs out....

9. Despite these claims, several methods exist by which a recipient can use tools outside of the application to save both photo and video messages, allowing the recipient to access and view the photos or videos indefinitely.

10. For example, when a recipient receives a video message, the application stores the video file in a location outside of the application's "sandbox" (*i.e.*, the application's private storage area on the device that other applications cannot access). Because the file is stored in this unrestricted area, until October 2013, a recipient could connect his or her mobile device to a computer and use simple file browsing tools to locate and save the video file. This method for saving video files sent through the application was widely publicized as early as December 2012. Snapchat did not mitigate this flaw until October 2013, when it began encrypting video files sent through the application.

11. Furthermore, third-party developers have built applications that can connect to Snapchat's application programming interface (API), thereby allowing recipients to log into the Snapchat service without using the official Snapchat application. Because the timer and related "deletion" functionality is dependent on the recipient's use of the official Snapchat application, recipients can instead simply use a third-party application to download and save both photo and video messages. As early as June 2012, a security researcher warned Snapchat that it would be "pretty

easy to write a tool to download and save the images a user receives" due to the way the API functions. Indeed, beginning in spring 2013, third-party developers released several applications on the iTunes App Store and Google Play that recipients can use to save and view photo or video messages indefinitely. On Google Play alone, ten of these applications have been downloaded as many as 1.7 million times.

12. The file browsing tools and third-party applications described in paragraphs 10 and 11 are free or low cost and publicly available on the Internet. In order to download, install, and use these tools, a recipient need not make any modifications to the iOS or Android operating systems and would need little technical knowledge.

13. In addition to the methods described in paragraphs 10–12, a recipient can use the mobile device's screenshot capability to capture an image of a snap while it appears on the device screen.

14. Snapchat claimed that if a recipient took a screenshot of a snap, the sender would be notified. On its product description pages, as described in paragraph 7, Snapchat stated: "We'll let you know if [recipients] take a screenshot!" In addition, from October 2012 to February 2013, Snapchat disseminated, or caused to be disseminated, to consumers the following statement on the "FAQ" page on its website:

> What if I take a screenshot?
>
> Screenshots can be captured if you're quick. The sender will be notified immediately.

15. However, recipients can easily circumvent Snapchat's screenshot detection mechanism. For example, on versions of iOS prior to iOS 7, the recipient need only double press the device's Home button in rapid succession to evade the detection mechanism and take a screenshot of any snap without the sender being notified. This method was widely publicized.

Snapchat's Collection Of Geolocation Information

(Count 3)

20. From June 2011 to February 2013, Snapchat disseminated or caused to be disseminated to consumers the following statements in its privacy policy:

> We do not ask for, track, or access any location-specific information from your device at any time while you are using the Snapchat application.

21. In October 2012, Snapchat integrated an analytics tracking service in the Android version of its application that acted as its service provider. While the Android operating system provided notice to consumers that the application may access location information, Snapchat did not disclose that it would, in fact, access location information, and continued to represent that Snapchat did "not ask for, track, or access any location-specific information . . ."

22. Contrary to the representation in Snapchat's privacy policy, from October 2012 to February 2013, the Snapchat application on Android transmitted Wi-Fi-based and cell-based location information from users' mobile devices to its analytics tracking service provider.

Snapchat's Collection of Contacts Information

(Counts 4 and 5)

Snapchat's Deceptive Find Friends User Interface

25. Snapchat provides its users with a feature to find friends on the service. During registration, the application prompts the user to "Enter your mobile number to find your friends on Snapchat!," implying—prior to September 2012—through its user interface that the mobile phone number was the only information Snapchat collected to find the user's friends.

26. However, when the user chooses to Find Friends, Snapchat collects not only the phone number a user enters, but also, without informing the user, the names and phone numbers of all the contacts in the user's mobile device address book.

27. Snapchat did not provide notice of, or receive user consent for, this collection until September 2012, at which time the iOS operating system was updated to provide a notification when an application accessed the user's address book.

Snapchat's Deceptive Privacy Policy Statement Regarding the Find Friends Feature

30. From June 2011 to February 2013, Snapchat disseminated or caused to be disseminated to consumers the following statements, or similar statements, in its privacy policy regarding its Find Friends feature:

> Optional to the user, we also collect an email, *phone* number, and facebook id for purpose of finding friends on the service. (Emphasis in original).

31. As explained in Paragraph 26, the Snapchat application collected more than email, phone number, and Facebook ID for purpose of finding friends on the service. The application collected the names and phone numbers of all contacts in the user's mobile device address book.

Snapchat's Failure to Secure Its Find Friends Feature

(Count 6)

34. Snapchat failed to securely design its Find Friends feature. As described in paragraph 25, Snapchat prompts the user to enter a mobile phone number that will be associated with the user's account. In addition, as described in paragraph 26, Snapchat collects the names and phone numbers of all the contacts in the user's address book. Snapchat's API uses this information to locate the user's friends on the service.

35. From September 2011 to December 2012, Snapchat failed to verify that the phone number that an iOS user entered into the application did, in fact, belong to the mobile device being used by that individual. Due to this failure, an individual could create an account using a phone number that belonged to another consumer, enabling the individual to send and receive snaps associated with another consumer's phone number.

36. Numerous consumers complained to Snapchat that individuals had created Snapchat accounts with phone numbers belonging to other consumers, leading to the misuse and unintentional disclosure of consumers' personal information. For example, consumers complained that they had sent snaps to accounts under the belief that they were communicating with a friend, when in fact they were not, resulting in the unintentional disclosure of photos containing personal information. In addition, consumers complained that accounts associated with their phone numbers had been used to send inappropriate or offensive snaps.

37. Snapchat could have prevented the misuse and unintentional disclosure of consumers' personal information by verifying phone numbers using common and readily available methods.

38. Indeed, in December 2012, Snapchat began performing short-message-service (SMS) verification to confirm that the entered phone number did in fact belong to the mobile device being used by that individual.

39. In addition, from September 2011 to December 2013, Snapchat failed to implement effective restrictions on the number of Find Friend requests that any one account could make to its API. Furthermore, Snapchat failed to implement any restrictions on serial and automated account creation. As a result of these failures, in December 2013, attackers were able to use multiple accounts to send millions of Find Friend requests using randomly generated phone numbers. The attackers were able to compile a database of 4.6 million Snapchat usernames and the associated mobile phone numbers. The exposure of usernames and mobile phone numbers could lead to costly spam, phishing, and other unsolicited communications.

40. From June 2011 to May 2012, Snapchat disseminated or caused to be disseminated to consumers the following statement in its privacy policy:

> The Toyopa Group, LLC is dedicated to securing customer data and, to that end, employs the best security practices to keep your data protected.

41. From May 2012 to February 2013, Snapchat disseminated or caused to be disseminated to consumers the following statement in its privacy policy:

> Snapchat takes reasonable steps to help protect your personal information in an effort to prevent loss, misuse, and unauthorized access, disclosure, alteration, and destruction.

42. From February 2013 to the present, Snapchat disseminated or caused to be disseminated to consumers the following statement in its privacy policy:

> We take reasonable measures to help protect information about you from loss, theft, misuse and unauthorized access, disclosure, alteration and destruction.

45. The acts and practices of respondent as alleged in this complaint constitute deceptive acts or practices in or affecting commerce in violation of Section 5(a) of the Federal Trade Commission Act, 15 U.S.C. § 45(a).

Therefore, the Federal Trade Commission this twenty-third day of December, 2014, has issued this complaint against respondent.

By the Commission.

Notes and Questions

1. Settlement. On the same day that the FTC published the complaint above, the FTC and Snapchat entered into a consent order, under which Snapchat admitted no liability but agreed to change certain practices and its disclosures as well as FTC supervision for a number of years. Under the Act, the FTC may not seek fines in an administrative matter, but it may go to court to seek fines if a party violates an administrative order, including a consent order. Does this strike you as a sufficient enforcement regime?

2. Tort Actions. A party whose privacy was invaded by an application could try to bring a tort action for invasion of privacy (or, in the case of a deceptive privacy policy, for breach of contract). In many cases, however, the person will have difficulty showing damages (or, if the claim is stated in contract, other parts of the user agreement may disclaim liability). And, even if a person has suffered identity theft, it may be difficult to tie it to a specific data breach. Indeed, that difficulty has caused some courts to dismiss private litigation for privacy or security breaches, finding that the plaintiffs lacked standing because they could not show a strong link between a particular breach and injury. *See, e.g.*, Reilly v. Ceridian Corp., 664 F.3d 38 (3d Cir. 2011).

3. Deceptive versus Unfair. Some of the FTC's charges against Snapchat were clearly based upon the service not working the way the company told its customers that it would. Others relied on implication. Others, such as the data security claim, seem to focus more on setting an objective standard of good practice, although the complaint does reference industry standards as well. FTC enforcement has principally focused on forcing a company to make clearer statements or to live up to the statements that it has made. Should the FTC take a more aggressive approach?

4. Other Internet Platforms. The FTC has brought privacy actions against some of the other large platforms, including an action against Google and multiple actions against Facebook. Again, these actions have largely been based on those services not making their privacy practices clear or failing to live up to stated privacy policies. In 2012, the FTC issued a comprehensive report on consumer privacy, and it singled out "large platform providers"—which included ISPs, browsers, large social networking sites, and others—as uniquely worthy of privacy concern. *See* Federal Trade Commission, Protecting Consumer Privacy in an Era of Rapid Change: Recommendations for Businesses and Policymakers (2012), https://www.ftc.gov/sites/default/files/documents/reports/federal-trade-commission-report-protecting-consumer-privacy-era-rapid-change-recommendations/120326privacyreport.pdf. Congress has not acted on the FTC's recommendations.

§ 13.D. Federal Statutory Privacy Protections

Federal statutes address privacy in specific contexts such as children online, health care, or financial information. In this section, we provide a few examples, far short of a comprehensive treatment, but as examples of the types of federal interventions that have been made.

§ 13.D.1. Communications Act Privacy

The Communications Act, as to the services that it covers, does consider the issue of customer privacy. Section 705 of the Act generally prohibits the disclosure or interception of all communications by wire or radio. 47 U.S.C. § 605(a). As to telecommunications, § 222 provides: "Every telecommunications carrier has a duty to protect the confidentiality of proprietary information of, and relating to, other telecommunication carriers, equipment manufacturers, and customers, including telecommunication carriers reselling telecommunications services provided by a telecommunications carrier." 47 U.S.C. § 222(a). As to cable television, the Act provides that cable operators must notify subscribers as to what personally identifiable information the cable system collects and must secure advanced consent before collecting or disclosing that information. 47 U.S.C. § 551.

In 2016, the FCC issued an order that both summarized its prior actions under § 222 (which we omit here) and extended privacy protections to broadband internet access providers.

Protecting the Privacy of Customers of Broadband and Other Telecommunications Services

Report and Order, 31 FCC Rcd. 13,911 (2016)

2. Broadband providers provide the "on ramp" to the Internet. These providers therefore have access to vast amounts of information about their customers including when we are online, where we are physically located when we are online, how long we stay online, what devices we use to access the Internet, what websites we visit, and what applications we use.

5. The privacy framework we adopt today focuses on transparency, choice, and data security, and provides heightened protection for sensitive customer information, consistent with customer expectations.

8. *Transparency.* Recognizing the fundamental importance of transparency to enable consumers to make informed purchasing decisions, we require carriers to provide privacy notices that clearly and accurately inform customers about what confidential information the carriers collect, how they use it, under what circumstances they share it, and the categories of entities with which they will share it. We also require that carriers inform their customers about customers' rights to opt in to or opt out (as the case may be) of the use or sharing of their confidential information.

9. *Choice.* We find that because broadband providers are able to view vast swathes of customer data, customers must be empowered to decide how broadband providers may use and share their data. In this section, we adopt rules that give customers of broadband Internet access service (BIAS) and other telecommunications services the tools they need to make choices about the use and sharing of customer PI, and to easily adjust those choices over the course of time. For purposes of the sensitivity-based customer choice framework we adopt today, we find that sensitive customer proprietary information (PI) includes financial information, health information, Social Security numbers, precise geo-location information, information pertaining to children, content of communications, web browsing history, application usage history, and the functional equivalents of web browsing history or application usage history. With respect to voice services, we also find that call detail information is sensitive information. We also adopt a tiered approach to choice, by reference to consumer expectations and context that recognizes three categories of approval with respect to use of customer PI obtained by virtue of providing the telecommunications service:

> *Opt-in Approval.* We adopt rules requiring carriers to obtain customers' opt-in approval for use and sharing of sensitive customer PI (and for material retroactive changes to carriers' privacy policies). A familiar example of opt-in practices appears when a mobile application asks for permission to use geo-location information.
>
> *Opt-out Approval.* Balancing important governmental interests in protecting consumer privacy and the potential benefits that may result from the use of non-sensitive customer PI, we adopt rules requiring carriers to obtain customers' opt-out approval for the use and sharing of non-sensitive customer PI.
>
> *Congressionally-Recognized Exceptions to Customer Approval Requirements.* Consistent with the statute, we adopt rules that always allow broadband providers to use and share customer data in order to provide

broadband services (for example to ensure that a communication destined for a particular person reaches that destination), and for certain other purposes.

10. *Data Security and Breach Notification.* At its most fundamental, the duty to protect the confidentiality of customer PI requires telecommunications carriers to protect the customer PI they collect and maintain. We encourage all carriers to consider data minimization strategies and to embrace the principle of privacy by design. To the extent carriers collect and maintain customer PI, we require BIAS providers and other telecommunications carriers to take reasonable measures to secure customer PI.

11. We also adopt data breach notification requirements. In order to ensure that affected customers and the appropriate federal agencies receive notice of data breaches that could result in harm, we adopt rules requiring BIAS providers and other telecommunications carriers to notify affected customers, the Commission, and the FBI and Secret Service unless the carrier is able to reasonably determine that a data breach poses no reasonable risk of harm to the affected customers.

Notes and Questions

1. Reclassification. As you know from Chapter 6, in 2018 the FCC reclassified BIAS to take it outside of Title II, and so these rules would have lost their effect on the basis of that reclassification.

2. Congressional Repeal. Even before reclassification could occur, Congress passed legislation in 2017 pursuant to the Congressional Review Act, 5 U.S.C. §§ 801–808 (which allows Congress via simple majority vote to send a bill to the President that, if signed, disapproves recently promulgated regulations) that nullified the order excerpted above. *See* Pub. L. No. 115-22, 131 Stat. 88 (2017). FCC Chair Ajit Pai responded by welcoming the resolution of disapproval. *See* Statement of FCC Chairman Ajit Pai on Congressional Resolution of Disapproval of FCC Broadband Privacy Regulations, 2017 WL 1165163. But even if a majority of FCC Commissioners did want to promulgate new broadband privacy regulations, the disapproval poses a major hurdle: By the terms of the Congressional Review Act, not only is the order repealed but also it "may not be reissued in substantially the same form, and a new rule that is substantially the same as such a rule may not be issued, unless the reissued or new rule is specifically authorized by a law enacted after the date of the joint resolution disapproving the original rule." 5 U.S.C. § 801(b)(2). So the FCC's broadband privacy regulations are not only gone but also difficult to resurrect.

3. Consent. Section 222 and the FCC rules allow carriers to seek consumer consent to the use of personally identifiable information. But, consistent with its view that ISPs could access significant amounts of information and consumers do not always have choice among ISPs, the FCC also prohibited "take it or leave it offers" and required providers to make enhanced disclosures if they offered customers a discount on service in exchange for their personal information.

4. Equivalence between ISPs and Edge Providers. ISPs fought the FCC's regulation on the ground that it handicapped them compared to internet platforms that would not be subject to equivalent regulation. Does it make sense to apply privacy regulations to BIAS providers and not large platforms? Surely, Google, Facebook, and many other internet-based services accumulate substantial information about users. Are you persuaded by the FCC's response that ISPs are uniquely positioned to gather private information?

5. The Federal Trade Commission. As noted above, the obvious alternative to FCC regulation is FTC regulation. The FTC has emphasized the wealth of information that can be gathered by what it has called "large platform providers . . . such as Internet Service Providers, operating systems, browsers, and social media." Federal Trade Commission, Protecting Consumer Privacy in an Era of Rapid Change: Recommendations for Businesses and Policymakers v, ix, 55–57 (2012), https://www.ftc.gov/sites/default/files/documents/reports/federal-trade-commission-report-protecting-consumer-privacy-era-rapid-change-recommendations/120326privacyreport.pdf. What are the tradeoffs between FCC and FTC regulating privacy?

§ 13.D.2. Other Federal Statutory Protections

One of the most important federal privacy regimes has emerged from the Health Insurance Portability and Accountability Act of 1996 (HIPAA), Pub. L. 104-191, 110 Stat. 1936, and the rules adopted pursuant to its authority. HIPAA is broader than privacy, covering issues such as insurance portability, and HIPAA rules apply to medical information whether or not it touches the internet. But as with most information, it often touches the internet. The following case is an example of HIPAA regulation in the context of electronic health records, with the interesting twist of its combination with other platform data.

Dinerstein v. Google, LLC

484 F. Supp. 3d 561 (N.D. Ill. 2020)

PALLMEYER, District Judge.

In 2017, Defendants The University of Chicago and The University of Chicago Medical Center (collectively "the University") and Google began a research partnership in which they used machine-learning techniques to create predictive health models aimed at reducing hospital readmissions and anticipating future medical events. As part of this research, the University disclosed to Google the "de-identified" electronic health records of all adult patients treated at its hospital from January 1, 2010 through June 30, 2016. Plaintiff Matt Dinerstein was an inpatient at the University in June 2015 and, asserting a variety of state-law claims, brings this suit on behalf of all patients whose medical information was disclosed for Defendants' research. The University and Google have both filed motions to dismiss. For the following reasons, Defendants' motions to dismiss are granted.

Background

Plaintiff Matt Dinerstein had two separate hospital stays as a patient at the University's hospital in June 2015. During his stays at the hospital and throughout 2015, Mr. Dinerstein maintained an account with Defendant Google and used a smartphone with Google applications on it, which, he alleges, collected and transmitted to Google his geolocation information. Also during these stays, the University generated and maintained health records for Plaintiff, which included such sensitive information as his demographic data, vital signs, diagnoses, procedures, and prescriptions. Mr. Dinerstein received two forms relevant to this sensitive information: the Admission and Outpatient Agreement and Authorization form, and the Notice of Privacy Practices.

The Admission and Outpatient Agreement and Authorization a copy of which was attached as an exhibit to the amended complaint, contains two paragraphs relevant to the present dispute:

> I understand and agree that my medical information in any form and any tissue, fluids, cells and other specimens that may be collected during this hospitalization and/or period of treatment may be used and shared for research that has been approved by the University of Chicago Institutional Review Board (IRB) and that has been found to pose a minimal risk. I acknowledge that such research by the University of Chicago Medical Center may have commercial value and, in that event, I understand that I will not be entitled to any compensation, regardless of the value of such research or any products or inventions developed therefrom.
>
> I understand that all efforts will be made to protect my privacy and that any use of my medical information will be in compliance with federal and state laws, including all laws that govern patient confidentiality, and the University of Chicago Medical Center Notice of Privacy Practices. I further understand that my identity and the identity of my medical records will not be included in any research findings or reports.

In early 2018, Defendants published a study discussing the results of their research and methodology. The article explains that the study used electronic health records provided by Defendant University and the University of California, San Francisco (UCSF) that included the following "de-identified" information: "patient demographics, provider orders, diagnoses, procedures, medications, laboratory values, vital signs, and flowsheet data . . . from all inpatient and outpatient encounters." Rajkomar et al., *Scalable and Accurate Deep Learning* at 6. The article notes that Defendant University—but not UCSF—included the "dates of service" as well as "free-text medical notes" in the EHRs provided to Google. *Id.* According to Plaintiff, disclosing such information is a *prima facie* violation of the Healthcare Insurance Portability and Accountability Act of 1996 (HIPAA), Pub. L. No. 104-191, 110 Stat. 1936 (1996). These records were not, the amended complaint alleges, sufficiently anonymized, and therefore put patient privacy at risk.

Plaintiff suggests that the risk of re-identification was in fact substantial because of the information Google already possesses about individuals through the other services it provides. Specifically, the amended complaint refers to Google as "one of the largest and most comprehensive data mining companies in the world, drawing data from thousands of sources and compiling information about individuals' personal traits (gender, age, sexuality, race), personal habits, purchases, and associations." *Id.* ¶ 76. Google has "create[d] detailed profiles of millions of Americans," including public and nonpublic information, and "possess[es] detailed geolocation information that it can use to pinpoint and match exactly when certain people entered and visited the University's hospital," according to the amended complaint. *Id.* ¶¶ 77–78, 80. In fact, for a user of Google applications like Mr. Dinerstein, Google can track the specific University hospital buildings or departments he visited and the time of his visits. Plaintiff alleges that the combination of such geolocation information and the EHRs, which include the date and time of hospital services, "creates a perfect formulation of data points for Google to identify who the patients in those records really are." *Id.* ¶ 87. The amended complaint does not allege, however, that Google has in fact used its extensive data to re-identify any EHRs.

* * *

Against the University, Plaintiff brings claims for violating the Illinois Consumer Fraud and Deceptive Business Practices Act (ICFA), 815 ILCS 505/1 *et seq.* (Count I), breach of express contract (Count II), breach of implied contract (Count III), and unjust enrichment (Count VII).

Discussion

II. Failure to State a Claim upon which Relief Can Be Granted

Defendants argue that Plaintiff's claims fail as a matter of law. As discussed here, the court agrees.

A. Express Contract Claim

1. Alleged Breaches

Plaintiff asserts that the University's disclosure of his medical information to Google violated four terms of the contract: (1) that "all efforts" would be made to protect his privacy, (2) that any use of his medical information would comply with federal law, (3) that any use of his medical information would comply with state law, and (4) that it would comply with its Notice and Privacy Practices.

b. Compliance with Federal Law

Plaintiff asserts that the University's disclosure of his medical information to Google violated HIPAA and, therefore, breached the Authorization's requirement that "any use of medical information will be in compliance with federal . . . laws." Three parts of the HIPAA Privacy Rule are at issue here. Two of these are safe harbors that permit the disclosure of medical information under certain circumstances: First, a covered entity, such as the University, may disclose a "limited data set" if it excludes certain direct identifiers; is used for "research, public health, or health care operations"; and the disclosure is made pursuant to a "data use agreement" that includes certain provisions governing the use of the medical information. 45 C.F.R. § 164.514(e). Second, a covered entity may disclose protected health information for research when approved by an Institutional Review Board (IRB), whose documentation is subject to numerous other requirements, so long as the recipient has made certain representations to the covered entity about its use of the data. 45 C.F.R. § 164.512(i). Plaintiff has not pleaded that Defendants failed to comply with the requirements of such regulations.

Indeed, the amended complaint contains facts supporting the application of these safe harbors. As noted, § 164.514(e) permits a covered entity to disclose a limited data set that has been stripped of certain identifiers listed in § 164.514(e)(2), so long as the disclosure is made for research purposes, and the disclosure is made pursuant to a data use agreement. Although Plaintiff has alleged that free text notes were not sufficiently anonymized, he never alleges that they, or any other part of the records, included the identifiers that are not allowed under this safe harbor. The amended complaint itself affirmatively asserts that the disclosure was made for research. And Plaintiff included with his amended complaint the agreement between the University and Google, which appears on its face to comply with the requirements in § 164.514(e)(4). As for the second safe harbor, documents referenced in the pleading confirm that the disclosure met those requirements as well. With respect to these two safe harbors, Plaintiff has not presented allegations "that raises a suggestion" of a HIPAA violation. Bell Atl. Corp. v. Twombly, 550 U.S. 544, 557 (2007).

The third relevant part of the Privacy Rule is more complicated. This component requires written authorization for the "sale of protected health information." 45 C.F.R. §§ 164.502(a)(5)(ii), 164.508(a)(4). Sales made pursuant to the research safe harbors discussed above are not prohibited sales if "the only remuneration received by the covered entity . . . is a reasonable cost-based fee to cover the cost to prepare and transmit the protected health information for such purposes." *Id.* § 164.502(a)(5)(ii)(B)(2)(ii). Putting "sale" and "remuneration" to the side for the moment, the court must first consider whether Plaintiff has alleged that his protected health information (PHI) was shared at all. A covered entity like the University "may determine that health information is not individually identifiable health information" in one of two ways. *Id.* § 164.514(b). An expert may determine that the risk of re-identification is "very small" by applying "generally accepted statistical and scientific principles and methods" and "[d]ocument[ing] the methods and results of the analysis that justify such determination." *Id.* § 164.514(b)(1). Alternatively, eighteen specific identifiers can be removed from the data, including — critically — "[a]ll elements of dates (except year) for dates directly related to an individual, including birth date, *admission date, discharge date*, date of death." *Id.* § 164.514(b)(2)(i) (emphasis added). Plaintiff alleges that an expert determination concerning the risk of re-identification of his data either was not made or was incorrect. And of course, he has alleged (and the published study appears to confirm) that the data turned over to Google did include the dates on which services were provided.

The University's arguments that Plaintiff has not pleaded that it engaged in an impermissible sale are unsatisfying. The University notes that the amended complaint contains no allegations about "a reasonable cost-based fee." Univ. Reply Mem. in Supp. of Mot. to Dismiss at 7 n.9. But the HIPAA regulation in question includes a broader definition of sale: "a disclosure of [PHI] by a covered entity . . . where the covered entity . . . directly or indirectly receives remuneration from or on behalf of the recipient of the [PHI] in exchange for the [PHI]." 45 C.F.R. § 164.502(a)(5)(ii)(B)(1).

3. Damages

As discussed above the court has concluded that Plaintiff's allegations state a claim for breach of a contract that was supported by consideration. Has he plausibly alleged that this breach caused him damages? In the amended complaint, Plaintiff alleges that he has suffered non-economic damages, such as anxiety and emotional distress. His response to Defendants' motions does not characterize these harms as part of his contract damages, however. As the University notes, Illinois does not recognize emotional distress damages for breaches of contract, "except where the breach was wanton or reckless and caused bodily harm, or where defendant had reason to know, when the contract was made, that its breach would cause mental suffering for reasons other than mere pecuniary loss." Parks v. Wells Fargo Home Mortg., Inc., 398 F.3d 937, 940–41 (7th Cir. 2005). Plaintiff has not pleaded that the University's conduct meets that standard. As for money damages, the Authorization contained the following provision in which Plaintiff disclaimed the right to receive compensation from the University's research: "I acknowledge that such research by the University of Chicago Medical Center may have commercial value and, in that event, I understand that I will not be entitled to any compensation, regardless of the value of such research or any products or inventions developed therefrom." Outpatient Agreement & Authorization § III. The University argues that this provision bars his claim for economics damages. Plaintiff responds that the University cannot take advantage of that provision because Illinois courts have said that "[a] party who materially breaches a contract cannot take advantage of the terms of the contract that benefit him." James v. Lifeline Mobile Medics, 792 N.E.2d 461, 464 (Ill. App. 4th Dist. 2003). [A]ccording to Illinois law, "[t]he determination of what constitutes a material breach is a question of fact which involves a fairly detailed inquiry, which should be left for the trial." Enter. Warehousing Sols., Inc. v. Capital One Servs., Inc., 2002 WL 406976, at *3 (N.D. Ill. Mar. 15, 2002). For pleading purposes, the court will therefore assume Plaintiff has alleged a material breach on the part of the University. The court concludes the claim nevertheless fails for another reason: none of his theories for money damages is adequate. He asserts that he is entitled to "restitution on the basis that he did not receive the full benefits of his payments to the University." Pl.'s Mem. in Opp'n to Defs.' Mots. to Dismiss at 20. At most, this allegation suggests that some indeterminate amount of the price he paid for his treatments represents the cost of the University's privacy practices. Alternatively, Mr. Dinerstein claims that the University owes him a reasonable royalty for the use of his PHI. [T]he court disagrees. A royalty is normally appropriate only for interference with a property right. And Plaintiff has not plausibly alleged that he has any such right in his PHI. Plaintiff has not adequately pleaded that the University's breach of contract caused him economic damages. His theories in support of his claim for money damages are inadequate. Because Mr. Dinerstein has not pleaded that the University's breach caused him economic damage, his express contract claim (Count II) is dismissed for failure to state a claim for relief.

Notes and Questions

1. Deanonymizing Data. The plaintiff's allegation that he could be personally identified arose from the combination of two datasets: the supposedly de-identified health records, which nevertheless included the dates of service, and Google's location data. The manner in which seemingly anonymized data can be reverse-engineered (deanonymized) to then identify individuals is a persistent one across many applications, and it further complicates the possibilities of privacy regulation. *See generally* Paul Ohm, Broken Promises of Privacy: Responding to the Surprising Failure of Anonymization, 57 UCLA L. Rev. 1701 (2010). For this reason, Ohm and others suggest that privacy regulation should be less focused on what information is collected and more focused on how collected information can actually be used by businesses and others. Is that a desirable approach?

2. Research. This case highlights the tradeoffs between greater privacy protections and the use of data for beneficial purposes. Although perhaps "better advertising" is a contestable benefit (though targeted advertising is valuable because it works), medical research advances have accelerated by using more sophisticated data analysis and related tools.

3. Co-Regulation. The HIPAA regime described here involves both institutional review boards, usually staffed at research universities, and independent experts to evaluate both the data practices and the research design. Government, which might have difficulty building and keeping comprehensive expertise, has therefore outsourced some of the key decisions. Can you think of other aspects of internet activity in which private bodies (existing or to be newly formed) might provide a better, more inclusive process for determining granular privacy protections?

4. Additional Provisions. The United States Department of Health and Human Services (HHS) has principal rulemaking and enforcement authority under HIPAA. HHS has compiled extensive resources at https://www.hhs.gov/hipaa, including a guide to the most important regulations.

Apart from HIPAA, we have already mentioned the most important other federal provisions. COPPA requires websites and online services that target children to receive consent of their guardians and to significantly limit data collection. 15 U.S.C. § 6502. The FTC has rulemaking authority under COPPA, and it also has enforcement authority. *See* 16 C.F.R. Part 312. In the financial services arena, the Gramm-Leach-Bliley Act, also known as the Financial Services Modernization Act of 1999, Pub. L. 106–102, 113 Stat. 1338, built on prior legislation to require financial institutions to protect and limit disclosure of personal financial information. The key provisions are contained in 15 U.S.C. §§ 6801–6809, 6821–6827, and in the FTC's rules in 16 C.F.R. Parts 313–314.

§ 13.E. Other Sources of Privacy Law

Privacy is regulated at the state level and by other countries internationally. Although many such laws exist, two jurisdictions have proved particularly consequential: the European Union (EU) and the state of California. Each is a huge market of its own, which even companies not domiciled in those jurisdictions wish to access. (California's would be approximately the fifth largest economy in the world if it were its own country.) Both the EU and California have adopted comprehensive privacy regulations, shaping online privacy practices.

More specifically, California has passed several statutes and created an agency regulator for issues of consumer privacy. Most notably, California's legislature enacted the California Consumer Privacy Act, Cal. Civil Code. § 1798.100ff (CCPA), in 2018 and in 2020 the state's voters approved, via ballot initiative, the California Privacy Rights Act (CPRA), which expanded the CCPA. The CCPA's scope draws in many companies not based in California, including all companies doing business in California that collect consumer information and (1) have gross revenues over $25 million/year; (2) buy, receive, or sell information on 50,000 or more California residents or households; or (3) derive more than 50% of their revenue selling California residents' data. (The CPRA thresholds are slightly higher.) The CPRA also created a new state agency, the California Privacy Protection Agency to implement California's privacy laws. Speaking generally, under California law, consumers now have the rights to know, to access, and to seek deletion of their PII from companies that collect and hold it. Consumers also have expanded consent rights and rights to tools to limit the use of certain sensitive information; companies are also required to respect signals from user-enabled privacy controls. Third-party sales of information are forbidden unless disclosed and consented to. Despite the breadth of protections, however, private remedies are limited, with enforcement principally flowing from the CPPA and the California Office of the Attorney General.

Turning to the European Union, it has enacted a number of general privacy regulations, the most important of which is the 2016 General Data Protection Regulation (GDPR). Regulation (EU) 2016/679 of the European Parliament and of the Council of 27 April 2015 on the protection of natural persons with regard to the processing of personal data and on the free movement of such data, and repealing Directive 95/46/EC (General Data Protection Regulation), 2016 O.J. (L 119) 1.

The EU regulations apply to all companies doing business in the EU or the European Economic Area (EEA). The U.S. Department of Commerce, International Trade Administration, has summarized the law's applicability:

- GDPR is broad in scope and uses broad definitions. "Personal data" is any information that relates to an identified or identifiable living individual (data subject) such as a name, email address, tax ID number, online identifier, etc. "Processing" data includes actions such as collecting, recording, storing and transferring data.
- A company that is not established in the Union may have to comply with the Regulation when processing personal data of EU and EEA residents (EEA countries are Norway, Lichtenstein and Switzerland):
  a) If the company offers goods or services to data subjects in the EU; or,
  b) If the company is monitoring data subjects' behavior taking place within the EU.
- The mere accessibility of a company's website in the EU is insufficient to subject a company to GDPR, but other evidence of the intent to offer goods or services in the EU would be relevant.
- As a general rule, companies that are not established in the EU but that are subject to GDPR must designate in writing an EU representative for purposes of GDPR compliance. There is an exception to this requirement for small scale, occasional processing of non-sensitive data.

U.S. Department of Commerce, International Trade Administration, European Union — Data Privacy and Protection, https://www.trade.gov/european-union-data-privacy-and-protection. As the Department of Commerce also reminds companies, "[f]ines in case of non-compliance can reach up to 4% of the annual worldwide revenue or 20 million euros — whichever is higher. Companies of all sizes and sectors should consider GDPR as part of their overall compliance effort." *Id.*

As to substantive requirements, the EU framework requires all controllers and processors of personal data to secure and be accountable for that data, to implement strong notice and consent procedures, to limit collection and disclosures (particularly the onward transfer of data), and to increase access and transparency. *See, e.g.*, Irene Loizidou Nicolaidou & Constantinos Georgiades, The GDPR: New Horizons, in EU Internet Law 3 (T.E. Synodinou, ed. 2017).

The following case presents a good general overview of the EU framework and of a particular issue arising from it, the so-called "right to be forgotten."

Google Spain SL v Agencia Española de Protección de Datos (AEPD)

ECLI:EU:C:2014:317 (May 13, 2014)
[European Court of Justice ("CJEU")]

Judgment

Legal context

4. Article 2 of Directive 95/46 [of the European Parliament] states that '[f]or the purposes of this Directive:

> (a) "personal data" shall mean any information relating to an identified or identifiable natural person ("data subject"); an identifiable person is one who can be identified, directly or indirectly, in particular by reference to an identification number or to one or more factors specific to his physical, physiological, mental, economic, cultural or social identity;
>
> (b) "processing of personal data" ("processing") shall mean any operation or set of operations which is performed upon personal data, whether or not by automatic means, such as collection, recording, organization, storage, adaptation or alteration, retrieval, consultation, use, disclosure by transmission, dissemination or otherwise making available, alignment or combination, blocking, erasure or destruction;'

6. Article 4 of Directive 95/46, entitled 'National law applicable', provides:

> '1. Each Member State shall apply the national provisions it adopts pursuant to this Directive to the processing of personal data where:
>
> > (a) the processing is carried out in the context of the activities of an establishment of the controller on the territory of the Member State; when the same controller is established on the territory of several Member States, he must take the necessary measures to ensure that each of these establishments complies with the obligations laid down by the national law applicable;'

7. In Section I (entitled 'Principles relating to data quality') of Chapter II of Directive 95/46, Article 6 is worded as follows:

> '1. Member States shall provide that personal data must be:
>
> > (a) processed fairly and lawfully;
> >
> > (b) collected for specified, explicit and legitimate purposes and not further processed in a way incompatible with those purposes. Further processing of data for historical, statistical or scientific purposes shall not be considered as incompatible provided that Member States provide appropriate safeguards;

(c) adequate, relevant and not excessive in relation to the purposes for which they are collected and/or further processed;

(d) accurate and, where necessary, kept up to date; every reasonable step must be taken to ensure that data which are inaccurate or incomplete, having regard to the purposes for which they were collected or for which they are further processed, are erased or rectified;

(e) kept in a form which permits identification of data subjects for no longer than is necessary for the purposes for which the data were collected or for which they are further processed. Member States shall lay down appropriate safeguards for personal data stored for longer periods for historical, statistical or scientific use.'

10. Article 12 of Directive 95/46, entitled 'Rights of access', provides:

'Member States shall guarantee every data subject the right to obtain from the controller:

(b) as appropriate the rectification, erasure or blocking of data the processing of which does not comply with the provisions of this Directive, in particular because of the incomplete or inaccurate nature of the data;'

The Dispute in the Main Proceedings and the Questions Referred For a Preliminary Ruling

14. On 5 March 2010, Mr Costeja González, a Spanish national resident in Spain, lodged with the [Agencia Española de Protección de Datos (Spanish Data Protection Agency) (AEPD)] a complaint against La Vanguardia Ediciones SL, which publishes a daily newspaper with a large circulation, in particular in Catalonia (Spain) ('La Vanguardia'), and against Google Spain and Google Inc. The complaint was based on the fact that, when an internet user entered Mr Costeja González's name in the search engine of the Google group ('Google Search'), he would obtain links to two pages of La Vanguardia's newspaper, of 19 January and 9 March 1998 respectively, on which an announcement mentioning Mr Costeja González's name appeared for a real-estate auction connected with attachment proceedings for the recovery of social security debts.

15. By that complaint, Mr Costeja González requested, first, that La Vanguardia be required either to remove or alter those pages so that the personal data relating to him no longer appeared or to use certain tools made available by search engines in order to protect the data. Second, he requested that Google Spain or Google Inc. be required to remove or conceal the personal data relating to him so that they ceased to be included in the search results and no longer appeared in the links to La Vanguardia. Mr Costeja González stated in this context that the attachment proceedings concerning him had been fully resolved for a number of years and that reference to them was now entirely irrelevant.

16. By decision of 30 July 2010, the AEPD rejected the complaint in so far as it related to La Vanguardia, taking the view that the publication by it of the information in question was legally justified as it took place upon order of the Ministry of Labour and Social Affairs and was intended to give maximum publicity to the auction in order to secure as many bidders as possible.

17. On the other hand, the complaint was upheld in so far as it was directed against Google Spain and Google Inc. The AEPD considered in this regard that operators of search engines are subject to data protection legislation given that they carry out data processing for which they are responsible and act as intermediaries in the information society. The AEPD took the view that it has the power to require the withdrawal of data and the prohibition of access to certain data by the operators of search engines when it considers that the locating and dissemination of the data are liable to compromise the fundamental right to data protection and the dignity of persons in the broad sense, and this would also encompass the mere wish of the person concerned that such data not be known to third parties. The AEPD considered that that obligation may be owed directly by operators of search engines, without it being necessary to erase the data or information from the website where they appear, including when retention of the information on that site is justified by a statutory provision.

Consideration of the Questions Referred

Question 2(a) and (b), Concerning the Material Scope of Directive 95/46 . . .

22. According to Google Spain and Google Inc., the activity of search engines cannot be regarded as processing of the data which appear on third parties' web pages displayed in the list of search results, given that search engines process all the information available on the internet without effecting a selection between personal data and other information. Furthermore, even if that activity must be classified as 'data processing', the operator of a search engine cannot be regarded as a 'controller' in respect of that processing since it has no knowledge of those data and does not exercise control over the data.

25. Article 2(b) of Directive 95/46 defines 'processing of personal data' as 'any operation or set of operations which is performed upon personal data, whether or not by automatic means, such as collection, recording, organisation, storage, adaptation or alteration, retrieval, consultation, use, disclosure by transmission, dissemination or otherwise making available, alignment or combination, blocking, erasure or destruction'.

26. As regards in particular the internet, the Court has already had occasion to state that the operation of loading personal data on an internet page must be considered to be such 'processing' within the meaning of Article 2(b) of Directive 95/46.

27. So far as concerns the activity at issue in the main proceedings, it is not contested that the data found, indexed and stored by search engines and made available to their users include information relating to identified or identifiable natural persons and thus 'personal data' within the meaning of Article 2(a) of that directive.

28. Therefore, it must be found that, in exploring the internet automatically, constantly and systematically in search of the information which is published there, the operator of a search engine 'collects' such data which it subsequently 'retrieves', 'records' and 'organises' within the framework of its indexing programmes, 'stores' on its servers and, as the case may be, 'discloses' and 'makes available' to its users in the form of lists of search results. As those operations are referred to expressly and unconditionally in Article 2(b) of Directive 95/46, they must be classified as 'processing' within the meaning of that provision, regardless of the fact that the operator of the search engine also carries out the same operations in respect of other types of information and does not distinguish between the latter and the personal data.

29. Nor is the foregoing finding affected by the fact that those data have already been published on the internet and are not altered by the search engine.

[The court then found that Google was a controller of the processing of personal data by its search engine because "the search engine operator which determines the purposes and means of that activity and thus of the processing of personal data that it itself carries out."]

Question 1(a) to (d), Concerning the Territorial Scope of Directive 95/46 . .

60. Article 4(1)(a) of Directive 95/46 is to be interpreted as meaning that processing of personal data is carried out in the context of the activities of an establishment of the controller on the territory of a Member State, within the meaning of that provision, when the operator of a search engine sets up in a Member State a branch or subsidiary which is intended to promote and sell advertising space offered by that engine and which orientates its activity towards the inhabitants of that Member State.

Question 2(c) and (d), Concerning the Extent of the Responsibility of the Operator of a Search Engine under Directive 95/46 . .

63. Google Spain and Google Inc. submit that, by virtue of the principle of proportionality, any request seeking the removal of information must be addressed to the publisher of the website concerned because it is he who takes the responsibility for making the information public, who is in a position to appraise the lawfulness of that publication and who has available to him the most effective and least restrictive means of making the information inaccessible. Furthermore, to require the operator of a search engine to withdraw information published on the internet from its indexes would take insufficient account of the fundamental rights of publishers of websites, of other internet users and of that operator itself.

80. It must be pointed out at the outset that . . . processing of personal data, such as that at issue in the main proceedings, carried out by the operator of a search engine is liable to affect significantly the fundamental rights to privacy and to the protection of personal data when the search by means of that engine is carried out on the basis of an individual's name, since that processing enables any internet user to obtain through the list of results a structured overview of the information relating to that individual that can be found on the internet — information which potentially concerns a vast number of aspects of his private life and which, without the search engine, could not have been interconnected or could have been only with great difficulty — and thereby to establish a more or less detailed profile of him. Furthermore, the effect of the interference with those rights of the data subject is heightened on account of the important role played by the internet and search engines in modern society, which render the information contained in such a list of results ubiquitous.

81. In the light of the potential seriousness of that interference, it is clear that it cannot be justified by merely the economic interest which the operator of such an engine has in that processing. However, inasmuch as the removal of links from the list of results could, depending on the information at issue, have effects upon the legitimate interest of internet users potentially interested in having access to that information, in situations such as that at issue in the main proceedings a fair balance should be sought in particular between that interest and the data subject's fundamental rights under Articles 7 and 8 of the Charter [of Fundamental Rights of the European Union]. Whilst it is true that the data subject's rights protected by those articles also override, as a general rule, that interest of internet users, that balance may however depend, in specific cases, on the nature of the information in question and its sensitivity for the data subject's private life and on the interest of the public in having that information, an interest which may vary, in particular, according to the role played by the data subject in public life.

82. [W]hen a request such as that at issue in the main proceedings is lodged with it, the supervisory authority or judicial authority may order the operator of the search engine to remove from the list of results displayed following a search made on the basis of a person's name links to web pages published by third parties containing information relating to that person, without an order to that effect presupposing the previous or simultaneous removal of that name and information — from the web page on which they were published.

84. Given the ease with which information published on a website can be replicated on other sites and the fact that the persons responsible for its publication are not always subject to European Union legislation, effective and complete protection of data users could not be achieved if the latter had to obtain first or in parallel the erasure of the information relating to them from the publishers of websites.

87. Indeed, since the inclusion in the list of results, displayed following a search made on the basis of a person's name, of a web page and of the information contained

on it relating to that person makes access to that information appreciably easier for any internet user making a search in respect of the person concerned and may play a decisive role in the dissemination of that information, it is liable to constitute a more significant interference with the data subject's fundamental right to privacy than the publication on the web page.

88. In the light of all the foregoing considerations . . . the operator of a search engine is obliged to remove from the list of results displayed following a search made on the basis of a person's name links to web pages . . . even, as the case may be, when its publication in itself on those pages is lawful.

Question 3, Concerning the Scope of the Data Subject's Rights Guaranteed by Directive 95/46

93. [E]ven initially lawful processing of accurate data may, in the course of time, become incompatible with the directive where those data are no longer necessary in the light of the purposes for which they were collected or processed. That is so in particular where they appear to be inadequate, irrelevant or no longer relevant, or excessive in relation to those purposes and in the light of the time that has elapsed.

94. Therefore, if it is found, following a request by the data subject pursuant to Article 12(b) of Directive 95/46, that the inclusion in the list of results displayed following a search made on the basis of his name of the links to web pages published lawfully by third parties and containing true information relating to him personally is, at this point in time, incompatible with Article 6(1)(c) to (e) of the directive because that information appears, having regard to all the circumstances of the case, to be inadequate, irrelevant or no longer relevant, or excessive in relation to the purposes of the processing at issue carried out by the operator of the search engine, the information and links concerned in the list of results must be erased.

97. [The rights of the data subject] override, as a rule, not only the economic interest of the operator of the search engine but also the interest of the general public in finding that information upon a search relating to the data subject's name. However, that would not be the case if it appeared, for particular reasons, such as the role played by the data subject in public life, that the interference with his fundamental rights is justified by the preponderant interest of the general public in having, on account of inclusion in the list of results, access to the information in question.

98. As regards [Mr. González], it should be held that, having regard to the sensitivity for the data subject's private life of the information contained in those announcements and to the fact that its initial publication had taken place 16 years earlier, the data subject establishes a right that that information should no longer be linked to his name by means of such a list. Accordingly, since in the case in point there do not appear to be particular reasons substantiating a preponderant interest of the public in having, in the context of such a search, access to that information, a matter which is, however, for the referring court to establish, the data subject may, . . . require those links to be removed from the list of results.

Notes and Questions

1. The Right To Be Forgotten. The right to require a search engine to de-link accurate but dated information goes beyond the right to protect nonpublic, personally identifiable information. How does it further a privacy interest? Could it be better characterized as a reputational or some other property interest? The United States does not recognize such a right writ large, both because the U.S. lacks privacy law of this kind and because of First Amendment concerns. Nevertheless, as Professor Amy Gajda has written, other parts of U.S. law, such as doctrines that consider the "newsworthiness" of published information (recall the *Jackson* case above), show a similar set of values to the right to be forgotten. *See* Amy Gajda, Privacy, Press, and the Right To Be Forgotten in the United States, 93 Wash. L. Rev. 201 (2018).

2. Splintering. Note that Google's compliance with the court's order requires it to either de-link worldwide or to effectively offer several versions of its search engine tied to geolocation. The EU's approach to competition law, as we saw in Chapter 8, similarly has placed differing legal requirements on Google in the U.S. and the EU, two of its biggest markets.

3. More Information? Do you think that privacy law ought to include a right to be forgotten? Does the EU structure consider the right factors in determining its application? How might someone respond to having old information linked other than seeking the de-linking of that information in relevant search engines?

4. Coordination with Europe. U.S. companies doing business in Europe have long sought a streamlined way to ensure they were complying with EU law in transferring data from the EU to the U.S., and for many years the U.S. Department of Commerce and the European Commission had agreed upon a framework known as the Privacy Shield. In 2020, however, the Court of Justice of the European Union declared that this framework was inadequate under EU law. Data Protection Commissioner v Facebook Ireland Ltd, Maximillian Schrems, Case No. C-311/18 [2020] (Grand Ct.).

5. International Fragmentation. Whatever the federal policy in the U.S., international privacy law will likely not be uniform. In the early days of the internet, some doubted the ability of governments to enforce laws in cyberspace. But it is now clear that, through a combination of technological tools and domestic seizure of assets and perhaps employees, countries often have the upper hand. On the flip side, the largest platforms are able to employ sophisticated geolocation technologies and vary their services to accommodate different rules in their largest markets.

6. What Jurisdictional Level? As these materials highlight, internet and telecommunications regulation can occur at the multinational, national, state, and/or local levels. Are some sorts of regulation better done by one level versus another? Which types of regulation are best for each level? What are the relevant considerations in making those choices?

Note that, in the United States, the trend in internet and telecommunications in the 20th and 21st centuries has been toward regulation at the federal level. Should privacy regulation, along with most all internet and telecommunications regulations, be at the federal rather than state level? Or is leaving so much to the federal government a mistake, such that privacy and many other aspects of internet and telecommunications regulation should be at the state (or international) level? If so, what else should move from federal to state regulation? Or, if not, should most internet and telecommunications regulation remain at the federal level, with the exception of privacy? If so, why should privacy be treated differently from other forms of regulation? Is your answer affected by your assumptions about the likelihood of comprehensive federal privacy legislation?

7. Privacy Regulation and Competition. To what extent might privacy regulation create barriers to entry? Extensive privacy regulation, if it multiplies record-keeping and dispute-resolution requirements, and significant limits on data usage might both increase costs to businesses, with the possible effect of limiting new companies and therefore competition. Indeed, some data from the first several months of the GDPR showed diminished investment in EU tech startups.[2] Should we be similarly skeptical of the occasional calls for privacy regulations from Facebook and Google and other companies best resourced to contend with new rules? One of the pillars of public choice economics is that private companies will sometimes seek regulation to reduce competition from new entrants. Professor Frank Pasquale has noted that "governmentally imposed privacy rules may prevent nonprice competition between companies." Antitrust in High Tech Industries, 19 Geo. Mason L. Rev. 1071, 1081 (2012). Indeed, if one concern is the size of current platforms, measures (whether antitrust or otherwise) that increase competition among platforms may lead to a greater diversity of privacy practices from which consumers can choose. Indeed, just as car manufacturers now compete in part over safety of their cars, could we expect platforms to compete over their privacy practices? Do you think consumers will respond? If not, what, if anything, should that tell us?

8. Are Privacy Regulations Constitutional? Recall that Sorrell v. IMS Health Inc., 564 U.S. 552 (2011), excerpted in Chapter 3, invalidated a fairly modest privacy law on First Amendment grounds (and the legislature's motives were irrelevant). In light of *Sorrell*, what privacy regulations will not run afoul of the First Amendment?

2. *See* Mark Scott, Laurens Cerulus, & Laura Kayali, Six months in, Europe's Privacy Revolution Favors Google, Facebook, poltico.eu (Nov. 23, 2018) (https://www.politico.eu/article/gdpr-facebook-google-privacy-data-6-months-in-europes-privacy-revolution-favors-google-facebook/).

Chapter 14

Copyright

Introduction

Much of the material transmitted on communications networks is copyrighted, and much of the consumer demand for internet and communications services is driven by demand for copyrighted materials—from movies and shows to music, to podcasts, and to other audio and video content. Individual voice calls are not copyrighted, because they are not "fixed in any tangible medium of expression," 17 U.S.C. § 102(a), but traditional broadcast and cable television content are, as is most internet content. Indeed, even individual Facebook posts and individual tweets are copyrighted.

In this chapter, we focus our attention on the interaction between copyright protections, on the one hand, and communications providers and internet platforms on the other. Traditional common carriers were immunized from the risk of copyright liability if others transmitted copyrighted works over their wires, so long as the carriers were not responsible for the transmission and had no specific control over it (which of course inheres in common carriage).[1] We start with a brief overview of U.S. copyright law, which is of course a broad, deep, and important subject in its own right, to set the stage for our specific discussion. Then, we discuss the copyright disputes between the owners of audiovisual works, broadcast television, and cable television companies as cable television began to grow in popularity, which were later replicated with the direct broadcast satellite services. They were ultimately settled, if not resolved, through legislation that created statutory licenses and allocated rights among the parties with a view towards regulation.

The internet's growth re-raised these controversies on an even greater scale, as digitization and the internet enabled fast and widespread replication of all kinds of content. The internet also created the possibility of applications and platforms that could enable widespread infringement. One of the earliest such applications was Napster, a service by which individual users could share music files (and potentially other files). In 2001, the Ninth Circuit affirmed a judgment against Napster for

1. 17 U.S.C. § 111(a)(3) ("The secondary transmission of a performance or display of a work embodied in a primary transmission is not an infringement of copyright if—made by any carrier who has no direct or indirect control over the content or selection of the primary transmission or over the particular recipients of the secondary transmission, and whose activities with respect to the secondary transmission consist solely of providing wires, cables, or other communications channels for the use of others.").

copyright infringement. A&M Records, Inc. v. Napster, Inc., 239 F.3d 1004 (9th Cir. 2001). In part, the court relied on Napster's having a central listing of the music files on its service, such that "Napster ha[d] *actual* knowledge that *specific* infringing material is available using its system, that it could block access to the system by suppliers of the infringing material, and that it failed to remove the material." *Id.* at 1022.

This question of what "knowledge" and what other activity creates liability for applications that enable users to share copyrighted material is where we focus our discussion of the interaction of copyright and the development of internet communications and services. In copyright doctrine, this goes under the heading of "secondary infringement." Congress has also sought to address this through statutory provisions, as we will see in the last section of this chapter.

As you proceed through this chapter, keep in mind the interdependence of the content owners and the communications providers and platforms. At bottom, this is a joint production problem. Although content producers (copyright owners) have some distribution that does not depend on communications networks (for example, bookstores, movie theaters, postal service), the overwhelming modern demand is for content carried over cable, satellite, and the wired and wireless internet. All the companies involved have both powerful interests to cooperate to make money and powerful interests to negotiate hard to maximize their share of the profits. Their ability to do so depends largely on their relative market power. Copyright is intended to create a form of monopoly that often confers market power, and communications companies have historically (and maybe still today) had some bottleneck or gateway power.

Two last introductory notes before we proceed: First, we do not cover conflicts over trademark as opposed to copyright, although these issues do sometimes arise with internet services. Most notably, trademark owners want to have control over the use of their trademarks in internet domain names. Although this was a significant problem in the early days of the internet, it has been addressed (though not entirely solved) by statute and changes in practices by the Internet Corporation for Assigned Names and Numbers (ICANN), a nonprofit that administers the domain name system.[2] Additionally, trademark owners have contended that search engines should not be permitted to sell advertising based on trademarks as keywords. In the United States at least, search engines have generally won this dispute, although it continues to be an area of controversy.[3] We do not cover trademark in this book because the controversies generally do not touch on telecommunications services.

---

2. *See* 15 U.S.C. § 1125(d) (codifying the Anticybersquatting Consumer Protection Act, Pub. L. 106–113, 113 Stat. 1501); ICANN, Uniform Domain-Name Dispute-Resolution Policy, https://www.icann.org/resources/pages/help/dndr/udrp-en.

3. *See, e.g.*, 1-800 Contacts, Inc. v. Lens.com, Inc., 722 F.3d 1229 (10th Cir. 2013); Rosetta Stone Ltd. v. Google, Inc., 676 F.3d 144 (4th Cir. 2012); 1-800 Contacts, Inc., v. Whenu.com, Inc., 414 F.3d 400 (2d Cir. 2005).

Second, the statutory provisions discussed here only address secondary liability for copyright infringement. In the next chapter, we tackle the question of online service providers' broader liability for the hosting of user generated content under 47 U.S.C. § 230, which creates an even broader and more controversial immunity.

§ 14.A. Copyright Basics

The Constitution grants Congress the power "[t]o promote the Progress of Science and useful Arts, by securing for limited Times to Authors and Inventors the exclusive Right to their respective Writings and Discoveries." U.S. Const., art. 1, § 8, cl. 8. Congress used this power early, passing the Copyright Act of 1790, Pub. L. 1–15, 2 Stat. 124, in the second session of the First Congress. Today, copyright law creates certain exclusive rights over all "original works of authorship fixed in any tangible medium of expression, now known or later developed, from which they can be perceived, reproduced, or otherwise communicated, either directly or with the aid of a machine or device." 47 U.S.C. § 102(a). "Works of authorship" include, though they are not limited to, literary works, musical works, motion pictures and other audiovisual works, sound recordings, and the like. *Id.* "Fixed in a tangible medium" means that the work "is sufficiently permanent or stable to permit it to be perceived, reproduced, or otherwise communicated for a period of more than transitory duration. A work consisting of sounds, images, or both, that are being transmitted, is 'fixed' for purposes of this title if a fixation of the work is being made simultaneously with its transmission." *Id.* § 101. This broad drafting is meant to encompass works written on paper, stored on magnetic tape, placed in digital storage, or fixed in any other media now existing or to be invented.

Copyright owners, who are the original authors or those to whom the original authors have transferred their copyright,[4] have the "exclusive rights" to reproduce, distribute, and publicly perform or publicly display their works, as well as the exclusive right to prepare derivative works, which are new works "based on one or more preexisting works." *Id.* § 106 (exclusive rights), § 101 (definition of derivative work). These exclusive rights are limited by statute in many ways, large and small. Perhaps the most significant is the right of "fair use." *Id.* § 107. Section 107 provides several nonexclusive examples of how fair use might arise, including uses "for purposes such as criticism, comment, news reporting, teaching (including multiple copies for classroom use), scholarship, or research." *Id.* But the statute also lists four factors that courts should consider in each case,[5] and even though a use fits in one of the

4. Copyright recognizes so-called "works for hire," and with these works the copyright vests in the author's employer or hirer instead of the author. Works for hire include works "prepared by an employee within the scope of his or her employment" and certain other works, in limited categories, if the parties agree in writing that the work is to be treated as a work for hire. 47 U.S.C. § 101.

5. Those four factors are: "(1) the purpose and character of the use, including whether such use is of a commercial nature or is for nonprofit educational purposes; (2) the nature of the copyrighted

categories (which is not required) it will not necessarily be a fair use. If the courts decide "too much" is taken or that the use is otherwise "unfair" after applying the factors they will find infringement, as some did in cases involving the reproduction and distribution of academic articles and other materials to university classes (the practice formerly known as "coursepacks").[6] Some of the cases below, involving communications and technology platforms, involve fair use, because if the underlying use by a consumer or user constitutes fair use, then the transmitting network, online host, or technology provider cannot be guilty of infringement, even under theories of secondary liability.

When a copyright owner proves infringement, remedies can include damages, disgorgement of profits, injunctions against continuing uses, costs and attorneys fees, and statutory damages. 47 U.S.C. §§ 501–505. Statutory damages are a particularly strong remedy and can range up to $150,000 per work infringed if the infringement is willful. *Id.* § 504(c).

As will be covered in more detail in the material that comes, copyright recognizes several doctrines of secondary liability, as do many other areas of law. Primary or direct infringement is the act of violating the exclusive rights of the copyright holder: making unauthorized copies, distributions, public performances, and the like. In one summary by the Supreme Court (not free from controversy as we will see), secondary infringement occurs by "intentionally inducing or encouraging direct infringement" (called "contributory infringement") or "by profiting from direct infringement while declining to exercise a right to stop or limit it" (called "vicarious infringement"). MGM Studios, Inc. v. Grokster, Inc., 545 U.S. 913, 930 (2005).

U.S. copyright law has principally been based upon an economic rationale, but one that balances the need to use an intellectual property monopoly to create incentives for authors to produce new (original) works with the need to limit that monopoly so that the public may effectively use those works and so that new authors can build on past works. As the Supreme Court has put it:

> The limited scope of the copyright holder's statutory monopoly . . . reflects a balance of competing claims upon the public interest: Creative work is to be encouraged and rewarded, but private motivation must ultimately serve the cause of promoting broad public availability of literature, music, and the other arts. The immediate effect of our copyright law is to secure a fair return for an "author's" creative labor. But the ultimate aim is, by this incentive, to stimulate artistic creativity for the general public good.

---

work; (3) the amount and substantiality of the portion used in relation to the copyrighted work as a whole; and (4) the effect of the use upon the potential market for or value of the copyrighted work." *Id.*

6. *See, e.g.*, Princeton Univ. Press v. Michigan Doc. Servs., 99 F.3d 1381 (6th Cir. 1996) (en banc); Basic Books, Inc. v. Kinko's Graphics Corp., 758 F. Supp. 1522 (S.D.N.Y. 1991).

Twentieth Century Music Corp. v. Aiken, 422 U. S. 151, 156 (1975). Copyright law, however, also can and does also promote certain noneconomic values, such as recognizing the author's personality and connection to works and maintaining the integrity of works. These values are more evident in the copyright laws of other countries, but they have some recognition in the U.S. due mostly to international copyright treaties. *See, e.g.*, 47 U.S.C. § 106A (rights of certain authors to attribution and integrity).

With this brief and incomplete primer, we turn now to copyright controversies and their interaction with communications and platform providers.

§ 14.B. Copyright and Traditional Communications Services

In Chapter 1, we discussed network effects and the manner in which they can pose a barrier to entry and competition in markets (a brief discussion you may wish to revisit now). For telephone networks, the necessity has been the ability to offer services to many or all of the other people and businesses that a subscriber wished to call. For a video service, the issue is having sufficient content to attract subscribers or viewers. As an historical and analytical matter, the regulatory questions are two: First, under what circumstances can entities be required to offer their content to other companies? And, second, under what circumstances can entities be required to carry the content of other entities? (As to this second question, recall the discussion in Chapter 3 of must-carry rules.) Depending on the circumstances, an entity — particularly a new entrant into a distribution market in which the existing distributors control all of the content — might love to have the legal right to present others' content. This was the problem when cable television first started (because content was associated with the broadcasters), and when the direct broadcast satellite (DBS) industry initially confronted cable's control over much content. In other circumstances, a company will want to have the right to require others to carry its content. This became the case when cable had grown so significantly, due in part to its ability to offer many channels, that broadcasters felt they needed to be on that platform. Historically, the major flashpoint has been the relationship between local television broadcasters and subscription video providers. The latter were mainly MVPDs. But, analytically, the issues remain the same with internet distribution schemes, as American Broadcasting Companies, Inc. v. Aereo, Inc. below highlights.

In light of the many disputes involving broadcasts, in this chapter first we focus on the copyright rules that govern access to broadcast content and mandate carrying of it. We start with the rules that apply to television programs in isolation, in essence asking whose permission is necessary if a cable company or a DBS provider wants to simulcast an episode of a show that is already being aired on a broadcast channel. Then we consider the somewhat overlapping rules that govern access to channels, by which we mean the stream of programs that a broadcaster strings together as part of an integrated offering.

§ 14.B.1. Individual Programs

§ 14.B.1.a. Compulsory Copyright Licenses

As the first entrant into the video marketplace, cable television providers tested the waters as to whether local broadcast programming could be retransmitted without permission. The first regulatory issue was copyright. As a matter of copyright law, the relevant programs were obviously protected. But cable operators were simply retransmitting content that had already been made public. Once the copyright holders had agreed to put their programs out for all to see, the question became whether they had a claim to additional royalties when a cable operator retransmitted that same program. Stated differently, the question presented to the courts was whether the cable company was acting as a passive conduit — like a viewer — or engaging in a public performance of the work.

In Fortnightly Corp. v. United Artists Television, Inc., 392 U.S. 390 (1968), the Supreme Court confronted this question. The facts were simple. A West Virginia cable operator had begun to retransmit five broadcast signals that were already available over the air in its local market. United Artists, which represented copyright holders that held rights in many of the programs being aired on those broadcast channels, sued the cable operator for infringement, arguing that the cable operator could not air copyrighted content without first obtaining licenses from the copyright holders. The Court ruled that there was no infringement. Just as a viewer was free to receive the broadcasts by antenna and then display the content on his home television, so cable operators, in the Court's view, were free to capture these signals by antenna and display them on the multiple television sets attached to the cable network.

In Teleprompter Corp. v. CBS, 415 U.S. 394 (1974), the Supreme Court reaffirmed and expanded on this logic. In this case, the cable provider was capturing broadcast signals in one community and then using microwave relays to transport those signals to its cable system hundreds of miles away. The issue, then, was not the local retransmission of broadcast signals (*Fortnightly*), but instead the importation of broadcast signals from distant communities. The Court recognized that a viewer might not be able to afford amplifying equipment that would provide access to those distant signals, but as in *Fortnightly* it held that that the cable provider was more like a viewer than a broadcaster. "The reception and rechanneling of [broadcast television signals] for simultaneous viewing is essentially a viewer function, irrespective of the distance between the broadcasting station and the ultimate viewer." *Id.* at 408. There was no copyright liability for the cable provider displaying those distant signals, just as there was no copyright liability for normal viewers.

None of this would remain good law for very long. The Copyright Act of 1976, Pub. L. No. 94-553 (codified as amended at 17 U.S.C. § 101 *et seq.*), changed a good many details of copyright law, and one of those changes effectively reversed *Fortnightly* and *Teleprompter.* Under the new Act, the retransmission of copyrighted broadcast content by a cable operator was defined to be copyright infringement.

See 17 U.S.C. §§101, 106(4), & 501(c). Home viewers were still implicitly licensed to capture broadcast signals off the air and display them privately, but cable operators could no longer borrow broadcast content with impunity.

Had the Copyright Act of 1976 stopped there—defining cable retransmission to be infringement but doing no more—then every time a cable operator wanted to retransmit a local signal, it would have had to acquire a license from every relevant content owner. If the local NBC affiliate was airing thirty copyrighted programs a day, that would mean that the cable operator would need thirty licenses to air the full day's content. This might have meant tracking down and negotiating with each and every copyright owner. Alternatively, some sort of clearinghouse organization (comparable to the role played by BMI and ASCAP in the music industry) might have emerged to handle these permissions en masse. Or, in what HBO ultimately managed to pull off (and became the norm for cable networks), TV stations could themselves obtain such permissions and offer cable distributors one-stop-shopping access to them.

Congress was unwilling to risk the possibility that the negotiated solution model would break down. Consequently, in addition to defining cable retransmission as infringement, Congress added to the Copyright Act what is today 17 U.S.C. §111. That provision establishes a system of compulsory licenses in favor of "cable systems" (i.e., cable operators) who want to retransmit copyrighted broadcast content. These are *compulsory* licenses: copyright owners have no choice but to authorize retransmission so long as the cable operators satisfy the terms of the licenses as set out by Congress. Particularly important among those conditions is §111(c)(3)'s stipulation that neither the content of the particular program at issue, nor any commercial advertising or station announcements transmitted by the primary transmitter immediately before or after the program's transmission, be "willfully altered by the cable system through changes, deletions, or additions." Under the royalty provision, cable operators enjoy a compulsory license for all retransmitted broadcast content and must pay royalties for their use of the programming. Cable operators, however, did win a crucial carve-out from the obligation to pay royalties; they need not pay royalties for either (1) network programming; or (2) local non-network programming.

DBS service confronted many of the same problems as cable when it first began, plus the added problem that cable was already distributing broadcast signals (which many consumers desired). In the early years of DBS's development, DBS providers relied on the Satellite Home Viewer Act of 1988, Pub. L. No. 100-667, 102 Stat. 3949 (SHVA), for compulsory licenses. This legislation provided a limited copyright license to retransmit the programming of "distant" broadcast stations to households that would otherwise be "unserved" by a local network affiliate. 17 U.S.C. §119(d)(10)(A). This exception allowed satellite carriers to deliver network programming to certain satellite dish owners without the copyright owners' permission. By enacting this provision, Congress sought to achieve two goals: (1) making network programming available to the small number of households that otherwise lack access to it; and (2) simultaneously preserving the existing national network/affiliate television distribution system by preventing satellite delivery of network programming to other households. In seeking to accommodate these goals, Congress limited the satellite compulsory license to "unserved households" for private home viewing. 17 U.S.C. § 119(a)(2)(B).

Under SHVA, the definition of an "unserved household" had two parts. First, it "cannot receive, through the use of a conventional outdoor rooftop receiving antenna, an over-the-air signal of grade B intensity (as defined by the [FCC])" from a local network station of the same network. 17 U.S.C. § 119(d)(10)(A). Second, to be "unserved," a household must not have recently received network stations via cable. 17 U.S.C. § 119(d)(10)(B).

DBS providers read this statutory authority broadly, and they used it to deliver network programming from ABC, CBS, Fox, and NBC to a large number of their customers. In particular, some providers offered the same network signal to all of their subscribers, rather than retransmit the signal of each local affiliate to the subscribers in that area. That is, a DBS provider would contract with a single television network affiliate (e.g., WRAL in Raleigh, North Carolina) and would then retransmit its signal nationwide.

The broadcast networks took the DBS provider to court to end this practice and ensure that the statutory requirements were adhered to appropriately. CBS Broadcasting Inc. v. PrimeTime 24 Joint Venture, 48 F. Supp. 2d 1342 (S.D. Fla. 1998). The court ruled for the broadcasters, concluding as follows:

> PrimeTime [the DBS service provider] or its distributors ask potential subscribers three questions: 1) whether they intend to use the programming for residential use; 2) whether they have subscribed to cable in the last 90 days; and 3) whether the household receives an acceptable picture through the use of a conventional rooftop antenna.[7] PrimeTime has always made its initial eligibility determinations exclusively on what the subscriber tells the customer service representative in response to these three questions.
>
> PrimeTime's efforts to comply with the SHVA [through] its use of questionnaires are insufficient to meet Congress' objective test. [A]sking potential subscribers about picture quality simply fails to provide evidence that such subscribers fit within Congress' definition of an "unserved household."
>
> Accordingly, the Court finds that PrimeTime has engaged in a nationwide willful or repeated pattern or practice of infringements.

Id. at 1349–57.

---

7. Before asking the third question, PrimeTime suggests that its distributors tell potential subscribers that, if they say that they receive an acceptable quality picture, they will not be eligible to receive network service.

Following the district court's decision, the satellite, cable, and broadcast industries took their arguments to Congress. Leaders in Congress made clear that they did not want to see three million Americans lose access to valued TV programming. At the same time, Congress recognized an opportunity to rationalize the regulation of DBS providers. In November 1999 (before a negotiated standstill was about to expire), Congress enacted the Satellite Home Viewer Improvement Act of 1999 (SHVIA), Pub. L. No. 106-113, 113 Stat. 1501 (codified at scattered sections of 17 U.S.C. and 47 U.S.C.) (SHVIA).

The general purpose of the Act was to make DBS regulation more consistent with cable regulation and, in that way, to promote competition between the two media platforms. In particular, the congressional reports suggested frustration with increased cable television prices but an unwillingness to re-impose the rate regulation on cable services that largely ceased April 1, 1999. SHVIA was therefore intended to increase competition by leveling the playing field and allowing DBS to offer local stations. *See, e.g.*, The Satellite Television Act of 1999, S. Rpt. 106-51, 1999 WL 320912 (May 20, 1999).

SHVIA made several important changes. First, in § 1002(a), it amended federal copyright law by adding a new section, 17 U.S.C. § 122, which made clear that "a secondary transmission of a performance or display of a work embodied in a primary transmission of a television broadcast station in the station's local market shall be subject to statutory licensing." In other words, DBS providers would enjoy a compulsory license to retransmit even copyrighted local broadcast content back into the local market. Subsection 1002(c) further provided that DBS providers do not have to pay any royalty in exchange for this compulsory license. Other provisions in this section established rules comparable to those in effect with respect to cable, for example prohibiting DBS providers from willfully altering the retransmitted signal.

Second, in § 1005, SHVIA addressed the issue of distant signal importation for the benefit of unserved households. The provision allowed the importation of distant signals for households not within the Grade B contour (the same technical test as applied under SHVA, without the requirement of a 90-day noncable waiting period). The section also grandfathered, but only until 2004, the households caught up in litigation like the *PrimeTime 24* case.

Third, §§ 1008 and 1009 of the Act created a retransmission consent requirement and a "carry one, carry all" rule for local stations.

In enacting SHVIA, Congress set an expiration date at the end of 2004. Congress continued to extend this basic structure through temporary extensions, until it was made permanent (though with some modifications) by the Satellite Television Community Protection and Promotion Act of 2019, and the Television Viewer Protection Act of 2019 (Titles XI and X of Division P, respectively, of the Further Consolidated Appropriations Act, 2020, Pub. L. 116-94, 133 Stat. 2534).

Notes and Questions

1. The *Fortnightly* Approach. Who was being hurt under the Supreme Court's interpretation of copyright law in *Fortnightly*? Local broadcasters? The copyright holders? Was the real problem just that the legal rule was unclear? That is, had copyright owners known that cable operators could retransmit their programs with impunity, could they have been fully compensated by raising the prices they charged broadcasters in the first place?

2. Drawing Distinctions. Was the Supreme Court's interpretation of copyright law defensible? Was it really that difficult to distinguish television viewers from cable operators for copyright purposes? Doesn't copyright law draw those sorts of distinctions all the time?

3. Compulsory Licenses. Why did Congress choose a compulsory licensing scheme as opposed to defining secondary transmission to be copyright infringement and then allowing the market to establish the terms and royalties for retransmission? Congress thought such a solution would have been impractical, but BMI and ASCAP have long successfully acted as copyright clearinghouses for the music industry, collecting royalties from radio stations, restaurants, and other entities that broadcast and otherwise perform musical compositions and then distributing those moneys to the appropriate copyright holders?

4. Internet Distribution. Throughout the 1980s and 1990s, cable television became an increasingly important distributor of video programming, including the programming originating on broadcast stations. Then, as the broadband internet took off, internet platforms—created by content producers, broadcasters, and third parties that acquired programming rights—became significant distributors as well. What does this mean for the compulsory license and retransmission consent scheme? Is there a continuing role for government? Of course, we ask this question throughout the book, but this is a particularly salient example.

§14.B.1.b. What Constitutes a Performance under Copyright Law?

The Copyright Act of 1976 granted broad exclusive rights to copyright holders that clearly applied to cable television service and thus effectively reversed *Fortnightly* and *Teleprompter*, but it did not disrupt the ability of viewers to use antennas to receive programs. What is the line between the viewer function of using an antenna and a public performance via antenna? Enter Aereo, Inc., which was designed to exploit *Fortnightly* and allow subscribers to stream broadcast content over the internet. Aereo attached many small antennas to an internet service that allowed anyone with an internet connection to select one of the antennas to receive broadcast content. Broadcast television networks were not amused (or compensated) and sued on copyright grounds, ultimately resulting in the opinion below.

American Broadcasting Companies, Inc. v. Aereo, Inc.

573 U.S. 431 (2014)

BREYER, J., delivered the opinion of the Court, in which ROBERTS, C.J., and KENNEDY, GINSBURG, SOTOMAYOR, and KAGAN, JJ., joined. SCALIA, J., filed a dissenting opinion, in which THOMAS and ALITO, JJ., joined.

JUSTICE BREYER delivered the opinion of the Court.

The Copyright Act of 1976 gives a copyright owner the "exclusive right[]" to "perform the copyrighted work publicly." 17 U.S.C. § 106(4). The Act's Transmit Clause defines that exclusive right as including the right to "transmit or otherwise communicate a performance . . . of the [copyrighted] work . . . to the public, by means of any device or process, whether the members of the public capable of receiving the performance . . . receive it in the same place or in separate places and at the same time or at different times." § 101.

We must decide whether respondent Aereo, Inc., infringes this exclusive right by selling its subscribers a technologically complex service that allows them to watch television programs over the Internet at about the same time as the programs are broadcast over the air. We conclude that it does.

I A

For a monthly fee, Aereo offers subscribers broadcast television programming over the Internet, virtually as the programming is being broadcast. Much of this programming is made up of copyrighted works. Aereo neither owns the copyright in those works nor holds a license from the copyright owners to perform those works publicly.

Aereo's system is made up of servers, transcoders, and thousands of dime-sized antennas housed in a central warehouse. It works roughly as follows: First, when a subscriber wants to watch a show that is currently being broadcast, he visits Aereo's website and selects, from a list of the local programming, the show he wishes to see.

Second, one of Aereo's servers selects an antenna, which it dedicates to the use of that subscriber (and that subscriber alone) for the duration of the selected show. A server then tunes the antenna to the over-the-air broadcast carrying the show. The antenna begins to receive the broadcast, and an Aereo transcoder translates the signals received into data that can be transmitted over the Internet.

Third, rather than directly send the data to the subscriber, a server saves the data in a subscriber-specific folder on Aereo's hard drive. In other words, Aereo's system creates a subscriber-specific copy — that is, a "personal" copy — of the subscriber's program of choice.

Fourth, once several seconds of programming have been saved, Aereo's server begins to stream the saved copy of the show to the subscriber over the Internet. The subscriber can watch the streamed program on the screen of his personal computer, tablet, smart phone, Internet-connected television, or other Internet-connected device. The streaming continues, a mere few seconds behind the over-the-air broadcast, until the subscriber has received the entire show.

Aereo emphasizes that the data that its system streams to each subscriber are the data from his own personal copy, made from the broadcast signals received by the particular antenna allotted to him. Its system does not transmit data saved in one subscriber's folder to any other subscriber. When two subscribers wish to watch the same program, Aereo's system activates two separate antennas and saves two separate copies of the program in two separate folders. It then streams the show to the subscribers through two separate transmissions — each from the subscriber's personal copy.

II

This case requires us to answer two questions: First, in operating in the manner described above, does Aereo "perform" at all? And second, if so, does Aereo do so "publicly"? We address these distinct questions in turn.

Does Aereo "perform"? *See* § 106(4) ("[T]he owner of [a] copyright . . . has the exclusive right[] . . . to *perform* the copyrighted work publicly" (emphasis added)); § 101 ("To *perform* . . . a work 'publicly' means [among other things] to transmit . . . a performance . . . of the work . . . to the public . . ." (emphasis added)). Phrased another way, does Aereo "transmit . . . a performance" when a subscriber watches a show using Aereo's system, or is it only the subscriber who transmits? In Aereo's view, it does not perform. It does no more than supply equipment that "emulate[s] the operation of a home antenna and [digital video recorder (DVR)]." Brief for Respondent 41. Like a home antenna and DVR, Aereo's equipment simply responds to its subscribers' directives. So it is only the subscribers who "perform" when they use Aereo's equipment to stream television programs to themselves.

Considered alone, the language of the Act does not clearly indicate when an entity "perform[s]" (or "transmit[s]") and when it merely supplies equipment that allows others to do so. But when read in light of its purpose, the Act is unmistakable: An entity that engages in activities like Aereo's performs.

B

In 1976 Congress amended the Copyright Act in large part to reject the Court's holdings in Fortnightly Corp. v. United Artists Television, Inc., 392 U.S. 390 (1968) and CBS v. Teleprompter, 415 U.S. 394 (1974). Congress enacted new language that erased the Court's line between broadcaster and viewer, in respect to "perform[ing]" a work. The amended statute clarifies that to "perform" an audiovisual work means "to show its images in any sequence or to make the sounds accompanying it audible." § 101. Under this new language, *both* the broadcaster *and* the viewer of a television program "perform," because they both show the program's images and make audible the program's sounds.

Congress also enacted the Transmit Clause, which specifies that an entity performs publicly when it "transmit[s] . . . a performance . . . to the public." § 101. Cable system activities, like those of the CATV systems in *Fortnightly* and *Teleprompter*, lie at the heart of the activities that Congress intended this language to cover. The Clause thus makes clear that an entity that acts like a CATV system itself performs, even if when doing so, it simply enhances viewers' ability to receive broadcast television signals.

Congress further created a new section of the Act to regulate cable companies' public performances of copyrighted works. *See* § 111. Section 111 creates a complex, highly detailed compulsory licensing scheme that sets out the conditions, including the payment of compulsory fees, under which cable systems may retransmit broadcasts.

Congress made these three changes to achieve a similar end: to bring the activities of cable systems within the scope of the Copyright Act.

C

This history makes clear that Aereo is not simply an equipment provider. Rather, Aereo, and not just its subscribers, "perform[s]" (or "transmit[s]"). Aereo's activities are substantially similar to those of the CATV companies that Congress amended the Act to reach. Aereo sells a service that allows subscribers to watch television programs, many of which are copyrighted, almost as they are being broadcast. In providing this service, Aereo uses its own equipment, housed in a centralized warehouse, outside of its users' homes. By means of its technology (antennas, transcoders, and servers), Aereo's system "receive[s] programs that have been released to the public and carr[ies] them by private channels to additional viewers." *Fortnightly,* 392 U.S., at 400. It "carr[ies] . . . whatever programs [it] receive[s]," and it offers "all the programming" of each over-the-air station it carries. *Id.* at 392, 400.

We recognize, and Aereo and the dissent emphasize, one particular difference between Aereo's system and the cable systems at issue in *Fortnightly* and *Teleprompter.* The systems in those cases transmitted constantly; they sent continuous programming to each subscriber's television set. In contrast, Aereo's system remains inert until a subscriber indicates that she wants to watch a program. Only at that moment, in automatic response to the subscriber's request, does Aereo's system activate an antenna and begin to transmit the requested program.

This is a critical difference, says the dissent. It means that Aereo's subscribers, not Aereo, "select[] the copyrighted content" that is "perform[ed]," and for that reason they, not Aereo, "transmit" the performance. Aereo is thus like "a copy shop that provides its patrons with a library card." A copy shop is not directly liable whenever a patron uses the shop's machines to "reproduce" copyrighted materials found in that library. And by the same token, Aereo should not be directly liable whenever its patrons use its equipment to "transmit" copyrighted television programs to their screens.

In our view, however, the dissent's copy shop argument, in whatever form, makes too much out of too little. Given Aereo's overwhelming likeness to the cable companies targeted by the 1976 amendments, this sole technological difference between Aereo and traditional cable companies does not make a critical difference here. The subscribers of the *Fortnightly* and *Teleprompter* cable systems also selected what programs to display on their receiving sets.

III

Next, we must consider whether Aereo performs petitioners' works "publicly," within the meaning of the Transmit Clause. Under the Clause, an entity performs a work publicly when it "transmit[s] . . . a performance . . . of the work . . . to the public." § 101. Aereo denies that it satisfies this definition. It reasons as follows: First, the "performance" it "transmit[s]" is the performance created by its act of transmitting. And second, because each of these performances is capable of being received by one and only one subscriber, Aereo transmits privately, not publicly.

We assume *arguendo* that Aereo's first argument is correct. But what about the Clause's further requirement that Aereo transmit a performance "to the public"? One and only one subscriber has the ability to see and hear each Aereo transmission. The fact that each transmission is to only one subscriber, in Aereo's view, means that it does not transmit a performance "to the public."

In terms of the Act's purposes, these differences do not distinguish Aereo's system from cable systems, which do perform "publicly." Viewed in terms of Congress' regulatory objectives, why should any of these technological differences matter? They concern the behind-the-scenes way in which Aereo delivers television programming to its viewers' screens. They do not render Aereo's commercial objective any different from that of cable companies. Nor do they significantly alter the viewing experience of Aereo's subscribers.

IV

We cannot now answer more precisely how the Transmit Clause or other provisions of the Copyright Act will apply to technologies not before us. We agree with the Solicitor General that "[q]uestions involving cloud computing, [remote storage] DVRs, and other novel issues not before the Court, as to which Congress has not plainly marked [the] course, should await a case in which they are squarely presented." Brief for United States as Amicus Curiae 34. And we note that, to the extent commercial actors or other interested entities may be concerned with the relationship between the development and use of such technologies and the Copyright Act, they are of course free to seek action from Congress.

JUSTICE SCALIA, with whom JUSTICE THOMAS and JUSTICE ALITO join, dissenting.

I. Legal Standard

There are two types of liability for copyright infringement: direct and secondary. As its name suggests, the former applies when an actor personally engages in infringing conduct. Secondary liability, by contrast, is a means of holding defendants responsible for infringement by third parties, even when the defendants "have not themselves engaged in the infringing activity." Sony Corp. of America v. Universal City Studios, Inc., 464 U.S. 417, 435 (1984).

Most suits against equipment manufacturers and service providers involve secondary-liability claims. This suit, or rather the portion of it before us here, is fundamentally different. The Networks claim that Aereo *directly* infringes their public-performance right. Accordingly, the Networks must prove that Aereo "perform[s]" copyrighted works, § 106(4), when its subscribers log in, select a channel, and push the "watch" button. That process undoubtedly results in a performance; the question is *who* does the performing. If Aereo's subscribers perform but Aereo does not, the claim necessarily fails.

The Networks' claim is governed by a simple but profoundly important rule: A defendant may be held directly liable only if it has engaged in volitional conduct that violates the Act. This requirement is firmly grounded in the Act's text, which defines "perform" in active, affirmative terms: One "perform[s]" a copyrighted "audiovisual work," such as a movie or news broadcast, by "show[ing] its images in any sequence" or "mak[ing] the sounds accompanying it audible." § 101. And since the Act makes it unlawful to copy or perform copyrighted works, not to copy or perform in general, *see* § 501(a), the volitional-act requirement demands conduct directed to the plaintiff's copyrighted material.

A comparison between copy shops and video-on-demand services illustrates the point. A copy shop rents out photocopiers on a per-use basis. One customer might copy his 10-year-old's drawings — a perfectly lawful thing to do — while another might duplicate a famous artist's copyrighted photographs — a use clearly prohibited by § 106(1). Either way, *the customer* chooses the content and activates the copying function; the photocopier does nothing except in response to the customer's commands. Because the shop plays no role in selecting the content, it cannot be held directly liable when a customer makes an infringing copy.

Video-on-demand services, like photocopiers, respond automatically to user input, but they differ in one crucial respect: *They choose the content.* That selection and arrangement by the service provider constitutes a volitional act directed to specific copyrighted works and thus serves as a basis for direct liability.

II. Application to Aereo

So which is Aereo: the copy shop or the video-on-demand service? In truth, it is neither. Rather, it is akin to a copy shop that provides its patrons with a library card.

Aereo offers access to an automated system consisting of routers, servers, transcoders, and dime-sized antennae. Like a photocopier or VCR, that system lies dormant until a subscriber activates it. When a subscriber selects a program, Aereo's system picks up the relevant broadcast signal, translates its audio and video components into digital data, stores the data in a user-specific file, and transmits that file's contents to the subscriber via the Internet—at which point the subscriber's laptop, tablet, or other device displays the broadcast just as an ordinary television would. The result of that process fits the statutory definition of a performance to a tee: The subscriber's device "show[s]" the broadcast's "images" and "make[s] the sounds accompanying" the broadcast "audible." § 101. The only question is whether those performances are the product of Aereo's volitional conduct.

They are not. Unlike video-on-demand services, Aereo does not provide a prearranged assortment of movies and television shows. Rather, it assigns each subscriber an antenna that—like a library card—can be used to obtain whatever broadcasts are freely available. Some of those broadcasts are copyrighted; others are in the public domain. The key point is that subscribers call all the shots: Aereo's automated system does not relay any program, copyrighted or not, until a subscriber selects the program and tells Aereo to relay it. Aereo's operation of that system is a volitional act and a but-for cause of the resulting performances, but, as in the case of the copy shop, that degree of involvement is not enough for direct liability.

* * *

We are told that nothing less than "the very existence of broadcast television as we know it" is at stake. Brief for Petitioners 39. Aereo and its amici dispute those forecasts and make a few of their own, suggesting that a decision in the Networks' favor will stifle technological innovation and imperil billions of dollars of investments in cloud-storage services. We are in no position to judge the validity of those self-interested claims or to foresee the path of future technological development. Hence, the proper course is not to bend and twist the Act's terms in an effort to produce a just outcome, but to apply the law as it stands and leave to Congress the task of deciding whether the Copyright Act needs an upgrade.

Notes and Questions

1. **The Threat to Broadcast Television.** The petitioners' brief that Justice Scalia quoted (joined by all major television broadcasters) presented Aereo's reading of copyright law as "threaten[ing] the very existence of broadcast television as we know it," because "Aereo has built an entire business around the unauthorized exploitation of broadcasters' copyrighted content. It seeks to siphon off cable and satellite subscribers by offering this content for a lower fee, which it can do only because, unlike its competitors, Aereo does not compensate copyright owners for its use." Petitioners' Brief at 39. On what constructions of copyright law should that affect the Supreme Court's holding?

2. The Threat to the Cloud. For its part, Aereo warned that acceptance of the broadcasters' reading of copyright law "would pervasively threaten the use of cloud technologies to store and access copyrighted content." Respondents' Brief at 49. What implications does the Supreme Court's ruling have for new and developing methods of storage and retrieval? Should the Supreme Court have said more about technologies beyond Aereo's? If so, what should it have said?

3. If It Looks Like Cable. . . . In a section of his dissent not excerpted above entitled "Guilt by Resemblance," Justice Scalia criticized the majority for creating a "cable-TV-lookalike rule," i.e., that a service that looks too much like cable "performs" under the statute. The majority gave some ammunition for this characterization when it rejected the dissent's copy shop analogy by emphasizing "Aereo's overwhelming likeness to the cable companies targeted by the 1976 amendments." In part this disagreement reflected different emphases on text and purpose—and, as a general matter, the dissenters were often more sympathetic to textual statutory interpretation and those in the majority more sympathetic to purposivist statutory interpretation. But this also has significant consequences for future technologies. If you were advising a company that was devising a system for remote storage and retrieval of broadcast television shows, would you advise them to be different than cable? What would that entail?

4. Does This Mean Aereo Is Entitled to a Compulsory License? In light of the holding that Aereo closely resembled a cable operator, is Aereo entitled to a compulsory license under 17 U.S.C. § 111? After all, § 111 creates a compulsory license for a "cable system," which it broadly defines as a facility that "receives signals transmitted or programs broadcast by one or more television broadcast stations licensed by the FCC, and makes secondary transmissions of such signals or programs by wires, cables, microwave, or other communications channels to subscribing members of the public who pay for such service." 17 U.S.C. § 111(f)(3). Unfortunately for Aereo, Congress designated the Copyright Office as the agency that administers § 111 (and thus courts look to its interpretations of § 111), and the Copyright Office has stated that "[e]xamination of the overall operation of section 111 proves that the compulsory license applies only to localized retransmission services regulated as cable systems by the FCC." 57 Fed. Reg. 3284, 3292 (1992); *see* WPIX, Inc. v. ivi, Inc., 691 F.3d 275 (2d Cir. 2012) (relying on the Copyright Office's construction of § 111 in concluding that an internet streaming service was not a "cable system" under § 111). And, in fact, shortly after losing in the Supreme Court, Aereo attempted to rely on 17 U.S.C. § 111, but the Copyright Office rejected that attempt, invoking the language quoted above from its regulation and the *WPIX* holding. Letter from Jacqueline C. Charlesworth, General Counsel and Associate Register of Copyrights, to Matthew Calabro, Aereo, Inc. (July 16, 2014), http://www.nab.org/documents/newsRoom/pdfs/071614_Aereo_Copyright_Office_letter.pdf. So unless the FCC regulates companies like Aereo as cable operators, the Copyright Office changes its interpretation, or a court rejects the Copyright Office's interpretation, companies like Aereo will not be entitled to compulsory licenses.

§ 14.B.2. Syndicated Exclusivity and Network Nonduplication

Overall, the Copyright Act of 1976 represented a compromise: cable operators had to pay for some of the content they retransmitted, but neither broadcasters nor copyright holders were able to deny cable operators the right to carry previously broadcast programming. Section 111, however, had an important exception: secondary transmissions were subject to compulsory licenses only "where the carriage of the signals comprising the secondary transmission [was also] permissible under the rules, regulations, or authorizations" of the FCC.

Prior to the 1976 Act, many FCC rules governed the respective rights of cable operators, broadcasters, and copyright holders. After the Act was passed, the FCC repealed most of those rules so as to not interfere with the compulsory licensing scheme devised by Congress. In 1988, the FCC reinstated the syndicated exclusivity rules. *See* Amendment of Parts 73 and 76 of the Commission's Rules Relating to Program Exclusivity in the Cable and Broadcast Industries, Report and Order, 3 FCC Rcd. 5299 (1988).

The syndicated exclusivity rules (sometimes called syndex) are companion rules to the network nonduplication rules (sometimes called network nondupe), which the FCC never lifted and which address closely related concerns. The FCC refers to these rules collectively as the exclusivity rules. The syndicated exclusivity rules apply to the syndicated programs that are distributed to and aired by independent broadcast stations. By contrast, the network nonduplication rules apply to programs that are distributed within and aired by the networks. In short, the syndicated exclusivity rules enable a local broadcaster to prevent a cable system from exhibiting that part of an imported distant broadcaster's signal that contains programs (or episodes from a television series) for which the local broadcaster has obtained exclusive broadcast rights, in that local area, from the copyright holder. The network nonduplication rules operate in a related fashion to give local broadcasters similar rights with respect to network programming for which they have obtained local exclusivity. (There are also similar rules protecting sports leagues' efforts to establish partial exclusivity in local markets.) The rules provide for FCC enforcement of these contractual arrangements. As the FCC explained, the rules "are grounded in the private contractual arrangements that exist between a station and the provider of network or syndicated programming. The Commission's rules do not create these rights but rather provide a means for the parties to the exclusive contracts to enforce them through the Commission rather than through the courts." Amendment of the Commission's Rules Related to Retransmission Consent, Notice of Proposed Rulemaking, 26 FCC Rcd. 2718, 2740–41, ¶ 42 (2011).

Congress did not mandate syndicated exclusivity and network nonduplication rules for cable television, but a section of SHVIA not discussed above requires the

FCC to apply rules like those developed for cable to DBS. Specifically, the Commission was directed to establish regulations applying network nonduplication, syndicated exclusivity, and sports blackout rules to DBS. Congress ordered the FCC to apply the network nonduplication and syndicated exclusivity rules to DBS only with respect to superstations (broadcasters, such as WTBS and WGN, that had established themselves as nationally distributed stations). 47 U.S.C. §§ 339(b) & (d). In the cable context, by contrast, the FCC's rules for cable television apply to any imported signal, be it superstation or not.

Why have these rules? As summarized by a D.C. Circuit opinion upholding the FCC's reinstatement of the syndicated exclusivity rules,

> [t]he Commission's decision to reinstate syndex rests on its finding that syndex rules will promote diversity in syndicated programming. In the report accompanying the rules, the Commission found that unrestricted importation of distant signals (i.e., no syndex protection) leads to duplication of programming in local broadcasting areas; this duplication lessens the value of syndicated programs to broadcast stations; that loss of value in turn lowers the price syndicated program suppliers will receive for their programs; and all of this ultimately reduces the incentive for syndicated program suppliers to produce programs, which translates into a reduction in the diversity of programming available to the public. On the basis of this scenario, the Commission concluded that syndex rules should be reinstated in order to promote diversity of programming.

United Video v. FCC, 890 F.2d 1173, 1178 (D.C. Cir. 1989).

That said, in 2011, and again in 2014, the Commission issued notices of proposed rulemaking asking whether the rules' benefits outweigh their costs and thus whether they should be eliminated. The Commission itself asked some of the key questions about the rules:

> Do these rules serve a useful purpose in today's marketplace? Should exclusivity in this area be left entirely to the private marketplace, without providing any means of enforcement through the Commission? Would there be a beneficial impact to removing these rules if the contractual provisions that the rules enforce stay in place? Would the elimination of the network non-duplication and syndicated exclusivity rules have a negative impact on localism? We seek comment on the impact of our network non-duplication and syndicated exclusivity rules on the distribution of programming by television stations. Do these rules provide stations and networks with any rights that cannot be secured through a combination of network-affiliate contracts and retransmission consent?

Amendment of the Commission's Rules Related to Retransmission Consent, Notice of Proposed Rulemaking, 26 FCC Rcd. 2718, 2742, ¶ 44 (2011).

Notes and Questions

1. The Logic of the Exclusivity Rules. What interests are these rules designed to protect? Suppose a major-market independent station (say, a non-network station in Washington, D.C.) is imported into a small market (Quincy, Illinois) by the Quincy cable system. Suppose further that both the imported D.C. station and a Quincy station hold rights to exhibit episodes of "NCIS." Is the D.C. station harmed by the importation of its signal? How about the Quincy station? Although the Quincy station may lose audience members to the Quincy cable system, won't it also be able to, as a consequence, obtain "NCIS" rights for a smaller fee? How about the producer of "NCIS"? Won't that firm now be able to charge higher prices to the D.C. station due to its expanded audience in Quincy?

2. Why Have *Rules*? The rules provide for FCC enforcement of contractual arrangements. Why not leave this up to the parties and courts? Is private enforcement via courts too inefficient or expensive? Whatever are the reasons for FCC rules enforcing these contractual arrangements, wouldn't those reasons apply to other contractual arrangements? That is, why shouldn't the FCC set up rules that will create enforcement mechanisms for a host of contractual arrangements, thus providing a comprehensive alternative to courts?

3. How Broad? The FCC's consideration of the exclusivity rules arose in its consideration of retransmission consent, as the title of the proceeding indicates: Amendment of the Commission's Rules Related to Retransmission Consent. Indeed, the paragraph excerpted above begins as follows: "We seek comment on whether eliminating the Commission's network non-duplication and syndicated exclusivity rules, without abrogating any private contractual provisions, would have a beneficial impact on retransmission consent negotiations. Would eliminating these rules help to minimize regulatory intrusion in the market, thus better enabling free market negotiations to set the terms for retransmission consent?" *Id.* ¶ 44. We will examine retransmission consent immediately below, but the quotation above raises larger questions. Examining rules in light of other rules seems to make sense, so that a regulator can try to craft coherent policies. But how far should that go? Should the FCC attempt to review all rules relevant to cable television in one big proceeding? All rules relevant to the provision of video (including broadcasters and MVPDs)? All rules relevant to telecommunications?

§ 14.B.3. Retransmission Consent

While both copyright law and the exclusivity rules focus primarily on program content, Congress created two additional rights under federal telecommunications law, both of which benefit TV broadcasters (at the expense of cable and DBS providers). First, 47 U.S.C. § 325(b) states that an MVPD (which includes cable and DBS operators) cannot retransmit a broadcaster's signal without that broadcaster's explicit permission. This retransmission consent provides a right for broadcasters to withhold the signals from cable and DBS providers, even if they enjoy the right of access under copyright law. This system allows broadcasters with desirable content to charge cable companies for the right to carry that content. Second, 47 U.S.C. §§ 534 and 535 give certain broadcasters the right to insist that their local signals be carried by the local cable system free of charge. This is known as the "must-carry" obligation, which prompted the First Amendment cases *Turner I* and *Turner II* excerpted in Chapter 3. Note that the must-carry obligations for DBS providers are different from those for cable providers. Section 338 provides that if a DBS operator carries a local broadcaster pursuant to a statutory compulsory license, it must carry all the local stations. This DBS provision is known as "carry one, carry all.".

More fundamentally, note that must-carry differs in an important way from compulsory copyright, which involves the terms under which a distributor has the legal right to offer content that the content owner might not wish to share. Must-carry entails a content provider having the legal right to demand carriage of content that a content distributor might not wish to distribute.

Retransmission consent refers to the permission a cable operator must receive in order to carry the signal of almost any broadcast station. Superstations are the only stations for which consent is not needed. Retransmission consent is required in addition to any permissions needed under copyright law. That is, retransmission consent recognizes a property right in the signal that is independent of, and in addition to, the intellectual property rights already recognized in the copyrighted content being transmitted by the signal. The provision gives broadcasters the power to negotiate with cable operators for a share of the revenues generated by the retransmission of broadcast signals.

So whose interests does retransmission consent protect? That, unfortunately, is not entirely clear. The copyright, syndicated exclusivity, and network nonduplication rules seem to already protect program suppliers. And if retransmission consent was designed to protect the additional value in a station's signal that is contributed by the station — for example, the value created when a station assembles a package of programs that provides a continuous sequence of entertainment — one still must explain why broadcasters could not be adequately compensated for this value in other ways, such as in the value of the advertising revenue they collect. The history of the retransmission consent right underscores that it provides broadcasters with a valuable threat to withhold programming in return for payments by cable companies (in dollars or in kind).

Retransmission consent took effect in 1993. In that year, the major networks had their first experience negotiating with cable providers and took different stances. CBS took a hard line and attempted to hold out for huge fees. Cable operators refused to pay, and ultimately CBS caved in and authorized retransmission at no charge. Meanwhile, NBC and ABC granted retransmission consent, but not for money. Instead, these networks gave their consent in exchange for space on the various cable systems. NBC used that space for an ultimately unsuccessful cable channel called America's Talking. ABC more profitably used its space for the sports channel ESPN2. (Fox also traded retransmission consent for system capacity, using its cable capacity to launch the cable channel FX.) The principal benefit to the broadcasters from this right (excepting CBS) was that they were able to introduce new cable channels that immediately reached upwards of 18 million subscribers.

Bargaining over retransmission consent grew increasingly contentious in subsequent rounds of these triennial negotiations. For example, in 1999, ABC took an aggressive stance with respect to retransmission consent, trying both to increase subscribership for its affiliated Lifetime network and to introduce a new movie channel. Negotiations went well past the expiration date of the then-existing retransmission consent agreement, and so for several weeks ABC's status on a number of major cable systems was precariously maintained through ad hoc extensions of the old deal. Indeed, in some negotiations, the two sides failed to make a deal by the expiration of their previous agreement and the broadcaster vanished from the cable lineup until the two sides reached an agreement. For example, in 2004, EchoStar (then owner of DISH Network) and Viacom similarly failed to reach an agreement by the relevant date, meaning that for a while Viacom's channels (CBS, MTV, and Nickelodeon, among others) were not available to EchoStar/DISH Network's DBS customers. In all of these cases, the disputes were ultimately settled, but it is worth noting that, without retransmission consent, such battles could not take place, as the compulsory license would set the terms of access.

Negotiations over retransmission consent have routinely involved broadcasters demanding a higher price and MVPDs complaining that the price is too high. Broadcasters say that they are merely demanding what they are worth. Cable and satellite companies complain that providing automatic carriage rights for some (must-carry) and the threat of hold-out for others (under retransmission consent) leaves them in the worst of all worlds. They particularly feel the pressure after the pre-existing agreement expires and valuable content is not available to their customers. In 2010, for example, Cablevision did not carry Fox for the first two games of the World Series because of a dispute over retransmission fees. Threats and occasional blackouts have continued, including of a Thursday Night Football game in 2019.

Notes and Questions

1. Good Faith Negotiation. The FCC's rules require that the broadcasters and MVPDs negotiate "in good faith" and create a complaint mechanism to enforce that requirement. *See* 47 C.F.R. § 76.65. But the FCC has also said that it does not have authority to order retransmission consent as a temporary or permanent remedy for bad faith negotiation. Amendment of the Commission's Rules Related to Retransmission Consent, Notice of Proposed Rulemaking, 26 FCC Rcd 2718, 2728 (2011). Why wouldn't parties always be able to negotiate terms? Who has the upper hand in these negotiations? And how will changes in market structure affect that conclusion?

2. Joint Negotiation. In 2014, the FCC issued an order forbidding joint negotiations by broadcast stations listed in the top four in any market. Amendment of the

Commission's Rules Related to Retransmission Consent, Report and Order and Further Notice of Proposed Rulemaking, 29 FCC Rcd. 3351, 3353, ¶ 6 (2014).

3. Relationship to the Exclusivity Rules. Cable operators, and the FCC, have connected retransmission consent with the exclusivity rules discussed in the previous section. Cable operators claimed that broadcasters use these rules to "extract supracompetitive prices for retransmission from small companies," whereas "broadcasters assert that eliminating the exclusivity rules would give MVPDs unfair leverage in retransmission consent negotiations," 29 FCC Rcd. at 3383–84, 3390–91, ¶¶ 54 & 65 (internal quotation omitted). On what basis should the FCC determine what constitutes unfair leverage, or supracompetitive prices?

The Commission's 2014 order also stated that "We note that upon elimination of our exclusivity rules, free market negotiations between broadcasters and networks or syndicated program suppliers would continue to determine the exclusivity terms of affiliation and syndicated programming agreements, and broadcasters and MVPDs would continue to conduct retransmission consent negotiations in light of these privately negotiated agreements, but without Commission intrusion in the form of a regulatory enforcement mechanism." *Id.* at 3391–92, ¶ 66. Is this important? Does it undermine the broadcasters' defense of the exclusivity rules (because they can achieve exclusivity without the rules) or the cable operators' attack against the exclusivity rules (because eliminating the rules will not change contractual exclusivity)?

§ 14.C. Copyright and Internet Platforms

We now turn to the potential copyright liability of internet services and platforms, starting with the doctrine of contributory infringement that we briefly discussed above. The starting point for the digital age is the Supreme Court's decision in Sony Corp. of America v. Universal City Studios, Inc., 464 U.S. 417 (1984). In that case, copyright holders sued Sony, the maker of Betamax video tape recorders, alleging that Sony contributed to copyright infringement by purchasers, who used the machines to record copyrighted movies and televisions shows while being broadcast. The Court first held that a user's recording of a copyrighted broadcast for the purpose of "time-shifting" would be a fair use, even though the user made a complete copy of the work, because it was for personal and noncommercial use. *Id.* at 447–56. Then, the Court held that producers of videotape machines were not secondarily liable for copyright infringement because the machines had "substantial noninfringing uses"—that is, the users' time-shifting of programs. *Id.* at 456.

Following *Napster*, several internet services that also allowed peer-to-peer file-sharing by users, but that maintained no central database, became popular. The Supreme Court confronted the liability of the providers of those services in the next case, which touches on the general problem of applications and platforms that allow user infringement.

Metro-Goldwyn-Mayer Studios Inc. v. Grokster, Ltd.

545 U.S. 913 (2005)

SOUTER, J., delivered the opinion for a unanimous Court. GINSBURG, J., filed a concurring opinion, in which REHNQUIST, C.J., and KENNEDY, J., joined. BREYER, J., filed a concurring opinion, in which STEVENS and O'CONNOR, JJ., joined.

JUSTICE SOUTER delivered the opinion of the Court.

The question is under what circumstances the distributor of a product capable of both lawful and unlawful use is liable for acts of copyright infringement by third parties using the product. We hold that one who distributes a device with the object of promoting its use to infringe copyright, as shown by clear expression or other affirmative steps taken to foster infringement, is liable for the resulting acts of infringement by third parties.

I A

Respondents, Grokster, Ltd., and StreamCast Networks, Inc., defendants in the trial court, distribute free software products that allow computer users to share electronic files through peer-to-peer networks, so called because users' computers communicate directly with each other, not through central servers. The advantage of peer-to-peer networks over information networks of other types shows up in their substantial and growing popularity. Because they need no central computer server to mediate the exchange of information or files among users, the high-bandwidth communications capacity for a server may be dispensed with, and the need for costly server storage space is eliminated. Since copies of a file (particularly a popular one) are available on many users' computers, file requests and retrievals may be faster than on other types of networks, and since file exchanges do not travel through a server, communications can take place between any computers that remain connected to the network without risk that a glitch in the server will disable the network in its entirety. Given these benefits in security, cost, and efficiency, peer-to-peer networks are employed to store and distribute electronic files by universities, government agencies, corporations, and libraries, among others.

Other users of peer-to-peer networks include individual recipients of Grokster's and StreamCast's software, and although the networks that they enjoy through using the software can be used to share any type of digital file, they have prominently employed those networks in sharing copyrighted music and video files without authorization. A group of copyright holders (MGM for short) sued Grokster and StreamCast for their users' copyright infringements, alleging that they knowingly and intentionally distributed their software to enable users to reproduce and distribute the copyrighted works in violation of the Copyright Act. MGM sought damages and an injunction.

Discovery during the litigation revealed the way the software worked, the business aims of each defendant company, and the predilections of the users. Grokster's eponymous software employs what is known as FastTrack technology. StreamCast distributes a very similar product except that its software, called Morpheus, relies on what is known as Gnutella technology. A user who downloads and installs either software possesses the protocol to send requests for files directly to the computers of others using software compatible with FastTrack or Gnutella. On the FastTrack network opened by the Grokster software, the user's request goes to a computer given an indexing capacity by the software and designated a supernode, or to some other computer with comparable power and capacity to collect temporary indexes of the files available on the computers of users connected to it. The supernode (or indexing computer) searches its own index and may communicate the search request to other supernodes. If the file is found, the supernode discloses its location to the computer requesting it, and the requesting user can download the file directly from the computer located. The copied file is placed in a designated sharing folder on the requesting user's computer, where it is available for other users to download in turn, along with any other file in that folder.

Grokster and StreamCast use no servers to intercept the content of the search requests or to mediate the file transfers conducted by users of the software, there being no central point through which the substance of the communications passes in either direction.

Although Grokster and StreamCast do not therefore know when particular files are copied, a few searches using their software would show what is available on the networks the software reaches. MGM commissioned a statistician to conduct a systematic search, and his study showed that nearly 90% of the files available for download on the FastTrack system were copyrighted works. Grokster and StreamCast dispute this figure, raising methodological problems and arguing that free copying even of copyrighted works may be authorized by the rightholders. They also argue that potential noninfringing uses of their software are significant in kind, even if infrequent in practice. Some musical performers, for example, have gained new audiences by distributing their copyrighted works for free across peer-to-peer networks, and some distributors of unprotected content have used peer-to-peer networks to disseminate files, Shakespeare being an example. Indeed, StreamCast has given Morpheus users the opportunity to download the briefs in this very case, though their popularity has not been quantified.

As for quantification, the parties' anecdotal and statistical evidence entered thus far to show the content available on the defendants' networks does not say much about which files are actually downloaded by users, and no one can say how often the software is used to obtain copies of unprotected material. But MGM's evidence gives reason to think that the vast majority of users' downloads are acts of infringement, and because well over 100 million copies of the software in question are known to have been downloaded, and billions of files are shared across the FastTrack and Gnutella networks each month, the probable scope of copyright infringement is staggering.

Grokster and StreamCast concede the infringement in most downloads, and it is uncontested that they are aware that users employ their software primarily to download copyrighted files. From time to time, moreover, the companies have learned about their users' infringement directly, as from users who have sent e-mail to each company with questions about playing copyrighted movies they had downloaded, to whom the companies have responded with guidance. And MGM notified the companies of 8 million copyrighted files that could be obtained using their software.

Grokster and StreamCast are not, however, merely passive recipients of information about infringing use. The record is replete with evidence that from the moment Grokster and StreamCast began to distribute their free software, each one clearly voiced the objective that recipients use it to download copyrighted works, and each took active steps to encourage infringement.

After the notorious file-sharing service, Napster, was sued by copyright holders for facilitation of copyright infringement, StreamCast gave away a software program of a kind known as OpenNap, designed as compatible with the Napster program and open to Napster users for downloading files from other Napster and OpenNap users' computers. Evidence indicates that "[i]t was always [StreamCast's] intent to use [its OpenNap network] to be able to capture email addresses of [its] initial target market so that [it] could promote [its] StreamCast Morpheus interface to them," App. 861.

StreamCast developed promotional materials to market its service as the best Napster alternative. One proposed advertisement read: "Napster Inc. has announced that it will soon begin charging you a fee. That's if the courts don't order it shut down first. What will you do to get around it?" *Id.* at 897. Another proposed ad touted StreamCast's software as the "#1 alternative to Napster" and asked "[w]hen the lights went off at Napster . . . where did the users go?" *Id.* at 836. StreamCast even planned to flaunt the illegal uses of its software; when it launched the OpenNap network, the chief technology officer of the company averred that "[t]he goal is to get in trouble with the law and get sued. It's the best way to get in the new[s]." *Id.* at 916.

The evidence that Grokster sought to capture the market of former Napster users is sparser but revealing, for Grokster launched its own OpenNap system called Swaptor and inserted digital codes into its Web site so that computer users using Web search engines to look for "Napster" or "[f]ree file sharing" would be directed to the Grokster Web site, where they could download the Grokster software. *Id.* at 992–93. And Grokster's name is an apparent derivative of Napster.

In addition to this evidence of express promotion, marketing, and intent to promote further, the business models employed by Grokster and StreamCast confirm that their principal object was use of their software to download copyrighted works. Grokster and StreamCast receive no revenue from users, who obtain the software itself for nothing. Instead, both companies generate income by selling advertising space, and they stream the advertising to Grokster and Morpheus users while they are employing the programs. As the number of users of each program increases, advertising opportunities become worth more. While there is doubtless some demand for free Shakespeare, the evidence shows that substantive volume is a function of free access to copyrighted work. Users seeking Top 40 songs, for example, or the latest release by Modest Mouse, are certain to be far more numerous than those seeking a free Decameron, and Grokster and StreamCast translated that demand into dollars.

Finally, there is no evidence that either company made an effort to filter copyrighted material from users' downloads or otherwise impede the sharing of copyrighted files. Although Grokster appears to have sent e-mails warning users about infringing content when it received threatening notice from the copyright holders, it never blocked anyone from continuing to use its software to share copyrighted files. StreamCast not only rejected another company's offer of help to monitor infringement, but blocked the Internet Protocol addresses of entities it believed were trying to engage in such monitoring on its networks.

B

After discovery, the parties on each side of the case cross-moved for summary judgment. The District Court held that those who used the Grokster and Morpheus software to download copyrighted media files directly infringed MGM's copyrights, a conclusion not contested on appeal, but the court nonetheless granted summary judgment in favor of Grokster and StreamCast as to any liability arising from distribution of the then-current versions of their software. Distributing that software gave rise to no liability in the court's view, because its use did not provide the distributors with actual knowledge of specific acts of infringement.

The Court of Appeals affirmed. In the court's analysis, a defendant was liable as a contributory infringer when it had knowledge of direct infringement and materially contributed to the infringement. But the court read Sony Corp. of America v. Universal City Studios, Inc., 464 U.S. 417 (1984), as holding that distribution of a commercial product capable of substantial noninfringing uses could not give rise to contributory liability for infringement unless the distributor had actual knowledge of specific instances of infringement and failed to act on that knowledge. The court also held that Grokster and StreamCast did not materially contribute to their users' infringement because it was the users themselves who searched for, retrieved, and stored the infringing files, with no involvement by the defendants beyond providing the software in the first place. The Ninth Circuit also considered whether Grokster and StreamCast could be liable under a theory of vicarious infringement. The court held against liability because the defendants did not monitor or control the use of the software, had no agreed-upon right or current ability to supervise its use, and had no independent duty to police infringement.

II A

MGM and many of the *amici* fault the Court of Appeals's holding for upsetting a sound balance between the respective values of supporting creative pursuits through copyright protection and promoting innovation in new communication technologies by limiting the incidence of liability for copyright infringement. The more artistic protection is favored, the more technological innovation may be discouraged; the administration of copyright law is an exercise in managing the tradeoff. The tension between the two values is the subject of this case, with its claim that digital distribution of copyrighted material threatens copyright holders as never before, because every copy is identical to the original, copying is easy, and many people (especially the young) use file-sharing software to download copyrighted works. As the case has been presented to us, these fears are said to be offset by the different concern that imposing liability, not only on infringers but on distributors of software based on its potential for unlawful use, could limit further development of beneficial technologies.

The argument for imposing indirect liability in this case is, however, a powerful one, given the number of infringing downloads that occur every day using StreamCast's and Grokster's software. When a widely shared service or product is used to commit infringement, it may be impossible to enforce rights in the protected work effectively against all direct infringers, the only practical alternative being to go against the distributor of the copying device for secondary liability on a theory of contributory or vicarious infringement.

One infringes contributorily by intentionally inducing or encouraging direct infringement, and infringes vicariously by profiting from direct infringement while declining to exercise a right to stop or limit it. Although "[t]he Copyright Act does not expressly render anyone liable for infringement committed by another," *id.* at 434, these doctrines of secondary liability emerged from common law principles and are well established in the law.

B

Despite the currency of these principles of secondary liability, this Court has dealt with secondary copyright infringement in only one recent case, and because MGM has tailored its principal claim to our opinion there, a look at our earlier holding is in order. In *Sony,* this Court addressed a claim that secondary liability for infringement can arise from the very distribution of a commercial product. There, the product, novel at the time, was what we know today as the videocassette recorder or VCR. Copyright holders sued Sony as the manufacturer, claiming it was contributorily liable for infringement that occurred when VCR owners taped copyrighted programs because it supplied the means used to infringe, and it had constructive knowledge that infringement would occur. At the trial on the merits, the evidence showed that the principal use of the VCR was for "'time-shifting,'" or taping a program for later viewing at a more convenient time, which the Court found to be a fair, not an infringing, use. There was no evidence that Sony had expressed an object of bringing about taping in violation of copyright or had taken active steps to increase its profits from unlawful taping. Although Sony's advertisements urged consumers to buy the VCR to "'record favorite shows'" or "'build a library'" of recorded programs, *id.* at 459 (Blackmun, J., dissenting), neither of these uses was necessarily infringing.

On those facts, with no evidence of stated or indicated intent to promote infringing uses, the only conceivable basis for imposing liability was on a theory of contributory infringement arising from its sale of VCRs to consumers with knowledge that some would use them to infringe. But because the VCR was "capable of commercially significant noninfringing uses," we held the manufacturer could not be faulted solely on the basis of its distribution. *Id.* at 442.

The parties and many of the *amici* in this case think the key to resolving it is the *Sony* rule and, in particular, what it means for a product to be "capable of commercially significant noninfringing uses." MGM advances the argument that granting summary judgment to Grokster and StreamCast as to their current activities gave too much weight to the value of innovative technology, and too little to the copyrights infringed by users of their software, given that 90% of works available on one of the networks was shown to be copyrighted. Grokster and StreamCast reply by citing evidence that their software can be used to reproduce public domain works, and they point to copyright holders who actually encourage copying. Even if infringement is the principal practice with their software today, they argue, the noninfringing uses are significant and will grow.

We agree with MGM that the Court of Appeals misapplied *Sony.* The Ninth Circuit has read *Sony's* limitation to mean that whenever a product is capable of substantial lawful use, the producer can never be held contributorily liable for third parties' infringing use of it; it read the rule as being this broad, even when an actual purpose to cause infringing use is shown by evidence independent of design and distribution of the product.

C

Sony's rule limits imputing culpable intent as a matter of law from the characteristics or uses of a distributed product. But nothing in *Sony* requires courts to ignore evidence of intent if there is such evidence, and the case was never meant to foreclose rules of fault-based liability derived from the common law. Thus, where evidence goes beyond a product's characteristics or the knowledge that it may be put to infringing uses, and shows statements or actions directed to promoting infringement, *Sony's* staple-article rule will not preclude liability.

The classic case of direct evidence of unlawful purpose occurs when one induces commission of infringement by another, or "entic[es] or persuad[es] another" to infringe, Black's Law Dictionary 790 (8th ed. 2004), as by advertising. Thus at common law a copyright or patent defendant who "not only expected but invoked [infringing use] by advertisement" was liable for infringement "on principles recognized in every part of the law." Kalem Co. v. Harper Brothers, 222 U.S. 55, 62–63 (1911) (copyright infringement).

For the same reasons that *Sony* took the staple-article doctrine of patent law as a model for its copyright safe-harbor rule, the inducement rule, too, is a sensible one for copyright. We adopt it here, holding that one who distributes a device with the object of promoting its use to infringe copyright, as shown by clear expression or other affirmative steps taken to foster infringement, is liable for the resulting acts of infringement by third parties. We are, of course, mindful of the need to keep from trenching on regular commerce or discouraging the development of technologies with lawful and unlawful potential. Accordingly, just as *Sony* did not find intentional inducement despite the knowledge of the VCR manufacturer that its device could be used to infringe, mere knowledge of infringing potential or of actual infringing uses would not be enough here to subject a distributor to liability. Nor would ordinary acts incident to product distribution, such as offering customers technical support or product updates, support liability in themselves. The inducement rule, instead, premises liability on purposeful, culpable expression and conduct, and thus does nothing to compromise legitimate commerce or discourage innovation having a lawful promise.

III A

The only apparent question about treating MGM's evidence as sufficient to withstand summary judgment under the theory of inducement goes to the need on MGM's part to adduce evidence that StreamCast and Grokster communicated an inducing message to their software users. The classic instance of inducement is by advertisement or solicitation that broadcasts a message designed to stimulate others to commit violations. MGM claims that such a message is shown here. It is undisputed that StreamCast beamed onto the computer screens of users of Napster-compatible programs ads urging the adoption of its OpenNap program, which was designed, as its name implied, to invite the custom of patrons of Napster, then under attack in the courts for facilitating massive infringement. Those who accepted StreamCast's OpenNap program were offered software to perform the same services, which a factfinder could conclude would readily have been understood in the Napster market as the ability to download copyrighted music files. Grokster distributed an electronic newsletter containing links to articles promoting its software's ability to access popular copyrighted music. And anyone whose Napster or free file-sharing searches turned up a link to Grokster would have understood Grokster to be offering the same file-sharing ability as Napster, and to the same people who probably used Napster for infringing downloads; that would also have been the understanding of anyone offered Grokster's suggestively named Swaptor software, its version of OpenNap. And both companies communicated a clear message by responding affirmatively to requests for help in locating and playing copyrighted materials.

Three features of this evidence of intent are particularly notable. First, each company showed itself to be aiming to satisfy a known source of demand for copyright infringement, the market comprising former Napster users. StreamCast's internal documents made constant reference to Napster, it initially distributed its Morpheus software through an OpenNap program compatible with Napster, it advertised its OpenNap program to Napster users, and its Morpheus software functions as Napster did except that it could be used to distribute more kinds of files, including copyrighted movies and software programs. Grokster's name is apparently derived from

Napster, it too initially offered an OpenNap program, its software's function is likewise comparable to Napster's, and it attempted to divert queries for Napster onto its own Web site. Grokster and StreamCast's efforts to supply services to former Napster users, deprived of a mechanism to copy and distribute what were overwhelmingly infringing files, indicate a principal, if not exclusive, intent on the part of each to bring about infringement.

Second, this evidence of unlawful objective is given added significance by MGM's showing that neither company attempted to develop filtering tools or other mechanisms to diminish the infringing activity using their software. While the Ninth Circuit treated the defendants' failure to develop such tools as irrelevant because they lacked an independent duty to monitor their users' activity, we think this evidence underscores Grokster's and StreamCast's intentional facilitation of their users' infringement.

Third, there is a further complement to the direct evidence of unlawful objective. It is useful to recall that StreamCast and Grokster make money by selling advertising space, by directing ads to the screens of computers employing their software. As the record shows, the more the software is used, the more ads are sent out and the greater the advertising revenue becomes. Since the extent of the software's use determines the gain to the distributors, the commercial sense of their enterprise turns on high-volume use, which the record shows is infringing. This evidence alone would not justify an inference of unlawful intent, but viewed in the context of the entire record its import is clear.

The unlawful objective is unmistakable.

B

In addition to intent to bring about infringement and distribution of a device suitable for infringing use, the inducement theory of course requires evidence of actual infringement by recipients of the device, the software in this case. As the account of the facts indicates, there is evidence of infringement on a gigantic scale, and there is no serious issue of the adequacy of MGM's showing on this point in order to survive the companies' summary judgment requests.

* * *

There is substantial evidence in MGM's favor on all elements of inducement, and summary judgment in favor of Grokster and StreamCast was error.

JUSTICE GINSBURG, with whom CHIEF JUSTICE REHNQUIST and JUSTICE KENNEDY join, concurring.

I concur in the Court's decision, which vacates in full the judgment of the Court of Appeals for the Ninth Circuit, and write separately to clarify why I conclude that the Court of Appeals misperceived, and hence misapplied, our holding in *Sony*. There is here at least a "genuine issue as to [a] material fact," Fed. Rule Civ. Proc. 56(c), on the liability of Grokster or StreamCast, not only for actively inducing copyright infringement, but also, or alternatively, based on the distribution of their software products, for contributory copyright infringement. On neither score was summary judgment for Grokster and StreamCast warranted.

The Ninth Circuit went astray when that court granted summary judgment to Grokster and StreamCast on the charge of contributory liability based on distribution of their software products. Although it acknowledged petitioners' (hereinafter MGM) assertion that "the vast majority of the software use is for copyright infringement," the court concluded that Grokster's and StreamCast's proffered evidence met *Sony's* requirement that "a product need only be *capable* of substantial noninfringing uses." Metro-Goldwyn-Mayer Studios, Inc. v. Grokster Ltd., 380 F.3d 1154, 1162 (9th Cir. 2004).

Even if the absolute number of noninfringing files copied using the Grokster and StreamCast software is large, it does not follow that the products are therefore put to substantial noninfringing uses and are thus immune from liability. The number of noninfringing copies may be reflective of, and dwarfed by, the huge total volume of files shared. Further, the District Court and the Court of Appeals did not sharply distinguish between uses of Grokster's and StreamCast's software products (which this case is about) and uses of peer-to-peer technology generally (which this case is not about).

JUSTICE BREYER, with whom JUSTICE STEVENS and JUSTICE O'CONNOR join, concurring.

I agree with the Court that the distributor of a dual-use technology may be liable for the infringing activities of third parties where he or she actively seeks to advance the infringement. I further agree that, in light of our holding today, we need not now "revisit" *Sony*. Other Members of the Court, however, take up the *Sony* question, and they answer that question by stating that the Court of Appeals was wrong when it granted summary judgment on the issue in Grokster's favor. I write to explain why I disagree with them on this matter.

When measured against *Sony's* underlying evidence and analysis, the evidence now before us shows that Grokster passes *Sony's* test—that is, whether the company's product is capable of substantial or commercially significant noninfringing uses. For one thing, petitioners' (hereinafter MGM) own expert declared that 75% of current files available on Grokster are infringing and 15% are "likely infringing." *See* App. 436–439, ¶¶ 6–17 (Decl. of Dr. Ingram Olkin). That leaves some number of files near 10% that apparently are noninfringing, a figure very similar to the 9% or so of authorized time-shifting uses of the VCR that the Court faced in *Sony*.

Importantly, *Sony* also used the word "capable," asking whether the product is "*capable of*" substantial noninfringing uses. Its language and analysis suggest that a figure like 10%, if fixed for all time, might well prove insufficient, but that such a figure serves as an adequate foundation where there is a reasonable prospect of expanded legitimate uses over time. And its language also indicates the appropriateness of looking to potential future uses of the product to determine its "capability."

Here the record reveals a significant future market for noninfringing uses of Grokster-type peer-to-peer software. Such software permits the exchange of *any* sort of digital file — whether that file does, or does not, contain copyrighted material. As more and more uncopyrighted information is stored in swappable form, it seems a likely inference that lawful peer-to-peer sharing will become increasingly prevalent.

The real question here, I believe, is not whether the record evidence satisfies *Sony*. Instead, the real question is whether we should modify the *Sony* standard, as MGM requests, or interpret *Sony* more strictly, as I believe Justice Ginsburg's approach would do in practice.

Sony itself sought to "strike a balance between a copyright holder's legitimate demand for effective — not merely symbolic — protection of the statutory monopoly, and the rights of others freely to engage in substantially unrelated areas of commerce." *Sony,* 464 U.S. at 442. Thus, to determine whether modification, or a strict interpretation, of *Sony* is needed, I would ask whether MGM has shown that *Sony* incorrectly balanced copyright and new-technology interests. In particular: (1) Has *Sony* (as I interpret it) worked to protect new technology? (2) If so, would modification or strict interpretation significantly weaken that protection? (3) If so, would new or necessary copyright-related benefits outweigh any such weakening?

The first question is the easiest to answer. *Sony's* rule, as I interpret it, has provided entrepreneurs with needed assurance that they will be shielded from copyright liability as they bring valuable new technologies to market.

Sony's rule is clear. That clarity allows those who develop new products that are capable of substantial noninfringing uses to know, *ex ante,* that distribution of their product will not yield massive monetary liability. At the same time, it helps deter them from distributing products that have no other real function than — or that are specifically intended for — copyright infringement, deterrence that the Court's holding today reinforces (by adding a weapon to the copyright holder's legal arsenal).

Sony's rule is strongly technology protecting. The rule deliberately makes it difficult for courts to find secondary liability where new technology is at issue.

Sony's rule is forward looking. It does not confine its scope to a static snapshot of a product's current uses (thereby threatening technologies that have undeveloped future markets).

Sony's rule is mindful of the limitations facing judges where matters of technology are concerned. Judges have no specialized technical ability to answer questions about present or future technological feasibility or commercial viability where technology professionals, engineers, and venture capitalists themselves may radically disagree and where answers may differ depending upon whether one focuses upon the time of product development or the time of distribution. Consider, for example, the question whether devices can be added to Grokster's software that will filter out infringing files. MGM tells us this is easy enough to do, as do several *amici* that produce and sell the filtering technology. Grokster says it is not at all easy to do, and not an efficient solution in any event, and several apparently disinterested computer science professors agree. Which account should a judge credit? *Sony* says that the judge will not necessarily have to decide.

Given the nature of the *Sony* rule, it is not surprising that in the last 20 years, there have been relatively few contributory infringement suits—based on a product distribution theory—brought against technology providers (a small handful of federal appellate court cases and perhaps fewer than two dozen District Court cases in the last 20 years). I have found nothing in the briefs or the record that shows that *Sony* has failed to achieve its innovation-protecting objective.

The second, more difficult, question is whether a modified *Sony* rule (or a strict interpretation) would significantly weaken the law's ability to protect new technology. Justice Ginsburg's approach would require defendants to produce considerably more concrete evidence—more than was presented here—to earn *Sony's* shelter. That heavier evidentiary demand, and especially the more dramatic (case-by-case balancing) modifications that MGM and the Government seek, would, I believe, undercut the protection that *Sony* now offers.

The third question—whether a positive copyright impact would outweigh any technology-related loss—I find the most difficult of the three. I do not doubt that a more intrusive *Sony* test would generally provide greater revenue security for copyright holders. But it is harder to conclude that the gains on the copyright swings would exceed the losses on the technology roundabouts.

Finally, as *Sony* recognized, the legislative option remains available. Courts are less well suited than Congress to the task of "accommodat[ing] fully the varied permutations of competing interests that are inevitably implicated by such new technology." *Sony,* 464 U.S. at 431.

I do not know whether these developments and similar alternatives will prove sufficient, but I am reasonably certain that, given their existence, a strong demonstrated need for modifying *Sony* (or for interpreting *Sony's* standard more strictly) has not yet been shown. That fact, along with the added risks that modification (or strict interpretation) would impose upon technological innovation, leads me to the conclusion that we should maintain *Sony,* reading its standard as I have read it. As so read, it requires affirmance of the Ninth Circuit's determination of the relevant aspects of the *Sony* question.

For these reasons, I disagree with Justice Ginsburg, but I agree with the Court and join its opinion.

Notes and Questions

1. Who Won? The defendants in this case lost, of course, based on the Supreme Court's holding that they induced copyright infringement. But did the copyright holders win a strong or a weak victory against companies that create peer-to-peer sharing networks? If you were advising a technology startup that created a peer-to-peer application, you would certainly advise them to avoid the kinds of statements and advertising on which the Supreme Court focused in this case.

2. Contributory and Vicarious Infringement. Did the Court clarify the standards for finding contributory or vicarious infringement? To what extent do you think, after this case, that a copyright case can be built simply by showing how users actually use the application?

3. Design Obligation. The Court said that the "evidence of unlawful objective is given added significance by MGM's showing that neither company attempted to develop filtering tools or other mechanisms to diminish the infringing activity using their software." Is there now a legal obligation to design software to minimize infringing activities? Is this true even if the software or application is otherwise capable of "substantial noninfringing uses"?

4. Justices Ginsburg and Breyer. Justice Breyer, in part responding to worries about amorphous design obligations, suggested a different interpretation from Justice Ginsburg, although both also join the Court's opinion. On what matters do they differ from the Court, and from each other? If the fundamental question is a balance between copyright protection — which seeks to incentivize innovation in content creation — and other technological innovation, which rule gets the balance right? Is there any chance that courts can make that balance?

5. The DMCA's Safe Harbors. The Digital Millennium Copyright Act (DMCA), passed in 1998 to implement certain copyright treaties, sought to address many of these problems of digital copyright, including applications and services provided on the internet. It did not specifically address standards of liability by, for example, specifying what would constitute contributory or vicarious infringement. But it did create a number of immunities and safe harbors. As to internet transmission by ISPs and others, the DMCA replicated and expanded slightly the protections given to common carriers by creating an immunity for both transmission and temporary caching. *See* 17 U.S.C. § 512(a), (b). An immunity for "information location tools" also protects internet services such as search engines. 17 U.S.C. § 512(d). For more detail on these immunities, the Copyright Office prepared a useful summary just after the Act passed. U.S. Copyright Office, The Digital Millennium Copyright Act of 1998 (Dec. 1998), https://www.copyright.gov/legislation/dmca.pdf.

The most difficult, and most litigated, of the DMCA's safe harbors covers "information residing on systems or networks at direction of users," 17 U.S.C. § 512(c) — that is, services that host and distribute user-generated content. The poster-child of such a business has been YouTube, but many cloud services and sites present the possibility of users posting copyrighted material, including social-networking sites, messaging services, and, in fact, any website that allows users to comment or provide reviews. The next case covers this safe harbor.

Viacom International, Inc. v. YouTube, Inc.

676 F.3d 19 (2d Cir. 2012)

Before: CABRANES and LIVINGSTON, Circuit Judges.[8]

Opinion for the court filed by Circuit Judge CABRANES, in which Circuit Judge LIVINGSTON concurs.

CABRANES, Circuit Judge:

This appeal requires us to clarify the contours of the "safe harbor" provision of the Digital Millennium Copyright Act (DMCA) that limits the liability of online service providers for copyright infringement that occurs "by reason of the storage at the direction of a user of material that resides on a system or network controlled or operated by or for the service provider." 17 U.S.C. § 512(c).

The plaintiffs in these related actions—Viacom International, Inc. (Viacom), The Football Association Premier League Ltd. (Premier League), and various film studios, television networks, music publishers, and sports leagues (jointly, the plaintiffs)—alleged direct and secondary copyright infringement based on the public performance, display, and reproduction of approximately 79,000 audiovisual "clips" that appeared on the YouTube website between 2005 and 2008. The District Court held that the defendants were entitled to DMCA safe harbor protection primarily because they had insufficient notice of the particular infringements in suit. Viacom Int'l, Inc. v. YouTube, Inc., 718 F. Supp. 2d 514, 523 (S.D.N.Y. 2010). In construing the statutory safe harbor, the District Court concluded that the "actual knowledge" or "aware[ness] of facts or circumstances" that would disqualify an online service provider from safe harbor protection under § 512(c)(1)(A) refer to "knowledge of specific and identifiable infringements." *Id.* The District Court further held that item-specific knowledge of infringing activity is required for a service provider to have the "right and ability to control" infringing activity under § 512(c)(1)(B). *Id.* at 527. Finally, the District Court held that the replication, transmittal, and display of videos on YouTube constituted activity "by reason of the storage at the direction of a user" within the meaning of § 512(c)(1). *Id.* at 526–27.

Background

A. The DMCA Safe Harbors

"The DMCA was enacted in 1998 to implement the World Intellectual Property Organization Copyright Treaty," Universal City Studios, Inc. v. Corley, 273 F.3d 429, 440 (2d Cir. 2001), and to update domestic copyright law for the digital age. Title II of the DMCA, separately titled the "Online Copyright Infringement Liability Limitation Act" (OCILLA), was designed to "clarif[y] the liability faced by service providers who transmit potentially infringing material over their networks." S. Rep.

8. The Honorable Roger J. Miner, who was originally assigned to the panel, died prior to the resolution of this case. The remaining two members of the panel, who are in agreement, have determined the matter.

No. 105-190 at 2 (1998). But "[r]ather than embarking upon a wholesale clarification" of various copyright doctrines, Congress elected "to leave current law in its evolving state and, instead, to create a series of 'safe harbors[]' for certain common activities of service providers." *Id.* at 19. To that end, OCILLA established a series of four "safe harbors" that allow qualifying service providers to limit their liability for claims of copyright infringement based on (a) "transitory digital network communications," (b) "system caching," (c) "information residing on systems or networks at [the] direction of users," and (d) "information location tools." 17 U.S.C. § 512(a)–(d).

To qualify for protection under any of the safe harbors, a party must meet a set of threshold criteria. First, the party must in fact be a "service provider," defined, in pertinent part, as "a provider of online services or network access, or the operator of facilities therefor." 17 U.S.C. § 512(k)(1)(B). A party that qualifies as a service provider must also satisfy certain "conditions of eligibility," including the adoption and reasonable implementation of a "repeat infringer" policy that "provides for the termination in appropriate circumstances of subscribers and account holders of the service provider's system or network." *Id.* § 512(i)(1)(A). In addition, a qualifying service provider must accommodate "standard technical measures" that are "used by copyright owners to identify or protect copyrighted works." *Id.* § 512(i)(1)(B), (i)(2).

Beyond the threshold criteria, a service provider must satisfy the requirements of a particular safe harbor. In this case, the safe harbor at issue is § 512(c), which covers infringement claims that arise "by reason of the storage at the direction of a user of material that resides on a system or network controlled or operated by or for the service provider." *Id.* § 512(c)(1). The § 512(c) safe harbor will apply only if the service provider:

> (A) (i) does not have actual knowledge that the material or an activity using the material on the system or network is infringing;
>
> (ii) in the absence of such actual knowledge, is not aware of facts or circumstances from which infringing activity is apparent; or
>
> (iii) upon obtaining such knowledge or awareness, acts expeditiously to remove, or disable access to, the material;
>
> (B) does not receive a financial benefit directly attributable to the infringing activity, in a case in which the service provider has the right and ability to control such activity; and
>
> (C) upon notification of claimed infringement as described in paragraph (3), responds expeditiously to remove, or disable access to, the material that is claimed to be infringing or to be the subject of infringing activity.

Id. § 512(c)(1)(A)–(C). Section 512(c) also sets forth a detailed notification scheme that requires service providers to "designate [] an agent to receive notifications of claimed infringement," *id.* § 512(c)(2), and specifies the components of a proper notification, commonly known as a "takedown notice," to that agent, see *id.* § 512(c)(3). Thus, actual knowledge of infringing material, awareness of facts or circumstances that make infringing activity apparent, or receipt of a takedown notice will each trigger an obligation to expeditiously remove the infringing material.

B. Factual Background

When YouTube announced the "official launch" of the website in December 2005, a press release described YouTube as a "consumer media company" that "allows people to watch, upload, and share personal video clips at www.YouTube.com." Under the slogan "Broadcast yourself," YouTube achieved rapid prominence and profitability, eclipsing competitors such as Google Video and Yahoo Video by wide margins. In November 2006, Google acquired YouTube in a stock-for-stock transaction valued at $1.65 billion. By March 2010, at the time of summary judgment briefing in this litigation, site traffic on YouTube had soared to more than 1 billion daily video views, with more than 24 hours of new video uploaded to the site every minute.

The basic function of the YouTube website permits users to "upload" and view video clips free of charge. Before uploading a video to YouTube, a user must register and create an account with the website. The registration process requires the user to accept YouTube's Terms of Use agreement, which provides, *inter alia,* that the user "will not submit material that is copyrighted . . . unless [he is] the owner of such rights or ha[s] permission from their rightful owner to post the material and to grant YouTube all of the license rights granted herein." When the registration process is complete, the user can sign in to his account, select a video to upload from the user's personal computer, mobile phone, or other device, and instruct the YouTube system to upload the video by clicking on a virtual upload "button."

Uploading a video to the YouTube website triggers a series of automated software functions. During the upload process, YouTube makes one or more exact copies of the video in its original file format. YouTube also makes one or more additional copies of the video in "Flash" format, a process known as "transcoding." The transcoding process ensures that YouTube videos are available for viewing by most users at their request. The YouTube system allows users to gain access to video content by "streaming" the video to the user's computer in response to a playback request. YouTube uses a computer algorithm to identify clips that are "related" to a video the user watches and display links to the "related" clips.

Discussion

A. Actual and "Red Flag" Knowledge: § 512(c)(1)(A)

The first and most important question on appeal is whether the DMCA safe harbor at issue requires "actual knowledge" or "aware[ness]" of facts or circumstances indicating "specific and identifiable infringements," *Viacom,* 718 F. Supp. 2d at 523.

1. The Specificity Requirement

Under § 512(c)(1)(A), safe harbor protection is available only if the service provider:

> (i) does not have actual knowledge that the material or an activity using the material on the system or network is infringing;

(ii) in the absence of such actual knowledge, is not aware of facts or circumstances from which infringing activity is apparent; or

(iii) upon obtaining such knowledge or awareness, acts expeditiously to remove, or disable access to, the material. . . .

17 U.S.C. § 512(c)(1)(A).

We are persuaded that the basic operation of § 512(c) requires knowledge or awareness of specific infringing activity. Under § 512(c)(1)(A), knowledge or awareness alone does not disqualify the service provider; rather, the provider that gains knowledge or awareness of infringing activity retains safe-harbor protection if it "acts expeditiously to remove, or disable access to, the material." 17 U.S.C. § 512(c)(1)(A)(iii). Thus, the nature of the removal obligation itself contemplates knowledge or awareness of specific infringing material, because expeditious removal is possible only if the service provider knows with particularity which items to remove. Indeed, to require expeditious removal in the absence of specific knowledge or awareness would be to mandate an amorphous obligation to "take commercially reasonable steps" in response to a generalized awareness of infringement. Viacom Br. 33. Such a view cannot be reconciled with the language of the statute, which requires "expeditious[]" action to remove or disable "*the material*" at issue. 17 U.S.C. § 512(c)(1)(A)(iii) (emphasis added).

On appeal, the plaintiffs dispute this conclusion by drawing our attention to § 512(c)(1)(A)(ii), the so-called "red flag" knowledge provision. *See id.* § 512(c)(1)(A)(ii) (limiting liability where, "in the absence of such actual knowledge, [the service provider] is not aware of facts or circumstances from which infringing activity is apparent"). In their view, the use of the phrase "facts or circumstances" demonstrates that Congress did not intend to limit the red flag provision to a particular type of knowledge. The plaintiffs contend that requiring awareness of specific infringements in order to establish "aware[ness] of facts or circumstances from which infringing activity is apparent," 17 U.S.C. § 512(c)(1)(A)(ii), renders the red flag provision superfluous, because that provision would be satisfied only when the "actual knowledge" provision is also satisfied. For that reason, the plaintiffs urge the Court to hold that the red flag provision "requires less specificity" than the actual knowledge provision. Pls.' Supp. Br. 1.

This argument misconstrues the relationship between "actual" knowledge and "red flag" knowledge. Contrary to the plaintiffs' assertions, construing § 512(c)(1)(A) to require actual knowledge or awareness of specific instances of infringement does not render the red flag provision superfluous. The phrase "actual knowledge," which appears in § 512(c)(1)(A)(i), is frequently used to denote subjective belief. By contrast, courts often invoke the language of "facts or circumstances," which appears in § 512(c)(1)(A)(ii), in discussing an objective reasonableness standard. The difference between actual and red flag knowledge is thus not between specific and generalized knowledge, but instead between a subjective and an objective standard. In other words, the actual knowledge provision turns on whether the provider actually or "subjectively" knew of specific infringement, while the red flag provision turns on whether the provider was subjectively aware of facts that would have made the specific infringement "objectively" obvious to a reasonable person. The red flag provision, because it incorporates an objective standard, is not swallowed up by the actual knowledge provision under our construction of the § 512(c) safe harbor. Both provisions do independent work, and both apply only to specific instances of infringement.

Based on the text of § 512(c)(1)(A), as well as the limited case law on point, we affirm the District Court's holding that actual knowledge or awareness of facts or circumstances that indicate specific and identifiable instances of infringement will disqualify a service provider from the safe harbor.

2. The Grant of Summary Judgment

The corollary question on appeal is whether the District Court erred in granting summary judgment to YouTube on the record presented. For the reasons that follow, we hold that although the District Court correctly interpreted § 512(c)(1)(A), summary judgment for the defendants was premature.

i. Specific Knowledge or Awareness

The plaintiffs argue that, even under the District Court's construction of the safe harbor, the record raises material issues of fact regarding YouTube's actual knowledge or "red flag" awareness of specific instances of infringement. To that end, the plaintiffs draw our attention to various estimates regarding the percentage of infringing content on the YouTube website. For example, Viacom cites evidence that YouTube employees conducted website surveys and estimated that 75–80% of all YouTube streams contained copyrighted material. The class plaintiffs similarly claim that Credit Suisse, acting as financial advisor to Google, estimated that more than 60% of YouTube's content was "premium" copyrighted content—and that only 10% of the premium content was authorized. These approximations suggest that the defendants were conscious that significant quantities of material on the YouTube website were infringing. But such estimates are insufficient, standing alone, to create a triable issue of fact as to whether YouTube actually knew, or was aware of facts or circumstances that would indicate, the existence of particular instances of infringement.

Beyond the survey results, the plaintiffs rely upon internal YouTube communications that do refer to particular clips or groups of clips. The class plaintiffs argue that YouTube was aware of specific infringing material because, *inter alia*, YouTube attempted to search for specific Premier League videos on the site in order to gauge their "value based on video usage." In particular, the class plaintiffs cite a February 7, 2007 e-mail from Patrick Walker, director of video partnerships for Google and YouTube, requesting that his colleagues calculate the number of daily searches for the terms "soccer," "football," and "Premier League" in preparation for a bid on the global rights to Premier League content.

The record in the *Viacom* action includes additional examples. For instance, YouTube founder Jawed Karim prepared a report in March 2006 which stated that, "[a]s of today[,] episodes and clips of the following well-known shows can still be found [on YouTube]: Family Guy, South Park, MTV Cribs, Daily Show, Reno 911, [and] Dave Chapelle [sic]." Karim further opined that, "although YouTube is not legally required to monitor content . . . and complies with DMCA takedown requests, we would benefit from *preemptively* removing content that is blatantly illegal and likely to attract criticism." He also noted that "a more thorough analysis" of the issue would be required. At least some of the TV shows to which Karim referred are owned by Viacom. A reasonable juror could conclude from the March 2006 report that Karim knew of the presence of Viacom-owned material on YouTube, since he presumably located specific clips of the shows in question before he could announce that YouTube hosted the content "[a]s of today." A reasonable juror could also conclude that Karim believed the clips he located to be infringing (since he refers to them as "blatantly illegal"), and that YouTube did not remove the content from the website until conducting "a more thorough analysis," thus exposing the company to liability in the interim.

Furthermore, in a July 4, 2005 e-mail exchange, YouTube founder Chad Hurley sent an e-mail to his co-founders with the subject line "budlight commercials," and stated, "we need to reject these too." Steve Chen responded, "can we please leave these in a bit longer? another week or two can't hurt." Karim also replied, indicating that he "added back in all 28 bud videos." Similarly, in an August 9, 2005 e-mail exchange, Hurley urged his colleagues "to start being *diligent* about rejecting copyrighted/inappropriate content," noting that "there is a cnn clip of the shuttle clip on the site today, if the boys from Turner would come to the site, they might be pissed?" Again, Chen resisted:

> but we should just keep that stuff on the site. i really don't see what will happen. what? someone from cnn sees it? he happens to be someone with power? he happens to want to take it down right away. he gets in touch with cnn legal. 2 weeks later, we get a cease & desist letter. we take the video down.

And again, Karim agreed, indicating that "the CNN space shuttle clip, I like. we can remove it once we're bigger and better known, but for now that clip is fine."

Upon a review of the record, we are persuaded that the plaintiffs may have raised a material issue of fact regarding YouTube's knowledge or awareness of specific instances of infringement.

We hasten to note, however, that although the foregoing e-mails were annexed as exhibits to the summary judgment papers, it is unclear whether the clips referenced therein are among the current clips-in-suit. By definition, only the current clips-in-suit are at issue in this litigation. Accordingly, we vacate the order granting summary judgment and instruct the District Court to determine on remand whether any specific infringements of which YouTube had knowledge or awareness correspond to the clips-in-suit in these actions.

ii. "Willful Blindness"

The plaintiffs further argue that the District Court erred in granting summary judgment to the defendants despite evidence that YouTube was "willfully blind" to specific infringing activity. On this issue of first impression, we consider the application of the common law willful blindness doctrine in the DMCA context. "The principle that willful blindness is tantamount to knowledge is hardly novel." Tiffany (NJ) Inc. v. eBay, Inc., 600 F.3d 93, 110 n.16 (2d Cir. 2010).

The DMCA does not mention willful blindness. The DMCA provision most relevant to the abrogation inquiry is § 512(m), which provides that safe harbor protection shall not be conditioned on "a service provider monitoring its service or affirmatively seeking facts indicating infringing activity, except to the extent consistent with a standard technical measure complying with the provisions of subsection (i)." 17 U.S.C. § 512(m)(1). Section 512(m) is explicit: DMCA safe harbor protection cannot be conditioned on affirmative monitoring by a service provider. For that reason, § 512(m) is incompatible with a broad common law duty to monitor or otherwise seek out infringing activity based on general awareness that infringement may be occurring. Accordingly, we hold that the willful blindness doctrine may be applied, in appropriate circumstances, to demonstrate knowledge or awareness of specific instances of infringement under the DMCA.

B. Control and Benefit: § 512(c)(1)(B)

Apart from the foregoing knowledge provisions, the § 512(c) safe harbor provides that an eligible service provider must "not receive a financial benefit directly attributable to the infringing activity, in a case in which the service provider has the right and ability to control such activity." 17 U.S.C. § 512(c)(1)(B). We hold that the District Court erred by importing a specific knowledge requirement into the control and benefit provision, and we therefore remand for further fact-finding on the issue of control.

1. "Right and Ability to Control" Infringing Activity

On appeal, the parties advocate two competing constructions of the "right and ability to control" infringing activity. 17 U.S.C. § 512(c)(1)(B).

The first construction, pressed by the defendants, is the one adopted by the District Court, which held that "the provider must know of the particular case before he can control it." *Viacom,* 718 F. Supp. 2d at 527. The trouble with this construction is that importing a specific knowledge requirement into § 512(c)(1)(B) renders the control provision duplicative of § 512(c)(1)(A). Any service provider that has item-specific knowledge of infringing activity and thereby obtains financial benefit would already be excluded from the safe harbor under § 512(c)(1)(A) for having specific knowledge of infringing material and failing to effect expeditious removal. No additional service provider would be excluded by § 512(c)(1)(B) that was not already excluded by § 512(c)(1)(A). Because statutory interpretations that render language superfluous are disfavored, we reject the District Court's interpretation of the control provision.

The second construction, urged by the plaintiffs, is that the control provision codifies the common law doctrine of vicarious copyright liability. The common law imposes liability for vicarious copyright infringement "[w]hen the right and ability to supervise coalesce with an obvious and direct financial interest in the exploitation of copyrighted materials—even in the absence of actual knowledge that the copyright mono[poly] is being impaired." Shapiro, Bernstein & Co. v. H. L. Green Co., 316 F.2d 304, 307 (2d Cir. 1963).

To adopt that principle in the DMCA context, however, would render the statute internally inconsistent. Section 512(c) actually presumes that service providers have the ability to "block . . . access" to infringing material. Indeed, a service provider who has knowledge or awareness of infringing material or who receives a takedown notice from a copyright holder is *required* to "remove, or disable access to, the material" in order to claim the benefit of the safe harbor. 17 U.S.C. § 512(c)(1)(A)(iii) & (C). But in taking such action, the service provider would—in the plaintiffs' analysis—be admitting the "right and ability to control" the infringing material. Thus, the prerequisite to safe harbor protection under § 512(c)(1)(A)(iii) & (C) would at the same time be a disqualifier under § 512(c)(1)(B).

Accordingly, we conclude that the "right and ability to control" infringing activity under § 512(c)(1)(B) "requires something more than the ability to remove or block access to materials posted on a service provider's website." Capitol Records, Inc. v. mp3tunes, LLC, 821 F. Supp. 2d 627, 645 (S.D.N.Y. 2011). The remaining—and more difficult—question is how to define the "something more" that is required.

To date, only one court has found that a service provider had the right and ability to control infringing activity under § 512(c)(1)(B). In Perfect 10, Inc. v. Cybernet Ventures, Inc., 213 F. Supp. 2d 1146 (C.D. Cal. 2002), the court found control where the service provider instituted a monitoring program by which user websites received "detailed instructions regard[ing] issues of layout, appearance, and content." *Id.* at 1173. The service provider also forbade certain types of content and refused access to users who failed to comply with its instructions. *Id.* Similarly, inducement of copyright infringement under Metro-Goldwyn-Mayer Studios Inc. v. Grokster, Ltd., 545 U.S. 913 (2005), which "premises liability on purposeful, culpable expression and conduct," *id.* at 937, might also rise to the level of control under § 512(c)(1)(B). Both of these examples involve a service provider exerting substantial influence on the activities of users, without necessarily—or even frequently—acquiring knowledge of specific infringing activity.

In light of our holding that § 512(c)(1)(B) does not include a specific knowledge requirement, we think it prudent to remand to the District Court to consider in the first instance whether the plaintiffs have adduced sufficient evidence to allow a reasonable jury to conclude that YouTube had the right and ability to control the infringing activity and received a financial benefit directly attributable to that activity.

C. "By Reason of" Storage: § 512(c)(1)

The § 512(c) safe harbor is only available when the infringement occurs "by reason of the storage at the direction of a user of material that resides on a system or network controlled or operated by or for the service provider." 17 U.S.C. § 512(c)(1). In this case, the District Court held that YouTube's software functions fell within the safe harbor for infringements that occur "by reason of" user storage. *Viacom,* 718 F. Supp. 2d at 526 (noting that a contrary holding would "confine[] the word 'storage' too narrowly to meet the statute's purpose"). We affirm that holding with respect to three of the challenged software functions—the conversion (or "transcoding") of videos into a standard display format, the playback of videos on "watch" pages, and the "related videos" function. We remand for further fact-finding with respect to a fourth software function, involving the third-party syndication of videos uploaded to YouTube.

Notes and Questions

1. Remand and Settlement. After remand, the District Court again granted summary judgment to YouTube, finding that the plaintiffs could not show the specific knowledge or willful blindness required under the standard set by the Court of Appeals. Viacom Int'l, Inc. v. YouTube, Inc., 940 F. Supp. 2d 110 (S.D.N.Y. 2013). The plaintiffs again appealed, but the case was settled during the appeal, the week before oral argument.

2. Notice and Takedown. Even if a site or platform qualifies for the safe harbor on the basis of the knowledge and control issues described here, it must comply with a "notice and takedown" regime in which, if a copyright holder gives specific notice of infringing content, the service provider must take down the allegedly offending content. 17 U.S.C. § 512(c)(1)(C), (c)(3). Copyright holders were not, of course, satisfied with this option, given both the monitoring costs and the extraordinarily large number of allegedly infringing uploads.

3. Content ID. Even prior to this litigation, YouTube developed and deployed a scanning technology known as "Content ID," which enables copyright holders to provide digital copies of copyrighted works from which YouTube makes signature files and then scans new uploads in order to identify copyright infringement in advance. Copyright holders have taken advantage of the system, which allows them to block uploads identified as containing infringing material or to allow the upload and "monetize" the use of their copyrighted material by adding advertising to the upload. Some users have claimed that the system is inaccurate and that they are penalized for false positives by YouTube.

But more importantly, the use of a Content ID-type system has become an expectation of the copyright industry and is required in Europe by the Copyright Directive of 2019. *See* Directive (EU) 2019/790 of the European Parliament and of the Council of 17 April 2019 on Copyright and Related rights in the Digital Single Market, PE/51/2019/REV/1, OJ L 130 (May 5, 2019). Content ID-type systems may impose barriers to entry to new video hosting services, due to their processing requirements and overall expense.

4. Design Again. Given the capability of Content ID, do you think the Court reached the right conclusion concerning the specific knowledge requirement? Even if it did, do you think Congress should modify the safe harbor to create a requirement that some or all platforms that host user-generated content should deploy a system such as Content ID? What would be the effect of such a requirement on new startups as opposed to established platforms such as YouTube and Facebook?

Chapter 15

General Protection for Intermediaries of User-Generated Content: Section 230

Introduction

Users can commit any number of other torts or illegal behavior on the internet. They can make threats, commit acts of discrimination, engage in criminal activity, and commit defamation, particularly where the platform enables anonymity. Common carriers are, in exchange for their decreased discretion over service, recognized as exempt from liability for defamation. *See* Restatement (Second) of Torts § 621 cmt. g (Am. L. Inst. 1977) ("Since it is the user of the telephone rather than the telephone company who is treated as transmitting a telephone message . . . the company is not subject to liability for a defamatory statement communicated by a customer."). The liability of internet platforms for user-generated content (apart from copyright) became part of Congress's consideration of pornography on the internet, as it formulated the Communications Decency (CDA), which became Title V of the Telecommunications Act of 1996. In Chapter 11 we addressed the Communications Decency Act's regulation of internet indecency and the Supreme Court's invalidation of that regulation in Reno v. ACLU, 521 U.S. 844 (1997). Here, we cover 47 U.S.C. § 230, which by contrast provides broad protection to internet platforms that host user-generated content. The relationship between pornography and this protection may not seem obvious. The connection arises largely due to Congress's reaction to Stratton Oakmont, Inc. v. Prodigy Servs. Co., 1995 WL 323710 (N.Y. Sup. Ct. May 24, 1995). That decision imposed liability on Prodigy because of Prodigy's practice of moderating content in various of its fora. A common carrier's immunity from liability flows from its lack of editorial control over user content, while others — such as newspapers and television stations — are treated as speakers and publishers of all of the content on their service by virtue of their editorial control. Congress perceived online platforms as being in a bind: platforms want to invite interactive communication with users but also want to occasionally moderate their content to make their platforms more appealing. Congress responded with § 230 to eliminate a perceived disincentive to online moderation and promote a safer internet.

One note before we proceed: Many § 230 cases, including some we excerpt here, arise in the context of extremely disturbing behavior, a matter which bears on the effect and interpretation of § 230, and which we try to grapple with throughout.

§ 15.A. Background and Foundation: Zeran v. America Online

One of the earliest cases interpreting § 230 involved America Online (AOL). In 1996, the United States had about 10 million internet service subscribers and about half of those used AOL. In addition, AOL had a web presence and 41 percent of all internet users checked it regularly.[1] The following case, which explains the general statutory structure, has remained one of the most influential decisions interpreting the scope of § 230.

Zeran v. America Online, Inc.

129 F.3d 327 (4th Cir. 1997)

Opinion for the court filed by Chief Circuit Judge WILKINSON, in which Circuit Judge RUSSELL and District Judge BOYLE concur.

WILKINSON, Chief Circuit Judge:

Kenneth Zeran brought this action against America Online, Inc. (AOL), arguing that AOL unreasonably delayed in removing defamatory messages posted by an unidentified third party, refused to post retractions of those messages, and failed to screen for similar postings thereafter. The district court granted judgment for AOL on the grounds that the Communications Decency Act of 1996 (CDA) — 47 U.S.C. § 230 — bars Zeran's claims. Zeran appeals, arguing that § 230 leaves intact liability for interactive computer service providers who possess notice of defamatory material posted through their services. Section 230, however, plainly immunizes computer service providers like AOL from liability for information that originates with third parties. Accordingly, we affirm the judgment of the district court.

I

"The Internet is an international network of interconnected computers," currently used by approximately 40 million people worldwide. Reno v. ACLU, 521 U.S. 844, 849 (1997). One of the many means by which individuals access the Internet is through an interactive computer service. These services offer not only a connection to the Internet as a whole, but also allow their subscribers to access information communicated and stored only on each computer service's individual proprietary network. *Id.* AOL is just such an interactive computer service. Much of the information transmitted over its network originates with the company's millions of subscribers. They may transmit information privately via electronic mail, or they may communicate publicly by posting messages on AOL bulletin boards, where the messages may be read by any AOL subscriber.

---

1. *See* Farhad Manjoo, Jurassic Web: The Internet of 1996 Is Almost Unrecognizable Compared with What We Have Today, Slate, Feb. 24, 2009, https://slate.com/technology/2009/02/the-unrecognizable-internet-of-1996.html.

On April 25, 1995, an unidentified person posted a message on an AOL bulletin board advertising "Naughty Oklahoma T-Shirts." The posting described the sale of shirts featuring offensive and tasteless slogans related to the April 19, 1995, bombing of the Alfred P. Murrah Federal Building in Oklahoma City. Those interested in purchasing the shirts were instructed to call "Ken" at Zeran's home phone number in Seattle, Washington. As a result of this anonymously perpetrated prank, Zeran received a high volume of calls, comprised primarily of angry and derogatory messages, but also including death threats. Zeran could not change his phone number because he relied on its availability to the public in running his business out of his home. Later that day, Zeran called AOL and informed a company representative of his predicament. The employee assured Zeran that the posting would be removed from AOL's bulletin board but explained that as a matter of policy AOL would not post a retraction. On April 26, the next day, an unknown person posted another message advertising additional shirts with new tasteless slogans related to the Oklahoma City bombing. Again, interested buyers were told to call Zeran's phone number, to ask for "Ken," and to "please call back if busy" due to high demand. The angry, threatening phone calls intensified. Over the next four days, an unidentified party continued to post messages on AOL's bulletin board, advertising additional items including bumper stickers and key chains with still more offensive slogans. During this time period, Zeran called AOL repeatedly and was told by company representatives that the individual account from which the messages were posted would soon be closed. Zeran also reported his case to Seattle FBI agents. By April 30, Zeran was receiving an abusive phone call approximately every two minutes.

Meanwhile, an announcer for Oklahoma City radio station KRXO received a copy of the first AOL posting. On May 1, the announcer related the message's contents on the air, attributed them to "Ken" at Zeran's phone number, and urged the listening audience to call the number. After this radio broadcast, Zeran was inundated with death threats and other violent calls from Oklahoma City residents. Over the next few days, Zeran talked to both KRXO and AOL representatives. He also spoke to his local police, who subsequently surveilled his home to protect his safety. By May 14, after an Oklahoma City newspaper published a story exposing the shirt advertisements as a hoax and after KRXO made an on-air apology, the number of calls to Zeran's residence finally subsided to fifteen per day.

II. A

Because § 230 was successfully advanced by AOL in the district court as a defense to Zeran's claims, we shall briefly examine its operation here. Zeran seeks to hold AOL liable for defamatory speech initiated by a third party. He argued to the district court that once he notified AOL of the unidentified third party's hoax, AOL had a duty to remove the defamatory posting promptly, to notify its subscribers of the message's false nature, and to effectively screen future defamatory material. Section 230 entered this litigation as an affirmative defense pled by AOL. The company claimed that Congress immunized interactive computer service providers from claims based on information posted by a third party.

The relevant portion of § 230 states: "No provider or user of an interactive computer service shall be treated as the publisher or speaker of any information provided by another information content provider." 47 U.S.C. § 230(c)(1). By its plain language, § 230 creates a federal immunity to any cause of action that would make service providers liable for information originating with a third-party user of the service. Specifically, § 230 precludes courts from entertaining claims that would place a computer service provider in a publisher's role. Thus, lawsuits seeking to hold a service provider liable for its exercise of a publisher's traditional editorial functions — such as deciding whether to publish, withdraw, postpone or alter content — are barred.

The purpose of this statutory immunity is not difficult to discern. Congress recognized the threat that tort-based lawsuits pose to freedom of speech in the new and burgeoning Internet medium. The imposition of tort liability on service providers for the communications of others represented, for Congress, simply another form of intrusive government regulation of speech. Section 230 was enacted, in part, to maintain the robust nature of Internet communication and, accordingly, to keep government interference in the medium to a minimum. In specific statutory findings, Congress recognized the Internet and interactive computer services as offering "a forum for a true diversity of political discourse, unique opportunities for cultural development, and myriad avenues for intellectual activity." *Id.* § 230(a)(3). It also found that the Internet and interactive computer services "have flourished, to the benefit of all Americans, with a minimum of government regulation." *Id.* § 230(a)(4). Congress further stated that it is "the policy of the United States . . . to preserve the vibrant and competitive free market that presently exists for the Internet and other interactive computer services, unfettered by Federal or State regulation." *Id.* § 230(b)(2).

None of this means, of course, that the original culpable party who posts defamatory messages would escape accountability. While Congress acted to keep government regulation of the Internet to a minimum, it also found it to be the policy of the United States "to ensure vigorous enforcement of Federal criminal laws to deter and punish trafficking in obscenity, stalking, and harassment by means of computer." *Id.* § 230(b)(5). Congress made a policy choice, however, not to deter harmful online speech through the separate route of imposing tort liability on companies that serve as intermediaries for other parties' potentially injurious messages.

Congress' purpose in providing the § 230 immunity was thus evident. Interactive computer services have millions of users. The amount of information communicated via interactive computer services is therefore staggering. The specter of tort liability in an area of such prolific speech would have an obvious chilling effect. It would be impossible for service providers to screen each of their millions of postings for possible problems. Faced with potential liability for each message republished by their services, interactive computer service providers might choose to severely restrict the number and type of messages posted. Congress considered the weight of the speech interests implicated and chose to immunize service providers to avoid any such restrictive effect.

Another important purpose of § 230 was to encourage service providers to self-regulate the dissemination of offensive material over their services. In this respect, § 230 responded to a New York state court decision, Stratton Oakmont, Inc. v. Prodigy Servs. Co., 1995 WL 323710 (N.Y. Sup. Ct. May 24, 1995). There, the plaintiffs sued Prodigy—an interactive computer service like AOL—for defamatory comments made by an unidentified party on one of Prodigy's bulletin boards. The court held Prodigy to the strict liability standard normally applied to original publishers of defamatory statements, rejecting Prodigy's claims that it should be held only to the lower "knowledge" standard usually reserved for distributors. The court reasoned that Prodigy acted more like an original publisher than a distributor both because it advertised its practice of controlling content on its service and because it actively screened and edited messages posted on its bulletin boards.

Congress enacted § 230 to remove the disincentives to self-regulation created by the *Stratton Oakmont* decision. Under that court's holding, computer service providers who regulated the dissemination of offensive material on their services risked subjecting themselves to liability, because such regulation cast the service provider in the role of a publisher. Fearing that the specter of liability would therefore deter service providers from blocking and screening offensive material, Congress enacted § 230's broad immunity "to remove disincentives for the development and utilization of blocking and filtering technologies that empower parents to restrict their children's access to objectionable or inappropriate online material." 47 U.S.C. § 230(b)(4). In line with this purpose, § 230 forbids the imposition of publisher liability on a service provider for the exercise of its editorial and self-regulatory functions.

B

Zeran argues, however, that the § 230 immunity eliminates only publisher liability, leaving distributor liability intact. Publishers can be held liable for defamatory statements contained in their works even absent proof that they had specific knowledge of the statement's inclusion. According to Zeran, interactive computer service providers like AOL are normally considered instead to be distributors, like traditional news vendors or book sellers. Distributors cannot be held liable for defamatory statements contained in the materials they distribute unless it is proven at a minimum that they have actual knowledge of the defamatory statements upon which liability is predicated.

Because of the difference between these two forms of liability, Zeran contends that the term "distributor" carries a legally distinct meaning from the term "publisher." Accordingly, he asserts that Congress' use of only the term "publisher" in § 230 indicates a purpose to immunize service providers only from publisher liability. He argues that distributors are left unprotected by § 230 and, therefore, his suit should be permitted to proceed against AOL. We disagree. Assuming arguendo that Zeran has satisfied the requirements for imposition of distributor liability, this theory of liability is merely a subset, or a species, of publisher liability, and is therefore also foreclosed by § 230.

Our view that Zeran's complaint treats AOL as a publisher is reinforced because AOL is cast in the same position as the party who originally posted the offensive messages. According to Zeran's logic, AOL is legally at fault because it communicated to third parties an allegedly defamatory statement. This is precisely the theory under which the original poster of the offensive messages would be found liable. If the original party is considered a publisher of the offensive messages, Zeran certainly cannot attach liability to AOL under the same theory without conceding that AOL too must be treated as a publisher of the statements.

Zeran next contends that interpreting § 230 to impose liability on service providers with knowledge of defamatory content on their services is consistent with the statutory purposes outlined in Part IIA. Zeran fails, however, to understand the practical implications of notice liability in the interactive computer service context. Liability upon notice would defeat the dual purposes advanced by § 230 of the CDA. Like the strict liability imposed by the *Stratton Oakmont* court, liability upon notice reinforces service providers' incentives to restrict speech and abstain from self-regulation.

If computer service providers were subject to distributor liability, they would face potential liability each time they receive notice of a potentially defamatory statement — from any party, concerning any message. Whenever one was displeased with the speech of another party conducted over an interactive computer service, the offended party could simply "notify" the relevant service provider, claiming the information to be legally defamatory. In light of the vast amount of speech communicated through interactive computer services, these notices could produce an impossible burden for service providers, who would be faced with ceaseless choices of suppressing controversial speech or sustaining prohibitive liability. Because the probable effects of distributor liability on the vigor of Internet speech and on service provider self-regulation are directly contrary to § 230's statutory purposes, we will not assume that Congress intended to leave liability upon notice intact.

For the foregoing reasons, we affirm the judgment of the district court.

Notes and Questions

1. Knowledge Requirement. The court held that AOL was immune, even after Zeran had given it specific notice of the false nature of the postings. Section 230 immunity holds, according to the court, even if the service provider has the specific knowledge that would, under § 512, be sufficient for copyright liability. AOL did not claim it could not take down the offending posts more quickly or prevent new posts from occurring.

2. A Direct Defamation Action. AOL's immunity under § 230 would not protect the original poster, and Zeran could bring a defamation action against them. But the internet makes such individuals difficult to find and prosecute in many instances. In theory, a website that allows comments to be posted can log the IP address from which the content is being posted, and a plaintiff can then seek the identity of the customer who used that IP address from the ISP that controls the address. But websites are not legally required to log the IP addresses of posters, and some websites intentionally do not (in order to protect the anonymity of their users). Moreover, the use of proxy servers and other techniques may allow a user to generate an IP address that would not be traceable to them.

3. The Value of Anonymity. Cases like *Zeran* (and even more cases such as the *Backpage* case below) make it easy to see the downside of anonymity on the internet. But anonymity can also protect those who post unpopular opinions that are not defamatory (because either true or at least contestable)—and those who criticize the government or the powerful. As you read the additional cases, think about whether we can address the downside without eliminating the benefits.

4. Moderation. Do you think that the court should or would have reached a different result if AOL had a practice of moderating—perhaps even one that tried to impose standards of civility and to pull out content that was questionably false or constituted personal attacks (as these posts would seem to be on their face)? Section 230 says that a provider is not a publisher even if it engages in some moderation of user-generated content.

§ 15.B. Attributing Authorship: The Problem of Joint or Separate Production

Section 230's core is protection for the online service provider's posting of user-generated content (and the moderation or editing of such user-generated content). Frequently, however, a site or service will be engaged with the content as well, either through structuring user submissions or commenting on user submissions. In such circumstances, the scope of § 230 is tested, for the online service provider might be the speaker or author itself, not merely a publisher.

Fair Housing Council of San Fernando Valley v. Roommates.com, LLC

521 F.3d 1157 (9th Cir. 2008) (en banc)

Opinion for the court filed by Chief Circuit Judge KOZINSKI, in which Circuit Judges REINHARDT, SILVERMAN, W. FLETCHER, FISHER, PAEZ, M. SMITH, JR. and N. SMITH concur. Opinion concurring in part and dissenting in part filed by Circuit Judge McKEOWN, in which Circuit Judges RYMER and BEA concur.

KOZINSKI, Chief Judge:

We plumb the depths of the immunity provided by section 230 of the Communications Decency Act of 1996 (CDA).

Facts

Defendant Roommate.com, LLC (Roommate)[2] operates a website designed to match people renting out spare rooms with people looking for a place to live. At the time of the district court's disposition, Roommate's website featured approximately 150,000 active listings and received around a million page views a day. Roommate seeks to profit by collecting revenue from advertisers and subscribers.

Before subscribers can search listings or post housing opportunities on Roommate's website, they must create profiles, a process that requires them to answer a series of questions. In addition to requesting basic information—such as name, location and email address—Roommate requires each subscriber to disclose his sex, sexual orientation and whether he would bring children to a household. Each subscriber must also describe his preferences in roommates with respect to the same three criteria: sex, sexual orientation and whether they will bring children to the household. The site also encourages subscribers to provide "Additional Comments" describing themselves and their desired roommate in an open-ended essay. After a new subscriber completes the application, Roommate assembles his answers into a "profile page." The profile page displays the subscriber's pseudonym, his description and his preferences, as divulged through answers to Roommate's questions.

Subscribers can choose between two levels of service: Those using the site's free service level can create their own personal profile page, search the profiles of others and send personal email messages. They can also receive periodic emails from Roommate, informing them of available housing opportunities matching their preferences. Subscribers who pay a monthly fee also gain the ability to read emails from other users, and to view other subscribers' "Additional Comments."

The Fair Housing Councils of the San Fernando Valley and San Diego (Councils) sued Roommate in federal court, alleging that Roommate's business violates

2. [The court uses Roommate.com and Roommate in the opinion, even though the party is Roommates.com in the case title—Eds.]

the federal Fair Housing Act (FHA), 42 U.S.C. § 3601 et seq., and California housing discrimination laws. Councils claim that Roommate is effectively a housing broker doing online what it may not lawfully do off-line. The district court held that Roommate is immune under section 230 of the CDA, 47 U.S.C. § 230(c), and dismissed the federal claims without considering whether Roommate's actions violated the FHA.

Analysis

Section 230 of the CDA immunizes providers of interactive computer services against liability arising from content created by third parties: "No provider . . . of an interactive computer service shall be treated as the publisher or speaker of any information provided by another information content provider." 47 U.S.C. § 230(c). This grant of immunity applies only if the interactive computer service provider is not also an "information content provider," which is defined as someone who is "responsible, in whole or in part, for the creation or development of" the offending content. *Id.* § 230(f)(3).

A website operator can be both a service provider and a content provider: If it passively displays content that is created entirely by third parties, then it is only a service provider with respect to that content. But as to content that it creates itself, or is "responsible, in whole or in part" for creating or developing, the website is also a content provider. Thus, a website may be immune from liability for some of the content it displays to the public but be subject to liability for other content.

In passing section 230, Congress sought to spare interactive computer services this grim choice by allowing them to perform some editing on user-generated content without thereby becoming liable for all defamatory or otherwise unlawful messages that they didn't edit or delete. In other words, Congress sought to immunize the *removal* of user-generated content, not the *creation* of content: "[S]ection [230] provides 'Good Samaritan' protections from civil liability for providers . . . of an interactive computer service for actions to *restrict* . . . access to objectionable online material. One of the specific purposes of this section is to overrule *Stratton-Oakmont*[sic] *v. Prodigy* and any other similar decisions which have treated such providers . . . as publishers or speakers of content that is not their own *because they have restricted access* to objectionable material." H.R. Rep. No. 104–458 (1996) (Conf. Rep.), *as reprinted in* 1996 U.S.C.C.A.N. 10 (emphasis added).

With this backdrop in mind, we examine three specific functions performed by Roommate that are alleged to violate the Fair Housing Act and California law.

1. Councils first argue that the questions Roommate poses to prospective subscribers during the registration process violate the Fair Housing Act and the analogous California law. Councils allege that requiring subscribers to disclose their sex, family status and sexual orientation "indicates" an intent to discriminate against them, and thus runs afoul of both the FHA and state law.

Roommate created the questions and choice of answers, and designed its website registration process around them. Therefore, Roommate is undoubtedly the "information content provider" as to the questions and can claim no immunity for posting them on its website, or for forcing subscribers to answer them as a condition of using its services.

Councils also claim that requiring subscribers to answer the questions as a condition of using Roommate's services unlawfully "cause[s]" subscribers to make a "statement . . . with respect to the sale or rental of a dwelling that indicates [a] preference, limitation, or discrimination," in violation of 42 U.S.C. § 3604(c). The CDA does not grant immunity for inducing third parties to express illegal preferences. Roommate's own acts — posting the questionnaire and requiring answers to it — are entirely its doing and thus section 230 of the CDA does not apply to them. Roommate is entitled to no immunity.

2. Councils also charge that Roommate's development and display of subscribers' discriminatory preferences is unlawful. Roommate publishes a "profile page" for each subscriber on its website. The page describes the client's personal information — such as his sex, sexual orientation and whether he has children — as well as the attributes of the housing situation he seeks. The content of these pages is drawn directly from the registration process: For example, Roommate requires subscribers to specify, using a drop-down menu provided by Roommate, whether they are "Male" or "Female" and then displays that information on the profile page. Roommate also requires subscribers who are listing available housing to disclose whether there are currently "Straight male(s)," "Gay male(s)," "Straight female(s)" or "Lesbian(s)" living in the dwelling. Subscribers who are seeking housing must make a selection from a drop-down menu, again provided by Roommate, to indicate whether they are willing to live with "Straight or gay" males, only with "Straight" males, only with "Gay" males or with "No males." Similarly, Roommate requires subscribers listing housing to disclose whether there are "Children present" or "Children not present" and requires housing seekers to say "I will live with children" or "I will not live with children." Roommate then displays these answers, along with other information, on the subscriber's profile page. This information is obviously included to help subscribers decide which housing opportunities to pursue and which to bypass. In addition, Roommate itself uses this information to channel subscribers away from listings where the individual offering housing has expressed preferences that aren't compatible with the subscriber's answers.

The dissent tilts at windmills when it shows, quite convincingly, that Roommate's *subscribers* are information content providers who create the profiles by picking among options and providing their own answers. There is no disagreement on this point. But, the fact that users are information content providers does not preclude Roommate from *also* being an information content provider by helping "develop" at least "in part" the information in the profiles. As we explained in Batzel v. Smith, 333 F.3d 1018, 1033 (9th Cir. 2003), the party responsible for putting information online may be subject to liability, even if the information originated with a user.

Here, the part of the profile that is alleged to offend the Fair Housing Act and state housing discrimination laws — the information about sex, family status and sexual orientation — is provided by subscribers in response to Roommate's questions, which they cannot refuse to answer if they want to use defendant's services. By requiring subscribers to provide the information as a condition of accessing its service, and by providing a limited set of pre-populated answers, Roommate becomes much more than a passive transmitter of information provided by others; it becomes the developer, at least in part, of that information. And section 230 provides immunity only if the interactive computer service does not "creat[e] or develop[]" the information "in whole or in part." *See* 47 U.S.C. § 230(f)(3).

Similarly, Roommate is not entitled to CDA immunity for the operation of its search system, which filters listings, or of its email notification system, which directs emails to subscribers according to discriminatory criteria. Roommate designed its search system so it would steer users based on the preferences and personal characteristics that Roommate itself forces subscribers to disclose. If Roommate has no immunity for asking the discriminatory questions, as we concluded above, it can certainly have no immunity for using the answers to the unlawful questions to limit who has access to housing.

It's true that the broadest sense of the term "develop" could include the functions of an ordinary search engine — indeed, just about any function performed by a website. But to read the term so broadly would defeat the purposes of section 230 by swallowing up every bit of the immunity that the section otherwise provides. At the same time, reading the exception for co-developers as applying only to content that originates entirely with the website — as the dissent would seem to suggest — ignores the words "development . . . in part" in the statutory passage "creation *or development* in whole *or in part*." 47 U.S.C. § 230(f)(3) (emphasis added). We believe that both the immunity for passive conduits and the exception for co-developers must be given their proper scope and, to that end, we interpret the term "development" as referring not merely to augmenting the content generally, but to materially contributing to its alleged unlawfulness. In other words, a website helps to develop unlawful content, and thus falls within the exception to section 230, if it contributes materially to the alleged illegality of the conduct.

In an abundance of caution, and to avoid the kind of misunderstanding the dissent seems to encourage, we offer a few examples to elucidate what does and does not amount to "development" under section 230 of the Communications Decency Act: If an individual uses an ordinary search engine to query for a "white roommate," the search engine has not contributed to any alleged unlawfulness in the individual's conduct; providing *neutral* tools to carry out what may be unlawful or illicit searches does not amount to "development" for purposes of the immunity exception. A dating website that requires users to enter their sex, race, religion and marital status through drop-down menus, and that provides means for users to search along the same lines, retains its CDA immunity insofar as it does not contribute to any alleged illegality; this immunity is retained even if the website is sued for libel based on these characteristics because the website would not have contributed materially to any alleged defamation. Similarly, a housing website that allows users to specify whether they will or will not receive emails by means of *user-defined* criteria might help some users exclude email from other users of a particular race or sex. However, that website would be immune, so long as it does not require the use of discriminatory criteria. A website operator who edits user-created content — such as by correcting spelling, removing obscenity or trimming for length — retains his immunity for any illegality in the user-created content, provided that the edits are unrelated to the illegality. However, a website operator who edits in a manner that contributes to the alleged illegality — such as by removing the word "not" from a user's message reading "[Name] did *not* steal the artwork" in order to transform an innocent message into a libelous one — is directly involved in the alleged illegality and thus not immune.

Here, Roommate's connection to the discriminatory filtering process is direct and palpable: Roommate designed its search and email systems to limit the listings available to subscribers based on sex, sexual orientation and presence of children. Roommate selected the criteria used to hide listings, and Councils allege that the act of hiding certain listings is itself unlawful under the Fair Housing Act, which prohibits brokers from steering clients in accordance with discriminatory preferences. We need not decide the merits of Councils' claim to hold that Roommate is sufficiently involved with the design and operation of the search and email systems — which are engineered to limit access to housing on the basis of the protected characteristics elicited by the registration process — so as to forfeit any immunity to which it was otherwise entitled under section 230.

3. Councils finally argue that Roommate should be held liable for the discriminatory statements displayed in the "Additional Comments" section of profile pages. At the end of the registration process, on a separate page from the other registration steps, Roommate prompts subscribers to "tak[e] a moment to personalize your profile by writing a paragraph or two describing yourself and what you are looking for in a roommate." The subscriber is presented with a blank text box, in which he can type as much or as little about himself as he wishes. Such essays are visible only to paying subscribers.

Subscribers provide a variety of provocative, and often very revealing, answers. The contents range from subscribers who "[p]ref[er] white Male roommates" or require that "[t]he person applying for the room MUST be a BLACK GAY MALE" to those who are "NOT looking for black muslims." Some common themes are a desire to live without "drugs, kids or animals" or "smokers, kids or druggies," while a few subscribers express more particular preferences, such as preferring to live in a home free of "psychos or anyone on mental medication." Some subscribers are just looking for someone who will get along with their significant other.

Roommate publishes these comments as written. It does not provide any specific guidance as to what the essay should contain, nor does it urge subscribers to input discriminatory preferences. Roommate is not responsible, in whole or in part, for the development of this content, which comes entirely from subscribers and is passively displayed by Roommate. Without reviewing every essay, Roommate would have no way to distinguish unlawful discriminatory preferences from perfectly legitimate statements. Nor can there be any doubt that this information was tendered to Roommate for publication online. This is precisely the kind of situation for which section 230 was designed to provide immunity.

The fact that Roommate encourages subscribers to provide *something* in response to the prompt is not enough to make it a "develop[er]" of the information under the common-sense interpretation of the term we adopt today. It is entirely consistent with Roommate's business model to have subscribers disclose as much about themselves and their preferences as they are willing to provide. But Roommate does not tell subscribers what kind of information they should or must include as "Additional Comments," and certainly does not encourage or enhance any discriminatory content created by users. Its simple, generic prompt does not make it a developer of the information posted.

* * *

In light of our determination that the CDA does not provide immunity to Roommate for all of the content of its website and email newsletters, we remand for the district court to determine in the first instance whether the alleged actions for which Roommate is not immune violate the Fair Housing Act, 42 U.S.C. § 3604(c).

REVERSED in part, VACATED in part, AFFIRMED in part and REMANDED.

McKEOWN, Circuit Judge, with whom RYMER and BEA, Circuit Judges, join, concurring in part and dissenting in part:

The majority's unprecedented expansion of liability for Internet service providers threatens to chill the robust development of the Internet that Congress envisioned. The majority condemns Roommate's "search system," a function that is the heart of interactive service providers. My concern is not an empty Chicken Little "sky is falling" alert. By exposing every interactive service provider to liability for sorting, searching, and utilizing the all too familiar drop-down menus, the majority has dramatically altered the landscape of Internet liability. Instead of the "robust" immunity envisioned by Congress, interactive service providers are left scratching their heads and wondering where immunity ends and liability begins.

Roommate neither "creates" nor "develops" the information that is challenged by the Councils, i.e., the information provided by the users as to their protected characteristics and the preferences expressed as to roommate characteristics. All Roommate does is to provide a form with options for standardized answers. Listing categories such as geographic location, cleanliness, gender and number of occupants, and transmitting to users profiles of other users whose expressed information matches their expressed preferences, can hardly be said to be creating or developing information. Even adding standardized options does not "develop" information. Roommate, with its prompts, is merely "selecting material for publication," which we have stated does not constitute the "development" of information. *Batzel*, 333 F.3d at 1031. The profile is created solely by the user, not the provider of the interactive website. Indeed, without user participation, there is no information at all. The drop-down menu is simply a precategorization of user information before the electronic sorting and displaying that takes place via an algorithm. If a user has identified herself as a non-smoker and another has expressed a preference for a non-smoking roommate, Roommate's sorting and matching of user information are no different than that performed by a generic search engine.

Displaying the prompt "Gender" and offering the list of choices, "Straight male; Gay male; Straight female; Gay female" does not develop the information, "I am a Gay male." The user has identified himself as such and provided that information to Roommate to publish. Thus, the user is the sole creator of that information; no "development" has occurred. In the same vein, presenting the user with a "Preferences" section and drop-down menus of options does not "develop" a user's preference for a non-smoking roommate. As we stated in Carafano v. Metrosplash.com, Inc., the "actual profile 'information' consist[s] of the particular options chosen" by the user, such that Roommate is not "responsible, even in part, for associating certain multiple choice responses with a set of [] characteristics." 339 F.3d 1119, 1124 (9th Cir. 2003).

The majority's definition of "development" epitomizes its consistent collapse of substantive liability with the issue of immunity. Where in the statute does Congress say anything about unlawfulness? Whether Roommate is entitled to immunity for publishing and sorting profiles is wholly distinct from whether Roommate may be liable for violations of the FHA. Immunity has meaning only when there is something to be immune *from,* whether a disease or the violation of a law. It would be nonsense to claim to be immune only from the innocuous. But the majority's immunity analysis is built on substantive liability: to the majority, CDA immunity depends on whether a webhost materially contributed to the unlawfulness of the information. Whether the information at issue is unlawful and whether the webhost has contributed to its unlawfulness are issues analytically independent of the determination of immunity. Grasping at straws to distinguish Roommate from other interactive websites such as Google and Yahoo!, the majority repeatedly gestures to Roommate's potential substantive liability as sufficient reason to disturb its immunity. But our task is to determine whether the question of substantive liability may be reached in the first place.

Applying the plain meaning of "development" to Roommate's sorting and transmitting of third-party information demonstrates that it was not transformed into an "information content provider." In searching, sorting, and transmitting information, Roommate made no changes to the information provided to it by users. Even having notice that users may be using its site to make discriminatory statements is not sufficient to invade Roommate's immunity.

The consequences of the majority's interpretation are far-reaching. Its position will chill speech on the Internet and impede "the continued development of the Internet and other interactive computer services and other interactive media." § 230(b)(1). To the extent the majority strips immunity because of sorting, channeling, and categorizing functions, it guts the heart of § 230(c)(1) immunity. Countless websites operate just like Roommate: they organize information provided by their users into a standardized format, and provide structured searches to help users find information. These sites, and their attendant display, search, and inquiry tools, are an indispensable part of the Internet tool box. Putting a lid on the sorting and searching functions of interactive websites stifles the core of their services.

Notes and Questions

1. No Liability. After remand and further litigation in the District Court, the case returned to the Ninth Circuit, where the court held (in an opinion again written by Judge Kozinski) that Roommate did not fall within the Fair Housing Act because that statute did not apply to shared dwellings. Fair Housing Council of San Fernando Valley v. Roommate.com, LLC, 666 F.3d 1216 (9th Cir. 2012). Thus, while the en banc opinion above held that § 230 liability does not immunize Roommate if it encourages illegal conduct, the court eventually held that its conduct was not illegal under the FHA.

2. Online/Offline Equivalence and Internet Exceptionalism. Even more than *Zeran*, which discusses the traditional "publisher" and "distributor" models, Judge Kozinski's opinion above argued that liability should be the same online as it is offline, and he resolved the case through analogies to offline liability. But § 230 is written only for the internet, and part of the Congress's intent was to create conditions for the internet to develop. Should we have different rules for the internet than we have for offline activities? If those rules were intended, in 1996, to help the internet develop, are they still needed?

3. Joint Development or Inducement? In the court's opinion, was Roommate liable because it had some hand in the development of the content and the content might have been actionable, or was Roommate liable because it specifically encouraged (or induced) actionable content? Is there a difference between these two holdings? For purposes of § 230 liability, consider whether liability in either situation is "publisher" liability. If you think that § 230 might cover both, what about the online version of The New York Times? Or a newspaper published only online? The following case raises the possibility of liability through inducement even more directly.

Jones v. Dirty World Entertainment Recordings LLC

755 F.3d 398 (6th Cir. 2014)

Opinion for the court filed by Circuit Judge GIBBONS, in which Circuit Judges GUY and GRIFFIN concur.

This case presents the issue of whether the Communications Decency Act of 1996 (CDA), 47 U.S.C. § 230, bars the state-law defamation claims of plaintiff-appellee Sarah Jones. Jones was the unwelcome subject of several posts anonymously uploaded to www.TheDirty.com, a popular website operated by defendants-appellants Nik Lamas-Richie and DIRTY WORLD, LLC (Dirty World), and of remarks Richie posted on the site. The website enables users to anonymously upload comments, photographs, and video, which Richie then selects and publishes along with his own distinct, editorial comments. In short, the website is a user-generated tabloid primarily targeting nonpublic figures.

Richie and Dirty World claimed that § 230(c)(1) barred these claims. The district court rejected this argument. The case was submitted to a jury, twice. The first trial ended in a mistrial upon a joint motion. The second trial resulted in a verdict in favor of Jones for $38,000 in compensatory damages and $300,000 in punitive damages.

Jones was found to be the object of defamatory content published on a user-generated, online tabloid; however, the judgment in her favor cannot stand. Under the CDA, Richie and Dirty World were neither the creators nor the developers of the challenged defamatory content that was published on the website. Jones's tort claims are grounded on the statements of another content provider yet seek to impose liability on Dirty World and Richie as if they were the publishers or speakers of those statements. Section 230(c)(1) therefore bars Jones's claims. Accordingly, we vacate the judgment in favor of Jones.

I

Richie is currently employed as the manager of DIRTY WORLD, LLC (Dirty World), which owns and operates the website www.TheDirty.com. The site then adopted a geographically neutral name—www.TheDirty.com. The website receives approximately six hundred thousand visits each day and eighteen million visits each month.

As the website grew, its focus and format changed. In the beginning, Richie created nearly all the content on the site, and users could not directly upload content. This is no longer true. For the past several years and currently, users of the site, who colloquially refer to themselves as "The Dirty Army," may submit "dirt"—*i.e.*, content that may include text, photographs, or video about any subject. Users may also post comments about the content submitted by others. The vast majority of the content appearing on www.TheDirty.com is comprised of submissions uploaded directly by third-party users.

The content submission form instructs users to "Tell us what's happening. Remember to tell us who, what, when, where, why." The content submission form requires users to submit a title and category for their submission as well as their city or college for indexing. Submissions appear on the website as though they were authored by a single, anonymous author—"THE DIRTY ARMY." This eponymous introduction is automatically added to every post that Richie receives from a third-party user. Many, but not all, of the submissions and commentaries appearing on the website relate to stories, news, and gossip about local individuals who are not public figures. The site receives thousands of new submissions each day. Richie or his staff selects and edits approximately 150 to 200 submissions for publication each day. The editing done to published submissions only consists of deletion. Richie or his staff briefly reviews each submission selected for publication to ensure that nudity, obscenity, threats of violence, profanity, and racial slurs are removed. Richie typically adds a short, one-line comment about the post with "some sort of humorous or satirical observation." Richie, however, does not materially change, create, or modify any part of the user-generated submission, nor does he fact-check submissions for accuracy. Apart from his clearly denoted comments appended at the end of each submission, which appear in bold-face text and are signed "-nik," Richie does not create any of the posts that appear on www.TheDirty.com. The bold-face text and signature are designed to distinguish editorial remarks from third-party submissions. Comments that appear in bold face and are signed "-nik" are only written and published by Richie.

Sarah Jones is a resident of northern Kentucky. Jones was a teacher at Dixie Heights High School in Edgewood, Kentucky, and a member of the Cincinnati Ben-Gals, the cheerleading squad for the Cincinnati Bengals professional football team. From October 2009 to January 2010, Jones was the subject of several submissions posted by anonymous users on www.TheDirty.com and of editorial remarks posted by Richie.

First, on October 27, 2009, a visitor to www.TheDirty.com submitted two photographs of Jones and a male companion and the following post:

> THE DIRTY ARMY: Nik, this is Sara J, Cincinnati Bengal Cheerleader. She's been spotted around town lately with the infamous Shayne Graham. She has also slept with every other Bengal Football player. This girl is a teacher too!! You would think with Graham's paycheck he could attract something a little easier on the eyes Nik!

Appearing directly beneath this post, Richie added:

> Everyone in Cincinnati knows this kicker is a Sex Addict. It is no secret . . . he can't even keep relationships because his Red Rocket has freckles that need to be touched constantly. — nik

Jones requested that the post be removed. Richie informed Jones that the post would not be removed.

Second, on December 7, 2009, a visitor submitted a photograph of Jones and the following post:

> THE DIRTY ARMY: Nik, here we have Sarah J, captain cheerleader of the playoff bound cinci bengals.. Most ppl see Sarah has [*sic*] a gorgeous cheerleader AND highschool teacher.. yes she's also a teacher.. but what most of you don't know is.. Her ex Nate.. cheated on her with over 50 girls in 4 yrs.. in that time he tested positive for Chlamydia Infection and Gonorrhea.. so im sure Sarah also has both.. whats worse is he brags about doing sarah in the gym.. football field.. her class room at the school she teaches at DIXIE Heights.

Appearing directly after this post, Richie remarked: "Why are all high school teachers freaks in the sack?nik"

Third, on December 9, 2009, a visitor submitted another photograph of Jones and a male companion and the following post:

> THE DIRTY ARMY: Nik, ok you all seen the past posting of the dirty Bengals cheerleader/teacher . . . well here is her main man Nate. Posted a few pics of the infected couple. Oh an for everyone saying sarah is so gorgeous check her out in these non photoshopped pics.

Appearing directly after this post, Richie added:

> Cool tribal tat man. For a second yesterday I was jealous of those high school kids for having a cheerleader teacher, but not anymore. — nik

Jones sent Richie over twenty-seven emails, pleading for Richie to remove these posts from the website, to no avail. Jones's father similarly wrote to Richie, also to no avail. She then sought legal help, and her attorney informed Richie that if the posts were not removed by December 14, 2009, Jones would file suit. The posts were not removed. [T]he lawsuit sparked national media attention, which precipitated further postings on www.TheDirty.com regarding Jones [omitted here].

[Jones sued Dirty World and Richie,] alleging claims of defamation, libel per se, false light, and intentional inflection of emotional distress. [The jury] returned a verdict in favor of Jones for $38,000 in compensatory damages and $300,000 in punitive damages.

II

A

The only claim that Dirty World and Richie raise on appeal is entitlement to immunity under the CDA.

B

Section 230(c)(1)'s grant of immunity is not without limits. It applies only to the extent that an interactive computer service provider is not also the information content provider of the content at issue. An "information content provider" is defined as "any person or entity that is responsible, in whole or in part, for the creation or development of information provided through the Internet or any other interactive computer service." 47 U.S.C. § 230(f)(3). A website operator can simultaneously act as both a service provider and a content provider. If a website displays content that is created entirely by third parties, then it is only a service provider with respect to that content — and thus is immune from claims predicated on that content. But if a website operator is in part responsible for the creation or development of content, then it is an information content provider as to that content — and is not immune from claims predicated on it. In short, immunity under the CDA depends on the pedigree of the content at issue.

Aware of this limit on § 230 immunity, courts have recognized that § 230 bars a claim if (1) the defendant asserting immunity is an interactive computer service provider, (2) the particular information at issue was provided by another information content provider, and (3) the claim seeks to treat the defendant as a publisher or speaker of that information. By contrast, a defendant is not entitled to protection from claims based on the publication of information if the defendant is "responsible, in whole or in part, for the creation or development of [the] information." 47 U.S.C. § 230(f)(3).

C

This case turns on how narrowly or capaciously the statutory term "development" in § 230(f)(3) is read. The district court held, and Jones maintains on appeal, that Dirty World and Richie are not immune under the CDA because Dirty World and Richie are information content providers with respect to the information underlying Jones's defamation claims because they *developed* that information. The district court set forth a test to measure whether a defendant is responsible for the development of the information grounding a plaintiff's state tort claim. According to the district court, "a website owner who intentionally encourages illegal or actionable third-party postings to which he adds his own comments ratifying or adopting the posts becomes a 'creator' or 'developer' of that content and is not entitled to immunity." Jones v. Dirty World Entertainment Recordings LLC, 965 F. Supp. 2d 818, 821 (E.D. Ky. 2013).

[T]his court has neither expounded the meaning of "development" in § 230(f)(3) nor addressed the scope of immunity that § 230(c) provides. Nevertheless, drawing inferences from these cases, it is not difficult to identify an overly inclusive and exclusive reading of "development." An overly inclusive interpretation of "development" in § 230(f)(3) would posit that a website operator is responsible for the development of content created by a third party merely by displaying or allowing access to it. But to read the term so broadly would defeat the purposes of the CDA and swallow the core immunity that § 230(c) provides for the "exercise of a publisher's traditional editorial functions." Zeran v. AOL 129 F.3d 327, 330 (4th Cir. 1997). Our recognition that the CDA affords immunity forecloses this overbroad reading of "development."

By contrast, an overly exclusive interpretation of "development" would exclude all the publishing, editorial, and screening functions of a website operator from the set of actions that the term denotes. Some courts have implied this interpretation, however. We have maintained that, despite the CDA, *some* state tort claims will lie against website operators acting in their publishing, editorial, or screening capacities.

Decisions from our sister circuits provide a workable measure of "development" that not only preserves the broad immunity the CDA provides for website operators' exercise of traditional publisher functions but also highlights the limited circumstances under which exercises of those functions are not protected. The leading case is Fair Housing Council of San Fernando Valley v. Roommates.com, LLC, 521 F.3d 1157 (9th Cir. 2008) (en banc). [T]he court applied a specific measure of development:

> [W]e interpret the term "development" as referring not merely to augmenting the content generally, but *to materially contributing to its alleged unlawfulness*. In other words, a website helps to develop unlawful content, and thus falls within the exception to section 230, if it contributes materially to the alleged illegality of the conduct.

Id. at 1167–68. A material contribution to the alleged illegality of the content does not mean merely taking action that is necessary to the display of allegedly illegal content. Rather, it means being responsible for what makes the displayed content allegedly unlawful.

D

Consistent with our sister circuits, we adopt the material contribution test to determine whether a website operator is "responsible, in whole or in part, for the creation or development of [allegedly tortious] information." 47 U.S.C. § 230(f)(3). And we expressly decline to adopt the definition of "development" set forth by the district court.

The district court read the foregoing decisions, identified *Roommates* as the guiding precedent, but derived a different rule. In its memorandum opinion explaining the denial of Dirty World's and Richie's Rule 50 motion, the district court gave two formulations of a rule providing when the CDA does not bar a plaintiff's claim. First, the district court said that a "website owner who intentionally encourages illegal or actionable third-party postings to which he adds his own comments ratifying or adopting the posts becomes a 'creator' or 'developer' of that content and is not entitled to immunity." *Jones,* 965 F. Supp. 2d at 821. Second, in a different formulation, the district court said that "if . . . [website] owners, as in the instant case, invite invidious postings, elaborate on them with comments of their own, and call upon others to respond in kind, the immunity does not apply." *Id.* at 822.

We do not adopt the district court's encouragement test of immunity under the CDA. [A]n encouragement test would inflate the meaning of "development" to the point of eclipsing the immunity from publisher-liability that Congress established. Many websites not only allow but also actively invite and encourage users to post particular types of content. Some of this content will be unwelcome to others—e.g., unfavorable reviews of consumer products and services, allegations of price gouging, complaints of fraud on consumers, reports of bed bugs, collections of cease-and-desist notices relating to online speech. And much of this content is commented upon by the website operators who make the forum available. Indeed, much of it is "adopted" by website operators, gathered into reports, and republished online. Under an encouragement test of development, these websites would lose the immunity under the CDA and be subject to hecklers' suits aimed at the publisher. Moreover, under the district court's rule, courts would then have to decide what constitutes "encouragement" in order to determine immunity under the CDA—a concept that is certainly more difficult to define and apply than the Ninth Circuit's material contribution test. Congress envisioned an uninhibited, robust, and wide-open internet, *see* §§ 230(a)(1)–(5), but the muddiness of an encouragement rule would cloud that vision.

The district court also suggested that when an interactive computer service provider adds commentary to third-party content that "ratifies or adopts" that content, then the provider becomes a "creator" or "developer" of that content and is not entitled to the CDA's protection. An adoption or ratification theory, however, is not only inconsistent with the material contribution standard of "development" but also abuses the concept of responsibility. A website operator cannot be responsible for what makes another party's statement actionable by commenting on that statement *post hoc*. To be sure, a website operator's previous comments on prior postings could encourage subsequent invidious postings, but that loose understanding of responsibility collapses into the encouragement measure of "development," which we reject. [T]he adoption theory of "development" would undermine the CDA for the same reasons as an encouragement theory.

III

We now apply the material contribution measure of "development" to the facts of this case. Jones's defamation claims target the statements that were posted by a third party on October 27 and December 7, 2009. Because Dirty World and Richie did not materially contribute to the illegality of those statements, the CDA bars Jones's claims.

Dirty World and Richie did not author the statements at issue; however, they did select the statements for publication. But Richie and Dirty World cannot be found to have materially contributed to the defamatory content of the statements posted on October 27 and December 7, 2009, simply because those posts were selected for publication. Nor can they be found to have materially contributed to the defamatory content through the decision not to remove the posts.

Further, Richie's comment on the December 7 post—*viz.*, "Why are all high school teachers freaks in the sack?"—although absurd, did not materially contribute to the defamatory content of the statements uploaded on October 27 and December 7, 2009. Richie's remark was made after each of the defamatory postings had already been displayed. It would break the concepts of responsibility and material contribution to hold Richie responsible for the defamatory content of speech because he later commented on that speech. Although ludicrous, Richie's remarks did not materially contribute to the defamatory content of the posts appearing on the website. More importantly, the CDA bars claims lodged against website operators for their editorial functions, such as the posting of comments concerning third-party posts, so long as those comments are not themselves actionable.

To be sure, Richie was an information content provider as to his comment on the December 7 post. But Jones did not allege that *Richie's* comments were defamatory. And the district court did not hold that Richie's comments were themselves tortious.

Because (1) the defendants are interactive service providers, (2) the statements at issue were provided by another information content provider, and (3) Jones's claim seeks to treat the defendants as a publisher or speaker of those statements, the CDA bars Jones's claims.

IV

We note that the broad immunity furnished by the CDA does not necessarily leave persons who are the objects of anonymously posted, online, defamatory content without a remedy. In this case, Jones conceded that she did not attempt to recover from the person(s) whose comments Richie elected to publish. She conceded that she did not attempt to subpoena Richie or Dirty World to discover who authored the defamatory posts. Instead, she sued Dirty World and Richie. But, under the CDA, Jones cannot seek her recovery from the online publisher where that publisher did not materially contribute to the tortious content. Congress envisioned a free and open internet, *see* §§ 230(a)(1)–(5), and the immunity provision of § 230(c)(1), which subverts common-law publisher-liability, serves that purpose. While some exercises of the considerable freedom that Congress allowed online publishers are regrettable, freedom and its uses are distinct. Congress enacted § 230(c)(1) to preserve a free internet, and that enactment resolves this case.

For the foregoing reasons, we vacate the judgment in favor of Jones and reverse the district court's denial of Dirty World's and Richie's motion for judgment as a matter of law with instructions to enter judgment as a matter of law in their favor.

Notes and Questions

1. Inducement Liability. Do you agree with the court's dismissing the plaintiff's argument that the inducement of the posts creates a separate ground for liability? As we saw in Chapter 14, the Supreme Court has held that "inducement" of a copyright violation will give rise to secondary liability for copyright infringement. Metro-Goldwyn-Mayer Studios, Inc. v. Grokster, Ltd., 545 U.S. 913 (2005). Was Jones seeking to hold the website liable for publication or for a separate act of inducing the publication? Wasn't Jones correct that inducing the development of content that defames and invades privacy is different from the publication of the content?

2. Analogies (Redux). As discussed in *Roommates*, defamation law imposes liabilities on newspapers and broadcasters because the content that they share is deemed to be their own content. Indeed, in defamation law, repeating a defamatory statement is its own publication of the statement. When Richie commented on the posted statements, wasn't he in fact adopting or endorsing their content? The court said no and therefore treated Jones's injury as arising only from the posts. But even if the better analogy is to a distributor such as a bookstore, Richie's comments showed that he knew what was being said in a post and, while he might not have known that it was defamatory, he was certainly put on notice that it might be. Should that affect the analysis?

3. Section 230 Policy? What are we trying to protect in § 230? The argument, discussed at length in *Zeran*, is that § 230 immunity is necessary to create the hosting and distribution services that revolutionize the ability of individuals to speak. Congress chose to protect hosts and other passive conduits, but also to protect them when they took down problematic material. Did Dirty World fit this model? Recall that Dirty World was affirmatively selecting a small number of posts, not hosting all that users submit. Isn't Dirty World's incentive (and business model) to select content most likely to draw an audience? And isn't that highly likely to be the most problematic content? Should that matter for the scope of § 230 immunity?

4. Creating Safer Experiences? Of course, while some online service providers might build their business models around the sharing of the kind of content in Dirty World, others might seek to create a content-sharing site that does not include such content. Or, at a minimum, an online service provider, even if it does not moderate postings in the first instance, might want to respond to complaints about content found on its site. The next case asks whether and how the law might address a provider's response to complaints.

Barnes v. Yahoo!, Inc.

570 F.3d 1096 (9th Cir. 2009)

Opinion for the court filed by Circuit Judge O'SCANNLAIN, in which Circuit Judges GRABER and CALLAHAN concur.

We must decide whether the Communications Decency Act of 1996 protects an internet service provider from suit where it undertook to remove from its website material harmful to the plaintiff but failed to do so.

I

This case stems from a dangerous, cruel, and highly indecent use of the internet for the apparent purpose of revenge.

In late 2004, Cecilia Barnes broke off a lengthy relationship with her boyfriend. For reasons that are unclear, he responded by posting profiles of Barnes on a website run by Yahoo!, Inc. (Yahoo). According to Yahoo's Member Directory, "[a] public profile is a page with information about you that other Yahoo! members can view. You[r] profile allows you to publicly post information about yourself that you want to share with the world. Many people post their age, pictures, location, and hobbies on their profiles." Through Yahoo's online service, computer users all over the country and the world can view such profiles.

Barnes did not authorize her now former boyfriend to post the profiles, which is hardly surprising considering their content. The profiles contained nude photographs of Barnes and her boyfriend, taken without her knowledge, and some kind of open solicitation, whether express or implied is unclear, to engage in sexual intercourse. The ex-boyfriend then conducted discussions in Yahoo's online "chat rooms," posing as Barnes and directing male correspondents to the fraudulent profiles he had created. The profiles also included the addresses, real and electronic, and telephone number at Barnes' place of employment. Before long, men whom Barnes did not know were peppering her office with emails, phone calls, and personal visits, all in the expectation of sex.

In accordance with Yahoo policy, Barnes mailed Yahoo a copy of her photo ID and a signed statement denying her involvement with the profiles and requesting their removal. One month later, Yahoo had not responded but the undesired advances from unknown men continued; Barnes again asked Yahoo by mail to remove the profiles. Nothing happened. The following month, Barnes sent Yahoo two more mailings. During the same period, a local news program was preparing to broadcast a report on the incident. A day before the initial air date of the broadcast, Yahoo broke its silence; its Director of Communications, a Ms. Osako, called Barnes and asked her to fax directly the previous statements she had mailed. Ms. Osako told Barnes that she would "personally walk the statements over to the division responsible for stopping unauthorized profiles and they would take care of it." Barnes claims to have relied on this statement and took no further action regarding the profiles and the trouble they had caused. Approximately two months passed without word from Yahoo, at which point Barnes filed this lawsuit against Yahoo in Oregon state court. Shortly thereafter, the profiles disappeared from Yahoo's website, apparently never to return.

Barnes' complaint against Yahoo is somewhat unclear, but it appears to allege two causes of action under Oregon law. First, the complaint suggests a tort for the negligent provision or non-provision of services which Yahoo undertook to provide. As Barnes pointed out in her briefs, Oregon has adopted section 323 of the Restatement (Second) of Torts (1965), which describes the elements of this claim. For the sake of brevity, we refer to this tort, which is really a species of negligence, as a "negligent undertaking." Barnes also refers in her complaint and in her briefs to Yahoo's "promise" to remove the indecent profiles and her reliance thereon to her detriment. We construe such references to allege a cause of action under section 90 of the Restatement (Second) of Contracts (1981).

Yahoo contended that section 230(c)(1) of the Communications Decency Act (the Act) renders it immune from liability in this case. *See* 47 U.S.C. § 230(c)(1). The district court granted the motion to dismiss, finding that the Act did in fact protect Yahoo from liability as a matter of law. Barnes timely appealed, claiming that, in the first place, the so-called immunity under section 230(c) did not apply to the cause of action she has brought and that, even if it did, Yahoo did not fit under the terms of such immunity.

II

Barnes did not contest in the district court that Yahoo is a provider of an interactive computer service, and we have no trouble concluding that it qualifies as one. Nor is there any dispute that the "information content"—such as it is—at issue in this case was provided by another "information content provider." The flashpoint in this case is the meaning of the "publisher or speaker" part of subsection (c)(1), and that is where we train our sights.

B

By its terms, then, section (c)(1) only ensures that in certain cases an internet service provider will not be "treated" as the "publisher or speaker" of third-party content for the purposes of another cause of action. The question before us is how to determine when, for purposes of this statute, a plaintiff's theory of liability would treat a defendant as a publisher or speaker of third-party content.

The cause of action most frequently associated with the cases on section 230 is defamation. But "a law's scope often differs from its genesis," Chi. Lawyers' Comm. for Civil Rights under Law, Inc. v. Craigslist, Inc., 519 F.3d 666, 671 (7th Cir. 2008), and the language of the statute does not limit its application to defamation cases.

III

Which leads us to whether Barnes, in her negligent undertaking claim, seeks to treat Yahoo as a "publisher or speaker" of the indecent profiles in order to hold Yahoo liable.

A

The Oregon law tort that Barnes claims Yahoo committed derives from section 323 of the Restatement (Second) of Torts, which states:

> One who undertakes, gratuitously or for consideration, to render services to another which he should recognize as necessary for the protection of the other's person or things, is subject to liability to the other for physical harm resulting from his failure to exercise reasonable care to perform his undertaking, if
>
> (a) his failure to exercise such care increases the risk of such harm, or
>
> (b) the harm is suffered because of the other's reliance upon the undertaking.

Barnes argues that this tort claim would not treat Yahoo as a publisher. She points to her complaint, which acknowledges that although Yahoo "may have had no initial responsibility to act, once [Yahoo,] through its agent, undertook to act, [it] must do so reasonably." According to Barnes, this makes the undertaking, not the publishing or failure to withdraw from publication, the source of liability. Under this theory, Barnes' cause of action would evade the reach of section 230(c) entirely because it treats Yahoo not as a publisher, but rather as one who undertook to perform a service and did it negligently.

We are not persuaded. As we implied above, a plaintiff cannot sue someone for publishing third-party content simply by changing the name of the theory from defamation to negligence. Nor can he or she escape section 230(c) by labeling as a "negligent undertaking" an action that is quintessentially that of a publisher. The word "undertaking," after all, is meaningless without the following verb. That is, one does not merely undertake; one undertakes *to do* something. And what is the undertaking that Barnes alleges Yahoo failed to perform with due care? The removal of the indecent profiles that her former boyfriend posted on Yahoo's website. But removing content is something publishers do, and to impose liability on the basis of such conduct necessarily involves treating the liable party as a publisher of the content it failed to remove. In other words, the duty that Barnes claims Yahoo violated derives from Yahoo's conduct as a publisher—the steps it allegedly took, but later supposedly abandoned, to de-publish the offensive profiles.

B

Barnes argues that, even if subsection 230(c)(1) applies to this tort in a general sense, it does not cover her claim because she is suing Yahoo as a distributor, not as a publisher. This argument asks us to join an ongoing academic debate, which has developed in response to the Fourth Circuit's *Zeran* opinion, on whether "publisher" in subsection 230(c)(1) means only "primary publisher" or both "primary publisher" and "distributor," also known as a "secondary publisher," for purposes of defamation liability. [Distributors are only liable for defamation if they know of the defamation content they are distributing.]

Primary publishers were held to a strict liability standard, whereas secondary publishers were only liable for publishing defamation with actual or constructive knowledge of its defamatory character. Secondary publishers came to be known as distributors.

In our view, however, we need not resolve the dispute at all, because it has little to do with the meaning of the statutory language. As noted above, section 230(c)(1) precludes courts from treating internet service providers as publishers not just for the purposes of defamation law, with its particular distinction between primary and secondary publishers, but in general. The statute does not mention defamation, and we decline to read the principles of defamation law into it. In any event, if the reach of section 230(c)(1) were fastened so tightly to the nuances of defamation law, our *Roommates* opinion, which dealt with a lawsuit under the Fair Housing Act, would simply have declared that the provision did not apply because there was no claim of defamation. We will not engage in an analysis so contrary to the reasoning, and even some of the holding, of our precedent.

C

Leaving no stone unturned, Barnes reminds us that the statutory purpose of [section 230] is to encourage websites affirmatively to police themselves, not to provide an excuse for doing nothing. This argument from statutory purpose has more force to it, because section 230(c) is, after all, captioned "Protection for 'good samaritan' blocking and screening of offensive material." It would indeed be strange for a provision so captioned to provide equal protection as between internet service providers who do nothing and those who attempt to block and screen offensive material.

A closer look at the whole of section 230(c), we believe, makes sense of this apparent contradiction. Subsection (c)(1), by itself, shields from liability all publication decisions, whether to edit, to remove, or to post, with respect to content generated entirely by third parties. Subsection (c)(2), for its part, provides an additional shield from liability, but only for "any action voluntarily taken in good faith to restrict access to or availability of material that the provider ... considers to be obscene ... or otherwise objectionable." § 230(c)(2)(A). Crucially, the persons who can take advantage of this liability shield are not merely those whom subsection (c)(1) already protects, but *any* provider of an interactive computer service. *See* § 230(c)(2). Thus, even those who cannot take advantage of subsection (c)(1), perhaps because they developed, even in part, the content at issue, *see* Fair Housing Council of San Fernando Valley v. Roommates.Com, 521 F.3d 1157, 1162–63 (9th Cir. 2008), can take advantage of subsection (c)(2) if they act to restrict access to the content because they consider it obscene or otherwise objectionable. Additionally, subsection (c)(2) also protects internet service providers from liability not for publishing or speaking, but rather for actions taken to restrict access to obscene or otherwise objectionable content.

Thus, we must reject Barnes' contention that it does violence to the statutory scheme to bar her suit for negligent undertaking. To summarize, we hold that section 230(c)(1) bars Barnes' claim, under Oregon law, for negligent provision of services that Yahoo undertook to provide. The district court properly granted Yahoo's motion to dismiss that cause of action.

IV

As we indicated above, Barnes' complaint could also be read to base liability on section 90 of the Restatement (Second) of Contracts, which describes a theory of recovery often known as promissory estoppel. At oral argument, counsel for Barnes acknowledged that its tort claim might be "recast" in terms of promissory estoppel. We think it might, and in analyzing it as such now we add that liability for breach of promise is different from, and not merely a rephrasing of, liability for negligent undertaking.

B

[W]e inquire whether Barnes' theory of recovery under promissory estoppel would treat Yahoo as a "publisher or speaker" under the Act.

As we explained above, subsection 230(c)(1) precludes liability when the duty the plaintiff alleges the defendant violated derives from the defendant's status or conduct as a publisher or speaker. In a promissory estoppel case, as in any other contract case, the duty the defendant allegedly violated springs from a contract—an enforceable promise—not from any non-contractual conduct or capacity of the defendant. Barnes does not seek to hold Yahoo liable as a publisher or speaker of third-party content, but rather as the counter-party to a contract, as a promisor who has breached.

How does this analysis differ from our discussion of liability for the tort of negligent undertaking? After all, even if Yahoo did make a promise, it promised to take down third-party content from its website, which is quintessential publisher conduct, just as what Yahoo allegedly undertook to do consisted in publishing activity. The difference is that the various torts we referred to above each derive liability from behavior that is identical to publishing or speaking: publishing defamatory material; publishing material that inflicts emotional distress; or indeed attempting to de-publish hurtful material but doing it badly. To undertake a thing, within the meaning of the tort, *is* to do it.

Promising is different because it is not synonymous with the performance of the action promised. That is, whereas one cannot undertake to do something without simultaneously doing it, one can, and often does, promise to do something without actually doing it at the same time. Contract liability here would come not from Yahoo's publishing conduct, but from Yahoo's manifest intention to be legally obligated to do something, which happens to be removal of material from publication. Contract law treats the outwardly manifested intention to create an expectation on the part of another as a legally significant event. That event generates a legal duty distinct from the conduct at hand, be it the conduct of a publisher, of a doctor, or of an overzealous uncle.

Therefore, we conclude that, insofar as Barnes alleges a breach of contract claim under the theory of promissory estoppel, subsection 230(c)(1) of the Act does not preclude her cause of action. Because we have only reviewed the affirmative defense that Yahoo raised in this appeal, we do not reach the question whether Barnes has a viable contract claim or whether Yahoo has an affirmative defense under subsection 230(c)(2) of the Act.

Notes and Questions

1. *Zeran* Redux. If the court here was correct that the online service provider could be sued for an unfulfilled promise to take down the material, could Zeran have made a similar claim? Do you think the *Zeran* court would have embraced that claim?

2. Where Is the Injury? If Barnes was injured by Yahoo's not taking down the material as it promised, that injury arose because of the continued publication of the material. Hence, the crux of the case is still liability for the (continued) publication of the material. Do you agree with the distinction the court is making when it says that liability arises from the promise and not from a step that could be considered publication?

3. What Now? If you are general counsel to an online service provider and you have read this decision, what advice do you give on how it should handle complaints? If a provider says nothing more than "we will check on it," does it face *any* liability for leaving something up or taking something down? In other words, doesn't this decision create an incentive not to respond at all to complaints and not to create terms of service that purport to limit the content that will be hosted?

4. Limits? *Barnes* involved a practice that has become known as "revenge porn." In 2013, laws in only three states expressly addressed the practice, but by 2017 38 states and Washington, D.C. had passed criminal prohibitions. *See* Mary Anne Franks, "Revenge Porn" Reform: A View from the Front Lines, 69 Fla. L. Rev. 1251 (2017). Nevertheless, § 230 continued to protect online service providers that host such content. *Id.* at 1291, 1294. When such an overwhelming consensus exists that the distribution of such speech should be more limited, should courts limit § 230's immunity?

§ 15.C. The Limits of Protecting Bad Content

Section 230 as originally written had two content-based exceptions, stating that it did not affect the enforcement of obscenity or child exploitation statutes. 47 U.S.C. § 230(e)(1). As the internet became more pervasive, parties sought other exceptions to the breadth of § 230. The next case pushes the question of whether § 230's immunity should have any limits.

Doe v. Backpage.com

817 F.3d 12 (1st Cir. 2016)

Opinion for the court filed by Circuit Judge SELYA, in which Circuit Judge BARRON and Associate JUSTICE SOUTER concur.

SELYA, Circuit Judge:

This is a hard case—hard not in the sense that the legal issues defy resolution, but hard in the sense that the law requires that we, like the court below, deny relief to plaintiffs whose circumstances evoke outrage. The result we must reach is rooted in positive law. Congress addressed the right to publish the speech of others in the Information Age when it enacted the Communications Decency Act of 1996 (CDA). *See* 47 U.S.C. § 230. Congress later addressed the need to guard against the evils of sex trafficking when it enacted the Trafficking Victims Protection Reauthorization Act of 2008 (TVPRA), codified as relevant here at 18 U.S.C. §§ 1591, 1595. These laudable legislative efforts do not fit together seamlessly, and this case reflects the tension between them. Striking the balance in a way that we believe is consistent with both congressional intent and the teachings of precedent, we affirm the district court's order of dismissal. The tale follows.

I. Background

Backpage.com provides online classified advertising, allowing users to post advertisements in a range of categories based on the product or service being sold. Among the categories provided is one for "Adult Entertainment," which includes a subcategory labeled "Escorts." The site is differentiated by geographic area, enabling users to target their advertisements and permitting potential customers to see local postings.

This suit involves advertisements posted in the "Escorts" section for three young women—all minors at the relevant times—who claim to have been victims of sex trafficking. Suing pseudonymously, the women allege that Backpage, with an eye to maximizing its profits, engaged in a course of conduct designed to facilitate sex traffickers' efforts to advertise their victims on the website. This strategy, the appellants say, led to their victimization.

Past is prologue. In 2010, a competing website (Craigslist) shuttered its adult advertising section due to concerns about sex trafficking. Spying an opportunity, Backpage expanded its marketing footprint in the adult advertising arena. According to the appellants, the expansion had two aspects. First, Backpage engaged in a campaign to distract attention from its role in sex trafficking by, for example, meeting on various occasions with hierarchs of the National Center for Missing and Exploited Children (NCMEC) and making "false and misleading representations" to the NCMEC and law enforcement regarding its efforts to combat sex trafficking. But this campaign, the appellants suggest, was merely a ruse.

The second aspect of Backpage's expansion strategy involved the deliberate structuring of its website to facilitate sex trafficking. The appellants aver that Backpage selectively removed certain postings made in the "Escorts" section (such as postings made by victim support organizations and law enforcement "sting" advertisements) and tailored its posting requirements to make sex trafficking easier.

In addition, the appellants allege that Backpage's rules and processes governing the content of advertisements are designed to encourage sex trafficking. For example, Backpage does not require phone number verification and permits the posting of phone numbers in alternative formats. There is likewise no e-mail verification, and Backpage provides users with the option to "hide" their e-mail addresses in postings, because Backpage provides message forwarding services and auto-replies on behalf of the advertiser. Photographs uploaded for use in advertisements are shorn of their metadata, thus removing from scrutiny information such as the date, time, and location the photograph was taken. While Backpage's automated filtering system screens out advertisements containing certain prohibited terms, such as "barely legal" and "high school," a failed attempt to enter one of these terms does not prevent the poster from substituting workarounds, such as "brly legal" or "high schl."

The appellants suggest that Backpage profits from having its thumb on the scale in two ways. First, advertisements in the "Adult Entertainment" section are the only ones for which Backpage charges a posting fee. Second, users may pay an additional fee for "Sponsored Ads," which appear on the right-hand side of every page of the "Escorts" section. A "Sponsored Ad" includes a smaller version of the image from the posted advertisement and information about the location and availability of the advertised individual.

Beginning at age 15, each of the appellants was trafficked through advertisements posted on Backpage. Jane Doe # 1 was advertised on Backpage during two periods in 2012 and 2013. She estimates that, as a result, she was raped over 1,000 times. Jane Doe # 2 was advertised on Backpage between 2010 and 2012. She estimates that, as a result, she was raped over 900 times. Jane Doe # 3 was advertised on Backpage from December of 2013 until some unspecified future date. As a result, she was raped on numerous occasions. All of the rapes occurred either in Massachusetts or Rhode Island. Sometimes the sex traffickers posted the advertisements directly and sometimes they forced the victims to post the advertisements.

Typically, each posted advertisement included images of the particular appellant, usually taken by the traffickers (but advertisements for Doe # 3 included some pictures that she herself had taken). Many of the advertisements embodied challenged practices such as anonymous payment for postings, coded terminology meant to refer to underage girls, and altered telephone numbers.

II. Analysis

The appellants, ably represented, have constructed a series of arguments. Those arguments are buttressed by a legion of amici (whose helpful briefs we appreciate). We review the district court's dismissal of the appellants' complaint for failure to state any actionable claim de novo, taking as true the well-pleaded facts and drawing all reasonable inferences in the appellants' favor. In undertaking this canvass, we are not bound by the district court's ratiocination but may affirm the dismissal on any ground apparent from the record. It is through this prism that we evaluate the appellants' asseverational array.

A. Trafficking Claims

The appellants challenge the district court's conclusion that section 230 of the CDA shields Backpage from liability for a course of conduct that allegedly amounts to participation in sex trafficking.

In holding Backpage harmless here, the district court found section 230(c)(1) controlling. Section 230(c)(1) can be broken down into three component parts. It shields conduct if the defendant (1) "is a 'provider or user of an interactive computer service'; (2) the claim is based on 'information provided by another information content provider'; and (3) the claim would treat [the defendant] 'as the publisher or speaker' of that information." Universal Communication Systems, Inc. v. Lycos, Inc., 478 F.3d 413, 418 (1st Cir. 2007) (quoting 47 U.S.C. § 230(c)(1)). The appellants do not allege that Backpage fails to satisfy either of the first two elements. Instead, they confine themselves to the argument that their asserted causes of action do not treat Backpage as the publisher or speaker of the contents of the advertisements through which they were trafficked. It is to this argument that we now turn.

The broad construction accorded to section 230 as a whole has resulted in a capacious conception of what it means to treat a website operator as the publisher or speaker of information provided by a third party. Courts have recognized that "many causes of action might be premised on the publication or speaking of what one might call 'information content.'" Barnes v. Yahoo!, Inc., 570 F.3d 1096, 1101 (9th Cir. 2009). The ultimate question, though, does not depend on the form of the asserted cause of action; rather, it depends on whether the cause of action necessarily requires that the defendant be treated as the publisher or speaker of content provided by another. Thus, courts have invoked the prophylaxis of section 230(c)(1) in connection with a wide variety of causes of action, including housing discrimination, negligence, and securities fraud and cyberstalking.

The appellants have an uphill climb: the TVPRA claims that they assert appear to treat Backpage as the publisher or speaker of the content of the challenged advertisements. After all, the appellants acknowledge in their complaint that the contents of all of the relevant advertisements were provided either by their traffickers or by the appellants themselves (under orders from their traffickers). Since the appellants were trafficked by means of these advertisements, there would be no harm to them but for the content of the postings.

The appellants nonetheless insist that their allegations do not treat Backpage as a publisher or speaker of third-party content. They rest this hypothesis largely on the text of the TVPRA's civil remedy provision, which provides that victims may bring a civil suit against a perpetrator "or whoever knowingly benefits, financially or by receiving anything of value from participation in a venture which that person knew or should have known has engaged in an act" of sex trafficking. 18 U.S.C. § 1595(a); *see id.* § 1591. Characterizing their allegations as describing "an affirmative course of conduct" by Backpage distinct from the exercise of the "traditional publishing or editorial functions" protected under the CDA, the appellants contend that this course of conduct amounts to participation in sex trafficking and, thus, can ground liability without treating Backpage as the publisher or speaker of any of the underlying content. This contention comprises more cry than wool.

We begin with the appellants' assertion that Backpage's activities do not involve traditional publishing or editorial functions, and are therefore outside the protective carapace of section 230(c)(1). In support, the complaint describes choices that Backpage has made about the posting standards for advertisements — for example, rules about which terms are permitted or not permitted in a posting, the lack of controls on the display of phone numbers, the option to anonymize e-mail addresses, the stripping of metadata from photographs uploaded to the website, the website's reaction after a forbidden term is entered into an advertisement, and Backpage's acceptance of anonymous payments. The appellants submit that these choices are distinguishable from publisher functions. We disagree.

As an initial matter, some of the challenged practices — most obviously, the choice of what words or phrases can be displayed on the site — are traditional publisher functions under any coherent definition of the term. And after careful consideration, we are convinced that the "publisher or speaker" language of section 230(c)(1) extends to the formulation of precisely the sort of website policies and practices that the appellants assail.

Without exception, the appellants' well-pleaded claims address the structure and operation of the Backpage website, that is, Backpage's decisions about how to treat postings. Those claims challenge features that are part and parcel of the overall design and operation of the website (such as the lack of phone number verification, the rules about whether a person may post after attempting to enter a forbidden term, and the procedure for uploading photographs). Features such as these, which reflect choices about what content can appear on the website and in what form, are editorial choices that fall within the purview of traditional publisher functions.

At oral argument in this court, the appellants placed particular emphasis on Backpage's provision of e-mail anonymization, forwarding, auto-reply, and storage services to posters. In the last analysis, however, the decision to provide such services and the parallel decision not to impose the same conditions on messaging services as are applied to "Escorts" section postings are no less publisher choices, entitled to the protections of section 230(c)(1).

Nor does the text of the TVPRA's civil remedy provision change this result. Though a website conceivably might display a degree of involvement sufficient to render its operator both a publisher and a participant in a sex trafficking venture (say, that the website operator helped to procure the underaged youths who were being trafficked), the facts pleaded in the second amended complaint do not appear to achieve this duality. But even if we assume, for argument's sake, that Backpage's conduct amounts to "participation in a [sex trafficking] venture" — a phrase that no published opinion has yet interpreted — the TVPRA claims as pleaded premise that participation on Backpage's actions as a publisher or speaker of third-party content. The strictures of section 230(c) foreclose such suits.

That ends this aspect of the matter. We hold that claims that a website facilitates illegal conduct through its posting rules necessarily treat the website as a publisher or speaker of content provided by third parties and, thus, are precluded by section 230(c)(1). This holding is consistent with, and reaffirms, the principle that a website operator's decisions in structuring its website and posting requirements are publisher functions entitled to section 230(c)(1) protection.

III. Conclusion

As a final matter, we add a coda. The appellants' core argument is that Backpage has tailored its website to make sex trafficking easier. Aided by the amici, the appellants have made a persuasive case for that proposition. But Congress did not sound an uncertain trumpet when it enacted the CDA, and it chose to grant broad protections to internet publishers. Showing that a website operates through a meretricious business model is not enough to strip away those protections. If the evils that the appellants have identified are deemed to outweigh the First Amendment values that drive the CDA, the remedy is through legislation, not through litigation.

We need go no further. For the reasons elucidated above, the judgment of the district court is affirmed.

Notes and Questions

1. "Publisher" Liability. Do you agree with the court that the plaintiffs sought to impose liability on Backpage for its publication of user-generated content? In a defamation case, liability is based on the speech and its effects. In *Roommates*, the plaintiffs alleged a violation of the FHA's prohibition on the publication of any advertisement "that indicates any preference, limitation, or discrimination based on race, color, religion, sex, handicap, familial status, or national origin." 42 U.S.C.

§ 3604(c). Although the FHA independently outlaws discriminatory rental practices, the violation charged was publishing the advertisements. The plaintiffs in this case alleged that the website affirmatively encouraged and enabled trafficking. While that enablement was by way of publication, the plaintiffs' focus was not on liability for the publication itself but for its relation to the underlying activity. Does this distinction hold water? What would its implications be for other online services and platforms?

2. Interpreting *Roommates*. Does this case help interpret *Roommates*, in the sense of choosing between "joint production" and "encouraging illegality" as the principal holding?

3. Content versus Structure. In *Roommates*, the website helped to structure the content of the advertisements and the content that the site itself provided was (arguably) impermissible under the FHA. Did Backpage provide any content of its own, such as headings, that might fit within a joint production argument? Could it be enough alone, or together with the architecture of the site, to say that Backpage was affirmatively publishing trafficking information?

4. Company Aftermath. In 2018, the U.S. Department of Justice unsealed an indictment of Backpage and several of its principals, charging a variety of crimes related to promoting prostitution. *See* Press Release, U.S. Dep't of Justice, Justice Department Leads Effort to Seize Backpage.Com, the Internet's Leading Forum for Prostitution Ads, and Obtains 93-Count Federal Indictment (Apr. 9, 2018), https://www.justice.gov/opa/pr/justice-department-leads-effort-seize-backpagecom-internet-s-leading-forum-prostitution-ads. At the same time, the DOJ and other law enforcement agencies seized the Backpage website and removed it from the internet. The Backpage CEO pled guilty to state charges in Texas and California, pursuant to an agreement with the federal government, turned over the website and related data permanently, and agreed to cooperate in the federal prosecution of Backpage's founders. *See* Maggie Astor, Backpage Chief Pleads Guilty to Conspiracy and Money Laundering, N.Y. Times (Apr. 12, 2018), https://www.nytimes.com/2018/04/12/us/backpage-plea-deal-ferrer.html.

5. FOSTA-SESTA. In the same week of 2018 that the Justice Department unsealed its indictment, the President signed a legislative package known as FOSTA-SESTA—the "Allow States and Victims to Fight Online Sex Trafficking Act of 2017." Pub. L. No. 115-164, 132 Stat. 1253. (SESTA was the "Stop Enabling Sex Traffickers Act," the name of a predecessor bill that merged with the FOSTA bill to result in the statute that eventually passed.) Congressional action was, in part, spurred by reaction to *Backpage*.

In the statute, Congress expressed its "sense" that § 230 "was never intended to provide legal protection to websites that unlawfully promote and facilitate prostitution and websites that facilitate traffickers in advertising the sale of unlawful sex acts with sex trafficking victims." *Id.* § 2. The statute further makes it a crime for anyone to "operate[] . . . an interactive computer service . . . with the intent to promote or facilitate the prostitution of another person." *Id.* § 3. The statute also creates civil remedies against such services, *id.*, and assures the enforceability of state and federal criminal laws against sex trafficking, *id.* § 4. In addition to the new criminal and civil liability provisions, FOSTA amended § 230 to eliminate immunity in the cases it authorized. *See* 47 U.S.C. § 230(e)(5).

In 2021, the U.S. Government Accountability Office published a 3-year assessment of the statute (as required by the statute itself). U.S. Gov't Accountability Off., GAO-21-385, Sex Trafficking: Online Platforms and Federal Prosecutions (2021), https://www.gao.gov/products/gao-21-385. The GAO found only a few criminal prosecutions had occurred and no awards of criminal restitution or civil damages. The DOJ explained that it had principally relied on other statutes. Assessing the general online environment, the GAO said, "The current landscape of the online commercial sex market heightens already-existing challenges law enforcement face in gathering tips and evidence. Specifically, gathering tips and evidence to investigate and prosecute those who control or use online platforms has become more difficult due to the relocation of platforms overseas, platforms' use of complex payment systems, and the increased use of social media platforms." *Id.*

6. Other § 230 Reforms. In 2020, President Trump issued an Executive Order on Preventing Online Censorship. Exec. Order 13,925, 85 Fed. Reg. 34,079 (2020), *revoked by* Exec. Order 14,029, 86 Fed. Reg. 27,025 (2021). Pursuant to the 2020 Order, the Department of Justice proposed a comprehensive set of amendments to reduce the scope of § 230's immunity, by, among other things, carving out "bad Samaritans," child abuse, terrorism, and cyber-stalking, and holding platforms liable in circumstances in which they had actual knowledge that content violated the criminal laws or court judgments. While these specific proposals did not survive the end of the Trump administration, proposals to change § 230 continued to have visibility. President Biden himself exclaimed that Facebook "is killing people" and instructed his administration to continue to review § 230. *See* Quinta Jurecic, The Politics of Section 230 Reform: Learning from FOSTA's Mistakes, Brookings (Mar. 1, 2022), https://www.brookings.edu/research/the-politics-of-section-230-reform-learning-from-fostas-mistakes/. More than 25 bills to alter or repeal § 230 were introduced in Congress. *See id.*; Meghan Anand, et al., All the Ways Congress Wants To Change Section 230, Slate.com (Mar. 23, 2021), https://slate.com/technology/2021/03/section-230-reform-legislative-tracker.html. These bills ranged from complete repeals of § 230; to more targeted limits on scope; to bills that sought to use § 230 to combat platform bias and private censorship, by making platform viewpoint neutrality a condition of immunity. Other legislative proposals would have imposed liability on platforms for the content they specifically promote, by considering their algorithms and content moderation practices. *Id.* Academic commentary arguing for reform is also extensive. Danielle Citron wrote an influential early book (Hate Crimes in Cyberspace) in 2014 calling for the statute to exclude the "very worst actors." As noted above, Mary Anne Franks and others have written extensively about harms to women and suggested changes to § 230. And Justice Thomas has questioned the broad interpretations lower courts have given § 230, saying that, "in an appropriate case, [the Supreme Court] should consider whether the text of this increasingly important statute aligns with the current state of immunity enjoyed by Internet platforms." Malwarebytes, Inc. v. Enigma Software Group USA, LLC, 141 S. Ct. 13, 14 (2020) (Thomas, J.) (statement respecting the denial of certiorari). This is only a sample of proposals, but their breadth reflects the importance and contested nature of § 230 immunity.

Conceptual Index and Glossary

1934 Act • An abbreviation for the Communications Act of 1934, the principal statute governing communications regulation in the United States. Most other communications statutes are actually just amendments to this Act. The Act is codified at 47 U.S.C. and is discussed throughout this text.

1984 Cable Act • An abbreviation for the Cable Communications Policy Act of 1984, a significant amendment to the 1934 Act which first added specific provisions addressing cable television. It is discussed primarily in Chapters 5, 7, 10, and 14.

1992 Cable Act • An abbreviation for the Cable Television Consumer Protection and Competition Act of 1992, a significant piece of legislation that amended the Communications Act of 1934 and also the Copyright Act of 1976. The 1992 Cable Act established many of the current rules governing cable service provision; it is discussed primarily in Chapters 5, 7, 10, and 14.

1996 Act • An abbreviation for the Telecommunications Act of 1996. This statute amended the Communications Act of 1934 and, among other things, established most of the rules under which the telephone industry is today regulated. The 1996 Act is analyzed extensively in Chapters 4 and 5, although provisions of the Act are discussed pervasively throughout the book.

Access Charges • Charges that are paid by IXCs to LECs to compensate LECs for their costs of originating and terminating interexchange calls. These charges have to date overcompensated LECs for those costs and in that way forced IXCs to contribute to LEC universal service obligations. This system is discussed in Chapters 4 and 5. *See also* Intercarrier Compensation, Reciprocal Compensation.

Advanced Services • A term used by both Congress and the FCC to refer to a wide range of technologies and services capable of delivering large quantities of data at high speeds. Examples include digital subscriber line (DSL) service and cable modem technology. Advanced services are considered in Chapter 6.

Amplitude Modulation (AM) • A method of modulating information on a radio wave by varying the strength (voltage) of some agreed-upon baseline signal. To take a simple example: the baseline strength might be 2 volts, and all parties might understand that every time the signal increases to 5 volts the sender intends to tell the receiver that a customer has entered the building. AM modulation is one of two common methods of encoding typically used for radio transmission. Modulation and modulation technologies are introduced in Chapter 9. *See also* FM, Carrier Wave.

Analog • A signaling method that uses continuous changes in the amplitude or frequency of a carrier wave to convey information. Analog signal transmission is discussed in Chapter 9. *See also* Carrier Wave, Digital.

Ancillary Jurisdiction • This doctrine provides the FCC with authority to regulate services "ancillary" to those services within its specifically authorized jurisdiction. This doctrine, which is relevant to the FCC's effort to regulate broadband communication, is discussed in Chapter 6.

Antitrust • Broadly speaking, antitrust refers to the competition law of the United States, including the federal antitrust laws (the Sherman Act and the Clayton Act, as amended), the Federal Trade Commission Act, and similar laws at the state level, together with their judicial interpretation. We discuss antitrust policy generally in Chapter 2 and more specifically in the context of networked industries in Chapter 8.

AT&T • An acronym for the American Telephone and Telegraph Company. The acronym is sometimes used to refer to the firm that ran most of the nation's telephone system prior to 1984 (which in this text we refer to as "Bell" or "Bell System"); but, in this text it is used to refer to the former Bell subsidiary that provided long distance service after the breakup of the Bell System. Note that, in 2006, SBC merged with AT&T and took the AT&T name; so now, once again, AT&T refers to a company that provides local telephone service, this time alongside wired and mobile broadband, multichannel video, etc. The breakup of Bell is discussed in Chapter 4.

Baby Bell • One of several terms for the LECs that were once part of the Bell System. The phrase sometimes refers to a single LEC, but it is more often used to refer to the Regional Holding Companies of which the LECs were a part. Baby Bells are particularly discussed in Chapter 4 . *See also* LEC, RBOC, RHC.

Band Plan • A set of decisions regarding how radio spectrum will be used. The band plan for a given block of spectrum typically establishes (1) which services can be offered, (2) how the block will be divided both across and within geographical areas, and (3) the rules for actually assigning licenses to use that spectrum to specific parties. Chapter 9 discusses the concept of the band plan and its role in spectrum management.

Bandwidth • The transmission capacity of a communications medium. Bandwidth is explained in Chapter 9.

Bell or Bell System • The firm built on Alexander Graham Bell's initial telephone patents. In this text, the word is used exclusively to refer to that company as it existed before divestiture. Bell is particularly discussed in Chapter 4.

Bell Operating Company (BOC) • One of several terms for the LECs that were once part of the Bell System. The creation of the BOCs under the MFJ is discussed in Chapter 4. *See also* Baby Bell, LEC, RBOC.

Bit • A contraction of the term "binary digit" which refers to the smallest unit of information that a computer processes. A bit has a value of either zero or one. Digital information is transmitted as a string of bits. The concept is discussed in Chapter 9 (p. 525). *See also* Digital.

Bottleneck • The point in a system or production process at which the traffic of competing providers must flow over facilities owned by a single provider. Bottlenecks raise concerns for competition policy because of the potential for the firm controlling the bottleneck to discriminate against competitors in access to the facility and thereby to exercise monopoly power over the good or service at issue. The concept is illustrated in, among other contexts, discussions of content access found in Chapters 5 and 8.

Broadband • Broadband is a descriptive term for evolving technologies that provide consumers with access to high-speed services. At present, the FCC defines broadband as the capability to provide 25 megabits per second (Mbps) for downstream internet traffic and 3 megabits per second for upstream internet traffic. Broadband is discussed in Chapters 1, 6, and 8. *See also* Advanced Services.

Broadband Internet Access Service (BIAS) • BIAS is a service, sold to consumers, enabling them to reach the internet (or, more specifically, all or substantially all of the other endpoints connected to the internet). Whether and to what extent BIAS should be regulated as a telecommunications service subject to common carrier requirements is the heart of the net neutrality debate. Chapter 6.

Carrier Wave • In situations where a radio wave or signal on a wire is being modified for the purposes of providing information on the wave, the "carrier wave" is the baseline, unmodified wave against which the modified waves are to be compared. A carrier wave is discussed in Chapter 9.

Clayton Act • The Clayton Antitrust Act of 1914 expanded the scope of the Sherman Act in a number of ways, most notably by adding private enforcement provisions, restricting mergers, and limiting price discrimination and exclusive dealing. We discuss the antitrust laws generally in Chapter 2 and merger law in Chapter 8.

Commercial Mobile Radio Service (CMRS) • The generic term for commercially available wireless services like mobile telephony, paging, and digital PCS. *See also* Mobile Telephony, PCS.

Common Carrier • A firm that sells its services to the general public and serves all comers for a set fee. A telephone carrier, for example, serves anyone who wishes to subscribe and does so on non-discriminatory terms. By definition, a provider of "telecommunications services" is subject to common carrier obligations unless the FCC lifts those obligations as a result of a forbearance determination. For further discussion of the implications of common carrier obligations and its role in the net neutrality debate see Chapters 1 (pp. 19–23) and 6 (pp. 230–241).

Communications Decency Act (CDA) • The CDA was a significant part (Title V) of the 1996 Act. The CDA generally sought to regulate pornography on the internet. That subject is addressed in Chapter 11. The CDA also included Section 230, which created an immunity from liability for internet hosts of user-generated content. That significant provision is discussed in Chapter 15. *See also* Section 230.

Comparative Hearing • The means by which the FCC for many years decided which among competing applicants would receive licenses to use the radio spectrum. This mechanism, as used to assign broadcast licenses, is discussed in Chapter 9 (pp. 491–502). *See also* Spectrum Auction.

Competitive Local Exchange Carrier (CLEC) • Firms that provide local telephone service in competition with the incumbent local exchange carrier (ILEC) in a given area. CLECs are discussed in Chapter 5. *See also* Incumbent Local Exchange Carrier (ILEC).

Computer Inquiries • The name given to the series of decisions, culminating in the *Computer III* decision, which set forth the rules governing the access of "information service providers" to "telecommunications services." Notably, the *Computer III* rules—explained in Chapter 4—historically required incumbent providers to make available telecommunications capability to information service providers at nondiscriminatory terms and conditions.

Convergence • Convergence occurs when a single infrastructure—a single network—is capable of carrying many services. It is used in contrast to the manner in which the public switched telephone network was designed for and largely carried voice traffic, spectrum carried radio and then television, and cable systems only carried linear video. A general purpose data network—such as those underlying the internet—can carry any digital service (and most services can be digitized). The concept and the consequences for communications regulation are discussed most explicitly in Chapter 1. *See also* Analog, Digital.

Copyright • Congress created copyright protection for "original works of authorship fixed in any tangible medium of expression." 17 U.S.C. § 102(a). The owners of such works have exclusive rights to reproduce, distribute, and perform those works, among other rights. As a result, content consumed through internet and telecommunications services is often copyrighted. Chapter 14 discusses the role of copyright in communications policy.

Cost-of-Service Regulation • *See* Rate-of-Return Regulation.

Cream Skimming • When a carrier seeks to serve only highly profitable customers, or to provide only highly profitable services, the strategy is called "cream skimming" or "cherry picking." Incumbent telephone firms have used the term to describe the strategies of new entrants into the telephone market, arguing that such strategies interfere with the incumbents' abilities to meet their universal service obligations. Cream skimming is examined most closely in Chapter 4 (p. 101).

Cross-Ownership Rules • Rules that restrict ownership across different communications services in an effort to foster competition. Discussion of the rules is found in Chapter 10. *See also* Multiple-Ownership Rules.

Customer Premises Equipment (CPE) • Products like ordinary telephones, fax machines, modems, computers, answering machines, and even private branch exchange (PBX) equipment that connect to the telephone network at a customer's home or business are discussed in Chapter 4 (pp. 91–108).

Department of Justice (DOJ) • The cabinet department entrusted with law enforcement. Relevant to this text, the DOJ, through its Antitrust Division, is one of the two agencies that enforces the antitrust laws and reviews large mergers prior to their closing. The DOJ is discussed generally in Chapter 2. *See also* Federal Communications Commission; Federal Trade Commission.

Digital • A signal consisting of binary code (a stream of ones and zeroes) to represent voice, video or data is discussed in Chapter 9 (p. 447–450).

Digital Millennium Copyright Act (DMCA) • The DMCA, passed in 1998, amended the Copyright Act to implement several treaties and to address questions of copyright law raised by the development of the internet and other digital technologies. One aspect of the DMCA is its regulation and protection of hosts of user-generated content that may infringe copyright. This issue is addressed in Chapter 14.

Direct Broadcast Satellite (DBS) • High-powered satellite transmission of signals intended for direct reception by the public. The signals are transmitted to small dishes (usually the size of a large pizza) mounted on homes or other buildings. The term DBS refers most often to satellite-based multichannel video services to which consumers can subscribe and which are competitors to conventional cable television service. Regulatory issues related to DBS are considered in Chapters 4, 7, 8, and 14.

Digital Subscriber Line (DSL) • A high-speed data service provided over conventional telephone networks. DSL refers to the technology that allows telephone carriers to attach certain electronics to the telephone line that can transform the copper loop that already provides voice service into a conduit for high-speed data traffic. Regulatory issues related to DSL and other advanced services are considered in Chapter 6. *See also* Advanced Services.

Divestiture • From the verb "divest" which means to separate or take away, this term refers to a structural change in a company to remedy an antitrust violation. The Department of Justice's 1974 antitrust prosecution resulted in significant divestitures and the breakup of the Bell System. Divestiture is considered extensively in Chapter 4.

Economy of Scale • An economy of scale is said to exist whenever the average cost of producing one unit of a good decreases over some range of increasing production (where the production of additional units has lower average cost). The concept is important to internet and telecommunications regulation because it gives an economic advantage to large companies over smaller competitors and can lead to a monopolized market. Scale economies are discussed further in Chapters 1 and 8 (pp. 12, 344, 435). *See also* Economy of Scope, Natural Monopoly.

Economy of Scope • An economy of scope is said to exist whenever a single firm can produce a given quantity of two or more goods more cheaply than could separate firms. Bell argued that economies of scope existed in the provision of local and long-distance telephone service and, thus, that it was desirable to have a single national telephone company. The concept is discussed in Chapter 4 (p. 90). *See also* Economy of Scale, Natural Monopoly.

Facilities-Based Competition • Under the 1996 Act, this phrase refers to competition from CLECs that build all or most of their own infrastructure. This form of local telephone competition is discussed alongside other forms—such as entry via resale, and entry via unbundled network elements—in Chapter 5.

Federal Communications Commission (FCC) • The federal agency in charge of communications regulation, created by the 1934 Act. Its actions are the core subjects of this text. The Commission's early history, structure and basic powers are considered in Chapter 1. *See also* FRC.

Federal Radio Commission (FRC) • The predecessor agency to the FCC, created by the Radio Act of 1927 and abolished by the 1934 Act. The history of the FRC is discussed in Chapter 1 (pp. 20–23).

Federal Trade Commission (FTC) • The FTC is an independent agency whose organic statute gives it authority (among other powers) to enforce the Sherman Act and to address "unfair methods of competition." It is one agency that reviews large mergers before they close. The FTC is discussed generally in Chapter 2. *See also* Department of Justice, Federal Communications Commission.

Financial Interest and Syndication Rules (Finsyn Rules) • The now-repealed finsyn rules prohibited the major TV networks from exercising certain types of control over already-broadcast television content. The concern motivating these rules was that the major networks could use this control to deny independent stations access to high-quality syndicated reruns. The finsyn rules are discussed in Chapter 5.

Frequency Modulation (FM) • A method of modulating information on a radio wave by varying the frequency of some agreed-upon baseline signal. To take a simple example: the baseline signal might reach its peak once every two seconds, and all parties might understand that every time the signal frequency drops below this level a customer has entered the building. FM modulation is one of two common methods of modulation typically used for radio transmission. Frequency modulation is discussed in Chapter 9 (pp. 446, 456). *See also* AM, Carrier Wave.

Horizontal Merger • A horizontal merger is a merger combining actual or potential competitors in a single market, those at (or potentially at) the same level of the supply system in a given market. Antitrust analysis is the focus of Chapters 2 and 8. *See* Horizontal or Horizontal Restraint.

Horizontal or Horizontal Restraint • In competition law analysis, a horizontal restraint is one that is made between two entities at the same level of the supply system in a given market—entities that are direct or potentially direct competitors in the relevant market. Antitrust, including horizontal restraints, are discussed throughout, but particularly in Chapters 2 and 8.

Incumbent Local Exchange Carrier (ILEC) • The established provider of local telephone service in a given area, which until the 1996 Act usually had a monopoly franchise. The regulation of ILECs, and the obligations put upon them under the 1996 Act, are discussed primarily in Chapter 5. *See also* Competitive Local Exchange Carrier (CLEC).

Information Services • The name given, under the 1996 Act, to services that use "telecommunications" to deliver a service—ranging from "Dial-A-Joke" to Lexis-Nexis to internet service—to the public. Information services, formerly called "enhanced services," are not subject to traditional common carriage regulation. These services are also exempt from access charges (i.e., they are treated as local and not long-distance calls). This regulatory category is discussed in connection with the FCC's decision to classify DSL and cable modem services as information services in Chapter 6 (pp. 241–248, 263–272, 280–281). *See also* Telecommunications Services.

Interexchange Carrier (IXC) • An IXC is a long-distance telephone company. The term comes from the fact that long distance carriers transport calls across the boundaries that separate one local exchange area from another. IXCs are introduced in Chapter 4 (p. 109–110). *See also* Local Exchange Carrier, Local Access, Transport Area.

Internet • The internet is a decentralized network of computer networks. The relevant regulations of internet services are introduced throughout.

Internet Backbone • Long-haul fiber optic networks that transport traffic among ISPs, content providers, online service companies, and other internet customers. Each backbone provider essentially creates a network over which customers and content providers can communicate. Its regulation, or lack thereof, is discussed in Chapter 6.

Internet Service Provider (ISP) • ISPs provide customers with access to the internet. An ISP is a firm that, at a minimum, receives and translates internet-bound data. The ISP takes data in whatever form it arrives and translates it into a form consistent with the communications protocols of the internet. Regulatory issues related to ISPs are considered in Chapter 6.

Internet Platform • An internet platform is an online service that facilitates interactions between two different but interdependent entities or types of entities which interact with the service through the internet. Examples of internet platforms include ridesharing platforms, which match drivers and riders; search engines;

social media networks; messaging platforms; online marketplaces; and the like. Internet platforms are discussed throughout the book.

Last Mile • The segment of a telecommunications network that connects directly to a customer's premises. The term often refers to the twisted pair of copper wires that connects a customer to a LEC's switch and over which a telephone call begins and ends its journey and is discussed in Chapter 6 (p. 264). Many people believe the "last mile" to be a bottleneck, although that belief is today less strongly held than it once was. *See also* Natural Monopoly.

Local Exchange • A geographical area in which customers receive service from a common central office or set of central offices. Sometimes an exchange is served by a single central office switch, in which case the switch itself is referred to as the "exchange." Local exchanges are explained in Chapter 4 (p. 238). *See also* LEC, ILEC, CLEC.

Local Exchange Carrier (LEC) • A provider of local telephone services. The term includes the BOCs, independent telephone companies, and also the CLECs that have entered the market since the effective date of the 1996 Act. Local exchange carriers are discussed in Chapters 4 and 5.

Loop • The part of a local exchange network connecting the customer to the carrier's switch; in essence, the loop is the customer's telephone line. (It was called a "loop" because, in telephony, there are actually two wires connected — one for sound in each direction.) Sometimes an entire local exchange network is referred to as "the local loop" for a given area. *See* Last Mile, Natural Monopoly. The local loop is discussed in Chapter 4 (p. 241).

Market Definition • In antitrust analysis, the process of market definition identifies the scope of competition, by identifying those products over which consumers will reasonably substitute and the geographies in which consumers will buy substitutes. The definition of a market precedes the question of whether an actor (or actors) in the defined market have market power. Market definition is discussed in Chapter 8. *See* Market Power; Monopoly Power.

Market Failure • The concept of market failure captures situations where private markets fail to produce a socially optimal mix of resources. This situation takes place when, for example, a monopolist controls a market and can withhold supply to raise its profits. The concept is discussed in Chapter 1.

Market Power • Often synonymous with monopoly power, an entity has market power within a defined market if it has the ability to raise prices above competitive levels in ways that injure consumers. The ability to raise prices must be the ability to do so for more than a transitory period, such that profits can be increased taking into account any loss of sales due to higher prices. Entities acting together can jointly exercise market power. Market power is discussed in Chapter 8. *See* Market Definition; Monopoly Power.

Mobile Telephony • Wireless telephone technology that divides the service area into small geographic "cells" each of which contains its own transmitter and receiver. As a caller moves from cell to cell, her call is handed off from the equipment in one cell to the equipment in the next, allowing the first cell to handle other callers' signals. In this way, callers moving around the same general area can use the same frequencies without interfering with one another. We consider mobile telephony throughout the book, but we discuss the basic technology in Chapter 4 and consider some spectrum allocation issues related to mobile telephony in Chapter 9. *See also* CMRS, PCS.

Monopoly Power • Antitrust cases brought under a monopolization theory usually refer to the question of the defendant's market power as monopoly power, and the Supreme Court has suggested that monopoly power is a greater degree of control than mere market power, such as the power to control price and exclude competition, though the line is not clear. The analytic process of market definition is the same. Monopoly power is discussed throughout the book, and in particular in Chapters 1 and 8. *See* Market Definition; Market Power.

Modification of Final Judgment or Modified Final Judgment (MFJ) • The 1982 consent decree between Bell and the Department of Justice, which took effect on January 1, 1984, and broke up the Bell System into AT&T long distance and seven independent Regional Bell Operating Companies (RBOCs) that would provide local exchange service. The MFJ also imposed line of business restrictions on the local Bell Operating Companies. "Modification" here refers to the fact that the decree technically "modified" the 1956 consent decree entered against Bell's Western Electric manufacturing subsidiary. The MFJ is considered extensively in Chapter 4 (pp. 98–112).

Multichannel Video Programming Distributor (MVPD) • An entity engaged in the business of selling multiple channels of video programming to paying subscribers. Such entities include, but are not limited to, cable operators, multichannel multipoint distribution services (MMDS, often called "wireless cable"), and direct broadcast satellite (DBS) services. MVPDs and relevant regulatory issues are considered in Chapters 7, 8, and 14.

Multiple Ownership Rules • Rules that restrict ownership within the same service or closely connected services, designed to foster competition. These rules can apply nationally or locally, and they can set caps by stipulating a maximum number of licenses/franchises, a maximum percentage of the relevant audience, or both. So, for example, the "local television ownership rules" limit the number of broadcast licenses that a single entity can hold in a given market; and the "national television ownership rules" limit the percentage of the national audience that a single broadcaster can reach through stations it owns or controls. These rules are discussed in Chapter 10.

Must-Carry Obligation • A 1992 Cable Act term referring to the statutory requirement that cable systems carry the signals of a certain number of commercial and noncommercial television broadcast stations that are "local" to the area served by the cable system. In the Satellite Home Viewer Improvement Act (SHVIA), a form of must-carry obligations was imposed on DBS providers. The must-carry obligations, and the First Amendment challenges to them, are discussed in Chapter 3.

Natural Monopoly • A natural monopoly is said to exist in any market where the costs of production are such that it is less expensive for demand to be met by one firm than it would be for that same demand to be met by more than one firm. For example, this occurs when, over a sufficiently large range of output, the addition of each new customer lowers the average cost of serving every other customer. The concept and its implications are explained in Chapters 1 and 5.

Network Effect or Network Externality • A condition that causes the value a given consumer places on an item to increase as the number of other consumers of that product increases. There is a network effect or network externality at work in the telephone industry because, the more subscribers, the more people to call, and hence the more each subscriber values his or her own telephone subscription. The concept of network effects and its implications are discussed in Chapter 1.

Network Neutrality or Net Neutrality • This phrase refers to a proposed regulatory regime under which the owners of internet infrastructure would be constrained in their ability to charge different prices to different content or service providers, for example, based on quality of service differences. Absolute network neutrality would require that all bits on the network be treated exactly the same. The network neutrality debate is considered in Chapter 6.

Network Nonduplication • Network nonduplication rules are companion rules to the syndicated exclusivity rules. They enable a local broadcaster to prevent a cable system from exhibiting that part of an imported distant broadcaster's signal that contains network programming for which the local broadcaster has obtained exclusive broadcast rights in that local area. The local broadcaster must acquire exclusive rights by contract with the network. Network nonduplication rules were later expanded to apply against retransmission by DBS providers as well. These rules are discussed in Chapter 14 (pp. 734–736). *See also* Syndicated Exclusivity.

Notice of Inquiry (NOI) • An administrative agency releases an NOI for the purpose of gathering information about a broad subject or as a means of generating ideas on a specific issue. The agency may issue an NOI *sua sponte*, or in response to an outside request. An NOI need not occur in order for a rulemaking to commence; that is, a rulemaking can begin with or without an NOI. NOIs are explained in Chapter 1 (p. 27–28). *See also* NPRM, R&O.

Notice of Proposed Rulemaking (NPRM) • Under the Administrative Procedures Act (APA), a rulemaking proceeding ordinarily begins with a Notice of Proposed Rulemaking. An NPRM contains a discussion of the issues to be addressed and proposed regulations in response to those issues. Readers are invited to comment on both the issues and the proposed rules. After reviewing comments on the NPRM, an agency might choose to issue a further Notice of Proposed Rulemaking—thereby providing an opportunity for the public to comment further on a related or specific proposal—or the agency might go ahead and release a final order (usually in the form of a Report and Order) that adopts some variant of the proposed rule, alters an existing rule, or decides not to take any action. This vocabulary is further introduced in Chapter 1 (pp. 27–28); NPRMs themselves are excerpted throughout the text. *See also* NOI, R&O.

Personal Communications Service (PCS) • A wireless communications service similar to mobile telephony, but transmitted at lower power and generally using digital rather than analog signals. The FCC licensed PCS providers in the mid-1990s to compete with the two mobile providers originally licensed in each geographic market. The history and division of spectrum allocation to PCS is discussed in Chapter 9 (p. 495). *See also* Mobile Telephony, CMRS.

Personally Identifiable Information • According to the the White House Office of Management and Budget, "Personally Identifiable Information (PII) means information that can be used to distinguish or trace an individual's identity, either alone or when combined with other personal or identifying information that is linked or linkable to a specific individual." (See p. 678). PII is the usual unit of protection in describing privacy policies, the focus of Chapter 13.

Plain Old Telephone Service (POTS) • Basic, traditional telephone service without any enhanced features like call-waiting, caller-ID, integrated voice messaging, internet service, and so on. POTS, which is sometimes also referred to as basic dial tone service, is discussed in Chapter 5 (p. 211).

Price Cap Regulation • A method of rate regulation that has largely replaced rate of return regulation for telecommunications carriers. Price cap regulation limits the prices firms can charge rather than limiting the returns a firm can earn. The theory behind price caps is that they give regulated firms incentives to reduce costs and become more efficient because, for at least some period of time before regulators readjust the caps, firms can thereby increase their profits. Price caps are discussed in Chapter 5 (pp. 117–123). *See also* Rate of Return Regulation.

Program Access Rules • The requirement that cable networks affiliated with cable distributors be offered, at non-discriminatory terms, to rival distributors. These rules are discussed in Chapter 8 (pp. 430–432).

Public Good • A term used to describe a product or service for which demand is "non-rivalrous" and from which consumers cannot be excluded. National defense is a classic example: one person's benefit from national defense does not preclude any fellow citizen's benefit from national defense, nor can anyone be excluded from the benefits it provides. The concept and economics of public goods is explained in Chapter 1 (pp. 12–13).

Public Interest Standard • The standard that the Communications Act directs the FCC to apply in a variety of settings, ranging from licensing broadcasters to authorizing service operations by telecommunications carriers. The phrase—"public interest, convenience, or necessity"—appears throughout the 1934 Act. This standard is discussed in Chapters 1, 8, and 9.

Public Switched Telephone Network (PSTN) • Usually refers to the incumbent local exchange network that offers service to all customers in its operating area. Connections over a PSTN are mentioned in Chapter 5 (p. 130).

Public Utilities Commission (PUC) • A state regulatory authority that oversees the intrastate aspects of telephone (and usually other utility) services. Sometimes called a "public service commission" (PSC) or another similar term. PUCs are often forced to share jurisdiction and authority with the FCC. PUCs and rate regulation are explained in Chapter 4 (pp. 91–92).

Ramsey Pricing • Ramsey pricing is a method of setting prices applicable in many situations, including situations where a single firm or entity must recover fixed costs and can do so by manipulating prices on more than one good. Ramsey pricing suggests that the most efficient way to recover those fixed costs is to set price levels for the goods such that, when comparing the goods, the good for which consumers are less sensitive to price is priced such that there is a greater difference between price and marginal cost than there is for the good for which consumers are more sensitive to price. We introduce this pricing strategy in Chapter 5 (pp. 124–126).

Rate of Return Regulation • A form of regulation under which firms are permitted to charge prices that both cover their total costs of providing a service and, in addition, pay a "reasonable" rate of return on their capital investments in providing the service. This form of regulation, which was for decades the primary means of regulating telephone rates, requires the regulator to determine the regulated firm's costs and then to decide what rate of return is reasonable for the firm to earn. Rate of return regulation is explained and discussed in Chapter 5 (pp. 117–123). *See also* Price Cap Regulation.

Reciprocal Compensation • Payment by one local exchange carrier to another for the additional, or marginal, costs of terminating calls that originated on the paying carrier's network. Reciprocal compensation is the general rule established by the Telecommunications Act of 1996 for interconnection among competing local exchange carriers. This regime is discussed in Chapter 5.

Regional Bell Operating Company (RBOC) or Regional Holding Company (RHC) • Term for each of the seven regional local exchange carriers created by the MFJ. An RBOC (or RHC) was a holding company generally consisting of several LECs. Thus, for example, Pacific Telesis (now part of SBC) was an RBOC that in turn consisted of several subsidiaries, such as Nevada Bell and Pacific Bell. Pacific Bell, in turn, owned and operated local telephone companies throughout California. The word "regional" distinguishes these firms from the Bell Operating Companies of which they are comprised. RBOCs and the MFJ are explained in Chapter 4 (p. 109). *See also* Baby Bell, Bell Operating Company.

Regulation by Raised Eyebrow • A form of implicit regulation where an agency—here, the FCC—does not use the rulemaking process to announce its policies but, instead, indicates its desires less formally and then threatens to enforce those desires through the exercise of its discretion. Regulation by raised eyebrow is discussed in Chapter 9 (pp. 493–494).

Regulatory Capture • Phrase used to describe situations where a regulatory agency falls under the influence of a powerful interest group. The paradigmatic case of capture arises when an agency does the bidding of the very parties it was originally designed to regulate and therefore stops regulating in the public's interest and starts, instead, regulating for the benefit of the regulated parties. This is not an uncommon allegation, especially because regulators necessarily work closely with the parties they regulate, for example gathering information from them, and thus at least some form of a relationship is bound to form. Moreover, regulators and regulatees in some sense rely on one another for their survival: should the industry disappear or become fully competitive, the regulators might find themselves without work; should the regulators become too strict, the regulatees might find themselves losing considerable profits and freedoms. All this intuitively could cloud a regulator's judgment. Regulatory capture is discussed in Chapter 1 (p. 17).

Report and Order (R&O) • The title of the document that the FCC or other agency customarily uses to take final action on a proposed rule. After considering comments to a Notice of Proposed Rulemaking (or further Notice of Proposed Rulemaking), the FCC issues a Report and Order. The R&O might establish new rules, amend existing rules, or announce a decision not to make any changes. We introduce this and related vocabulary in Chapter 1 (p. 27). *See also* NOI, NPRM.

Resale • One of the means by which Congress and the FCC have attempted to introduce competition into the local telecommunications market. A key example is the 1996 Act's mandate that ILECs make their services available at wholesale rates to new entrants such that those new entrants can, in turn, resell those services directly to consumers. This mode of entry and its regulation is discussed in Chapter 5.

Retransmission Consent • A requirement of the 1992 Act that cable operators receive consent from the relevant broadcaster before retransmitting that broadcaster's signal to cable subscribers. A broadcaster has a choice between demanding carriage under the 1992 Act's must-carry provisions or demanding that a cable operator obtain its consent for carriage. Similar obligations are also imposed on DBS providers. This regime is discussed in Chapter 14 (pp. 734–739).

Satellite Home Viewer Act of 1988 (SHVA) • An Act that, among other things, granted satellite carriers a statutory license to retransmit network television programming to "unserved households" even without copyright permission from the relevant copyright holders. The Act has since been significantly mooted by the Satellite Home Viewer Improvement Act of 1999 (SHVIA); both Acts are discussed throughout Chapter 14.

Satellite Home Viewer Improvement Act of 1999 (SHVIA) • An Act that established for DBS a regime of rules and licenses similar to that which governs retransmission of broadcast signals over cable television. For example, the Act establishes a retransmission consent requirement, must-carry obligations, and statutory licenses under which DBS providers can, in certain circumstances, retransmit copyrighted content without the relevant copyright holder's permission. This Act is discussed in Chapter 14.

Secondary Liability • In general, secondary liability refers to the derivative liability of a party other than the one committing the direct legal violation, because the secondary party contributes to, facilitates, or otherwise is responsible for aiding the direct violation. In Chapter 14, we discuss the secondary liability of internet platforms and other communications services for copyright infringement. In Chapter 15, we discuss the immunity that § 230 provides online service providers from much primary and secondary liability that might arise from hosting user-generated content.

Section 230 • An abbreviation for 47 U.S.C. § 230, which was added to the 1934 Act by the CDA, and which provides some immunity to online hosts of user generated content. This important provision is discussed in Chapter 15.

Separations • The regulatory division of facilities or costs between interstate and intrastate telecommunications services, usually for the purpose of drawing the line between state and federal regulatory jurisdiction. This division is explored in the context of access charge reform in Chapter 5 (p. 198).

Sherman Act • The Sherman Antitrust Act of 1890 was the first general federal competition law, forbidding agreements in restraint of trade and monopolization of markets. We discuss the Sherman Act, and competition laws generally, most intensively in Chapters 2 and 8.

Spectrum • The electromagnetic radio frequencies used in the transmission of television and other signals carrying video, sound, and data through the air. One of the FCC's major tasks is spectrum management. We discuss spectrum regulation most intensively in Chapter 9. *See also* Band Plan, Comparative Hearings.

Spectrum Auction • Spectrum auctions, distinguished from comparative hearings, are the allocation of spectrum licenses to parties with the highest bid in structured auctions. Auctions have been used to allocate much of the mobile and broadband spectrum and are discussed in Chapter 9. *See also* Comparative Hearings.

Syndicated Exclusivity • Syndicated exclusivity ("syndex") rules are companion regulations to the network nonduplication rules. Syndex rules enable a local broadcaster to prevent a cable system from exhibiting that part of an imported distant broadcaster's signal that contains programs (or episodes from a television series) for which the local broadcaster has obtained exclusive broadcast rights in that local area from the copyright holder. These rules, discussed in Chapter 14 (pp. 734–737), were later applied against DBS providers as well. *See also* Network Nonduplication.

Syndication • The process of licensing television programming for rebroadcast after the program's primary network run has ended. Syndication is explained in Chapter 14 (p. 760). *See* Finsyn, Syndicated Exclusivity.

Tariff • The document filed by a telecommunications provider (usually filed with the FCC or a PUC) describing a particular service and the terms, including price, under which that service will be offered. A "tariffed service" is one for which a service provider is required to file a tariff and, thus, one that is regulated by either state or federal authorities. Tariffs in general are introduced in Chapter 5 (p. 122). Tariffed service is discussed in Chapter 5 (pp. 182–183).

Taxation by Regulation • Phrase that refers to any situation where the government imposes a financial burden on a regulated party not directly, but instead by requiring a particular unprofitable behavior. The phrase is designed to remind policymakers to consider the explicit alternative: actually taxing the regulated party in that same amount and then using the money to further the policy goal at issue. Taxation by regulation is introduced in Chapter 1.

Telecommunications Services • This regulatory category governs all services provided under Title II of the 1934 Act and subjects such services (unless otherwise deregulated through a forbearance process) to common carrier regulation. We discuss telecommunications service, as distinguished from an information service, in Chapter 6.

Total Element Long-Run Incremental Cost (TELRIC) • The rule that the FCC adopted in 1996 for determining the price at which an ILEC must sell unbundled network elements to CLECs. TELRIC is explained and discussed in Chapter 5 (pp. 128, 180–196).

Ultra High Frequency (UHF) • A phrase that refers to television stations occupying frequencies above the 30 to 300 MHz bands used by VHF stations. Historically, UHF signals were weaker than VHF signals and could deliver a high-quality television picture only over a comparatively smaller geographic range. Broadcast stations thus for a long-time preferred VHF licenses over UHF licenses, although because cable can retransmit VHF and UHF equally well, the "UHF handicap" is less important in modern times. We discuss UHF in Chapter 9.

Unbundled Network Element (UNE) • A part ("element") of a telephone network, such as a switch or customer loop, that the 1996 Act requires ILECs to lease to CLECs at cost-based rates. The UNE regime is discussed in Chapter 5. *See also* TELRIC, Resale.

Universal Service • Historically, a set of policies designed to keep rates for local telephone service affordable and reasonably homogenous for subscribers. At times, the phrase refers more broadly to any subsidy or program designed to assist low-income or otherwise disadvantaged telecommunications consumers access services, including now broadband services. This concept is discussed in Chapter 5.

Unlicensed Spectrum • Spectrum that is authorized for use without a license under the FCC's Part 15 Rules, which require merely that certain power limits are respected. The authorization of the use of spectrum without a license allowed a number of technologies (including WiFi) to develop. The concept of unlicensed spectrum is discussed in Chapter 9 (pp. 462–488). *See also* White Spaces.

User-Generated Content (UGC) • User-generated content is that content produced and contributed (posted) to a communications service, internet platform, or other online service provider by a user of the service. We discuss the potential liability of communications and internet providers for user-generated content that may infringe copyright in Chapter 14 and their liability for other forms of user-generated content in Chapter 15.

Vertical Merger • A vertical merger is a merger combining companies at different levels of the supply system and connects separate markets. Vertical mergers and merger law are principally discussed in Chapters 2 and 8. *See also* Vertical Restraint.

Vertical Restraint • In competition law analysis, a vertical restraint is one undertaken between entities at different levels in a supply system, such as a manufacturer's requirement that its retailers only sell at certain prices (resale price maintenance) or that its customers purchase multiple goods from it in order to have access to any good (tying or bundling). A vertical restraint that limits competition is said to effect vertical foreclosure. We discuss these sorts of restrictions in Chapters 2 and 8.

Very High Frequency (VHF) • A phrase that refers to the part of the radio spectrum from 30 to 300 MHz. These bands are used to broadcast (among other things) television channels. We discuss VHF in Chapter 9. *See also* UHF.

Western Electric • The equipment manufacturing subsidiary of Bell before divestiture in 1984. Western Electric's history is described in Chapter 4 (pp. 96–104).

White Spaces • This term describes the unused parts of the wireless spectrum. It is specifically used to describe the bands of unused spectrum dedicated to over the air TV broadcasting. The FCC used this term in an order enabling the unlicensed use of white spaces in the TV bands. The concept is discussed in Chapter 9 (pp. 480–486). *See also* Unlicensed Spectrum.